THE NEW
BOOK OF KNOWLEDGE

A
volume
1

THE NEW
BOOK OF
KNOWLEDGE

GROLIER
INCORPORATED
DANBURY, CONN.

Library of Congress Cataloging in Publication Data
Main entry under title:

The New Book of Knowledge.

Includes indexes.

1. Children's encyclopedias and dictionaries
[1. Encyclopedias and dictionaries]

AG5.B64   1981   031   80–82958
ISBN 0–7172–0512–6

The publishers wish to thank the following for permission to use copyrighted material:
Harcourt, Brace & World, Inc., and Alfred J. Bedard for "The Emperor's New Clothes" from
It's Perfectly True and Other Stories by Hans Christian Andersen, translated by Paul Leyssac,
copyright 1938 by Paul Leyssac.
Little, Brown and Company for excerpt from *Little Women* by Louisa May Alcott.
David McKay Company, Inc., for excerpts from *Arabian Nights,* edited by Andrew Lang, new
edition 1946, copyright 1898, 1946, Longmans Green and Company, Inc., now David McKay
Company, Inc.
Harcourt Brace Jovanovich, Inc., for excerpt on measuring star distances from *Space in Your
Future* by Leo Schneider, copyright 1961 by Leo Schneider.

PREFACE

THE NEW BOOK OF KNOWLEDGE is uniquely related to the needs of modern children, both in school and at home. It is written for the children of today, who are standing on the threshold of a new world. Knowledge in every field is bursting its bonds. Old "truths" are becoming invalid; new "truths" are opening vistas never before imagined. The encyclopedia is addressed to the children of this new world.

Today's children need an encyclopedia as different from those that have gone before as today's world is different from that of yesterday. Over one thousand advisers and contributors, together with a staff of two hundred editors, artists, and related personnel, worked for six years to complete an alphabetically arranged, curriculum-oriented encyclopedia, a reference set designed for today's world . . . THE NEW BOOK OF KNOWLEDGE.

SCOPE

THE NEW BOOK OF KNOWLEDGE will be useful to a wide range of readers, starting with preschool children and including students in school up to the age when they are ready for an adult encyclopedia. For the very young child there are carefully selected illustrations that will catch attention and provide early background, as will the various games and activities and the story material composed of recognized classics. Parents will find material to read aloud to preschool children, both for pleasure and as answers to their questions. Students will find a wealth of information and a clarification of concepts that will be useful in their schoolwork. Activities, projects, and experiments are incorporated in order to increase the educational value of subject articles. The content of the encyclopedia was selected by educators who analyzed the curriculum requirements of school systems across the nation and by librarians familiar with the research needs of children. The encyclopedia is designed for the library and the classroom as well as for educational use at home.

AUTHORITY

The articles in THE NEW BOOK OF KNOWLEDGE are written or reviewed by scholars and experts eminent in their fields. All articles a page or more in length are signed—as are many of the shorter ones. The contributor's or reviewer's position appears with his signature so that readers can see immediately the writer's authority. Many articles are signed not only by an author but also by a reviewer. This is true of the articles on the countries of the world, for example, which have been written by experts in geography and then reviewed by distinguished nationals of the particular countries. The short, unsigned articles are written by staff editors, many of whom, in addition to being editors and subject-matter specialists, are authors in their own right. A complete list of contributors, consultants, reviewers, and staff writers appears in Volume 20.

ACCURACY

To insure utmost accuracy, every article, map, drawing, photograph, diagram, and chart is checked by skilled researchers. Wherever possible, information is checked against primary sources. Where authorities disagree or information is unknown, the reader is so informed. An underlying principle of editorial policy is the presentation of fact, not opinion.

READABILITY

The Dale-Chall readability formula is used to test the reading level of every article in THE NEW BOOK OF KNOWLEDGE. Professor Jeanne Chall of Harvard University serves as reading consultant to the encyclopedia. Under her direct supervision articles were tested with children to make certain the material was comprehensible, informative, and interesting. The reading level of articles whose subjects appeal to younger children is lower, whereas other articles, especially those with a technical vocabulary, are written at a higher level. The chief purpose of the encyclopedia is to provide accurate information. But the editors make every effort to present this factual information in a style of writing that will capture the interest and imagination of its readers. The type in which the set is printed was chosen after careful research in typeface legibility.

ARRANGEMENT and AVAILABILITY of INFORMATION

THE NEW BOOK OF KNOWLEDGE is organized alphabetically in unit letter volumes. Each volume contains an Index that is cross-referenced to the entire contents of the set. Blue paper is used for the Index pages so that they can be easily identified. The Index, in addition to the usual Index entries, includes thousands of short, informational items which will be found particularly useful for quick references. Articles and Index entries are arranged in alphabetical order, letter by letter to the comma, ignoring hierarchical orders. In addition to the extensive use of See Also references following articles, the encyclopedia includes 700 external cross-references for those items that are most appropriately covered in comprehensive articles. Other devices employed to facilitate the finding of information include: placing word guides at the bottom of each page close to the page number; placing a page number on every page, or, where this is not possible, on every double spread of pages; organizing long articles into shorter units through the copious use of sideheads; and presenting information in concise form as fact summaries, chronologies, and lists of foreign words.

MAPS

THE NEW BOOK OF KNOWLEDGE presents a unique map program planned especially to meet the needs of children. Maps are prepared by skilled cartographers in collaboration with geographers, experienced teachers, and subject editors. The maps are clear, accurate, informative, attractive, and easy to understand. Information of various kinds is presented on different but related maps, not crowded into one map. Pictorial symbols, decorative insets, and rich color make the maps appealing to the eye and also provide additional information. There are more than 1,000 maps of all kinds in the encyclopedia; most are in color.

ILLUSTRATIONS

THE NEW BOOK OF KNOWLEDGE is printed on a full-color press designed and built especially for this project so that color can be available wherever it serves a useful purpose. There are more than 13,000 color illustrations in the set. All of the 22,400 photographs, pictograms, and maps were selected to complement and extend the text and were as carefully checked for accuracy as the text itself. The illustrations appear on the same pages as the information they illustrate; and they are large enough to show details clearly. All of the art work and many of the photographs were commissioned especially for this publication.

BIBLIOGRAPHY

A comprehensive bibliography is provided, pointing the way to further reading on over 1,000 topics. The recommended readings are graded by level—primary, intermediate, and advanced. The encyclopedia must be considered a springboard that will stimulate the curiosity and interest of children and lead them to further research.

The Editors

Theodore C. Hines, M.L.S., Ph.D.
Professor of Library Science,
School of Education,
University of North Carolina at Greensboro

Daniel Jacobsen, Ph.D.
Professor of Geography,
Montclair State College (New Jersey)
and Michigan State University

John Jarolimek, Ph.D.
Professor of Elementatry Education and
Associate Dean, Undergraduate Studies,
University of Washington

Hyman Kublin, Ph.D.
Professor of History, Brooklyn College

Nancy Larrick, Ed.D.
Author, *A Parent's Guide to Children's
Reading*

John F. Lounsbury, Ph.D.
Professor of Geography and Director,
Center for Environmental Studies,
Arizona State University

Vincent H. Malmstrom, Ph.D.
Associate Professor of Geography,
Middlebury College

Lowell A. Martin, Ph.D.
Former Dean, Graduate School of Library
Service, Rutgers—The State University
(New Jersey); former Professor of Library
Services, Columbia University

Alexander Melamid, Ph.D.
Professor of Economics,
New York University

Charles Moritz, M.A.
Editor, *Current Biography*

Robert Rienow, Ph.D., Litt.D.
Professor of Political Science,
Graduate School of Public Affairs,
State University of New York at Albany

Daniel Roselle, Ph.D.
Editor, *Social Education* magazine;
Director of Publications, National
Council for the Social Studies

Herman Schneider
Author, *Health Science Series*

Philip Sherlock, Ph.D.
Secretary General, Association of
Caribbean Universities and Research
Institutes

Isidore Starr, Ph.D.
Professor Emeritus of Education,
Queen's College, City University of
New York

Monsignor George E. Tiffany, Ph.D.
Editor in Chief, *The Contemporary Church*

Aa Aa

A, the first letter of the English alphabet, was also the first letter of the Phoenician, Hebrew, and Greek alphabets. The Hebrews called it *aleph* and the Greeks changed it slightly, calling it *alpha*. The word "alphabet" itself comes from joining the Greek names for the first two letters—*alpha* (A) and *beta* (B). Thus the first two letters have come to stand for all the rest, just as "learning your ABC's" really means learning your DEFGHIJ's as well.

The shape of the letter A has changed slightly from time to time. The legs have been shorter or longer, the crossbar more crooked. But even the earliest traces of the letter look familiar to us. The Phoenician picture symbol for A was probably an ox's head with two long horns. It looked like this:

Some of the oldest forms of the letter, which date as far back as the 11th century B.C., lie on their sides in this way:

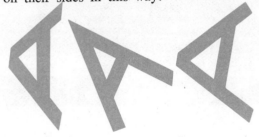

The later Greek forms stand up straight. By the time the Romans had adapted the Greek alphabet, the A looked very much as it does today.

A is a vowel, as are E, I, O, U, and sometimes Y. A vowel is a speech sound made by vibrating the vocal cords and allowing a free passage of breath through the mouth. A, like the other vowels, stands for different sounds. Pronounce these words: *fate, bare, am, farm, grass.* You will notice that each A has a different sound. The most common sounds are the long A, as in *fate;* the short A, as in *am;* and the broad A, as in *farm.*

A is a word in itself. It is found before the name of a thing to show that this thing is one of a particular class or kind: a tree, a bird, a worm.

In Phoenician, Hebrew, and Greek, the letter A also meant the number 1. In English too, A has come to mean the first or best. Some schools give A as the highest grade. Grade-A milk and grade-A eggs mean top quality. When we say something is A-1, we mean that it is in excellent condition.

In music A is a note; in chemistry A sometimes stands for the element argon. Two of our most common abbreviations employ the A—A.D., for the Latin *anno Domini,* is used with dates and means "in the year of our Lord"; A.M., for *ante meridiem,* is used with time and means "before noon."

Reviewed by MARIO PEI
Author, *The Story of Language*

See also ALPHABET.

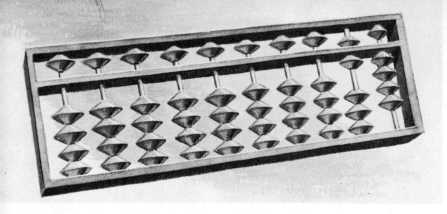

At left is a modern Japanese abacus. Single counters above bar stand for 5, 50, 500, and so on. For example, to count in units row, you move up the four counters for 1,2,3,4. Then you move down the single counter for 5. You leave the single one down and return the others to their original position. You use them to go on counting 6,7,8,9. You move up the top counter in the second, or tens, column for 10. Abacus in drawing shows counters at 64.

ABACUS

The abacus is a simple calculating machine that is used for doing arithmetic. A modern abacus is made of beads, rods, and a frame. The rods are fastened in the frame, and each stands for a place in the decimal system. One rod stands for units, one for 10's, one for 100's, and so on. The beads are counters. Numbers are added or subtracted by moving the beads on the rods.

▶ WHY THE ABACUS WAS INVENTED

The abacus was invented thousands of years ago. It offered a way of doing arithmetic without using written numerals. And it was used in many ancient civilizations.

The numerals of ancient times were very awkward for doing arithmetic. The trouble was that they did not express zero or place value.

For example, compare our numerals with the Roman ones. Our numeral 5 can stand for 5, 50, or 500, depending on the place it is given. In the number 555 each 5 has a different value. The Romans used letters as numerals and expressed place by using a different letter. 5, 50, and 500 were written as V, L, and D. Without the idea of zero and place, there was no way that the same numeral could be made to stand for more than one number. That is, V could not be made to stand for any number except 5.

This system of numerals made written arithmetic very difficult. So the Romans, like other ancient peoples, used the abacus. The idea of place was built into the abacus. One counter could be made to express 1, 10, or 100, according to its place on the abacus.

The abacus offered a quick and easy way of adding and subtracting. It could also be used for multiplication and division. Multiplication was done by adding equal groups. Division was done by subtracting equal groups.

▶ HOW TO MAKE AND USE AN ABACUS

The abacus is still widely used today. For example, it is used in China and Japan. There numerals do not express place. People who are used to the abacus can do arithmetic on it very quickly. A Japanese abacus can be

Children in Peking, China, learn to use the abacus in primary school.

bought in almost any toy store or five-and-ten. The instructions that come with it explain how it works.

However, it is very simple to make an abacus like those of ancient times. You can draw four lines in sand, dust, or soil and use pebbles as counters. Or you can rule heavy lines on a piece of paper or cardboard. Use buttons, bottlecaps, dried beans, or pebbles as counters.

The lines, from right to left, stand for 1's (or units), 10's, 100's, and 1,000's. For example, if you want to express 2,222, you put two counters in each row. If you want to express 2,220, you put two counters in three of the rows and none in the units row. Make up some numbers of your own and express them.

Now suppose you want to add 271 and 302. Set up one of the numbers; then set up the second number. A glance at the abacus gives you the sum.

This is how to subtract 271 from 394. Set up the larger number on the abacus and take away the counters that represent the smaller number.

The drawings on this page show you how to exchange 10 counters for 1 in addition and 1 counter for 10 in subtraction.

See also NUMBERS AND NUMBER SYSTEMS.

Adding 2,365 and 572

A. Place the counters in rows so that they express the number 2,365.

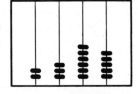

B. Add the number 572. Note that the 10's row now contains too many counters. Its 13 10's add up to too great a number to be expressed in this row.

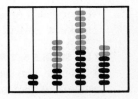

C. However, 10 counters in the 10's row equal 1 counter in the 100's row. So you remove 10 counters from the 10's row and add 1 to the 100's row.

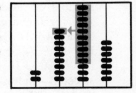

D. The abacus now shows the correct sum: 2,937.

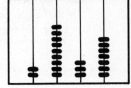

Subtracting 539 from 2,574

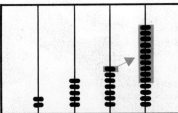

A. Set up the larger number, 2,574, on the abacus. Now, starting to subtract, you find you must take away 9 counters from 4. This is impossible. But one counter in the 10's row equals 10 counters in the 1's row. So you borrow a 10, which becomes 10 1's.

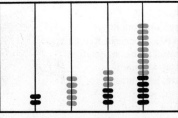

B. Now it is possible to take away 9 from the 1's row. You also take 3 from the 10's row and 5 from the 100's row.

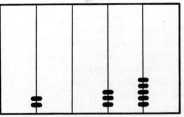

C. The remainder is shown on the abacus.

ABBREVIATIONS

Abbreviations are shortened forms of words and phrases. In the past, when all writing was done by hand, abbreviations saved time and space. Today, when so much is printed about so many subjects, they serve the same purposes. In government, business, the armed forces, sports, the sciences, and other fields of writing, the abbreviated forms make a sort of language within a language.

▶ NO SINGLE SET RULE FOR ABBREVIATIONS

There are various ways of abbreviating words. A part of the whole word followed by a period may be used. It is often the first syllable or letters, as in Mon. for Monday, Jan. for January, co. for company or county. Some words are shortened to the first and last letters—pr. for pair, yr. for year, Mr. for Mister. In other cases key letters are selected—mdse. for merchandise, pkg. for package. Modern abbreviations often use initials, and many omit periods.

Initials for Latin phrases are used in our language. Here the period is retained. The letters i.e. stand for the Latin *id est*, which means "that is." There are many other Latin abbreviations—for example, No., meaning number, goes back to *numero*, the Latin word meaning "by number."

People often make up their own abbreviations, and some of these, like VIP (very important person), come into general usage. Your notebook may contain abbreviations that you have made yourself.

▶ ACRONYMS

An acronym is a word formed from the initial letters in a phrase or title. It is pronounced as a single word, not as a series of letters. CARE and NATO, two such forms, stand for the names of organizations. These acronyms, like many others, omit periods.

Some common abbreviations and acronyms are listed below. Others may be found in the dictionary, generally in the regular alphabetical order of words. Some dictionaries list abbreviations in a special appendix.

ISABELLE FORST
Former Assistant Superintendent of Schools
New York City

AAA American Automobile Association.
A.A.U. Amateur Athletic Union.
abbr. abbreviation.
ABC ABC powers (Argentina, Brazil, Chile); American Broadcasting Company.
AC alternating current.
acct. account; accountant.
A.D., A.D. anno Domini (Latin, in the year of [our] Lord; used with dates in the Christian Era).
ad, advt. advertisement.
adj. adjective.
adm. administration.
ADP automatic data processing.
AFL-CIO American Federation of Labor and Congress of Industrial Organizations.
agt. agent.
alg. algebra.
alt. altitude.
A.M., A.M., a.m. ante meridiem (Latin, before noon).
AMA American Medical Association.
amt. amount.

Angl. Anglican.
anon. anonymous (giving no name).
ans. answer.
ANZAC Australian and New Zealand Army Corps.
AP Associated Press.
APO army post office.
Apr. April.
apt. apartment.
ARC American Red Cross.
assn., assoc. association.
asst. assistant.
att., atty. attorney.
attn. attention
Aug. August.
av., avdp., avoir. avoirdupois (a system of weights).
Ave. (also **Av.**) Avenue.
AWOL absent without leave.

b. born.
B.A. (also **A.B.**) Bachelor of Arts.
Bap., Bapt. Baptist.
BBC British Broadcasting Corporation.
bbl. barrel(s).
B.C., B.C. before Christ.

bf boldface.
biog. biography.
biol. biology.
bk. book.
bldg. building.
blvd. boulevard.
bot. botany.
bros. brothers.
B.S., B.Sc. Bachelor of Science.
BSA Boy Scouts of America.

C. century.
c. circa (Latin, about).
cal. calendar.
cap. capital.
Capt. Captain.
CARE Co-operative for American Relief to Everywhere.
Cath. Catholic.
CBS Columbia Broadcasting System.
cent. century; centuries.
cf. confer (Latin, compare).
chap. chapter.
chg. charge; change.
Cmdr. Commander.
CO Commanding Officer.
c/o care of.

co. company; county.
C.O.D. cash on delivery.
Col. Colonel.
col. college; column.
con. continued.
conj. conjunction.
cont., contd. continued.
cop., © copyright.
CORE Congress of Racial Equality.
corp. corporation; corporal.
cr. credit.
cu. cubic.

d. died.
D.A. District Attorney.
D.A.R. Daughters of the American Revolution.
DC direct current.
D.D. Doctor of Divinity.
D.D.S. Doctor of Dental Surgery.
Dec. December.
dec. deceased.
Dem. Democrat.
dept. (also **dep.**) department.
DEW Distant Early Warning.
D.F.C. Distinguished Flying Cross
dia., diam. diameter.
dict. dictionary.
doz. dozen.
DP displaced person.
Dr. Doctor.
dr. debtor.
D.S.C. Distinguished Service Cross.
D.S.M. Distinguished Service Medal.
D.S.O. Distinguished Service Order.
DST daylight saving time.

ed. edited; edition; editor.
e.g. exempli gratia (Latin, for example).
elec. electric.
elev. elevation.
ency., encyc. encyclopedia.
enl. enlarged; enlisted.
eq. equal; equation.
Esq. Esquire.
est. established; estimate.
et al. et alii (Latin, and others); et alibi (Latin, and elsewhere).
etc. et cetera (Latin, and the rest).

FBI Federal Bureau of Investigation.
FCC Federal Communications Commission.
Feb. February.
fed. federal.
fem. feminine.
ff. following (pages).
FHA Federal Housing Administration.

Fig. Figure.
FOB free on board (price includes charge of loading).
Fri. Friday.

G.A.R. Grand Army of the Republic.
Gen. General.
geog. geography.
geol. geology.
geom. geometry.
GHQ General headquarters.
GI government issue.
G.O.P. Grand Old Party, nickname for present Republican Party in the United States.
Gov. Governor.
Gov.-Gen. Governor-General.
GSA General Services Administration; Girl Scouts of America.

H.E. His Eminence; His Excellency.
hist. history; historical.
H.M.S. His (or Her) Majesty's Service; His (or Her) Majesty's Ship.
Hon. Honorable; Honourable (British usage).
hosp. hospital.
H.P., HP, h.p. horsepower.
hr. hour(s).
H.R.H. His (or Her) Royal Highness.
ht. height.

ibid. ibidem (Latin, in the same place).
ICC Interstate Commerce Commission.
i.e. id est (Latin, that is).
IHS symbol meaning Jesus, formed by a contraction of Greek letters.
ill., illus. illustrated; illustration.
inc. incorporated; including.
incl. including; inclusive.
I.N.R.I. Iesus Nazarenus Rex Iudaeorum (Latin, Jesus of Nazareth, King of the Jews).
ins. insurance.
inst. instant (used to denote the present month); institute.
intro., introd. introduction.
IOU I owe you.
IQ intelligence quotient.
IRS Internal Revenue Service.

Jan. January.
J.P. justice of the peace.
Jr. Junior.
Jul. July.
Jun. June.
juv. juvenile.

KO knockout.
KP kitchen police.
kwhr., kwh. kilowatt-hour(s).

L, £ pound(s) (British money).
l., ll. line, lines.
lab. laboratory.
lang. language.
Lat. Latin.
lat. latitude.
leg. legal; legislative.
Lieut., Lt. Lieutenant.
liq. liquid.
lit. literary.
lon., long. longitude.
Ltd. limited.

M. meridies (Latin, noon).
m. married.
M.A. (also **A.M.**) Master of Arts.
Maj. Major.
Mar. March.
masc. masculine.
math. mathematics.
max. maximum.
M.C. member of Congress.
M.D. Doctor of Medicine.
mdse. merchandise.
med. medical; medicine.
met., metrop. metropolitan.
mfg., manuf. manufacturing.
mgr. manager.
min. minimum; minute(s).
misc. miscellaneous.
Mme. Madame.
mo. month(s).
Mon. Monday.
MP military police.
M.P. member of Parliament.
mph miles per hour.
Mr. Mister.
Mrs. Mistress (the original term for a married or unmarried woman).
M.S. Master of Science.
Ms. Miss or Mrs.
Ms., MS., ms. manuscript.
Msgr. Monsignor.
Mt., mt. mount; mountain.

n. noun.
NASA National Aeronautics and Space Administration.
nat. national; native.
NATO North Atlantic Treaty Organization.
N.B. nota bene (Latin, note well).
NBC National Broadcasting Company.

NCO noncommissioned officer.
neut. neuter.
no. north, number.
nom. nominative.
Nov. November.
N.P. Notary Public.

OAS Organization of American States.
ob. obiit (Latin, he [or she] died).
obj. object; objective.
Oct. October.
O.K. correct; approved.
op. cit. opere citato (Latin, in the work cited).
OPEC Organization of Petroleum Exporting Countries.
O.S. Old Style (calendar).

p., pp. page; pages.
par. paragraph; parallel.
pd. paid.
Pfc. Private, First Class.
Ph.D. Doctor of Philosophy.
phil., philos. philosophy.
phys. physical; physics.
pk. park.
pkg. package.
pl. plural.
P.M., P.M., p.m. post meridiem (Latin, after noon).
P.O. Post Office.
pop. population.
poss. possessive.
POW prisoner of war.
pr. pair.
prep. preposition; preparation.
pres. president.
prin. principal.
prof. professor.
pron. pronoun.
Prot. Protestant.
pro tem. pro tempore (Latin, for the time being; temporarily).
prov. province.
P.S. postscript; Public School.
pseud. pseudonym.
pt. part.
PTA Parent-Teacher Association.
pub. public; publisher; published.

Q.E.D. quod erat demonstrandum (Latin, which was to be shown or proved).
QM Quartermaster.
quot. quotation.
q.v. quod vide (Latin, which see).

RA Regular Army.
R.A. Rear Admiral.
RAF Royal Air Force.
R.C. Red Cross; Roman Catholic.
Rd., rd. road.
rd. rod(s); round.
recd. received.
ref. referee; reference; referred.
rep., rept. report.
ret. retired; returned.
Rev. Reverend.
rev. revenue; revised.
R.F.D. rural free delivery.
R.N. Registered Nurse.
rpm revolutions per minute.
R.R. railroad.
R.S.V.P. Répondez, s'il vous plaît (French, please reply).
rte. route.

SAC Strategic Air Command.
Sat. Saturday.
sch. school.
sci. science.
sec., secy. secretary.
Sen. Senator.
Sept. September.
seq., seqq. sequentia (Latin, the following).
serg., sergt., sgt. sergeant.
sing. singular.
soc. society.
sp. spelling; species.
SPCA Society for the Prevention of Cruelty to Animals.
SPCC Society for the Prevention of Cruelty to Children.
sq. square.
Sr. Senior.
SST supersonic transport.
St. Saint; Street.
st. stanza.
sta. station; stationary.

Ste. Sainte (French, feminine of Saint).
subj. subject.
Sun. Sunday.
supt. superintendent.
syn. synonym.

tbs. tablespoon(s).
tech. technical.
tel. telegraph; telephone.
temp. temperature.
terr. territory.
Thurs. Thursday.
TNT trinitrotoluene (a high explosive).
trans. transportation; translation.
treas. treasury; treasurer.
tsp. teaspoon(s).
Tues. Tuesday.
TV television.

U., univ. university.
ult. ultimo (Latin, in the month preceding the present month).
U.N. United Nations.
UNESCO United Nations Educational, Scientific and Cultural Organization.
UNICEF United Nations International Children's Emergency Fund.
UPI United Press International.

v. verb; verse.
VA Veterans Administration.
vid. vide (Latin, see; used to direct attention, as *vide p. 40*).
VISTA Volunteers in Service to America.
viz. videlicet (Latin, namely).
vocab. vocabulary.
vol. volume.
vs. versus.

Wed. Wednesday.
WHO World Health Organization.
wk. week(s).
wt. weight.

yr. year(s).

For abbreviations of state names, see articles on individual states and the article POST OFFICE. For symbols of measurement, see the article WEIGHTS AND MEASURES.

There are also abbreviations for ordinal numbers, or numbers that indicate order or succession:

1st first.	**5th** fifth.	**9th** ninth.	**100th** (one) hundredth.
2nd second.	**6th** sixth.	**10th** tenth.	**200th** (two) hundredth.
3rd third.	**7th** seventh.	**20th** twentieth.	**1,000th** (one) thousandth.
4th fourth.	**8th** eighth.	**21st** twenty-first.	**1,000,000th** (one) millionth.

ABOLITIONISTS. See Negro History; Civil War, United States; Underground Railroad.

ABORIGINES, AUSTRALIAN

The Australian aborigines are the native people of Australia—its earliest known inhabitants. For thousands of years they roamed all parts of the vast continent, hunting and gathering food. Today most aborigines live in cities and towns. Only a few live as their ancestors did in prehistoric times.

The term "aborigine" comes from Latin words that mean "from the beginning." It can be applied to the first people of any region. The Australian aborigines form an ethnic group called Australoid. Most of them have brown skin and eyes and wavy, dark hair.

There are many ideas about how, when, and from where the aborigines traveled to Australia. It seems most likely that they first lived in India and the Malay Peninsula, perhaps more than 30,000 years ago. They may have traveled across the Indian Ocean to Australia by raft or dugout canoe.

▶ **TRADITIONAL WAY OF LIFE**

Over centuries, the aborigines spread out across Australia. Eventually each tribe—actually an extended family—claimed its own territory. Within each territory was a watering place that was very important to the tribe for two reasons. Water is scarce in Australia, and the aborigines believed that the spirits of their ancestors remained near the watering place where the tribe had first settled.

The aborigines were nomads—they moved from place to place within their territory to hunt, fish, and gather food. Their journeys, called walkabouts, gave them detailed knowledge of their territory and every kind of animal and plant in it.

Each tribe was made up of several clans. Members of these clans lived in family groups of 30 to 40 people. Each clan had a totem or emblem—perhaps an animal, a plant, or a fish. It served as a reminder of the clan's common ancestry and was painted on shields and weapons. And the totem animal or plant was honored as a member of the clan. The aborigines believed that all things—people, animals, plants, and even rocks—were important parts of nature and of the spirit world.

A painting on tree bark by a present-day artist.

The aborigines have left a rich heritage of cave paintings and rock carvings. And they were one of the few early peoples to make use of the principle of the lever. They used it in the design of the woomera, a spear-thrower. They also used the returning boomerang, made from a curved piece of wood. When thrown properly, the boomerang returned in a perfect arc. Different boomerangs were designed for fighting, hunting, and other uses.

By adapting to Australia's often harsh conditions, the aborigines survived for thousands of years. In 1788, when the first European settlers arrived, there may have been as many as 300,000 of these native people.

▶ **ABORIGINES IN MODERN AUSTRALIA**

As the new settlers spread out, many aborigines were forced to change their way of life. In the 19th century, many were killed by settlers or disease. Others were driven into outlying areas or became workers on cattle and sheep ranches.

Today there are fewer than half as many aborigines as there were when Europeans first arrived, and fewer than half of these are considered pure-blooded. Since the 1940's, the Australian Government has worked to improve opportunities for the aborigines. They now have the same rights—and many of them, the same way of life—as other Australians. But often their incomes are lower. Several aborigine groups are trying to preserve some form of the old, nomadic way of life.

CAROL PERKINS
Author, *The Sound of Boomerangs*

See also Australia.

Abraham receiving God's promise of a son, as depicted by a 13th-century Christian artist.

ABRAHAM

Abraham is called the father of the Jews and is considered to be the founder of their religion. He was the first to believe in one all-powerful God instead of many gods.

Abraham's story is found in the book of Genesis, the first book of the Bible. When Abraham was 75 years old, God commanded him to leave Haran in search of a new home. God promised that a great nation would arise in the new land. Abraham set out with his wife, Sarah, his nephew Lot, and some followers. They traveled into the land of Canaan. God told Abraham that this was the land He would give to Abraham's descendants. Abraham journeyed on, always toward the south. When a famine came, he went into Egypt. He grew rich in cattle, silver, and gold.

When Abraham and his followers left Egypt, both Abraham and Lot grew very prosperous. They acquired so many sheep that their shepherds quarreled over grazing land. Abraham and Lot agreed to separate and live in different places.

Abraham settled in Hebron. Lot and his family settled in Sodom. When Sodom was attacked by the armies of four great kings, Lot was taken captive. Abraham went to his rescue with 318 men and brought Lot and all his goods back to Sodom.

The people of Sodom and neighboring Gomorrah grew very wicked. God told Abraham that he would destroy both cities because no righteous people could be found in them. But God warned Lot to escape with his wife and two daughters, forbidding them to look behind as they fled. Lot's wife looked back, and she became a pillar of salt.

When Abraham and Sarah had grown very old and were still childless, God promised them a son. God also said that Abraham would have as many descendants as there were stars in the sky and that one day they would dwell in the Promised Land. In time, a son was born and was named Isaac. The name means "he laughs." God told Abraham that he would keep his promise with Isaac and his descendants.

While Isaac was still a boy, God tested Abraham again. He told Abraham to take Isaac to the top of a mountain and sacrifice him. Abraham loved his son, but he could not disobey God's command. At the place of sacrifice, Isaac asked, "Where is the lamb for a burnt offering?" Abraham answered that God would provide it. Then he built an altar, laid wood on it, bound up Isaac, and laid him on top of the wood. Just as he was about to put the knife to his son, God stopped him. God said, "Lay not thine hand upon the lad, neither do thou any thing unto him: for now I know that thou fearest God, seeing thou hast not withheld thy son, thine only son, from me." Abraham looked up and saw a ram caught in a thicket. He offered the ram in sacrifice. God blessed Abraham for his obedience.

When Sarah and Abraham died, they were buried in the cave of Machpelah in Hebron. After Abraham's death God blessed Isaac.

Christians and Muslims also honor Abraham and trace their belief in one God back to him. The Arabs claim descent from Ishmael, who was Abraham's son by Hagar, Sarah's handmaiden. When Sarah thought she would have no children, she gave Hagar to Abraham.

Abraham's life is regarded as an example of the proving of faith through trial. Because Abraham listened to God, he is called the Friend of God. His "leaning upon God's word" is taken as proof of genuine righteousness.

Reviewed by MORTIMER J. COHEN
Author, *Pathways Through the Bible*

ACCIDENTS. See FIRST AID; SAFETY.

ACCOUNTING. See BOOKKEEPING AND ACCOUNTING.

ACIDS. See CHEMISTRY, SOME TERMS OF.

ACNE. See DISEASES.

ACOUSTICS. See SOUND AND ULTRASONICS.

ACTION PROGRAMS

Millions of people around the world need help in different ways—help in finding health care, housing, or legal advice; help in learning a skill; or help in simple things, such as writing a letter or going to the store. Many agencies try to bring this help to people who cannot afford to pay for it. ACTION, established by the U.S. Government in 1971, is one such agency. Through ACTION programs, volunteers help people meet their basic needs. The volunteers work full- or part-time and in some cases receive an allowance to cover their expenses.

▶ TYPES OF PROGRAMS

ACTION's international service program, the Peace Corps, helps people outside the United States. An article about the work of the Peace Corps around the world is included in Volume P.

In the United States, ACTION programs include Volunteers in Service to America (VISTA) and several programs for students and for older persons. The agency also directs specialized volunteer programs in criminal justice, mental retardation, income counseling, and many other fields.

Volunteers in Service to America (VISTA). VISTA, created by Congress in 1964, became part of ACTION in 1971. Volunteers are U.S. residents and are at least 18 years old. After a short training period, they work full-time for one to two years in poverty-level urban and rural communities. The volunteers share their talents and skills in such fields as education, health and nutrition, community development, energy, legal aid, and housing.

Student Volunteer Programs. University Year for ACTION (UYA) gives college students a chance to earn academic credit by serving in low-income communities. UYA volunteers concentrate on health, housing, and legal aid. The National Student Volunteer Program (NSVP) provides guidance and training for directors of student volunteer programs in high schools and colleges.

Programs for Older Volunteers. Through these programs, volunteers 60 years old and over serve their communities on a part-time basis.

The Retired Senior Volunteer Program

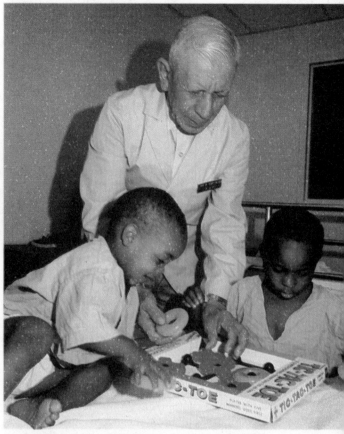

In ACTION's Foster Grandparent Program, volunteers work individually with children who have special needs.

(RSVP) offers older adults the opportunity to share their skills and experience in local schools, libraries, and other community centers. In the Senior Companion Program (SCP), volunteers give personal care and companionship to other adults. They provide such services as shopping, reading, and letter writing. The Foster Grandparent Program (FGP) is staffed by adults who work individually with children who have special needs or who are emotionally, physically, or mentally disabled. The volunteers help feed and dress the children, read to them, play games, and provide speech and physical therapy.

The most important idea behind all ACTION programs is that of people helping one another. These people share, care, and work together to improve the quality of life for others.

Sam Brown
Director, ACTION

JOHN ADAMS (1735–1826)

2ND PRESIDENT OF THE UNITED STATES

ADAMS, JOHN. Of all the early presidents of the United States, John Adams has been the least understood or appreciated by his countrymen. His reputation, both during his lifetime and after, has suffered from this lack of understanding. Yet he was a remarkable man who contributed greatly to the creation of the United States. Appreciation of him has been growing, although slowly, in recent years.

▶ EARLY YEARS

Adams was a descendant of sturdy New England farmers and clergymen. He was born on October 30, 1735, in Braintree (now Quincy), Massachusetts, where the Adamses had deep roots. His great-grandfather Henry Adams had come from England in the 17th century. But his father, John Adams, and his grandfather Joseph Adams were born in Braintree. His mother came from the same neighborhood. She was Susanna Boylston, daughter of a Boston doctor.

Adams grew up on his father's farm, doing the usual country chores, including feeding the horses, milking the cows, and chopping wood. He attended a local school and a "private Academy," as he called it. In 1751, at the age of 16, he entered Harvard, then a small college, and graduated 4 years later. He then moved to Worcester, where he taught school during the day and studied law at night. In 1758 he became a lawyer. Perhaps his most famous case, which showed Adams' characteristic courage, was his successful defense of the British soldiers who were arrested after the Boston Massacre in 1770.

In 1764 Adams married Abigail Smith, the 20-year-old daughter of William Smith, a Massachusetts clergyman. She was an intelligent and sprightly woman. Her letters are still a source of interesting information. The marriage was happy and successful. It lasted 54 years, until Abigail Adams' death in 1818 at the age of 74. Their eldest son, John Quincy, later became the sixth president.

▶ POLITICAL CAREER

Altogether, Adams spent about 25 years in public life. He became interested in politics quite early in his career as a lawyer. In 1765 a crisis arose when the British Government passed the Stamp Act. This was an unpopular tax on public documents, newspapers, licenses, insurance policies, and even playing cards. Adams wrote powerful articles against the tax in the Boston *Gazette*. These articles helped to establish his reputation as a learned writer and champion of individual rights. The Stamp Act was repealed in 1766.

Adams was among the first to favor independence from Great Britain and referred to himself as John Yankee. He spoke out eloquently against what he called the "Design of Great Britain to deprive us of our Liberties." In 1771 he was elected to the Massachusetts House of Representatives and in 1774 to the Continental Congress.

At the Continental Congress in Philadelphia, Adams was a member of at least 90 different committees and chairman of about 25. His arguments for independence, in the face of many who were still reluctant to break with Britain, were brilliant and persistent.

It was Adams who in 1775 recommended George Washington to be commander in chief of the new Continental Army. A year later, on June 7, 1776, Adams seconded Richard Henry Lee's historic resolution: "That these United Colonies are, and of right ought to be, free and independent States . . . ." He was then named to a committee to draft a public declaration explaining the reasons for independence. The result was the famous Declaration of Independence. Though the declaration was written by Thomas Jefferson, Adams bore the burden of defending it on the floor of Congress. It was adopted on July 4, 1776.

▶ DIPLOMATIC SERVICE

Adams' diplomatic career began in 1778 when he was sent to France to help conclude a treaty of alliance. In 1780 he returned to Europe as minister to arrange for loans and trade agreements in France and the Netherlands. Two years later Adams, together with Benjamin Franklin and John Jay, signed the preliminary peace treaty with Great Britain. This Treaty of Paris, finally concluded in 1783, ended the Revolutionary War. It crowned Adams' long struggle for American independence.

In 1785 Adams was appointed minister to Great Britain. In London he tried to win British friendship and commercial co-operation, but without success. For one thing, John Yankee was too outspoken in his defense of American interests. For another, Great Britain was not sympathetic to a republican form of government. Adams' efforts were met coldly. He was happy to return home in the spring of 1788. That was the end of his diplomatic career. But the experience of 10 years abroad was to be invaluable at home when he became president.

▶ VICE-PRESIDENT AND PRESIDENT

In the election of 1788 George Washington received 69 electoral votes and was elected president. Adams received 34 and became vice-president. Both were re-elected in 1792.

Despite his general agreement with Washington's policies, Adams was impatient with his position as vice-president. Adams was eager to lead and to act. Instead he had to confine himself largely to the more or less ceremonial job of presiding over the Senate. He described the vice-presidency as "the most insignificant office that ever the invention of man contrived or his imagination conceived."

His frustration was ended by the election of 1796. In that year Adams ran as the Federalist candidate against the Democratic-Republican Jefferson. He received 71 electoral votes to Jefferson's 68 and became the second president of the United States.

John Adams was the first president to occupy the White House. He and Abigail moved in near the end of his term, in the fall of 1800. The President's Palace, as it was then known, was still unfinished and littered with building debris. Abigail Adams wrote of it: "We have not the least fence, yard, or other convenience without [outside], and the great unfinished audience-room I make a drying-room of, to hang the clothes in."

Adams' one term as president was marked by troubles, both international and domestic. The foreign affairs crisis involved American neutrality at a time when the British and the French were at war. The French raided American ships. This stirred up a warlike atmosphere in the United States, even inside Adams' own Cabinet. The situation was aggravated by the so-called XYZ Affair.

The XYZ Affair. Adams had sent a three-man diplomatic mission to Paris to arrange a treaty. There the diplomats were visited by three agents of the French foreign minister Talleyrand. These agents, known as X, Y, and Z, asked for a bribe of $240,000. When news of this XYZ Affair reached America, it caused an uproar and led to an undeclared war between the United States and France. But despite immense pressure, including that of members of his own Federalist Party, President Adams knew that the United States was not strong enough to fight the French Empire. He persisted in his efforts for peace, which was finally achieved by the Convention of 1800. Adams considered it his great accomplishment. He said, "I desire no other inscription over my gravestone than: 'Here lies John Adams, who took upon himself the responsibility of the peace with France in the year 1800.'"

Adams' courageous but unpopular peace policy and his stubborn independence in other political matters cost him the support of his own party. The leading Federalists, including the powerful Alexander Hamilton, turned bitterly against him. This led to a hopeless split in their party.

The Alien and Sedition Acts. President Adams' unpopularity was aggravated by the Alien and Sedition Acts. These acts were a direct result of the excitement over the trouble with France. The country was divided into pro-French and pro-British groups. Adams' Federalist Party was strongly anti-French. The opposition Democratic-Republican Party, led by Jefferson, was just as strongly anti-British.

The Federalists were convinced that opposition against them was aroused by the French and Irish living in America. They were sure that the country swarmed with French spies.

The Federalists controlled Congress. In 1798 they decided to crush the opposition through legislation that came to be known as the Alien and Sedition Acts.

The Alien Act contained three provisions. One required that the period of naturalization for foreigners be changed from 5 to 14 years. The second authorized the president to deport all aliens considered dangerous to the peace and security of the country. The third gave the president the power to imprison or banish citizens of an enemy country in time of war.

More serious was the Sedition Act, which was aimed at American opponents of the government. It made it a crime to oppose the administration directly or indirectly. Even those who merely voiced criticism in print were made subject to harsh penalties.

The Sedition Act resulted in the prosecution of 25 persons and the conviction of 10 of them. All were prominent Democratic-Republicans.

These acts were violently unpopular. They were considered an attack on the basic liberties of the American people. President Adams was not personally responsible for them, but they were passed by his party and he signed them. Therefore the blame fell upon him. In the election of 1800, Adams and his party suffered disastrous defeat. The Federalist Party never recovered.

On March 4, 1801, after the inauguration of President Jefferson, Adams retired from public life. He returned to Braintree and devoted the remaining 25 years of his life to

The White House, from a drawing of about 1800.

John Adams (*standing, in rust-colored suit*) and the four other members of the drafting committee present the Declaration of Independence to the Second Continental Congress.

intellectual pursuits, mainly reading (philosophy, religion, political thought, science) and letter writing. He resumed his friendship and correspondence with Thomas Jefferson in 1812. The two men had been separated for 12 years because of political differences. On July 4, 1826—the 50th anniversary of the Declaration of Independence—John Adams died at Quincy. That same day Jefferson died at Monticello, Virginia.

▶ HIS POLITICAL PHILOSOPHY

Adams expressed his ideas in a number of essays and books, as well as in his letters. There are three main elements in his philosophy. One is Adams' view of human nature. Another is his conception of inequality. The third is his idea of government.

```
IMPORTANT DATES IN THE LIFE OF
           JOHN ADAMS

1735   Born at Braintree (now Quincy), Massachusetts,
       October 30.
1755   Graduated from Harvard College.
1758   Began practicing law.
1764   Married Abigail Smith.
1765   Attacked the Stamp Act in articles in the Boston
       Gazette.
1774–  Served in the Continental Congress.
1777
1780   Minister to the Netherlands.
1782   Went to Paris (with John Jay and Benjamin
       Franklin) to arrange peace treaty with Great
       Britain ending the Revolutionary War.
       Treaty of Paris concluded 1783.
1785–  Minister to Great Britain.
1788
1789–  Vice-president of the United States.
1797
1797–  2nd president of the United States.
1801
1826   Died at Quincy, Massachusetts, July 4.
```

Adams did not agree with democrats like Jefferson that men were naturally good and decent. On the contrary, he believed that human beings were basically selfish and only good because of necessity.

Adams also denied the democratic idea of equality. He pointed out that among all nations the people were "naturally divided into two sorts, the gentlemen and the simple men." The gentlemen, being superior in abilities, education, and other advantages, were therefore qualified to rule.

These views underlay Adams' philosophy of government. Since men were greedy and selfish, it was necessary for society to keep them in check. The average human being, he felt, could not be entrusted with power.

Adams believed in liberty and was opposed to tyranny. Though he was sometimes accused of being a monarchist, he actually preferred a republic. But instead of a Jefferson-type democracy, Adams favored a republican government run by an aristocracy of talented men.

Such views, expressed with his typical bluntness, gained Adams unpopularity and even hostility among the American people. But he was not one to seek popular favor. He died as he had lived, an independent, tough-minded, somewhat opinionated and irritable Yankee—but always a courageous patriot and scholar.

SAUL K. PADOVER
Editor, *The World of the Founding Fathers*

JOHN QUINCY ADAMS (1767–1848)

6TH PRESIDENT OF THE UNITED STATES

ADAMS, JOHN QUINCY. Many Americans have sought the office of president of the United States and have deliberately shaped their lives to that end. John Quincy Adams' parents prepared him for the presidency from boyhood. But though Adams achieved his goal, his term in the White House was overshadowed by his two other political careers—as America's greatest diplomat and as its greatest defender of human freedom in the House of Representatives.

▶ AN UNUSUAL CHILDHOOD

John Quincy Adams was born on July 11, 1767, at Braintree (now Quincy), Massachusetts. His father was John Adams, later to become the second president of the United States. His mother, Abigail Smith Adams, was the most accomplished American woman of her time. Young John Quincy grew up as a son of the American Revolution. In 1775, when not yet 8 years old, he stood at his mother's side atop Penn's Hill in Braintree and watched the Battle of Bunker Hill in the distance. His father was then in Philadelphia attending a meeting of the Continental Congress.

John Quincy's education began in the village school. The schoolmaster soon went off to war, and young John studied under his mother's guidance. His education was inspired by his father's letters from Philadelphia. Abigail told her son that the state would someday rest upon his shoulders.

During the Revolution, John Quincy accompanied his father on two diplomatic missions to Europe. He studied at schools in Paris and later at the University of Leiden in the Netherlands. French became his second language. In 1781, at the age of 14, he acted as French interpreter on a mission to Russia. In 1783 John Quincy served as secretary to his father. The elder Adams was then minister to France. Young Adams was present at the signing of the Treaty of Paris, which ended the Revolutionary War.

It was in Paris that John Quincy Adams began his famous diary. He was to continue it for over 60 years. On the title page of the first volume was the proverb that ruled his life: "Sweet is indolence and cruel its consequences." Adams never had a lazy day.

Young Adams returned to Massachusetts in 1785 to complete his education at Harvard College. He graduated in 1787 and then studied law.

WHEN JOHN QUINCY ADAMS WAS PRESIDENT
The 220-foot-high Bunker Hill Monument was begun on the site of the famous battle. The Erie Canal was opened in 1825. Canalboats linked the Great Lakes with the Hudson River, 362 miles away. An early steam locomotive had a speed of 13 miles an hour. Adams' birthplace was in Braintree, Massachusetts.

He had barely developed a law practice when the French Revolution broke out. Articles Adams wrote for a Boston newspaper attracted the attention of President George Washington. In 1794 Washington appointed the 28-year-old John Quincy Adams minister to the Netherlands. Adams' official dispatches and his letters from the Dutch capital at The Hague convinced the President that this young man would one day stand at the head of the American diplomatic corps.

In 1797, while on a mission from the Netherlands to England, Adams married Louisa Catherine Johnson, daughter of the American consul in London.

From The Hague Adams (whose father was now president) was assigned to the Court of Prussia. There he negotiated a treaty of friendship and commerce. He continued his letters and dispatches about the war of the French Revolution. Because of political reasons, John Adams recalled him after Thomas Jefferson was elected president in 1800.

Adams' experiences had convinced him that the United States must never be caught in the "vortex" of European rivalries and wars. This lesson guided him through his later diplomatic career and influenced United States policy for a century afterwards.

▶ A SHORT TERM IN THE SENATE

When he returned to Boston, Adams found the practice of law frustrating. He had a strong desire to enter politics. In 1803 the Massachusetts legislature elected him to the United States Senate. Though elected as a Federalist, Adams felt that party politics stopped at the ocean's edge. To the disgust of Massachusetts Federalists, he voted for President Jefferson's Embargo of 1807. The embargo was aimed at protecting United States neutrality in the wars between England and France. It stopped all American trade with the two countries. Adams' vote in favor of the embargo cost him his Senate seat. The legislature held a special election ahead of time to replace him with a more faithful Federalist.

▶ DIPLOMAT AGAIN

In 1809 President James Madison appointed Adams the first American minister to Russia. Adams was in Russia when the War of 1812 broke out between the United States and Great Britain. He served on the delegation that brought about the Peace of Ghent in 1814. The following year he became minister to Great Britain, where he served until 1817.

By now Adams was in his 50th year. He was without question the most experienced man in the United States diplomatic service. Because of his European experience Adams had become a confirmed isolationist. He felt that the future of the United States lay in expansion across the North American continent rather than in European alliances.

▶ SECRETARY OF STATE

In 1817 President James Monroe called Adams home to become secretary of state. The most important achievements of Secretary Adams were the treaties he negotiated, which brought much of the Far West under American control. The famous Transcontinental Treaty of 1819 (ratified 1821) with Spain gave the United States access to the Pacific Ocean. This was the greatest diplomatic triumph ever achieved by one man in the history of the United States. Adams was also responsible for treaties with the newly independent countries of Latin America.

The Monroe Doctrine

John Quincy Adams had a major role in forming the Monroe Doctrine. Adams' words in that famous document made it clear that the United States would not tolerate any new European colonization in the Americas. The doctrine properly bears President Monroe's name. For it was Monroe who in 1823 first declared its principles to the world as American foreign policy.

The Election of 1824

Adams was never a dynamic politician. But his accomplishments brought him before the people in the national election of 1824. There was no real party contest. The old political parties had disappeared during the so-called Era of Good Feeling of Monroe's administration. It was a contest of men.

General Andrew Jackson, the hero of the battle of New Orleans during the War of 1812, received a majority of the popular vote. But no candidate received the necessary ma-

The 79-year-old Adams sat for this photograph in 1847, a year before he died.

In 1824 John Quincy Adams (*right*) gave a magnificent ball in honor of Andrew Jackson (*center*) on the 10th anniversary of the battle of New Orleans. But soon after, Adams and Jackson became bitter enemies.

jority in the electoral college. Jackson had 99 electoral votes; Adams, 84; William H. Crawford of Georgia, 41; and Henry Clay of Kentucky, 37. Under the Constitution the election had to be decided by the House of Representatives. The voting there was by states and was limited to the first three candidates. On February 9, 1825, Adams was elected president by a bare majority of states.

John Adams, then 90 years old, was delighted at his son's victory. But Abigail Adams did not live to see the presidency come to rest on her son's shoulders. She had died in 1818.

HIS TERM AS PRESIDENT

President John Quincy Adams appointed Henry Clay secretary of state. Clay had thrown the votes of his supporters in the House of Representatives to Adams rather than Jackson. At once Jackson and his followers raised the cry of "corrupt bargain." That there was a political deal seems fairly certain. But there is nothing to show that it was dishonest.

The charge of corrupt bargain was the beginning of a quarrel with Jackson that marred Adams' administration. Jackson had strong support among the voters of the newly admitted states. Adams, after all, had not received a majority of the popular vote. The Jacksonians were out to get rid of Adams and seize office themselves.

The 4 years of Adams' presidency were prosperous and generally happy years for the United States. Adams' ambition was to govern "as a man of the whole nation," not as the leader of a political party. He believed in liberty with power. He favored more power for the federal government in the disposal of public lands and in building new roads and canals to keep up with the westward movement. He supported federal control and protection of the Indian tribes against invasion of their lands by the states.

This program hit at the narrow interpretation of the Constitution under the old Jeffersonian concept of states' rights. It thus aroused Adams' opponents. In the election of 1828 Andrew Jackson was elected president by an overwhelming majority.

With his term as president over, Adams' career seemed finished. He returned sadly to

Quincy, Massachusetts. However, he was still willing to serve his country in any office, large or small. In 1830 he was elected to the House of Representatives. Nothing could have been more pleasing to Adams, for the ghost of the presidency still haunted him. He hoped for the nomination again. But these hopes soon faded.

▶ "OLD MAN ELOQUENT"

During Adams' years in the House of Representatives, the stormy issue of slavery faced the United States. At heart Adams was an abolitionist: he wished to do away completely with slavery. But he was politically prudent, and did not say so publicly. He became a leader of the antislavery forces in Congress but limited his efforts to constitutional means. He sought to abolish slavery in the District of Columbia. He opposed its expansion into the territories of the United States. And he championed the right of petition to Congress for abolition of slavery.

As secretary of state and as president, Adams had tried to obtain Texas from Mexico. But in Congress he resisted to the last the movement for annexation of Texas. By that time the entry of Texas into the Union would have meant the creation of one or more new slave states. On the other hand, he championed the annexation of Oregon, where slavery did not exist. "I want the country for our Western pioneers," he said.

Adams was a patron and supporter in Congress of scientific activities, especially in the fields of weights and measures, and astronomy. He led the movement for establishment

A lithograph of Adams after his collapse in the House of Representatives in 1848.

of the Smithsonian Institution, in Washington, D.C., one of the nation's foremost centers of learning.

"Old Man Eloquent," as Adams was called, opposed the war with Mexico that followed the annexation of Texas in 1845. He considered it an unjust war. On February 21, 1848, while protesting the award of swords of honor to the American generals who had won the war, Adams collapsed on the floor of the House of Representatives. He died two days later in the Capitol.

During most of his early career as a diplomat, Adams was little known throughout the country. His term as president was unpopular. Always a reserved man, he seemed cold and aloof to the people. His career in the House of Representatives made him a violently controversial figure—"Madman of Massachusetts," the pro-slavery people called him. It was not until the final years of his life that Adams won esteem and almost affection, especially in the hearts and minds of the millions who hated slavery. Representatives of both political parties journeyed to Quincy, Massachusetts, for his funeral. Not until his death did John Quincy Adams at last seem to belong to the whole nation.

SAMUEL FLAGG BEMIS
Author, *John Quincy Adams*

IMPORTANT DATES IN THE LIFE OF JOHN QUINCY ADAMS

1767	Born at Braintree (later Quincy), Massachusetts, July 11.
1787	Graduated from Harvard College.
1794	Appointed minister to the Netherlands.
1797	Married Louisa Catherine Johnson.
1797–1801	Minister to Prussia.
1803–1808	Served in the United States Senate.
1809–1814	Minister to Russia.
1814	Headed American delegation that negotiated the Peace of Ghent, ending the War of 1812.
1815–1817	Minister to Great Britain.
1817–1825	Secretary of state.
1825–1829	6th president of the United States.
1831–1848	Served in the House of Representatives.
1848	Died at Washington, D.C., February 23.

In a fiery speech to a group of Boston patriots, Samuel Adams angrily denounced the British Stamp Act.

ADAMS, SAMUEL (1722–1803)

Samuel Adams was a Boston patriot and signer of the Declaration of Independence. As an organizer of the American Revolution, he did much to arouse the colonists against the British rule.

Adams was born into a well-to-do family in Boston on September 27, 1722. He attended the Boston Grammar School and was a graduate of Harvard College.

▶ ORGANIZER OF REVOLUTION

Adams studied law, but gave it up and devoted much of his time to politics. In 1765 he was elected to the Massachusetts legislature and soon became a leader of the radical (anti-British) party. He wrote many angry articles and letters protesting against British laws such as the hated Stamp Act.

As a political leader in Massachusetts, Adams tried to keep anger against British rule always at the boiling point. He denounced the royal governor as an enemy of liberty. Adams insisted that colonial legislatures were not subject to Parliament. He discussed his revolutionary ideas and plans for action with John Hancock, Joseph Warren, Paul Revere, and many others who are remembered for the parts they played in the American Revolution.

Adams organized the Sons of Liberty to protest unjust British acts. He delivered fiery speeches in which he declared that England was reducing the colonies to a state of slavery, misery, and poverty.

When British troops were stationed in Boston, Adams led the protest against them. On the night of March 5, 1770, a large crowd of Bostonians yelled insults and threw snowballs at a detachment of British troops. The soldiers fired into the crowd, killing five Bostonians. Adams used this Boston Massacre as another weapon against British rule.

The British tried to quiet unrest in the colonies by repealing most taxes that angered the colonists. However, Adams continued to warn the people that their liberties were in danger. The British continued the tax on tea, and Adams led protests against paying the tax. He wanted the ships to leave Boston harbor with the tea, but Governor Thomas Hutchinson refused to permit ships to return to England. In 1773 Adams' "Indians" dumped the tea overboard in the now-famous Boston Tea Party.

It was not difficult for Adams to get Bostonians to work against British rule. But long distances, poor roads, and few newspapers prevented colonists from keeping in touch with each other. Adams played a major role in overcoming these obstacles to unity. He organized a "committee of correspondence . . . to state the rights of the Colonists . . . and to communicate the same to the several towns and to the world." His object was to spread news of events in Boston by letter to the other towns. By 1773 about 80 committees had been organized in the towns of Massachusetts. Soon committees of correspondence from Massachusetts to Georgia were helping to speed the colonies toward unity and independence.

Adams' influence troubled the British. Since he was poor, they tried to bribe him, but Adams refused to be silenced by British gold. General Thomas Gage was then ordered to capture Adams on the charge of high treason.

In April, 1775, Adams and Hancock, who was also charged with treason, were in hiding at Lexington, Massachusetts. Gage secretly sent some of his soldiers from Boston to Lexington, where he hoped to capture the rebels and a store of ammunition that patriots had hidden nearby. Paul Revere learned of Gage's plan and rode out to warn Adams, Hancock, and other patriots. Adams and Hancock escaped. As they fled they heard the shots that marked the beginning of the American Revolution. It was a moment of triumph for Adams.

▶ INDEPENDENCE AT LAST

In 1776 Samuel Adams was one of the signers of the Declaration of Independence. His work as an organizer of the revolution was complete. He played a minor role as a member of the Continental Congress during the Revolutionary War. In the peace that followed, fiery old Samuel Adams lived in honorable poverty in Boston. Many people thought he was too much of a firebrand for the new nation. However, Adams did serve as lieutenant governor and one term as governor of Massachusetts before retiring in 1797. Adams died six years later, on October 2, 1803, in Boston.

Reviewed by RICHARD B. MORRIS
Editor, *Encyclopedia of American History*

ADAMS FAMILY

One of the most distinguished families in American history is the Adams family of Massachusetts. The first Adams to come to the colony was Henry, a farmer from England. For about three generations his descendants were simple, hard-working farmers. Then early in the 18th century the family became prominent. Since then there have been Adamses in government, politics, art, and education.

Almost all members of the Adams family recorded their impressions of the times in which they lived. Their diaries, letters, and books are sources for study of the early history of the United States. Their family home at Quincy, Massachusetts, is a national historic site.

Here are brief biographies of some of the leading members of the family. You will also want to read the longer articles about Samuel Adams, John Adams, and John Quincy Adams.

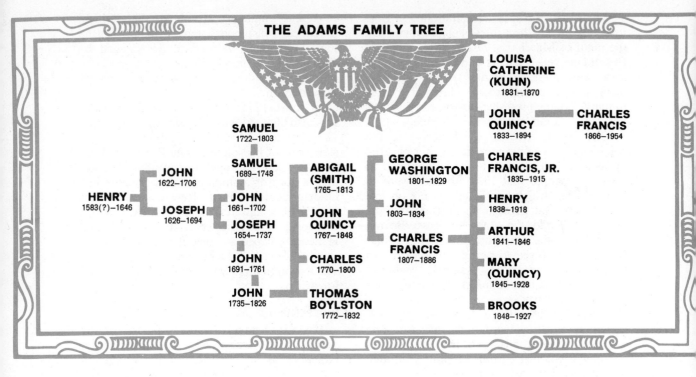

THE ADAMS FAMILY TREE

HENRY
1583(?)–1646

JOHN
1622–1706

JOSEPH
1626–1694

SAMUEL
1722–1803

SAMUEL
1689–1748

JOHN
1661–1702

JOSEPH
1654–1737

JOHN
1691–1761

JOHN
1735–1826

ABIGAIL
(SMITH)
1765–1813

JOHN
QUINCY
1767–1848

CHARLES
1770–1800

THOMAS
BOYLSTON
1772–1832

GEORGE
WASHINGTON
1801–1829

JOHN
1803–1834

CHARLES
FRANCIS
1807–1886

LOUISA
CATHERINE
(KUHN)
1831–1870

JOHN
QUINCY
1833–1894

CHARLES
FRANCIS, JR.
1835–1915

HENRY
1838–1918

ARTHUR
1841–1846

MARY
(QUINCY)
1845–1928

BROOKS
1848–1927

CHARLES
FRANCIS
1866–1954

Henry Adams (1583?–1646) came to New England from Somerset, England, in 1636 and became a farmer at Braintree (now Quincy), Massachusetts. His two famous great-great-grandsons were Samuel and John Adams.

Samuel (1722–1803) is called the father of the American Revolution because of his efforts to make the United States independent. He helped organize the Boston Tea Party and the committees of correspondence. He was a signer of the Declaration of Independence.

John (1735–1826), Samuel's cousin, was also a signer of the Declaration of Independence and a delegate to the Continental Congress. He was vice-president under George Washington and served as the second president of the United States (1797–1801). He was married to Abigail Smith.

John Quincy (1767–1848) was the best-known son of Abigail and John Adams. He served the United States as a diplomat, secretary of state, senator, sixth president (1825–1829), and representative to Congress. He married Louisa Johnson.

Charles Francis (1807–1886) was the distinguished son of John Quincy Adams. He won fame as a diplomat and statesman. He was a leader in politics, served in Congress, and was Lincoln's ambassador to Great Britain during the Civil War. He had three famous sons:

Charles Francis, Jr. (1835–1915) was an economist and historian. He was president of the Union Pacific Railroad for a number of years but was also active in public school reform.

Henry (1838–1918) was a well-known historian. His two most famous books are *The Education of Henry Adams* and *Mont-Saint-Michel and Chartres*.

Brooks (1848–1927) was also a historian. He believed that western Europe was losing importance and that the United States and Russia would be the great powers of the future.

Charles Francis (1866–1954), great-grandson of John Quincy, was a lawyer, businessman, yachtsman, and from 1929 to 1933 served as secretary of the navy under President Herbert Hoover.

ADDAMS, JANE (1860–1935)

Jane Addams was the founder of Hull House, one of America's first settlement houses. She also crusaded for world peace and for the right of women to vote.

Jane Addams was born in Cedarville, Illinois, on September 6, 1860. Her family was a large and wealthy one with a tradition of public service. Jane wanted to be a doctor, but she was not well enough for the hard study of medical school. To improve her health, her family sent her to Europe.

While traveling, Jane wondered what she could do to help people. Remembering the Chicago slums she had seen as a child, she thought of starting a settlement house to provide education and recreation for the poor. Jane traveled to London to study the famous English settlement house, Toynbee Hall. When she returned to Chicago in 1889, Jane and her friend Ellen Gates Starr rented an old house that had once belonged to the Hull family. This became Hull House.

Between 1870 and 1900 millions of immigrants came to the United States. Many found life very hard in the new country. Jane Addams welcomed them warmly to Hull House. Some came to play games. Some listened to poetry readings or took classes in painting, music, or acting. Others studied English and citizenship. A day nursery cared for children whose mothers worked. Hull House became a center of the community.

Shortly after opening Hull House, Jane Addams began working for laws that would end child labor, so that children could go to school. She was angry because women could not vote, so she campaigned for woman suffrage. Jane Addams' fame spread, and when her book *Twenty Years at Hull House* was published in 1910, she won nationwide recognition for her work.

From 1914 until her death Jane Addams pleaded for a world that would be free from war. She served as president of the Women's International League for Peace and Freedom, and as chairman of the Woman's Peace Party. In 1931 she won the Nobel peace prize (with Dr. Nicholas Murray Butler). Four years later, on May 21, 1935, Jane Addams died, mourned by thousands of people.

ADDITION. See ARITHMETIC.

ADDRESS, FORMS OF

If you were to meet a governor, a rabbi, or an archbishop, how would you address that person? If you wanted to write to the president of the United States, how would you begin your letter?

Forms of address are ways of addressing people in speech or in writing. In everyday life we use some forms of address quite naturally. Aunt, Uncle, and Cousin are forms of address that are familiar to us, as are Grandpa and Grandma or Grandfather and Grandmother. The family physician is addressed as Doctor, as are many people in the academic world. We address adult acquaintances as Mr., Mrs., or Miss.

History and Use of Present-day Titles

Most titles used today come from other times and places. Mister (Mr.) comes from the old title Master, just as Mrs. and Miss come from Mistress. These words were once used to emphasize the high social position of particular persons. Today they serve as courtesy titles for all. The term Mr. applies to all men, Mrs. to all married women, Miss to unmarried women and girls. Some people prefer the title Ms. for all women, whether married or unmarried.

The courtesy title Honorable, given to many government officials, is used in written address and in formal introductions. It is never used by officials in speaking of themselves or by others in social conversation.

Esquire, first used for an attendant to a knight, continued in use as a form of address for gentlemen. Placed after a name—Ernest Johnston, Esquire—it takes the place of Mr. In British usage this title belongs by birth to certain eldest sons. Lawyers and justices of the peace in the United States formerly received the title out of politeness. Some law firms still use the form in correspondence with their clients.

OFFICIAL	ADDRESS IN WRITING	SALUTATION OF LETTER	INTRODUCED AS OR REFERRED TO	SPEAKING TO
President	The President The White House	Dear Mr. *or* Madam President	The President *or* Mr. *or* Madam Adams	Mr. President *or* Sir *or* Madam
Vice-President	The Vice-President United States Senate	Dear Mr. *or* Madam Vice-President	The Vice-President *or* Mr. *or* Madam Jones	Mr. Vice-President *or* Sir *or* Madam
Cabinet Members[1]	The Honorable Albert Cox *or* Ann Graham Secretary of Labor[1]	Dear Sir *or* Madam	The Secretary of Labor[1] Mr. Cox *or* Mrs. Graham	Mr. *or* Madam Secretary, Mr. Cox *or* Mrs. Graham
Senators[2]	The Honorable Carl Day *or* Maria Montez United States Senate	Dear Senator Day *or* Senator Montez	Senator Day *or* Senator Montez	Senator Day *or* Senator Montez
Representatives[3]	The Honorable David Bell *or* Edna Lane House of Representatives	Dear Mr. Bell *or* Mrs. Lane	Mr. Bell *or* Mrs. Lane	Mr. Bell *or* Mrs. Lane
Speaker of the House	The Honorable John Lawson Speaker of the House of Representatives	Dear Mr. Lawson	The Speaker, Mr. Lawson	Mr. Speaker *or* Mr. Lawson
Chief Justice, Supreme Court	The Chief Justice The Supreme Court	Dear Mr. *or* Madam Chief Justice	The Chief Justice	Mr. *or* Madam Chief Justice
Associate Justices, Supreme Court	Mr. *or* Madam Justice Fein The Supreme Court	Dear Mr. *or* Madam Justice	Mr. *or* Madam Justice Fein	Mr. *or* Madam Justice *or* Mr. *or* Madam Justice Fein
American Ambassadors	The Honorable Leo St. John *or* Ada James American Ambassador The American Embassy	Dear Mr. *or* Madam Ambassador	The American Ambassador	Mr. *or* Madam Ambassador
Foreign Ambassadors in America	His Excellency David Brice *or* Her Excellency Joan Johnston Ambassador of Canada	Dear Mr. *or* Madam Ambassador	His (*or* Her) Excellency, the Ambassador from Mexico	Mr. *or* Madam Ambassador
Governors	The Honorable Henry Harris *or* Lucy Stone Governor of Maine	Dear Governor	The Governor *or* Governor Harris *or* Stone	Governor Harris *or* Stone
Mayors	The Honorable Irving Ames *or* Susan Brown Mayor of Detroit	Dear Mayor Ames *or* Mayor Brown	Mayor Ames *or* Brown, *or* the Mayor	Mayor Ames *or* Brown, Mr. *or* Madam Mayor
Judges[4]	The Honorable Kenneth Lee *or* Laura Rossi Judge of _____ Court	Dear Judge Lee *or* Rossi	Justice Lee *or* Rossi	Justice Lee *or* Rossi

Madam was originally a title of quality given to a woman of high rank or to a nun. It comes from *ma dame,* French for "my lady." Today it is used in addressing office-holders (Madam President, for example). Married women who are not from English-speaking countries are addressed as Madame.

Excellency, once used only in reference to kings and princes, now serves as a title for certain high dignitaries of state (as a governor or an ambassador) and church (as a Roman Catholic archbishop or bishop). Two American states—Massachusetts and New Hampshire—have officially adopted the term Excellency for use in referring to their governors. The term may be used as a courtesy title for the governor of any state.

Eminence, formerly a title of honor for various church ranks, is now used only in addressing a cardinal.

In writing to officers and enlisted personnel of the United States Army or Navy,

RELIGIOUS ORDERS

OFFICIAL	ADDRESS IN WRITING	SALUTATION OF LETTER	INTRODUCED AS OR REFERRED TO	SPEAKING TO
JEWISH				
Rabbi with Doctor's Degree	Rabbi Nathan Stein, D.D.	Dear Rabbi Stein *or* Dear Dr. Stein	Rabbi Stein *or* Dr. Stein	Rabbi Stein *or* Dr. Stein
Rabbi without Doctor's Degree	Rabbi Abram Cohn	Dear Rabbi Cohn	Rabbi Cohn *or* Rabbi	Rabbi Cohn *or* Rabbi
PROTESTANT				
Bishop, Episcopal[5]	The Right Reverend Henry Bronson Bishop of Dallas	Right Reverend Sir *or* Dear Bishop Bronson	Bishop Bronson *or* Dr. Bronson, the Bishop of Dallas	Bishop Bronson
Minister with Doctor's Degree	The Reverend James Cleves *or* Elsie Ray	Reverend Sir *or* Madam Dear Dr. Cleves *or* Dr. Ray	The Reverend Dr. Cleves, The Reverend Mr. Cleves, Dr. Cleves, *or* Mr. Cleves	Dr. Cleves *or* Dr. Ray
Minister without Doctor's Degree	The Reverend Charles Moore *or* Doris Hart	Reverend Sir *or* Madam My dear Mr. Moore *or* Miss (Mrs., Ms.) Hart	The Reverend Charles Moore *or* Doris Hart	Mr. Moore *or* Miss (Mrs., Ms.) Hart
ROMAN CATHOLIC				
Pope	His Holiness, the Pope, *or* His Holiness Pope John Paul II Vatican City	Your Holiness *or* Most Holy Father	His Holiness, *or* The Pope, *or* The Holy Father, *or* The Pontiff	Your Holiness *or* Most Holy Father
Cardinal	His Eminence James, Cardinal Flynn Archbishop of New York	Your Eminence	His Eminence James, Cardinal Flynn	Your Eminence
Archbishop (or Bishop)	The Most Reverend John Erhart Archbishop (or Bishop) of New York	Your Excellency	The Most Reverend John Erhart *or* His Excellency, Archbishop (or Bishop) Erhart	Your Excellency, Archbishop (or Bishop) Erhart
Monsignor	The Right (or Very) Reverend Monsignor Volpe	My dear Monsignor Volpe *or* Dear Monsignor Volpe	Monsignor Volpe	Monsignor Volpe
Priest	The Reverend Patrick Foley	Reverend Father *or* Dear Father Foley	Father Foley	Father Foley
Sisterhood, Member of	Sister Mary Rose Hayes, S.C.	Dear Sister *or* Dear Sister Mary Rose	Sister Mary Rose	Sister Mary Rose

[1]Exception—The Attorney General is addressed or referred to as the Attorney General of the United States, not as Mr. *or* Madam Secretary. [2]Members of state senates—Same as for U.S. senators. [3]Members of state houses of representatives (or assemblies)— Same as for U.S. representatives. [4]Exception—The Presiding Justice of an Appellate Division is addressed as "Dear Mr. *or* Madam Justice." [5]Bishops of other denominations are addressed as "The Reverend ———," not as "The Right Reverend ———."

use the person's title and name: General George Thompson; Sergeant Margery Hall; Commander Virgil Beasley; Donald Lambert, Machinist's Mate 2. (Note that a Navy petty officer's title follows the name.) Dear Sir or Madam is the proper salutation of a letter to an officer or enlisted person in the Army or Navy.

Courtesy demands that we use the proper title and form when speaking or writing to people who hold certain positions. Envelopes carrying letters should be properly addressed, with a title such as Mr., Mrs., or Ms. or with a special courtesy title. Such a title is, in a way, part of a name.

ISABELLE FORST
Former Assistant Superintendent of Schools
New York City

See also LETTER WRITING.

ADEN. See YEMEN (ADEN).

ADHESIVES. See GLUE AND OTHER ADHESIVES.

ADJECTIVE. See PARTS OF SPEECH.

ADOLESCENCE

The time of growing up from childhood to adulthood is known as adolescence. It is a period of physical growth. But it is more than that. It is a time for the maturing of mind and behavior as well. The length of time for this period of development varies. Adolescence can start at 9 and end at 18. It can start at 14 and end at 25.

Young people may grow quickly in some ways and more slowly in others. This is why children who may be only 9, 10, or 11 years old may be adolescents in some ways already, while teenagers of 13 or 14 may just be reaching adolescence.

For example, 11-year-old Sue is already 163 centimeters (5 feet 4 inches) tall. Her body is fully developed, and people often think she is 15 or 16. But sometimes she acts very babyish. She has not yet learned to concentrate, so her schoolwork is far below that of others in her class.

On the other hand Ricky, at 14, is quite thin and short. He looks much younger than he is. But he is the brightest boy in his class. He is editor of his school newspaper, and his teachers and friends know that he is reliable and capable.

Sue is adolescent because of her physical growth, and Ricky because of his maturity of mind and behavior. When they "catch up with themselves," they will be well on the way to adulthood.

During adolescence young people begin to find out about themselves and what they want to do, what kind of people they want to be.

Adolescence can be a time of creative energy and vitality, of great zest for living. It can also be a time for self-expression, curiosity, and exploration, a time of discovery and adventure. Slowly but surely boys and girls accept more and more responsibility for their own behavior. If they do not expect too much of themselves too quickly, they find adolescence an exciting and rewarding time of life.

▶ **THE BODY BEGINS TO CHANGE**

Only a short time ago, the adolescent boy or girl had the body of a child. Now many physical changes begin to take place. Girls become aware that their breasts are developing. They begin to have more of a waist-line, and there are signs of pubic hair as well as hair under their arms. Boys may notice that their voices are becoming deeper and that there are signs of hair on their faces as well as on their bodies.

Before, during, or after some of these changes, girls will begin to menstruate and boys will begin to mature sexually. These are normal glandular changes. They show that the organs of reproduction are being prepared for the part they will some day play.

Both boys and girls may feel that their arms and legs are growing too fast for the rest of their bodies. They may feel clumsy and awkward. Glandular changes sometimes cause acne, a skin disturbance. The skin may become oily, and pimples may appear. It is natural for young people to feel strange and uncomfortable about these physical changes. They often seem to occur before the boy or girl feels ready for them. But part of growing during adolescence is getting acquainted with the new self that is appearing and gradually accepting the changes that are taking place.

▶ **FEELINGS ARE CHANGING, TOO**

These body changes affect feelings as well as appearance. The glands and hormones that are bringing about external physical changes are also working toward a new internal balance. This is hard work for the body. There are times when adolescents feel very tired and seem to need a lot of sleep. At times they may feel happy and lively, at other times gloomy and depressed. Ups and downs are natural during adolescence. As the physical changes within become more stable and balanced, boys and girls begin to have more control over their feelings.

Adolescents still feel unsure of themselves, so they are annoyed at anything that makes them feel exceptional or different, whether it is wearing glasses or braces or having too many freckles. As young people gain self-confidence through all the experiences of growing and learning, they are able to accept themselves as they are. Then being different becomes a pleasure instead of a disaster.

▶ **ADOLESCENTS CAN HELP THEMSELVES**

An adolescent boy or girl is not merely a spectator who just stands by and watches as all these changes in body and feelings take place.

The adolescent is directly involved. The changes are happening to him or her. Boys and girls can help themselves a great deal during this time. If they have periods of fatigue, they can plan their homework and social activities so that they get extra sleep and relaxation. If they feel full of energy, they can participate in sports at school or go bowling or dancing. They can eat sensibly and take proper care of their bodies.

They can also help themselves by seeking information and advice about the things that are troubling them. At this time a number of questions and worries come up in the minds of adolescents. They want to be free and independent, but they still need the strength and support their parents give them. They are concerned about their future roles as mature men and women. Soon they will be ready to choose careers and adult relationships. Adolescents are often troubled by their suddenly awakened feelings about sex. It is quite normal for people at this age to begin to feel strong physical desires.

Both boys and girls need reassurance and information. They can get information from reading. Or they can talk to their parents. Sometimes it is hard for young people to talk freely and openly with their parents, because the relationship is so close. Then an understanding adult who is not part of the family may be able to help. It may be easier to confide in a favorite teacher or camp counselor. The person whose advice an adolescent seeks should be someone whom she or he trusts and who has enough background and experience to be of help.

If boys and girls feel guilty and unhappy about some of their thoughts, if they keep all their fears and confusions to themselves, they will make this an unnecessarily difficult period.

▶ **GROWING UP WITH OTHERS**

This is a time that will influence a boy's or girl's choice of adult companions, of a vocation, and even of a marriage partner.

Friends

Making friends and learning how to be a friend take on special importance during adolescence. At first the most important thing is popularity. Boys and girls want to be well liked. They want to do what their friends want to do, and be what their friends want to be. This is all part of feeling unsure.

Later on, young people become more selective about their friends. They begin to choose those who have the same ideas and interests or those who are interesting because they have different backgrounds. As boys and girls develop their own standards popularity becomes less important to them than the genuine affection of individuals they admire.

Young people often need to make friends among those of their own sex before they feel ready for relationships with the opposite sex. It is natural to feel more at ease with those who are having the same experiences and feelings. Then, as girl-boy friendships begin and become more intense and personal, a girl or a boy has to face some important issues and make some important decisions.

Dating is one problem. Should girls and boys date only one person because it makes them feel safe and popular or because everyone else in the crowd is dating only one person? Or should they go out with many different kinds of people in order to learn more about themselves, to find out what relationships give them the most satisfaction?

The intimacy that develops between a girl and a boy who go out only with each other often brings another problem. How far should an adolescent girl and boy permit this intimacy to lead them? The sexual drive in young people can be very strong. It is a powerful and often disturbing feeling. Girls and boys are also very curious about sex. It is a great unknown. They have certain worries and fears about it, too. Both girls and boys hope that they will be attractive and appealing to members of the opposite sex, but they feel confused and uncertain about just how this can be accomplished.

As boys and girls mature they try to understand their feelings about sex. They try to find answers to their questions so that they can set standards for their own behavior. The more responsible and mature they become, the more they think about long-range goals. They are willing to give up immediate satisfactions for something that is more important to them in the future. The more they care about their own feelings and needs, the more sensitive they are to other people. They understand the need for making choices seriously, rather than on a sudden impulse, to avoid hurting themselves and others.

Family

All adolescents have mixed feelings about their families. There are times when boys and girls feel that they could manage very well if only their parents would leave them alone. At other times young people feel uncertain and inexperienced and confused. They wish their parents would take over and tell them what to do.

Many conflicts with parents come up over social relationships. Teenagers are often so eager to belong to a group that they do not always use good judgment in making dates. Then their parents have to step in and help them by keeping some control over their activities. This is especially true when matters of health and safety are concerned. But when boys and girls show signs of greater maturity and sounder judgment, parents usually have more confidence in them and allow them to make more decisions and choices.

Family chores and responsibilities are other common causes of conflict. Teenagers are very much involved with their own interests, and they are apt to forget that as members of the family group they have certain obligations. At times they feel they are being nagged at about everything. Their rooms are untidy, their clothes are not neat, they sleep too late, they talk on the phone too much, they go to bed too late, they are careless with money, they do not allow enough time for homework. At times teenagers feel overwhelmed with criticism. But at other times they may sense that all their parents' comments are really signs of loving and caring.

Sometimes younger brothers and sisters seem to be a nuisance. Teenagers resent babysitting. It interferes with their privacy and cuts into their free time. Older sisters and brothers may tease teenagers, and this makes them feel young and foolish. But all this is only one side of the picture. Adolescents still need their families and the special kind of love a family gives, and their families still need them.

Some rebellion against adult authority is healthy—within limits. An adolescent wants to become a strong and independent person, and that is right. But this is not accomplished by fighting against adults. Learning to be an understanding, co-operating member of the family is, in the long run, the biggest sign of growing up.

But adolescents cannot grow up alone. They need the help and understanding of the adults who are closest to them. Parents can help their teenagers as they mature. One of the best ways is simply by acting as parents. This means being strong and firm when the occasion calls for it. Children may call their parents old-fashioned. They may say, "You don't understand me." But wise parents overlook such expressions. They know that many times teenagers ask for permission to do something they are not ready for. They ask because the whole crowd is asking, and they do not want to be different. But secretly the teenagers want their parents to say "No," to set limits for them. They need to feel that their parents have authority and will use this authority wisely. Teenagers also need to know that their parents will not take a firm stand one day and then give in the next day. They want their parents to be consistent.

Being firm, of course, does not mean being too strict, and being consistent does not mean being stubborn. Understanding parents give their teenagers love and encouragement and let them feel that they are free to grow but have not been set adrift.

▶ LOOKING AHEAD

A young child finds it hard to imagine being grown up. Adulthood seems so far away and strange. To a child what happens each day matters most. The child is not really interested in what will happen next month, next year, or in the next ten years.

During adolescence all that changes. The subjects boys and girls study in school and the marks they get have a great deal to do with their plans for a vocation. Their friendships with other boys and girls and their dating have a clear relationship to adult love and the choice of a marriage partner.

One of the most exciting things about adolescence is that it suddenly brings the future so much closer. Growing up makes adolescence a very special time.

EDA J. LeSHAN
Author, *You and Your Feelings*

ADOPTION

Adoption is a way for children who cannot be cared for by their natural parents to become members of another family. Certain laws and procedures create the same legal relation between adoptive parents and a child as the one that exists between natural parents and a child. Adoption ends the child's ties to his natural parents. After adoption the child has a new and permanent home.

▶ WHY CHILDREN NEED ADOPTION

In most countries children are brought up in their natural families, which are made up of a father, a mother, and the children born to them. Some natural parents, however, cannot give the love and care that every child needs. They are often very young and unmarried. They did not think ahead of time about the responsibilities of being parents. These parents may decide, after much sorrow, to give up the child for adoption. They want the child to have a chance to grow up in a real family.

Other children may lose their parents by death, accident, illness, war, or some other disaster. Sometimes parents with serious personal problems neglect or abandon a child. Children may be left for a long time in temporary foster homes or institutions. Then it may become clear that their parents will never be able to take them home. In all these cases someone responsible for the child, instead of the parents, has to decide that adoption will be best for the child.

Families have to be found for children who no longer have parents to care for them. There are, fortunately, many childless people who wish to adopt. They have a great desire to love and bring up a child and to have a child who loves them. Also, some parents who already have children want to share their love and family life with another child who needs parents.

▶ WHO IS ADOPTED

The children who are adopted in the United States are mostly white babies. They go into their new homes shortly after birth. It has usually been difficult to find families for older, handicapped, or nonwhite children. Recently, however, a greater number of these children—especially black, American Indian, and Asian children—are being adopted.

The total number of children adopted each year, which had been steadily increasing for years, has begun to level off. It is estimated that in the United States more than 150,000 children are adopted each year.

About half are adopted by a stepparent, by grandparents, or by other relatives. The others are adopted by unrelated people.

▶ HOW ADOPTION TAKES PLACE

Children needing families and people seeking children may be brought together in several ways. Most of the adoptions by nonrelatives now take place through social agencies.

Physicians, lawyers, clergymen, and other well-meaning individuals have frequently arranged adoptions. Sometimes a dishonest person tries to make money by finding a child for someone willing to pay a high price.

Arrangements by individuals have in some cases been harmful to a child, to natural parents, or to adoptive parents. An individual cannot usually give the time, help, and protections needed in adoption. Many difficulties are prevented when social agencies are responsible for planning adoption and selecting adoptive parents.

Social agencies are established and supported by concerned people in a community or by state governments. Some agencies have been given the duty by law to protect children and to provide adoption and other social services. Such agencies are known as child-welfare agencies, children's aid societies, or family and children's services.

▶ ADOPTION SERVICES

The purpose of an adoption service is to help children and, also, natural parents and adoptive parents. Social workers, who have special training, skills, and experience, provide the service. They know how to study children and find out what may be best for each child. They work with physicians, psychologists, and lawyers. They use the advice of other experts in selecting suitable parents for a particular child. Then they help adoptive parents take the necessary steps to complete a legal adoption. Agencies usually charge a fee for this service, based on ability to pay.

Parents and older children especially may need continuing help as they become a family. Most problems that occur are the usual ones that all parents and children have. Some of the problems have to do with adoption. For example, adoptive parents are encouraged to help a child understand, as soon as the child is able, what it means to be adopted. It is not easy to explain about adoption. Many adoptive parents would like to keep it a secret. Sooner or later, however, adopted children discover that they have not been born to their parents. Many become upset about it. They wonder why their natural parents gave them up. They may imagine that they would have been happier with those other parents. They are curious about their heredity.

It takes time for children to feel comfortable about being adopted. They have to learn that real parents are the ones who help a child grow up and feel loved. They have to know why parents give up a child. Usually it is because the parents care about the child and want him or her to have a better family life than they could ever provide.

▶ LEGAL PROCESS

An adoption must take place according to law. In each state and in most countries, laws have been passed that say how the relationship of parent and child can be ended and a new one created. The laws require certain procedures to be followed. These are designed to protect the various people, and especially the child, involved in an adoption.

The parent-child relation is very important in our society. The law requires that a judge must decide whether it should be broken. A judge must also grant an adoption decree to make the adoption legal and final. The adoptive parents must go to court and ask that lasting family ties between the child and them be established. They must first wait until the child has lived with them for a set period of time. Then the judge has to make sure that the adoption is likely to benefit the child. The judge considers all the facts obtained in a study of the case and talks with a child if he is old enough to understand. After the decree all court records are sealed. No one can see these without a court order. Then a new birth certificate for the child is issued with the names of the adoptive parents. Lawyers are used in an adoption to see that all legal procedures are properly carried out.

▶ TRENDS IN ADOPTION

Adoption is mentioned in ancient legends, myths, and stories. The Bible, for example, describes the adoption of Moses by Pharaoh's daughter. The Roman general Julius Caesar adopted his grand-nephew Octavius.

Formerly the purpose of adoption was to provide a childless family with an heir to inherit property or to continue a family name. It was not until 1851, in Massachusetts, that the first adoption law to protect children was passed. Since then people have become more concerned about the child's welfare in adoption.

Gradually ideas about adoption have changed. Adoption is now considered a way to find families for children. Communities and social agencies are trying to give more children the benefits of adoption. One reason is the belief that every child has a right to a family.

The number of white infants who need adoptive homes has been decreasing. At the same time many other children are waiting to be adopted. Social agencies are using new methods to find families who can enjoy caring for an older child or for a child with handicaps. People who are black or members of other minority groups are encouraged to consider adopting children. In some states the law allows single persons to adopt children, and this practice is becoming more and more common. Legislation has been advocated to help families who choose to adopt children with special problems. The adoptive parents of such children would be given allowances to help them pay their expenses.

National and international organizations, including national associations of doctors, lawyers, hospitals, and state governments, have prepared guides and models to improve adoption practices.

In addition various organizations are engaged in research. They are trying to find out how to make adoption as satisfactory as possible for children and adoptive families.

ZITHA R. TURITZ
Former Director, Standards Development
Child Welfare League of America, Inc.

ADVERTISING

Advertising is part of our daily lives. To realize this fact, you have only to leaf through a magazine or newspaper or count the radio or television commercials that you hear in one evening. Most people see and hear several hundred advertising messages every day. And people respond to the many devices that advertisers use to gain their attention.

Advertising is a big business—and, to many people, a fascinating business, filled with glamour and excitement. It is part literature, part art, and part show business. Many young people want to work in advertising. The rewards can be great, but the work is hard, and the hours are often long. Advertising is more than an exciting game in which clever people spend their time writing catchy slogans and entertaining clients.

▶ **WHAT IS ADVERTISING?**

Advertising is the difficult business of bringing information to great numbers of people. The purpose of an advertisement is to make people respond—to make them react to an idea, such as helping to prevent forest fires, or to make them want to buy a certain product or service.

At the beginning of the 20th century, advertising was described as "salesmanship in print." If this definition were expanded to include radio and television, it would still stand today. The most effective way to sell something is through person-to-person contact. But the cost of person-to-person selling is high. Because it takes a great deal of time, it increases the cost of the product or service. Advertising distributes the selling message to many people at one time.

▶ **THE MEDIA**

To bring their messages to the public, advertisers must use carriers, such as newspapers, magazines, radio, and television. The carrier of a message is called a medium of communication, or simply a **medium**. The four media (plural of medium) just mentioned are the ones most commonly used. Other media include billboards, posters, printed bulletins, films, skywriting, and even the old-fashioned "sandwich boards"—signboards that were once commonly paraded up and down the streets.

An example of public service advertising. Woodsy the Owl promotes an antipollution campaign.

Unusual methods that have been used to attract attention include messages painted on the sails of boats or trailed from high-flying kites.

When advertisers select a medium or a group of media to carry a message, they must think of the kind of product they are selling and the kind of people who are most likely to buy it. Then they must figure out how to reach the largest possible number of these people at the lowest possible cost. The cost of reaching a thousand people—the "cost per thousand"— is different in each medium. In print media such as newspapers and magazines, advertisers buy **space** in which to display their messages. In the broadcast media—radio and television— they buy **time** in which to present them.

Most magazines, newspapers, and radio and television stations in the United States depend on advertising for their support. Without advertising, radio and television would have to charge their listeners and viewers directly or be supported by the government. Newspapers and magazines would have to charge much higher rates to their readers. In most cases the

This Canadian poster teaches the metric system. An average-sized hamburger weighs about 100 grams.

price would be so high that the average reader would not want to pay it, and the magazine or paper would go out of business.

Magazines

Magazines cover a wide range of audiences. There are general magazines that reach several million people with varied interests. And there are hundreds of magazines for readers with special interests. They offer the advertiser a good way to reach a particular group of likely customers. An advertiser who is trying to sell washing machines, for example, would choose a magazine for homemakers rather than one for hunters or boat owners. And an advertisement for fishing rods would be placed in a fishing magazine rather than in a general magazine or a newsmagazine.

Newspapers

Most newspapers reach an audience that is concentrated in one geographical area—a town, a city, or a county. Most are published daily or weekly. Because of these two facts, newspapers have several advantages for advertisers. Ads placed in newspapers often bring quick results. And advertising can be placed in newspapers on very short notice. Usually ads can be placed for a specific day—to announce a sale, for example. If the ad had to be published a week or a month in advance, many people would forget about the sale before it took place. An advertiser can also choose to place an ad in a special section of the newspaper, such as the sports section or the food section, or in the classified pages, where ads of similar kinds are grouped together.

Local businesses depend on newspapers to reach customers in their neighborhoods. Newspapers also carry a great deal of advertising for nationally sold products, sometimes mentioning local dealers' names.

Radio and Television

Nothing has had so profound an effect on advertising as the development of the broadcast media—radio and television. Radio took words off the printed page and gave them a voice and a sound of urgency. It lacks the advantage of a visual image, but it reaches into places that other media do not, such as automobiles. Television is the most dramatic of the media. Because it combines sight, sound, and motion, it gives advertisers many ways of catching customers' attention.

Radio and television use every dramatic device possible to get their messages across. Commercials may be presented as short plays that tell how a new detergent can make washday pleasant or how a headache remedy can transform someone who is grouchy and ill-tempered into a cheerful, lovable person. Jingles help plant the name of the advertiser's product in the listener's mind. In radio, tones of

Television commercials are an important part of advertising. These actors promote a pudding.

A huge outdoor billboard advertises a special museum exhibition.

voice and sound effects—like breaking glass or slamming doors—attract the listener's attention. In addition to the devices used by radio, television uses elaborate sets, picturesque costumes, and amusing cartoons to help put the message across. Filming commercials has become a business in itself.

To attract listeners on a nationwide or regional basis, advertisers **sponsor** programs— that is, they pay the costs of producing the program. An advertiser who does not wish to sponsor an entire program may sponsor part of a program or may purchase **spot announcements** between or during programs. Television has become advertising's glamour medium, and today a minute's time on television may cost advertisers hundreds of thousands of dollars.

Outdoor Advertising

Outdoor advertising is one of the oldest media. It is usually colorful and strong on illustration, and it has short selling messages. It consists mainly of billboards and posters. Billboards are placed in locations where surveys have shown that they will be seen by large numbers of people. They range from the common **showing**, or **panel**, of lithographed paper sheets pasted together, through the more permanent and more expensive **painted bulletin** (painted on the billboard or side of a building), to the eye-catching and very costly **spectacular**, which uses flashing lights to attract attention. By flashing the lights in proper sequence, the spectacular can create the effect of motion, such as a coffee cup being filled or

an animated cartoon. Because of their high cost, it is not practical to use painted bulletins or spectaculars for products with slogans that change frequently.

Posters are often placed in train stations and in buses and railroad trains. This is called **transit** advertising.

Direct Mail and Direct Response

In direct mail advertising, the advertiser mails material to potential customers, urging some action, such as buying a product or subscribing to a magazine. You or members of your family have probably received such material, perhaps addressing you by name. This kind of advertising is effective because it is almost like person-to-person selling. In most cases, the advertiser can select the audience. Direct mail specialists assemble their lists of names and addresses from such sources as telephone books and lists of automobile registrations, magazine subscriptions, and book club memberships. For selling automobile equipment, for example, a list of automobile registrations would be a good choice.

Direct mail advertising asks for a direct answer. This makes it easy for advertisers to measure their response. They can compare how much money was spent on a mailing with how much money the mailing brought in. Then they can decide whether the advertising approach was successful.

Direct response advertising is radio or television advertising that invites people to call or write "right now" for information or to order a product. It is the broadcast equivalent of direct mail advertising.

▶ NATIONAL AND RETAIL ADVERTISING

From the marketing, or selling, point of view, advertising has two main divisions.

National advertising is used to promote products or services that are sold all over the country or over large areas. Examples are products such as automobiles, soft drinks, and household appliances, as well as services such as insurance and air travel. Such products and services are advertised in magazines with nationwide circulation and on nationwide radio and television programs.

Retail advertising is used by local businesses. Unlike most national advertising, retail advertisements give specific prices and dealers' addresses. Department stores, drugstores, automobile dealers, and banks are typical retail advertisers. Most retail advertisements are carried by newspapers, direct mail, and local broadcasting stations. They are usually prepared by the business that is doing the advertising or by a local agency. Some large businesses have special departments to handle retail advertising.

In the United States, about 45 percent of advertising money is spent on retail advertising, and 55 percent on national advertising. Of the two types, national advertising has a more direct influence on the products and services the consumer buys. The rest of this article will therefore deal with national advertising. For simplicity's sake, services will be considered products.

▶ THE AGENCY

In most cases, manufacturers and other national advertisers do not produce their own advertising. Instead, they rely on specialists—the advertising agencies. These agencies bring together a number of people with specialized talents in various fields. To be in close touch with business activities, the agencies are usually located in major cities and may have branch offices.

The advertising agency is a service company. It earns its income from planning, creating, researching, producing, and placing printed advertisements and broadcast commercials for its clients.

Large agencies employ a wide variety of specialists, including writers, artists, photographers, moviemakers, musicians, actors, producers, directors, sociologists, and psychologists. There are also experts in economics, law, accounting, marketing, management, and research.

Each client of the agency is served by an account team representing most of these specialties. The team's job is to create the client's advertising. But everything the team does must be approved by the client—the kind of advertising that is chosen, the media that are used, and the amount of money that is spent. To do this, the person in charge of the team, called the **account manager** or **account executive**, meets often with the client. The account executive may also confer periodically with the client's sales manager to determine whether the campaign has increased sales.

Research

The first step in preparing an advertising campaign is to conduct research on the possibilities of the product. The members of the agency team must find out what qualities of the client's product are most likely to appeal to the buying public. They must know how the product compares with competing products. They learn where the product can be bought and how it is sold. The team also investigates the age, sex, occupation, income, and special interests of the product's best customers—or prospective customers, if the product is a new one. Even such factors as climate, season of the year, and holidays have a bearing on sales. For instance, umbrellas sell best in rainy seasons; cold remedies, in winter; turkeys, around Thanksgiving; and soft drinks, in warm weather.

Nearly every product has a selling pattern of this sort. The client and the agency must be sure that the right selling message reaches the right people in the right place at the right time.

The Consumer Proposition

After studying this information, the team's writers and artists, working with the **creative director**, explore different advertising approaches. Finally, they arrive at a consumer proposition—a simple, convincing statement about the product that will make it stand out

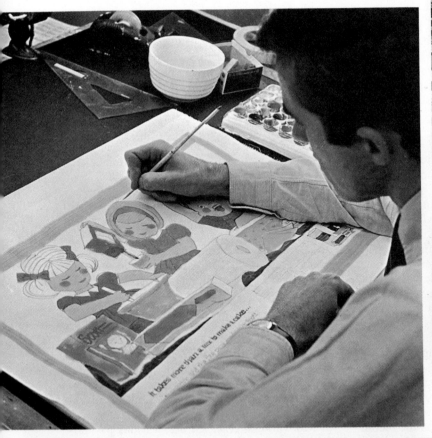

Left: An artist works on the rough for a new advertisement. Above: Artist and art director discuss changes for the comp, or second stage. Below: The final ad.

It takes more than a mix to make a cake...
teamwork, and the fine paper products by Scott

To wipe up the spills that occur, no matter how efficient the teamwork, ScotTowels with extra drying power.

To cover the cake once it's baked (a precaution against frosting-snitching fingers) Cut-Rite Wax Paper, triple-waxed and extra strong.

To wipe off sticky little fingers (when the frosting gets snitched anyway):

Scott Family Napkins, the paper napkins that are strong and absorbent... yet are soft, like cloth.

To blot the tears of the "uninvited." Scotties. They float up one at a time, or you can reach in for a nice handful. Amazing, isn't it, how many times a day you reach for a fine paper product made by Scott?

SCOTT MAKES IT BETTER FOR YOU

from competing products. The basic idea of the consumer proposition may be that the product is good for you, tastes good, is a bargain, lasts a long time, works well, or looks attractive. There are many themes that can be developed. Sometimes several propositions are developed and tested on consumers to see which has the most appeal.

Creating the Advertisement

When the consumer proposition has been agreed upon, it is converted into actual advertisements. Whatever idea has been chosen, the ad must express it clearly and in such a striking way that the consumers will remember it.

The proposition is expanded into the **copy platform**, which sets up the advertisement as it will appear. Layouts are made for printed media such as newspapers, magazines, and posters. Scripts are prepared for radio commercials. A storyboard—a series of pictures with captions for spoken dialogue or written messages—is set up as rough copy for a live television commercial. Writers and artists work together in producing this material.

When the rough draft is ready, the account manager presents it to the client for approval. Usually the team designs one ad as the recommended approach, as well as several alternative ads so that the client can see different possibilities. The alternatives are in rougher form than the recommended ad, but the client still gets a good idea of what they would look like in final form. This preliminary draft is called a **comp**, or **comprehensive**.

When the client has approved the advertisement, it is put into final form. Finished art or photography is prepared, and type is set for printed advertisements. This material is then sent to an engraver or a printer. Films and tapes for the broadcast media are produced by specialists outside the agency.

Meanwhile, media planners at the agency determine the size, color, and dates for printed advertisements, the time periods for broadcast commercials, and the costs in each case. These must also be approved by the client. The materials for the completed advertisement are then shipped to the media owners with authorization for their use on specific dates or for specific periods of time at agreed-upon rates or prices.

The agency checks to make sure that each advertisement or commercial actually appears in the proper form and at the proper time. If everything is satisfactory, the agency then bills the client and pays the media. The agency deducts a 15 percent commission for its services when it pays the media, so that it is actually paid by the media, not by the client. A few agencies work for flat fees rather than commissions. Under this system, the client pays the agency a sum of money in addition to the cost of producing the advertising.

▶ WHAT MAKES CUSTOMERS BUY?

Advertisers and their agencies have spent great amounts of time, money, and effort trying to determine what makes potential customers want a product. There is no single answer. To find the special quality of a product that will cause people to buy, advertisers often turn to research.

Several kinds of research are employed in advertising. **Marketing research** explores sales patterns, problems, and possibilities for a product. **Product research** is designed to discover how the public feels about a product. **Copy research** discovers how well an advertisement gets its message across.

Motivational research uses various psychological techniques to uncover unexpected motives that can be appealed to in advertising. (Motives are thoughts or feelings that make people act.) Motivational researchers have discovered that very often the reasons customers give for buying a particular product are not the real reasons. In fact, many of the customers' true motives are not reasonable at all. For instance, many people do not buy automobiles for convenient and reliable transportation, although this is the reason they will usually give if asked. They buy a certain type of car because they feel that it will make them look important.

But not all advertising appeals to these kinds of motives. When owners of businesses buy trucks for making deliveries, they are not concerned with seeming important. They are looking for trucks that do the job efficiently without breaking down. Industrial advertising is generally straightforward and factual.

Similarly, a consumer may buy a certain brand of soap because it is used by a glam-

Imaginative copy and a striking picture draw attention to this magazine advertisement.

orous movie star or sports figure. But when selecting a new refrigerator, that same consumer does not expect glamour. More important are such matters as how much food it will hold, whether the food is easy to reach, and how efficiently a particular model uses energy.

Printed advertisements may use either or both of these approaches. Some may appeal to the rational mind through straightforward presentation of facts about a product. Others, which appeal more to the emotions, may concentrate on the headline and illustration, with very little text. Many advertisements combine rational and emotional approaches. For example, some automobile ads feature glamorous illustrations but also describe the car's good handling qualities or efficient use of fuel.

ADVERTISING AS A CAREER

The average advertising agency has a need for people with many different kinds of experience and talent. But opportunities are not unlimited. Some estimates suggest that there are probably not more than a few thousand places for newcomers in advertising each year.

There is no one talent that guarantees success in advertising. But it is essential to be genuinely interested in the process of selling.

And people who work in advertising must believe in the importance of what they are doing.

Most advertising jobs require the ability to use language with skill and imagination. Other important qualities are curiosity and the ability to use imagination in analyzing problems and situations. Retail selling experience is excellent preparation for a career in advertising. But more and more, agencies are seeking people with college training. The American Association of Advertising Agencies, in New York City, offers information about careers in advertising.

HISTORY

Advertising is very old. It can be traced back as far as the public criers of ancient Greece—who, for a fee, shouted out messages about their clients' wares to one and all. But it first became important in the late 15th century, when the merchants of the rapidly growing cities and towns needed a way to tell people where their goods could be bought.

The first printed advertisement in the English language appeared in 1478, more than a century before Shakespeare's first play was produced. This early ad was the work of William Caxton, England's first printer, who used it to advertise religious books from his own workshop. Caxton posted small printed notices along London's main streets. Besides advertising his product, he identified his shop with a red-striped shield so that customers could find it easily.

This same sort of simple, informational advertising is still used. Examples are the roadside signs that tell travelers that they can buy fresh corn just down the road or that there is a restaurant in the next town.

The Industrial Revolution, in the 18th and 19th centuries, brought a new kind of advertising. Large factories took the place of small workshops, and goods were produced in large quantities. Manufacturers used the newly built railroads to distribute their products over wide areas. They had to find many thousands of customers in order to stay in business. They could not simply tell people where shoes or cloth or tea could be bought—they had to learn how to make people want to buy a specific product. Thus modern advertising was born. Advertising created new markets and helped to raise standards of living as people came to feel that they had a right to new and better products.

Advertising agencies began to develop in the United States just after the Civil War. At first these agencies merely sold space in the various media, mainly newspapers and magazines. But they soon added the service of writing and producing advertisements. From these beginnings, advertising has developed into a highly specialized profession.

▶ PROS AND CONS OF ADVERTISING

Advertising has received a great deal of criticism from various sources. Its critics say that it appeals to unworthy motives like vanity, snobbery, and the fear of being "left out." And they say that high-pressure advertising makes people buy some things that they do not really need and cannot afford. Another common criticism is that some advertising is deceitful or downright dishonest.

Most advertising people regret abuses of their profession. Advertising agencies and media work against deceptive practices by setting standards within the industry. In the United States there is also some government regulation. Consumer interests are protected by such agencies as the Federal Trade Commission, the Federal Communications Commission, and the U.S. Postal Service. State and local agencies, as well as private organizations, work to prevent false or misleading advertising.

Defenders of advertising say that it stimulates the economy by helping to keep production and employment high. Without advertising, they say, industries that today can produce more goods than ever before would grind to a halt for lack of customers to buy their products.

Advertising is used for public service messages as well as for commercial ones. Smokey the Bear, who warns the public against the dangers of forest fires, is a creation of the advertising industry. Advertising agencies produce the campaigns of organizations such as the Red Cross, helping them to gather money for their work. And advertising is an efficient way of telling large numbers of people about new ideas, useful inventions, and scientific discoveries.

Advertising is an important part of modern society. Its importance is likely to grow as more countries become industrialized.

DON JOHNSTON
Chairman and Chief Executive Officer
J. Walter Thompson Company

This 18th-century advertisement, simply listing products, shows how advertising has changed.

Paul Revere & Son,

At their BELL *and* CANNON FOUNDERY, *at the North Part of* BOSTON,

CAST BELLS, of all sizes; every kind of Brass ORDNANCE, and every kind of Composition Work, for SHIPS, &c. at the shortest notice; Manufacture COPPER into SHEETS, BOLTS, SPIKES, NAILS, RIVETS, DOVETAILS, &c. from Malleable Copper.

They always keep, by them, every kind of Copper fastening for Ships. They have now on hand, a number of Church and Ship Bells, of different sizes; a large quantity of Sheathing Copper, from 16 up to 30 ounce; Bolts, Spikes, Nails, &c of all sizes, which they warrant equal to English manufacture.

Cash and the highest price given for old Copper and Brass.   march 10

AENEID

The most famous work in Latin literature is the *Aeneid,* an epic poem about the hero Aeneas. Epic poetry tells a powerful story of conflict and is written in a noble, complex style. Publius Vergilius Maro, whom we call Vergil, began the *Aeneid* about 29 B.C. at the request of the Emperor Augustus. Vergil worked on it for over 10 years. He meant to spend 3 more years revising the poem, but he died in 19 B.C. before he could complete it. On his deathbed he asked for his manuscript, intending to burn it because he felt it was imperfect, but his friends refused to give it to him. It was published as Vergil left it.

The 12 parts (called books) of the *Aeneid* tell the story of Aeneas, a legendary ancestor of Augustus. At the end of the Trojan War, when his native city, Troy, was destroyed by the Greeks, Aeneas escaped with his father, Anchises; his son, Ascanius; and a band of followers. He intended to build a new Troy, and searched long for a site. After founding several settlements (which failed) and having many adventures, he and his party were shipwrecked in North Africa and were given shelter in the city of Carthage.

Carthage was ruled by the beautiful Queen Dido, who fell in love with Aeneas and wanted him to marry her. But the gods had chosen him to go on to Italy, where his descendants would found the Roman nation. The messenger of the gods, Mercury, came to Aeneas and reminded him of his destiny. So Aeneas left Dido, who killed herself in despair.

Aeneas and his men sailed across the Mediterranean and landed at Cumae, in Italy. There he met the sibyl, a prophetess who guided him to the underworld so that he could consult the spirit of his father. Anchises told his son that he was to establish a city in central Italy and that his descendants were to be the founders and citizens of Rome. Then he showed him the souls of the great Romans of the future, waiting for their time to be born; among them was Vergil's own friend and patron, the Emperor Augustus.

The last six books of the *Aeneid* tell of the settlement in Italy and the warfare between the Trojans and some of the Italians, who rise against the invaders. The poem ends with a fierce duel between Aeneas and his chief enemy, Turnus. Turnus is killed, and Aeneas' triumph is assured.

Tales of Aeneas and Rome had been told by the older Roman poets Naevius and Ennius. Vergil owes something to them. He also owes a debt to Homer, from whose *Iliad* and *Odyssey* he borrowed freely, intending to create a Roman epic that would rival Homer's work. The wanderings of Aeneas in the first six books are like the wanderings of Odysseus in the *Odyssey;* the fighting in the last six books of the *Aeneid* is like the savage battles of the *Iliad.*

Vergil also follows Homer in using gods as characters in the story. The gods struggle against one another to help or hinder Aeneas. This means that he was not merely a wanderer, but a man with a great mission. Even with a spiteful goddess opposing him, he succeeded, and worked out the will of fate.

The *Aeneid* is a proudly national epic, showing Rome as the chief carrier of civilization. Its poetry is magnificent. It has many fine phrases, such as the opening line, "Arms and the man I sing," the warning, "I fear the Greeks even when they bring gifts," and the advice to Rome, "Spare the conquered and crush the proud." Its scenes and symbols stir our imagination: the golden bough that opens the path to the underworld, the shield of Aeneas decorated with the battles and the champions of future Rome, the description of the fall of Troy, and the mystical vision of heaven filled with noble and happy souls.

The *Aeneid* was the greatest achievement in the golden age of Latin literature, and it has continued to influence poets through the centuries. Dante Alighieri, the greatest Italian poet of the Middle Ages, called Vergil his master and his model. English poetry also has been shaped by Vergil. Shakespeare read him at school, and quotes him several times. Chaucer, Spenser, Milton, Tennyson, all imitated him, each in his own way. Poets in French, German, Spanish, and other European languages also felt his power and tried to equal his artistry. Although he himself had imitated Homer, he was one of the great creators of Western literature.

GILBERT HIGHET
Author, *The Speeches in Vergil's Aeneid*
See also VERGIL.

AERODYNAMICS

Aerodynamics is the science that tells what happens when air, or any other gas, moves rapidly. Its name comes from two Greek words meaning "air" and "power." Aerodynamics sometimes deals with air moving against an object—like wind filling the sails of a boat. Sometimes it deals with an object moving through air—like an airplane flying through the sky. The same laws apply in both cases.

▶ PUTTING AIR TO WORK

Long before anything was known about aerodynamics, people noticed that moving air pushed things. The wind scattered leaves and bent tree branches. Strong winds could uproot trees and knock down houses. Hunters could run faster and throw spears farther when the wind was behind them.

In time people learned how to put the wind to work. They built sailboats and windmills. Today we still use the wind in these ways. But an understanding of aerodynamics has opened up many other ways of using the power of moving air. For example, it is an understanding of aerodynamics that has made possible all heavier-than-air craft. This includes airplanes, helicopters, hovercraft—in fact, all aircraft except balloons, which are lighter than air and float in it.

The Dream of Human Flight

The first flying machines made a very old dream come true, for people have always envied birds their ability to fly through the air. Since ancient times there have been myths and legends about people who could fly like birds. Perhaps the best-known story tells of Daedalus, the Greek craftsman who was imprisoned with his son Icarus. Using birds' feathers and wax, Daedalus made two pairs of wings. When he and Icarus put the wings on, they were able to fly away from the prison. But Icarus flew so close to the sun that the wax in his wings melted. The feathers dropped out, and Icarus fell into the sea and drowned.

The flight of Daedalus and Icarus was only a story, but the idea of flying like a bird seemed possible to people for hundreds of years. It was a long time before anyone realized that the human body is simply not built in a way to allow birdlike flight.

Powered flight in a heavier-than-air craft had to await several things. One was an understanding of aerodynamics. And this began more than 200 years ago with a discovery made by a Swiss mathematician who was studying, not flight, but the flow of water in pipes.

▶ BERNOULLI'S PRINCIPLE

The Swiss was Daniel Bernoulli, who came from a family of famous scientists and mathematicians. In the 1730's Bernoulli began to investigate what happened to water flowing through pipes that were partly blocked. He experimented by putting obstacles of different sizes in pipes and keeping track of differences in the speed and pressure with which the water flowed (Fig. 1).

The first thing Bernoulli discovered was that the water flowed faster as it went past an obstacle. Then he discovered that wherever the water flowed faster, it lost some of its normal pressure. On the far side of the obstacle the flow of water slowed down again and pressure returned to normal.

The explanation is that steadily flowing water has a constant amount of energy. This energy depends on both the speed and the pressure of the water. If more of the energy goes into speed, then there is less for pressure; if less goes into speed, then there is more for pressure. To put it another way, where the speed is great, the pressure is small. This idea is known as Bernoulli's principle.

Other scientists became interested in what Bernoulli had discovered. They began to experiment with what happened inside pipes of different shapes. One of the first to do

Figure 1. Bernoulli investigated what happened to water flowing through pipes that were partly blocked.

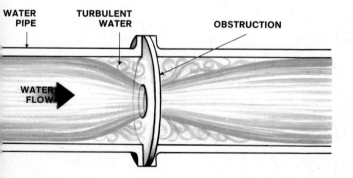

WATER PIPE TURBULENT WATER OBSTRUCTION

WATER FLOW

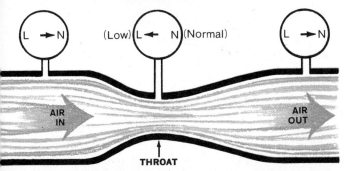

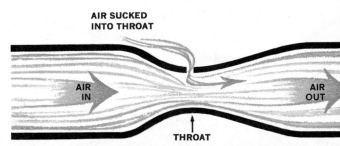

Figure 2. When air passes through the throat of a venturi tube, it moves faster. When the air moves faster, its pressure decreases. With air as with water, the greater the speed is, the smaller the pressure is.

Figure 3. Normal air pressure outside tube is greater than air pressure in the throat. Therefore outside air is forced in through a small hole in the throat. The force increases as air in throat flows faster.

this was an Italian scientist named Giovanni Venturi. Later a pipe invented for such experiments was named the venturi tube, in his honor.

▶ THE VENTURI TUBE

The drawing in Figure 2 shows a venturi tube. Notice that its shape resembles the path taken by the water through the pipe in Bernoulli's original experiment.

Experiments with the venturi tube revealed an important fact: Air passing through the tube behaves the same as water. When air passes through the tube's throat (narrow section), it moves faster. When the air moves faster, its pressure decreases. That is, the greater the speed of the air, the smaller its pressure. At sea level, still air presses down with a force of 1.036 kilograms per square

centimeter (14.7 pounds per square inch). But when air passes through the throat of a venturi tube, its pressure is less than that.

Now suppose air is moving through a venturi tube that has a small hole in its throat (Fig. 3). Tiny bits of paper scattered near the hole will be pushed into the tube because the outside air pressure is greater than the pressure in the throat. The outside air forces its way in, carrying the bits of paper along. The faster the air flows in the throat, the greater this inward force becomes.

The venturi tube has been put to use in many ways. A paint sprayer, a perfume atomizer, and an automobile carburetor are three devices that depend on it. In each a liquid is made to move by a difference in air pressures. The liquid is broken into drops that are driven forward by the airstream (Fig. 4).

Figure 4. Difference in air pressure forces paint up into sprayer tube.

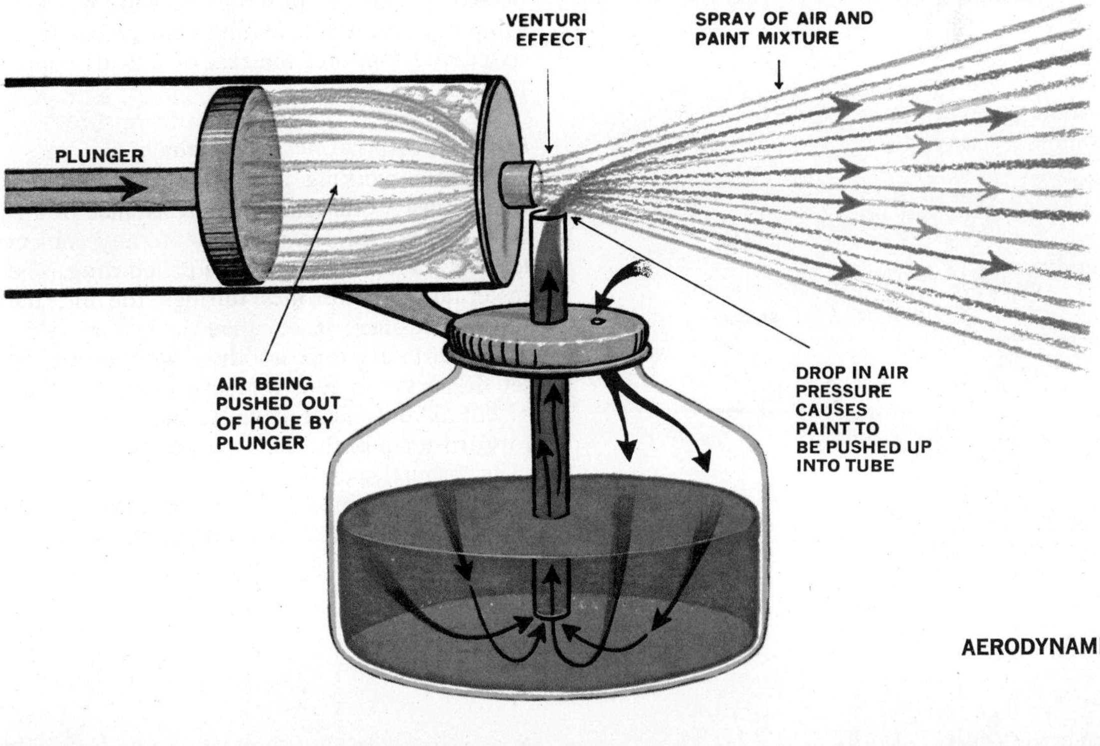

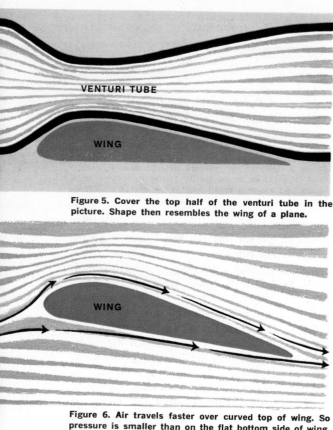

VENTURI TUBE

WING

Figure 5. Cover the top half of the venturi tube in the picture. Shape then resembles the wing of a plane.

WING

Figure 6. Air travels faster over curved top of wing. So pressure is smaller than on the flat bottom side of wing. The greater pressure on bottom causes wings to rise.

Figure 7. You can demonstrate lift this way.

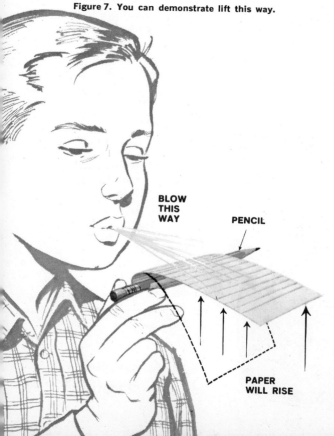

BLOW THIS WAY

PENCIL

PAPER WILL RISE

The principle of the venturi tube also applies to an airplane in flight.

▶ WHAT KEEPS A PLANE UP IN THE AIR?

Cover the top half of the venturi tube in Figure 5. Notice that the shape of the tube resembles the curved top surface of a cross section of an airplane wing. The bottom of the wing is flat (Fig. 6). This means that the top surface is longer than the bottom. As the plane wing rushes through the air, the particles of air are separated. They move over or under the wing and meet again behind the wing. The air that passes over the wing has a longer way to go, so it must move faster. As we saw, more speed means less pressure. So the pressure above the wing is lower than the pressure beneath the wing. The wing, and the plane it is attached to, are forced upward. The upward force is called **lift**, and it offsets the downward force of **gravity**. As a plane's speed increases, so does the lift of the plane's wings.

You can demonstrate lift by curling a piece of paper around a pencil (Fig. 7). Blow across the top of the paper, and it rises. This happens because you make air move above the paper. The pressure of the moving air above is less than the pressure of the still air below. So the piece of paper, like the airplane wing, rises.

A wing develops lift in a second way. The wing is set into the plane at a slight angle. Air that hits the bottom of the wing is deflected downward, pushing the wing upward. About two thirds of a wing's lift comes from its curved top, and the rest of the lift comes from the bottom.

Other Forces That Act on a Plane

Besides working against gravity, an airplane must work against the resistance of air. Air resists the movement of any object through it. This resistance is called **drag**. The faster an airplane flies through the air, the more drag there is.

An airplane opposes drag with **thrust**. A jet or rocket engine forces a powerful blast of hot air out of the back, to move the plane forward against the air's resistance.

In propeller-driven planes, thrust is provided in another way. The engine turns a propeller rapidly. The propeller pulls its

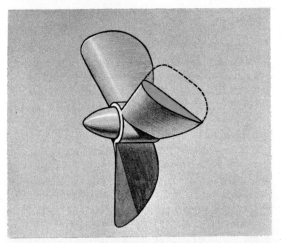

Figure 8. A propeller blade is shaped like a wing. Because of curved surface, there is less pressure in front of the propeller blades than behind them.

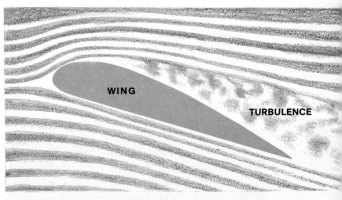

Figure 9. Smoke is used to make streamlines visible in wind tunnel. If the smooth, gently curving streamlines break up and become irregular, turbulence results.

way through air somewhat as a wood screw pulls itself through wood. But a propeller turns much faster, and there is a great deal of slipping.

As Figure 8 shows, a propeller blade is shaped like an airplane wing—flat on the back side and curved on the front side. As a blade revolves, air passes over the two sides. Its speed is greater when it passes over the curved side, and so the pressure is less. This means that there is less pressure in front of the propeller than behind it. The propeller moves forward, pulling the rest of the plane with it.

Stalling Speed and Turbulence

There is a certain minimum speed that an airplane must have if the amount of lift is to be greater than the force of gravity. This minimum speed is called the airplane's stalling speed. A plane must be moving faster than its stalling speed to take off. It cannot stay up in the air if it flies slower than its stalling speed.

An airplane also loses lift if the smooth flow of air over its wings is disturbed. This disturbance is called turbulence. Turbulent air swirls in eddies above the wings.

▶ STREAMLINING

Drag is a special problem for designers of high-speed planes because drag increases much faster than speed does. If a plane is to fly at 200 kilometers (125 miles) an hour, the engines' thrust must overcome a certain amount of drag. But at twice that speed the drag is four times as great, and at three times that speed the drag is nine times as great.

To reduce drag as much as possible, all parts of an airplane exposed to the air are streamlined. Streamlining helps to make the air flow over an airplane as smoothly as possible. A scientist thinks of streamlines as imaginary lines along which particles of air flow smoothly. Streamlines can be made visible in a wind tunnel by letting small tubes blow thin lines of smoke into the airstream (Fig. 9). If the streamlines are smooth, gentle curves, the airflow is called **laminar**. Laminar airflow causes the least amount of drag. If the streamlines break up and become irregular, turbulence results.

The perfect streamlined shape is neither round like a ball nor pointed like an arrowhead. The shape that causes the least amount of drag is a teardrop. But airplane wings cannot be shaped like teardrops. With the perfect streamlined shape, there is no difference in pressure between air flowing above and underneath an object. This means there is no lift. So airplane wings are shaped like half teardrops (Fig. 10). This shape provides the most lift with the least drag.

Figure 10. Airplane wings are shape of half teardrop.

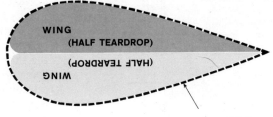

TEARDROP SHAPE

▶ THE SOUND BARRIER

The designers of modern high-speed planes must also take into account what happens when a plane passes the speed of sound. At sea level the speed of sound is about 1,225 kilometers (760 miles) an hour. At higher altitudes the particles of air are farther apart and the speed of sound is less. As it reaches the speed of sound, an airplane is said to meet the sound barrier.

Air flows smoothly past the wing of a plane flying at less than the speed of sound. But at the speed of sound, the wing and other parts of the plane produce a thin, cone-shaped wave of compressed air, called a **shock wave**. There is turbulence around the wave, and this increases drag, destroys lift, and shakes the plane violently. A plane must be specially designed to go through the sound barrier safely. Even so, pilots try to go through it as quickly as possible into the smooth flight of **supersonic** (faster than sound) speeds.

Figure 11. Shock wave occurs as air piled up in front of high-speed airplane wing is forced to part.

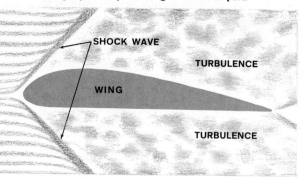

A shock wave spreads out like the wave formed by the bow of a ship. Just as the ship's wave strikes the shore, the shock wave may sweep along the ground below the plane. It causes a thunderlike noise called **sonic boom**. If a plane is flying low enough, the boom may break windows and shake houses.

Speeds of fast-moving planes are measured in units called **Mach numbers**. The numbers are named after Ernst Mach (1838–1916), an Austrian scientist. A plane traveling at the speed of sound is said to fly at Mach 1. For a plane flying at twice that speed, the Mach number is 2. A space capsule re-entering the earth's atmosphere may travel at Mach 20 or higher.

▶ OTHER CRAFT

The principles of aerodynamics apply to several kinds of craft.

Lighter-Than-Air Craft

Lighter-than-air craft such as dirigibles and balloons do not require forward motion to produce lift. They rise because they are filled with a gas that is lighter than air. However, the design of such craft must take drag into account. And for controlled, forward motion, the craft must provide its own thrust.

Gliders

Gliders have no engines and so have no thrust. For launching they must be pulled forward or shot into the air to overcome gravity. But once in the air, glider pilots use the changing currents to gain lift. By control-

---

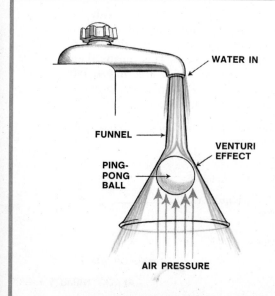

BERNOULLI'S PRINCIPLE

Here is a way to demonstrate that pressure decreases as speed increases. You will need a funnel and a ping-pong ball.

First turn on a medium flow of cold water into the sink. Place the ping-pong ball in the flow. Let the ball go. It will be carried down to the sink.

Next hold the funnel upside down at a water faucet so that water runs through the funnel. Put the ping-pong ball up into the funnel and let it go. The ball will be suspended in the stream of water and it will not fall down. The explanation is that the shape of the funnel allows the water to go around the ball. In going around the ball, the water must flow faster. Therefore, the pressure of the water drops at the obstacle. The water now has less pressure than the air has, and the ball is held in place by air pressure.

British-built hovercraft is 8 meters (27 feet) long, carries 10 passengers, has top speed of about 100 kilometers (60 miles) an hour.

Ryan X-13 was world's first VTOL jet. It could rise straight up, hover, fly, and land vertically on a column of jet-hot gas.

U.S. Navy's first hydrofoil—a boat with underwater wings. Forward movement provides lift. Wings rise like a plane's, raising hull. With less resistance, speed increases.

ling the relation between lift and drag, glider pilots can stay aloft for many hours. Gliders are sometimes compared to birds. But in many ways birds are more like airplanes, since they create "thrust." Only when birds soar can gliders be compared to them.

Helicopters

Helicopters also use the basic aerodynamic forces. Helicopters have no recognizable wings. But the rotating blades—called rotors —are a combination of wings and propeller. As they revolve, the rotors act like wings by creating lift. By using the controls to tip the rotors slightly, the pilot can make the helicopter travel forward or backward, go up and down, and hover (stand still) in the air.

VTOL Aircraft

VTOL aircraft (vertical takeoff and landing aircraft) have the advantages of both standard airplanes and helicopters. They can fly through the air like propeller or jet airplanes and can take off and land like helicopters. Engine thrust is used for a straight-up takeoff, then for forward movement, at speeds greater than those of a helicopter.

Hovercraft

A hovercraft is meant not to fly high but to hover just above the surface of water or land. The propeller is on the bottom of the craft. When the propeller turns, it pushes air down, against the surface. A "skirt" around the edge of the craft helps to confine the air, allowing the hovercraft to ride a short distance above the surface. A second source of thrust moves the craft forward. Instead of using the lift of a wing, the hovercraft rides on a cushion of air.

IRA M. FREEMAN
Rutgers, The State University of New Jersey

See also AVIATION; BALLOONS AND BALLOONING; GLIDERS; HELICOPTERS; SUPERSONIC FLIGHT.

AERONAUTICS. See AVIATION.

AESOP. See FABLES.

AFGHANISTAN

Afghanistan was once known as the "forbidden kingdom" of Central Asia because few foreigners were allowed to cross its borders. This rugged, mountainous country was isolated until recent times. In 1978, Communists took power. They were opposed by many Afghans, and in 1979, Soviet troops entered the country to put down a rebellion.

▶ **THE PEOPLE**

Most Afghans belong to one of five different groups. The Pushtuns, who live in the south, and the Tajiks, who live in the northeast and around the city of Kabul, are the most numerous. They speak languages very much like Persian. The Uzbeks and the Turkomans live on the northern plains. And the Hazaras live in the mountains. The Uzbeks and the Turkomans speak languages similar to Turkish, but the Hazaras have adopted one of the Persian languages. Most Afghans are Muslims. They follow the teachings of Mohammed. More than 500,000 people live in and around Kabul, the capital city of Afghanistan.

FACTS AND FIGURES

DEMOCRATIC REPUBLIC OF AFGHANISTAN is the official name of the country. Afghanistan means "Land of the Afghans."

CAPITAL: Kabul.

LOCATION: Central Asia. **Latitude**—29° 22′ N to 38° 30′ N. **Longitude**—60° 28′ E to 74° 52′ E.

AREA: 647,497 km² (250,000 sq mi).

POPULATION: 15,500,000 (estimate).

LANGUAGE: Pushtu and Persian.

GOVERNMENT: People's republic. **Head of government**—president. **International co-operation**—United Nations, Colombo Plan.

NATIONAL ANTHEM: *Soroode Meli* ("National Anthem").

ECONOMY: Agricultural products—grain, cotton, fruits, wool, karakul pelts. **Industries and products**—cotton and wool textiles, rugs, carpets. **Chief minerals**—coal, iron ore, oil, natural gas, salt, lapis lazuli. **Chief exports**—natural gas, fresh and dried fruits, karakul pelts, cotton, wool. **Chief imports**—cloth, sugar, petroleum products, motor vehicles, tea. **Monetary unit**—afghani.

Way of Life

In the past most Afghans were nomads. Some people still make their living this way. They are always on the move, searching the dry plains and plateaus for water and fresh pasture for their sheep and camels.

In recent times many nomads have given up the nomadic life and have settled down to make a living as farmers. Their farms are very small, and they use only the simplest hand tools. It is quite usual to see farmers plowing their fields with wooden plows or cutting their wheat crops by hand with sickles. Threshing machines are unknown, and cattle are walked back and forth across the threshing floor to separate the grain from the stalks.

Some farmers and nomads have moved to the cities in recent times. Kabul, Kandahar, and Herat are the largest cities. The managers, civil servants, and mechanics who are making Afghanistan a modern country live in the cities. City people live in stone or mud-brick houses. The roofs are often made of mud plastered over wooden poles. This is a protection when an earthquake occurs because the wood bends with the shock. But the roofs sometimes leak on rainy days when the mud is washed away. Homes of the wealthy have tiled or marble floors, but the homes of the poorer people usually have mud floors. Furniture and thick rugs add comfort to the homes of the well-to-do Afghans. In the simpler homes quilts are spread on the floor for beds, and floor pads and cushions are used for chairs.

Farmer, nomad, and city dweller meet and mingle in Afghanistan's colorful markets and bazaars. In the bazaars, tobacco, snuff, luscious fruits, spices, rugs, and carpets are displayed in small shops along winding streets. Until the summer of 1959, Afghanistan's women visited the bazaars only when wearing a *chaderi* over their usual clothes. This is a tentlike garment that covers everything but the feet. Today, thanks to a change in government policy, many women have discarded the *chaderi*. In the cities, especially, women wear Western clothes.

Many city men wear Western suits. But

the brimless karakul hats on their heads add a distinctive Afghan touch. Farmers and nomads cling to their old styles of clothing. Turbans wound around their heads give protection from the cold in winter and from the blazing sun in summer. Long, baggy pantaloons and long, quilted coats complete their costumes. One sign of the changing times in Afghanistan is the sight of a turbaned man wearing a Western suit jacket over his traditional pantaloons.

Today's young girls are growing up in a fast-changing Afghanistan and will lead lives very different from those of their mothers. More schools are being built so that all girls and boys can have at least 6 years of elementary education. Many women today hold jobs outside their own homes.

The boys enjoy playing Western games like soccer and hockey, but it is every boy's ambition to ride well enough to play the national game, called buz-kashi. Buz-kashi is a form of polo. Instead of using a ball as in polo, buz-kashi players use a calf's or goat's carcass. The horses used for this game are swift and well-trained.

Every boy also learns the vigorous national dance called attan. The music and frenzied dancing of this warlike dance remind both dancer and watcher alike of Afghanistan's long and hard fight for freedom and independence.

▶ THE LAND

Afghanistan is a land-locked Asian country wedged between Pakistan, Iran, and the Central Asian republics of the Soviet Union. Its area is somewhat larger than that of France and slightly more than twice that of Italy.

About two thirds of Afghanistan is mountainous. The snowcapped Hindu Kush mountain range and the Pamir mountains rise in the northeast. The highest point in Afghanistan is Nowshak, which rises to 7,485 meters (24,557 feet). The mountains are lower in the southeast. Here the twisting Khyber Pass, about 1,050 meters (3,450 feet) above sea level, links Afghanistan with Pakistan. Dry, dusty plains lie north of the mountains, along the shores of the Amu Darya. In the west and south are barren lowland desert areas.

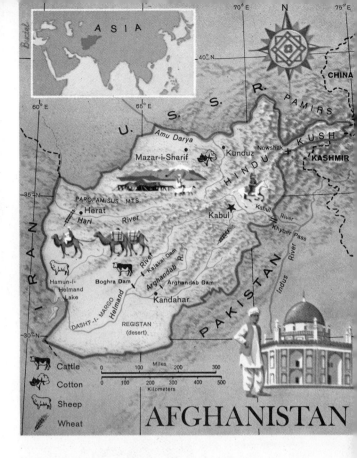

AFGHANISTAN

For centuries herders in Afghanistan have lived nomadic lives. In summer they herd their sheep, goats, and camels on mountain pastures. In the winter they return to the warmer lowlands.

There are textile mills in Afghanistan, but some spinning is still done by hand.

Although new factories have been built in Afghanistan, much remains unchanged.

Cattle are still widely used to thresh grain.

The only navigable river is the Amu Darya, formerly called the Oxus. Barges bring oil from the Soviet Union along this river. Other imports from the Soviet Union are ferried across the river. The Amu Darya and the Helmand, as well as all the other large rivers, are used for irrigation of farm crops and orchards. The Kabul River joins Pakistan's Indus River and flows to the Indian Ocean.

The mountains and high plateaus are cold and snow-covered in winter, but they are pleasant places in the summertime. The surrounding plains are hot and dry in summer. In winter the northern plains are very cold and snowy, but the southern plains, sheltered by the mountains, are cool, with some rain.

Brass and copper metalware and jewelry are sold at the bazaars of Kandahar, a trading center.

THE ECONOMY

Afghanistan's soils are eroded and not always fertile. Only a small percentage of the land is cultivated each year, and most of it must be irrigated. In spite of this, Afghanistan is mainly an agricultural country. Most of the people still earn their living as farmers and shepherds. They raise sheep and grow grains, cotton, and fruits. The pelts of karakul sheep, used as fur, are a leading export. There are thousands of fruit and wild nut trees and many vineyards. Afghanistan's former forest wealth is almost gone because most of the trees that once grew in the mountains have been cut down.

Afghanistan is known to have mineral resources. But their full extent remains to be discovered, and most of the known resources remain to be developed. The minerals found in the country include coal, iron ore, copper, chromium, natural gas, oil, lapis lazuli, and small amounts of gold, silver, and rubies. Coal mining is carried on, and natural gas discovered in the north is now being piped to the Soviet Union. Commercial production of oil, also found in the north, has not yet begun.

In the past, most of Afghanistan's industry was based on its agricultural raw materials. Textile mills, sugar refineries, and fruit-processing plants were the most important factories. But science and technology are changing and expanding industry. Afghanistan is striving to make better use of its mineral resources. Hydroelectric plants are producing valuable power to light Afghan homes and run the factories that are springing up all over the country.

HISTORY AND GOVERNMENT

The Afghans were ruled by many different rulers before the 18th century. One of these was Alexander the Great, who added Afghanistan to his empire in the 4th century B.C. Another was Genghis Khan, who led his Mongol army into the country in the 13th century. Tamerlane conquered Afghanistan in the 14th century, and Baber conquered it in the 16th century on his way to India. Nadir Shah of Persia was the last invader.

After many years of foreign rule, the Pushtun tribes made Afghanistan independent in 1747. After independence the young kingdom fought hard to keep its freedom. But in 1879 the British defeated Afghanistan and took control of the country's foreign policy. For nearly 40 years thereafter, Afghanistan served as a "buffer state" between the British Empire in India and the Russian Empire in Central Asia. In 1919 Afghanistan finally regained its independence and recovered control of its foreign affairs.

After World War II, Afghanistan and Pakistan were occasionally on unfriendly terms. Pakistan sometimes refused to let the Afghans use its port of Karachi. This forced the Afghans to become friendly with the Soviet Union to obtain badly needed imports.

Afghanistan was a kingdom until 1973, when political dissatisfactions and poor economic conditions led to a military coup that toppled the monarchy. The country was declared a republic, and parliament was dissolved. The coup leader, General Mohammad Daoud Khan, was elected president and prime minister. Daoud was killed during another military coup in 1978. The constitution was annulled, and martial law was imposed. The military council soon turned power over to a leftist civilian group led by Noor Mohammed Taraki. The new government signed a treaty of peace and friendship with the Soviet Union.

But many groups in Afghanistan opposed the new government. These included Muslim religious leaders, non-Pushtun tribes, and farmers protesting the government's land-reform policy. The Soviet Union sent arms and military advisers to help the government. But by mid-1979, rebel forces controlled most of the countryside. Taraki was overthrown and Premier Hafizullah Amin became president.

President Amin was unable to control the spreading rebellion and was killed in a coup in December, 1979. Thousands of Soviet troops were airlifted into Afghanistan, and former Deputy Premier Babrak Karmal returned from exile in Eastern Europe to head the new government. In 1980, Soviet forces struck hard at rebels inside Afghanistan. Over 500,000 refugees fled into Pakistan, and the rebels mounted fresh attacks on the Soviet Army and the Afghan Government.

ALOYS A. MICHEL
University of Rhode Island
Reviewed by ROBERT I. CRANE
Syracuse University

AFRICA

"... geographers, in Afric maps,
With savage pictures fill their gaps,
And o'er unhabitable downs
Place elephants for want of towns."

These words were written by Jonathan Swift, the author of *Gulliver's Travels*. He wrote them more than 200 years ago. Swift was pointing out how little the Europeans of his day knew about Africa. It was a "dark continent" to them—huge and vast and unknown. It remained so for centuries.

Today the spotlight of world attention is focused on Africa. Exciting events have been taking place on this continent. Almost all the African nations once ruled by Europeans have won their independence. They are determined to control their own destinies. Some of their leaders are among the most important people of our time. Africa's great store of natural resources is envied by many of the industrial nations of the world. The continent is rapidly developing its own industries and trying to make life better for all of its people by improving housing, health care, agriculture, and education. The continent's importance in international affairs is clearly recognized.

FACTS AND FIGURES

LOCATION AND SIZE: Mainland Africa extends from: **Latitude**—37° 21′ N to 34° 50′ S. **Longitude**—51° 24′ E to 17° 32′ W. **Area**—approximately 30,313,000 km² (11,703,860 sq mi). **Highest point**—Kibo Peak (Kilimanjaro), Tanzania, 5,963 m (19,565 ft). **Lowest point**—Qattara Depression, Egypt, 134 m (440 ft) below sea level.

POPULATION: 424,000,000 (estimate).

CHIEF LAKES: Victoria, Tanganyika, Malawi, Chad, Turkana, Albert, Tana, Kivu, Edward.

CHIEF RIVERS: Nile, Congo (Zaïre), Niger, Zambezi, Orange, Kasai, Limpopo, Senegal, Gambia, Volta.

CHIEF MOUNTAIN RANGES AND PEAKS: Kilimanjaro (Kibo Peak, Mawenzi); Kenya; Meru; Elgon; Cameroon; **Ruwenzori**—Margherita, Alexandra; **Simen**—Ras Dashan; **Virunga**—Karisimbi, Mikeno; **Atlas**—Djebel Toubkal, Bou Naceur; **Drakensberg**—Thabana Ntlenyana; **Tibesti Massif**—Emi Koussi; **Ahaggar**—Tahat.

CHIEF DESERTS: Sahara, Arabian, Kalahari, Nubian, Libyan, Namib.

▶THE LAND

Africa is the world's second-largest continent. Only Asia is larger. Africa is large enough to hold nearly four continents the size of Australia.

This giant continent straddles the equator, stretching both north and south about 35 degrees. But because of Africa's shape, the bulk of its land lies between the Tropic of Cancer and the Tropic of Capricorn. This means that most of Africa is in the tropics. Indeed, Africa is the most tropical of the continents.

Landforms

This great continent has all four of the major types of landforms—mountains, hills, plains, and plateaus. Near the equator snowcapped mountain peaks rise above the warm, tropical lowlands. The Congo and the Nile, Africa's greatest rivers, are among the largest in the world. Tremendous rift valleys—deep, long, narrow valleys—contain some of the world's largest lakes.

The most important of all of Africa's landforms are its plateaus. Indeed, Africa is frequently called the plateau continent. These plateaus are highest in the east and south. They average over 1,500 meters (about 5,000 feet) above sea level.

There is very little coastal plain around this plateau continent. In some places the steep land rises up from the sea with no coastal plain at all. As a result, the continent does not have many good harbors for its size. At many ports ships must anchor offshore to be unloaded. But there are a few excellent harbors on the Mediterranean and in southern Africa.

Across the entire width of northern Africa stretches the Sahara, the largest desert of the world. Two mountain ranges rise in the center of this desert land. Their tallest peaks are snow-covered several months of the year. Only small areas of the Sahara are covered by shifting sand dunes and bare, rocky land. Most of the desert is covered with plains of gravel and rough boulders. The Atlas Mountains separate the fertile plains along the Mediterranean Sea from the deserts of the inland region.

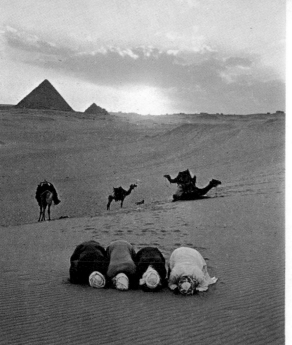
Muslims in Egypt bowing toward Mecca in prayer.

Rain forest in central Africa near the equator.

Pondoland in the Republic of South Africa.

The famous Victoria Falls on the Zimbabwe-Zambia border.

Zebras roam grasslands at the foot of Kilimanjaro, Africa's highest peak.

To the southeast of this vast desert land are the highest parts of the African continent. In Tanzania towers Africa's highest peak, Kilimanjaro.

In eastern Africa is another important and unique landform. This is the Great Rift Valley. It was created ages ago, when the land was pulled apart by geologic forces. The crust of the earth sank down to form a great canyon extending from present-day Syria through the Red Sea, and south through Africa to Mozambique.

Southern Africa also has highland areas. In many cases these "mountains" are really the tilted edges of plateaus. The Drakensberg Mountains are the largest in southern Africa. They are chiefly a part of the plateau edge, but have also been built up higher by outpourings of volcanic rock.

Western Africa has a low coastal plain. Much of it is wet and swampy. Inland from the coast are highland areas where rainfall is not so heavy. Like so much of Africa, this is chiefly a plateau area, although there are also hills and mountains. The highest parts of western Africa are the volcanic Cameroon Mountains and the Guinea highlands.

Rivers and Lakes

Central Africa, the most tropical portion of this tropical continent, is a land of heavy rainfall and high plateaus. Here is where most of Africa's great rivers begin.

As the rivers drop toward the coasts, they form huge waterfalls and rapids. Few of Africa's rivers are navigable near the coasts. Thus, central Africa was still unexplored long after the coastline had been fully mapped.

The Nile is the world's longest river. Ancient Egyptian civilization thrived on its banks thousands of years ago. The Nile has two main branches—the White Nile and the Blue Nile. The White Nile rises in Lake Victoria in east central Africa. The Blue Nile rises in Lake Tana in Ethiopia.

Africa's second longest river is the Congo (called the Zaïre River in Zaïre). It carries even more water than the Nile. The Congo's vast drainage area in central Africa is seven times as large as France. Another major river is the Niger. It rises in the Guinea highlands, flows northeastward to the edge of the Sahara, then turns southward to the Gulf of Guinea.

INDEPENDENT AFRICAN COUNTRIES

COUNTRY	CAPITAL	GOVERNMENT	ADMISSION TO THE UN
Algeria	Algiers	Republic	1962
Angola	Luanda	Republic	1976
Benin	Porto-Novo	Republic	1960
Botswana	Gaborone	Republic	1966
Burundi	Bujumbúra	Republic	1962
Cameroon	Yaoundé	Republic	1960
Cape Verde	Praia	Republic	1975
Central African Republic	Bangui	Republic	1960
Chad	N'Djemena	Republic	1960
Comoros	Moroni	Republic	1975
Congo	Brazzaville	Republic	1960
Djibouti	Djibouti	Republic	1977
Egypt	Cairo	Republic	1945
Equatorial Guinea	Malabo	Republic	1968
Ethiopia	Addis Ababa	Military Council	1945
Gabon	Libreville	Republic	1960
Gambia, The	Banjul	Republic	1965
Ghana	Accra	Republic	1957
Guinea	Conakry	Republic	1958
Guinea-Bissau	Bissau	Republic	1974
Ivory Coast	Abidjan	Republic	1960
Kenya	Nairobi	Republic	1963
Lesotho	Maseru	Monarchy	1966
Liberia	Monrovia	Republic	1945
Libya	Tripoli	Republic	1955
Madagascar (Malagasy Republic)	Antananarivo	Republic	1960
Malawi	Lilongwe	Republic	1964
Mali	Bamako	Republic	1960
Mauritania	Nouakchott	Republic	1961
Mauritius	Port Louis	Monarchy	1968
Morocco	Rabat	Monarchy	1956
Mozambique	Maputo	Republic	1975
Niger	Niamey	Republic	1960
Nigeria	Lagos	Republic	1960
Rwanda	Kigali	Republic	1962
São Tomé and Príncipe	São Tomé	Republic	1975
Senegal	Dakar	Republic	1960
Seychelles	Victoria	Republic	1976
Sierra Leone	Freetown	Republic	1961
Somalia	Mogadishu	Republic	1960
South Africa	Pretoria Cape Town Bloemfontein	Republic	1945
Sudan	Khartoum	Republic	1956
Swaziland	Mbabane	Monarchy	1968
Tanzania	Dar es Salaam	Republic	1964
Togo	Lomé	Republic	1960
Tunisia	Tunis	Republic	1956
Uganda	Kampala	Republic	1962
Upper Volta	Ouagadougou	Republic	1960
Zaïre	Kinshasa	Republic	1960
Zambia	Lusaka	Republic	1964
Zimbabwe (Rhodesia)	Salisbury	Republic	1980

Southern Africa has two major rivers. The Orange River flows across semi-desert on much of its trip to the Atlantic Ocean. Parts of the river dry up completely during dry periods of the year. Southern Africa's other large river is the mighty Zambezi, which flows into the Indian Ocean on the eastern side of Africa. On the Zambezi River are the famous Victoria Falls. These great waterfalls are about 120 meters (400 feet) high—more than twice the height of Niagara Falls in North America.

The great lakes of the continent are located in eastern Africa. Most of them occupy portions of the Great Rift Valley. They include lakes Edward, Albert, Malawi, and Tanganyika (one of the deepest lakes in the world). The largest of the lakes, Lake Victoria, is not in the Rift Valley but on the East African Plateau, between the eastern and western branches of the Rift Valley. Although Lake Victoria is quite shallow, it is the world's second largest freshwater lake. Only Lake Superior, in North America, is larger.

Lake Chad is in the drier, upper central part of Africa. Many rivers of the region flow into Lake Chad instead of going to the sea. Because these rivers often come from regions that have wet and dry seasons, the size of Lake Chad changes with the seasons.

Climate

Africa is a mostly tropical continent. But there is great variety in its weather and climate. Some of the world's highest temperatures have been recorded in the Sahara. The world's record high, 58°C (136°F), was registered at Azizia, in Libya. The tropical forest and grassland areas also have high temperatures the year round, but they are never as high as the desert's. Although most of Africa does not have a true winter season, there are high mountain peaks that are covered with ice and snow all year. Kilimanjaro, the highest mountain in Africa, is almost on the equator. Yet its crest is always snowcapped.

There are also great contrasts in precipitation. The central portion, or heart, of Africa generally has heavy rainfall all year. Some places receive well over 2,500 millimeters (100 inches) of rain a year. In the savanna grassland regions, farther from the equator, there is a rainy season and a dry season. The desert and semi-desert areas are dry almost all year. Over half the continent receives less than 500 millimeters (20 inches) of rain a year. Of course, the Sahara receives much less than this. Most of the precipitation falls in the form of heavy showers. Africa has snow only in the higher regions.

Plants and Animals

High year-round temperatures and abundant rainfall provide ideal conditions for plant growth. Central Africa possesses these ideal conditions. As a result, this equatorial region is a land of vast, lush, tropical rain forests. Its hundreds of species of trees include such valuable hardwoods as ebony and mahogany.

The dense tropical forests provide fine homes for monkeys, chimpanzees, gorillas, and a variety of birds. Throughout the tropical lowlands roam gnu (large African antelope), buffalo, and wild pigs.

Beyond the tropical rain forests of central Africa are the grasslands. North and south of the equatorial region the climate becomes drier, and there is a gradual change from forest to grassland. The wetter portions of the grassland are dotted with trees. This tree-dotted grassland is called savanna. Some of the coarse grasses of the savanna grow to be twice the height of a human being. It is difficult to travel in such areas except by cutting paths through the grass.

The savanna is the home of great herds of animals—antelope of many varieties, zebras, giraffes, elephants, and rhinoceroses. All of them live on the grass and the leaves of trees of this area. The savanna is also the home of meat eaters—lions, leopards, and hyenas—which feed on the grass eaters.

North and south of the grasslands are deserts. Parts of the deserts are so dry that no vegetation grows at all. Where a little rain falls, grass and desert shrubs appear. Typical desert animals are the gazelle, the fox, and the hare. All these can survive in regions of little water, little shade, and high daytime temperatures.

In the northern and southwestern coastal portions of Africa, there are areas covered with Mediterranean-type vegetation. Mediterranean vegetation consists of rather dense brushland of woody evergreen plants. These plants usually have thick and leathery or shiny leaves. Such leaves protect the plants from

Giraffe.

Hippopotamuses.

Lions.

Elephants.

Impalas.

Animals of the east African highlands attract tourists and photographers from all parts of the world.

the long, hot, dry summers that are typical of this region.

Throughout Africa are several thousand species of birds, including the world's largest flightless bird, the ostrich. Africa also has a large number of reptiles. One of the most dangerous is the crocodile, which lives in and beside the streams of most of the continent. There are various kinds of snakes. Some of them, such as cobras and mambas, are poisonous. The largest of the snakes is the python. Many kinds of lizards are also found.

Africa's wildlife is an important natural resource. Its animals, birds, and reptiles are known all over the world. But there is real danger that many species will soon be extinct if greater care is not taken to protect them from hunters and poachers. Many African nations are studying ways of better conserving their wildlife. Kenya, for instance, has outlawed big-game hunting. Africa has some of the world's largest national parks.

Soils

Africa, like all large landmasses, has many types of soil. But most of its soils are only average in fertility, and some are quite poor. Poor soils are typical of many tropical areas. And Africa has a larger tropical area than any other continent.

Leaves and branches fall to the floor of the tropical rain forest, where they slowly decay. This enriches the soil and nourishes the forest growth. But tropical soils are more easily destroyed than those of temperate regions. Once the forest vegetation has been cleared, the heavy rainfall leaches out the minerals needed by agricultural crops and washes away the thin layer of topsoil. Some tropical soils can be farmed productively for only two or three years. They must then be left uncultivated for years to restore their fertility.

Africa's best soils are alluvial soils. These are soils that have been deposited by rivers, chiefly when they flood and overflow their banks. Most of the crops of Egypt and Sudan are grown on the alluvial soils of the Nile River. In western Africa, some of the best soil is found along the Niger River. The same is true in the valleys of the Zambezi, the Congo (Zaïre), and other rivers.

Many desert portions of Africa lack true soil. Such areas may be covered by sand or pebbles or may have a bare, rocky surface. The only true soils found in African deserts are known as red desert soils. These soils often have many of the minerals needed for plant growth, and there is not very much rainfall to wash the minerals out of the soil. All that is needed for good crops is water.

The soils of the Mediterranean climatic regions are usually better than the true tropical soils. Some of the higher and cooler parts of southern and eastern Africa also have better-than-average soils. There are prairie soils in the veld region of southern Africa. Natal Province, in the southeastern part of the Republic of South Africa, has fertile red-yellow soils. Red-yellow soil is the type found in the southeastern portion of the United States. Africa has no large areas of good soil to compare with the corn- and wheat-growing areas of North America, the Soviet Union, and eastern Asia.

Mineral Resources

Africa is rich in minerals of many kinds. Its mineral wealth includes diamonds and precious metals such as gold, as well as bauxite (used in making aluminum), copper, iron, cobalt, manganese, vanadium, uranium, lead, zinc, asbestos, and phosphate.

Africa, especially southern Africa, leads the world in the production of diamonds and gold. The Republic of South Africa is the world's largest producer of gold. Johannesburg, in the heart of the great Witwatersrand goldfield, has been nicknamed "the city of gold." When Ghana was a British colony, it was called the Gold Coast. Ghana still has major gold deposits. South African diamonds are world famous. Kimberley has been called "the diamond city." Diamonds, which are used in industry as well as for jewelry, are also found in Zaïre, Ghana, Angola, Sierra Leone, Liberia, Tanzania, the Central African Republic, and Namibia (South-West Africa).

Copper is a very important mineral product of Africa. The major sources are in Zaïre, the Republic of South Africa, Uganda, and Zambia. Huge deposits of high-grade iron ore are also found on the continent. The major iron-ore fields are located in northern Africa, Liberia, Guinea, Mauritania, and the Republic of South Africa.

Western Africa has tremendous reserves of bauxite, particularly in Guinea and Ghana. Zaïre is the world's principal supplier of cobalt, which is used in hardening steel. Large deposits of uranium are found in South Africa, Zaïre, Niger, and Gabon.

Power Resources

Power resources include coal, petroleum, waterpower, and nuclear energy. Although Africa is not one of the major coal-producing continents, there are significant deposits in South Africa, Nigeria, Zaïre, Tanzania, and Zimbabwe (Rhodesia).

In recent years, large deposits of petroleum have been discovered in Africa, especially in the dry regions of the north. Prospectors have explored the Sahara, sometimes with air-conditioned trucks and airplanes, searching for petroleum. Oil is now being extracted from wells in Algeria, Libya, Egypt, Nigeria, Gabon, and Angola.

Africa has more potential for producing power from water than any other continent. The water is used to turn huge turbines to make electricity. In some areas, hydroelectric power is generated at the natural sites of waterfalls and rapids. In other cases, large dams have been constructed to regulate the flow of water. Some of the most important dams are the Kariba Dam on the Zambezi River, the Aswan High Dam in Egypt, and the Volta Dam in Ghana.

Africa also has large deposits of uranium. Uranium is used in nuclear power plants. Thus, the continent has many alternative sources of energy, although it lacks coal.

▶ THE PEOPLE

It is difficult to give exact population figures for Africa. In many parts of the continent, no accurate census has ever been taken. But the continent has over twice as many people as the United States.

On every continent, people tend to gather in the places with the best climate, resources, and location. Large areas of Africa that are made up of desert, semi-arid land, mountains, or dense tropical forest are sparsely populated. But there are certain areas that are very crowded.

Millions of people live in the valley and delta area of the Nile River. Here the soil is fertile, and water is available. There are also many people living along the coast of northern Africa. This region is well located for trade with Europe and has a pleasant climate.

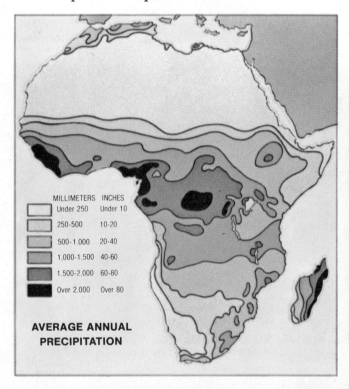

MILLIMETERS	INCHES
Under 250	Under 10
250-500	10-20
500-1,000	20-40
1,000-1,500	40-60
1,500-2,000	60-80
Over 2,000	Over 80

AVERAGE ANNUAL PRECIPITATION

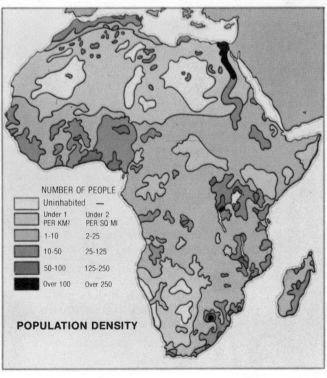

NUMBER OF PEOPLE	
Uninhabited	—
Under 1 PER KM²	Under 2 PER SQ MI
1-10	2-25
10-50	25-125
50-100	125-250
Over 100	Over 250

POPULATION DENSITY

A Mossi dignitary of Upper Volta.

A Marrakesh merchant in Morocco.

A man from the Niger Republic.

A Zulu girl of South Africa.

A girl from the Republic of Chad.

An Ethiopian scholar.

Children of Botswana.

Large numbers of people are found in western Africa south of the Sahara. Some of the continent's largest kingdoms of the past developed in this region. Many people live in parts of the cool, high plateaus of eastern Africa and in the cooler, better-watered parts of southern Africa. In contrast, such arid regions as the Sahara and the Kalahari Desert (in southern Africa) can support only a few people. Tropical central Africa has a larger population than the desert regions, but it has a lower population density than some other areas of Africa.

Most Africans live in small towns and villages. The percentage of Africa's population that lives in cities is very low in comparison with most continents. But the rate of recent urban growth is very high. As in many other parts of the world, large numbers of people are moving to the cities. Often there are not enough jobs and housing for all those who want work and places to live.

Population Groups

Africa's people can be divided into two major groups—the black African and the Caucasoid. Black Africans are by far the largest population group of the continent. They occupy most of Africa, with the exception of northern Africa. Black Africans usually have dark brown hair and skin and may be divided into many subgroups. Some, notably the Tutsi of east central Africa, are very tall. The Pygmies, who live mostly in tropical central Africa, are one of the shortest peoples in the world. The Bushmen and Hottentots of southern Africa are also short in stature. But they are not considered true black Africans. They belong to the most ancient peoples in Africa, the Khoisan.

North Africa has more Caucasians than black Africans. Besides the small number of Europeans who have settled there, there are two major subgroups of Caucasians—the Arabs and the Berbers. Both groups are Muslims (followers of the Islamic religion). The Arabs and Berbers form a majority in all north African nations.

A large number of Caucasians from Europe have settled in southern Africa, particularly in the Republic of South Africa, where they control the government and the economy. The earlier European settlers were mostly Dutch and French, while the more recent immigrants were British.

In addition to the Caucasians of European background, there are a number of Caucasians of Asian background. Most of them are Indians who live in Kenya and other parts of eastern Africa and in southern Africa, especially in the Natal Province of South Africa. Many Indians once lived in Uganda. But they were forced to leave the country in the early 1970's.

In the northern parts of western Africa and in many parts of eastern Africa, most of the people are of mixed black African and Caucasian stock. Some of these mixed racial types have become distinct population groups. The best known of them are the so-called Cape Coloureds of South Africa. They are a mixture of European and black African peoples.

Languages

Africa is a continent with a multitude of languages. In tropical Africa alone some 800 to 1,000 different languages are spoken. This has long been a serious problem. To make communication easier, many African nations kept English or French as their national languages when they became independent.

Arabic, a Semitic language, is the dominant language of northern Africa. It is also used in parts of eastern Africa where there are fairly large numbers of Arabs or where the Arabs have traded for centuries. Berber, a Hamitic language, is also widely spoken in northern Africa. The languages of Ethiopia are mainly Semitic. In Somalia most of the languages belong to the Cushitic family.

The Sudanic language group is dominant in the large grassland region south of the Sahara. Sometimes it is referred to as the language of the savanna. It is spoken by people who are scattered from the upper Niger region in western Africa to Tanzania in eastern Africa. It includes the Kanuri, Nubian, and Nilotic languages.

Bantu languages are spoken throughout central and eastern Africa and are dominant in parts of southern Africa. There are over 80 different Bantu languages. Zulu, spoken by the Zulu people of South Africa, is one of the chief Bantu languages. Swahili is a Bantu language that includes words from other languages. It is often used as a "lingua franca," or trading language, in eastern Africa and parts of central Africa. Swahili is one of the most important languages south of the Sahara.

Hausa, another trading language, is spoken widely in western Africa. It is also an important language in the grassland region around Lake Chad. Fulani, Mande, and Kwa are the major languages of western Africa. The languages of the Hottentots of southern Africa and the Bushmen of the Kalahari Desert region of southern Africa have distinctive "click" sounds.

A number of European languages are also spoken in Africa. For example, French is used widely in parts of northern Africa and in former French colonies in western and central Africa. Many people in former British colonies speak English. In South Africa, people of British descent speak English. Those with a Dutch background speak Afrikaans, a Germanic language that is derived from 17th-century Dutch.

Religions

A majority of the African people practice tribal religions. These tribal religions have been handed down from generation to generation for many centuries. The followers of most of the tribal religions believe in spirits. For this reason they often worship the dead or the spirits that they believe are in things such as stars, mountains, and trees. Another important ingredient of most African tribal religions is magic. It is sometimes used for healing. This is why priests of African tribal religions are often called medicine men. Although most of these tribal religions do not deny the existence of many minor gods, a great many of them believe in one supreme god.

Islam, the religion founded by Mohammed, is the chief religion north of the Sahara. It is the religion of the Arabs. Followers of Islam are called Muslims. During the past century Islam has been very successful in winning converts in the neighboring non-Arab regions immediately south of the Sahara.

Christianity also has many followers in Africa. Some African Christians are members of the Ethiopian Orthodox Church, in Ethiopia. There are also a number of Christians who belong to the Coptic Church, the ancient Christian church of Egypt. But outside of northeastern Africa, most African Christian communities are of recent origin. Large numbers of Christian missionaries went to Africa from Europe and America in the beginning of the 19th century. Thousands of missions were established in Africa after that. They did much to develop education and improve medical standards. Today, African Christian leaders have control of many religious institutions.

The European population of Africa is mostly Christian. The Indians are mostly Hindu. Hinduism was introduced into Africa by Indian traders centuries ago, but the Hindus have never made any effort to spread their religion in Africa. There are also a number of Jews in Africa.

Ways of Life

For centuries the basic organization of the African community has been the tribe. People of the same tribe usually speak the same language, wear the same kind of clothing, eat the same kind of food, and live in the same kind of dwelling. They are said to have a dis-

INDEX TO AFRICA MAP

tinctive culture. Although some tribes are small in number, more commonly they consist of many millions of people. Most of the large African tribes would be called "nations" or nationalities if they lived in Europe.

The tribal society is the basic pattern for the African way of life. It is the center of an individual's life. It offers social and economic security and regulates life through tribal laws and customs, so that tribe members can live

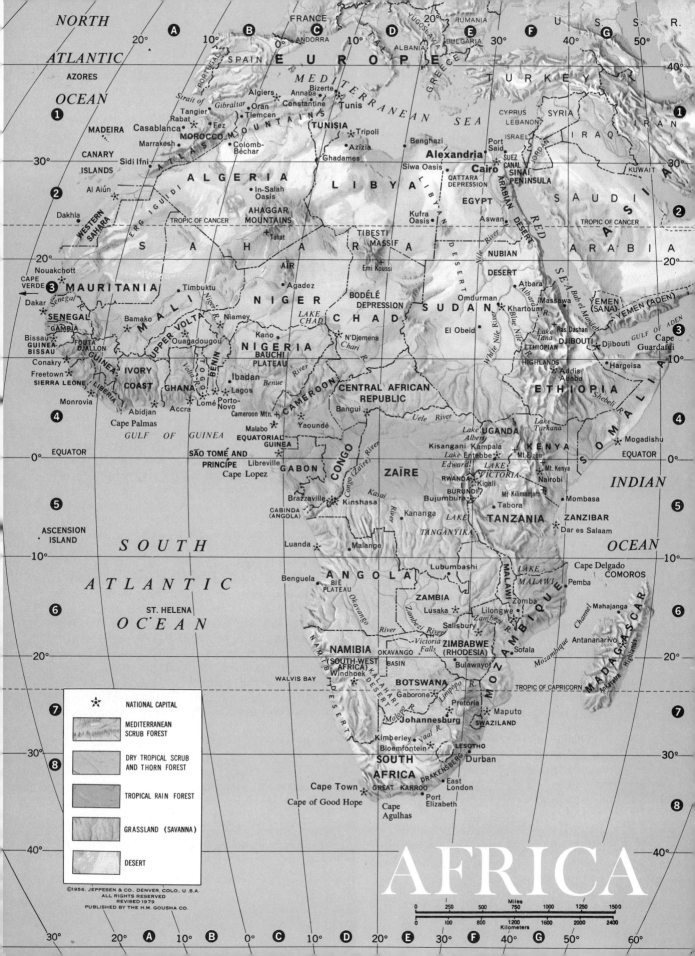

AFRICA

peacefully with one another. The tribe takes care of its members in time of need. It protects them from hostile outsiders. In return, individuals offer their services to the tribe.

A tribe is usually ruled by a chieftain or a tribal council or, sometimes, by both. In some areas, tribes with similar cultural backgrounds band together under a paramount chief. But the borders of these tribal "nations" do not always correspond with those of the African nations. The border between Togo and Ghana, for instance, cuts through the traditional homeland of the Ewe tribe. This is because most of the national borders were drawn by colonial powers who had little knowledge of traditional tribal boundaries.

In some cases, this situation has led to bloodshed. For example, Somali tribespeople in the Ogaden and Eritrea regions attempted to secede from Ethiopia in the 1970's. And Katangese rebels attempted to separate Shaba province from Zaïre. But most African leaders have opposed redrawing national boundaries to conform to tribal ones. They fear that doing so might plunge the continent into chaos. It will probably be many years before the disruption of tribal units will be resolved and people in Africa will feel a greater loyalty to their national governments than to their tribes.

Since there are hundreds of tribes in Africa, there are naturally many different ways of doing things. In almost every tribe, respect for elders and ancestors is an important value. Their spirits seem very close and ever watchful. Most tribal societies also are closely attached to their land. Perhaps this is because most people in Africa have always lived off the land. The land normally belongs to everyone in the tribe—the living, the dead, and the unborn.

Throughout tropical Africa, the men have traditionally hunted and fished, herded cattle and goats, and done heavy work such as building homes. They have been the protectors of the village and, when necessary, the warriors that defended it. The women have cared for the children, cooked, and woven cloth. They have also done most of the planting, selling the extra produce at the market. Children were given chores to do when they were quite young. The boys tended to the animals, went hunting and fishing with the men, and helped clear the land. Girls worked with their mothers, taking care of the house and of the younger children.

This traditional way of life is changing. Some 200 years of European development and settlement have profoundly influenced the thinking and life of many Africans. The introduction of industry and spread of education have opened up new ways of earning a living for both men and women. Bicycles, automobiles, railroads, radio, and television have brought the outside world ever closer to tribal society. Each year more and more people move from their tribal villages to the cities in search of more education and better jobs in factories, offices, and mines.

Many Africans are reluctant to leave the traditional rural way of life and the security it offers. Those who do venture into the cities cannot always find work and housing. The governments of the African nations, most of which have won independence since World War II, are not always able to meet the needs of their people. They have built more hospitals and schools, encouraged the growth of industry and the use of new agricultural methods to improve production, and attempted to wipe out diseases that kill thousands of people each year. But the changes often are not rapid or smooth enough to satisfy people's demands. Economic and social dislocation and political strife are often the result.

Food and Drink

Most rural African families grow their own crops and raise their own animals. A few peoples of Africa, such as the Pygmies of central Africa, still get their food by hunting and by gathering berries in the forest. But most Africans are either farmers or cattle raisers.

Desert dwellers get food and drink from the camels and goats they raise. They often trade for fruits, grains, and vegetables that are grown on oases. Dates are a staple food in many parts of northern Africa. This way of life is being seriously threatened in the **Sahel**, a semi-arid region that forms a transition zone between the Sahara to the north and the savanna to the south. The desert seems to be expanding southward into the Sahel. This may be caused partly by changes in climate, such as the severe drought conditions that made headlines in the 1970's. But human

Breadmaking in Uganda.

Nigerian girls sorting cotton.

At the market place in Ouagadougou, Upper Volta.

The Songhai tribe depends on the Niger River for its water supply and transportation.

Colorful designs decorate many homes
of the Ndebele tribe in South Africa.

A village of thatched houses in Zaïre.

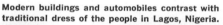

Ugandan tribal leader meets with his tribesmen.

Modern buildings and automobiles contrast with
traditional dress of the people in Lagos, Nigeria.

factors, such as overgrazing, have played an important role in the southward encroachment of the Sahara. Many animals have died. Millions of nomads have been forced to abandon their traditional way of life and move southward in search of food.

The grassy plains of the northern savannas are well suited to raising cattle. The people who live there have meat to eat and milk to drink. They grow millet (a kind of grain), groundnuts (peanuts), yams, beans, rice, and peas.

Many kinds of fruit grow well in the southern rain forest. There the people eat oranges, guavas, grapefruit, pineapples, limes, mangoes, and bananas. They drink the milk of the coconut. They also eat yams, rice, cassava, potatoes, and maize (corn). But diseases kill animals in these rainy, humid regions, and the people do not have enough milk and meat.

Maize is one of the most important foods in many parts of Africa. The grain is ground into meal. The meal is then boiled with water in a big kettle. When it is cooked, it makes a corn porridge, often served with beans.

Cassava is another important plant. It can be stored for a long time and prepared in several different ways. One cassava dish is called *gari*. The roots are dug up, peeled, and soaked in water for a few hours. They are then chopped up. The pieces are put into a bag with heavy weights on top. After three days, the bag is opened and the cassava is spread in the sun to dry. Palm oil is added, and the cassava is roasted. *Gari* is ready to eat when it is crisp and dry.

Today more and more African families are moving from their farming villages into the towns and cities. An increasing amount of the continent's food is being grown on large farms and plantations.

Dress and Dwelling

The types of clothing Africans wear and the types of houses they live in depend greatly upon where they live and the kind of life they lead. The nomads of northern Africa must wear clothes that protect them from the wind, dust, and very high and very low temperatures of the desert. They wear simple hooded cloaks and baggy trousers of camel's hair, turbans on their heads, and slippers on their feet. Their homes must be simple, too, for they move from place to place. They live in tents made from camel's hair. They have little furniture except rugs to cover the dirt floor for sleeping.

The people who live along the rivers of the central rain forest must clear away the thick jungle to build their homes, so they build them close together. They make their houses out of the bamboo stalks, palm branches, and broad leaves that they find about them. Because it is hot and rainy, these people wear little clothing. Like people all over the world, they wear jewelry. Their necklaces are made of beads and animal teeth.

In some parts of western Africa, the people build square houses with walls of red mud and roofs of bamboo covered with palm leaves. In the middle of the house is a court where the family relaxes after the day's work is done. Attached to the house is a type of barn for storing or drying food and for keeping domestic animals. In one corner of the barn is a bathhouse fenced off with bamboo mats.

West Africans often wear brightly colored clothes. Most men wear narrow tunic-shirts called *bubu* and narrow trousers called *sokoto*. Over these they wear long, flowing gowns called *sapara*. They also wear small square or pointed caps. The women wear dresses called *irobirin*. They are made from long pieces of colored material wrapped around and tucked in, apron style, around the hips. On their heads women wear turbans known as *gele,* which they twist into many styles.

But many African people do not live in tribal villages or wear traditional African dress. In large towns and cities they may live in housing developments and frequently wear European-style clothing.

▶ THE ECONOMY

The average yearly income of most Africans is low. But people who grow most of their own food, build their houses from the material at hand, and make their own clothing do not need to buy many things with cash. Africa is a wealthy continent in terms of its natural resources, but many of them have not yet been fully used.

Farming

Most people in Africa make their living from agriculture. But a number of serious problems plague the African farmer. Soils are not very fertile in many parts of the continent. Rainfall is unevenly distributed. Plant diseases, insects, and foraging wild animals limit farm production. The use of newer farming methods could help produce more food for Africa's growing population.

A variety of crops is grown in northern Africa. Wheat, barley, and grapes flourish in the Mediterranean coastal region. In the desert all farming is carried on at the oases. There a "three-story" type of agriculture is often practiced because the people must grow all they can on small pieces of land. The "top story" consists of tall date palms. Sunlight filters through the feathery tops of the date palms, and smaller trees such as peaches, apricots, and figs can be grown between them. On the ground level, the main crops are wheat, barley, cotton, and vegetables.

Western Africa is an important agricultural region. In the rainy tropical region near the Gulf of Guinea, the chief food crops are yams, rice, and cassava. Plantation products include rubber and palm oil. Cocoa and coffee are grown on small farms and on some plantations. Palm oil is the chief export of much of the rain forest. In the drier savanna, important crops include groundnuts, millet, sorghum, maize, cotton, and vegetables.

Wheat, maize, millet, cassava, and vegetables are the major food crops of eastern Africa. There are a large number of plantations in this region, where various crops are grown for export. The chief plantation products are cotton, sisal, coffee, tea, and pyrethrum (used in making insecticides).

The region around Cape Town, South Africa, has a Mediterranean climate with hot, dry summers and mild, wet winters. Winter wheat, grapes, and various kinds of fruit are grown there. Sugarcane is an important crop in the coastal region of Mozambique and along the eastern coast of South Africa. Maize, wheat, tobacco, and groundnuts are other important crops in southern Africa.

Hunting, Herding, and Fishing

Farming is not the only way the people of Africa make a living. Some African people get all or part of their food by hunting and gathering wild plants. The Pygmies of central Africa and the Bushmen of the Kalahari Desert depend on hunting for most of their food supply. The Pygmies trade part of their catch with their farming neighbors for agricultural crops to vary their diet. While hunting is their most important economic activity, these peoples also gather wild plants that can be used as food. But most hunting is done by African farmers who add meat to their diets by catching wild game where it is available.

Animal raising is a major occupation in some parts of Africa, particularly in the grasslands. In very dry regions such as the Sahara, shepherds must constantly move about with their animals in search of pasture. In more humid areas with better pastures, people raise sheep, goats, and cattle on their farms. Camels and horses are raised in northern Africa. Chickens and pigs are raised in many farming villages and are an important source of meat in much of the continent.

Eastern Africa is known for its cattle culture. The ownership of cattle is taken as a sign of a person's weath and prestige. The Masai, a cattle-raising tribe of Kenya, keep their cattle in kraals (enclosures made of thorns) to protect the cattle from wild animals. Many other cattle-raising people in eastern and southern Africa also protect their animals in this fashion.

Sheep are important in South Africa, one of the world's leading exporters of wool. Another major sheep-raising area is the hilly region of northwestern Africa. Cattle and horses do not thrive in most areas where the climate is extremely tropical. And in such regions, they are subject to the disease-carrying tsetse fly.

The rivers and lakes of Africa provide fish in large quantities to help make up for the lack of meat in the diet of most Africans. There are many fishing villages along these inland waters and along the seacoast.

There are important fishing grounds off the coasts of South Africa, Namibia (South-West Africa), and Angola, where the cold Benguela Current attracts many fish. Another major fishing region is the Gulf of Guinea, off western Africa. Part of the catch is used locally for food, and part is processed for export.

Lumbering and Mining

Africa has vast areas of forest, especially tropical rain forest. There are many tall, valuable trees such as mahogany. But the cutting and marketing of these trees is not always

Many people are needed to pull in the fishing nets from the ocean off the coast of Ghana.

Ghanaian prepares cocoa beans for marketing.

Dyers' market place in Morocco.

Cow turning waterwheel for irrigation in Egypt.

Sisal being loaded in Kenya for transport to factories.

63

Gold mining in South Africa. Some of these mines are over 3,300 meters (about 11,000 feet) deep.

easy. Many of the trees of commercial value are scattered widely throughout the forest. Cutting must be selective, and selective cutting is costly. Most of these trees also are far from rivers or other means of transportation. One of the most important lumber-producing areas of the continent is the region between central and western Africa, including Nigeria, Cameroon, the Central African Republic, Gabon, Zaïre, and the Congo.

Lumber is not the only commercial product that comes from trees. Extracts from the bark of the wattle tree are used in tanning leather. Rubber trees are important in western and central Africa, and more than half of the world's cocoa comes from trees in Ghana and Nigeria. Coffee and palm trees are also important. Many experts feel that "tree farming" is one of the best ways to use African land, especially in the rainy tropical regions.

Africa is rich in mineral resources. Old and new mining centers dot the continent. Large diamond and gold mines are found in southern Africa. Diamonds and gold are also mined in other parts of Africa. Zaïre is a leading producer of uranium and cobalt. Nigeria is an important exporter of tin. Bauxite is exported from Guinea and Ghana. Some coal is mined in southern Africa and in Morocco. There are oil fields in Algeria, Libya, Egypt, Nigeria, Gabon, and Angola. Iron, copper, phosphates, and chrome are other important minerals exported from Africa.

Industry

South Africa is the most highly industrialized nation in Africa. Egypt, Algeria, and Zaïre are also important manufacturing centers. Many nations in eastern and western Africa are developing industry, among them Ghana, the Ivory Coast, and Kenya.

Local industries have been important for centuries in all parts of Africa. They include the making of tools, weapons, clothes, and boats. Important newer industries in many African countries include food processing (such as canning), the refining of minerals, and the manufacturing of textiles, chemicals, and clothing. Many of Africa's new industries are located near rivers that provide electricity to run their machinery.

Transportation

Scorching deserts, teeming jungles, irregular terrain, and disease have combined to hinder the development of transportation in Africa. In view of the vastness of the continent and the large number of countries it contains, the development of transportation will necessarily be slow and painstaking.

Roads. Although new highways are constantly being built in Africa, the continent still has very few roads compared with Europe or North America. Most roads are not paved, and many are impassable during the rainy season. The use of private automobiles is not widespread, but it is growing. Trucks and buses are more common. It is difficult to build and maintain roads in the rainy tropical areas. The deserts present different problems. They are extremely hot and lack water. Generally speaking, southern Africa and the Mediterranean area have the best-developed road systems. Paths and trails link villages throughout the continent. People travel on foot or by bicycle.

Railroads. In many parts of Africa, it is even more difficult to build railroads and keep them in good condition than it is to build roads. There is a lack of wood for making railroad ties in the deserts and grasslands. Flooding is a constant threat in rainy regions.

Most of Africa's railroads are found in coastal areas and therefore are of comparatively short length. They usually serve only to connect plantations or mining areas to local seaports. The densest network of railroads on the continent is found in southern Africa. One of the most famous of Africa's longer railroads extends from the Kenyan port of Mombasa to the copper-mining region of western Uganda. Quarrels between nations and tribes have disrupted rail transport in some places.

Water Transportation. Water transportation is often more important in Africa than highways or railroads. The many rivers and lakes of Africa provide natural transportation routes and are used by canoes, small boats, and steamers. The chief inland waterways of Africa are the Nile, Congo (Zaïre), and Niger rivers and the large lakes of eastern Africa.

For its size, Africa has few good natural harbors. In many areas goods must be transferred from large oceangoing ships to small boats and then be taken ashore. Artificial harbors—such as Tema, the port of Accra, Ghana—have also been built.

There are good natural harbors in Africa at Dakar, Freetown, and Cape Town, on the Atlantic Ocean; at Durban, Maputo, Mombasa, and Zanzibar, on the Indian Ocean; and at Alexandria, Algiers, Tangier, and Casablanca, on the coasts of northern Africa.

Air Transportation. The airplane has become an important means of transportation in Africa. It can get to places that are difficult to reach by any other means of transportation. Today the major African cities and many smaller ones are connected to other parts of the continent and to the rest of the world by air routes. Many international airlines operate regular flights to Africa. Some of the leading airports are located at Cairo, Khartoum, and Algiers, in northern Africa; Dakar, Accra, and Kano, in western Africa; Kinshasa and Brazzaville, in central Africa; Nairobi, in eastern Africa; and Johannesburg, in southern Africa.

Other Means of Transportation. The camel is still "the ship of the desert." Camels, and sometimes horses and donkeys, are important means of transportation for people and products in northern Africa. But specially equipped vehicles that can travel over the desert sand are being used increasingly.

In other parts of Africa, there are few animals that can be used for transportation. Dutch settlers brought the ox and ox wagon to southern Africa. But few are left today.

The bicycle is a widely used means of transportation in Africa. Bicycles are not very expensive and can be used on paths or in open country as well as on good roads.

Trade

For many years, Africa's trade was limited by poor means of transportation and lack of export commodities. Most regions produced only a limited number of goods for export. The continent's colonial rulers were more interested in exporting raw materials for use in European factories than in developing African industry. In recent years, African nations have been trying to diversify their economies. Many of them are now producing a variety of goods for export.

Today Africa still imports fuel, textiles, and other consumer products. Electrical equipment, machinery, and automobiles are also major import items.

Africa has a favorable balance of trade because of the agricultural and mineral products it exports. In other words, the value of the goods exported from Africa is greater than that of the goods imported.

In the past, foreign trade was almost entirely conducted by foreign merchants—Europeans in western and southern Africa, Arabs in northern Africa, and Indians in eastern Africa. And Europeans ran many of Africa's mines, factories, and large farms and plantations during the colonial period. Although foreign advisers and technicians still play important roles in some nations and industries, Africans have been taking over positions of leadership in both commerce and industry.

▶ **CITIES**

Most of Africa's people live in villages and small towns, but there are a number of large and flourishing cities on the continent. Africa's largest city—Cairo, in Egypt—has been called the Arab capital of the world. Two other large cities in northern Africa are Alexandria, Egypt, and Casablanca, Morocco, a port of call for ships from all over the world.

Other leading cities in Africa include Addis Ababa, in Ethiopia; Lagos and Ibadan, in Nigeria; Kinshasa, in Zaïre; and Johannesburg and Cape Town, in South Africa. Many other African cities are growing in importance as trade, administrative, mining, transportation, or industrial centers.

Roman amphitheater in El Djem, Tunisia.

▶ HISTORY

The earliest humans on the earth may have lived in Africa. Until the late 1950's, there was proof only that early people dated back 700,000 to 800,000 years. Then, in 1959, at Olduvai Gorge in Tanzania, Louis and Mary Leakey discovered remains of humanlike creatures who lived there some 1,750,000 years ago.

Since then, other scientists have found even earlier remains of our human ancestors in Kenya and Ethiopia. Many scholars now believe that human beings have lived in eastern Africa for at least 3,500,000 years—and perhaps for as long as 5,000,000 years. Africa, which has been incorrectly called "the continent without a history," may well have the longest human history in the world.

Early History of Northern Africa

Northeastern Africa is the home of one of the world's earliest civilizations—the Egyptian civilization. It was established more than 4,000 years before Christ.

The Phoenicians, from the eastern Mediterranean, settled in northern Africa. In 1100 B.C. they founded Utica in present-day Tunisia. And in 814 B.C. they established the famous city-state of Carthage. But by the 2nd century A.D., the Roman Empire had gained control of the entire northern coast of Africa from Morocco to Egypt.

Between the 7th and 11th centuries, the Arabs conquered northern Africa. They introduced Islam. The religion gradually spread southward into the neighboring savanna region. Later the Arabs traded and settled along the coast of eastern Africa.

IMPORTANT DATES

About 2600 B.C.	Great Pyramids of Egypt are built.
814 B.C.	Phoenicians settle the colony of Carthage on the Mediterranean coast.
About 600 B.C.	Greece replaces Phoenicia in trade and exploration of Africa.
350 B.C.– 710 A.D.	The kingdom of Axum (later Ethiopia) was most powerful during the 4th century A.D.
264– 146 B.C.	Punic Wars: Roman Empire fights Carthage for control of Mediterranean trade. Roman armies destroy Carthage.
168 B.C.	Romans conquer Egypt.
A.D. 300–1076	Kingdom of Ghana flourishes.
333	Ethiopia converted to Christianity.
429–439	Vandals conquer northern Africa.
About 500	Decline of Vandals; northern Africa becomes part of the Byzantine Empire.
640– 710	Arab conquest of northern Africa; introduction of Islam and Arabic language.
11th Century	Mali kingdom conquers Ghana.
1415	Henry the Navigator sends Portuguese expeditions down the west coast of Africa.
1445	Dinis Dias rounds Cape Verde.
1487– 1488	Bartholomeu Dias of Portugal discovers Cape of Good Hope.
1497– 1498	Vasco da Gama sails around the Cape of Good Hope to India.
About 1500	Songhai kingdom overthrows Mali.
1517	Turks conquer Egypt.
1520– 1526	Francisco Alvarez of Portugal explores Ethiopia.
1535	Spain conquers Tunis.
1541	Portuguese expel Somalis from Ethiopia.
1595	First Dutch settlement on the Guinea Coast.
1626	French settle in Senegal.
1652	Cape Town founded by the Dutch.
1660	Rise of the Bambara kingdoms on the upper Niger.
1697	France completes conquest of Senegal.

Early Kingdoms of Western Africa

Several ancient African kingdoms flourished in the Niger River valley in western Africa. These kingdoms engaged in trade with the Arabs of the north and became centers of Muslim learning and culture.

Three of the larger kingdoms were Ghana, Mali, and Songhai. The kingdom of Ghana flourished from the 3rd or 4th century A.D. to the 11th century. It was then conquered and succeeded by the Mali kingdom. The Songhai kingdom, which replaced the Mali kingdom, was powerful during the 16th century. Timbuktu was a center of trade and learning in the Songhai kingdom.

West African peoples today are very proud of these ancient kingdoms. Two African nations, Ghana and Mali, have taken their names from these old kingdoms.

European Exploration

European exploration along the coast of Africa began with the Portuguese, who were looking for a safe water route to India. Bartholomeu Dias rounded the Cape of Good Hope at the southern tip of Africa in 1488. Another Portuguese explorer, Vasco da Gama, visited the eastern coast and reached India in 1498. Soon afterward, the Portuguese established coastal settlements and began trading in gold, spices, ivory, and slaves.

Other European powers began to compete

1768–1773	James Bruce explores Ethiopia.
1787	Home for freed slaves set up in Sierra Leone.
1792	Denmark becomes the first country to abolish slave trade.
1795, 1805	Mungo Park of Scotland explores the Niger River.
1807, 1811	Great Britain abolishes slave trade.
1814	Cape Colony becomes a British possession.
1815	France, Spain, Portugal abolish slave trade.
1822	Liberia established as a home for freed American slaves.
1830–1847	France conquers Algeria.
1834	Great Britain frees all slaves in its colonies.
1836–1840	Great Trek of Boers to interior of southern Africa.
1841	Livingstone begins exploration of Africa.
1847	Liberia becomes the first independent black republic.
1849	The French establish a home for emancipated slaves at Libreville in Gabon.
1850's	Richard Burton and John Speke explore source of the Nile.
1866	Diamonds are found in South Africa.
1869	Suez Canal opens.
1871	Stanley finds Livingstone in Tanganyika.
1871	Cecil Rhodes starts building his fortune.
1884	Germany annexes South-West Africa, gains control of Togoland and the Cameroons.
1885	King Leopold II of Belgium establishes the Congo Free State as his personal property. Germany gains control of Tanganyika. Berlin Conference on African Affairs: nations agree to work for abolition of slavery, slave trade.
1886	Gold discovered in South Africa—gold rush begins.
1898	Fashoda Crisis: Anglo-French confrontation at the upper Nile brings the two powers to the brink of war.
1899–1902	The Boer War; Great Britain gains control of South Africa.
1908	Congo Free State is turned over to the Belgian Government and renamed the Belgian Congo.
1910	The British colonies in South Africa are united to form the Union of South Africa.
1922	Egypt gains independence from Great Britain.
1935	Italy invades Ethiopia.
1941–1943	North African campaign of World War II.
1948	South Africa formally adopts apartheid.
1951	Libya gains independence.
1954–1962	Algerian war of independence.
1956	Tunisia, Morocco, Sudan gain independence. Egypt nationalizes the Suez Canal, touching off a serious Middle East crisis.
1957	Ghana (Gold Coast) gains independence.
1958	Guinea gains independence.
1960	Cameroon, Central African Republic, Chad, Congo (Brazzaville), Congo (Kinshasa), Dahomey, Gabon, Ivory Coast, Malagasy Republic, Mali, Mauritania, Niger, Nigeria, Senegal, Somalia, Togo, and Upper Volta gain independence. Congo crisis erupts.
1961	Sierra Leone and Tanganyika gain independence. South Africa becomes a republic.
1962	Algeria, Burundi, Rwanda, and Uganda gain independence.
1963	African leaders meet in Addis Ababa to form the Organization of African Unity (OAU). Zanzibar and Kenya gain independence.
1964	Zanzibar and Tanganyika become Tanzania. Malawi and Zambia gain independence.
1965	The Gambia gains independence. Rhodesia unilaterally declares independence.
1966	Botswana and Lesotho gain independence.
1967	Civil war breaks out in Nigeria.
1968	Equatorial Guinea, Mauritius, and Swaziland gain independence.
1970	Nigerian civil war ends with defeat of Biafra.
1971	Formal opening of Aswan Dam (Egypt).
1974	Guinea-Bissau, formerly Portuguese Guinea, gains independence.
1975	Comoros, Mozambique, São Tomé and Príncipe, Angola, and Cape Verde gain independence.
1976	Seychelles gains independence.
1977	Djibouti gains independence.
1980	Rhodesia becomes the independent nation of Zimbabwe, under black majority rule.

with Portugal. They also established forts and trading posts along the African coast. But the Europeans did not explore the inland regions. Dense jungles, tropical diseases, waterfalls, rapids, and hostile Africans kept European explorers from the interior.

The Arabs had long been established in the slave trade. By the 16th and 17th centuries, the British, Dutch, and French—as well as the Portuguese—had joined them. Millions of men, women, and children died in slave raids and in captivity.

European exploration of the interior of Africa began in the latter half of the 18th century. In 1770 a Scottish explorer, James Bruce, explored the region of the Blue Nile, one of the two main branches of the Nile River. Later, Mungo Park, a Scottish doctor, traveled down the Niger River. One of the most famous 19th-century explorers was the Scottish missionary and doctor, David Livingstone. In the 1850's and 1860's, Livingstone explored central Africa and the lake region of southeastern Africa. He was joined by the journalist Henry Morton Stanley, who later explored the Congo region.

Early History of Southern Africa

Southern Africa's history is somewhat different from that of the rest of Africa. Because this region had a better climate than other parts of the continent, Europeans went there to settle permanently. Dutch settlers began to come to the region in the 17th century. They were followed by British settlers in the 18th century. When diamonds and gold were dis-

Many new buildings like this one have been built in Dakar, the capital of Senegal.

The University of Ibadan, in southwestern Nigeria, attracts students from many nations.

This oil refinery is at Hassi Messaoud, Algeria, in an important petroleum-producing region.

Uranium is being processed for export in this factory at Franceville, Gabon.

covered in southern Africa in the latter half of the 19th century, more British settlers came.

The Dutch settlers, called Boers, did not get along well with the British settlers. In 1836, large numbers of Boers loaded their belongings onto ox wagons and began what is known as the Great Trek into the interior of southern Africa. They met with little resistance because the black African population had been greatly reduced by a series of bitter tribal wars. The Boers settled in the veld (grassland) and established two independent republics, the Transvaal and the Orange Free State. Later, after the Boers were defeated by the British in the Boer War (1899–1902), the Union (now Republic) of South Africa was established.

Imperialism in Africa

The "scramble for Africa" really began in the mid-19th century. During the next 50 years, the continent came almost completely under European domination. France gained control of large parts of northern and western Africa, as well as a vast area between western and central Africa known as French Equatorial Africa. Britain established colonies in western, eastern, and southern Africa. The king of Belgium became the ruler of the Congo region. Germany became the master of Togoland, the Cameroons, Tanganyika, and South-West Africa. Large parts of Africa came under the control of Spain, Portugal, Italy, and Turkey. At the outbreak of World War I, the only nations in Africa that were still independent—besides European-dominated South Africa—were Ethiopia and Liberia.

The March Toward Independence

Africa's great march toward independence began in the late 1950's. In 1960 alone, seventeen African nations became independent. Most African nations have now achieved independence. Independence was generally gained peacefully. One exception, however, was Algeria, where years of guerrilla war preceded independence.

The transfer of authority was usually orderly. In a few colonies, such as the Belgian Congo (now Zaïre) and Nigeria, independence was followed by civil war. The goal of independence for all of Africa came closer in the mid-1970's, when Portugal gave up its vast African territories. But Africa still faces many problems. Black Africans are struggling for control of their own affairs in white-dominated South Africa and Namibia (South-West Africa). A cease-fire agreement was reached in war-torn Zimbabwe (Rhodesia). It returned temporarily to the status of a British colony until a new, black-ruled government for an independent Zimbabwe was formed in 1980. There are independence movements in the Canary Islands, Western Sahara, and parts of Ethiopia. Tribal loyalties that sometimes conflict with European-drawn national boundaries have also created problems.

Africa's Present and Future

Africa is a great continent, rich in both natural and human resources. Schools and hospitals are being built. Natural resources, industry, and new methods of farming are being developed. African nations are working hard to raise the standard of living of their peoples.

There is still much to be done. Average incomes for most Africans are very small. There are not enough schools or teachers. There are relatively few hospitals and doctors compared to Africa's vast size and population.

The traditional ways of life have been increasingly disrupted by contact with the rest of the world and by the massive migration to the cities. Despite many political, social, and economic advances, governments are burdened with demands that they lack the resources to meet.

Africa has become increasingly important in world affairs. In 1963, most of the independent nations of Africa banded together to form the Organization of African Unity. African nations have swelled the membership of the United Nations. When the world organization was founded in 1945, only four of the original members were African countries. Today about one out of every three member nations is African. These African nations are now making their influence felt.

DONALD J. BALLAS
Indiana University of Pennsylvania
Reviewed by E. A. BOATENG, author, *A Geography of Ghana;* HUGH C. BROOKS, Director, Center for African Studies, St. John's University (New York); L. GRAY COWAN, Director, Institute of African Studies, Columbia University.

AFRICAN-AMERICANS, HISTORY OF. See NEGRO HISTORY.

This wooden headpiece of the Bambara people (Sudan) was used in religious dances.

The Ashanti people of West Africa are famous for delicately carved gold weights.

AFRICAN ART

No one seems to know exactly how old the art of Africa is. We do not know where it started, how it grew, or how much it was influenced by other cultures. We do know, however, that African art has developed from traditions as old as those of European and Asiatic art.

Africa and its art were once thought of as being primitive. But generations before, England, France, and the United States had become great powers, Africa had known the rise and fall of many great kingdoms. The organization, discipline, laws, and religions of these ancient kingdoms show that Africa has been civilized for many centuries.

▶ GEOGRAPHY AND ART

Africa is often divided into two parts, and each part is studied separately. To the north of the Sahara Desert are the peoples known as Arabs, living in such countries as Morocco, Algeria, and Egypt. To the south of the desert are the groups referred to as black Africans. The term "African art" is used to mean the art of black Africans.

South of the Sahara the land varies greatly. The Victoria Falls, in Rhodesia, and snow-capped mountains like Kilimanjaro are in sharp contrast to the dry plains and deep jungles of the continent. The differences in climate, in addition to the differences of kingdoms, created many different kinds of cultures. Each culture has developed a separate artistic tradition.

▶ THE UNCERTAIN HISTORY OF AFRICAN ART

Visitors to Africa have always had a great interest in the carvings, sculpture, jewelry, and trinkets of the people. These works of art were regarded as interesting curiosities but were usually considered nothing more than the crude and grotesque expressions of savage people.

Toward the end of the 19th century, there was a sudden change in the attitudes of the Western world toward African art. European artists discovered in the art of Africa a directness, a rhythm, a vitality, and a use of distortion to accent certain elements that had been missing from recent Western art.

A story is told about the artist Pablo

Picasso when he first discovered the beauty of African art. Early in the 20th century, he was dining at the apartment of another great artist, Henri Matisse, and it was there that Picasso saw his first piece of African sculpture. It is said that Picasso sat silently, as though hypnotized, holding the sculpture throughout the evening. When he went home, he began a painting and worked on it through the night and all during the next day. In it he used the basic forms of the African sculpture. This was probably the very moment—if such a moment can be fixed—that African art, previously called "savage," began to influence the art of our century.

The Beginnings of African Art

Although it has not yet been proved, many scholars think that some of the rock paintings recently discovered in the Ahaggar Mountains of Algeria and in southwest Libya may have been done by black Africans. This area is north of the Sahara, but there is a theory that blacks once lived there and were driven to the south by Asians. These paintings were probably done over 4,000 years ago.

We can be more certain of the origins of African art if we begin with the cave and rock paintings of the San (Bushmen) of South Africa. These pleasant paintings depict mostly animals, for the San have always been great hunters. In southwest Africa the San paintings depict human figures. Strangely, the physical characteristics of the men can be easily recognized as European and Asiatic as well as African.

In Northern Nigeria archeologists have found several sculpted heads made of terra cotta, a red clay. The heads are not in very good condition, but after they were tested, it was discovered that originally they were parts of larger statues and are about 2,000 years old.

Ifé and Benin

There are great gaps in the history of African art. This is largely because most of the art was carved from wood, which did not last. Wooden objects could easily have been destroyed during a religious ceremony, by rotting, or by termites. But metal lasts longer, and in several areas in Africa, metal was known and used for art.

In the midwestern part of what is now

A bronze plaque of a queen and her attendants made by artisans in the kingdom of Benin.

Nigeria, two ancient kingdoms existed, Ifé and Benin. Artists in Ifé were using metal by the 12th century; Benin artists learned about it late in the 13th. First they made their statues out of beeswax; then they dipped them into thick, wet clay. When the clay was thoroughly dry, the statue was heated, causing the wax to melt and run out. Then hot, molten metal was poured into the clay mold, where the wax had been. When the metal cooled and turned hard, the clay mold was broken away, leaving a metal statue.

The famous Ifé heads and the carvings in ivory and metal castings from Benin represent as high an artistic achievement as anything done anywhere in the world at that time. Unlike most other African art, Ifé and Benin sculpture was naturalistic—the work of art resembled the actual object it was meant to represent. For subject matter the artists used animals, birds, bearded and clothed leaders, human heads, and even some Portuguese warriors (indicating that Ifé and Benin may have traded with European countries). Ivory was also used frequently, especially by Benin.

Ifé and Benin art is closer to classical Western art than any other ever created in Africa. As the Benin kingdom gradually died out, naturalism died with it. We do not know what the influences were that resulted in naturalism, but whatever they were, they disappeared.

THE FUNCTIONS OF AFRICAN ART

Very little African art bears the stamp of an individual artist. Artists were sometimes requested to do a specific work for a king or leader, but for the most part works of art were created by several tribal artists working according to tradition. Yet, in spite of his restrictions, the African artist managed to express his own imagination and technique. If a new technique proved to be good, it became part of an ever-growing tradition.

Much of the world's art is religious. So too is African art. Ancestor worship, spirits, magic, and other aspects of the religion of African tribes are reflected in the art. Art was also created for ceremonies of marriage, for funerals, and for the festive celebrations of the people.

We in the Western world can value a work of art for its beauty alone. But in Africa every line, every form, and every arrangement of shapes on a work of art has a meaning. An African sculptor seldom creates art just for the pleasure of doing so, just for the purpose of creating something beautiful. Nearly everything has a function, or purpose.

Statues are carved to honor ancestors, kings, and gods. Masks are created for festive occasions. Jewelry, trinkets, and beads are sometimes used to indicate wealth, growing up, authority, or marriage. Guardian figures are fastened to coffins to invite good spirits to protect the dead and to chase away evil demons. Combs, spoons, bowls, stools, and other useful items are carved to make them decorative. But an object of art is always meant to be useful first and beautiful only second.

Masks

The use of masks was an important part of the spirit world that existed in the lives of the African people. They were used at initiations, for example, when a boy was accepted as an adult hunter. Their main purpose was to scare away evil intruders.

Among the masks most widely admired—at least by people in the Western world—are those of the Bambara of the Sudan region. They have graceful lines and a smooth finish, which show the craftsmanship of the artists. Sometimes they are covered with feathers or other decorations. Often worn on top of the head instead of over the face, the designs of the masks are usually based on the horns of an animal, reaching heavenward.

Gold Weights

An important type of metal sculpture in Africa is the gold weight. Made of gold, bronze, brass, or copper, these small cast figures were of various sizes and weights. Their purpose was to measure quantities of gold. Most of these gold weights were made on the Gold Coast, in what is now Ghana, for here gold was important for trade. The Ashanti people, who probably produced more gold weights than any other, made their figures in a wide variety of subjects, including medicine men, birds, fish, reptiles, trees, plants, insects, pots and stools, swords, drums, animals, and plain rectangular blocks decorated with geometric designs.

Jewelry

Africans have always appreciated the beauty of gold. Little girls while still infants wear tiny gold earrings through their pierced ears. African women wear gold trinkets for ornamentation. Men, too, on great occasions wear long gold chains and heavy pendants. The African goldsmith is a masterful craftsman. Working in 18-karat gold, he creates intricate work of the finest detail.

Handicrafts

Africans, weaving their own textiles, create striking and well-made rugs, shopping bags, robes, and other decorative products. The artists who create these fabrics are usually women; all other art is left to the men. Patterns on cloth are sometimes geometrical designs. Often animals or birds are repeated throughout. The variety of color and the frequent inclusion of silk or other glossy threads within the weave of the fabric prevent the designs from becoming monotonous.

Pottery has always been an important craft in Africa. Bowls and jars are usually very functional and simple in design. It is this simplicity that makes them so interesting.

1. Drinking vessel made from the shell of an ostrich egg by Bushmen artists. 2. Ivory head carved in the 16th century in Benin. 3. Stone stool, Ifé kingdom, 13th century. 4. Tree of iron made by Yoruba tribe of Nigeria. 5. Ashanti gold ornament. 6. Musical instrument known as *kundi*, made of animal skins, animal hairs, and fiber, Mangbetu tribe, Congo.

1

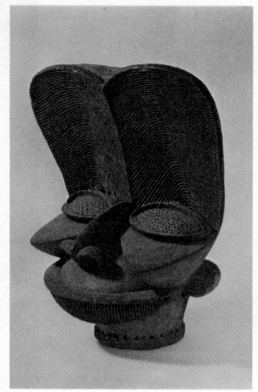

2

3

Masks for religious ceremonies are an important form of
African art. 1. Bobo buffalo mask, Sudan region. 2. Mask
for dancing, Bacham people, Cameroon grasslands. 3.
Kagba mask, Senufo people, Sudan region. 4. Ogowe River
spirit mask, Gabon. 5. Abstract mask of the Bateke people,
Lower Congo.

4

5

1. Guardian figure of wood and copper, Bakota tribe. Congo region. 2. Wooden statue of high-ranking person, Basundi tribe, Lower Congo. 3. Head from wooden figurine of Baule tribe, Guinea Coast. 4. Wooden hippopotamus from the Barotse tribe, Zambia. 5. Copper guardian figure to protect tombs, Bakota tribe, Congo. 6. Wooden bird, probably a hornbill, about 4 feet high, Senufo tribe, Ivory Coast.

Baskets, briefcases, shoes, and even fans and rugs are made of a coarse cloth called *samfos* or a strawlike fiber known as raffia.

Sculpture

Sculpture is Africa's greatest art. Wood is used far more than any other material, not only because it is easy to carve but because the Africans feel that a tree represents the force of life.

The three principal cultural regions in Africa south of the Sahara are the Sudan, the Guinea Coast, and the Bantu. Within each region many very different styles of sculpture exist, but in most cases there are characteristics that link the art of one tribe to the art of another. The best way to understand this is to study the illustrations.

Sudan. The Sudan, a strip of land just south of the Sahara, extends roughly from the Atlantic Ocean to the Red Sea. Ideas in Sudanese sculpture are represented by reducing a form to its simplest state. A geometric shape, such as a cone or a cylinder, may be used to stand for the horns of an animal. This type of art, called abstract, is new to the Western world, but to the Sudanese it is part of an old tradition.

The most influential—and perhaps the finest—art of the Sudan is created by the Bambara tribe. The finish of Bambara sculpture is smooth and highly polished; the forms are flowing and graceful. The Dogon tribe today creates sculpture that is the extreme of the style; nearly all of their forms are purely geometric.

Guinea Coast. South of the Sudan, along the coast of the Gulf of Guinea, is the area known as the Guinea Coast. The most interesting thing about much Guinea sculpture is its sharp contrasts. Rounded, graceful forms are stopped abruptly by flat, massive shapes.

The sculpture of the Yoruba of Nigeria exaggerates or simplifies human features. A torso may be long and curved, ending abruptly at a flat neck or square foot. The Yoruba are noted for their use of color. Sculpture is often painted in bright colors. Other peoples noted for the quality of their sculpture are Baule, Ibibio, and Fang. In Fang sculpture the parts of the body are sometimes turned into massive spheres or squares.

Bantu Africa. The rest of southern Africa, from Cameroon across the continent to the Indian Ocean and southward to the tip of the continent, is known as Bantu Africa. Bantu is the name of the family of languages spoken there. Bantu sculpture is noble and beautifully finished. The faces on most of the figures are meant to be those of ancestors. Living people are not used as models.

The sculpture of the Bushongo and Baluba tribes shows fine workmanship. Carving is done in the direction of the grain of a hardwood, no carving scars are left, and each piece is highly polished. Many of these people, especially the Baluba, are very slender. This is reflected in the sculpture, where big, majestic heads representing those of ancestors are placed on very long, thin bodies. Unlike most other African sculpture, art in the northern Bantu region is quite stony and without a feeling of movement.

▶ AFRICA OUT OF THE DARK

The art of Africa, which is very old and is neither savage nor uncivilized, has had a great impact on modern art. In our time the peoples and tribes of what used to be called the dark continent are working together to form new nations. One by one these nations are becoming part of the political world and are sharing the problems of other nations.

Africa's participation in the forming of a new face for the art of our time began long before its participation in world politics. If art is a hint—and it often is—then Africa will help give a needed new face to today's world and to better worlds yet to come.

J. NEWTON HILL
Director, Lagos Office, African-American Institute

The Yoruba of Nigeria used this wooden mask for religious ceremonies. At left is the front of the mask, and at right, the back.

Storytellers have kept the traditional spoken literature of Africa alive for centuries.

AFRICAN LITERATURE

An African philosopher once said, "Whenever an old man dies, it is as though a library had been burned to the ground." The philosopher said this because for centuries, the traditional literature of Africa was not written down. It was performed, and it was handed down from parent to child by word of mouth.

This article concerns the literature of black Africa (the part of the continent south of the Sahara) in its traditional and modern forms. The African nations that border the Mediterranean Sea belong to a different cultural tradition. Their literature and the literature of Europeans who settled in Africa will not be discussed here.

▶ THE ORAL TRADITION

Literature, as we think of it, is written. But the traditional forms of African literature—stories, poems, and proverbs—are spoken and chanted. Something basic in the African approach to life and art resists the very notion of alphabets and written records.

Africans believe that the spoken word is much more powerful than the written word. The spoken word is also an art and a celebration of life, to be shared by all who live in the community. Like life, this art constantly changes. When a story is repeated, it will be different. The storyteller's costume will have changed, and new verses will have been added to the song. And the audience, joining in singing and clapping, will be different, too. Each listener will be older and wiser than the last time.

Art in Africa is never just for fun. It has a purpose. Stories and poems are used to teach the duties and beliefs of the community. This knowledge is taught by the older people. Some of the truths that people have always lived by are dramatized in spoken performances, in masquerades, and in rituals. The members of the audience understand according to their ages. A story may mean one thing to a grandmother who tells it in the cool of the evening. It may mean another to the children eagerly listening. Everyone laughs, and everyone learns something appropriate.

Small children are encouraged to sharpen their wits by exchanging riddles such as "Going, they talk a lot; coming back, they keep silent." (Answer: water gourds. Empty gourds rattle together—"talk"—on the way to be filled. Full gourds do not rattle.) As the children grow older, they learn to tell stories well. They also flavor their everyday speech with proverbs, such as "Speed ends, distance continues." Beautiful and polite speech is required of adults. But not everyone goes on to become a famous storyteller. Those who do become storytellers must learn to play musical instruments—usually a guitar or harp—because music is an important part of this oral literature.

▶ FORMS OF ORAL LITERATURE

There are many different kinds of traditional spoken literature in Africa. Trickster tales are very popular. These stories are about clever characters who outwit people and animals and humorously escape difficult situations. In western Sudan and in southern Africa, such stories are told about the hare. The spider, Anansi, is the mischievous, greedy hero of trickster tales in Ghana, Liberia, and Sierra Leone. In Nigeria and Cameroon, the tortoise is the cleverest animal. Sometimes, as in Benin (Dahomey) and Tanzania, the trickster is a human, or partly human, being. A god may also be a trickster. The Yoruba of Nigeria call this god Elegba.

Trickster stories were carried to the New World by Africans. The hare became Brer Rabbit. Anansi stories are still told in Jamaica, Surinam, and Belize (British Honduras). In the Carolinas and Georgia in the southern United States, Anansi became Aunt Nancy, a clever old woman.

Certain songs that are sung and stories that are told by young girls (like those about pale fox told among the Dogon of Mali) encourage young men to think of marriage. Tales of heroic ancestors, sung on the eve of battle, will inspire young men to perform brave deeds in war. Poems praising the gods and spirits are meant to persuade them to bring good fortune to the community.

In some parts of Africa south of the Sahara, heroic or epic poetry still exists. (An epic is a long poem that tells the story of a legendary hero and often weaves the ideals and traditions of a people into the story.) The singing or chanting of these long poems may take hours or even several days. Such poetry requires an excellent memory. It also requires the ability to improvise (to make up as you go along). These things are beyond most people's skill. For all these reasons, the people who recite African epics are professional singers and storytellers.

Often these professionals are members of a special family or social group. In Mali, they are known as *djeli;* in eastern Zaïre, they are called *karisi*. In Cameroon and in Gabon, the bards, or heroic singers, bear the same name as the instrument they play and the type of tale they recite—*mvet*.

In return for an exhausting performance, the grateful community gives these professional bards food, money, and praise. But the performers must be good. African audiences expect the best and are critical. Many singers have to please an invisible as well as a visible audience. In Nigeria, the professional Bini storyteller sings special songs for the witches and spirits of the night, who dance to the music and are thought to be angry if the songs end before they have finished their dances.

Sundiata is the national epic of the Malinke people of Mali. It honors the founder of the Mali empire, who was unable to walk until he was 7 years old but grew up to be a remarkable hunter, warrior, and magician. *Lianja* tells the fabulous story of the epic hero of the Mongo people of Zaïre. Liyongo, the spear lord, gives his name to an epic sung in the languages of eastern and central Africa. These are only three of the many epics that represent African imaginations at their greatest power.

Today some of these heroic poems have been written down. Times have changed in Africa, and there is a danger that young people who have talent for the profession will not choose to become bards. Several versions of *Sundiata* have been translated into English, as have stories of the deeds of Chaka, the Zulu warrior chief, and parts of *Lianja*. To the ruling class of Ethiopia, the written word was always more important than the spoken word. In Ethiopia the epic story of Solomon and Sheba, called *The Glory of Kings,* has been read for many centuries.

▶ AFRICAN LITERATURE IN EUROPEAN LANGUAGES

With the coming of European missionaries in the 18th and 19th centuries, African languages were written down. European schools were started in which Africans learned to read and write not only their own languages but also European languages. This learning produced a new literature—short stories, poems, and novels that were never meant to be recited and plays that were meant to be performed on a stage rather than in a village square.

Some of these literary forms, new to Africans, have been explored by African writers in their own languages. But those who write in English and French can hope for more readers.

For this reason most recent African literature has been written in these languages. African writing in French developed in the regions once occupied by the French. African literature in English comes from countries in eastern, western, and southern Africa, where for a time English-speaking people ruled.

Because African societies are quite different from one another, some African writers have asked themselves this question: Is it possible to speak of the "African" qualities of literature? In other words, can literature express ideas that truly reflect all of black Africa? Those who have answered "yes" are known as the negritude poets and novelists. Most of them write in French.

The Spirit of Negritude

It was a West Indian from the island of Martinique, Aimé Césaire, who first used the word "negritude." Césaire had been in-

---

TRADITIONAL AND MODERN AFRICAN LITERATURE

Benin (Dahomey)
Dahomean Narrative: A Cross-Cultural Analysis by Melville J. Herskovits and Frances S. Herskovits.

Cameroon
Houseboy by Ferdinand Oyono.
Old Man and the Medal by Ferdinand Oyono.

Ethiopia
Fire on the Mountain and Other Ethiopian Stories by Harold Courlander and Wolf Leslau.
Shinega's Village by Sahle Sellassie; translated by Wolf Leslau.

Ghana
The Adventures of Spider by Joyce Cooper Arkhurst.
Guardians of the Sacred Word, edited by Kofi Awoonor.
More Adventures of Spider by Joyce Cooper.
Vulture- Vulture- by Efua T. Sutherland.

Guinea
The Dark Child by Camara Laye.

Kenya
The River Between by James Ngugi.
Weep Not Child by James Ngugi.

Mali
Sundiata: An Epic of Old Mali by D. T. Niane.

Nigeria
Arrow of God by Chinua Achebe.
The Calabash of Wisdom and Other Igbo Stories by Romanus Egudu.
Lion and the Jewel by Wole Soyinka.
My Life in the Bush of Ghosts by Amos Tutuola.
The Palm-Wine Drinkard by Amos Tutuola.

Poetic Heritage: Igbo Traditional Verse by Romanus Egudu and Donatus Nwoga.
Sweet Words: Storytelling Events in Benin by Dan Ben-Amos.
Things Fall Apart by Chinua Achebe.
Yoruba Poetry by H. U. Beier.
Yoruba Proverbs by Bernth Lindfors and Oyekan Owomoyela.

Senegal
Selected Poems by Léopold S. C. Senghor.
Tales of Amadou Koumba by Birago Diop.

South Africa
Chaka: An Historical Romance by Thomas Mofolo; translated by F. H. Dutton.
Down Second Avenue: Growing Up in a South African Ghetto by Ezekiel Mphahlele.
Lion on the Path and Other African Stories by Hugh Tracey.
Zulu Poems by Mazisi Kunene.

Zaïre
The Mwindo Epic from the Banyanga by Daniel Biebuyck and Kahombo C. Mateene.
Myths and Legends of the Congo by Jan Knappert.

Anthologies
African Assertion: A Critical Anthology of African Literature, edited by Austin J. Shelton, Jr.
African Myths and Tales, edited by Susan Feldman.
Leaf and Bone: African Praise Poems, edited by Judith Gleason.
Poems of Black Africa, edited by Wole Soyinka.
Yes and No: The Intimate Folklore of Africa by Alta Jablow.

fluenced by the American literary movement of the 1920's known as the Harlem Renaissance. His greatest poem, *Return to My Native Land,* was published in 1939. In this poem, he defined negritude as a celebration of blackness. The title of the poem points to a desire for a non-European way of life in the place where he grew up.

Césaire's friend Léopold Sédar Senghor became the president of Senegal and the most important writer of his generation. Senghor defined negritude as the cultural heritage, the values, and the spirit of black African civilization. In his poems, Senghor longs to be a child again, looking up into the peaceful face of his mother.

To the negritude writers, education in Paris —or even in French-language schools in Africa—meant that a person was changed by the European world and was not so African as before. Such a person would be less able to understand African problems. The works of Tchicaya U Tam'si, a poet from the Congo, reflect the desire to return to an understanding of his own suffering and the suffering of his people.

Césaire wrote of return to his native land; Senghor, of return to cultural heritage; and Tchicaya, of return to understanding. But in a novel called *The Dark Child,* by Camara Laye of Guinea, the going-back aspect of negritude is most simply and beautifully expressed. From this novel the reader may learn how it feels to grow up in an African village. And one may learn how it feels to say goodbye, perhaps forever, to the land of one's ancestors.

Another feeling expressed by negritude authors is anger. It is an anger that attacks the white world for inhumanity—for racism, for concern with wealth and material things, and for pretending one thing but being another. This anger, close to that of the United States author Richard Wright, may be seen in the novels of Ferdinand Oyono from Cameroon, especially in *Houseboy,* the story of an African servant in a white household.

Other Attitudes

Wole Soyinka, a Nigerian playwright, has a different view. To him, for a black person to insist on negritude is as silly as for a tiger to insist on "tigritude." Soyinka wrote *A Dance of the Forests* for the celebration of Nigerian independence in 1960. This play is a fantasy in which traditional gods and spirits call up a small group of ancestors to accuse them of participating in the European slave trade. "Do not romanticize old Africa," the play is saying.

This no-nonsense attitude is shared by Ezekiel Mphahlele, an exiled South African writer, and by most Africans writing in English. To them, Senghor's homesickness has seemed self-indulgent, and his idea of traditional African life unrealistic.

The Nigerian novelist Chinua Achebe has recorded the strife within the traditional African community. He says it is useless to deny social change—the problem is how to meet it. His novels ask whether modern Nigerian leaders can develop the strength of character of certain old chiefs and priests who resisted European ways. *Things Fall Apart* (1958) and *Arrow of God* (1964) both deal with such heroic old men in a time of social change.

▶ **AFRICAN LITERATURE AS WORLD LITERATURE**

The question remains—is it possible to speak of the African qualities of this literature? The pain of feeling separated from one's own people has been expressed by writers in many parts of the world, as well as by African writers. And Soyinka's humor and richness of language are sometimes like Shakespeare's. Thus, African writing is a part of world literature.

On the other hand, African literature, traditional or modern, is about a place many people have never visited, even in imagination. It is a place worth getting to know. The sights and sounds are unique. The rain beats heavily on tin roofs and thatched roofs. When the rain stops, a small bird begins to sing in a mango tree. Then people come out, talking. On their way they meet others and stop for a while to talk some more. The conversation may be in any one of the more than 800 languages spoken on the continent, but it is undeniably African. In the spoken word may be found the quality that some African writers have called the genius of black civilization. And in the spoken word there is magic. The spoken word, always fresh, is the source of all African literature.

JUDITH GLEASON
Author, *Orisha: The Gods of Yorubaland*

AFRICAN MUSIC

Every time you turn on your radio or listen to television or a juke box, there is a good chance that the music you hear will be at least partly African in origin. This is because the music of Africa has strongly influenced the music of Europe and America. It began when black Africans were transported to America as slaves, taking their songs and dances with them. Gradually, as they became accustomed to their new home, they combined their own music with the folk music and American Indian music they heard in the New World. The result was a new and original American folk music. Largely out of this grew jazz, one of the most popular forms of music today.

African music is considered primitive because it comes from people who do not have a written language; songs are passed on by word of mouth rather than by the use of written notes. Yet it does not seem right to call this music primitive, since some of it is more highly developed than the folk music of Europe and America.

▶ MUSIC IN AFRICAN LIFE

To the black Africans south of the Sahara, music is a vital part of everyday life. It means more to them than merely listening pleasure.

Wind instruments are sometimes made from the horns of animals.

As in most primitive societies, it is primarily associated with religious and ceremonial life. Besides ceremonial and prayer songs, there are songs appropriate only for certain times of the year, songs for the important events in a person's life (birth, coming of age, marriage, death), songs for curing the sick, bringing rain, for religious dances, and so on. The Tutsi tribe of Rwanda has songs for boasting, songs for young women when they meet together, songs to flatter girls, songs for children, working songs, songs about cattle, and many other kinds.

In contrast to the people of Western societies, everyone plays an active part in the musical life of the tribe. In a typical tribe of Nigeria, for instance, it is taken for granted

The most familiar of African musical instruments are the drums.

that every member has musical talent. Despite the fact that there are some professional musicians who are paid for their special skills, most members of a typical African tribe know and can sing their music as a matter of course.

Music is ultimately tied to the things that are most important to the welfare of the tribe. For example, to the Tutsi tribe of Rwanda, cattle are extremely important because they are the tribe's chief source of food. Therefore, as you might expect, cattle are popular subjects for a wide variety of songs. There are ceremonial songs about cattle, songs in which men boast about their cattle, flute pieces that keep cattle thieves away at night, children's cow songs, and songs that tell of historical events in which cattle have taken part. There are work songs to sing while the cowherd prepares to take cattle home in the evening, others to sing during the journey home, still others to sing while the cowherd draws water. This shows the many kinds of songs connected with only one aspect of tribal life. Can you imagine how many other different kinds of songs there must be in the life of this tribe? How wonderful it would be if music played as vital a rôle in our everyday lives as it does in the lives of African children.

▶ CHARACTER OF THE MUSIC

Africa is a huge continent with hundreds of tribes. Its people sing and play many different kinds of music. Some peoples, such as those of the southern African deserts, have very simple songs. Others, such as those of the Congo (Zaïre) River basin, have complicated singing and instrumental music. The East Africans specialize in music played on xylophones, while the tribes of the West Coast have developed the art of drum playing to a very high level of skill.

Once you have heard African music, it is surprising how easy it is to recognize, in spite of all its variety. Perhaps this is due mainly to its unforgettable rhythm. It has a very steady beat that may not change in tempo for hours. Many African musicians have developed an extraordinary rhythmic ability that helps them to keep up a tempo without the slightest variation over enormous time spans. They can perform rhythmic feats on their drums that are truly amazing.

The melodies are usually short and simple and use fewer notes of the scale than our music does. These melodies are not like ours, which can be sung through from beginning to end; rather they consist of short bits of melody repeated over and over. In performance the singers or players may change them at will, so that what you hear is something like a theme with many variations. Often such music is sung or played by two separate groups, or by one group and its leader, each singing a bit of the melody in alternation with the other. Africans sometimes distort their voices to make them sound like instruments or like the cries of wild animals.

The people of many tribes south of the Sahara have developed a highly refined sense of harmony. Although they probably do not hear music in terms of chords, as we do, they do think in terms of several voices singing different melodies at the same time. In some pieces there are so many rhythms and melodies going on at once that you can hardly distinguish them all as you listen. Often the same melody is sung by separate groups on different pitches at the same time.

Africans also sing rounds, as people do in other countries. (Examples of rounds that are often sung in Western countries, in and out of school, are "Three Blind Mice" and "Frère Jacques.") Some songs are accompanied by instruments. The accompaniment may be either chords or short melodic patterns that are repeated over and over.

When a group of singers performs, sometimes one person in the chorus will suddenly begin to improvise, or make up a special version of the melody, while the other singers continue the original melody. To be able to improvise, or to make up your own version of the music as you go along, is considered good musicianship. This is a practice that has survived in American black folk music and in jazz, since these also allow you to improvise and make variations of the melody while performing.

▶ INSTRUMENTS

Almost any musical instrument you can think of has its related form in Africa. The most famous ones are the drums, and there are many kinds, shapes, and sizes. Some are so large and heavy that they must be set on the ground. Others can be held between the player's legs or under the arm. Some are small enough to be hung from the player's neck or shoulders. When drumsticks are not used, Africans beat the drums with their hands and fingers. They have developed a highly sensitive technique, so that the different fingers can make the drum give out a variety of sounds, and the various parts of the drum make different kinds of noises. Drums are played singly or in groups of up to five.

Perhaps the most characteristic African instrument, which is not found on any other continent, is the sansa, or *mbira,* sometimes called the thumb-piano. It consists of a wooden board or box over which several tongues of metal or bamboo are tied. Each of these tongues is plucked gently, making a buzzing or tinkling sound. There are from 8 to over 20 such tongues on the sansa. Often a large gourd is tied under the sansa to make it more resonant. The sansa is played as a solo instrument, or in groups, or with other types of instruments. It is also used to accompany singing.

The sansa is a relative of the xylophone, another typical African instrument. Xylophones were probably first brought to Africa from Java and Bali, where they had already existed many centuries before. African xylophones vary greatly in size. Some are small enough to be held by a child; others (in Liberia, for example) are so large that the slabs must rest on two small tree trunks lying parallel on the ground. Like the sansa, it is also played as a solo instrument, in groups, with other instruments, or as accompaniment to singing.

Stringed instruments are of many kinds. Most of them are plucked rather than bowed. Some are tall like harps with many strings; others are simple like the musical bow, which has only one string that is plucked or struck with a small stick. The most common wind instruments are the flutes, the horns made from animals' horns or of wood, and the panpipes. But it is the rattles and the bells that receive the widest use and that are so essential to the great rhythmic vitality of the music. Although they do not have orchestras, as we do, Africans do have something very much like chamber music. For example, a harp, a sansa, and a rattle may be played together in a piece; or a bell, horns, and a chorus, or a

Large gourds are filled with water and beaten with spoons and drumsticks.

group of three xylophones may form an ensemble.

Musical instruments are also used for purposes other than music making in some tribes. They are sometimes used to signal information over long distances. Since instruments usually can be heard over greater distances than shouting or singing, some tribes have made up codes based on the melodic movement of speech. Many African languages are called tone languages because the pitch, high or low, on which you speak a word or a syllable determines the meaning of the word. In the signaling codes the melodic pitches of a word are often played on a slit drum made from a hollowed log pounded with a stick, and people far away can understand what the drum says. In Liberia, xylophones are sometimes used in this way to signal messages.

BRUNO NETTL
Wayne State University

AGASSIZ, JEAN LOUIS RODOLPHE (1807–1873)

Long ago the glaciers of the earth began to grow. Great sheets of ice ground their way south from the Arctic. Huge rivers of ice crept down from lofty mountains into the valleys. As thousands of years passed, the ice reached out and covered lands we know today as green and fair.

The man who first drew this picture of a strange and vanished past was a young Swiss scientist named Louis Agassiz. It was Agassiz who realized that there had been an ice age.

Agassiz was born on May 28, 1807, in Môtier-en-Vully, Switzerland. As a boy he showed a strong interest in animals and plants. His mother encouraged him, letting him collect specimens and carry out experiments. His father was a minister, and although far from rich, was determined that his bright son receive a good education. At 10 Louis was sent away to school. Later he studied at several universities.

While at the University of Munich, he began work on the classification of fishes, both living and fossil. His research soon drew the attention of scientists all over Europe. It also helped Agassiz make a decision. He would not practice medicine, as his father wished. He would work in the natural sciences.

By 1832 he was teaching at Neuchâtel, in Switzerland. The 14 years he spent there set the pattern for his life: his home became his workshop. Life was not easy for his wife, Cécile; funds were always low, yet the house was always full of co-workers who lived and ate with the Agassiz family.

In the summer of 1836, Agassiz and two friends climbed one of the great Alpine glaciers. What Agassiz observed caught his curiosity and his imagination. Studies of other glaciers soon convinced him that ice had played a major role in sculpturing the earth. Within a year he announced that a large part of the earth had once been covered with ice.

The geologists of his day were furious. Who was Agassiz to talk about geology? Why didn't he stick to his fishes? Agassiz, however, was sure he was right. Year after year he went back up the Alps, gathering the evidence that proved his case.

In 1845 Agassiz was invited to lecture in America. He accepted, and as things turned out, spent the rest of his life in the United States. In his new home Agassiz became famous as a lecturer and teacher.

In 1848 he became a professor at Harvard University. His wife, whom he had had to leave in Switzerland, was now dead. So Agassiz sent for his children and soon remarried. His second wife was Elizabeth Cabot Cary, a remarkable woman, who later became a founder of Radcliffe College. Mrs. Agassiz encouraged her husband in his work and added to their income by setting up a girls' school on the top floor of the house.

Agassiz was an extraordinary teacher. He treated his students as co-workers. He believed that they should learn to gather facts, rather than learn facts already gathered. The first summer school for studying animals in their natural environment was set up by Agassiz on an island in Buzzards Bay, Massachusetts. He also founded the first natural history museum in America. It is the Museum of Comparative Zoology at Harvard (often known as the "Agassiz museum").

Agassiz's enthusiasm for natural history overflowed. For him no audience was too small—he would lecture to the man driving him to his hotel or to a fisherman in a rowboat. His desire to learn as well as to teach endeared him to his students. One wrote, after his death on December 14, 1873, that Agassiz "had been a student all his life long, and when he died he was younger than any of them."

PATRICIA G. LAUBER
Author and editor, field of science

See also ICE AGES.

Agassiz lecturing in the United States on animals like starfish, sea urchins, sea anemones, and jellyfish.

In 1513 Ponce de Leon searched Florida in vain for fabled Fountain of Youth.

AGING

Everybody knows that old people are more likely to die than young people. We know it from experience. We can find the facts and figures in life insurance tables. For example, in a well-fed, advanced country only about one in every 1,000 children dies during his or her 12th year. But one in every 20 men aged 70 will die before his 71st birthday.

The risk we run of dying at any particular age is called the **force of mortality** for that age. The force of mortality has been carefully worked out for all ages of people—this is what life insurance rates are based on. Naturally, it grows steadily greater with age. If we kept all through life the same force of mortality that we had at 12—never becoming any more likely to die than we were then—we could all hope to live several hundred years, unless we were very unlucky or careless. The fact that people do not live several hundred years (and only rarely reach 100) is due to a process called **aging**.

We can recognize aging by the gray hair, weakened muscles, wrinkled skin, loss of hearing, and other signs that it produces. It also has a more important effect on us. It reduces our power of staying well and of getting better if we fall ill. A head cold may not be serious in a young person, but its complications may lead to death in an old person.

This loss of the power to stay healthy (and the increase in the likelihood of dying) happens at about the same rate in everybody. As we get older, we tend to be like an old radio or an old automobile—more and more things go wrong with us. There comes a time beyond which it is very difficult to stay alive at all. The least thing may be enough to finish us. This is the end of our **life span**.

▶ **LIFE SPANS IN MEN AND WOMEN**

People and other animals that age have fixed life spans, or characteristic ages of death. Some individuals may die sooner, while strong or lucky ones live longer. But most individuals of a species have about the same length of life. In countries with good food and medical services, the most common length of life in people is between 70 and 80 years. Where there is hunger or little medical care, many people die young. Often death among babies, or infant mortality, is very high. For those who survive, the expectation of life is low—perhaps 40 to 45 years.

Women, for reasons we do not yet understand, live a little longer on the average than men. Some people, especially if they have come from long-lived families, live longer than others. Some are able to live as much as 20 years beyond the usual limit of life. For example, here are the figures for England, Canada, and the United States. In these countries about three out of every 100 babies born will live to be 90 years old; about one out of every 1,000 will live to be 100.

A few people live longer still, up to 107 or 108 years. There is a great deal of argument about the highest age ever reached by a person.

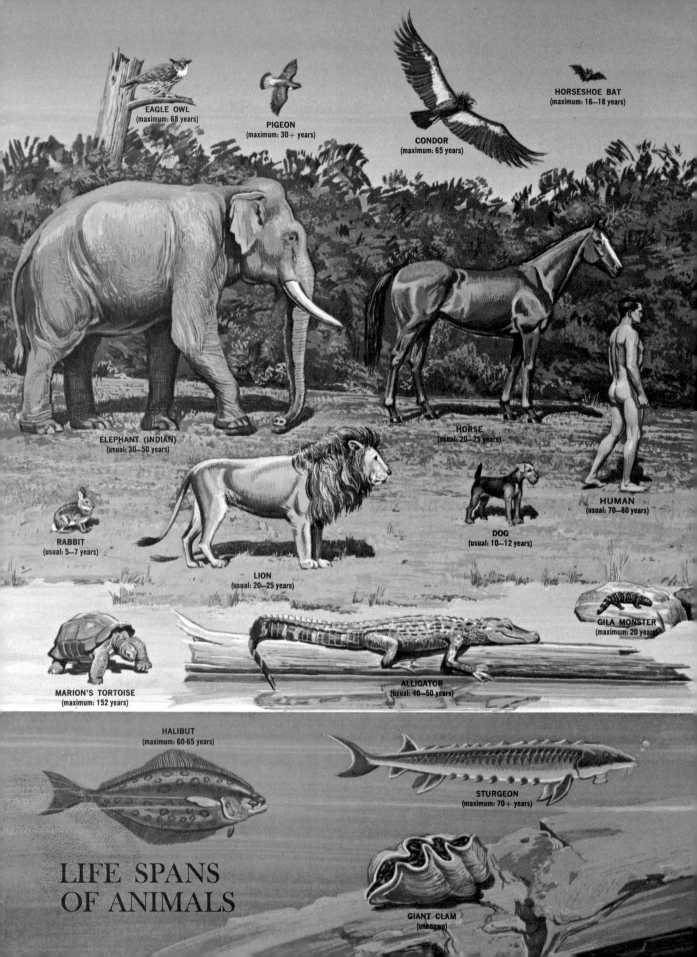

EAGLE OWL
(maximum: 68 years)

PIGEON
(maximum: 30+ years)

CONDOR
(maximum: 65 years)

HORSESHOE BAT
(maximum: 16—18 years)

ELEPHANT (INDIAN)
(usual: 30—50 years)

HORSE
(usual: 20—25 years)

HUMAN
(usual: 70—80 years)

RABBIT
(usual: 5—7 years)

LION
(usual: 20—25 years)

DOG
(usual: 10—12 years)

GILA MONSTER
(maximum: 20 years)

MARION'S TORTOISE
(maximum: 152 years)

ALLIGATOR
(usual: 40—50 years)

HALIBUT
(maximum: 60-65 years)

STURGEON
(maximum: 70+ years)

LIFE SPANS
OF ANIMALS

GIANT CLAM
(unknown)

HOW LONG THEY LIVE
(arranged by maximum age in years)

	USUAL	MAXIMUM
Marion's tortoise	—	152 or more
Human	70–80	Perhaps 120
Box turtle	—	Over 100
Alligator	40–50 in zoos	Possibly 100
River mussel	—	60–100 (some sorts)
Elephant (Indian)	30–50	77
Sturgeon	—	Certainly over 70
Eagle owl	—	68
Condor	—	65
Halibut	—	60–65
Cockatoo	—	At least 60
Silurus (a catfish)	—	60
Giant salamander	—	Over 50
Whale	—	Probably not much over 50
Carp	—	50
Goose	—	50
Ostrich	—	50
Horse	20–25	40–42
Chimpanzee	15–20	40
Clam	—	40
Giant clam	Not known, but may be no longer than for small clams.	
Goldfish	—	40
Lion	20–25	40
Large toad	—	36
Newt	—	35
Polar bear	16	33
Cow	— *	Over 30
Pigeon	—	Over 30
Cat	9–10	27–31
Most snakes	—	20–30
Chaffinch	—	29
Dog (depends on breed)	10–12	26?
Sheep	— *	Over 20
Gila monster	—	20
Giant spider	—	11–20
Queen ant	—	16–19
Horseshoe bat	—	16–18 in the wild
Rabbit	5–7	15–18
Frog	—	12–16
Gray squirrel	9	15
Guinea pig	4–5	10–12?
Earthworm	—	10
Large beetle	Up to 10 years as adults (larval life may be very long).	
Guppy	2	5–6
Queen bee	—	5 or more
Mouse	1½	3¼
Mayfly	½ day	1 week or more

* No "usual" life given because many are eaten while still relatively young.

Probably it is just short of 120 years. For instance, a man who said he was 117 and the last survivor of the Confederate Army died in Texas in 1959. People who have claimed to be older than 120 have never been able to prove it. Some old people are jokers who tell tremendous tales about their age. Other people are willing to believe these tales because they like the idea of living a long time.

▶ LIFE SPANS IN ANIMALS

We are used to the idea that we will age. We are so used to this that it comes as a surprise to find that there may be some animals that do not age. Sea anemones are an example. Some have been kept for nearly a century without showing any signs of losing vigor. Some kinds of marine worm can even "grow backwards." If starved and kept in the dark, they get steadily smaller. They finally end as a ball of cells, looking rather like the egg from which they came. Under favorable conditions the ball will turn back to a worm and start growing again. One could probably keep them growing and "un-growing" indefinitely.

An animal that does not age is not immortal. That is, it is not deathless. Some individuals will die by accident or from disease every year. But such animals do not get *more likely* to die with age. The force of mortality stays the same in them.

It is sometimes said that small wild animals and birds do not age. What really happens is that they do not have a chance to age. Nearly all die by accident before they have a chance to get really old. Few small birds in the wild survive more than a couple of years. But in a cage, protected from hunger and enemies, they can live as long as 20 years and then die of old age.

Most animals are like us in having fixed life spans. The chart on this page shows some of these. From it you will see that the large species in any group generally live longer than the small. (There are exceptions. Many bats are about the size of mice but live much longer.) Birds live longer than mammals of the same size. Fish and reptiles, which are cold blooded, live longer still. Not only do they live long but, unlike us, they keep growing. An English ship once caught a halibut about 3 meters (10 feet) long. Experts could tell from its scales that it was more than 60 years old. The fish was full of eggs and still growing. At one time it seemed that because they go on growing, these big fish and reptiles might not "age" at all. However, recent studies on fish suggest that they age much as we do, only the big kinds do so more slowly.

Tortoises (land turtles) and sturgeon are probably the two longest-lived vertebrates (animals with backbones). Human beings are the longest-lived mammals. The elephant is the only other mammal that approaches our life span. In spite of what you read in many books, whales and elephants do not live for hundreds of years. The figures in the chart represent the most recent knowledge about animal life spans.

▶ THE DREAM OF LONGER LIFE

People have never liked to think that they would get old or that their lives would end around a fixed age. So there have always been stories about miraculously long lives and about people who regained their youth. A Greek myth tells us of Eos (Aurora), goddess of the dawn, who prayed that her husband, Tithonus, be made immortal. The prayer was granted, but unfortunately she had forgotten to ask that he stay eternally young. So he grew older and older and more and more decrepit until he prayed to be allowed to die.

Poets in the Middle Ages wrote of a Fountain of Youth in which one could bathe and become young. The fountain was a fiction invented by the poets. But there was, at the same time, another group of people called alchemists. They were the inventors of chemistry, though they mixed a great deal of magic in with it. The alchemists took over the dream of eternal youth. They made it one of their three great projects: to change lead into gold, to travel to the moon, and to discover the elixir of life, which would make old people young.

The alchemists failed to achieve these goals. Time passed and scientific knowledge grew. In the light of the new knowledge, the three old dreams seemed less and less likely ever to be realized. Scientists left them to lunatics and frauds. But then more time passed, and the modern age of science arrived. In it the old dreams have started to come true.

Today we can change one metal into another in the atomic pile. Astronauts have visited the moon and returned safely. The third of the alchemists' projects, the slowing down of aging, remains the hardest. It has not been achieved. It may be that this is an impossible task, so that it will never be achieved. But many scientists, backed by a number of governments and by various universities, are now planning and carrying out serious research on aging.

▶ INVESTIGATIONS OF AGING

Work on aging is the new science of **gerontology**. (The name comes from the Greek *gerōn,* "an old man.") The aim of this work is to collect as much knowledge as possible about aging in people and animals. The scientists who work in it want to find out how and why aging happens. Eventually, if they can, they want to find out how to slow aging down and make people stay healthy longer.

We do not yet know why people and animals lose vigor with age. There seem to be three main possibilities.

First, aging may be due to the dying-off of cells we cannot replace. The animals that do not age are mostly kinds that can replace all their cells. In people and other vertebrates, cells of the skin, blood, and liver are renewed. But this renewal slows down with age. Other cells, like those of the brain, cannot divide and are never renewed. We keep the same brain cells all our lives, but they get fewer as we get older. Aging may be due simply to a loss of cells or structures that we cannot renew.

A second possibility has to do with cell formation. Aging may be due to a change in the cells that are newly produced throughout life. Perhaps the new cells formed by an old man are different from, and not so good as, new cells in a baby.

The third possibility is that aging is more complicated than this. It may be the result of development. Chemical changes in the body make us grow up. Perhaps these same chemical changes eventually damage the body in some way and make it grow old.

Those are only three of the theories that have been suggested to explain aging. Nobody yet knows for certain which, if any, of them is right.

Two important facts have already been discovered, however. One concerns very

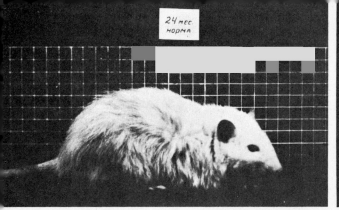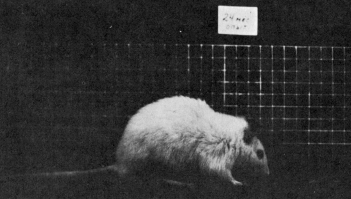

In a Russian experiment on aging, some rats were fed normally, while others were under-fed. Normally fed rats aged normally, like the rat at left. It is 24 months old and has reached old age. Rat at right is same age but looks younger because of underfeeding.

small doses of radiation (X rays and the rays given off by radium, called gamma rays) given to mice. The doses shorten the lives of mice in a way that strongly suggests they are hastening the normal aging process. This is very interesting. It does not mean that aging is due wholly to the "background" radiation to which we are exposed all the time. But it may mean that the changes in aging animals and the changes brought about by radiation are similar. If this is right, it will be a big step toward understanding aging. And it raises another possibility. There are drugs that can protect us against radiation effects. Perhaps similar drugs could protect us against aging.

The other discovery is that aging can be slowed down. It can be slowed by slowing growth and development. A great many animals (cockroaches, for instance) have shorter lives if they are fed heavily and made to grow as fast as possible. They live longer if they eat less and grow more slowly. Dr. Clive M. McCay, at Cornell University, found that this was also true of rats. Other scientists have repeated his experiments. Litters of young rats are divided at random into two groups. One group is fed a normal rat diet; the other gets everything it needs except enough energy-giving food (calories) to grow. The fully fed group grow up, become adult, live their lives, and die of old age. During the same period of time, the underfed group stay apparently young. And they can be made to grow long after their fully fed brothers and sisters are dead of old age. This means that aging can be made to "mark time." Aging is not simply a matter of passing weeks and months, but also of the rate of living. McCay's experiment does not mean, of course, that starving people will live longer than the well

fed. Starvation in people is a shortage of everything. The rats were short only of enough energy foods for growth.

In McCay's experiment both growth and development were affected. The rats stayed small and did not become able to breed. Fish that are underfed stay small but become adult and able to breed. However, they too live longer than fish that grow fast. It seems that slowing of growth slows down aging in a great many animals. Some body materials, such as the collagen in the tendons, stay chemically "young" in the slowed-down animals.

Most research on slowing down aging is now concerned with the brain. Certain parts of the brain are known to act as the "clocks" that control growing up and becoming adult. There is much evidence that while many "aging processes" are going on in different parts of the body, it is the brain—in a region called the hypothalamus—that controls and organizes life span. The effects of changed diets on the life span are probably brought about by this controlling action of the brain.

One of the difficulties in trying to slow aging in people is the long wait involved. It would take a lifetime, 70 to 80 years, to conduct experiments in aging. But researchers are studying certain factors that might be useful in measuring aging. Skin elasticity and mental performance, for example, change with age. If reliable tests of these and other factors can be worked out, it will be possible to do experiments directly on people, aimed at prolonging their lives.

▶ OTHER KINDS OF RESEARCH ON AGING

There is still another type of research on aging. This is the collection of facts about ages and growth rates in animals. It is very

Fish fins have bony rods called fin rays. These may reveal age. A cross section from haddock's fin ray (*above left*) shows seven growth zones. Waxlike plug (*above*) from whale's ear shows yearly growth. This plug, 15 centimeters (6 inches) long, is from 28-year-old whale.

Certain animals reveal their own ages to scientists. Scallop shell grows slowly in winter and quickly in summer, creating pair of bands a year. Shell is about 10 years old.

Number of rings in sheep's horn increases as animal grows older.

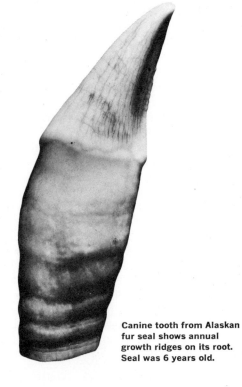

Canine tooth from Alaskan fur seal shows annual growth ridges on its root. Seal was 6 years old.

hard to study the force of mortality in animals by keeping them for life and recording when they die. The reason is that many live half as long as we do ourselves.

What we need to find out is the force of mortality at different ages in a mixed population of animals. This means we must know the age of each one—but wild creatures do not have birth certificates. For the most part we must rely on records, though the records are far from complete. In a few cases, however, we can tell the ages of animals by some structure that grows regularly. The shells, bones, or teeth of certain animals lay down a fixed number of marks or rings every year. We can tell the ages of these animals just as we can tell the age of a tree by counting its rings.

Yet another kind of research in aging is concerned with grafting. Grafts are pieces of tissue taken from one animal and put into another. For example, Peter Krohn of the University of Birmingham in England transplanted a mouse ovary into a succession of young mice. He found that the ovary did not stay "young" any longer than it would have in the animal from which it was taken. Experiments like these may tell us how much organs age when they are taken from the animal of which they are a part.

Would our skin or our liver age if it was not joined to the rest of us? One possible way to find out is by making an age chimera. This is an animal containing tissue of two different ages—an old mouse with a young ovary implanted in it, for example. (The chimera was a mythical animal made up of parts of many different creatures: eagle's head, lion's feet, and so on.) One way of making an age chimera is to take tissue from a young animal and store it in a deep freeze until that animal is old; then we can put the tissue back and see what happens.

It is sometimes said that grafts could be used as "spare parts" in people. But this is not so. Even if it could be done freely, the use of such parts in people would not stop them from aging. Old people, like old automobiles, are defective in many parts. We would not know what to replace. Besides, grafts in people will usually live only if the person who gives the graft and the one who receives it are identical twins. Since twins are exactly the same age, this does not help. But for animal ex-

periments we can breed mice that are as alike as twins; they can exchange grafts. Tissue from infant mice can be put into old mice. Tissue from old mice can be put into young mice. And the effects can be studied.

Scientists also study aging in cells taken from the body. The cells seem immortal, for they continue to live and grow in the laboratory. But the cells are not normal. They are more like cancer cells. Why do cells fail to reproduce normally after a time? Learning the answer to this question might bring researchers closer to an understanding of aging.

Within the cell, certain molecules known as nucleic acids are able to make new parts for the cell. But faults sometimes appear in the structure of the nucleic acids. As time passes, more faults collect. The results of the ever-increasing number of faults in the cell may be the aging that is observed. It may be that radiation, by increasing the number of faults in the nucleic acid, shortens the life of the cell.

▶ **SHOULD PEOPLE LIVE LONGER?**

Gerontologists are sometimes asked if they really think that it is a good idea to make people live longer. Obviously it would raise many population problems, but all big new discoveries give rise to problems, as the airplane and nuclear energy have done. Certainly if we only made people live longer, like Tithonus, it would not be a good thing. On the other hand, there are some people of 80 who are ill or crippled because of age, while others are hale and active. If we could all be hale and useful at 80, that would be a great improvement, even if we lived no longer in the end. Now we spend nearly a third of our lives learning our jobs. If we lived longer, we could do more work in a lifetime. We could carry out bigger and better plans.

The possibility of lengthening life raises some difficult questions, though we do not need to solve them yet. At the moment we do not know for certain whether we can ever hope to change the rate of aging. Yet everyone should think about the problems because scientists are making a serious attempt to find the means of slowing aging. It seems reasonable to think they will succeed eventually—but when and by how much nobody can yet say.

ALEX COMFORT
Author, *A Good Age*

AGRICULTURE

If you ask the average person what agriculture is, he will probably reply, "Why, it means farming, of course." He will be partly right, for raising crops is a branch of agriculture. So also are livestock raising, dairy farming, fruit growing, chicken raising, and even fur farming. Agriculture includes the raising of every kind of plant and animal that is useful to man.

With all its many branches, agriculture is the world's most important industry. It supplies the food we eat and many of the materials from which we make our clothing. Modern agriculture also provides business for many other industries. Farmers buy tractors, plows, seeders, and many other kinds of equipment. They buy supplies such as fertilizer, chemical sprays, and animal feed. The manufacturers from whom they buy these things in turn buy raw materials from other industries. Grocery stores and supermarkets, restaurants and lunch counters, and companies that can and freeze food would have nothing to sell without agriculture. Railroads and truck lines that carry farm products to market are among the other industries that depend directly or indirectly on agriculture.

▶ TYPES OF FARMING

Farms are classified according to the type of farming that is done and the kinds of crops and livestock that are raised. They may be classified in several different ways, such as general, specialized, intensive, and extensive farms.

A farm may fall into more than one classification at the same time. For example, it may be both extensive and specialized.

General Farming

A farm where a variety of things are raised is called a general farm. On such a farm there may be a herd of dairy cows whose milk the farmer sells. There may also be hogs, sheep, or poultry to provide extra income and supply some of the family's needs. The farmer may raise some of the hay and grain for feeding his animals. There may be some "cash crop" such as tobacco, soybeans, or vegetables. Cash crops, as the name indicates, are raised to be sold rather than for use on the farm.

Specialization

There are many factors that influence the types of crops and livestock that a farmer raises. One of the most important is climate, which includes temperature, length of growing season, sunshine, and rainfall. Another is the type of soil. A third is the amount of water available for irrigation. Other factors are the terrain (whether the land is level and easily cultivated or steep and rocky), distance to markets, perishability of the product, and demand for the product.

By concentrating on the particular crops or animals that fit in best with his situation, the specialized farmer hopes to use his land in the most efficient and profitable way.

For example, farmers in the semi-arid western plains of the United States and Canada specialize in raising wheat and other drought-resisting grains. The reason is that these plants will survive there while moisture-loving crops would fail. The land is generally level and the soil is free from large stones, so that it is practical to use large machines for cultivation and harvesting. Farmers in this region of vast natural grasslands could also raise cattle if they wished, but grain pays them better.

West of the plains there are vast mountainous regions where the land is too steep and rocky to cultivate. However, there are natural grasses that cattle and sheep can eat. Mountain streams provide a water supply. Here ranching takes the place of farming, for livestock can be raised profitably but plant crops cannot.

Many farmers in New England, New York State, and Pennsylvania have found it profitable to specialize in producing fresh milk for the towns and cities of the northeastern states. The relatively cool summers and heavy rainfall are almost ideal conditions for pasture land, hay, and other feed crops. And markets are within easy trucking distance.

There are many other kinds of specialized farming. One example is the raising of pure strains of seeds of all sorts for farms, gardens, and lawns. Another example is the growing of nursery stock—trees and shrubs—for landscaping homes. The boom in the building of new homes has made it a big business. Coffee production in warm, moist regions of South America, raising fish in farm ponds in the

Middle East, and raising fur-bearing animals on "ranches" in northern Europe, the United States, and Canada are still other examples of specialization in response to natural conditions and buyers' demands.

Intensive and Extensive Agriculture

When a farmer devotes a great deal of labor to a piece of land, he is practicing **intensive** agriculture. If he works a large area of land with relatively little labor, he is practicing **extensive** agriculture.

Intensive agriculture usually goes together with small farms. (However, intensive agriculture can also be practiced on a large scale, as on large fruit or vegetable farms. The old-time southern plantations were examples of large-scale intensive agriculture.) A great deal of careful work is always involved in intensive agriculture. Often this work must be done by hand. Vegetables, small fruits, and other crops that have a comparatively short growing season are produced by intensive agriculture. In some cases more than one crop a year is grown on the same land. Commercial egg production, where thousands of hens may be kept in buildings on a lot the size of a city block, is another type of intensive agriculture. Intensive agriculture demands a great deal of labor and high expenses for each acre of land. The yield per acre is also usually high. The farmer hopes to get a high return in dollars

ANCIENT EGYPT, ABOUT 1500 B.C

WESTERN EUROPE, ABOUT A.D. 1400

COLONIAL AMERICA, 18TH CENTURY

MODERN FARMER

AMERICAN AGRICULTURE

Wheat fields stretch for mile after mile across the fertile, level soils of the Great Plains. Combine crews travel from farm to farm to do the harvesting.

Picking tangerines in a Florida grove. Florida's year-round warm climate and plentiful rainfall make the state a center of citrus production.

Cowboys drive a herd of cattle across a stream in Arizona. Cattle are important in the dry, rugged Southwest, where water and level land for farming are scarce.

Grain fields and rolling
countryside surround this
Midwestern farm. Large barn
and tall silo for storing
feed are typical.

A field of colorful flowers
being raised for seed.
Seed production is a limited
but very important branch
of agriculture.

91

per acre, but this depends on the market for his crop.

Extensive agriculture is usually practiced on large farms or ranches where most of the work is done by machinery. The large farms that raise wheat and other grain crops in the midwestern United States and Canada's prairie provinces are good examples of extensive agriculture. There is work at planting time and harvest time. Otherwise the crops need little attention.

Raising cattle on the range is another type of extensive agriculture. Extensive agriculture does not yield as great a return per acre of land as intensive agriculture, but it requires much less work per acre.

THE MODERN FARM

Agriculture in the United States and Canada has gone through many changes since the days when most of the work on the farm was done by the muscles of men and animals. A hundred years ago a farmer produced enough food for his family, with a little left over to sell. Today one full-time farm worker produces enough food to feed over 55 people.

The modern farm is much larger, and the farmer depends heavily on machinery. He plants improved varieties of seeds for better crops. He practices better methods in the control of diseases and insects. He understands soil management and the use of fertilizer better than his father and grandfather. The modern farmer constantly uses knowledge gained from scientific research. He also makes use of the latest improvements in machinery to help him manage his farm.

In a modern dairy farm, for example, the cows are fed a scientifically balanced diet. Careful records of their production are kept. One farmer may milk 50, 60, or more cows—not by hand, but with machines. In many cases the milk is piped directly to a refrigerated tank, where it is held until it is picked up by a large tank truck. Then the milk is taken to a distribution center for processing and bottling before it is delivered to consumers in the cities.

Even getting in the hay to feed the cows in winter is a thoroughly mechanized process from beginning to end. The farmer mows and bales the hay with tractor-operated machines. A mechanical loader lifts the bales onto trac-

tor-drawn wagons or trucks. At the barn another machine lifts the bales into the loft for storage.

These examples of the use of machinery apply to all types of agriculture. Machines are now doing most of the heavy work on the modern farm. They make it possible to do more work and do it faster. But farm machines are expensive. To pay for them the farmer must raise large quantities of produce to sell. This is one of the reasons why today's farms are becoming larger. Modern agriculture is no longer a way of life in the country. Instead it is a business enterprise.

AGRICULTURE IN OTHER LANDS

Agriculture in some form is carried on in all countries. In the less developed countries, the ways of farming are very primitive. Much of the work is done by men and women. The fields are plowed with a crooked stick pulled by poorly nourished oxen, burros, or camels. Grain is reaped and threshed by hand. Practically no machines are used. Women do much of the work and carry loads on their heads or backs. Lack of knowledge about modern ways of farming is one of the reasons why these countries continue to follow their centuries-old agricultural practices. Another reason is the vast population that presents a problem in many parts of the world. If machines were introduced, many people would be out of work.

Rice and vegetables are the basic crops in most of the countries of eastern and southeastern Asia. The farms are small, and much of the work is done by hand, with the water buffalo supplying power to plow the rice fields.

In the dry Middle East, farming is generally limited to places where water is available from river, wells, or springs. There are many people and little good farmland. Because of this, labor is cheap. Most work is done by hand with crude implements. However, scientific methods of farming are beginning to replace traditional ones, and machinery is gradually coming into use. Israel has been a pioneer in scientific farming and the use of machinery.

Farming methods in Europe are quite advanced and can be compared to those of the United States and Canada. However, the farms are generally smaller and do not lend themselves to the use of large machines. In the more rugged mountainous regions, such as Switzerland and parts of the Scandinavian countries, it is impossible to use machinery. The farmers specialize in raising livestock for meat, milk, butter, and cheese.

▶ THE LAND

Agriculture depends on land. This may seem obvious, but it is none the less true. About three tenths of the surface of the earth is land. The rest is covered by the oceans.

Not all of the land surface of the earth is suitable for agriculture. Some land is covered by snow and ice. Some is dry, barren rock and sand. Some is too wet and swampy.

The proportion of land that can be used for raising crops is quite small. For example, the total land area of Canada is about 2,279,000,000 (billion) acres, but only about 95,000,000 acres (about 4.1 percent) are used for raising crops. The total land area of the United States is about 2,266,000,000 (billion) acres. Of this, about 287,000,000 acres (about 13.2 percent) are used for raising crops. Lakes and streams, mountains and deserts, rocky wastelands, towns, suburban housing developments, cities, and highways all occupy their share of the total area. The last four often take up good farming land. They are occupying more and more each year.

Management of the Land

Because such a small portion of the earth's surface can be used to produce crops, it is very important that farmers do a good job of managing the soil, that is, taking care of it so that it does not become exhausted and is not eroded away by rain and wind. The wise farmer follows these rules:

He never leaves land bare. After a cultivated crop is harvested, he sows a **cover crop.** A cover crop covers the soil and helps protect it from blowing or washing away. Some of the main cover crops are grass, clover, and rye and other grains. Many of these crops are planted in the fall to protect the soil over the winter. Then they are plowed under in the spring; this also enriches the soil.

He **rotates** his crops so that the land has a crop of grass or hay every 2 or 3 years. This helps build up the soil as well as protects against erosion.

He plants crops along the **contour levels** of sloping land; that is, the crop rows run horizontally along the slope instead of up and down. This allows water to sink into the soil instead of running off down the slope. In some cases he may terrace the land to control the flow of water and reduce gullying.

He may practice contour **strip cropping.** This is a method of growing crops in alternate strips or bands that follow the contour levels of the land. He usually plants a cultivated crop and a close-growing crop. For example, a sloping field may be planted with alternating strips of corn and grass. Cultivation means that the soil around the plants is kept bare and the plants are spaced well apart. This leaves the soil poorly protected. The strips of close-growing crops between the cultivated strips help cover and bind the soil.

He never plows a steep hillside. Such land should be kept in grass for pasture or planted with trees.

He manages his pastures so that the livestock does not eat the grass too close to the ground.

Soil management includes irrigation, drainage, and fertilization. Irrigation has long been used in dry lands where there is not enough rainfall for crops. Nowadays many farmers in humid regions are beginning to use irrigation because the natural rainfall may be undependable. With irrigation farmers can be sure of giving their crops the right amount of water at the right time.

Drainage is just as important as irrigation. If the soil is full of water, there is no room for air, and most plants cannot grow without air around their roots. Drainage has turned great areas of swamp into productive farmland. The most usual types of drain are open ditches or tile pipes laid end to end in channels dug in the soil. Drainage channels are laid out parallel to each other. They empty into a main ditch or pipe that carries the water away.

Every time that a crop is grown on a piece of land, some of the plant food in the soil is used up. This plant food must be replaced to keep the soil fertile. Manure and animal and plant wastes were the earliest fertilizers. The use of fertilizers was known even to primitive people. When the first settlers came to New England, they found that the Indians placed dead fish in each hill of corn to make the corn grow better. Today man has learned to make artificial fertilizers. These supply the same plant foods as natural fertilizers and they are easier to store and to apply. Scientific soil tests have been devised so that the farmer can test soil from any part of his land and find out just what plant foods he must supply. This is important because different plants have different food requirements.

If crops are grown on the same land year after year without fertilization, the plant food becomes exhausted. In past years many farmers in the United States would farm a piece of land in this way until it was worn out. Then they moved on to new land. This practice is known as "robbing the soil" or "soil mining."

▶ GOVERNMENT AID AND CONTROLS

Government aid to agriculture takes many forms. Governments have often used high import taxes to protect farmers against the competition of lower-priced crops from other countries. Sometimes they have paid bounties for growing special crops like tobacco or mulberry leaves for feeding silkworms. This was done in order to build up a domestic supply of these products and avoid importing them from other nations.

During the 19th century, governments began to realize that the farmers of their countries needed help other than bounty payments and protective tariffs. One by one they began to set up special government departments to take care of farm problems.

The United States Department of Agriculture was established on May 15, 1862. It started out in a very modest way. Its first duties were mainly distributing free seeds for farmers to try out. Soon the public demanded increased government service to farmers. Congress expanded the department during the 1880's. The first secretary of agriculture was appointed in 1889. This step gave recognition to the importance of agriculture in the national economy.

The task of the new department was to give leadership in the development of agriculture and to administer the laws and regulations affecting agriculture. Its duties have grown as agriculture has become more scientific and government responsibilities have increased. Today the Department of Agriculture is one of the largest departments in the government. Its responsibilities include soil conservation, crop-control programs, inspecting and grading farm products, and making loans to farmers for improving their land. It also conducts research to develop improved practices in all areas of farming.

The Department of Agriculture provides services to help the public as well as the farmer. Department of Agriculture inspectors examine meat to make sure that it is free from disease and also grade it for quality. The Department has also established standards of quality for eggs, fruits, vegetables, milk, and other farm products. If the consumer buys Grade A eggs, he knows that he is getting good value for his money.

Another very important job of the Department is to inspect seeds and plants that are brought in from foreign countries. This is done to prevent destructive insects or plant diseases from entering the country. Many such pests were introduced in shipments of plant materials before the inspection program began. The Japanese beetle, the European corn borer, the Dutch elm disease, and the chestnut blight, which has practically wiped out the native American chestnut tree, are a few of these unwelcome guests.

In 1914 the United States Congress passed the Smith-Lever Act, establishing the Cooperative Extension Service in agriculture and home economics. Perhaps the most important aspect of this act was the county agent system. The county agent is a trained agricultural expert who serves the farmers in the county or district where he is stationed. He visits farmers and gives them free advice about their problems. He gives demonstrations of new techniques for such matters as preventing soil erosion, destroying insect pests, and caring for and feeding animals. He informs farmers about improved varieties of seeds. He conducts soil tests and sends out bulletins telling the farmers when it is time to spray their crops. He keeps them informed of new developments. He may also advise them on marketing their products. These are some of the many services for which farmers depend on their county agents.

AGRICULTURAL EDUCATION

Until the 19th century agricultural education was limited to whatever practical information and folklore a father might hand down to his son. England led the way in scientific agricultural education by establishing an experimental station in 1843 and an agricultural college in 1845. Other European countries soon followed suit. Agricultural education had a hard time winning acceptance. Many farmers were unwilling to change the methods they were used to, and many also disliked and distrusted "book learning."

One of the leaders in the movement to establish agricultural education in the United States was Senator Justin S. Morrill (1810–98), the son of a Vermont blacksmith. It was he who introduced the bill, signed by President Lincoln in 1862, which provided for the establishment of agricultural colleges in every state. Money for these colleges was to come from the sale of public lands granted to the states by the federal government. For this reason these agricultural colleges are known as "land-grant" colleges. Some of the leading universities in the United States began as small land-grant colleges.

Research stations that worked closely with the land-grant colleges were established soon after. They quickly proved their value by the contributions they made to agricultural knowledge. They also were important in developing better types of animals and plants.

The county agents played an important part in bringing the knowledge of the agricultural colleges and research stations to the ordinary farmer. Their on-the-spot demonstrations probably did more than anything else to convince farmers that "book learning" was truly practical.

Typical subjects taught in agricultural colleges nowadays include plant and animal biology, genetics, soil conservation, soil chemistry and the use of fertilizers, bacteriology, entomology and pest control, agricultural engineering, and marketing.

HISTORY

To tell the whole story of agriculture in every part of the world would take many books the size of this volume. Here we shall only cover the highlights.

Nobody knows exactly when or where agriculture began. But scientists now believe that it began 8,000 years ago or more when people discovered that the wild grass seeds that they ate as part of their diet would grow if they were placed in the ground at the right time of year. Not only did the seeds grow but each one produced many more seeds to fill the stomachs of the tribe. This may seem like a small thing to modern people, but for these primitive men it was a truly revolutionary discovery. Up until then they had depended for their very lives on their luck in hunting and fishing and finding wild plants that they could eat. Being able to grow a part of their own food meant that starvation was no longer such a danger.

As men learned more about raising crops they came to depend more and more on farming and less on hunting to keep themselves alive. In addition to the wild grasses, from which our present-day grains are descended, these early men learned to grow many other plants, the ancestors of today's vegetables.

Permanent settlements grew up where the land was good for farming. As time passed and the population increased, some of these settlements grew into large towns and eventually cities. People who were especially skilled at making things, such as pots, cloth, or tools and weapons, began to work full time at their specialties. This was the beginning of division of labor, which is so important to our economy today.

Agriculture was developed independently by different groups of people in widely separated parts of the world. The knowledge probably spread slowly from each little group of farmers to their neighbors. Some tribes never made the change to agriculture. They preferred to remain wandering hunters and food gatherers, just as their ancestors had always been.

Two of the very earliest places where we know that agriculture was practiced were the valley of the Nile River, in northeastern Africa, and the region called Mesopotamia, along the Tigris and Euphrates rivers in southwestern Asia. The little farming settlements of the Nile Valley grew into the mighty civilization of Egypt. A whole series of countries, from Ur of the Chaldees to Babylonia, flourished in Mesopotamia.

Primitive farming methods were extremely

crude. Seeds were planted in little holes in the ground made with a sharp stick. Grain was harvested with flint knives or flint-edged sickles or was sometimes pulled up by the roots. The invention of the spade and the hoe made it possible to cultivate the ground. This helped the crops by loosening the soil and keeping down weeds. At first the work in the fields seems to have been done by women, while the men watched the herds, hunted occasionally, and defended the village against its enemies.

Domestic animals were probably kept at first for hunting (such as dogs) or food (such as cows, sheep, and pigs). Eventually it was discovered that some of them could be used to carry loads or pull a plow. This was another great step forward. The first plows were little more than forked sticks pulled through the soil to stir it up. They were hard to pull and did not work very well by modern standards. Still, they made it possible to cultivate more land with less work than had ever been possible with only hand tools.

The Egyptians, the Mesopotamians, and the Chinese developed advanced systems of agriculture. They knew the value of fertilization, irrigation, and drainage. They developed improved varieties of plants and animals by selective breeding. The Chinese, in particular, were skilled at getting the most possible use out of every inch of land. By comparison Europe lagged far behind. The Romans developed fairly advanced methods of farming around the beginning of the Christian Era, but most of their knowledge was lost when the Roman Empire fell apart during the 5th century A.D.

Farming methods in Europe during the Middle Ages were generally crude, wasteful, and inefficient. Very few farmers owned their own land. Most of the land was owned by noblemen or the Church. It was worked by tenant farmers who were little better off than slaves. On each estate, or **manor,** much of the land was kept as forest, where the nobles hunted for sport. The less fertile land was used as pasture. Hay was gathered from swampy meadows. The cultivated land was divided into three large sections. Crops were grown on two of these sections, while the third lay **fallow**; that is, nothing was grown on it. This allowed the land to recover a little

of its fertility. Each year a different section lay fallow. In the sections that were cultivated, each peasant was allotted a certain amount of land. The fields were usually long, narrow strips rather than squares because this shape made plowing easier. The plow did not need to be turned around so many times at the end of the furrow. The peasant's land strips were usually scattered in different parts of the big field. The average size of the individual allotments was as much as one man could plow in one day. Our word "acre" comes from the Latin word *ager,* meaning "field." So does the word "agriculture."

Deep-rooted customs forced all the peasants on a manor to plant the same crops and do their plowing, planting, and harvesting together. Thus there was very little chance for trying out new crops or new farming methods.

Agricultural machinery was unknown, and all farm work except for plowing and harrowing was done by hand. The harrow of those days was an implement like a large rake. It was pulled over the ground after plowing to break up the clods and smooth the surface somewhat. Sometimes a large bundle of brush was used instead. Seeds for grain crops, the main food of the people, were **broadcast** (scattered by hand) over the ground. Since they were not covered, many were eaten by birds. Much grain was also lost by inefficient harvesting and storage. Domestic animals were usually small and scrawny from lack of food. The swamp meadows did not yield enough hay to support many animals over the winter; so most of them were slaughtered in the fall. The lack of domestic animals meant that there was never enough manure for the fields. This kept crop yields very low. Under these conditions starvation was never very far around the corner.

The revival of European agriculture really began in the Low Countries (now the Netherlands and Belgium) around the 16th century A.D. The Dutch and Flemish (Belgian) farmers had begun to cultivate two new "wonder crops"—clover and turnips. Clover enriched the soil by adding nitrogen and made very nutritious hay. Turnips made good winter feed for animals. They fitted in well with the primitive scheme of crop rotation. With plenty of feed the farmers could keep herds of animals over the winter. Furthermore, ani-

Costa Rican plantation workers spread coffee beans to dry.

In parts of Norway the land is too steep and rugged for machines. Much hard work must still be done by hand.

A tractor lightens work for an Irish farmer.

Forkful by forkful, workers on a big Polish farm build a giant haystack.

Women cultivate pineapples by hand on a large plantation in South Africa.

Spain's famous wines are made from grapes like these.

Dairy cows wait to be milked in northern Germany.

A Nepalese woman shakes wheat in a sieve to separate the uneatable chaff from the heavier grain.

A Taiwanese farmer plows his rice field before transplanting seedlings.

An elderly French farmer carefully tends his young orchard.

Camels make good work animals in the harsh desert land of Libya.

mals could be kept in farmyards during the rest of the year so that the manure could be easily collected. The manure was carefully put on the fields to maintain their fertility. With more and better food, the animals soon improved in size and quality. Historians call this discovery the Agricultural Revolution.

The new methods spread slowly. But more advances were made in 18th-century England. Pioneer experimenters developed horse-drawn farming machines, improved systems of crop rotation and fertilization, and better breeds of sheep and cattle.

Meanwhile, Europeans were exploring the New World. They returned home with crops previously unknown in Europe—white and sweet potatoes, corn, pumpkins, and tomatoes. Most of these remained little more than curiosities for many years. But one plant, the potato, was found to grow well in cold, damp climates and on poor soils. It soon became an important food item in northern Europe.

Similarly, crops and animals native to Europe and Asia were carried to North America by early explorers and colonists. Later, crops were exchanged between other lands. Coffee, a native of northern Africa, was taken to Brazil and Indonesia. Peanuts, native to South America, were carried to Africa.

As trade between the various countries of the world increased, there was a growing exchange not only of plants and animals but also of agricultural practices and technologies.

Scientific agriculture in the United States had its beginnings in the 1700's. Benjamin Franklin promoted the use of lime to improve acid soils. George Washington and Thomas Jefferson were leading experimenters in scientific farming. Their work was continued by a few wealthy landowners, who corresponded with one another and with like-minded people in Europe.

In the 1800's, the government began to become involved in helping farmers. Agricultural experiment stations were set up. The establishment of land-grant colleges and other institutions brought knowledge of scientific methods and improved techniques within reach of ordinary farmers.

Another advance during the 1800's was the discovery that chemicals could be used as fertilizers. These substances, produced cheaply and in large quantities, increased crop yields even on poor soil. The development of machines like the reaper, binder, and thresher also increased production. Steel plows replaced the less efficient cast-iron plows. The use of power, at first steam and then gasoline, took much of the physical labor out of agriculture.

In the 1900's the major advances have been in three areas—chemistry, breeding, and technology. Modern farming depends heavily on chemical fertilizers and insect-killers. Other chemicals fight plant diseases and kill weeds. Synthetically produced vitamins, hormones, and antibiotics speed the growth of livestock and chickens and control the tenderness of meat and the amount of fat in it.

Plant and animal breeders, building on the discoveries of geneticists, developed improved breeds of plants and animals. Some plant breeds produce much higher yields per unit of land than earlier breeds. This has been particularly valuable in basic crops such as wheat, rice, and corn. Corn hybrids, for example, enable farmers of today to get three or four times more corn per hectare of land than farmers of 60 years ago.

Power-driven machinery and the electrification of farms has also greatly increased production. This has led to an increase in the size of farms and a decrease in the number of farm workers. One person operating large, efficient equipment can produce much more than a group of workers without machines.

But many problems remain. Modern agricultural methods have not reached all the farmers of the world. Fuel is becoming scarcer and much more expensive. Some farmers cannot afford the costly fertilizers needed to grow high-yield crops. Soil is being misused or covered with roads and houses. Yet more and more food is needed to feed the ever-growing human population. Agriculture, the one industry on which human survival depends, must continue to develop and improve.

CHARLES H. THOMPSON
Emeritus Leader of Extension Agents
State of New Jersey

See also CONSERVATION; EROSION; FARM LIFE; FARM MACHINERY; FERTILIZERS; INSECT CONTROL; IRRIGATION; NATURAL RESOURCES; SOILS; names of products, as CORN, WHEAT; kinds of farming, as DAIRYING; and the agriculture sections of continent, country, and state articles.

AIR. See AERODYNAMICS; ATMOSPHERE.

AIR CONDITIONING

In 1900 there was very little people could do during a hot spell except grumble about the weather or—if they could afford it—go away to the mountains or the seashore. Today air conditioning has changed this. With air conditioning you can be comfortable anywhere indoors on even the hottest, stickiest day of the year. You will almost certainly find air conditioning in the movie theaters you attend, in many of the stores where your family shops, and in the restaurants where you eat. It may even be in your own home.

▶ WHAT IS AIR CONDITIONING?

You know that air conditioning makes you feel cool. But air conditioning is more than just cooling. It means keeping the temperature and humidity (moisture content) of air in an enclosed space, whether it is one room or an entire building, at just the right level for the comfort of the people inside. It also means circulating the air with fans and removing dust from it with filters. In winter it means heating the air and adding moisture if necessary. In summer it means removing moisture by passing the air over cold pipes that collect water from the air, much as drops of water condense on a cold water glass on a hot, damp day. In fact, we might almost say that air conditioning means creating an artificial, comfortable climate. In this article we shall discuss only cooling.

In dry climates air can be cooled simply. The cooler may be no more than a large fan that draws hot, dry air through a water-soaked fiber mat. The air is cooled as it evaporates the water. It is so dry to begin with that the added moisture will not cause discomfort. (This is not the case in humid climates.)

▶ THE MANY USES OF AIR CONDITIONING

Air conditioning has many uses besides keeping us comfortable. Many industries depend on it to keep the air in their plants clean, cool, and at the right moisture level. For example, textile fibers such as wool and cotton will stretch or shrink as the moisture content of the air changes. This causes variations in the quality of the cloth. Too much moisture in the air—or even on a worker's fingertips—will cause delicate metal parts such as rocket components or precision instruments to corrode. The wrong temperature can spoil a batch of antibiotic culture. Proper air conditioning prevents these mishaps.

The deep diamond and gold mines of South Africa use air conditioning to enable miners to work in what would otherwise be suffocating heat, thousands of feet below ground. With air conditioning, atomic submarines can cruise for weeks under water without coming up for air. Air conditioning is involved in every part of the United States space program, from making missiles to tracking them through the atmosphere.

This odd-looking costume was a 19th-century design for an air-cooled suit. Adjustable slats could be raised to admit cooling breezes. The hat was similarly equipped.

▶ HISTORY

Inventors have tinkered with methods of air conditioning for years. Ancient Egyptians and Romans got some relief from the heat by hanging woven mats soaked with water across the entrances to their houses, so that incoming air would be cooled by evaporation. In the 15th century A.D., the famous artist and inventor Leonardo da Vinci built a water-powered fan.

As men's interest in science grew so did the number of schemes for getting cool. There were hundreds of ideas, but none of them really worked. In fact, many of the schemes made people feel worse because they added large amounts of water to the air. Air is like a sponge. It will soak up water and make people feel sticky and uncomfortable, especially in hot weather. When the air is very moist, we say the humidity is high. When the air is dry, the humidity is low and we feel better.

The first machine that kept the humidity low and cooled the air at the same time was developed in 1902 by Willis H. Carrier, who is often called "the father of air conditioning." Carrier built this machine for a printing plant in Brooklyn, New York, that had trouble printing in color. Paper stretches when the air is damp and shrinks when the air is dry. Since each color had to be printed separately, printings of different colors on the same sheet of paper did not line up accurately because the paper changed size between printings. Carrier's machine kept the moisture level of the air constant by drawing the air over a row of cold pipes that condensed the excess moisture. This kept the paper at one size and also made the people in the plant feel cool. Carrier's invention marked the beginning of scientific air conditioning.

Air conditioning was soon being used in many factories, such as the plants that made ammunition during World War I. But people generally did not know about this invention until the 1920's, when hundreds of movie theaters, department stores, and restaurants had air conditioners installed. People often came into these places just to get relief from the hot, muggy air outside.

As air conditioning became more popular during the 1930's, central air conditioning systems were developed. These could cool a whole office or apartment building from one centrally located unit, just as buildings were heated from one big furnace in the basement instead of by little stoves in each room. During the same period small units that could air-condition a single room were developed. After World War II large numbers of small units began to be used in private homes. A

Air conditioners like this are used to cool rooms in houses. Follow steps 1 through 6 to see how heat in the air is removed by the air conditioner.

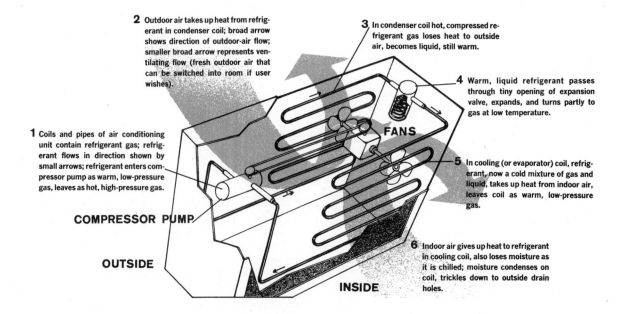

2 Outdoor air takes up heat from refrigerant in condenser coil; broad arrow shows direction of outdoor-air flow; smaller broad arrow represents ventilating flow (fresh outdoor air that can be switched into room if user wishes).

3 In condenser coil hot, compressed refrigerant gas loses heat to outside air, becomes liquid, still warm.

4 Warm, liquid refrigerant passes through tiny opening of expansion valve, expands, and turns partly to gas at low temperature.

1 Coils and pipes of air conditioning unit contain refrigerant gas; refrigerant flows in direction shown by small arrows; refrigerant enters compressor pump as warm, low-pressure gas, leaves as hot, high-pressure gas.

FANS

5 In cooling (or evaporator) coil, refrigerant, now a cold mixture of gas and liquid, takes up heat from indoor air, leaves coil as warm, low-pressure gas.

COMPRESSOR PUMP

OUTSIDE

INSIDE

6 Indoor air gives up heat to refrigerant in cooling coil, also loses moisture as it is chilled; moisture condenses on coil, trickles down to outside drain holes.

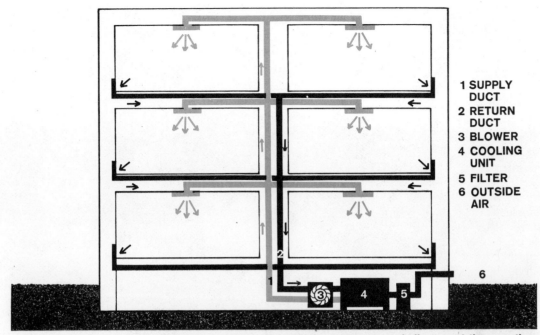

Large buildings use central air conditioning systems to cool all rooms at the same time. Arrows show the path of the air as it travels through filter, cooler, and ducts to rooms. Cool, filtered air comes out of vents in ceilings, returns to air conditioner through openings near floors.

later development, used increasingly in both public buildings and private homes, combined heating and cooling units in one system.

▶ **HOW DOES AIR CONDITIONING WORK?**

An air conditioning unit does not "add coolness" to the air. It removes heat. An air conditioner works on the same basic principle as a refrigerator—though it is not designed to produce such low temperatures. Heat is taken from the air by the rapid expansion of a refrigerant (cooling substance) as it turns from a liquid at high pressure to a gas at low pressure. An accompanying illustration shows the cycle of operations of a small home-type air conditioner. Here the air is cooled directly by the machine. For the sake of simplicity, filters and motors are not shown in this diagram. In large, central installations, such as those in office buildings and schools, a machine chills water that is piped to a series of coils. Air from the building is drawn over these coils and circulated through the building by blowers.

To be practical, an air conditioning unit must be able to maintain a steady tempera-

ture. Otherwise people would have to turn their units off and on continually as the temperature became too cold or too hot. A steady temperature is maintained by a temperature-regulating device called a thermostat. The thermostat is set at the desired temperature. It then switches the cooling unit on and off as needed.

The air conditioning systems of the future may work by what is known as **thermoelectricity.** A thermoelectric unit is very small and very quiet. It is made up of tiny "couples," each couple consisting of a pair of semiconductors and connected in parallel to an electric current. These couples produce cooling at one end and heating at the other when direct current flows through them. This is called the Peltier effect. When the current is reversed, the cooling and heating effects also reverse. When a way is found to produce these tiny thermoelectric units cheaply, they may cool and heat your whole house.

RUSSELL GRAY
President, Carrier Air Conditioning Company
See also HEAT; HEATING; REFRIGERATION.

AIR FORCE. See UNITED STATES AIR FORCE; CANADIAN ARMED FORCES.

A radio-controlled aerobatic (stunt) plane is readied for flight.

AIRPLANE MODELS

No one knows who built the first model airplane. Models of birds, carved from wood and able to fly like gliders, have been found in ancient Egyptian tombs. Early inventors such as Leonardo Da Vinci (1452–1519) built models of their concepts of "flying machines." But the modern hobby of model-airplane building did not really begin until after World War I. The war proved that the airplane was an exciting and practical way to transport people and products. The romance of air travel, together with a natural creative desire, led many people of all ages into the hobby of building miniature models of real airplanes.

▶ NON-FLYING MODELS

The easiest-to-build and least expensive model airplanes are constructed from plastic kits. They are made up of pre-molded plastic parts. The parts are very detailed. When they are glued together and painted, the result is a very realistic model of an airplane. They are simple to build, but serious modelers have been known to spend hundreds of hours in research and construction. They try to dupli-

cate, as nearly as possible, an actual aircraft—perhaps one flown by a specific pilot in a particular battle. Many modelers go one step further. They build realistic settings, complete with trees and shrubs, buildings, and even miniature people, to create museumlike displays for their airplanes.

In the days before plastic kits, it was common practice to carve models from blocks of wood. That type of construction is mostly limited now to experienced modelers who wish to duplicate an airplane for which no kit is available. It is quite enjoyable to whittle an airplane from a piece of wood. And it is good practice for going on to the next step in model building.

▶ FLYING MODELS

This is the part of model-airplane building where the real excitement begins. An airplane is not truly an airplane unless it flies.

There is great variety in the types of models built for flight. They range from the simplest hand-launched glider to very complicated radio-controlled helicopters. Some are scale models of real airplanes. But others are special aircraft designed for contests in which the models are judged for flight duration, precision maneuvers, or speed.

Flying models are classified according to the way they are controlled in flight. The three categories of flying models are free flight, control line, and radio control.

Free Flight

The very early model airplanes were all free-flying. That is, once they were launched, there was no way to control their flight. Free flight remains a very popular activity today. To many modelers there is nothing quite so beautiful as the sight of a model drifting freely on a gentle breeze.

But it is not fun to lose a model if it flies too far. The wise free-flight flier sets the rudder on the airplane to produce a gentle turn. This keeps the model flying in circles overhead.

Free-flight models can be divided into three types—gliders, rubber-powered, and engine-powered. Gliders are relatively simple. They are launched into the air either by being thrown or by being towed on a string (like a kite) and then released for free flight. The towline is attached to a hook on the bottom of the glider. When it reaches altitude, the line is slackened, allowing it to slide off the hook. The glider is then free to soar like a bird.

Rubber-powered models have propellers that are turned by wound-up rubber bands. When the rubber unwinds, it turns the propeller, which causes the airplane to move forward through the air. Some rubber-powered models are very small, with wingspans of no more than 30 centimeters (12 inches). Others have wingspans of close to 2 meters (6 feet). A very special type of rubber-powered model is designed to be flown in large rooms indoors. These super-lightweight models can fly for almost an hour at a time.

Engine-powered models, sometimes called gas models, are powered by engines similar to those used in lawn mowers. But they are small enough to fit in the palm of your hand. These miniature engines produce a great deal of power for their small size. They can fly a model airplane to amazing heights. Once the model rises high enough, the motor is shut off by a timing mechanism, and the airplane is free to glide back to earth.

Free-flight models have one disadvantage. They require large open spaces in which to fly. This was one of the factors that led to the invention of a means of controlling the flight in a small area.

Control Line

Control-line airplanes are flown in circles at the end of two thin steel wires connected to a handle that is held by the pilot. The two wires are usually about 20 meters (65 feet) long. They are attached to a mechanism inside the airplane that controls the up-and-down direction of flight. By moving the handle, pilots can make the airplane do loops, figure eights, and other stunts. They can also control the takeoff and landing.

Control-line airplanes are all powered by miniature engines. There are contests for stunt flying, speed flying, and racing and for scale models.

Radio Control

Remote-control airplanes are the most realistic because they can be controlled in flight without wires or connections of any sort. Every maneuver that a real airplane makes can be duplicated by a radio-controlled model. Sometimes it is difficult to tell whether a model or a real plane is in the sky.

To understand how radio control works, think of your radio or television set. Somewhere outside your house there is a radio or television station transmitting radio waves through the air. You cannot see them or feel them or hear them. But your radio or television is designed to receive these waves and turn them into sound and pictures. Different kinds of radio waves are sent out on different channels, and you can tune your receiver to pick up these waves.

In a radio-control system for model airplanes, there is a transmitter, a receiver, and small electric motors (called servos) to move the airplane's controls. The pilot, using a hand-held transmitter, moves various levers and buttons to transmit different signals on different channels. Inside the airplane, the receiver picks up these signals and activates the servos to move the controls that steer the plane.

On simple radio-controlled models, the only control is the rudder, which steers the airplane right or left. On the most complex models, all the controls of a real airplane are duplicated. These include retractable landing gear, engine throttle, sky-writing smoke in stunt planes, bomb-dropping in war planes, parachute drops, and just about anything else you can think of.

Radio-controlled models come in all types and sizes. There are gliders with wingspans of more than 3 meters (over 10 feet) that can soar for hours when the skillful pilot takes advantage of rising air currents. There are racing planes that fly at almost 200 kilometers (125 miles) per hour. Aerobatic airplanes can loop, roll, spin, and do everything a real air-show plane can do. And there are helicopters that hover and fly backward and sideways just like the real ones. In fact, radio-controlled models can be quite realistic in appearance and flight. Many have been used in motion pictures when it would have been too danger-ous or expensive to use real aircraft.

Remember that flying models are not mere toys. Many of them are fast-moving objects that can fall and cause injury or damage. Care should be taken to fly them only under com-pletely safe conditions.

▶ROCKETS

As the space age has developed, model rock-ets have become an exciting part of the model-ing hobby. But model rockets are not strictly model airplanes. They are not toys, either. They are miniature missiles powered by real solid-fuel rocket motors.

Scale model rocket.

Model rockets are generally constructed of a basic cardboard tube for the body, with a balsa wood or plastic nose cone and balsa tail fins. There are many kits available, and it is best to start with a kit. They are prop-erly designed and built to be completely safe in operation. A homemade rocket can be dan-gerous.

The rocket motor itself is a small cylinder that fits into the rear of the rocket body. Model-rocket motors are dangerous when they are not used properly. In certain places it is necessary to have a license to purchase them. For example, in California, in the United States, you must be at least 14 years of age to get a license. Your local hobby shop can give you full details on how to get a license.

Model-rocket motors are ignited by wires. These are attached at one end to the rocket and at the other end to an electric ignition device placed some distance away for safety. When electricity flows through the wires, the ignition wire in the rocket motor gets hot, just as the wires in a toaster do. This causes the rocket fuel to burn. When the fuel burns, the rocket does not go off like a firecracker. In-stead, a hot, rapidly expanding gas is released. It shoots out through the motor nozzle at a very high speed and pushes the rocket up with a great deal of thrust (power).

A single rocket motor burns for just a few seconds. But it will push the model rocket to altitudes of more than 100 meters (over 325 feet). Multistage rockets use two or more mo-tors, burning one after the other, to get to much greater heights.

Just before the motor burns out, the last little bit of gas pressure actually blows out through the front of the motor. This causes the nose cone of the rocket to pop off and release a parachute. The model rocket then comes down very gently on its parachute, ready for another blast-off.

As with airplanes, model rockets can be scale models of actual rockets and missiles. Or they can be original designs made up by the builder. Contests are often held on military bases, where the models can be tracked by radar to determine how high they fly.

▶YOU CAN DO IT, TOO

When the model-airplane hobby first started, very little equipment was available in

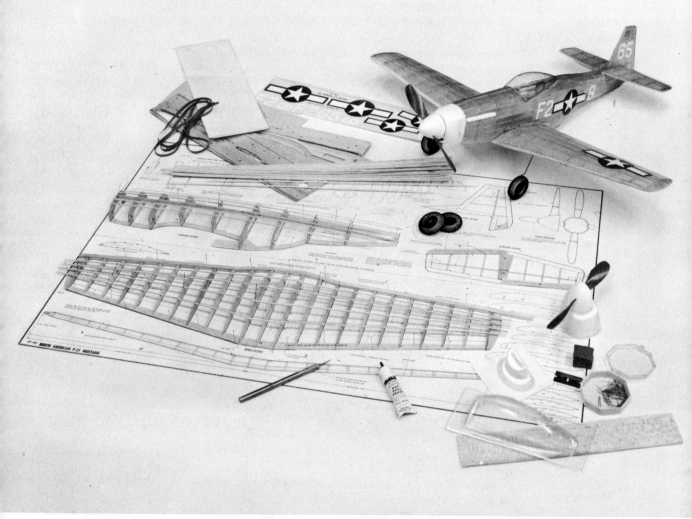

Construction plan and materials for model of U.S. Army Air Force P-51 Mustang. The completed model, also shown, can be flown either by rubber-band power or a small gas engine.

stores. Now, most cities and towns have well-stocked hobby shops, and construction kits are available for all types of airplanes.

The most common construction material is still lightweight balsa wood. But plastics are also popular, especially for complex shapes such as engine cowlings (housing for the engine) and wing tips. Some flying models are all plastic and are almost ready to fly right out of the box.

If you are just becoming interested in model airplanes, the best way to begin is with a well-proved kit of a simple airplane. It is not wise to start off with a big, complex model just because it looks exciting. Start with a model that is within your ability to build. You will soon progress to that big, fancy airplane. If at all possible, try to get advice from an experienced modeler. Read some of the model magazines that are available on newsstands and in hobby shops. If you wish to join a model-airplane club, your local hobby shop will know whether there are any clubs in your area. The Academy of Model Aeronautics in Washington, D.C., can give you information on flying-model contests.

Above all, be patient. Don't rush in building a model. If you work carefully and neatly, all your airplanes will fly like birds.

DON TYPOND
Editor, *Model Airplane News*

AIRPLANES. See AVIATION.

Industrial plants pollute the air with smoke and gases that pour from their smokestacks.

AIR POLLUTION

Wherever you go, whatever you do—inside, outside, on top of a mountain, deep in a coal mine—you are always surrounded by a sea of gases. This sea is called the air, or the atmosphere.

The gases of the atmosphere cannot be seen, and we are rarely aware of them. But they are of the greatest importance. Without the atmosphere, people, animals, and plants could not live. Of almost equal importance is the quality of the atmosphere—whether it is pure or **polluted** (meaning impure).

The atmosphere is made up mainly of the gases oxygen and nitrogen, together with water vapor and smaller amounts of carbon dioxide and other gases. But all air contains small amounts of impurities. In rural areas, far removed from factories and heavy traffic, the air may contain pollen from plants, dust from the soil, and even bacteria. These impurities are usually in such small amounts that they are not important.

Air is said to be polluted when it contains enough harmful impurities to affect the health, safety, or comfort of living things. The impurities, or **pollutants**, could be tiny particles of matter or gases not normally found in air.

When people breathe, pollutants in the air may be deposited in the lungs or absorbed into the body. And polluted air can harm animals and plants as well as people. For this reason, our air supply should be closely watched and managed to assure its good quality.

▶ CAUSES OF AIR POLLUTION

There are two main types of air pollution—natural pollution and pollution caused by people. Natural pollutants are windblown dust, pollen, fog, and the like. There have been instances when the ash from volcanic eruptions has been blown across large areas of the earth. And early in the 1950's, forest fires in the southeastern United States blanketed huge areas of the country with smoke so intense that air flights had to be canceled as far away as New York City. Acts of nature such as these are often beyond human control.

The chief concern is the second and perhaps more serious form of air pollution—the pollution caused by people. Most of this pollution is produced by industry and by vehicles such as cars, trucks, and airplanes. It becomes worse as society becomes more industrialized—as more automobiles are driven, new factories are built, and existing factories are expanded. And it is most severe in cities, where people and industries are concentrated in large numbers.

The millions of people who live in cities need heat, hot water, light, electric power, and transportation. Burning coal and fuel oil to produce these essentials creates much of the pollution from which cities suffer. City dwellers produce vast quantities of waste paper and other refuse, which are burned in incinerators. This also produces air pollution. The exhausts from vehicles in city traffic fill the air with still more pollutants. Sometimes the work at factories creates waste chemicals that escape into the air. Smoke from cigarettes can pollute the air in a closed room. And all kinds of surfaces grind against one another, sending tiny particles of dust into the air. Even ordinary wear and tear on brakes and tires produces dust, as do sanding, grinding, and drilling operations.

Some of these pollutants, such as exhaust gases from cars and trucks, are discharged into the air at street level. Others, such as smoke from power plants and factories, enter the atmosphere at higher levels. When smoke and other pollutants combine with fog, they form **smog**. An article on fog and smog is included in Volume F.

The amount of air pollution is affected by atmospheric conditions such as temperature and air pressure. Because the air near the earth's surface is normally warmer than the air at higher altitudes, air currents usually rise. The rising air currents carry pollutants to the upper atmosphere, where they are dispersed, or scattered. But sometimes the air above the earth's surface is warmer than the air at the surface. When this happens, the warm air stops the flow of rising air currents. This condition is called a **temperature inversion**. The pollutants are trapped close to the surface, where they do the most harm.

Cool air containing smoke and gases is trapped under warm air. This is called a temperature inversion.

High Cost of Air Pollution

The damage caused by air pollution is enormous. In money alone it represents a loss of billions of dollars each year. Many flower and vegetable crops suffer ill effects from car exhaust gases. Trees have been killed by pollution from power plants. Cattle have been poisoned by the fumes from smelters that recover aluminum from ore. Air pollution causes rubber tires on automobiles to crack and become porous. Fine buildings become shabby, their walls blackened with soot that has settled on them. Building surfaces may actually deteriorate because of air pollution.

But the high cost of air pollution is most strikingly illustrated in its damaging effects on the human body. Air pollution causes eye irritations, scratchy throats, and respiratory illnesses. It also contributes to a number of serious diseases. In both the United States and Europe, periods of high levels of air pollution were linked to an increased number of deaths.

Much direct harm is done by air pollution.

Exhausts from a jet airplane pollute the air.

SOME MAJOR POLLUTANTS

Particulate matter is made up of tiny solid or liquid particles. Dust, whether natural or produced by human activity, is particulate. Another example is fly ash, which results from the burning of fuels. Beryllium, used in rockets, and asbestos, used for insulating against heat, are among the materials listed as particulate pollutants.

Oxides of sulfur are gases. They are produced when sulfur-containing fuels, such as coal or oil, are burned. They are also produced in factories where sulfur is used in manufacturing processes. Oxides of sulfur irritate the breathing passages and can damage the lungs.

Carbon monoxide is a poisonous gas produced by the incomplete burning of the carbon in such fuels as gasoline, coal, and oil. Most of the carbon monoxide in the air comes from the exhausts of automobiles and other vehicles that burn gasoline.

Oxides of nitrogen are also produced by automobile engines and other engines. Nitrogen makes up about 78 percent of the air, and oxygen, about 21 percent. Normally these gases do not combine chemically in the air. But in engines that run at very high temperatures, such as those in automobiles, they combine to form gases called oxides of nitrogen.

Photochemical oxidants are formed when oxides of nitrogen combine with other substances present in automobile exhaust. Sunlight promotes the combining process. The photochemical oxidants are the main ingredient of smog, which irritates the eyes and breathing passages.

Scientists are also concerned about the possibility that the increased smoke and dust discharged into the air may, in time, reduce the amount of heat that the surface of the earth receives from the sun. Reduction in the amount of heat from the sun might affect clouds and rainfall.

There is also concern that a certain pollutant may destroy the atmospheric layer that protects us from harmful kinds of solar energy. This pollutant, which belongs to a group of chemicals called fluorocarbons, has been used in spray cans. The substance is also used as a refrigerant and a cleaner.

▶ **CONTROL OF AIR POLLUTION**

There are three basic approaches to the control of air pollution—**preventive measures**, such as changing the raw materials used in industry or the ingredients of fuel; **dispersal measures**, such as raising the heights of chimneys and smokestacks; and **collection measures**, such as designing equipment to trap

Clouds of dust and smoke pour from two stacks of steel-making furnaces before control devices are installed to remove most of the "red dust."

With control devices installed, smoke is no longer visible from the furnace stacks. Factories and plants have been serious sources of air pollution.

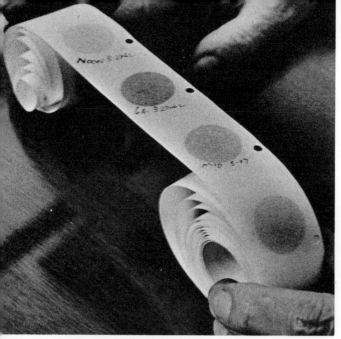

The solids in the air are sampled by being sucked through filter paper. The color of the spots indicates the amount of impure substances in the air.

Chemical pollutants in the air have eaten away the surface of these 17th-century stone statues that decorate the Palace of Versailles, near Paris.

pollutants before they escape into the atmosphere.

Nearly all the highly industrialized countries of the world are working to prevent and control air pollution. Among the many countries in which some type of control legislation exists are Belgium, Bulgaria, Canada, France, West Germany, Italy, Japan, the Soviet Union, the United Kingdom, and Yugoslavia.

In the United States, control of air pollution is basically the responsibility of the state and local governments. All the states have air quality management programs, which are patterned after federal laws.

In 1970, the U.S. Congress passed the Clean Air Act. Under this law, the federal Environmental Protection Agency set standards for air quality. The agency also placed limits on the amounts of pollutants that could be given off by cars, factories, and other sources of pollution. The states and industries such as the automobile industry were asked to meet a first set of standards by 1975, after which stricter standards were to be applied. Many areas could not meet the deadline, and it was extended several times. In 1978 the government declared a partial ban on the use of fluorocarbons, which sharply reduced their use in spray cans.

Air quality programs have brought improvements in many areas. For example, burning low-sulfur coal and oil in factories and power plants has lowered pollution in many cities. To meet federal standards, new cars are equipped with devices such as the catalytic converter, which changes pollutants into harmless substances. Because of this, air pollution from car exhaust has also been reduced.

It is not easy to bring about the new developments needed to control air pollution. Many people—physicians, engineers, meteorologists, botanists, and others—are involved in research, seeking new ways. Permanent observatories have been established to measure gradual changes in the atmosphere over long periods of time. The first observatory of this type was established near Mauna Loa, in Hawaii.

Vast sums of money will have to be spent in the future to clean the air and to keep it clean. Often pollution control means higher prices—to cover the cost of control devices on new cars, for example. But to most people, the cost is justified. Perhaps the day will come when people can breathe pure air in cities where the sunlight is no longer blocked by an umbrella of pollution.

FRED H. RENNER, JR.
Office of Regional Programs
U.S. Environmental Protection Agency

See also ENVIRONMENT.

AIRPORTS. See AVIATION.

ALABAMA

After the battle came the night. It was the night of March 27, 1814. The soldiers stretched wearily by the campfires. General Andrew Jackson sat in his tent at Horseshoe Bend and thought of the great victory. At last he had broken the power of the Creek Indians. Hundreds of warriors lay dead in the sweeping bend of the Tallapoosa River.

Across the river, deep in the forest, a man stood motionless and alone. He was William Weatherford, also known as Red Eagle, a leader of the Creeks. He had escaped from the battle, and he would be hunted.

Yet Red Eagle did not flee. He thought of the Creek women and children hiding in the forest without food or protection. He sighed and made a decision. He would offer his life in exchange for food and safety for his people.

Red Eagle crossed the dark river and stood before Jackson, waiting for death. But Jackson, admiring his courage, allowed Red Eagle to leave in peace. Before long the Creeks and other tribes left Alabama, and settlers took the land.

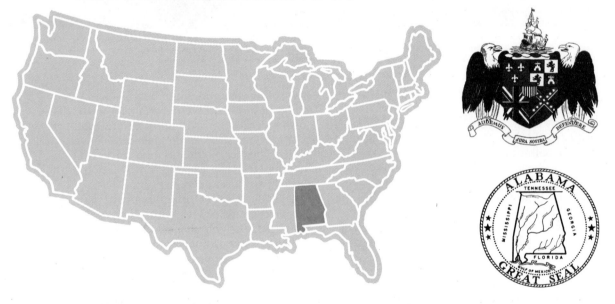

One of Alabama's nicknames, Heart of Dixie, comes from the fact that the state is located in the heart, or center, of the South. There are several stories about the origin of the word "Dixie." Perhaps it came from the French word *dix,* meaning "ten." This word was printed on $10 bills used in the state of Louisiana before the Civil War. The bills were called dixies, and the name Dixie, or Dixie Land, came to be used for all the cotton-growing states.

Alabama has a long history as a farming area. The Indians were its first farmers. Long before European settlers came to the New World, the Indians cleared the thickets—thick growths of shrubs, bushes, and vines—along Alabama's rivers and carried on agriculture. Then settlers took the land, and fields of fluffy cotton began to stretch across Alabama. For years the state was known as a land of cotton. But the time came when Alabama's farmers realized that it was not wise to depend on a single crop. They began to grow many different kinds of crops and to raise hogs, cattle, and chickens. Today leaders of the state say that Alabama's farms can produce enough foods to give every one of its citizens a well-balanced diet without having to repeat a menu for 30 days.

Roaring blast furnaces at Birmingham show that factories as well as farms are important in Alabama. Birmingham is known as the Pittsburgh of the South because of its steel mills. It is the largest of Alabama's industrial cities. There are many others.

The U.S. Army's Redstone Arsenal, located at Huntsville, took Alabama into the space age. Here scientists worked on the Jupiter C rocket. This rocket hurled the nation's first successful satellite into orbit. Huntsville is also known for the Redstone III rocket and the Saturn. The Redstone III boosted the nation's first astronaut into outer space. The Saturn enabled U.S. astronauts to land on the moon. Later, the space shuttle was tested at Huntsville.

The map on the state seal proudly displays Alabama's rivers. They have always been important for transportation. Dams in some of the rivers have great power plants. These plants supply electric power to help light Alabama's farms and cities and to run its factories. The dams also create strings of sparkling lakes, where residents and visitors can enjoy fishing, boating, and other forms of recreation. Besides its rivers and lakes, Alabama has a share of the Gulf of Mexico. Mobile, on beautiful Mobile Bay, is one of the important ports of the nation.

Timber from the forest and fish from the sea add to Alabama's wealth. Many of the people still raise cotton and corn, but agriculture alone is no longer the main concern of the state.

STATE BIRD: Yellowhammer, or flicker.

STATE FLOWER: Camellia.

STATE TREE: Longleaf pine tree.

STATE FLAG.

ALABAMA

CAPITAL: Montgomery.

STATEHOOD: December 14, 1819; the 22nd state.

SIZE: 133,667 km² (51,609 sq mi); rank, 29th.

POPULATION: 3,444,165 (1970 census); rank, 21st.

ORIGIN OF NAME: From the Alibamu, or Alabamu, tribe of Indians, members of the Creek Confederacy. The name may have come from words in the Choctaw language, *alba ayamule*, meaning "I clear the thicket."

ABBREVIATIONS: Ala.; AL.

NICKNAMES: Heart of Dixie, from its location in the center of the Deep South. Yellowhammer State, from Civil War times, when troops from Alabama were called Yellowhammers.

STATE SONG: "Alabama," by Julia S. Tutwiler; music by Edna Goeckel Gussen.

STATE MOTTO: *Audemus jura nostra defendere* (We dare defend our rights).

STATE SEAL: A map of Alabama showing the bordering states, the Gulf of Mexico, and the major rivers.

STATE COAT OF ARMS: The shield in the center contains the emblems of five governments that have ruled over Alabama—France (upper left), Spain (upper right), Great Britain (lower left), the Confederacy (lower right), and the United States (center). The eagles on each side of the shield represent courage. They stand on a banner that carries the state motto. The ship above the shield shows that Alabama borders on water.

STATE FLAG: A crimson cross of St. Andrew on a white field.

Spanish moss hanging from trees is a common sight in Alabama and other southern states.

The Appalachian Highlands include three areas. They are the Appalachian Plateau, the Appalachian Ridge and Valley Region, and the Piedmont Plateau. The average elevation of the highlands varies from 150 to 200 meters (500 to 700 feet), with most of the highest points in the Ridge and Valley Region.

The Appalachian Plateau, also known as the Cumberland Plateau, enters the northeast corner of the state and extends southwestward. This plateau is rather rugged. It has some good farmland, but it is mainly an area of lumbering and mining.

The Appalachian Ridge and Valley Region is made up of narrow valleys between steep mountain ridges. It is known for its mineral riches and forests of oak and pine.

The Piedmont Plateau is a wedge-shaped area southeast of the Ridge and Valley Region. It gets its name from the word *piedmont,* which means "lying at the base, or foot, of mountains." This region is generally hilly, with some rolling land. The most rugged part is in the northwest, where Cheaha Mountain rises to 734 meters (2,407 feet).

The Gulf Coastal Plain is mainly a flat to rolling plain. Ages ago it was covered by oceans. The part adjoining the Appalachian

▶ THE LAND

Alabama is one of the East South Central group of states. It could be called an Appalachian state or a Gulf state. The southern end of the Appalachian Mountain system extends into Alabama and covers the northeastern part of the state. The Gulf of Mexico forms a small but important part of Alabama's southern border.

Landforms

Within the state of Alabama there are three major landforms. They are the Interior Low Plateau, the Appalachian Highlands, and the Gulf Coastal Plain. The Gulf Coastal Plain is the largest of the three regions. It lies south of a line that begins in the northwestern corner of the state, runs southeastward through the city of Tuscaloosa, and continues to Phenix City, on the eastern border.

The Interior Low Plateau enters Alabama from the state of Tennessee and covers a small area in the extreme northwest. The average elevation of this part of Alabama is 210 meters (700 feet). It is a region of knobby hills, cut through by the broad valley of the Tennessee River.

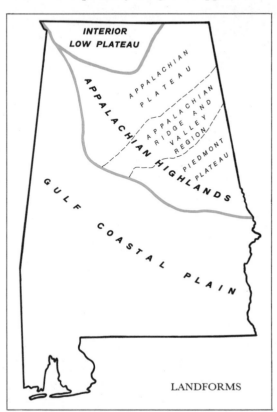

LANDFORMS

Highlands is called the Upper Coastal Plain. This is the oldest part, as well as the highest in elevation. South of it is a strip of nearly level land known as the Black Belt because of its dark-colored soils. The southeastern quarter of the state is known as the Wire Grass area because it was once covered with a kind of coarse grass called wire grass.

For many years the Coastal Plain was the heart of the cotton fields. It is changing gradually to an area where livestock graze and many different crops are grown.

Rivers, Lakes, and Coastal Waters

Alabama is drained by three major river systems. The Tennessee River dips down into Alabama from the state of Tennessee. It flows westward through northern Alabama and then northward to join the Ohio River. The other major rivers of Alabama flow toward the Gulf of Mexico. The Mobile River system is made up of several important rivers. The Tombigbee River and its main tributary, the Black Warrior River, drain the western part of the state. The Coosa and the Tallapoosa rivers flow through east central and eastern Alabama. They join near Montgomery to form the Alabama River, which flows southwestward toward the Tombigbee. North of Mobile, the Alabama and the Tombigbee rivers join to form the Mobile River, which drains southward into Mobile Bay. The Chattahoochee is the major river of southeastern Alabama. Guntersville Lake is the largest of the many lakes in the state.

The Tennessee-Tombigbee (Tenn-Tom) Waterway project was designed to provide a water route from the Tennessee Valley to the Gulf of Mexico, by way of the Tombigbee River. It includes a canal in the northeastern corner of Mississippi that links the rivers.

Alabama's general coastline on the Gulf of Mexico is 85 kilometers (53 miles) long. If the shorelines of inlets, bays, and offshore islands are added, the total shoreline is 977 kilometers (607 miles).

Climate

People sometimes think of Alabama as an uncomfortably hot, tropical state, but this impression is false. Actually, there is a wide variety of climate from the highlands of the north to the beaches of the Gulf of Mexico.

Winter temperatures in the southern half of the state rarely drop below freezing. Snow is so rare that many children have never seen a snowfall. In the northern part of the state, winters are not so mild. Northwest winds bring cold snaps, but they are usually short and are followed by mild weather.

Summer temperatures tend to be about the same over the state. The summer is long, but extended heat waves are almost unknown. Along the coast the hot days are relieved by frequent breezes blowing in from the Gulf of Mexico. Nights are cool and comfortable even in midsummer. In the north, summer temperatures are relieved by the higher altitudes and by cool forest shade. Spring and autumn are long and delightful. Autumn extends from early September to well after Thanksgiving.

THE LAND

LOCATION: Latitude—30° 13′ N to 35° N. **Longitude**—84° to 53′ W to 88° 28′ W.
Tennessee to the north, Mississippi on the west, the Florida panhandle and the Gulf of Mexico to the south, Georgia on the east.

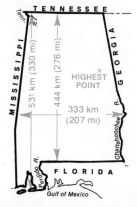

ELEVATION: Highest—Cheaha Mountain, 734 m (2,407 ft). **Lowest**—Sea level, along the Gulf of Mexico.

LANDFORMS: Highlands (the Interior Low Plateau and the Appalachian Highlands) in the northern part of the state; lowlands (the Gulf Coastal Plain) in the south and west.

SURFACE WATERS: Major rivers—Tennessee; Tombigbee, with its main tributary, the Black Warrior; Coosa and Tallapoosa, which join to form the Alabama; Mobile, formed by the joining of the Alabama and the Tombigbee; Chattahoochee. **Major artificial lakes**—Pickwick, Wilson, Wheeler, and Guntersville, on the Tennessee River; Lay, Mitchell, Weiss, and Jordan, on the Coosa; Martin and Thurlow, on the Tallapoosa; Holt Reservoir on the Black Warrior.

CLIMATE: Temperature—July average, about 27°C (80°F) statewide. January average, about 7°C (44°F) in north, 12°C (53°F) in south. **Precipitation**—Rainfall average, 1,350 mm (53 in); varies from 1,320 mm (52 in) in north to 1,730 mm (68 in) along the coast. **Growing season**—Varies from about 200 days in north to 300 days in south.

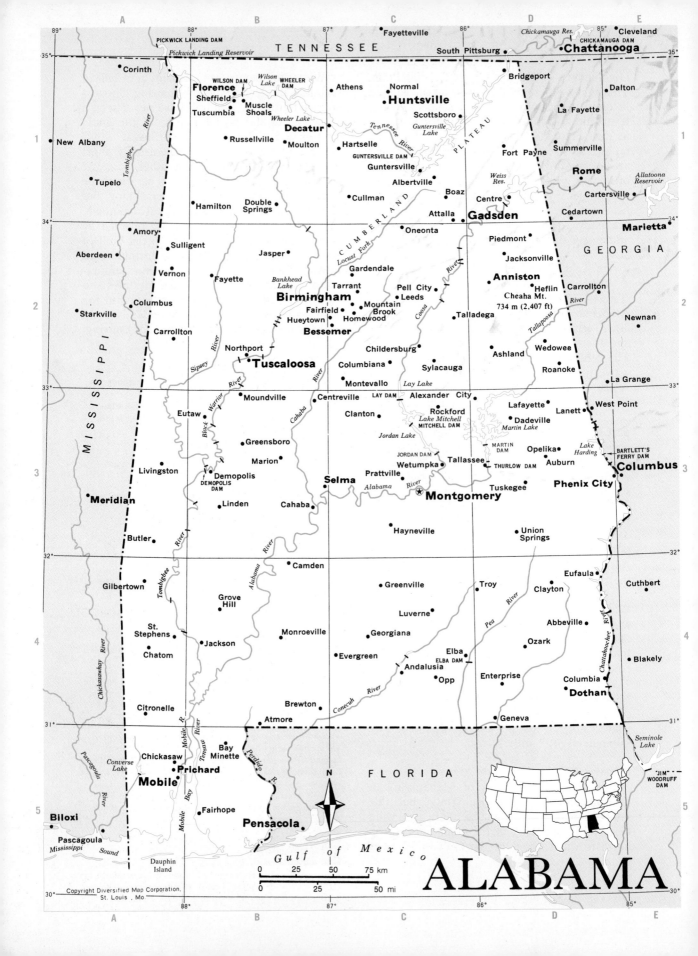

Natural Resources

Leaders of the state like to say that Alabama has more natural resources than any other area of its size in the world. These resources include soils, minerals, forests, and water.

Soils. Alabama may be divided into several major soil areas. Along the Coosa and the Tennessee rivers, there are valleys called limestone valleys. The soils in these valleys are mainly red clay loams. They were formed by the weathering of limestone rock. The soils of the Appalachian Plateau are mainly sandy loams. Red sandy loams and clay loams cover much of the Piedmont Plateau. The soils of the Gulf Coastal Plain were formed from sediment laid down in the oceans that once covered the plain. Most of these soils are sandy loams or clay soils.

Long years of growing cotton and corn lowered the fertility of Alabama's soils. The abundant rainfall also caused the topsoil to be washed away. In many places, especially in the Piedmont Plateau and the Black Belt, farms are now planted in grasses to improve the soil and provide pasture for cattle.

Forests. About 60 per cent of all the land of Alabama is forested. Many kinds of trees are found, but the soft pine is the most common. It is also the most valuable for wood pulp, which is used for making paper. The pine forests grow mainly in the central and southern parts of the state.

To improve worn-out soils, farmers have developed many tree farms for future harvest. Paper companies, farmers, and the government all help in a continuing program of reforestation.

Minerals. Most of Alabama's minerals are in the northern half of the state. Coal and iron ore are found in the Appalachian Plateau and in the Ridge and Valley Region. One of the largest deposits, or fields, of coal is the Warrior field. It extends through all of Walker County and parts of Fayette, Tuscaloosa, and Jefferson counties. Some of the best beds of iron ore are in the Birmingham area.

Limestone occurs in the Tennessee Valley and in the Ridge and Valley Region, as well as in areas of the Gulf Coastal Plain. Marble is found in Coosa and Talladega counties.

Petroleum is the most important mineral of the Gulf Coastal Plain. It has been found in the extreme southwestern counties. There are important salt deposits north of Mobile. Henry and Barbour counties, as well as other parts of the state, have deposits of bauxite, a claylike mineral from which aluminum is obtained.

Waters. Alabama's water is one of its most valuable resources. The supply is abundant. Mainly it is soft, pure water that does not require treatment before being used in homes and industries.

Hydroelectric plants line the Coosa, Tallapoosa, Tennessee, Chattahoochee, and Black Warrior rivers. Along the rivers there are also steam power plants, fed by Alabama's coal. Additional plants are now being built or planned. They will provide ample power for years to come.

Wildlife. Alabama has more than 300 species of birds. Among the largest are bald eagles, hawks, ospreys, and wild turkeys, ducks, and geese. Rabbits, squirrels, raccoons, foxes, and white-tailed deer are found in most of the state, and black bears in some areas. Fresh-water fish include bass, perch, bluegill, and trout. Some fisheries have been closed by mercury pollution.

In 1955 the tarpon was named the state salt-water fish. It is a big fighting fish found in the warm, blue waters of the Gulf of Mexico. It has no commercial value. The main products of the sea fisheries are shrimp, oysters, and crabs.

▶ THE PEOPLE AND THEIR WORK

There are very few foreign-born people living in Alabama. The majority are descendants of European settlers who came to the area in colonial times. About one third of the people are blacks whose ancestors were brought to the South as slaves. Among the people of Indian heritage, the most active organized group is the Creek Nation East of the Mississippi, at Atmore.

In 1960, for the first time, more Alabamians lived in cities than in rural areas. The number of persons who worked on farms dropped steadily during the years from 1940 to 1960. The number who worked in manufacturing plants increased greatly.

Industries and Products

The growth of industry in Alabama had been so rapid that by the early 1960's the value of manufactured products was far greater than the value of agricultural products. Minerals ranked third in value.

Manufacturing. The most important industries are the ones that manufacture metals, textiles, chemicals, and forest products. Many of the industries make use of Alabama's own raw materials.

The areas around Birmingham and Gadsden are the only places in the nation where iron ore, coal, and limestone are found close together. These are basic raw materials needed in the making of steel. About 90 per cent of all the steel making in the South is carried on in Alabama, mostly in and around Birmingham, Anniston, and Gadsden. New factories that make products from iron and steel continue to spring up throughout the state, mainly along the water routes.

Around Mobile, as well as in other areas, there are plants that extract aluminum from bauxite. These plants provide metal for factories in the Tennessee Valley that make aluminum products. A large copper-tubing plant at Decatur, on the Tennessee River, is a new development for Alabama.

The textile industry produces yarn and thread, woven fabrics, clothing, and other goods. Textile mills are spread throughout the state.

WHAT ALABAMA PRODUCES

MANUFACTURED GOODS: Metals, textiles and apparel, chemicals, paper and related products, foods.

AGRICULTURAL PRODUCTS: Broilers, cattle and calves, eggs, milk, hogs, soybeans, cotton.

MINERALS: Coal, iron ore, cement, stone, petroleum.

Many communities have sawmills (*above*) and lumber companies. Alabama is a leading producer of lumber and wood pulp.

Many of the chemical industries make use of coal tar, a tar that is left from the process of making coke. Some of the by-products of coal tar are medicines, explosives, dyes, and plastics. The salt deposits near Mobile provide raw material for the making of chlorine products, such as bleaches, disinfectants, and water purifiers. At Muscle Shoals in northwestern Alabama there is a federal plant where fertilizers and munitions are developed for the benefit of agriculture and industry.

Alabama ranks among the first five timber producers in the nation. The forests supply lumber for furniture and other wood products as well as wood pulp for the paper industries. The first pulp and paper plant in the state was built at Tuscaloosa in 1929. Other cities that now have large pulp mills are Mobile and Brewton, in southern Alabama, and Demopolis, in the western part of the state. Most of the pulp is made into finished products such as newsprint, stationery, corrugated boxes, and kraft paper. Kraft paper is the strong brown paper used in grocery bags.

Agriculture. In Enterprise, Alabama, there is a monument to the boll weevil. It is perhaps the only monument in the world to an insect pest. The monument was erected in 1919 after the boll weevil destroyed the cotton crops. It reminds Alabama's farmers of the part that the boll weevil played in

Peanuts are piped into a silo for storage. Peanuts are an important crop in southeastern Alabama.

teaching them not to depend on cotton alone for their living.

For a long time cotton ranked first among Alabama's crops, but today cotton brings only a fraction of the total income from crops. Alabama also produces substantial amounts of soybeans, peanuts, corn, hay, sweet potatoes and other garden vegetables, and fruits and pecans. Some crops are identified with particular areas. Soybeans are grown extensively in the Black Belt and around Mobile Bay. Peanuts are a main crop in the Wire Grass area. Strawberries are grown commercially around Cullman in Cullman County, Clanton in Chilton County, and Georgiana in Butler County. Clanton is also known for peaches. Truck farming is carried on in many areas.

An interesting fact about Alabama's agriculture is that since 1958 livestock sales have brought more income than crops. Cattle are raised chiefly in the Black Belt and hogs in the Wire Grass area. Poultry raising is concentrated north of Birmingham. Dairying is carried on throughout the state.

Mining. Alabama is well-known for its production of coal, cement, and limestone. A number of other minerals are produced in varying quantities including petroleum, iron ore, clays and shale, mica, sand and gravel, bauxite, gold, silver, and manganese. Marble from Alabama's quarries is sold throughout the United States.

The first producing oil well began operating near Gilbertown, in Choctaw County, in 1944. Later, oil was found in Escambia County and near Citronelle, in Mobile County. There are more than 200 producing wells in southwestern Alabama. In the northwest a large natural gas field is being developed.

Transportation and Communication

Waterways, railroads, highways, and airways connect Alabama to other parts of the nation. The port of Mobile connects the state to the seaports of the world.

Waterways. Alabama has the finest river system in the nation. The U.S. Corps of Engineers classifies large portions of its rivers as suitable for navigation. Millions of dollars have been spent to develop the harbor and build docks at Mobile, to widen and deepen the channels of the rivers, and to build public docks along the waterways.

The Black Warrior and Tombigbee waterway extends all the way from the port of Mobile to Jefferson and Walker counties. This waterway carries great quantities of limestone as well as millions of tons of cargo for the industries of Birmingham and other cities along the rivers. The Alabama River provides water transportation between Mobile and the capital city, Montgomery. The Tennessee River is the main water route of northern Alabama. The Chattahoochee waterway, on the east border of the state, serves the cities of Columbia, Eufaula, and Phenix City.

Railroads and Highways. Alabama was among the pioneers in railroad building. Its first railway, between Decatur and Muscle Shoals, was completed in 1832. Today Alabama's railroads are used largely for freight. Hubs of state, federal, and interstate highway systems are Birmingham and Montgomery.

Airlines. Several airlines provide commercial flights to cities in different parts of the state. Frequent daily schedules are available from major centers. Most of the interstate traffic uses the airports at Birmingham, Huntsville, and Mobile. Alabama's system of local airfields, with paved and lighted runways for smaller planes, is considered to be among the best in the nation.

Newspapers, Radio, and Television. Almost every city has its own local newspaper. More than 100 newspapers are published in the state, but only about 20 are dailies. Among the more influential daily newspapers are the *Alabama Journal* and the *Montgomery Advertiser,* both published at Montgomery, and the *Birmingham News.* The *Mobile Press-Register,* originally the *Gazette,* is one of the oldest newspapers in the state. It was founded in 1815.

Birmingham had the state's first licensed radio station, WBRC, in 1925, and the first television stations, WABT and WBRC-TV, both in 1949. In 1955 Alabama began operating one of the first state-owned educational television networks (ETV) in the nation. Stations of this network are capable of reaching almost all the people in the state.

▶ **EDUCATION**

Alabama is proud of its natural resources and its industrial development in recent years. State and community leaders also recognize the importance of developing its educational and cultural institutions.

Schools and Colleges

The first teachers in Alabama were probably French and Spanish priests who gave instruction to the Indians. In 1799 a New England cotton merchant, John Pierce, opened a school for the children of wealthy settlers in the Mobile Bay area. It was the kind of pioneer school known as a blab school because the pupils studied by repeating their lessons aloud.

When Alabama became a state in 1819, an attempt was made to establish a system of public schools. The attempt failed, as did others in later years, largely because of a lack of money. Private schools sprang up to educate the children of parents who could afford to pay. It was not until after the Civil War that the state was able to make progress toward establishing its present system of public elementary schools, high schools, and colleges.

Alabama has more than 50 institutions of higher education. About half of these are 2-year institutions, mainly state-supported junior or community colleges. The others are universities and senior colleges.

The University of Alabama at Tuscaloosa (post office address, University) is Alabama's oldest college. It was established by the legislature in 1820. Other state-supported universities are located at Auburn, Birmingham, Florence, Huntsville, Jacksonville, Livingston, Mobile, Montevallo, Montgomery, Normal, and Troy. Tuskegee Institute, the famous school established by Booker T. Washington in 1881, is partly supported by the state.

Libraries

Throughout the state there are many public and private libraries. The largest public libraries are in Birmingham, Montgomery, and Mobile. The Amelia Gayle Gorgas Library, on the campus of the University of Alabama, is one of the largest libraries in the entire South.

Fine Arts and Museums

Most high schools and junior high schools in the state have bands or orchestras. The Birmingham Civic Symphony gives annual concerts in the city. It also tours the state.

Before the Civil War, architecture was one of the most important fine arts. Some of the beautiful homes that were built before the war may be seen in the older cities, such as Selma, Huntsville, Eufaula, Greensboro, Mobile, Tuscaloosa, and Montgomery.

The Art Museum at Birmingham and the Museum of Fine Arts at Montgomery have large collections of paintings. The following are among the other noted museums:

The **Alabama Museum of Natural History,** at the University of Alabama, has an excellent display of rocks and minerals.

Mound State Monument, a state park and museum at Moundville, near Tuscaloosa, preserves ancient mounds that Indians built for their temples, council houses, and burial places. Relics from the grounds in the park, such as skeletons, tools, ornaments, and pottery, are displayed in the museum.

The **Regar Museum of Natural History,** at Anniston, contains an unusual display of 900 specimens of birds, with nests and eggs.

▶ PLACES OF INTEREST

Some of the many other interesting places have been made by people. Some, such as mountains, forests, and white sand beaches, are nature's own work.

Historic Places

Many historic treasures are preserved in Alabama's museums. The following are a few of the historic places in various parts of the state:

Horseshoe Bend National Military Park, on the Tallapoosa River, marks the site of General Andrew Jackson's victory over the Creek Indians.

The **Natchez Trace Parkway** crosses the northwestern corner of Alabama. It extends from Natchez, Mississippi, to Nashville, Tennessee. The parkway commemorates a famous Indian trail and pioneer highway.

Russell Cave National Monument, at Bridgeport in northeast Alabama, was established in 1961. In the cave, scientists have found records of almost continuous human habitation from at least 6000 B.C. to about A.D. 1650.

Tuskegee Institute National Historic Site includes Tuskegee Institute, the George Washington Carver Museum, and Booker T. Washington's home. The museum includes displays of African art and George Washington Carver's agricultural experiments.

The **Cathedral of the Immaculate Conception,** at Mobile, stands on land that the first settlers used as a burying ground.

The **State Capitol,** Montgomery, is a stately building, similar in appearance to the National Capitol. For the first few months of the Civil War, it served as the capitol of the Confederacy.

Jefferson Davis' Home, in Montgomery, is known as the first White House of the Confederacy because it was here that President Davis lived when Montgomery was the Confederate capital.

Parks and Forests

Alabama has four national forests. The Talladega National Forest has two sections, one in the central part of the state and the other in the east. The William B. Bankhead National Forest, formerly the Black Warrior National Forest, is in the northwest. The Tuskegee, smallest of the national forests, is in the east, and the Conecuh is in the south.

State parks and forests total about 30. They are planned to conserve the natural beauty of the state and to provide places where people may go for outdoor recreation—picnicking, camping, hiking and nature study, fishing and other water sports.

Other Attractions

The following are among other places that attract visitors from all over the nation and the world:

Ave Maria Grotto, at St. Bernard, near Cullman, displays more than 100 small reproductions of famous religious buildings of the world.

The **Azalea Trail,** in Mobile, is a 55-kilometer (35-mile) trail of flowers that leads through residential parts of the city, past historic homes and buildings.

Bellingrath Gardens and Home, south of Mobile, is a beautifully landscaped estate. Here the finest flowers, shrubs, and trees have been brought together in a setting of great natural beauty. The home is noted for its rich furnishings and priceless art objects.

Cathedral Caverns, north of Guntersville, contains a large forest of stalagmites and one cavern 27 meters (90 feet) deep.

Ivy Green, in Tuscumbia, is Helen Keller's birthplace and childhood home.

Vulcan Statue, at the summit of Red Mountain, Birmingham, is a statue of the god of fire. It was made of iron from the local area and is said to be one of the largest statues in the world.

Annual Events

Many of Alabama's annual events center upon sports, the products of the state, and the interests and traditions of the people. From the early French settlers, Mobile inherited the celebration of Mardi gras. Mobile's Mardi gras festival is the oldest such celebration in the United States. It begins on the Friday before the first day of Lent and reaches its high point on the night of Shrove Tuesday, or Mardi gras.

Mobile celebrates the azalea season from late February to early April, when thousands of visitors tour the Azalea Trail. The Deep-Sea Fishing Rodeo, at Mobile and Dauphin Island, climaxes the fishing season, usually late in July or early in August.

Other events include the state fair at Birmingham, in September, and the River Boat Regatta at Guntersville, in August.

▸ CITIES

No one region claims all or most of the cities. Large cities are found in each part of the state—central, north, and south.

Montgomery

Besides being the capital, Montgomery is a center of agricultural trade and the leading cattle market of southeastern United States. The large ranches and herds of cattle in the area remind one of Texas. Industries of the city include textile mills, meat-packing plants, and furniture factories.

Montgomery has several institutions of higher education, including Alabama State University, campuses of Troy State and Auburn universities, and Huntingdon College, a private senior college. The Air University at Maxwell Air Force Base is a national center for research and for education and training of U.S. Air Force personnel.

Birmingham

Alabama's largest city is located at the southern end of the Ridge and Valley Region. It is sometimes called the Magic City because of its rapid growth. In less than 80 years, it grew from the small town of Elyton into a metropolitan area serving more than 600,000 people. It is the South's only major producer of iron and steel. The hundreds of other industries in the area manufacture such items

The Bellingrath Gardens and Home, south of Mobile, are a major year-round tourist attraction in the South.

Dexter Avenue in Montgomery is one of the city's oldest and busiest streets.

ALABAMA
PLACES OF INTEREST

This part of the Alabama State Capitol was built before the Civil War. Wings have been added since that time.

tion increased to more than 135,000. In 1960 a part of the arsenal was transferred to the National Aeronautics and Space Administration. This part was named the George C. Marshall Space Flight Center.

Tuscaloosa, the home of the University of Alabama, is located on the Black Warrior River at the edge of the Appalachian Plateau. Its name comes from the Indian words *tuska,* meaning "black," and *lusa,* meaning "warrior." The city's many industries include a large paper mill, a rubber-tire plant, textile mills, oil refineries, and plants that make metal products.

Gadsden, northeast of Birmingham, is an important iron and steel center, as well as a distribution point for livestock and grain produced in the surrounding area.

Dothan, leading city of southeastern Alabama, is located in a rich farming area. The main crop is peanuts. Industries in the city manufacture such products as peanut oil, hosiery, and cigars.

▸ **GOVERNMENT**

The legislative department of the state government is made up of the Senate and the House of Representatives. The members of both bodies serve 4-year terms. An amendment to the state constitution, adopted in 1975, provided for annual legislative sessions, beginning in 1976. Before that, regular sessions had been held every other year.

The state's chief executive is the governor, who is elected to a 4-year term. The people also elect a lieutenant governor, secretary of state, attorney general, treasurer, auditor, superintendent of education, and commissioner of agriculture and industry.

The highest state court is the supreme court. It consists of a chief justice and eight associate justices elected statewide for 6-year terms. The court of appeals is divided into two courts, one to hear civil appeals and one to hear criminal appeals. The major trial courts in Alabama are its numerous circuit courts.

as cast-iron pipe, heavy machinery, chemicals, textiles, and wood and paper products.

Birmingham is a leading educational and cultural center. It is also noted for mountain scenery and places of outdoor recreation.

Mobile

The second-largest city and only seaport is known as Alabama's Gateway to the World. It was founded by the French and was named for the Mobile Indians, who lived in the area. Today it is a busy industrial center with chemical plants, shipyards, and seafood industries. It is also a gracious and beautiful resort city, known for its flowers and ancient oak trees draped with Spanish moss.

Other Cities

The following are some of the other important cities:

Huntsville, now the Rocket City, was one of Alabama's first settlements. It remained a small farming community for more than 125 years. Its population was only 16,000 in 1950. About that time the Army began to develop a rocket and guided-missile center at the Redstone Arsenal at Huntsville. Thousands of scientists and other workers came to the area. So did dozens of new industries. Within 20 years Huntsville's popula-

---

GOVERNMENT

Capital—Montgomery. **Number of counties**—67. **Representation in Congress**—U.S. senators, 2; U.S. representatives, 7. **State Legislature**—Senate, 35 members; House of Representatives, 105 members; all 4-year terms. **Governor**—4-year term. **Elections**—Primary elections to select candidates, first Tuesday in May; general and state elections, Tuesday after first Monday in November.

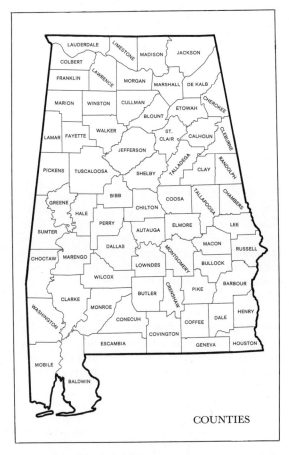

COUNTIES

The state is divided into 67 counties. Each county is governed by a commission, presided over by a judge of probate.

▶ FAMOUS PEOPLE

Alabama claims many persons who did important work in government, education, the law, military affairs, business, and the arts. The following are some of the honored names:

William Wyatt Bibb (1781–1820) was Alabama's only territorial governor and the first governor of the state. He was born in Georgia.

Josiah Gorgas (1818–83), born in Pennsylvania, was a teacher and an army officer. He became an Alabamian after his marriage to Amelia Gayle, daughter of John Gayle, governor of Alabama from 1831 to 1835. During the Civil War, Josiah Gorgas was chief of military supplies, and eventually a brigadier general, in the Confederate Army. Later he served for a year as president of the University of Alabama. His son, William C. Gorgas (1854–1920), who was born near Mobile, is world famous as the U.S. Army surgeon and sanitation expert who stamped out yellow fever in the Canal Zone and made possible the building of the Panama Canal.

Julia Strudwick Tutwiler (1841–1916) was born in Greene County. She established several girls' vocational schools and secured admission of women to the University of Alabama. She was also active in prison reform. The words for the state song were written by her.

Booker T. Washington (1856–1915) is known throughout the world as the founder of Tuskegee Institute and as an educator, author, and lecturer. He was born in Virginia and was educated at Hampton Institute. His biography is included in Volume W.

George Washington Carver (1864–1943), botanist and agricultural scientist, gained international fame for his work in agricultural research at Tuskegee Institute. He taught improvement of the soil and developed hundreds of products from the peanut, sweet potato, and soybean. A biography of George Washington Carver, who was born in Missouri and educated in Iowa, is included in Volume C.

William Brockman Bankhead (1874–1940) was born in Moscow (now Sulligent), Alabama. He served in the U.S. House of Representatives from 1917 to 1940. He was speaker of the House from 1936 to 1940. His daughter, Tallulah Brockman Bankhead, became one of America's best-known actresses. His father, John H. Bankhead, and his brother, John H. Bankhead, Jr., were both U.S. senators.

Helen Adams Keller, who was born in Tuscumbia in 1880, lost both sight and hearing before she was 2 years old. Because she could not hear, she also lost the ability to speak. In spite of her handicaps, she learned to speak, gained an education, and then spent her life lecturing and writing to raise money for the training of other handicapped persons. Her biography is included in Volume K.

George Corley Wallace (1919–   ) was born in Clio, Alabama. He was a judge and state legislator before his election in 1962 as governor of Alabama. He was re-elected to that office in 1970 and 1974. He was also a presidential candidate in 1964, 1968, and 1972. A bullet from an assassination attempt during the 1972 campaign left him crippled.

Three Alabamians have become justices of the U.S. Supreme Court. Justices John McKinley and John A. Campbell, who served during the 1800's, were born in other states. Hugo L. Black, who became a justice in 1937, was born in Clay County, Alabama.

Writers, musicians, and entertainers who were born in Alabama include novelists Nelle Harper Lee (Monroeville) and Borden Deal

(Tuscaloosa), composer William C. Handy (Florence), and singer Nat "King" Cole (Montgomery).

Famous names in sports include heavyweight champion Joe Louis (born Joe Louis Barrow, Lafayette); baseball players Henry "Hank" Aaron (Mobile), Frank Lary (Northport), and Willie Mays (Fairfield); and sports announcer Mel Allen (born Melvin Allen Israel, Birmingham).

▶ **HISTORY**

At the time of Columbus, Alabama was inhabited by four main groups of Indians. They were the Cherokees, Creeks, Choctaws, and Chickasaws. Sometimes there were skirmishes resulting from border disputes. But usually the Indians lived in peace, hunting, fishing, and raising corn and vegetables on small plots of land.

Exploration and Settlement

During the early 1500's Spanish explorers sailed along the coast of the Gulf of Mexico. But Europeans were not seen in the interior of Alabama until 1540, when Hernando de Soto passed through with a band of well-armed soldiers. De Soto forced the peaceful Indians to provide him with food and servants, and his harsh methods stirred up resentment. When he reached the land governed by the gigantic Choctaw chieftain, Tuskaloosa, he ran into trouble. De Soto captured the chief and took him to the tribe's strongly fortified village. Here the Indians rose up to free their chief. For many hours the bloody battle raged. The Spanish soldiers slaughtered Indian men, women, and children alike. When the battle was over, the village was in ruins and its population was destroyed. De Soto's troops also suffered heavy losses. Later, in 1559, Spanish colonists started a settlement on Mobile Bay, but storms and other troubles caused the settlers to leave.

English traders from the Carolinas and Georgia traded with the Indians during the late 1600's, but the English made no permanent settlements in Alabama at that time. In 1702 the French established Fort Louis on Mobile Bay. This settlement was moved, in 1711, to the present site of Mobile. It became the first permanent white settlement in what is now Alabama.

During the 1700's the French and the British fought over the territory of which Alabama was a part. After the French and Indian War, the Treaty of Paris, in 1763, gave the territory to England. Spain, Georgia, and the Carolinas still argued over who owned the land. It was not until 1813 that all of what is now Alabama passed into undisputed possession of the United States and became part of the Mississippi Territory.

After 1800 more and more settlers came into Alabama from the states on the Atlantic Coast. The invention of the cotton gin and the growth of the cotton textile industry in England made cotton a valuable crop. The settlers grew cotton on most of the land that they cleared. But settling the territory was not without its perils. Much of the good farmland was already being used by the Indians, whose ways of living easily adapted to the settlers' ways. The Indians resisted the theft of their lands. The Creeks, who held more than half the land in the territory, were

---

IMPORTANT DATES

1540	Hernando de Soto marched across Alabama, exploring and searching for gold.
1559	Tristán de Luna, Spanish colonizer, started a temporary settlement on Mobile Bay.
1699	An expedition under the French explorer Pierre Lemoyne, Sieur d'Iberville, explored the coast and claimed the area for France.
1702	Pierre Lemoyne's brother, Jean Baptiste Lemoyne, Sieur de Bienville, founded Fort Louis de la Mobile.
1711	The French moved Fort Louis to the present site of Mobile.
1763	At the end of the French and Indian War, France gave the area east of the Mississippi River, including Alabama, to Great Britain.
1783	After the Revolutionary War, Great Britain gave the Mobile area to Spain and the rest of Alabama to the United States.
1813	United States captured Mobile and added it to the Mississippi Territory.
1814	General Andrew Jackson defeated the Creek Indians.
1817	Congress created the Alabama Territory.
1819	Alabama admitted to Union December 14, as 22nd state.
1847	Montgomery became state capital.
1861	Alabama seceded from the Union January 11 and formed the Republic of Alabama, which lasted until February 8, when Alabama joined the Confederacy.
1868	Alabama re-admitted to the Union.
1875	A new constitution adopted, ending the period of Reconstruction.
1888	First steel produced in Birmingham.
1901	Present state constitution adopted.
1944	First petroleum produced near Gilbertown.
1949	Redstone Arsenal, at Huntsville, became a center for rocket and missile research.
1970	Black Alabamians won seats (two) in the state legislature for the first time since Reconstruction.
1976	State legislature began to hold annual, rather than biennial, sessions.

especially bitter. They sided with the British in the War of 1812. The Indians raided Fort Mims and killed several hundred settlers. In a final battle at Horseshoe Bend, the Creeks were defeated, and before long they were moved out of the territory. The Cherokees, who had remained neutral in the war, were later moved from their lands. They were the most progressive of the Indian tribes. They lived in brick houses, grew cotton, raised cattle, and even had a written language.

Alabama Becomes a State

When Mississippi became a state in 1817, the eastern half of the Mississippi Territory was removed and made the Alabama Territory. Its capital was St. Stephens, a small town to the north of Mobile. At that time settlers were found mainly in three regions—in the Tennessee Valley, around Huntsville; along the Tombigbee and Black Warrior rivers, with centers at St. Stephens and Tuscaloosa; and along the Alabama and Coosa rivers, near such towns as Wetumpka and Montgomery.

Alabama was not a territory very long. With the approval of Congress, leading citizens met at Huntsville on July 5, 1819, and drafted Alabama's first constitution. Soon after, on December 14, 1819, Alabama became a state. The capital was situated at Cahaba, a town built for just this purpose at the junction of the Cahaba and the Alabama rivers. The choice of this town was bad. It lay in low, swampy land that flooded regularly. In 1825 the session of the legislature could be held only on the second floor of the capitol, and the legislators had to get there by rowboat. Because of this situation the state capital was moved in 1827 to Tuscaloosa, where it stayed for 20 years. In 1847 the increase in wealth and political strength of the cotton planters of the Black Belt caused another move of the state capital—this time to Montgomery, where it is today.

King Cotton, Slavery, and the Civil War

Between 1820 and 1860 Alabama's economy was closely tied to slavery. The large cotton plantations could not be worked profitably without slaves. In the 1840's Alabama was one of the wealthiest states in the Union. In 1860 forces in the North moved toward the abolition of slavery. The leaders of Alabama opposed federal interference in the affairs of their state. They proposed secession. After a special election among the people, a convention was held in Montgomery on January 7, 1861. On January 11 a resolution of secession was adopted, and Alabama invited all the other southern states to meet in Montgomery to form a new union.

On February 4, 1861, the convention met and drew up the constitution for the Confederate States of America. Jefferson Davis was sworn in as the president on February 18, 1861.

During the Civil War there were many minor battles in the state. No major battles took place within its borders, but the state was badly hurt by the fighting. When the war was over, Alabama's economy was destroyed.

Between 1865 and 1875 Alabama lived under a partly military government called the Reconstruction. These were harsh times— times of agricultural failures, general poverty, and great political confusion. In 1875 a new constitution was adopted and approved by Congress. Between 1875 and 1900 Alabama went through a period of economic recovery. Cotton was still king, but industry grew.

Modern Times and the Future

After the Reconstruction era, blacks in Alabama were stripped of their newly won civil rights, including the right to vote. They had to attend different schools from whites. Racial segregation of many kinds was the law in Alabama for a long time.

In the 1960's, however, federal legislation enabled blacks in Alabama to vote in large numbers. Progress has also been made against many forms of racial segregation. Much of this progress in Alabama resulted from peaceful protest conducted under the leadership of Martin Luther King.

Alabama has undergone many other changes recently. Industry has grown rapidly. The state's waterways are being enlarged and improved. With its abundance of raw materials, and its vital people, Alabama should continue to be the industrial heart of the New South.

H. D. HAYS and WALTER F. KOCH
University of Alabama

ALAMO. See TEXAS; MEXICAN WAR.

ALASKA

The story of Alaska's flag begins in 1926. Because Alaska had no flag of its own, the American Legion sponsored a flag contest in October of that year. All Alaskan boys and girls in grades 7 to 12 were invited to enter.

At a school near Seward was an orphan whose name was Benny Benson. Thirteen-year-old Benny loved his land and often dreamed of its greatness. Out of his love and dreams came the winning design. Below his sketch Benny wrote these words:

"The blue field is for the Alaskan sky and the forget-me-not, an Alaskan flower. The North Star is for the future state of Alaska, the most northerly of the Union. The Dipper is for the Great Bear, symbolizing strength."

On May 2, 1927, Benny's design became Alaska's official flag. A prize of $1,000 was put aside for Benny's education. When Alaska was preparing for statehood in 1955, the delegates to the constitutional convention publicly honored Benny Benson. Later the town of Kodiak named a street for him.

Alaska is the largest, the next-to-youngest, and the most sparsely populated state of the Union. It contains Point Barrow, the northernmost point in the United States, and Mount McKinley, the highest mountain peak in all North America. About one third of this huge state lies north of the Arctic Circle.

Like Florida, in the extreme southeastern United States, Alaska is a peninsula. The mainland of Alaska juts out at the northwest corner of the North American continent like a huge thumb on a doubled-up fist. At one point on the western side, Alaska is about 90 kilometers (55 miles) from Asia. Thousands of years ago, the mainlands of the two continents were connected. Now they are separated by the Bering Strait, where Russia's Big Diomede Island lies within 5 kilometers (3 miles) of Little Diomede Island, owned by the United States. The international date line runs between the two islands. Sunday on Little Diomede is Monday on Big Diomede.

Alaska includes thousands of islands. One chain of islands, the Aleutians, stretches beyond the 180th meridian into the Eastern Hemisphere. Attu Island, at the tip of the chain, is in the same longitude as New Zealand.

Among Alaska's people are the native inhabitants of "The Great Land"—Eskimo,

Aleuts, and Indians. The rest of the people represent all parts of the nation and many countries of the world. Mainly they are young, adventurous people who have answered the challenge of developing the last United States frontier.

For many years Alaska had no government of its own to conserve and develop its natural resources. People rushed into this vast land to strip it of furs, fish, and gold, and then rushed out again to spend somewhere else the profits from their plundering.

Russia owned Alaska for more than 100 years. During this time the fur seals were killed so wastefully that only a fraction of

them survived. The sea otter was almost exterminated. Then, in 1867, the United States bought Alaska, and the land lay almost forgotten until its wealth in fish, especially in salmon, attracted a new kind of fortune hunter.

In 1896 the cry of "Gold!" rang out in the Klondike region of Canada's Yukon Territory. This cry shifted attention from fish to gold. Thousands of people poured through Skagway, Alaska, on their way to the Klondike. Others hurried to Alaska's own gold fields. Many of the gold seekers were disappointed. But many who struck it rich returned "outside"—anywhere outside Alaska—to

STATE FLOWER: Forget-me-not.

STATE BIRD: Willow ptarmigan.

STATE TREE: Sitka spruce.

STATE FLAG.

ALASKA

CAPITAL: Juneau.

STATEHOOD: January 3, 1959; the 49th state.

POPULATION: 302,173 (1970 census); rank, 50th.

SIZE: 1,518,807 km² (586,412 sq mi). Rank, 1st. Almost one fifth the size of the other 48 continental states.

ORIGIN OF NAME: From the Aleut word *alakshak*, meaning "peninsula"; used by the Aleuts in referring to the part of the mainland that is now known as the Alaska Peninsula.

ABBREVIATION: AK.

NICKNAME: None official; often called The Great Land, The Land of the Midnight Sun, or The Last Frontier.

STATE SONG: "Alaska's Flag," by Marie Drake; music by Elinor Dusenbury.

STATE MOTTO: North to the Future.

STATE SEAL: The sun in the background casts brilliant rays over coastal mountains, which seem to rise from the water's edge. The ships at the right represent activities on the waters that surround three sides of the state. Pictures on the left and in the foreground stand for activities on the land—mining, forestry, and agriculture. The fish and the fur seal in the border show two of Alaska's products.

STATE FLAG: See the story of the flag on page 128.

spend their wealth, leaving little of permanent value. At the end of the gold rush, some Alaskans compared their land to the storybook Cinderella, whose riches turned to rags at the stroke of midnight.

Finally, on January 3, 1959, Alaska gained statehood and control of its resources. Those resources have proved considerable, including what may be the largest oil deposits in North America. The problem for Alaska today is how to exploit its natural wealth without despoiling its natural beauty.

▶ **THE LAND**

Alaska's coastline is ragged, with many bays, inlets, and sounds. Some of these bodies of water cut deeply into the coastline, forming peninsulas between them. Seward Peninsula, between Kotzebue and Norton sounds, is a prominent feature of the western coast of the state.

A long, carrot-shaped piece of land, the Alaska Peninsula, dangles from the southern coast. From the tip of this peninsula, the Aleutian Islands extend southwestward in a graceful curve. North of the Aleutian chain, in the Bering Sea, are other Alaskan islands. Among them are the Pribilof Islands, summer home of the fur seals.

The Kenai Peninsula is another important peninsula along the southern coast. South of Kenai Peninsula is Kodiak Island, one of the homes of the huge brown bear. Kodiak Island is due north of Hawaii.

On the east the border between Alaska and the Yukon Territory of Canada extends in a straight line from the Arctic Ocean to within a short distance of the Gulf of Alaska. The boundary then starts a jagged course southeastward. It slices off a thin strip along the Canadian province of British Columbia. Along this coast is the Alexander Archipelago, a group of more than 1,000 islands. These islands are the tops of submerged mountains, with deep channels between them. The channels form part of a long sheltered waterway—the famous Inside Passage—between Seattle, in the state of Washington, and Skagway, in Alaska.

The Alexander Archipelago and the thin strip of mainland are known as Southeastern Alaska, or the Panhandle. This part of Alaska is closest to the other 48 continental states.

Landforms

Alaska includes four major landforms. They are the Pacific Mountain Region, the Interior Plateau, the Brooks Range, and the Arctic Slope.

The Pacific Mountain Region. The mountains of southern Alaska are a continuation of mountain systems that extend through California, Oregon, Washington, and British Columbia. It is interesting to notice that in Alaska these mountains form a huge arc, or part of a circle, all around the Pacific coast of the state. They include the Coast Mountains, in the southeast; the Alaska Range, forming the broad top part of the arc; and the Aleutian Range, sweeping southwestward through the Alaska Peninsula and the Aleutian Islands.

On the side toward the sea, the Coast

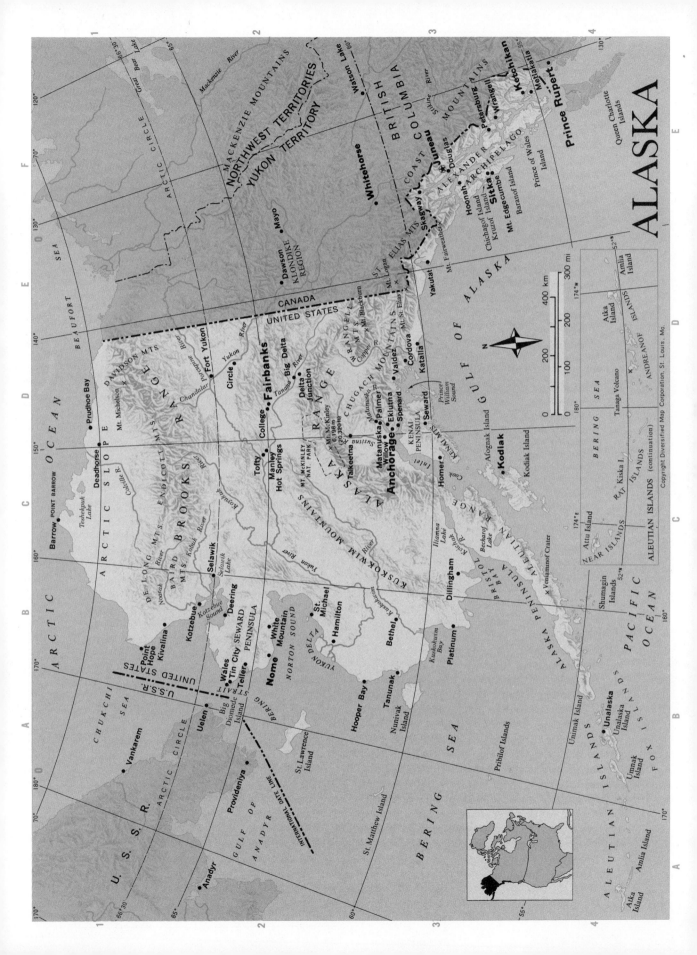

Mountains seem to rise straight from the water's edge. At many points they are deeply cut by fiords—long, narrow bays between high cliffs. Travelers on the Inside Passage say that these fiords remind them of the fiords of Norway. The Alaska Range is known for its high peaks and its many glaciers and rivers. Mount McKinley is in this range. Many of the mountains in the Aleutian Range are volcanic.

Northwest of the Panhandle there are other mountains—the St. Elias, Wrangell, Chugach, and Kenai mountains. These mountains curve around the coast of the Gulf of Alaska. Many of the snow-capped peaks rear up from vast fields of ice. Mount St. Elias, the peak first sighted by explorer Vitus Bering, is about 5,500 meters (18,000 feet) high. South of this peak is Alaska's largest glacier, the Malaspina Glacier. It spreads out over the coastal plain, covering an area about equal to the state of Rhode Island.

It might seem that people could not establish homes and make a living in a land of mountains, volcanoes, and glaciers. But there are broad river valleys, hundreds of islands, and many level areas along the coast and between the mountains. Most of the people of the state live in the south central and southeastern parts of the Pacific Mountain Region.

In March, 1964, an earthquake caused great damage along the south central coast. Each year many quakes are recorded in the Pacific Mountain Region. Usually they are very light.

The Interior Plateau. The central part of Alaska is mainly a plateau, with many low hills and valleys. It extends from the Alaska Range on the south to the Brooks Range on the north. The highest elevations are in the east, near the Canadian border. The best-known feature of this vast region is the Yukon River, which flows across the entire width of the state.

The valleys in the eastern and central parts of the region are forested. In some places the water in the subsoil remains frozen throughout the year. Permanently frozen subsoil is called permafrost. In areas of permafrost the trees do not grow very tall because the roots cannot reach down through the frozen subsoil. Parts of the Interior Plateau are flat and almost treeless but covered with a dense growth of low vegetation. A great network of twisting, snake-like waterways extends throughout the region.

The Brooks Range. A chain of mountains, known as the Brooks Range, enters Alaska from Canada and stretches across the state north of the Interior Plateau. This range is a continuation of the Rocky Mountain system of North America. The highest peaks are in the eastern and east central parts. Much of this region of Alaska is rugged and little known.

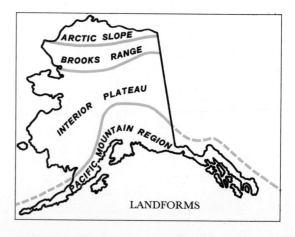

LANDFORMS

Mount McKinley, highest peak in North America, was named for William McKinley, 25th President of the United States. The native name for this peak is Denali, the Great One.

The Arctic Slope. From the foot of the Brooks Range, a low coastal plain slopes northward to the Beaufort Sea and the Arctic Ocean. It is flat and treeless, with permanently frozen subsoil. This kind of plain in northern arctic lands is known as tundra. Several rivers and many small waterways extend across the plain. The north central part of the tundra is dotted with lakes and ponds. The largest lake found in this region is Teshekpuk Lake.

During the long winter the frozen surface of the land is brown or snow-covered. But during the time of continual sunlight, the topsoil thaws enough for plants to spring to life. Because the moisture cannot drain down through the permafrost, the surface becomes very wet. The Eskimos, who live in villages along the sea, use river routes when traveling inland.

Rivers, Lakes, and Coastal Waters

The Yukon is the great river of Alaska. It winds across the Interior Plateau for more than 1,900 kilometers (1,200 miles) and empties through a huge, swampy delta into the Bering Sea. The largest of the Yukon's tributaries in Alaska are the Porcupine, the Koyukuk, and the Tanana rivers. The Kuskokwim River drains the southwestern part of the Interior Plateau. The main rivers of the Pacific Mountain Region are the Susitna, the Matanuska, and the Copper rivers, which flow into the Gulf of Alaska. The Colville is the best-known river of the Arctic Slope.

Alaska has many natural lakes. The largest, Iliamna Lake, covers about 2,600 square ki-lometers (1,000 square miles) at the northern end of the Alaska Peninsula. Becharof Lake, south of Iliamna, is the next largest.

Alaska's general coastline—10,684 kilometers (6,640 miles)—is longer than the general coastline of the other continental states. The total shoreline—including offshore islands, bays, and inlets—is about 54,700 kilometers (34,000 miles) long.

A fishing boat navigates through Endicott Arm, a fiord near Juneau. The icy cliff behind it is Dawes Glacier.

Caribou search for food along the Alaska Range in Mount McKinley National Park.

Climate

In 1867 many people in the United States objected to the purchase of Alaska. They knew little about it, but from its position on the map, they supposed it to be a huge "icebox." Since that time people have learned a great deal about Alaska, including the fact that it has different kinds of climate.

Climate 1. The Panhandle and the coastal plain along the Gulf of Alaska have moderate temperatures and heavy precipitation. High mountains protect these areas from cold northerly winds, and warm ocean currents circle around the shores. The prevailing southeasterly winds reach the coast full of moisture from the Pacific Ocean. They lose this moisture in passing over the coastal mountains. Average yearly precipitation is 2,400 millimeters (94 inches). In some places, the precipitation is twice that much. The average annual temperature is 5°C (41°F). July temperatures average 13°C (55°F), but summer days are often warmer.

Climate 2. The climate of the Aleutian Islands is influenced by contrasting bodies of water—the warm Pacific Ocean and the cold Bering Sea. The average annual temperature is about the same as along the Gulf of Alaska, but there is only half as much precipitation. Usually the weather is wet and foggy, and fierce winds lash the islands. The winds, called williwaws, are of hurricane force, but they travel in gusts or waves, not steadily as a hurricane does.

Climate 3. In the Copper River, Cook Inlet, and Bristol Bay areas, the average summer temperatures are about the same as along the Gulf of Alaska. But the winters are somewhat colder, and the average yearly precipitation is much lower—about 560 millimeters (22 inches). The growing season in the Matanuska Valley is about 100 days.

Climate 4. Interior Alaska is an area of extremes. It has the highest as well as the lowest temperatures in the state. Several weather stations have recorded summer highs of 35°C (95°F) and winter lows of −55°C (−67°F). The average for January is −18°C (0°F) or below. Average annual precipitation is 380 millimeters (15 inches). The growing season in the Tanana Valley near Fairbanks averages only about 100 days, but long hours of summer sunlight help to make up for the short season.

Climate 5. From south to north in Alaska, winters become longer and summers, shorter. Arctic Alaska has ten months of winter and two of summer. The average yearly precipitation is 180 millimeters (7 inches). But the climate is not dry because cold air keeps the moisture from evaporating. Frosts are frequent.

Natural Resources

Alaska's traditional natural resources were fur, fish, and gold. Now Alaska looks to petroleum and natural gas as major resources.

In December, 1978, President Carter proclaimed millions of hectares of Alaska wild land as national monuments, to be administered chiefly by the National Park Service. Since then Congress has considered various proposals for new national areas in Alaska.

Forests and Other Vegetation. There are two kinds of forests in Alaska, the coastal forests and the interior forests. The coastal forests begin in the Panhandle and extend around the Gulf of Alaska coast as far as Kodiak Island. These are dense, towering forests, mainly of hemlock, Sitka spruce, and cedar. The interior forests are found in river valleys in the interior and as far north as the eastern and central parts of the Brooks Range. Here the timber is mainly aspen and willow. Much of it is stunted because of permafrost and the short growing season.

The kind of vegetation known as tundra vegetation is common to much of Alaska. This is a spongy mass of plant life—cranberry vines, crowberries, grasses, and various mosses and lichens. The dead plants decay slowly because of dampness and low temperatures. Year after year the old plants pile up and new plants grow up through them. True arctic tundra, with no trees or shrubs, is found on the Arctic Slope and Seward Peninsula. The tundra vegetation in other parts of the state may include bushes and dwarf species of trees. The only extensive grazing lands are on the Aleutian Islands.

Animal Life. In an area the size of Alaska, with different kinds of climate and natural shelter, one would expect differences in wildlife. Sitka deer, mountain goats, a few moose, and brown and black bears are among the large animals of Southeastern Alaska. A bit farther north moose become more plentiful than deer, and grizzly bears and Dall sheep

appear. Caribou replace deer in the interior and increase in numbers toward the north until they travel in herds of thousands. The polar bears of the far north spend most of their time out on the ice packs hunting food. Animals that have been brought to Alaska include reindeer throughout the arctic areas, elk on Afognak Island, musk oxen on Nunivak Island, and bison at Big Delta, southeast of Fairbanks. To conserve animal life, the federal government is setting up wildlife ranges and refuges.

Wolves and foxes are found in most of the state. Animals that are valued for their fur include marten, mink, and beaver. Ducks, geese, grouse, and ptarmigan are among the birds found commonly in Alaska. The principal game fish are rainbow trout and grayling. Commercial fisheries depend mainly on salmon, cod, herring, and halibut and such shellfish as crabs, shrimp, clams, and scallops.

Minerals. Deposits of gold and silver are known to exist in almost every region of the state. Petroleum and natural gas are being produced in the south at Cook Inlet and on the Kenai Peninsula and in the far north at Prudhoe Bay. Geologists believe that petroleum exists in many parts of the state. The Panhandle is known to have such important minerals as iron, lead and zinc, copper, nickel, and tungsten. Mineral deposits of the Gulf of Alaska coast and interior Alaska include coal, copper, platinum, antimony, tin, and mercury. Seward Peninsula has tin, tungsten, and iron. The Brooks Range contains copper and antimony. The Arctic Slope has coal and enormous reserves of petroleum.

Alaska has a plentiful supply of sand and gravel and stone. Deposits of molybdenum, flourite, sulfur, graphite, and bismuth have also been found.

Water. There are a few hydroelectric plants in southern Alaska, but production of hydroelectric power is still largely undeveloped. Many possible sites are known to exist both in the south and in the interior.

▶THE PEOPLE AND THEIR WORK

When the Russians discovered Alaska in 1741, they found it occupied by three groups of native peoples—Eskimos, Aleuts, and Indians. Descendants of these natives still live in Alaska.

Native Peoples

Scientists believe that the native peoples went to Alaska from Asia over a period of thousands of years. Probably the last to enter Alaska were the ancestors of the Eskimo.

Eskimo. The Eskimo are the most numerous of the different groups of native peoples. They call themselves the *Inuit,* or *Yuit,* meaning "the people." Alaskan Eskimo live along the coasts of the Arctic Ocean and the Bering Sea and as far south as Bristol Bay.

Eskimo have long been known for their ability to survive and adapt in one of the world's harshest environments. Expert hunters, they have depended upon seals, walruses, sea otters, fish, and caribou for their living. In the 1890's, reindeer were brought from Siberia as an additional means of livelihood. The Eskimo are also fine artisans. They have produced distinctive ivory carvings and other arts and crafts.

Today many Eskimo live in frame houses heated by fuel oil. They once lived in sod and driftwood houses heated by seal-oil lamps. They did not build snow igloos, except for emergency shelter. They are also finding opportunities for schooling and for employment in trades and professions. They have representatives in the state legislature.

Aleuts. The Aleutian Islands and the Alaska Peninsula are the homelands of the Aleuts. Like many of the Eskimo, the Aleuts have always depended on the sea for food. Some present-day Aleuts operate fishing boats. Others are employed in fish canneries. A group of Aleuts on the Pribilof Islands helps with the government-controlled seal herds.

Indians. There are two major groups of Indians—the Indians of the Interior Plateau and the Indians of Southeastern Alaska.

The Indians who live in the interior came to Alaska from Canada. They belong to the Athapascan language family. Originally they were hunters. Some of them still live by hunting, fishing, and trapping. Others have moved to towns, where they live and work as do other present-day Alaskans.

The Indians of southeastern Alaska are sometimes known as the maritime Indians, or Indians who live near the sea. They are the Tlingit (or Tlinkit), the Tsimshian, and the Haida. The Tlingit are by far the most numerous, as well as the oldest. They have

POPULATION			
TOTAL: 302,173 (1970 census). **Density**—20 persons to each 100 square kilometers (52 to each 100 square miles).			
GROWTH SINCE 1890			
Year	**Population**	**Year**	**Population**
1890	32,052	1939	72,524
1900	63,592	1950	128,643
1920	55,036	1960	226,167
1929	59,278	1970	302,173
Gain Between 1960 and 1970—33.6 per cent.			
CITIES: Populations of Alaska's largest cities, according to the 1970 census.			
Anchorage	48,081	Kenai	3,533
Fairbanks	14,771	Sitka	3,370
Ketchikan	6,994	Nome	2,488
Juneau	6,050	Bethel	2,416
Kodiak	3,798	Petersburg	2,042

been in Alaska for hundreds of years. They live in towns and villages throughout the Panhandle and the south central coastal areas. The Haida, the smallest and next-oldest group, migrated to Prince of Wales Island shortly before the Russian discovery of Alaska. They came from the Queen Charlotte Islands of British Columbia, where many of their people now live. The Tsimshian migrated from British Columbia in 1887 and settled at Metlakatla, on Annette Island.

Carving and basket making are among the crafts of the maritime Indians. They are known for their totem poles. From earliest times they depended on fish, especially salmon, for their living. Today they are efficient business people who operate commercial fishing boats and canneries. They also follow other occupations such as logging, shopkeeping, and working in government offices. Like the Eskimo, they have representatives in the state legislature.

Alaska Native Claims Settlement Act. In 1971, Congress passed the Alaska Native Claims Settlement Act. This was in response to native peoples' claims that their land had been taken away from them illegally. The act set aside land and money to be divided among 200 native peoples' villages. Each village became a corporation, and 13 regional corporations were formed to administer the land, money, and resources received in the settlement. The land that the native peoples received has some of the world's richest resources. The people are using some of the profits from these resources to establish their own businesses and social services.

Occupations, Industries, and Products

Between 1960 and 1970, the population of Alaska increased by nearly 35 percent. Because Alaska is vital to the nation's defense, many people have moved to the state to serve at military posts and defense installations. Not including military personnel, almost 40 percent of Alaska's labor force is employed by the federal, state, or local government. But opportunities for employment in other fields, such as business and industry, are expanding steadily.

Manufacturing. The waters and forests of Alaska provide raw materials for two kinds of manufactured products—canned and frozen fish and logs and wood pulp. Now, as in the past, canned salmon is the main product of most canneries. But canned king crab is also increasing in value. Other major products are herring, fresh and frozen crab, and halibut. Wood processing is also an important part of Alaska's economy. The majority of logging operations are in the coastal forests. But the lumber industry has also begun activities in the interior forests. There are pulp mills in operation at Sitka and Ketchikan, and sawmills can be found in many of the forested areas of Alaska.

Mining. Two minerals—gold and copper—are prominent in the history of mining in Alaska. The famous copper mines in the Copper River area around Cordova began operating before World War I. They yielded millions of dollars' worth of ore before the deposits were exhausted and the mines closed in the late 1930's. Gold has been produced each year since the 1880's, although the value has varied greatly from time to time.

By far the most important development in recent decades has been the discovery of im-

Alaskan farmers take pride in the size and the quality of their cabbage and other products.

mense oil reserves in the state. Oil drilling began in earnest in Alaska during the late 1950's. In the 1960's the state's production of crude oil increased spectacularly, with drilling concentrated around Cook Inlet and on the Kenai Peninsula. Then, in 1968, came another exciting development. Oil companies announced discovery of perhaps the largest oil field in North America, near Prudhoe Bay in the Arctic Slope region. Fifteen companies bid some $900,000,000 to lease from the state parcels of oil-rich land in that area.

Late in 1973, Congress authorized the construction of a 1,300-kilometer (800-mile) oil pipeline, from Prudhoe Bay to the ice-free southern port of Valdez. Work on the Trans-Alaska Pipeline began in early 1974. Some conservationists strongly opposed the project and demanded special measures to help prevent damage to the environment. On June 20, 1977, oil flowed through the pipeline for the first time. It arrived at Valdez on July 28.

Agriculture. Farming is limited mostly to three areas. They are the Matanuska Valley, northeast of Anchorage; the Tanana Valley, near Fairbanks; and the western coast of the Kenai Peninsula. The Matanuska Valley is the most productive area.

Fertile soils and long hours of summer sunlight in the farming regions cause vege-

---

WHAT ALASKA PRODUCES

MINERALS: Petroleum, sand and gravel, coal, natural gas, and other minerals including gold, gem stones, and mercury.

MANUFACTURED GOODS: Canned and cured seafoods; lumber and wood products.

FISH: Salmon, king crab, halibut, sardines, herring.

AGRICULTURAL PRODUCTS: Milk, eggs, potatoes, cattle and calves, miscellaneous vegetables, livestock feed crops.

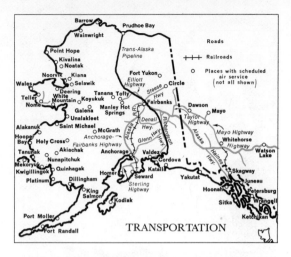

TRANSPORTATION

tables and berries to grow to unusually large sizes. There is no doubt that agriculture can be carried on in Alaska, but there are several reasons for the small production at present. One reason is the high cost of clearing the land. Other reasons are the short growing season and the problems of transporting produce to markets. New methods of farming in northern lands and improved transportation may bring changes.

Furs. Alaska's fur trade is no longer a major industry. But some people still earn a living by trapping. Seals are also hunted from government-owned rookeries on the Pribilof Islands.

Transportation and Communication

Alaska has waterways, airways, highways, railroads, and even several hundred kilometers of dog-sled trails. With improvements in transportation, thousands of people visit Alaska each year. Tourism is becoming an important industry.

Air Transportation. Alaskans are called the "flyingest" people in the world. The first commercial flights in Alaska were made in the early 1920's, and since that time planes have filled the air. Every part of the state can be reached easily and quickly by air. There are hundreds of airports and numerous seaplane facilities. Helicopters are used everywhere for exploring, mapping, transporting heavy equipment, and doing rescue work. Anchorage's international airport is one of the busiest airports in the nation.

Railroads. The first railroad in Alaska was the White Pass and Yukon Railroad. It was started in 1898 and is still in operation, mainly as a tourist attraction. It is a narrow-gauge line that runs between Skagway, in Alaska, and Whitehorse, in the Yukon Territory of Canada. At Whitehorse, the White Pass and Yukon Railroad connects with the Alaska Highway.

The Alaska Railroad, operated by the U.S. Department of the Interior, is the main railroad of the state. It provides rail transportation between Seward, on the Gulf of Alaska, and Fairbanks, in the interior. Passengers may ask to get off at any point along the route. The train will then stop and let the passengers off, and a conductor will instruct them on how to signal another train when they are ready to be picked up.

Highways. The Alaska Highway, originally called the Alcan Military Highway, was built for military purposes during World War II. When the Alaska Highway was opened to the public after the war, improvement of local highways became necessary. Now major roads connect towns on the Gulf of Alaska with Fairbanks, in the interior. All of them lead into the Alaska Highway.

The Alaska Highway starts at Dawson Creek, British Columbia, and ends officially at Delta Junction, Alaska. At Delta Junction it connects with the Richardson Highway, which continues to Fairbanks. The total distance from Dawson Creek to Fairbanks is 2,450 kilometers (1,523 miles). From the northern border of the other 48 continental states, the distance to Fairbanks is approximately 3,780 kilometers (2,350 miles).

Two sections of the Alaska Highway are paved—the first 149 kilometers (93 miles) from Dawson Creek and all the Alaska portion, 486 kilometers (302 miles). The rest is a two-lane gravel and clay road. The highway is open all year, but the best time for travel is June through September. For most of the distance, lodges and service stations are spaced at regular intervals. Camping is popular along the way, and a number of campgrounds are available for tourists who bring their own equipment and supplies.

Waterways. One of the most satisfying ways to enter Alaska is through the beautiful Inside Passage. Cruise ships from Canada and the United States use that route. There is also a state-operated ferry system on the Alaska Marine Highway, which runs between Seattle, Washington, and Skagway. Prince Rupert,

British Columbia, at the approximate center of the route, has connections with major Canadian and United States railroads and highways. There is also a ferry that runs between Cordova, Kodiak, and Homer.

Newspapers, Television, and Radio. Alaska has seven daily newspapers and numerous other weekly publications and magazines. All the large towns have television and radio stations. Local radio networks provide a special service for villages that have no telephones. Messages are collected during the day and are broadcast at a specified time. The program at Fairbanks is called Tundra Topics.

▶ EDUCATION

The first schools in Alaska were established by the Russians after the settlement of Kodiak Island in 1748. These schools were intended mainly to teach religious beliefs to Russian children. Native Aleuts and Indians were encouraged to attend. Many of them were converted to the Russian Orthodox faith, which was the national religion of Russia at that time. Some people still worship in churches built by the Russians.

After the United States purchased Alaska in 1867, educational work among the native peoples was carried on by mission schools, which were established by various religious groups from the States. Gradually, as settlers went to Alaska during the 1880's and 1890's, the federal government began to establish public schools.

Present-day Schools

Education for all its people is one of Alaska's most important goals. Many new schools have been built, and others are

"So that's where I live?" A schoolgirl in Barrow talks with her teacher about the geography of her native state.

planned. A system of locally controlled public schools has been established. This replaces the federal- and state-operated system. All students in the state are now able to attend school through grade 12 in their home communities. Mission schools, regional high schools, vocational training centers, and a boarding program are also available to students from remote areas of Alaska.

Universities and Colleges

The present-day University of Alaska Fairbanks Campus was established in 1917 as the Alaska Agricultural College and School of Mines. It is part of a state-supported university system that includes the University of Alaska Anchorage Campus and the University of Alaska Southeastern Senior College, at Juneau. These institutions offer advanced degrees and attract students from other states as well as foreign countries. The university system also includes ten community (two-year) colleges, which are situated throughout the state.

Alaska Methodist University is in Anchorage, and Sheldon Jackson College (a senior college) is in Sitka. A unique university, the Inupiat University of the Arctic, opened in Barrow in 1975. Its aim is to provide educational opportunities for the Inupiat Eskimo and other residents of the far north.

Libraries and Museums

Most of Alaska's larger towns have community libraries. The state library service supplies books to towns that do not have libraries and to persons who live in isolated places. The University of Alaska system and Sheldon Jackson College have large libraries.

The Alaska State Museum, at Juneau, is noted for its historical books and records and its displays of Eskimo life, Indian and Aleut arts and crafts, pioneer life, minerals, and wildlife. The museum at the University of Alaska Fairbanks Campus contains valuable relics of arctic life, exhibits of animals, and many examples of native arts and crafts. The Sheldon Jackson Museum, at Sitka, has collections, mainly of Eskimo life, made by Sheldon Jackson when he was superintendent of education in Alaska during the late 19th century. Anchorage has a historical and fine arts museum.

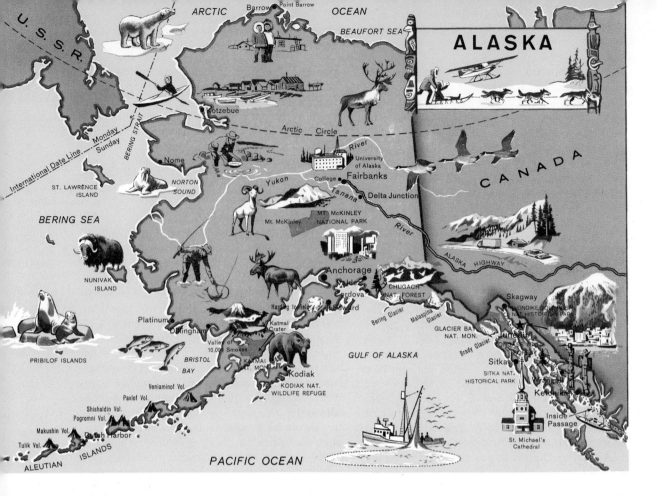

▶ PLACES OF INTEREST

The following are only a few of Alaska's many places of scenic and historic interest, including national forests, national monuments, national historical parks, and a national park:

Barrow is the northernmost town in the United States. It is an important Eskimo village, as well as the site of a scientific center, the Arctic Research Laboratory. A memorial nearby marks the place where the humorist Will Rogers and his pilot Wiley Post were killed in a plane crash in 1935.

Chugach National Forest is on Prince William Sound, and **Tongass National Forest** is in the Panhandle. Both national forests have campsites, hiking trails, towering trees, and many species of wild flowers and ferns.

Eklutna, site of a large hydroelectric plant, is interesting also for relics of early-day Indians, including tiny models of houses filled with precious possessions that the Indians placed on the graves of their dead.

Glacier Bay National Monument, at the northern end of the Panhandle, includes many large glaciers that extend between mountain peaks to the inlets of Glacier Bay. At the water's edge, the glaciers form huge cliffs of ice. The bay is filled with floating ice that has broken off the cliffs. The area is of special interest to scientists, who visit it to study the glaciers.

Katmai National Monument, on the eastern shore of the Alaska Peninsula, includes the scene of a violent volcanic eruption in 1912 that turned green lands into the Valley of Ten Thousand Smokes. The area is remarkable for scenery and wildlife, as well as for volcanoes.

Klondike Gold Rush National Historical Park, at Skagway, preserves the Chilkoot Trail and the White Pass Trail. Prospectors trekked along these trails during the Alaska gold rush. An interpretive center is located at Seattle, Washington.

Mount McKinley National Park, midway between Anchorage and Fairbanks, contains the highest peak in North America. The park includes deep lakes, glaciers, tall mountains, and many species of wildlife.

St. Michael's Cathedral, at Sitka, a Russian church built in 1848, was destroyed by fire on January 2, 1966. It has since been rebuilt. It contained art treasures and objects of historic religious significance.

Sitka National Historical Park, at Sitka, preserves the site of a stockade where the Sitka tribe of Tlingit Indians made their last stand against the Russian settlers in 1804. The park also includes beautiful spruce and hemlock trees and a fine collection of totem poles from the old villages of the Haida Indians.

Annual Events

Alaskans love celebrations. The following are a few of the popular annual events:

February—Fur Rendezvous at Anchorage, with world championship sled-dog races and other events.

March—Winter Carnival at Fairbanks, featuring North American championship sled-dog races.

May—King Crab Festival at Kodiak; "Little Norway" Festival at Petersburg.

June—Alaska Festival of Music at Anchorage; Midnight Sun Festival at Nome.

July—Golden Days celebration at Fairbanks, commemorating the gold strike in 1902; Golden North Salmon Derby at Juneau.

August-September—State Fair at Palmer.

October—Alaska Day Festival at Sitka, commemorating the transfer of Alaska from Russia to the United States.

▶ CITIES

Most of Alaska's largest cities and towns are in the southern part of the state on the main transportation routes. Villages dot the interior and the coast of the Bering Sea.

Juneau

Alaska's capital is located near the northern end of the Panhandle in one of the most beautiful settings in the state. It was founded by gold miners in 1880 and was named for Joe Juneau, one of the prospectors who discovered gold in the area. The gold mines were productive for many years, but they are no longer in operation. Juneau today is the seat of government and an important tourist center. Its industries include fishing, lumbering, and transportation.

Across Gastineau Channel, directly opposite Juneau, is Douglas, on Douglas Island. During gold-rush days Douglas was an important mining community. Today it is a residential suburb connected to Juneau by the Gastineau Channel bridge. The ski bowl on Douglas Island is a popular sports center.

Alaskans enjoy the sun at a lake near Anchorage.

Anchorage

The largest city of Alaska is situated in a V-shaped area of land formed by the two extensions, or arms, of Cook Inlet. About one half of all Alaskans live in Anchorage or its immediate vicinity. Anchorage is the state's more important commercial air center and a center of rail and highway transportation, trading, and national defense systems. Fort Richardson and Elmendorf Air Force Base are located nearby.

Anchorage had its beginnings in 1915, when the Alaska Railroad was under construction. The Department of the Interior, the builder of the road, chose this site for its headquarters and shops. The opening of farmlands in the Matanuska Valley spurred the city's growth in the 1930's. It grew rapidly as a defense center during World War II.

The earthquake of 1964 destroyed many of Anchorage's homes and part of its business section. But new construction has given the city more dwellings than before the quake, and the downtown area has been modernized.

Fairbanks

The second largest city is located near the geographic center of the state. It is the northern terminus of the Alaska Railroad and of the major highways of the state. Fairbanks' busy airport handles international traffic as well as flights to all parts of the state. The city was founded after Felix Pedro discovered gold in the area in 1902. It is a main trading center for the Yukon Valley. Nearby are the University of Alaska Fairbanks Campus and important military bases.

▶ **GOVERNMENT**

In 1955, the people of Alaska elected 55 Alaskans to draft a proposed constitution for what they hoped would soon be the state of Alaska. The president of the constitutional convention was William A. Egan of Valdez, who later became the first elected governor of the state. The constitution of Alaska was approved in 1956. It became effective on January 3, 1959.

Alaska has only two elected executive officers, the governor and the lieutenant governor. The legislature consists of the Senate and the House of Representatives. In 1974, Alaskans voted to move the state capital from Juneau to a more central location. In 1976, they chose Willow as the site. But the move is opposed by those who feel it would be too costly.

The highest state court in Alaska is called the Supreme Court. It is made up of five judges, who are appointed initially by the governor then later re-elected by the voters. The major trial courts are called superior courts. Below them are the district courts and magistrate courts.

The Alaska state constitution provides for local governmental units called boroughs. They are similar to the counties of other states. As of 1970, there were nine organized boroughs in Alaska, containing all the state's major population centers within them.

▶ **FAMOUS PEOPLE**

The following are among the many persons whose names are associated with Alaska's history and its development.

Vitus Bering (1680–1741) discovered Bering Strait, Bering Sea, and the mainland of Alaska. A biography of Bering is included in Volume B.

Alexander Baranof (1747–1819) served as the manager of the Russian-American Company when it was established in 1799 and as the first Russian governor of Alaska.

Sheldon Jackson (1834–1909) was appointed in 1885 as the first U.S. superintendent of education for Alaska. He founded schools and was responsible for having reindeer brought from Siberia to save Eskimos from starvation. Jackson, a Presbyterian missionary, was born in New York.

James Wickersham (1857–1939), born in Illinois, came to Alaska in 1900 as a U.S. district judge. He served as Alaskan delegate to Congress, helped Alaska gain territorial status, and also helped found the University of Alaska.

Carl Ben Eielson (1897–1929) was one of the pioneers of commercial flying in Alaska. In 1924 he served as the first airmail pilot in the territory. In 1928 he flew as pilot with the British explorer Sir George Hubert Wilkins from Point Barrow to Spitsbergen, a distance of more than 3,200 kilometers (2,000 miles). Eielson went to Alaska from North Dakota.

▶ **HISTORY**

Most of North America was discovered by western Europeans coming across the Atlantic Ocean. Alaska was discovered by Russians coming across the Pacific. In 1741 Vitus Bering, a Dane who had been exploring far northeastern Siberia for Russia, led an expedition from the Siberian coast toward Alaska. In mid-July of that year he sighted the St. Elias Mountains on the eastern side of the Gulf of Alaska.

Russian Occupation and Settlement

As a result of Bering's expedition, Russian fur traders learned of the valuable sea otters in Alaskan waters. During the following years the traders flocked to southern Alaska and nearby islands. The first Russian settlement was made at Three Saints Bay, on Kodiak Island, in 1784.

Other nations were also interested in Alaska. Spanish expeditions claimed the coast for Spain. The English explorer and navigator Captain James Cook explored the waters of southern Alaska in 1778. Another English explorer, Captain George Vancouver, surveyed much of the coastline in 1792–94. Many of Alaska's Russian, Spanish, and English place names come from this period in its history.

While other nations explored and traded

in Southeastern Alaska, the Russians had become firmly established on the Aleutian Islands, on the Pribilofs, and on Kodiak Island. The fur traders enslaved the native Aleuts and treated them cruelly. In 1799 the czar of Russia established a single fur-trading company, called the Russian-American Company, and appointed Alexander Baranof as manager. Baranof extended the fur trade eastward into the Alexander Archipelago. He built a fort near the present location of Sitka, on Baranof Island. In 1802 the native Tlingit Indians rose up and destroyed the fort, but in 1804 Baranof subdued them and built another settlement, New Archangel. This became the capital of Russian America, as Alaska was then called. Later the name of the settlement was changed to Sitka. It remained the capital of Alaska until 1900. Juneau officially became the capital in that year, but the government offices were not moved from Sitka until 1906.

Purchase by the United States

By 1854 the supply of furs, as well as the demand for them, was greatly reduced. Russia offered to sell Alaska to the United States. It was due largely to the efforts of Secretary of State William H. Seward that the purchase was finally made in 1867. The price was $7,200,000. At that time there were only 37 states in the Union. The Civil War had ended only two years before, and the nation had great problems to solve. Many people thought that the purchase of Alaska was foolish. Newspapers of the day referred to the new possession as Seward's Folly, Icebergia, Seward's Icebox, and other names.

Gold in Alaska

For some time after the purchase, there was no provision for the governing of Alaska. Law and order were administered at various times by the Army, the Navy, and the Treasury Department. In 1884 the United States began to provide a small measure of government. The laws governing the state of Oregon were applied to the new district of Alaska, and a governor was appointed.

When gold was discovered in 1896 in the Yukon Territory of Canada, people became excited about Alaska. Just after the great Yukon gold rush, there were rich strikes at Nome, in 1899, and at Fairbanks, in 1902. Alaska was no longer called Seward's Folly. In 1912, Alaska became a territory, with a limited form of territorial government.

Statehood

The first bill asking for statehood was introduced in the U.S. Congress in 1916. It failed to pass, as did others at later times. In 1942, during World War II, Japan invaded islands in the Aleutian chain, but the islands were recaptured in 1943. Because of the nearness of the Soviet Union and the Far East, Alaska became increasingly important as a defense area after World War II. Finally, in 1958, a bill asking for statehood was approved. On January 3, 1959, President Dwight D. Eisenhower proclaimed Alaska the 49th state.

Rich natural resources should ensure continued economic growth in Alaska. But development of these resources must go hand in hand with protection of the environment. Development versus environmental protection continues to be the subject of a great debate.

LOIS L. JENSEN
Reviewed by LILLIAN P. STINSON
University of Alaska Fairbanks Campus

IMPORTANT DATES

1741 Russian expedition under Vitus Bering made first recorded sighting of Alaska's mainland.

1784 Russians made first permanent settlement in Alaska, on Kodiak Island.

1799 Russian czar granted fur-trade charter to the Russian-American Company.

1804 Capital transferred from Three Saints Bay, on Kodiak Island, to Sitka, on Baranof Island.

1867 United States purchased Alaska from Russia.

1878 First salmon canneries built.

1880 Gold discovered in Juneau area.

1884 District of Alaska began to be governed by the laws of Oregon.

1896 Gold discovered in Klondike region.

1899 Gold discovered on beaches at Nome.

1900 Juneau designated as capital; government offices not moved from Sitka until 1906.

1902 Gold mining began at Fairbanks.

1912 Congress authorized limited territorial government for Alaska; first territorial legislature met, 1913.

1923 The Alaska Railroad completed.

1935 Farmers from midwestern part of the 48 states settled in Matanuska Valley.

1942 Japan invaded Aleutian Islands; Alaska Highway completed.

1943 Islands recaptured from Japan.

1956 Alaska adopted a proposed state constitution.

1959 Alaska became 49th state on January 3.

1964 A severe earthquake on March 27 damaged Anchorage and other places.

1968 One of the largest oil fields in North America was discovered on the Arctic Slope.

1974 Alaskans voted to move the state capital from Juneau; in 1976 they chose Willow as the site.

1977 Trans-Alaska Pipeline was completed and in use as of June 20.

ALBANIA

Albanians call themselves Shqyptarë, which means "sons of the eagle." This is an appropriate name because so many Albanians live in the high mountains just as eagles do. For thousands of years these fiercely independent mountain dwellers fought bravely against Albania's many conquerors. Albania became independent in 1912. A Communist government took control after World War II. Albania received aid from the People's Republic of China for years, but that aid was stopped in 1978.

ALBANIA

▶ THE PEOPLE

Albania's population today is divided into two major groups. These are the Gegs, in the north, and the Tosks, in the south. The Shkumbî River is the dividing line between the two groups. Each group has its own dialect and customs. The Gegs and Tosks form 98 percent of the Albanian population. Greeks, Vlachs, Serbs, Bulgars, and Gypsies make up the remainder.

Most of the people live in and around the cities of Tirana, Scutari, Koritsa, and Durazzo. Tirana, the capital and largest city, has a population of about 175,000.

FACTS AND FIGURES

SOCIALIST PEOPLE'S REPUBLIC OF ALBANIA is the country's official name (Shqypní or Shqipëri in Albanian).

CAPITAL: Tirana.

LOCATION: Southeast Europe, west coast of the Balkan Peninsula. **Latitude**—39° 38′ N to 42° 41′ N. **Longitude**—19° 16′ E to 21° 03′ E.

AREA: 28,748 km² (11,100 sq mi).

POPULATION: 2,600,000 (estimate).

LANGUAGE: Albanian.

GOVERNMENT: People's republic. **Head of state**—chairman of the Presidium. **Head of government**—chairman of the Council of Ministers. **International cooperation**—United Nations.

NATIONAL ANTHEM: *Rreth Flamúrit te per bashkuar* ("The flag that united us in the struggle").

ECONOMY: Agricultural products—grain, cotton, tobacco, sugar beets, sheep, goats, cattle, pigs. **Industries and products**—food processing, cement, textiles, oil and sugar refining. **Chief minerals**—petroleum, lignite, chromium, copper, asphalt, bitumen. **Chief exports**—metal ores, crude petroleum, coal. **Chief imports**—industrial equipment, fuels and raw materials, food. **Monetary unit**—lek.

About 1,000,000 Albanians live outside their country. Most of these live in Yugoslavia, but about 50,000 live in the United States.

Way of Life. In spite of many centuries of foreign occupation, the traditional Albanian way of life was preserved in the high mountain region. In the more isolated areas, the feudalistic clan system, based on family kinship, survived until the present century. The families in the clan lived together in a fortress-like stone house called a *kula*. But these old-fashioned ways are now rapidly changing. After the Communists took over Albania in 1944, they broke up the clan system and seized the land owned by the landlords. The land was divided into small farms, which were later combined into collectives. The government owns and operates more than 90 percent of all the farms in Albania.

Striking contrasts between old and new are seen in all Albania's cities. The huge new sports stadiums and factories are modern in appearance. They are very different from the narrow, cobblestone streets and oriental-looking bazaars in the older parts of the cities.

Language. Albanian is one of the Indo-European group of languages, but it is quite unlike any other language spoken in Europe. The Gegs speak one dialect and the Tosks another. Some Greek is spoken in the southern part of Albania.

Religion. Although the government does not encourage religion, about 70 percent of the Albanians are said to be Muslims, 20 percent are members of the Eastern Orthodox Church, and 10 percent are Roman Catholics. Albania is the only predominantly Muslim nation in Europe.

Education. When the Turks ruled Albania, there was no organized schooling and the majority of people were illiterate. After independence, in 1912, the government built a number of primary schools for children between the ages of 6 and 11. In 1947 the school system was modeled after that of the Soviet Union. All children now go to school until they are 14. Albania's first university was opened in Tirana in 1957.

▶ THE LAND

Albania lies on the west coast of the Balkan Peninsula, in southeastern Europe. The smallest Balkan country, it extends about 320 kilometers (200 miles) from north to south and about 100 kilometers (60 miles) from east to west. On the west are the Adriatic Sea and the Strait of Otranto. Across the Strait of Otranto is the heel of Italy's boot. Yugoslavia borders Albania on the north and east. Greece is on the south.

Albania has three natural regions. They are the coastal lowland in the west, the mountains in the east, and a central hilly belt.

The Coastal Lowland. Along the coast is a narrow, marshy lowland. Fast-running streams flow from the mountains onto this plain and often flood the land. Until recently mosquitoes thrived in the stagnant water, and few people lived here because of the dangers of malaria. Now the land is being reclaimed.

The Hilly Belt. A narrow strip of hilly land stretches across central Albania, where the mountains and the coastal lowlands meet. At this point the mountains are quite low, and their lower slopes are terraced and planted with tree crops. Here, too, the narrow mountain valleys widen into broad basins. The soils of these basins are fertile and are carefully cultivated. Tirana, Scutari, Elbasan, and Berat are important cities in this region.

The Mountains. Nearly three fourths of Albania is mountainous. The highest mountain is Mount Korab, which rises to 2,763 meters (9,066 feet) in northeastern Albania. In the north the mountains are deeply fissured. In the central and southern parts of the country, they are more rounded and often open up into broad, fertile basins. The city of Koritsa is located in one of the largest basins.

Lakes and Rivers. Albania has three large lakes. They are Scutari, in the north, and Ochrida and Prespa, in the southeast. The rivers are short and swift and are not navigable except for short stretches.

Natural Resources. Oak or scrub oak forests are found in the southern part of the country. Forests of pine, oak, and poplar trees grow along the rivers and in the lowlands. Pine, oak, and chestnut grow at higher elevations. A Mediterranean scrub growth called maquis grows in the drier areas.

Albania's mineral resources include bitumen, asphalt, lignite, chromium, copper, bauxite, clay, and kaolin. All metal deposits except chromium are small. Its reserves of petroleum and natural gas are shrinking.

Climate

The coastal lowland and the hilly belt have a Mediterranean type of climate. But in Albania summers are more humid than summers in other Mediterranean lands. A cold wind called the bora sometimes blows from the mountains to the lowlands, bringing very cold days in winter and cool days in summer. The mountains have a continental type of climate. Summers are cool and winters cold and snowy. This part of Albania has an annual rainfall of up to 4,000 millimeters (about 160 inches).

▶ THE ECONOMY

Most of the people continue to make their living as farmers. Less than half of them work in industry. In recent years the government has made great progress in industrializing the country. But more industry is needed.

Agriculture. Sheep raising is especially important. Sheep's milk is made into a cheese called *kackaval,* which is one of the main foods of the Albanians. Cheese, wool, and sheepskins are exported.

Corn and wheat are the leading agricultural crops. Apricots, peaches, and figs are grown in the central part of the country. Olives and citrus fruits are raised in the south. Tobacco and cotton are important cash crops.

Industry. Food processing, oil refining, sugar refining, cement manufacture, and textile production are the chief industries of the country. Albania's petroleum, lignite, bitumen, asphalt, and chromium ore deposits have been developed greatly since 1945.

Tirana, the capital of Albania, is an industrial and transportation center. It was founded by the Turks, and Turkish influence can still be seen in its architecture.

Transportation and Communication. Radio, telegraph, telephone, the postal system, and all transportation are government controlled. The most important railroad connects the port of Durazzo with Tirana, Peqin, and Elbasan. There are asphalt roads, but many parts of the country have only dirt or gravel roads. Many people still travel on horseback and in oxcarts.

▶ HISTORY AND GOVERNMENT

The territory that is now Albania has been invaded over and over again. These invasions took place because Albania is located on important east-west routes across the Balkan Peninsula. In 1385 the Turks invaded the country. They held it, except for one short break in the 15th century, until the early 20th century. In 1443 Gjergj Kastrioti, called Skënderbeg or Skanderbey, united the country against the Turks. He led the resistance for 24 years, but when he died, the Turks again took control of the country.

Turkish power began to decline in the 19th century, and Albania declared its independence on November 28, 1912. The years between World War I and World War II were stormy. Ahmet Zogu, a political leader, was named president in 1925. Three years later he gave himself the title of King Zog I. Zog fled when the Italian dictator Mussolini in-

vaded Albania on April 7, 1939. In 1943 the German Army took over the troubled land.

At the end of World War II, a Communist government took control of the country. Albania is entirely controlled by one party— the Albanian Labor Party (the Communist Party). The chief legislative body is the People's Assembly, whose members are elected by all citizens over 18. But the assembly does its work in the course of a few days each year when it approves the laws proposed by the Presidium. The Presidium is made up of a number of high-ranking ministers. The chairman of the Presidium is the head of state. The head of government is the chairman of the Council of Ministers, the government's highest executive body. Real power is in the hands of the first secretary of the Albanian Labor Party. Enver Hoxha has headed the party since 1943.

After World War II Albania received economic and military aid from the Soviet Union, but the two nations broke diplomatic relations in 1961. Albania later received aid from Communist China. In the 1970's, Albania signed trade agreements with Yugoslavia, Greece, and other countries. In 1976, under a new constitution, the country was renamed the Socialist People's Republic of Albania.

GEORGE W. HOFFMAN
University of Texas at Austin

ALBERTA

Alberta is one of Canada's three Prairie Provinces. It stretches from British Columbia and the towering, snow-clad Rocky Mountains in the west to the province of Saskatchewan in the east; and from the thinly settled Northwest Territories in the north to the state of Montana in the south. Within the boundaries of Alberta, fields of grain extend farther than the eye can see, and cattle ranches dot the foothills of the Rockies.

▶ THE LAND

Alberta has a varied landscape that falls into three landform regions: the Canadian Shield, the Interior Plains, and the Mountains and Foothills.

The Canadian Shield. The northeast corner of Alberta lies in the Canadian Shield. This region occupies 3 percent of the land area of the province. Elevations in the Shield are below 400 meters (1,300 feet). Bare rock outcrops are found throughout the area. Only in a few places do patches of soil cover the rocks. The soils are thin and rocky and of little use for agriculture. Many rivers and lakes formed during the Great Ice Age are found in the Shield region.

The Interior Plains. The Interior Plains occupy almost 90 percent of the land. The plains lie between the Shield in the northeast and the Mountains and Foothills in the southwest. Elevations range from about 200 to 1,200 meters (700 to 4,000 feet).

Contrary to popular opinion about the flatness of the plains, they have a highly varied local relief. The land is flat only in places once covered by ancient glacial lakes. Elsewhere, the plains region is typically rolling. Deep river valleys and a number of hilly areas contrast sharply with the surrounding plains. Some of the valleys are now dry (coulees), but at one time they carried away the meltwaters from the retreating ice sheets. The hills are flat-topped remnants of land that was eroded (worn away) by the rivers. The Cypress Hills in the southeast, the Swan Hills south of Lesser Slave Lake, and the Caribou Mountains in the north all rise at least 370 meters (1,200 feet) above the countryside. In a few areas the streams have cut deeply into softer rocks. Small sections of deeply eroded land called badlands have resulted. The Red Deer Valley contains the major area of badlands. In addition to the weird landforms in this valley, the badlands are the biggest storehouse of dinosaur fossils in Canada.

The Mountains and Foothills. This region is located along the southwestern margin of the province. The mountains form the boundary between Alberta and British Columbia. They also act as a continental drainage divide between waters flowing into the Pacific Ocean on the one hand, and the Arctic Ocean, Hudson Bay, and the Gulf of Mexico on the other.

Between the plains and the eastern wall of the Rockies lie the rolling foothills, which reach elevations of up to 1,800 meters (6,000 feet). West of the foothills tower the ranges of the Rocky Mountains. Here the landscape is composed of jagged, snow-clad peaks and broad, U-shaped valleys. Many small lakes and swift streams are found high in the rocky basins of the mountains. Thirty of these peaks are at least 3,300 meters (11,000 feet) high. Many

---

FACTS AND FIGURES

LOCATION: Latitude—49° N to 60° N. **Longitude**—110° W to 120° W.

JOINED CANADIAN CONFEDERATION: September 1, 1905 (with Saskatchewan, as the 8th and 9th provinces).

POPULATION: 1,838,037 (1976 census). **Rank among provinces**—4th.

CAPITAL: Edmonton.

PHYSICAL FEATURES: Area—661,188 km² (255,285 sq mi). **Rank among provinces**—4th. **Rivers**—Athabasca, Pembina, Smoky, Peace, and Hay, flowing north; North and South Saskatchewan, Oldman, Bow, and Red Deer, flowing east; Milk River, flowing south. **Lakes**—Athabasca, Claire, Lesser Slave, la Biche, Cold, Utikuma, Beaverhill. **Highest mountains**—Mt. Columbia, 3,747 m (12,294 ft); other peaks above 3,520 m (11,550 ft)—The Twins (north and south peaks), Alberta, Assiniboine, Forbes, Temple, Lyell, Hungabee, Snow Dome.

INDUSTRIES AND PRODUCTS: Mining, agriculture, manufacturing (especially oil refining and meat processing), hydroelectric power, lumber, fur, fishing.

GOVERNMENT: Self-governing province. **Titular head of government**—lieutenant governor appointed by Governor-General in Council. **Actual head of government**—premier, elected as a member of legislative assembly by the people. **Provincial representation in federal parliament**—6 appointed senators; 21 elected members of the House of Commons. **Voting age for provincial elections**—18.

PROVINCIAL FLOWER: Wild rose.

An Alberta wheat field. In the background are homes and grain elevators.

Left: An oil field, with derrick and storage tank, near Blackie, southeast of Calgary. Right: Badlands in southern Alberta, with the Milk River in background.

of them have glaciers similar to those that once covered the neighboring plains. The mountains are a favorite tourist attraction and offer the visitor some of the most spectacular scenery in the world.

Rivers and Lakes

All the important rivers of the province begin in the snow and ice fields of the Rocky Mountains. Most of the rivers in central and southern Alberta flow eastward to Lake Winnipeg and then northward to form part of the Hudson Bay drainage system. The Milk River flows about 160 kilometers (100 miles) in Alberta near the southern border. It is a tributary of the Missouri, and is part of the Gulf of Mexico drainage. The large rivers of northern Alberta flow northward and form part of the Arctic Ocean drainage.

There are thousands of lakes in Alberta. The largest is Lake Athabasca, although only one third lies in Alberta. The remaining two thirds is in Saskatchewan. Because of its beauty and the large number of tourists who visit it, Lake Louise in Banff National Park is perhaps the best known lake in Alberta.

Climate

Alberta has a continental climate with long cold winters and short warm summers. In winter, the cold is sometimes broken by warm dry winds from the mountains. The Indians call these winds "chinooks," or "snow-eaters." The chinook can cause temperatures to rise sharply in less than an hour.

Except in the Rocky Mountains, annual precipitation in Alberta averages 400 millimeters (16 inches). Westerly winds from the Pacific Ocean lose most of their moisture crossing the mountains. The Rockies thus have a higher annual precipitation—usually over 1,270 millimeters (50 inches). Precipitation there falls mostly as winter snow.

In the plains, most of the precipitation falls as rain in the summer, when it is needed for crops. Autumn is fairly dry, which is good for harvesting grain. The growing (frost-free) season varies from about 120 days in the southwest to about 60 days in the northwest.

Natural Resources

Soils. Alberta's rich soil is one of its major resources. The black soils of the parkland are among the most fertile in the world. The brown soils of the prairies are also fertile, but they are located in the drier parts of the province. Ranching, dryland agriculture, and irrigation agriculture are important in this soil zone. The gray forest soils, which occupy the northern half of the province, are the least suited for agriculture.

Vegetation. The foothills, the eastern slopes of the Rocky Mountains, and large portions of northern Alberta are forested. The forest lands comprise one of the province's important natural resources.

Between the forests and the prairie lies the parkland. Parkland is a region of mixed trees and grassland. To the south and east of the parkland lie the prairies. Almost all the agriculture is located in the prairie and parkland regions.

Minerals. The most important of Alberta's widespread mineral deposits are the mineral fuels—oil and gas. Geologists estimate that there are at least 950,000,000 cubic meters (6,000,000,000 [billion] barrels) of crude oil and over 1,500,000,000,000 (trillion) cubic meters (52,000,000,000,000 cubic feet) of natural gas in the rock formations. Every year new oil and gas fields are discovered. Sulfur is an important by-product of the natural gas in the province.

The Athabasca tar sands (sands filled with thick, tarry oils), located along the Athabasca River, contain the richest reserves in the province. But recovery of the oil is costly. Two plants are now in production, and others have been planned.

Alberta has almost half of Canada's minable coal reserves. Most of the coal is bituminous (soft) coal. It underlies much of the plains area, and also occurs in the foothills and along the eastern slopes of the Rockies.

Good-quality sand and gravel occur throughout most of the province; limestone is abundant in the Rockies, and clay and shale are found in the Medicine Hat area. Large deposits of low-grade iron are available in the Peace River district. Alberta also has deposits of gypsum, phosphate, salt, sodium sulfate, and silica sand.

▶ THE PEOPLE

Alberta is one of the fastest-growing provinces in Canada. Its population, like those of the other Prairie Provinces, is made up of people from different backgrounds. The greatest number are British in origin. In addition there are large groups of German, Ukrainian, Scandinavian, French, Dutch, or Polish background. Smaller ethnic groups include Russians, Hungarians, Italians, Rumanians, Yugoslavs, Finns, Chinese, and Japanese. There are also about 30,000 native Indians.

At the beginning of the 20th century almost 85 percent of the people lived on farms or in rural villages. Today, the five major cities—Edmonton, Calgary, Lethbridge, Medicine Hat, and Red Deer—contain more than two thirds of the population of Alberta.

Agriculture was once the leading occupation in Alberta. Today less than one fourth of the people earn their living by agriculture. Increased use of farm machinery requires fewer people to operate the farms. Higher wages offered in other industries also account for the movement away from the farms.

More than half of the people now employed in Alberta work in service industries—education, health, welfare, entertainment, recreation, transportation, communication, finance, and personal services. Many people are employed in wholesale and retail trades. Manufacturing, construction, mining, forestry, fishing, and trapping are other occupations.

▶ **EDUCATION**

Schooling is free for all children in the province and is compulsory for those between the ages of 7 and 15.

Alberta has four universities—the University of Alberta and Athabasca University in Edmonton, the University of Calgary, and the University of Lethbridge. There are 13 community colleges and technical schools. The Banff School of Fine Arts in Banff holds classes in the summer.

Alberta has more than 100 public libraries. Museums include the Provincial Museum in Edmonton and Glenbow Museum in Calgary. Art galleries and other cultural institutions are widely distributed.

▶ **PLACES OF INTEREST**

Banff National Park, in the Canadian Rockies, is noted for its majestic scenery and its wildlife preserve. An article on Banff National Park appears in Volume B.

Elk Island National Park, near Edmonton, is a preserve for buffalo and other plains animals.

Jasper National Park is also in the Rockies. An article on this park appears in Volume J.

Waterton Lakes National Park, bordering on Montana, is a recreational area. It shares the International Peace Park with Montana.

Wood Buffalo National Park, in northeast Alberta and the Northwest Territories, is famous for its herds of buffalo and other wild animals.

There are also many provincial parks that offer a wide variety of recreational opportunities. Best known are **Dinosaur Park**, which contains the fossil remains of prehistoric dinosaurs; and **Writing-on-Stone**, which features monumental stones with inscriptions by prehistoric peoples.

▶ **INDUSTRIES AND PRODUCTS**

Mining. Alberta ranks first among the provinces in mineral production. It produces over 85 percent of Canada's oil and natural gas, making the nation approximately self-sufficient in these mineral fuels.

The most important oil fields are at Pembina, Leduc-Woodbend, Redwater, Swan Hills, and Rainbow Lake. Development of the vast Athabasca tar sands deposits began in 1964. The first oil was produced in 1967. A second and larger development started operating in 1978. Production from conventional oil wells has peaked and will now slowly decline. Deposits in the tar sands will be increasingly important.

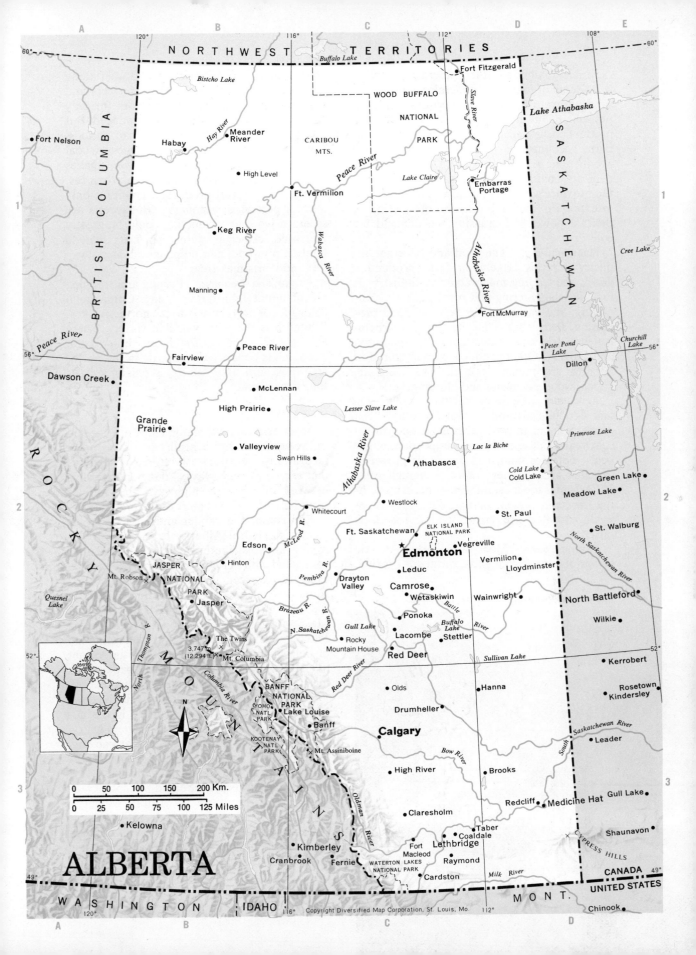

ALBERTA

Much of Alberta's other mineral production is made up of industrial minerals such as clay, sand, gravel, limestone, gypsum, salt, and phosphate. Sulfur, a by-product of natural gas production, is becoming more important. Alberta accounts for most of Canada's sulfur production. Although Alberta has vast coal deposits, coal makes up less than 4 percent of the province's mineral production. But growth in exports to Japan and in the production of thermal power is increasing the demand for coal.

Manufacturing. The food and beverage industry depends largely on farm production and is the leading manufacturing industry. It includes slaughtering and meat-packing, flour milling, and various other types of food processing. Petroleum refineries and petrochemical industries are located mainly in Edmonton and Calgary. Other products manufactured in Alberta are metals, cement and concrete, paper, wood products, and clothing.

Agriculture. Grain is still the most important agricultural product, but there has been a steady trend toward general farming in recent years. Cattle ranching is important. Sugar beets, potatoes, and feed crops are grown in irrigated areas. Where there is enough rainfall, wheat is the most important grain crop. In the parkland region, barley, oats, rye, rapeseed, and flax are grown and livestock is raised.

Electric Power. Most of Alberta's electric power plants use coal and natural gas for fuel.

Valley of the Ten Peaks, Banff National Park.

Hydroelectric power plants are located along the Bow and North Saskatchewan rivers and their tributaries. These now account for only 12 percent of the electric power produced. But they are important during peak-load periods. Power generated from huge supplies of coal and gas, together with waterpower, makes Alberta one of the most energy-rich provinces.

Forestry. Forest products account for only a small part of the economy. But forests are so extensive that production could be greatly increased. Alberta's forest products include lumber, plywood, and pulp, as well as railway ties and Christmas trees.

Fishing and Trapping. Fishing and trapping are of minor importance today. Commercial fishing is confined largely to the northern lakes. Whitefish is the most valuable variety. There are several hundred fur farms in Alberta. Trapping is conducted primarily in the northern forest and, like fishing, is chiefly a part-time occupation.

▶ **CITIES**

Most of Alberta's major cities are located in the southern and central part of the province. Many were first established near rivers that served as waterways. Today an extensive network of railways, highways, and airlines serves all the urban centers of the province.

Edmonton, the capital and largest city, is located in central Alberta. It serves as a collecting and distributing center for industries connected with agriculture and petroleum. Because of its excellent transportation facilities, Edmonton also serves the mining centers in the Northwest Territories and the Yukon. Meat-packing and other food processing, oil refining, metal production, and the production of petrochemicals are some of the important industries. Edmonton has grown rapidly. Its metropolitan population is now over 600,000.

Calgary, the second largest city, is the chief city of southern Alberta. Calgary is the administrative center of Alberta's oil industry. Food and beverage processing, meat-packing, flour and feed milling, and the production of dairy products are important industries. The annual Calgary Exhibition and Stampede (rodeo) attracts thousands of visitors. Calgary's metropolitan population is over 500,000.

Lethbridge, with a population of more than 45,000, is a major center for food processing

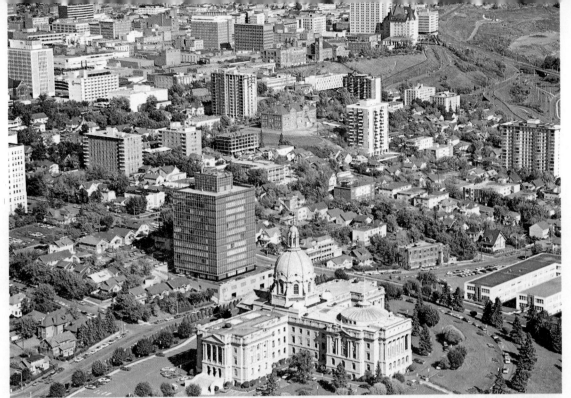

Edmonton, capital of Alberta. In the foreground is the Legislative Building.

—especially vegetable canning based on irrigation agriculture. Lethbridge lies in the center of the chinook belt and thus enjoys relatively mild winters. Early settlers included many Mormons, Hutterites, and Mennonites.

Medicine Hat, a city of about 30,000, is noted for clay products and pottery. The ample supply of natural gas serves as fuel for factories and for heating Medicine Hat's thriving greenhouse industry.

Other important cities are Red Deer, Fort McMurray, Grande Prairie, Camrose, Wetaskiwin, Lloydminster, and Drumheller.

▶**TRANSPORTATION AND COMMUNICATION**

Since most of the people live in the southern part of Alberta, transportation is more highly developed there. However, new roads are being built in remoter areas to aid in economic development and to attract tourists. Transpor-

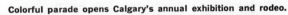

Colorful parade opens Calgary's annual exhibition and rodeo.

146g

tation by truck is important, and Alberta has a higher percentage of automobiles in proportion to population than other provinces.

Railways. Alberta is served by two transcontinental lines that provide year-round access to world markets for Alberta's products. Feeder lines serve most of the communities in the province. One of the latest additions—the Great Slave Railway—will have far-reaching effects on the northern areas through which it passes.

Aviation. Aircraft are used to transport people, machinery, and supplies to the north, where there are few roads and railways. All of the major cities have regular passenger and air freight services, and various airlines link Alberta with the rest of Canada and the world.

Water Transport. Freighting by river was once the only means of shipping heavy goods in Alberta. It is of minor importance today. Water routes still in use today are the Athabasca River from Waterways to Lake Athabasca, and the Slave River between Athabasca and Great Slave Lake in the Northwest Territories. In summer, power barges haul heavy freight bound for northern settlements.

Pipelines. Pipelines are the most economical means of transporting the oil and gas produced in Alberta. Oil is transported by pipelines from Edmonton to Superior, Wisconsin; to Sarnia and Port Credit in Ontario; and to the Pacific coast.

Alberta has eight daily newspapers. Of these, the Edmonton *Journal* has the largest circulation. Numerous weeklies are also published. The province has ten television and 13 radio stations. Telephone and telegraph service are provided throughout the populated areas.

▶ GOVERNMENT

Alberta is a self-governing province. Like the other provinces, it is headed by a premier who represents the controlling party in the provincial assembly. A lieutenant governor, appointed by the Governor-General in Council, is the titular head of the province. He represents the Crown. Alberta is represented in the federal parliament by 6 senators appointed by the Governor-General and by 21 elected members of the House of Commons. The voting age for provincial elections is 18.

▶ HISTORY

The first European to set foot in Alberta was probably Anthony Henday. In 1754 he set out from Hudson Bay to trade for furs with the Indians. Henday explored large tracts of unknown land, including a large portion of southern Alberta.

After the surrender of New France to the English in 1763, fur traders from eastern Canada and the United States began to tap the rich fur resources of the Canadian west.

Peter Pond, an American from Connecticut, was the first of these men to reach Alberta. He established a trading post on the Athabasca River in 1778. In 1789 Alexander Mackenzie began his famous explorations to the Arctic Ocean; and, in 1793, to the Pacific Ocean.

The Hudson's Bay Company and the North West Company competed for the fur trade of the Canadian west. Soon much of the country between Hudson Bay and the Rocky Mountains was dotted with rival trading posts. Competition was so fierce that there was sometimes bloodshed. But the rivalry ended when the companies united in 1821 under the name of the Hudson's Bay Company.

IMPORTANT DATES

1691	Henry Kelsey of the Hudson's Bay Company reached the eastern border of Alberta.
1754–1755	Anthony Henday of the Hudson's Bay Company was the first white man to enter Alberta.
1778	Peter Pond established the first trading post in Alberta.
1789	Alexander Mackenzie went down the Mackenzie River from Chipewyan to the Arctic Ocean.
1793	Alexander Mackenzie crossed Alberta via the Peace River.
1794	Fort Augustus founded on the site of Edmonton.
1861	St. Albert Mission founded by Father Lacombe.
1870	Canada acquired Alberta from the Hudson's Bay Company.
1874	North West Mounted Police posts established.
1882	The District of Alberta was created.
1883	The Canadian Pacific Railway main line was built across Alberta.
1905	Alberta admitted to Canadian Confederation.
1923	Alberta Wheat Pool organized.
1924	Turner Valley began producing oil.
1947	Oil discovered at Leduc.
1949	Mackenzie Highway to Hay River in the Northwest Territories completed.
1950–1953	Interprovincial Pipeline built between Edmonton and Sarnia, Ontario.
1951	Completion of the St. Mary Dam near Spring Coulee provided irrigation for southeastern Alberta.
1956	Trans-Canada Pipe Line began to carry natural gas from Alberta to eastern Canada.
1964	Development of oil sands at Athabasca began.
1969	Alberta Resources Railway completed.
1976	The Alberta Heritage Fund established to invest oil and gas revenues and thus provide for Alberta's future welfare.
1979	Charles Joseph (Joe) Clark of Alberta became prime minister of Canada.

In 1870 the Dominion of Canada acquired title to the company's lands, and 5 years later the area known today as Alberta became part of the newly organized Northwest Territories.

Before the transfer of land to Canada, most of the settlers in Alberta were traders, Indians, métis, and missionaries. The best known mission was St. Albert Mission, founded by Father Lacombe in 1861. It was the first successful agricultural settlement in the province.

In 1873 the Canadian Government organized the North West Mounted Police. Mounted Police posts were established in Alberta at Fort Macleod, Fort Saskatchewan, and Fort Calgary. The "Mounties" brought law and order to the region. One of their first acts was to stamp out an illegal whiskey trade that was conducted by traders among the Indians of southern Alberta.

The Canadian Pacific Railway reached Calgary in 1883. This was the turning point in the growth of settlement. The first settlers to take advantage of the rail line were ranchers who settled on the rich grazing land in the south.

Toward the end of the 19th century, Canada encouraged immigration by offering land to homesteaders. This, together with more railway construction in western Canada, attracted many settlers. They came from eastern Canada, the United States, and Britain and other European countries. The population of Alberta rose rapidly from about 73,000 in 1901 to more than 375,000 in 1911.

In 1905 Alberta became a separate province. Following World War I, the Depression and drought of the 1930's slowed up economic growth. However, population doubled in the years between World War I and World War II. The discovery of oil at Leduc in 1947, followed by even larger oil discoveries elsewhere, touched off the greatest period of economic growth in Alberta's history. Population continues to increase. Rising energy prices since the early 1970's have resulted in continued rapid economic growth in Alberta.

D. WAYNE MOODIE
University of Manitoba
Reviewed by A. H. LAYCOCK
University of Alberta

ALCHEMY. See CHEMISTRY, HISTORY OF.

ALCOHOL

Around A.D. 1100 an unknown alchemist, probably in southern Italy, distilled some wine. He got a clear, colorless fluid with a strange odor. Though this strange new fluid looked like water, it did not behave at all like water. It had a burning taste. When it was drunk, it had powerful intoxicating effects. Strangest of all, it burned—with a hot, blue flame. This mysterious "burning water," which the alchemists believed was the spirit of the wine, was ethyl alcohol.

Today hundreds of different alcohols are known. Some are clear, colorless fluids that mix freely with water. They evaporate quickly in open air. They have low freezing points. Ethyl alcohol freezes at about −117°C (−179°F). Other alcohols behave quite differently. They are thick, oily fluids that hardly mix with water at all. Some are even solid at room temperature.

Alcohols are made up of atoms of carbon, hydrogen, and oxygen. The carbon atoms form a kind of framework around which the hydrogen and oxygen atoms are arranged.

In industry, alcohols are used as raw materials for making many other chemicals. They are also used to dissolve fats, oils, and many other organic (carbon-containing) substances, including some plastics. Another use is to extract flavoring oils, perfumes, and drugs from plant and animal materials. Some alcohols are burned as fuels in rockets. Scientists are testing the use of alcoholic fuels in automobiles and other land vehicles.

In the home, ethyl alcohol is found in antiseptics, flavorings, perfumes, and liquor. Colored red for visibility, it is used as the fluid in outdoor thermometers. Isopropyl alcohol is used as rubbing alcohol.

All the alcohols except glycerol are more or less poisonous. Methyl alcohol (wood alcohol) is extremely poisonous, and even a small amount can cause blindness or death. **Denatured** alcohol is ethyl alcohol that has been made undrinkable by adding poisons or unpleasant-tasting chemicals to it.

ALCOHOLISM

Alcoholism is a disease in which the drinking of alcoholic beverages interferes with some aspect of life. A person who drinks alcohol in spite of the fact that it results in loss of health, job, or good relationships with family, friends, and colleagues is said to be suffering from alcoholism.

There is a great difference between casual, or social, drinkers and alcoholics, or compulsive drinkers. The social drinkers drink because they choose to. The compulsive drinkers drink because they must, in spite of knowing that drinking is affecting their lives in a harmful way.

Alcohol is one of a large group of sedative drugs, which includes barbiturates, bromides, and chloroform. A sedative drug is one that causes sleep when used in large enough quantities. Alcohol was one of the earliest sedative drugs used.

Doctors are not sure why people become alcoholics. There does not seem to be a particular type of personality likely to become an alcoholic. Alcoholism may affect people of all races and religions. It may affect both men and women, the old and the young, the rich and the poor.

Health authorities are disturbed by the great increase in the use of alcohol among young people in recent years. Alcohol is by far the most common substance causing drug dependency among the teenage population.

The idea that the alcoholic is a person of bad character and poor morals is no longer widely held. Through the efforts of the National Council on Alcoholism, the American Medical Association, and other organizations, alcoholism is now generally recognized as a disease. The alcoholic is an ill person who needs help and treatment.

Effects of Alcohol

People drink alcohol only for the effect it has on the way they feel. The social drinkers may get a feeling of relaxation and freedom from tension. The alcoholics often show a great change in personality. They may become angry and argumentative, or quiet and depressed. Often a small amount of alcohol causes persons with alcoholism to feel even more anxious, sad, tense, and confused. They then seek relief by drinking more. This is how the alcoholic gets caught up in a web of ever-increasing need for and dependency on alcohol.

Many medical problems affect alcoholics. Serious damage to the liver, heart, stomach, and other organs can result from the overuse of alcohol. Many alcoholics do not eat properly, and some of their ills are caused by poor nutrition as well as by the direct effects of alcohol on the body.

The most tragic effect of alcohol, however, is the damage it causes to the brain. Patients find it difficult to concentrate, their memories are affected, and a few suffer even more serious brain damage.

Alcoholism has become a leading cause of death in the young adult population of the United States. This grim statistic is based on accidental deaths resulting from drunken driving; from fires started by carelessly dropped cigarettes; and from overdosage with other sedatives while under the influence of alcohol.

Treatment for Alcoholism

Even though the exact cause of alcoholism is not known, the problems associated with this illness can be treated. For the alcoholic, the use of alcohol in any form must be forever avoided.

To achieve this aim, organizations like Alcoholics Anonymous give patients guidance, support, and hope. Doctors, psychologists, and trained counselors can help motivate the patient to enter into a plan for recovery. Private rehabilitation centers have been established to help the alcoholic recover. Many large businesses have also set up programs to help their employees who are alcoholics.

Two programs were established to help the families of alcoholics better understand their problems. Al-Anon is for the family and friends of alcoholics. Alateen, a division of Al-Anon, is for young people 12 to 20 years of age who live in an alcoholic family situation.

It is essential that research into better treatment methods, and, more important, into methods of prevention, be continued. Only in this way can progress be made in dealing with this major health problem.

STANLEY E. GITLOW, M.D.
Chairman, Committee on Alcoholism
Medical Society of the State of New York

ALCOTT, LOUISA MAY (1832–1888)

Louisa May Alcott, best known as the author of *Little Women,* was among the first authors to write novels for young readers. She was born in Germantown, Pennsylvania, on November 29, 1832. Her father, Bronson Alcott, was a noted educator and lecturer, famous for fresh ideas and idealistic projects. When Louisa was 2 years old, the family moved to Boston, Massachusetts, where her father opened a school. Six years later, the Alcotts moved to Concord, a beautiful, historic town near Boston.

There were five children in the Alcott family—Anna, Louisa, Elizabeth, Abba, and a boy who died in infancy. The four girls went to their father's school. Later Louisa said that her father was the best teacher she ever had. Louisa's mother taught her to sew. And as Louisa later recounted, "At 12 I set myself up as a dolls' dressmaker, with my sign out and wonderful models in my window." She also liked "to run races, climb trees, and leap fences."

The Alcott barn was a wonderful place for giving plays. At first the girls acted out fairy tales, but before long Louisa began to write original plays. The neighbors were invited to see the plays, and they praised Louisa's talents as a playwright and actress.

Many famous people of Concord were friends of the Alcotts. Henry David Thoreau, Ralph Waldo Emerson, and Oliver Wendell Holmes were among those from whom Louisa gathered ideas about the rights of women and the need for social reform.

For the Alcott girls, childhood was not all play and fun. Bronson Alcott's projects failed, one after another, and money became scarcer and scarcer. Louisa realized that she must find a way to help her family. She tried dressmaking, had a job caring for two elderly people, and then became a teacher.

When she was 16, she began writing and sending out her stories for publication. When she was 17, one of her plays was accepted, and a part was promised to her. But the play was never produced, and she never got a real part in the theater.

As a teacher, Louisa made up fairy stories to tell her pupils. These were published in 1854 as *Flower Fables,* her first book.

During the Civil War, Louisa May Alcott served as a nurse in a Union Army hospital in Washington, D.C. She wrote about her experiences in the book *Hospital Sketches,* published in 1863.

She wrote her most famous book, *Little Women,* while she was editor of a magazine for girls. She based the story on the Alcotts' family life in Concord. The book was published in two parts, in 1868 and 1869. It sold so well that at last she was able to take care of her family. She continued the story in *Little Men* and *Jo's Boys.* Her other books for young readers include *An Old-Fashioned Girl* and *Eight Cousins.*

Louisa May Alcott died on March 6, 1888, in Boston.

LOUISE HALL THARP
Author, *The Peabody Sisters of Salem*

▶ LITTLE WOMEN

In the following scene we meet Jo, her sister Meg, and their neighbor Laurie.

"What in the world are you going to do now, Jo?" asked Meg, one snowy afternoon, as her sister came tramping through the hall, in rubber boots, old sack and hood, with a broom in one hand and a shovel in the other.

"Going out for exercise," answered Jo, with a mischievous twinkle in her eyes.

"I should think two long walks this morning would have been enough! It's cold and dull out; and I advise you to stay, warm and dry, by the fire, as I do," said Meg with a shiver.

"Never take advice! Can't keep still all day, and, not being a pussy-cat I don't like to doze by the fire. I like adventures, and I'm going to find some."

Meg went back to toast her feet and read "Ivanhoe"; and Jo began to dig paths with great energy. The snow was light, and with her broom she soon swept a path all round the garden, for Beth to walk in when the sun came out; and the invalid dolls needed air. Now, the garden separated the Marches' house from that of Mr. Laurence. Both stood in a suburb of the city, which was still country-like, with groves and lawns, large gardens, and quiet streets. A low hedge parted the two estates. On one side was an old, brown house, looking rather bare and shabby, robbed of the vines that in summer covered its walls, and the flowers which then surrounded it. On the other side was a stately stone mansion, plainly betokening every sort of comfort and luxury, from the big coach-house and well-kept

A scene from *Little Women*. The "little women" are the March daughters—Meg, Jo, Amy, and Beth. Their mother reads a letter from Mr. March, away in the Civil War.

grounds to the conservatory and the glimpses of lovely things one caught between the rich curtains. Yet it seemed a lonely, lifeless sort of house; for no children frolicked on the lawn, no motherly face ever smiled at the windows, and few people went in and out, except the old gentleman and his grandson.

To Jo's lively fancy, this fine house seemed a kind of enchanted palace, full of splendors and delights, which no one enjoyed. She had long wanted to behold these hidden glories, and to know the "Laurence boy," who looked as if he would like to be known, if he only knew how to begin. Since the party, she had been more eager than ever, and had planned many ways of making friends with him; but he had not been seen lately, and Jo began to think he had gone away, when she one day spied a brown face at the upper window, looking wistfully down into their garden, where Beth and Amy were snowballing one another.

"That boy is suffering for society and fun," she said to herself. "His grandpa does not know what's good for him, and keeps him shut up all alone. He needs a party of jolly boys to play with, or somebody young and lively. I've a great mind to go over and tell the old gentleman so!"

The idea amused Jo, who liked to do daring things, and was always scandalizing Meg by her queer performances. The plan of "going over" was not forgotten; and when the snowy afternoon came, Jo resolved to try what could be done. She saw Mr. Laurence drive off, and then sallied out to dig her way down to the hedge, where she paused, and took a survey. All quiet, —curtains down at the lower windows; servants out of sight and nothing human visible but a curly black head leaning on a thin hand at the upper window.

"There he is," thought Jo, "poor boy! all alone and sick this dismal day. It's a shame! I'll toss up a snowball and make him look out, and then say a kind word to him."

Up went a handful of soft snow, and the head turned at once, showing a face which lost its listless look in a minute, as the big eyes brightened and the mouth began to smile. Jo nodded and laughed, and flourished her broom as she called out,—

"How do you do? Are you sick?"

Laurie opened the window, and croaked out as hoarsely as a raven,—

"Better, thank you. I've had a bad cold, and been shut up a week."

"I'm sorry. What do you amuse yourself with?"

"Nothing; it's as dull as tombs up here."

"Don't you read?"

"Not much; they won't let me."

"Can't somebody read to you?"

"Grandpa does, sometimes; but my books don't interest him, and I hate to ask Brooke all the time."

"Have some one come and see you then."

"There isn't any one I'd like to see. Boys make such a row, and my head is weak."

"Isn't there some nice girl who'd read and amuse you? Girls are quiet, and like to play nurse."

"Don't know any."

"You know us," began Jo, then laughed, and stopped.

"So I do! Will you come, please?" cried Laurie.

ALEXANDER THE GREAT
(356–323 B.C.)

Alexander III of Macedonia was the greatest general of ancient times. His armies conquered most of the civilized world. Alexander never lost a battle, although the difficulties he faced were tremendous. But Alexander was more than a warrior. He introduced new ideas for governing conquered countries. He helped to spread Greek ideas in science and art. He was a legend in his own time and a hero to those who came after him.

Alexander was born in 356 B.C., in Macedonia, a small country north of Greece. His father, King Philip II, had changed Macedonia from a poor, unknown country to the most powerful nation in Europe. Philip conquered the city-states of Greece and ruled over much of the land to the north and northwest of Macedonia as well.

When Alexander was a boy, his father bought a wild horse named Bucephalus. No one was able to ride the horse. Alexander boasted that he could tame him. Philip allowed him to try, with the condition that Alexander pay for the horse if he should fail.

Alexander noticed that Bucephalus was terrified by the movement of his shadow on the ground. He turned the horse so that Bucephalus could not see his shadow. Then with one bold jump Alexander mounted the horse and triumphantly rode to his father. Philip was very proud of Alexander and supposedly said, "My son, look for a kingdom worthy of yourself. Macedonia is too small for you."

▶ ALEXANDER'S EDUCATION

When Alexander was 13 years old, his father engaged a new teacher, Aristotle. He was one of the greatest thinkers of all time—a perfect teacher for a future king.

Aristotle made Alexander hungry for knowledge and taught the Prince to study the world around him carefully. Alexander dreamed of a world empire held together by common customs, ideas, and traditions, not by force.

King Philip was murdered by his enemies when Alexander was 20. Alexander succeeded to the throne of Macedonia.

After Philip's death many of the people he had conquered rebelled. For the next 2 years Alexander traveled through the countries we now call Yugoslavia, Bulgaria, Rumania, and Greece, calming the rebellious people. When he conquered the once-powerful city-state Thebes, the rest of Greece surrendered to Alexander's leadership. Then he turned to the countries of the East.

▶ ALEXANDER'S ARMY

In Alexander's time the great Persian Empire of King Darius III was a threat to Greece. The empire of Darius extended from the Dardanelles strait to India. Its army was huge—some say it had 1,000,000 foot soldiers and 40,000 cavalry. Alexander had only 30,000 foot soldiers and 5,000 cavalry, but they were better organized and trained than the Persians. King Philip had built the Macedonian army on the model of the Greek infantry, called the phalanx, which consisted of deep rows of armored foot soldiers, equipped with shields and long spears. Under Alexander's leadership the Macedonian phalanx became invincible in battle.

Alexander used many new methods for waging war. One of the most effective was the siege train. A siege train was made up of several high towers that could be rolled on wheels to the walls of a city. From the towers the walls could easily be attacked and the city conquered.

He also developed new weapons. One of these was the torsion catapult, which could hurl large stones or fire big arrows more than 180 meters (200 yards).

▶ THE DEFEAT OF THE PERSIANS

In 334 B.C. the 22-year-old king began his invasion of Asia. It lasted for 11 years. Alexander's soldiers traveled 17,500 kilometers (11,000 miles), sometimes marching 65 kilometers (40 miles) a day.

Alexander fought three great battles against the Persians. The first took place in Asia Minor, at the Granicus River. When the two armies met, Alexander led the Macedonian advance. He was in the thick of the fighting and would have been killed if it had not been for the bravery of his friend Clitus. Clitus rushed to Alexander's aid and saved the young king's life. Alexander defeated the Persians and they fled inland.

His army camped at a town called Gor-

The army of Alexander the Great attacks a Persian city. Alexander's genius and his well-trained Macedonian soldiers made him master of much of the ancient world.

dium, in what is now Turkey. Here, according to an old legend, was the chariot of an ancient king, Gordius. King Gordius had tied a complicated knot to the pin that fastened the chariot to the harness. He proclaimed that whoever could untie the knot would one day rule over all Asia. Some say Alexander did not even try to untie the knot but sliced it in half with his sword. Others say he pulled out the pin, thus loosening the knot so that he could untie it easily.

In order to complete his conquest, Alexander seized the Mediterranean bases held by the Persian navy. When the lands along the Mediterranean coast were safely in his power, Alexander returned to his Persian campaign. He won a great victory over the Persian army, led by King Darius, at Issus in 333 B.C. Alexander again led the Macedonian assault. His cavalry charge was so fierce that he broke through the Persian lines and almost captured King Darius. Only the brave stand of the royal bodyguard saved the King, who fled from the battlefield. Alexander then went on to conquer Syria, Palestine, and Egypt. In Egypt, Alexander ordered a great city built. This city, Alexandria, became a center of learning and trade.

The final defeat of the Persians came in 331 B.C. At the battle of Gaugamela (sometimes called the battle of Arbela) the Persian army was completely defeated.

▶ KING OF ASIA

Alexander and his men spent the next winter in Persepolis, the home of Persia's kings. Here they found great treasures taken from the lands the Persians had conquered.

In Persepolis, Alexander at last fulfilled the prophecy of the Gordian knot. Sitting on the great golden throne of the Persian kings, he became king of Asia. The following spring Alexander set fire to Persepolis. The whole world then knew that Persia had been defeated.

But Alexander, king of Asia, was not satisfied. His ambition and curiosity would not let him rest. He decided to take his army into eastern Persia and then on into India. Some say he believed he would reach the great ring of water that was supposed to surround the earth. Others say Alexander wanted to be king of the whole world.

Alexander's soldiers marched through some of the most desolate and barren land in the world. They entered India through the

dangerous passes of the Hindu Kush Mountains. Alexander's last great victory took place in India against the Indian rajah Porus. The Rajah's army was accompanied by elephants. These huge beasts, which were unknown in Europe, frightened Alexander's men. But in spite of their fear, the well-disciplined army triumphed.

▶ ALEXANDER'S DEATH

At the time Alexander's army entered India, they had been on the march for 8½ years. Only one fourth of the original army was still alive. The men were exhausted by years of battle and hardship. Disease, thirst, and hunger had been their constant companions. At last the soldiers refused to go on. Alexander gave in to his army.

The homeward march began in 326 B.C. In the same year his faithful horse Bucephalus died. Alexander ordered a city built in India and named it Bucephala, after his old friend. Alexander, too, was exhausted, and finally became ill and died in Babylon, in October, 323 B.C. He was only 32 years old. His body, wrapped in golden cloth and enclosed in a glass coffin, was buried in Alexandria.

▶ ALEXANDER'S DREAM: ONE WORLD

Alexander's empire lasted only a short time after his death. Since he had no heir, his empire was divided among his generals. Soon they began to fight with each other over their share of the spoils. The empire finally crumbled into many small kingdoms. However, Alexander had accomplished his dream of spreading Greek ideas to the countries under his rule. Greek culture lived on long after the empire perished.

Alexander had another ambition: to unite people by their common interests rather than to separate them by their differences. Alexander was the first world leader to hope that someday men would be united under one government. Unlike most Greeks of his time, he did not believe that all non-Greeks were barbarians, fit only for slavery. Instead of making slaves of all the people he conquered, Alexander used some as officers in his army and in the governments he established. He married a Persian princess and sometimes wore Persian clothes. Plutarch, the Greek historian, said of Alexander that he wished "to mix all men together as in a loving cup."

Reviewed by KENNETH S. COOPER
George Peabody College

ALFRED THE GREAT (849–899?)

Only one king in the history of the English people has been called "Great." This was Alfred, who ruled the land of the West Saxons.

Alfred, the youngest son of King Aethelwulf of Wessex, was born in 849 in Wantage, a town in south central England.

Alfred's father was a very religious Christian and a friend of Pope Leo IV. Twice before his 10th birthday, Alfred traveled to Rome. Those visits made a lasting impression on the little boy. Alfred came to respect education, and in later years learned to speak and read Latin.

During Alfred's youth Danish sea rovers, whom we now call Vikings, were raiding the English coast. The Danish invaders even made settlements on the English coast and used these bases for raids farther inland.

▶ ALFRED BECOMES KING

Alfred's father died in 858. Soon afterward two of Alfred's older brothers were killed in battle. Aethelred, Alfred's last surviving brother, was king when a new invasion of Danes menaced the West Saxon kingdom in the year 870. The next year has been called "Alfred's year of battles" because he fought against the Danes in nine different places. The most important battle took place at Ash-

down in January, 871. The Saxons defeated the Danes, but Aethelred was wounded and died in the spring. Alfred, the last of the brothers, then became ruler of the war-torn kingdom. He was 22 years old.

The next 7 years saw times of peace and times of war. In the winter of 878, a Danish force attacked the castle where Alfred was celebrating Christmas. Alfred and a small band of loyal soldiers escaped and hid in the forest until Easter.

Alfred spent this time training and rebuilding his armies. Many legends have grown up about Alfred's adventures during those trying times. The most famous is the story of Alfred and the cakes. According to that legend, he took refuge in a forest hut. An old peasant woman who lived there asked him to watch the cakes baking in her oven while she went about her work. Alfred was so busy worrying about his kingdom and planning new battles that he let the cakes burn. When the woman returned, she gave Alfred a severe scolding. But he did not embarrass her by telling her that he was the king.

In 876 Alfred defeated the Danes at Edington. All the nobles of England now turned to Alfred as their leader. Alfred and Guthrum, the pagan Danish chief, signed a peace treaty at Wedmore. Guthrum and many of his followers settled in England, and were

Alfred the Great built monastery schools to encourage education in his kingdom. Here, while visiting one of the schools, he asks a young student about his lessons.

converted to Christianity. This was an important step toward uniting England. However, in 886 other Danish invaders attacked England, but Alfred defeated them, too.

Alfred turned his attention to strengthening England. English laws were rewritten and clarified. New forts and walls were built to protect towns. But Alfred's most important work was in restoring the learning and education that had existed in England before the Danish invaders swept through the country.

With the help of scholars, Alfred translated several books from Latin to English. These were among the first books ever written in the language of the country, and were the foundation of English literature. Alfred also encouraged the historians of the time to continue a record of events that had been started many years earlier, *The Anglo-Saxon Chronicle*.

When Alfred died, about 899, an unknown chronicler wrote, "There passed away Alfred the king . . . the famous, the warlike, the victorious, the careful provider for the widow, the helpless, the orphan and the poor; the most skilled of Saxon poets, most dear to his own nation, courteous to all, most liberal . . . most watchful and devout in the service of God."

Reviewed by KENNETH S. COOPER
George Peabody College

ALGAE

Algae are simple plants. Most kinds of algae live in water. All the various kinds take their name from the Latin word for seaweed—alga (the plural is algae, *also* algas). The green scum that floats on ponds is made up of algae. So is the green material that sometimes covers the walls of aquarium tanks.

Algae are found in great numbers all over the world. They occur in so many different shapes and sizes that it is hard to think of all of them as related. Except for certain seaweeds, algae do not look like the familiar plants. But because of their basic forms and way of life, all algae are classed as flowerless plants. (The other major groups of flowerless plants are the fungi, mosses, and ferns.) Flowerless plants also lack some of the other familiar plant parts, such as fruits and seeds. The simple forms and life processes of the flowerless plants have not changed much through millions of years. That is why they are called primitive plants.

For a long time scientists were puzzled as to how plants without flowers or seeds could reproduce themselves. It is now known that algae reproduce in several ways. Here are the three main ways. Some algae produce male and female cells. When two join, a new cell is formed and grows into the new alga. Other algae have seedlike cells called spores. Once set free, the spores grow into new plants wherever they settle. Other algae reproduce by dividing into two or more parts. Each part then grows into a new plant.

Like all green plants, algae make their own food. They can do this because they have chlorophyll. This is the green coloring matter that, in the presence of sunlight, enables a plant to make its own food.

Although classed as green plants, most algae do not appear green. Other coloring matter blocks out the green. The algae in the ocean are chiefly brown, red, yellow-brown, or blue-green. Green algae are usually found in fresh water or on land.

Algae differ greatly in size and shape as well as in color. Some are so small that they can only be seen under a microscope; these include the single-celled algae. Many algae are simply rows of cells; they appear as thread-like forms called filaments. Some

Tiny green algae form scum that adds oxygen to fresh-water ponds.

Like all seaweed, kelp is classed with the algae. This kind is almost 2 meters (about 6 feet) long.

algae grow with spiky branches; at the bottom of a pond they look like dwarf trees. Some algae grow to a large size. One of the largest plants on earth, a brown seaweed called kelp, may be 30 meters (about 100 feet) long.

Algae are able to live almost anywhere. They can survive in salt water and fresh water, in hot or cold. Some live in hot springs. A small, bright red alga grows in polar snow and ice; these algae are a cause of "red snow."

Relatives of the fresh-water algae also live on land. These are usually greenish algae that cling to soil, trees, or rocks. They get their water from the damp ground and moist air. If the soil dries up, these algae stop growing but may remain alive for years.

Certain algae form a partnership with fungi, another of the primitive plants. These algae and fungi live so closely together that they seem to form a single plant. This plant is called a lichen. Other algae live on animals such as turtles or the three-toed sloth.

The best-known algae are the seaweeds. Seaweeds grow in many different shapes. Some look like land plants, such as moss, asparagus, or mushrooms. There is a light-

Diatoms are algae. A diatom is rarely bigger than 0.5 millimeter (1/50 inch). It has a thick shell. Each diatom is a single cell that reproduces by dividing. But cells sometimes remain attached and form a chain of cells, as shown in the photograph. The organisms that cause red snow are usually described as algae, but they are actually a mixture of algae, fungi, and bacteria growing together. They are found only in polar regions. *Nitella* is the most complex kind of algae and the closest to the higher plants. It has what look like roots, stems, leaves, and even seeds. These parts are different in their anatomy from true roots, stems, leaves, and seeds. But they do serve similar purposes.

Nitella, magnified 10 times.

Diatoms, magnified 375 times.

Red snow near Wilkes Station, Antarctica.

green sea lettuce that looks like regular leaf lettuce. One seaweed, the sea palm, looks like a little palm tree. And the gulfweed looks as if it had berries; actually, the "berries" are little bladders that keep the plant afloat.

Most of the algae mentioned so far are harmless or helpful to people, but some others can be dangerous. There are algae that spoil water supplies by producing a bad-tasting oil. When certain algae decay in water, they may give off poisons that will kill fish and animals that drink the water. Other algae are poisonous to fish and people. The mysterious, fish-killing "red tides" are made up of tiny organisms that may be algae.

But most algae benefit us, directly or indirectly. Algae and lichens that grow on the land help to keep the soil from washing away. And when these algae decay, they fertilize the plants that people and animals eat.

Algae are especially important to life in the sea. Diatoms, a type of alga, make up a large part of plankton, the floating mass of tiny plants and animals on which fish and other sea creatures feed. Algae also supply oxygen to the animal life in the water.

In some parts of the world, especially in Asia, people eat certain seaweeds. Elsewhere livestock are fed seaweeds. From kelp come substances used in making such things as ice cream and rubber tires. And from certain red algae comes the gelatin-like agar-agar. This is the material in which bacteria are cultivated in research laboratories.

In the future algae may become far more important as a food. Scientists have succeeded in growing a single-celled alga, Chlorella, in tanks of water exposed to sunlight. The plants grow very fast, using human wastes as their only source of needed materials. Chlorella cells contain a great deal of protein. They also provide carbohydrates, fats, and vitamins. As the world's population grows, Chlorella and other algae may provide a means of overcoming food shortages.

Reviewed by THOMAS GORDON LAWRENCE
Formerly, Erasmus Hall High School, New York
See also FERNS, MOSSES, AND LICHENS.

ALGEBRA

Algebra, like arithmetic and geometry, is a branch of mathematics. In addition to arithmetic's symbols of 1, 2, 3, and so on, algebra uses letters to represent numbers. The use of letters makes it easier to study relationships among numbers and to discover general laws that are true for *all* numbers.

For example, when we write $3 - 3 = 0$, all we are saying is that 3 subtracted from 3 gives 0. But when we write $a - a = 0$, we are saying that *any* number subtracted from itself gives a remainder of 0. Similarly, $5 \div 1 = 5$ means that when 5 is divided by 1, the quotient is 5. But $a \div 1 = a$ means that when *any* number is divided by 1, the quotient is the number itself.

For those reasons, algebra can be thought of as generalized arithmetic.

▶ALGEBRA IN PROBLEMS

The letters used in algebra do not always stand for numbers in general. In problem-solving, a letter may be made to represent one particular, unknown number. (The letter x is often used as an unknown. So to avoid confusion, $\times$ is rarely used as a multiplication sign in algebra. We write xy or $x \cdot y$ or $(x)(y)$ to express x times y.)

The use of letters makes it easier to handle problems. For instance, consider this problem: A boy and girl collected $19 for the Red Cross. The girl collected $3 more than the boy. How much money did each collect?

In algebra we say: Let x represent the number of dollars collected by the boy; then $x + 3$ represents the number of dollars collected by the girl. Then we can express the problem by writing $x + x + 3 = 19$; this tells us that the boy and girl together collected $19.

▶USE OF EQUATIONS

Expressions like $x + x + 3 = 19$ or $16 - a = 7$ or $2y - 1 = y + 2$ are called equations. The study of equations is an important part of algebra. An equation can be thought of as a balanced seesaw or a scale in balance: $10 = 10$

In working with equations, we combine like units: $x + x$ is stated as $2x$. And we simplify. In simplifying, we must keep the equation in balance. Here are four ways of simplifying an equation:

1. Make both sides larger by the same number. $\quad 10 + 2 = 10 + 2$

2. Make both sides smaller by the same number. $\quad 10 - 2 = 10 - 2$

3. Multiply both sides by the same number. $\quad (3)(10) = (3)(10)$

4. Divide both sides by the same number. $\quad$ ½ of 10 = ½ of 10

Let us see how these rules help in solving the equation $x + x + 3 = 19$:

First combine the like units and change $x + x$ to $2x$.

Make both sides smaller by the same number—subtract 3 from each side.

Now divide both sides of the equation by the same number—divide by 2.

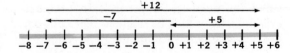

The equation is solved: $x = 8$.
The last equation tells us that the boy brought in $8; the girl $(x + 3)$ brought in $11.

This same problem can be solved by arithmetic, but it is more easily solved by using the letter language of algebra. More complicated problems that are solved with great difficulty by arithmetic are easily solved by algebra.

▶ NEW NUMBERS

Algebra uses various kinds of numbers. Among these are **signed numbers: positive** $(+4)$ and **negative** (-3). Note that for clarity such numbers are often written within parentheses. This keeps the number sign distinct from the sign that says add, subtract, multiply, or divide.

You have often used positive or negative numbers. For instance, a gain of $7 can be written as $+7$, while 7 degrees below zero can be written as -7. Such numbers can be pictured by the number line:

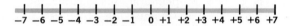

Here are a few examples of how negative and positive numbers are added:

1. $(+7) + (+3) = +10$
A 7° rise in temperature followed by a 3° rise is the same as a 10° rise.

2. $(+7) + (-3) = +4$
A 7° rise followed by a 3° drop amounts to a 4° rise.

3. $(-7) + (-5) = -12$
A 7° drop followed by a 5° drop amounts to a 12° drop.

4. $(-7) + (+12) = +5$
A 7° drop followed by a 12° rise amounts to a 5° rise.

Again, a number line is helpful in picturing these calculations. For example,

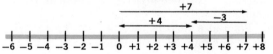

shows that $+7$ followed by -3 gives $+4$.

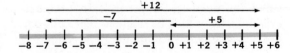

shows that $+12$ followed by -7 gives $+5$.

In arithmetic we say $5 - 3 = 2$ because we must add 2 to 3 to get 5. A similar process is followed in algebra:

1. $(+7) - (+3) = +4$

To get from $+3$ to $+7$, there must be a rise of 4. Or to put it another way, we must add $+4$ and $+3$ to get $+7$.

2. $(+7) - (+8) = -1$

To get from $+8$ to $+7$, there must be a drop of 1.

3. $(-7) - (-2) = -5$

To get from -2 to -7, there must be a drop of 5.

4. $(-7) - (-10) = +3$

To get from -10 to -7, there has to be a rise of 3.

Both multiplication and division follow the same rules: If the signs of two numbers are alike, the result is a positive number. If the signs are different, the result is a negative number.

1. A positive number multiplied by a positive number gives a positive product:

$(+) \cdot (+) = (+)$ or $(+7) \cdot (+5) = +35$

2. A negative number multiplied by a negative number gives a positive product:

$(-) \cdot (-) = (+)$ or $(-7) \cdot (-5) = +35$

3. A positive number multiplied by a negative number gives a negative result:

$(-) \cdot (+) = (-)$ or $(-7) \cdot (+5) = -35$

$(+) \cdot (-) = (-)$ or $(+7) \cdot (-5) = -35$

How would you phrase the rules for the following situations in division?

$$(+8) \div (+4) = +2$$
$$(+8) \div (-4) = -2$$
$$(-8) \div (+4) = -2$$
$$(-8) \div (-4) = +2$$

▶ NEW PROCESSES

In arithmetic, multiplication is a short way of adding equal groups. 5×3 stands for $3 + 3 + 3 + 3 + 3$.

In algebra there is a similar procedure when all numbers to be multiplied are alike. For instance:

2^2 is a short way of saying $2 \times 2 = 4$.

2^3 is a short way of saying $2 \times 2 \times 2 = 8$.

2^4 is a short way of saying $2 \times 2 \times 2 \times 2 = 16$.

2^7 is a short way of saying

$$2 \times 2 \times 2 \times 2 \times 2 \times 2 \times 2 = 128.$$

2^2 is read: two squared or 2 to the second power.

2^3 is read: two cubed or 2 to the third power.

2^4 is read: 2 to the fourth power.

2^7 is read: 2 to the seventh power.

The little upper numbers (^{2}, ^{3}, ^{4}, ^{7}) are called **exponents.** The larger-sized lower number is called the **base.** The exponent tells that there is to be a multiplication, and it tells how many times the lower number, or base, has to be repeated.

This is how these numbers are used in multiplication:

$$(2^2) \cdot (2^3) = 2^5$$

because 2^2 means $(2) \cdot (2)$ and 2^3 means $(2) \cdot (2) \cdot (2)$, and so $(2^2) \cdot (2^3)$ means $(2 \cdot 2) \cdot (2 \cdot 2 \cdot 2)$, which is 32, or 2^5.

The rule: When multiplying numbers with the same base, copy the base and add the exponents.

In division the rule is different: When the numbers have the same base, copy the base and subtract the exponents:

$$(2^5) \div (2^3) = 2^2, \text{ or } 4$$

Sets

In modern mathematics the idea of **sets,** or collections, is important. Sets may consist of similar things, like a set of books on a shelf; they may be different things, like a set of toys in a toy chest; they may be people, like the set of children in a class; and they may be numbers, like the set of all numbers from 1 to 100.

▶ THE MEANING OF "ALGEBRA"

The word "algebra" comes from a book written about A.D. 825 by an Arab named Al-Khwárizmì. Its title was *Hisab al-jabr w'al-muqabala,* probably meaning "the science of equations." *Al-jabr* or "algebra" became the name for all topics studied in algebra.

Algebra includes many other processes besides those described in this article. It is a very useful branch of mathematics. The invention of radio and the development of space-ships and computers all required the use of algebra.

JACK ENGELHARDT
Brooklyn Friends School

See also ARITHMETIC; MATHEMATICS.

ALGERIA

On July 3, 1962, after seven years of struggle, the Algerian people became independent. The Algerian Revolution, which began on November 1, 1954, was part of the vast movement for the liberation of former colonial peoples that has swept Asia and Africa during the last half of the 20th century.

The new nation that emerged is a land of rich and varied contrasts. The old culture and traditions of this North African Arab nation live side by side with the modern industries of the 20th century. Alongside the modern steel and glass skyscrapers of Algiers, the capital city, lies the ancient Casbah with its winding, narrow streets.

▶ **THE PEOPLE**

The first people known to live in Algeria were the nomadic Berbers of North Africa. The Arabs came in the 7th century. Algeria, although nominally attached to the Ottoman Empire, existed as a state and maintained diplomatic relations with many countries. In 1830 a French expeditionary force invaded Algeria, and France gradually gained control of the country. French settlers, or *colons*, came to Algeria, which was declared a part of France in 1848 but was in effect a colony, a part of the French colonial empire.

FACTS AND FIGURES

DEMOCRATIC AND POPULAR REPUBLIC OF ALGERIA is the official name of the country.

CAPITAL: Algiers.

LOCATION: Northwest Africa. **Latitude**—19° **N to** 37° 05′ N. **Longitude**— 8° 40′ W to 12° E.

AREA: 2,381,741 km² (919,593 sq mi).

POPULATION: 18,500,000 (estimate).

LANGUAGE: Arabic (official), French.

GOVERNMENT: Republic. **Head of government**—president of the Council. **International co-operation**—United Nations, Arab League, Organization of African Unity (OAU), Organization of Petroleum Exporting Countries (OPEC).

NATIONAL ANTHEM: *Kassaman* ("We take this oath").

ECONOMY: Agricultural products—wheat, barley, grapes, vegetables, cotton, citrus fruits, olives, figs, sheep, goats, cattle, camels. **Industries and products**—food processing, textiles, leather goods, petroleum products, cement. **Chief minerals**—petroleum, natural gas, iron, phosphates, zinc, lead. **Chief exports**—petroleum, natural gas, iron ore, wine, phosphate, citrus fruits, vegetables. **Chief imports**—textiles, sugar, iron and steel, coal, fuel oils, machinery. **Monetary unit**—Algerian dinar.

Most of the people who live in Algeria today are Arabs and Berbers who follow the Muslim faith. Arabic is the national and official language, but French is still widely used.

More than three fourths of the people live in cities and towns along the Mediterranean coast. The others live inland in small villages, on patches of fertile ground in the desert called oases, or in the desert itself. The traditional Algerian house is built around an open courtyard that has a garden and a fountain. The house has thick walls and is built to keep the sun out and keep the interior cool. In an oasis village, houses are built of mud-brick and enclosed by high mud-brick walls. Nomads in the desert live in dark-colored tents.

▶ **THE LAND**

Algeria, in North Africa, is bordered on the north by the Mediterranean Sea; on the west by Morocco; on the east by Tunisia and Libya; and on the south by Niger, Mauritania, and Mali. After Sudan, it is the second largest country in Africa.

Two almost parallel ranges of the Atlas Mountains, called the Tell Atlas and the Saharan Atlas, divide Algeria into three physical regions: the Tell, the High Plateau region, and the Sahara.

The Tell. The Tell (Arabic for "hill") lies along the Mediterranean. Lowlands on the coast make up a fertile region of farms and orchards. Forests grow on the lower slopes of the hills, and sheep and goats graze higher up. Most of Algeria's major cities are located in the Tell.

The High Plateau. South of the Tell and north of the Sahara lies the High Plateau. Here and there on the plateau are **shotts**— shallow salt lakes that are dry part of the year. Coarse, prickly drinn and tall esparto grasses grow on the High Plateau.

The Sahara. *Sahara* is the Arabic word for "desert." This is also the name of the largest part of Algeria. The Sahara is mainly a rocky plateau, or **hammada**, flanked by areas of giant sand dunes called **ergs**. During the brief rainy season, streams flow through valleys called **wadis**. When the rains stop, the wadis dry up. Oases are scattered throughout the monotonous desert. These areas of greenery are watered by springs and wells.

The Tell has mild, rainy winters and dry, hot summers. It gets about 750 millimeters (30 inches) of rain a year. On the High Plateau summers are also hot and dry, but winters are colder. Rainfall here is much less than on the Tell. The Sahara is hot by day, but temperatures drop sharply at night Rainfall is very scanty. In the spring the **sirocco**—a hot, dry wind from the south —blows across the desert, causing fierce sandstorms.

Algeria has valuable mineral resources. It has deposits of phosphates, high-grade iron ore, bituminous coal, lead, and zinc. In the 1950's petroleum and natural gas were discovered in the Sahara. Natural gas is piped from the desert to coastal cities. The government controls the oil and gas industries.

Forests of pine, cedar, and cork oak grow in northern Algeria. Also along the coast grow olive trees, evergreens, and shrubs that look like those grown on the European side of the Mediterranean.

The High Plateau is a treeless plain. Some palm trees grow in the Saharan oases, and thorny plants survive on the dry desert.

Algeria has many animals like those of southern Europe—deer, otters, and weasels. There are also some animals—gazelles, jackals, and wild pigs—that are typical of Africa. Monkeys, hyenas, and panthers still live in the remote highlands.

▶ **INDUSTRIES AND PRODUCTS**

Less than 10 percent of Algeria's land can be farmed. Yet most of the Algerian people are farmers. On the Tell they grow bountiful crops of grain, wine grapes, tobacco, citrus fruits, olives, and figs.

On the High Plateau the farmers—mainly Berbers—grow wheat and barley and raise livestock. On the sparse grazing lands of the Sahara, Arab nomads breed sheep and goats for wool, meat, and hides, and camels for transportation. In the Saharan oases farmers grow dates and other fruits, cereal grains, and cotton.

Fishing boats on the Mediterranean return to Algerian ports with large catches of sardines, tuna, and anchovies. Most of these are

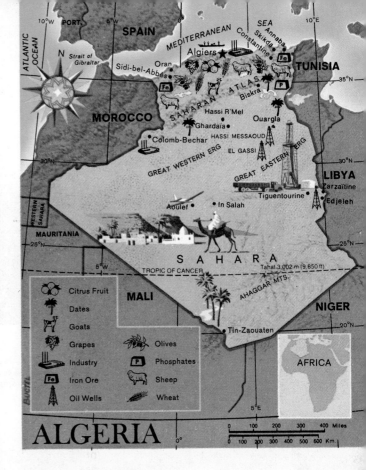

ALGERIA

sold at dockside fish stands or sent to canning factories.

Petroleum is Algeria's single most important natural resource, and petroleum and natural gas represent its most valuable exports. Algeria's industry is limited. The chief manufactured products include processed foods, textiles, leather goods, cement, and petroleum products. Paper is made from the esparto grass that grows on the High Plateau. Cork is harvested from cork oak trees.

Wine, iron ore, citrus fruits, and other Algerian products are exported to foreign countries. From other nations Algeria imports machinery, metal goods, and paper products. After independence France became Algeria's best customer and chief supplier.

Algeria has a well-developed road system. Railroads connect the coastal cities with Tunisia and Morocco. The biggest airfields are at Algiers, Oran, Annaba, and Aoulef. The chief ports are Algiers, Oran, and Annaba.

The government owns and runs the telephone and telegraph services and the radio stations. A telephone cable linking Algeria with Spain has recently been completed.

The rugged Kabylia district of the Atlas Mountains is Algeria's main cork-producing area.

A mosque tower rises over Ghardaïa, a desert city. In the foreground is the lively market place.

Veiled Muslim women and modern skyscrapers are both part of Algiers, the capital of Algeria.

▶ CITIES

Most of Algeria's large cities are on the Mediterranean coast.

Algiers. The capital, Algiers, with a population of over 900,000, is Algeria's largest city. It is a major seaport and an important center of transportation, industry, and culture. The winding, hilly streets of the city rise from the half-moon-shaped bay. In the bustling, modern harbor, wine is piped automatically from warehouse tanks to ships tied up at the piers. The 19th-century French architecture, colorful sidewalk cafés, and well-stocked bookstalls give the city a feeling of Marseilles or Paris. New building programs have begun; new roads are being constructed. Even some of the narrow Casbah streets have been transformed into broad boulevards.

Oran. An important port and industrial city, Oran has over 300,000 people. It was ruled by the Spanish for 2 centuries.

Constantine. The largest inland city, Constantine has over 250,000 people. It was named after the first Christian emperor of ancient Rome. Constantine's port, Skikda (formerly Philippeville), lies on the Mediterranean, 50 miles to the northeast.

▶ **HISTORY AND GOVERNMENT**

The Berbers, an ancient nomadic people, were the first people known to live in Algeria. In the 1100's B.C. the Phoenicians began to set up colonies along the North African coast. Some of these colonies were in Algeria, but the biggest, Carthage, was in Tunisia. After Rome destroyed Carthage in 146 B.C., it took over Algeria as well.

The Vandals replaced the Romans in A.D. 429. But their reign was brief. A hundred years later they were conquered by the Byzantine, or East Roman, Empire.

The Arabs began their conquest of the area during the 600's. For a time early in the 16th century (and into the late 18th in some places) the Spanish held major ports. From 1518 to 1830 Algeria was part of the Ottoman Empire. In 1830 the French invaded Algeria and occupied it after many years of armed resistance by the Algerians. The country then became a part of the French Empire.

Early in World War II France surrendered to Germany. Through the Vichy French puppet government, Germany controlled Algeria. In 1942 the Allied armies recaptured Algeria, and General Charles de Gaulle set up his headquarters there.

On May 8, 1945—V-E Day (Victory in Europe Day)—45,000 Algerian men, women, and children were killed in the repression of a peaceful demonstration for freedom in Algeria. From that day on, a time was foreseen when armed struggle would be required, no other means of expression being allowed. Thus, the Algerians formed the Front of National Liberation (FLN), the organization that on November 1, 1954, began the struggle for Algerian independence and brought it to a successful conclusion 7 years later. Following the long and difficult French-Algerian negotiations at Evian, a truce was signed bringing to an end French-Algerian hostilities. But with the truce and the announcement that Algeria was to be independent, revolt from another quarter sprang up. This was a rebellion by the Secret Army Organization (OAS), made up of French army men and French civilians who claimed that "Algeria is French." After a long and bloody fight, the OAS was defeated.

The long years of struggle and the efforts of the people and the government since independence have brought about radical changes in the lives of the people. Agrarian reform, nationalization of many industries, and the social and economic reforms that have taken place are bringing new possibilities of life to a country which previously knew only the great extremes of prosperous *colons* and impoverished Algerians. In particular, the government has made great efforts to overcome illiteracy, to provide adequate schooling for all children, and to change the patterns of the past through education and industrialization. Although much has been done, much remains to be accomplished. Many people still lack basic education, and a number of economic problems are still unsolved.

Algeria became independent in 1962. Ahmed Ben Bella, a leader in the struggle for independence, became the first premier and, later, president. He served until 1965, when a military coup led by Colonel Houari Boumedienne, then defense minister, ousted him. The constitution was suspended and the legislature dismissed. Boumedienne became the leader of the country.

In 1976 a new constitution was adopted. It declares that Algeria is a socialist and Islamic country and that the National Liberation Front is the only political party. The chief executive is the president, who is elected directly for a 6-year term. The legislature, the National People's Assembly, is also elected for 6 years. Boumedienne was elected president and continued to lead the country until his death in 1979.

ROBERT S. CHAUVIN
Stetson University

ALGONKIN INDIANS. See INDIANS OF NORTH AMERICA.

Alice in Wonderland

Some authors do not use their real names when they write a book. Charles Lutwidge Dodgson was such a man. This shy professor of mathematics used the pen name Lewis Carroll when he wrote *Alice's Adventures in Wonderland, Through the Looking-Glass,* and other delightful stories.

Dodgson, or Carroll, made up the stories for a friend's three young daughters—Alice, Lorina, and Edith Liddell. He even gave his heroine the name Alice. While picnicking with the children, the professor invented the White Rabbit, the Cheshire Cat, the March Hare, and all the other strange creatures that appear in *Alice's Adventures in Wonderland.* There is a scholarly caterpillar, for instance, who listens while Alice recites a poem, which goes like this:

"You are old, Father William," the young man said
"And your hair has become very white;
And yet you incessantly stand on your head—
Do you think, at your age, it is right?"

"In my youth," Father William replied to his son,
"I feared it might injure the brain;
But, now that I'm perfectly sure I have none,
Why, I do it again and again."

"You are old," said the youth, "as I mentioned before.
And have grown most uncommonly fat;
Yet you turned a back-somersault in at the door—
Pray, what is the reason of that?"

"In my youth," said the sage, as he shook his grey locks,
"I kept all my limbs very supple
By the use of this ointment—one shilling the box—
Allow me to sell you a couple?"

"You are old," said the youth, "and your jaws are too weak
For anything tougher than suet;
Yet you finished the goose, with the bones and the beak—
Pray, how did you manage to do it?"

"In my youth," said his father, "I took to the law,
And argued each case with my wife;

Father William balances an eel on the end of his nose.

And the muscular strength, which it gave to my
    jaw
Has lasted the rest of my life."

"You are old," said the youth, "one would
    hardly suppose
That your eye was as steady as ever;
Yet you balanced an eel on the end of your
    nose—
What made you so awfully clever?"

"I have answered three questions, and that is
    enough,"
Said his father. "Don't give yourself airs!
Do you think I can listen all day to such stuff?
Be off, or I'll kick you down-stairs!"

Alice's Adventures in Wonderland was
published in 1865, *Through the Looking-
Glass* in 1872. For both books Sir John Tenniel did the drawings, two of which appear on
this page. Tenniel was an artist on *Punch,* a
British magazine devoted to humor. He
worked closely with Carroll, and his drawings are almost as famous as the stories they
illustrate.

Through the Looking-Glass carries Alice
on further adventures. In this story Alice explores the world that lies on the other side of a
mirror. There she finds Humpty Dumpty; she
reads about the Jabberwock; she meets
Tweedledum and Tweedledee, the Red
Queen and the White Queen. These two
queens try to teach Alice how to be a queen,
and they criticize her for not learning lessons
in manners.

"Manners are not taught in lessons," said
Alice. "Lessons teach you to do sums, and things
of that sort."

"Can you do Addition?" the White Queen
asked. "What's one and one and one and one
and one and one and one and one and one and
one?"

"I don't know," said Alice. "I lost count."

"She ca'n't do Addition," the Red Queen interrupted. "Can you do Subtraction? Take nine
from eight."

"Nine from eight I ca'n't, you know," Alice
replied very readily: "but—"

"She ca'n't do Subtraction," said the White
Queen. "Can you do Division? Divide a loaf by
a knife—what's the answer to *that?*"

"I suppose—" Alice was beginning, but the
Red Queen answered for her. "Bread-and-Butter,
of course. Try another Subtraction sum. Take a
bone from a dog: What remains?"

Alice considered. "The bone wouldn't remain,
of course, if I took it—and the dog wouldn't remain: it would come to bite me—and I'm sure *I*
shouldn't remain!"

"Then you think nothing would remain?" said
the Red Queen.

"I think that's the answer."

"Wrong, as usual," said the Red Queen: "the
dog's temper would remain."

"But I don't see how—"

"Why, look here!" the Red Queen cried. "The
dog would lose its temper, wouldn't it?"

"Perhaps it would," Alice replied cautiously.

"Then if the dog went away, its temper would
remain!" the Queen exclaimed triumphantly.

Alice said, as gravely as she could, "They
might go different ways." But she couldn't help
thinking to herself, "What dreadful nonsense we
are talking!"

Alice receives a lesson in how to be a queen.

ALIENS

People who are not citizens of the country in which they live are called aliens. Some aliens are temporary visitors. Others have made a complete break with the past—they have become permanent residents of the new country. They may have left their home country because of poverty or lack of freedom. Or they may have been drawn to the new country by the allure, real or imagined, of a better life.

The laws governing aliens vary from country to country, but usually an alien may become a citizen after a period of time. In the United States, the period is five years; in Canada, three years. The Immigration and Naturalization Service is the main agency for alien affairs in the United States. This agency is also responsible for dealing with illegal aliens, who have entered the country without permission.

In Canada, the Ministry of Employment and Immigration enforces regulations covering aliens. Aliens living in Canada are usually called landed immigrants.

Aliens who commit illegal acts or do not comply with regulations can be excluded (barred from entering the country) or deported (required to leave the country). The U.S. Government has had the power to deport aliens since 1798, when Congress enacted the Alien Act. The Alien Enemies Act of the same year gave the government the right to restrict the activities of aliens from enemy countries during time of war.

The United States admits aliens in three categories—temporary visitors, permanent residents, and refugees.

Several million **temporary visitors** travel to the United States each year. They obtain permits called visas from the Department of State. The visas allow them to visit, go to school, or conduct business for a set period of time. Temporary visitors must leave when their visas expire. They are not allowed to take permanent jobs.

There are nearly 5,000,000 people who are registered as **permanent resident aliens** in the United States. They have many of the rights, duties, and privileges of citizens. They attend public schools, run businesses, work, and own property. They pay taxes and sometimes serve in the armed forces. But resident aliens are not allowed to vote, hold public office, or serve on juries. They are usually not allowed to hold public service jobs.

Resident aliens must report their addresses each January. Those over 14 years of age must be registered and fingerprinted. Aliens who are over 18 years of age must carry an identification card that is commonly known as a green card.

Refugees are people forced to leave their country—by war, persecution, or some other cause. Hundreds of thousands of refugees—including many from Cuba and from Vietnam—have settled in the United States.

Most of these refugees have been admitted under a special procedure called **parole**. A refugee on parole is not considered a permanent resident, and the parole may be revoked at any time. Many refugees have achieved the status of permanent resident aliens through special legislation. Others have been admitted as **conditional entrants**. Their status is like that of refugees on parole, but they automatically become eligible for permanent resident status after two years.

An **illegal alien** is a person who enters a country by crossing the border secretly, having false entry documents, or breaking the conditions of a visa. Because illegal aliens are not registered, it is impossible to know how many there are in the United States. Some estimates place the number at 12,000,000 or more.

In parts of the country—the Southwest and West, for example, where many Mexicans enter illegally to work—illegal aliens have created a complex problem. It is argued that the aliens take jobs away from citizens and place a burden on schools, medical facilities, and other social services, while paying no taxes to support these services. A solution to the problem seems difficult. But it is possible that the number of illegal aliens can be reduced if conditions in the home countries are improved and if people there are made aware of the problems and shortcomings of life in the new country.

ROBERT RIENOW
Author, *The Great Unwanteds: Illegal Aliens and the American Challenge*

See also CITIZENSHIP; IMMIGRATION AND EMIGRATION; NATURALIZATION; PASSPORTS AND VISAS.

ALLEN, ETHAN (1737?–1789)

Ethan Allen was a hero of the American Revolution and a leader in the fight for Vermont's independence and statehood.

Allen was born in the frontier settlement of Litchfield, Connecticut, on January 10, 1737 or 1738. When he was only 16 years old, his father died. As the oldest child, Ethan became the head of the family.

His mother chose well when she picked the biblical name Ethan (meaning "strong") for her first son. Ethan's strength and daring inspired legends that are still told. It is said that he could lift a large bag of salt with his teeth and throw it over his shoulder. His voice calling the settlers to a big wolf hunt would echo over the hills and spur men to brave deeds.

Ethan had the same urge to conquer the frontier that made his great-great-grandfather Samuel leave England in 1632 to settle in America. When Ethan heard that land was selling for a penny an acre in the New Hampshire grants (now Vermont), he left his wife and young son to explore the region.

▶ THE GREEN MOUNTAIN BOYS

Trouble began in the new territory when the colonial governors of New York and New Hampshire both claimed the land that lay between their two colonies. Ethan felt that the settlers from New Hampshire who wanted to build homes and farms in the wilderness had a better claim to the land. He became the leader of the Green Mountain Boys, a group of fighting settlers and farmers who were determined to protect their homes.

Meanwhile trouble was brewing between the American colonies and England. In 1775 the Revolutionary War began. News of battles with British soldiers at Lexington and Concord reached Allen at Bennington. Ethan and his Green Mountain Boys set off to capture the British fort at Ticonderoga, on Lake Champlain. They were joined by a force under the command of Benedict Arnold and succeeded in taking the fort.

The victory at Ticonderoga was not enough for Allen. He wanted to capture Montreal. He gathered a small force of men. By chance, Allen and his recruits met another troop, under the command of John Brown. Together, with about 300 men, they planned to attack Montreal. But when Allen arrived outside the city, Brown and his men failed to appear. Allen was left stranded with less than half the men. A British force of 500 marched on them. Allen's troops fought bravely, but they were outnumbered and finally defeated.

The British general considered Allen a prize rebel and sent him to England to be hanged. He was never put on trial but was kept a prisoner there for several months before being sent back to New York on parole.

In 1778 Allen was released from parole and returned home to Bennington, Vermont. There he found that many changes had taken place. Vermont had declared itself independent in 1777, but the Continental Congress refused to recognize its claims to statehood. Ethan and his brother Ira turned all their energies to keeping Vermont separate from New York and New Hampshire. At one point they even discussed the possibility of Vermont's joining Canada. The end of the Revolution put a stop to that idea, and in 1784 Allen retired from politics.

The courageous and colorful leader of the Green Mountain Boys died on February 12, 1789, at Burlington, Vermont. Two years later, on March 4, 1791, Vermont became the 14th state of the Union.

Reviewed by RICHARD B. MORRIS
Editor, *Encyclopedia of American History*

ALLERGY. See DISEASES.

ALLIGATORS. See CROCODILES AND ALLIGATORS.

ALLOYS

An alloy is a substance formed by combining a metal with other metals or non-metals. Brass is an alloy made with the metals copper and zinc. Steel is an alloy made with a metal—iron—and a non-metal—carbon. Alloys are usually made by melting the ingredients and mixing them together.

The special characteristics of a metal, such as its flexibility, hardness, strength, and resistance to corrosion, are called **properties.** Alloying makes it possible to create materials with just the right combination of properties for a particular use.

Almost every metallic substance used today is an alloy of some kind. But the idea of making alloys is not new. It was known by men in ancient times.

Thousands of years ago men discovered that they could use copper instead of stone to make their tools. Copper was easier to work with than stone and was fairly easy to obtain. Perhaps the only trouble with copper was that it was not hard enough for some uses. About 3500 B.C. it was found that if tin, another fairly soft metal, was combined with copper, a very hard material was produced. This material was the alloy called bronze.

The discovery of how bronze is made was probably accidental, but it turned out to be an important event. Bronze was a better material for many purposes than either of the two metals that composed it. The alloy was so widely used that this period of history became known as the Bronze Age.

Bronze is only one example of an alloy that is used because it does a certain job better than many pure metals. Airplanes must be built of material that is both light and strong. Aluminum is light enough, but it is not strong enough for this purpose. Steel is strong enough, but it is too heavy. But combining aluminum with copper, magnesium, and other metals yields an alloy that is light, yet strong enough to stand up to the stresses of flight. Similarly, adding nickel, vanadium, chromium, and other metals to steel produces a stronger metal. This saves weight by making it possible to reduce the thickness of parts.

Steel itself is one of the most versatile and useful metallic materials. In the United States alone about 100,000,000 tons of steel are produced each year for use in everything from skyscrapers to saucepans.

Alloying steel with other metals produces materials called **alloy steels,** which are suitable for a wide variety of purposes. Manganese alloy steels are used to make machines such as rock crushers and power shovels, which must withstand extremely hard use. Stainless steel, which contains chromium and sometimes nickel and manganese, is a hard, strong substance that resists heat and corrosion. Stainless steels are used for such things as jet engines, automobile trim, knives, forks, and spoons, and kitchen equipment.

▶ CLASSES OF ALLOYS

Alloys are divided into two main classes: ferrous and non-ferrous. The term **ferrous** (from the Latin word *ferrum,* meaning "iron") applies to alloys, such as steel, whose base metal is iron. Alloys that contain little or no iron, such as aluminum and copper alloys, are called **non-ferrous.**

There is an important difference between alloys and impure metals. Both are mixtures, but alloys are mixtures that have been deliberately combined in definite proportions. Impure metals are accidental mixtures that vary greatly in their make-up.

▶ ALLOY STRUCTURES

Why does an alloy have different properties from the metals that compose it? To understand the answer to this question, something must be known about how atoms line up to form the inner structure of metals.

When a metal is melted, the atoms of the metal move about freely. When the metal cools and becomes solid, the atoms form clusters of a certain shape, called **crystals.** There are three main types of crystal structure. Two of these crystal structures are shaped like cubes, with the atoms at various places on the cubes. The third type is a more complicated structure that has a six-sided, or hexagonal, shape.

These clusters of atoms, or crystals, also form larger groups called **grains.** These grains can be seen with the aid of a microscope. In a pure metal, such as copper, all the grains look alike.

Certain metals can mix together so closely when they are melted that the grains all look

Grain structure of pure copper (magnified 150 times). Darker areas are caused by uneven reflection of light.

Grain structure of copper-zinc alloy (magnified 150 times) shows two different types of crystals.

alike when the alloy becomes solid, just as they do in a pure metal. When two metals are so completely mixed, they are said to be in **solid solution.** One such solid solution is the alloy of copper and nickel called cupronickel. In this alloy copper is the base metal; that is, more copper than nickel is used in making the alloy. Cupronickel is stronger and harder than copper but less able to conduct heat or electricity. The addition of nickel to the copper has created new properties that neither copper nor nickel alone has.

These new properties are created by the difference in the sizes of the atoms of copper and the atoms of nickel. When the nickel atoms enter the crystal structure of the copper, they replace some copper atoms. Because the nickel atoms are of a different size, the crystals of copper are distorted, or warped out of their normal shape. Although the grains of the alloy appear to have the same shape as the grains of the base metal (copper), the smaller units, the crystals, have been changed. This change in the shape of the copper crystals is the reason the alloy has different properties from the copper and nickel of which it is made. Every metal has atoms of different size from those of all other metals. Thus, whenever a solid-solution alloy is formed, a distortion of the crystal structure of the base metal will always take place, and new properties will be created.

Some metals do not mix completely with each other. These metals are said to be **partially soluble** in each other. They form two or more different kinds of grains when the

alloy solidifies. The different kinds of grains are called **phases.** They are actually solid solutions containing different proportions of the two metals. Some kinds of brass, an alloy composed of copper and zinc, have this kind of structure.

There is a third type of constituent in some alloys. The metals combine to form an **intermetallic compound,** which has a crystal-and-grain structure quite different from either of the pure metals. In an aluminum-copper alloy, for instance, a small amount of copper goes into solid solution with the aluminum. The rest of the copper combines with aluminum atoms to form an intermetallic compound composed of two atoms of aluminum and one atom of copper. Thus, the aluminum-copper alloy is made up of three components: a large amount of aluminum, a small quantity of copper in solid solution, and tiny particles of the intermetallic compound.

Although intermetallic compounds are usually hard and brittle, their presence in an alloy in small amounts is very valuable. Such alloys combine the toughness of solid solutions with the hardness of intermetallic compounds.

We owe jet airplanes, television, and many other technical marvels to alloys. These metal mixtures made it possible to turn engineers' and scientists' ideas into reality.

JOHN A. RING
Union Carbide Corporation

See also BRONZE AND BRASS; IRON AND STEEL; METALS AND METALLURGY.

ALMANACS. See REFERENCE BOOKS.

ALPHABET

An alphabet is a list of letters arranged in a definite order and used in writing a language. We use the alphabet of the Romans of 2,000 years ago. The Romans based their letter names and forms upon those of the Etruscans, who got their alphabet from the early Greeks. The Greeks had borrowed from the Phoenician alphabet. But the Phoenicians had no help. They invented the idea of writing with an alphabet and established names and letter forms.

This invention was perfected over 30 centuries ago, probably at the seaport city of Gebal on the eastern shore of the Mediterranean Sea. Centuries later Gebal was called Byblos, meaning "city of paper"—that is, "city of books." The Lebanon Mountains rise steeply behind the narrow strip of coastal plain that was the land of ancient Phoenicia, where Gebal was located. Forests of fir, spruce, and cedar covered the mountains. With a great deal of timber nearby and with workmen skilled in the handling of wood, Gebal became the greatest boat-building port in the world of that time. Its sea captains and navigators were the ablest and the boldest.

Gebal needed a writing plan, but until the invention of the alphabetic way of writing, there was no plan suitable for Phoenician words. True, Egypt had a hieroglyphic type of writing consisting of about 600 picture symbols. It was designed for, and could be used with, Egyptian words only. Chaldea and the Babylon country had been using a cuneiform type of writing for 1,000 years or more. Designed for Chaldean words, it made use of about 300 picture symbols, made with a wedge-ended stylus in damp clay. Neither the hieroglyphic nor the cuneiform kind of writing could be applied very easily to Phoenician.

▶ CONSONANTS AND VOWELS

Word sounds are divided into consonants and vowels. The consonant sounds start with the tongue pressed tightly against the roof of the mouth, as in T and D, or the lips pressed together, as in P and B, or in some other position of teeth, tongue, and lips to make explosive, gruff, throaty, or hissing sounds.

Vowel sounds are made with the mouth open, the tongue not touching the roof of the mouth or the lips. We may think of vowels as singing sounds.

Phoenician words started with consonant sounds, ended with consonant sounds, and often had other consonant sounds in between. Vowel sounds were used but these were so unimportant that no letters were provided.

▶ THE PHOENICIAN ALPHABET IS FORMED

The Phoenician alphabet, then, had to stand for the consonant sounds that made up all Phoenician words. There were 22 of these sounds. For each sound the Phoenicians chose a sign that was actually a picture. The 22 pictures showed 22 different objects, all familiar—an ox, a house, a camel, and so on. An object was selected because the first sound in its name was one of the consonant sounds. In writing a word containing three consonants, for example, three pictures would be put down in a row.

We refer to these 22 pictures as **letters.** The names of the letters are the names of the objects. For easy handling in learning to write, the Phoenicians put the letters in a list that started with *'aleph.* (The ' represented a sound that we cannot pronounce and for which we have no letter.) The second letter was *beth.* The list, then, was called the *'aleph-beth,* or, as we would say, the Phoenician **alphabet.**

The pictures as letters were designed for writing on papyrus with a stubby brush dipped in thick black watercolor paint. The papyrus was prepared from the pithy center of the stalks of a Nile River plant, and the brush was made from the stalks of a river reed. Writing started at the right side of a papyrus sheet and moved toward the left. Short vertical lines separated words.

The Phoenicians' 22 letter pictures, and the names of the objects they stood for, passed to the Greeks, the Etruscans, the Romans, and us. Let us carefully examine the letter forms and names.

The letters will seem to be drawn backward. But it is ours that are backward; the

PHOENICIAN letter names: 'ALEPH, BETH, GIMEL, DALETH, HĔ, WAW, ZAYIN, KHETH, TETH, YODH, KAPH, LAMED, MEM, NUN, SAMEKH, 'AYIN, PE, TSADE, QOPH, ROSH, SHIN, TAW

CLASSICAL GREEK letter names: ALPHA, BETA, GAMMA, DELTA, EPSILON, ZETA, ETA, THETA, IOTA, KAPPA, LAMBDA, MU, NU, XI, OMICRON, PI, RHO, SIGMA, TAU, UPSILON, PHI, CHI, PSI, OMEGA

FINAL ROMAN Z — (placed last)

Greeks did the reversing when they began to write from left to right. We would not know the meanings of the Phoenician letters without some help. Look at each sketch. Beside the sketch is the Phoenician letter, and below it is the Phoenician word for the letter. The A, B, C, D, E, and H letters of today were, in the Phoenician originals, pictures of objects common to the homes and highways of Phoenicia: an ox, house, camel, tent door, comb for carding wool, and a barred gate.

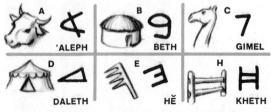

The letters we write as I, K, O, P, R, and S pictured body parts: a hand, palm, eye, mouth, face, and molar tooth. The Q pictured a monkey, with the curved line its tail.

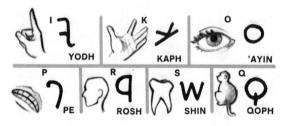

The letters we put down as L, M, N, T, Y, and Z were objects found along the seacoast or in seaside shops: an overseer's rod, waves tossing a boat, a fish head, an owner's mark on a package, a metal hook, and a simple balance used in weighing bundles.

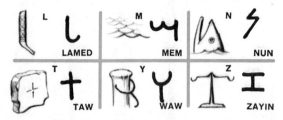

The remaining three letters of the Phoenician list found a place in both the Greek and Etruscan alphabets, but not in that of the Romans, so we have no letters like them. The pictures were those of a ball of yarn, a supporting pillar, and a fishing pole and line.

THE GREEK ALPHABET

In a few centuries the Phoenician letter plan spread to all peoples east of the Mediterranean having word sounds like those of the Phoenicians. In particular this meant the Hebrews, Moabites, and Syrians.

Several hundred years after the first use of the plan, the new way of writing with letters reached the Greeks. These people were Europeans, and their language was very different from the Phoenicians'. Greek vowels had a more singing tone; the lips-tongue-teeth sounds of the consonants were less important. And the vocabularies of the two peoples were as unlike as the people themselves.

The task of adjusting the Phoenician way of writing to Greek use was no easy matter. It demanded the thoughtful efforts of one familiar with both the Phoenician and the Greek ways of speaking. Greek legend has given credit for this to Cadmus, a Phoenician prince who reached Greek islands in search of a kidnaped sister. He stayed on, founded the city of Thebes, and married a Greek girl. After learning to speak some Greek, Cadmus explained to interested Greek friends how the 22 Phoenician letter symbols were used in writing. He explained that each symbol had a name, that it was only the first sound in the name that was important, and that words could be shown as sounds by putting the symbols in the right order.

To Cadmus, a Phoenician, all of the 22 letter names were easy to pronounce. But to the Greeks half the names were easy, some rather difficult, and some impossible. The Phoenician names are listed in alphabetical order, with the Greek names below.

'aleph	beth	gimel	daleth	hĕ		waw	zayin
*	**beta**	**gamma**	**delta**	*			**zeta**

kheth	teth	yodh		kaph	lamed	mem	nun
*	(theta)			**kappa**	**lambda**	**mu**	**nu**

samekh	'ayin	pe		tsade	qoph	rosh	shin	taw
(xi)	*	**pi**		(san)	(kōppa)	**rho**	(sigma)	**tau**

The names in bold type were easy for the Greeks to pronounce. The Greek names in parentheses indicate letter sounds of the Greeks that were not quite the same as those of the Phoenicians. The Phoenician names with stars beneath them had consonants the Greeks could not pronounce, so they made each name that of a vowel. For example, the marks at the beginning of 'aleph and 'ayin represented consonant sounds. The Greeks found them impossibly difficult. So they changed 'aleph to *alpha,* and 'ayin to ŏ-ĕ (or *omicron,* meaning "little o"). Pronouncing *hĕ* and *kheth* also gave the Greeks trouble, so *hĕ* became *ĕ* (or *epsilon,* meaning "merely e") and *kheth* became *eta.*

The remaining two letters, *yodh* and *waw,* became vowel sounds in the Greek way of pronouncing these words—with the mouth open. Their name for the first was *i-o-ta.* For the second, pronounced with puckered lips that did not come together, they got a sound about like ōō-ĕ. Their name for the letter was *upsilon,* or "merely ü."

That was the way the Greeks got an alphabet having six vowels. The vowels seem to be there almost by accident. And yet, strangely enough, how complete that alphabet turned out to be for the vowel and consonant sounds of the Greek language. The Western Greeks also had a letter that was to develop into our letter F. They called it *digamma.*

𐤟𐤟𐤟𐤟𐤟𐤟𐤟𐤟𐤟𐤟𐤟

ABϞΔEHIKOPϘ

WQ𐤥ϞϞϞΥIΦ𐤟M

ΣQ𐤥MϞΤΥIΦ𐤟M

▶ THE ROMAN ALPHABET

Ancient Rome was a fortress city that guarded the bridge across the swift Tiber River. The Romans' only neighbors were the rich and cultured Etruscans. The language of these people differed from that of the Phoenicians, Greeks, and Romans. The Etruscans wrote with the letter forms used by the Greeks, but from right to left, as the Phoenicians did. Their letter names were short, like the Romans' el, em, en, es, and tē.

The alphabet produced by the Romans from the Etruscan letters had one very peculiar feature. It had three letters for the single sound of soft K. Two of these (K and Q) came from the Phoenician alphabet sounds for soft K and emphatic K, letters called *kay* and *koo* by the Etruscans. The other letter for the soft K (C) got in by mistake. The Phoenician word *gimel* matches our word "camel." Pronounce the two words one after the other and notice how little difference there is. The Etruscans thought that the letter for the *gimel* sound was pronounced like a K. And the Romans, after them, also pronounced their third letter—C—like a K.

By the year 300 B.C. the Etruscan influence on the Roman alphabet was a thing of the past. The Romans were coming in contact with a Greek world where the writing was from left to the right, and great attention was paid to vowels. At that time the G went in for the *gimel* sound, and the X, Y, and Z were placed at the end of the alphabet. Also, two letters began doing double duty. The letter I stood for the consonant sound Y as well as the vowel sound I; the letter V served as consonant sound V and vowel sound U.

By the time of the Roman Empire, the Roman alphabet had taken its final form, but it contained only 23 letters. Today, with the addition of J, U, and W over the years, there are 26.

The 26 letters of the Roman alphabet have two forms today: capitals, or big letters, and small letters. At first there were only capitals. The Romans applied them to the inscriptions cut in stone, to papyrus writing, and later to a writing material called parchment. Prepared in a special way from the skins of sheep, parchment took ink marks well, and the writing remained unchanged for centuries.

For 1,000 years books were made by writing on parchment and then fastening sheets of parchment together. Most of the writing consisted of capitals, but there gradually developed the smaller, more rounded letter forms known as small letters. These small letters were easier to make than capitals, and they took up less space on expensive writing material. By the mid-15th century, printing presses in Italy had adopted the large and small Roman letters known to us today.

Keith Gordon Irwin
Author, *The Romance of Writing*

See also individual letters of the alphabet; Writing.

ALPS

The snow-crowned Alps are probably the most famous range of mountains in the western world. These Alpine ranges begin on the Mediterranean coasts of southern France and northwestern Italy. They lie in a rough half circle across parts of Switzerland, southern West Germany, Austria, Yugoslavia, and Albania. The best-known Alpine ranges are the Bernese Alps, in Switzerland; the Maritime Alps, in Italy and France; the Bavarian Alps, in Austria and West Germany; the Tyrol Alps, in Italy and Austria; and the Dolomites, in Italy.

Climate in the Alps depends chiefly on altitude. Temperatures are mild in the southern foothills and on the southern slopes of the mountains. Grapes and other fruits grow on the sides of the lower mountains. Hardwood trees grow until the mountains reach altitudes of 1,200 to 1,500 meters (4,000 to 5,000 feet). Only evergreens grow above this to the timberline, at about 2,100 meters (7,000 feet). Above the timberline are pastures where cattle, sheep, and goats graze in summer. Alpine flowers grow on the rocky crags and icy ledges of the timberline.

The snow line begins between 2,400 and 3,000 meters (8,000 and 10,000 feet). Snow and ice never melt above this altitude.

The moist westerly winds bring abundant rain and snow to the Alps. As the altitude increases, the temperature grows colder and snow piles up. In many places snow turns into ice that flows slowly down the mountain as frozen rivers, or glaciers. There are more than 1,200 glaciers in the Alps. The largest is the Aletsch Glacier, in the Bernese Alps.

Hundreds of peaks in the Alps rise to more than 3,000 meters (10,000 feet). The tallest —Mont Blanc, in France—rises to 4,810 meters (15,781 feet). Two very high peaks in the Swiss Alps—the Jungfrau and the Matterhorn—are famous for their unusual shapes.

Winding roads lead up to passes between towering Alpine peaks. There are about 50 of these passes. Some of them have been used for thousands of years by armies entering Italy. The lowest pass is the Brenner, at 1,371 meters (4,495 feet), which connects Italy and Austria. The highest pass is the Stelvio, at 2,757 meters (9,048 feet), across northern Italy. The most-traveled pass is the Mont Cenis, between Italy and France.

A tunnel extending 19.8 kilometers (12.3 miles) under the Simplon Pass is the longest railroad tunnel in the world. It links Italy and Switzerland. The 14-kilometer (8.7-mile) Arlberg highway tunnel in Austria was opened in 1978. The 16-kilometer (10-mile) St. Gotthard tunnel in Switzerland later surpassed the Arlberg tunnel as the longest highway tunnel in the world.

Reviewed by DANIEL JACOBSON
Michigan State University

A young shepherd tends his sheep on a high Alpine pasture in Switzerland. Flocks often graze within sight of glaciers.

Mont Blanc, the highest mountain in western Europe, looms above a small village. Tourists come here from all over the world to ski in winter and go mountain climbing in summer.

The majestic Matterhorn towers over an Alpine village.

The Jungfrau in the Swiss Alps is eternally snow-capped.

ALUMINUM

In the 19th century people already knew that aluminum was the most abundant metal in the earth's crust. They had even been able to extract the bluish-white metal from its ores. But the cost of refining it was still so high that Emperor Napoleon III of France still had his finest dinner spoons made of it in the 1860's. Metallurgists were in the position of having discovered a great treasure house of extremely useful metal without having found the key that would unlock it. When a way was found to refine the metal cheaply in 1886, aluminum became an important part of nearly every industry in the world.

Aluminum makes up between 7 and 8 per cent of the earth's crust. Although it is so abundant, its existence was not suspected for a long time. This is because it is never found in nature as a pure metal but is combined with other chemical elements in compounds that are very hard to break down.

Aluminum compounds are found in many minerals, and all clay contains aluminum. Many of the most beautiful precious stones are basically nothing but colored aluminum compounds. Rubies and sapphires, for example, are aluminum oxide with traces of other elements. Emeralds contain aluminum along with beryllium, chromium and silicon.

The most important ore of aluminum is bauxite, a type of clay. It generally contains from 40 to 60 per cent aluminum oxide.

The existence of aluminum was predicted in 1808 by the English scientist Sir Humphry Davy. However, he was unable to solve the problem of extracting the metal from its ore. In 1825 the Danish scientist H. C. Oersted produced the first aluminum metal the world had ever seen—but in an amount too small even to conduct experiments. The German scientist Friedrich Wöhler succeeded in extracting aluminum in powder form in 1845 and made the first discoveries about aluminum's properties.

Aluminum's career as a luxury item ended in 1886 with the simultaneous discoveries of Charles M. Hall in the United States and Paul Héroult in France. They had independently hit upon the same solution to the problem of converting aluminum ore into the metal aluminum cheaply enough for everyday use.

The Hall-Héroult process is basically the same one used in today's two-step process of aluminum refining. Bauxite ore is refined to produce aluminum oxide, a white powder, which is also called alumina. Alumina in turn must be further processed to produce aluminum. It was this second step that held back aluminum production for so many years.

Hall and Héroult found that alumina could be dissolved in molten cryolite, an icy-looking mineral found in Greenland, and then broken down by passing an electric current through the molten mixture. The current separates the alumina into aluminum and oxygen. The aluminum settles at the bottom of the cell and is drawn off periodically. More alumina is added from time to time to keep the process going. About 2 kilograms of alumina are needed to make 1 kilogram of aluminum metal.

Aluminum's many characteristics combine to make it suitable for many products. One of its most important characteristics is its light weight. Aluminum weighs two thirds less than such common metals as iron, copper, nickel, or zinc. Its lightness makes aluminum useful in the manufacture of building materials, bus and truck bodies, and automotive and airplane parts. About 90 per cent of the total weight of a typical four-engine aircraft is aluminum.

Aluminum also conducts electricity well. For this reason it has replaced copper for high-voltage electric transmission lines. Since it is lighter than copper, electric lines of aluminum need fewer supporting towers.

Because it is a good conductor of heat, aluminum makes good cooking utensils. If just one edge of an aluminum pan is heated,

---

FACTS ABOUT ALUMINUM

Chemical symbol: Al

Atomic weight: 26.9815

Specific gravity: 2.70 (a little over 2½ times as heavy as water).

Color: silvery-white with a bluish tinge.

Properties: soft, easily shaped, resists corrosion, non-magnetic, good conductor of heat and electricity, forms compounds that are hard to break down.

Occurrence: third most abundant element in the earth's crust (after oxygen and silicon); most abundant metal in earth's crust.

Chief ore: bauxite (named after town of Les Baux, in southern France, where it was first mined).

In England and certain other countries, aluminum is called "aluminium."

Many activities go on at once in a busy aluminum refinery. As melting pot at left is filled with raw material, man in right foreground casts molten aluminum into blocks. In rear, giant ladle is filled with molten metal. Finished blocks are trucked away.

the heat will spread evenly through the pan. With many other metals, "hot spots" that cause food to stick and burn may form.

Besides being a good conductor of heat, aluminum is also a good insulator. This is not as confusing as it seems. The metal's shiny surface reflects heat rays away.

Another important characteristic of aluminum is its resistance to corrosion. The protective coatings that iron and steel need, such as red lead or paint, are not necessary with aluminum.

Why doesn't aluminum rust? It would seem that aluminum's quickness to react with the oxygen in the air would make it subject to corrosion. But actually it is this very quickness to react with oxygen that protects aluminum against corrosion. When aluminum is exposed to the air, it immediately combines with some of the oxygen to form a thin, tough, colorless film that protects the metal against further chemical action and thus prevents rusting.

Aluminum also stands up well against most acids, but it is attacked by strong solutions of alkalies, such as lye and ammonia, and of salts, including common table salt. Salt solutions cause pitting and form a dull film on the metal. Aluminum boats that are used in salt water need a protective coating, usually of clear plastic. Aluminum cooking vessels do not usually show this pitting and dulling because in most homes they are shined with abrasive pads after use.

Although aluminum is naturally light and flexible, it is not especially strong for a metal. There are two ways to increase its strength. One is by cold-working (hammering or rolling the metal at room temperature). This compresses the metal and makes it harder. When very high strength is needed, the other method—alloying—must be used.

The metals most frequently alloyed with aluminum are copper, manganese, nickel, magnesium, zinc, iron, and silicon. Because of its higher strength, most of the aluminum used for structural parts in airplanes, automobiles, and buildings is in the form of alloys. Aluminum for machine parts and other industrial uses is also generally alloyed.

The aluminum industry has grown steadily as new uses for aluminum have developed. To help ensure a sufficient supply of aluminum in the coming years, efforts are being made to recycle, or re-use, aluminum products such as soft-drink cans. In addition to conserving ore supplies, recycling uses much less energy than does refining.

ROBERT E. ABBOTT
Senior Associate Editor
Product Engineering Magazine

The Amazon was once famous for rubber trade. Boats now carry household goods and machinery up the river and bring back jute, lumber, and other forest products.

When the heavy rains come, the river overflows its banks for miles. This is why the wooden huts of the river settlements are built on stilts.

AMAZON RIVER

The Amazon is South America's most important river. A Spaniard named Francisco de Orellana made the first explorations of the river in 1541. The Amazon carries more water than the Mississippi, the Yangtze, and the Nile together. In a single second the Amazon pours more than 60,000,000 gallons of water into the Atlantic Ocean. The muddy river stains the ocean brown for 200 miles. This tremendous flow is caused by heavy tropical rains and melting snow in the Andes mountains. The Amazon's huge basin extends for about 2,700,000 square miles.

The Amazon is almost 4,000 miles long. It begins in the snow-fed Andean lakes of Peru, 18,000 feet above sea level, and then flows eastward across the low plains of Brazil. On its journey the Amazon gathers additional water from hundreds of rivers. The Negro, Madeira, Purus, and Juruá are major branches. Each one is between 1,000 and 2,000 miles in length.

The Amazon is only 200 feet above sea level at the Peru-Brazil border. It flows slowly on its lengthy journey to the Atlantic. Sometimes the river is so wide that one cannot see the opposite shore. During the rainy season the flood waters spread for miles over the jungle lowland. It is no wonder that the Amazon is sometimes called the River Sea.

Where the river empties into the Atlantic Ocean a strange thing happens. Twice a day,

How did the Amazon River get its name?

The Amazon River was named by Francisco de Orellana. In 1542 Orellana was exploring the river from one of its tributaries all the way to the Atlantic Ocean. He and his group were attacked by a tribe of fierce women and barely managed to escape. Orellana thought they must be descendants of the legendary Amazons. So he named the broad river the Amazon.

According to an ancient Greek legend, the Amazons were a race of women warriors who lived in Asia Minor. They ruled their own country and had their own army. No men were permitted to stay in their land. When the Amazons had children, they kept only the girl babies. The Amazons were fierce fighters who battled the Greeks in the Trojan War. Supposedly, they were all wiped out in an attack on Athens, but their fame lives on.

when the tide rises, 12-foot tidal waves called "bores" rush upstream. The current of the river is reversed for as much as 400 miles.

Ocean-going ships can travel 1,700 miles up the Amazon from Belém, Brazil, at the river's mouth. Smaller steamers can reach Iquitos, in Peru, 2,300 miles inland. Ships pass through some of the most densely forested land in the world.

Reviewed by DANIEL JACOBSON
Montclair College

Manaus, Brazil, is a fully grown city with floating wharves. During the floods the water level may rise 33 feet.

Belém is the main port and largest city on the Amazon Delta. The kegs in the foreground, called *garrafôes*, are used to hold alcohol or kerosene.

A little boy, like any boy who lives near a river, plays on a raft. Rafts are used for transportation on some parts of the Amazon.

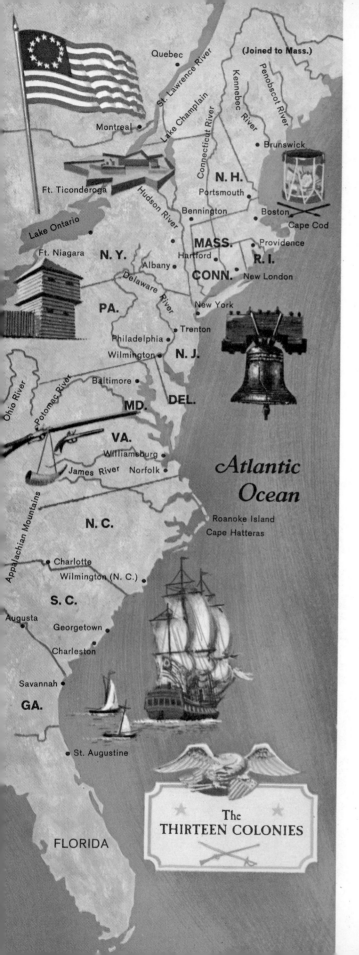

The THIRTEEN COLONIES

AMERICAN COLONIES

The winter of 1587 was past, and spring had come to England. The countryside was fresh and green with new leaves on the trees and flowers in bloom. Farmers were planting their fields. Newborn lambs, still unsteady on their long, knobby legs, frolicked in the pastures.

This year, however, one group of Englishmen had no time to enjoy the beauty of the spring. This group of men, women, and children were about to sail for America. Sir Walter Raleigh was sending them to build what he hoped would be the first successful English colony in the New World.

Sir Walter Raleigh

Sir Walter Raleigh was a born leader. Handsome, intelligent, and wealthy, he was afraid of nothing. It is not surprising that he was one of Queen Elizabeth's favorites. Raleigh hoped that some day England would become a mighty empire with many colonies across the seas.

In 1583 an expedition commanded by Raleigh's half brother, Sir Humphrey Gilbert, sailed to Newfoundland. Sir Humphrey had been looking for a place to start a colony. On the return voyage from Newfoundland, however, Gilbert's ship and all on board were lost at sea.

Raleigh asked the Queen for permission to carry on the work Sir Humphrey had started. The Queen gave him the right to build colonies in North America. In April, 1584, Raleigh sent an expedition to America to explore the coast and find the best location for a colony. Avoiding the cold, bleak shores of Newfoundland, Raleigh's expedition explored the coasts of what are now North Carolina and Virginia.

The Virginia Colony

The expedition returned to England with glowing reports of the New World. They said that America was a rich land. The soil was the best in the world. The trees were larger than any they had ever seen. Clusters of wild grapes hung from the vines, and herds of deer roamed the forests. The Indians were "gentle, loving, and faithful."

Raleigh was delighted with the good news.

The country was named Virginia to honor Queen Elizabeth, who was sometimes called the Virgin Queen.

Raleigh was now ready to start his colony. He chose Sir Richard Grenville and Ralph Lane to lead the expedition. With 108 men aboard their ships, Grenville and Lane sailed from England in April, 1585. They reached Roanoke Island, off what is now the North Carolina coast, in July. Grenville then returned to England with the ships, leaving Lane in charge of the settlement.

Roanoke. Up to this point Raleigh had been successful in one venture after another. Now he ran into a series of misfortunes that left him penniless and landed him in prison.

The first blow came in the summer of 1586. The settlers on Roanoke Island abandoned the settlement and returned to England.

The men admitted that they had spent most of their time exploring and looking for gold and jewels. They had killed an Indian chief and the Indians were no longer friendly. Then in the spring of 1586, an English ship captained by Sir Francis Drake had sailed into the harbor. Drake was on his way back to England after raiding Spanish islands in the Caribbean Sea. When he offered to take the settlers home, they quickly accepted.

In spite of this blow, Raleigh did not give up hope. He sold more of his property and borrowed from friends in order to raise money for another expedition. This time, however, he decided to send entire families to the New World. Raleigh's colonists sailed from England early in May, 1587, and reached Roanoke Island late in July.

Several weeks after they landed, the wife of Ananias Dare gave birth to a daughter. She and her husband named the baby Virginia in honor of her birthplace and her queen. Virginia Dare was the first English child born in what is now the United States.

From the day they landed, the colonists were in trouble. Some of the Indians were still friendly, but most had learned to fear and hate the English. The colonists had to be on guard day and night. There was no time to build houses and plant crops, as Raleigh had ordered them to do. Finally, driven to desperation, they asked John White, the leader of the colony, to return to England and bring back more men and supplies.

The "Lost Colony." White left Roanoke in August, 1587. When he reached home he learned that a huge Spanish fleet was preparing to sail for England. The Spaniards intended to land an army on English shores and conquer the country. The English needed all their ships to defend their coasts. No rescue ships could be spared.

The Spanish fleet (Spanish Armada) was defeated in 1588. White was at last able to get help. But 3 years had passed since he had left America. Late one night in the summer of 1590 his rescue ship reached Roanoke Island. Through the darkness the crew saw the light of a campfire burning on shore. White and some men rowed ashore. The ashes from the fire were still warm, but the beach was deserted. They fired their guns to let the settlers know that help had arrived. There was no answer. The houses and the fort were in ruins. Broken furniture and scraps of books and maps littered the ground. The colonists had vanished. The only clue was the word CROATOAN, which someone had carved on a doorpost. Croatoan was the name of a nearby island inhabited by friendly Indians. White wanted to search for the lost colony, but the captain of the ship insisted on returning to England before the fall and winter storms began. No one ever learned what had become of the colonists.

▶ **THE SETTLERS AND WHY THEY CAME**

In 1606 the east coast of North America was an almost unbroken wilderness. A handful of Spaniards lived in the small fort at St. Augustine, Florida. And some French people, who had first settled at St. Croix, New Brunswick, lived in Port Royal, Nova Scotia. From Florida to Canada, there was only an immense forest. Here and there along the shores of the rivers and lakes, the Indians had built their villages.

In all this vast and nearly empty wilderness, no European footprint marked the earth. No European voice echoed down the Indian trails through the forest. There was only the sound of the surf rolling upon the shore and the murmur of the wind through the trees. North America still belonged to the first Americans, the American Indians.

In 1607, however, great changes began to take place. Between 1607 and 1733 English-

The Pilgrims march through the snow to Sunday services.

men established 13 prosperous colonies along the east coast of North America. By 1750 nearly 2,000,000 men, women, and children were living in the 13 colonies. Raleigh's dream had come true. Between New France in the north and Spanish Florida in the south, the eastern coast of North America was indeed "an English nation." Many people came from many lands. During the first 150 years of colonial history, most of those who settled in America came from the British Isles. They came from England, Scotland, Ireland, and Wales. Many came from other countries in Europe, too. Still others came from Africa. Most of the Africans were transported to the New World as slaves.

From the very first days of settlement, the British colonies in America became "a melting pot." Here, in the immense wilderness of the New World, men, women, and children from many countries learned to live together. They built a new way of life.

America: Land of Opportunity

Why did they come? Why did they leave their homes and their friends in the Old World to come to a strange and distant land?

Opportunity was the magic word that drew people to America. It drew English nobles who dreamed of carving great new estates out of the wilderness. It drew carpenters, masons, bakers, tailors, and other skilled workmen who could not find work in England. Most of all, it drew the poor and the homeless from the farmlands and villages of Europe. It offered people a chance to live a better life than they could hope for in the Old World.

At the time Sir Walter Raleigh was trying to build his colony in Virginia most people in England were farmers. A few wealthy nobles owned most of the land. The owners of these large estates rented small areas of land to farmers. These tenant farmers lived in thatch-roofed huts, just as their fathers and grandfathers had before them.

But England was changing. Many of the rich landowners could make more money by raising sheep than they could by renting their land to tenant farmers. The landowners turned the plowed fields of the small farms into pastures. As a result, the tenant farmers and their families lost their houses and their way of making a living.

Some of the homeless farmers found work in the towns and cities. But there were not enough jobs for all of them. Many homeless people wandered the roads of England looking for work. For these people America was indeed a land of hope in which there would be work for everyone.

America: Promise of Religious Freedom

Many settlers came to the English colonies in search of religious freedom. They wanted the right to worship God in their own way in their own churches.

In Europe at this time each nation had an official state church. In most European countries the Roman Catholic Church was the official, or established, church. In England the Church of England, or Anglican Church, was the official church. The government collected taxes to support the state church. Every citizen had to pay these taxes, even if he did not want to worship in that way. The government also expected every citizen to attend the state church. Those who refused were sometimes fined or sent to prison.

Many people were unhappy with this situation. For example, Roman Catholics in England did not want to attend the Anglican Church. Methodists, Baptists, Presbyterians, Quakers, and other religious groups in England wanted to attend their own churches. Many discontented religious groups started their own colonies in America. These colonies attracted people from all over Europe as well as from England.

Each man and each woman who crossed the sea had his own reason for beginning life again in the New World. Some came to improve their fortunes. Others came in search of land and jobs. Still others came in search of freedom. But for all of them America was the land of opportunity.

▶ VIRGINIA: THE FIRST SUCCESSFUL COLONY

Englishmen built their first successful colony in Virginia, in the same general area where Sir Walter Raleigh had earlier tried and failed.

In 1606 King James gave two business companies the right to settle and trade along the Atlantic coast. To the London Company he gave the right to settle all the land from what is now Cape Fear, North Carolina, northward to Long Island. To the Plymouth Company he gave the right to settle all the land from what is now Maine southward to Chesapeake Bay.

These two grants overlapped. Both companies had the right to build and trade in the area between what are now the states of Virginia and New York. In order to prevent trouble, the King ruled that neither company could build a settlement within 160 kilometers (100 miles) of the other's settlement.

Shortly after the King made his grants, the directors of the London Company met to make their plans. They decided to build their first settlement in the south, where the climate was warm. They planned to sell shares of stock to anyone who was willing to buy them. As for the settlers, in 1606 many Englishmen were more than willing to risk their lives with the hope of improving their fortunes.

By December the directors had completed their plans. Three ships—the *Goodspeed,* the *Sarah Constant,* and the *Discovery*—swung at anchor in the Thames River, ready for a long voyage. New sails had been neatly folded and stored in lockers. The ropes and rigging had been tarred to protect them from the weather. Casks of fresh water and barrels of food had been packed in the holds. The colonists, 120 men in all, had said good-by to their friends in London and were waiting to sail.

Finally the moment arrived. Captain Christopher Newport gave the order to raise the anchors. One by one the vessels swung into

John Smith is said to have been saved from death by Pocahontas, daughter of an Indian chief.

the ebbing tide and began to float down the Thames toward the sea.

For 4 months the three ships moved slowly across the Atlantic Ocean. Day after day and week after week the passengers and crews saw only the immense dome of sky above them and the immense expanse of sea on every side. Sixteen men died during the long voyage. At last, late in the month of April, the vessels sailed between two capes of land into the mouth of Chesapeake Bay.

Captain Newport named the capes Cape Henry and Cape Charles, in honor of King James's two sons. Then, after crossing the bay, he sailed up a river that he named the James, in honor of the King himself.

The directors of the London Company had given the colonists strict orders to build their settlement well inland. There the settlers would be safe from Spanish warships that might try to destroy the colony. Captain Newport sailed about 50 kilometers (30 miles) up the river to a marshy island. He and the other leaders decided to build their settlement on the island. They named the future colony Jamestown.

It was springtime, and the weather was mild. The colony might have prospered, but in their ignorance the colonists made many mistakes. These mistakes cost them dearly. By the end of the year only one third of the men who had sailed from London were still alive. Some had been killed by Indians. Most had died from hunger and disease.

The first serious mistake was the poor location of the colony. To be sure, the island could be defended easily against attack by Indians. But the settlers could not defend themselves against the mosquitoes. Day and night clouds of insects carrying deadly malaria swarmed out of the surrounding marshes.

The settlers made other, equally bad mistakes. Instead of digging a well to get pure water, they drank from the river and swamps. Instead of planting gardens and raising food for the coming winter, they explored the surrounding country in search of gold and jewels. As a result, when winter came those who were still alive were poorly sheltered and had little food to eat.

The settlers were not entirely to blame for their troubles. The directors of the company in London were also to blame. They should have sent skilled workmen to build the colony. Instead they sent men who had never held a saw or an ax or a hoe in their hands before. Even when they tried, these men did not know how to build houses and plant gardens. And many did not try.

The directors made another mistake when they ordered that all supplies must go into a common storehouse. All of the men shared equally whether they worked or not. This discouraged those who were willing to work hard. Why should they work, they asked, when other men were roaming the forest in search of gold or resting in the shade of a tree?

If it had not been for John Smith, every one of the first settlers might have died. When the situation became desperate, Smith made himself the leader of the colony. He was a hard ruler. He took charge of the lazy men and made them work whether they wanted to or not. Every morning he lined them up in front of the little fort. Then, in military fashion, to the beat of a drum, he marched them to their jobs. He made them dig a well, build shelters, and plant gardens. The men grumbled, but John Smith's rule was no work, no food, and so the men worked. In the meantime Smith himself traveled to nearby Indian villages, where he traded glass beads and iron knives and kettles for corn, meat, and fish.

During the winter and spring of 1608, ships from England brought new settlers and more supplies. Under John Smith's leadership, conditions improved. But after he returned to England, in the autumn of 1609, the situation became more desperate than ever. The winter of 1609–10 was the darkest period in Jamestown's history. So many died during that terrible winter that the survivors called it the starving time.

In the spring of 1610 the survivors decided to abandon the colony. Just then, however, ships from England brought new settlers and fresh supplies of food, clothing, and tools. Up to this point the colony of Jamestown had been a bitter disappointment to the directors and stockholders of the London Company. Instead of making a profit on their investment, they had lost a great deal of money. Fortunately, during these years the directors learned several important lessons.

For one thing, they realized that men worked harder when they had land of their own to farm. As a result, the London Company made each settler responsible for a particular area of land. After this the men no longer had to take everything they produced to the common storehouse. They turned part of it over to the company and kept the rest for themselves.

The directors also realized that married men made the best settlers. In 1621, therefore, the company sent the first shipload of women to America. The women soon married and began to raise families. They made homes out of the bare cabins, planted flowers in the gardens, and helped their husbands in the fields. The colony that began as a business undertaking was transformed into a community of families.

In 1619 the directors of the London Company made another very important decision. They gave the settlers a share in their own government. By then more than 1,000 settlers were living in Virginia. Their settlements stretched along the James River for about 30 kilometers (20 miles). In each settlement the men were allowed to elect two of their number to represent them in the government. These representatives traveled to Jamestown to meet with the colonial governor and help to make the laws. In this way representative government had its beginnings in America in the colony of Virginia.

Virginia Begins to Prosper

Both the London Company and the settlers in Virginia were learning the lesson John Smith had once tried to teach them. From the beginning Smith believed that the true wealth of Virginia lay in its forests and fertile soil. While he was still in Jamestown he warned the directors, "There is nothing to be gained here except by hard work." John Smith was right.

Tobacco was the settlers first "money crop"; it transformed the struggling settlements into a prosperous colony. American Indians had been smoking long before the first Europeans arrived in the New World. When tobacco was introduced to the Old World, many Europeans at first objected. King James of England warned that smoking was "hateful, harmful to the brain, and dangerous to the lungs." But each year Englishmen bought more tobacco. As the demand for tobacco increased, the price climbed higher and higher.

One of the early Jamestown settlers, John Rolfe, decided to try growing tobacco. He planted the first seeds in 1612 and discovered that this valuable plant grew well in the soil and the mild, moist climate of Virginia. Other settlers quickly followed his example. Within a few years Englishmen began to call Virginia their tobacco colony.

As the years passed, King James became dissatisfied with the way the London Company was managing Virginia. Finally, in 1624, he took Virginia away from the company and made it a royal colony.

▶ NEW ENGLAND

In 1607, only a few weeks after the first settlers landed at Jamestown, another band of Englishmen arrived off the coast of what is now Maine. They had been sent by the Plymouth Company to start a colony. They built a fort and a few huts near the mouth of the Sagadahoc River, later called the Kennebec. But they were no better prepared to build a settlement in the wilderness than the men who first landed at Jamestown. To make matters worse, the winter was bitterly cold. Many of the hungry, half-frozen men died. The survivors returned to England.

The Pilgrims

Meanwhile, a small group of Englishmen who lived in the farming village of Scrooby were having their own troubles. These were Separatists, who wanted to separate from the Church of England. We know them as the Pilgrims because they traveled from place to place seeking a place to worship God in their own way.

Their troubles began when the English Government adopted a law compelling all Englishmen to attend the Church of England. The Pilgrims refused to obey this law. They gathered secretly in one another's homes to worship in their own way. Those who were caught were fined and thrown into jail. In 1608 they fled from England to Holland.

The Pilgrims lived for a year in Amsterdam and then moved to the smaller city of Leyden. In Holland they were allowed to worship as they chose. The Dutch, a tolerant people, gave shelter to religious and political refugees from many nations.

But the Pilgrims were not completely happy in the Netherlands. Most of them had been farmers in England. They found it hard to earn a living at other trades. It disturbed them to see their children growing up as Dutchmen instead of as Englishmen. So the Pilgrims decided to move again, this time to America.

The Voyage to the New World. The Pilgrims could not afford to hire ships and to buy supplies for their colony. Fortunately, a company of English businessmen was looking for colonists. The company was willing to finance the venture. In return the Pilgrims agreed to work for the company for a period of 7 years. During this period all the profits from trade with the Indians and from fishing, lumbering, and farming were to belong to the company. It was a hard bargain, but the best the Pilgrims could make.

The Pilgrims left Holland and sailed first to the English seaport of Southampton. There they joined another group of Pilgrims. On August 15, 1620, they sailed for America on two vessels, the *Speedwell* and the *Mayflower*. But the smaller of the two ships, the *Speedwell,* sprang a leak, and both ships turned into the port of Dartmouth. As soon as repairs had been made the Pilgrims sailed again. The *Speedwell* still leaked, however, and the vessels turned back a second time, this time to the port of Plymouth. There the Pilgrims decided to abandon the *Speedwell*. Leaving 20 of the passengers behind, the remaining travelers—101 in all—crowded on board the *Mayflower*.

On September 16 the *Mayflower* left Plymouth and headed west into the open sea. In one terrible storm a main beam of the ship split wide open. The vessel seemed doomed. But the Pilgrims and the crew managed to repair the damage, and the *Mayflower* continued on its way.

At last, on November 19, after more than 2 months at sea, the Pilgrims caught their first glimpse of land. In the distance they saw the long, sandy peninsula of Cape Cod. They had intended to settle much farther south, but winter was close at hand. They decided to land and begin their colony as soon as possible.

The next day the *Mayflower* rounded the tip of the cape and anchored in what is now the harbor of Provincetown. There, before they landed, the Pilgrims made a solemn promise to each other. One by one the men stepped forward in the ship's tiny cabin and signed an agreement known as the Mayflower Compact. They pledged each other to obey all the laws that they themselves would adopt. With this agreement the Pilgrims took a long step along the road to self-government and democracy.

Plymouth Colony

The next day was Sunday, and the Pilgrims spent the time aboard ship in prayer and thanksgiving. But early on Monday they landed. While some of the men stood on guard with loaded muskets the women washed clothes and the children played on the beach.

The *Mayflower* remained in Provincetown harbor for several weeks. During this period Captain Miles Standish and a number of the men explored the coast. Finally they chose Plymouth as the place to build their colony. Captain John Smith had visited the site of Plymouth in 1614 and had given it the name it bears to this day. It was an ideal location, with a good harbor, brooks of clear water, and fields cleared by the Indians.

Late in December the *Mayflower* crossed Massachusetts Bay and anchored in Plymouth Harbor. On December 25 the men began work on the first building, a "common house." During the following weeks the first rough cabins began to take shape. But the Pilgrims suffered from the bitter cold and sickness. At one time only seven people were able to work. Before spring arrived only half of those who sailed in the *Mayflower* were still alive. But not one of the survivors returned to England when the *Mayflower* sailed for England in April.

All through that cruel winter the Pilgrims had lived in constant fear of the Indians. Guards stood on watch day and night. The little graveyard on the hill grew larger and larger. But only the Pilgrims knew it was there, for they had carefully covered the scarred earth with leaves and grass. They did not want the Indians to learn how many of their number had died and how few were left.

The Pilgrims land at Plymouth. The *Mayflower* is anchored in the harbor.

Toward the end of winter, however, the settlers learned that the Indians living around Plymouth were friendly. They taught the Englishmen how to make the best use of the forest, sea, and soil. They showed them how to hunt game and trap fish. They told them what berries and nuts were good to eat. They gave them seeds of pumpkins, squash, beans, and corn, and taught them how to plant and cultivate the crops.

With the Indians helping them, the Pilgrims began to prosper. They caught and dried fish. They cut down trees and sawed the logs into planks. They traded with the Indians and collected bundles of furs. All these were carefully stored until they could be sent to the company in England. When autumn came, seven houses and a church faced the street that led to the water. Three other buildings, all storehouses, were filled with the harvest from the fields and with fish, furs, and lumber.

By November, 1621, the Pilgrims had been in the New World an entire year. A ship from England had just landed 30 new settlers and fresh supplies. The storehouses were filled to overflowing. William Bradford, the governor, decided to set aside several days for recreation and giving thanks to God. And so, with nearly 100 Indians for company, the Pilgrims held the first Thanksgiving celebration in America.

After 1621 other ships brought more men, women, and children to the Plymouth Colony. Plymouth itself grew larger. New villages sprang up nearby. There on the shores of Massachusetts Bay the Pilgrims found the religious freedom and the new way of life they had been seeking for themselves and their children.

Massachusetts Bay Colony

The Pilgrims led the way. The Puritans soon followed. The Puritans, like the Pilgrims, were dissatisfied with the Church of England. Unlike the Pilgrims, however, they were willing to remain members of the church. But they wished to simplify and purify the church service. This is why they were called Puritans. Finally they decided to move to the New World. They did not wish to go to Virginia, because there the Church of England had already been established as the official church. They decided, therefore, to follow the Pilgrims to New England.

In 1629 the Puritan leaders secured a charter from the King of England. This charter gave them a grant of land in New England and the right to build a colony. The leaders of the Massachusetts Bay Company, as it was called, then began to make plans to settle in America.

In 1628, even before the King gave a charter to the company, a number of Puritans had moved to New England. About 40 settlers, led by John Endecott, had started the village of Naumkeag, later called Salem, on the northeast coast of Massachusetts.

The first large group of Puritans sailed for the New World in the spring of 1630. They were led by John Winthrop, their first governor. There were nearly 1,000 men, women, and children aboard the fleet of ships that carried them on their great venture.

Many of the Puritans were well educated. Many were wealthy. They brought with them to the New World everything they needed to start a successful colony. They brought large supplies of food and equipment—plows and other tools, seeds, cattle, horses, and oxen. They brought furnishings for the homes they planned to build.

During the next few years thousands of other Puritans arrived in America. By 1640

Roger Williams talks with his friends the Narragansett Indians. He was always welcome in their villages.

more than 20,000 settlers were living in the growing towns of Boston, Charlestown, Newtown (Newton), and other settlements.

Representative Government and Town Meetings. During the first few years, John Winthrop and other Puritan leaders tried to keep the control of the colony in their own hands. They refused to allow people of other religions to settle in the colony. They punished Puritans who did not agree with them, sometimes whipping them in public, sometimes driving them out of the colony. They permitted only a small, select group of settlers to vote and to hold public office.

Many settlers objected to this strict rule. They demanded the right to share in the government. Finally, as the protests increased, the leaders agreed to meet these demands. They allowed all Puritan men to vote. They gave each town the right to send representatives to the legislature of the colony. And they gave each town the right to govern itself through town meetings. At these town meetings the citizens assembled and reached decisions by a majority vote. So in Massachusetts Bay Colony, as earlier in Virginia, the settlers began to develop a democratic form of government.

Rhode Island

Massachusetts Bay Colony was only a year old when, in 1631, a young man named Roger Williams arrived in New England. He began to trade with the Indians around Narragansett Bay and soon learned their language. Because he was always fair in his dealings with them, the Narragansetts became his firm friends.

On Sundays Roger Williams preached in a church in Salem. From the beginning he was in trouble with the Puritan leaders. He taught that the settlers had no right to the land unless they bought it from the Indians. He made the Puritan leaders even angrier when he insisted that they had no right to compel the colonists to attend the Puritan church. He argued that every individual had the right to worship in his own way and to say what he believed to be true. The Puritan leaders repeatedly warned Roger Williams that he must stop teaching these beliefs. When he refused to be silent, the Puritans decided to send him back to England.

On a cold, wintry night a friend knocked on the door of Roger Williams' home. He warned Williams that officers were on the way to arrest him. Williams hastily gathered a few belongings and fled into the forest. He made his way through the snow-covered wilderness to his friends, the Narragansett Indians, and lived with them during the rest of the winter.

In the spring Roger Williams bought land from the Indians. With a group of friends from Massachusetts he started the settlement of Providence on the shores of Narragansett Bay. Other exiles from Massachusetts built other villages around the bay. In 1644 the King of England gave Roger Williams a charter for the colony of Rhode Island.

Rhode Island became a model of freedom. Every man had the right to vote and to hold public office. Every individual could worship as he pleased. Every person was free to say what he believed without fear of being arrested.

Connecticut

In 1636, the same year that Roger Williams started Rhode Island, another group of people from the Massachusetts Bay Colony settled on the banks of the Connecticut River. This group of about 100 men, women, and children had heard of the rich soil in the Connecticut Valley. Led by Thomas Hooker, the pastor of their church, they traveled westward along Indian trails through the forest. On the banks of the Connecticut River they built a village called Hartford.

Other pioneers soon started settlements nearby. In 1662, after 15 towns had been settled, the English king gave the new colony a charter. This charter gave the Connecticut colonists the right to govern themselves.

Maine and New Hampshire

As early as 1622 the King gave Sir Ferdinando Gorges and John Mason the right to settle the vast wilderness area that in time became the states of Maine and New Hampshire. Seven years later the two men divided the land. Gorges took the northern, or Maine, section. Mason took the New Hampshire area.

During the 1630's pioneers from Massachusetts Bay Colony moved northward and started the towns of Portsmouth, Exeter, and Hampton, in New Hampshire. Other pioneers built farms and villages in the New Hampshire hills and valleys. Like the settlers of Rhode Island, many of these people were escaping from religious persecution. It was not until 1679, however, that New Hampshire became a separate colony.

During these same years fishermen, traders, and pioneers from Massachusetts started a number of villages and towns in Maine, mostly along the coast. But Massachusetts claimed the entire area, and Maine never became a separate colony.

▶ THE MIDDLE COLONIES

Settlers from the Netherlands and from Sweden, not from England, first built settlements in the area that later became the middle colonies—New York, New Jersey, Pennsylvania, and Delaware.

New Netherland

In 1609, when Jamestown was only 2 years old, a Dutch ship called the *Half Moon* sailed from the Netherlands. Henry Hudson, the captain of the ship, was an Englishman. He had been hired by a company of Dutch businessmen, the Dutch East India Company, to explore the Atlantic coast of the New World. The owners of the company hoped that Hudson would find a passage through America that would give them a shorter trade route to the East Indies.

Henry Hudson failed to find the passage. But he did discover two rivers, the Delaware and the river that bears his name, the Hudson. He also discovered that the land around these rivers was more fertile than any he had seen in Europe. Even more important, the Indians were friendly and eager to trade their furs for European goods.

The Dutch claimed all the territory Hudson had explored and called it New Netherland. Dutch businessmen immediately organized a new trading company, the Dutch West India Company. Since the King of England had granted the same land to a company of London businessmen, there was certain to be trouble in the future. But at the time the land belonged to the Indians, and no European settlements had been started.

During the next few years, traders sent out by the Dutch West India Company built forts

Peter Stuyvesant, the stern, peg-legged governor of New Netherland (*left*), turns over control of the colony to the British commander (*right*) in a ceremony at New Amsterdam.

and trading posts along the Delaware, Hudson, and Connecticut rivers. They built their largest fort and trading post on an island near the mouth of the Hudson. The Indians called the island *Manahatta,* which meant "the heavenly land." The Dutch called the fort and the land around it New Amsterdam. In 1626 Peter Minuit, the governor of the colony, bought all of this area from the Indians with knives, beads, colored cloth, and food, worth about $24 in all.

The Dutch West India Company was eager to strengthen the colony of New Netherland. It offered huge areas of land along the Hudson River to any member of the company who would settle at least 50 tenants on his land at his own expense. The patroons, as the wealthy landowners were called, soon built a number of large estates along the banks of the Hudson River. But most Dutchmen were not willing to give up the freedom they had in the Netherlands to work as tenants for wealthy landowners in America. As a result, New Netherland grew only slowly.

New Sweden

The Swedes as well as the Dutch were interested in building trading posts in the New World. In 1638 two Swedish ships sailed up the Delaware River. On the site of present-day Wilmington, the men landed and started a settlement called Fort Christina, in honor of the Queen of Sweden. They gave the name New Sweden to this and several other forts and trading posts they later built along the Delaware River.

New Sweden lasted only a few years. Dutch traders resented the competition from the Swedes. In 1655 Dutch troops seized the Swedish settlements.

England Conquers New Netherland

In the meantime, English settlers in the New World were becoming more and more concerned about the growth of New Netherland. The English insisted that the Dutch had no right to be there and that the land belonged to England.

In 1664 a powerful fleet of English warships sailed into the harbor of New Amsterdam. The commander of the fleet ordered the Dutch to surrender. The Dutch looked at the warships and at their own weak defenses. They realized that it would be hopeless to fight. Sadly the Dutch governor, Peter Stuyvesant, hauled down the Dutch flag, which for

50 years had flown over New Netherland. So, without a shot being fired, the colony passed into the hands of the English.

New York and New Jersey

The King of England gave all of what had once been New Netherland to his brother James, the Duke of York. The new colony was named New York in his honor. The old Dutch city of New Amsterdam was renamed New York City. The Duke of York then made a gift of some of the land to two of his friends, Lord John Berkeley and Sir George Carteret. Carteret had once been governor of the island of Jersey in the English Channel. In honor of this English island, he named the colony New Jersey.

New York City had a splendid harbor and a central location. It grew rapidly and soon became one of the largest English seaports in America. New Jersey grew as settlers moved in from New England and from the Old World.

William Penn Founds Pennsylvania

William Penn, who started the colony of Pennsylvania, was the son of a wealthy admiral in the English Navy. He devoted his life to helping others less fortunate than himself and to defending the cause of religious freedom.

Penn was still a young man when he left the Church of England. He believed that everyone had the right to worship in his own way. His father was shocked at his son's behavior. He was even more shocked when, a few years later, the young man joined the Society of Friends, or Quakers. The Quakers believed that in the eyes of God all men were equal. They wore plain dress and refused to take off their hats even in the presence of the King.

Because he was a Quaker, Penn was jailed several times. On one occasion the officials told him that they would keep him in prison for the rest of his life unless he abandoned his Quaker beliefs. Penn refused. "My prison

William Penn (*center*) trades food and tools and other valuable supplies with an Indian chief (*right*) in return for a tract of his tribe's land.

shall be my grave before I will budge one jot," he said.

When his father died William Penn became a rich man. He decided to build a colony where the Quakers could worship as they pleased. He asked the King, Charles II, for a grant of land in America. The King had owed Penn's father a large sum of money, and Penn offered to cancel the debt and take the land instead. This was an easy way for King Charles to pay off his debt. It was also an easy way for him to get the troublesome Quakers out of England.

In 1681 the King gave Penn a large grant of land that stretched westward from the Delaware River. The King himself named the land Penn's Woods, or Pennsylvania, in honor of William Penn's father. Penn was disappointed that his colony did not have a coastline. In 1682 the King's brother, the Duke of York, solved this problem by giving Penn another grant of land, on Delaware Bay, south of Pennsylvania. This land, at first called the lower counties, in time came to be known as Delaware.

From the beginning Penn invited people from many different countries to settle in his colony. He wanted honest and hard-working people. He gave them land, as much as 200 hectares (500 acres) a family. He promised them that in Pennsylvania they could worship in their own way and share in the government.

The first group of settlers started Philadelphia, The City of Brotherly Love, on the banks of the Delaware River. Others followed by the hundreds and then by the thousands. Many who came were Quakers, but there were also large numbers of other Protestant groups as well as Catholics and Jews. They came from England, Scotland, Wales, and Ireland. They came from France, Holland, Germany, Switzerland, and other European countries.

One of the largest groups was made up of German and Swiss farmers from the Rhine Valley. After they arrived in Pennsylvania, the colonists from the Rhineland continued to speak German, or *Deutsch,* as they called it. According to one story, their English-speaking neighbors misunderstood them and thought they said "Dutch." So it was that the German-speaking settlers in Pennsylvania came to be known as the Pennsylvania Dutch.

William Penn kept his promises, not only to the colonists but to the Indians as well. He had promised the Indians that he would buy land from them and not take it by force. As a result, for many years the colonists lived at peace with their Indian friends and the colony prospered.

▶ **THE SOUTHERN COLONIES**

While New England and the Middle Colonies were growing, other Englishmen started other colonies in the warmer, milder regions to the south. One of these was George Calvert, whose title was Lord Baltimore.

Lord Baltimore Founds Maryland

George Calvert was a good friend of the English king, Charles I. Calvert was a Roman Catholic. He wanted to build a colony in which all Christians, including Catholics, could worship in their own way. The King gave him a large land grant just north of Virginia.

George Calvert died before he could send out his first group of settlers. But his son, Cecilius, the second Lord Baltimore, carried on the work his father had started. He named the colony Maryland in honor of Henrietta Maria, the wife of King Charles I.

The first group of about 200 settlers, including Catholics and Protestants, arrived in America in 1634. Their leader was Leonard Calvert, Cecilius Calvert's younger brother. They landed near the mouth of the Potomac River and called the settlement St. Mary's.

The Calverts had learned from the earlier experience of the settlers in Jamestown. As a result, Maryland, with Leonard Calvert as its first governor, prospered from the beginning. The settlers bought land from the Indians. They cleared the land and built large farms, called plantations, along the banks of the Potomac and other rivers. As in Virginia, tobacco became the most important cash crop.

In 1649 Lord Baltimore urged the Maryland legislature to adopt a law that came to be known as the Toleration Act. This act guaranteed religious freedom to all Christians who settled in Maryland.

North and South Carolina

In the meantime, restless pioneers from Virginia had been moving into the wild, un-

Members of Virginia's House of Burgesses arrive in Williamsburg for a meeting.

settled country to the south of their colony. They built log cabins and cleared a little land. They lived by hunting, fishing, and raising crops in the forest clearings.

The early settlers had moved into country where there was no government. Some of them lived wild, lawless lives. The rivers and creeks came to be favorite hiding places for pirates.

But most of the settlers were hard-working men and women. Some of them planted small patches of tobacco, which they sold as a cash crop. Others earned a living by selling forest products to shipbuilders in England. They sold lumber and tall, straight pine trees for shipmasts. They sold resin and turpentine, which they got from the sap of the pines.

In 1663 the King of England renamed this region Carolina. He gave it to eight of his friends, all wealthy noblemen. The new owners advertised for settlers, offering land on easy terms to all who came to the colony.

The southern area of Carolina at first attracted most of the new settlers. They built a seaport, which they named Charles Town (later shortened to Charleston). Charleston soon became the most prosperous of all the southern seaports. Settlers from many different countries and of many different religious beliefs moved to the city and into the surrounding countryside.

Many of the wealthy settlers started large rice plantations on the rich swampland along the coast. Before long they began to bring in slaves to work on the plantations. By this time the owners of tobacco plantations in Maryland, Virginia, and the northern part of Carolina were also using slave labor. So in the early years of colonization slavery became firmly established in the southern colonies.

Although Carolina became a thriving colony, the proprietors had difficulty governing it from overseas. Finally they returned it to the King, who divided it into two royal colonies. In 1721 he created South Carolina, and 8 years later, in 1729, he created North Carolina.

Georgia, Last of the 13 Colonies

Three years after North Carolina became a separate royal colony, James Oglethorpe started the last of the 13 colonies along the Atlantic coast. Oglethorpe was a wealthy

James Oglethorpe, accompanied by a surveyor, starts to block out the tracts of land he will give to the settlers of his Savannah colony.

Why were forests important in the American colonies?

Forests were valuable resources in the American colonies. Many things needed by the colonists were made of wood—houses, kitchen utensils, furniture, wagons, sleds, canoes, and tools. Wood was needed to make the charcoal that provided the hot fire for the blacksmith's forge. The bark of oak trees was used for tanning leather. Cedar was used for shingles. Tall spruce trees furnished the masts for sailing vessels. And timber was used to build ships for fishing, and transporting goods.

Vast amounts of wood were needed for heating as well as cooking. Torches from pitch pine (called candlewood) burned over the hearth. Colonial housewives saved wood ashes to make lye for soap. Walnut, hickory, and chestnut trees supplied nuts for food, and maple trees were tapped for syrup. Wild animals and birds inhabited the forest; and hunting in the woods provided the colonists with much of their meat.

Englishman. He and a number of his friends were deeply troubled over conditions that existed in English prisons. In those days debtors (men who owed money they could not repay) were sent to jail until they repaid their debts. But since they could not earn money in prison, those who had no friends to lend them the sum they owed remained behind bars for years.

Oglethorpe had visited such prisons. He knew that many of the unfortunate prisoners were poor but honest. He realized that they could become good citizens and live happy lives if they were given a chance. And so he decided to start a colony where debtors could begin life again.

In 1732 the King of England gave Oglethorpe and several of his friends a large grant of land. This land, known as Georgia, lay between South Carolina and the Spanish colony of Florida. The King realized that English settlements in Georgia would help to protect the other English colonies from Spanish attack.

James Oglethorpe himself led the first group of debtors to the new colony. They arrived in 1733 and settled at a site they called Savannah. Each person received 20 hectares (50 acres) of land. Oglethorpe and the other owners (trustees) were determined to make Georgia a model colony. They refused to allow slavery or the sale of rum and other alcoholic drinks.

Settlers from New England and from Europe, as well as debtors from English prisons, moved to Oglethorpe's colony. Savannah became a thriving seaport. Farms and farming villages of free people spread inland. In 1752 Georgia became a royal colony.

In 1606 the coast of North America was a wilderness, except for the settlements in Florida and Canada. Less than 150 years later, the English flag was flying over 13 colonies along the coast. These 13 colonies were the new homeland of nearly 2,000,000 men, women, and children. The colonists were building a new way of life in the New World. Although they did not know it, they were building a new nation, one that in time would become the United States of America.

LEWIS PAUL TODD
Author, *New Ways in the New World*
See also COLONIAL LIFE IN AMERICA.

AMERICAN LITERATURE

From the beginning of American history to the present day, American literature has recorded the story of a search, or quest. At different times the quest has taken different forms. In the 16th century, Europeans went to the New World in search of the lost continent of Atlantis. They went looking for the cities of gold that haunted the imagination of Francisco Vásquez de Coronado. They searched for the fabled Northwest Passage to Asia.

These fantastic dreams changed in time to more down-to-earth dreams of success. These dreams brought millions of young men and women from farms and small towns to cities in the hope of winning fame and fortune. At times the quest was a religious pilgrimage. For example, the Puritans hoped the New World would become a place where a chosen people might at last build a society of which God would approve. The Mormons who trekked across the plains to Utah were inspired by a similar vision. Other pioneers—and many later Americans as well—were pulled westward by neither financial nor religious ambitions. They were simply restless. Whether they traveled by covered wagon or by automobile trailer, they believed that being on the road was better than staying put. The quests of the American people have indeed become parts of a drama. In one way or another, their questing has always been a "pursuit of happiness." American literature is the continuous narrative of that pursuit.

▶ THE COLONIAL PERIOD

The earliest American writing was a sort of advertising. It was written by English people who tried to interest other English people in the real estate of a howling wilderness. Of these writers the most famous was Captain John Smith (1580–1631). In 1606 Smith sailed for America with an expedition financed by the Virginia Company of London, a land-development company. Two years later Smith published an account of his experiences in the Jamestown settlement. He called it *A True Relation of . . . Occurrences and Accidents . . . in Virginia*. The book was in many ways an amazingly exact description of the region. It also contained many exaggerations of how easy life was for the settlers. In these exaggerations the **tall tale** of American humor was born.

Pilgrim and Puritan Writings

In sharp contrast to Smith were the voyagers on the *Mayflower,* who were religious seekers. The Pilgrims, as they called themselves, dropped anchor in 1620 in Plymouth Harbor, in what is now Massachusetts. They wished to separate themselves from the Church of England so they could worship God in their own way. Although the Church of England was nominally Protestant, it did not satisfy the Pilgrims. They felt the Church had too many traces of Catholic ritual and too little emphasis on sermons and Bible readings. The second governor of the Plymouth Colony, William Bradford (1590–1657), described in his *History of Plymouth Plantation,* the epic journey of the Pilgrims from England to Holland and then to America, and the hardships they suffered in setting up their colony. The straightforward style of Bradford's history fits in with the plainness that governed all aspects of Pilgrim life. Ornament had no place in writing or in everyday life.

Ten years after the landing of the *Mayflower,* another group of English settlers established Massachusetts Bay Colony. They settled first at Salem and then at Boston. These people, called Puritans, shared many of the Pilgrims' religious beliefs. The Puritans, however, wished to remain members of the Church of England in order to "purify" it, instead of leaving the Church as the Pilgrims had. Because the Puritans had more wealth than the Pilgrims, came in greater numbers, and possessed more intellectual leaders, they quickly dominated New England. Like Bradford, many of the early Puritans wrote histories of their "errand into the wilderness." Among these histories were *New-Englands Plantation* (1630), by Francis Higginson (1586–1630); *Wonder-Working Providence of Sions Saviour in New England* (1654), by Edward Johnson (1598–1672); and *New Englands Memoriall* (1669), by Nathaniel Morton (1613–86). The most important account was the *Journal* of Governor John Winthrop (1588–1649), made available to the public in 1790.

The Puritans believed that their church

should govern and have complete control over the colony. This belief was set forth by many writers, but most colorfully by Nathaniel Ward (1578?–1652). He wrote a **satire**— a form of writing that makes fun of habits, ideas, or customs. Ward's *Simple Cobler of Aggawamm* (1647) laughed at the idea that the Puritans should grant religious toleration to Quakers, Baptists, and others who did not share the Puritans' beliefs. Roger Williams (1603?–83) was a Puritan who came to believe that all organized churches were an obstacle to the truly religious life. He established a colony in Rhode Island in which all people were free to worship as they pleased. In a stirring manifesto—a declaration of beliefs —called *The Bloudy Tenent of Persecution* (1644), he wrote against religious intolerance.

But it was under Puritan rule, not in Williams' freer settlement, that the most important writers of the period flowered. Life in Massachusetts Bay was serious and narrow, as the poems of Michael Wigglesworth (1631–1705) and Anne Bradstreet (1612?– 72) prove. Wigglesworth's *Day of Doom* (1662) is a graphic account of the joys of heaven and the terrors of hell. Written in jingly meter, or verse pattern, and often reprinted throughout the colonial period, it was one of the first American best sellers. Anne Bradstreet's collection of poems was titled *The Tenth Muse Lately Sprung Up in America* (1650). It deals with the everyday, if no less gripping, problems of being a wife, a mother, and an American.

Somewhat lighter sides of Puritan life may be seen in the writings of Samuel Sewall (1652–1730) and Thomas Morton (1590?– 1647). In his *Diary,* published between 1878 and 1882, Sewall gives a hilarious account of his courtship, at the age of 68, of Madam Winthrop. Morton's *New English Canaan* (1637) mixes prose and poetry to poke fun at his joyless neighbors in what is now Quincy, Massachusetts.

Probably the most sensitive Puritan literary artist was Sewall's Harvard classmate Edward Taylor (1644–1729). A minister in the frontier town of Westfield, west of Boston, Taylor lived a lonely life. As a means of forgetting his loneliness, he wrote poems that explored deeply and beautifully the relationship between God and people. But Taylor's poems were not published in his lifetime, and he died unknown.

If the Puritans themselves had been asked who their finest writer was, most would have named either Cotton Mather (1663–1728) or Jonathan Edwards (1703–58). Both men were of well-educated families, and both were highly intelligent. Mather was the author, among many other works, of numerous **biographies**, or histories of people's lives. This form of writing fascinated the Puritans, who believed that the events of people's lives were the key to the state of their souls. In his *Magnalia Christi Americana* (1702), Mather combined biography with history to produce an unforgettable picture of the New England mind.

Edwards, like Taylor, knew the hardships of life in western Massachusetts. For 24 years he was the minister at Northampton. Then, after a dispute with his congregation, he became a missionary to the Indians at Stockbridge. In 1758 he became president of the College of New Jersey, later Princeton University, but died 2 months after taking office. Possessed of a brilliant mind, Edwards was able to bring into harmony the historic beliefs of the Puritans with the newer learning of his own time. His best-known work is *Freedom of the Will* (1754). A superb preacher, Edwards became famous throughout New England—and is chiefly remembered today—for his sermon *Sinners in the Hands of an Angry God* (1741).

Virginia's William Byrd

The 18th-century South produced only one writer of importance before the time of the Revolutionary War (1775–83). This was William Byrd II (1674–1744). The master of Westover, a famous estate in the Tidewater country of Virginia, Byrd brought to American life the style and manners of an English gentleman. His secret diary was not published until almost 200 years after his death. It is the record of a man who acted as if he were living in the shadow of Buckingham Palace rather than managing a Virginia tobacco plantation in America. For example, Byrd kept up with all the latest books from London. To the Royal Society in England he sent facts about the plant life in America. His *History of the Dividing Line,* published

Puritan ministers preached long sermons. If churchgoers dozed off, they were awakened by the tickle of a feather or the sharp rap of a light metal ball.

in 1841, contains some delightfully snobbish descriptions of the southern backwoods people Byrd met while he was helping to survey the boundary line between Virginia and North Carolina.

▶ THE AGE OF REASON

Born in the Boston of Cotton Mather's day, Benjamin Franklin (1706–90) moved to Philadelphia when he was 17. With this move he turned his back on the Puritan point of view, except for its stress on good works. The Puritans had emphasized human sinfulness. Franklin, along with many other 18th-century thinkers, emphasized human reason. By the exercise of intelligence and powers of reason, Franklin insisted, people could master their environment. Practicing what he preached, Franklin invented bifocal spectacles, the lightning rod, and the Frankin stove. In addition he founded the first circulating library in America and the first fire insurance company. He interested himself in a variety of reforms, among them improved methods of paving city streets. During the Revolution he was America's chief diplomatic representative in Europe. His *Poor Richard's Almanack,* a collection of useful information and pithy

proverbs published between 1733 and 1758, made Franklin widely known throughout the colonies. His fine *Autobiography* brought him everlasting fame. For of all the autobiographies that have been written by Amer-

At 65 Benjamin Franklin began his *Autobiography.* Of school he wrote: "I failed in the arithmetic . . . ."

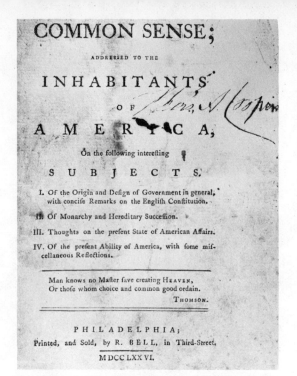

Paine's *Common Sense* spoke for American independence.

icans, Franklin's is the greatest—the frankest, the funniest, the most inspiring.

Another writer who argued for the "reasonableness" of all things was Thomas Paine (1737–1809). His *Age of Reason* (1794) attempted to prove that God had constructed the universe as carefully as a watchmaker would a watch. Then God departed, leaving in charge people who were able to think and reason. Whatever Paine's merits were as a philosopher, he was a marvelous propagandist, a man who gave time and effort in spreading certain opinions. Although born an Englishman, Paine was an enthusiastic supporter of American independence. His pamphlet *Common Sense* (1776), followed by the 16 issues of *The American Crisis* (1776–83), spoke for the colonists who were angry with the mother country, England. Paine wrote with unforgettable feeling. Other arguments in favor of the American cause were advanced by John Dickinson (1732–1808) in *Letters from a Farmer in Pennsylvania* (1767–68), Benjamin Franklin in *Rules by Which a Great Empire May be Reduced to a Small One* (1773), and Francis Hopkinson (1737–91) in *A Pretty Story* (1774). Surpassing all, however, was the noble Declaration of Independence (1776), by Thomas Jefferson (1743–1826).

Another fine autobiography of these years was the *Journal* (1774) of the Quaker preacher John Woolman (1729–72). But most Americans at the end of the 18th century were less interested in examining their souls than Woolman was. *Travels* (1791), by William Bartram (1739–1823), appreciatively described the wonders of American nature. St. John de Crèvecoeur (1735–1813) analyzed the problem of the American character in *Letters from an American Farmer* (1782). The framers of the Constitution of the United States (1787), led by James Madison (1750–1836), debated the question of federal versus state power.

The first American novel was written by William Hill Brown (1765–93). His *Power of Sympathy* (1789) is a shrewd imitation of the sentimental fiction being written in England at the time. Susanna Haswell Rowson (1762?–1824) followed the same formula in *Charlotte Temple* (1791), as did Hannah Foster (1759–1840) in *The Coquette* (1797). Hugh Henry Brackenridge (1748–1816) reworked Cervantes' *Don Quixote* in an American setting in *Modern Chivalry*. The final version of this novel was published in 1815. With the writings of Charles Brockden Brown (1771–1810), America acquired its first novelist of original talent. *Wieland* (1798), *Arthur Mervyn* (1799), *Ormond* (1799), and *Edgar Huntly* (1799) are gripping stories of violence and terror. They look forward to the short stories of Poe.

The Contrast (1787) is the only American play worth recalling from this period. The playwright Royall Tyler (1757–1826) satirized the British and praised the homespun American. In poetry the situation was somewhat better. Timothy Dwight (1752–1817) and Joel Barlow (1754–1812) wanted to give the youthful nation poetry to match its natural grandeur. With mixed results they wrote epics, long poems telling of the great adventures of great heroes. Dwight composed *The Conquest of Canaan* (1785), and Barlow wrote *The Columbiad* (1807). Only the more modest verse of Philip Freneau (1752–1832), however, which addressed itself to "The Wild Honeysuckle," "The Indian Burying Ground," and "To a Caty-did," had the unfailing honesty of feeling that lasting poetry must have.

The United States grew as settlers moved west during the early 1800's. At the same time—with Irving, Bryant, Cooper, and other writers—American literature also grew.

THE FIRST FLOWERING OF AMERICAN LITERATURE

Barlow, Dwight, and others writing after the Revolutionary War ended in 1783 tried to create a literature with a definite American flavor. Their work was extremely self-conscious. Possibly the writers failed because they tried so hard. Not until the generation of Washington Irving (1783–1859) and James Fenimore Cooper (1789–1851) came of age did a more relaxed attitude become evident. The nation had cause for a feeling of self-confidence. The vast Louisiana Territory was acquired in 1803. Andrew Jackson's glorious victory over the British at New Orleans came in 1815. The publication of Lewis and Clark's thrilling *History* (1814) of their expedition to the Far West stirred the popular imagination, as did the appearance of Robert Fulton's steamboat the *Clermont* in 1804. Such things were witnesses to the physical daring and imaginative energy of a rising people.

Irving, Cooper, and Bryant

Writers of the post-Revolutionary period had been embarrassed that America did not have much of a history. Washington Irving solved this problem by inventing a history. His *History of New York* (1809) is sup-

posedly an account of the Dutch settlement of Manhattan Island. With this work Irving furnished America with its first myth-hero, Father Knickerbocker. In "Rip Van Winkle" and "The Legend of Sleepy Hollow," both of which were published in *The Sketch Book*

Ichabod Crane is the superstitious schoolmaster in Washington Irving's "The Legend of Sleepy Hollow." A headless horseman frightens Ichabod out of his wits.

(1819–20), Irving contributed even more memorable characters to his legendary recreation of the American past: Rip Van Winkle, Brom Bones, and Ichabod Crane. In his accounts of his European travels, his biography of Columbus, and his history of *The Alhambra* (1832), the fabulous palace of the Moors in Granada, Spain, Irving also demonstrated that an American writer need not write only about America in order to remain a patriot.

His *Tour on the Prairies* (1835) showed Irving's interest in the literary possibilities of the West. But writing about the West was more the specialty of his fellow New Yorker James Fenimore Cooper. Cooper's novel *The Spy* (1821) was an exciting story of espionage in New York during the Revolution, but he did not really hit his stride as an author until he turned to *The Pioneers* (1823). This was the first of the five great romances known as the "Leatherstocking Tales." Surpassing Irving as a mythmaker, Cooper introduced in *The Pioneers* the fabulous woodsman, Natty Bumppo. He was the forerunner of all heroic forest scouts, bear hunters, and cowboys of later American novels and films. *The Last of the Mohicans* (1826), *The Prairie* (1827), *The Pathfinder* (1840), and *The Deerslayer* (1841) pursued Natty's career both forward and backward in time, from the first flush of manhood to his death as an old man on the western plains.

The "Leatherstocking Tales" measured the conflicting values of nature and civilization —and found civilization wanting. In other works, such as *The American Democrat* (1838), Cooper continued his examination of American civilization in a more direct fashion. Some of his critical remarks made him unpopular. Readers of his books did not understand that Cooper's criticisms were a sign of how deeply he cared about America.

Another New York writer who celebrated the virtues of nature was William Cullen Bryant (1794–1878). For 50 years Bryant was the editor of the New York *Post,* and he was as caught up in the life of the city as most big-city newspaper editors are likely to be. But Bryant's poetry does not deal with the life of the city. Drawing on the memories of his youth in the Berkshire Hills of western Massachusetts, he instead wrote poems like "Thanatopsis" and "To a Waterfowl." These poems declare that natural beauty is a source of moral strength.

Southern Novelists and Poe

The first southern novelist of any consequence was John Pendleton Kennedy (1795–1870). His *Horseshoe Robinson* (1835) did for southern history what Cooper's *Spy* had done for New York. Kennedy's *Swallow Barn* (1832), a series of verbal sketches of plantation life, viewed the society of the Old South in a mellow light, as did at least two novels. These were *The Kentuckian in New York* (1834), by William Alexander Caruthers (1802–46), and *The Virginia Comedians* (1854), by John Esten Cooke (1830–86). A far more skillful novelist was William Gilmore Simms (1806–70). His *Yemassee* (1835) is the most exciting story of Indian warfare on the southern frontier that has ever been written. Simms was also an eloquent defender of the southern way of life, as was his fellow South Carolinian John C. Calhoun. Although James Kirke Paulding (1778–1860) was a New Yorker born and bred, he too was charmed by the graciousness of southern ways, which he described in numerous stories and essays.

By far the greatest southern writer in pre-Civil War America was Edgar Allan Poe (1809–49). He was the master of the tightly wound tale of psychological horror, such as "The Fall of the House of Usher," "William Wilson," and "The Pit and the Pendulum." He invented the detective story, and his detective-hero, Dupin, foreshadows Sherlock Holmes. Poe developed a theory of poetic composition. This theory emphasized tightness of form and unity of tone, and had a significant effect on several later American poets, particularly Amy Lowell and Ezra Pound. Poe's own poetry, once highly regarded, is now considered by some critics to be the weakest aspect of his art. They feel that there is too much jingling and clanging in "The Bells," that the haunted atmosphere of "The Raven" is overly theatrical.

Emerson, Thoreau, and Hawthorne

Although Poe loved the South, he spent much of his life in New York. He was a professional writer who lived by his pen, and he

Concord, Massachusetts, was settled in 1635. Emerson, Thoreau, and Hawthorne lived there 200 years later and made it the center of American intellectual thought.

wanted to be close to the literary heart of the nation. Yet in the era when Poe was a resident of New York, the true literary heart of America was a small town northwest of Boston. Never before had Concord, Massachusetts, been known as an intellectual community. But now it was the home of Ralph Waldo Emerson (1803–82), Henry David Thoreau (1817–62), and—for a time—Nathaniel Hawthorne (1804–64).

While the 18th-century writers had emphasized the head as the source of all wisdom, Emerson emphasized the heart. The true genius was not merely a person who used reason and intelligence but a person of deep feeling whose five senses were very much alive to the wonders of life. Believing this, Emerson constructed essays not as exercises in reason but as inspirational appeals. Such essays as *Nature, The American Scholar, Self-Reliance,* and *Experience* were designed to quicken the imaginations of his readers and of his listeners. (Emerson often delivered his essays as lectures.) Blending fact and fancy, Yankee common sense and a spiritual joy, Emerson gave his audience a thrilling confidence in the power of the individual American to control his or her own fate. "Know thyself," said Emerson. "Every heart vibrates to that iron string."

In many ways Emerson's ideas struck at the roots of everyday thought and action. Thoreau carried the ideas even farther. He went to jail rather than pay a tax to the government to support a military campaign (the Mexican War) of which he disapproved. His essay *Civil Disobedience* (1849) insisted that individual protest was the most revolutionary force in the world. Such protest could bring about social justice more swiftly and more completely than governmental action.

In the most famous act of his life, Thoreau retired to a cabin beside Walden Pond. There he lived alone for 2 years because he "wished to live deliberately, to front only the essential facts of life." *Walden* (1854) is the record of that experience and is his finest work. The joys of living close to nature have rarely if ever been described so enchantingly. His other books include *A Week on the Concord and Merrimack Rivers* (1849), *The Maine Woods* (1864), and *Cape Cod* (1865).

Emerson and Thoreau were also poets and journal keepers. It would be hard to decide which writer's journal is the more fascinating document, for both men used their journals as a means of confessing their innermost thoughts. But in poetry Emerson was clearly the superior artist. Such poems as "Brahma" and "The Rhodora" delicately observe the presence of God in nature. Almost every schoolchild knows "Concord Hymn," Emerson's tribute to the minutemen of Concord who "fired the shot heard round the world."

Hawthorne's *Scarlet Letter* (1850) is one of the greatest American novels. Although Hawthorne could not accept the religion of his Puritan ancestors, he nevertheless shared their interest in the problem of sin. In his masterpiece he probed into the guilty consciences of two lovers, Hester Prynne and Arthur Dimmesdale. In *The House of the Seven Gables* (1851), he examined how the evil done by one generation affects the lives of later generations. *The Blithedale Romance* (1852), a picture of life in an experimental community, stems from Hawthorne's brief stay at Brook Farm. A settlement in West Roxbury, Massachusetts, Brook Farm attempted to prove that society would work more effectively if property were owned jointly and manual labor were performed by all citizens. *The Marble Faun* (1860) is a novel about another sort of colony—an American artists' colony in Rome. Like Poe, Hawthorne was a superb short-story writer. His best-known collections are *Twice-Told Tales* (1837) and *Mosses from an Old Manse* (1846). Hawthorne also wrote books for children, including *A Wonder Book* (1851) and *Tanglewood Tales* (1853).

Dana and Melville

The decades before the Civil War began in 1861 were the last days of the great sailing ships. Many American writers were attracted by their waning glory. In 1840 Richard Henry Dana (1815–82) told an exciting tale of *Two Years Before the Mast.* Eleven years later Herman Melville (1819–91) published *Moby Dick,* America's greatest sea tale, which was to become one of the most famous and most discussed works in the English language.

Melville had gone to sea as a cabin boy on a ship bound for Liverpool when he was still in his teens. Later he went to the South Seas on the whaler *Acushnet,* then jumped ship and lived for a time on the Marquesas Islands. Eventually he reached Hawaii. There he enlisted in the U.S. Navy and did a tour of duty on a frigate. *Typee* (1846) and *Omoo* (1847), his first two books, achieved great popularity with the public. They were exciting adventure stories based on the author's first-hand experience of the South Seas. *Mardi* (1849) also had a South Seas setting, but it puzzled readers. It introduced philosophical issues concerning the moral nature of the universe into a story of a chase. What the public did not know was that in *Mardi* Melville was warming up for *Moby Dick.*

For *Moby Dick* is also the story of a chase. Captain Ahab searches for the white whale that in a previous encounter had sheared off one of his legs. But it is more than just the story of a fish that got away. It is also a dramatization of good and evil and of the everlasting human desire to understand the mysteries of creation. Through Captain Ahab, Melville set himself against the universe, yet at the end of his days he wrote *Billy Budd* (1891). In this short, beautiful novel, Melville expressed both the tragedy of life, and his renewed faith in the beauty and basic strength and power of the human spirit.

Historians and Poets

Nineteenth-century American literature was particularly rich in historical writing. William Hickling Prescott (1796–1859) told the dramatic story of the Spanish conquest in the New World in *The Conquest of Mexico* (1843) and *The Conquest of Peru* (1847). George Bancroft (1800–91) saw the United States of America as the model for all future societies in the world and set forth in detail how American society had come into being. His massive *History of the United States from the Discovery of the American Continent* (1834–74) is undeniably thorough. John Lothrop Motley (1814–77) chose the Netherlands for his subject because he could see similarities between the Dutch and the American ways of life. His *Rise of the Dutch Republic* (1856) was popular on both sides of the Atlantic.

Top honors in the historical field go to Francis Parkman (1823–93). For a time Parkman lived with the warlike Sioux in order to gather facts for *The Oregon Trail* (1849). His later books deal with the struggle between France and England for control of North America. Like Cooper, Parkman weighed the conflicting claims of nature and civilization. Unlike Cooper, Parkman made his Indians seem like real people, not ideal types.

Next to Emerson, the leading nature poet of New England was John Greenleaf Whittier (1807–92). In poems like "The Barefoot Boy," "Telling the Bees," and "Snow-Bound," Whittier recalled his youth on a Massachusetts farm. The ballad "Barbara Frietchie" retells the story of a brave old lady defending the honor of her country's flag.

After a voyage that almost circles the globe, Captain Ahab and his crew of the whaler *Pequod* sail within sight of the giant whale Moby Dick.

Oliver Wendell Holmes (1809–94) was a professor of medicine and an essayist as well as an accomplished poet. In 1830 he saved the frigate *Constitution* from the scrap pile with his stirring poem "Old Ironsides." Holmes's serious side also appears in "The Last Leaf" and "The Chambered Nautilus." Yet Holmes was at his best as a humorist. "The Deacon's Masterpiece, or, The Wonderful 'One-Hoss Shay' " is a wonderfully comic account of the decline of New England Puritanism. This poem first appeared as part of an essay—one of the many delightful prose pieces that make up *The Autocrat of the Breakfast-Table* (1858).

James Russell Lowell (1819–91) studied law in his youth and held government posts in Spain and England during his last days. In the time between he edited the *Atlantic Monthly* for 4 years, taught at Harvard, and wrote poems and essays. In *The Biglow Papers* (1848) he made use of comic Yankee dialect in verses that ridiculed the Mexican War and the slave system of the South. His best-known poem was "The Vision of Sir Launfal," which tells of a knight's search for the Holy Grail. In "A Fable for Critics," he expressed his opinions of fellow American writers. In this work Lowell used **rhymed couplets**, pairs of lines whose end words rhyme.

The most popular poet of the era was Henry Wadsworth Longfellow (1807–82). His major works are three long narrative poems—that is, poems that tell a story. Each one dips into the North American past for its subject. *Evangeline* (1847) is set in Nova Scotia and Louisiana in the mid-1700's. *The Song of Hiawatha* (1855) goes back to American Indian legends, and *The Courtship of Miles Standish* (1858) borrows its theme from colonial times.

Shorter poems, just as popular as the long ones, include "The Children's Hour," "The Village Blacksmith," and "The Psalm of Life." Critics tend to dismiss Longfellow as a good but not great poet. Readers have always liked him, however, for his poems' melody, clearness, and story content.

The poetry of Walter (Walt) Whitman (1819–92) differed greatly from that of all other American poets of his time. His poems rarely had rhyme. The lines were of unequal length. The meter, or pattern of verse, was irregular. Whitman wrote in this free and flowing style because he felt it suited the democratic informality and the large, loose organization of American life. The first edition of *Leaves of Grass* was published in 1855. Throughout the rest of his life, Whitman added poems to the volume and revised the ones he had already published. A nurse in various military hospitals around Washington during the Civil War, Whitman also composed a number of touching poems about the wounded soldiers whom he was tending. At the end of the war he wrote the beautiful "When Lilacs Last in the Dooryard Bloom'd" in memory of President Lincoln. More than any other poet, Whitman comes the closest to being the voice of American democracy.

Civil War Writers

The Civil War touched other writers besides Whitman. Both Henry Timrod (1829–67) and Paul Hamilton Hayne (1830–86) championed the cause of the South. They wrote significant poems in defense of Dixie. However, the war cost them their health as well as their fortune, with the result that neither poet fulfilled his early promise. The same fate befell Sidney Lanier (1842–81). His collection of *Poems* (1884) and his novel, *Tiger Lilies* (1867), might have led to even better work if 4 years in the Confederate Army had not permanently weakened him.

The most explosive work produced by the years of the slavery crisis and the War Between the States was *Uncle Tom's Cabin* (1852), by Harriet Beecher Stowe (1811–96). A powerful and exciting story, filled with vivid characterizations, *Uncle Tom's Cabin* was no mere propaganda tract. It blamed northerners as well as southerners for the evils of slavery. It portrayed the slaves as human beings—some of whom were good and some of whom were bad. An enormous best seller, Mrs. Stowe's novel aroused the conscience of the civilized world.

▶THE LITERATURE OF A CONTINENTAL NATION

The writing of the period after the Civil War was as varied ‘as the American landscape. There were tales about the village and rural life of different sections, known as **local color** stories. There were regional poets. And there were novelists who dealt with the cities of the East, the South, and the West.

For America had a new sense of itself as a nation. It had come through a bloody war still united. In the years following, the rest of the West, which was still in Indian hands, came under United States control. When railroad workers from the West and from the East met at Promontory, Utah, in 1869, and drove a golden spike into the last tie of the first transcontinental railroad, they literally bound the nation together as never before.

Local Color Writers

The best of the New England local color writers were Sarah Orne Jewett (1849–1909)

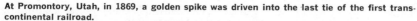

At Promontory, Utah, in 1869, a golden spike was driven into the last tie of the first transcontinental railroad.

Tom Sawyer tricks friends into whitewashing a fence.

and Mary E. Wilkins Freeman (1852–1930). Miss Jewett's *Country of the Pointed Firs* (1896) had a down East Maine setting; Mrs. Freeman's *New England Nun and Other Stories* (1891) focused on Massachusetts. Both writers emphasized the narrowness— and yet the beauty—of life in New England small towns. The dreary existence of the pioneers who broke the sod of the prairies in the Middle West was the theme of the *Main-Travelled Roads* (1891) of Hamlin Garland (1860–1940).

In the South, Joel Chandler Harris (1848–1908) drew on his knowledge of Georgia blacks and their folk legends for his Uncle Remus stories. New Orleans and its Creoles —descendants of French and Spanish settlers in Louisiana—furnished George Washington Cable (1844–1925) with material for *Old Creole Days* (1879) and *The Grandissimes* (1880).

California in the gold-rush days inspired Bret Harte (1836–1902). "The Luck of Roaring Camp" and "The Outcasts of Poker Flat" recapture the danger and the excitement and the laughter of the Far West in a wide-open era. The poetry of Joaquin Miller (1839–1913) also caught some of the color and energy of post-Civil War California. This is especially true of *Pacific Poems* (1870) and *Songs of the Sierras* (1871).

Mark Twain and Other Humorists

California also gave Samuel Langhorne Clemens (1835–1910)—Mark Twain, that is—his literary start. "The Celebrated Jumping Frog of Calaveras County," Twain's first success as a humorist, was set in a California mining camp. *Roughing It* (1871) recalled Virginia City, Nevada, at the height of the silver boom. *The Innocents Abroad* (1869) turned to Europe for its local color. Europe was also the setting of *The Prince and the Pauper* (1882) and *A Connecticut Yankee in King Arthur's Court* (1889). Twain was at his best, however, when he relived his years on the mighty Mississippi—in *The Adventures of Tom Sawyer* (1876), *Life on the Mississippi* (1883), and *The Adventures of Huckleberry Finn* (1884). What could be funnier than Huck and Tom walking in on their own funeral, more exciting than the arrival of a gaudy steamboat at the town dock, more beautiful than the scene where Huck and Jim are drifting down the river on a raft and gazing up at the stars?

Whatever his subject or scene, Twain was thoroughly American. His characters' speech, ideas, and behavior borrowed little from European models. With equal ease Twain gave a fresh, American approach to a novel about King Arthur's knights.

There were other humorists of the age.

Charles Farrar Browne (1834–67) used the pen name Artemus Ward. Henry Wheeler Shaw (1818–85) called himself Josh Billings. David Ross Locke (1833–88) became famous as Petroleum Vesuvius Nasby. Unlike these men, Mark Twain was basically serious. Underneath his jokes there was a sharp commentary on American society. In his old age he became very bitter. His last book, *The Mysterious Stranger* (1916), portrays the destruction of the universe.

Emily Dickinson and Henry James

The poetry of Emily Dickinson (1830–86) also mixed gaiety and gloom. During the last 25 years of her life, she rarely left the grounds of the Dickinson household in Amherst, Massachusetts. But her imagination took her on long flights of fancy. Her verses are filled with the names of faraway, exotic places that she visited only in imagination. On the other hand, she could make poetic drama out of things close at hand—a cracked plate on a shelf in the dining room or the sound of a honeybee in the garden. She was fascinated by life. She was also more than a little in love with death. Of the 1,500 poems she composed, more than 600 have to do with dying. Almost all of her poems are brief, rarely more than 12 or 15 lines long. But into small spaces she packed an emotional charge of surprising force. In the great line of New England poets that leads from Edward Taylor to Robert Frost, Emily Dickinson is one of the greatest.

One of the most distinguished novelists of the post-Civil War era was Henry James (1843–1916). He excelled at "international" novels and stories about Americans living in Europe. *The American* (1877), *Daisy Miller* (1878), and *The Portrait of a Lady* (1881) are among his treatments of this theme. Whereas Mark Twain's books about Europe had concentrated on descriptions of people and places, James was more interested in the psychology of his characters—that is, in their thoughts and emotions. He also wrote a number of ghost stories, including the famous short story *The Turn of the Screw* (1898).

Realism and Naturalism

While his good friend Henry James wrote about Americans abroad, William Dean Howells (1837–1920) published novels about Americans at home. Howells was a **realist**. His main aim as a writer was to give a true picture of ordinary, everyday life. He portrayed an unfortunate marriage in *A Modern Instance* (1882), a businessman's ruin in *The Rise of Silas Lapham* (1885). Howells also wrote a number of **Utopian novels**—that is, novels set in a society of the future in which there was no social injustice and everyone lived happily.

Utopian novels were in fact turned out by a number of writers. This period of the 1880's and 1890's was a time of great unrest in American life. There were stock-market crashes, strikes, falling farm prices. It was only natural that people should dream about a better America of the future. The best of the Utopian novels was *Looking Backward* (1888), by Edward Bellamy (1850–98).

To show the difference between their extreme realism and the milder realism of Howells and James, Frank Norris (1870–1902) and Stephen Crane (1871–1900) called themselves **naturalists**. Their wish was to portray people and their environment in a coldly objective and scientific manner. Crane had trouble getting a publisher for his first novel, *Maggie: A Girl of the Streets* (1892). The heroine's life in the New York slums was too grim. *The Red Badge of Courage* (1895) is Crane's finest book. It describes the terrified state of mind of a young Civil War soldier under fire for the first time. Crane was also a poet and very gifted short-story writer.

In *McTeague* (1899) Frank Norris told an unforgettable story of how the greed for gold leads a San Francisco dentist and his wife to destruction. Norris planned three books that would make up a trilogy called "The Epic of the Wheat," but he finished only two of them. *The Octopus* (1901) presents the struggle between the wheat growers of California and the railroad owners. *The Pit* (1903) is concerned with the buying and selling of the huge American wheat crop.

Realism and naturalism did not claim all writers. There were best-selling authors like Lew Wallace (1827–1905). He specialized in **romances**—novels having scenes, incidents, and adventures not usually found in everyday life. Wallace's *Ben-Hur* (1880) is a story of the time of Christ.

AMERICAN LITERATURE IN THE 20TH CENTURY

Henry Adams (1838–1918) was the grandson of John Quincy Adams and great-grandson of John Adams, both presidents of the United States. Henry Adams spent most of his life seeking order in what he considered a world of chaos. By the early 1900's industry and the sciences had made gigantic alterations in American life. How could people adjust to all the changes? How could their lives have meaning when everything was unfamiliar?

Henry Adams addressed himself to these questions in two books. *The Education of Henry Adams* (1907) contrasts modern America with its 18th-century past. *Mont-Saint-Michel and Chartres* (1904) makes the Middle Ages the standard of measure for the contemporary world. In looking backward, both books forecast trouble in the 20th century.

Two world wars, the depression of the 1930's, the development of the nuclear bomb, wars in Korea and Vietnam, and the civil rights struggle have made Henry Adams an accurate prophet. Yet national and international problems have by no means stopped American writers from producing. In the midst of all the troubles of the 20th century, American literature has had another flowering.

Novels and Short Stories

Theodore Dreiser (1871–1945) and Sherwood Anderson (1876–1941) belonged to the Chicago group of writers who were active before and following World War I. Dreiser wrote of life as he saw it, holding back nothing. *Sister Carrie* (1900), his first novel, and *An American Tragedy* (1925), his finest work, are grim and bitter narratives. Awkwardly written, they nevertheless have great emotional power.

Psychology took on new importance during the 1920's, with the theories of Sigmund Freud and others. Some authors began to explain characters in a new way. Thus Sherwood Anderson examined the private problems of small-town Middle Westerners in *Winesburg, Ohio* (1919) and other books. As Anderson portrayed them, these people led unfulfilled and twisted lives.

Indiana's Booth Tarkington (1869–1946) looked at life in a different way. The hero of *Penrod* (1914) and *Penrod and Sam* (1916) gets into all sorts of scrapes at home and at school, and Willie Baxter is amusing as he woos Lola Pratt in *Seventeen* (1916). In his more serious work, Tarkington showed the effect of industrial growth on residents of a quiet, pleasant city. *The Turmoil* (1915) and *The Magnificent Ambersons* (1918) both have this theme.

The prairies, farther west, inspired two writers. Ole Rölvaag (1876–1931), in *Giants in the Earth* (1927), described the hardships of Norwegian farmers in the Dakota Territory. Willa Cather (1873–1947) wrote about immigrant pioneer farmers in Nebraska in *O Pioneers!* (1913) and *My Ántonia* (1918). Stories of struggle, defeat, and enduring courage, these novels are written in the clear, beautiful prose that is the mark of all Miss Cather's work. Of her later novels the finest is *Death Comes for the Archbishop* (1927), a story of two French priests in the American Southwest.

Other 20th century writers wrote of the "Wild West." Owen Wister (1860–1938) wrote stories of cowboys. His novel *The Virginian* (1902) is a classic example of the popular Western tale. Zane Grey (1875–1939) wrote 54 novels, including the famous *Riders of the Purple Sage* (1912).

Sinclair Lewis (1885–1951), the first American writer to win the Nobel prize for literature, "photographed" small-town Middle Western life. He spared no detail of the tension between a doctor and his bored wife in *Main Street* (1920). Lewis gave equally sharp pictures of George F. Babbitt's unhappiness in *Babbitt* (1922) and of a religious leader's hypocrisy in *Elmer Gantry* (1927). All these were works of satire.

Sinclair Lewis won a Nobel prize for his novels.

Two other Middle Western writers of the 1920's and 1930's were Zona Gale (1874–1938) and Ruth Suckow (1892–1960). Miss Gale used Wisconsin small-town life as the background for *Miss Lulu Bett* (1920). Miss Suckow described Iowa scenes in *The Folks* (1934).

The writings of Edith Wharton (1862–1937) and Ellen Glasgow (1874–1945) mirror different backgrounds. Edith Wharton was a member of the wealthy New York society she described in *The House of Mirth* (1905), *The Age of Innocence* (1920), and other novels. She clearly saw the good and bad effects that wealth can have on human character and recorded her observations with skill and grace. Another side of her talent is shown in *Ethan Frome* (1911), a stark tragedy set in rural New England.

Although Ellen Glasgow belonged to an old Virginia family, she was not sentimental about the historic South. In *The Battleground* (1902), *Barren Ground* (1925), and *Vein of Iron* (1935) she faced social changes squarely. Her novels present realistic pictures of all the classes that composed the South.

Upton Sinclair (1878–1968) wrote novels calling for social reform. *The Jungle* (1906) described the terrible conditions in Chicago's meat-packing industry. Partly as a result of this novel, the federal government passed pure-food laws.

The roots of black American literature go back as far as the poetry of Phillis Wheatley in the 18th century. But in the 20th century, black writers began to express their own experience in a way that commanded the attention of all Americans. In the 1920's, a number of talented black novelists and poets gathered together in Harlem, a community in New York City. This period came to be known as the Harlem Renaissance. Among the novelists, Jean Toomer (1894–1967) wrote about American black life in *Cane* (1923). Claude McKay (1890–1948) wrote *Home to Harlem* (1928), the story of a black soldier's return home after World War I.

Two tremendously popular writers in the early years of the 20th century were William Sydney Porter (1862–1910), who used the pen name of O. Henry, and Jack London (1876–1916). O. Henry wrote short stories about people from every walk of life. Many of the stories ended with an unexpected twist, a form that has come to be called the O. Henry ending. His most famous story is called "The Gift of the Magi."

At the height of his fame, Jack London was the highest paid, most popular writer living. The violence and adventure in such stories as *The Sea Wolf* (1904) and *The Game* (1905) shocked and thrilled readers. Probably his best book is *The Call of the Wild* (1903), an exciting tale of a man and a dog in Alaska and the Yukon during gold-rush days.

Two writers known for their humor and their use of slang were Damon Runyon (1880–1946) and Ring Lardner (1885–1933). During his long career as a newspaperman, Runyon wrote essays and stories. His best-known collection of stories is *Guys and Dolls* (1932), which later was the basis of a highly successful musical comedy. Lardner, also a newspaperman, wrote humorous and often biting articles and short stories.

Poetry

At the end of the 19th century, most American poets were content to imitate past masters. The exceptions were few. Stephen Crane's poems showed originality as did those of William Vaughn Moody (1869–1910), but both men died young. Then in 1897 a volume of poems called *The Children of the Night* appeared. The author, Edwin Arlington Robinson (1869–1935), had nothing but scorn for the tradition of "pretty" poems. He presented honest portraits of men who were misfits or outcasts. The words and rhythm of his poems matched the New England speech of the day. Robinson continued to write in this way for many years, but not until *The Man Against the Sky* (1916) did he receive adequate recognition of his genius. Like Mark Twain, Robinson was also attracted to King Arthur's England, and he wrote a number of long poems about the Knights of the Round Table, among them *Tristram* (1927).

Thanks to *Poetry: A Magazine of Verse*, the poets of the generation that followed in Robinson's footsteps had a sympathetic outlet for their work. *Poetry* was founded in Chicago in 1912 by Harriet Monroe. Early issues of the monthly carried work by Edgar Lee Masters (1868–1950), Vachel Lindsay

(1879–1931), Carl Sandburg (1878–1967), and Ezra Pound (1885–1972).

Masters is best known for a book of free-verse poems entitled *Spoon River Anthology* (1915). The former residents of the imaginary town of Spoon River speak from their graves and sketch out the story of their frustrated lives. The bitter truth to be found in Masters' book attracted many readers, who made it the first best seller of the new age of poetry.

Vachel Lindsay believed that poetry should be spoken and sung. He often traveled around the country, earning money by reciting "Abraham Lincoln Walks at Midnight," "General William Booth Enters into Heaven," "The Congo," and others of his poems. With his colorful, musical language and his knowledge of American folk legends, Lindsay brought a certain freshness to poetry.

Although Carl Sandburg was often called the Chicago poet because he celebrated that city's strength, he was far more than a city poet. Like Whitman, Sandburg sang of all America. A few of Sandburg's titles show the variety of his work: *Chicago Poems* (1916), *Cornhuskers* (1918), *Smoke and Steel* (1920), and *Good Morning, America* (1928). Sandburg also edited a collection of folk ballads called *The American Songbag* (1927) and wrote a lengthy biography of Lincoln that many consider his best work. Young readers particularly enjoy his *Rootabaga Stories* (1922).

Ezra Pound headed a group of poetic experimentalists. They called themselves **imagists**. This means they expressed themselves through a series of clear, exact images, or likenesses. Of the group, two besides Pound are outstanding—Amy Lowell (1874–1925) and Hilda Doolittle (1886–1961), who signed her work H. D.

Pound also possessed a rare ability to recognize talent in others. From 1912 to 1919 Pound was foreign correspondent for *Poetry* magazine. He sent Harriet Monroe contributions by two then-unknown Americans living abroad—Robert Frost (1874–1963) and T. S. Eliot (1888–1965).

Frost's first books of verse were *A Boy's Will* (1913), *North of Boston* (1914), *Mountain Interval* (1916), *New Hampshire*

Robert Frost at work in the study of his Vermont home.

(1923), and *West-Running Brook* (1928). They shed a magic light, half humorous, half tragic, on the stone-filled fields and snowy woods of Vermont and New Hampshire. They give us haunting glimpses of the people who live on the lonely farms or tramp the muddy roads. Poems like "Birches," "Mending Wall," and "The Death of the Hired Man" fulfill Frost's definition of a poem. To him a poem was an expression that "begins in delight and ends in wisdom."

The poetry of Thomas Stearns Eliot is both traditional and modern. To recall the cultural glories of the past, he included in his poems quotations from Shakespeare, Saint Augustine, the playwrights of 5th-century (B.C.) Greece, and many other writers. Yet Eliot was in many ways boldly original. Poems like "The Love Song of J. Alfred Prufrock" (1917) and *The Waste Land* (1922) had new poetic rhythms. New meanings were given old words. Eliot stated in these poems that the modern world was spiritually bankrupt. He influenced a whole generation of younger American writers, including Ernest Hemingway, F. Scott Fitzgerald, and William Faulkner.

Eliot was also an influential essayist in the 1920's and 1930's. His praise of John Donne, Dante, and the playwrights of 17th-century England helped to form the taste of many readers in those decades. Eliot's later work was in the field of poetic drama. From *Murder in* the Cathedral (1935) to *The Cocktail Party* (1950) and *The Confidential Clerk* (1954), his plays were often popular as well as critical successes.

Sara Teasdale (1884–1933) and Elinor Wylie (1885–1928) excelled in writing lyric, or songlike, poetry, as did Edna St. Vincent Millay (1892–1950). Miss Millay's *Renascence and Other Poems* was the literary sensation of 1917. With her poems about love, she became a symbol of "flaming youth" in the 1920's. She was especially well-known for her intense, deeply felt, and at the same time controlled sonnets.

The strong, brooding poems of Robinson Jeffers (1887–1962) expressed an even grimmer outlook on life than did Eliot's. Jeffers' favorite theme was the grandness of nature in contrast to the meanness of people. He wrote long narrative, or story, poems, some of them set on the wildly beautiful California coast where he lived. Stephen Vincent Benét (1898–1943), on the other hand, expressed a mellow feeling for American life in *John Brown's Body* (1928) and *Western Star* (1943).

Both Archibald MacLeish (1892–   ) and Hart Crane (1899–1932) were influenced by Eliot's poetry. Crane borrowed some of Eliot's methods and techniques of writing poetry, but he spoke of a different world. Crane was especially interested in the sea and in ships and in the past and present of the United States. In his most famous poem, *The Bridge* (1930), using New York City's Brooklyn Bridge as a poetic metaphor, Crane tells an emotional and spiritual history of his country. MacLeish's best poetry is strikingly similar to Eliot's, both in theme and manner. Again like Eliot, MacLeish has had success in the theater in his later years. His play *J. B.* (1958), based on the Biblical story of Job, enjoyed a long run when it was produced in New York.

Edward Estlin Cummings (1894–1962) was the author of one of the best prose narratives to come out of World War I, *The Enormous Room* (1922). He was also a skillful painter. But primarily he was a poet. In an effort to make his poetry fresh and natural, he used punctuation in unusual ways. He avoided capital letters—he signed his name e. e. cummings—and he placed words on a page in a seemingly helter-skelter way. Cummings' satires of the American business world are very funny, and his love poems are full of a special sense of sweetness and beauty that is characteristic of the poet.

Twentieth-century black poetry began with the easy lyrics of Paul Laurence Dunbar (1872–1906). James Weldon Johnson (1871–1938) was first known for his song lyrics, and he later also distinguished himself for his poetry, especially *God's Trombones* (1927). In the outspoken poems of Langston Hughes (1902–1967), protests against white racism employ the musical rhythms of jazz and the blues. Hughes's collections of poetry include *Shakespeare in Harlem* (1942) and *Fields of Wonder* (1947). Countee Cullen (1903–1946) used more traditional European verse forms, especially in *Copper Sun* (1927) and *The Ballad of the Brown Girl* (1927).

Wallace Stevens (1879–1955) was a **symbolist**, which means that words in his poems frequently carry special meanings. The moon, for instance, is usually for Stevens a symbol of the imagination. Stevens had a taste for the strange and foreign, and his most memorable poems are set in the lush world of the Caribbean. Stevens' friend William Carlos Williams (1883–1963) used settings for his poems that were as matter-of-fact as Stevens' were poetic. Most often Williams wrote about the industrial city of Paterson, New Jersey, his home town. Associated with the imagists for a time, Williams always tried to present a series of clear pictures in his poetry.

Marianne Moore (1887–1972) came to know Williams when she was an undergraduate at Bryn Mawr and he a medical student at the University of Pennsylvania. She shared his poetic interest in "objects," but developed a subtle technique of expression that was entirely her own.

The regional problems of the South, as well as more general human problems, have been set forth in the poetry of three outstanding southern writers—John Crowe Ransom (1888–1974), Allen Tate (1899–1979), and Robert Penn Warren (1905–   ). All three have also written important literary criticism, and Warren is a talented novelist as well.

Several young poets emerged during the 1940's and 1950's. From the war experiences of Karl Shapiro (1913–   ) came *V-Letter* and Other Poems (1944). This collection expressed the longings, fears, and hopes of the ordinary soldier. Lord Weary's Castle (1946), which won Robert Lowell (1917–77) the Pulitzer prize, also established him in the front rank of American poets. He maintained this position with several distinguished collections of poetry, including The Mills of the Kavanaughs (1951) and Life Studies (1959), and with distinguished verse dramas as well. Lowell's technique combined a masterful command of the traditional ways of writing poetry, a gift for character analysis and storytelling, and a keen awareness of the American past. With The Beautiful Changes (1947) and Ceremony and Other Poems (1950), Richard Wilbur (1921–) proved himself a traditional lyric poet of high order. Theodore Roethke (1908–63), Randall Jarrell (1914–65), John Berryman (1914–72), Denise Levertov (1923–), Sylvia Plath (1932–63), and Anne Sexton (1928–74) also made original and interesting contributions to contemporary poetry.

Allen Ginsberg (1926–) was one of the most famous poets of the "beat generation" of the 1950's. The "beats" satirized the way of life of middle-class America. Beat poets put special emphasis on reciting poetry aloud. They made poetry a public performance instead of words on a page. There was also an interest in the connection between poetry and modern music such as jazz. Some notable collections of beat poetry are Ginsberg's Howl and Other Poems (1956), A Coney Island of the Mind (1958) by Lawrence Ferlinghetti (1919–), and The Happy Birthday of Death (1960) by Gregory Corso (1930–).

Free verse and the street language of blacks are used in sharp and forceful ways in poems by Gwendolyn Brooks (1917–) and in Preface to a Twenty-Volume Suicide Note (1961) by Leroi Jones (1934–), who later changed his name to Imamu Baraka. In her poetry, Nikki Giovanni (1943–) expresses her feelings about being a young black person in America.

The Later Novelists and Short-Story Writers

The writer-critic Gertrude Stein (1874–1946) left America in 1903 and spent the rest of her life in France. Americans abroad flocked to her, especially writers living in Paris in the 1920's. Stein coined a phrase for these people. She called them members of the "lost generation"—young people lost and embittered in a world that had been shaken to its foundations by World War I. Gertrude Stein did not influence all the postwar writers. Nevertheless, her term "lost generation" applied to a great many of them.

Among the novelists who voiced the spiritual restlessness of the 1920's was F. Scott Fitzgerald (1896–1940). Born in St. Paul, Minnesota, he attended Princeton University before joining the Army. His first novel, This Side of Paradise (1920), expressed perfectly the feverish, excitement-craving lives of the youth of the "jazz age." His finest book, though, was The Great Gatsby (1925). Gatsby, a man at the end of his youth, is striving to recapture a beautiful dream he once believed in. He sees the dream turn into a nightmare. Like a great many writers of the era, Fitzgerald was attempting in this book to say something about what had happened to American life.

The same effort was made by John Dos Passos (1896–1970). His emphasis was political in the three related novels that make up U.S.A. (1930–37). Dos Passos' trilogy is also interesting for its style. The three books attempted to introduce into fiction the sweep of scenes and the quick shifts of focus that one often finds in movies. Other novels by Dos Passos include Thee Soldiers (1921)—a novel of World War I—and Manhattan Transfer (1925). He also wrote travel books and works on American history.

William Faulkner (1897–1962) wrote about a mythical Mississippi town called Jefferson, in a mythical county called Yoknapa-

William Faulkner in his native Oxford, Mississippi.

John Steinbeck wrote of people struggling to survive.

tawpha. He traced the varied lives and fortunes of the Compson, Sartoris, and Snopes families, among others. These people's stories revealed profound truths about the South and about human fate in general. If there is darkness and tragedy in such novels as *The Sound and the Fury* (1929), *Light in August* (1932), *Absalom, Absalom!* (1936), *The Hamlet* (1940), and *A Fable* (1954), there is laughter in these books, too. Like Shakespeare, Faulkner was a master of both comedy and tragedy. In 1949 he was awarded the Nobel prize for literature.

Another Nobel winner (1954) was Ernest Hemingway (1899–1961). Hemingway was above all famous for his literary style, which was spare, understated, and direct. He was at his best describing physical activity, and his descriptions of bullfights, lion hunts, and fishing trips have no equal in world literature.

Hemingway's first novel was *The Sun Also Rises* (1926). The book tells of the sadness and isolation of young Americans living in Paris after World War I. *A Farewell to Arms* (1929) recalls the suffering and destruction of World War I. The love story of an American officer and a British nurse who meet in war-torn Italy, this book was based in part on Hemingway's own experiences on the Italian front. Books on bullfighting—*Death in the Afternoon* (1932)— and big-game hunting— *The Green Hills of Africa* (1935)—preceded

an important novel about the Spanish Civil War, *For Whom the Bell Tolls* (1940). Perhaps most at home in the short-story form, Hemingway is the author of such famous stories as "The Killers" and "The Snows of Kilimanjaro."

In his four principal novels, Thomas Wolfe (1900–38) told the story of himself. *Look Homeward, Angel* (1929) is about Wolfe's North Carolina boyhood and parents. The hero in *Of Time and the River* (1935) studies at Harvard, teaches in New York City, travels in Europe—all of which Wolfe did. *The Web and the Rock* (1939) and *You Can't Go Home Again* (1940) also parallel Wolfe's private life. In his enthusiasm for American life, Wolfe poured forth a torrent of words. His novels are poetic but sprawling works.

During the depression of the 1930's, fiction that dealt with social and economic themes came to the fore. The Studs Lonigan novels of James T. Farrell (1904–79) are important examples of this kind of fiction. The outstanding author in this field, however, is John Steinbeck (1902–68). *The Grapes of Wrath* (1939) tells of the Joad family's westward flight. Forced by drought to leave their farm in Oklahoma, they travel in a ramshackle truck to California. They are hired for miserable wages to work in the fruit groves. Yet their courage endures. In *Of Mice and Men* (1937) Steinbeck unfolded the moving story of a mentally retarded man, Lennie, who cannot cope with the world around him. Possessed of a fine sense of humor, Steinbeck looked at the lighter side of depression conditions in *Tortilla Flat* (1935) and *Cannery Row* (1945). In yet another display of his many-sided talents, Steinbeck wrote *The Red Pony* (1938). This story of a boy and his horse is a favorite of young readers. In 1962 Steinbeck received the Nobel prize for literature.

Pearl Buck (1892–1973) received the same award in 1938. Her specialty was Chinese life. Through her best-known novel, *The Good Earth* (1931), as well as through her other books, essays, and children's stories, the reader can gain a picture of life in China under the emperors.

Scenes of rural Florida life attracted Marjorie Kinnan Rawlings (1896–1953). *The*

Yearling (1938), her best book, is a touching story about a boy and his pet deer. John P. Marquand (1893–1960) sketched sharply observed, dryly humorous portraits of upper-class New Englanders in *The Late George Apley* (1937), *H. M. Pulham, Esq.* (1941), and many other novels.

Death cut short two promising careers. Nathanael West (1904–40) probed the emptiness and the evil of contemporary life in *Miss Lonelyhearts* (1933). *A Death in the Family* (1957), by James Agee (1909–55), beautifully recaptures this talented author and critic's childhood and family life in Knoxville, Tennessee.

The plight of blacks in America forms the basis of *Native Son* (1940), by Richard Wright (1908–60). *Invisible Man* (1952), by Ralph Ellison (1914–   ), follows a black man from a southern background to the horror of a race riot in New York's Harlem. Harlem is also the setting of *Go Tell It on the Mountain* (1953), a strong yet graceful story of a boy's religious conversion, by the essayist and novelist James Baldwin (1924–   ). Baldwin's essay on racial conflict in the United States, *The Fire Next Time* (1963), was a major contribution to the understanding of one of the country's most serious problems.

Historical novels were especially popular during the 1930's and 1940's. Kenneth Roberts (1885–1957) wrote exciting stories about colonial times, including *Arundel* (1930), *Northwest Passage* (1937), and *Oliver Wiswell* (1940). In *Drums Along the Mohawk* (1936), by Walter D. Edmonds (1903–   ), early settlers of the state of New York fight the British, the Indians, and the wilderness. Margaret Mitchell (1900–49) used the backdrop of the Civil War for her hugely successful *Gone With the Wind* (1936). This novel is best remembered for its two leading characters, Scarlett O'Hara and Rhett Butler. Almost as popular, and even longer than *Gone With the Wind,* was *Anthony Adverse* (1933), by Hervey Allen (1889–1949).

World War II did not bring about an abrupt break with previous literary practice as World War I had. Novels that came out of the second global conflict broke no new ground, violent as some of them were.

Norman Mailer (1923–   ) told the story of the war in the Pacific in *The Naked and*

James Baldwin's essays stirred America's conscience.

the Dead (1948). John Horne Burns (1916–53) wrote about Naples under Allied occupation in *The Gallery* (1947). In *A Bell for Adano* (1944), John Hersey (1914–   ) narrated a sympathetic story of American soldiers in a small Italian town. His *Hiroshima* (1946) is a gripping account of the atomic bombing of that Japanese city. *Guard of Honor* (1948), a novel by James Gould Cozzens (1903–78), gives an excellent picture of three action-packed days at a Florida air base.

The conflicts between officers and men aboard a navy minesweeper come vividly alive in *The Caine Mutiny* (1951) by Herman Wouk (1915–   ). This novel eventually became a highly successful play and movie. In *From Here to Eternity* (1951), James Jones (1921–77) described peacetime army life in Hawaii before the attack on Pearl Harbor. Though not a war story, the novel is violent and tragic. A later book of Jones's, *The Thin Red Line* (1962), depicts a company of soldiers struggling to win a Pacific island hill.

The subject of World War II continued to be a significant one into the 1960's, when Joseph Heller (1923–   ) published *Catch-22* (1961), a satire on the military and on war. In the 1970's, Herman Wouk's *The Winds of War* (1971) and *War and Remembrance* (1978) showed that the impact of the war was still strong.

Other novelists have dealt with problems

of postwar living. Saul Bellow (1915–) followed the adventures of a restless young man who will not conform in *The Adventures of Augie March* (1953). A sense of wonder and a sense of fear mark the delicate work of Eudora Welty (1909–), particularly *The Ponder Heart* (1954). The same may be said of *Other Voices, Other Rooms* (1948) and of *The Grass Harp* (1951), by Truman Capote (1924–). In 1965, Capote's masterful "non-fiction novel," *In Cold Blood,* the detailed study of an actual murder in the American Midwest, received great acclaim from the critics and the reading public. *Lie Down in Darkness* (1951), by William Styron (1925–), is' as violent—and occasionally as exciting—as Faulkner. A deep understanding of the crippled and lonely distinguishes the novels of Carson McCullers (1917–67), especially *The Heart Is a Lonely Hunter* (1940) and *The Member of the Wedding* (1946). With *On the Road* (1957), Jack Kerouac (1922–69) became a spokesman for the "beat generation"—the people who refuse to join the "rat race" of middle-class life.

Welty and McCullers were part of a group of writers who wrote brilliantly about the South. The most famous, of course, was William Faulkner. Robert Penn Warren wrote *All the King's Men* (1946), a novel that told of the tragic rise and fall of a Louisiana politician. Flannery O'Conner (1925–64), like McCullers, wrote of her native Georgia, particularly in short stories. Many of these "Southern" novels and short stories are about characters haunted by loneliness and violence.

Two writers with a fine ear for American speech and a bitter sense of humor are Dorothy Parker (1893–1967) and John O'Hara (1905–70). Parker is the author of *Here Lies* (1939) and other collections of short stories. John O'Hara's many books include *Appointment in Samarra* (1934)—generally considered his best—and *The Cape Cod Lighter* (1962).

O'Hara's tight style contrasts with the loosely woven prose of William Saroyan (1908–), who often substitutes warmth of feeling for carefulness of craftsmanship. This colorful writer is at home with the short story ("The Daring Young Man on the Flying Trapeze," 1934) or the novel (*The Human Comedy,* 1943).

The short stories in *Flowering Judas* (1930) and *Pale Horse, Pale Rider* (1939) established the literary reputation of Katherine Anne Porter (1890–1980). Her novel, *Ship of Fools* (1962), added to her stature. Doom awaits the passengers of the ship (which represents the world) as it crosses the ocean in 1931, bound for Germany.

Bernard Malamud (1914–) became known for his sympathetic portrayals of ordinary people struggling with life. Among his most important works are *The Assistant* (1957), the story of a poor shopkeeper and his helper; *The Magic Barrel* (1958), a collection of short stories; and *The Fixer* (1966), a novel.

J. D. Salinger (1919–) skyrocketed to fame with *The Catcher in the Rye* (1951). This novel is about Holden Caulfield, a teenager puzzled and alone on the path between childhood and adulthood. *Nine Stories* (1953) and *Franny and Zooey* (1961) further proved Salinger a gifted storyteller with a sure sense of how young people talk and what they feel. The poems, short stories, and novels of John Updike (1932–) show a dazzling flair for language. His novel *Poorhouse Fair* (1959) is an excellent example of his work. Philip Roth (1933–) made a favorable impression with his short-story collection, *Goodbye, Columbus,* published in 1959. His first novel, *Letting Go,* appeared in 1962. It was followed by the novels *When She Was Good* (1967) and *Portnoy's Complaint* (1969).

Saul Bellow continued his earlier success with such novels as *Herzog* (1964), *Mr. Sammler's Planet* (1970), and *Humboldt's Gift* (1975). Bellow was awarded the Nobel prize in 1976. Polish-born Isaac Bashevis Singer (1904–) went to the United States in 1935. He wrote mostly in Yiddish, though many of his works were translated into English. His writings concerned the difficulties encountered by European-born Jews in adjusting to American life. Singer was awarded the Nobel prize in 1978.

Joyce Carol Oates (1938–) wrote of the violence in American life in *Them* (1969) and *Do With Me What You Will* (1973). Satire and social criticism were the themes of *Lolita* (1957) by Vladimir Nabokov (1899–1977) and of *One Flew Over the Cuckoo's Nest* (1962) by Ken Kesey (1935–).

The 1960's and 1970's saw the popularity of "black humor," an irreverent attack upon many aspects of the American dream. Novelists who wrote in this vein were Kurt Vonnegut, Jr. (1922–), in *Cat's Cradle* (1963) and *Breakfast of Champions* (1973); Joseph Heller, in *Catch-22* and *Something Happened* (1974); John Barth (1930–), in *Giles Goat-Boy* (1966); and Thomas Pynchon (1937–), in *V* (1963) and *Gravity's Rainbow* (1973). Donald Barthelme (1931–) wrote of life's absurdity in short story collections such as *Guilty Pleasures* (1974).

Nonfiction

History, biography, essays, philosophy, and criticism form a significant part of 20th-century American literature.

At the beginning of the century, the scientist Booker T. Washington (1856–1915) published his autobiography, *Up From Slavery* (1901). In 1903, *The Souls of Black Folk,* a series of essays by W. E. B. DuBois (1868–1963), was published. Both these books called attention to the problem of the "color line" in the United States.

The history of American life was fascinatingly re-created by Charles Beard (1874–1948) and his wife, Mary (1876–1958), in *The Rise of American Civilization* (1927). Colonial life is reconstructed in *The Founding of New England* (1921), by James Truslow Adams (1878–1949), and in *Paul Revere and the World He Lived In* (1942), by Esther Forbes (1894?–1967). The meaning of Puritanism was brilliantly analyzed by Perry Miller (1905–63) in *The New England Mind* (1939). *The Age of Jackson* (1945), by Arthur M. Schlesinger, Jr. (1917–), portrays not only a president but an era. In *Across the Wide Missouri* (1947), Bernard De Voto (1897–1955) described pioneer exploration of a vast territory. *A Stillness at Appomattox* (1953) is one of several compelling Civil War narratives by Bruce Catton (1899–1978).

Historical writing has great variety. Hendrik Willem Van Loon (1882–1944) in *The Story of Mankind* (1921) combines scholarship with informality. The same is true of two books by Frederick Lewis Allen (1890–1954) that picture American life of the 1920's and 1930's, *Only Yesterday* (1931) and *Since Yesterday* (1940). In *Main Currents in American Thought* (1927–1930), Vernon Louis Parrington (1871–1929) examined the development of American ideas and how they were expressed in literature. *The Ordeal of Mark Twain* (1920) and *The Flowering of New England* (1936) are two important works of American literary history by Van Wyck Brooks (1886–1963).

The journalists of America have supplied interesting and valuable books about the changing world and its crises. Notable in this field are John Gunther (1901–70), with his *Inside Europe Today* (1961), and William L. Shirer (1904–), with his monumental study of Nazi Germany called *The Rise and Fall of the Third Reich* (1960).

But history does not always deal with world-shaking events. The story of one acre of soil is told in *A Prairie Grove* (1938), by Donald Culross Peattie (1898–1964). Joseph Wood Krutch (1893–1970) gives his impressions of the American Southwest desert country in *The Desert Year* (1952). Rachel Carson (1907–64) combines a beautiful style and a wealth of information in *The Sea Around Us* (1951).

Through biography, historical figures receive new dimension. *Grover Cleveland* (1932), by Allan Nevins (1890–1971), *Robert E. Lee* (1934), by Douglas Southall Freeman (1886–1953), *Benjamin Franklin*

Rachel Carson was a naturalist as well as a writer.

"All Right, Have It Your Way—You Heard a Seal Bark!"

Writer James Thurber was also a talented cartoonist. Here is one of his most famous cartoons.

(1938), by Carl Van Doren (1885–1950), and *John Paul Jones* (1959), by Samuel Eliot Morison (1887–1976), are but a few of the books that shed new light on the past.

Some people write their own life stories, or autobiographies. Dutch-born Edward Bok (1863–1930) called his story *The Americanization of Edward Bok* (1920). Charles A. Lindbergh (1902–74) titled his autobiography after the plane in which he made the first nonstop flight across the Atlantic—*The Spirit of St. Louis* (1953). Biography and autobiography, like history, are not limited to the stories of great events and world-famous people. A good example of the intimate autobiography, concerned with everyday life, is *Memories of a Catholic Girlhood* (1957), by the well-known novelist and critic Mary McCarthy (1912–).

Two essayists with the gift for the right word or phrase are James Thurber (1894–1961) and E. B. White (1899–). In *The Thurber Album* (1952) and *Thurber Country* (1953), Thurber gave affectionate accounts of his home town, Columbus, Ohio. White's *One Man's Meat* (1944) and *The Points of My Compass* (1962) are representative of his graceful literary manner.

Will Durant (1885–) has done much to make both philosophy and history popular. He is scholarly but readable in *The Story of Philosophy* (1926) and in the later books that make up his large-scale *Story of Civilization* (1935–1967).

Some of the best literary work of the present era has come from critics—that is, from authors who compare and judge the works of other authors. Henry L. Mencken (1880–1956), with his slashing, brilliant style, was the terror and the delight of writers and readers in the 1920's. Edmund Wilson (1895–1972) and Alfred Kazin (1915–) have, more recently, contributed brilliant critical writing, Wilson with *Axel's Castle* (1931) and *The Shores of Light* (1952), and Kazin with *On Native Grounds* (1942) and *Contemporaries* (1962).

In nonfiction, the civil rights and black power movements found expression in the essays of James Baldwin and in the powerful autobiographies *Manchild in the Promised Land* (1965) by Claude Brown (1937–) and *The Autobiography of Malcolm X* (1965) by Malcolm X (1925–1965) with Alex Haley (1921–). Haley traced his family's history back to Africa in *Roots* (1976).

Modern American Drama

William Dunlap (1766–1839) was America's first professional playwright, but his work merely copied European dramas. James A. Herne (1839–1901) broke away from foreign influence with *Margaret Fleming,* produced in 1890. This realistic play opened the way for modern American drama.

America's most renowned playwright is Eugene O'Neill (1888–1953), winner of the Nobel prize for literature in 1936. Insight into character, emotional power, strong and poetic language—these are keys to O'Neill's greatness. The scope of his plays is enormous. *The Emperor Jones* (1920) is a study in the psychology of fear. *Mourning Becomes Electra* (1931) gives Greek tragedy a New England setting. *Ah, Wilderness!* (1933), by contrast, is a lighthearted comedy about a young boy and his family. *Long Day's Journey into Night* (1956) is one of O'Neill's longest and most serious plays. It is basically the story of a young writer's attempt to understand and eventually escape from his nightmarish home. This is one of the most moving portrayals of an unhappy family to appear in the American theater. It is doubly touching because the play is, in part, the story of a period in O'Neill's own life.

If O'Neill towers over other American

playwrights, he does not completely overshadow them. Elmer Rice (1892–1967), in *The Adding Machine* (1923), drew a sharp portrait of Mr. Zero, society's "little man" ruined by the machine age. Social criticism also appears in *Dead End* (1935), by Sidney Kingsley (1906–   ); the play contrasts the lives of slum dwellers and their rich neighbors. *The Little Foxes* (1939), the work of Lillian Hellman (1905–   ), is a chilling drama about a southern family's self-destructive greed. In *Awake and Sing!* (1935), Clifford Odets (1906–63) wrote warmly of the poverty and problems of a family in the Bronx, New York.

Maxwell Anderson (1888–1959) wrote historical dramas, including *Elizabeth the Queen* (1930) and *Mary of Scotland* (1933), that are distinguished by their moments of poetic beauty. Robert Sherwood (1896–1955) wrote *Abe Lincoln in Illinois* (1938). Thornton Wilder (1897–1975) in *Our Town* (1938) pictured life in a typical New England village. Lorraine Hansberry (1930–65) wrote with insight and warmth about the problems of a black, urban family in *Raisin in the Sun* (1959).

Comic playwriting is best represented by the work of Philip Barry (1896–1949), George S. Kaufman (1889–1961), and Moss Hart (1904–61). Barry's *Philadelphia Story* (1939), a comedy of manners, deals with a society family. Kaufman and Hart's *You Can't Take It with You* (1936) is about a family of zanies. Neil Simon (1927–   ) became a popular playwright of the 1960's and 1970's with such plays as *The Sunshine Boys* (1972).

Tragedy is the major theme in several modern American dramatists' work. Tennessee Williams (1914–   ) writes poetically of the isolated and lonely people of American society. He is especially expert at creating sympathetic women—the faded southern belle in *The Glass Menagerie* (1945), the pathetic Blanche in *A Streetcar Named Desire* (1947), the touching spinster in *The Night of the Iguana* (1961). Williams is also gifted with a keen sense of humor that comes into play even in his most serious works. A sense of failure drives Willy Loman to suicide in *Death of a Salesman* (1949), a powerful tragedy by Arthur Miller (1915–   ). Among this play-

Lillian Hellman's plays explored powerful ideas.

wright's later works are *The Crucible* (1953), *After the Fall* (1963), and *Incident at Vichy* (1964). William Inge (1913–73) reflected life in the Middle West in a series of touching dramas including *Picnic* (1953), which won a Pulitzer prize. The tragic conflicts of two modern married couples form the central theme of *Who's Afraid of Virginia Woolf?* (1962), a drama by Edward Albee (1928–   ). Albee rapidly gained recognition as one of America's leading dramatists.

Revivals of a number of past stage successes were produced in the early 1970's. In addition, a group of promising new playwrights appeared, expressing a concern with present-day society and the problems it faces. The group included Charles Gordone (1925–   ) with *No Place to Be Somebody* (1970), Jason Miller (1930–   ) with *That Championship Season* (1972), and David Rabe (1940–   ) with *Sticks and Bones* (1972).

KENNETH S. LYNN
Author, *Visions of America: Eleven Literary Historical Essays*

AMERICAN REVOLUTION. See REVOLUTIONARY WAR.

AMMUNITION. See GUNS AND AMMUNITION.

AMOEBA. See MICROBIOLOGY.

AMPHIBIANS. See FROGS, TOADS, AND OTHER AMPHIBIANS.

ANATOMY. See BODY, HUMAN.

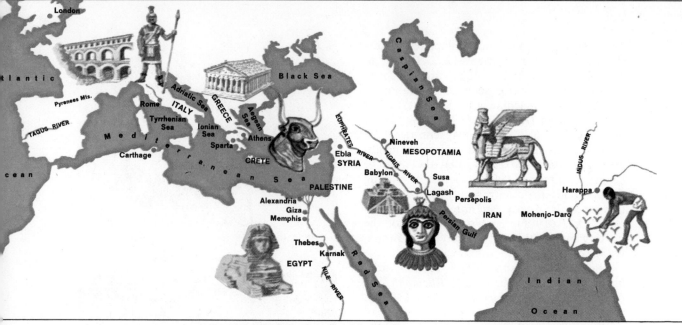

Many ancient civilizations flourished in the area between the Atlantic and Indian oceans.

ANCIENT CIVILIZATIONS

In a museum in Paris there is a small carved stone tablet. It was found on the broad plain between the Tigris and Euphrates rivers in the country of Iraq. The tablet shows the king of Lagash and his sons. If you look at a map of modern Iraq, you will not find Lagash. It was a city that disappeared long ago, for this tablet is at least 4,500 years old.

Words carved on the tablet in a strange script say that the king of Lagash brought timber from the mountains to build temples for the gods. But this is not all the tablet tells us. It also tells us that the people of this land lived in cities, had governments, built temples, and —most important of all—knew how to write. In brief, the tablet tells us that people living on the plains of the Tigris and Euphrates rivers had a civilization 4,500 years ago, before 2500 B.C.

Visitors to Egypt usually go to see the huge stone pyramids that are about as old as the tablet from Lagash. The pyramids, too, tell a story. They tell us that the Egyptians had architects who understood enough mathematics to plan these enormous structures with amazing accuracy. The pyramids tell of the many skilled stonecutters and masons and the thousands of people who lifted, tugged, and pushed these stones into place. The Egyptians had to have rulers to command and direct the labor of so many people. Such a government would have required scribes to keep records, and we know from other carved stones that the Egyptians did have writing. The pyramids, temples, and tombs tell us that the Egyptians, too, had a civilization 4,500 years ago.

A library of clay tablets, discovered in 1975 in Syria, gives us information about the ancient city of Ebla, which existed more than 4,000 years ago. It was thought to be a lost city until the clay tablets were discovered.

On the island of Crete, there are traces of another civilization over 4,000 years old.

This stone tablet was found in the ruins of Lagash, one of the oldest cities of the ancient world.

Carved stone seals and the remains of palace walls have been found there. Piles of bricks on the plains of the Indus River in Pakistan tell of cities that stood there, too.

It is possible that people living in North China on the Hwang Ho (Yellow River) had a civilization 4,000 years ago. But no carved stones or ruins have been found that tell of it.

People today speak of these civilizations as ancient civilizations because we think of the centuries before A.D. 500 as ancient times. But ancient times do include most of human history. Civilization grew old even within what we now call ancient times. For example, a king who reigned in 540 B.C. took much interest in digging up ruins of temples built hundreds of years earlier, in what he regarded as ancient times. The time span between the building of the pyramids and the birth of Christ is greater than the time from the birth of Christ to the present.

▶ THE CIVILIZATION OF THE SUMERIANS AND BABYLONIANS

Civilization was not new 4,500 years ago in the lands along the Tigris and Euphrates rivers. Much earlier, the Sumerian people had settled there and had begun to build cities. The Sumerians first entered the plain before 3000

B.C. Semites, people from the dry grasslands south and west of the Euphrates, also settled along the rivers. The Semites adopted many Sumerian ways of living.

Each city had its own ruler, who governed the city within the walls, as well as the areas nearby. As the number of cities and people increased, each city tried to get more land. Sometimes, cities quarreled about land and water for irrigation. At times the quarrels led to war, and the more powerful cities gained more lands. Babylon, one of the Semite cities, conquered and ruled the whole plain known as Babylonia—the land of Babylon.

Temple Cities and Priests

The Sumerians built their cities around temples, called **ziggurats**. These were large towers that looked like pyramids. At the top of the ziggurat was a shrine that held an image of the city's god. At different seasons of the year, priests made offerings to the god. The Sumerians believed that their crops, their health, and the safety of their city depended on the favors of the god. The priests said that they acted for the god. They collected such things as grain, wool, and silver from the people to offer the god. These payments to the god were a form of tax.

While a Sumerian sculptor makes a figure for a temple, his apprentice drills a stone vase.

Hammurabi's code, one of the oldest sets of laws, was inscribed about 4,000 years ago on this tablet. It is now in the Louvre museum, in Paris. Detail below.

Building Cities with Clay

There was little timber or stone on the river-bottom land where the Sumerians built their cities. But clay was plentiful. They packed moist clay into molds and dried the clay in the sun. In this way they formed flat bricks that could be stacked upon each other to build the walls of houses, shops, palaces, and the ziggurat. The main disadvantage of the sun-dried bricks was that they crumbled after a time, even in a dry climate. But the builders discovered that if they baked the moist bricks, the heat hardened the clay. The bricks then remained firm even in wet weather. A wall built of fire-baked bricks set together with asphalt would stand for a very long time. The Sumerians and Babylonians used fire-baked bricks for their more important buildings.

Writing on Clay Tablets

The Sumerians wrote on clay. They pressed the end of a stick into the soft clay, making little three-cornered marks. They combined these three-cornered marks to form signs that stood for words. Since the marks looked like wedges, this form of writing is called cuneiform, which means "wedge-shaped." The Babylonians, as well as other peoples, borrowed cuneiform writing from the Sumerians. For more than 2,000 years people in this part of the world wrote with these little wedge-shaped marks.

Clay tablets were heavy and awkward to handle, but they lasted for centuries. A paper book buried in the ground for 3,000 years would have rotted away completely. But a clay tablet, carefully dug up, remains in good condition. Scholars in modern times have found thousands of the Sumerian and Babylonian tablets. These tablets tell many things about this ancient civilization. They tell of business and trade, for there are letters from merchants to their agents. There is a "farmer's almanac," which gives instructions about each season's work in the fields. A Sumerian physician wrote down some favorite medical remedies. One of the most interesting tablets describes what children did in school 4,000 years ago. They hurried to school because their teacher would beat them with a cane if they were late. The teacher also used the cane to punish children for talking, leaving the school without permission, and not doing lessons properly.

The Oldest Written Laws in the World

People living together in cities must have laws. The Sumerians and Babylonians wrote their laws on tablets of clay and stone. These are some of the oldest known written laws. One law provided that people would have to pay a certain amount of silver if they entered an orchard that was not their own and were caught there for stealing. The most famous collection of early laws was issued by Hammurabi, king of Babylon, around 1750 B.C. His code declared that Hammurabi was like a real father to his people. He gave them laws "to cause justice to prevail in the land, to destroy the wicked and evil, that the strong might not oppress the weak." Most of our knowledge of the code comes from a tablet found in Susa, Iran, in 1901.

All people were not equal in Babylon. Some people were aristocrats, some were commoners, and some were slaves. People were not treated in the same way by the laws. If a free man knocked out the eye of another free man, he could lose his own eye as punishment. Slaves were still less fortunate. The laws treated them like property. The Sumerians and Babylonians were not the only slave owners in ancient times. Almost all ancient civilizations allowed slavery. Frequently prisoners of war were kept as slaves rather than killed.

More Trade and Better Products

People living in a city did not have to make everything they used. Instead, they could spend their time making one kind of product that they traded for things they needed. A weaver would make cloth and trade it to the potter for dishes, to the merchant for grain, and to the metalsmith for tools. Since weavers spent their time doing only one kind of job, they learned to do it well. They made much finer cloth than part-time weavers could. The same was true of potters, smiths, barbers, and people with other skills.

In the Sumerian and Babylonian cities, artisans devoted themselves to their special jobs. The fine metalwork, jewelry, and stone carving that they produced show the skill of these specialized workers.

▶ EGYPTIAN CIVILIZATION

Civilization in Egypt is older than the oldest pyramid. About 3200 B.C. a king named Menes (also called Narmer) brought the land along the Nile River under his rule. For more than 3,000 years, Egypt remained one of the richest and most civilized lands in the world.

The Egyptians had a system of writing. Instead of using clay tablets, they wrote on sheets of papyrus. These were made from strips of the papyrus reed, which grew along the Nile. Papyrus does not last as well as clay tablets. But since the Egyptian climate is dry, many ancient writings have survived. There is a letter from a boy-king to one of his captains, asking that the captain bring back a dancing dwarf from central Africa. There are collections of wise sayings, including one that advised a young man to "think much, but keep thy mouth closed." One essay by a soldier tells how difficult it is to serve in a cold, foreign land. Such writings tell the thoughts of people who lived thousands of years ago.

The God-Kings and Their Officials

The Egyptians thought of their kings, whom they called pharaohs, as gods who had power over the Nile River. The Nile flooded each year and brought water to the fields. Since the prosperity of the people depended on the king, they had to give the king a part of what they produced.

The king supposedly ruled the entire land. But no one person could actually manage so large a kingdom alone. Egypt was in fact ruled in the king's name by an army of officials. The king's chief assistant, called a vizier, appointed the most important officials. They in turn appointed other officials, who appointed still lesser ones. Every district had its official, who was the government representative best known to the common people. The district official served as chief of police, judge, overseer of the irrigation canals, and tax collector.

Tombs and Temples

Stone was plentiful in the Nile Valley. And Egyptian builders had a good supply of material to build tombs and temples for the god-kings and their officials. The pyramids were tombs designed to protect the bodies of the kings. The bodies were placed in the burial chambers within these huge heaps of stone.

This gold-covered statue of the goddess Selkis (Selket) was found in the tomb of Tutankhamen, an Egyptian king.

This gold death mask of Tutankhamen was also found in the tomb. The king died at 18 or 19, in about 1325 B.C.

The first pyramid was designed by the architect Imhotep for King Zoser. The largest was built by King Khufu (called Cheops by the Greeks). It took more than 2,000,000 blocks of stone, each with an average weight of more than 2 metric tons, to build Cheops' Great Pyramid. This pyramid stood close to the Nile River, so that during the high-water season barges could float across to it. The pyramid was about 145 meters (480 feet) high. It was the tallest structure in the world for more than 4,000 years. People spoke of it as one of the seven wonders of the world.

Later, kings built other kinds of tombs. Some were cut from solid rock cliffs. Rooms inside the tombs were furnished like rooms in a palace, so that the dead would not want for anything in the next life. Beds, benches, clothing, food, tools, and even games were placed in the tombs. Painters covered the walls with pictures that showed familiar scenes of people working in shops or in the fields or boating on the river. Some of the tombs were never opened until recent years. Thus people today can still see the furnishings and paintings made so long ago.

The Egyptians also built temples such as the temple for the god Amon-Re at Karnak. This temple is famous for its huge carved stone columns.

Science of the Egyptians

Science grows partly out of the need to know. The Egyptians, for example, needed to know how to mark time so that they would know when to expect the Nile's yearly flood. The river rose in early summer and left behind a rich deposit of soil in which farmers planted crops. The Egyptians discovered that they could keep a record of time by observing the position of the stars and the sun. They invented a calendar that was divided into 12 months of 30 days each. They used the remaining 5 days of the year for religious rites.

Egyptian physicians learned some things about the human body, and they tried to cure diseases. They knew that the pulse was caused by the beating of the heart and that the brain controlled the arms and legs. Egyptians, like most ancient peoples, believed that evil spirits caused sickness. They tried to drive the evil spirits out by magical spells and words. Physicians also made medicines of olive oil, honey, and many kinds of herbs and other ingredients. It is hard to say whether any of these medicines worked. If patients believed that a medicine or magic would help them, it may actually have done so. The Egyptians did set broken bones successfully. They used splints and casts made of linen, glue, and plaster.

Statues Large and Small

Egyptian sculptors were among the best of ancient times. They carved both wood and stone. They made small busts and huge statues of kings as high as seven-story buildings. The Great Sphinx of Giza has the head of a king on the body of a lion. At its tallest point, the figure is 20 meters (66 feet) high.

The portrait statues were remarkably lifelike. Some years ago workers who found a wooden statue of an official called it "sheikh of the village" because they thought it looked like their village mayor. Queen Nefertiti died more than 3,300 years ago. But people can still admire her beauty because of the skillful artists who carved her portrait. Her husband was Amenhotep IV.

A Woman Ruler, a Conqueror, and a Religious Reformer

Nefertiti is not the only famous Egyptian woman. Queen Hatshepsut ruled the country for over 20 years. She put up monuments throughout the land on which she referred to herself as pharaoh, or ruler. One monument tells of an expedition that she sent to Somaliland, on the Red Sea. The expedition returned with rare spices, sweet-smelling woods, gold, ivory, ebony, and apes.

Hatshepsut's nephew, Thutmose III, ruled after her death. He tried to wipe out all memory of the woman who had ruled as pharaoh. Thutmose had his aunt's statues smashed and her monuments covered over with stone walls. But after a time, the walls fell down, revealing Hatshepsut's words.

Thutmose was a soldier who was not content to rule only Egypt. He conquered the cities and kingdoms of Palestine and Syria and made a large empire for himself in the 1400's B.C. Thutmose was one of the most famous military leaders of ancient times.

Amenhotep IV, who ruled in the 1300's B.C., was not a soldier, but he is as famous as Thutmose the conqueror. Amenhotep, unlike most Egyptians, did not worship many gods. Instead he believed only in Aten (or Aton), the sun god. Amenhotep changed his name to Akhenaten (or Akhnaton). He wrote hymns in praise of the sun god. He also tried to stop the worship of the old gods, but he did not succeed. After his death the old worship was restored. Later records written by priests who served the old gods always referred to Akhnaton as "that criminal."

▶ EBLAITE CIVILIZATION

Ebla was one of the ancient world's important trading cities from about 2400 to 2000

This carving is of Nefertiti, one of the most famous of Egyptian queens, who lived in about 1360 B.C.

This painting was found in a tomb at Thebes, the capital of ancient Egypt.

B.C. Today Ebla is only a large mound in northern Syria, about 55 kilometers (34 miles) southwest of Aleppo. We would know little about Eblaite civilization if there had not been a fire in the palace library 4,000 years ago. It may seem strange that a fire preserved a library. Fire destroys paper books and records. But this was a library of clay tablets. The fire that destroyed the palace baked the tablets so that they became as hard as bricks. Nearly 15,000 of the hardened tablets lay buried until 1975, when an Italian archeologist discovered them.

What the Tablets Tell about a Trading City

About 30,000 people lived within the walls of the ancient city of Ebla. Most of the city-dwellers were probably officials and their families. Tablets list the amounts of wheat, barley, and wine collected to support the large number of officials. The fact that there were many officials suggests that Ebla was the center of a large kingdom. Kings ruled the land with the help of a council of high officials. The tablets give the names of some kings. It is thought that each king was elected for a term of 7 years.

The tablets prove that Ebla was a great trading center for timber, fine cloth, rare gems, and metalwork. Eblaite traders carried goods to distant places—to Egypt, the Sumerian cities, the island of Cyprus, and even to Iran.

Scribes kept business records with cuneiform marks on clay tablets. Ebla had a school where scribes learned this Sumerian way of writing. Some students' tablets have been found with the names of the students who wrote on them and of the teachers who corrected the mistakes. Scribes wrote the Sumerian language as well as Eblaite. When the tablets were first found in 1975, no one could read Eblaite. Fortunately, the discovery of word lists with both Sumerian and Eblaite words provided a key. These word lists made it possible for scholars to learn that Eblaite is the oldest known language of the Semitic group. Hebrew and Arabic also belong to this group.

The Eblaites appear to have had many gods. They worshipped more than 500, many of them borrowed from other peoples.

The tablets tell that Eblaite kings conquered other cities. And remains in the mound show that Ebla itself was conquered several times. The burning of the palace library took place when a rival king captured the city about 2250 B.C. The conquest did not destroy Eblaite civilization, for the Eblaites rebuilt their city. But it may have weakened the city. Even through a later war with the Amorites, about 2000 B.C., Ebla remained a trading city. It was conquest by the Hittites, about 1650 B.C., that finally destroyed Ebla. After that date, Ebla was almost forgotten.

▶ INDUS CIVILIZATION

A hundred years ago historians could not have written about the ancient civilization on the plains of the Indus River. The story of that civilization still lay buried in mounds. The first hint of buried cities came in the 19th century. Workers digging for a railroad bed found some unusual carved stone seals. No one paid much attention to the seals at that time. After 1920, scholars unearthed the ruins of buried cities on the Indus Plain. Then they

The ox-drawn cart and the little clay dog from Mohenjo-Daro were toys for children of that ancient city.

Farmers in the Indus Plain paid taxes by bringing part of their grain crop to the city granary.

realized that the strange seals were but a few of the things left behind by people who lived about 4,000 years ago.

Cities with Sewers

The Indus cities were fairly large. It is thought that Mohenjo-Daro and Harappa, two of the main cities, each had as many as 20,000 inhabitants. The cities were laid out in regular blocks with streets and alleys. The remains of brick walls and platforms mark where the buildings once stood. Houses were generally built around an unroofed court. The rooms of the house opened onto the court. Some houses had bathrooms with drains connected to sewers that ran beneath the paved streets. A thick-walled fort served as a place of safety for the people in time of danger. Mohenjo-Daro had a large pool that may have been used for religious ceremonies.

The World's First Cotton Farmers

The Indus people were the world's first cotton farmers. They also grew wheat, barley, and melons and kept livestock—sheep, cattle, water buffalo, camels, horses, and donkeys.

The Indus farmers paid their taxes in grain. One of the most important buildings in the city was a large granary (a storehouse for grain). It was built of timber on a brick platform. This made it high enough to keep the grain safe from the river's floodwaters. The granary served as the ruler's "bank," where the wealth collected from the people was kept.

Weapons, Tools, and Toys

Most of the people were farmers, but there were artisans in the Indus cities. They must have spent most of their time working at a single craft. Metalsmiths made fine bronze weapons such as swords, knives, daggers, and spearheads. They also made things for everyday use such as razors, hairpins, fishhooks, axes, hammers, and saws.

The cities had toymakers who made playthings for children. They made rattles, marbles, little clay carts, and animals on wheels that could be pulled by a string. Perhaps the

This stone seal of an elephant was found at Mohenjo-Daro. The picture writing on top has never been deciphered.

Indus children had the world's first toy with moving parts—a little clay bull with a head that moved when someone pulled a string.

Trade with Faraway Lands

Beads were found in the Indus ruins. This tells us that the people liked ornaments and that they traded with faraway lands. Some of the beads are like those worn by the Sumerians and Babylonians. Silver, gold, asphalt, and precious stones show that there was trade with Afghanistan, Iran, and southern India.

Writing That No One Can Read

A great many carved stone seals have been found since the first ones were dug up more than a century ago. The Indus people probably used the stones to mark lumps of clay, which were used to seal goods. Each person may have had an individual mark. The seals usually have animals carved on them and some strange writing. No one today can read this writing.

What Happened to the Cities?

How could cities with thousands of people disappear and be completely forgotten? Scholars know only that about 1500 B.C. some disaster struck the Indus cities. Perhaps invaders conquered them. People died in the streets of one of the cities, and no one was left to bury the bodies. After a time, walls fell down and covered the bones. The winds of many centuries blew dust over the mound of ruins. People of later times seeing the mounds never guessed that a city once stood there. It was only when people began to dig that the secret came out.

▶ ASSYRIAN AND PERSIAN CIVILIZATIONS

A thousand years after the time of Hammurabi, Babylon was no longer a great power. Other peoples had grown strong. Among them were the Assyrians, who lived in the hilly country north of the Babylonian plain. In 710 B.C. the Assyrians conquered Babylon and then went on to conquer other lands. The Assyrian king Ashurbanipal, who ruled from 669 to 626 B.C., had an empire that included Egypt as well as Babylonia.

Fierce Warriors and Iron Weapons

Assyrian kings boasted of their fierceness and the terrors they inflicted upon those who opposed them. One king grimly declared that he dyed the mountain red with the blood of his foes.

The Assyrian army was both fierce and well armed. Soldiers no longer fought with bronze weapons. They used iron swords, lances, and axes, and they wore iron helmets and armor. Iron dulled the best bronze blade. Assyrian horsemen drove swift battle chariots. It is no wonder that the Assyrian kings conquered an empire.

The King's Library

King Ashurbanipal boasted of his victories, but he was at least as proud of his learning and his library. He probably declared that he had mastered the noble art of writing. It is said that he could even read the beautiful writings of the Sumerians. The Assyrians used

This detail of a carving made in ancient Persia shows Darius I with a servant holding a parasol over him.

the cuneiform writing of the Babylonians. Ashurbanipal's library consisted of thousands of clay tablets. He instructed his officials to search for any old writings in the cities of the empire. It is said that one official wrote from Babylon that he had found an original tablet that Hammurabi the king prepared. Much of what we know about Sumerian and Babylonian writings comes from the tablets found in the ruins of Ashurbanipal's palace.

The Assyrian scribes produced histories of the reigns and wars of their kings. From these writings, we have learned a great deal about the terrors of their conquests. Other armies were probably as brutal, but they left few records of their horrors.

The Assyrian Empire came to a sudden end. Their fearful methods did not keep the conquered peoples quiet. A few years after Ashurbanipal's death, Babylonia revolted. With others, the Babylonians captured and destroyed Nineveh, the Assyrian capital, in 612 B.C.

The Coming of the Persians

Babylon did not long remain free. In 538 B.C. it was conquered by the army of Cyrus the Great, king of the Persians. The Persians were an Iranian people who gave their name to the high land east of Babylonia. The Persians went on to conquer still more lands. Darius I, who ruled from 521 to 486 B.C., controlled an empire that reached from the Indus River to the Aegean Sea. It included Egypt as well as Babylonia. Assyria had never ruled so large an empire.

The Teachings of Zoroaster and the Rule of an Empire

Darius followed the teachings of a Persian prophet called Zoroaster (or Zarathustra). Zoroaster taught that life was a constant struggle between a god of good, Ahura Mazda, and a spirit of evil. Wise people, said Zoroaster, should put themselves on the side of good and justice. For rulers this meant that they should keep peace and order throughout their realm. Darius tried to follow Zoroaster's teachings in at least this one respect. He allowed the people he conquered considerable freedom as long as they remained peaceful. He allowed them to manage most of their own affairs. Athough they had their own kings, Darius was recognized as the "king of kings," and taxes were paid to him. To be sure of this, he placed a governor and a general in every district of his empire. To keep watch on these officials, he sent special agents to travel about their districts.

The Persians built roads between the main cities of the empire. About every 23 kilometers (14 miles) there were rest stations with inns and stables. Royal messengers changed horses at each station so that they could cover long distances rapidly. They could carry a message from Sardis to Susa, a distance of 2,400 kilometers (1,500 miles) in less than two weeks.

The Persian Empire was the largest empire the world had yet seen. It included the lands that are now the countries of Turkey, Egypt, Israel, Jordan, Lebanon, Syria, Iraq, Afghanistan, and part of Pakistan.

An Assyrian wall carving, dating from the 7th century B.C., depicts a victory by the soldiers of King Ashurbanipal.

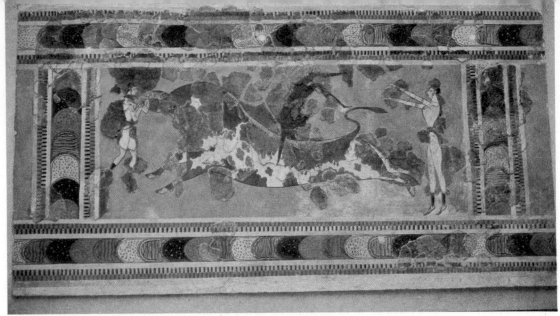

A wall painting in the palace of Minos at Knossos depicts the acrobatic bull-fighters of ancient Crete. The painting dates from the Middle Bronze Age.

▶ CRETAN CIVILIZATION

Four thousand years ago the people of Crete depended on the sea for both their wealth and safety. Crete is an island in the Mediterranean Sea, well situated for trade. The Cretans traded wheat, wine, linen, olive oil, and cypress timber for goods from Egypt, Syria, Italy, and lands still farther away. They also depended on the sea for defense. They built no walls around cities because they counted on their navy to keep enemies from their shores.

A statue of a young man, dating from the 6th century B.C., in a temple of the god Apollo in Boeotia, Greece.

Knossos and the King's Palace

Knossos was the greatest of the Cretan cities. Thousands of people lived there. The king's palace was a rambling structure covering 2 hectares (5 acres). It contained an open court, a throne room, chapels, and apartments for the king and his attendants. There were rooms where wheat and olive oil were stored in jars nearly as tall as a human adult. Paintings showing scenes from daily life decorated the walls. Bits of the paintings that remain show us how these people looked.

The people of Knossos watched performances in outdoor theatres. They liked active sports such as boxing. They had an unusual exhibition in which acrobats turned somersaults in midair, coming down on the backs of charging bulls. "Bull leaping" would have made most rodeo contests of today look tame.

Throughout Knossos there were signs of the city's wealth. Women wore gold jewelry and elaborately ruffled skirts. The palaces and houses contained fine pottery and carved stone figures. The king and the nobles had chariots complete with spare wheels, which were necessary because of the rough cobblestone streets.

Trade was important in Crete, but most people were not traders. They worked on the land, growing wheat, olives, figs, and grapes. They tended goats and sheep and drove ox teams. The people gave the oxen such names as Dapple and Darkie, Blondie and Bawler.

Disaster Strikes: A Civilization Forgotten

The prosperity of Knossos came to an end about 1400 B.C. Disaster struck the city, but just what happened is not clear. Perhaps the sea no longer kept invaders away. People continued to live at Knossos, but the great days were past. After 1100 B.C. the old civilization disappeared and was almost entirely forgotten within a few hundred years. The world has learned of the ancient cities only since 1900, when scholars digging among the ruins found the walls of palaces and houses. Among other things, diggers found a number of clay tablets with writing on them. It was clear that there were two different kinds of writing, but both were in an unknown script. It was 1952 before anyone could read these tablets. Then scholars discovered that these ancient writers used an early form of Greek on one group of tablets. But the other writing still remains a complex mystery.

This wall carving of the Greek goddess Athena dates from the 5th century B.C.

▶ GREEK CIVILIZATION

Athens in the year 447 B.C. was not the largest city in the ancient world. But it was surely one of the liveliest and most interesting. In that year builders began working on the Parthenon, the beautiful temple built in honor of the goddess Athena. The Parthenon stands on the high rocky hill called the Acropolis. Some of the most brilliant people of the ancient world were in Athens in those days, writing books and plays and teaching. There was interesting talk in the homes, on the streets, or wherever people gathered.

Athens was a leader of the Greek cities. This does not mean that Athens ruled Greece, for in those days each city ruled itself. The separate city-states might unite to some extent in times of war, as they did in 490 and 480 B.C. when the Persians invaded Greece. But the cities sometimes fought among themselves. The great Peloponnesian Wars (431–404

Greek vase from the 6th century B.C. depicts the legendary heroes Achilles and Ajax playing dice.

The citizens of Athens often discussed the news of the day in the Agora, or market place. The temples of the Acropolis and the statue of the goddess Athena rise above the city.

B.C.) brought two groups of cities into conflict. Athens led one group. Sparta led the other.

The Democracy of Athens

Athens had an early form of democracy, with government by the citizens. But only men could hold citizenship. Five hundred men made up the council, which had direct charge of city affairs. This council met about three times a month. The men discussed and voted on laws and such important matters as going to war or making peace. Every year a new group of 500 was chosen by drawing names. In this way all men had a chance to serve on the council. The Athenians drew names for all officials except the generals. These were elected each year and could be re-elected any

number of times. Pericles was elected general every year except one from 461 to 429 B.C. He was so important as a leader that these years are called "the age of Pericles."

Sparta—A City of Soldiers

Sparta differed from Athens in many ways. In both cities, all men served in the army in wartime, but in Sparta military service was the main duty of all males. A boy began his military training at age 7 and continued it until he was an old man. The laws of Sparta closely regulated what a citizen did. Since a citizen was always a soldier, he did not carry on trade in a foreign land or travel without permission. Perhaps it was feared that the citizen-soldiers might lose interest in their job if they were allowed too much liberty.

The Spartans paid great attention to military training because they were afraid. They had conquered their neighbors and enslaved them, and they feared that their numerous slaves might revolt.

Things of Beauty

The Greeks did not build the largest structures of ancient times. No Greek building could compare in size with the pyramids. But the Greeks did erect some of the most beautiful buildings of any time. An example is the Parthenon, at Athens. Only the ruins of the Parthenon stand today. It was blown up during a battle in A.D. 1687. Yet even in ruins the Parthenon remains one of the world's most famous and lovely buildings.

The Greeks produced many things of beauty—pottery, metalwork, and sculpture. It was said that the sculptor Phidias " made marble breathe."

Poets and Playwrights

Most Greek children studied Homer's *Iliad* and *Odyssey,* long epic poems that tell of the gods and heroes. The Greeks admired different kinds of poetry, including the verses of a woman named Sappho.

Greek playwrights wrote about subjects well known to their audiences. This did not matter, for the Greeks judged a play by the beauty of its language rather than the

originality of its plot. In the 5th century B.C., the great age of playwriting, Aeschylus, Euripides, and Sophocles moved people deeply with their tragic plays. Aristophanes made them laugh with his uproarious comedies.

Sports and the Olympic Games

The Greeks held games in honor of the gods. Athletes from all the Greek cities took part in the Olympic Games, held in August every four years. They wrestled, boxed, threw the discus and javelin, and ran races. The prize for a victor was only a wreath of leaves. But the honor of winning the wreath was so great that the athletes trained for years to compete for it.

The Desire To Know

The Greeks were eager to learn about the heavens, the world, and themselves. Some searched to discover the elements from which all matter is made. Others studied the sky and carefully observed the sun, moon, and planets. The Greeks knew that the earth was round, and they were not far wrong in their estimations of its size.

The Greeks learned about different peoples and their history. In the 5th century, Herodotus traveled among the Persians, Babylonians, and Egyptians and wrote a history of the world he knew. At the same time Hip-

During the time of Pericles, the great temple known as the Parthenon was built in Athens, Greece. These sculptures were part of the temple's magnificent decorations.

This sculpture shows Aristotle and his teacher, Plato, two of the greatest of the Greek philosophers.

pocrates studied diseases. He described cases he had observed and suggested remedies. He drew up rules of ethics (morals) for those who practiced medicine, which doctors still respect.

Wisdom is more than knowledge alone. Those Greek thinkers who searched for deep understanding called themselves philosophers —"lovers of wisdom." Socrates, his student Plato, and Plato's student Aristotle were among the greatest Greek philosophers.

Greek Civilization Outside Greece

The Greeks were a restless people. They established colonies around the shores of the Mediterranean and Black seas. In 334 B.C., Alexander the Great, the Greek-speaking ruler of Macedonia, waged war against the Persian Empire. Within ten years Alexander conquered the Persians and ruled an empire that extended from Greece east to the Indus River. Alexander established cities through-

out his empire that became centers of Greek civilization. After Alexander's death a Greek ruler of Egypt established the Museum, a kind of university, at Alexandria. There many famous Greek thinkers studied and wrote. Among the scholars of the Museum was the mathematician Euclid, who developed a form of geometry that people still study.

The fact that people still study the ideas of such Greeks as Euclid, Socrates, Plato, and Aristotle tells something important about Greek civilization. The ideas and teachings of the Greeks have lasted longer than many of their ancient stone monuments.

▶ ROMAN CIVILIZATION

When Alexander was conquering his empire in the east, Rome was fighting wars to control Italy in the west. In the years from 265 B.C. to A.D. 14, the Romans won control of the lands around the Mediterranean. For hundreds of years Rome ruled a great empire, which included Egypt and Greece.

Roman conquest did not mean that Roman ways replaced those of the conquered peoples. It was often the other way. The Romans conquered the Greek cities, but they adopted many Greek ideas and ways of thinking. The Romans had no real philosophy. If they wished to study this subject, they had to have Greek teachers. They found the

Cameo portrait of an emperor of Rome.

View of the Roman Colosseum and, in front of it, the Arch of Constantine.

literature of the Greeks more interesting than their own. In fact, the poet Vergil, who lived from 70 to 19 B.C., modeled his great epic poem, the *Aeneid,* on the epics of Homer. The Romans produced important histories and writings about politics, such as those by Cicero.

The Romans as Engineers and Builders

The Romans were excellent engineers. They built a network of good roads. Official messengers and troops moved rapidly over swamps, rivers, and mountains because of good bridges, paved causeways, and tunnels. A Roman bridge still spans the Tagus River in Spain.

Good engineers provided Rome with a better water supply than almost any other ancient city. Stone aqueducts brought pure water from springs sometimes more than 64 kilometers (40 miles) away. Rome had a huge arena, the Colosseum, where over 45,000 people could watch athletic contests, combat between gladiators, chariot races, and other spectacular events. The huge dome on one of ancient Rome's most famous buildings, the Pantheon, still stands.

An aqueduct in Segovia, Spain—one of more than 200 built by the Romans.

These Roman coins picture, from left to right, Neptune, god of the sea; the emperors Julius Caesar and Augustus Caesar; and Apollo, the god of poetry and music.

Above: Ruins of the ancient Roman city Pompeii. The city was covered with ash by the eruption of Mt. Vesuvius (background) in A.D. 79. Below: A mosaic from Pompeii depicts the Academy of the Greek philosopher Plato.

Peace and Justice

The Roman Empire included many different peoples, each with its own language, religion, and customs. The Romans did not force people to give up their own ways so long as they did not interfere with the welfare of the empire. They allowed people to worship their own gods, and they let them manage many of their local affairs. But the Romans could not, of course, use everybody's language. Latin, the Roman tongue, served as the language of government wherever Rome ruled. In some areas Latin came to replace other languages. Portuguese, Spanish, French, Romanian, and Italian all developed from Latin.

The Romans also developed a system of law for the empire. They learned that a law was more likely to be obeyed when it was fair. Roman laws grew increasingly reasonable and fair in the course of time. The Romans saw that the purpose of law is justice. What is justice? The Romans said that it was giving people what was due them. The fact that Roman law lasted so long shows how well they did this. A number of modern countries base their law on that of the Romans.

The Romans did not give the ancient world its greatest art or philosophy, but their contribution was not small. The Roman Empire gave the peoples of that time a peaceful world that allowed them to prosper.

KENNETH S. COOPER
George Peabody College

See also ALEXANDER THE GREAT; ANCIENT WORLD, ART OF THE; BYZANTINE EMPIRE; CITIES; EGYPTIAN ART AND ARCHITECTURE; GREEK ART AND ARCHITECTURE; GREEK MYTHOLOGY; POMPEII; ROMAN ART AND ARCHITECTURE; ROMAN EMPIRE; TROJAN WAR; WONDERS OF THE WORLD; ZOROASTRIANISM.

ANCIENT WORLD, ART OF THE

On the shores of the eastern Mediterranean Sea, where Europe meets Asia and Asia meets Africa, are the remains of ancient cities. These cities lay buried for centuries. When the ruins were dug up, the works of art that were found revealed that this region was one of the first in which civilization was known.

Some of the earliest sculpture of civilized people was created in Mesopotamia, the land between the Tigris and Euphrates rivers. Much of this sculpture was carved on stone slabs, and the slabs served as backgrounds. This kind of sculpture is known as relief. Sculpture-in-the-round—three-dimensional sculpture, free from background—was also created, but it has not survived so well.

Ancient Mesopotamia was the home of many different nations. Certain characteristics of art lasted for thousands of years and were present in the art of every nation. These characteristics were established by the Sumerians, the first civilized people of Mesopotamia. They developed one of the first known empires in history, and their art influenced the Egyptians as well as all later Mesopotamian civilizations.

▶ SUMER (3200–2000 B.C.)

Most of the art that survives from the first 500 years of Sumerian civilization has been found in the ruins of temples. Several bronze statuettes of animals prove that these ancient people knew and used metal. White stone statues of human figures were decorated with

These panels of many-colored stones and shells once decorated a temple in the ancient Sumerian city of Ur. British Museum, London.

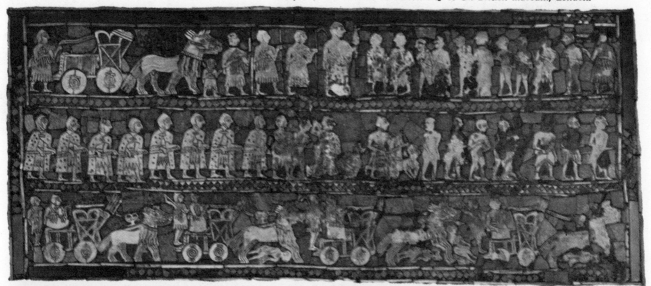

These small ancient statuettes were found buried beneath an altar of a Sumerian temple. Oriental Institute, University of Chicago; Iraq Museum, Baghdad.

colored stones. Bowls, vases, bottles, and other containers (called vessels) were made of stone for religious use. The outsides of the vessels were decorated with relief carvings of animals and plants.

Around 3000 B.C. the Sumerians entered their first truly great age, called the Early Dynastic period. Sculpture during this period was created to stand in the temple of the god of the city. Sculptured worshipers stood with their hands clasped in front of their bodies—a gesture of respect before the god. Sometimes the figure held a cup that may have contained an offering to the god. Clothing was solid and stiff; there was no suggestion that a body was beneath it. Most of the artist's skill was concentrated on the head. Eyes were enormous and bulging. The long beards of men had heavy, crosswise ridges. If the figure had hair, it was long and braided, but often heads were shown shaved.

Sumerian sculpture was carved from stone, which had to be imported. There was very little stone in Mesopotamia. The most popular stone was gypsum, which is soft, satiny, and white, and looks like mother-of-pearl.

During this period sculpture gradually became more delicate and lifelike. The rocklike clothing was replaced by more natural-looking skirts, and beards were formed with hundreds of tiny curls. The mouths of these statues are slightly upturned and give life to the face.

Sumerian art reached a peak during the rule of the famous King Gudea. The sculptures made of Gudea and his family were among the greatest achievements of Sumerian art. Sometimes the statues were seated and sometimes they were standing. Gudea's body was a heavy mass of stonelike drapery as in early Sumerian sculpture. An attempt may have been made to carve a likeness of Gudea's features on the statues.

Sumerian Architecture

Mesopotamia was a land without stone or forests. The usual materials for buildings were mud and reeds. Homes were built of reeds from the marshlands. Sometimes the reeds were tied in great bundles and set in two rows. The tops were bent together and tied. Other homes were rectangular and constructed of woven reed. Often the reed building was entirely covered with mud and painted.

The only other buildings that we know about are temples. They were built of bricks made of mud and dried in the sun. Platforms raised the brick walls from the ground, and

An example of Sumerian sculpture at its peak is this small stone statue of King Gudea, who ruled over 4,000 years ago. Louvre, Paris.

Babylonian sculpture was more lifelike than the Sumerian. Heads such as this one—probably of King Hammurabi—are among the first portraits in history. Louvre, Paris.

great staircases were constructed from the ground to the platform. The walls were held up by brick structures called buttresses, which were built against the walls.

Sumerian architects developed the style of temple that became the main form of ancient Mesopotamian architecture: the **ziggurat**. The ziggurat was built in many stages in the shape of a mountain. On top of the "mountain" was a shrine to the city-god enclosed within a great wall. As far as we know, the ziggurat at Warka was the first. The brick walls of ziggurats were often decorated with colored stones, mother-of-pearl inlays, large paintings, and rows of animals forged from copper. The ziggurat built for the moon-god in the city of Ur during the Neo-Sumerian period has remained in better condition than earlier ones. This is because its architects had learned that bricks baked in an oven were much stronger than bricks simply dried in the sun. However, nothing survives of the shrine.

▶ BABYLONIA (2000–1100 B.C.)

Three centuries of war followed the end of the Sumerian Empire. City-states within Mesopotamia fought with each other, and barbarian tribes invaded the Tigris-Euphrates region. Finally in the 18th century B.C., Hammurabi, ruler of the city of Babylon, became the ruler of Sumer and Akkad and united the warring city-states.

Sculpture during the time of Hammurabi was more naturalistic (lifelike) than ever before in Mesopotamia. Although it is not certain, the stone heads that have been found were probably meant to represent Hammu-

rabi. The king was shown as a bearded man with very large eyelids and wearing a cap. Portraiture was unusual in Mesopotamia, but in Egypt—the great nation to the west—royal portraits were being created. It is likely that Egypt influenced Babylonian art.

Hammurabi recorded his famous laws on a large stone called a **stela**. The laws were written on the lower three quarters of the stone; the top quarter was carved in bold relief, with a figure of a seated god before whom Hammurabi stood. The scene was intended to give religious authority to the laws.

Like the Sumerians, the Babylonians used bronze as well as stone for their sculpture. One bronze statue from the First Dynasty was of a kneeling man. His face was covered with gold. On the base of the statue a carved inscription requested long life for the king, perhaps Hammurabi. Other surviving bronze statues include one of a spirited group of wild

Frescoes—paintings on wet plaster—decorated the walls of the Minoan palace at Knossos. The most important figure was the king-priest.

Painted pottery statuettes known as snake-goddesses were created by the Minoans around 1600 B.C. Herakleion Museum, Crete.

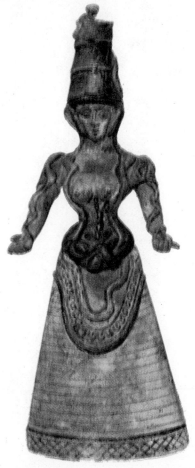

goats standing on their hind legs and another of a ram bearing an inscription to a god.

The Kassites, mountaineers from the east, slowly pushed their way into Babylon after the death of Hammurabi. The First Dynasty fell around 1600 B.C., and the Kassite barbarians made themselves masters of Babylonia. Although they adopted Babylonian culture, the Kassites produced very little art—certainly nothing of importance.

Babylonian Architecture

Only a few ruins remain of the architecture of the First and Kassite dynasties. Many Sumerian buildings were rebuilt, and the architecture of new buildings was copied from Sumerian styles. The Kassite royal palace was larger than most earlier buildings. Around 1450 B.C. a new temple was built at Warka for the worship of the mother-goddess. It was not on a ziggurat, but was small and rectangular. Reliefs in brick depicting huge gods formed a continuous band of decoration on the outside walls of the temple.

The Kassite Dynasty fell to the Assyrians in about 1100 B.C. Until the 6th century B.C., the Babylonians were attacked, overrun, crushed, and conquered many times. But they survived to rise again and to make Babylon one of the great cities of the ancient world.

▶ MINOAN CIVILIZATION (2000–1200 B.C.)

More than 5,000 years ago the Mediterranean island of Crete was inhabited by people known as the Minoans. The Minoans developed a civilization around the same time that the Sumerians began theirs. Nothing was known about this civilization until the 20th century, and little is certain about its history and earliest art.

The sculpture of the Minoans—at least what has survived—is small and very different from the sculpture of Mesopotamia. Figures of animals and people were made of bronze, stone, ivory, or terra-cotta (red clay). The Minoans sometimes baked clay statuettes and painted them. In contrast to Mesopotamian sculpture, Minoan figures were shown in motion: representations of worshipers had upraised arms; animals were shown running; an acrobat was depicted jumping over a bull. Slender young men and women were portrayed with impossibly small waists and nar-

Most Minoan carving was done on stone vessels such as this 3,500-year-old *Harvester Vase*. Herakleion Museum, Crete.

row hips. Figures of men had arms crossed on their chests. Women wore narrow corsets beneath their breasts, flaring skirts, and high headdresses.

Around 1600 B.C. the Minoans created statuettes known as snake-goddesses. However, these sculptures probably represented priestesses rather than goddesses. Made of painted pottery, these figures are similar to earlier Minoan work—they are dressed in the same skirts and headdresses and have tiny waists—but their outstretched arms have snakes coiled around them.

Ivory figurines were originally enriched with gold details now lost. Common subjects were young athletes leaping over bulls, a child at play, or a child attended by nurses. Bronze sculpture almost always represented a Minoan at prayer.

Relief sculpture on a large scale was probably unknown to the Minoans. Most carving in relief was done on stone vessels. Subjects included farmers marching and singing, and people boxing, wrestling, bull leaping, or just standing. The Minoans also created a great many delicate, tiny seals carved on gems. Some scholars believe that all adult Minoans had their own seal designs.

Minoan Architecture

The Minoans did not build temples. Religious ceremonies were conducted outdoors or in the palaces. The palace was the center of the Minoan community. It was, of course, the residence of the royal family and the seat of government, but it was also used as a storehouse for merchandise and contained workshops where goods were manufactured.

The palace was usually built on a hillside and was made up of many low, rectangular units. Roofs were flat, and foundations were made of stone. Two or three stories was the usual height; the first story was stone and the ones above were probably of mud bricks.

A great court paved with stones was built in the center of the palace. Religious ceremonies were conducted in this court. It is thought that this central court was planned first, and as new parts were needed they were built around it. Corridor walls were decorated with large frescoes—paintings done on wet plaster. Because the building was constructed in separate parts, many staircases and corridors were needed. Walls and sometimes even floors may have been covered with alabaster. Ceilings were held up by painted wooden columns, which were circular or oval. They were unusual because they were smaller at the base than at the top. No one is certain why the columns were made in this way.

Comfort was important to the Minoans. Their palaces and country houses sprawled over large areas, and there were many passageways and windows. Sunlight poured into every part of the buildings, and there was a great feeling of spaciousness. Elaborate bathrooms—undoubtedly the first in Europe—contained terra-cotta tubs, drains, and toilets.

In the course of many centuries, the great Minoan palaces were destroyed several times. Scholars cannot be absolutely certain of the causes, but earthquakes, tidal waves, or fires were among the natural causes. There may also have been uprisings and invasions. But each time, the Minoans rebuilt their palaces. Then, around the year 1200 B.C., the Minoan civilization came to a sudden end. The Dorian tribes from the north took over Crete along with much of the Greek mainland. The Minoan buildings, along with all Minoan art, were lost for the next 30 centuries.

▶ THE HITTITES (1400–1200 B.C.)

Anatolia, a land in Asia Minor, was the home of the ancient peoples known as the Hittites. Around 1400 B.C. the Hittites extended their empire eastward as far as Mesopotamia.

Except for their statuettes in bronze, the Hittites made no sculpture-in-the-round that we know of. Hittite sculpture, in fact, was so completely a part of Hittite architecture that the two arts must be discussed together.

The Hittites built on an enormous scale. Unlike Mesopotamia, Anatolia was rich in stone and wood. The foundations of their military, civil, and religious buildings were of stone. In early Hittite buildings, stones 3 meters (10 feet) high were used in rough blocks. Later, stone that had been trimmed was used. Above the stone first level, the buildings were constructed with bricks and wood. Parts of the structure that received the most use—such as window sills and thresholds—were reinforced with stone.

Hattusas, the capital city of the Hittite Empire, was enclosed in a great wall. One of the gates was guarded by two stone lions, one on each side. The lions had been carved in very high relief from huge stones, and the remaining part of the boulders rose as high as 3 meters above the lions. Other gates were protected by sphinxes (lions with human heads) that were carved in the same way. The lions and sphinxes appeared to have grown out of the stone.

Marching figures carved in relief from stone slabs were placed along the walls of Hittite buildings on the ground level. The slabs were of either limestone or dolerite, a coarse-grained stone that had to be coated with plaster or gesso (chalk mixed with glue) to create a smooth surface. The marching figures represented a religious procession. Most of these reliefs were at Yasilikaya, which was probably a holy shrine or religious center. Gods were shown wearing flowing robes and often standing on sacred animals.

Great stone lions over 3,000 years old still stand at the ruins of Bogazkoy, a meeting place of the ancient Hittites.

Some of these reliefs were carved on the sides of cliffs at Yasilikaya, and elaborate buildings with open courts and great staircases led to the cliffs. Egyptian and Minoan designs were often included in the reliefs, a sign of trade and communication between empires. Yasilikaya may have been the coronation place of the Hittite kings.

Hittite art did not have a chance to develop fully. In the 13th century B.C., the empire was overwhelmed by invasions of barbarians from the north and by an army of mysterious peoples called the Peoples of the Sea, whose origins are unknown.

▶ ASSYRIA (900–600 B.C.)

In the centuries that followed the decline of the Hittites, the Assyrians gradually built a great empire. The Assyrians were similar to the Babylonians in language, law, and religion, but they were much more brutal. Their civilization was based on the army, and their art reflected their love of war and vio-

Marching figures were carved on the sides of cliffs at Yasilikaya, a Hittite religious center.

lence. Only a few sculptures-in-the-round have been found. One is of an early emperor, Ashurnasirpal II. In style it resembled sculpture from the Early Dynastic period of Sumer.

In the long, rectangular rooms of Assyrian buildings, there were large gypsum slabs carved in relief. The carvings often showed fierce battles or hunting scenes. Complicated and horrible scenes of torture and bloodshed and of vicious animals may have been highlighted with black, red, and yellow paint.

Assyrian reliefs give us a picture of cities, fortresses, costumes, and daily life of a people forever lost to us. From these reliefs we know the kind of furniture the Assyrians used, although only bits and pieces of real furniture have been found.

The Assyrians also carved reliefs of gigantic human-headed bulls, each with five legs. These huge creatures always appear in pairs as guardians of a palace. Placed near an entrance, they were sometimes combined with figures of men of superhuman size.

Reliefs of ivory were used by the Assyrians to decorate chests, thrones, chairs, and other furniture. Often the reliefs were gilded (coated with gold) and inlaid with colored glass and stones. Common subjects of the sculpture were plants, real and imaginary beasts, musicians, and a woman standing at a window.

Assyrian Architecture

The chief cities of Assyria were Nimrud, Khorsabad, and Nineveh, the capital. Following an ancient custom, cities were enclosed within great walls to keep enemies out. The buildings in the cities of Assyria were made of mud bricks and looked much like the buildings of Sumer. The buildings were not very high, but were spread over a large area and contained a great many rooms.

Only the ziggurat towered high over the city walls. At Khorsabad the Assyrians erected a spectacular ziggurat reaching as high as a twelve-story building of today. It was probably built in seven levels, and each one was painted a different color.

Inside and outside of every important Assyrian structure, color played an important part. Colorful glazed bricks in various patterns decorated the walls. Sometimes the outside walls were whitewashed and the inside decorated with frescoes. Ceilings were held up by wooden columns resting on stone bases. The combination of wooden columns, glazed brick, stone reliefs, and frescoes of flowers and animals created rich and impressive effects that never grew monotonous.

Assyrian stone carvings frequently illustrated battle scenes. British Museum, London.

Limestone statue of the Assyrian emperor Ashurnasirpal II, dating from the 9th century B.C. British Museum.

Five-footed winged bulls protected the gates of Assyrian palaces. British Museum, London.

In 640 B.C. the Assyrian Empire controlled more of the Middle East than it ever had before. Yet, less than 30 years later the empire no longer existed. In 612 B.C. it was invaded and crushed by a combined army of Chaldeans and Medes.

▶THE CHALDEANS (615–539 B.C.)

When the Chaldeans and Medes divided the Assyrian Empire in two, southern Mesopotamia and the lands west of the Euphrates River became the Chaldean, or Neo-Babylonian, Empire. The Chaldeans were the descendants of the Babylonians, who had ruled the ancient world before the rise of the Hittites and Assyrians.

Babylon was restored as the capital of a great empire. Temples from the old First and Kassite dynasties were rebuilt. The best-known Chaldean king, Nebuchadnezzar, built the Hanging Gardens of Babylon. His palace was built in levels, and each level had a terrace planted with flowers and shrubs. The pillars that supported each level were hollow and were used as wells.

Little remains of the art of the Chaldeans. Their famous ziggurat is hardly more than rubble today. It is likely that this ziggurat was the Tower of Babel mentioned in the Bible, for it was Nebuchadnezzar who conquered and destroyed Jerusalem, enslaved the Hebrews, and carried them to Babylonia. The ziggurat and palace were made of baked bricks. The exteriors were decorated with

Left: Part of a relief sculpture at Persepolis, showing subjects bringing gifts to the king.
Right: The Persians used this gold-and-silver winged ibex as a handle for a vase.

reliefs in glazed brick. Bright yellow bulls and sparkling white dragons were set against backgrounds of rich blue or green. Babylon during this period became a glowing expression of its luxury-loving people.

▶THE PERSIAN EMPIRE (550–332 B.C.)

In the middle of the 6th century B.C., the Persians conquered all of Mesopotamia. The Persian Empire eventually spread to Egypt and Europe in the west and into India in the east. The Persians permitted religious freedom —they returned the Hebrews to Palestine— developed an alphabet, and introduced simple systems of arithmetic.

Persia's religion (Zoroastrianism) did not require temples. Services were conducted at an altar in the open. The chief royal palaces were at Susa and Persepolis. The Persians continued the ancient Mesopotamian custom of building their palaces on platforms or terraces of mud brick. Persepolis, which was started about 520 B.C., was built on a series of these

platforms. The throne hall and the audience hall were separate buildings of immense height and were built with forests of tall columns— many more than were needed. Elaborately carved and painted, the columns were topped by enormous capitals (tops of columns) carved with bulls or dragons. The architects continued the earlier Mesopotamian use of huge stone statues of bulls and human-headed bulls as guardians of gates. At Susa reliefs of molded and glazed bricks representing lions and dragons were used as wall decorations in the palace. They date from early in the 4th century B.C.

Sculpture-in-the-round was almost unknown in Persia. A few heads of men, all of them small, were created, and some sculptures found in Egypt may be of Persian origin. But relief sculpture was made for the exteriors of buildings and to line the walls of staircases. The majority of the reliefs were made of limestone often almost black in color. But even this handsome stone was enriched with paint

One of the few remaining monuments of the ancient Chaldeans is the Ishtar Gate. Berlin Museum.

in a wide range of colors, and details were gilded.

Egyptians and other foreign craftsmen were brought to Persepolis to sculpt the reliefs. Foreign influences can be detected, but the work must have been closely supervised by Persians. These very decorative reliefs represent the king receiving foreign envoys bearing tribute. Sometimes the king is shown in combat with a demon. Persian art was very decorative, but was not especially original.

In 331 B.C. the Greek conqueror Alexander the Great overran the Persian Empire and destroyed the palace of Persepolis. The defeat of the Persians marks the end of the great cultures of the ancient Middle East. The rise of the Greeks marks the beginning of modern civilization.

JOHN D. COONEY
Author, *Late Egyptian and Coptic Art*

See also ANCIENT CIVILIZATIONS; ARCHITECTURE; EGYPTIAN ART AND ARCHITECTURE; SCULPTURE; WONDERS OF THE WORLD.

ANCIENT WORLD, MUSIC OF THE

In primitive times, music was a means to an end. People used it as a bridge to power. They used it to call in the gods of healing. They used music to bring rain to ensure a good harvest. Hunters expected added strength and accuracy after chanting the correct magic words and melody.

Dramatic changes took place in music about 6,000 years ago. The advanced civilizations of the Sumerians and the Egyptians appeared on the historic scene at this time and set music on a new path. Music received a new personality. No longer was it primarily a tool for religion and magic or for the daily functions of life. Music became an end in itself, an art to be appreciated for its own sake. The change was not abrupt, for primitive people sometimes danced, sang, and played instruments for the sheer joy of making music. But music truly became an art when it was taken over by professional musicians.

Kings, princes, and nobles demanded entertainment in their leisure time. They supported a great many professional singers, dancers, and instrumentalists. These musicians were trained from childhood, and they became highly skilled. They raised music to the level of a special trade or profession. Female musicians were particularly popular. They were often attached in large numbers to the royal courts. Pharaoh's daughter, for example, brought 1,000 "music girls" and instruments as part of her dowry when she married King Solomon.

Professional musicians were also heard in the temples, since religion still made use of music. The priests, who could read and write, were often also scholars. They were trained in mathematics, science, and philosophy. (Such subjects were not developed among primitive peoples because they had no written language.) The well-educated priests applied their knowledge to music and made other dramatic changes in this art. For the first time music could be written down, since the priests developed a special music notation. In addition, they looked for the mathematical and scientific bases of music. Their search resulted in the first organized music theory. Such theory contained information

An Egyptian wall painting shows female musicians playing the double oboe, long-necked lute, and harp.

A mosaic dating from about 2800 B.C. shows a musician of ancient Sumeria playing a lyre.

A double-reed instrument is shown in an ancient Etruscan wall painting.

on the types of scales, melodies, and rhythms the professional musician had to learn and guided him in tuning his instruments.

The Sumerians

In the ancient cities of Mesopotamia, near the Tigris and Euphrates rivers, Sumerian and later Babylonian court musicians sang and played their harps and long-necked lutes. Temple musicians participated in ceremonies honoring Shamash, the sun god; Ningirsu, the god of war; and other gods. The sacred prayers were sung by large choirs trained at the temple schools. The priests wrote their theories of religion, science, and music on clay tablets in wedge-shaped symbols. They also wrote down many prayers and hymns, often with the accompanying music written alongside the text. Unlike modern Western notation, each special sign for writing the music represented groups of notes rather than single notes. The written prayers, religious myths, and sacred music were probably kept secret and hidden from the eyes of those outside the clergy.

In addition to the harp and long-necked lute, the Sumerians favored another string instrument, the lyre. Instead of a neck the lyre has two separate arms connected by a crossbar. The flute and oboe also appeared, although wind instruments were generally not as popular as strings. Two oboes were usually bound together in a V shape and played at the same time. One of the pair probably played the melody, and the other droned a single continuous note. This melody-and-drone style of music has persisted to modern times in the Middle East and in India, where the double-wind instrument is still found.

Many of the Sumerian instruments were played at the religious ceremonies. For example, the god of wisdom, Ea, was worshiped in a sacrificial bull ritual featuring a large, goblet-shaped metal drum. Special hymns at this ceremony were accompanied by the double oboe.

The Egyptians

The civilization of ancient Egypt first appeared along the Nile River about 4000 B.C., perhaps a few hundred years later than that of Sumer. Like the Sumerian and Babylo-nian kings, the Egyptian pharaohs had many professional musicians. These are often shown on tomb paintings and sculptures playing, singing, and dancing in groups rather than as soloists. A typical musical group of about 2500 B.C. might have had several of the Egyptians' favorite instrument, the large curved harp, standing upright. There might also have been some flutes and a double clarinet consisting of two clarinets glued together. However, the most important part of the group was the singers, who were also conductors. These conductors accomplished more than conductors of modern times, for their special finger, hand, and arm motions were a special sign language. By holding the palm upward or making a circle of the thumb and forefinger, for example, they could indicate to the accompanists what melodies and rhythms to play. A similar sign language is still used today in Egypt and India.

Many musicians were exchanged as gifts between the kings of ancient times. Pharaoh Pepi II, who ruled Egypt for more than 90 years in the 26th and 25th centuries B.C., even received presents of skilled Pygmy dancers from the Congo. Much later, when Egypt became a conquering nation, many such gifts began to pour in. The pharaohs received hundreds of music girls and their instruments from Mesopotamia and other parts of southwest Asia after conquering this region in about 1500 B.C. Among the new instruments were the lyre, long-necked lute, double oboe, and tambourine. The girls seem to have brought with them a more exciting style of music, which the Egyptians soon adopted.

Little is known of the melodies and rhythms of the ancient Egyptians. However, their harps were tuned to one of the most popular scales of ancient times (and of modern Japan). This is one of the pentatonic, or five-note, scales, which can be illustrated on the piano by the tones A F E C B. No doubt other scales were also used by the Egyptians. Like the Sumerians, the Egyptians enjoyed a touch of harmony in their music, such as the drone. The drone is a steady, continuous note with a hypnotic effect. However, it was always merely a backdrop to the more important part of the music, the melody.

The sistrum, a rattle with jingling cross-bars, was played at the festivals of the

Egyptian cow-headed goddess Hathor. Although the goddess is no longer worshiped, an instrument similar to the sistrum is still played in Ethiopian Coptic churches.

The Hebrews

Although the ancient Sumerian and Egyptian civilizations faded away in history, ancient Hebrew traditions continue to the present day. Some modern Hebrews, such as those in Yemen and Iraq, have lived alone and have not been influenced by surrounding people. Their religious music, therefore, is probably very much like the music of King Solomon's temple from the 10th to 6th centuries B.C.

In this temple professional male choirs sang at daily and special ceremonies. They sang the psalms of David and other religious texts, often in the form of two choruses answering each other. There was also a soloist who chanted the different parts of the Old Testament and at certain points was answered by the congregation. Most of the melodies

Ancient Greek singers sometimes accompanied themselves on the kithara.

sung at the temple were made up of tiny melodic patterns of a few notes each. Like little formulas, these patterns could not be changed in themselves. They could, however, be strung together in different ways to form a large variety of melodies. This idea is connected with the old Sumerian music notation described above and with some later Hebrew and Christian music notation. In such types of notation, a single written sign stands for a group of musical tones that make up a tiny melodic pattern. In fact, some of the melodies of the early Christian Church are exactly like some Hebrew religious melodies sung today in Yemen, Iraq, and Iran.

The ancient Hebrews played many instruments. In the temple large professional orchestras of harps, lyres, and cymbals accompanied the choirs. Horns and metal trumpets were played by the priests. The sound of the 120 trumpets played by the priests at the opening of Solomon's temple, an event described in the second chapter of Chronicles, must really have been shattering. Outside the temple shepherds and other people played the lyre, which was King David's favorite instrument, the flute, and the oboe. Women played the tambourine, often dancing and singing as they played.

The Greeks

In the 9th century B.C., when Homer wrote his great poems the *Iliad* and the *Odyssey,* Greece was on the way to becoming a great civilization. Like Sumeria, Egypt, Persia, and nearby nations, Greece shared in the general Oriental culture of the Middle East. Through royal gifts, conquests, and migrations, musicians and instruments were interchanged throughout this entire area. As a result the music of these ancient civilizations had many things in common. One of these was the melody patterns. Another was the lack of any real harmony, a feature that developed much later in Europe, after the Middle Ages. Melody and rhythm were strongly emphasized in the ancient world, as they still are in the Middle East and India.

The Greeks were so interested in melody and rhythm that of all the ancient nations they developed the most elaborate theories on these subjects. Since all melodies are based on scales, the Greek scientists soon set to work in this direction. The great mathematician Euclid was one of the first to organize all the important Greek scales in one system, in the 4th century B.C. These scales, or modes as they are often called, had seven notes each. Earlier the Greeks had favored five-note scales, the most important resembling the ancient Egyptian harp scale A F E C B. In fact, two famous hymns of the 2nd century B.C., sung to Apollo at his shrine in Delphi, still had sections in this very old scale. The popular Greek aulos, a shrill double oboe often heard at the exciting spring rites of the god Dionysus, was also frequently played in this five-note scale, even as late as the 2nd century A.D.

When the seven-note modes were organized, they received the names of various people and places in Greece, such as Dorian, Phrygian, and Lydian. All of these modes can to some extent be played on the white keys of the piano. The C major scale is a good example of the Lydian mode, and all the white keys between any two E's on the piano give the Dorian. In the Middle Ages the Christian Church used the same Greek names for its own musical scales.

The Greeks were very fond of psychology. They felt that mental and physical health could be directly influenced by different scales and rhythms. The philosopher Aristotle, for example, said the Phrygian mode should be used to inspire enthusiasm, and the Dorian to produce calm in a person. Many of these ideas were applied to musical education, which in Arcadia, Sparta, and other places was required for most people from childhood on.

The lyre was the national instrument of Greece. Amateurs usually played a light type of lyre made of a tortoise shell. Professionals played the famous kithara, a heavier lyre said to be Apollo's favorite instrument. Composers often wrote their lyre melodies in a special notation in which each note was represented by a letter of the alphabet.

As in other ancient nations, singing was very popular in Greece. Professional soloists, especially poets who sang their own poetry, were in great demand by the nobility. Even more important were the choruses, some of which contained hundreds of singers. Choruses sang hymns to the gods and sang at athletic competitions, where they won prizes. Resembling opera, Greek drama usually included choruses that also danced and acted. A chorus leader would beat out the rhythm with a special sandal having a loose, flapping sole. His conducting was very helpful to the musicians, since Greek poetry and music had complicated rhythmic patterns made up of long and short beats.

Ancient music left many traces in early Europe, particularly in its instruments and in the Gregorian chant of the Christian Church. Eventually Europe broke away from its heritage from other parts of the world and developed its own musical ideas.

ROSE BRANDEL
City University of New York, Hunter College

ANDERSEN, HANS CHRISTIAN (1805–1875)

When I was a very young boy, just discovering the world of books and stories, Hans Christian Andersen was a magic name to me. I used to laugh and cry over his tales—especially *The Ugly Duckling*. You see, I was a gawky, lonely child, too, and now that I have found my place in the world, I think of the story as *my* story.

When I was chosen to play Hans Andersen in the movie and went to Denmark to learn as much about him as I could, I found out from townspeople whose grandparents had been Andersen's neighbors that *The Ugly Duck-* ling was really Hans's story. This made me feel a great kinship for him and gave his story special meaning.

In many ways his life was like a fairy tale. Out of the poverty of his boyhood, out of years of hardship, loneliness, and ridicule he came to be one of the honored men of his time. He was a friend of all the great people of his day and a welcome guest in the palaces of princes and kings. Yet the purity of his heart, his simplicity, his faith in God and man, never changed. Throughout his life he saw the world with the clear and innocent eyes of childhood. He understood children, and they loved to sit at his feet while he wove a spell of enchantment and wonder.

Yet he was a man, not a child. He had seen and learned many things that became part of his stories. He himself said, "I tell the story for the young ones, remembering all the time that father and mother are listening and we must give them something to think about too."

On a sunny September day in 1819, when Hans was only 14, he left his home town of Odense to seek his fortune in the great capital city of Copenhagen. He was very tall, gawky, and awkward, with yellow hair. He had a big head and a big nose. He wore a long coat, wooden shoes, and a peaked cap. He carried his few belongings in a tiny bundle. In his pockets was enough money to last him a day or two, until he became, as he was sure he would, an actor in the Royal Theatre.

With high hopes he said good-by to his mother and grandmother—the two people in the world who loved him and whom he dearly loved. As the coach that took him to the boat rumbled away he may have been thinking not only of the unknown experiences ahead but of the life he was leaving behind.

In the one-room cottage where he had lived with his parents was his father's cobbler's bench, but no one was beside it now. His father had died several years before. In the new house, not much better than the old, where Hans had lived after his mother had remarried, was the toy theater his father had made. The little figures wore costumes that Hans himself had cut out of bits of cloth while the shoemaker, working at his trade, told his son stories from *The Arabian Nights* and old Danish legends.

Left behind too was the church where he had been confirmed only a few weeks before. Wearing new shoes outside his trousers so that people could see them, he had walked down the aisle, proud when his shoes creaked but later ashamed that all through the service he had thought only of his shoes. Many years later he wrote *The Red Shoes*, about a selfish girl who behaved in much the same way. She was also vain, like the woman in Odense who had refused to accept or pay for the red shoes his father had made for her. Hans put many pieces of his own life into his fairy tales. He never forgot that his mother as a young girl had been forced to go begging and, frightened, had hidden herself under a bridge on a cold winter day. This led him to write *The Little Match Girl*, so full of compassion for the unfortunate ones of this earth. His own story, *The Ugly Duckling*, points out that sometimes the qualities that make you feel lonely, different, and out of place are the very qualities that, when properly used, can make you shine.

The people of Odense had never known what to make of Hans. He was different, and they thought he might be a little "touched," like his poor grandfather. When he recited long passages from plays or did a clumsy dance or insisted on singing, they could hardly help laughing. Everyone advised him to learn a trade, but this he could not do.

He had no doubts at all about himself. He was forever saying that he was going to be famous, that he knew he would have to suffer hardships like all heroes but in the end God would make his dreams come true. His belief in himself caused some of the wiser people of Odense to be kind to him, but others with less understanding made fun of him. It comforted Hans to remember what the old woman in Odense had prophesied when his superstitious and worried mother had asked her to foretell the future: "He will be a wild, high-flying bird, and one day the whole of Odense will be illuminated for him."

When Hans got off the little boat at Copenhagen, he sought the shelter of a nearby wall and, dropping to his knees, prayed to God to give him strength and help. His first disappointment—the first of many—shows how young and inexperienced he was. He went to the home of a great lady of the theater to seek her help. To the lady's astonishment and fright, he tried to dance the Cinderella role from the ballet in which she had starred. Instead of helping him she had him hastily shown out.

Many people of the theater and wealthy families of the city tried to help him, without much success. His dancing master gave up, and so did his singing teacher. Directors of the Royal Theatre sympathized with his efforts to write plays but finally concluded that, despite his imagination, he lacked education, for he had had practically no schooling in Odense. A purse was raised, and at 17 Hans was sent away to school. The next few years were the unhappiest of his life. He was much older than the other students, and the schoolmaster, jealous of his connections with important people, found endless ways to make fun of him. Finally, when word of Hans's plight reached his benefactors in Copenhagen, he was removed from the school and put into the hands of a private tutor.

Not until Hans was 30 did he write any fairy tales. He spent many years in travel and in continued efforts to write poems, books, and plays, which met with enough success to give him some reputation in Danish cultural circles. For the most part he was supported by small grants from the king and the assistance of friends. The first small book of fairy tales became popular almost immediately, however, and from then on his fame grew rapidly, spreading from country to country. Hans had found himself at last. The rest of his life was a happy and busy one.

In 1867 he returned to Odense to be honored by the great of his country. Standing on the balcony of the hall where the ceremonies had been held, he saw below him the city square, full of people who cheered him, and bright with thousands of candles burning in the windows of all the buildings. The prophecy of the old woman was fulfilled.

DANNY KAYE

Here is one of Hans Christian Andersen's best-loved fairy tales.

▶ THE EMPEROR'S NEW CLOTHES

Many years ago there lived an Emperor who was so exceedingly fond of fine new clothes that he spent all his money on being elaborately dressed. He took no interest in his soldiers, no interest in the theater, nor did he care to drive about in his state coach, unless it were to show off his new clothes. He had different robes for every hour of the day, and just as one says of a King that he is in his Council Chamber, people always said of him, "The Emperor is in his wardrobe!"

The great city in which he lived was full of gaiety. Strangers were always coming and going. One day two swindlers arrived; they made themselves out to be weavers, and said they knew how to weave the most magnificent fabric that one could imagine. Not only were the colors and patterns unusually beautiful, but the clothes that were made of this material had the extraor-

The Emperor's new clothes exist only in his mind. Two swindlers have pretended to weave a fabric of silk and gold thread.

dinary quality of becoming invisible to everyone who was either unfit for his post, or inexcusably stupid.

"What useful clothes to have!" thought the Emperor. "If I had some like that, I might find out which of the people in my Empire are unfit for their posts. I should also be able to distinguish the wise from the fools. Yes, that material must be woven for me immediately!" Then he gave the swindlers large sums of money so that they could start work at once.

Quickly they set up two looms and pretended to weave, but there was not a trace of anything on the frames. They made no bones about demanding the finest silk and the purest gold thread. They stuffed everything into their bags, and continued to work at the empty looms until late into the night.

"I'm rather anxious to know how much of the material is finished," thought the Emperor, but to tell the truth, he felt a bit uneasy, remembering that anyone who was either a fool or unfit for his post would never be able to see it. He rather imagined that he need not have any fear for himself, yet he thought it wise to send someone else first to see how things were going. Everyone in the town knew about the exceptional powers of the material, and all were eager to know how incompetent or how stupid the neighbors might be.

"I will send my honest old Chamberlain to the weavers," thought the Emperor. "He will be able to judge the fabric better than anyone else, for he has brains, and nobody fills his post better than he does."

So the nice old Chamberlain went into the hall where the two swindlers were sitting working at the empty looms.

"Upon my life!" he thought, opening his eyes very wide, "I can't see anything at all!" But he didn't say so.

Both the swindlers begged him to be good enough to come nearer, and asked how he liked the unusual design and the splendid colors. They pointed to the empty looms, and the poor old Chamberlain opened his eyes wider and wider, but he could see nothing, for there was nothing. "Heavens above!" he thought, "could it possibly be that I am stupid? I have never thought that of myself, and not a soul must know it. Could it be that I am not fit for my post? It will never do for me to admit that I can't see the material!"

"Well, you don't say what you think of it," said one of the weavers.

"Oh, it's delightful—most exquisite!" said the old Chamberlain, looking through his spectacles. "What a wonderful design and what beautiful colors! I shall certainly tell the Emperor that I am enchanted with it."

"We're very pleased to hear that," said the two weavers, and they started describing the colors and the curious pattern. The old Chamberlain listened carefully in order to repeat, when he came home to the Emperor, exactly what he had heard, and he did so.

The swindlers now demanded more money, as well as more silk and gold thread, saying that they needed it for weaving. They put everything into their pockets and not a thread appeared upon the looms, but they kept on working at the empty frames as before.

Soon after this, the Emperor sent another nice official to see how the weaving was getting on, and to enquire whether the stuff would soon be ready. Exactly the same thing happened to him as to the Chamberlain. He looked and looked, but as there was nothing to be seen except the empty looms, he could see nothing.

"Isn't it a beautiful piece of material?" said the swindlers, showing and describing the pattern that did not exist at all.

"Stupid I certainly am not," thought the official; "then I must be unfit for my excellent post, I suppose. That seems rather funny—but I'll take great care that nobody gets wind of it." Then he praised the material he could not see, and assured them of his enthusiasm for the gorgeous colors and the beautiful pattern. "It's simply enchanting!" he said to the Emperor.

The whole town was talking about the splendid material.

And now the Emperor was curious to see it for himself while it was still upon the looms.

Accompanied by a great number of selected people, among whom were the two nice old officials who had already been there, the Emperor went forth to visit the two wily swindlers. They were now weaving madly, yet without a single thread upon the looms.

"Isn't it magnificent?" said the two nice officials. "Will Your Imperial Majesty deign to look at this splendid pattern and these glorious colors?" Then they pointed to the empty looms, for each thought that the others could probably see the material.

"What on earth can this mean?" thought the Emperor. "I don't see anything! This is terrible. Am I stupid? Am I unfit to be Emperor? That would be the most disastrous thing that could possibly befall me.—Oh, it's perfectly wonderful!" he said. "It quite meets with my Imperial approval." And he nodded appreciatively and stared at the empty looms—he would not admit that he saw nothing. His whole suite looked and looked, but with as little result as the others; nevertheless, they all said, like the Emperor, "It's perfectly wonderful!" They advised him to have some new clothes made from this splendid stuff and to wear them for the first time in the next great procession.

"Magnificent!" "Excellent!" "Prodigious!" went from mouth to mouth, and everyone was exceedingly pleased. The Emperor gave each of the swindlers a decoration to wear in his buttonhole, and the title of "Knight of the Loom."

Before the procession they worked all night, burning more than sixteen candles. People could see how busy they were finishing the Emperor's new clothes. They pretended to take the material from the looms, they slashed the air with great scissors, they sewed with needles without any thread, and finally they said, "The Emperor's clothes are ready!"

Then the Emperor himself arrived with his most distinguished courtiers, and each swindler raised an arm as if he were holding something, and said, "These are Your Imperial Majesty's knee-breeches. This is Your Imperial Majesty's robe. This is Your Imperial Majesty's mantle," and so forth. "It is all as light as a spider's web, one might fancy one had nothing on, but that is just the beauty of it!"

"Yes, indeed," said all the courtiers, but they could see nothing, for there was nothing to be seen.

"If Your Imperial Majesty would graciously consent to take off your clothes," said the swindlers, "we could fit on the new ones in front of the long glass."

So the Emperor laid aside his clothes, and the swindlers pretended to hand him, piece by piece, the new ones they were supposed to have made, and they fitted him round the waist, and acted as if they were fastening something on— it was the train; and the Emperor turned round and round in front of the long glass.

"How well the new robes suit Your Imperial Majesty! How well they fit!" they all said. "What a splendid design! What gorgeous colors! It's all magnificently regal!"

"The canopy which is to be held over Your Imperial Majesty in the procession is waiting outside," announced the Lord High Chamberlain.

"Well, I suppose I'm ready," said the Emperor. "Don't you think they are a nice fit?" And he looked at himself again in the glass, first on one side and then the other, as if he really were carefully examining his handsome attire.

The courtiers who were to carry the train groped about on the floor with fumbling fingers, and pretended to lift it; they walked on, holding their hands up in the air; nothing would have induced them to admit that they could not see anything.

And so the Emperor set off in the procession under the beautiful canopy, and everybody in the streets and at the windows said, "Oh! how superb the Emperor's new clothes are! What a gorgeous train! What a perfect fit!" No one would acknowledge that he didn't see anything, so proving that he was not fit for his post, or that he was very stupid.

None of the Emperor's clothes had ever met with such a success.

"But he hasn't got any clothes on!" gasped out a little child.

"Good heavens! Hark at the little innocent!" said the father, and people whispered to one another what the child had said. "But he hasn't got any clothes on! There's a little child saying he hasn't got any clothes on!"

"But he hasn't got any clothes on!" shouted the whole town at last. The Emperor had a creepy feeling down his spine, because it began to dawn upon him that the people were right. "All the same," he thought to himself, "I've got to go through with it as long as the procession lasts."

So he drew himself up and held his head higher than before, and the courtiers held on to the train that wasn't there at all.

ANDERSON, MARIAN (1902 –   )

Visitors at a small church in Philadelphia, Pennsylvania, were amazed by the beautiful voice of a 6-year-old girl singing in the choir. She was Marian Anderson, born in Philadelphia on February 17, 1902. As a child, she loved to sing all kinds of songs, but her favorites were the hymns she sang in church. This little girl eventually became known all over the world as one of the greatest singers of her time.

It was not easy for Marian Anderson to acquire a musical education because her family was very poor. But when she won a scholarship in 1930, she was able to study and travel in Europe. Her European debut in Berlin was triumphant, and her fame spread quickly. She delighted many heads of state as well as huge audiences in every major city of Europe with her singing. The great composer Jean Sibelius dedicated a song to her when she visited him in Finland.

News of Marian Anderson's success in Europe reached America. When she sang at her homecoming concert in New York City in 1935, she received thunderous applause. But her highest acclaim came on Easter Sunday in 1939. When she was prevented from singing at Constitution Hall in Washington, D.C., she gave a free concert for an audience of 75,000 from the steps of the Lincoln Memorial.

As her fame increased, Marian Anderson toured all parts of the world. In 1955 she became the first black singer to appear with the Metropolitan Opera. A beloved international figure, she was sent by the U.S. State Department on a goodwill tour of Asia in 1957. The following year she served as a U.S. delegate to the United Nations.

The hardy llama can survive the cold and rare atmosphere of the lofty Peruvian Andes.

In the Andes travel is difficult. Even trains must creep slowly through the winding mountain passes.

Balsas, boats made of light, strong reeds, are a popular means of transportation on Lake Titicaca.

Snowcapped Cotopaxi (19,344 ft.), in Ecuador, is one of the highest active volcanoes in the world.

ANDES

The Andes form the longest and one of the highest mountain ranges in the world. Only the Himalayas in south central Asia are taller and more rugged. The Andes Cordillera (Andes Range) stretches nearly 4,500 miles along the west coast of South America, from the Caribbean Sea in the north to Tierra del Fuego, an archipelago at the southern tip of South America. The Andes are in every South American republic except Brazil, Paraguay, Uruguay, and Guyana.

Within the Andean regions are many different kinds of life and lands. There are great modern cities and small Indian villages where people live much as they did centuries ago. There are dense forests and barren plains, fertile farmlands, and stony soil where little grows. About a third of all the people in South America live in the Andean regions, most of them in crowded cities and towns. Four South American capitals lie high in the Andes—Caracas, Venezuela; Bogotá, Colombia; Quito, Ecuador; and La Paz, Bolivia.

Many peaks in the Andes are over 20,000 feet high—taller than any peak in North America. Aconcagua (22,835 ft.), in Argentina, is the highest mountain in the Western Hemisphere. Many of the Andean mountains are volcanic. Some are inactive, although a number of them still erupt from time to time and cause great damage.

The northern Andes lie in Colombia, Venezuela, and Ecuador. Much of South America's fine coffee is grown on the lower slopes of the northern Andes.

The central Andes are in Bolivia, Peru, northern Chile, and northern Argentina. The mountains in some parts of the central Andes are extremely high and wide, making transportation difficult. For example, to reach La Paz, Bolivia, the railroad must cross the mountains at an elevation of nearly 14,000 feet.

The southern Andes, at the tip of the continent in Argentina and Chile, are the lowest range. This is a sparsely populated area.

Many of the people who live in the Andes of Bolivia, Peru, and Ecuador are the descendants of the ancient Incas and other Indians who inhabited the area before the Spanish conquest in the 16th century. Many of these people still speak an Indian tongue, such as Quechua. The Spanish language is unknown to them.

The Andes act as a great barrier to transportation and communication. From the Caribbean Sea to the Strait of Magellan there are few passes through the mountains. Deep gorges, steep slopes, and towering heights make roads and railroads difficult and costly to build. Within recent years, however, the airplane and some modern highways have opened up areas that were previously cut off from the outside world.

Two major river systems of South America —the Amazon and the Orinoco—begin in the Andes. High in the mountains between Bolivia and Peru is Lake Titicaca. It is the largest lake in South America and the highest large lake in the world.

The climate in the Andes changes with the elevation above sea level. At the lowest elevation, below 3,000 feet, the climate is tropical. Here are dense green jungles and rivers filled with crocodiles. This is called the *tierra caliente,* or "hot land."

The climate is cooler from 3,000 feet to 7,000 feet. At 7,000 feet the cold land, or *tierra fría,* begins. Evergreen trees and wheat grow well at this elevation.

Between 10,000 feet and 13,000 feet is the *puna.* Only potatoes and barley and a few other hardy crops will grow on these high mountainsides. The top level, between the *puna* and the snowfields, is called the *páramo.* Nothing grows here except mosses and lichens.

The mines of the Andean regions provide the world with many important minerals. Among them are copper, tin, and petroleum. Gold and silver are mined in smaller amounts. The supply of coal is limited in most areas.

Many interesting animals live in the Andes. There are llamas, guanacos, alpacas, and vicuñas—all members of the camel family. The chinchilla is highly prized for its valuable fur. There is the fierce cougar, or mountain lion, and the small deer, or guemal. Tiny humming birds, brilliantly colored, dart about in the Andean forests. Soaring high above the towering, snowcapped Andes are the huge condors, the largest of the vultures. They are also the world's largest flying birds.

Reviewed by DANIEL JACOBSON
Montclair College

Andorra is a tiny country in the eastern Pyrenees mountains, between France and Spain. Although it is an old country, few people know much about it.

THE PEOPLE

The original inhabitants of Andorra can be traced back to a tribe that settled in the area in Roman times. Almost all Andorrans speak Catalan, a language like French in some ways and like Spanish in others. The population today includes a large number of Spaniards and a small French minority.

In the summer months, men and women work from sunrise to sunset in fields high on the mountain slopes. The leading crops are oats, barley, tobacco, and fruit. But sheep are more important than field crops. Many hills are dotted with flocks of sheep.

By autumn the sheep are fat from grazing and ready to be taken to France, where they are sold. This is the busiest season. The corn and tobacco must be harvested and the apples, grain, and hay stored away for the winter. Even the children are needed to milk the cows and watch the animals. Schools do not open until October, when the major part of the work is finished. Classes are conducted in either French or Spanish.

THE LAND

Andorra is a rugged country. Surrounded by the high peaks of the Pyrenees mountains, it is broken by deep gorges and narrow, irregular valleys. Andorra is drained by the Valira River and its tributaries.

Andorra's isolation, beautiful mountain scenery, and cool climate have made it a popular tourist resort. There are no railroads, but roads link Andorra with France and Spain. There are fine spots for winter skiing and mineral springs at the village of Les Escaldes. Because only about one fourth of Andorra's area can be used to grow crops or pasture livestock, tourism has replaced agriculture as the chief source of income.

THE ECONOMY

Andorrans pay no income taxes, and there is no national debt. Several hydroelectric plants supply power to Spain. Andorra must import much of its food. Mining, stone quarrying, and lumbering are carried out on a limited scale. Cigars, cigarettes, matches, anisette, and sandals are manufactured and exported. Many items are imported into Andorra, which has no customs duties, for sale to tourists at low prices. Goods shipped between France and Spain are often smuggled through Andorra's mountains.

Stamp collectors are familiar with Andorran stamps. These are an important source of income. Radio Andorra, which plays mostly music and broadcasts in both French and Spanish, provides additional revenue.

HISTORY AND GOVERNMENT

According to tradition, Andorra was established late in the 8th century when Charlemagne granted the people a charter of independence for their aid in driving out the Moors. Charlemagne's son, King Louis I (called the Pious and the Debonair), is said to have confirmed the charter in 815. For years the French counts of Foix and the Spanish bishops of Urgel contested the territory. Finally, in 1278, a treaty was signed at Les Escaldes, a small town near Andorra la Vella, the

---

FACTS AND FIGURES

VALLEYS OF ANDORRA (Valls d'Andorra) is the official name. It is called Les Vallées d'Andorre in French, Los Valles de Andorra in Spanish.

CAPITAL: Andorra la Vella.

LOCATION: On the southern slope of the Pyrenees mountains, between France and Spain. **Latitude**—42° 27' N to 42° 30' N. **Longitude**—1° 25' E to 1° 30' E.

AREA: 453 km² (175 sq mi).

POPULATION: 29,000 (estimate).

LANGUAGE: Catalan (official), French, Spanish.

GOVERNMENT: Republic, principality, suzerainty. **Head of government**—first syndic (syndic procureur des vallées).

NATIONAL ANTHEM: El Gran Carlemany Mon Pare ("Great Charlemagne my father").

ECONOMY: Agricultural products—tobacco, hay, barley, oats, potatoes, garden vegetables, olive trees, grapes, cattle, sheep, goats. **Industries and products**—tourism, cigars, cigarettes, matches, anisette, sandals, lumber. **Chief minerals**—iron, lead, building stone. **Chief exports**—stamps, tobacco products, anisette, handicraft goods. **Chief imports**—foodstuffs, manufactured items. **Monetary unit**—French franc, Spanish peseta.

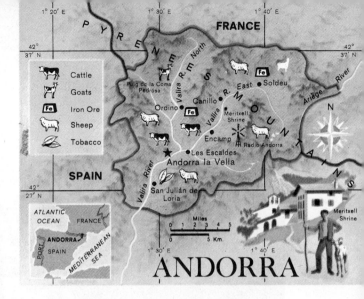

ANDORRA

capital. By this treaty, the count of Foix and the bishop of Urgel were made co-princes of Andorra. The rights of the count of Foix were inherited by the kings of France and later by the French presidents when France became a republic.

Under the treaty of Les Escaldes, a "tribute" has been paid by Andorra to its co-princes since the 13th century. Every year at Christmastime the bishop of Urgel receives two plump capons, four cheeses, and two hams from each of the six Andorran districts. The mayor of each district must see that the capons are plump enough, that the cheeses are not spoiled, and that the hams are not too dry. It is a serious affair, for occasionally part of the tribute has been found unsuitable and has been sent back. Every year the bishop receives a cash tribute of 460 pesetas as well as the food. The president of France, whose dining table is farther away from Andorran kitchens, receives a cash tribute of 960 francs every year.

Because of its ties with Spain and France, Andorra escaped invasion during both World Wars and the Spanish Civil War. It was an important escape route for Allied troops during World War II. With the growth of tourism, Andorra is emerging from its centuries-old isolation. Women were given the right to vote in 1970. Many people have moved to the rapidly growing urban areas.

Andorra has the distinction of being the only nation in the world that is a republic, a principality, and a suzerainty. It is a republic because it is a self-governing country with laws made by the 24-member General Council. It is a co-principality because executive power is divided between the Spanish bishop of Urgel and the president of France. It is a suzerainty because it has overlords.

Reviewed by FRENCH EMBASSY PRESS AND INFORMATION DIVISION

ANEMIA. See DISEASES.

The high Pyrenees surround little Andorra. Every bit of farmland is carefully cultivated.

One of the main streets in Andorra la Vella. The signs on the building are in Catalan.

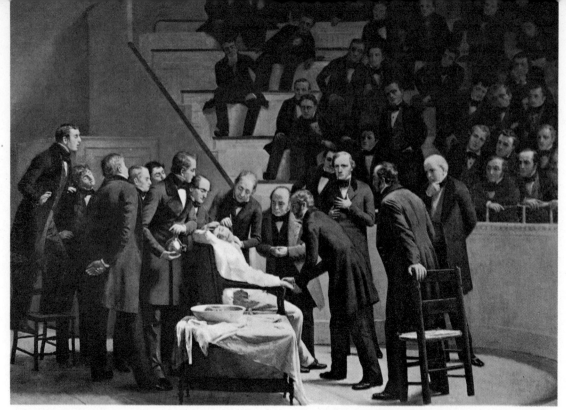

Ether as an anesthetic during surgery was first demonstrated in public by Morton in 1846.

ANESTHESIA

Nowadays when a person undergoes surgery, he is given an anesthetic. It keeps him from feeling pain. Anesthetics affect the nervous system. Some prevent the nerves from sending messages of pain; others affect the brain. In either case no pain is felt. Such anesthetics have been known and used for only a little more than 100 years.

▶ PAIN RELIEVERS OF OLD

Human pain is as old as man. And so from the earliest times men have sought ways of relieving pain. They discovered that drugs made from certain plants could be used to kill pain. Doctors then tried using the same drugs during operations. Sometimes the juice of the plants was drunk. Other times the fumes were breathed in. Among these drugs were opium, mandrake, and hashish. But none of them were really very good. Small amounts had little effect. Large amounts often killed the patient.

Alcoholic drinks such as wine or whiskey were tried as a means of making the patient unconscious. But the patient often came to as soon as the first cut was made.

Even as late as the 1840's there seemed to be no safe and satisfactory way of putting a patient out of pain during an operation. So in most cases the patient was simply held or tied down and the doctor worked as quickly as possible. Operations were limited to those that could be done in a few minutes. The best surgeon was the one who could work the fastest. Even so, many patients did not survive the pain and shock.

▶ THE START OF MODERN ANESTHETICS

The story of modern anesthetics begins with scientific studies of gases and ways they could be used. As early as 1799 the English chemist Humphry Davy had described nitrous oxide as a man-made gas that was "capable of destroying physical pain." But many years passed before anyone used it as an anesthetic.

Probably the first man to use a gas as an anesthetic was an English doctor, Henry Hill Hickman. He had been experimenting with carbon dioxide. By 1824 he had successfully anesthetized animals. He then tried to persuade surgeons to use gases as anesthetics on human patients, but no one would listen.

In the meantime people had discovered that breathing small amounts of nitrous oxide produced a pleasant sensation. In fact, nitrous oxide was known as laughing gas. By the 1840's people had also discovered the pleasures of breathing in ether. (Ether is a liquid that quickly turns into a gas when exposed to air.) They held parties called "ether frolics." Such parties were silly, but one good came from them. Many medical students and doctors were introduced to these gases at the parties.

One doctor who learned about ether at a frolic was Dr. Crawford W. Long of Jefferson, Georgia. In 1842 he painlessly removed tumors from the neck of a patient who had breathed in ether. This was probably the first truly effective anesthetic ever used in an operation on a human being. But Dr. Long failed to report the event, and other doctors did not learn of his success.

By this time, however, many men were experimenting with anesthetic gases. Dr. Horace Wells, a dentist in Hartford, Connecticut, was working with nitrous oxide. Unfortunately, when he tried to demonstrate it in public, something went wrong. The patient screamed with pain as his tooth was pulled out. Dr. Wells fled to the sound of boos.

Success came to Wells's former partner, Dr. William T. G. Morton. At the Harvard Medical School, Morton met Dr. Charles T. Jackson, who suggested trying ether. Morton did. First he tried it on animals, including his own dog. Then he tried it on himself. It proved to be a safe and effective anesthetic.

By 1846 Morton was ready to demonstrate how ether could be used in surgery. He persuaded Dr. John C. Warren of the Massachusetts General Hospital to try operating on a patient who had been given ether. The day set was October 16. A group of doctors and students had been invited to observe. Many of them were sure that the ether would not work and had only come to laugh at Morton.

The patient was strapped to a chair in the usual way. Dr. Morton placed a tube in his mouth. The tube was connected to a glass globe filled with ether. Breathing the fumes into his lungs, the patient fell asleep.

Dr. Warren began to operate. Expecting the usual outcry, he made the first cut. There was silence. The doctor finished the operation. When the patient became conscious, he announced he had felt no pain.

The news of Dr. Morton's success spread quickly. The operation was reported in medical journals. The way to modern surgery was open. Operations could be performed without pain.

Meanwhile, Oliver Wendell Holmes, an American doctor and poet, applied the term "anesthesia" to the condition produced by ether. The word is from the Greek and means "not feeling."

The search for more and better anesthetics was stepped up. Dr. James Simpson, an English doctor, was dissatisfied with ether because it irritated the lungs. Seeking a substitute, he found that chloroform had an anesthetic effect. In 1847 he gave it to a woman during childbirth and she suffered no pain. Chloroform became very popular after 1853, when Queen Victoria took it during delivery of her seventh child.

Since then many anesthetics have been developed, each with its own special properties. New ones continue to be made in laboratories. Today's medical men can choose from

Modern equipment is complex (left). At right, hypothermia blanket lowers body temperature.

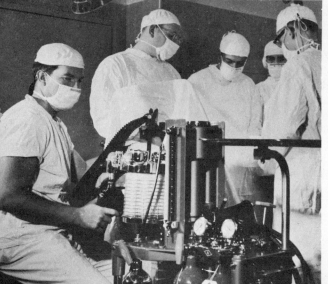
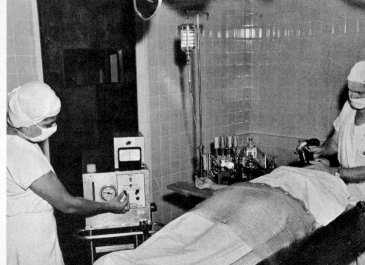

many anesthetics the one best suited to the patient and the operation.

► GENERAL AND LOCAL ANESTHETICS

There are two main types of anesthetics: general and local.

A general anesthetic makes the patient lose consciousness. All senses are temporarily cut off.

A local anesthetic affects only part of the body. It leaves the patient awake and con-

scious. The only loss of feeling is in the anesthetized area.

The General Anesthetic

A general anesthetic works by first entering the bloodstream. The blood carries the drug to the central nervous system. Once there, the anesthetic acts on the nerve cells of the brain. These cells lose their ability to send and receive messages. No sensations are felt, and the patient loses consciousness.

General anesthetics are usually given either as a gas to be breathed in or as a liquid to be injected into a vein. The anesthetic may be given by an anesthesiologist, a physician who specializes in this work. Sometimes it is given by an anesthetist, a specially trained nurse or technician. Monitoring, or watching, the patient's vital signs is a very important part of giving an anesthetic. This means close observation of the pulse, blood pressure, color of the skin, and appearance of the eyes to check the depth of anesthesia.

The Local Anesthetic

A local anesthetic blocks the nerves at the area of the operation. The chemical may be applied to the surface of the body, to act on the nerve endings in the skin. Or it may be injected with a needle, to block nerve impulses to the brain and thus prevent the feeling of pain. Tooth extractions are often done in this way, with the anesthetic injected into the gum.

A method called spinal or regional anesthesia may be used for some abdominal operations or for the delivery of a baby. Nerves to the lower part of the body branch from the spinal cord. A single injection into the fluid surrounding the spinal cord blocks large numbers of nerves. The patient remains conscious and relaxed and feels no pain.

► WHY A RANGE OF ANESTHETICS IS NEEDED

Every anesthetic has both advantages and disadvantages. There is no single all-purpose anesthetic. Doctors choose what seems best for the patient and the kind of operation. They may choose one particular anesthetic. Or they may use several together.

Any good anesthetic must free the patient from pain, be safe and dependable, and prevent struggling movements. In most cases the

---

SOME WELL-KNOWN ANESTHETICS

These are all chemical anesthetics, identified by names in common usage. All are made in a laboratory.

GENERAL ANESTHETICS

CHLOROFORM: Clear liquid with a sweet odor. Quickly changes into gas. Stronger than ether, but not as safe in large amounts. Unlikely to burn or explode. Can damage liver. An early anesthetic, now rarely used.

CYCLOPROPANE: Colorless, sweet-smelling gas. Produces quick and deep anesthesia. Useful especially in diseases of the heart and respiratory system, when a high level of oxygen must be provided to the tissues. But its use is limited because it can explode.

ETHER: The chemical ethyl ether or diethyl ether. A colorless liquid that quickly changes into gas. Produces deep but safe anesthesia for long operations. Strong odor. Irritates breathing passages and lungs. Leaves patient feeling sick after operation. Burns and explodes easily. An early anesthetic, now replaced by newer ones.

FLUOTHANE: Trade name for the chemical halothane. A liquid that quickly changes into gas. Stronger than ether. May cause liver damage in a few patients. No unpleasant aftereffects. Unlikely to burn or explode. Now the most widely used anesthetic.

NITROUS OXIDE: Colorless, sweet-smelling gas. Produces unconsciousness quickly. No unpleasant aftereffects. Unlikely to burn or explode. Produces light anesthesia and must be used with stronger drugs. Used often in dental work or short operations. One of the first anesthetics. Also known as laughing gas.

PENTOTHAL: Trade name for thiopental sodium. A chemical solid that is dissolved in liquid before being injected into veins. Puts patients to sleep and makes them forget operation. Not a true anesthetic, so must be used in combination with other anesthetics for long operations. Few unpleasant aftereffects, but not safe for people with heart or lung trouble.

LOCAL ANESTHETIC

NOVOCAIN: Trade name for the drug procaine hydrochloride. Injected into area of pain. Commonly used in dental work and minor operations. Related anesthetics include those known by trade names Carbocaine, Metycaine, Nupercaine, Pontocaine, and Xylocaine.

muscles must be relaxed by anesthetics or by other drugs in order for an operation to be performed successfully.

Ideally an anesthetic should also be pleasant to take, put the patient to sleep rapidly, have the smallest possible effect on the heart and lungs, and wear off quickly, leaving no unpleasant aftereffects.

▶ **OTHER KINDS OF ANESTHESIA**

The anesthetics described so far are drugs that act chemically on the nerves of the body. But there are other ways to produce anesthesia.

One method is to lower the temperature of some part of the body by packing it in crushed ice. As the temperature goes down, sensation is dulled. The same effect can be produced by spraying certain fast-evaporating chemicals, such as ethyl chloride, on the area. The quick evaporation causes the skin to become so cold that all sensation is lost.

You may have read about operations where an internal organ, or even the whole body, is cooled. This technique, called **hypothermia**, does produce anesthesia, but that is not why it is used. As the body is cooled down to 25.5°C (78°F), various changes take place. For example, the body's need for oxygen is low, and the heart action is reduced. This allows surgeons to perform difficult brain and heart operations because the part under surgery is nearly bloodless.

Hypnosis is another and a very old way of producing a state of anesthesia. The hypnotist-doctor suggests to the patient that no pain will be felt. The sensation of pain is then absent until the patient is awakened. But not everyone can be successfully hypnotized. And hypnosis cannot be used in major operations.

Acupuncture is a method that is used to prevent pain during surgery. It was developed in China, where it is routinely used in place of conventional anesthesia. Now it is being used in other parts of the world. In acupuncture, fine needles are inserted under the skin and twirled. More than 500 specific acupuncture points on the body are known. In acupuncture anesthesia, the patient remains conscious and relaxed and does not suffer the nausea or other unpleasant aftereffects of chemical anesthesia.

Anesthesia has done away with the nightmare of pain in surgery. Today anesthesia makes possible long and difficult life-saving operations that were never before dreamed of. The search for new and better anesthetics and methods of anesthesia still goes on. So does the effort of scientists to learn more about the way in which anesthesia works.

SARAH R. RIEDMAN
Author, science books for children
See also DRUGS; MEDICINE, HISTORY OF.

ANGELICO, FRA (1387?–1455)

One of the most beloved artists in history was the Italian painter Fra Angelico. He was so saintly that many legends were made up about him. For example, one story relates that when he fell asleep while working on a painting, the angels came down from heaven to finish it for him.

Fra Angelico was born in Tuscany. His real name was Guido di Pietro. When he was about 20, he entered the monastery at Fiesole, where he became famous for his paintings and illuminated manuscripts.

In 1436 Fra Angelico was transferred to the San Marco monastery in Florence. It is said that when Pope Eugene IV saw San Marco after Fra Angelico had redecorated it, he was so impressed that he offered to make the artist archbishop of Florence. But Fra Angelico refused, explaining that he could better serve the Church by painting.

Fra Angelico's most important work can be seen today in the Vatican and in Florence, especially at San Marco. His frescoes (wall paintings done on wet plaster) use soft, yet clear, colors and graceful lines to tell Biblical stories, and his madonnas and saints reflect the tenderness of this gentle and religious man. The names Fra Angelico, which means "the angelic brother" in Italian, and Il Beato, "the blessed one," were given him after his death because he was so devout—in his life and in his art.

ANGLO-SAXONS. See ENGLAND, HISTORY OF; ENGLISH LANGUAGE.

Angola is situated on the western coast of Africa, south of the equator. In area, it is larger than France, Portugal, the United Kingdom, and West Germany combined. It includes a small enclave called Cabinda. This enclave (a territory enclosed within a foreign land) is separated from the rest of Angola by the nation of Zaïre.

THE PEOPLE

The people of Angola are related to the Bantu of central, southern, and eastern Africa. The Angolans are composed of many groups. One of the largest is the Ovimbundu, who occupy the Benguela highland in the center of Angola. The Ovimbundu are famous as traders and are skilled ironworkers. The Kimbundu live between the cities of Luanda and Malange. They have been influenced by European ways because they live and work in or near these cities, which were long under Portuguese control. A third important group is the Bakongo of northwestern Angola. Many of the Bakongo are coffee growers. There are also a number of people of mixed ancestry in Angola. Most of the skilled European workers in Angola left the country after independence.

Angolans speak various Bantu languages and Portuguese. Most of the people follow tribal religions. But there is a large Roman Catholic minority. Primary education is compulsory. There is a shortage of teachers and schools, but the government is working to expand the educational system. The University of Angola at Luanda opened in 1963.

Most Angolans live in rural areas. Traditional villages may have as few as 5 households or as many as 500. The heads of the households are usually related. Angolan houses are either round or square, with thatched roofs shaped like cones. Near the houses there are often granaries and chicken coops built on stilts. There may also be pens for pigs, goats, and sheep and gardens of maize (corn), beans, and tobacco.

Most of the Europeans in Angola lived in the coastal cities. The hotels, cafés, and office buildings in the busy ports of Luanda, Lobito, Benguela, and Moçâmades resemble those of Portugal.

THE LAND

Most of Angola is a great plateau. The highest part is called the Bié Plateau. There is a narrow strip of lowland along the coast. The coastal zone has a hot, dry climate and scrubby desert vegetation. The plateau is cooler and receives more rain. The tropical rain forests in the northeast are part of the Congo River basin. In the south is the northern edge of the vast Kalahari Desert, which covers much of southern Africa.

THE ECONOMY

Most people in Angola are farmers who grow only enough food for their own use. Coffee, cotton, sisal (a fiber used in making rope), tobacco, maize, sugarcane, beans, and cacao are among the crops grown on the plateau. Cattle, sheep, and goats are also raised there. The chief export crop is coffee.

Minerals are an important part of Angola's exports. Diamonds are mined in the northeast. Iron ore is produced near Huambo (Nova Lisboa), in the west central part of the country. There are rich deposits of oil off the coast of Cabinda and of uranium on the border with Namibia (South-West Africa).

Fish and fish products are important exports. Fishing is a thriving industry along the southern coast, where the cold Benguela Cur-

---

FACTS AND FIGURES

PEOPLE'S REPUBLIC OF ANGOLA is the official name of the country.

CAPITAL: Luanda.

LOCATION: West coast of southern Africa. **Latitude**— 4° 28′ S to 17° 26′ S. **Longitude**—11° 40′ E to 24° 4′ E.

AREA: 1,246,700 km² (481,351 sq mi).

POPULATION: 6,800,000 (estimate).

LANGUAGE: Portuguese, Ovimbundu, Kimbundu.

GOVERNMENT: Republic. **Head of government**—president. **International co-operation**—United Nations, Organization of African Unity (OAU).

ECONOMY: Agricultural products—coffee, cotton, sisal, tobacco, maize, livestock, palm oil, sugarcane, beans, cacao. **Industries and products**—fishing, processed foods, textiles, beverages. **Chief minerals**—diamonds, iron ore, petroleum. **Chief exports**—coffee, diamonds, fish, iron ore, oil, sisal, cotton. **Chief imports**—transportation equipment, iron and steel goods. **Monetary unit**—kwanza.

rent attracts many fish. Other industries process locally grown crops. Angola's rivers provide hydroelectric power.

Angola's well-developed network of roads and railroads was badly damaged during the civil war that followed independence. The Benguela Railway, linking the mineral-rich Katanga province of Zaïre to Angolan ports, was closed in 1975. The two countries agreed to reopen the railroad in 1978.

▶ HISTORY AND GOVERNMENT

The Bantu peoples moved into Angola from central Africa in the 14th and 15th centuries. The country was named for Ngola, the ruler of an ancient Kimbundu kingdom.

The Portuguese explorer Diogo Cão reached the mouth of the Congo River in 1482 while searching for a sea route from Europe to India. The Portuguese founded the capital city, Luanda, in 1575. Disease, the tropical climate, and the hostility of the Africans prevented the Portuguese from gaining complete control of the region until 1918.

Most African countries became independent in the late 1950's and early 1960's, but Portugal refused to grant independence to Angola at that time. The Angolans, like other Africans, wanted to rule themselves. Armed revolts took place in 1961, and Angolan guerrillas waged a long war against the Portuguese in the northern part of the country. Portugal's government was toppled by a military coup in 1974. The new government recognized the right of Angola and other Portuguese terri-

tories in Africa to independence. Angola gained its independence in 1975.

But independence did not bring peace. A long-standing power struggle between three rival liberation groups led to civil war. The war was finally won by the Popular Movement for the Liberation of Angola (MPLA), with the aid of Soviet arms and Cuban troops. The leader of the group, Agostinho Neto, served as Angola's president until his death in 1979. The following year, the MPLA announced that a People's Assembly would be established to rule the country.

HUGH C. BROOKS
St. John's University (New York)

Fishing boats at Luanda, capital of Angola, with modern buildings in the background.

261

ANIMALS

If you asked someone to list names of animals, you would probably get such answers as dog, horse, squirrel, lion, and mouse. Very few people would think of snakes, clams, robins, or earthworms. Yet all are members of the vast and wonderful kingdom of animals. We are members of it. So are amoebas, herrings, elephants, and penguins.

The big animal kingdom is divided into groups called classes. Birds form one class. Insects are another class. So are fishes. Still other classes include lobsters, clams, worms, and jellyfish. Snakes belong to one class. Frogs belong to another. We ourselves belong to the class called mammals—along with dogs, horses, elephants, monkeys, and many others. (Mammals are animals that nurse their young on milk.)

Together the members of the animal kingdom offer a wondrous variety of life.

▶ THE LARGE AND THE SMALL

The largest animals that have ever lived are still in existence. They are the great whales—mammals, as it happens. The biggest of these is the blue whale, which may grow more than 30 meters (100 feet) long. A fair-sized blue whale weighs about 105 metric tons, as much as 1,500 adult males.

Next to whales the largest living animals are the whale shark and the basking shark.

ELEPHANT

GRASSHOPPER

OSTRICH

SQUIRREL

ROBIN

MOUSE

LOBSTER

They are classed with the fishes. The whale shark may be 15 meters (50 feet) long, while the basking shark is slightly shorter.

The largest land animal now living is the African elephant. African elephants have been known to grow as tall as 4 meters (13 feet). Indian elephants are only slightly smaller. Some may stand 3 meters (10 feet) tall and weigh more than 5 metric tons.

Dinosaurs were the largest animals that ever lived on land. The biggest dinosaur was more than 25 meters (about 85 feet) long. Another, which ran about on its hind legs, stood 6 meters (20 feet) tall. Yet there were other dinosaurs only 30 centimeters (1 foot) or so long. (All the dinosaurs died out about 65,000,000 years ago.)

Dinosaurs, classed as reptiles, were related to the distant ancestors of living reptiles such as crocodiles and snakes. Among the largest living reptiles are the giant sea turtle, which may be 2.5 meters (8 feet) long and weigh almost a ton, and the American and Orinoco crocodiles, which may grow 7 meters (23 feet) long. The largest snakes are boas and pythons, members of the same family. Among these the largest is probably the anaconda, a South American boa. It may grow to a length of more than 11 meters (37 feet).

The largest bird is the ostrich, which cannot fly but can run fast. Among the largest flying birds are the condors of South America and California. But the albatross has the larg-

FROG

PORTUGUESE MAN-OF-WAR

SPIDER

SPONGE

SNAKE

FISH

CAT

THE ANIMAL KINGDOM
INVERTEBRATES (Animals Without Backbones)

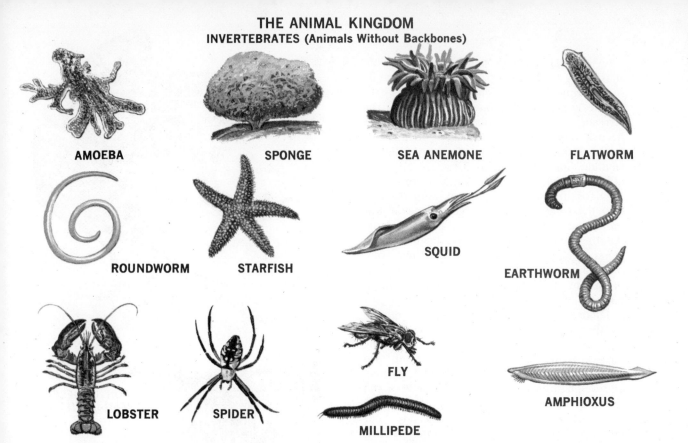

AMOEBA

SPONGE

SEA ANEMONE

FLATWORM

ROUNDWORM

STARFISH

SQUID

EARTHWORM

LOBSTER

SPIDER

FLY

MILLIPEDE

AMPHIOXUS

VERTEBRATES (Animals With Backbones)

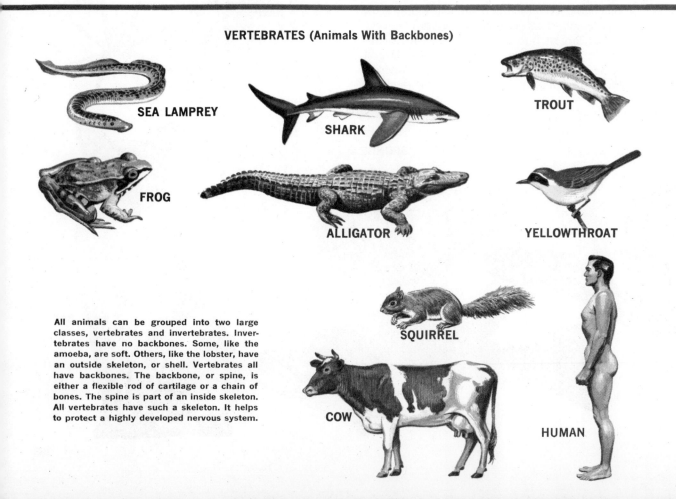

SEA LAMPREY

SHARK

TROUT

FROG

ALLIGATOR

YELLOWTHROAT

SQUIRREL

COW

HUMAN

All animals can be grouped into two large classes, vertebrates and invertebrates. Invertebrates have no backbones. Some, like the amoeba, are soft. Others, like the lobster, have an outside skeleton, or shell. Vertebrates all have backbones. The backbone, or spine, is either a flexible rod of cartilage or a chain of bones. The spine is part of an inside skeleton. All vertebrates have such a skeleton. It helps to protect a highly developed nervous system.

est wingspread. From the tip of one wing to the other, it may measure almost 3.5 meters (11 feet). Among the heaviest birds that can fly is the male trumpeter swan, weighing 17 kilograms (38 pounds). The U.S. national bird, the bald eagle, never weighs much more than 5 kilograms (11 pounds).

As well as whales and sharks, other large animals inhabit the oceans. A giant squid with its arms outstretched may be 15 meters (50 feet) long. Its body is about one third of this length. There is a tropical giant clam that grows to 1.5 meters (5 feet) in diameter and weighs 225 kilograms (500 pounds). The giant jellyfish found in the North Atlantic may weigh nearly a ton. It has an umbrella, or body, 2.5 meters (8 feet) wide and tentacles almost 37 meters (120 feet) long.

The Small Animals

The smallest mammals are the shrews. The smallest of all is the Etruscan shrew, of southern Europe. It weighs less than a dime.

Every class of animals has its very tiny members. Among the most remarkable are certain wasplike insects. Though only about 0.2 millimeter ($\frac{1}{125}$ inch) long, they have four wings, six legs, feelers, eyes, numerous muscles, a brain, and a complex nervous system. These tiny insects are smaller than some one-celled animals. For example, there is a giant amoeba, called *Chaos,* that sometimes stretches out to 5 millimeters ($\frac{1}{5}$ inch) in length.

The smallest forms of animal life are one-celled creatures that can be seen only with a microscope. Some are so small that they can live inside blood cells. The creatures that cause the disease kala-azar, widespread in parts of Asia, are so small that 2,400 of them placed side by side would measure only 1 centimeter (6,000 to 1 inch).

▶ SEPARATING PLANTS FROM ANIMALS

With creatures as tiny as these it is sometimes impossible to tell which are plants and which are animals. Therefore, many scientists prefer to group these forms into a separate division called micro-organisms. Another name for the same group is "protists."

With larger forms of living things, it is much easier to tell the animals from the plants. We look for the answers to two key questions. First, does the living thing move? If it moves itself about, it is probably an animal. Second, does it eat? If a living thing takes in and digests food, it is probably an animal. There are exceptions to both of these rules, but for the most part they hold true.

▶ HOW ANIMALS MOVE

We have seen that there is a wondrous variety in the sizes of animals. We observe that same variety in the ways in which animals move on land, in the air, and in water.

Animal Movement on Land

Land-dwelling mammals walk, run, and jump. Lizards, turtles, and salamanders also walk, although they are often said to crawl. Ants, termites, and some other insects walk a great deal. Grasshoppers and crickets are jumpers, but they may walk about slowly when they are eating. Even flying birds must be able to walk or hop on land.

Next time you are in a garden, look for a snail and note how smoothly it moves. The snail rows itself about. It produces a watery liquid that serves as a private lake. The snail rows through the "lake" by contracting muscles that move its skin.

Many animals live in the ground and must get from place to place. Moles and mole crickets dig their way rapidly with their shovel-like forelegs. Earthworms often eat their way through. When the soil is loose, they push through it in much the same way that they move on the surface of the ground. They have little bristles, or stiff hairs, in their skin. A worm moves about by digging these into the ground and making itself first longer and then shorter. In that way it pulls itself ahead.

Animals That Fly

Several kinds of animals fly through the air. Certain others—known as flying squirrels, flying frogs, flying lizards, and flying fish—do not really fly. Instead they glide through the air. The best gliders are the flying fish. They leap from the water with such force that they can glide as far as 45 meters (150 feet).

A true flying animal propels itself through the air by beating its wings against the air. Only four groups of animals have ever produced many kinds that could really fly. These are the birds, the bats, the insects, and the flying reptiles that died out with the other dinosaurs. Each group has its own kind of wing. However, the wings of birds, bats, and the flying reptiles are alike in having bones. An insect's wing, like an insect's body, has no bones. The veins that strengthen its wing are really air tubes with strong walls.

Animal Movement in Water

A great many animals live in the water, chiefly because there is much more room for them than on land. A few kinds of mammals, such as whales and dolphins, live only in the water. Other mammals, such as seals, spend most of their lives in the water. Many birds do a great deal of paddling about in the water. Reptiles, like the turtles, and amphibian animals, like frogs, are also good swimmers.

Most of the swimming animals belong to the class of fishes. A fish normally propels itself through the water by moving its tail fin. Yet many fish can swim even if most of the tail fin is bitten or cut off. These fish push themselves through the water by twisting their bodies from side to side. Some fish can move forward or backward by means of their side fins.

Several animals move through the water by jet propulsion. Squids and cuttlefish, for example, suck water into their bodies and then squirt it out. This shoots them forward. Jellyfish also swim by jet propulsion. They slowly open their jellylike umbrellas and then rapidly close them. A stream of water jets out, pushing the jellyfish forward.

Some tiny animals row themselves through the water. They have thousands of tiny hairs, called cilia. The cilia act as oars. Other tiny sea creatures have whiplike threads with which they pull themselves forward.

There are still more curious ways in which animals move about. Some ride from place to place on other animals. For example, the remora (or shark sucker) is a fish with a sucker on the top of its head. It fastens onto sharks or other big fishes and sometimes onto a big sea turtle. When a shark kills another fish, the remora frees itself to go after part of the meal.

Animals' Eating Habits

Animals have a great range of eating habits. Human beings can eat many different kinds of food, although some eat nothing but plant foods and seeds. Others, like some Eskimos, eat almost nothing but meat and fish.

Some animals—such as chickens, rats, pigs, and bears—eat both animal and vegetable foods. Such animals are called **omnivores** (eaters of everything). Lions and tigers live almost entirely on meat. They are called **carnivores** (eaters of meat). Cattle, horses, and sheep, which eat only vegetable matter, are **herbivores** (eaters of plants).

Some animals eat only a few kinds of food. The koala, a pouched mammal found in Australia, eats the leaves of the eucalyptus tree. Silkworms, the young of the silkworm moth, depend on the leaves of the mulberry tree. Anteaters live on ants and termites, which they capture with their long, wormlike tongues. The female mosquito lives on blood. To get it, she pierces the skin of her victim with her needle-like mouth tube. Male mosquitoes live on flower juices.

Other animals also have eating habits that seem strange to us. The praying mantis and many fishes will eat young of their own kind, including their own offspring. They seem to have no way of knowing that the young ones are their own. Hyenas and carrion vultures rarely attack anything, but sit at a safe distance, waiting for a wounded or sick animal to die. Hyenas also wait for a lion to finish eating and then gobble up what is left.

When one shark attacks a big fish, other sharks often dash at the prey and fight wildly for a bite. But the fiercest fish is the small piranha, of South America. Hundreds of these fish will gather and strip all the flesh off a large fish or some other animal in a few minutes. If one piranha is cut, the others eat it in a few seconds.

Elephants may knock down trees to strip off all the leaves. Grasshoppers and caterpillars usually nibble along the edge of a leaf instead of biting into the middle. Some caterpillars eat by tunneling their way through a leaf, leaving the skin of the leaf on each side of them.

Some flies and wasps inject poison into leaves or stems. This makes the plant tissue grow into galls (blisterlike swellings). The insects lay their eggs in these galls, and the young then have a ready food supply.

Most ants are hard-working insects and often travel great distances to find food. But

ANIMALS OF THE FOREST

TIGER

CHIMPANZEE

CENTIPEDE

TURTLE

ROSE-BREASTED GROSBEAK

WOLVERINE

FAWN

RACCOON

SNAIL

ANIMALS OF POLAR REGIONS

POLAR BEAR

LEMMINGS

KING PENGUIN

WALRUS

CARIBOU

ARCTIC TERN

SIBERIAN HUSKY

ANIMALS OF THE PRAIRIES

GIRAFFE

ZEBRA

LION

KANGAROO

COYOTE

PRAIRIE DOG

BLACK-TAILED JACKRABBIT

MEADOWLARK

DIAMONDBACK RATTLESNAKE

ANIMALS OF THE DESERT

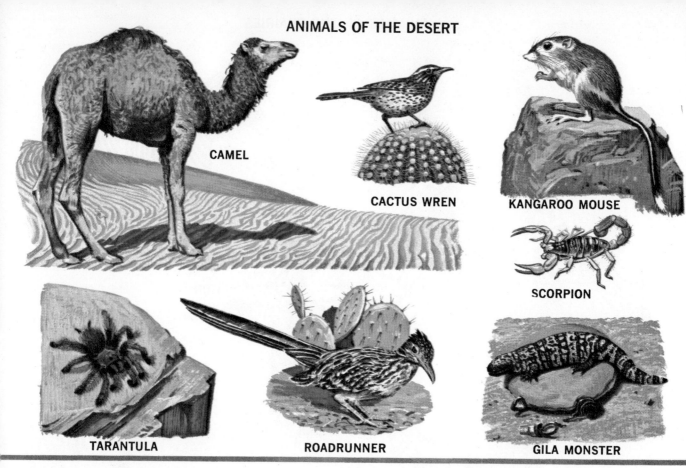

CAMEL

CACTUS WREN

KANGAROO MOUSE

SCORPION

TARANTULA

ROADRUNNER

GILA MONSTER

ANIMALS OF THE SEA AND SEASHORE

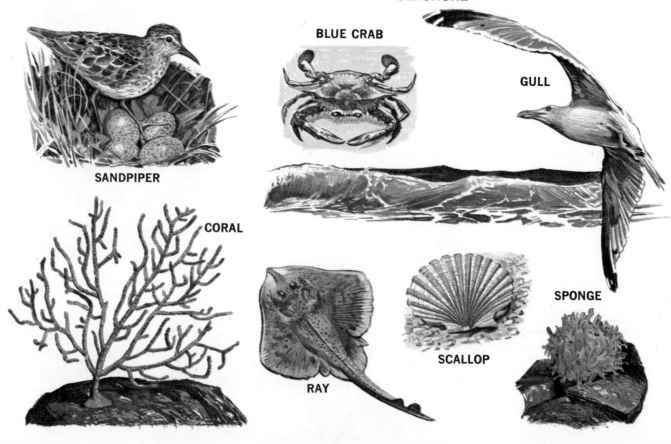

BLUE CRAB

GULL

SANDPIPER

CORAL

RAY

SCALLOP

SPONGE

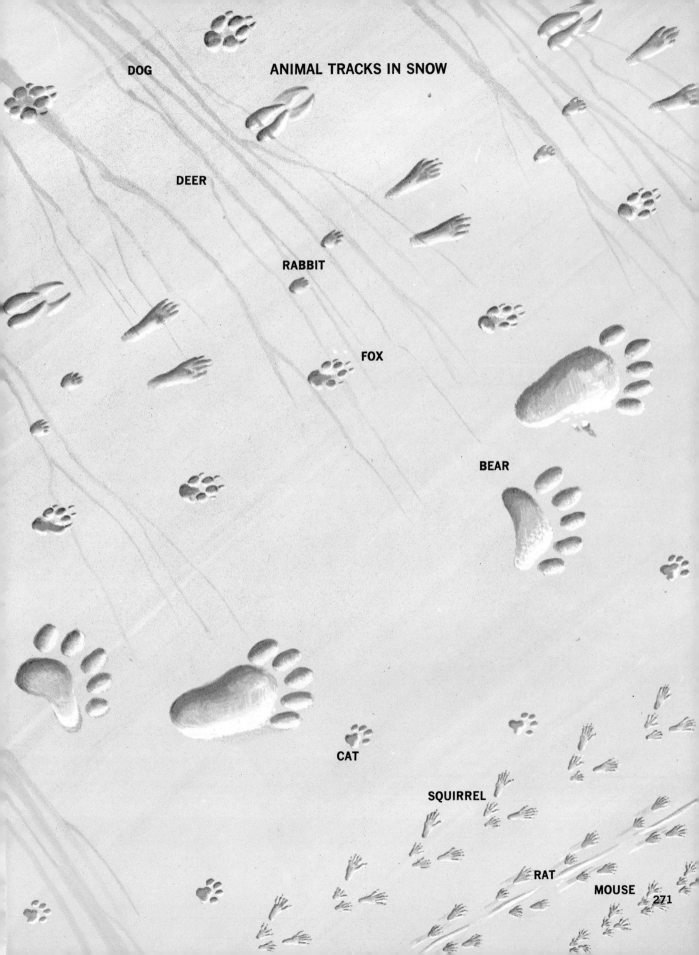

ANIMAL TRACKS IN SNOW

DOG

DEER

RABBIT

FOX

BEAR

CAT

SQUIRREL

RAT

MOUSE

271

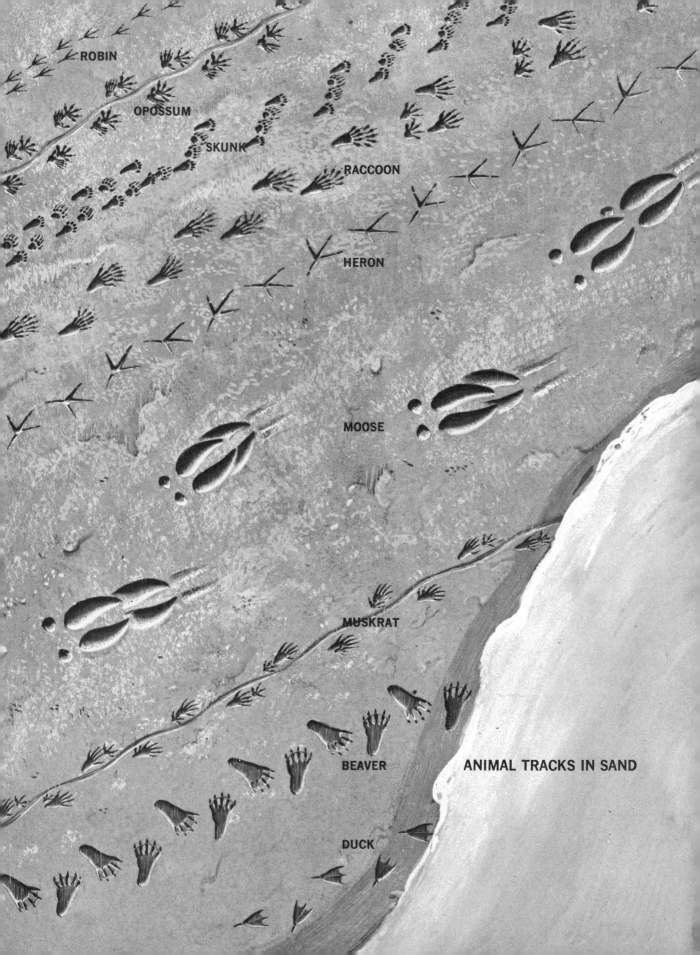

ROBIN

OPOSSUM

SKUNK

RACCOON

HERON

MOOSE

MUSKRAT

BEAVER

ANIMAL TRACKS IN SAND

DUCK

ANIMAL HOMES

BOWERBIRD

SQUIRREL

TURTLE

BEAVER

CHIPMUNK

CICADA

HONEYBEE

MAGPIE

BEAR

273

ANIMAL FEEDING HABITS

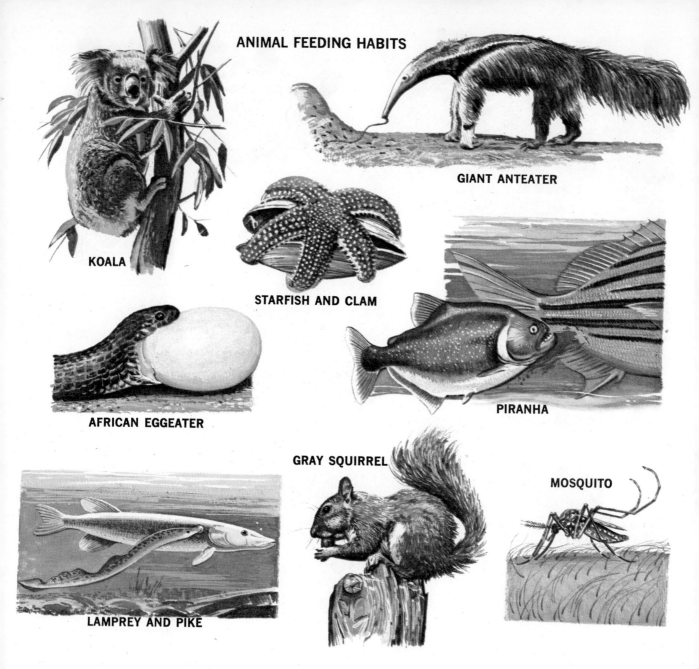

KOALA

GIANT ANTEATER

STARFISH AND CLAM

AFRICAN EGGEATER

PIRANHA

GRAY SQUIRREL

MOSQUITO

LAMPREY AND PIKE

there are ants that make slaves of other ants. Some slave-owning ants would starve if the slaves did not provide them with food.

Many animals capture small animals and plants by what is called filter feeding. These animals make currents of water that bring them victims smaller than themselves. Among the animals that filter their food in this way are sponges, coral animals, clams, oysters, and certain kinds of worms.

The one-celled amoeba eats in still another way. It is always changing its shape, and it simply flows around smaller animals and plants and digests them.

There are many kinds of animals, and they eat many kinds of food. But all eat for the same reason—food is necessary for life.

THOMAS GORDON LAWRENCE
Erasmus Hall High School

See also ANIMALS: LOCOMOTION; BIRDS; FISHES; FROGS, TOADS, AND OTHER AMPHIBIANS; GIANTS OF NATURE; INSECTS; KINGDOMS OF LIVING THINGS; LIFE; LIFE, ADAPTATIONS IN THE WORLD OF; MAMMALS; MICROBIOLOGY; REPTILES; WORMS.

ANIMALS: COMMUNICATION AND SOCIAL ORGANIZATION

For years people have watched snake charmers in Indian bazaars play music to their cobras. The watchers have marveled at the way the snakes seem to move in response to the music. But a little research shows that a snake cannot hear high-pitched sounds. If a cobra is blindfolded, you can play music on a pipe for hours and the snake will sit still. Remove the blindfold and wave your arms about; the snake will raise its head and spread its hood. A cobra responds not to the music, but to the movements the snake charmer makes as he plays.

It is difficult to enter the world of animals. Too often we think of animals as if they were human beings. It is hard to realize that they do not see as we see, smell as we smell, or hear as we hear. Yet anyone who does not realize this is bound to make mistakes.

To find out how animals communicate, we must observe them carefully; we must note just what signals pass from one animal to another and bring forth a response. Scientists have studied the ways in which animals communicate. They have watched the animals in their natural environments, as well as in zoos, aquariums, and laboratories. Some scientists have gone to lonely islands to study the breeding colonies of birds and seals. Others have traveled to tropical jungles to explore the social life of monkeys and apes. Some have spent months on remote mountaintops, following herds of deer and elk or watching the ways of wolves. With binoculars, cameras, and notebooks, they have recorded exactly what they saw.

In recent years they have had a new tool: the battery-operated tape recorder. This is a great improvement over written reports of animal sounds. The cry of a gull may sound like *ga-ga-ga* to one person; to another it sounds like *kek-kek-kek*. Now it is no longer a question of what each person hears. All the grunts, barks, howls, cries, and songs of the animal world can be recorded on tape. Other electronic instruments can turn these songs into pictures on paper. The pictures are called sound spectrograms. They can be examined and compared. Human hearing plays no part in the study.

Cobra is responding to movements of the snake charmer and not to sound of music, as most people think.

Many observers of animal life have also been able to do experiments in the field. But that is difficult. Most experiments must be done in the laboratory, where conditions can be controlled. If you change some factor in the life of a group of animals, how will the animals respond? And how does this behavior compare with the behavior of a control group kept in normal surroundings? Scientists are very careful to make sure that the animals are reacting only to the sights and sounds provided and not to something else. Even the experimenter himself can ruin an experiment. One scientist was studying how geese responded to a cardboard model of an enemy. The enemy was a bird of prey sailing overhead. Before each test he had to climb a tree to fasten the model overhead. Very soon the geese were giving an alarm call every time the experimenter started to climb the tree. Some other method of setting up this experiment had to be found.

Observations and experiments have shown that all kinds of animals have a "language." It is not a language like ours, for animals do not communicate with words and sentences. But they do have many signals—a twitch of the tail, a flick of the ears, a low bark, a chirp, a special odor, or a flutter of wings are

Many mother animals and their young exchange vocal signals. Hen calls chicks with three distinct signals.

follow her. When she finds food, she makes a series of quick noises that sound like *kuk-kuk-kuk-kuk,* and her chicks come running. When she settles down for the night on her roost, she calls the chicks close to her with a long, low, purring sound.

Young chicks are able to give distress calls 15 minutes after they are hatched from the eggs. When the hen hears this call, she immediately moves toward the chick. This sound (and not the sight of her chick) is the important signal. A scientist proved this by hiding a chick from its mother hen. The chick could be heard but not seen. When the hen heard the chick's distress call, she went toward the sound. Then the scientist put the chick under a glass jar. This time no sound could be heard, although the chick could easily be seen through the glass. The hen paid no attention to the chick.

Young robins are born with their eyes closed. Their feeding signal is a slight jarring movement of the nest, like the one made by a parent robin as it lands. This makes them open their mouths. Later, when their eyes open, young robins recognize other signals. They open their mouths only when they see their parents or hear a light, low whistle—the feeding call. The young robins respond with a food-begging call. This call is important later. When the robins leave the nest, the call makes it possible for the parent robins to find their young, who may be hidden from sight by overhanging leaves.

just a few. Any one signal may produce a response in another animal perceiving it. And these signals may play an important part in the social life of the animals. Most of the signals have to do with parent-young relationships, with food, enemies, the meeting of the sexes, and with keeping in touch with other members of a group.

▶ PARENT-YOUNG RELATIONS

Vocal (voice) signals are constantly exchanged between many mother animals and their young.

The hen calls her chicks with three different signals. When she clucks, the chicks

These are sound spectrograms. They serve as pictures of the sounds made by animals, and they can be readily examined and compared. Spectrograms were made by electronic instruments from tape recordings of sounds.

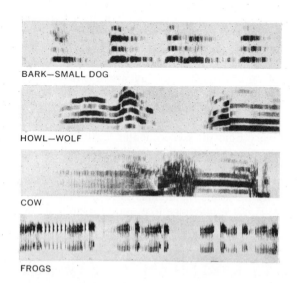

BARK—SMALL DOG

HOWL—WOLF

COW

FROGS

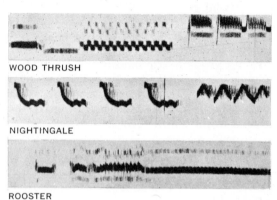

WOOD THRUSH

NIGHTINGALE

ROOSTER

Many mother ducks have calls that draw the young to them. A mother blue-winged teal duck is one of these. She makes a steady, soft *pe-tunk, pe-tunk* sound as the family travels through thick grass. The baby ducks may lose sight of their mother, but they are able to follow her. The young ducks have a peep call that helps them find each other when they are separated.

There is a constant calling back and forth between baby and mother among deer, elk, cows, sheep, and goats. When little rabbits cry *qua-a-a,* mother rabbit comes running. Baby opossums cry, and mother opossum rushes back to the nest. She has a special clicking signal that attracts her young to her. If she clicks before leaving the nest, the baby opossums enter their mother's pouch or climb onto her fur. If she does not click, the young stay behind.

Sound and smell help a mother fur seal to recognize her own pup. Thousands of pups are born every year on the Pribilof Islands, near Alaska. A mother seal stays with her pup for about a week after its birth. Then she returns to the sea, where she feeds. Once a week she comes up on land to let her pup nurse. When she comes ashore, she bleats like a sheep. All the hungry pups in the area bleat back and move toward her. When they are close, the mother seal sniffs at their noses. She finds her own pup by its smell, singling it out from all the others. In this way she feeds only her own pup.

▶FOOD CALLS

When a herring gull sees food, it gives a special three-note call. The call brings gulls streaming in from all directions. When this call is played on a tape recorder along the seacoast, gulls gather in a few minutes. Ducks and many other birds also have a call that signals food.

Animals that hunt other animals may have special hunting cries. For instance, the gray wolf hunts in packs. When one wolf finds food, it calls to the pack with a long smooth howl. While the hunt is on, short rapid barks keep them together. When they close in for the kill, their call is like a short bark and howl combined. While the prey is being pulled down, they howl and snarl like a bunch of dogs.

When parent robin lands, nest is jarred. This is the signal for young to open their mouths for food.

When some gulls discover source of food, their cries attract many other gulls. Here gulls follow boat.

ALARM AND DISTRESS CALLS

A call of alarm or distress can send a whole flock of birds into the air. So can a special kind of movement. Similar signals can make a herd of animals rush away from the source of danger.

Herring gulls have an alarm call that works in this way. First other herring gulls draw near the gull that is giving the alarm. Then they all rise into the air and circle away. To test this call, a tape of it was broadcast through a loudspeaker at a garbage dump crowded with hundreds of shrieking gulls. In a few minutes the dump was deserted. Even while still inside the egg, a gull chick stops squeaking when it hears these alarm calls. Newly born gull chicks respond to it by crouching down in the nest. When they are a few days old, they respond in a different way. They leave the nest and crouch some distance away. They are hidden by the camouflage of their brownish-gray color against the sand.

Gulls are often pests on the landing strips of airfields. So the playing of these alarm calls may be a means of getting rid of them. Distress calls of starlings, used in the same way, frighten the starlings away from their roosts on public buildings.

Many kinds of deer have barks, hisses, or coughs that warn the herd of danger. Alarm calls by baby monkeys and apes bring the parents to their side. Warning calls by prairie dogs and marmots are signals for these animals to dash into their burrows.

Even fish and frogs have danger signals. Suppose a minnow is caught by bigger fish, and wounded. Its cut skin then gives off a chemical that frightens all other minnows nearby. It makes them huddle together into a tight school. In the case of frogs, the alert is a warning grunt plus the sound of the splash made as the frog dives into the water to escape an enemy.

COMMUNICATION BETWEEN THE SEXES

Insects, fishes, frogs and toads, reptiles, birds, and mammals—all have ways of attracting members of the opposite sex when they are ready to mate.

Male goby fish make thumping sounds that attract females. The belly of the three-spined stickleback turns a bright red when he is ready to mate. This acts as a sight signal to the female stickleback. When she approaches, the male does a zigzag dance. The female responds by swimming toward him with her head up. This signal makes the male lead her to the nest he has prepared. The female lays her eggs inside it. Then the male enters and fertilizes the eggs.

Male frogs and toads trill, peep, and croak. These sounds attract females to the ponds where the males are calling. Experiments with recorded sounds have proved this. When a loudspeaker plays these calls, females move toward the source of the sound. Moreover, they move toward sounds made by their own species. That is how a female frog finds her own kind in a pond where many different species of male frogs are calling.

Female snakes attract males by their movements and their odor.

Odor is the signal that brings male moths to the side of female moths. A male moth may be a mile away from a female. But the wind carries tiny scent particles from the female moth. The smell organs on the antennae of the male moth pick up the signal. He heads straight into the wind that carries the scent. He flies nearer and nearer to the female, following the scent that grows stronger and stronger.

Fireflies have light signals that attract members of the opposite sex. Many different kinds of fireflies may be active at the same time of night. Even so, the female firefly can tell her own kind by the rhythm of the flashing and the length of each flash.

Many male insects make noises that serve as calling sounds to the females. Grasshoppers, katydids, crickets, and cicadas fill warm summer nights with sounds they make by rubbing one part of the body against another. Each kind of insect makes its own particular kind of buzz, scrape, or rattle. Only its own females answer to the sound.

The beautiful songs that birds sing are territory songs. Male birds sing them to keep other males away from the chosen nest site (or territory) and to attract females. Females generally arrive at nesting areas after the males. They locate mates by songs. Once males and females have found each other, the amount of singing drops by 90 per cent.

Not all birds sing. Those that do are usually small. They are likely to be hidden in the un-

Male birds sing to keep other males away from territory chosen as nest site and to attract females. Little green heron (*above*) is not very green, in spite of name.

Red-bellied male stickleback is ready to mate. Below left, he rises from stony nest he has prepared to chase away another fish. Below right, courtship ended, male guides female to nest. She will lay eggs, which he will fertilize.

Spring peeper is giving his mating call. Balloon-like extension of throat serves to magnify sound.

derbrush or among the branches of trees. Bigger birds—like gulls, ducks, and geese—generally exchange calls rather than songs.

Many mammals are voiceless. They locate each other by scent signals. Often there are special glands in the skin that give off powerful smells. The smells, which may be deposited on mud, rocks, or trees, are followed by animals hunting for mates.

▶ INTER-GROUP SIGNALS

Hundreds or thousands of fish may swim together in schools. The signal that attracts members of the group seems to be light. Blind fish do not school. If the light over a tank of schooling fish is turned off, the group breaks up. When the light is turned on again, the fish arrange themselves in a tight school within 5 minutes. Other signals may also play a part, for we know that some fish school at night. These fish may respond to the water currents set up by fish swimming nearby.

Flocks of songbirds communicate with each other by sound as they move through the bushes or trees. Have you heard the *chick-a-dee-dee* of the black-capped chickadee? This sound tends to bring together members of a scattered flock. In the air, Canada geese make a loud honking that keeps the flock together. On the ground a low-pitched grunt serves the same purpose.

Bermuda chub, like other fishes, swim in groups called schools. Signal that attracts them seems to be light.

Many monkeys and apes have signals that keep a group together as they move through thick jungle. The howler monkey is a good example. A clan of howler monkeys may be feeding together in trees. When the group is ready to move on, all the males look for good passageways through the trees. The one who finds such a route gives a deep hoarse cluck. Then the other members of the clan move toward the leading animal and follow him through the trees.

▶ COMMUNICATION LEADS TO ORGANIZATION

The signals by which animals communicate play definite parts in their social life. Some of the amazing social relationships that exist among animals are dependent on the signals. For example, there are social dominance orders. In these one animal bosses another who bosses others—and so on down to the lowliest member of the group. Some groups of animals live together "free and equal." Some have "follow-the-leader" societies. Others have complicated social organizations in which labor is divided.

A Norwegian psychologist, T. Schjelderup-Ebbe, discovered the dominance order in flocks of chickens. One hen dominates all the others; she pecks all members of the flock without being pecked back. The hen next below her in rank pecks all except the top hen. Hen number three pecks all below her (but not the two top hens). And so it goes. The pecking order ends with a poor hen who is pecked by all and can peck no other hen. Experiments have shown that this social order in hens reduces fighting. It makes flock life more peaceful.

There are dominance orders among many other kinds of animals. When a number of cats are put together, for example, one cat dominates the group. It seizes all available food first. But there is no social order below the leader. The rest of the cats are about equal in rank. When the dominant cat is removed, the next most aggressive cat in the group takes over.

Some monkeys have dominance orders, too. This is true of baboons, ground monkeys with doglike faces. They live in Africa in troops of 10 to several hundred members. Among baboons, adult males hold the highest rank. They take the best feeding and resting

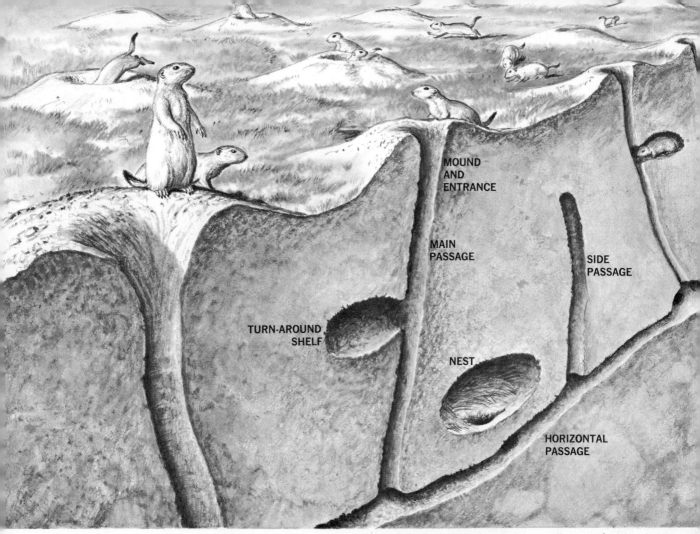

MOUND
AND
ENTRANCE

MAIN
PASSAGE

SIDE
PASSAGE

TURN-AROUND
SHELF

NEST

HORIZONTAL
PASSAGE

Prairie dogs live in huge "towns." But real social unit is the coterie, a small group of perhaps 10 members who live together and share burrows, as shown.

places. They mate with the most females. Less dominant animals always move out of the way of the more dominant ones.

But animals also live together in other ways. In tropical forests small apes called gibbons live together in families. Male and female are equally dominant. Howler monkeys live in clans; here females outnumber the males by two to one. But there is no dominance order. The adult males feed together without fighting. They share the females. They work together in leading and defending the group.

Many animals, like sheep and deer, live in large herds where "follow the leader" is the rule. This pattern of social life usually begins with strong bonds between mother and offspring. The young generally follow the mother, who continues to follow her mother, who follows her mother. The pattern con-

tinues up to the oldest female in the flock, who is the leader.

A few animals live in great communities called "towns." The prairie dog is one of these. Although the towns are huge, the real unit of social life is the coterie. This is a group of about 10 members who share burrows and live with one another on a friendly basis. Members of neighboring coteries are treated as enemies. Only one thing unites the whole town—a danger signal. All members of the town obey a warning call announcing an enemy. They respond to it by dashing into their underground burrows.

Insect societies also exist. Bees and ants form complicated ones where labor is divided.

MILLICENT E. SELSAM
Author, science books for children

See also ANTS; BEES.

ANIMALS: INTELLIGENCE AND BEHAVIOR

Think a little about the word "intelligence." Are you certain of its meaning? What is meant by saying that an animal is intelligent? And how can we tell whether animals are intelligent? After all, animals cannot speak, and they do not use words. They cannot express ideas. They cannot learn history or spelling.

Still, animals do many things. Perhaps your pet goldfish swims to the surface looking for food when you move near its tank. The cat may ring the doorbell when it wants to enter the house. Many other animals can do tricks and tasks. Circuses are filled with dancing bears, playful sea lions, prancing horses, and hard-working elephants.

Such behavior is often wrongly interpreted as signs of intelligence. As you will see, performing tricks or tasks is not truly a sign of intelligence. Intelligence is the ability to rea-son. It is the sudden flash of an idea. It is the ability to solve a new problem directly and also by using previous experiences. Performing tricks and tasks does not require the ability to reason, to think, to have ideas.

Tricks and tasks can be mastered through special kinds of learning. One way of learning them is through trial-and-error methods. Another is through conditioned responses. These are actions stemming from repeated experiences—things that happen over and over again. For example, if a bell is rung every time an animal is fed, the animal soon learns to look for food when it hears the bell.

It is important to understand how such learning behavior works. Then you will be able to understand the differences between it and truly intelligent behavior.

Behavior and intelligence in animals and people are studied by scientists known as psychologists. One of the hardest problems for psychologists is to figure out ways to test intelligence. This article will tell you about some of the ways that scientists study behavior and intelligence and what they are learning.

▶ CONDITIONED RESPONSES

Conditioned responses are not signs of intelligence. Nevertheless, they are part of the

Sea lion balances a ball on its nose while walking a tight-rope at a circus. Sea lions are among the many animals that are easily tamed and trained.

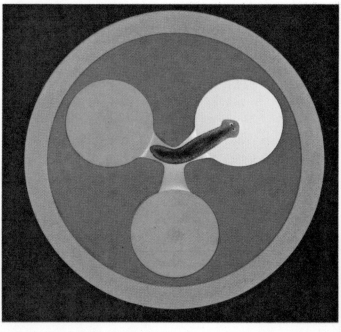

Planarian worm in maze consisting of three plastic wells connected by a Y-shaped tunnel. One well is brightly lighted. Worm needs water. It gets water only if it enters lighted well. After several trials planarian learns to find water by choosing lighted well.

animal's behavior. And so they may help psychologists to compare differences among animals and how animals learn. Conditioning takes place through special training. The animal learns to connect a new activity with behavior that he already has. For example, in an experiment with *Nereis,* a kind of sand worm, a light was flashed every time the worm was fed from a tube. After 60 times the worm learned that the flash of light meant feeding time. Later the same worm was taught to come to the tube when the light was off.

Animals can be conditioned in another way. They can learn to avoid a place or an object by being given a mild, harmless electric shock. Some can even be forced to change their normal behavior. For example, cockroaches usually come out only in the dark. They hide in dark places during the daytime. In one experiment some cockroaches were placed in a box; one half was lighted and the other half dark. As expected, the cockroaches scurried into the dark half. Once inside the dark half, they were given a shock, which they didn't like. After a number of electric shocks, they kept away from the dark and stayed in the light. This was against their nature. But they disliked the electric shocks even more than they disliked the light.

Almost all animals from the flatworm up can be conditioned. A few scientists think that even the *Paramecium,* a tiny, one-celled animal, can be conditioned. Fishes, frogs, turtles, birds, and mammals can be trained in this way. Mammals can be conditioned to complicated situations, worms to very simple ones.

▶ TRIAL AND ERROR

Another kind of learning takes place through trial and error, or "fumble and find." Trial-and-error methods are very popular ways of studying learning. Some scientists think that trial-and-error methods help to show how intelligent an animal is. The most famous kind of trial-and-error method is the maze.

The Maze

Mazes are thousands of years old. But it was only in the early 1900's that scientists first began to put animals in mazes to test learning ability. (Some scientists think that mazes can also be used to indicate intelligence.

However, this depends on how complicated the maze is.)

These mazes are all based on the same idea. An animal is placed in an entrance, and it must find the exit. As it proceeds it finds a series of branches, or forks. The animal must make a choice at each fork. If it chooses the wrong one, the animal comes to a dead end. Then it must go back and take the other path. After a time the animal learns to go through the maze. After a number of times it can run through the maze without making mistakes. The reward at the end is a tasty piece of food for the hungry animal.

The maze is very important to psychologists. It can have a simple design or a very difficult one. In the simple design the animal is called upon to make one turn, such as in a box shaped like the letter T. In the difficult ones animals may meet 25 separate turning points.

Experiments show that ants can master very complicated mazes. Many other animals can also master mazes, among them crabs, cockroaches, toads, frogs, goldfish, snakes, turtles, chickens, cowbirds, pigeons, bluebirds, rats, monkeys, chimpanzees, guinea pigs, and mice. But great differences are found among them in ability. For example, *Formica* ants need about 40 trials to master a maze with 6

Pigeon has been trained to peck at brighter of two spots of light. Here, spots are the same but dark background makes left-hand spot seem brighter.

Canary has learned that seeds are contained only in jar with white lid. It removes lid by pulling string.

forks. Rats can master a similar maze in 12 trials or fewer.

The only mammal that has been tested very much in mazes is the white rat. Rats have been tested on many, many kinds of mazes. In one test rats and college students were compared. The rats had to learn to find their way through a maze. Blindfolded college students did the same thing, using their hands. Twenty-seven white rats made a better showing than 38 college students. The rats could run through the maze without a single mistake after fewer tries than the students needed. But does this mean that rats are more intelligent than college students? Of course not. Learning a maze depends only on memory of trial and error. It does not require reasoning.

For some types of learning there is no advantage to being very intelligent. Since a maze is a trial-and-error test, it is not a good way of measuring higher intelligence, such as

Harvester ant in one type of maze learns to take shortest route from start to food. Can you solve this maze?

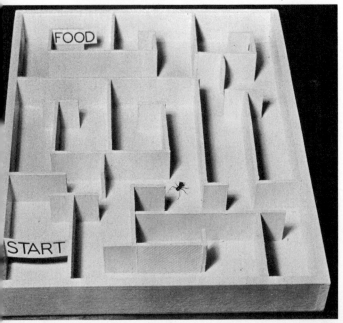

is found in humans. But a maze is useful in studying how learning takes place. Many of our activities involve learning, which contributes to intelligence.

The Problem Box

Another way to study trial-and-error learning is to place an animal in a box. A bit of food is placed outside, and the animal can reach the food only by unlocking a door. Or the food may be put into the box. Then the animal must open the door to get into the box. In both cases the problem is the same: opening a door to get food.

For many years people thought that door opening was a sign of great intelligence, but no one knew how animals learned to open doors. Scientists decided to study door opening by animals. Careful study showed that door opening is another form of trial-and-error learning. It is no more a proof of great intelligence than running through mazes.

One scientist carefully watched a number of cats. He found that they all acted just about the same. A cat was placed in a cage (a kind of problem box) and a fish placed outside. The cage door could be opened by pulling a string. The cat bit and clawed at all parts of the cage. Finally it began to claw and chew near the string. It pulled the string and the door opened. This was, of course, pure chance. Also by chance, other cats turned handles or pushed down levers that opened doors. In time the cats learned to concentrate only on the lock. They had learned that the lock was related to the food. But their success was only through trial and error.

Squirrels learned to enter problem boxes for food. So did porcupines. They learned to raise a hook, pull a plug, or turn a button to open a box. Dogs did not do too well with these problems, although some dogs did better than others. Several dogs learned to open a food box by pushing down a handle. After they had learned to work the handle, the box was turned partly around. Strangely, the dogs kept pawing at the place where the handle had been before the box was turned. They had to learn the method of opening all over again after the box was turned.

Sparrows learned to enter a cage by pulling a string. Pigeons, redheaded woodpeckers, cowbirds, juncos, bluebirds, crows, and Balti-

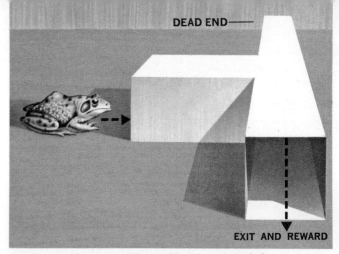

DEAD END——

EXIT AND REWARD

Frog is placed in a covered T-maze. When it comes to fork, it must choose path to exit and reward. If it turns left, it comes to a dead end. Then it must go back and try again. After several trials frog will usually turn right.

more orioles opened doors to get at food. To test these birds, the scientist first trained them to feed in the box with the door open. After they got used to feeding inside, the door was closed. It could be opened only by pulling a string or lifting a latch.

Raccoons can learn to open really complicated locks. They can open a door with seven separate locks—pushing down pedals and pulling strings, lifting latches, sliding bolts back, undoing hooks, and pressing down a thumb latch. Tests showed that when they learned to open all the locks, they could get out of a cage in 8 seconds. Raccoons can be very quick once they have mastered the locks because their front paws work like hands. In fact, they do almost as well as monkeys in these tests.

Monkeys learned to open locks in a special order. That is, they had to open lock 1 before they could open lock 2. They had to open lock 2 before lock 3, and so on. Once monkeys learned (and they learned fairly fast), they became interested in any lock. If they were presented with a new one, they immediately tried to open it.

Monkeys are sometimes difficult to work with because they have bad tempers. One scientist placed a banana in a problem box with several locks on it. The monkey couldn't manage the locks. He went into a tantrum, picked up the box, and smashed it against the wall. He ate his banana, but next time the scientist bolted the box to the floor.

At first humans took as long as monkeys to open locks in a special order. But once they learned, they were much faster. The reason humans took so long is a fairly simple one. There is no way to figure out the order by looking at the locks. Learning the order is a form of trial-and-error learning. Insight or reasoning does not help here any more than with mazes. Thus, in the first stages of trial-and-error learning, humans are not fast either.

Multiple-choice Tests

In multiple-choice experiments, an animal is placed in a box with several doors. The doors are next to one another. The animal (a hungry one, as usual) learns that it can get food on the other side of one of the doors. All but one of the doors are always locked. The food can be found behind the one unlocked door. The next time another door is unlocked, and so the same door is never unlocked two times in a row. That is what the animal must learn. It must learn to stay away from the door that was unlocked the time before.

In one experiment humans, monkeys, dogs, cats, and horses were tested. Humans and some monkeys quickly learned to stay away from the door that had been open the time before. The other animals did not. They tried

Chimpanzee is learning to open locks. If it opens them in the correct order, it will be rewarded with food. A chimp learns to solve such problems very quickly.

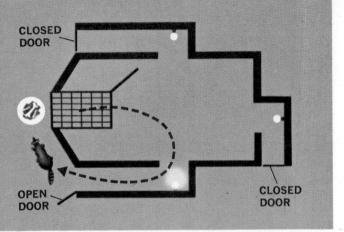

Raccoon learns that door at end of lighted passageway will be open, allowing animal to get food. Later, light is turned on and off in a different passageway. To get food raccoon must remember which passage was lighted.

each door once or twice until they had tried all. Cats and dogs tried a door once or twice and then moved on to another door. Horses kept trying the same doors over and over again.

▶ DELAYED REACTION

Another way scientists have tried to discover differences in intelligence is known as the delayed-reaction (response) test.

This test is concerned with the ability of an animal to develop an "idea." A hungry animal is stimulated by food in a box. A light is placed over the box. The animal soon learns that food is in the lighted box.

After the animal is trained, a light is turned on over a box and then turned off. But the animal is not allowed to go to the box for a short time after the light is turned off. Thus

Food is placed outside a picket fence. Hungry animal is left inside fence. Hen runs back and forth along fence near food. If opening in the fence is large enough, hen may see how to get food. Dog goes around fence right away.

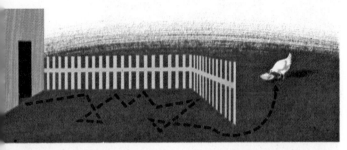

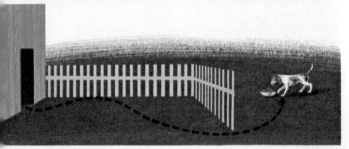

the animal has to have the "idea" that light means food and then remember which box was lighted. Scientists watch to see how long they can delay the animal and still have it make the right choice.

Scientists have discovered that rats could not find the right box if they waited for more than 10 seconds. Dogs could wait as long as 5 minutes, but each had to keep its head pointed to the right box. If the dog was turned around, it couldn't find the right box. A raccoon could wait for 25 seconds, and it didn't have to keep pointing at the box. Children 2½ years old could wait 25 minutes without keeping their eyes on the right box.

Animals that had to look at the box during the whole delay time were not considered to have ideas. But some scientists have suggested that those that could wait and not point may have formed the "idea" that light meant food.

Other experiments were done in different ways. Monkeys were trained to find food under a cup. They could remember that there was food under a cup and remember the right cup up to 24 hours later in some experiments. The monkeys could even remember what kind of food was under the cup. For example, some monkeys were trained to a banana. If lettuce was placed under the cup instead, the monkeys went into a rage. Clearly, they could associate food with the cup and also remember what the food was.

Such tests do tell something about the animal's ability to associate different things. They also tell us how long the animal can be delayed before it forgets the associations. But we are not sure that these tests measure an animal's ability to have "ideas." They do not measure its adaptability—its ability to work out new solutions to problems.

▶ ADAPTABILITY

Adaptability is one of the features of reasoning. Animals that are adaptable can vary their behavior. They will try to solve problems in different ways. If one way doesn't work, they try another.

Animals lower than mammals are apparently not adaptable. They cannot vary their behavior very much. For example, a hungry octopus is separated by glass from a juicy crab. It can see the crab but can't reach it. The octopus stretches out its arms only to find the way blocked. Since the glass partition is small, the octopus can slither around it but never does. It cannot change its behavior easily. Perhaps if it loses sight of the crab, it can't remember where the crab was. In similar experiments a chicken will also fail to get the food, but a dog will succeed.

Primates

The primates are the most adaptable of all animals. Man heads the list, followed by monkeys, apes, and their relatives. Several kinds of primates show what scientists consider to be truly intelligent behavior. You can see that the way monkeys solve problems is more than a trial-and-error effort.

A scientist presented monkeys with objects of different color, size, and shape, in different combinations. If the monkeys picked up the right ones, they found sweet raisins. The objects were moved around. The monkeys were trained to many different combinations of objects. They always eventually picked the right object, through trial and error. But, interestingly enough, each time they were given new problems, they solved the problems faster and faster. Finally they could solve problems in one trial. The scientist concluded that monkeys showed insight, which is necessary for intelligent behavior. He said that monkeys "learned to learn." Once they had mastered this kind of problem, they could remember the answers and how to do the problem for a year or more.

▶ USE OF TOOLS

The use of tools is often regarded as a sign of the highest intelligence. Of course, hands are very important for the use of tools. Horses or dogs could not be expected to hold tools, because they don't have hands. Since monkeys and chimpanzees do have hands, it is possible to see how well they can use tools.

If a monkey wanted to get a banana that was out of reach, it would not approach the problem as a chimpanzee would. Monkeys will not go look for a box they have seen earlier. Chimpanzees, on the other hand, will pile box on box and climb up on them to reach the food. One *Cebus* monkey used sticks and other objects to pull in food lying out of reach. It even used a short stick to

Playing with two short sticks of bamboo, this *Cebus* monkey notices one stick can be fitted inside the other. With the two sticks shoved together, monkey can get food beyond reach of either stick.

reach a long stick. Then the monkey used the long stick as a tool to reach the food. Other monkeys, after training, did learn how to stack boxes. At first these were poorly stacked, and in the wrong places. Through practice the monkeys improved. When boxes and sticks are used in this way, they are tools.

Chimpanzees show some insight and reasoning, which lead to remarkable behavior. For instance, suppose a banana is placed high out of reach. A few things to help in reaching the banana are present—sticks, boxes, a hanging rope. Chimpanzees will stack boxes and climb up on them. They will use a long stick as a jumping pole to reach bananas. They will swing on a rope until the banana is reached. One chimp even climbed on the shoulders of the scientist to reach the banana.

Chimpanzee tried various ways to get bananas hung from ceiling. Then it stacked boxes. Boxes fell over. Soon chimp discovered how to stack boxes properly. The next time it meets a similar problem, it will not need a period of trial and error. It will remember this solution.

Still another gnawed the end of a bamboo pole. Then he stuck it into the end of a second pole to make a long stick. With this he could reach the food.

One interesting study done with chimps has become known as the Chimp-O-Mat tests. Six chimps were trained to operate a special vending machine. One ripe grape came out for each white poker chip put into the slot. At first the chimps did not consider the poker chips valuable. But when the chimps learned to buy grapes with them, the chips did become valuable. The chimps even took to stealing chips from one another. And they would accept poker chips as a reward.

After a while the scientist gave them chips of other colors. A blue chip bought 2 grapes; a red chip bought a drink of water; and a yellow chip bought a return to the home cage.

The chimps lost interest in the white chips. They wanted the blue ones, which bought twice as many grapes. They took a red chip when thirsty. The yellow chip didn't interest them much.

The importance of these experiments is that they show that chimps can understand symbols. The use of symbols here is a very simple one—colored chips stand for other things. But the use is important.

Porpoises and Whales

One group of animals thought to be highly intelligent are the porpoises and whales. We know more about porpoises than about whales because they are easier to keep in captivity. However, it is not yet possible to say much about intelligence in porpoises. Porpoises are wonderful to watch and are quick to learn new tricks. But we can't be sure how intelligent they really are because so far no ways have been found to test them.

Below man and some other primates we have not found that reasoning occurs. What is called intelligent behavior in animals is usually the result of training, trial-and-error learning, and conditioning. Animals can be lovable and wonderful companions, but we are not sure that they show true reasoning ability, insight, and truly intelligent behavior.

EVELYN SHAW
The American Museum of Natural History
See also PSYCHOLOGY.

A fish sweeps its tail from side to side as it swims. Its speed depends partly on shape and slant of tail fin.

From top to bottom: Trout, herring, barracuda, shark. Their tail fins differ, but they all have streamlined bodies.

ANIMALS: LOCOMOTION

The word "locomotion" means "moving from place to place." It comes from two Latin words: *locus,* meaning "place," and *motio,* meaning "movement." Animals move from place to place in water, on land, or in the air. Such movement requires work. The body must be lifted or moved forward or both.

You may have noticed this yourself. When you walk, you feel the weight of your body. As you lift each foot, you are working against the downward pull of gravity.

When you swim, the water supports your weight almost entirely. The downward pull of gravity is balanced by the upward lift of the surrounding water. However, you have to work to push through the water. The water resists your moving body. On land the air resists your movement very little. You hardly notice the resistance.

Thus animals that live in water work mainly to overcome the resistance of their surroundings. Animals that live out of water work to lift the weight of the body against the pull of gravity. Locomotion is naturally very different in the two cases.

▶ LOCOMOTION IN WATER

A fast-swimming fish, such as a trout or mackerel, has an ideal shape for moving swiftly through the water. The body tapers at the front and tail ends, more toward the tail than the head. This shape meets little resistance from the surrounding water. Since water streams smoothly over the surface of the body, this shape is called streamlined. It is also the shape of large sea mammals, such as whales and porpoises. It is the shape man chooses for his submarines.

An animal, particularly if it is large, needs a streamlined shape for rapid movement through water. It also needs stiffening and power. In a fish the backbone stiffens the body and helps it keep its shape. Also, the backbone is loosely jointed and can bend from side to side. The muscles of the trunk and tail supply the power. They pull the tail fin sideways and

A dolphin drives forward through the water by sweeping its powerful tail up and down.

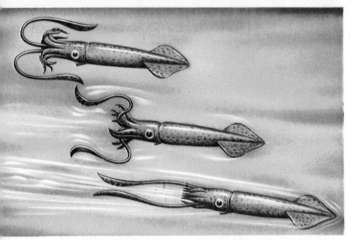

Squid squirts out jets of water and shoots backward.

backward against the surrounding water. When the muscles on the left side of the backbone contract, or shorten, the tail sweeps to the left side. When the muscles on the right side contract, the tail moves to the right. As a result, all the force of the contracting muscles acts against the water.

The force of the forward push depends on the size, shape, and slant of the tail fin. (In most fishes the other fins are used mainly for balancing and steering. In a few they also are used for power.) The force also depends on the rate at which the tail moves.

The body's speed through the water depends on the body's size, too. A trout about 1½ inches long, with its tail beating 24 times a second, swims at a rate of about 1½ miles an hour. A larger trout about 11 inches long, with its tail moving much more slowly, swims at more than 6 miles an hour. The fastest fish known is the barracuda. This is a sharp-toothed, tropical ocean fish that preys on other fish. A 20-pound barracuda 4 feet long may swim as fast as 27 miles an hour.

Since the fin movements of such animals are too swift for our eyes to follow, scientists use slow-motion moving pictures to study them. (They use similar photographs to study locomotion in land and flying animals.)

It is somewhat easier to study locomotion in sea mammals, such as porpoises and dolphins. (Mammals are warm-blooded animals that give birth to and nurse their young.) One reason is that these animals breathe air and must come to the surface for it. Also, dolphins and porpoises enjoy riding the bow wave of a ship. As a result, many people are able to watch them.

A porpoise or a dolphin 6 feet long can swim easily at 20 miles per hour—as fast as most ships travel. Its body shape is streamlined like that of a fast-swimming fish. But its body and tail sweep up and down rather than from side to side. A very thin, loose, rubbery skin covers the body. This skin adjusts to the flow of the surrounding water and so reduces the resistance.

However, the surface of the body does meet some resistance from the water. Because of this resistance an increase in the size of the animal results in little or no increase in speed. Huge whales about 100 feet long cruise along no faster than their smaller porpoise relatives. Some middle-sized whales can put on short bursts of higher speed. This is particularly true of the savage killer whale, which can swim as fast as 35 miles an hour for a short time. Except when the animal is attacking its prey or escaping an enemy, such high speeds demand more effort than the body can afford. It is interesting that in fish, porpoises, giant whales, submarines, and ocean liners the top cruising speed is almost the same.

Other sea animals move through water much more slowly. Some, such as worms and snails, glide along the bottom. Turtles and other animals paddle.

Jellyfishes move by a kind of jet propulsion. A jellyfish swims in a series of short spurts. It gently fills its hollow, bell-shaped body with water. Then by contracting the bell, it rapidly squeezes the water out. A jellyfish usually repeats this process many times a minute. With each contraction the jellyfish moves ahead a short distance.

The squid, an animal related to the octopus and the clam, swims by somewhat the same method. Its body is streamlined, but more like a torpedo than a fish. Water is taken gently into a hole at the front end of the body and then forced out violently through a narrow tube. This causes the body to shoot quickly backward.

▶LOCOMOTION ON LAND

On land most kinds of animals move from place to place by means of legs. Working against the pull of gravity, legs lift and support the weight of the body. They carry it forward. Most kinds of animals can move along with their bodies clear of the ground.

The number of legs may be many or few. The common centipedes, for example, have 15 pairs of short, slender, jointed legs. Spiders and scorpions have 4 pairs of longer, jointed legs. Insects have 3 pairs. Lizards, mice, and most other vertebrates (animals with backbones) have 2 pairs of legs. Some, like men, can balance and move on 1 pair. This leaves the front pair free for other uses.

For rapid locomotion over the ground a few pairs of longer legs seem better than lots of short legs. A spider can move across a table faster than a millipede can, and a mouse can move faster than a spider.

The fewer and longer the legs are, however, the better the body must be balanced. In an insect, for example, the body is carefully balanced, with the six legs attached to and supporting the middle part of the body. The insect moves only three legs at a time. The other three are used for support. An insect's head weighs about the same as its hind end. Thus an insect can stand and move along without falling over on its head or tail. Although good for balance, this arrangement is not as good for fast locomotion as the vertebrate plan.

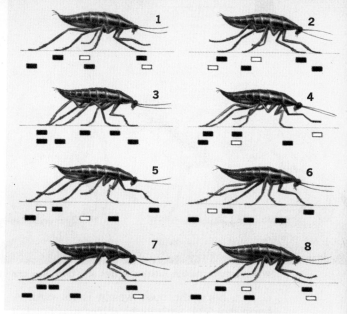

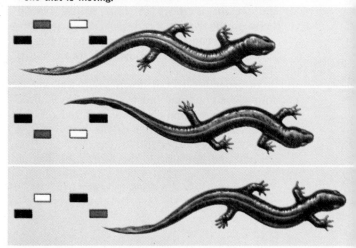

When walking, insect (*above*) must balance on at least three of its legs. Black squares represent feet on ground; white squares, raised feet. Salamander (*below*) lifts one foot after another, always in a certain order. Red square indicates the foot that has just moved; white, the one that is moving.

Walking

In most land vertebrates four legs support the body and move it from place to place. In some animals, such as the salamander, the legs are at the sides. These animals wriggle along like fish. They move their bodies and tails from side to side as if swimming. And in fact, they swim this way when in water. In reptiles, such as the lizard, and even more so in mammals, such as the cow, the legs are under the body and can raise it clear of the ground.

When standing, some vertebrates place their body weight on their front legs. Some place it on their hind legs. Still others place it evenly on both pairs of legs.

When walking, lioness raises one foot at a time. She can stop suddenly without falling.

In a horse the body weight is forward. A horse can kick with its hind legs and not fall down. In rabbits, squirrels, and bears the weight is more on the hind legs. These animals can sit on their haunches and use their front legs somewhat like hands and arms. In a dog the weight is more or less evenly placed between the two pairs of legs. With encouragement a dog can stand either on its front legs or on its hind legs. But it must shift its weight to do so.

In order not to fall down when walking, a four-legged animal must always have three feet on the ground. No foot is lifted off the ground unless the center of the body weight lies over the other three feet. Three legs support the body while the fourth leg swings forward into a new position. One leg moves after another in a certain order.

For instance, if movement begins with the right front leg, the left rear leg steps next. Then the left front leg moves, followed by the right rear leg. This pattern is the same for a salamander, turtle, sheep, dog, elephant, or human infant on all fours. (Man walking on two legs must support and balance the body with one leg while the other swings forward.) By walking this way, a four-footed animal can stop suddenly at any moment without falling down.

Running

It takes time to replace each foot on the ground before raising the next one. An animal

When a human baby is crawling, he balances on three "feet" and moves the fourth one forward.

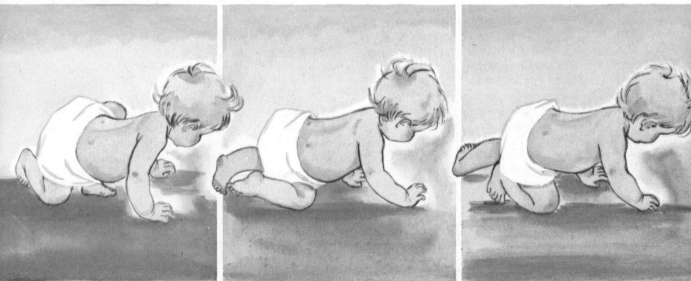

Mule stands with weight well forward. It can kick out hind feet without falling.

cannot move very quickly this way. What happens when the animal starts to run?

When running, a four-footed animal lifts each foot just before putting down the one ahead of it. Only two feet are on the ground at the same time.

Since two legs will not support the body weight for long, you might expect the animal to lose its balance. However, locomotion is so fast that the right front and left rear legs take the body weight from the left front and right rear legs before the animal falls. Nevertheless, when the body is not fully supported, it does tip forward a little or roll to one side.

To make up for this tipping, the leg muscles must continually lift the body. The larger the animal is, the greater the weight that the

muscles must lift. The leg muscles and bones of a horse are especially suited for lifting its body at top running speeds. A horse can run as fast as smaller and lighter animals, such as rabbits and foxes. Other large animals, such as elephants, cannot run at the same high speed.

The complete movement—from the lifting of the right front foot, say, to the putting down of the right hind foot—is called a stride. The length and the rate of stride determine an animal's speed. A mouse moves its legs at a rapid rate. But the legs are so short that the mouse has a short length of stride. On the other hand, a giraffe moves quickly. Its legs are long, even though they move at a slow rate. A racehorse has long legs and the legs move fast. This animal's running speed is very fast

When galloping, elk brings hind legs under body. At one point all feet are in the air.

The looper, or inchworm, alternately loops and stretches, as if it were measuring the object on which it moves.

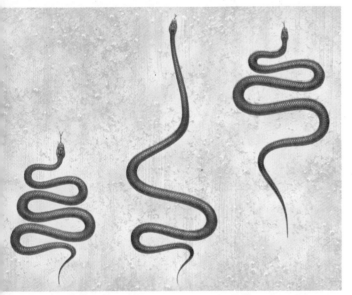

At left, snake is coiled. Then tail part presses against ground, head pushes forward. At right, head part presses ground, and rest of body is pulled up.

indeed—about 45 miles an hour. And it can keep up this speed for a long time. Cheetahs and some other big cats can run even faster for short spurts.

Forty-five miles an hour is almost top running speed on land, whether for horses or rabbits. Greater speeds for long periods demand too much work—they are more than the body framework can bear.

Walking and running are not the only means of locomotion on land. Even quite large animals, such as bears, can climb trees. Apes and monkeys move from tree to tree, their bodies swinging from their hands. A kangaroo leaps on its two hind legs, using its long, stout tail for balance. Other animals move from place to place in other ways.

Creeping

Earthworms, snakes, and some other land creatures travel without the use of legs at all. But as in all other animals, locomotion depends on muscle power.

A snake may find its food in the long, narrow, underground burrows of small animals, such as mice and shrews. The long, muscular body wriggles almost as though the snake were swimming. The snake presses against the solid earth. Muscular contractions move the body. Part of the body pushes forward while the other part holds its place. The scales covering the underside also prevent slipping. A snake can probably move at a speed of 2½ miles an hour.

▶ LOCOMOTION IN AIR

Bats, most birds, and many insects can fly. Some other animals can travel short distances in air. But true flight is possible only for animals with wings.

Wings beating the air upward and downward raise the body against the pull of gravity. Wings drive the body forward through the air. The faster a bird flies, the more lift it gets from its wings. If it stops, it usually begins to sink toward the ground.

Flying animals need legs as well as wings. For no creature can remain in the air all the time. A flying creature must land once in a while and move about on the ground. It must be able to take off again.

A very small, light creature, such as an insect, can take off from the ground much more easily than a large one, such as a bird. And an insect uses up less energy to keep flying. A small bird can take off from the ground much more easily than a large bird. A sparrow, for example, jumps into the air and is off. A swan is about as heavy as a bird can be and still fly. To gather enough speed to become airborne, it must run 100 feet or more. A heavy airplane also needs a long runway.

To take off, an airplane must work against

Heavy birds like these flamingos must run to gain the speed needed to fly.

the force of gravity. The plane rolls along the runway very fast. Air rushing over the curved tops of its wings creates an upward push called lift. As the plane rolls faster, enough lift is built up so the plane can rise. Like airplanes, creatures that fly must also build up lift to take off.

Most birds—particularly small, very light ones—get up air speed by flapping their wings. Larger birds flap their wings more slowly. A large heron flaps its wings 2 times a second, a gull flaps its wings 5 times a second, a pigeon 10 times. A hummingbird flaps its wings more than 50 times a second. In fact, by changing the angle and motion of its wings, a humming-bird can fly forward, hover, and even fly backward.

Birds keep up air speed by flapping their wings or by gliding. When gliding, a bird stretches out its wings. It moves them only to change the shape or the angle of the wings. By holding the wings this way, the bird keeps up forward motion with very little fall, although gliding is always slightly downward. You can see this if you watch birds gliding in still air. Sooner or later a bird will glide to earth.

But as a rule the air is not still. Rising air currents carry the bird upward. This kind of gliding is called soaring. The largest birds, such as eagles and vultures, usually soar. These birds have very broad wings. Other large birds, such as the man-o'-war and the albatross, have long narrow wings. These birds glide low over the water.

Watch a bird as it flies. It is a living flying machine, fitted for flight in many ways. Its wings are moved by powerful breast

The narrow wings of the albatross limit its ability to ride the rising air currents.

muscles. Its feathers are light, yet arranged in a way to provide strong strokes against the air.

A bird's skeleton is made of very strong bones. Yet the skeleton of a bird is light, because the bones are hollow. For example, the man-o'-war bird, with a 7-foot wingspread, has a skeleton weighing only 4 ounces.

It takes a lot of energy to fly. The warm blood of birds, their good breathing systems, and their ability to digest their food quickly are important in providing energy.

Although a bat appears to flutter aimlessly, it is an efficient flier.

The tiny ladybug flaps its wings very rapidly in order to fly.

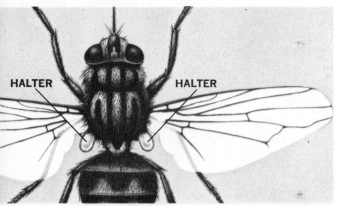

HALTER   HALTER

Close-up of fly's wings. Larger front wings are used for flying, small back wings (halteres) for controlling flight.

The wings of bats are different from those of birds. A bat is a hairy mammal. Its wing is a sheet of skin stretched out between the extremely long fingers of its front feet, or hands, and down the sides of the body to the hind legs.

Compared to a bird's movements in air, a bat's movements look fluttering and clumsy. Actually the bat has great control of its movements. It turns and twists in order to capture flying insects.

Insect wings are different from those of both birds and bats. Instead of developing from one pair of walking legs, their wings grow from the upper surface of the body's midsection. An insect may have one or two pairs of wings. In most insects with two pairs, the wings on each side move together. This is true in dragonflies, butterflies, and moths, for example.

A few insects, such as the larger butterflies, both flap their wings and glide. Others, like bees and midges, fly only by flapping their wings. The movements are so rapid as to be invisible. Again, slow-motion moving pictures help the scientist study locomotion.

Swallowtail butterflies flap their wings about 5 times a second, bees about 200 times. A certain small midge flaps its wings about 1,000 times a second.

As a rule, insects take off into the wind, as an airplane does. The larger kinds may even have to warm up for a few minutes before taking off. They do this either by fluttering their wings or by sitting in the sun. The fastest insects, such as dragonflies and hawk moths, cruise at about 25 miles an hour and can reach speeds of about 35 miles an hour.

The greatest acrobats of the insect world are the flies, as you know if you have ever tried to catch one. The front wings of a fly are used for flight. Behind each of the familiar wings is a halter, a small knoblike structure. These structures are believed to act as controls that help the fly to balance itself in flight. As a result, a fly can twist and turn easily and even fly upside down at times.

Animals that move through the air without wings, such as flying squirrels and frogs, usually live in trees. Flaps of skin along their sides aid in gliding from tree to tree. By spreading out their legs and extending their tails, they can control direction.

N. J. Berrill
McGill University

See also Bats; Birds; Dolphins and Porpoises; Feet and Hands; Fishes; Hoofed Mammals; Insects; Snakes.

Some famous cartoon characters. Left to right: Mickey Mouse, Pluto, Spiderman, Mr. Twiddle and Wally Gator, and Woody Woodpecker with Splinter and Knothead.

ANIMATED CARTOONS

When we go to the movies and see a cowboy jump on his horse and ride off in a cloud of dust, we know that we are seeing pictures of a real man, a real horse, and real dust. But when Mickey Mouse appears on the screen, we know that he isn't a real mouse at all, but a drawing of a mouse. Yet, like the cowboy, he moves and talks.

How can a drawing move around on the screen, tell jokes, and do tricks? In order to understand how drawings can be made to behave like living creatures, we must first understand how pictures of real people are made to move on the screen.

When the hero of a Western jumps on his horse, every movement he makes is photographed by a high-speed camera. The photographs are taken one after another on a long roll of film. In only 1 second, 24 separate pictures are taken.

After the film has been developed, the photographs are projected on a screen in the order in which they were taken, and at the same speed. The pictures are flashed on the screen so fast that to the human eye the cowboy and his horse seem to move naturally and smoothly.

▶ MOVIES WITH ACTORS OF INK AND PAINT

Animated cartoon movies, such as *A Boy Named Charlie Brown, Cinderella,* and *The Aristocats,* are not made by photographing real actors and actresses. The characters in the films are drawings. Every movement we see on the screen is photographed from many different drawings.

Hundreds of thousands of drawings are used in a full-length animated cartoon feature. Hundreds of artists must work for several years to produce a film like *Cinderella.* One artist could never make a film alone, for it would take one person over 200 years of steady work to complete.

▶ A STORY COMES TO LIFE

The first thing needed to produce a good animated cartoon movie is a good story. After a story has been selected, studio writers write the script (movie version) of the story. The script is divided into sections, and each section is illustrated separately. When it is finished, the script looks like a giant comic strip with the dialogue—what the characters are saying—written under each picture.

Music needed for the movie is specially composed and fitted into the script. Actors and singers are selected to give voices to the

The story board is the script for a cartoon feature. Rough sketches suggest all of the important action planned for the film.

drawn characters. Then the whole script is recorded.

After the story has been given life with sounds and words, work begins on giving the characters life through movement. The art director makes a chart listing the length of time and the number of frames needed for each word, sound, and action in the entire script. Studio artists design the backgrounds and make sketches showing how large the figures should be and where on the background the figures should move. The artists who animate, that is, give life to, the characters study the director's chart and the background sketches before beginning to draw.

The animator must follow the chart exactly. If the chart indicates that a particular action or word takes 30 frames of film, the animator

Walt Disney's *Cinderella* is an animated movie made for the wide screen.

It only takes Donald Duck a moment to tip his hat. At right are five of the many different drawings needed to show a moment's gesture on the screen.

must make certain that 30 pictures are drawn. For example, if a scene in *Cinderella* shows the Fairy Godmother waving her magic wand and singing, the first picture the animator draws is the Fairy Godmother standing perfectly still, with her mouth closed. Then he draws a second picture almost exactly like the first by tracing the first drawing, with a slight difference. In the second picture the Godmother's arm is slightly raised, and her mouth barely open. A third drawing, traced from the second, shows her arm still higher, her mouth open a little wider. Drawing after drawing is made in this way, until the action has been completed in 30 pictures.

When the drawings are completed, they are sent to the inking and painting department. There they are traced onto sheets of clear plastic and painted. In another department artists are painting the backgrounds. After the transparent sheets are painted, they are placed over the proper background and photographed by a motion-picture camera. Each photograph becomes a frame of film. When all the sheets have been photographed, the film is cut to make it the right length and to eliminate unnecessary material.

There is much more to an animated cartoon movie than drawings. A special department must create the appearance of rain, shadows, sparkles on jewels, dust, smoke, and so on. The sound-effects department creates special sounds. For example, cellophane, berry boxes, and bottle caps are rattled together to sound like a forest fire. Peas are shaken in a barrel to sound like rain on the roof. A broom sloshed across water makes the sound of Donald Duck swimming.

Cartoon short subjects about such favorites as the Incredible Hulk are made in the same way as feature-length cartoons. But because they are shorter, they are usually completed in six to nine months rather than three years. Instead of 300,000 drawings, only 30,000 are needed.

WALT DISNEY

ANTHROPOLOGY

Why are people in some parts of the world called by their mother's family name instead of their father's? Why do people in widely separated parts of the world speak related languages? What did human beings look like when they first began to use tools or make pottery? Such questions are dealt with by the science of anthropology. Scientists who work in this field are called anthropologists.

The word "anthropology" comes from two Greek words—*anthropos* ("human being") and *logos* ("study"). Anthropology, then, is the study of human beings and human culture. It is a young science, which took formal shape only in the mid-1800's. Until that time, few individuals had made a serious scientific study of different peoples. European explorers had long been bringing back stories about peoples of Africa, Asia, and the Pacific islands. These peoples were of many different sizes and colors. They brought up their children and ran their societies in ways unknown to Europeans. Their languages had sounds that Western peoples had not heard before. To most Westerners such customs were strange, wrong, or uncivilized. They thought that the best thing that could happen to these distant peoples would be to learn about European ways. The goal was not to understand these peoples and their ways but to change them.

By the middle 1800's some Westerners were beginning to hold rather different ideas. Perhaps what was best for one group of people might not be best for another. Perhaps it was not desirable to make everyone over in the European image. Perhaps other peoples and their ways should be studied for their own sakes. From such ideas grew the science of anthropology. It deals with peoples of the past and peoples of the present, with us as well as with faraway peoples.

Because the science is young, it is still developing its methods. But, in general, an anthropologist specializes in one of two main areas—the cultural or the physical nature of human beings. Anthropology also overlaps with and uses the techniques of several other sciences. One is archeology, which deals with the material remains of past life. Another is linguistics, the study of languages.

African Bushmen hunting for spring hares.

All over the world people hunt and fish for food. They have many different ways of doing so. Left, an Eskimo fishes through the ice. Below, American hunters use a gun to shoot wild duck.

▶ CULTURAL ANTHROPOLOGY

To an anthropologist the culture of a people includes their whole way of life. It takes in everything a group of people has, makes, thinks, believes, and passes on to its children. Such things are never exactly the same in any two groups, even groups that live as close together as Buffalo and Toronto and are in close communication with each other. The scientists who study such differences are known as cultural anthropologists.

The Beginnings of Cultural Anthropology

The first cultural anthropologists began their studies with some of the primitive peoples who lived in faraway lands. These were peoples who had not developed writing, the use of metals, or cities. Such cultures seemed

Fishing with big nets in the Philippines.

Fishermen on the Congo casting their nets.

Indian hunting with blowgun in Panama jungle.

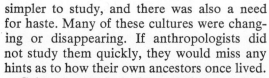

simpler to study, and there was also a need for haste. Many of these cultures were changing or disappearing. If anthropologists did not study them quickly, they would miss any hints as to how their own ancestors once lived.

Cultural anthropologists usually went alone to some distant island or village. Perhaps they were sent by their government because it was responsible for the people. Perhaps they came from a university that wanted to know about such people.

Anthropologists had to win the friendship of people who viewed their customs as strange. The people might think they were crazy or were evil spirits because they wore clothes and could write. Anthropologists tried to learn about the customs and the language. If the people accepted them, the anthropologists settled down and perhaps were even adopted into a family. Then the anthropologists were ready to study all the different sides of such a culture. The findings of cultural anthropologists can be classed under several main areas.

A People's Livelihood

What do people do for a living—hunt, fish, farm, trade? The answer may be simple, but the work affects every aspect of their lives. The way of living then comes to affect the character of the people themselves. For example, in Siberia there used to be people whose total way of life depended on their herds of horses, sheep, and yaks. Because the livestock needed fresh pasture, the people could not have a settled home. With their tents and all their belongings, they moved about, living

Thatched cottage in the English countryside.

Concrete termite-proof house in Puerto Rico.

Tents of Mongolian nomads.

Adobe pueblo of Taos Indians in New Mexico.

on milk and meat. They had no central government and no big ceremonies, for the groups could not plan on getting together. Like early American cowboys they defended their grazing lands against strangers and so were known as fighters.

The Tewa Indians of New Mexico, on the other hand, depended on the corn, beans, and squash they raised. Because their fields were near their home village, they could live there all year round. These Indians had officers who lived in the village all the time and who planned ceremonies months in advance. The Tewa Indians had little need to fight, and so they became known as peaceful people. Yet if their way of life had been like that of the Siberians, they might have developed into very different people.

The Family

Many people have the same way of life, but anthropologists learn not to expect the same rules of conduct everywhere. Human groups go through all sorts of experiences that make them behave in different ways. Even a basic group like the family may change from area to area.

Most North Americans think of the family as made up of a father, mother, and children. Yet among the Zulu in Africa, a family may consist of one man with five or six wives. Each wife lives in her separate hut, with her garden and her children. The women get along together like teachers in a school with a flock of children to look after.

Among the Iroquois of Six Nations Reserve, Canada, "family" used to refer to the people in a "longhouse." This was a large house where an old lady lived with her husband, her married daughters and their husbands, and all the children of these different families. Women did the farming in the old Iroquois life, while the men went off hunting and fighting. It was natural for women to have a home near the fields and to own the house and tools. Children took the name of their

Straw houses of Zulus in Natal, South Africa.

Straw houses built on stilts in the Philippines.

Eskimo igloo built of snow in northern Canada.

In different parts of the world people build their houses from different materials. Materials used are those that are abundant locally. Houses fit the climate where the people live and are suited to the people's way of life.

Thatched mud houses on the Ivory Coast, Africa.

mother's family, for that showed where they lived.

There are many other family matters that interest anthropologists. For instance, how is marriage arranged—by the young couple themselves, by the parents, by an uncle or a brother? How are children brought up to fit them for the culture of their particular group? How are old people treated—are they neglected and sometimes left to die, or are they looked up to as guides and teachers? The answer usually depends on how the group is living and whether the people have any means of taking care of the weak. Anthropologists have learned that the family cannot be studied unless the total way of life of a people is studied as well.

Government

Families may gather into clans, large groups who think of themselves as related and owing duties to one another. Clans sometimes form larger groups, such as tribes, and tribes or other large groups form nations. Such changes come about slowly and may be accompanied by many problems among the people. The anthropologist tries to learn who really holds the power in a new grouping. Is it the new chief? Or are the people turning in secret to an older person or to a religious leader?

War and Games

The anthropologist observes all the activities carried on by the group. War is one such activity, for there has rarely been a group in human history that did not fight. But why do people fight? For land? For slaves? To defend themselves? To avenge an insult? Does war involve many ceremonies? Do the warriors believe themselves protected by friendly spirits? Anthropologists see how a people's beliefs about war are related to livelihood, education, and religion.

Much can also be learned from a people's games. They show whether a people likes to

Children all over the world use rope or string to amuse themselves in different ways. Left: In practice for adult life, children of Lapland use rope to lasso boy pretending to be a reindeer. Right: Indian boy makes calabash whistle on string.

Left: An Eskimo woman delights her grandchild with a toy made of string. Right: American children jumping rope in a game called double dutch.

count and calculate. They reveal character, which may be competitive or peaceful. Primitive people, old and young, play group outdoor games more than moderns do. The games may be connected with religion and played in honor of some god. Or the people may believe that the outcome of a game tells something about the future.

Knowledge

The anthropologist needs to become familiar with everything that a people knows. What do they understand about the earth, the stars, the animals? Can they write? Can they count? If not, how do they record their knowledge? That question takes anthropologists into the subject of picture writing and counting by knots or sticks. They learn, too, how people become educated by memorizing what others tell them instead of by reading.

Religion and Mythology

A people's religion is one of the most difficult subjects for anthropologists to gather information about. Early visitors often thought that primitive tribes had no religion. Later students of the same tribes have suggested that these peoples believed in a Great Being who created them but lived far away and was never seen. Some peoples had a great number of spirits to whom they could pray. All peoples have some kind of religion—a window to the Great Beyond, which others may find hard to see through. However, most people do not readily reveal their religious beliefs to strangers.

Connected with religion is mythology, the ancient tales about spirits, gods, and other superhuman beings. To learn these, anthropologists may sit crouched on the floor along with a crowd of people while an old person tells their tale of the beginnings of the world. The researcher listens to the tales and perhaps to singing accompanied by the tapping of a drum or the scraping of sticks.

How Cultural Anthropologists Work Today

Matters such as the family, games, and religion have always been the concern of anthropologists. Today universities and governments also see a great need for understanding those people with whom we trade and to whom we send help. Clearly no single investigator could ever find out all that needs to be known about a group of people. So anthropology has had to develop new methods.

More and more, a team of anthropologists goes out. Among them may be specialists in psychology, music, or language; a physical anthropologist; and perhaps a doctor. Women anthropologists may have greater success in making friends with the women and girls, whose lives are often different from those of the men and boys. The team need not all work together. Members will be busy with their own specialties. But they consult often and combine their findings. They have tape recorders and cameras so that they can record the words the people speak, hear their music, and photograph them in action.

Such a group cannot walk into a village or a camp and settle down to ask questions, as the single worker did in the early days of anthropology. Generally modern anthropologists talk to the chief or the council and ask permission, explaining that their studies will provide a history of the people's culture. Often the people are glad that someone really wants to understand their ways. Several Indian groups in the United States have even asked for anthropologists to make such a study.

Change

People of developing nations have come to appreciate the work of anthropologists who help them adjust to new ways. Old ways are being given up almost everywhere. People who wore straw sandals two years ago may have leather shoes today. Where people used to cook on campfires, they may now be using electricity.

Cultural anthropologists have a great chance to help with such changes because they can see where new ways would fit and where they would not work just yet. For instance, flat, open countryside may look good for tractors. But tractors would be of no use if every family has its little patch of land and does not believe in joining with the others.

Modern Groups and Cultures

Many of the differences that once separated simple agricultural cultures from industrial cultures are now smaller. And anthropologists have learned much from their studies that can be applied to industrial cultures. A team of anthropologists can be useful in a factory, a hospital, or a section of a city. The people who work and live there may never have stopped to consider who is the real leader of their group, how the young people marry, or what happens to the old people. Modern people are learning a great deal from anthropologists' studies of their own life.

▶ PHYSICAL ANTHROPOLOGY

One expert who is needed in the study of any people is the physical anthropologist, who studies the physical characteristics of people. This is the oldest branch of anthropology. In Europe the word "anthropology" still refers only to physical anthropology. The study of cultures is called ethnology.

Physical anthropologists are interested in humanlike creatures and early humans. Heads shown below are based on studies of skulls.

AUSTRALOPITHECUS   PITHECANTHROPUS   NEANDERTHAL   CRO-MAGNON

Left: L. S. B. Leakey compares skulls of humanlike creatures found in Africa with other ancient skulls. Right: Alakaluf Indian with one foot in ice water as part of a test.

Ancient People

The physical anthropologists started with an interest in the ancient skeletons or parts of skeletons dug up in different parts of the world. They studied the shapes of heads, sizes of brain cases, lengths of limbs. All such measurements give hints about how the human race has changed since its beginning. For example, the anthropologists noticed that ancient jaws were bigger than the jaws of modern people. This shows that ancient people must have eaten coarse, raw food.

Physical anthropologists have been working for more than a century with the bones of ancient people. They have found bones in Africa, Palestine, Java, and southern China. There is much disagreement on when the human species actually began. Some anthropologists think it began with the first creatures who stood on two legs. They think such folk evolved at least 3,500,000 years ago. Other anthropologists trace the human species to a later beginning. They date the start of humankind about 2,300,000 years ago. Bones found in the Americas are not nearly so ancient. The oldest found there so far are hardly more than 12,000 to 20,000 years old.

Modern People

The physical anthropologist is also interested in modern people's physical traits, such as types of skin, eyes, hair, blood, and diseases. Some of the basic information comes from the work of biologists and physicians. Physical anthropologists combine their findings and look for new patterns. Are several inherited physical traits related to one another?

In what way do these traits differ from people to people around the world?

The anthropologist's first job is to record all such information. Eventually the physical traits are related to other conditions. For example, certain traits are of special advantage to people living in a particular region or climate. Through thousands of years the individuals with the special traits tended to survive, passing on the traits to their descendants. Today many groups of people have physical features that seem to be especially well adapted to the surroundings.

One such group is the Alakaluf Indians, who live near the southernmost tip of South America. The climate there is subarctic, with snow and cold through much of the year. The Alakaluf Indians live along the coast, where they hunt and fish the animals of the sea.

The Indians spend much of their time in and around the water, but they seem to be unaffected by the cold and wet. Babies may walk naked in the snow. People go barefoot in water of 4°C (40°F). And sometimes they swim in this cold water.

Scientists have long known about these Indians and their ability to withstand the cold. Only recently several scientists, including a physical anthropologist, went to study the Indians. The first thing the visitors noted was the unusual shape of the Indians' feet. They are short and wide—almost square—with a thick pad of fat on the arch. The ankles are also unusually thick and fleshy. The form of their feet seems to equip these Indians for wading around in water.

Next, the scientists measured the body temperature of the Indians under various conditions. One Indian swam in the cold water for eight minutes while his temperature was being recorded. Another Indian man kept only his foot in ice water while the body temperature was recorded. Another spent the night outdoors in the cold air while instruments recorded his body's reactions. All the measurements showed that the Indians' bodily fuel-burning processes work as much as twice as fast as those of Europeans (of the same height and weight). When exposed to cold and wet, the Indians' bodies are able to keep up their normal temperature.

This is an extreme case of a people whose physical traits make them well adapted to their surroundings. Physical anthropologists are interested in all kind of adaptations. They may even try to relate the physical traits to the behavior and personalities of humans. In the end, the physical anthropologist tries to relate people's physical traits to their total way of life. And if anthropologists can find out how much people have changed in the past, they may be able to suggest how people may adapt in the future.

▶ ARCHEOLOGY AND ANTHROPOLOGY

The work of anthropologists often overlaps with the work of archeologists. Archeologists dig up and study the things made by people in early periods of history. But skeletons and bones are often found among the ruins. The archeologist photographs the bones just where they were found, for the benefit of other students. The archeologist also records how deep in the earth the bones were found and whether any other objects were found with them. Such facts help to give a complete picture of ancient human beings and their way of life.

Then the bones are taken out of the site as carefully as possible. Ideally a physical anthropologist works with an archeological expedition. Otherwise, the bones are sent to a laboratory, usually at some distant museum or university. The anthropologists there study the bones and make plaster casts of them to be sent to other experts. Perhaps these experts will discover that the bones are like others from Africa or China or France. Along with the findings of the archeologist, the information supplied by the anthropologist helps to tell the story of early people.

Anthropologists study physical traits of all kinds of people. Below are types of people from many parts of the world. Notice the differences in head shapes and other features.

ESKIMO

CELTIC

SCANDINAVIAN

CHINESE

MEDITERRANEAN

NEW GUINEA

INDIAN

SOUTH AMERICAN

AFRICAN

One of the most important discoveries about early humans involved a famous set of bones. These bones were found in a cave near Peking, China, in the late 1920's and early 1930's. Along with the bones was some charcoal. This meant that the people who had lived in the cave—300,000 years earlier—could make fire. The anthropologists working in China made plaster casts of the Peking bones. At the start of World War II, the bones were being sent to a museum for further study. Somewhere along the way they were lost. They were never found. But archeologists and anthropologists have co-operated to piece together quite a bit of ancient history from the casts.

▶ LINGUISTICS AND ANTHROPOLOGY

There is another specialist who is needed to help anthropologists complete their picture of people. This is the linguist, a person trained in the history and nature of speech. The linguist is especially valuable to cultural anthropologists working among people who speak a little-known language.

Analyzing Sound

Linguists must be able to write down any sound that human beings can make, even though they have never heard it before. An international system, which has a symbol for each sound, is used. After the linguist has recorded the sounds, the stream of sounds is divided into words and sentences. This work is done with the help of native speakers. Today, too, much work is done with tape recorders, which can reproduce the sounds for later study and comparison.

Grammar

When a linguist has recorded the sounds—with their clicks, whispers, high tones and low tones—it is time to analyze the grammar. It was once thought that many little-known languages had no grammar. In fact, most of these languages have precise, complicated grammars. But they differ from the familiar, more widely spoken languages.

In some of these languages, for example, someone who wanted to say "We go . . ." would have to use different forms of the verb that mean "We two go," "We three go," and so on. There may be at least two ways to indicate the plural. One way refers to many things bunched together, like a sack of grain. The other refers to many things scattered, like sheep on a hillside.

The linguist must work out all these points by trial and error, for the people who speak the language are not used to explaining it. When the general shape of the language begins to emerge, perhaps the linguist can relate it to other languages.

Language Families

Languages may seem very different. But they can be grouped into several "families," which have the same general sounds and kinds of grammar. There seem to be innumerable African languages. Some have never been completely recorded. But they are grouped into eleven families by the latest classification system. The same may be said of American Indian languages, which have been grouped into six large families.

Most of the languages of modern Europe can be placed into one family. Greek, Latin, French, German, English, Slavic, and the Scandinavian languages all belong to the same family, called Indo-European. There was probably once a main language from which these languages branched. This happened at different times as groups of people moved away and learned other habits. Tracing the history of languages throws light on human history.

The same sort of study can be made with languages of many different peoples and cultures. Linguistics also helps anthropologists learn other things. The customs of different peoples can be pictured from the things they talk about. For example, the Arabic language has dozens of special words to describe the behavior of camels. Just from studying the language, an anthropologist can learn that the camel plays an important part in the life of Arabs.

▶ PREPARING FOR A CAREER IN ANTHROPOLOGY

Very little anthropology is taught in high schools. An anthropologist usually begins formal training in college. A young person wishing to study anthropology should look over the catalogs of various colleges to see what courses they offer. Some colleges may not have separate departments of anthropology but may offer courses in other departments.

Students who have decided to concentrate on anthropology must choose additional courses related to their specialties. Cultural anthropologists need a good background in history, sociology, and psychology. Physical anthropologists must know a great deal of biology and physiology.

The Basic Approach to Anthropology

No matter which areas they plan to concentrate in, all students must begin with an introductory course that traces human history. The course starts with the earliest people and follows them out of their caves and into their first houses of straw or mud. It studies what is known of their hunting and fishing, their drawings and paintings on rocks, the first boats, and new tools. It studies clues to their religion and government.

Next comes an account of how people in different parts of the world found wild plants good for food. These were gathered by the women while the men were away hunting. Then various peoples got the idea of planting seeds or bulbs for future harvesting in a place where they often lived. This was an important discovery, for it led people to settle down in villages. They built larger houses and held regular ceremonies.

Around the same period people began to tame wild sheep, goats, cattle, and pigs. They then had more time for inventing new things and for developing earlier discoveries. Only when people had settled down did the big advances occur—pottery, weaving, the wheel, metals, and writing.

The Next Steps in Anthropology

With writing, recorded history begins. The student anthropologist wants to know as much as possible about ancient history because all of it gives hints to understanding people of today.

The students also take courses describing anthropologists' work among different preliterate peoples—those who have not developed writing. Later, when they visit such a group, they will be able to compare its culture with those of similar peoples. They can notice where their group is different and work out the reasons. The people, too, will appreciate the students' being familiar with their ways.

Some of the reading and course work can be done only in graduate school. During this

Model shows people who lived in France 8,000 years ago hunting with dogs, clubs, and flint-tipped spears.

work—if students show promise—they may be allowed to join a team of anthropologists on a project. Finally, they may make an investigation of their own. That is the goal of all anthropologists. In living with one group of people, anthropologists learn a great deal about all people, including themselves and their own culture.

Cultural Anthropology Today

A knowledge of cultural anthropology is useful to people in many professions. Almost anyone who deals with people can use some of it as a background. Workers sent by governments to help people in other countries can make errors if they have never studied anthropology. Training in anthropology is useful for those who serve in consulates, embassies, and trade delegations or work as technical advisers. A knowledge of various cultures prevents people from thinking that their way is the only way. It helps them understand when and how a people might change its ways for the better, as well as when no change is necessary.

LOUITA D. WILSON
University of Colorado at Boulder
RUTH M. UNDERHILL
Formerly, University of Denver
Reviewed by RALPH M. ROWLETT
University of Missouri—Columbia

See also ANCIENT CIVILIZATIONS; ARCHEOLOGY; PREHISTORIC PEOPLE.

ANTIBIOTICS

At one time or another, almost everyone has used an antibiotic, like penicillin or Terramycin. You may use an antibiotic ointment for bad scrapes or cuts. The doctor may order an antibiotic to help you get over pneumonia, scarlet fever, boils, and other infections.

Antibiotics work so well against so many infections that they are often called "miracle drugs." But a more accurate name would be "microbe drugs," for that is what antibiotics are.

Microbes are tiny living things. Bacteria are microbes. So are molds. There are many, many kinds of microbes in the world. Some of these microbes are used by man to make antibiotics.

Antibiotics are chemicals. When the chemicals are put into your body, they kill or stop the growth of certain kinds of germs. They help your body fight disease. That is why these medicines are called antibiotics. The name was first applied to these medicines in 1942. It comes from two Greek words meaning "against life." Antibiotics work against many of the forms of life that we call germs.

▶ MICROBE AGAINST MICROBE

Like other living things, microbes produce complex chemicals within their bodies. Some of the chemicals made by one kind of microbe may kill other kinds of microbes. In making antibiotics, scientists take advantage of this killing ability. They choose microbes whose chemicals work against the microbes that cause disease. If these chemicals can be made in large enough quantities in laboratories, they may be used as antibiotics.

Microbes are found just about everywhere, in immense numbers. Scoop up a handful of moist, rich soil, and you are also holding millions of bacteria and molds that live in the soil. These microbes are far too small to be seen without a microscope. But when the molds grow in colonies, the colonies are large enough to be seen with the unaided eye. Spots of gray, green, or pink fuzz are sometimes seen growing on bread, cheese, or fruit. The spots are colonies of molds.

One mold may produce millions of microscopic cells called spores. The light, tiny spores may be carried far from the parent mold by currents of air. One spore can produce a new mold if it settles in a place where living conditions are right. In a short time, the mold may grow into a colony.

▶ THE FIRST ANTIBIOTICS

More than 3,000 years ago ancient peoples stumbled on the discovery that some molds could cure. The Egyptians, the Chinese, and Indians of Central America used molds to treat rashes and infected wounds. However, they did not understand either diseases or treatments. Many of them thought in terms of magic. They believed that molds drove away evil spirits that caused disease.

As time passed, men slowly gained some knowledge of disease. But true understanding began only in fairly recent times. In the 1860's the French scientist Louis Pasteur showed that many diseases are caused by bacteria. Later he also said that man might learn to fight germs with other microbes.

Two German doctors were the first men to make an effective medicine from microbes. The doctors, Rudolf Emmerich and Oskar Löw, carried out their experiments in the 1890's. Among other things, they proved that the germ that causes one disease may cure another.

The two men took germs from infected bandages and grew them in test tubes and bottles. They managed to isolate a particularly vicious germ that caused green infections in open wounds. The germ was a bacterium called *Bacillus pyocyaneus*. Then they put some of these germs into test tubes containing other known disease germs. A strange thing happened. The *Bacillus pyocyaneus* wiped out the other disease germs, which were causes of cholera, typhoid, diphtheria, and anthrax.

Emmerich and Löw used *Bacillus pyocyaneus* to make a medicine, which they called pyocyanase. It was the first antibiotic to be used in hospitals, but unfortunately it was ahead of its time. No one yet knew how to control production or how such a chemical worked. Also, the medicine did not have the same effect on all patients. Many people were cured of typhoid, diphtheria, and the plague, but others only became sicker. So pyocyanase was abandoned.

Other scientists went on looking for a safe

and effective antibiotic. They tried hundreds of microbes, but none produced the magic cure-all they hoped to find.

The first real breakthrough was made in the summer of 1928 by a research scientist named Alexander Fleming. It was made because Fleming grasped the meaning of a small mishap in his laboratory.

▶ THE DISCOVERY OF PENICILLIN

At the time, Fleming, a Scottish bacteriologist, was on the staff of a hospital in London, England. He was studying a germ called *Staphylococcus aureus,* which caused many ailments from boils to brain disease. In order to study the germs, Fleming grew colonies of them in small glass plates called petri dishes. Each dish held a gelatin food to nourish the germs.

One day Fleming found a spot of green mold in one dish. It was growing on the gelatin among the germs. He realized that a spore from some mold must have settled on the dish while it was uncovered. But Fleming did not throw out the spoiled dish, because something unusual caught his attention.

There was a clear, germ-free ring of gelatin around the mold. This meant that the mold had killed the staphylococcus germs there. Fleming watched the mold grow for several days. As the green mold spread, it killed more and more germs.

Many earlier workers had made this same observation. But Fleming, studying the mold with great care, suspected he had found a remarkable medicine. But there was much he had to learn before he could be sure. Could he extract the chemical used by this mold to destroy the bacteria? Would the same chemical kill other germs? Would this chemical prove to be "friendly" to the human body? If so, could it be produced in quantity?

Fleming set out to find the answers. For the rest of the summer he gave all his attention to the mysterious mold. It grew and grew. Fleming noticed tiny drops of liquid on the surface of the mold. Perhaps this was the chemical that was destroying the germs.

Fleming drew off the liquid, drop by drop. He found that this liquid could kill germs in a test tube. Since the name of the mold was *Penicillium notatum,* he called the liquid penicillin. Other scientists showed later that pen-icillin could cure certain infections in mice and rabbits, without harming the animals.

Fleming published his findings in a British medical journal in 1929. Strange as it now seems, the article attracted little attention. Scientists thought it would take too much time and money to produce a useful amount of penicillin. Like pyocyanase, penicillin had been discovered before scientists were ready to develop it.

The Sulfa Drugs

Then, too, a "wonder drug" was discovered shortly afterwards in Germany. It was Prontosil, a substance used as a dye. When taken into the body, Prontosil changes into an active germ-killing drug called sulfanilamide. It was found that this drug could cure pneumonia, scarlet fever, and blood poisoning.

During the early 1930's, laboratories began to make other drugs in the same family. These were known as sulfa drugs and were powerful weapons against disease. But the sulfa drugs had serious drawbacks. Too small a dose could make a disease worse. Too large a dose could upset the body's defense system

Circles of blotting paper are soaked in new antibiotic and placed among germs growing in petri dish. Dark rings indicate germ-killing power of the antibiotic.

and prevent a cure, because sulfa drugs did not kill germs. They weakened germs and gave the body's defenses a chance to kill the germs. So scientists continued to search for an effective antibiotic. One of them was Dr. René Dubos of the Rockefeller Institute (now Rockefeller University) in New York City.

▶ ANTIBIOTICS FROM SOIL MICROBES

Dubos, a French-born scientist, was seeking a cure for pneumonia. He was seeking it in the soil, which scientists had long viewed as a possible source of germ killers. Dubos was determined to take microbes from the soil and see whether they could be made to work for people.

Experimenting with microbes from a New Jersey cranberry bog, Dubos obtained a substance he called tyrothricin. This chemical killed pneumonia germs in test tubes with amazing speed. Hopefully, he tested it on mice and rabbits. But it proved harmful to the animals as well as to the germs. The search for a pneumonia cure would have to continue. Still, progress had been made. Dubos had shown that antibiotics could be obtained from microbes in the soil.

▶ SUCCESS WITH PENICILLIN

Meanwhile, two scientists in England had taken up Fleming's work with penicillin. By 1939 Dr. Howard Florey and Dr. Ernst Chain were convinced that penicillin could save countless lives—if a way could be found to make it in quantity. They wanted to grow the mold in large tanks. But Fleming himself pointed out: "The mold does not like growing in tanks. You cannot simply put it into a tank and expect good results. It just grows on top and you get a poor yield. It likes plenty of air, so you have to blow in air and keep the fluid moving, and you have to blow in air without microbes. . . ."

It was a difficult problem in chemical engineering. Also, by this time World War II had begun and England was under heavy attack. So, in 1941 Dr. Florey traveled to the United States and asked for help. Government laboratories and private drug manufacturers co-operated to find a way to produce penicillin in large amounts. Within 2 years they had found it. Soon drug companies were producing penicillin in huge tanks. Then an American researcher found a new kind of penicillium mold on an over-ripe canteloupe. It grew much faster and produced 200 times more penicillin than the mold Fleming had found. By 1945 the United States was making enough penicillin to treat several million patients a year.

▶ THE SEARCH FOR OTHER ANTIBIOTICS

Penicillin had proved its worth against pneumonia, scarlet fever, abscesses, and several other diseases. It was also highly effective against yaws, a disease that affects many people in the tropics. But it had no effect on germs that caused typhoid, poliomyelitis, influenza, and many other diseases. Research scientists continued their hunt for antibiotics.

One of the leaders in the search was an American, Dr. Selman A. Waksman. Turning to microbes of the soil, he looked for a cure for intestinal diseases like dysentery and typhoid. Finally he discovered streptomycin. This drug proved effective against many diseases that penicillin could not cure, such as bubonic plague, a deadly epidemic disease.

Now medical science had penicillin and streptomycin, each effective against particular diseases. But doctors wanted a **broad-spectrum** antibiotic—that is, a single antibiotic that could cure many different diseases.

Research scientists began a worldwide search for more helpful soil microbes. Anybody who traveled was asked to pick up samples of soil. Airline pilots, tourists, missionaries, students, and soldiers all co-operated. Thousands of samples poured in to be tested.

The tests produced results. One laboratory discovered Aureomycin, an antibiotic that does the work of both penicillin and streptomycin. Another laboratory discovered Chloromycetin; it proved effective against many diseases including typhus, typhoid, whooping cough, and certain intestinal ailments.

Then, in 1949, a laboratory that had run off more than 100,000 tests turned to a sample of soil from Indiana. From that test came Terramycin, one of the most effective antibiotics ever found. Terramycin can be used against many bacterial diseases.

Even so, the search goes on. Drug companies continue to seek new antibiotics in nature. And their chemists are learning to make

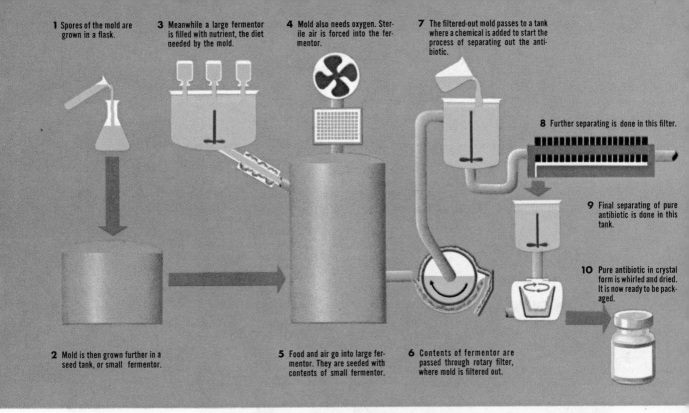

1 Spores of the mold are grown in a flask.

3 Meanwhile a large fermentor is filled with nutrient, the diet needed by the mold.

4 Mold also needs oxygen. Sterile air is forced into the fermentor.

7 The filtered-out mold passes to a tank where a chemical is added to start the process of separating out the antibiotic.

8 Further separating is done in this filter.

9 Final separating of pure antibiotic is done in this tank.

10 Pure antibiotic in crystal form is whirled and dried. It is now ready to be packaged.

2 Mold is then grown further in a seed tank, or small fermentor.

5 Food and air go into large fermentor. They are seeded with contents of small fermentor.

6 Contents of fermentor are passed through rotary filter, where mold is filtered out.

This flow chart shows the main steps taken in the production of Terramycin, one of the most effective antibiotics known. Here biology, chemistry, and engineering are all at work.

or **synthesize** some antibiotics without the help of microbes. These synthetic antibiotics are made from chemicals in the laboratory. Chloromycetin and cycloserine are two antibiotics from microbes that scientists are able to make synthetically. But with many antibiotics, it is difficult for chemists to imitate the work of the microbes. So microbes are used to make half of the antibiotic molecule, and chemists attach the other half. Antibiotics made in this way are called **semi-synthetics**.

Scientists have also learned how to improve antibiotics that are already in use. In hospitals, for example, antibiotics are sometimes combined. Sometimes scientists treat an antibiotic with chemicals to change it into a new one. In the laboratory, scientists are "educating" microbes to make special antibiotics. They do this by changing the microbes' living conditions, such as food, light, or temperature. The change in living conditions may cause a change in the chemicals that the microbes produce.

▶ **WHY MORE ANTIBIOTICS?**

Perhaps it seems odd that scientists keep trying to find new or different antibiotics when they already know so many. But there are several good reasons for this.

One is that scientists are never content with what they know. They always want to learn more, to explore the unknown.

A second reason has to do with the problems created by antibiotics themselves. A third concerns the discovery of new uses for antibiotics.

Problems with Antibiotics

For a number of years antibiotics seemed to be winning the battle against disease. Then doctors noticed that some germs were not being killed. Some kinds of bacteria were no longer affected by an antibiotic that used to kill them.

For example, doctors had expected streptomycin to conquer tuberculosis, but the antibiotic was not doing the job. It killed some kinds of tuberculosis germs but not others. Some of the bacteria even seemed to make a nourishing meal out of the poison that should have destroyed them. It was as if a new race of super-germs had developed—and they probably had.

When an antibiotic attacks a colony of

Penicillium chrysogenum, a mold that yields penicillin.

Power of a new antibiotic is tested against six different kinds of germs (*left*); of four antibiotics tested against a single germ species (*right*), two were effective.

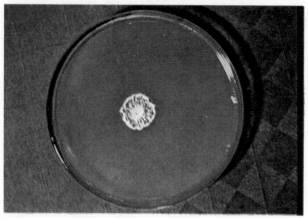

Streptomyces rimosus, used in making Terramycin.

Streptomyces griseus, used in making streptomycin.

Some living molds and microbes, like *Penicillium* and the *Streptomyces*, produce germ-killing substances that are harmless to people. Scientists use these substances in antibiotic medicines to cure hundreds of diseases, some formerly incurable.

germs, it usually destroys all of them. But if some survive, they are the ones best able to resist the antibiotic. The super-germs then multiply, producing more super-germs. Soon a new army of germs exists, and they are germs that the antibiotic cannot destroy.

A second problem has also resulted from the use of antibiotics. Microbes, you remember, compete for food, water, and living space. The winners thrive and spread. The losers become few in number and are not very active. Now suppose something wipes out the winners, which is what antibiotics are doing. The former losers suddenly have room to develop. They become active—and people begin to suffer from new kinds of infections.

The best way to attack such problems is with new or different antibiotics. If one anti-

biotic cannot control a germ, perhaps another can.

New Uses for Antibiotics

Farmers have put antibiotics to work in different ways. They add small amounts of antibiotics to the feed of pigs and chickens. The antibiotics speed up growth, so that the animals are ready for market earlier. Exactly why this happens is not fully understood. Today scientists do not agree about the wisdom of using antibiotics to promote growth.

Farmers have also found that antibiotics are of great value in keeping their animals in good health. There was a time when fatal diseases used to sweep through barnyards. Today these epidemics are rare. And the usefulness of antibiotics does not end with the animal's lifetime. Antibiotics are also used as preservatives. In some parts of the world, although not in the United States, antibiotics are used to keep meat and fish from spoiling on the way to market.

On many farms, fruit trees and vegetable plants are sprayed with antibiotics to prevent certain diseases.

Those are a few of the new uses that have been found for antibiotics. Because of these uses, many people have an interest in new antibiotics and what they can do.

▶ **FUTURE RESEARCH**

The field of antibiotics holds many unanswered questions. For example, no one is sure how or why microbes produce antibiotic chemicals. Do they always produce these chemicals, under all conditions? Or do they produce the chemicals only under laboratory conditions? Many scientists now believe that only "captive" microbes make antibiotics. They think that the laboratory diet may stimulate the microbes to produce these chemicals. But no one is sure.

Do microbes use antibiotic chemicals themselves? Again no one knows. If microbes produce these chemicals under natural conditions, they may also make use of the chemicals. Such chemicals may be a weapon in the war among microbes. Or the chemicals may cause faster growth. Then the faster-growing microbes crowd out the others.

How Antibiotics Work

Other questions have to do with the way that antibiotics work inside our bodies. How do antibiotics cure diseases? What actually happens when an antibiotic overcomes a microbe? Why does a particular chemical kill some kinds of microbes without killing others?

So far, these questions have not been fully answered. In spite of all the antibiotics that have been used successfully, no one knows the full story of how they work.

For instance, disease germs multiply so fast that a few can become a billion in 24 hours. One germ splits into two. Two become four, and the four become eight. This continues until a whole population of germs spreads over an infected wound or into the bloodstream. Given in time, an effective antibiotic stops this growth. How does the antibiotic do this?

Emmerich (*left*) made a crude antibiotic in 1890's. Chain (*right*) helped develop penicillin in 1940's.

Florey (*above left*) shared Nobel prize with Fleming and Chain. Dubos (*above right*) found germ killers in the soil. Below left, Waksman, discoverer of streptomycin, is visited by Fleming, penicillin pioneer.

Scientists have learned some facts about the way that antibiotics do their work against bacteria. In one group of experiments, penicillin was added to a liquid in which bacteria were growing. The bacteria began to bulge. Their cytoplasm, or living material, spilled out, and the bacteria died. Evidently the penicillin affected the cell wall, a stiff outer layer that holds the bacterial cell in shape. Another antibiotic, Terramycin, was used in other experiments. It prevented the bacteria from making substances they must have in order to live. These experiments show how some antibiotics work in the laboratory. Scientists believe they probably work the same way within the body.

Antibiotics for Virus Diseases

Many diseases are caused not by bacteria but by viruses. Among the diseases caused by viruses are polio, influenza, the common cold, measles, and perhaps some kinds of cancer. Research scientists have tested the anti-virus power of antibiotics in experiments with eggs and mice. They were able to slow the growth of the viruses in these cases. Some medical scientists hope that they will be able to develop antibiotics to control virus diseases in people.

BARBARA LAND
Formerly, Columbia University

Reviewed by TIMOTHY H. CRONIN
Central Research, Pfizer Inc.

GROWING PENICILLIUM MOLDS

Step 1: Wipe a piece of stale bread lightly across a windowsill or the kitchen floor. The bread will pick up microbes, even though you can't see them.

Step 5: Get a clean, fresh orange. Then pass a sharp knife blade through the penicillium mold on the bread. Using this knife, make 4 deep cuts in the orange skin.

Step 2: Sprinkle the bread with water. An eyedropper or laundry sprinkler is good for this. Microbes need moisture to grow. *Step 3:* Place bread in a large, wide-mouthed jar and cover with a lid or aluminum foil. Microbes will have enough air for growth. Put jar in a warm, dark cupboard. *Step 4:* In a few days look at bread. Although most bread contains chemicals to slow the growth of molds, there will probably be several different molds growing. If not, wait a few days and look again. Soon you will see mold colonies growing. And if one of these colonies is blue-green, it is probably penicillium mold.

Step 6: Thoroughly wash and dry the jar. Put the orange in it. Add a wet piece of cotton and cover jar. Store in a warm, dark place. **Step 7:** Examine orange each day. In a week or so you may see green mold growing along the cuts. A few days after that, tiny drops of gold liquid may form. Penicillin is made from this liquid. *Other things to do:* With other pieces of bread, grow penicillium molds under different conditions. For example, omit step 2. Change step 3 by putting jar in refrigerator or in strong light. Try wrapping bread tightly in plastic. Under what conditions does mold grow best?

ANTIBODIES AND ANTIGENS

The human body is quick to recognize foreign organisms that enter it. "Foes" must be attacked or otherwise got rid of. The most common of these foes are viruses, bacteria, and other microscopic organisms. The body recognizes these foes by the chemicals within them called **antigens**. To counteract these foreign invaders, the body produces its own chemicals, protein molecules called **antibodies**. Each kind of antigen causes the production of a specific kind of antibody. Antibodies appear in the body fluids such as blood and lymph and in the body's cells.

Doctors learned to make use of the antibody system for defense long before they had any idea that antibodies existed. As early as 1796, Edward Jenner, an English country doctor, discovered that if he gave people a case of the mild disease cowpox, he prevented them from getting the serious disease smallpox. What Jenner did not know is that the diseases are caused by closely related viruses. They are so closely related that the cowpox antibody will counteract the smallpox antigen.

Injecting an antigen to start the production of antibodies is now called **vaccination**. (It is one kind of immunization—making a person immune.) The antigen injected is a **vaccine**. These terms are based on *vacca,* the Latin word for "cow," because Jenner's vaccine was made from the cowpox virus.

Today doctors know of several ways that people become immune to diseases. Some people inherit a natural resistance to certain diseases. Over the years they build up an immunity that keeps them from ever getting certain diseases. But most antibodies are acquired only after the body has been exposed to a known antigen. The antigen may be carried by some organism that enters the body on its own, or the antigen may be artificially injected with a needle.

When a specially prepared antigen is injected into a person, it is called **active immunization**. The person actively produces the antibodies that fight off the foreign matter. The antibody defense system then remains on the alert, ready to deal with any later invasion. This procedure can be used to protect people against tetanus, typhoid, cholera, polio-

White—ANTIBODIES   **Black—ANTIGENS**

Diagram represents reaction between antibodies (shown as white) and antigens (shown as dark). Antigen is put out of action when antibody locks with it.

myelitis, typhus, Rocky Mountain spotted fever, smallpox, yellow fever, diphtheria, whooping cough, and plague.

Antibodies may also be produced in animals by injecting them with antigens. The antibodies are then transferred directly to a person. These antibodies are immediately ready for action. This is called **passive immunization** because the person plays no part in the production of antibodies. Passive immunization disappears within a few weeks. Active immunization gives much more lasting protection.

The substance taken from the immunized animal or person for passive immunization is called **antiserum**. If used early enough, it can prevent such diseases as measles and tetanus. Sometimes an antiserum can be used after the antigen has entered a person's body, as in measles, tetanus, and diphtheria. Antiserums against bee and snake venom have also been developed.

Both antigens and antibodies are large molecules. Scientists believe that the antibody molecule combines with a particular antigen molecule, the two fitting like a key and a lock. In the chemical reaction that takes place, the antigen loses its power to cause the disease.

L. D. HAMILTON
Brookhaven National Laboratory

See also IMMUNOLOGY.

ANTIDOTES.   See POISONS AND ANTIDOTES.

ANTIGUA AND BARBUDA

Beautiful beaches, calm waters, and sunny skies make the Caribbean nation of Antigua and Barbuda a popular resort. The country is part of the Leeward islands in the Lesser Antilles. It includes the islands of Antigua and Barbuda and tiny, uninhabited Redonda.

▶ THE LAND

Antigua, the largest island, is mostly flat, with rolling green hills, tropical vegetation, and many gardens. The nation's high point, Boggy Peak, rises to 405 meters (1,330 feet) in western Antigua. The capital, St. John's, is on Royal Cove in Antigua, the nation's chief harbor. The wooded island of Barbuda, north of Antigua, is noted for its superb beaches of pink and white sand.

The country is relatively dry. Rainfall averages only 1,070 millimeters (42 inches) a year. Additional water is provided by desalinization plants. Temperatures are pleasant all year, ranging from 22 to 30°C (71 to 86°F).

▶ THE PEOPLE AND THE ECONOMY

Over 90 percent of the people are of black African descent. The rest are of British, Portuguese, Lebanese, or mixed ancestry. English is the official language. Most of the people live on the island of Antigua.

ANTIGUA AND BARBUDA

Tourism is the chief economic activity. Sugar was the mainstay of the economy until the mid-1960's, but the nation has since ceased to be a sugar producer. Cotton and vegetables are grown, and a number of light industries have recently been established.

▶ HISTORY AND GOVERNMENT

Christopher Columbus visited the island now known as Antigua in 1493. The islands were first settled by Arawak Indians from Venezuela. But there were few Indians left when British settlers from nearby St. Christopher (now St. Kitts) arrived in 1632. The islands were briefly under French control during the 17th century. Nelson's Dockyard, built on English Harbour in 1764, served as headquarters for the English admiral Horatio Nelson.

Tobacco, the first commercial crop, soon gave way to sugar. Many black Africans were brought to the sugar plantations as slaves. They were freed in 1834, when slavery was abolished in the British colonies. In 1967, Antigua became one of the West Indies Associated States, with full internal self-government. Plans for full independence were made in 1979.

The British monarch, represented by a governor-general, is head of state. A prime minister is head of government. The legislature has two houses, one elected by universal adult suffrage and the other appointed.

HOWARD A. FERGUS
University of the West Indies (Montserrat)

ANTILLES. See CARIBBEAN SEA AND ISLANDS.

FACTS AND FIGURES

ANTIGUA AND BARBUDA is the official name of the country.

CAPITAL: St. John's.

LOCATION: Caribbean Sea. **Latitude**—17° N to 18° N. **Longitude**—61° W to 62° W.

AREA: 442 km² (171 sq mi).

POPULATION: 71,000 (estimate).

LANGUAGE: English.

GOVERNMENT: Constitutional monarchy. **Head of state**—British monarch, represented by governor-general. **Head of government**—prime minister. **International cooperation**—United Nations, Commonwealth of Nations, Caribbean Community (CARICOM), Organization of American States (OAS).

ECONOMY: Agricultural products—cotton, vegetables. **Industries and products**—tourism, rum, wine, textiles, handicrafts, assembled equipment. **Chief exports**—beverages. **Chief imports**—machinery, petroleum, foodstuffs, raw materials. **Monetary unit**—Eastern Caribbean dollar.

Collectors attend an antique furniture auction. Items are sold to the highest bidders.

ANTIQUES AND ANTIQUE COLLECTING

Antiques are things that were once in everyday use around the home or farm.

For centuries, skilled artisans have made beautiful furniture, silver, pottery, and glassware. You may see these things in historic houses and in museums where period rooms show the way homes looked many years ago. You may also see antiques in shops and in many private houses. Perhaps there are interesting antiques in your own home.

It is true that auction galleries hold sales at which expensive antiques are bought by collectors. But this need not discourage the beginning collector, for it is not necessary to be an authority on costly art objects or furniture to enjoy collecting antiques.

Paperweights, miniature tea sets, penny banks, dollhouse furniture, old glassware, and buttons are fun and inexpensive to collect.

▶ANTIQUE FURNITURE

One of the most attractive items to many collectors is beautiful furniture. The furniture most in demand is that of the 18th century.

English furniture made in the period from 1714 to 1820 is called Georgian after the reigning monarchs of that time. The leading furniture makers were Chippendale, Hepplewhite, Sheraton, and Adam.

In early 18th-century France, cabinetmakers designed small, graceful pieces with curved lines. Later, furniture was based on classic designs using straight lines and a light, dainty style.

Much of the furniture seen today is copied or adapted from older styles. The really old, or period, pieces are often in museums and public collections, but there are many still in private homes.

▶THE WONDERFUL WORLD OF GLASS

Antique glass ranges from glass tumblers and goblets, vases and pitchers, to plates and candlesticks, and might even include colored glass beads once used for bartering, or trading. It would be impossible to list here the hundreds of colors, patterns, and kinds of glass made by each country. Glass colors can be any shade from deep red to violet, or the sparkling clear glass that reflects light like a diamond. A collection of glass might begin with a very small object, such as a tiny glass figure of a rabbit or a reindeer.

All glass is divided into two kinds, lead or lime. Lead glass is also called flint glass. It has a high luster, but it is brittle and easily scratched. Lime glass is less breakable and is used for windows and mirrors.

Antique markets are often set up outdoors. Expensive as well as inexpensive items are put up for sale.

A dealer's booth at an antique show. Many dealers specialize in antiques from a specific period.

A pontil is an iron rod used to handle the hot glass while it is being shaped. When the shaped object is broken off the pontil, a rough mark is left on the base. Pontil marks make it possible to identify handmade blown glass—early or modern. Even when smoothed over, the mark shows in the form of a hollow.

Another sign of old glass is that it is often irregular in shape. Also, the pattern in reverse may show through on the inside of the glassware unless it is made of very thick glass.

Often old glass will show signs of wear on the base, and long exposure to light may have discolored it. Sometimes you will see glass that has a crackled look. This is due to age and is called crizzling.

There is really no easy way to tell old glass from new. Study and experience are needed to place an accurate date on any antique.

Although modern manners frown upon drinking tea out of a saucer, in the early 1800's it was quite correct. But it was a problem to know where to put the cup while drinking from the saucer. Manufacturers found the answer. They made a special flat plate on which to place the cup. The most valuable cup plates are made of Sandwich glass. Sandwich glass, first made in 1825 in the town of Sandwich, on Cape Cod, Massachusetts, by a man named Deming Jarves,

was a molded, or pressed, glass. The molds were so deeply carved that Sandwich glass looks as if it had designs cut into it. The cup plates are 10 centimeters (4 inches) or less across. The patterns include steamboats, log cabins, and portraits of famous people. Once the cup plates cost 5 cents each. Today they cost much more because collectors prize them.

Also of interest to collectors are the historical and portrait flasks in several small

Left: An English Wedgwood butter-dish. Right: Covered glass sugar bowl made about 1825 by an unknown American artisan.

sizes in many shades of green, blue, and yellow. These portraits in glass are of George Washington, the Marquis de Lafayette, Benjamin Franklin, and many other famous people. There are also patriotic designs and pictures of ships, railroads, and historical events. In fact, bottles and flasks tell the story of their time just as prints and etchings do.

There are even very small bottles that were shaped like animals, birds, and fish, and were used for medicines and perfume. These are called character bottles.

▶ **POTTERY**

Clay can be shaped and baked into plates, cups, and other useful articles; this is called pottery. Pottery that is given a thin, glassy coating is called glazed ware. The coarser, often unglazed kinds of pottery are usually called earthenware or, if very hard, stoneware. The finest kind of pottery is porcelain (also called china because it first came from China). It is hard and translucent—that is, light will show through it.

Pottery pieces that might be fun to collect are cow-shaped cream pitchers, or water pitchers that have animal tails for handles. There are fanciful animals, too—lions with flowing china manes and deer with branching antlers. There are statuettes of famous people —Thomas Jefferson, Queen Victoria—and Toby mugs, which are shaped like fat people and portray characters from literature.

Tiffany lamps are popular antiques. The lampshades are made of colored glass arranged in attractive patterns.

Stoneware was very practical in colonial times. Artisans made jugs and jars, crocks and churns, bottles and milk pans. But the ware had to be pretty as well as useful. The gray or tan pottery often had a transparent salt glaze with the designs in cobalt blue.

Slipware is pottery decorated in colors in the same way that a baker decorates the top of a cake. The cream-thick slip (fine clay mixed with water and coloring) is placed in a funnel. Then the decorator uses the funnel to apply designs on the pottery.

Potters have marked their ware with many different signs. A well-known mark is the

Left: Early 19th-century tin coffeepot, japanned with painted decorations that imitate oriental lacquer. Center: An 18th-century Sèvres (French) plate. Right: A Meissen (German) saucer of the same period.

crossed swords that appear on Meissen china (also called Dresden).

The marks scratched, indented, or painted on porcelain tell us who made the piece and from what country it came. Marks appear on the bottom of a plate or cup or vase. But sometimes the makers put their marks on the outer part, the way painters sign their pictures where their names can be seen.

But many old pieces of china are unmarked. For this reason, a collector also judges the value and age of a piece by its glaze and modeling as well as by its shape and decoration. In identifying marked pieces, a handbook of old pottery marks is useful.

Since 1891 all goods imported into the United States have been required to show the country of origin. If a piece of china is marked "Made in England" or in any other country, you will know that it was made later than 1891. *Déposé* is the mark seen on French goods. It is the same as the mark "Registered" on English ware and "Patented" on American products.

From 1842 until 1883 the British Patent Office required a register mark on pottery. The mark was a diamond shape with various code letters inside it. English china made after 1883 bears the mark "Rd." and a number.

▶ SILVER

In the 17th century the English standard for silver coin (sterling) was 925 parts of silver for each 1,000 parts of metal. In those days all silver was made to order from the silver coins a customer brought in to a silversmith. The objects most often made were cups, tankards, and mugs. They were stamped with a mark that showed the quality of the silver. Since 1544, except for a short time of some 20 years, the symbol for the standard has been a lion passant (walking with right forepaw raised). This mark shows the piece has been made from sterling coin silver. Later silversmiths made tea sets and knives and forks and other tableware.

The marks on English silver are called hallmarks because they were stamped on at the Goldsmiths' Hall in London. The Goldsmiths' Guild was formed to protect the interests of gold- and silversmiths just as modern unions protect their workers today. The guild required that silver be stamped with the maker's mark, the town mark, and a date letter. For instance, between the years 1784 and 1890, a silver spoon might have had the following marks: the lion passant and a side-view likeness of King George III or perhaps Queen Victoria to show that the duty had

Left: Antique Uncle Sam money bank. When a coin is put in Sam's hand and the button on his umbrella pressed, the bag opens and the coin drops into it. Center: Flask of about 1850 shows head of George Washington. Right: Pottery wine cask dated 1820.

Mark of John Coney, Boston, Mass., early 1700's.

Mark of Benjamin Wynkoop, N. Y., early 1700's.

Hallmark of John Wakelin & William Taylor, London, late 1700's, showing king's head, date letter K, lion, leopard's head, and makers' mark.

A silver tankard by patriot-silversmith Paul Revere.

been paid; the maker's mark and initials; the town mark, which for London was a leopard's head, for Edinburgh two towers, for Dublin a harp; and the date letter, which might appear in many ways—the London date letter for 1776 is a small roman "a."

Thousands of marks are explained in books to which anyone may refer to learn the date and maker of a piece of silver.

In 1743, Thomas Boulsover, a knifemaker of Sheffield, England, discovered that a thin coating of silver could be made to stick to a thicker sheet of copper by a proper use of heat. When this baking was done, the two pieces could be hammered or shaped as a single piece of metal. Sheffield plating, as the new process was called, was less expensive than making sterling silver. Today good examples are prized by collectors.

▶ ANTIQUES MADE OF OTHER METALS

Metals have been formed into a variety of interesting objects that have a place in antique collections.

Ironwork. All early ironwork was fashioned by blacksmiths. They did not just make horseshoes. They made latches and hinges for doors and gates. They also made andirons for fireplaces and iron pots and pans for cooking. A collection of ironwork might include some wonderful old locks and keys.

Pewter. If you mix 90 percent copper and 10 percent tin, the result is bronze. By changing the mixture to 90 percent tin and 10 percent copper, you make pewter. Other substances mixed with tin will also form pewter. Among them are antimony and bismuth.

Pewter fiddleback teaspoons, so called because the handle was shaped like a violin, are of interest to collectors, as are pewter plates and teapots and coffeepots.

The eagle is a trademark on American pewter made after the Revolution. English ware is often marked with a rose and crown.

Brass. Brasswork was used in old times just as it is today, for fireplace tools and door handles and furniture hardware.

Copper. This metal has long been used for pots and pans. Another copper utensil was the warming pan, used to take the chill out of bedclothes. In the days before furnaces, these flat, round copper containers with long handles were filled with hot coals and rubbed quickly over the cold sheets to warm the bed.

Tinware. Tin was often shaped into candlesticks, lanterns, and all kinds of boxes.

Sometimes the antiques we come upon are neither beautiful nor rare. But they do give a picture of the people and customs of other times. Follow your interests and let them lead you into the adventures of collecting.

DOROTHY DRAPER
Formerly, Dorothy Draper Company, Inc.

ANTISEPTICS. See DISINFECTANTS AND ANTISEPTICS.

ANTITOXINS. See VACCINATION AND INOCULATION; DISEASES, PREVENTION OF.

ANTONY, MARK. See MARK ANTONY.

ANTONYMS. See SYNONYMS AND ANTONYMS.

ANTS

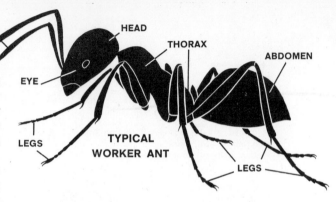

ANTENNAE HEAD THORAX ABDOMEN EYE LEGS **TYPICAL WORKER ANT** LEGS

Some people think of ants as pests. It is true that ants searching for food at a picnic or in the kitchen can be pests. Ants that bite or sting can be a serious problem. So are those that strip the leaves off trees. But most ants are not pests. Some are harmless to people. Others are helpful. They keep down various insect pests. And all ants offer a fascinating study to anyone who will take the trouble to observe them.

Ants are among the most interesting insects. As seen by us, they are always busy and they go about their work in an organized way. This busyness made them one of the first insects to attract the attention and admiration of people. They are even mentioned in the Bible—in Proverbs we find: "Go to the ant, thou sluggard; consider her ways and be wise."

The same kind of ant still thrives in the Holy Land. And a close relative, the harvester ant, lives on the Great Plains of North America. This tells you something else about ants: They are found almost everywhere in the world except in the coldest regions. As a result, over millions of years they have adapted to a wide variety of living conditions. Take, for example, the matter of food.

Many ants capture and eat other insects. Some gather plant seeds and store them underground for food. Other ants eat a mold that grows on leaves they carry into their underground nests. Still other ants feed on the sweet matter that certain plants, flowers,

Mushroom ant. This soldier ant is easily recognized by its huge jaws. Soldiers defend colony from invaders.

and insects secrete (give off). Certain ants guard plant lice, or aphids, which are called "ants' cows." The ants feed on the sweet honeydew that the aphids secrete.

The Ant Family

Scientists estimate that there are about 8,000 different species, or kinds, of ants. They all belong to the insect family known as the Formicidae. Their closest relatives are the bees, wasps, and hornets. Ants differ from all these in having small projections that extend upward from their narrow waists.

Like all insects ants have bodies covered with a shell, which is really an outer skeleton. The body is divided into three parts: the head; the abdomen, or stomach; and the thorax, which lies between the head and the abdomen. The worker ants, which are the ones most commonly seen, have no wings. But most other ants have two pairs of wings. Like all insects ants have three pairs of legs. They are air breathers, and they reproduce by laying eggs.

▶ ANT COLONIES AND SOCIAL BEHAVIOR

Ants are called social insects because they live together in colonies. A colony may contain a dozen ants or many thousands. The size of the colony depends on the species of ant.

The Classes of Ants

Like those other well-known social insects, the honeybees, ants are divided into three castes (classes): males, workers, and queens. Some ant colonies have a group known as soldiers. They usually have large jaws, and their task is to defend the colony. Soldiers are actually a special kind of worker. Like other workers their life span is usually a few months to a year.

Male ants develop from unfertilized eggs. They are produced only at certain seasons. Short-lived, they serve one function. They are mates for queens.

Both workers and queens develop from fertilized eggs. The queens receive special food and develop into perfect, or egg-laying, females. The workers do not receive this special food and so are not able to lay eggs. Workers are considered to be imperfect females.

Life Cycles of Ants

At certain times of the year, usually in spring, a number of males and queens develop in a nest. Winged, they soon swarm out and fly off. During or at the end of the flight, they mate. Afterward each male seeks shelter. He does not return to the nest. He may fly around for a while, but within a few days he dies.

Each queen, however, flies off to select a site for her nest. One of her first acts there is to bite off her wings. Wings will not be of any use in her future life. The queen ant is then ready to establish a new colony by laying eggs.

The young queen takes care of the first generation of ants she produces. After the larvae (young ants) are hatched, she feeds them. In time the larvae become full grown and change to the pupal (resting) stage. Sometimes the pupae are enclosed in white cases, known as cocoons. The cases are what people often call "ant eggs." Actually, the true eggs are almost microscopic in size and are seldom seen by the average person.

After a while adult ants emerge from the pupal cases. This period varies from one to several weeks. This first generation of ants usually consists entirely of female workers. They at once take over the duties of food gathering and colony defense. Later they will care for the new young ants. As the colony grows the queen's only function is to lay eggs. Having mated just once, the queen is able to lay fertilized (as well as unfertilized) eggs for the rest of her life. Some queens live many years.

Nest Construction

Ants build their nests in a great variety of locations. Many kinds dig their nests under-

Male red ant. Male ants develop from unfertilized eggs. Queen and worker ants develop from fertilized eggs.

ground, where they are safe from enemies and bad weather. Other ants build nests under rocks or in rotten logs. Some dwell inside living plants.

Certain ants have become very skillful at nest construction. For example, in the United States the acrobatic ants build shelters around twigs to protect their insect "cows." Their shelters are made of vegetable fibers that the ants chew into a pulp and then let dry. The finished material is like the paper made by hornets. These are called "carton" nests. They are also constructed by various ants in tropical countries.

Probably the most unusual method of nest construction is that used by the weaver ants of southeastern Asia. They fasten growing tree leaves together with silk threads. If a space separates the leaves, the workers grasp the edges with their jaws and pull them into place. If the leaves are far apart, a number of ants join in chains. Then they slowly draw the leaves together.

In the meantime other workers have come out of a nest. Each worker carries a larva, or young ant, in its jaws. The larvae provide the silk for joining the leaves.

Adult weaver ants cannot secrete silk. Only the larvae can. So the adults use the larvae as tiny spools. Adult workers move the larvae back and forth between the leaf edges while the larvae secrete threads of silk from their mouths. The moist threads glue the leaves together.

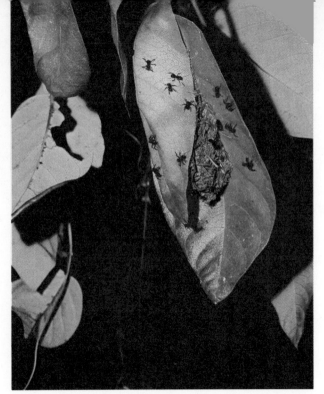

Weaver ants build a nest by sewing together two leaves. The "thread" is silk made by larvae (young ants).

How Ants Find Their Way

Ants must often travel great distances in search of food. Scientists have long studied how the ants find their way back to the home colony. Some ants get their bearings from landmarks. Others use the direction of the sun's rays.

It has also been found that some ants lay scent trails as they walk along, by touching the tips of their abdomens to the ground from time to time. As they do this they secrete the scent.

In some cases scent patches also have a shape that tells other ants the direction in which the first ant was traveling. This can be demonstrated by reversing a chip or some such object over which a column of ants is passing. The ants at once become confused. It is as if an arrow had been turned backward.

Communication Among Ants

The ability to lay and follow scent trails is really a form of communication. For certain kinds of ants that are blind, scent is especially important. It is also a means of communication for many kinds of sighted ants. Most recognize others of the same colony by their scents. (Honeybees and other social insects have this same ability.) To signal danger, certain ants give off poison from the tips of their abdomens. The scent "excites" and warns nearby ants.

Some ants also communicate by sounds. An ant rubs one part of its armor-like body against another. Sounds made in this way are called stridulations. A number of ants have stridulating organs. The sounds they produce are like those made by crickets and katydids. If one of the large workers of the Texas leaf-cutting ants is held near the ear, a squeaking sound can be heard.

▶ANTS' RELATIONSHIPS WITH OTHER ANT SPECIES

In general, ants that live and work together belong to the same species. But there are also many interesting relationships among ants of different species.

Thief Ants

Turn over a stone under which a colony of large ants is located. You may find a second colony of tiny yellow ants near the cells and tunnels of the larger ants. These yellow ants are called thief ants because they invade the tunnels of the larger ants and steal food. The thief ants escape into their own tiny tunnels. These are so small that the larger ants cannot follow and destroy them.

Ant Slaves

Several species of ants make slaves of other ants. In North America, for example, there is a species of large red ant that keeps as slaves a closely related but smaller species of black ant. The red ants make slave-hunting raids on nests of the smaller ants, and carry off the young. The kidnaped ants grow up as slaves, doing the work of the red-ant colony. In many cases a colony that starts out with red ants ends up with three times as many slaves as slave hunters. The red ants can get along without slaves, but they usually have them.

An Unusual Case of Ant Slaves

The amazon ants, however, must have slaves because they have completely lost the ability to take care of themselves. The amazons make regular slave-hunting raids on more timid ants. Curiously enough, the enslaved ants become somewhat like their captors. Their nature changes and they become aggressive. Sometimes they go out on slave-hunting raids with the amazons. They may even accompany the amazons when the raids are against their own kind.

Since the queen of the amazon ants cannot take care of herself or her offspring, she establishes a new colony in an unusual way. After mating, she invades a nest of slave ants. The amazon queen kills the queen of the slave ants and establishes herself as the egg-laying queen mother. The slave ants take care of her young, and in time her young take over the nest completely. They carry on the colony with the aid of the captured slaves.

ANTS' RELATIONSHIPS WITH OTHER INSECTS

Ants often play host to other insects. There are hundreds of kinds of beetles and other insects that find homes and food in ant colonies. The small insects that live in ant colonies are rarely found anywhere else.

Insects Living in Ant Colonies

Among the insects that live in ant colonies are tiny crickets. The crickets are very agile and can dodge the jaws of their hosts. One kind of cricket is associated with the American fire ant. Another cricket is found in the large mound nests of the prairie harvester ant. Still another and larger cricket lives in rotten wood with the large carpenter ant.

Tiny cockroaches are also found in ant colonies. For instance, cockroaches are usually found in the large underground nests of the leaf-cutting ant in the southern parts of Texas and Louisiana. Strangely, the antennae (feelers) of the cockroaches are always clipped short. It is not known whether the ant hosts do this or not.

Ant "Pets"

Sometimes ants allow guest insects into their nests, taking care of them as if they were pets. In at least one case the guest insects get more attention than the ants' own young. It may be that the guests give off some attractive substance. The neglected young ants become undernourished and deformed.

Why "foreign" insects are accepted by ants is something of a mystery. In some cases the guests turn out to be vicious, killing and eating the young ants. But most ant "pets" do little or no harm to their hosts.

ANTS AND PLANT LIFE

Among the many kinds of ants are several "farmer" species that cultivate their own food gardens. Unknown to most people, these ants are found in many parts of the United States. The food they grow is a fungus, a very simple plant that grows on other forms of plant life.

One of the most common fungus-growing ants is the *Trachymyrmex*. These ants are unusual in appearance because their small bodies are covered with many short spines. The ants dig out underground holes about the size of an orange. They gather material such as bits of leaves, flower petals, or caterpillar droppings from the ground. They carry this into the nest and make it into a bed in which they cultivate their fungus "garden."

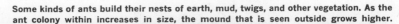

Some kinds of ants build their nests of earth, mud, twigs, and other vegetation. As the ant colony within increases in size, the mound that is seen outside grows higher.

The Leaf-cutting Ants

Of all the fungus-growing ants, the large leaf cutters, or *Atta* ants, are the most spectacular. They are common in the tropical areas of South and Central America and are also found in southern Texas and Louisiana. Their leaf-cutting activity makes them serious pests—they have been known to strip the leaves off a large tree or destroy a garden.

The leaf-cutting ants are somewhat larger than most ants. The largest workers may be from 10 to 15 millimeters (about ½ inch) long. They do not sting, but they have sharp jaws with which they can give a painful bite.

The leaf-cutting ants gather large quantities of leaves, which they carry to their underground nests. The nests are holes, often as large as watermelons, filled with a gray fungus. Here the ants chew up the leaves into a substance that fertilizes the fungus. The growing fungus provides food for the ants. The fungus is a special kind that grows nowhere else. It is carefully tended by very small worker ants. Their special duty is to weed out the other fungi that have been carried in on the ants' bodies or on leaves.

The leaf-gathering raids of these ants often take place at night during favorable weather. Columns of ants come out of their underground tunnels and follow well-worn ant trails to some tree or bush. There the ants cut off leaf sections. Then they return to the nest, each carrying a piece of leaf as big as itself over its head. (For this reason these ants are often called "parasol ants.") In the returning columns the ants hurry along, bumping into obstacles and into each other. They crowd into the tunnels, each ant still carrying its load.

The queen of the leaf-gathering ants founds a new colony in an interesting way. After mating and selecting a spot for the colony, her first act is to bite off her wings. Next she digs a small hole in the ground and seals herself in. From her mouth she then takes out a bit of fungus, which she has brought from the parent colony. She lays a few eggs on the fungus and settles down to guard them until they hatch. Meanwhile the fungus begins to grow, fed by waste matter from the queen's body. When the eggs hatch, the young are fed on the fungus. During this period the queen does not eat fungus. But she—and her young—may eat some of the more recently laid eggs. After several weeks the young become adult ants. They open an entrance to the ground and go out to gather leaf bits for use in the fungus garden.

The queen now has a labor force to carry on the work of the colony. She herself becomes a mere egg-laying machine. A queen may live for a number of years, during which the colony continues to grow. Such a colony is fairly permanent, since newly mated queens are taken in to contribute their egg-laying activity. In this way the life of the colony continues beyond the life of the original queen.

Eventually a colony may contain several million ants living in many large underground holes. These holes are all connected by tunnels that may lie as deep as 4.5 meters (15 feet) below the surface of the ground.

Seed-gathering Ants

Anyone who has traveled across the plains of North Texas, Oklahoma, Kansas, Colorado, or Wyoming has noticed certain neat mounds of earth. These are the homes of the harvester ants. There are other kinds of harvester ants that live as far south and east as Florida. They do not construct so neat a cone

A harvester ant, shown dragging a seed. Ants can carry or drag objects that are far heavier and larger than themselves.

The abdomen of this ant is swollen with liquid deposited there by other worker ants. A living storage tank, ant is called a "replete." Liquid will be eaten later by colony.

as their relatives on the Great Plains, but otherwise their habits are similar.

On the Great Plains each mound is located at the center of a cleared space about 3 meters (10 feet) in diameter. The mound, which is made of coarse sand, has many tunnels that run one above the other. The lowest tunnels are usually about 1 meter below the ground.

Watch one of these mounds closely and you will see the ants continually coming and going. They go in and out of the mound through a hole at the base. Careful observation also reveals that many of the homeward-bound ants are carrying seeds in their jaws.

The ants gather seeds from various plants. Inside the nest they remove the seeds' husks, or outer coverings. They then carry the husks out to the edge of the cleared space and leave them there. The seeds are stored in certain tunnels, which are set aside as grain bins. (The bins are often robbed by various small animals such as kangaroo rats.)

The seeds are the ant colony's food supply. Harvester ants have tongues like rough files. They scrape off the starchy material of the seeds with their tongues. This material is the basic part of their diet.

Liquid-gathering Ants

Storing seeds is not difficult for ants. Storing liquids is not so easy. Yet in several parts of the world there are ants that collect liquid for food. Honeybees, of course, collect a liquid and store it in wax cells in their hives. But ants cannot secrete wax for making cells. They solve the problem of storing liquid in another way.

The liquid collected by ants is the honeydew given off by certain insects and plants. An ant carries this honeydew in its "honey stomach," a tiny storage pouch in its abdomen. Back at the nest the ant feeds the liquid to certain worker ants, which become storage tanks.

It is not known how worker ants are chosen for the role of food storage. At the start of the summer, these workers are the normal 8 millimeters (⅓ inch) long. After they become filled with honeydew, they are almost twice that size. They weigh several times as much as their normal sisters and can no longer move about. Their abdomens are swollen to the size of small grapes. These living storage tanks are called "repletes."

Liquid-storing ants are found in Australia and in North America. In America they are found in the fairly high regions and semi-desert areas from Mexico City north to Idaho. Their region in Australia has about the same kind of land and climate. These are dry regions, where food can be harvested only during a short period of the year. The ants' unusual method of storing food is an adaptation to these special conditions.

Ants and the Bull-horn Acacia

A remarkable ant-plant relationship involves the ants that live with the bull-horn acacia trees of Central America and Mexico. The bull-horn acacias are small, shrubby trees that thrive mostly in the coastal areas. There are several varieties of these acacias, but all have heavy, thorn-like structures growing from twigs. The thorns, which resemble small bull's horns, are thin-walled and filled with a soft, spongy material.

Anyone who examines an acacia thorn closely is likely to see a small hole near its tip. Cutting open the thorn will show that the spongy matter is gone. In its place is a colony of small, quick-moving ants.

The acacia does more than provide the ants with shelter. The tree gives off a sweet secretion that the ants eat. At the tip of the leaves is a small reddish "fruit" that the ants also eat. This means that the ants are continually exploring the tree in search of food. While searching, the ants guard the tree against other insects. There are caterpillars and beetles, for example, that like to eat the leaves of the acacia tree. Hundreds of ants attack these insects if they approach the tree. One of the chief enemies of the acacia is the leaf-cutting ant described earlier. The leaf cutters are driven off by the standing army of the acacia tree.

The bull-horn acacia trees are not the only plants that attract guardian ants. Several common plants such as partridge peas, elderberries, and castor beans give off sweet secretions that are desirable food for ants. The ants keep off other, destructive insects. No plant, however, does as much as the bull-horn acacia, which provides both food and shelter.

An ant enters hole on thorn of bull-horn acacia tree. A colony of ants lives inside the hollowed-out thorn.

Other Ants in Trees

Other ants also live in plants, using holes and hollows as secure locations for nests.

Queen ant below belongs to kind known as carpenter ants because they chew holes in wood. Note queen's wings; worker ants, the most familiar class, have no wings.

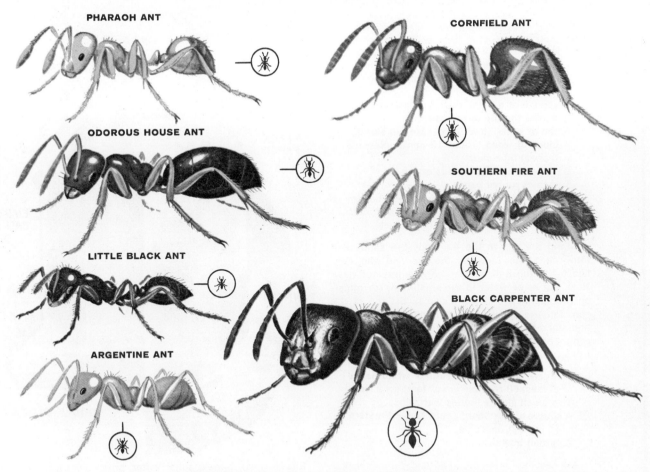

PHARAOH ANT

ODOROUS HOUSE ANT

LITTLE BLACK ANT

ARGENTINE ANT

CORNFIELD ANT

SOUTHERN FIRE ANT

BLACK CARPENTER ANT

Pictured above are seven common ants of the New World. Actual size of each kind is shown within the circle nearest the ant.

Some, such as the medium-sized acrobatic ants, establish nests almost anywhere—in holes in trees or cracks in bark. Large carpenter ants dig out tunnels in dry or rotting wood. (So do termites, but they are not ants.) Other ants seek out small holes bored in trees by beetles.

The *Colobopsis* ant is probably the best adapted to living in plants. These ants make their homes inside the twigs of such trees as sumac and white ash, and they are found in many parts of the United States and Europe. Their food is the honeydew collected from aphids, tiny insects that feed upon the tree leaves.

The *Colobopsis* colonies are small. They consist of a queen, a dozen or so workers, and a few soldiers. It is the soldier caste that is of special interest. The chief task of the soldiers is to guard the entrance to the nest. The soldier's head is shaped like a plug. The soldier stays inside the twig and uses the flat front of its head to plug the entrance. When one of the workers from the nest returns, it is apparently recognized by its odor. The soldier backs away and lets the worker enter. No other ants or ant enemies are admitted.

▶ THE IMPORTED FIRE ANTS

The fire ants are natives of South America. They were first seen in the United States in 1930, and have spread from Alabama to several other southern states. They feed mainly on insects and other small creatures, but their painful sting can make humans sick. The nests of the fire ants are high mounds of earth that interfere with the mowing of hay fields. Several states, with the aid of the

HOW TO BUILD AN ANT OBSERVATION NEST

To build a nest, you will need these things:

A large glass jar with a screw top. (An empty pickle jar is very good for this purpose.)
A tall, thin, empty can that can stand inside the jar.
A sponge or a small dish for water, to rest across the top of the can.
A pan of water, in which the jar can stand.
A block of wood, about 12 centimeters (5 inches) on a side.
Dark paper for the outside of the jar.
Two thick rubber bands.
Enough sandy soil to fill about one half of the space between the jar and the can. The sand should be slightly moist.

Stand the can in the jar. Pour the sandy soil into the space between the jar and the can. Leave the top half of the space empty for now. Next, put some water in the small dish (or moisten the sponge), and put it across the top of the can. Put the block of wood in the pan of water and stand the jar on the block. This is so the ants cannot escape as you put them into the nest.

To collect ants, you will need:

A square piece of white cloth or white paper at least 60 centimeters (2 feet) on a side.
Two small plastic bottles with caps.
A square of cardboard about 15 centimeters (6 inches) on a side.
A garden trowel.

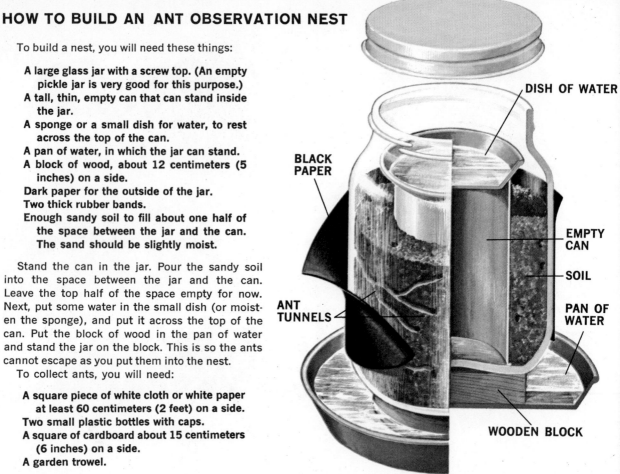

DISH OF WATER

BLACK PAPER

EMPTY CAN

SOIL

PAN OF WATER

ANT TUNNELS

WOODEN BLOCK

Ant nests are often found outdoors under rocks. Lift some rocks until you find ants scurrying around under one. Black or gray ants are harmless and will not sting.

Lay one of the bottles on its side, near the ants, and guide them with the cardboard into the bottle. When you have collected about 100, screw the cap on the bottle.

Collect a queen by digging deep under the rock where you found the ant nest. Take the soil you have dug and spread it on the white sheet. One ant larger than the rest will probably show up against the white. This is the queen. (You may have to dig a foot or more to find a queen.) Guide her into the other bottle and close it. In this way you can be sure not to lose her.

Carry some soil from the ant nest back with you. Put it into your nest, filling most of the space left between the jar and the can. Put the ants and the queen into the nest and screw the cap on the jar. Fasten dark paper around the jar with rubber bands. (Ants like the dark. They will build their tunnels close to the glass, where you can observe them, if the glass is covered with dark paper.)

Feed the ants by putting different kinds of food on top of the soil. Try bread or cake crumbs, bits of meat, honey, sugar water, small pieces of vegetables, and dead insects. Always remove unused food before adding new food. Keep the dish on top of the can filled with water, or if you use a sponge, keep it moist. If the soil gets very dry, moisten it a little, using a dropper.

Place the observation nest in a warm place, but not in direct sunlight. After a few days you can remove the jar from the pan of water. The ants will have settled down in their new home.

Watch the activity of the ants in the nest. You may find it helpful to use a magnifying glass to get a better view of them. You may be able to see them build tunnels, keep these tunnels clean, move eggs and larvae from one place to another, and do many other things. See if you can find out how they communicate with each other.

Try some experiments with the ants. Take some out of the nest and put them in a different place, such as a jar of soil. See what happens in the nest when you put them back after a few days.

Introduce some new ants from outdoors into the nest and watch what happens.

Set up a regular time to feed the ants, and see how soon they learn when it is feeding time.

How many other experiments can you think of doing with the ants in your observation nest?

federal government, are trying to wipe out these serious pests.

▶ THE ARMY ANTS

The so-called army ants are famous the world over, though found largely in the tropics. In Africa they are known as driver ants. In the American tropics they are called legionary ants. The habits of these ants are similar. Most people are surprised to hear that some varieties of army ants are also found in the United States. But their habits are much less spectacular.

Both the driver ants and the legionary ants travel in armies of thousands, and they are bold fighters. As they travel through the forest or jungle they eat insects of all kinds and sizes. They will eat domestic animals like chickens and pigs. They may even attack wild creatures of any size, especially if the animals are injured or unable to escape. African driver ants have killed and eaten a caged leopard in one night. But army ants usually eat insects. They will feed on any insects— cockroaches, grasshoppers, spiders—that lie in their path.

A colony of legionary ants in the American tropics may have up to 150,000 workers and soldiers. They are almost 10 millimeters (⅜ inch) long. The queen may be twice as long. Unlike most queen ants, she is wingless.

The army ants do not set up permanent homes. They settle for a short time, then move on again in columns that may stretch for hundreds of meters. The common legionary ants of the American tropics march for about 17 days. During the day they search for food. At night they form a huge cluster in a hollow log, or beside a tree or stone.

At the end of the 17 days of wandering, the ants stop. They form a cluster, usually in some well-protected location. Within this cluster the queen lays thousands of eggs. The workers get food by making short raids in the area around the cluster. As the larvae grow they need more food. The workers must go out on longer and more intensive hunting raids. The period during which the eggs are laid and the young are reared lasts about 20 days. At the end of this stationary period, the ants start their wanderings again.

The American and the African army ants

Variation in size of American army ants is seen when large-jawed soldier ant is beside worker ants (*above*). American army ants hook onto one another's legs and form cluster that serves as shelter (*below*).

share an unusual feature. Although sensitive to light, some have no eyes and many others cannot see well. This may seem strange in ants that are always on the move and live by hunting. But since individuals survive only as part of a large group, a lack of vision may actually help by discouraging individual action.

Ross E. Hutchins
Author, *The Ant Realm*

See also ANIMALS: COMMUNICATION AND SOCIAL ORGANIZATION; INSECTS.

APACHE INDIANS. See INDIANS OF NORTH AMERICA.

APES. See MONKEYS, APES, AND OTHER PRIMATES.

| Bartholomew | Andrew | | Simon Peter | | Jesus | Thomas | Philip of Bethsaida | | Jude |
| James the Younger | | Judas Iscariot | | John | | James the Elder | | Matthew | | Simon the Cananaean |

This famous painting, *The Last Supper*, was painted by Leonardo da Vinci on a wall of Santa Maria delle Grazie, a church in Milan, Italy.

APOSTLES, THE

The Apostles were 12 men especially appointed by Jesus Christ "that they should be with him, and that he might send them forth to preach, and to have power to heal sicknesses, and to cast out devils." Later Jesus sent them forth two by two. He "gave them power over unclean spirits; and commanded them that they should take nothing for their journey, save a staff only; no scrip, no bread, no money in their purse."

The word "apostle" comes from a Greek word meaning "to send away." Today it is sometimes used for religious missionaries.

Christ's 12 Apostles came from different backgrounds. Four were fishermen. Matthew, a tax collector, was the only wealthy man.

Like people everywhere, the Apostles had different personalities. Peter was a dependable leader with an independent nature. James the Younger was strict and severe, but respected for his justice. Philip liked to ask questions. Christ nicknamed James the Elder and his brother John "Sons of Thunder" because they had quick tempers. Thomas is known as "Doubting Thomas" because at first

he would not believe that Christ had risen from the dead. Some of the Apostles were quiet men, content to listen and to learn. Others were impatient. Because Peter, James the Elder, and John had a deeper understanding of Jesus' teachings, they were chosen to be with Jesus at the most important times.

Following Jesus' lifetime the Apostles traveled near and far. It is believed that Thomas went to India and Andrew reached what is now Russia. The teachings of Christ were spread throughout Asia Minor and most of the Roman Empire. The experiences of some of the Apostles are recorded in the New Testament.

According to a custom of the time, some of the Apostles were given new names when they took up their new responsibilities. The 12 Apostles are usually named in this order:

Simon, renamed Peter; a fisherman. Christ said, "Thou art Peter, and upon this rock I shall build my church."

Andrew, a fisherman; brother of Simon Peter. Saint Andrew's cross is so named because of the traditional belief that Andrew died on a cross made in the form of an X. He is the patron saint of Scotland, Greece, and Russia.

James the Elder (also called James the Greater), a fisherman; son of Zebedee. James was the first to die as a martyr in Jerusalem.

John, a fisherman; brother of James the Elder; author of the Fourth Gospel. He was known as "the disciple whom Jesus loved."

Philip of Bethsaida, who, when he became an Apostle, led his friend Nathanael (renamed Bartholomew) to Christ.

Bartholomew, Philip's friend. He was the son of Talmai (Bar Talmai in Hebrew). It is thought that his new name, Bartholomew, came from Bar Talmai.

Matthew, a tax collector. He preached in Judea, and is the traditional author of the First Gospel. Tradition also says that he brought Christianity to the East.

Thomas (also called Didymus, which means "twin"). He showed great faith by offering to accompany Jesus to Jerusalem, where some sought to stone him.

James the Younger (also called James the Less, or James the Little). Some scholars say that this is the James who welcomed Saint Paul to Jerusalem when many were suspicious of Saint Paul's conversion to Christianity.

Jude, or Judas (also called Thaddaeus), brother of James the Younger (though some scholars think he was the son of James).

Simon the Cananaean, martyred in Persia. "Cananaean" means one who is zealous or eager. Simon was so named for his devotion to Judaism before becoming a Christian.

Judas Iscariot. He betrayed Jesus for 30 silver coins. When Jesus was condemned to death, Judas repented and hanged himself.

Matthias was chosen by the 11 Apostles to replace Judas Iscariot. Tradition says he brought Christianity to ancient Ethiopia and Macedonia.

Paul of Tarsus (originally named Saul) was not one of the chosen 12, but is called an Apostle and is as respected as the others.

Reviewed by JAMES I. McCORD
President, Princeton Theological Seminary

APPALACHIAN MOUNTAINS. See NORTH AMERICA.
APPENDICITIS. See DISEASES.

APPLE

The apple is the most important tree fruit of the temperate regions of the world. Apples have been grown and used as food since the dawn of history. Charred remains found in Stone Age lake dwellings in central Europe show that prehistoric people ate apples. There are carvings of apples on ancient tombs and monuments in the Middle East.

The apple appears often in the myths and folklore of ancient civilizations. In Greek mythology Hercules traveled to the end of the world to bring back the golden apples of the Hesperides. A golden apple—the apple of discord—caused a quarrel that led to the Trojan War. A Norse myth tells of magic apples that kept people young forever. The Halloween game of dipping for apples had its beginning among the ancient Celts as a way of foretelling the future.

Apples were brought to America by the earliest European settlers. At first apples were used mainly for cider, which was a popular beverage in England and northern France, where most of the early colonists came from. Cider is another name for apple juice. Hard cider is apple juice that has fermented. It contains a small percentage of alcohol—about as much as beer.

As the frontier moved westward across the continent, apple trees followed. One of the first things a settler did after clearing the land and building a cabin was to plant a few apple trees in the yard.

▶ **ORIGIN OF THE APPLE**

Although there are numerous kinds of wild, or crab, apples native to different

---

SCIENTIFIC CLASSIFICATION

FAMILY: Rosaceae (rose family).

GENUS: *Pyrus* (pear); sometimes classified as *Malus* (apple).*

SPECIFIC NAME: *Pyrus malus.**

RELATED FRUITS: Pear (close); peach, plum, cherry (less close).

There are many species of crab apple. Nine species are native to North America, of which the best known are *P. ioensis* and *P. baccata.*

* Scientists do not agree on the proper name for the apple.

parts of the world, the kind from which the familiar cultivated apple developed came from the mountains of southwestern and central Asia, between the regions of the Black and Caspian seas and eastward from there. This ancestor of the modern apple, which still grows wild, is smaller and more sour than our present fine varieties, but the tree on which it grows resembles our present cultivated trees.

People selected the best fruit from the wild trees for eating and used seed from the better fruit for planting. In this way the quality of apples was gradually improved.

▶ VARIETIES

A number of distinct varieties of apple were raised in the lands north of the Mediterranean Sea several centuries before the time of Jesus. Since then thousands of varieties have been named and grown in different parts of the world. Most of these have now disappeared from commercial production, although many different varieties are still grown in various parts of the world.

In the United States and Canada, about 25 varieties are grown extensively, although there are small plantings of many other kinds. Apple varieties must meet certain requirements before growers are willing to invest time, money, and labor in them. First of all, the trees must be productive. Second, the fruit must be attractive-looking and of good size. Its flavor and texture must appeal to most people. Finally, the fruit must keep well in storage. This is why so few varieties are grown on a large scale.

Nearly all our present important varieties originated as chance seedlings. Since about 1900 scientific breeding work has resulted in the development of some fine new varieties. Most of these are not yet widely grown.

The leading variety of apple in the United States is the Delicious, which originated from

a seedling tree found on a farm at Peru, Iowa, about 1881. Most of the Delicious apples are now raised in the northwest Pacific states and British Columbia, though some are grown in nearly all apple-growing regions.

The McIntosh is the leading variety in Canada, New York, and the New England states. McIntosh trees are all descended from one chance seedling found on a pioneer farm in Ontario in 1796. The original tree survived, bearing apples, until 1908, although it was badly damaged by a fire.

Other leading varieties include the Golden Delicious, Rome Beauty, Jonathan, Stayman, York Imperial, and Winesap. The Northern Spy is a favorite in Canada. Some of these varieties are also grown in Europe, Japan, South America, and Australia along with the local kinds.

▶ THE TREE

The apple grows on a medium-sized tree. In good soils unpruned trees will reach 9 to 12 meters (30 to 40 feet) in height. But when apples are grown for market, the trees are pruned to prevent them from becoming this tall. The trees in most commercial orchards are kept to a height of less than 6 meters (20 feet).

The apple tree is "rounded"—that is, it is about as broad as it is high. The branches are twisted and spreading. The fruit of most commercial varieties is red, but there are also varieties that bear yellow, green, russet, and striped fruit. Apple wood is dense, hard, and heavy. Because the tree has a short trunk and many branches, it is not used for lumber. Apple wood is sometimes used for carved ornaments, in furniture, and in lasts, or forms, for making shoes.

Apple trees generally do not begin to blossom and bear fruit until they are 5 to 8 years old. They reach maximum production at about 20 years, and commercial orchards are generally replaced when the trees are 35 to 40 years old. Although the trees would live much longer, the fruit produced on old trees is generally smaller and poorer in appearance and more expensive to care for.

▶ MANAGING THE APPLE ORCHARD

A great deal of intensive work must be performed in the commercial orchard. Each year

---

Was the "apple" in the Garden of Eden really an apple?

The Bible simply speaks of the fruit of the tree of knowledge, without naming any particular fruit. The apple probably came to be the popular symbol for the fruit of the knowledge of good and evil because of the magical qualities attributed to it in many mythologies. Some archeologists now believe apricots or quinces may have been the "apples" in the Garden of Eden.

the trees should be pruned, usually in late winter. This prevents them from becoming too tall or too thick and bushy and results in larger, better-colored fruit. Proper pruning also makes it easier to spray the trees and pick the fruit. The trees must be fertilized to make them grow and bear properly. Nearly all apple orchards need nitrogen fertilizers. Other elements such as potassium, magnesium, zinc, and boron may also be needed.

Frost, insect pests, and fungus diseases are among the most serious problems the apple grower faces. Open apple blossoms are killed when the temperature drops a few degrees below freezing, and crops are often lost because of spring frosts that kill the blossoms. Commercial orchards generally are planted on slopes or high ground to reduce this danger, since cold air tends to sink. Some apple growers protect their orchards with heaters where frost occurs in blossom time.

Many insects and diseases attack the apple tree. One of the worst is the codling moth, which lays its eggs on or near the fruit. When the eggs hatch, the larvae bore into the fruit and a "wormy" apple results. Other insect pests include scales, aphids, and mites. Certain fungi also spoil the appearance of the fruit or cause it to rot.

Repeated spraying is necessary to keep the fruit free of insects and diseases because these appear at different times of the year. In some

Fragrant white blossoms in the spring (*right*) are followed by shiny, colorful fruit in the fall. Modern commercial apple-growing is a large-scale business. Spraying is too big a job to be done by hand. Below, a powerful machine blasts spray at trees to cover them thoroughly.

areas 12 to 14 sprays per year may be necessary. Sprays must be applied at just the right time for each pest.

▶ PROPAGATION

Apple trees do not "breed true." That is, new trees grown from seeds do not produce fruit that is exactly like the parent tree's. Trees for orchards are therefore produced by budding or grafting. A bud or a short piece of a twig taken from a parent tree is inserted into a young seedling tree so that it grows and forms the top of the new tree. The new tree

LEADING APPLE VARIETIES OF THE UNITED STATES AND CANADA

BALDWIN
canning, home cooking

McINTOSH
dessert, home cooking

ROME BEAUTY
mainly canning, cooking

CORTLAND
dessert, home cooking

NORTHERN SPY
dessert, cooking; late keeper

YELLOW NEWTOWN
dessert, canning; late keeper

GOLDEN DELICIOUS
dessert, canning, home cooking

RED DELICIOUS
mainly dessert

YORK IMPERIAL
commercial canning

JONATHAN
dessert, cooking

RHODE ISLAND GREENING
commercial canning

WINESAP
dessert, canning, cooking; late keeper

will then produce fruit exactly like that of the tree from which the bud was taken.

By budding or grafting onto certain kinds of roots, it is possible to produce trees that never become very large. Such trees are called dwarfs. Dwarf trees, besides being easier to spray, prune, and harvest, usually bear fruit earlier. Dwarf trees are popular for home planting and are used commercially on a large scale. Since they can be planted together, the yield of fruit per acre is generally increased by using dwarf trees.

▶ HARVESTING AND STORAGE

Some varieties of apples mature in midsummer, others in late fall. Most kinds are ready for picking in September and October. The fruit must be picked by hand and carefully handled, for it will spoil if it is bruised.

The fruit is firm when picked but softens quite rapidly after picking unless it is put into cold storage. Apples will soften as much in one day at room temperature as they will in ten days in cold storage. Therefore, if the fruit is to be held for winter or early spring markets, it must be put at once in cold storage and cooled rapidly to about 0°C (32°F). It is held there until time for marketing.

Apples will keep even better in "controlled atmosphere" storage. The fruit is put into airtight rooms, and the oxygen level in the room is reduced from the 20 percent present in normal air to about 3 percent. At the same time the carbon dioxide content, normally present only in trace amounts, is increased to 2 to 5 percent. (The exact figures vary for different kinds of apples.) This slows down the life processes of the fruit cells and helps keep the fruit from softening. The controlled atmosphere, together with low temperatures, can keep some kinds of apples in good eating condition up to a year. But very few apples are stored more than nine months.

▶ LEADING APPLE AREAS

Apples can be grown in nearly all the temperate areas of the earth. Most kinds can endure winter temperatures down to −29°C (−20°F), and some kinds can withstand temperatures as low as −40°C (−40°F).

In the United States, Washington, New York, Michigan, Pennsylvania, and California are leading producers of apples. In Canada,

Apple pickers with long ladders harvest the ripe fruit. Canvas-bottomed pails protect apples from bruising.

British Columbia, Ontario, and Nova Scotia lead. Apples are the leading tree-fruit crop in most of Europe. Australia, New Zealand, Japan, Chile, and Argentina also produce many apples. Apples do not thrive in the tropics, for the trees require a period of cold and dormancy to grow and bear fruit properly.

▶ USES OF APPLES

Apples have many uses. They are eaten fresh, cooked, dried, and canned. Their juice is used for drinking and for making vinegar. Apples furnish valuable minerals and vitamins and add bulk to the diet. Fresh apples help clean the teeth and reduce tooth decay.

Almost 49,000,000 metric tons (160,000,-000 bushels) of apples are produced each year in commercial orchards in the United States alone. About 60 percent of the crop is sold as fresh fruit. The rest is canned commercially as applesauce and sliced apples, is frozen, or is crushed and pressed for apple juice or vinegar. Apple pie is a favorite dessert in the United States and Canada.

Reviewed by MORRIS INGLE
West Virginia University

See also FRUITGROWING.

APRIL

No one really knows how April, the fourth month, got its name. Some people think April was named for Aphrodite, the Greek goddess of love. Others think that the name came from a Latin verb meaning "to open" or a Greek word meaning "the opening." In fact, the Greeks called the season of spring "the opening."

In the Northern Hemisphere spring officially starts on March 21 (the vernal equinox). But April really ushers in the spring. It is a month of growth for all nature. The winter snows have melted, and plants begin to appear. Early spring flowers, such as the daisy, forsythia, lady's-slipper, primrose, and Bermuda lily (also called the Easter lily), burst into full bloom. Pear and cherry blossoms make a brief appearance. April showers nourish the young plants.

For the animal kingdom, too, April is a month of awakening. The animals that have slept all winter appear dressed for spring. The weasel's winter coat of white fur is now brown. The snake sheds his old skin for a new one. Stags are busy rubbing the velvet coating from their new horns.

Birds have returned from the warmer climates to build nests and lay eggs. In the woods newly born animals are taking their first wobbly steps. Speckled fawns, copying their mothers, learn what to eat in order to grow strong.

In the northern United States and Canada, April is a time for planting, spring-cleaning, and the opening of the baseball season. But in the Southern Hemisphere things are just the opposite. April is the beginning of fall. It is the end of the apple harvest and the beginning of winter-wheat planting.

Some April festivals are celebrated throughout the world. It is a month for the nonsense of April Fool's Day. But it is also a time for the religious holidays of Easter and Passover.

For all the world April is a month of work and play. Man and nature alike are getting ready for new seasons.

Place in year: 4th month.
Number of days: 30.
Flower: Sweet pea and daisy.
Birthstone: Diamond.
Zodiac signs:
Aries, the Ram
(March 21-April 19)
and
Taurus, the Bull
(April 20-May 20).

Holidays

April

1 April Fool's Day.

4 Hungarian Liberation Day.

6 Army Day (United States entry into World War I on Allied side, 1917).

14 Pan American Day.

21 San Jacinto Day (Texas victory over Mexican Army, 1836, which led to Texan independence).

Holidays that may occur in either April or March: Palm Sunday, Holy Week and Easter, Passover.

Historical Firsts

April

2 United States Mint established, 1792.

3 Pony express begun in United States, 1860.

12 Soviet Major Yuri A. Gagarin orbited the earth, 1961.

24 United States Library of Congress established, 1800.

30 George Washington inaugurated as 1st president of the United States, 1789.

Birthdays

April

1 William Harvey, English physician, 1578.
Otto von Bismarck, Prussian statesman, 1815.
Sergei Rachmaninoff, Russian composer, 1873.

2 Charlemagne, first Holy Roman emperor, 742.
Hans Christian Andersen, Danish writer, 1805.
Emile Zola, French writer, 1840.
Walter P. Chrysler, American industrialist, 1875.

3 Washington Irving, American writer, 1783.
John Burroughs, American naturalist, 1837.

4 Dorothea Lynde Dix, American prison reformer, 1802.

5 Elihu Yale, benefactor of Yale University, 1648.
Joseph Lister, English physician, 1827.
Algernon Swinburne, English poet, 1837.
Booker T. Washington, American educator, 1856.
Chester Bowles, American statesman, 1901.

7 William Wordsworth, English poet, 1770.

9 Charles P. Steinmetz, American electrical engineer, 1865.

10 Matthew C. Perry, American naval officer, 1794.
William Booth, English founder of the Salvation Army, 1829.
Joseph Pulitzer, American newspaperman, 1847.

11 Charles Evans Hughes, Chief Justice of the United States, 1862.
Dean Acheson, American statesman, 1893.

12 Henry Clay, American statesman, 1777.

13 Thomas Jefferson, 3rd president of the United States, 1743.

14 Arnold Toynbee, English historian, 1889.

15 Leonardo da Vinci, Italian artist, 1452.
Henry James, American writer, 1843.

16 Anatole France, French writer, 1844.
Wilbur Wright, American inventor, 1867.
Charles Chaplin, American actor, 1889.

17 Nikita Khrushchev, Russian premier, 1894.

20 Marcus Aurelius, Roman emperor, A.D. 121.
Adolf Hitler, German dictator, 1889.

21 Charlotte Brontë, English writer, 1816.
Elizabeth II, Queen of England, 1926.

22 Isabella I, Queen of Castile and Aragon, 1451.
Immanuel Kant, German philosopher, 1724.
Lenin, Russian Bolshevik leader, 1870.

23 William Shakespeare, English writer, 1564.
James Buchanan, 15th president of the United States, 1791.

25 Oliver Cromwell, English general and statesman, 1599.
Guglielmo Marconi, Italian inventor, 1874.

26 John James Audubon, American ornithologist and artist, 1785.

27 Edward Gibbon, English historian, 1785.
Samuel Morse, American inventor, 1791.
Ulysses S. Grant, 18th president of the United States, 1822.

28 James Monroe, 5th president of the United States, 1758.

29 Duke of Wellington, English general, 1769.
Harold C. Urey, American physicist, 1893.

30 Juliana, Queen of the Netherlands, 1909.

Historical Events

April

4 American flag adopted, 1818.
North Atlantic Treaty signed, 1949.

6 Church of Jesus Christ of Latter-Day Saints (Mormon) founded, 1830.

8 Ponce de León claimed Florida for Spain, 1513.

10 London and Plymouth companies chartered by King James I of England, 1606.
United States patent system established, 1790.

11 Napoleon I abdicated, 1814.

12 Civil War began at Fort Sumter, 1861.

13 Edict of Nantes freed the French Huguenots, 1598.

14 Abraham Lincoln shot by John Wilkes Booth, 1865.

18 Paul Revere's ride, 1775.
Great earthquake and fire in San Francisco, 1906.

20 United States abandoned the gold standard, 1933.

21 Legendary founding of Rome, 753 B.C.

22 Oklahoma Territory opened to settlers, 1889.

24 British burned Washington, D.C., 1814.

28 Mutiny of the British ship Bounty, 1789.

30 Louisiana Purchase, 1803.
Louisiana became the 18th state, 1812.
War in Vietnam ended, 1975.

AQUARIUMS

Even a beginner can have a successful home aquarium, with crystal-clear water, beautiful plants, and colorful fishes. There are just a few principles involved in keeping an aquarium. If you learn what they are and follow them, you will be able to avoid the mistakes that people often make when they set up an aquarium.

▶ CHOICE AND LOCATION OF THE TANK

It is best to buy a rectangular tank that is at most about 7 or 8 centimeters (3 inches) higher than it is wide. Globes or tall, narrow tanks are not good because there is too little water surface open to the air. A wider tank has more open water surface, and the water can take in more oxygen. This is important for the health of the fish. The water takes in oxygen from the air, and the fish breathe this oxygen through their gills. Fish give off a gas called carbon dioxide, just as people do when they breathe. The carbon dioxide given off by the fish must escape into the air through the surface of the water, or the fish will suffocate.

It is important to keep metal out of a fish tank. The slightest bit of metal in the water can be poisonous to fish. Paints, soaps, detergents, and certain plastics and chemicals must also be kept out of the tank. Insecticides are especially deadly to fish. Limestone products, such as marble chips, seashells, coral, and coral sand, should be avoided. They dissolve and make the water too hard. The best minerals for use in an aquarium are quartz, sandstone, and granite.

For protection, a glass cover should be kept on the tank. Do not worry that the fish will not get enough air. No tank cover fits so tightly that it keeps out the necessary air.

Finding the proper location for the tank is important, too. An aquarium should not stand in a drafty spot or near a radiator. Sudden changes in temperature are bad for fish.

Direct sunlight should be avoided except for short periods of time. Artificial lighting is just as satisfactory for fish as daylight. But too much light encourages the growth of tiny plants called algae, which turn the water green. Too much direct sunlight may also overheat the water.

A tank filled with water is very heavy. A 50-liter (13-gallon) tank weighs more than 50 kilograms (110 pounds) when filled. That is why the aquarium needs a firm resting place and why a filled tank should never be moved. It is impossible to move a full tank without cracking its glass or making it leak.

▶ GRAVEL, WATER, AND PLANTS

The gravel, water, and plants put in the tank are all important to the health of the fish and the beauty of the aquarium.

Gravel or sand is not necessary except when using rooted plants. But it makes a more natural-looking setting for the fish. Material about the size of bird gravel or a little larger is best. Too fine a sand packs tightly and holds back the growth of plants. If gravel is used, it should be carefully washed.

The most important single element of an aquarium is the water, and unless it is kept in good condition, neither fish nor plants will stay healthy. The best water for fish is water in which they have already lived. This is called "conditioned water." Fish are unusual in the following respect. The living quarters of most domestic animals must be cleaned regularly. But the water in a standing aquarium need not be changed. The waste products of the fish actually make the water more suitable for them to live in.

People who keep aquariums speak of two kinds of dirt in a tank: clean dirt and dirty dirt. Clean dirt means the waste products of the fish themselves. This need not be removed. Dirty dirt means such things as uneaten food and the bodies of dead fish. This kind of dirt should be removed.

Beginners will have to start with plain tap water in the tank. Letting it stand until it comes to room temperature will get rid of any chlorine that may have been added to the water to purify it. Chlorine is harmful to fish. The fish may be placed in the water as soon as it has reached room temperature. At first the water may look slightly cloudy or milky. But this is typical of water in a new aquarium. If the fish are fed very little for the first two weeks, the water should clear up and stay crystal clear for an unlimited time.

Plants are important in a home aquarium but not so important as many people believe. Plants do not "balance" an aquarium by pro-

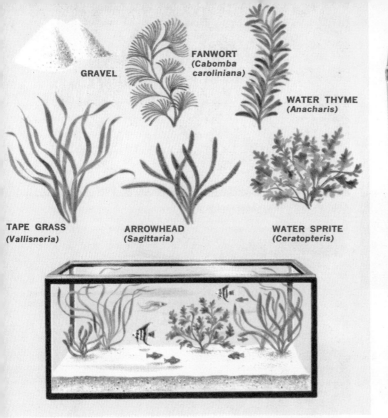

GRAVEL

FANWORT
(Cabomba
caroliniana)

WATER THYME
(Anacharis)

TAPE GRASS
(Vallisneria)

ARROWHEAD
(Sagittaria)

WATER SPRITE
(Ceratopteris)

Sand or gravel about the size of bird gravel and plants are important in a home aquarium.

It is better to have too few fish in the tank than too many. Overcrowding can be fatal.

viding the fish with all the oxygen they need and using up all the carbon dioxide they give off. In spite of everything you may have heard, fish in the usual aquarium do as well without plants as they do with plants, as far as breathing is concerned.

Plants add oxygen to the water and use up carbon dioxide only when they are actively making food. Green plants make their own food by taking in the carbon dioxide and changing it chemically so that they are able to use it. Then they give off oxygen. This process, called photosynthesis, takes place only in the presence of sunlight.

But underwater plants add a great deal to the beauty of an aquarium. Plants that grow in water also provide more natural surroundings for the fish. The fish can hide in the leaves of the plants and lay their eggs on them. In addition, well-planted tanks are less apt to develop green water.

Remember that plants in an aquarium should be placed along the back of the tank so that they make a background for the fish.

The amount of light the tank receives has much to do with the kinds of plants that will grow well in it. It is best to experiment with several different types to discover which ones will do best. Plants for an aquarium will be found in shops that sell fish and other aquarium supplies. Fanwort (*Cabomba caroliniana*) and waterweed or water thyme (*Anacharis* or *Elodea*) require strong light. Tape grass or eelgrass (*Vallisneria*), arrowhead (*Sagittaria*), and floating fern or water sprite (*Ceratopteris*) need somewhat less. Cryptocorynes, which have broad, heart-shaped leaves, do well with still less light. Tanks that depend on artificial light will require a light for 8 or 9 hours a day.

▶ FEEDING THE FISH

More pet fish die from overfeeding than from any other cause. Cats and canaries must be fed every day, but not fish. If you feed them every day, the uneaten food accumulates in the tank. It blackens the sand and produces harmful gases and other poisons. Most fish can go for a week without your feeding them because they feed on microscopic plants and animals that live in the aquarium.

Fish should be fed only three times a week.

Cardinal tetra.

Pyjama Apogon.

Common veiltail goldfishes.

Killifish (*Nothobranchius rachovi*).

Black scarftail guppy.

Rock beauty (*Holocanthus tricolor*).

Red tuxedo swordtails.

At a single feeding they should be given only as much food as they can eat up completely in 10 minutes. You can judge the correct amount by feeding the fish from the flat end of a toothpick and standing by to see that each bit of food is totally eaten up before giving any more.

Snails or catfishes can be added to the tank to act as scavengers. They will eat a certain amount of leftover food and decaying leaves of underwater plants, but no scavenger alive can handle the problem of overfeeding if it goes on day after day.

When feeding fish, use as many different foods as possible. In addition to the dried foods that are already packaged, try finely chopped raw lean meat, liver, raw fish, shrimp, clams, the yolk of hard-boiled eggs, cooked oatmeal, boiled spinach, and fresh lettuce. **Tropical fishes** and many kinds of fishes that live in colder water relish all these foods.

Fish also enjoy some living food once a week. In a pet shop you can find live *Daphnia* (water fleas), enchytraeids (white worms), and *Tubifex* (red worms). Earthworms, chopped up for small fish, are excellent.

▶ **SELECTING THE FISHES**

Before setting out to buy fishes, it is important to understand that some of them can live only in water that is kept at a certain temperature. The water in which many tropical fishes live must be kept at a temperature that ranges from 22 to 27°C (72 to 80°F). For certain tropical fishes, an electric heater with a thermostat is required to control the temperature of the water.

Goldfish usually do not need any temperature control. Minnows, certain darters, sunfishes, catfishes, suckers, sticklebacks, gars, and mud minnows do not need it either. But they must not have sudden changes in temperature. None of these fishes should be kept in a room in which the temperature drops more than 5°C (10°F) at night.

When buying fishes for the first time, it is best to get the less expensive kinds. The **guppy**, a small tropical fish that bears living young, is probably the best of all fishes for beginners because of its color, strength, and the number of young fish it bears. Although it is a tropical fish, the guppy does not need specially treated water.

Other strong fishes that are not quite as sturdy as guppies are the brightly colored platyfishes, swordtails, and black mollies. They are in the same family as guppies and also have living young. Tetras, *Corydoras* catfishes, Siamese fighting fish, and angelfish are also good fish for beginners to raise.

Not all fishes get along well together. Many, like the sunfishes, crappies, paradise fish, and Siamese fighting fish, are fighters, especially at breeding time. Guppies, platyfishes, danios, tetras, and *Corydoras* catfishes are the best fish to buy if you plan to keep several kinds in one tank.

Be sure your tank is large enough for the number of fish you plan to buy. Next to overfeeding, overcrowding kills most pet fish. When fish come to the top of the tank gasping, it is a sign of overcrowding. For goldfish a safe rule is to allow 3 liters of water for each centimeter (2 gallons for each inch) of the fish's length, not counting the tail. North American fishes, such as sunfishes or minnows, need at least this much water. For tropical fishes allow one fourth of this amount. It is better to start an aquarium with too few fish and add to it gradually than it is to start with a crowded tank.

When one of the fish acts sick, it should be put into a small aquarium by itself so that the other fish do not become sick, too. The most common disease of tropical fish is white spots, or ichthyophthirius ("ich" for short). It is hard to cure a sick fish, but you can ask about remedies at your pet shop.

If there are both male and female fish in the tank, the female may lay eggs. They often look like seed pearls, and settle on the plants. These eggs should be placed in a separate aquarium, too, before the larger fish eat them up. This is done by taking out the part of the plant on which the eggs have settled and putting it in another tank. When the eggs develop into tiny fish, they may be fed very small amounts of hard-boiled egg yolk, crushed fine.

If you follow these suggestions, you should be able to start a successful home aquarium of your own. You can have many moments of pleasure watching your fish swim lazily along or dart quickly about in your tank.

JAMES W. ATZ
Former Curator, New York Zoological Society

AQUEDUCTS

Many places need more water than they have naturally. This is particularly true for big cities and for farms in dry areas. Usually, water is brought to such cities and farms by means of aqueducts. An aqueduct is a channel built to carry water from one place to another. The word "aqueduct" comes from the Latin word *aquaeductus,* which means "carrier of water."

The ancient Romans built huge aqueducts that ran for long distances through tunnels and over bridges. Eleven aqueducts were built to bring water to the city of Rome. Others were built all over the Roman Empire. Some of these Roman aqueducts are still standing in Italy, France, Spain, and Greece. About 500 years before any of the Roman aqueducts were built, the Assyrians built an aqueduct that carried water 80 kilometers (50 miles) to their capital city, Nineveh.

Modern aqueducts are usually long systems of pipes, ditches, canals, and tunnels. In some cases, the water moves downhill under the force of gravity. In other cases, the water is pumped along level ground or upward.

One of the major aqueducts in the United States is the California Aqueduct, which carries water from northern California to southern California. It is about 720 kilometers (450 miles) long and consists mostly of concrete-lined canals and pipelines. Pumping plants move water into the aqueduct west of San Francisco. When it crosses the Tehachapi Mountains, the water is pumped up to about 945 meters (3,100 feet) above sea level. It then passes through a series of four tunnels that are lined with concrete and supported by an outer steel shield. On the south side of the mountains, the aqueduct branches and runs downhill toward reservoirs to the north and west of Los Angeles.

AQUINAS, SAINT THOMAS (1225?–1274)

Saint Thomas Aquinas, patron saint of all Catholic universities, colleges, and schools, had a powerful influence on the thinking of his time. Yet as a student in Cologne, his silence in the classroom and his heavy build earned him the nickname of "dumb ox." His fellow students and professors soon discovered, however, that he was not stupid, but a deep and humble thinker.

Thomas was born in the castle of Rocca Secca near Aquino, Italy. His father was Landulf, Count of Aquino, and his mother was Theodora, Countess of Teano. He had four older brothers and several sisters. When he was 5, he was taken to the abbey of Monte Cassino for his schooling. He stayed there until he was about 13 and later was sent to the University of Naples, where he studied for 5 years.

In Naples, Thomas often went to church to pray, and when he was about 19, he entered the Dominican order. This displeased his mother, who did not wish him to enter a mendicant, or begging, order. His brothers, who were then soldiers, captured him while he was fleeing with Dominican friars and kept him prisoner for nearly 2 years. Then his family gave up trying to change his mind and let him complete his studies in Paris and Cologne.

Thomas studied under Albertus Magnus, the most renowned professor in the Dominican order. When Thomas began preaching and teaching, traveling from place to place to explain and defend Christian truth, people were more anxious to hear him than they had been to hear Albert. He was always clear, brief, accurate, and powerful in what he said.

About 1266, Thomas began writing his most famous work, the *Summa theologica,* a scientifically arranged study of theological teaching and Christian philosophy. He never finished it. On December 6, 1273, he experienced such a spiritual revelation at Mass that he could write no more. The revelation made all his writings appear as nothing to him.

Thomas died on March 7, 1274. He was made a saint in 1323 and a doctor of the Church in 1567. His writings fill 20 thick volumes and include much on Aristotle. Thomas is especially remembered for the way he always sought guidance through prayer.

HARRY J. CARGAS
Editor, *The Queen's Work*

ARABIA. See MIDDLE EAST; SAUDI ARABIA.

ARABIAN NIGHTS

Hundreds of years ago professional story-tellers in India and the Middle East made up the stories now known as *The Arabian Nights*. Later on, groups of these stories were put together. One group was translated from Arabic to French by Antoine Galland in the early 1700's. His *Mille et une nuits,* or *A Thousand and One Nights,* introduced these Oriental tales to the Western world.

All the collections have one thing in common. A heroine, Scheherazade, tells the different stories. She recites the tales for a very good reason: she must save her life.

Scheherazade was married to Sultan Shah-riyar, who had killed his first wife when she was unfaithful to him and then all his later wives in revenge against women. Scheherazade did not want to suffer the same fate. On her wedding night she began to tell her husband a story and stopped just before she reached the end. The Sultan allowed her to live another day in order to hear the end of her tale. The next night she finished the story and began another one even more fascinating than the first. Again she stopped before the ending, gaining another day of life.

And so it went, for a thousand and one nights. Finally the Sultan realized that Scheherazade was a good and faithful wife, and the couple lived happily ever after.

The stories supposedly told by Scheherazade are understandably popular. Nowhere does one find treasures more magnificent, beasts more fabulous, or magicians more cunning. For example, in "Aladdin and the Wonderful Lamp" a magician poses as a long-lost uncle to the unsuspecting Aladdin. The two leave the city and arrive at a secret place, where the magician kindles a fire, throws powder on it, and says some magic words. The earth trembles and opens, revealing a flat stone with a brass ring to raise it by. With the help of more magic words, the stone is moved and some steps appear.

"Go down," said the magician. "At the foot of those steps you will find an open door leading into three large halls. Tuck up your gown and go through them without touching anything, or you will die instantly. These halls lead into a garden of fine fruit trees. Walk on till you come to a niche in a terrace where stands a lighted lamp. Pour out the oil it contains and bring it to me." He drew a ring from his finger and gave it to Aladdin, bidding him prosper.

Aladdin found everything as the magician had said, gathered some fruit off the trees and, having got the lamp, arrived at the mouth of the cave.

The magician cried out in a great hurry, "Make haste and give me the lamp." This Aladdin refused to do until he was out of the cave. The magician flew into a terrible passion, and throwing some more powder on the fire, he said something, and the stone rolled back into its place.

The magician left Persia forever, which plainly showed that he was no uncle of Aladdin's, but a

Aladdin, snatching the lamp, said boldly, "Fetch me something to eat."

cunning sorcerer who had read in his magic books of a wonderful lamp which would make him the most powerful man in the world. Though he alone knew where to find it, he could only receive it from the hand of another. He had picked out the foolish Aladdin for this purpose, intending to get the lamp and kill him afterward.

For two days Aladdin remained in the dark, crying and lamenting. At last he clasped his hands in prayer, and in so doing rubbed the ring, which the magician had forgotten to take from him.

Immediately an enormous and frightful genie rose out of the earth, saying, "What wouldst thou with me? I am the slave of the ring and will obey thee in all things."

Aladdin fearlessly replied, "Deliver me from this place," whereupon the earth opened, and he found himself outside. As soon as his eyes could bear the light he went home, but fainted on the threshold. When he came to himself he told his mother what had passed, and showed her the lamp and the fruits he had gathered in the garden, which were in reality precious stones. He then asked for some food.

"Alas, child," she said, "I have nothing in the house, but I have spun a little cotton and will go and sell it."

Aladdin bade her keep her cotton, for he would sell the lamp instead. As it was very dirty she began to rub it, that it might fetch a higher price. Instantly a hideous genie appeared and asked what she would have.

She fainted away, but Aladdin, snatching the lamp, said boldly, "Fetch me something to eat!"

The genie returned with a silver bowl, twelve silver plates containing rich meats, two silver cups, and a bottle of wine.

Another *Arabian Nights* favorite is "The Forty Thieves." The hero, Ali Baba, is a poor woodcutter. Here is how he finds out what the forty thieves are up to.

One day, when Ali Baba was in the forest, he saw a troop of men on horseback, coming toward him in a cloud of dust. He was afraid they were robbers and climbed into a tree for safety. When they came up to him and dismounted, he counted forty of them. They unbridled their horses and tied them to trees.

The finest man among them, whom Ali Baba took to be their captain, went a little way among some bushes and said, "Open, Sesame!" so plainly that Ali Baba heard him. A door opened in the rocks and, having made the troop go in, he followed them and the door shut again of itself.

They stayed some time inside and Ali Baba, fearing they might come out and catch him, was forced to sit patiently in the tree. At last the door opened again and the forty thieves came out. As the captain went in last he came out first, and made them all pass by him; he then closed the door, saying, "Shut, Sesame!" Every man bridled his horse and mounted, the captain put himself at their head, and they returned as they came.

Then Ali Baba climbed down and went to the door concealed among the bushes and said, "Open, Sesame!" and it flew open. Ali Baba, who expected a dull, dismal place, was greatly surprised to find it large and well lighted, and hollowed by the hand of man in the form of a vault, which received the light from an opening in the ceiling. He saw rich bales of merchandise—silk stuffs, brocades, all piled together, gold and silver in heaps, and money in leather purses. He went

Ali Baba was surprised to find silk stuffs, brocades, gold, and silver.

An eagle rescues Sinbad from the valley of diamonds.

in and the door shut behind him. He did not look at the silver but brought out as many bags of gold as he thought his asses, which were browsing outside, could carry, loaded them with the bags, and hid it all with fagots. Using the words, "Shut, Sesame!" he closed the door and went home.

One of the most famous *Arabian Nights* stories, "Sinbad the Sailor," tells of seven voyages made by Sinbad, a wealthy merchant. On one journey he is trapped in a valley strewn with diamonds. Here Sinbad describes his escape.

At last, overcome with weariness, I sat down upon a rock, but I had hardly closed my eyes when I was startled by something which fell to the ground with a thud close beside me.

It was a huge piece of fresh meat, and as I stared at it several more pieces rolled over the cliffs in different places. I had always thought that the stories the sailors told of the famous valley of diamonds, and of the cunning way which some merchants had devised for getting at the precious stones, were mere travellers' tales invented to give pleasure to the hearers, but now I perceived that they were surely true.

These merchants came to the valley at the time when the eagles, which keep their eyries in the rocks, had hatched their young. The merchants then threw great lumps of meat into the valley. These, falling with so much force upon the diamonds, were sure to take up some of the precious stones with them, when the eagles pounced upon the meat and carried it off to their nests to feed their hungry broods. Then the merchants, scaring away the parent birds with shouts and outcries, would secure their treasures.

Until this moment I had looked upon the valley as my grave, for I had seen no possibility of getting out of it alive, but now I took courage and began to devise a means of escape. I began by picking up all the largest diamonds I could find and storing them carefully in the leathern wallet which had held my provisions; this I tied securely to my belt. I then chose the piece of meat which seemed most suited to my purpose, and with the aid of my turban bound it firmly to my back; this done I lay down upon my face and awaited the coming of the eagles. I soon heard the flapping of their mighty wings above me, and had the satisfaction of feeling one of them seize upon my piece of meat and me with it, and rise slowly toward his nest, into which he presently dropped me.

Luckily for me the merchants were on the watch and, setting up their usual outcries, they rushed to the nest scaring away the eagle. Their amazement was great when they discovered me, also their disappointment, and with one accord they fell to abusing me for having robbed them of their usual profit.

Reviewed by CAROLYN W. FIELD
The Free Library of Philadelphia

ARBITRATION. See INTERNATIONAL RELATIONS; LABOR AND MANAGEMENT.

ARBOR DAY. See HOLIDAYS.

Painting from Mayan Indian vase from Guatemala.

Pottery shards (fragments) from Anatolia.

This selection of artifacts is from various cultures and periods. Some of these objects were decorative works of art; others were simple everyday objects. Some of these artifacts hint at how people lived; some give direct evidence. Together they are typical of what archeologists study to put together a picture of past cultures.

Egyptian wooden statuette.

Harp from Mesopotamia.

Centuries-old bird-feather cape from Peru.

Early Greek safety pin.

Pompeian mosaic, made of colored stones.

ARCHEOLOGY

Archeologists are detectives who investigate the past. They are interested not in crimes and criminals but in discovering how people used to live.

Using all the clues available, archeologists try to piece together a picture of the people they are investigating. The goal is to learn what sort of environment the people lived in. If the people lived in houses, the archeologist wants to know how they built and furnished their houses. The archeologist is also interested in what they ate, how they obtained and prepared food, and what kind of tools they used. The archeologist tries to discover something about their relations with neighbors—whether they were friendly and exchanged goods or were enemies and fought each other—and something about their customs and about their religious and political practices.

▶ THE STUDY OF PHYSICAL REMAINS

The word **archeology** comes from two old Greek words—*archaios* ("ancient") and *logos* ("study" or "talk"). From these two words you can see that "archeology" means the study of the past. Archeologists base their study on physical remains—the objects that people leave behind. They may find an arrowhead, a stone axe, or a clay tablet with writing on it. These objects are called **artifacts**, and archeologists study them for clues to how people lived in the past. Archeologists also find animal and plant remains. A charred basket full of seeds, a burned wooden post, or the bones of animals can tell the archeologist something about the physical environment the people lived in, what they ate, and perhaps how they got their food.

Some archeologists are concerned only with early peoples who had not discovered how to write. These are the peoples that we know the least about. But some ancient peoples left written records that tell about their times. Archeologists may excavate places where such people lived.

Together, archeologists and historians who can read the writings piece together a picture of the people—the archeologists study the physical remains, and the historians study the writings.

▶ KINDS OF ARCHEOLOGISTS

When you think of an archeologist, you may think of a person in a sun helmet who digs up gold and mummies. You may think of someone who works with the Indian arrowheads or pueblos of the southwestern United States. These people are both archeologists, but each has specialized in something that is of personal interest.

Archeologists usually decide as students what they want to specialize in. Sometimes it is a particular region or people. They may be interested in the Western Hemisphere—perhaps in the Indians of the American Southwest or the ancient Aztecs of Mexico. They may choose a specialty in the Eastern Hemisphere—the Biblical peoples of the Middle East, the ancient Egyptians, or the classical Greeks and Romans. Often archeologists decide to study a particular time period or a particular problem. The interest may be in the time when people were using stone tools or when people first learned how to plant and grow their own food. Or the archeologist may be interested in the problem of how cities first began or how writing was invented. Most archeologists read with interest about what goes on in areas that are not their own.

Of course, there are differences in what archeologists must study to become specialists in their fields. A classical archeologist interested in ancient Greece or Rome will study much art history, classical literature, ancient Greek and Latin, and history. Students interested in prehistory (that is, before writing was invented) will spend their time studying methods of excavation and analysis, as well as anthropology. (Anthropology is the science that is concerned with how people developed over the years. It studies the different social customs that existed in the past and those that are present today in various parts of the world.)

▶ WHY ARCHEOLOGY EXISTS

There are many reasons for the existence of archeology. People have always been curious about how other people lived in the past. They have wanted to know how certain skills and practices developed. For example, how and why did people first start writing, and where did the alphabet come from? When did people start using metal instead of stone to

Statuette from Egyptian tomb shows man making loaves of bread much as many people around the world still do.

Here are two great archeological discoveries of the past 100 years or so. One of the most famous discoveries was made by Heinrich Schliemann, who excavated the site of ancient Troy, basing his search on his reading of Homer's *Iliad*. Illustration above shows earliest digging at the site. The great mound at Ur, when cleared, turned out to be a ziggurat, or temple tower (*below*); it has helped to reveal much about early civilization of Mesopotamia.

Model of original ziggurat.

make tools? And how did people begin to develop certain forms of organization—such as kinship and governments? People have been fascinated by such questions for a long time.

Archeologists can study the way people have behaved over thousands of years. Such a long time range allows archeologists to see the many similarities between ourselves and the people of long ago. For example, thousands of years ago bread was made from flour that was ground from wheat, mixed with water, and then baked near an open fire. Today we may buy our bread in supermarkets, but it is still made chiefly of flour and water. There are many examples like this. In studying them, we come to understand ourselves and our own problems better.

▶ HISTORY OF ARCHEOLOGY

Archeology as we know it today is a young science. But for several hundred years people have been interested in digging up the past.

Around 1770, Thomas Jefferson excavated an Indian burial mound in Virginia and carefully wrote down what was contained in the mound. Jefferson was probably the first American digger who could be called scientific. He not only wrote down what was coming out of the ground but also noted the order in which the objects were found. Other people could

Site at Higgins Flat, in New Mexico (*left*), was only slight mound that meant little except to archeologists. Excavation uncovered an Indian pueblo, shown in photo at right.

then read his report and understand what he had found and where. This kind of careful reporting is extremely important in archeology, but more than 100 years passed before it became the generally accepted thing to do.

Another famous man with an interest in archeology was Napoleon Bonaparte. When he made his conquering expedition to Egypt, he took along skilled artists and scientists as well as his army. He wanted these people to investigate, record, and draw all the artifacts of ancient Egypt that they could find. He established a place for studying artifacts in Cairo. The objects were meant for the Louvre museum in Paris. But because of an English victory over the French in 1801, the artifacts all went to the British Museum in London.

Both Jefferson and Napoleon were ahead of their time in archeology. Many important finds were made in the 1800's, but most of them were not recorded as carefully as the finds of these two men. Many people working at this time had no formal training in archeology. Some were European government officials who were working in foreign countries such as Iraq, India, or Egypt. They became interested in archeology as a hobby. Some were wealthy people who could afford to organize and conduct their own expeditions. Sometimes these excavations were conducted like fancy picnics—especially in England and France, where there were many Roman ruins dating from the time when Rome ruled Britain and Gaul. Lovely mosaic floors (made of tiny bits of colored stones), Roman burial grounds, and the ruins of villas were all fascinating to

the picnic-diggers. But these people viewed their finds only as pretty or curious objects. They gave little thought to the fact that the objects and their positions might be clues to understanding the lives of the people who had made them.

Archeologists must know the order in which things have come out of the ground and which groups of things were found together. Only then can they accurately reconstruct the scene of life in the past. No detective wants the clues removed from the scene of the crime before they can be studied in their relationship to one another. And no archeologist can use clues that have been removed and mixed up.

▶ **CHOOSING A PLACE TO DIG**

Archeology today is not at all what it was at the time of Jefferson, Napoleon, or the picnic-diggers. Archeologists today choose as students what they want to specialize in. They choose a specific problem to work on and a geographic area where they may find the answers. The area may be Europe, with the beautifully painted caves of southern France and Spain or the Roman ruins of Britain. Or it may be Asia, which holds much Biblical material—as well as traces of the first farmers, who lived long before Biblical times. In Africa some archeologists search for signs of the first humans, and others study Egyptian pyramids. In the Western Hemisphere, they investigate the many kinds of American Indians who lived in straw huts, mud houses, or tepees—depending on their part of the country and the tribe to which they belonged. In Mexico an archeologist can work with the ancient Aztec civilization. And in what are now Guatemala and Yucatán, the Mayans once had an extensive civilization, as did the Incas of Peru.

How an Archeologist Finds a Site

Once archeologists have defined the questions they want to answer and chosen the place where they think the answers will be found, they must obtain permission from the government of that country. Next, a **site** must be picked. A site can be any place where people in the past have lived, worked, built something, buried someone, or done anything that has left a trace. It may be in a cave or in the open. The national museum of the country (or, in the United States, the museum of the state) may make suggestions. It may know of a site that might yield artifacts from the period of time in which the archeologist is interested. Or perhaps another archeologist who is interested in a different period has found such a site and will give it up. But usually the archeologist and the staff must go out and search for a site themselves.

The search may begin with a study of aerial photographs of an area in which the archeologists are interested. They know that people of long ago had to have water and so probably built their villages along or near banks of rivers. These rivers may still exist today, or there may be simply the dried-up beds of what once were rivers. But the old beds, like the rivers, will show up in a detailed aerial photograph. The archeologist may decide to start the search for a site near the rivers or the old riverbeds. If so, the team sets out, probably in jeeps if the country is rough and the roads are bad or few.

What Remains at a Site

A mound like those found in the Middle East is a good example. People of long ago generally built their houses of wood, reed, stone, unbaked mud, or mud brick. In heavy rain or wind storms, these houses gradually melted down or fell in. But the houses had been built in a certain place for a reason. The place was close to water or good land or was easy to defend. And as other people came along, they also liked the location and built their houses in the same spot. Houses kept falling in, and people kept building new houses in the same place. Gradually a mound of earth and artifacts rose up above the level of the surrounding ground. The mounds do not look like natural hills. In some cases, if the water supply has remained good, there may still be a village on top of a mound. But usually a change in water supply, an attack by neighbors, or some other mishap drove away the people who lived in a village hundreds or thousands of years ago. All that remains to be seen is a mound itself—an unnatural hump on the landscape.

All the people who lived on these mounds did some digging, perhaps to make a foundation for a new house or to bury garbage. In doing this, they dug up pieces of pottery or tools from the layers of houses below.

Mayan Indian tomb from Palenque, Mexico.

Then, when people no longer lived on the mound, nearby farmers came. They plowed the earth for crops, turning it over and mixing it more. Because of all this, a few artifacts from the various layers of the mound worked up to the surface. They lie in the fields and pastures of present-day farmers.

When archeologists are out looking for a site, they ask farmers whether they have noticed any hills with stray bits of pots and tools. If so, the farmers may take the archeologists to look at the places where the artifacts were seen. Otherwise, the archeological team must carefully examine the area in which it is interested, traveling by car, by donkey, and on foot.

Archeologists seek sites with artifacts that look as though they belonged to the people or the time range that interests them. When some are found, a site is chosen for digging. Part of the archeologist's training was to come to know the great variety of things that men and women made in the past. Just as you can tell the difference between an automobile made years ago and one made today, so can archeologists recognize broken bits and pieces of artifacts made at different times. For instance, if the people they are interested in had not yet discovered how to harden pottery by baking, the archeologists will not dig a site that seems to have many pieces of baked pottery on the surface. People who made such pottery lived too recently for the period of time being studied.

▶ DIGGING A SITE

After an archeologist has decided upon a site, the excavation is begun. In countries

Stone Age walls of Jericho, in Jordan.

Hadrian's Wall, built by Romans in Britain.

Archeologists have a choice of many parts of the world and many kinds of sites to investigate. And each find usually reveals something about past peoples. Tomb at far left contains artifacts intended to ease the life after death. Excavated walls at left are evidence of one of the earliest towns. The wall above confirms recorded history. Cliff dwellings below reflect the society of Pueblo Indians.

Indian Cliff Palace, Mesa Verde, Colorado.

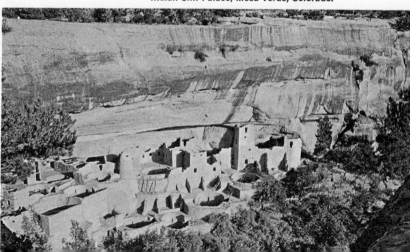

Inca city of Machu Picchu, Peru.

Pre-Aztec pyramid, Veracruz, Mexico.

Each of these great archeological discoveries casts much light on some ancient culture. The remains of the city of Machu Picchu (*above*) hint at the extent of Inca civilization. The temple pyramid (*left*) is the work of one of the Indian cultures that preceded the Aztecs in Mexico. The paintings below were found in caves in southern France. They are among the most dramatic reminders of Stone Age people. The ruins of Pompeii (*facing page*) revealed many details of everyday life in the ancient world. Discovery of Knossos was first evidence that Greek legends about Minos were based on fact.

Cave paintings at Lascaux, France.

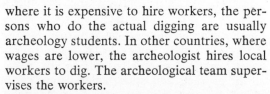
Bakery millstones in Pompeii.

Ruins of King Minos' palace at Knossos, Crete.

where it is expensive to hire workers, the persons who do the actual digging are usually archeology students. In other countries, where wages are lower, the archeologist hires local workers to dig. The archeological team supervises the workers.

The site, whether a cave or a mound, is usually made up of many layers. The people who inhabited the bottom layers were the earliest. The people who lived in the top layers came later. The layers may have been built one right after another, with a new house being constructed as soon as the old one fell down. Or people may have moved away from the site, leaving it unoccupied until other people settled there some time later. When people lived steadily on a site, one layer is much like the next. Only small

changes occur in the shape of pots and tools and in ways of doing things. But in the second case, there may be very great changes from one layer to another. The great changes are caused in part by the longer amount of time between the building of layers, during which people may have discovered different ways of doing things. The changes are also caused by the fact that a different group of people may have moved in, with their own way of doing things. An early group of people may not have known how to bake pottery to make it hard. A later group may have made very good pottery. Thus, small and orderly changes tell an archeologist that there probably was continual life on the site. But a sharp change in the way things were made or done indicates that there was a gap in living on the site or

Giant circular mound, made by Indians in Louisiana, was unknown until this aerial photograph revealed it.

a strong influence from some outside group. When archeologists begin to dig, they may have to go through several layers of artifacts before they find any from the period being studied.

Choosing the Most Promising Area To Dig

Once a site is found, archeologists must decide where to dig. Excavating the whole site would be expensive and unnecessary—the archeologist can get a good idea of what life at the site was like by carefully choosing places to dig. First, test pits are dug. The test pits may reveal the size of the settlement, interesting buildings, and areas that did not have many houses at all. One deep cut may also be dug into the side of the mound. The side cut shows approximately how many layers are in the site.

How the Digging Is Done

When the test diggings have shown the most promising areas, the archeologists are finally ready to begin a full excavation. With surveying equipment, they divide the site into smaller units, marked on the ground with stakes and rope. The archeological team then digs away the soil in the chosen areas. The excavators search the dirt carefully for clues. Sometimes the dirt is sifted through screens to recover small bits of bone and stone. Sometimes it is put in big tanks of water to recover plant material such as small seeds. After all the artifacts and other materials are carefully collected, the dirt goes to a dumping area near the site.

When the soil has been removed from the top of the digging area, the archeologist begins to see the different layers. Sometimes they are natural layers of mud or clay left by heavy rainstorms. Sometimes they are cultural layers (layers deposited by people)—broken pots left on a floor inside a house, for example. The archeologist tries to find and uncover each layer.

If archeologists are excavating a site with

many buildings, they may see the outlines of the lower parts of walls. Some walls made of packed mud or mud brick are very much like earth, but they are slightly harder. Careful excavators can feel this extra hardness. Using special small, light picks, they can usually tell by feel what they are hitting—a pot, a skeleton, or the wall of a house. Excavators also have trowels, brushes, and other special tools. They may use very delicate tools, like those of a dentist, to excavate a burial or uncover pieces of burned wood.

If the archeologist is excavating a settlement with houses, the area inside each room is carefully cleared down to the floor. When this job is done, a whole house may appear or, if the area is large enough, several houses.

When the houses have been cleared, the archeologist records the layout of the settlement. The staff photographer takes pictures of the houses, perhaps from a high photographic tower. Someone else draws an architect's plan of the houses, which includes careful measurements. Such records must be accurate and complete because once they are made, the walls and floors are cleared away, and this layer is gone forever.

The whole site may be excavated in this way. A representative sample of each layer is carefully dug out and recorded. If time and funds allow, the earliest layer may be reached.

▶ **THE STAFF AND ITS JOBS**

The staff of an archeological expedition is made up of students and full archeologists. It must include people with a variety of talents and special knowledge. It needs people to dig and to supervise the digging on the site. It needs people who have specialized in the study of pottery, stone or metal tools, clay figures, and so on. It also needs a photographer and a person skilled in making architectural drawings. There may be a need for someone who can read what was inscribed on ancient tablets, scrolls, or stone, if the site is expected to have such things. There may also be some natural scientists—such as zoologists, geologists, and botanists—whose specialized knowledge is necessary to complete the picture of how people lived in the past. And finally, there is a camp manager, who takes care of bookkeeping, running the household, and supervising the kitchen.

Test pits at Jarmo, Iraq, show how archeologists locate buried remains without digging up whole area.

Above: Diggers carefully remove and search through dirt at Jarmo. In background, workers carry dirt to dump. Below: Trench allows archeologists to record layers as they are cleared at Tepe Sarab, Iran—a site like Jarmo.

Sorting and Labeling

Every expedition must have special large tents or workrooms where the materials can be cleaned, sorted, labeled, and recorded. Small and delicate objects are taken to this workplace at the end of each day's digging. Other artifacts—like broken pottery, heavy stone objects, or animal bones—may first be cleaned and sorted in a cleared area near the site.

All the material is carefully labeled according to where it was found, and a written description of these finds is made each day. The materials are then carefully put in bags or boxes for further study.

For example, here is what happens to the pieces of broken pottery, called **shards**. The pottery specialist cleans the pieces as well as possible and then studies them to see whether any pieces might fit together to make a whole pot. Next, the unusual pieces are picked out, and the specialist selects enough of the other pieces to make a small sample of the whole pile. These pieces are labeled in waterproof ink to indicate exactly where they were found. They are put aside for further study by the archeologists at the end of the digging season.

Meanwhile, work on the smaller and more delicate objects goes on in the indoor workroom. The specialists in bone tools, stone or metal tools, clay figures, and the like sort, clean, and label their artifacts. A record is kept of all of these objects, and the particularly interesting ones are drawn and photographed.

▶ FINANCING AND FINISHING A SITE

The season of digging goes on until its time runs out. Often this is at the end of summer, when students and teachers must go back to school. In some places, the digging is done in the fall and winter months because the summer is too hot for work. Most archeologists work for either a museum or a university, and they must do something besides digging and studying what they find. If they are employed by a university, archeologists are expected to teach some classes and perform other academic duties.

Then, too, there is the problem of money. Archeologists can dig only so long as funds are available. All the money for an expedition usually does not come from a university or a museum. Part of it may come from wealthy people who are interested in archeology. Some may come from a foundation. In the United States, several large private foundations have special funds for scientific work of various kinds. The United States Government also has such a foundation. Well-trained

Archeologist's tools include spade, pick, gloves, soft brush, bucket, measuring tape, sifting screen.

Bits of broken pottery excavated at Jarmo are piled near site for sorting. They reveal much about past.

archeologists who have carefully prepared and worthwhile research designs, or plans, may get money from one or more foundations. But because an expedition is very expensive, the money is usually spent quickly.

Because archeologists have other work to do and because it is not always easy to obtain the necessary money, digging seasons are seldom long. An expedition that lasts as long as nine months will probably dig only every three or four years. Many archeologists dig each year, but for just two or three months. Sometimes archeologists can finish digging a site in the time allowed. But more often the team must go back again in the next digging season. Some large and complex sites, such as Babylon and Jericho, have been dug for many seasons and are still not finished.

When the digging is finished, the team must check all the records, drawings, photographs, and notes to be sure there is a complete set for use in the final study. If the team is working in a foreign country, the director of the country's museum will list all those artifacts that the expedition may keep. Each country has its own laws. Some national museums claim most of the artifacts an expedition finds but allow the archeologists to borrow some to study at home. Archeologists never know until the last minute which artifacts they will be allowed to keep—if any at all. For this reason, the records must be thorough if they are to complete their study.

When the archeologist learns what may be kept, the fragile objects are wrapped in soft tissue or cotton wool, and everything is packed in large crates. If the archeologist intends to go back to the same area, the house or tent equipment is stored nearby. The expedition is then ready to return home and begin the long study of what has been found.

▶ STUDYING ARCHEOLOGICAL EVIDENCE

The excavation is only the first part of an archeologist's work. At the site, the archeologist mainly gathers information. After the excavation, the archeologist must analyze and interpret the finds.

During this period of study, the archeologist really begins to find out what life was like in the time being investigated. Drawings on pieces of pottery may show the kinds of clothing the people wore. If they lived before the time of pottery, a bone needle may show that they sewed skins together for clothing or had some sort of woven fabric of wool or flax. Two kinds of rubbing stones probably mean that they knew how to grind wheat into flour.

Other Scientists Aid the Archeologist

The natural scientists mentioned before are very important in this final study of artifacts. Some of the artifacts will be pieces of grain or impressions of pieces of grain in floors. It is also likely that there will be many pieces of animal bone, with some made into needles, spoons, and beads.

Botanists who are experienced in this sort of work study the plant remains—often charred seeds or their impressions (if the seeds have disintegrated). They can tell what kinds of plants grew in the area, what kinds of food the people ate, and whether they grew the food themselves. If there are impressions of a fabric, the botanist can sometimes tell whether it was a vegetable fabric (like cotton or linen) and if so, what sort of plant was used.

The zoologist examines the bones to find out what kinds of animals lived in the area. These findings are compared with the findings of the botanist. Together, they can reconstruct a picture of what the natural environment was like at the time being studied. The zoologist can suggest which animals the people

An archeologist works under light from lamp in a cave. He wears mask to filter out dust. Note that delicate work of unearthing skeleton is done with simple tools such as a soft paintbrush.

ate and whether they kept cows, sheep, and goats. If there are impressions of a fabric that was made of animal hair, the zoologist can tell what animal the hair came from.

The geologist identifies the main kinds of stones that the people used to make tools and ornaments. Some of these stones may come from places far away. The archeologists then know that the people they are studying either traded or traveled over long distances for this material. The geologist's work is also important in understanding many aspects of the ancient environment.

If archeologists use the information that the natural scientists supply, they will learn a great deal about the people being studied. Botanists and zoologists, along with geologists, can even tell how many trees and animals there may have been. They can tell what the weather was like from evidence such as tree rings. And there are many other things they can deduce about the countryside in ancient times.

Using all the information, archeologists finally write reports or books describing the investigations. These reports let other people know what has been learned. The report of one archeologist can help others with a problem. Suppose, for example, that archeologists discover an object that cannot be identified. Through reading, they may learn that someone else has found a similar object under circumstances that made it clear how the object

was used. In one case, archeologists had found a certain kind of flint blade. They were unable to determine its use. Finally, some of the blades were found set into handles. Archeologists realized that the blades formed part of a sickle or scythe. Possibilities like this make it very important for all archeologists to publish their findings. Only through co-operation can the fullest picture of life long ago be formed.

▶ DATING A SITE

How do archeologists date the people being studied? There are many ways. But it is important to remember that dates given for times before writing was common are approximations. The approximations may be bolstered by the newest scientific methods, but archeologists cannot be sure that they are exact.

Dating by Comparison

Comparing a site with others is the oldest and most commonly used method for dating. The material that has been discovered may be similar to that found in other sites already dated. This suggests an approximate date for the new find. There are several reasons why the date can only be approximate. For one thing, different styles of decorating pottery or making tools lasted for different amounts of time in different places. So it is not certain that the two sets of artifacts were made at the same time. In ancient days, ideas spread

Greek vase below is more than 3,000 years old. Drawings on it show how soldiers of the period dressed. At left is Chinese vase of the same period from later Shang dynasty. By comparing similar objects from different countries, archeologists can compare how two cultures advanced.

Flint blade below was one of many such objects excavated at Jarmo, Iraq. It was saved by archeologists (see box at right) but could not be identified. Later, finds from other sites, such as fresco from Egyptian tomb above, revealed blades were used to cut grain.

slowly. They were carried from one village to another by merchants. This means, for example, that people did not learn to make the same kind of pottery at the same time. One group learned first. Later, the idea spread to another group.

Archeologists study how the ways of making and decorating things developed through time. It does not surprise them that a carpenter's saw from Colonial Williamsburg, in Virginia, is a much cruder tool than a saw now sold in hardware stores. You yourself could easily tell which was the older and which the newer of the two saws.

Dating by Scientific Methods

Many different scientific methods are available to archeologists. At the excavation, they cannot use laboratory equipment for dating. But they can take many samples to send to laboratories for analysis. These samples must be taken carefully if the results of the analysis are to be useful in dating.

Perhaps the most common samples taken by archeologists are carbon-14 samples. All living things receive a set amount of radioactive carbon (carbon-14, or C-14) from the outer atmosphere. When a plant or animal dies, the carbon-14 begins to leave it at a known rate. Scientists can measure—in a machine called a counter—the amount of radioactive carbon left in any artifact made of material that was once alive (such as wood, grain, and bone). Then, by figuring backward, they can set an approximate date for the artifact. Scientists are working to make the carbon-14 method more exact. But it is useful even now for comparing objects less than 50,000 years old with other objects that have also been dated by the carbon-14 method.

The potassium-argon method is another way of dating with radioactivity. This method can be used only when the site has been covered with volcanic rock soon after people lived on it, because the date represents the time when the volcanic rock cooled. Radioactive changes turn potassium into argon over a very long

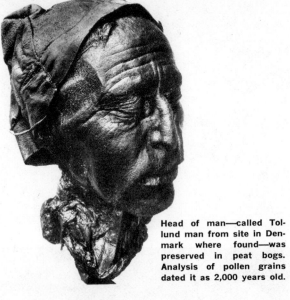

Head of man—called Tol-lund man from site in Den-mark where found—was preserved in peat bogs. Analysis of pollen grains dated it as 2,000 years old.

time. Therefore, archeologists can use this method only when studying very ancient fossils from sites covered with volcanic rock. The potassium-argon method could not be used, for example, to date a recent site like Pompeii, which was covered with lava in A.D. 79. But Roman records tell us about Pompeii.

Counting tree rings is another method of dating. If wood was used in building houses and it has not rotted away, its rings may be very useful in estimating the age of the wood, as well as the weather in the area over a period of time. Tree rings grow wide or narrow, depending on each year's weather. Based on the comparison of bands of many trees, a master chart is made. It shows the weather for every year in a particular region. When a piece of wood from an ancient site in the region is found, its pattern of bands can be matched against the master chart. In this way an archeologist can tell when the wood was cut and first used.

The study of pollen grains provides another way of dating. The kinds of trees and shrubs that grow in a particular area change over long periods of time. Scientists drill into the ground, or into a lake bottom, using long, hollow metal tubes. They bring up cylinders, or cores, of material that contains pollen grains from ancient vegetation. Then they study the pollen grains from the different levels in a core. This gives an overall picture of the kinds of plant life that grew in the area, when each kind grew, and what changes in climate occurred in the area.

In trying to date an ancient site, scientists analyze the kinds of pollen grains found there. Comparing these grains with grains in the overall picture of the area, as recorded in a master chart, provides a clue to the age of the site.

Still another method of dating depends on the study of magnetic particles in clay. These particles line up with the earth's magnetic field, like millions of tiny compasses. Scientists know that the earth's magnetic field has shifted many times in the past, and they know when these shifts took place. During such a shift, the magnetic particles in the clay also shift, re-aligning themselves with the new direction of the earth's magnetic field.

But this re-alignment does not occur in clay that has been heated to a very high temperature. The magnetic particles in the floor of an ancient clay oven, for example, are fixed in the pattern that they had when the oven was first fired. By comparing this pattern with the known shifts in the magnetic field, scientists can calculate the age of the oven.

Using these various methods of dating, an archeologist can get a fairly good idea of when a certain people lived. And scientists are working on still other ways to help the archeologist date materials.

Archeology, as a scientific profession, is relatively new. There are many problems in human development and human history yet to be solved. But the methods by which they can be solved are becoming more and more scientific.

Even so, each problem that is solved often raises new problems, and new ways of solving these need to be found. The radioactive-dating methods were not even dreamed of until the late 1940's. And it is probable that future years will bring other new and important changes for archeology.

▶ THE TRAINING OF AN ARCHEOLOGIST

As archeology changed from a hobby and a picnic sport to a scientific profession, more and more importance was laid on the training of archeologists. In particular, an archeologist must know how to define an important problem. An archeologist does not go out and dig just anywhere for the pleasure of discovering artifacts. There must be a purpose—

Modern archeology draws upon many other sciences. Piglets above give zoologist clues to ancient animal life of a region. Below, cores containing pollen will be analyzed by botanist for clues to plant life of the past.

Above: Pyramid of the Sun is among vast remains left by pre-Aztec culture at Teotihuacán, near Mexico City. Below: Archeologists from many countries co-operated to save ancient monuments that would have been lost under a lake formed by a new dam on Egypt's Nile River. Shown are the temples of Abu Simbel, built by Ramses II. Tents belong to workers who were measuring the temples.

an archeological problem that needs solving. The expedition is carried out in a careful and studious manner, and the results are published for others to study.

It takes many years of hard work to become an archeologist. The training may begin as early as high school. Young people who are interested in archeology should realize that both a college and a graduate degree are needed. It may be necessary to read and speak several foreign languages, depending on where the students wish to work. Many important reports are published in French and German. Future archeologists start one of these modern languages in high school. Latin and Greek are necessary if one is interested in classical archeology. Students may also learn to type, and they may study mechanical drawing.

It is best to start with a well-planned liberal arts course. Students should learn to express ideas in writing easily and well, so that they can prepare clear and interesting reports. Particularly useful for students of prehistory are courses in geology, geography, botany, and zoology, to help them understand the natural environment. They need at least one year each of chemistry, physics, and biology so that they can understand methods for dating and the information the natural scientists will supply later on. In college, the students continue with foreign languages. They may try to learn the languages of the countries in which they are interested so that they can talk with workers there. They may also study ancient scripts such as Sumerian, Akkadian, or Egyptian, if they are interested in these periods. Finally, the archeologist should have a good foundation in anthropology, history, and art history.

The Archeologist Studies Anthropology

A study of anthropology helps the archeologist to see how other peoples are different from ourselves. What is important to us may not matter at all to someone who lives in a different part of the world or has a different cultural background. Certainly the objects used in daily life in Arctic regions differ from those used near the equator. Archeologists must realize that people today, like those in the past, do not necessarily all think and behave in exactly the same ways. Through anthropology, students of archeology can learn

how different peoples live and feel and think about things. This is very important because archeologists depend heavily on their understanding of the present when they reconstruct how people lived in the past.

The Archeologist Studies Recorded History

In the same way, an archeology student needs to learn as much history as possible, especially the history of the chosen area. Usually we think of history as coming from the writings of an earlier people themselves. But these people probably did not describe everything they did, or how they lived, or what their countryside looked like. In ancient times—before the invention of paper, pens, and pencils—writing was difficult. Only a few scribes wrote what the priests and kings told them to write. These people may have left us only descriptions of battles, hymns to the gods, and a few business letters. Nevertheless, interesting ideas did slip in, and the archeology student must learn as much as possible about these writings. From what the people wrote of themselves (and from the knowledge gained through anthropological training), the arche-

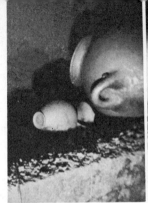

NEW TECHNIQUES: Left, diver using modern aqualung lifts amphora (vase) from Roman ship that sank some 1,900 years ago off the coast of Turkey. Right, periscope is sunk into underground tomb of Etruscans, an early Italian people. Then camera takes photos (*above*) that show if tomb is worth excavating.

ologist forms a better picture of their lives. These writings may also show what the ancient people took to be good or bad, useful or worthless. All this helps archeologists understand what they find.

For example, archeologists study Greek writings about foreign trade carried on by ships. Now suppose that an archeologist, working as a skin diver, discovers the underwater wreck of a Greek trading ship. The description of the ship can be recorded as well as the type of cargo. The direction in which the ship was headed may also be deduced. Such discoveries add much to Greek history as recorded by the Greeks themselves.

The Archeologist Studies Art History

Most of the artifacts an archeologist finds are everyday tools and objects. But occasionally, some art objects may be found—things that must have had special value to the people who owned them. This is why the study of art history is important. Greek vases and Egyptian tomb paintings, for example, often have wonderful pictures of Greeks or Egyptians doing all kinds of things. In the pictures, they are actually using many of the tools, weapons, and objects that the archeologist finds. It would be foolish to guess at the use of an artifact if an ancient picture shows how people actually used it.

Rounding Out the Training

On their own, archeology students can learn much by trying to do and make many things in simple ways. They can try to chip stone into a rough tool and use it to cut a small log. This was once the only kind of tool available. Or they could take wet clay, make a simple pottery bowl, dry it in the sun, and then bake it over an open fire. Students can grind a point on a sliver of bone and then drill a needle's eye in it. These projects help them understand how ancient people did things.

During the summers, archeology students will probably work on one of the digs that most large universities run. This gives them a chance to learn how digging should be done. At the same time, the students will learn photography and architectural drawing, as well as how to handle artifacts.

After college, the archeology student usually enters a graduate school to work toward a doctoral degree. If possible, the graduate program should be one in the student's field.

Archeologists may find work with a university or museum after graduate school. After working with older and more experienced archeologists on their digs, the young archeologists may eventually have digs of their own and their own students working with them.

ROBERT J. BRAIDWOOD
GRETEL BRAIDWOOD MANASEK
University of Chicago
Reviewed by MAGGIE DITTEMORE
University of Chicago

See also ANTHROPOLOGY; PREHISTORIC PEOPLE; RADIOACTIVE DATING.

ARCHERY

People have been shooting bows and arrows for at least 20,000 years. Some famous paintings of archers are at least that old. These paintings, showing people hunting huge deer and bison with bows and arrows, were found on cave walls in France and Spain.

In the earliest days people depended upon hunting for food and clothing. Even today there are people in the jungles of South America and Africa who rely on their skill in archery to obtain some of their food. For many centuries the bow was a weapon of war, and nations rose and fell because of it. American Indians were still hunting with the bow in the late 1800's. It may surprise you to learn that many hunters today pursue deer, bear, and other animals with bows and arrows. These archers are called bow hunters.

Archery is a sport enjoyed by people everywhere. Most archers shoot at targets of various kinds. Many schools, playgrounds, parks, camps, and organizations such as the Boy Scouts and Girl Scouts have archery programs in which young people are taught to shoot the bow. The National Archery Association sponsors the Junior Olympic Archery Development Program, in which thousands of boys and girls are enrolled.

Whether you shoot in the backyard or anywhere else, remember this: Used properly, bows and arrows are not dangerous. But you must be careful. As far as safety is concerned, there is no such thing as a toy bow.

▶ **EQUIPMENT**

Most bows now used by young people are made of a material called fiberglass. Bows of wood are also available, but they do not stand up as well. The all-fiberglass bows are very sturdy and almost impossible to break. Most champion archers, including many young archers, prefer bows made of layers of fiberglass and wood. Such bows are called **composite**, or **laminated**, bows.

Almost every bow is graded according to weight. But the number that you see written on a bow does not give the weight of the

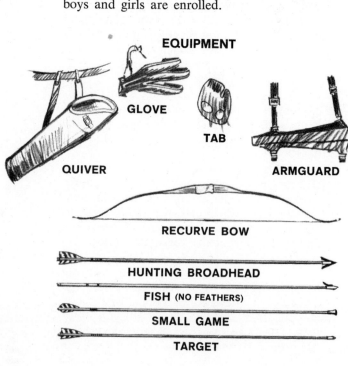

EQUIPMENT

QUIVER

GLOVE

TAB

ARMGUARD

RECURVE BOW

HUNTING BROADHEAD

FISH (NO FEATHERS)

SMALL GAME

TARGET

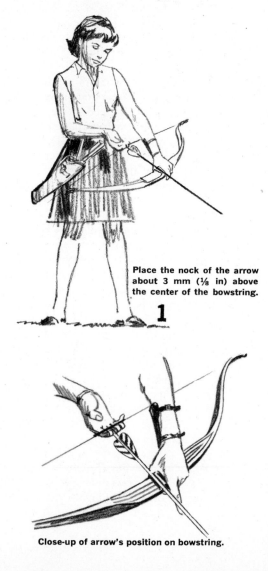

Place the nock of the arrow about 3 mm (⅛ in) above the center of the bowstring.

1

Close-up of arrow's position on bowstring.

bow. It stands for the amount of force needed to pull back the string. Young archers usually shoot bows that are between 7 and 14 kilograms (15 and 30 pounds).

Most arrows are made of fragrant Port Orford cedar from Oregon. But many experts prefer arrows made of aluminum tubing or fiberglass. Turkey feathers are generally used for the **fletching** (feathers on an arrow). Most arrows have steel points, but hunters shoot arrows with sharp-bladed tips called **broadheads**. These should only be used for hunting.

All archers should wear a leather or plastic armguard. This is worn on the arm above the hand in which the bow is held. Its purpose is to prevent the string from hitting or slapping the arm. All archers wear a three-fingered glove or a piece of leather called a **tab** on the fingers used to draw back the bowstring. Arrows are carried in a leather **quiver**, worn at the archer's side or on the back. Many archers use a **bow sight**, attached above the handle. It consists of a metal bar on which a pin can be moved up or down depending on the distance of the target.

▶ **SHOOTING**

If you have never shot a bow and arrow, it is best to get some personal instruction. This is provided by schools, clubs, and other organizations. Sporting goods and archery stores often will teach you the first steps or provide booklets on the subject.

When you are learning to shoot, stand sideways to the target and about 3 meters (10 feet) from it. If you are right-handed, hold your bow in your left hand. Left-handed archers should hold the bow in the right hand. Grip the bow's handle firmly, but not too tightly. Use the same sort of grip you would employ if you were picking up a suitcase.

Place the arrow's slotted plastic **nock** (the string notch at the end of the arrow) about 3 millimeters (1/8 inch) above the center of the bowstring's length. Most archers make a little knot of thread there so they can place the arrow at the same spot for every shot. Now place your three middle fingers on the string, bending them at the first joint of each finger, with the nock between the index and middle fingers. Do not clamp down on the nock with your fingers. Simply hold it firmly.

Place the forward part of the arrow on the little shelf above the bow's handle. If you are right-handed, this means on the left side of the bow.

Now you are ready to draw back the string. As you start to do this, push your left arm out in front of you. Draw the string straight back to your face. Do not twist your fingers around

Stand sideways to target, with bow arm straight out. Do not grip bow handle too tightly.

2

Draw bowstring back until it is against your jaw, your fingers at corner of your mouth.

3

Let arrow go by opening your string fingers, pulling them back slightly. Keep this position until arrow strikes target.

4

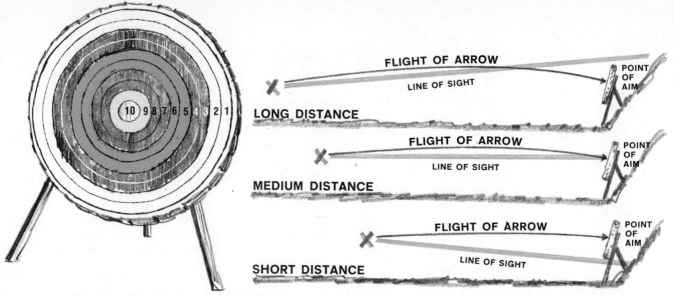

LONG DISTANCE — FLIGHT OF ARROW / LINE OF SIGHT — POINT OF AIM

MEDIUM DISTANCE — FLIGHT OF ARROW / LINE OF SIGHT — POINT OF AIM

SHORT DISTANCE — FLIGHT OF ARROW / LINE OF SIGHT — POINT OF AIM

Targets are made of paper and are fastened to tightly woven mats of special grass or to hay bales. The circles and bull's-eye are numbered as shown, and points are scored according to where the arrows hit.

Because the path of the arrow in flight is curved, the height of your bow arm must be adjusted to distance from the target.

the string. Bring your fingers to the corner of your mouth. Look at the target. If the target is close, as it should be when you are learning, make sure your left arm is pointed below the bull's-eye. If you are shooting from about 9 to 12 meters (30 to 40 feet), your left hand should be pointed directly at the bull's-eye. The farther back you go, the higher you will need to hold your left hand.

When you think your hand is properly aimed—and you will need to shoot a few arrows before you are certain—let the arrow go by simply opening your string fingers and pulling them back slightly. Follow through—that is, keep that position until the arrow strikes the target. Expert archers often use mechanical aids to help them see the target clearly and to release the arrows smoothly.

▶ **GAMES, ROUNDS, TARGETS**

Target backstops usually are round, tightly woven mats of a special grass, or simply hay bales. Many backyard archers use bales and tie balloons to them for targets. Two basic forms of archery have long been popular—target archery and field archery.

In target archery you shoot most often at a 122-centimeter (48-inch) target. It has five rings—gold, red, blue, black, and white—each divided into two scoring areas. The center area of the gold circle counts 10 points, and the rest of the ring counts 9.

The two scoring areas in the red ring count 8 and 7 points, in the blue ring 6 and 5, in the black ring 4 and 3, and in the white ring 2 and 1.

You always shoot six arrows in a series, or **end**, and then score them. An archery match is called a **round**. For young archers, a round consists of 4 to 24 ends (24 to 144 arrows) shot at distances as short as 18 meters (20 yards) and as long as 55 meters (60 yards). The National Archery Association in Lancaster, Pennsylvania, sends information about rounds to young people all over the world.

In field archery the targets are smaller and are usually black and white. The bull's-eye and the ring next to it count 5 points per arrow. The third and outer rings count 3 points. Targets are set up in the woods at different distances. The archer shoots four arrows at each target.

Field archery clubs in the United States, Canada, Australia, New Zealand, and many other countries shoot under the rules of the National Field Archery Association.

Parks, schools, and camps have other games and rounds that will help you sharpen your skill and afford you much fun. But no matter where or when you shoot a bow and arrow, always be very careful. Remember, there is no such thing as a toy bow!

WILLIAM STUMP
Author, *Archery Handbook*

ARCHIMEDES (287?–212 B.C.)

"Give me a place to stand, and I can move the world." The man who is supposed to have spoken those words was Archimedes, a Greek mathematician and inventor who lived some 2,200 years ago. It was not an idle boast. Archimedes was one of the first men to develop the science of mechanics. He understood that a man with a mechanical device such as a lever could move many times his own weight. Challenged by the king to prove his point, Archimedes did so. He arranged a device that allowed the king to move a large ship all by himself.

Archimedes was born about 287 B.C., in Syracuse, a Greek settlement on the island of Sicily. Little is known about his personal life except that his father was an astronomer and may have been related to the king of Syracuse. Also, at some time in his life Archimedes studied in Alexandria, Egypt, a center of Greek culture.

Archimedes is best known for his many inventions. Among other things, he invented a compound pulley; a sphere that imitated the motions of the heavenly bodies; and a water screw to raise water. He himself most valued his work in mathematics and scientific theory. But his fame rests on inventions and the legends that grew up around him.

One legend tells how Archimedes made his most important discovery.

The king, it seems, had ordered a new crown. It was supposed to be made of solid gold, but the king suspected that the jeweler had cheated him. He asked Archimedes to tell him if the crown was solid gold.

At first Archimedes could not think how to do this. Then one day the solution came to him as he was getting into his bath. Legend has it that he rushed naked into the streets shouting, "Eureka [I have found it]!"

What had happened was very simple. The bath was full, and it overflowed as Archimedes climbed into it. This started him thinking about the way objects displace water. And he suddenly saw how to solve his problem.

First he took a quantity of gold and a quantity of silver, each equal in weight to the crown. The weights of gold and silver were equal, but their volumes were not. The silver, being less dense, was bulkier than the gold.

Next Archimedes took two vessels filled to the brim with water. He placed the gold in one and the silver in the other. The silver, being bulkier, caused more water to overflow. Archimedes concluded that when a solid sinks in water, it displaces its own volume of water.

Finally he tested the crown against the equal weight of gold. When placed in water, the crown caused more overflow. Therefore, the crown had to contain metal other than gold. This metal made it bulkier and caused the greater overflow.

Further experiments resulted in what is known as Archimedes' principle: An object in a fluid is buoyed up by a force equal to the weight of the displaced fluid.

When Archimedes was an old man, the Romans attacked Syracuse. He turned his mind to defense, and invented several engines of war that held off the enemy. It is claimed that he built a huge burning mirror. When it was used to focus the sun's rays on the Roman fleet, the ships were set on fire. Syracuse, however, was defeated in 212 B.C., and Archimedes was killed. The story goes that he was drawing mathematical figures in the sand when a Roman soldier struck him down. Archimedes was so highly respected that the Roman commander buried him with full honors.

JOHN S. BOWMAN
Author, *Prehistory and Early Civilization*
The Golden History of the World series

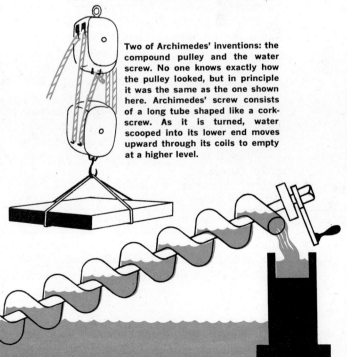

Two of Archimedes' inventions: the compound pulley and the water screw. No one knows exactly how the pulley looked, but in principle it was the same as the one shown here. Archimedes' screw consists of a long tube shaped like a corkscrew. As it is turned, water scooped into its lower end moves upward through its coils to empty at a higher level.

The apse of the basilica church of Sant' Apollinare in Classe, in Ravenna, Italy, is covered with a mosaic picture of Christ as the Good Shepherd.

ARCHITECTURE

Architecture is the art of building. Unlike sculpture, painting, or music, it is an art that has a practical basis. Each building serves a definite and special purpose. People living in different ways have developed different styles of architecture to suit their special needs.

Every age demands its own style of architecture, for buildings must suit the way of life of the people who use them. We are living in an exciting period of this art, a time of great experimentation. New engineering techniques and new materials are making possible buildings that never could have been built before.

The American architect Frank Lloyd Wright proposed a building 1.6 kilometers (1 mile) high. R. Buckminster Fuller, an American engineer and designer, suggested the possibility of making a kind of roof, or dome, big enough to cover a whole city or even a region. By using such a dome, he thought, we could control climate and make frozen lands or deserts into livable places. These plans are still dreams. But during your lifetime you will see new kinds of buildings designed for new ways of living.

Every day we move in and out of buildings designed to suit the way we live—our homes, schools, the stores where we shop. We take these buildings for granted, but just like the factories and office buildings necessary to industry, and the courthouses, city halls, and post offices necessary to government, they reflect the life of our times. Airports and railroad stations fulfill the needs of modern systems of transportation. Towering skyscrapers and tall apartment buildings are the result of our large cities.

Architecture is an art. But as every picture is not a work of art, neither is every building. To create real architecture the architect—the designer of the building—must succeed in certain ways. First, the practical requirements of the building must be met. It must be strong, of sound construction, and suitable to its function. It must also be satisfying to look at. The different parts of a building must be in harmony with each other. Much of the beauty of architecture comes from its proportions—the balance of size and shape of its different parts. An architect has to be an artist and a technician.

Construction is a science. The various possible ways to build a structure have been worked out by experiment. Builders of the past had to discover the nature of materials —which ones were strong and which were weak. They had to find out how much weight a material could bear and whether it would resist sun and rain. They had to learn from experience how to hold materials together. The development of architecture has been a long, long process.

▶ THE EARLIEST ARCHITECTURE

At first, people lived in caves. Then, experimenting with whatever material they could find—wood, mud, stone, plants—they started to build homes to protect themselves and their families from weather and danger.

Building was much easier after people learned what could be done with mud. Formed into cubes, cylinders, and many other shapes, mud could be dried in the sun or baked in a fire to make a hard, strong building material. And mud was easy to repair and was durable.

The first builders learned that round or oval buildings were the simplest kind to construct. All they needed to do was lay stones of nearly equal size in a circle or oval on the ground, using enough mud for mortar. Mortar can be made of many materials—sand, straw, or pebbles mixed with mud or clay. Its purpose is to bind together stones or bricks in a strong and lasting way.

Making a roof was one of the first problems. A circular building was roofed by leaning branches or other plant material from the top of the low walls toward the center. On a rectangular building branches could rest on the long sides of the walls and meet at an angle to make a roof called a gable. For a very wide building, it was necessary to put a row of posts down the center of the room to support the roof. These posts took up space inside the room.

Wood easily catches fire, so important buildings meant to be permanent were often built of stone. The first great stone buildings were probably made in Egypt.

▶ EGYPTIANS BUILT TOMBS AND TEMPLES TO LAST FOREVER

The ancient Egyptians believed that their kings, called pharaohs, were gods. This belief affected their architecture. The pharaohs' palaces were used only during their lifetimes. The palaces did not have to be sturdy. They could be made of mud brick. But a pharaoh's tomb would be used forever. It had to withstand time and weather. For their eternal homes the pharaohs built great stone pyramids that are still standing after 5,000 years.

The first pyramid was built around 2700 B.C. Built in the form of six great steps, it was about as high as a 20-story building. This step pyramid was the tomb of King Zoser and was built by the architect Imhotep. This is the earliest record we have of both architect and client. Nothing had ever before been built on so large a scale.

The pyramids were surrounded by small rectangular buildings called **mastabas**. These were the tombs of court officials. A sloping passage connected each pyramid with the riverbank, where there were temples in honor of the kings.

Egyptian Temples

The pharaohs built many temples to the gods during the New Kingdom (1580– 1100 B.C.). A good example is one at Karnak, where there is a series of temples built and rebuilt over a period of 1,200 years, from 1550 to 323 B.C.

Egyptian temples were surrounded by a high wall. There was one great gate, placed between two towers called **pylons.** The statue of the god was placed at the back of the temple, and approaching it must have been a dramatic and awe-inspiring experience. The few worshipers who were allowed inside went from large, light courtyards through ever smaller and darker rooms until they reached the last one, where the god's face was lighted by only a tiny shaft of light. The massive walls were about 8 meters (25 feet)

A model of the hypostyle hall, part of the Great Temple of Amon-Re at Karnak, Egypt. The hall had 134 stone columns. The central columns were 21 meters (69 feet) high.

thick. Many huge stone columns supported the ceilings of the large halls. Walls and columns were often decorated with designs carved into the surface of the stone and brightly painted.

▶ MESOPOTAMIANS BUILT "MOUNTAINS" OUT OF MUD BRICK

While the Egyptians were building pyramids and temples of stone, the people living between the Tigris and Euphrates rivers (the area called Mesopotamia) were building towns and temples of mud brick and reeds. There was little timber and stone in Mesopotamia. The people often covered the outsides of buildings with glazed tiles. The glazes were made from the same ingredients as glass, melted at a high heat and fused with the bricks to make a hard, shiny surface.

Houses were built in a row on a street and had only one entrance on the street side. The rooms were arranged around an open central courtyard and the windows looked into it. There were usually no windows at all on the outside street walls.

These thick-walled houses were one or two stories high. The rooms on the upper floor opened onto a balcony. The plan of many small rooms had to be exactly the same on both stories because the walls of the first story supported the walls and floors of the second story. The outsides of the houses were covered with mud, and they were sometimes whitewashed.

Ziggurats

Because the Mesopotamians lived on a flat plain, high places came to have a religious meaning to them. Therefore they built their temples, called **ziggurats**, to look like miniature mountains. On a huge foundation they added terrace after terrace, each one smaller than the one beneath, until the top of the mountain was reached. These terraces were made of solid brick. On the very top of the ziggurat was a small building for the use of the god. The outside walls of the ziggurat were covered with glazed and molded brick. But the ziggurats have not lasted as well as the stone temples of Egypt. When the glazed exterior bricks were destroyed, the sun-dried bricks crumbled into a great dusty mound.

A great flight of steps leads to the ruins of the audience hall of the Persian palace at Persepolis. The stairway is lined with marching soldiers carved in stone.

▶ASSYRIANS BUILT PALACES OF STONE

Temples and towns much like those of the Mesopotamians were in use for several thousand years. Then, about 1200 B.C., a new nation of builders, the Assyrians, came into Mesopotamia. They built royal palaces of brick, decorated with stone carved and painted with scenes of court life. Our knowledge of their architecture is from these carved pictures, for most of the palaces were destroyed by wars.

▶PERSIAN PALACES SHOW THE GREATNESS OF THE KINGS

In the 6th and 5th centuries B.C., the Persians built great cities. One of the most famous is Persepolis, begun by King Darius I about 500 B.C. and continued by Xerxes I. This city was really one gigantic royal palace. Built on the plain on a huge stone foundation, it could be seen from a great distance. Everything about the palace was planned to impress people with the grandeur of the Persian ruler. A great flight of steps led up to the entrance. Of the many large rooms in the palace, the greatest was the throne room.

It was an impressive sight, its flat roof held up by 100 very tall, slender stone columns. The capitals of these columns were carved in the shape of the heads of horses and bulls.

Persepolis is important not only for its size and beauty but also for its influence on the architecture of other countries.

▶MINOANS BUILT LUXURIOUS PALACES

The Minoans, who lived on the island of Crete, in the Mediterranean Sea, were a seafaring people. By 2000 B.C. the Minoan kings had such strong navies that they were able to build unfortified palaces, and to consider comfort and elegance rather than safety.

The great palace of Knossos, which was built over a long period of time, covered about 1.6 hectares (4 acres). It was built around a large courtyard. Each wing of the palace was about 120 meters (400 feet) long and at least two stories high. Each had a special use. The rooms included a shrine for the god-king, his living quarters, and the quarters of the queen. All parts of the palace were connected by a very complicated system of passageways and stairs.

The stones of an ancient Greek gate at Mycenae are so large that later Greeks thought it was built by giants.

The pleasure-loving Minoan court lived in luxurious and cheerful surroundings. Large windows let sunlight into the rooms. Floors were covered with gypsum, a mineral that has a satin-like sheen, and walls were painted with brightly colored pictures. The elegant palace at Knossos was destroyed about 1400 B.C., but we do not know whether by fire, earthquake, or enemy invasion. No one ever returned to live there again, and the ruins became a great grass-covered mound. The palace was not discovered until the 20th century, when Sir Arthur Evans, an English archeologist, dug it out and reconstructed it.

▶ GREEKS BUILT FORTIFIED CITIES

About the time that Knossos was destroyed, a new civilization with different ideas about architecture was developing on the Greek mainland. Because inland cities needed strong fortifications, the Greeks from very early times built their cities on hills.

The city of Mycenae, built about 1300 B.C., was surrounded by massive stone walls. The gates of the city were set back in the walls so that attackers would be caught in a small space. Only the foundations of the houses remain, but the Mycenae gate is still standing. Built about 1250 B.C., it is a fine example of **post-and-lintel** construction.

In post-and-lintel construction, a pair of upright posts supports a horizontal beam called a lintel. It is one of the basic kinds of construction and is used for doors, windows, or the entire frame of a building. The stone posts of the Mycenae gate support a gigantic stone lintel. One piece of stone is 5 meters (16 feet) long and 2.4 meters (8 feet) wide.

The highest area of a Greek city was called the **acropolis.** In each city the acropolis came to represent two ideas: safety and a sacred area for the gods. If a king needed a big house, it followed that a god needed a bigger one. So temples were the largest buildings and were placed in the center of a city.

Greek architects wanted the proportions and the shapes of their buildings to be clearly visible. Egyptian temples were most often placed so that only the front could be seen and the viewer was not able to tell the building's size or shape. But the Parthenon, the great temple of the goddess Athena in Athens, is so placed that when Greeks entered the great gate of the acropolis, they saw the corner and two sides of the building. At one glance they knew exactly what its shape and dimensions were.

Although the Greeks built many kinds of buildings, the most important to them, and to later ages, was the temple. Almost always rectangular, the temples were built on a foundation of stone. Three or more steps led up to the temple, and the outside walls were surrounded by columns. Inside the columns was a walk that led all around the **cella**, or inner chamber. The cella was often divided into two parts that did not open into each other, but only to the outside. In one room was a statue of the god, in the other the god's treasures. The most famous of all Greek temples is the Parthenon, built in the middle of the 5th century B.C. by the architects Ictinus and Callicrates. Built of marble, its perfect and graceful shape dominated the Athens acropolis. It was decorated with magnificent sculpture that was brightly painted.

The Architectural Orders and New Techniques

Among the great contributions the Greeks made to architecture were the orders, de-

The Parthenon, the great temple of the goddess Athena in Athens, was built in the 5th century B.C. in the Doric style.

veloped from the post and lintel. The orders are styles for a column and its parts (shaft, capital, and usually a base) and the entablature (architrave, frieze, and cornice) that it supports. There were three Greek orders—**Doric**, **Ionic**, and **Corinthian**. Later the Romans and others added more, and the orders have been used in architecture ever since.

Architectural ideas and new methods of construction often spring from the discovery of new materials. Wooden posts and lintels, sun-dried brick, and cut stone all played their parts in the development of architecture. When people began to use metal, a further change occurred.

By using molten metal the Greeks learned how to bind a horizontal line of stones together. They cut T-shaped slots into the top edge of each stone opposite a similar slot in the next stone. This made an H shape into which they poured molten lead. When the lead hardened, the stones were held firmly together. Later iron was added to the lead.

For buildings too wide to roof in stone, the Greeks used cut timber to make a truss for the roof. A truss is really a triangle made by two slanting rafters meeting at the top and held by a tie beam at the bottom side of the triangle. The Greeks covered the truss with clay tiles baked at a high heat.

▶ROMAN ENGINEERS RAISED HUGE BUILDINGS

Because the Greeks were fighting disastrous wars among themselves toward the end of the 5th century B.C., they had little time to develop new ideas in architecture. But in Italy the Romans began to build a great city filled with enormous public buildings. An acropolis and an **agora** (marketplace) had been the main open spaces of the Greek cities. In Rome the chief feature was a **forum** (public square). The Romans introduced their architecture into the many countries they conquered. Towns and cities all around the Mediterranean were built according to Roman designs.

Every Roman city had at least one forum, and the great cities, like Rome, often had many. In the forum were the temples, law courts, senate house, and other public buildings. The market area was usually alongside the forum.

The great buildings of Rome were not only complicated feats of engineering and planning but were beautiful as well. The Romans made their buildings suit their functions.

They used different plans for temples, markets, theaters, palaces, amphitheaters, and public baths.

The Arch and Vault

The Roman masons, who were very skillful in using brick and stone, developed a roof form called the **arch and vault**. An arch is made by using wedge-shaped stones, later called **voussoirs**, placed with the narrow end on the inside of the arch, the wide end on the outside. An arch may be round, pointed, or a combination of these. It may be used as an entrance, repeated along a wall as decoration, or used to support a heavy roof.

A connected series of arches built one behind the other forms a **barrel** or **tunnel vault**. When two barrel vaults intersect, they form a **groined vault**. Roman engineers mastered the problem of roofing wide areas by using great arched vaults supported on piers (pillars). In the Basilica of Constantine (built about A.D. 300), they were able to roof an open space 23 meters (75 feet) wide.

Roman engineers also succeeded in building **domes**. Domes are really a development of the arch. A dome can take many shapes, but it is basically like a teacup put upside down over an open circle. In one of the largest Roman temples, the Pantheon, the

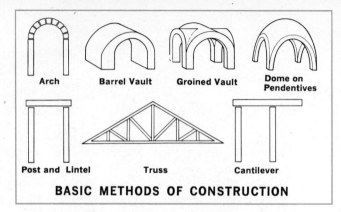

BASIC METHODS OF CONSTRUCTION

dome spans an opening of 43 meters (142 feet). The use of a new material—concrete—was one of the reasons that Roman engineers were able to build large domes.

▶THE FIRST CHURCH BUILDERS ADOPTED ROMAN FORMS

The Emperor Constantine made Christianity the official religion of the state in A.D. 326. This meant that many churches were required in a very short time.

Christian worship demanded a style of architecture very different from the religious architecture of Greece and Rome. Temples had served as a house for the god, a storehouse for treasures, and as a background for outdoor ceremonies. Christians worshiped together inside their churches. Therefore the builders of the first churches adopted the design not of temples, but of the Roman public halls called **basilicas**. The basilica plan provided the open space necessary for Christian worshipers to gather and windows to light the interior. Many churches are still built in this style today.

The plan of a basilica is a rectangle divided lengthwise into three parts. The widest part in the center is called the **nave**. On either side of the nave are two aisles, which are usually not as high as the nave. A line of columns divides the nave on either side from the aisles and supports the upper walls of the nave, known as the **clerestory**. The church is lighted by windows cut into the walls of the side aisles and into the clerestory. At one end of the building is a semicircular projection called an **apse**.

The exteriors of the first basilica churches were usually simple and undecorated; it was the inside that was important. To focus attention on the altar, which was the center of the rites, the builders placed it toward the

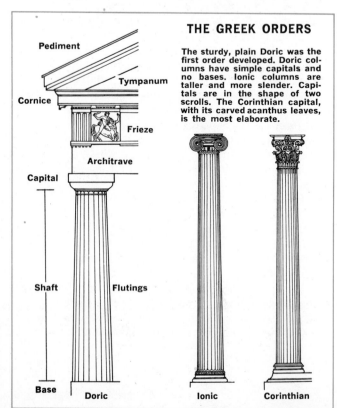

THE GREEK ORDERS

The sturdy, plain Doric was the first order developed. Doric columns have simple capitals and no bases. Ionic columns are taller and more slender. Capitals are in the shape of two scrolls. The Corinthian capital, with its carved acanthus leaves, is the most elaborate.

Pediment

Tympanum

Cornice

Frieze

Architrave

Capital

Shaft

Flutings

Base

Doric

Ionic

Corinthian

end of the long, low building. The lines of columns seem to march toward the altar, leading the eye of the worshiper to the most important place. As church architecture developed, every part of the church came to have a special function, even the decoration. Sculpture, mosaics, or wall paintings were intended to teach the Bible stories.

▶ BYZANTINE CHURCHES HAVE DOMES AND RICHLY DECORATED INTERIORS

Barbarian invasions weakened the Roman Empire. In 410, Rome itself fell to invaders from the North, and Roman traditions died out in the West. But for eleven centuries a civilization based on Greek and Roman ideas was kept alive in what remained of the empire in the East. The capital of the Eastern Empire was the rich city of Constantinople (now Istanbul, Turkey), on the shores of the Bosporus. The city had once been called Byzantium, and Byzantine is the name that we give to the architecture that developed in this area.

Byzantine churches were usually built in the form of a Greek cross, a cross with four equal arms. Domes made of brick and mortar were the most common form of roof, and Byzantine architects became expert in making them. They learned how to raise a round dome over a square space. They did this by means of **pendentives**, triangular forms with curved sides that look as though they were cut out of a ball. Pendentives are built up from the corners of the square space. The base of the dome rests on their uppermost edges.

The interiors of Byzantine churches were richly decorated with colored marble and with bands of lacy stone carving. Walls and domes were often covered with brilliant mosaics—designs and pictures made of pieces of colored glass stuck into plaster.

The greatest church in the Byzantine style is Hagia Sophia, in Istanbul. It was begun by the Emperor Justinian in 532. The dome of this church, which is covered with gold mosaics, is one of the most magnificent ever made. A person standing beneath it feels a sense of great open space. The light falling from windows cut in the bottom of the dome casts a shimmering light throughout the church.

The Byzantine style spread to Greece, Russia, and finally through Venice to western Europe.

▶ CHARLEMAGNE COPIED ROMAN AND BYZANTINE BUILDINGS

The year 800 is usually considered the beginning of Western architecture. In that year, in Rome, Charlemagne was crowned emperor of the Holy Roman Empire. This empire covered much of Europe. The event was important to architecture because Charlemagne wanted to revive the glory of the old Roman Empire. On his way back and forth between Aachen, his German capital, and Rome, he visited Ravenna, where he saw Byzantine buildings. In Nîmes, in the South of France, he saw a Roman temple and amphitheater. All the lessons that Charlemagne learned from Rome and Byzantium were applied on a simpler scale in his own lands. Although most of these buildings were destroyed, we know about them from excavations and old records. At Aachen he built an eight-sided domed chapel and a large palace. Compared to the buildings of ancient Rome, Charlemagne's chapel was crudely made, for over the centuries techniques of construction had been forgotten.

▶ THE ROMANESQUE ERA WAS A PERIOD OF DEVELOPMENT

About the year 1000 a revival of building began in Europe. All the buildings built between 1000 and 1200 bear the general name **Romanesque**. They all have certain characteristics in common, such as thick walls, small windows, round arches, short, thick columns, and a heavy and massive appearance. But there is great variety in different countries and even within each country. The greatest amount of building was done in France, and there every section of the country had its own local style of church.

During the Romanesque era the simple basilica plan was made more elaborate. To provide more altars, chapels were built off the side aisles and the apse. A semicircular aisle called an **ambulatory** was placed between the apse and its chapels. **Transepts** were extended on either side of the nave to make the church into the shape of a cross. Architects began to make the main façade of the church into an important architectural feature. The doors were placed inside arches, and these arches were covered with carved decoration. Towers were raised on either side of the entrance. By the end of the 11th century, most churches also had a tower above the crossing of nave and transepts.

The Development of Rib Vaulting

Architects had learned that a long, rectangular building could be roofed with a barrel vault, a groined vault, or a series of domes. But the masons in France were not satisfied with any of these systems, for the buildings were too heavy, low, and dark. By experimenting they learned how to push up the center of the roof to make a pointed vault. To do this the interior of the church was divided into rectangles of nearly equal size. Next a wooden centering (a temporary wooden support) in the shape of a pointed vault was built to hold the stones in place until the mortar set.

The great achievement of the architects of the Romanesque era was the development of rib vaulting for ceilings.

To make a **rib vault**, architects divided the nave of the church into rectangles. They used a pier at each of the four corners of the rectangle and constructed ribs to a central point. The ribs supported a thin web of ceiling, but the real weight of the roof was carried down the ribs and through the piers into the ground.

At first there were four ribs for each vault. But this arrangement was too heavy, and in France a vault with six, rather than four, ribs made possible a higher, lighter, and more beautiful vault. As architects became more skillful the vaults were divided into more and more parts, and the ribs were decorated with carving. Together with the six-part vault, the French architects used a pointed arch that made the building higher than the old, round arch.

The French church builders also began to use a new type of **buttress**. A buttress is a support to strengthen the walls of a building by receiving the thrust from the vaulting. At first buttresses were built flat against the walls. The new kind was called a **flying buttress**, because it arched away from the outside of the church. The flying buttress pushed in against the walls and balanced the weight of the roof, which pushed out.

▶ **GOTHIC CHURCHES SOAR INTO THE SKY**

By 1150 the masons and architects in northern France had discovered three building techniques that they combined to form a new style called **Gothic**: the rib vault, the pointed arch, and the flying buttress. All these building methods aided the architects in building higher and higher churches and in stressing the vertical line in the design. Steeply slanting roofs, pinnacles crowning the flying buttresses, slender spires, all make the Gothic churches look as though they are reaching into heaven.

Cathedrals

Large churches called cathedrals were built in the cities where bishops had their thrones. In France, Spain, Italy, Germany, and England, masons made the roofs of these great churches higher and higher and the walls thinner. This meant that a great deal of engineering and machinery was necessary. It also made possible large windows that, filled with stained glass, flooded the churches with color.

During the Romanesque and Gothic eras, masons and architects traveling from one job to another spread the new ideas and building techniques. This led to a kind of international style of building in Europe. However, there was still a great deal of local variety.

In England the churches were longer and lower than in France. Some of the most important cathedrals there are those at Canterbury, Lincoln, and Salisbury. In Spain and Germany the Gothic style was also important. But in Italy many architects continued to use designs inspired by buildings of the ancient Roman Empire.

Monasteries

At the same time that churches and cathedrals were rising in the towns and cities monasteries were being built in the countryside. Because of the different kinds of buildings needed by the religious orders, the monasteries were almost like towns. There was a church, a dormitory where the monks slept, a kitchen, a guesthouse for visitors, an

The high vaults of the Gothic cathedral of Notre Dame in Paris are supported by flying buttresses.

infirmary for the sick, and a writing room. An important feature of monastic architecture was the **cloister**, a covered passage built around an open court. There the monks could walk sheltered from the sun and rain.

Castles

During the Middle Ages people lived in houses or castles. Castles were built to be

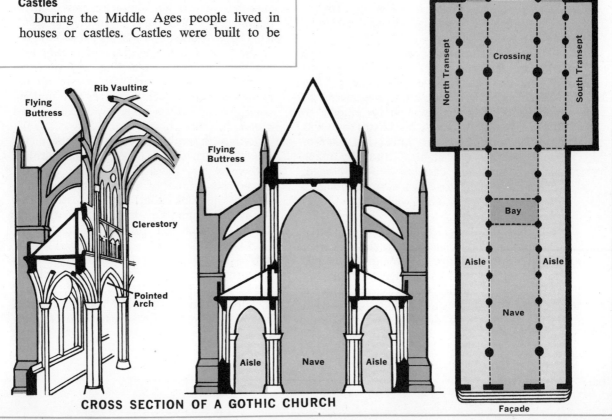

BASILICAN PLAN OF A GOTHIC CHURCH

Apse
Chapel
Choir
North Transept
Crossing
South Transept
Bay
Aisle
Aisle
Nave
Façade

Flying Buttress
Rib Vaulting
Clerestory
Pointed Arch
Flying Buttress
Aisle
Nave
Aisle

CROSS SECTION OF A GOTHIC CHURCH

Like most medieval palaces, the Palazzo Vecchio, Florence, Italy, was built to be defended against attacks.

the towns as well as in the countryside. Even though the towns were surrounded by walls, rich citizens built their houses to be as strong as castles. For extra protection these houses usually did not have windows on the ground floor. Many of them had fortified towers. A good example is the Palazzo Vecchio, or Old Palace, built in Florence between 1298 and 1314. Built around a courtyard, it had one large, easily defended entrance and a tower.

Castles were so strongly built that they seldom fell to attackers except through treachery or after a long siege. But the owners of the castles were always at war with each other. As towns grew up and local wars decreased a new style of architecture was developed to fit a new way of living.

▶ RENAISSANCE ARCHITECTS IMITATED ROMAN BUILDINGS

The **Renaissance** began about 1400 in Italy, in the city of Florence. Renaissance means rebirth. Throughout Europe there was a rebirth of interest in the art and literature of ancient Greece and Rome. In architecture there was a rebirth of interest in the ancient Roman ruins so common in Italy. For 500 years beautiful buildings were built in the Renaissance style: palaces for kings, large houses for nobles and rich merchants, town halls, law courts, marketplaces, theaters, and churches. The main characteristics of these buildings are order and balance. The architect Leon Battista Alberti (1404–72) described the Renaissance idea of beauty in a building. Alberti wrote that beauty came from "the harmony and concord of all the parts achieved in such a manner that nothing could be added or taken away or altered except for the worse."

Renaissance architects used few new methods of construction or new materials, but they had many new ideas about what a building should be. Many of them published their theories in books that are still useful. One of the most important ideas was that people should feel their full size in a building.

Italy

During the 15th century an architect named Brunelleschi (1377–1446) designed the first Renaissance buildings in Florence. The very first was the Hospital of the In-

safe and strong. Little was done to make them comfortable to live in. Some castles were just outposts to house a garrison of soldiers, but others were the homes of knights and their families.

By the 13th century there were thousands of castles in France and England. The earliest castles were called **mottes and baileys**. They were made very simply, by digging a circular ditch and piling the earth in the middle to make an artificial hill. A crude structure was built on top, at first of timber but later of stone if it was available. Gradually much more complicated castles were developed. These had high stone walls surrounding a courtyard. Usually the walls had towers placed at intervals.

During the Crusades knights of Christian Europe fighting on the eastern shores of the Mediterranean learned new building methods from the fortifications of the Arabs. After they returned home, the crusaders applied these new techniques in building their castles.

In Italy fortified dwellings were built in

nocents, for orphans. This building is different from most of those that had been built before. When people looked at a Gothic cathedral, their eyes wandered from one part to another. They saw the parts of the building separately. Brunelleschi's building is meant to be seen as a whole. The facade has a series of delicate columns that support graceful arches. On the second floor, square windows are placed above the arches. Instead of a feeling of great weight, there is a feeling of lightness. People could feel important here, not small and weak as they might feel in a medieval building.

Brunelleschi designed the church of Santo Spirito around squares and according to a mathematical pattern. When people step into the church, they can tell that the nave is twice as high as it is wide and that the ground floor and the clerestory are the same height. The theory of beauty based on arithmetic was carried further by other architects in Italy.

Italian Renaissance Palaces. An important Renaissance contribution to architecture was made in the design of palaces. The palaces built in Florence in the 15th century were constructed of great blocks of stone. The façades were generally divided into equal sections and were usually three stories high. The proportions were based on the proportions of a human being—a supposedly ideal division into two dimensions: foot to waist and waist to head. These proportions were so popular that they were used in buildings throughout Europe and the Americas.

One of the most interesting palaces was that of the powerful Medici family, begun in 1444 by an architect called Michelozzo. It had three main doors, and a row of double windows in both the second and third stories. The third-floor windows were lighter and more delicate than the ones below. The plan of the palace was a series of large rooms opening into arcades that looked into a large courtyard. On the ground floor were guard rooms and a grand staircase leading to the upper floors.

St. Peter's. In 1506 Pope Julius II asked an architect named Donato Bramante to rebuild the church of St. Peter, in Rome, which was badly in need of repair. The foundation of what was to become an entirely new church was laid in the same year. Many of the great artists of the 16th and 17th centuries contributed to the design of St. Peter's. Raphael, Peruzzi, the Sangallos, and Michelangelo were the most important of these artists. The immense dome that dominates the building was designed by Michelangelo, who modeled it after the dome in Florence that had been designed by Brunelleschi. Higher than a football field is long, the dome of St. Peter's is supported by only four gigantic piers. The church and its magnificent dome is one of the greatest achievements of the Renaissance.

France

The new Renaissance style begun in Italy rapidly spread north over the Alps. One reason why this happened was that masons, architects, and clients traveled. Also, at the end of the 15th and at the beginning of the 16th centuries, several kings of France went to Italy to try to conquer part of that country. Their wars were unsuccessful, but they liked the new style of architecture and persuaded Italian architects to work for them in France.

Châteaux. King Francis I of France (ruled 1515–47) built large palaces called **châteaux** that were influenced by Italian designs. Usually built near the Loire River, these châteaux served as residences for the court, which traveled from one part of the country to another. A major difference between French and Italian Renaissance buildings was that the French continued to use some Gothic forms, such as steep roofs.

During the 16th century not only the king and nobles but also well-to-do members of the middle class built châteaux in France. Many of these people also built large houses in the towns, where they carried on their business in comfortable and handsome surroundings.

The Palace of Versailles. In the last half of the 17th century, Louis XIV, king of France, built a huge palace outside of Paris, in the village of Versailles. The palace is so large that 5,000 people were able to live in it. It is over 0.4 kilometers (¼ mile) long. It was meant to impress everyone who saw it with the power of France. Other European kings competed with each other in imitating the palace on a smaller scale, but none of them was able to build on such a grand scale.

Aerial view of the Palace of Versailles and its magnificent gardens. In the days of King Louis XIV, as many as 5,000 people could live in the palace at one time.

The Palace of Versailles is surrounded by immense gardens decorated with sculpture showing scenes from the life of Apollo, the ancient god of the sun. The interior of the palace is decorated with gilded symbols of the sun surrounded by glittering rays. This was meant to convey the idea that as Apollo had given light to the ancient world, so was Louis XIV the center of light in France.

England

The 16th century was a period of great building activity in England. Some of the most important structures were large country houses. These houses reflected ideas brought back to England by English people who had traveled to the Low Countries (now Holland and Belgium), to France, to Germany, and to northern Italy, especially Venice.

But the Renaissance style came later to England than to other countries. The earliest part of Hampton Court Palace, which was begun about 1520, is still medieval in style. But when a new wing was added, toward the end of the 17th century, it was built in the Renaissance style.

In 1616 Inigo Jones (1573–1652) designed an important house at Greenwich for the queen. It was one of the first times in England that a small private house was built for an important person. A significant feature was that the rooms were arranged so that the queen was able to have more privacy than in her palace. Designed in the form of a bridge, the queen's house is two stories high and has a road running between the two ground-floor wings. On the second floor the wings are joined together by a large room. The house was imitated all over England, and engravings and plans were taken to the English colonies in North America, where they were much copied.

St. Paul's Cathedral. Sir Christopher Wren was one of the greatest English architects. After the Great Fire of London, in 1666, which destroyed much of the city, he set about rebuilding the churches. Wren designed 52 new churches, which are known for their simplicity and the ingenious designs of their different steeples. Architects in the English colonies in America were very much influenced by these churches, and they imitated the style.

The most magnificent of all the buildings designed by Wren is St. Paul's Cathedral, in London. Its dome is a masterpiece of calculation and construction.

▶ BAROQUE ARCHITECTS TRIED TO GIVE THE IMPRESSION OF MOVEMENT

During the wars and revolutions in 17th-century Europe, many buildings were destroyed. But a surprising number of new ones were built. Many of the buildings designed during this unsettled period are in a new style called **baroque**. The main characteristic of baroque architecture is movement. Architects wanted their buildings to be exciting and to give the impression of activity. They did this by making dramatic contrasts of light and shadow and by using curved shapes. To give the illusion of movement to the exterior of buildings, they made the façades of the buildings curve, as an S does. Light striking these curves makes them appear to move.

Architects tried to outdo each other in using new and dramatic shapes. They designed columns, arches, and vaults that were more and more elaborate than the Renaissance forms on which they were based. For example, instead of straight columns they often used twisted ones. The interiors of baroque churches are decorated with fantastic shapes modeled out of stucco and stone and often painted and gilded. Domes and ceilings are painted with clouds and flying figures of angels. If you look up at these ceilings, you get the illusion that there is no roof and that you are looking right up into the sky. The baroque style was most popular in Austria, Germany, Italy, and Spain.

▶ ITALIAN VILLAS AFFECTED ARCHITECTURE IN ENGLAND AND THE UNITED STATES

The works of some architects have had a great influence, either while they were living or after they died. Such an architect was Andrea Palladio (1508–80), of Vicenza, in Italy. Palladio's buildings tended to be symmetrical and sometimes identical when seen from any of their four sides. If you were to draw a cross through the center of a Palladian plan, you would, generally, end up with four identical quarter plans. Palladio not only built beautiful country houses near Venice but he published his designs and wrote about them. In 1715, over 100 years after Palladio's death, his designs were published in England. A young Englishman, Richard Boyle, earl of Burlington, saw these designs and was so pleased with them that he went to Italy to look at the houses. With him he took an architect named William Kent to study Palladio's houses on the spot. When they returned to England, Burlington and Kent made the Palladian style very popular. Following Palladio's work they designed spacious, well-arranged houses with simple exteriors.

In the middle of the 18th century the Palladian style was also popular in the English colonies, especially in Virginia and through-

The Baroque church San Carlo alle Quattro Fontane in Rome has a dramatic façade that curves in and out.

The Villa Capra, a Renaissance country house in Vicenza, Italy, was built by Palladio, who studied the buildings of ancient Rome.

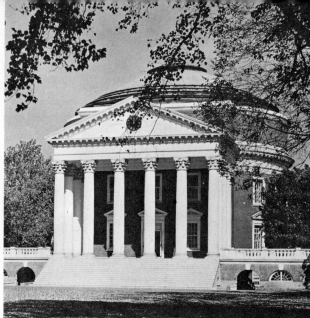

The Rotunda of the University of Virginia, designed by Thomas Jefferson, shows the influence of Roman architecture and the work of Palladio.

out the South. Plantation houses like Westover, built about 1730 on the James River, were Palladian adaptations in brick. When he rebuilt Mount Vernon, George Washington used the Palladian style.

Thomas Jefferson, the third president of the United States, was an architect as well as a statesman. He thought that the new republic should have a suitable style of architecture. While Jefferson was the American minister to France in the late 18th century, he visited Nîmes. Like Charlemagne, who had been there 1,000 years before, Jefferson admired the Roman temple called the Maison Carrée. The temple was actually built later, but Jefferson probably thought that it had been built during the time of the Roman Republic, whose laws he admired. He had a model of the temple made and sent it back to Virginia, and so the state capitol in Richmond came to look like a Roman temple.

▶ MOST NINETEENTH-CENTURY ARCHITECTS COPIED BUILDINGS OF OTHER TIMES

Architects soon began to imitate building styles besides those of ancient Rome. In Europe and America, buildings were designed in the styles of ancient Greece and Egypt and of the Middle Ages. In the early years of the Renaissance, architects had copied earlier styles too, but in a very different way. The difference came from two important changes.

In the 1800's, for the first time in centuries, new building materials were available. And new kinds of buildings—such as factories, railroad stations, and high office buildings—were needed. The new materials included cast iron, steel, reinforced concrete, and large sheets of glass. Toward the end of the 1800's, young architects rebelled at using the styles of the past for these new materials and buildings.

The Beginning of a Modern Style

One of the first buildings in a modern style was built in the United States by the architect Louis Sullivan (1865–1924). It was the Guaranty Building, in Buffalo, New York, built in 1894. It had a steel frame. On the upper floors, which house offices, the windows are all alike to show that similar work is done in all of them. The roof projects on all sides so that a person can see exactly where the top of the building is. Sullivan believed that a building should show how it is constructed. "Form follows function," he said. This means that the shape, or form, of a building must contribute to its usefulness, or function. Sullivan did not try to hide the fact that his office buildings were constructed on a steel frame. Other architects were combining the new steel-frame construction with the old styles.

Reviewed by PETER BLAKE, A.I.A.
Former Managing Editor, *Architectural Forum*

▶ THE TWENTIETH CENTURY REVOLUTIONIZED ARCHITECTURE

The twentieth century is one of the greatest periods in the history of architecture. It brought a revolution in the design of buildings that has seldom, if ever, been matched in earlier times. Twentieth century architecture can be divided into three periods, separated by the two world wars.

Before World War I

Between 1900 and 1914 a few architects broke decisively with traditional architectural styles and ways of planning interior spaces. The Austrian architect Adolph Loos (1870–1933) helped influence the course of contemporary architecture. Loos wrote an essay, *Ornament and Crime* (1908), in which he proclaimed that architectural ornamentation of any kind is immoral in modern society. Ornament had always been a major part of architectural design. After Loos, it was not.

The break with tradition was made possible in part by improvements in building materials. In Germany, Walter Gropius (1883–1969) designed the Fagus Shoe Last Factory (1911), using products of new technology—especially steel, plate glass, and reinforced concrete. Concrete, reinforced with wire mesh or steel rods, is a very strong material. Used as a floor slab, it will support itself even if extended beyond the posts that hold it up. Gropius took advantage of this characteristic. He did away with the usual corner post and replaced it with panes of glass that were held in place by thin pieces of steel. The result was a building that seemed to weigh very little—even to float.

In the Chicago area, Frank Lloyd Wright (1869–1959) experimented with new possibilities for interior spaces. Wright disliked the boxlike rooms of most houses. He therefore used fewer partitions between rooms. In this way, the whole interior seemed to flow together into one large, continuous space. Most of his designs, such as the Robie House (1909) in Chicago, had long, low silhouettes that were in harmony with the flat Midwestern landscape.

The rebellion against tradition took other forms as well. In Italy, a group of artists was fascinated by speeding cars, trains, and airplanes. The artistic movement of this group

The Seagram Building, New York City, was designed by Ludwig Mies van der Rohe and Philip Johnson.

was called **futurism**. Antonio Sant'Elia (1886–1916), a futurist architect, thought that old cities should be destroyed and replaced with tall concrete towers connected on many levels by bridges and roads.

In Germany, an artistic movement called **expressionism** was based on a desire to create strong emotional reactions. One expressionist designer imagined the earth covered by buildings of colored glass. An important example of expressionist architecture was an observation tower built in 1919 by Eric Mendelsohn

Falling Water, designed by Frank Lloyd Wright, fits into the landscape and seems to become part of it.

(1887–1953) in Potsdam (now in East Germany) for the scientist Albert Einstein. Its vigorous curves sought to express the power and newness of Einstein's ideas.

In Russia, artists of another movement, **constructivism**, designed buildings that showed the way the building was put together and how it operated. Very few futurist, expressionist, or constructivist designs were actually built. But the designs helped revolutionize architecture.

Between World War I and World War II

After World War I, the rebellion against tradition resulted in the development of a new architectural style. This style was marked by simple, geometric lines and the use of concrete, steel, and large areas of glass. The leaders in its development were Gropius, Le Corbusier, and Mies van der Rohe. In the 1930's, architectural historians gave the name **international style** to the movement.

Gropius founded a design school, called the Bauhaus, located in Weimar (now in East Germany). He wanted to train a new generation of designers who were well informed about many fields of art. He felt that machine tech-

nology required a certain kind of rational design that used pure geometric shapes and smooth surfaces. In 1926, Gropius designed a new building to house the school in Dessau. The flat-roofed building was arranged in a pinwheel plan. It expressed the different activities taking place inside by the different treatments given the five major parts of the building. The workshops, which needed a great deal of light, had glass walls. The office and classroom blocks had smaller windows set in white stucco walls.

The most important architect in France after World War I was Swiss-born Charles Édouard Jeanneret (1887–1965), who took the name Le Corbusier. In 1923 he published a book called *Towards a New Architecture,* which became a basic source of the modern movement. Le Corbusier sought to set standards for modern architectural design based on those developed for cars, airplanes, and ocean liners. He felt that engineers had a better understanding of how to use modern materials than did architects.

In 1925, Le Corbusier produced a plan for Paris that involved tearing down much of the old city (but leaving certain historical buildings) and erecting great steel and glass towers, widely separated by gardens and highways. This vision of urban renewal was not carried out. But it became the source for most housing projects involving tall buildings.

In the late 1920's, Le Corbusier designed a series of houses, the most famous of which is the Savoye House, at Poissy-sur-Seine, near Paris. This rectangular stucco house is raised up on thin pillars, called *pilotis.* It appears to hover over the field in which it was built. Long, thin windows light the interior.

The third founder of the new style was the German-born American architect Ludwig Mies van der Rohe (1886–1969). He used glass extensively in buildings with precise, angular lines. He expressed his design principles in the saying "Less is more." The architecture of Mies van der Rohe is often considered the most elegant of the 20th century.

In the late 1930's, some architects began to use heavier materials such as stone and brick, often in combination with steel, glass and concrete. The Kaufmann House (1937–39) at Bear Run, Pennsylvania—designed by Frank Lloyd Wright—is one of the most impressive of the houses designed in this period. Called Falling Water, the house extends out from a rocky slope and hovers over a waterfall. Its reinforced concrete platforms, or "trays," form a dramatic composition that blends architecture and landscape.

After World War II

After World War II almost the whole world came to embrace the international style. The masters of the style, each moving in a new direction, took the lead in the immediate postwar years. Gradually, architecture began to move away from the boxlike severity of the years between the wars.

Le Corbusier expanded the use of reinforced concrete. In the late 1940's, he designed the Unité d'Habitation, a big apartment building in the French city of Marseilles. He put the building on thick concrete legs instead of thin stilts. He made the entire structure of reinforced concrete, which was left rough to show the marks of the wooden boards that held the wet concrete in place while it dried. On top of the building he placed large concrete ventilators that look like big pieces of sculpture.

But the building that really pointed the way to new concrete forms was Le Corbusier's chapel Notre Dame du Haut at Ronchamp, France, designed in 1950. Its boldly curved roof is made of a thin shell of reinforced concrete held together by concrete struts, like the metal struts inside the wing of an airplane.

Another great achievement of Le Corbusier's is the city of Chandigarh, India. The architect planned this whole new city and built its civic center out of raw concrete.

In the early 1950's, Mies van der Rohe designed the Lake Shore Drive Apartments in Chicago. These were among the first big rectangular steel and glass towers. They set a standard for the steel and glass commercial buildings that came to dominate the skylines of cities all over the world during the great postwar building boom. A notable example is the 38-story Seagram Building (1956–58) in New York City, designed by Mies and Philip Johnson (1906–   ). The metal parts on the outside are bronze, and the glass is tinted gray. Because Mies was looking for general solutions that would fit almost any problem, he could design apartment and office buildings that are almost identical.

The Finnish architect Alvar Aalto (1898–1976) came to occupy a very important place in world architecture in the postwar years. Aalto moved away from the international style to develop buildings in which people would

The chapel Notre Dame du Haut at Ronchamp, France, was designed by Le Corbusier.

The Guggenheim Museum, New York City, designed by Frank Lloyd Wright. Its spiral design was revolutionary for an art museum.

feel at ease. His buildings featured open, sky-lit spaces, curving lines, and natural materials such as pale birch wood. The best known of his designs were civic buildings constructed in Europe. Aalto's buildings often have unexpected shapes. These shapes reflect the purposes that the buildings serve. Baker Hall (1948), a dormitory at the Massachusetts Institute of Technology, is an example. The dormitory has a curved facade facing the Charles River to give every room a view of the water. The other side, facing the campus, is angular. It reflects the lounges, staircases, and bathrooms inside and is in keeping with the shapes of buildings nearby.

The differences among the types of buildings designed by Corbusier, Mies van der Rohe, and Aalto set the stage for the incredibly varied architecture of the years after 1950. The uses of reinforced concrete continued to expand dramatically. Thin concrete vaults spanned enormous spaces, especially in the stadiums and arenas designed by the Italian architect Pier Luigi Nervi (1891–1979). Concrete was also used to create bold, expressive forms, such as the Trans World Airways terminal at Kennedy International Airport in New York City, designed by Eero Saarinen (1910–61). Other examples are the sail-like vaults of the Sydney Opera House, in Sydney, Australia, designed by the Danish architect Joern Utzon (1918–   ), and Frank Lloyd

Pier Luigi Nervi used Y-shaped buttresses for the Little Sports Palace in Rome.

Wright's spiral design for the Guggenheim Museum in New York City.

Concrete was also used by Louis I. Kahn (1901–74), an important architect working in the 1950's and 1960's. His design for the Salk Institute for Biological Studies in La Jolla, California, used concrete piers and a concrete truss system. This created large, open laboratory spaces, in which scientists could arrange their equipment in any way they wished. Above each laboratory floor is a floor that does nothing but hold all the mechanical equipment for the laboratories below. Each scientist also has a private study that looks out onto a quiet interior court and has a view of the Pacific Ocean.

Two other important architects of the period were Edward Durell Stone (1902–78) of the United States and Oscar Niemeyer (1907–) of Brazil. Stone's best-known buildings include the Museum of Modern Art in New York City and the John F. Kennedy Center for the Performing Arts in Washington, D. C. Niemeyer was the chief architect of Brasília, the new capital city of Brazil constructed during the 1950's.

Some architects of the 1950's and 1960's broke completely with the simplicity that was the mark of the international style. In 1966, Robert Venturi (1925–) published a book called *Complexity and Contradiction in Architecture*. He was dissatisfied with the bland, repetitive look of many modern buildings. Architecture, he argued, should be complex and filled with contradictions, as is life itself. Venturi's buildings use architectural forms for the ideas they carry with them. A house designed for his mother in Chestnut Hill, Pennsylvania, in 1961, has a big peaked roof to present the idea of shelter. The peak is broken by a large gap over the front door, and the door itself is crowned by a curving archlike line. These forms emphasize the idea of entering. Above this playful combination rises a chimney, much bigger than it need be, to make people aware of the warm fireplace inside.

Recent Trends in Architecture

Architects have developed as many new ways to use steel and glass as they have concrete. R. Buckminster Fuller (1895–) makes what he calls geodesic domes with very light steel rods, put together in triangles.

Stadium by Alvar Aalto for the Polytechnical School in Otaniemi, Finland.

These can be covered with thin sheets of glass or plastic to keep the rain out. Fuller has even designed a geodesic dome that, if built, would cover the whole of Manhattan Island in New York City.

The triangle is considered the most stable structural form. It can also be one of the most beautiful forms, as shown in I. M. Pei's design for the East Building of the National Gallery of Art (1978) in Washington, D.C. Pei used the triangle as the basic form of his design and

Robert Venturi was the architect of this house in Chestnut Hill, Pennsylvania.

Above and left: Inside the Pompidou Center, Paris. This building has an unusual design with transparent escalators, glass walls, and visible heating and electrical systems. Below: Habitat, an apartment building in Montreal, designed by Moise Safdie. All the units, made of concrete, were prefabricated and lifted into place by crane.

repeated it in skylights, courtyards, and other details.

One of the most spectacular of the recent steel and glass buildings is the Georges Pompidou National Center for Art and Culture in Paris. This building, also known as the Beaubourg, opened in 1977. It was designed ten years earlier by Renzo Piano and Richard Rogers. The front is dominated by an escalator, enclosed in a glass and steel tube, that moves visitors up to all the floors through the thin steel struts that form the structural system.

The Georges Pompidou Center has given new life to an old part of Paris, just as the remodeling of the 19th-century Quincy Markets has done for an old part of Boston. Both projects deal successfully with the important issue of bringing the centers of old cities back to life.

Early in the 1900's architects talked of destroying the architecture of the past. During the 1950's many cities, particularly in the United States, undertook or became involved in urban renewal programs. Many older buildings were destroyed to make way for blocks of high-rise buildings. Today, architects want to preserve older buildings that are of historic importance and make them useful once again —or to design new buildings so that they fit comfortably with the old. Architects seem to have realized that past and present can live side by side, to their mutual benefit.

In the 25 years immediately following World War II, most buildings were designed with little thought to energy conservation. Then, in the 1970's, it became more apparent than ever before that fuel resources were limited. People wanted homes, offices, and public buildings that used fuel economically. Architects turned toward designs that include using solar energy and better insulating materials. There was also a renewed emphasis on relating new structures to their environment.

EUGENE J. JOHNSON
Williams College

See also ANCIENT WORLD, ART OF THE; BAROQUE ART AND ARCHITECTURE; BUILDING CONSTRUCTION; BYZANTINE ART AND ARCHITECTURE; CATHEDRALS; GOTHIC ART AND ARCHITECTURE; GREEK ART AND ARCHITECTURE; ISLAMIC ART AND ARCHITECTURE; RENAISSANCE ART AND ARCHITECTURE; ROMANESQUE ART AND ARCHITECTURE.

ARCTIC. See POLAR REGIONS.

Citicorp, New York City. The wedge at the top of the building was designed as a solar energy collector.

ARGENTINA

More than 400 years ago (1526), Sebastian Cabot explored some of the waterways of southern South America. Friendly Indians went down to greet him when he landed on the riverbanks. Like other explorers Cabot was excited when he saw the silver jewelry worn by the Indians. Cabot believed he had discovered a land rich in silver. Thrilled by his "discovery," he gave the name Río de la Plata, "river of silver," to a great estuary. The surrounding country was later named Argentina, which means "land of silver." These names have remained, even though the disappointed Spanish later learned that the silver had come from the mountains of Peru, more than 1,600 kilometers (1,000 miles) away.

Argentina is a land of great contrasts.

Tierra del Fuego, the group of islands at its southern tip, is a cold, wet land where penguins thrive. In the hot, humid Chaco, the lowland region of the north, giant anteaters, jaguars, pumas, and other animals of the subtropics abound. In the west are the towering Andes mountains. They thrust their snow-capped peaks to more than 6,700 meters (22,000 feet) above sea level. In the east are the flat, prairielike plains of the Pampa.

But it is not only Argentina's land and climate that vary from place to place. Cities and other parts of the landscape made by people vary as well. There are hundreds of tiny villages that are seldom visited by strangers and bustling cities like Buenos Aires, the capital of Argentina. It is one of the world's largest and most cosmopolitan cities.

FACTS AND FIGURES

ARGENTINE REPUBLIC is the official name of the country. Argentina means "land of silver." Nicknames for the country are "Land of the Pampa" and "Land of the Plata."

CAPITAL: Buenos Aires.

LOCATION: Southern South America. **Latitude**—21° 47′ S to 55° 03′ S. **Longitude**—53° 40′ W to 73° 30′ W.

PHYSICAL FEATURES: Area—2,766,889 km² (1,068,297 sq mi). **Highest point**—Aconcagua, 6,960 m (22,835 ft), highest point in the Western Hemisphere. **Lowest point**—40 m (131 ft) below sea level. **Chief rivers**—Río de la Plata system (Uruguay, Paraguay, and Paraná rivers), Río Negro, Bermejo. **Chief mountain peaks**—Aconcagua, Ojos del Salado, Mercedario, Tupungato.

POPULATION: 26,500,000 (estimate).

LANGUAGE: Spanish.

GOVERNMENT: Republic (under military rule). **Head of government**—president. **International co-operation**—United Nations, Organization of American States (OAS), Latin American Free Trade Association (LAFTA).

NATIONAL ANTHEM: *Oid, mortales, el grito sagrado Libertad* ("Hear, O Mortals, the sacred cry of liberty").

ECONOMY: Agricultural products—wheat, corn, livestock, sunflower and linseed oil, sugarcane, rye, oats, barley, cotton, fruits and vegetables, tobacco, soybeans, yerba maté. **Industries and products**—meat and other animal products, food processing, textiles, beverages, wine, plastics, iron and steel, machine tools, chemicals, paper, tobacco products, automobiles, tourism, fishing, tannin. **Chief minerals**—petroleum, sulfur, silver, tin, coal. **Chief exports**—grain, livestock and livestock products, foodstuffs, wine. **Chief imports**—minerals, chemicals, machinery, various manufactured goods. **Monetary unit**—Argentine peso.

▶ THE PEOPLE

Most of the people in Argentina are of European stock. The remainder are mestizos (persons of mixed European and Indian ancestry) and a few pure-blooded Indians. Most Argentines live on the eastern plains. The dry western and northwestern provinces are sparsely populated. Most people live in towns and cities rather than rural areas.

Between the years 1858 and 1930, more than 6,000,000 people left their homes in Europe to settle in Argentina. Immigrants still arrive in large numbers. As a result, many of the people are of European birth or descent. People of Spanish and Italian ancestry are the most numerous. There are also many descendants of French, Swiss, Austrian, German, Russian, English, and Scottish settlers. Many recent immigrants have come from Poland and other countries of eastern Europe.

When the Spanish first came there were relatively few Indians in Argentina. Wars broke out when the Spaniards tried to seize their land, and many Indians were killed. Most of the tribes were unfriendly, and there was little intermarriage. As a result, Argentina has far fewer mestizos than any other Latin American country.

The gaucho is the cowboy of Argentina.

During Argentina's early days the gauchos played an important part in the settlement of the country. Many stories were written about the way they lived and their heroic deeds. Today they tend the herds of cattle on the great plains of the Pampa.

In cities and suburbs people live in comfortable houses or apartments. The demand for washing machines and other conveniences is growing rapidly. In the rural areas there are *estancias* (ranches) and *quintas* (farms). Wages for household help are low, and most middle-income families have servants.

Food and Dress

The gauchos' clothes are colorful and distinctive. Gauchos wear full, billowing trousers called *bombachas*. These are tucked into leather boots adorned with big spurs. They wear bright neckerchiefs and bright sashes or wide leather belts decorated with coins. On cold days they drape shawls, or ponchos, of sheep or llama wool around their shoulders. The *facon,* a highly decorated knife with many uses, is worn sheathed at the back of the belt. The gauchos often use it at mealtimes to cut strips of raw beef to be broiled over an open campfire.

Many of the ranch owners and men in small towns also wear the *bombachas,* leather boots, sash, and neckerchief of the gaucho. The men drape long shawls over their shoulders in the cool season. The cheaper shawls are woven from sheep and llama wool, but the more prized ones are woven from the wool of the alpaca.

Argentines who live in the large cities dress in Western fashion. People on the streets of Buenos Aires look very much like Parisians or New Yorkers. Many women still have their own dressmakers, and men often have their suits made to order. But the number of good clothing stores is growing. The trend among young people is to buy their clothes readymade in fashionable new shops.

Argentines eat their dinner very late. Although the children may eat early in the evening, adults seldom eat dinner until 8 o'clock. Many families begin their meal as late as 9 or 10 o'clock. Nearly every lunch and dinner starts with homemade soup. The second course is frequently Argentine beef. Macaroni, spaghetti, vermicelli, and other *pastas*

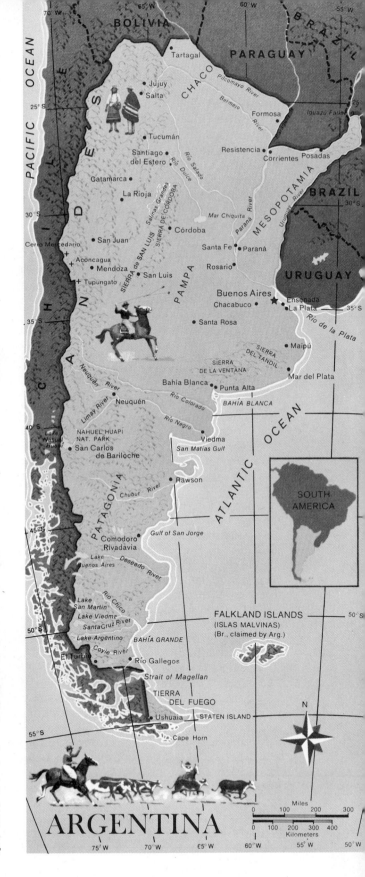

ARGENTINA

made popular by Italian immigrants are often served. Nearly everyone drinks wine with lunch and dinner.

Religion

Most Argentines are members of the Roman Catholic Church. The government helps to support the church, and the constitution requires that the president be a Roman Catholic. But all religious groups are guaranteed religious freedom.

Education and Culture

The Argentines are proud of their school system. The nation has one of the highest literacy rates in all of Latin America. Public education is free and separate from the church. But many parents send their children to private parochial schools.

All boys and girls between the ages of 6 and 14 must attend elementary school. The schoolchildren wear knee-length smocks, called *delantales,* over their everyday clothes. The boys button their smocks down the front. The girls' smocks button down the back. President Domingo F. Sarmiento, who served from 1868 to 1874, made wearing smocks a law so that rich and poor children could feel equal in school.

When they are 14, boys and girls choose the type of secondary school they wish to attend. Students who plan to go to college have to attend high school for five years. In high school they work for a diploma called a *bachillerato.* To prepare for business careers, they may then attend *La Escuela Comercial* (The Commercial School) and work for a diploma called a *perito mercantil.* If they wish to acquire other skills, they go to industrial or trade schools.

Argentina has several national universities. The largest is the University of Buenos Aires. There are also numerous provincial and private universities located in various parts of the country.

Symphony concerts and opera, the theater, and ballet are all very popular in Argentina. The Teatro Colón, or Columbus Theater, in Buenos Aires is the largest and most elaborate theater. It is decorated in rose and gold. Six tiers of boxes and balconies look down on the large stage. The opera series held there every year is one of the major cultural events in Buenos Aires. It is always well attended. Famous North American and European singers often appear in the Teatro Colón.

When Argentine music is discussed, most people think of the tango, but the *chacarera,* the *zamba,* and the *milonga* are also popular. The folk tunes are a combination of Spanish and Indian music. The most popular musical instrument is the guitar. Many people learn to play the guitar when they are children.

Among Argentina's earliest authors was a mestizo named Ruy Díaz de Guzmán. His work, *La Argentina,* is a history of the early days of settlement. Domingo Sarmiento wrote a book called *Facundo,* an attack against dictators. In 1872 José Hernández wrote a long epic poem called *Martín Fierro.* This tale about the life of the early gauchos has become a classic. The works of several present-day writers have been translated into other languages and have become known throughout the world.

Argentina is today the leading book and newspaper publisher in Latin America because of the high literacy rate. Newsstands and bookshops abound in Buenos Aires and other large cities. *La Prensa* ("The Press") and *La Nación* ("The Nation") are important newspapers. *La Prensa* became known throughout the world for its independent editorials. Its offices were once closed because it opposed President Juan Perón.

▶THE LAND

Argentina occupies most of South America's long tip and is somewhat triangular in shape. It extends for 3,700 kilometers (2,300 miles) from north to south and varies in width from 1,450 kilometers (900 miles) in the north to less than 16 kilometers (10 miles) on Tierra del Fuego.

Among Latin American countries, Argentina ranks second to Brazil in area. The mainland of Argentina is about one third the size of Brazil. Argentina claims an additional 1,190,000 square kilometers (460,000 square miles) of territory. Most of it is in Antarctica. Additional claims include the Falkland Islands, in the Atlantic Ocean, and the nearby South Georgia, South Sandwich, South Shetland, and South Orkney islands. Argentina's claim to these islands is not recognized by the British, who presently occupy them.

Argentina's western neighbor is Chile. Uruguay and Brazil are to the east. The Uruguay River and the Río de la Plata separate Argentina from Uruguay. Bolivia and Paraguay are to the north.

Natural Regions

There are five natural regions in Argentina. These are the Andean region, the Chaco, Mesopotamia, the Pampa, and Patagonia.

Andean Region. The Andes mountains form most of Argentina's western border with Chile. The highest and most impressive peaks are found midway in the range, not far from the beautiful city of Mendoza. Snow-capped Aconcagua, the highest mountain in the Western Hemisphere, towers to 6,960 meters (22,835 feet). Nearby Cerro Mercedario and Tupungato are nearly as high. West of Tucumán, on the border with Chile, is Ojos del Salado, the hemisphere's second highest mountain.

The northern Andes are high and dry. The mountains rise from a high, windswept plateau called the Puna. Some of the rivers of this region empty into salt lakes in the mountains and foothills. Some lakes have dried up and left great salt flats called *salinas*. The largest salt flat is the Salinas Grandes, in a deep depression between the foothills of the Andes and the Sierra de Córdoba.

The Plaza de Mayo, one of Buenos Aires' busiest squares, also serves as a playground for school children.

In the southern Andes, the mountains are lower and rise to about the level of the Puna. The southern Andes remind visitors of the Swiss Alps and are often called the Alps of Argentina. San Carlos de Bariloche is the center of one of Argentina's most popular tourist areas. Thousands of tourists visit nearby Nahuel Huapí National Park in summer. Skiers and other winter sports enthusiasts visit it in winter.

The Chaco. The most northerly of Argentina's lowland regions, the Chaco is a very wide, wooded plain. Four broad rivers—the

Gauchos prepare their daily meal of beef and maté (herb tea).

Above, San Carlos de Bariloche in Nahuel Huapí National Park is one of Argentina's favorite vacation resorts. Below, the snowcapped peaks of the Andes rise above fertile fields in western Argentina.

Paraná Plateau in the northeast. Waterfalls are formed as rivers tumble down from this plateau. The Iguazú Falls on the Iguazú River are the largest. They are 64 meters (210 feet) high and 4 kilometers (2½ miles) wide.

The Pampa. The Pampa lies south of the Chaco and stretches to the Río Colorado. This is the heart of Argentina's ranch country. The Pampa forms a huge semicircle of lowlands, centering on Buenos Aires. In the east is the humid Pampa. In the west is the dry Pampa. The land rises gradually toward the west. There are few hills or trees, and the land appears perfectly level. The only relief features are the Sierra del Tandil and the Sierra de la Ventana. These hills rise to more than 1,200 meters (4,000 feet) just north of Bahía Blanca.

Patagonia. Patagonia is the name given to the cold, dry, and windy plateaus south of the Río Colorado. The name comes from the Spanish word *patagones,* which means "big feet." The early Spanish explorers noticed the big feet of the local Indians. They called the land Patagonia, or "The Land of People with Big Feet." Tierra del Fuego, the bleak and windswept island at the southern tip of Argentina, is a part of Patagonia. Argentina owns the eastern part of the island, and Chile controls the west.

Climate

The Pampa has a healthful, temperate climate. Mild temperatures and regular rainfall make it one of the best farming regions in Argentina. Summer comes in January because

Pilcomayo, Bermejo, Salado del Norte, and Dulce—cross the Chaco. These rivers often overflow their shallow banks in the wet season (October through April) and flood large areas of the Chaco.

Mesopotamia. Mesopotamia lies between the Paraná and Uruguay rivers. The name comes from a Greek word meaning "between the rivers." The region includes a portion of the

Argentina is in the Southern Hemisphere. In the summer, temperatures average 21°C (70°F). Winter temperatures (July) average 9°C (49°F). Rainfall varies from over 970 millimeters (38 inches) a year in the eastern, humid Pampa to less than 500 millimeters (20 inches) in the western, dry Pampa.

Since northern Argentina lies in the subtropics, both the Chaco and Mesopotamia have hot summers and warm, frost-free winters. Summer temperatures average 27°C (80°F), and winter temperatures average 13°C (55°F). Mesopotamia, the wettest place in Argentina, receives over 1,500 millimeters (60 inches) of rain a year. Less rain falls in the west and south. Tucumán, Córdoba, Mendoza, and other places farther west are too dry for farming without irrigation.

In Patagonia, winters are cold, with temperatures slightly above freezing. Summer temperatures are around 18°C (65°F). Strong winds sweep across Patagonia and make the winter seem colder than it really is. Rainfall is light, especially in the east. Most places receive less than 280 millimeters (11 inches) of rain a year.

Natural Resources

The Pampa is Argentina's most valuable resource. It produces most of the country's agricultural wealth and provides nearly all its exports. The hardwood forests of the Chaco and Mesopotamia are also important. One valuable tree is the red quebracho. The bark of this tree is used in tanning leather.

Argentina does not have many valuable mineral resources except oil. Oil and natural gas are now the top-ranking mineral products. There is a major oil field near Comodoro Rivadavia, in northern Patagonia, and offshore oil deposits were discovered in 1979. Coal is mined in Patagonia and near Mendoza. Some silver, tin, copper, iron, manganese, gold, nickel, lead, tungsten, and zinc are also mined. Sulfur, salt, and other chemicals are taken from the *salinas*.

Argentina has many waterfalls and swift streams. They are beginning to be harnessed for hydroelectric power, but in general they are too far from the population centers of the Pampa. The Iguazú Falls and the snow-fed streams from the Andes are the greatest future sources of power.

▶ THE ECONOMY

Traditionally, Argentina has been an agricultural country. The economy is still based largely on meat, wool, and cereals. But manufacturing and trade are of growing importance to the nation's economy.

Agriculture

Agriculture is big business in Argentina. Cattle raising is one of the oldest and still one of the leading industries. Wheat, grown mainly on the Pampa, is the major crop.

Wheat did not become a major crop in Argentina until the last decades of the 19th century. During the presidential term of Domingo Sarmiento millions of hectares of meadowlands were converted into wheat fields. Sarmiento encouraged the farmers to grow the crop. By the beginning of the 20th century Argentina had become one of the world's major wheat exporters. Other important grain crops are corn, grown near Rosario, and barley, oats, and rye, grown on the drier edges of the Pampa.

Cotton is the most important crop in the subtropical north, where many rivers irrigate the land. Most of the cotton is grown without artificial irrigation in the provinces of Chaco and Formosa.

Yerba maté, a tea made from the leaves of the yerba maté bush, is a special crop grown in the northeast. The tea brewed from maté leaves is a favorite beverage of the people of Argentina and neighboring Paraguay.

Irrigation has turned parts of western Argentina into vast gardens. The irrigated sugarcane fields at Tucumán have given this city the name "Garden of the North." Hundreds of orchards and vineyards are found in the western regions. Table and wine grapes, olives, apples, pears, and peaches are the leading fruits. Citrus fruits are grown just north of Buenos Aires. Oilseeds, tobacco, and soybeans are other important crops.

Cattle once roamed the Pampa in wild herds. They were used mostly for their hides. But the development of a way to ship meat in refrigerated compartments opened new markets for Argentina's beef. Improved strains of beef cattle and scientific methods of cattle raising were introduced. Cattle raising is most important in the Pampa and Mesopotamia, where cattle are raised on huge ranches. Alfalfa is widely grown throughout the Pampa. It is used mainly as feed for cattle.

Sheep are also raised in the east and in Patagonia and other parts of the country. Argentina has more than two head of cattle and more than one sheep for every person. Horses, goats, and poultry are also raised.

Manufacturing and Trade

Manufacturing is concentrated in the east, particularly around the cities of Buenos Aires and Rosario. Many other cities have industries that serve nearby farms and ranches.

The chief industries are based on livestock —meat processing and packing and the making of such products as leather goods from hides and textiles from wool. Wine making and the processing of sugar, oilseeds, grains, fruit, and other foodstuffs are also important. The plastics, iron and steel, machine tool, engineering, and chemical industries are expanding rapidly. Many kinds of consumer goods are manufactured, including paper, tobacco products, beverages, automobiles, and clothing.

Grain is Argentina's chief export, followed by animals and animal products, other foodstuffs, and wine. Europe, the United States, Japan, Brazil, and Chile are the chief markets for Argentina's products. Imports include minerals, chemicals, and machinery and other manufactured goods, mostly from the United States and Europe.

Other Industries

Argentina has sufficient petroleum and natural gas to satisfy most of its own needs. Small quantities of other minerals are extracted, mostly for local use. The government controls mining activity. Fishing is important in coastal areas.

Tourism is a growing industry. Among the popular tourist spots are the Andean resorts, the lake district around San Carlos de Bariloche, seaside resorts like Mar del Plata along the Atlantic coast, the spectacular Iguazú Falls, and the city of Buenos Aires. Most tourists are from other Latin American nations.

Transportation and Communication

Argentina's railroads are government-owned. They link Buenos Aires with almost every part of the country and with Chile, Bo-livia, Peru, and Paraguay. Buses and trucks are increasingly important as Argentina's roads improve. But most paved roads are still in the eastern part of the country. The Río de la Plata system (the Paraná, Uruguay, and Paraguay rivers) is the only important navigable waterway. Domestic air transport covers most of the country. Buenos Aires is served by many international airlines, including the state-owned Aerolíneas Argentinas.

▶ CITIES

Buenos Aires, on the Río de la Plata, is Argentina's capital and by far its largest city. Greater Buenos Aires is the home of about one third of the nation's people. Most of Argentina's manufacturing, ocean shipping, and commercial businesses are located there. An article on Buenos Aires is included in Volume B.

Rosario, on the Paraná River, is Argentina's second largest city. At Rosario the Paraná River is deep enough to permit the docking of oceangoing ships. This has made the city an important manufacturing, commercial, and export center for the Pampa.

Córdoba is Argentina's third largest city. Its university, one of the oldest in the Western Hemisphere, was founded in 1613. La Plata and Tucumán are important industrial centers, and Mendoza is famous as the center of Chile's wine-growing region.

▶ GOVERNMENT

According to the constitution adopted in 1853, Argentina has a republican, representative, and federal system of government. Each of the provinces has its own constitution, but the powers of the provincial governments are sharply limited by the federal government.

The National Congress was dissolved and most public officials were dismissed when the military took control of the country in 1976. Supreme power now rests with a junta made up of the heads of the army, navy, and air force. The head of the executive branch of government is the president, who is appointed by the junta. The president must be native-born and a Roman Catholic. The junta appoints Supreme Court judges, and the president appoints lower court judges and provincial governors. A special commission advises the junta on legislative matters.

In 1978 the president retired from the army and became a civilian president with increased powers. An eventual return to civilian rule, with an active role for the armed forces, was promised.

▶ HISTORY

Juan Díaz de Solís, a Spanish navigator, is said to have been the first European to visit Argentina. He visited the shores of the Río de la Plata in 1516 but was killed by unfriendly Indians. His companions beat a hasty retreat. Other explorers, including Sebastian Cabot, followed.

During the 16th and 17th centuries, Argentina was a part of the Spanish colony of Peru. A Spanish colonial law required that all trade from Argentina pass westward through Peru and Bolivia. This law made the west the most important part of the country. Trade prospered in the western cities of Santiago del Estero (founded in 1553), Tucumán (1565), Córdoba (1573), Mendoza (1561), San Juan (1562), Salta (1584), La Rioja (1591), Jujuy (1594), and San Luis (1596). These cities were the centers of Argentina's Spanish colonial life.

In 1776, Spain divided its empire and made Argentina a part of the viceroyalty of the Río de la Plata. Buenos Aires became the capital of the viceroyalty. This new colony included all Argentina, Uruguay, and Paraguay, and the southern part of Bolivia.

But the eastern parts of the country made little progress under Spanish rule. By the end of the 18th century, the *porteños* (as the inhabitants of Buenos Aires were called) had grown very restless. The *porteños* took advantage of Napoleon's invasion of Spain and revolted on May 25, 1810. On July 9, 1816, the western provinces joined Buenos Aires, and independence was formally declared. Under the leadership of General José de San Martín, the Argentines drove the Spanish from neighboring Chile and Peru.

Independence from Spain did not lead to immediate peace and prosperity. For many years there were bitter disputes between the central government in Buenos Aires and the *caudillos,* or leaders of the interior provinces. These disputes resulted in years of civil war. Juan Manuel de Rosas came to power in 1829 and finally united the country. He ran

Mar del Plata, Argentina's most luxurious Atlantic resort, attracts tourists from all over the world.

Argentina for more than 20 years. But the people, discontented with his dictatorial ways, drove him out of power in 1852. The following year the country adopted a constitution similar to that of the United States.

During the 19th century Argentina developed many new industries and became one of the wealthiest countries in Latin America. The steel plow, which was invented in 1837, greatly helped Argentine farmers. The farmers used this plow to cut through the thick sod of the Pampa to plant wheat and corn in the fertile soils. By the end of the century, Argentina had become one of the world's leading producers of wheat and corn.

Cattle raising also prospered. For many years cattle had grazed on the open Pampa. But the cattle were valuable only for their hides and for tallow. Before refrigeration was invented, there was no way to market the meat abroad. The industry changed in 1877 when the first refrigerator ship called at Buenos Aires to take on a cargo of chilled and frozen meat for the countries of Europe.

Other inventions also helped the cattle industry. Well-drilling machinery, invented in 1859, made it possible to set up ranches in the dry Pampa. The underground sources of water in the Pampa could be used for cattle. Barbed wire, invented in 1873, enabled the ranchers to fence huge *estancias,* where they could improve their cattle.

Argentina also advanced in other ways. In 1868, President Domingo F. Sarmiento made schooling compulsory for all children. He also encouraged Europeans to settle in Argentina. In later years as many as 200,000 immigrants arrived each year.

In 1946, Juan Perón took control of the government. He appealed to the working people, vowing to make Argentina a strong industrial nation. He raised the workers' wages, but at the expense of the farmers. Many farmers went out of business. Farm production fell so low that Argentina was on the brink of bankruptcy. As Argentina grew poorer, the people divided into two opposing groups. On the one hand were Perón's followers—the Peronistas—and on the other the anti-Peronistas.

Continuing economic problems and political conflicts weakened Perón's control. In 1955 he was removed from office and forced into exile. The military took over, and an election in 1958 put Arturo Frondizi in office. Frondizi's efforts to redevelop the nation's economy failed, and he was overthrown in 1962.

After a decade of political confusion, Perón returned from exile. In 1973 he was elected president, and his wife, Isabel Perón became vice-president. When Perón died in 1974, Isabel Perón became the first woman head of government in the Western Hemisphere. Her administration was marked by soaring inflation and political violence. In 1976 she was replaced by a military junta.

Since taking power, the junta has been criticized for violations of human rights. Inflation remains high, making life especially hard for city dwellers. But the economy has improved, and terrorist activities have been curbed.

ROBERT L. CARMIN
Ball State University

ARISTOTLE (384–322 B.C.)

Aristotle was one of the most important men of ancient Greece. He never won a battle or held a political office, but he gained fame as a teacher and as one of the greatest philosophers who ever lived.

Only a few facts are known about Aristotle's childhood. We know he was born in Stagira, a town in northeastern Greece, in 384 B.C. His father was court physician to Amyntas II, King of Macedonia, who was the grandfather of Alexander the Great. It seems likely that Aristotle learned something about science from his father.

▶ ARISTOTLE THE STUDENT

When Aristotle was about 17 years old, he went to study in Athens, an important Greek city-state. He became a pupil of the finest teacher of his day, the philosopher Plato.

The young men at Plato's Academy spent several years studying mathematics, astronomy, and government. When the youths had mastered these studies, they were asked to think about some of the problems at the heart of Greek philosophy: What is happiness?

What is the good life? What is a man's duty to his country? Plato's method of teaching stressed learning how to think clearly.

Aristotle studied under Plato for about 20 years. He was an excellent student. Plato called him "the mind of the school." When Plato died in 347 B.C., Aristotle left the Academy and began to develop his own method of teaching.

There was nothing, it seemed, that did not capture Aristotle's interest. How does the mind work? How can we learn what is true and what is false? What is the best form of government? These were only a few of the problems with which Aristotle wrestled.

Aristotle tried to find the answers by observing the world around him and gathering facts. He believed that every event had a logical explanation, and he was one of the first men to form conclusions from investigation and observation.

▶ ARISTOTLE THE TEACHER

Aristotle's fame was great by the time he left Plato's school. When King Philip II of

Macedonia was looking for a teacher for his son Alexander, he chose Aristotle. It is hard to know how much Aristotle influenced Alexander the Great, but we do know that teacher and pupil became lifelong friends.

After Alexander became king of Macedonia, Aristotle returned to Athens. In 335 B.C., with money contributed by Alexander, Aristotle opened a school called the Lyceum. It is from Aristotle's school that the high schools of France and Italy take their names: *lycée* and *liceo*.

Many subjects were taught at the Lyceum, and there were various aids for learning. Aristotle collected the first large library of ancient times. There was a museum of natural science, a garden, and a zoo.

After the morning classes Aristotle lectured to anyone who wanted to listen while he paced up and down the covered walk (called the *peripatos*) outside of his school. For this reason those who accepted his philosophy were called **Peripatetics**.

Aristotle lived and taught in a world that was very different from the one that Plato knew. In Plato's time every citizen understood the part he was to play in the life of Athens and his responsibility to the government of the city-state.

While Aristotle taught at the Lyceum, Athens lost its independence and became only a small part of Alexander's empire. As citizens of an empire, the Athenians had to adjust to a new form of government.

Aristotle urged each man to seek his own place in the world by learning how to live a good and useful life. A happy life could be found by living according to the "golden mean." By the "golden mean" Aristotle meant the middle way between two extremes. For example, he said the middle way "between cowardice and rashness is courage."

Twelve years after Aristotle opened his school, word reached Athens that Alexander the Great had died. At that time the people of Athens were divided into two groups—those who had learned to live under Alexander's rule and those who still hated it. When news of his death came, Alexander's enemies turned on his friends. Aristotle was prosecuted, like Socrates, for offending against religion. Rather than stand trial, he left Athens. He died soon afterward, in 322 B.C.

Copied from a Greek original, this Roman statue of Aristotle is in the Spada Gallery, Rome.

▶ **ARISTOTLE'S BOOKS**

Of the 400 books that Aristotle is said to have written, only a small number have come down to us. But they are remarkable books. Aristotle's works seem to have been an encyclopedia of Greek learning of the 4th century B.C. There are books on astronomy, physics, poetry, zoology, oratory, biology, logic, politics, government, and ethics.

Aristotle's books were studied after his death. They were used as textbooks in the great centers of learning: Alexandria, Rome, and the universities of medieval Europe. No other man influenced the thinking of so many people for so long.

Even today Aristotle's books are an important influence because we still use his method of investigation and observation. He classified and related all the knowledge of his time about the world. Modern scientists have found that many of the observations he made more than 2,000 years ago are correct. He showed us that every statement should be supported by evidence. Aristotle's key to knowledge was logic and his basis for knowledge was fact.

Reviewed by GILBERT HIGHET
Author, *The Classical Tradition*

ARITHMETIC

Arithmetic is the science of numbers. It is concerned with the meanings of numbers, with their symbols, and with ways of working with them. It is a branch of the larger science of mathematics, as are algebra, geometry, trigonometry, and calculus.

▶ KINDS OF NUMBERS

The earliest arithmetic ideas have to do with quantity, not with counting. Children too young to count know that four pieces of candy are more than two. They know that the four are more simply by looking. Very early peoples had the same kind of **number sense**. They could not count, but they could tell by looking that they had picked enough berries. A hunter could tell by looking that he had lost a spear.

But, as time passed, it was not enough to have only a sense of number. People needed numbers and number names. Herders needed to keep track of their animals. Farmers needed to keep track of the seasons. And so at some unknown time, long ago, the first numbers and number names were invented. These are counting numbers, which we also call **whole numbers** or natural numbers.

For a long time, counting numbers were all that were needed. Then it turned out that these were not enough. There was a need for a number that was less than 1 or for a number that was, for example, somewhere between 3 and 4. And so "in-between," or "broken," number symbols were developed. These are **fractions**. Today we express them in several ways: ¼, .25, and 25% are all ways of expressing the same fraction.

Much later, still other kinds of numbers came into use. One of these was **negative numbers**, like −2 or −7. The idea of negative numbers was very hard to work out. In ancient Greece it was known that if you took 5 from 7 you had 2 left. But was it possible to take 7 from 5? The Greeks decided it was not. To take 7 from 5 would leave less than nothing, and they could not imagine a number that is less than nothing.

Not until the 1500's did people begin to see that there could be a number that was less than nothing. The idea is easy to understand. Suppose you have $2 and you owe a friend $3.

You pay him the $2 and promise to give him the $1 as soon as possible. Now you have less than no money, because you are $1 in debt. Take 3 from 2 and you have 1 less than 0. Take 7 from 5 and you have 2 less than 0, or −2.

All of the above kinds of numbers are important in arithmetic. The numbers that you use most often, though, are the whole, or natural, numbers. These are the numbers with which you often add, subtract, multiply, and divide.

▶ OPERATIONS OF ARITHMETIC

Addition, subtraction, multiplication, and division are the four basic processes, or operations, in arithmetic. Counting is basic to all of these processes.

If there are only a few things in a group, the number can be "seen" without counting.

Just by glancing at the above group you can see that there are four birds in the group. If there are more things in a group, you must count them to get the number.

Addition

Addition is a way of operating with numbers. It is the process of putting groups together. It is also a quick way of counting forward. In the example 34 + 5, you can get the sum by:

Counting forward		or	Adding	
34	35, 36, 37,		34	addend
	38, 39		+5	addend
			39	sum

Adding is much quicker than counting forward. In order to add you must know the basic addition facts (see Table I). An addition fact is made up of two **addends** (numbers from 0 to 9) and their **sum** (answer).

$$8 + 2 = 10 \qquad 9 + 8 = 17$$

In the first example, 8 and 2 are the addends and 10 is the sum. In the second example, 9 and 8 are the addends and 17 is the sum.

How do the addition facts help you to add 34 and 5? After all, 34 is not in the table. To add these numbers, think: 4 + 5 = 9. So 34 + 5 = 39.

TABLE I

ONE HUNDRED ADDITION FACTS

0 +0 — 0	0 +1 — 1	0 +2 — 2	0 +3 — 3	0 +4 — 4	0 +5 — 5	0 +6 — 6	0 +7 — 7	0 +8 — 8	0 +9 — 9
1 +0 — 1	1 +1 — 2	1 +2 — 3	1 +3 — 4	1 +4 — 5	1 +5 — 6	1 +6 — 7	1 +7 — 8	1 +8 — 9	1 +9 — 10
2 +0 — 2	2 +1 — 3	2 +2 — 4	2 +3 — 5	2 +4 — 6	2 +5 — 7	2 +6 — 8	2 +7 — 9	2 +8 — 10	2 +9 — 11
3 +0 — 3	3 +1 — 4	3 +2 — 5	3 +3 — 6	3 +4 — 7	3 +5 — 8	3 +6 — 9	3 +7 — 10	3 +8 — 11	3 +9 — 12
4 +0 — 4	4 +1 — 5	4 +2 — 6	4 +3 — 7	4 +4 — 8	4 +5 — 9	4 +6 — 10	4 +7 — 11	4 +8 — 12	4 +9 — 13
5 +0 — 5	5 +1 — 6	5 +2 — 7	5 +3 — 8	5 +4 — 9	5 +5 — 10	5 +6 — 11	5 +7 — 12	5 +8 — 13	5 +9 — 14
6 +0 — 6	6 +1 — 7	6 +2 — 8	6 +3 — 9	6 +4 — 10	6 +5 — 11	6 +6 — 12	6 +7 — 13	6 +8 — 14	6 +9 — 15
7 +0 — 7	7 +1 — 8	7 +2 — 9	7 +3 — 10	7 +4 — 11	7 +5 — 12	7 +6 — 13	7 +7 — 14	7 +8 — 15	7 +9 — 16
8 +0 — 8	8 +1 — 9	8 +2 — 10	8 +3 — 11	8 +4 — 12	8 +5 — 13	8 +6 — 14	8 +7 — 15	8 +8 — 16	8 +9 — 17
9 +0 — 9	9 +1 — 10	9 +2 — 11	9 +3 — 12	9 +4 — 13	9 +5 — 14	9 +6 — 15	9 +7 — 16	9 +8 — 17	9 +9 — 18

You use the basic addition facts in:

(1) Adding a single column of numbers, such as

$$3$$
$$2 \qquad 3 + 2 = 5$$
$$4 \qquad 5 + 4 = 9$$
$$\overline{9}$$

The numbers on the right show how the steps in the addition are carried out.

(2) Adding several columns of numbers.

Thousands	Hundreds	Tens	Ones
1	2	6	8
	1	5	9
1	4	2	7

You add by columns from right to left. Begin in the ones column and move left from column to column.

The largest number you may write in any column is 9. What do you do when the sum in a column is more than 9?

In the above example, the sum in the ones column is 17. You must think of 17 as 1 ten and 7 ones. You then write 7 in the ones column and add the 1 ten to the other numbers in the tens column.

Now add in the tens column: $1 + 6 + 5 = 12$. Think of this as 1 hundred and 2 tens. Write 2 in the tens column. Add 1 to the hundreds column.

Adding the hundreds column, you get $1 + 2 + 1 = 4$. Write 4 in the hundreds column. There is nothing to carry over to the thousands column, so you just add that column. Since there is only one number in that column, write it at the bottom of the column. The answer is 1,427.

You can see that keeping straight columns is important, for each column has a different value.

Subtraction

Subtraction is the opposite of addition. It is a quick way of counting back. In the example $39 - 5$, you can get the answer by:

Counting back		or		Subtracting	
39	38, 37, 36,			39	minuend
	35, 34			−5	subtrahend
				34	remainder, or difference

You subtract from the **minuend**. The number you subtract is the **subtrahend**. What's left over is the **remainder**, or **difference**.

To use the faster subtraction method, you must know the basic subtraction facts. For every addition fact there is a related subtraction fact.

Addition Fact	Related Subtraction Fact
$34 + 5 = 39$	$39 - 5 = 34$
34	39
+5	−5
39	34

From the addition table you can make your own table of subtraction facts.

Here is a way to think in subtraction:

$$92 = \text{9 tens and 2 ones}$$
$$-35 = \text{3 tens and 5 ones}$$

The 9 tens and 2 ones can be written as 8 tens and 12 ones. All you do is change 1 ten into 10 ones. This gives:

92 = **8 tens and 12 ones**	minuend
−35 = **3 tens and 5 ones**	subtrahend
57 or **5 tens and 7 ones**	difference

You can easily check your results by adding the remainder to the subtrahend. You should get the minuend.

You can use addition to do subtraction. A store clerk often does this when giving you your change after you make a purchase. Suppose your purchase costs $2.60 and you give the clerk a $5.00 bill. The clerk thinks:

$$\text{\$2.60 to \$3.00} = \text{\$ .40}$$
$$\text{\$3.00 to \$5.00} = \text{\$2.00}$$
$$\overline{\text{\$2.40 (change)}}$$

Subtraction is also used to express the idea of difference. Suppose you compare the temperatures of a 19-degree day and a 35-degree day to find out how much warmer the second day was. You think: What number added to 19 will make 35?

19 to 20	=	1 degree
20 to 30	=	10 degrees
30 to 35	=	5 degrees
		16 degrees

On paper the quick operation is subtraction:

35 degrees
−19 degrees
16 degrees

Multiplication

Multiplication is a quick way of adding when the groups are equal. A package contains 24 pieces of candy. How many pieces are there in 3 packages? You can get the answer by:

Adding equal groups	or	Multiplying	
24		24	multiplicand
24		×3	multiplier
24		72	product
72			

To do multiplication, you must know the basic multiplication facts. For example, 3 × 8 = 24 is a basic multiplication fact. Read it as "3 eights equal 24." Another basic

TABLE II

ONE HUNDRED MULTIPLICATION FACTS

0 ×0 0	0 ×1 0	0 ×2 0	0 ×3 0	0 ×4 0	0 ×5 0	0 ×6 0	0 ×7 0	0 ×8 0	0 ×9 0
1 ×0 0	1 ×1 1	1 ×2 2	1 ×3 3	1 ×4 4	1 ×5 5	1 ×6 6	1 ×7 7	1 ×8 8	1 ×9 9
2 ×0 0	2 ×1 2	2 ×2 4	2 ×3 6	2 ×4 8	2 ×5 10	2 ×6 12	2 ×7 14	2 ×8 16	2 ×9 18
3 ×0 0	3 ×1 3	3 ×2 6	3 ×3 9	3 ×4 12	3 ×5 15	3 ×6 18	3 ×7 21	3 ×8 24	3 ×9 27
4 ×0 0	4 ×1 4	4 ×2 8	4 ×3 12	4 ×4 16	4 ×5 20	4 ×6 24	4 ×7 28	4 ×8 32	4 ×9 36
5 ×0 0	5 ×1 5	5 ×2 10	5 ×3 15	5 ×4 20	5 ×5 25	5 ×6 30	5 ×7 35	5 ×8 40	5 ×9 45
6 ×0 0	6 ×1 6	6 ×2 12	6 ×3 18	6 ×4 24	6 ×5 30	6 ×6 36	6 ×7 42	6 ×8 48	6 ×9 54
7 ×0 0	7 ×1 7	7 ×2 14	7 ×3 21	7 ×4 28	7 ×5 35	7 ×6 42	7 ×7 49	7 ×8 56	7 ×9 63
8 ×0 0	8 ×1 8	8 ×2 16	8 ×3 24	8 ×4 32	8 ×5 40	8 ×6 48	8 ×7 56	8 ×8 64	8 ×9 72
9 ×0 0	9 ×1 9	9 ×2 18	9 ×3 27	9 ×4 36	9 ×5 45	9 ×6 54	9 ×7 63	9 ×8 72	9 ×9 81

multiplication fact is: Any number multiplied by 0 is 0. You can find the basic multiplication facts in Table II.

Division

Division is the process of splitting a group into equal parts or groups. It is the opposite of multiplication. For example, 24 children are to be divided into eights for a folk dance. To find the number of groups, we can:

Take away, or subtract, groups of 8	or	Divide by 8
24		3 quotient
−8	divisor	8)24 dividend
16		
−8		
8		
−8		

You can check your results easily by multiplication. Multiplying the **quotient** and the **divisor** should give you the **dividend**.

In division you cannot divide by zero. Here's why. Take any number, say 24. Try to divide it by zero:

$$\begin{array}{r} ? \quad \text{quotient} \\ \text{divisor} \quad 0)\overline{24} \quad \text{dividend} \end{array}$$

It cannot be done. For when you multiply the divisor and the quotient, you should get the dividend. What number multiplied by 0 gives 24? There is no such number. Therefore division by 0 has no meaning in arithmetic.

ANOTHER WAY OF DOING DIVISION

Suppose you are asked to divide 639 by 3. First you divide the 6 by the 3. What you are doing is dividing 600 by 3, because this is what the 6 stands for in 639. You are finding out how many 3's are in 600. There are 200. This is the first answer you write down when you divide.

$$\begin{array}{r} 200 \\ 3)\overline{639} \\ 600 \\ \hline 39 \end{array}$$

The remainder is 39. When you divide 39 by 3, you are first dividing 30 by 3. You are finding out how many 3's are in 30. There are 10. You write this second answer above the first one and carry out the division.

$$\left.\begin{array}{r} 3 \\ 10 \\ 200 \end{array}\right\} 213$$
$$\begin{array}{r} 3)\overline{639} \\ 600 \\ \hline 39 \\ 30 \\ \hline 9 \\ 9 \\ \hline 0 \end{array}$$

Now the remainder is 9. When you divide 9 by 3, you are finding out how many 3's there are in 9. The answer is 3. You write this final answer above the other two. Now add up all the answers in the **number pyramid** you have made: $200 + 10 + 3 = 213$.

This way of dividing numbers is sometimes called **ladder division**. Ladder division shows you what you are doing with numbers during each step in the division.

▶**THINKING WITH NUMBERS**

Arithmetic is not only a way of operating with numbers. It is also a way of thinking with numbers. Here are a few illustrations:

(1) You have discovered a law of addition when you realize that the order in which you add numbers does not change the sum. If you find it more convenient, you can change $11 + 37$ to $37 + 11$. If you add a column of numbers down, you check the sum by adding up.

Does the law work in multiplication? Does $4 \times 5 = 5 \times 4$?

Does it work in subtraction? Does $8 - 4 = 4 - 8$?

(2) Examine the addition example below to get an estimate before you do it. Round off two-place numbers to the nearest 10; round off three-place numbers to the nearest 100; round off four-place numbers to the nearest 1,000.

1,029	1,029 is rounded to 1,000
836	836 is rounded to 800
89	89 is rounded to 90
1,920	1,920 is rounded to 2,000

Now it's easy to see that the sum will be close to 3,900. This estimate will tell you whether your computed answer is reasonable.

(3) Make up problems without numbers. Figure out how to solve them, then supply the numbers. You will often have need to solve problems like this. For example, you wish to buy a camera. You don't have enough money. How much more money do you need?

You must know the price of the camera and the amount of money you have. Then you can find the difference.

Price of camera	———	$24.95
Amount you have	———	−13.75
Amount you need	———	$11.20

(4) There are many ways to think about any number. Here are some ways of thinking about the number 9:

5+4 4+5 3×2+3 45÷5 3×3 ⅓ of 27

Continue expressing 9 in other ways.

When you think with and about numbers, arithmetic becomes an exciting and interesting subject.

ESTHER MARCUS
Board of Education of the City of New York
See also ALGEBRA; MATHEMATICS; NUMBERS AND NUMBER SYSTEMS.

ARIZONA

A strange caravan made its way across the sun-baked wilderness. Hadji Ali, whom all the soldiers called Hi Jolly, signaled that it was time to rest the camels. Lieutenant Edward F. Beale of the United States Army agreed.

The year was 1857. The place was a desert, but not in Africa or Asia. This was a desert in Arizona. Lieutenant Beale and his men were surveying a wagon road to California. Lieutenant Beale was also in charge of an experiment to find out whether camels could be used for transportation in the arid Southwest. Congress had supplied money for the purchase of 75 camels in Egypt and Turkey. Hadji Ali, a native of Syria, was hired as a camel driver.

Hi Jolly signaled again, and the caravan moved on. The camels did get to California. Some officials thought that they proved their worth, but the experiment was dropped and the camels were offered for sale. Hi Jolly settled in Arizona. A memorial to him and his camels now stands in Quartzsite, where he died in 1902.

STATE FLAG.

STATE BIRD: Cactus wren.

STATE FLOWER: The blossom of the saguaro cactus.

STATE TREE: Paloverde.

Arizona is one of the newest states, but it has one of the longest histories. Remains left by ancient Indians—weapons, tools, and ruins—show that people lived in Arizona hundreds of years before the time of Columbus. In these remains Arizona has much of the nation's important pre-Columbian treasure. Descendants of some of those ancient Indians still live in the state.

Arizona's modern history is also long and colorful. It began with the Spaniards, who were the first Europeans to enter Arizona. They remained for many years and left their names and their language and customs in the land. After the Spaniards came rugged American pioneers—trappers, traders, scouts, prospectors, miners, and cattle ranchers. With

them came the outlaws and the sheriffs of frontier days. Those days have passed, but Arizona still contains many reminders of the Old West.

Nature has given Arizona some of the nation's most spectacular scenery as well as a climate unsurpassed for healthful living. For many years tourists from all over the world have come to see the Grand Canyon and the other natural wonders for which Arizona is famous. For many years people have also come to gain health or to enjoy retirement in Arizona's warm, dry air.

Vast irrigation projects have made Arizona an important agricultural state. It is also rapidly becoming an industrial state. Increasingly manufacturers, scientists, artists, educators, and engineers are discovering that the southwestern part of the United States is the nearly perfect place in which to work and live. Within a few hours' drive by modern superhighways, people in Arizona may swim or ski. They may see desert browns and forest greens, cattle ranches and copper mines, ancient cliff dwellings and ultramodern homes.

The 48th state is booming. Its people believe that it has just begun to grow.

▶ **THE LAND**

Arizona is one of the largest states in area. It lies in the southwestern United States, about 65 kilometers (40 miles) from the Gulf of California and 235 kilometers (145 miles) from the Pacific Ocean. Its northeast corner is part of the Four Corners, the only point in the nation common to four states—Arizona, New Mexico, Colorado, and Utah.

Landforms

The three main landforms of Arizona are the Colorado Plateau in the north, the Arizona Highlands, or mountains, extending diagonally through the central part of the state, and the Basin and Range Region in the south.

The Colorado Plateau is a huge tableland that covers nearly 40 percent of the state's

ARIZONA

CAPITAL: Phoenix.

STATEHOOD: February 14, 1912; the 48th state.

SIZE: 295,025 km² (113,909 sq mi); rank, 6th.

POPULATION: 1,772,482 (1970 census); rank, 33rd.

ORIGIN OF NAME: Not yet really proved, but possibly from Papago Indian words for "small springs," which the Spanish fitted to their own pronunciation.

ABBREVIATION: Ariz.; AZ.

NICKNAME: Grand Canyon State.

STATE SONG: "Arizona," by Margaret Rowe Clifford; music by Maurice Blumenthal.

STATE MOTTO: *Ditat Deus* (God enriches).

STATE SEAL: Mountains in the background represent one of Arizona's important landforms. A storage reservoir, a dam, irrigated fields, and cattle stand for agriculture. A quartz mill and a miner represent mineral wealth.

STATE FLAG: A copper star, standing for Arizona's most important mineral, rises from a field of blue into the rays of a setting sun. The setting sun represents Arizona as a western state. The 13 rays stand for the original 13 states of the Union. Blue and gold are Arizona's colors.

LANDFORMS

western movies have been filmed at this site.

The Arizona Highlands extend across the central part of the state from northwest to southeast. In the northwestern part of this region, there are three tiers, or rows, of mountains separated by filled basins. One of these tiers, the Hualpai range, is called the Desert Alps of Arizona. Parts of it are carpeted with grass and flowers and covered with forests of aspen, fir, and pine. The southeastern part of the highlands is made up of several tiers of mountain ranges, all trending in a southeast-northwest direction. One of these tiers is the Santa Catalina range, northeast of Tucson. Mount Lemmon in this range is more than 2,700 meters (9,000 feet) high. The mountains in the central part of the region are not like those in the northwest or the southeast. They are not arranged in tiers or lined up in one direction but are somewhat jumbled together. The Mazatzal Mountains are of this kind.

Most of Arizona's dams and water-storage projects are in the mountain region, where deep, narrow canyons and the underground rock structure make ideal sites for dams. Much of the mineral wealth is also in this region.

The western part of the **Basin and Range Region** is known as the Sonora desert subregion. It is very dry, and it has very little soil that is suitable for farming, except in the river valleys around the city of Yuma. It is attractive mainly for desert scenery and for recreation on the Colorado River.

The rest of the Basin and Range Region is a partly desert area, known as the Gila semidesert subregion. Like the Sonora area, it is made up of small block ranges with basins in between. The many tiers of mountains extend in a northwest-southeast direction.

The Gila subregion is the most important part of Arizona. The main rivers are the Gila and its tributaries, such as the Agua Fria, Salt, Verde, and Santa Cruz. Large irrigation projects supply water to the fertile river basins. One of these basins, called the Valley of the Sun, holds the city of Phoenix and nearly half the population of the state.

Rivers and Lakes

The Colorado, the principal river of Arizona, drains more than 90 percent of the

total area. Upon this tableland, overlooking the town of Flagstaff, are high volcanic mountains known as the San Francisco Peaks. One of these, Humphreys Peak, is the highest point in the state. It contrasts sharply with the deep gorge of the Grand Canyon, 80 kilometers (50 miles) to the northwest. The Grand Canyon is but one of the great natural wonders of the plateau. Others include the Painted Desert and the Petrified Forest.

The Four Corners area, in the eastern part of the plateau, is the site of Hopi and Navajo Indian reservations. North of the Grand Canyon is a series of small plateaus called the Strip. This is a very dry area, isolated and undeveloped. Early inhabitants were Paiute Indians. Later, cattle ranchers brought their herds to the Strip. But the pasturelands were soon badly overgrazed. Today cattle and sheep are permitted to graze in the higher and better-watered area of the Kaibab National Forest.

The southern edge of the Colorado Plateau is mainly an escarpment—a steep slope or cliff—known as the Mogollon Rim. It extends to the White Mountains near the eastern border of the state. Here the rim of the tableland was hidden ages ago by great flows of lava that built the White Mountains. Baldy Peak, in these mountains, is the second highest point in the state. Dense forests and many small natural lakes lie along the edge of the plateau, and colorful canyons cut into the rock walls. Oak Creek Canyon, near Sedona, is noted for its superb colors. Many

land area. It winds across the northwestern part of the state and then turns south, forming the western boundary. Its main tributaries in Arizona—the Little Colorado, the Bill Williams, and the Gila rivers—are dry most of the year, as are many of the other rivers. Rivers in Arizona flow mostly after a heavy rain or when snow melts in the mountains.

Small natural lakes are found in or near the San Francisco Peaks and along the Mogollon Rim, but most of Arizona's lakes are artificial.

Climate

Generally, southern Arizona is warm and sunny. The highlands and the plateau usually have cooler temperatures.

Summer is the time of heaviest rainfall. The higher elevations receive as much as 750 millimeters (30 inches) of rain each year. The southwest corner of the state receives less than 125 millimeters (5 inches). During the winter, snow falls in northern Arizona as well as on the higher elevations elsewhere, such as Mount Lemmon, near Tucson. The amount varies from only a trace to more than 150 centimeters (60 inches).

Eight out of every 10 days in Arizona are sunny days. The humidity is generally quite low. Sunshine and low humidity help explain why people come to Arizona for health.

Natural Resources

A healthful climate and magnificent scenery have long been two of Arizona's most important natural resources. Others include its alluvial soils, minerals, and forests.

In its attempts to conserve its resources and protect the natural environment, Arizona faces at least one unusual problem—the theft of desert plants by persons who sell them for landscaping. Especially endangered by this thievery is the magnificent saguaro cactus, which produces the state flower.

Soils. More than half of Arizona's soils are gray desert soils, which are not very productive. The mountain soils are stony and are suitable only for pasture and forests. The very best soils for agriculture are in the dry Basin and Range Region. The basins in this region are filled with alluvial materials— sand and mud—that have been washed down from the highlands.

Minerals. Arizona is famous for its copper. This is the most important of the many mineral resources, which include zinc, lead, gold, silver, uranium, molybdenum, and asbestos.

Vegetation. The plant life in a given area of Arizona depends upon the amount of rainfall. The rainfall increases as the elevation of the land increases. In areas of low elevation where the precipitation is relatively low, the land is covered with typical desert plants. These include the mesquite bush, the paloverde tree, and prickly pear, saguaro, and other kinds of cacti. Sycamore and cottonwood trees are often found along dry stream beds.

Yellow and white pine, live oak, juniper, and piñon trees grow in higher elevations where the precipitation is greater. Still higher, there are forests of golden aspen, white fir, and Engelmann spruce.

THE LAND

LOCATION: Latitude—31° 20′ N to 37° N. **Longitude**—109° 03′ W to 114° 49′ W.
Utah to the north, Colorado River on the west forming part of the border with Nevada and all of the border with California, the Republic of Mexico to the south, New Mexico on the east, Colorado to the northeast.

ELEVATION: Highest—Humphreys Peak, 3,853 m (12,633 ft). **Lowest**—Along Colorado River in southwest corner of state, about 21 m (70 ft).

LANDFORMS: Colorado Plateau in the north and northeast; Arizona Highlands, or mountains, extending diagonally through the central part of the state; Basin and Range Region in the south and southwest.

SURFACE WATERS: Major rivers—Colorado River and its main tributaries in Arizona, Little Colorado, Bill Williams, Gila. **Major artificial lakes**—Mead, Mohave, Havasu, Roosevelt, Powell. **Largest natural lake**—Mormon.

CLIMATE: Temperature—Flagstaff's yearly average, 7°C (44.6°F); January average, 3°C (27.2°F); July average, 18°C (65.2°F). Phoenix's yearly average, 21°C (70.5°F); January average, 11°C (51.8°F); July average, 32°C (90.3°F). **Precipitation**—Yearly average at Flagstaff, 47 mm (18.47 in); at Phoenix, 181 mm (7.12 in). **Growing season**—10 to 11 months in the south; 4 months on the Colorado Plateau.

ARIZONA

INDEX TO ARIZONA MAP

The Mogollon Rim is covered with one of the largest stands of virgin timber remaining in the United States. The trees are mainly ponderosa pine. Other heavily forested areas are the Kaibab Plateau, the San Francisco Peaks, and the White Mountains. Most of the forests are included in national forest lands. They are valuable for lumber as well as for recreation and for conservation of water, soil, and game animals.

Wildlife. Some of Arizona's largest native animals—the grizzly bear, the timber wolf, and the elk—have been hunted almost to extinction. The native elk have been replaced by elk brought to Arizona from Jackson Hole, Wyoming. Other large Arizona animals include desert bighorn sheep, deer of several kinds, brown and black bears, bobcats, and mountain lions. The eagle and the wild turkey are the largest of many kinds of native birds.

Water. Control of water from its rivers and conservation of water and soil are among Arizona's most important problems. Roosevelt Dam and other dams on the Salt River store water for the important Salt River Project. This project is part of a vast program for conservation of soil and water that was begun in Arizona by the federal government more than 50 years ago. Coolidge Dam, on the Gila River, provides water for Casa Grande, Coolidge, and other communities.

Hoover Dam, on the Colorado River, creates Lake Mead, the world's largest reservoir. Power generated at Hoover Dam is sold to Arizona, Nevada, and California. Downstream from Lake Mead is Davis Dam. Lake Mohave, behind Davis Dam, is widely used for recreation, as are other artificial lakes. Imperial Dam and Laguna Dam, on the lower Colorado, supply water for irrigated farming around Yuma. Glen Canyon Dam, north of the Grand Canyon, forms Lake Powell.

In 1968, Congress authorized construction of a huge reclamation project for Arizona, called the Central Arizona Project. When completed, it will divert water from the Colorado River to the Phoenix and Tucson metropolitan areas.

▶ **THE PEOPLE AND THEIR WORK**

Between 1960 and 1970 the population of Arizona increased by 36.1 per cent, a rate surpassed only by Florida's and Nevada's. About half of Arizona's new residents during these 10 years came from other states. Many came to work in the new industries that were locating in the state. Some came to establish businesses of their own. Others were older, retired people.

Arizona's Indian population, which numbers about 96,000, is one of the largest in the country. Most of the Indians in the state live on reservations. Many of them are descended from the original people of Arizona. The largest of the tribes are the Navajo, the Hopi, the Apache, the Papago, and the Pima.

Where the People Live

The early settlers of Arizona made their living mainly from mining and from stock raising and a limited amount of irrigated agriculture. They lived in small settlements in the mountains and valleys. Today more than half the people live in two great irrigated areas in the Basin and Range Region —the areas around Phoenix and Tucson.

Industries and Products

It is often said that words beginning with the letter *c* are the keys to Arizona's economic life. Some of these words are copper, cotton, cattle, citrus, and climate. To them should be added at least one more word— manufacturing, which now surpasses mining and agriculture in value.

Mining. For more than 50 years Arizona has been the leading producer of copper in the United States. Clifton, Morenci, Globe, and Prescott are among the chief copper-mining communities. Copper accounts for about 85 percent of Arizona's mineral production. The state produces a significant amount of molybdenum, a metal used for hardening and strengthening steel. Silver and gold are also mined. Asbestos, a mineral used for fire-resisting fabric, is mined on the Fort Apache and the San Carlos Indian reservations. Cement, sand and gravel, building stone, and gypsum are abundant as well as valuable for the construction industries. The mountain region is the most important for mining, but copper and other minerals are found elsewhere in the state.

The Four Corners area has deposits of low-grade coal, which the Indians mine for their own use. Some radioactive minerals are found in this part of the plateau, and the deposits of helium gas are of high quality. Years ago panning for gold brought rich yields from the lower Gila and the Colorado river valleys, but today this part of the Basin and Range Region produces only small amounts of manganese, fluorite, and tungsten. Ajo, near the Papago reservation, has huge deposits of low-grade copper. Mining began here as early as the year 1750, and it is still an important industry.

Agriculture. Maricopa County, in the Salt River Project, ranks within the first five counties in the United States for value of agricultural production. Pima County is the center of another great irrigated farming area. These are the counties where Phoenix and Tucson are located. Cotton lint and cottonseed, cattle, vegetables, livestock feeds, citrus fruits (oranges, lemons, grapefruit), and sheep are the most important agricultural products in these counties. Around Yuma, in the western part of the Basin and Range Region, farmers grow large crops of cotton, citrus fruits, and vegetables.

It's roundup time on Oak Bar Ranch near Nogales. Beef cattle are among Arizona's main agricultural products.

Molten copper flows into a ladle at a smelter in San Manuel. Arizona is the nation's leading copper producer.

The mountain region has fine cattle ranches where great herds of Hereford and Brahman cattle graze. Leading cattle-producing areas are the upper San Pedro and the San Simon valleys. Kingman, in the northwest part of the mountain region, and Benson and Willcox, in the southeast, are important centers from which cattle are shipped to various parts of the nation.

In the mountain region there is little soil that is suitable for farming except in the extreme southeast, where cotton, vegetables, livestock feeds, and melons are grown.

Most of the Indian tribes raise some livestock and grow small crops of corn, beans, squash, and melons.

Forest Industries. Arizona's most important forest product is ponderosa pine, a fine-grained wood in demand for doors, flooring, and general millwork. Lumber from the Mogollon Rim is sawed at Flagstaff, Winslow, Heber, and Show Low.

Manufacturing. The increase in manufacturing has been one of the most spectacular developments in Arizona in recent years. The state's leading manufactures are electrical equipment and supplies (particularly electronic devices), machinery, food products, primary metals, and military equipment.

Other Industries. Tourism is a year-round business in Arizona. The rapid growth of the tourist industry, as well as a great increase in population, has stimulated the growth of such businesses as banking, insurance, retail selling, and building.

Transportation and Communication

For many years railroads were the chief means of transportation to and within Arizona. During the 1920's Arizona pioneered in air travel. Today a network of airways, highways, and railroads covers all parts of the state.

Railroads and Highways. Railway building began in Arizona about 1880. By 1883 two transcontinental railways spanned the area. The Santa Fe crosses Arizona from Lupton to Topock. The Southern Pacific crosses the state from San Simon to Yuma by way of Tucson and Gila Bend. There is also a network of lesser rail lines.

Arizona is well served by federal and interstate highways, especially those that run in an east-west direction. North-south traffic is by U.S. Highway 89 north of Flagstaff and connecting interstate highways south of that city. Paved highways connect all the more important centers and make it easy for people to reach the main scenic and recreational areas. Off the highways and major roads, there are many dirt roads that may become impassable after a rain. An unexpected rain or a light snow often isolates deer hunters.

Airports. In 1919 Tucson established a city-owned airport, one of the first in the nation. By 1927 a passenger and express service linked Tucson, Phoenix, and Los Angeles. During World War II the federal government established military air bases at Luke, Davis-Monthan, Williams, and other flying fields, and these military bases speeded the growth of air transportation. By the early 1960's Phoenix's Sky Harbor Airport ranked among the top 10 airports in the United States. Several major airlines link Arizona's cities with other points in the nation and the world.

Publications. The first Arizona newspaper, the *Weekly Arizonian,* appeared in Tubac in 1859. It went out of existence in 1871 after having been moved to Tucson, to Prescott, and back to Tucson. Several other newspapers were founded during the 1860's and the 1870's. The early papers were very informal. Much space was given to local and personal news and to discussions of ways to handle the Indians. After statehood the papers broadened their coverage of news.

Some of the territorial papers are still publishing. The *Arizona Republic,* established in 1890 as the *Arizona Republican,* ranks as one of the better newspapers in the nation. Today Arizona publications include about 15 daily newspapers, more than 50 weekly papers, and numerous magazines. *Arizona Highways,* the monthly publication of the Arizona Highway Department in Phoenix, is famous internationally for its color photography and its other excellent qualities.

Radio and Television. Arizona's first commercially licensed radio station, KTAR, began broadcasting in Phoenix on June 21, 1922. Television broadcasting began, also in Phoenix, when KPHO-TV went on the air on December 4, 1949. Today there are 85 radio broadcasting stations and 11 television stations in Arizona.

The University of Arizona at Tucson (*left*) is a leading educational center of the Southwest.
At right Tucson spreads over a desert valley near the Santa Catalina Mountains.

► EDUCATION

In the early days of Arizona's history, education was sketchy and haphazard. Settlers were few, and they were scattered over a wide area. Often children were taught in the home. Well-to-do families sent their children to eastern boarding schools.

Anson P. K. Safford, third territorial governor (1869–77), is regarded as the founder of Arizona schools. He presented plans for a public school system and worked for the establishment of schools. The first schools were opened during the 1870's, but it was not until much later that Arizona was able to develop an adequate system of public education. Today the educational and cultural institutions of the state rank among the best in the nation.

Colleges and Universities

Arizona had four institutions of higher learning while it was still a territory. Two were founded in 1885. They were the University of Arizona, at Tucson, and the Arizona Territorial Normal School, now Arizona State University, at Tempe. Northern Arizona Normal School was established at Flagstaff in 1899. It is now Northern Arizona University. Eastern Arizona College, at Thatcher, was founded by the Mormon Church as an academy in 1891. Today it is a public two-year college. Other such colleges have been established in every section of the state. One of these, the Navajo Community College, is on the Navajo Indian reservation. Grand Canyon College and Southwestern College, in Phoenix, are private senior colleges.

Libraries and Museums

Most of the larger towns have their own public libraries. Bookmobiles carry library service to very small towns and remote areas.

Arizona has a variety of museums. The museum of the Arizona Historical Society, in Tucson, has collections from pioneer days. The Arizona State Museum, on the University of Arizona campus in Tucson, specializes in the study of American Indian activities in the Southwest from prehistoric times. The Museum of Northern Arizona, near Flagstaff, includes exhibits that show changes in the earth and in the way Indians have lived in northern Arizona since prehistoric times. Museums in Phoenix include the Heard Museum, which specializes in anthropology and primitive art; the Phoenix Art Museum, with collections of painting and sculpture; and Pueblo Grande, a Hohokam Indian archeology museum.

The Arizona-Sonora Desert Museum, near Tucson, displays desert animals and plants. This museum is unusual in that most of its displays are alive. Important collections of desert plants are found also in the Desert Botanical Garden, in Papago Park, Phoenix, and in the Boyce Thompson Southwestern Arboretum, near Superior.

► CITIES

Arizona has two major cities, Phoenix and Tucson. Eleven other communities had populations of more than 10,000 in 1970.

Phoenix

Arizona's capital and largest city was named for the mythical bird, the phoenix. It stands on the site of ancient Indian ruins, where the Hohokam Indians built a canal system and carried on irrigated farming long before the time of Columbus. Part of this ancient canal system is in use today. Phoenix became the territorial capital in 1889 and the state capital in 1912. Today it is the center of agriculture, industry, commerce, and tourism in the state. It has three colleges and numerous parks, botanical gardens, and museums.

Tucson

The second largest city is located on the Santa Cruz River in the south central part of the state. The name Tucson is a corruption of a Pima Indian word, *Stjukshon,* meaning "foot of the black hill." The community was begun by the Spanish about the year 1700. From 1867 to 1877, Tucson was the territorial capital. It grew rapidly after the building of the Southern Pacific Railroad and the development of mining, ranching, and irrigated agriculture in the 1880's. By 1890 it was a university town and the center of local trade. Tucson is the gateway to an area of varied attractions such as Saguaro National Monument, Coronado National Forest, Misson San Xavier del Bac, and Kitt Peak National Observatory, a major solar observatory.

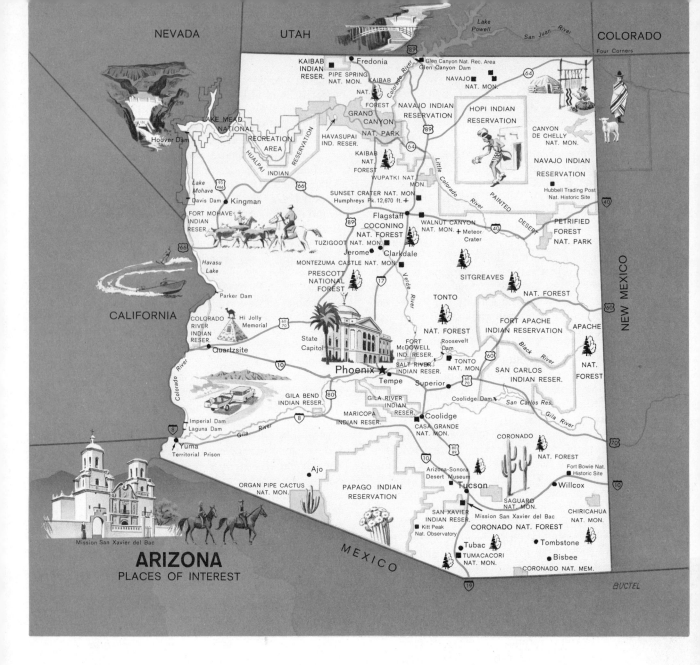

NEVADA   UTAH   COLORADO

Four Corners

Lake Powell

San Juan River

KAIBAB INDIAN RESER.

Fredonia

Glen Canyon Nat. Rec. Area
Glen Canyon Dam

NAVAJO NAT. MON.

PIPE SPRING NAT. MON.

KAIBAB NAT. FOREST

HOPI INDIAN RESERVATION

NAVAJO INDIAN RESERVATION

CANYON DE CHELLY NAT. MON.

Colorado River

LAKE MEAD NATIONAL RECREATION AREA

Hoover Dam

GRAND CANYON NAT. PARK

HAVASUPAI IND. RESER.

KAIBAB NAT. FOREST

NAVAJO INDIAN RESERVATION

Hubbell Trading Post Nat. Historic Site

HUALPAI INDIAN RESERVATION

WUPATKI NAT. MON.

SUNSET CRATER NAT. MON.
Humphreys Pk. 12,670 ft.

Little Colorado River

PAINTED DESERT

Lake Mohave

Davis Dam   Kingman

FORT MOHAVE INDIAN RESER.

Flagstaff
COCONINO NAT. FOREST

WALNUT CANYON NAT. MON.
Meteor Crater

PETRIFIED FOREST NAT. PARK

NEW MEXICO

TUZIGOOT NAT. MON.

Jerome   Clarkdale

MONTEZUMA CASTLE NAT. MON.

SITGREAVES NAT. FOREST

Havasu Lake

PRESCOTT NATIONAL FOREST

Verde River

TONTO NAT. FOREST

FORT APACHE INDIAN RESERVATION

APACHE NAT. FOREST

Parker Dam

CALIFORNIA

COLORADO RIVER INDIAN RESER.

Hi Jolly Memorial

State Capitol

FORT McDOWELL IND. RESER.

Roosevelt Dam

TONTO NAT. MON.

Black River

Quartzsite

Phoenix
Tempe   Superior

SALT RIVER INDIAN RESER.

SAN CARLOS INDIAN RESER.

San Carlos Res.

Gila River

Colorado River

GILA BEND INDIAN RESER.

GILA RIVER INDIAN RESER.

Coolidge Dam

Imperial Dam
Laguna Dam

MARICOPA INDIAN RESER.

Coolidge

CASA GRANDE NAT. MON.

CORONADO NAT. FOREST

Gila River

Yuma
Territorial Prison

Ajo

PAPAGO INDIAN RESERVATION

Arizona-Sonora Desert Museum

Tucson

SAGUARO NAT. MON.

Fort Bowie Nat. Historic Site

Willcox

ORGAN PIPE CACTUS NAT. MON.

SAN XAVIER INDIAN RESER.

Kitt Peak Nat. Observatory

Mission San Xavier del Bac

CORONADO NAT. FOREST

CHIRICAHUA NAT. MON.

Mission San Xavier del Bac

MEXICO

Tubac

TUMACACORI NAT. MON.

Tombstone

Bisbee

CORONADO NAT. MEM.

ARIZONA
PLACES OF INTEREST

BUCTEL

Other Cities

Several important cities have grown up to the east of Phoenix. Scottsdale, the center of a popular resort area, calls itself "The West's Most Western Town." Only western-style construction is allowed in the downtown section. Mesa was founded by the Mormons in 1878. It is a winter resort, surrounded by a rich agricultural area. Tempe, the home of Arizona State University, was known as Hayden's Ferry when it was founded on the Salt River in 1872 by Charles Trumbull Hayden. Glendale is situated on the northwestern edge of Phoenix. Nearby are Luke Air Force Base and the American Graduate School of International Management.

Flagstaff lies just south of the San Francisco Peaks near the southern edge of the Colorado Plateau. Beautiful mountain scenery, pine forests, and cool temperatures have made Flagstaff a well-known tourist and recreation center for northern Arizona. It is also a university city. Lumbering is a major industry. Lowell Observatory, near Flagstaff, is the observatory from which Clyde W. Tombaugh discovered the planet Pluto in 1930.

Prescott is the seat of Yavapai County, in west central Arizona. At two different times, 1864–67 and 1877–89, it was the territorial capital. In the early 1900's it was the center of a mining area. Today it is resort center in a mining and ranching area.

Yuma, on the Colorado River in the southwestern part of the state, is a port of entry into California. Since the development of the Yuma irrigation project, it has become the center of a rich agricultural district. It was named for the Yuma Indians.

▶ **PLACES OF INTEREST**

Nearly three fourths of Arizona's total area has been set aside for use as Indian reservations and as national areas.

Indian Reservations

When the Spanish arrived, there were 14 Indian tribes in Arizona. They were of four types:

(1) Pueblo dwellers: Hopi (and Tewa), Zuñi.
(2) Desert herdsmen and farmers: Pima, Papago, Maricopa, Mohave, Yuma.
(3) Plateau herdsmen and farmers: Paiute, Havasupai, Hualpai, Yavapai, Chemehuevi.
(4) Nomad hunters: Navajo, Apache.

The establishment of present-day reservations in Arizona corresponds roughly with the areas inhabited by the various tribes before 1850. Altogether there are 19 reservations.

On the Hopi and Navajo reservations in Four Corners, the Indians raise sheep and grow small crops for their own needs. Some families improve their income by making silver jewelry and weaving beautiful rugs for tourists. The ancient Indian community of Oraibi, on the Hopi reservation, is thought to be the oldest continuously inhabited community in the United States.

The mountains of central Arizona contain two large reservations, the Fort Apache and the San Carlos. Both are for the Apaches. Once feared as raiders and fighters, the Apaches today raise cattle and cut much reservation-held timber. The Apache reservations have many camping sites and recreational facilities for tourists.

About a fifth of the Basin and Range Region is set aside for Indian reservations. The Papago, Pima, and Maricopa Indians who live in this region carry on a little irrigated agriculture and raise some cattle.

The most isolated are the Havasupai Indians, who live in Cataract Canyon, a side canyon of the Grand Canyon. Their isolation made it easier for them than for the other tribes to keep their age-old culture.

A Navajo child watches his mother prepare wool for the weaving of a blanket.

Rodeos are popular in Arizona. Cowboys compete in more than 100 rodeos held in the state each year.

National Areas

There are seven national forests in Arizona. The largest, Tonto National Forest, is in the central part of the Arizona Highlands, north of Roosevelt Dam. Other national forests in the highlands are the Apache, which Arizona shares with New Mexico; the Sitgreaves, near Holbrook; the Coconino, near Flagstaff; and the Prescott, near the town of Prescott. The Kaibab National Forest is in the plateau region near the Grand Canyon. The Coronado is in the southeast.

Two of Arizona's best-known natural features have been preserved as national parks. Grand Canyon National Park includes the spectacular canyon of the Colorado River. An article on this park is included in Volume G. In the Petrified Forest National Park, visitors see ancient logs of great size that have turned into beautifully colored stone. A museum in the park shows the process in detail.

Arizona shares the Glen Canyon National Recreation Area with Utah and the Lake Mead National Recreation Area with Nevada.

Arizona has about one fifth of all the national monuments in the United States. They are described in the following list, along with national historical areas.

Canyon de Chelly National Monument, in the northeast corner of the state, contains prehistoric Indian ruins built at the base of cliffs and in caves.

Stone logs in the Petrified Forest are the remains of giant trees that grew more than 150,000,000 years ago.

White House and Antelope House are among the most interesting. Mummy Cave gets its name from the fact that well-preserved human bodies hundreds of years old were found there.

Casa Grande National Monument, at Coolidge, preserves a ruined adobe tower that was built 600 years ago by Indians.

Chiricahua National Monument, southeast of Willcox, is called the Wonderland of Rocks because of the fantastic shapes of the rocks.

Coronado National Memorial, on the Mexican border near Bisbee, marks the place where Coronado entered what is now the United States.

Fort Bowie National Historic Site, northeast of Willcox, preserves the site of military operations against the Apache chief Geronimo.

Hohokam Pima National Monument, southwest of Chandler, preserves the remains of a Hohokam Indian village known as Snaketown.

Hubbell Trading Post National Historic Site, at Ganado on the Navajo reservation, preserves a trading post that is still active.

Montezuma Castle National Monument, south of Flagstaff, includes one of the best-preserved cliff dwellings in the country.

Navajo National Monument, on the Navajo reservation, is made up of three different parts containing the largest and most interesting of known cliff dwellings.

Organ Pipe Cactus National Monument, south of Ajo, on the Mexican border, contains cacti and other desert plants found nowhere else in the nation. It gets its name from a cactus that has as many as 30 arms resembling organ pipes.

Pipe Spring National Monument, a historic site near Fredonia, contains a fort and other structures built by Mormon pioneers about 1879.

Saguaro National Monument, east of Tucson, preserves one of the state's richest desert areas. Here the visitor sees the saguaro cactus, which grows as high as 15 meters (50 feet) and branches into weird shapes. It blossoms in May, and in June it bears a purple fruit, which the Papago and the Pima Indians use for food. There are many other kinds of cacti and also desert animals.

Sunset Crater National Monument, in the San Francisco Peaks, preserves a crater from which molten lava spewed forth about 900 years ago. The cone is colored as if by the glow of sunset.

Tonto National Monument, near Roosevelt Dam, contains cliff dwellings where Indians lived and farmed in the Salt River Valley during the early 1300's.

Tumacacori National Monument, south of Tucson, preserves a historic Spanish mission built about the year 1700. It is near the site first visited by Father Kino in 1691.

Tuzigoot National Monument, near Clarkdale,

contains ruins of a large prehistoric pueblo where people lived as long ago as A.D. 1000.

Walnut Canyon National Monument, east of Flagstaff, preserves a group of small cliff dwellings in shallow caves. These cliff dwellings were built by Pueblo Indians about 800 years ago.

Wupatki National Monument, north of Flagstaff, contains red sandstone pueblos built by a group of farming Indians. They are thought to be the ancestors of the modern Hopi Indians.

Other Places of Interest

Among the many other places of interest in Arizona are San Xavier del Bac, a beautiful Spanish mission church on the Papago Indian reservation south of Tucson; Dinosaur Canyon, north of Flagstaff, where footprints of dinosaurs are preserved in sandstone; and the "ghost" mining towns of Jerome and Tombstone. London Bridge, which once spanned the Thames River in London, England, now spans an artificial river in Arizona. The bridge was taken apart, transported to Arizona, and rebuilt at the resort community of Lake Havasu City, south of Topock.

The Territorial Prison, at Yuma, is one of the historical, scenic, or recreational sites preserved in the state park system.

Annual Events

The following are a few of Arizona's many annual events that are eagerly awaited by tourists and residents alike:

February—Parada del Sol (Parade of the Sun), Scottsdale.

March—Major league exhibition baseball games, Mesa, Phoenix, Scottsdale, Tucson, Apache; World's Championship Rodeo, Phoenix.

Easter—Sunrise Service, Grand Canyon.

July—All-Indian Powwow, Flagstaff.

August—Hopi Indian snake dances, Hopi villages.

September—Navajo Tribal Fair, Window Rock.

November—Arizona State Fair, Phoenix.

GOVERNMENT

Capital—Phoenix. **Number of counties**—14.
Representation in Congress—U.S. senators, 2; U.S. representatives, 4. **State Legislature**—Senate, 30 members; House of Representatives, 60 members; both 2-year terms. **Governor**—4-year term; no limit on number of terms. **Elections**—General and state, Tuesday after first Monday in November.

COUNTIES

▶ **GOVERNMENT**

The state constitution was drafted by members of the constitutional convention that met in Phoenix from October 10 to December 9, 1910. On February 2, 1911, the constitution was approved by the people of Arizona. The proposed constitution found favor in Congress, but it was not acceptable to President Taft, who objected to the provision that judges could be recalled by popular vote. Finally, after the constitution had been amended, the President approved Arizona's admission into the Union on February 14, 1912.

The executive branch of the state government is made up of the governor and several other officers. All executive officers serve a term of 4 years.

The legislative branch consists of the Senate and the House of Representatives. In 1966 the legislature was re-apportioned to provide equal representation according to population. The legislature meets in January of each year.

There are 5 justices in the Supreme Court, elected for terms of 6 years. Superior Court judges are elected for 4-year terms, as are justices of the peace in rural areas.

Counties in Arizona are administered by county boards of supervisors. Most towns operate under the city-manager type of government.

Arizona has not had the time or the population to produce many persons of international fame. The following are among the adopted and native-born citizens of Arizona who have made important contributions to the state and the nation:

Pauline Weaver (1800–67), born in Tennessee, was one of the early mountain men, explorers, and prospectors in Arizona. As a scout and guide, he served often as a go-between for the Indians and the settlers. Weaver, who was part Cherokee Indian, was named Paulino but was known as Pauline.

Charles D. Poston (1825–1902), a native of Kentucky, worked to help Arizona become an organized territory and then served as the first territorial delegate to Congress. He is remembered also as one who helped develop the mining industry in Arizona and as an explorer, author, and the territory's first superintendent of Indian affairs.

George W. P. Hunt (1859–1934) served as a member of the Arizona territorial legislature and as president of the state constitutional convention in 1910. He was elected first governor of the state. Afterward he served several more terms as governor. He was born in Missouri.

William O. "Bucky" O'Neill (1860–98), an editor, soldier, and famous frontier sheriff, came to Arizona from Washington, D.C. He enlisted in the Rough Riders of the Spanish-American War and was killed at San Juan Hill.

Frank Luke, Jr. (1897–1918), of Phoenix, was the first aviator in World War I to receive the Congressional Medal of Honor. A monument to Luke stands on the capitol grounds in Phoenix.

Barry M. Goldwater (Phoenix) was elected to the United States Senate in 1952. In 1964 he was the Republican nominee for president of the United States. Other well-known persons born in Arizona are Carl T. Hayden (Tempe), who served in Congress for more than 50 years; Stewart Udall (St. Johns), who was U.S. secretary of the interior from 1961 to 1969; Morris Udall (St. Johns), who was an unsuccessful candidate for the Democratic presidential nomination in 1976; Helen Hull Jacobs (Globe), tennis champion of the 1930's; and Romana Acosta Bañuelos (Miami), treasurer of the United States from 1971 to 1974.

Noted persons to whom Arizona lays claim, although they were not born in the state, include Zane Grey, author of western fiction; James H. McClintock, historian; and Frank Lloyd Wright, architect, whose school of architecture, Taliesin West, is near Phoenix.

Arizona's two most famous Indian chiefs were Cochise and Geronimo. Both were great Apache warriors and able leaders.

▶ HISTORY

Tools, weapons, and ruins of different kinds show that Arizona has been inhabited by people for some 20,000 years. The Hohokam first lived in southern Arizona about 500 B.C. They settled along the valleys of the Salt and the Gila rivers, developed a remarkable system of canals, and carried on irrigated agriculture. Sometime about A.D. 1400 the Hohokam deserted their land. No one knows where they went. The present-day Pima Indian term *Ho-ho-kam* means "those who are gone." It is thought that perhaps these people are the ancestors of modern Pima and Papago Indians.

Arizona was explored quite early, but lack of water and other problems discouraged settlement for some time. There are four periods in the modern history of Arizona.

Spanish Exploration and Settlement

Marcos de Niza, an Italian in the service of Spain, entered Arizona in 1539. He is thought to have been the first European to enter the area. He was searching for the Seven Cities of Cibola, as was Coronado, who explored eastern and northeastern Arizona from 1540 to 1542. These explorers were followed by many others and by missionaries, soldiers, and colonists. The most famous mission builder was Father Kino, a Jesuit priest and a native of Austria who established the major missions in southern Arizona between 1692 and 1711.

Some of the Indian tribes accepted the work of the missions. Other tribes were hostile, and between 1737 and 1769 Indian troubles destroyed the work of Father Kino and other missionaries. In 1752 Spain established a garrison at Tubac to protect miners and colonists in the area. In 1776 the garrison was moved to Tucson for greater protection. But continued Indian uprisings discouraged Spanish settlement, and Arizona became a neglected land.

Mexican Rule

In 1821 Mexico won independence from Spain, and for more than 20 years a Mexican governor ruled the Territory of New Mexico, which included the present states of Arizona and New Mexico. The capital was at Santa Fe. In 1846 war broke out between Mexico and the United States. Soon the United States flag replaced the Mexican flag over the governor's palace, in Santa Fe.

American Territorial Period

The Mexican War ended with the Treaty of Guadalupe Hidalgo in 1848. This treaty, together with the Gadsden Purchase a few years later, gave the land that is now Arizona to the United States. Arizona remained a part of the Territory of New Mexico until, in February, 1862, it joined the Confederacy as a territory. The only battle of the Civil War to be fought in Arizona occurred in April of that year at Picacho Peak, northwest of Tucson. It was a minor skirmish, involving fewer than 20 men on each side. In 1863 President Abraham Lincoln signed a bill establishing Arizona as a territory of the United States.

During the territorial period, cattlemen brought their herds to Arizona's grazing lands, and prospectors carried on a vigorous search for minerals. Gold was found on the Gila and the Colorado river. In 1863 Henry Wickenburg developed the famous Vulture Mine at Wickenburg. Mining activities brought many towns into existence. Some grew; others became ghost towns when the mineral deposits proved to be small. Indian troubles continued until the Apache chief Geronimo surrendered in 1886. By 1900 many of Arizona's towns had been founded.

Statehood

Arizona applied for admission as a state several times before it finally gained statehood in 1912. Even before statehood the federal government had helped Arizona solve its water problems. The (Theodore) Roosevelt Dam on the Salt River was completed in 1911. Other dams brought irrigation and hydroelectric power to undeveloped areas.

During World War I many new farms were developed in Arizona. Mining flourished, and by 1929 millions of tourists were on the roads for the first time. Southern Arizona developed as a favored winter playground. Northern Arizona became a choice summer recreation area. World War II brought an industrial boom to the state, and the years between 1940 and today have brought a startling growth of population.

The Future

The first 50 years of statehood, 1912–62, were marked by agricultural and industrial development. Climate and scenery have stimulated tourism in the state. People have come to Arizona to work, play, and retire. During the next 50 years, Arizona is likely to experience even greater growth, but much of its future growth depends on obtaining additional water from the Colorado River and on the desalting of ocean water.

GEORGE T. RENNER, 3RD
Formerly, Arizona State University

IMPORTANT DATES

1539	Marcos de Niza is thought to have been the first European to enter Arizona.
1540–1542	Francisco Vásquez de Coronado explored eastern and northeastern Arizona.
1692–1711	Eusebio Francisco Kino established missions in southern Arizona.
1752	Spanish garrison established at Tubac.
1776	Garrison of Tubac moved to present site of Tucson.
1824	Mexico formed the Territory of New Mexico (including Arizona), with its capital at Santa Fe.
1848	Mexico signed the Treaty of Guadalupe Hidalgo, giving lands, including most of Arizona, to the United States.
1854	Ratification of Gadsden Purchase added land south of Gila River to Territory of New Mexico.
1857	Lieutenant Edward F. Beale and his survey party used camels in Arizona.
1862	Only battle of the Civil War in Arizona fought at Picacho Peak.
1863	Congress created the Territory of Arizona.
1880–1883	Two railroads spanned Arizona.
1886	Geronimo, Apache chief, surrendered to the U.S. Army.
1889	Phoenix became the capital of Arizona.
1911	Completion of (Theodore) Roosevelt Dam on Salt River marked the beginning of large-scale irrigation projects.
1912	Arizona admitted to the Union, February 14, as the 48th state.
1930	Arizona entered an era of tourism, population increase, and industrial growth.
1963	A decision by the U.S. Supreme Court gave Arizona a major share of Colorado River water.
1975	Raul H. Castro took office as the state's first Mexican-American governor.
1977	Legislature passed a law providing tax incentives for use of solar-energy devices.

ARKANSAS

One day in 1906, while walking across his land near Murfreesboro, John W. Huddleston noticed some pebbles shining on the earth. He held them in his hand and watched them shine. He watched and wondered, for he had suddenly remembered something. Hadn't geologists said that rocks in this neighborhood might contain diamonds?

Huddleston saved the pebbles and asked the opinion of experts. The experts replied, "They're diamonds."

People were astonished. "In Arkansas?" they asked. "Nobody ever found diamonds in Arkansas. It can't be true."

It was true. The mines near Murfreesboro were the first and only true diamond mines ever to be discovered and worked in all North America. No mining is done today, but people are welcome to visit the diggings and search for diamonds.

STATE FLAG.

STATE TREE: Shortleaf pine tree.

STATE BIRD: Mockingbird.

STATE FLOWER: Apple blossom.

▶ **ARKANSAS OR ARKANSAW?**

Should the name be spelled *Arkansas,* or should it be spelled *Arkansaw?* Should it be pronounced ar KAN zus, or should it be pronounced ARK un saw? These were important and troublesome questions in the history of Arkansas. In 1880 the state appointed a committee to make a study and give a report.

The early settlers had no doubt about the name. It was a word that sounded like ARK un saw, and that was what they said. It had been spelled in different ways. By 1880 the spelling usually was *Arkansas,* and by this time many people were insisting that the pronunciation should be ar KAN zus.

The committee asked the opinion of learned persons, including the poet Longfellow. Longfellow replied that he preferred ARK un saw. It was more musical, he thought, than ar KAN zus.

The committee also reviewed the history of the name. In 1673 French explorers came paddling down the Mississippi from Canada. Near a river that flowed into the Mississippi, they found an Indian tribe that called itself the Akansea, or Akansa. These Indians were known later as the Quapaws, or the Arkansas Indians. The explorers spelled the name in various ways, but soon the French were using *Arkansa* and then *Arkansas.*

When the United States bought Arkansas as part of the Louisiana Purchase, in 1803, the Americans took over the French pronunciation of the name. Sometimes they spelled it *Arkansaw,* because that was the way it sounded. At first the name of the territory was spelled in this way. But when the territory became a state, in 1836, it was admitted to the Union as *Arkansas.*

The committee made its report. In 1881 the state legislature passed a law declaring that the spelling was to be *Arkansas* but that the pronunciation was to be ARK un saw.

The people of Arkansas are proud of their heritage from the early settlers. At the same time they look to the future of their state. In 1953 they gave it a new nickname, The Land of Opportunity.

Arkansas is indeed a land of opportunity. Its natural resources provide for agriculture, manufacturing, mining, lumbering, and commerce. Many of the resources have not been used to their fullest extent, and they offer a wide range for future development.

Visitors find much to see and enjoy in Arkansas—mountains, lakes, and swift, clear streams in the Ozark and the Ouachita highlands; cotton and rice fields in the Coastal Plain; countless springs, waterfalls, and caves in many parts of the state.

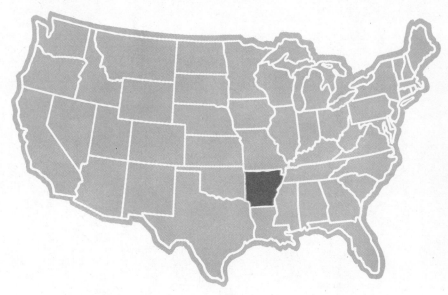

ARKANSAS

CAPITAL: Little Rock.

STATEHOOD: June 15, 1836; the 25th state.

SIZE: 137,540 km² (53,104 sq mi); rank, 27th.

POPULATION: 1,923,295 (1970 census); rank, 32nd.

ORIGIN OF NAME: From local Indians, the Quapaws, meaning "downstream people." Called Arkansa by the French.

ABBREVIATION: Ark.; AR.

NICKNAME: Land of Opportunity.

STATE SONG: "Arkansas."

STATE MOTTO: *Regnat populus* (The people rule).

STATE SEAL: The American eagle holds in its beak a scroll with the state motto and in its claws an olive branch and arrows representing the powers of peace and war. The shield over the eagle's breast stands alone, showing that Arkansas depends on its own strength. A steamboat, a plow and a beehive, and a sheaf of wheat on the shield are symbols of wealth and industry. The goddess of liberty is above the eagle. The sword of justice is on one side and the angel of mercy on the other.

STATE FLAG: A large white diamond on a red field and bordered in blue shows that Arkansas is the only state that yields diamonds. The 25 white stars indicate that Arkansas is the 25th state. The blue star above the name of the state shows that it belonged to the Confederacy. The other three blue stars represent the nations that have owned the land—France, Spain, and the United States. They also tell that Arkansas was the third state created from the Louisiana Purchase.

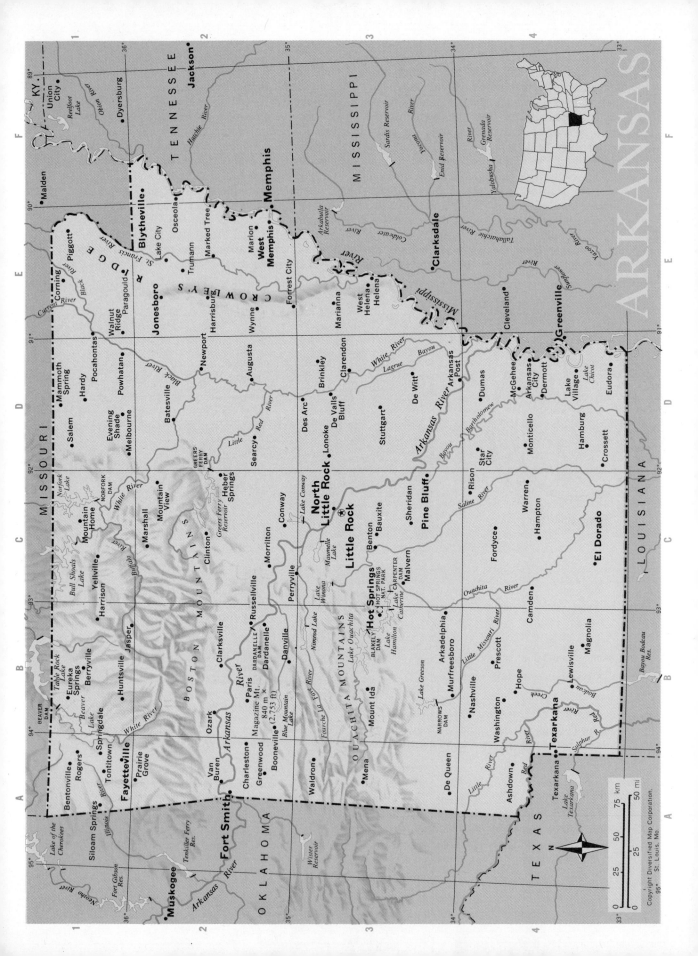

INDEX TO ARKANSAS MAP

• County Seat   Counties in parentheses   ★ State Capital

▶THE LAND

Arkansas is located in the Upper South, among the West South Central group of states. It is usually thought of as a southern state. It shares the Cotton Belt with its neighbors to the south and east. But Arkansas is also somewhat like the Midwest and the West. It produces grain and cattle. Fort Smith, on the western side of the state, holds a rodeo along with its annual livestock show.

Landforms

The landforms of Arkansas are of two kinds—highlands in the northwest half of the state and lowlands in the southeast half. The highlands are made up of the Ozark Plateaus and the Ouachita Highlands. The lowlands consist of the Mississippi Alluvial Plain and the Gulf Coastal Plain.

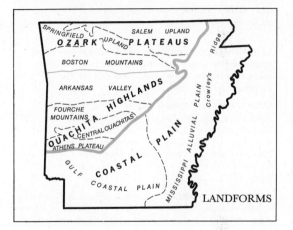

LANDFORMS

Highlands. The Ozark area is often called the Ozark Mountains. Actually, this area is made up of three plateaus of different elevations, or heights. Geographers call these plateaus the Salem Upland, the Springfield Upland, and the Boston Mountains.

The Salem Upland is located mainly north of the White River. It is a land of rolling plains and low hills that rise as high as 300 meters (1,000 feet). The Springfield Upland, which is somewhat higher, lies west and south of the Salem Upland. It is chiefly a plain. The Boston Mountains form the southern edge of the Ozarks. They are rugged hills and low mountains, which rise more than twice as high as the Salem Upland.

The Ouachita Highlands are divided into

THE LAND

LOCATION: Latitude—33° N to 36° 30′ N. Longitude—
89° 38′ W to 94° 37′ W.
Missouri to the north, Oklahoma and Texas on the
west, Louisiana to the south, Mississippi River on the
east separating Arkansas from Tennessee and
Mississippi.

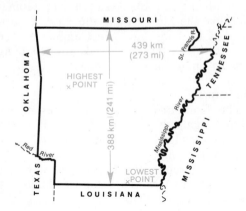

ELEVATION: Highest—Magazine Mountain, 840 m (2,753
ft). Lowest—Along Ouachita River near southern border,
17 m (55 ft).

LANDFORMS: Highlands (the Ozark Plateaus and the
Ouachita Highlands) in northwest half of state; low-
lands (the Mississippi Alluvial Plain and the Gulf
Coastal Plain) in southeast half.

SURFACE WATERS: Major rivers—White, Buffalo,
Black, Little Red, St. Francis (part of boundary with
Missouri), Arkansas, Red (part of boundary with Texas),
Ouachita, Saline. Major artificial lakes—Ouachita,
Greeson, Blue Mountain, Nimrod, Maumelle, Conway, Bull
Shoals, Norfork, Greers Ferry, Beaver. Largest natural
lake—Chicot.

CLIMATE: Temperature—Summer average, 26°C (79°F).
Winter average, 2°C (36°F) in north, 9°C (48°F) in south.
Precipitation—Rainfall average, 1,000–1,500 mm (40–60
in). Snowfall, from 25 cm (10 in) in north to a trace in
south. Growing season—In the north 180 days; more
than 230 days in south.

sippi Alluvial Plain lies to the east. The entire lowland area is relatively flat to gently rolling. There is much swampland along all the main rivers.

A very interesting feature of the Mississippi Valley is Crowley's Ridge, a long, narrow ridge extending through southeastern Missouri and northeastern Arkansas to Helena. Long ago the Mississippi River flowed along the west side of Crowley's Ridge. The Ohio River was on the east, and the two rivers met near the present site of Helena, Arkansas. Then the Mississippi cut its present course through the north end of the ridge. The two great rivers joined at what is now Cairo, Illinois, and left the ridge standing above the old floodplains.

Rivers and Lakes

The surface waters are among Arkansas' most interesting and useful features. The Mississippi River forms most of the eastern border. The Arkansas River flows southeastward through the center of the state and empties into the Mississippi. Both of these great rivers are important for transportation. All the rivers and streams are valuable as homes for wildlife and as places for recreation.

Dams have been built in the rivers, creating large artificial lakes. These lakes are chiefly in the highlands. They provide flood control, waterpower, and recreation. No one knows the exact amount of surface water. It increases almost year by year as dams are built and new lakes fill.

Climate

The climate of Arkansas is described as a humid subtropical climate. This means that the state has long, hot summers and short, cool winters. It is far enough north and inland to receive cold air masses from the heart of the continent in winter and hot air masses in summer. It is also far enough south to receive warm, moisture-laden winds from the Gulf of Mexico.

Because of the mild climate, people find that costs of building, heating, and lighting are lower in Arkansas than in states farther north. Usually snow and ice do not hinder transportation because they do not last long.

The weather during the summer is about the same in all parts of the state. Temperatures

four parts—the Arkansas Valley, the Fourche Mountains, the Central Ouachita Mountains, and the Athens Plateau. Most of the hills and mountains in these highlands extend in a east-west direction. The Arkansas Valley includes both the Arkansas River and an area of widely spaced mountains and broad valleys on both sides of the river. In the Fourche Mountains and the Central Ouachitas, the mountains are closer together and the valleys are more narrow. The Athens Plateau is a rolling plain.

Lowlands. The Gulf Coastal Plain lies to the south of the highlands, and the Missis-

Norfork Lake was formed by a dam on North Fork, a tributary of the White River. The lake helps prevent floods and provides fishing and other recreation all year round.

are generally comfortable, but there can be days of extreme heat. The highlands have cooler summer nights than do the lowlands because of the breezes that blow along the slopes of hills and mountains.

Winter temperatures vary considerably, although the north is usually somewhat colder than the south. Once in a while there are periods of extreme cold, when the temperature drops well below freezing in both parts of the state.

The mountains receive more precipitation than do other parts of the state, but all areas receive enough moisture for crops. Most of the precipitation falls as rain.

In the north some snow falls during the winter. In the south there is little snow. Children who have sleds may be able to use them only once in 5 or 6 years.

The growing season permits a wide range of crops, including cotton. This crop is grown commercially in areas having more than 200 frost-free days.

Natural Resources

Arkansas' natural resources include its soils, forests, minerals, waters, and wildlife. These resources provide the raw materials for the economic life of the state. Arkansas therefore devotes much effort to soil and water conservation. Dams and reservoirs help to prevent floods and soil erosion. And some of the reservoirs help ensure a supply of water for homes and industries.

Soils. The most fertile soils are the limestone and the alluvial soils. Limestone soils are located in the extreme northern part of the state. Alluvial soils are found along the rivers and streams, especially the Mississippi River. Most of Arkansas' soils will produce many different crops when they are properly fertilized and cultivated.

The Ouachita River flows through scenic Ouachita National Forest in west central Arkansas.

A power shovel dumps a big bite of bauxite-bearing earth in central Arkansas. Bauxite is the raw material from which aluminum is made.

The soils in the rice-growing areas are especially interesting. They have a subsoil that will not let water drain down easily. As a result, water will stand on the surface for long periods and irrigate the rice.

Forests. The early settlers had to clear land for crops because nearly all of Arkansas was once a forest. The softwood forest, shortleaf and loblolly pine, is in the southern part of the state. The hardwood forest, mainly oak and hickory, is in the northern part of the state, in the Mississippi Valley, and along streams in the south. The forests supply lumber and wood products. They are important also as homes for wildlife, as protection for the soil against erosion, and as pasture for livestock.

Minerals. Most of the important minerals are located in the Gulf Coastal Plain and the Arkansas Valley. Minerals in these areas include petroleum, natural gas, natural-gas liq-

uids, clays, coal, and diamonds. Bauxite, a claylike mineral from which aluminum is obtained, is found in the center of the state. Manganese, lead, and zinc are found in the north central part. But these are no longer mined. Sand, gravel, and stone are plentiful almost everywhere.

Waters. Ground and surface waters are sufficient to supply people's needs in most parts of the state. The larger cities have had to build reservoirs to meet their greater need for water. Most of the dams have equipment for generating hydroelectric power, but only about a fifth of the waterpower is being used.

Wildlife. Many forms of wildlife are found in Arkansas. Deer, fish, and migrating ducks and geese are the most important. Deer are especially plentiful in the mountains and in the river lowlands in the eastern part of the state. Trout, largemouth bass, and smallmouth bass are the most popular game fish. Fishing for gar provides great sport in the rivers of the lowlands. Migrating waterfowl are attracted to the rice fields for food as they journey southward.

▶ **THE PEOPLE AND THEIR WORK**

Arkansas was settled as part of the westward movement in the United States. Most of the early settlers came from land directly to the east. Nearly all of them were descendants of southern colonists who had come from northwestern Europe during colonial days. Some of the early settlers of Arkansas married Indians, especially Cherokees. As cotton growing spread throughout the lowlands, large numbers of slaves were brought in. Today fewer than 1 percent of the people are foreign born and most were born in the state.

POPULATION

TOTAL: 1,923,295 (1970 census). **Density**—14 persons to each square kilometer (36.2 persons to each square mile).

GROWTH SINCE 1820

Year	Population	Year	Population
1820	14,273	1920	1,752,204
1840	97,574	1940	1,949,387
1860	435,450	1960	1,786,272
1900	1,311,564	1970	1,923,295

Gain Between 1960 and 1970—7.7 percent.

CITIES: Population of Arkansas' largest cities according to 1970 census.

Little Rock	132,483	Fayetteville	30,729
Fort Smith	62,802	Jonesboro	27,050
North Little Rock	60,040	West Memphis	25,892
Pine Bluff	57,389	El Dorado	25,283
Hot Springs	35,631	Blytheville	24,752

Where the People Live

About half the people live in urban areas (places of 2,500 residents or more); the other half, in rural areas. The lowlands have more people than the highlands because the soils in the lowlands are more productive, transportation is easier, and most of the mineral wealth is in this region. Many retired people from other states have come to the highland areas because of the scenery, the moderate cost of living, and the pleasant climate.

The censuses of 1950 and 1960 showed that Arkansas had lost population. People were moving from rural areas to cities, where they could find jobs in industry, but many people were leaving the state to find jobs. However, with the growth of industry in Arkansas, the trend was reversed. The 1970 census showed a gain in population.

Industries and Products

In earlier times Arkansas depended on farm products for most of its income. These products (crops, livestock, and poultry) are still very important. But in recent years agricultural products have ranked second in value. Manufactured products are first, and minerals are third.

Agriculture. From the early days of the state, the lowlands were developed as part of the Cotton Belt. Here the farmers grew a single crop (cotton) and sold it for cash. Farmers in the highlands grew various kinds of crops, mainly for their own use. Sometimes they had very little left for sale. This situation is changing.

Cotton remains a major agricultural product, and Arkansas ranks among the top producers of cotton in the nation. But farmers in the Cotton Belt are now using the soil to grow other crops as well—soybeans, corn, and hay. Arkansas has become one of the chief soybean-producing states. Rice is a third major crop.

Rice farmers have found ways to get additional income from their land. They rent hunting privileges when ducks and geese migrate over the rice lands in the fall. Fish farming is a new idea that the farmers are trying. To keep the soil fertile, they allow the land to lie idle every year or two. During this year the fields are kept flooded and fish are raised. The fish are used for fertilizer.

WHAT ARKANSAS PRODUCES

AGRICULTURAL PRODUCTS: Poultry and poultry products, cattle and calves, milk, soybeans, rice, cotton, vegetables, fruits, wheat, corn.

MANUFACTURED GOODS: Food and related products, electrical equipment and supplies, paper and related products, lumber and wood products, chemicals and related products, rubber and plastics products, clothing and other textile products, metal products.

MINERALS: Crude petroleum, natural gas and natural-gas liquids, bauxite, stone, bromine, sand and gravel, barite, coal.

The highlands have turned to cattle raising. Both the highlands and the lowlands produce poultry, fruits, and vegetables for the market. Rogers, in northwestern Arkansas, is well-known for poultry, especially broilers. Tontitown is known for grapes, Clarksville for peaches, and Marshall for strawberries. Hope, in southwestern Arkansas, is called the watermelon capital of the state. Monticello, in the southeast, is known for tomatoes.

Forest Industries. Arkansas' forests provide the raw materials for many manufacturing industries. These industries produce such things as lumber, wood pulp, paper, railroad ties, and furniture.

Lumber is the major forest product. It comes from the pine forest in the southern part of the state. Pine is also used for wood pulp, which in turn is made into paper. The oak and hickory forest of the highlands is used for furniture, barrel staves, railroad ties, and other wood products.

Forest industries can be almost any size. Lumber mills in the highlands may employ only a few persons, and the mills may be moved frequently. Big paper mills have several hundred employees, and the locations of the mills remain fixed.

Mining. Crude petroleum was first produced in Arkansas in 1921. Today it ranks first in value among Arkansas' minerals. The state is the nation's leading producer of bauxite, the principal source of aluminum. More than 90 percent of all the bauxite ore mined in the United States comes from central Arkansas. Arkansas is also a leading producer of barite, a mineral used in the manufacture of paper, rubber, and other products.

Arkansas' first natural gas was produced in the western part of the state, near Fort Smith, in 1901. Today natural gas is produced in both the west and the south. Some coal is mined in the western Arkansas Valley, but coal mining is not so important as it once was.

The industries that process minerals (refine them or separate them from other substances) are usually located near the supply. Oil refineries are at El Dorado and Magnolia, near the oil fields. Bauxite is processed into aluminum at Benton and Bauxite, near the bauxite mines. Natural gas is processed in southern Arkansas to make such important by-products as natural gasoline, butane, sulfur, and propane.

Other Industries. In recent years, industries that prepare foods have become very important. These industries involve mainly the canning of fruits and vegetables and the processing of poultry and various livestock products. Most of the foods are grown in the areas near the factories.

Industries that make electrical equipment are also of great importance. Among their many products are electric motors, refrigerators and ranges, air conditioners, television sets, and light bulbs. Many towns and cities have factories that produce clothing, plastic or metal products, and chemicals.

Transportation and Communication

Little Rock is the hub of the federal interstate highways that cross Arkansas and of most of the other major highways, which serve all sections of the state.

The Mississippi River is the greatest river transportation system in the United States. From earliest days Arkansas has benefited from use of this famous waterway. The Arkansas River has always been used for a limited amount of river traffic. Federal funds totaling $1,200,000,000 were used to make the Arkansas navigable to Catoosa, a suburb of Tulsa, Oklahoma. The project, completed in 1970, provides a major waterway through the Arkansas Valley.

Most of the cities, especially in the lowlands, have railroad freight service. Trucks and buses provide freight and passenger service throughout the state.

There are over 100 airports and airfields, with several major commercial companies serving the state.

Every large town has a local newspaper. The *Arkansas Gazette,* published in Little Rock, is the major paper of the state. It is also the oldest newspaper in continuous publication west of the Mississippi River. It was first issued at Arkansas Post in 1819.

Radio and television stations are fairly widespread. There are more than 100 radio stations and 8 television stations.

▶ EDUCATION

Arkansas is well supplied with schools and other educational and cultural institutions.

Schools and Colleges

The best-known early school was established for the Cherokees in 1822. Its founder was Cephas Washburn, a Protestant missionary from New England. Catholic missionaries had been active in teaching the Indians before that time.

When Congress created the Arkansas Territory in 1819, it set aside a section of land in each township for the support of public schools. In 1843 the legislature established a system of public education, but there were few public schools until after the Civil War. Private schools and academies provided schooling for a small percentage of the people. The present public school system is largely the system that was established by the state constitution of 1868.

Arkansas has a number of state-supported and private institutions of higher education. Most of the colleges and universities are small. The largest is the University of Arkansas, which has its main campus at Fayetteville and other campuses at Little Rock, Monticello, and Pine Bluff. The University of Arkansas Medical Sciences Campus is in Little Rock.

Libraries

Arkansas' first public library was established early in the 1800's, but the growth of public libraries was slow, partly because the people lived in widely scattered rural areas.

The State Library Commission was created in 1935. It maintains a book collection at Little Rock from which volumes are sent by mail to individuals, schools, and organizations. Bookmobiles operate throughout the state. Most of the counties have some type of library service, and most of the cities support free public libraries. The major historical library is maintained by the Arkansas History Commission, Little Rock.

Fine Arts and Museums

The fine arts are represented in Arkansas by various activities. Little Rock has a Fine Arts Club and a Palette Club. The Arkansas Poets hold regional meetings and an annual Poets' Day. The Arkansas Federation of Music Clubs, which was established in 1908, has branches in several cities. Little Rock has a choral society, an opera company, and a philharmonic society. Fort Smith, Fayetteville, and El Dorado have symphony orchestras. Clarksville, Conway, and Fayetteville have youth orchestras.

The following are among the leading museums:

The **Arkansas Arts Center**, in MacArthur Park, Little Rock, contains the state's most important collection of paintings and other fine arts. The **Museum of Science and Natural History**, also in MacArthur Park, occupies the building in which General Douglas MacArthur was born.

The **El Dorado Fine Arts Association**, El Dorado; **Fort Smith Art Center**, Fort Smith; and **Southeast Arkansas Arts and Science Center**, Pine Bluff, all have fine arts collections. They also sponsor lectures, drama, and arts festivals.

The **University of Arkansas Museum**, Fayetteville, contains Arkansas Indian material and many science and natural history exhibits. The **Arkansas State University Museum**, State University (Jonesboro), is a history, science, and technology museum.

Folklore

The most famous folk tale of Arkansas is the one entitled *The Arkansas Traveler*. This story has given much amusement to many people, but it has left the impression that the natives of Arkansas are lazy and uneducated. The story goes that the traveler lost his way and came at last upon a cabin. In front of the cabin, which was badly in need of repair, sat the settler, playing the same unfinished tune over and over again on his fiddle. At his side were his dogs. All around him was work waiting to be done. In the conversation that followed, the traveler offered to finish the tune, and in gratitude the settler let him spend the night. The story and the tune are famous, but both have injured the reputation of the state and its people among those who take the tale too seriously.

The mountains are full of legends that are now being written down and saved for future generations. The University of Arkansas library has an unusual Arkansas folklore collection, including a large quantity of tape-recorded material gathered in the state. Usually the tales are about some local person or some event of early times. Like all such tales, they have been enlarged upon until much of the truth is gone. But they add a romantic touch to life and are part of the heritage of the frontier, which still lingers in many areas.

▶ PLACES OF INTEREST

Each year the state increases its efforts to preserve and improve the many places of interest. They range from important historic sites to roadside picnic areas.

Historic Places

Most of the historic sites are related to pioneer settlement or to the Civil War.

Arkansas Post National Memorial, near the mouth of the Arkansas River, marks the first permanent French settlement (1686) in the Lower Mississippi Valley.

Arkansas Territorial Capitol Restoration, Little Rock, is a group of buildings that have been restored to give a picture of life in territorial days.

Fort Smith National Historic Site, Fort Smith, preserves the site of one of the first U.S. military posts in the Louisiana Territory. The fort was founded in 1817.

Pea Ridge National Military Park commemorates the greatest battle west of the Mississippi during the Civil War. The park is near Rogers.

Parks and Forests

Besides the national areas listed above, Arkansas has one national park, Hot Springs (see "Cities," in this article), and three national forests. The national forests are the Ozark National Forest, in the northwestern part of the state; the Ouachita National Forest, in the west, extending into Oklahoma; and the St. Francis National Forest, in the east. The Buffalo National River, established in 1972, preserves the scenic Buffalo as a free-flowing, unpolluted river and as a major recreation area.

The system of state parks includes about 30 areas, most of which provide for picnicking, camping, and a variety of activities for young and old. The following are among the state parks that attract large numbers of people:

Bull Shoals State Park, located on the White River at the foot of Bull Shoals Dam, is a favorite for campers. Visitors may tour the dam and fish for trout in the waters released through the dam.

Crater of Diamonds State Park preserves the area where diamonds once were mined. It attracts diamond hunters from all over the country.

Petit Jean State Park, in west central Arkansas atop Petit Jean Mountain, has spectacular mountain views and many recreational facilities. Nearby is Winrock Farm, an experimental farm established by Winthrop Rockefeller.

Other Attractions

Many tourists come to Arkansas to enjoy the scenery in the highlands. The hills and mountains are not of great height, but they are very rugged and colorful. The roads twist and turn, bringing an ever-changing scene into view. In the spring people come to see the redbud and the dogwood. In the autumn the foliage is a major attraction.

Each year more and more tourists come to both the highlands and the lowlands to enjoy a particular activity. They fish in the many lakes and streams, hunt wildfowl, hike in the forests, search for diamonds at the diamond mine near Murfreesboro, or explore caves. Diamond Cave, near Jasper, contains many passages. It has no diamonds, but the quartz crystals give a spectacular effect. Special events such as homecoming and folk pageants also attract many visitors.

Annual Events

Arkansas has many annual events that are based on products of the state or that

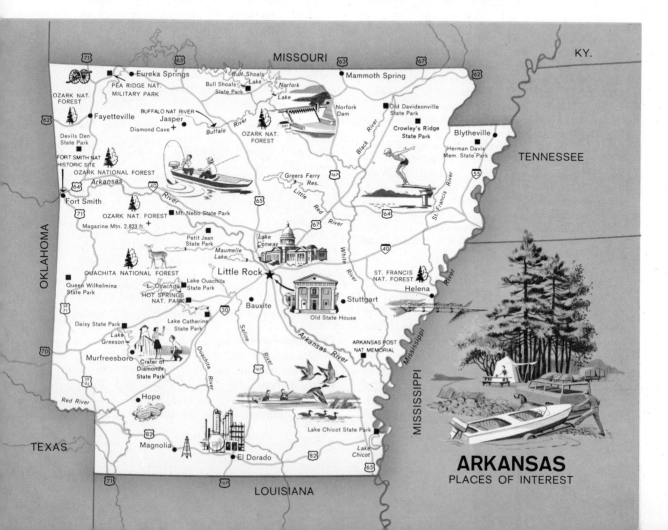

ARKANSAS
PLACES OF INTEREST

The city of Hot Springs, surrounding Hot Springs National Park, is one of the nation's best-known resorts.

The state capitol at Little Rock was built mainly of Arkansas stone and marble.

emphasize the people's interests or talents. Some of the events are of local interest. Others attract national attention.

February, March—Horse racing, Hot Springs.
March—Oil Jubilee, Magnolia.
May—Rodeo and livestock show, Fort Smith.
October—Annual State Fair and Livestock Show, Little Rock; National Cotton Picking Contest, Blytheville; National Wild Turkey Calling Contest, Yellville; Folk Festival, Eureka Springs.
November—Homecoming, University of Arkansas and most of the other colleges; Rice Carnival and World's Championship Duck Calling Contest, Stuttgart.

▶ **CITIES**

The following are three of Arkansas' best-known cities:

Little Rock

The state capital and largest city was founded in 1820. It is located on the Arkansas River near the center of the state. Its central location and its political functions make it the most important city. It is a major market for cotton, soybeans, and other agricultural products of the surrounding area; the leading transportation and trade center; and the home of a large number of industrial plants. In 1970 the Arkansas River Navigation Project was completed. This created a major waterway through the Arkansas Valley and meant increased port activity for Little Rock.

Across the Arkansas River from Little Rock is the city of North Little Rock. Together these cities are the center of a metropolitan area that contains approximately one fifth of all the people of the state.

Hot Springs

Hot Springs is located in the Central Ouachita Mountains. The city is a well-known tourist center and health resort surrounding Hot Springs National Park. It is noted for its 47 mineral springs. The naturally hot water from the springs is collected into a central system and is distributed to bathhouses, where it is used in the treatment of certain ailments.

The Indians used the hot waters long before the city was settled in 1807. Early travelers brought the springs to national attention, and in 1832 the U.S. Government made a health resort of the area. Hot Springs National Park was established in 1921. Besides the thermal springs, it includes wooded hills and valleys, with scenic drives, forest trails, and bridle paths. The beautiful scenery and the many recreational activities, such as boating, fishing, and horse racing, attract many visitors all year round.

Fayetteville

The home of the University of Arkansas is located on hills at the edge of the Boston

Mountains, overlooking the Springfield Upland. It was on the Butterfield stage route, and it developed early as an important trade center and the home of wood industries. Today Fayetteville's industries include the processing of poultry and the manufacture of clothing and of wood products. Its main point of interest is the university. The countryside is famous for scenery and for apples and strawberries.

Other Cities

The following are among the largest cities of Arkansas. Each has a population of more than 20,000 (1970 census).

North Little Rock is an industrial city. Among its products are lumber, fertilizer, and textiles.

Fort Smith, a market center on the Arkansas River, serves the livestock and truck-farming region of western Arkansas and eastern Oklahoma. It is also a leading industrial center, producing glass, paper cups, light metal products, furniture, coal, and natural gas.

Pine Bluff is a commercial center, also on the Arkansas River, in a rich agricultural region downstream from Little Rock. It has lumber and textile mills, cotton gins, and cottonseed-oil mills. Pine Bluff is the home of one of the campuses of the University of Arkansas.

El Dorado, principal city in southern Arkansas, is called the oil capital of the state.

Jonesboro is the largest city in northeast Arkansas. It is a trading center, with rice mills and a variety of other industries. It is the home of Arkansas State University.

Blytheville is a trade center, near Jonesboro, in a highly productive area. It has light industry.

▶ GOVERNMENT

The government of Arkansas is organized under the constitution adopted in 1874 and its various amendments. This is the fifth constitution that the state has had. The first was adopted in 1836, when Arkansas became a state. The second was adopted when Arkansas withdrew from the Union in 1861. Others were adopted in 1864 and in 1868 as a result of the Civil War and the difficult period of Reconstruction. All the constitutions have provided for three branches of government, with largely separate powers.

The Three Branches

The legislative branch makes the laws. This branch is a General Assembly consisting of two bodies, the Senate and the House of Representatives. The members of the Senate are elected by the people for 4-year terms. The members of the House are elected for 2-year terms. The lieutenant governor is the presiding officer of the Senate. The House has a presiding officer called the speaker, who is elected by the members. A bill may be introduced into either body. To become a law, it must be approved by a majority of both houses.

The executive branch enforces the laws. This branch consists of a governor and six other state officers, all elected by the people. Governors may succeed themselves. But only two of Arkansas' governors have served more than two terms.

The judicial branch interprets and applies the law. Four kinds of state courts make up this branch. They are the minor courts, the circuit courts, the chancery courts, and the supreme court. The supreme court consists of a chief justice and six associate justices.

Local Government

County and city governments have authority in various local matters, including taxation. Important county officers are the county judge, county and circuit clerks, sheriff, assessor, collector, and treasurer.

COUNTIES

The following persons are among Arkansas' native-born or adopted citizens who became well known in public affairs:

Albert Pike (1809–91) is remembered as a teacher in one of Arkansas' early schools, a newspaperman, a general in the Confederate Army, and Indian commissioner for the Confederacy. He led a brigade of Cherokee Indians in the battle of Pea Ridge. Pike came to Arkansas when he was a young man. He was born in Massachusetts.

Augustus H. Garland (1832–99) was born in Tennessee but was brought up in Washington, Arkansas. He was governor of the state from 1874 to 1877, a U.S. senator from 1877 to 1885, and U.S. attorney general in the cabinet of President Grover Cleveland. Garland City was named for his father, Rufus Garland.

Joseph Taylor Robinson (1872–1937) was born in Lonoke. He was elected governor in 1912 while serving in Congress. He was inaugurated as governor, but within 2 weeks the General Assembly elected him to the U.S. Senate. He remained in the Senate until his death. Senator Robinson was the candidate for vice-president when Al Smith ran for the presidency in 1928.

James William Fulbright was born at Sumner, Missouri, in 1905, but his family moved to Fayetteville in 1906. He was president of the University of Arkansas from 1939 until 1941. From 1943 to 1945 he was a member of the U.S. House of Representatives; and from 1945 to 1975, a member of the U.S. Senate. He became known in many parts of the world as the sponsor of the Fulbright Act of 1946. Under this act the U.S. Government provides money for an exchange of scholars between the United States and other countries.

The names of many other Arkansans are well known in state or national affairs. The two governors who served more than two terms were Jeff Davis and Orval Eugene Faubus. Governor Davis served for three terms, from 1901 to 1907. He was also a U.S. senator. Governor Faubus was reelected to a fifth term in 1962. The first woman to be elected to the U.S. Senate came from Arkansas. She was Mrs. Hattie Wyatt Caraway, who was elected in 1932. General Douglas MacArthur and former Secretary of the Army Frank Pace, Jr., were born in Little Rock. Winthrop Rockefeller, an adopted son of Arkansas, was governor of the state (1967–71) and a leader in civic affairs and agriculture.

Arkansas' writers include biographer Katharine Susan Anthony (Roseville), poet and novelist John Gould Fletcher (Little Rock), short-story writer Thyra Samter Winslow (Fort Smith), and novelist Charles Morrow Wilson (Fayetteville). Opera singer Mary Lewis was born in Hot Springs. Fayetteville was the birthplace of Edward D. Stone, one of America's best-known architects.

Actors and actresses who came from Arkansas include Fay Templeton (Little Rock), Dick Powell (Mountain View), and Alan Ladd (Hot Springs). Radio comedian Robin (Bob) Burns was born in Greenwood, but he claimed Van Buren as his home.

▶ HISTORY

The original inhabitants of Arkansas were members of the Osage, the Quapaw, and the Caddo Indian tribes. These tribes wandered from place to place, using the land mainly for hunting and fishing.

Discovery and Exploration

The first Europeans to see Arkansas were Spaniards under Hernando de Soto, who crossed the area in 1541. They found no gold or other treasure, and Europeans did not visit the area again for more than 100 years.

In 1673 two French explorers came south along the Mississippi to the mouth of the Arkansas River. They were Father Jacques Marquette, a Jesuit priest, and Louis Jolliet. They stayed for a short time with the friendly Quapaw Indians and then returned to Canada. They were followed in 1682 by a party under Robert Cavelier, Sieur de la Salle. La Salle explored the valley of the Mississippi, named it Louisiana, and claimed it for France. In 1686 one of La Salle's lieutenants, Henri de Tonti, returned and founded the settlement of Arkansas Post. It was located a few miles upstream from the mouth of the Arkansas River. The French called it *Aux Arcs,* a name that later became "Ozarks."

In 1762 France gave the Louisiana Territory to Spain. Spain kept it for 38 years, until 1800, and then gave it back to France.

Early Settlement

During French and Spanish ownership, little was done to settle Arkansas. Spain promised many things to American colonists who would settle there, but very few of the colonists were interested.

In 1803 the United States acquired the area as part of the Louisiana Purchase. American settlers began to look upon it more favorably, but for a time there was still a great deal of land east of the Mississippi. People did not find it necessary to look for homesteads farther west.

The presence of Indians was another thing that delayed settlement. The native Osage Indians lived north of the Arkansas River, and the Quapaws lived to the south. Between 1808 and 1828, treaties were made, and the native Indians were removed to areas in what is now Oklahoma. At first much of the Osage land was granted to Cherokee Indians, who were being forced out of their homes east of the Mississippi. Much of the Quapaw land was given to the Choctaw Indians. Then white settlers began to arrive in Arkansas, and the Cherokees and the Choctaws were forced to move on to the west.

The process of settlement was very slow. People came mainly by waterways. They lived on homesteads far from other settlers or in very small villages near the rivers. The town of Arkansas Post was the only major settlement for more than 100 years. Gradually people spread out along the rivers in the northeastern part of the state and through the Arkansas Valley. Small settlements were made along the edges of the mountains and in the valleys. In 1820 there were about 14,000 people in the territory.

Arkansas Becomes a State

Congress created the Arkansas Territory in 1819, and the first territorial legislature met at Arkansas Post on July 28 of that year. Two years later the capital was moved to Little Rock. On June 15, 1836, Arkansas became a state.

At the time of the Civil War, the people of Arkansas were divided in their feelings, especially in the northern part of the state. Arkansas joined the Confederacy on May 16, 1861, and many battles were fought on its soil. The battle of Pea Ridge, sometimes known as Elkhorn Tavern, was the greatest battle of the war west of the Mississippi. It was fought in March, 1862.

Arkansas was re-admitted to the Union in 1868, but a responsible state government did not come until 1874. Since that time Arkansas has been as prosperous as most southern states, but it has lagged behind the nation as a whole.

The Future

Future development will depend upon fuller use of natural resources and upon adjustments of various kinds. Farms in the highlands need to be larger to provide enough income for farm families. Industry is growing, and more factories and plants are needed to provide more jobs in the towns and cities. The mountains, lakes, parks, and forests can be made to attract far more tourists. Arkansas' people think the future looks bright.

O. ORLAND MAXFIELD
University of Arkansas

ARLINGTON NATIONAL CEMETERY. See NATIONAL CEMETERY SYSTEM.

ARMADA, SPANISH. See BATTLES IMPORTANT IN WORLD HISTORY.

ARMENIA. See UNION OF SOVIET SOCIALIST REPUBLICS.

IMPORTANT DATES

1673	Marquette and Jolliet, French explorers, came down the Mississippi River to the mouth of the Arkansas River.
1686	Henri de Tonti established Arkansas Post.
1762	France ceded area to Spain as part of Louisiana.
1800	Spain ceded Louisiana back to France.
1803	United States bought area as part of Louisiana Purchase.
1806	Southern part of New Madrid District set off as District of Arkansas.
1811	Earthquakes at New Madrid, Missouri, in 1811 and 1812 caused people from that area to flee to Arkansas.
1812	Arkansas included in Missouri Territory.
1813	Arkansas County created as part of Missouri Territory.
1819	Territory of Arkansas established; first meeting of territorial legislature; first issue of *Arkansas Gazette*, oldest newspaper west of Mississippi River.
1836	June 15, Arkansas admitted to Union as 25th state.
1861	Arkansas seceded to join Confederacy.
1868	Arkansas re-admitted to Union.
1871	Arkansas Industrial University founded, later to become the University of Arkansas.
1874	Present constitution adopted.
1896	First bauxite mined.
1906	First diamonds found.
1921	First petroleum produced.
1932	Arkansas became first state to elect a woman, Hattie Wyatt Caraway, to the U.S. Senate for a full term.
1970	Arkansas River Navigation Project completed.
1972	First black state legislators (four) in 20th century elected.
1975	First woman state supreme court justice appointed.
1977	"Sunset" law passed, requiring state agencies to undergo periodic review to justify their existence.

ARMOR

When primitive people began to use weapons, they were faced with new problems. Their bodies needed more protection. They learned to use shields of wood or tough animal hide to protect themselves from the enemy's clubs or stone axes. This was the earliest armor.

Later the ancient Egyptian and Assyrian soldiers wore heavy cloth jackets or shirts to add to their protection. These were made of many layers of quilted linen.

▶ METAL ARMOR

The first metal armor was made of bronze. It was probably used by the Greeks about 2000–1800 B.C. They hammered bronze into helmets to protect their heads. They also covered their wooden shields with thin metal sheets.

The Romans were the first to make wide use of iron for armor. Roman soldiers protected their bodies with leather vests covered with thin strips of bronze or iron. Sometimes they covered their legs with metal shin guards. Helmets shielded the head. Roman helmets had broad, curving metal sidepieces to protect the cheeks. Brims came down to cover the forehead and the back of the neck.

Steel was not used in armor much before the Middle Ages. Armor made of steel was even stronger and more flexible than that made of iron. Whole suits of steel protected the medieval knight from head to toe.

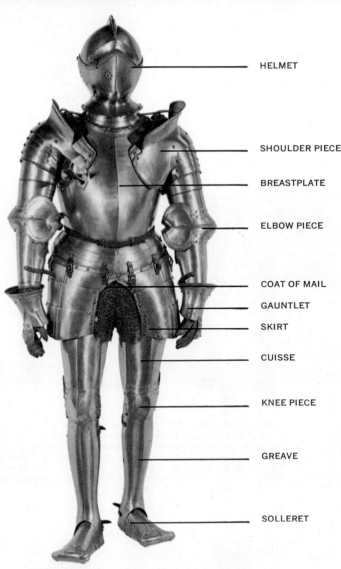

HELMET

SHOULDER PIECE

BREASTPLATE

ELBOW PIECE

COAT OF MAIL

GAUNTLET

SKIRT

CUISSE

KNEE PIECE

GREAVE

SOLLERET

Suits of 16th-century armor, with etched decoration, for rider and horse.

Sleeves, shin guards, and even gloves with jointed fingers were carefully shaped from thin metal plates. Hinges, joints, and rivets fastened the suits to make them flexible. Helmets had movable visors, or lids that dropped over the face when fighting began.

Some knights wore flexible armor of chain mail. Such armor was made of hundreds of tiny steel rings linked together to form a kind of steel cloth. Shirts of chain mail slipped over the head and reached to the knees.

Plate armor had to be carefully fitted to the body. The armorer heated the metal and shaped it with tools. Working like a tailor, the armorer measured, shaped, tried on, and shaped again. Sometimes beautiful designs were etched into the steel. The shield was usually decorated with inlaid metal in several colors.

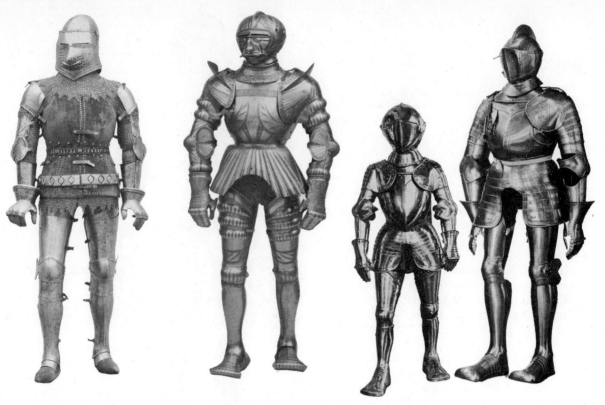

When knights rode to battle they wore armor of many styles. Shown above (left to right) are 15th-century Italian armor decorated with velvet, 16th-century German Maximilian armor with steel ruffles that copied formal court dress, pageboy's armor, and a heavy suit of 16th-century Italian armor. Shown below (left to right) are ornate French parade armor (not worn in battle), armor used in tournaments (with a metal rest on the breastplate to hold the lance), 17th-century German three-quarter armor that was lighter for horse and rider than a full suit, and new armor that protects astronauts in space against the forces of nature.

Italian parade helmet, 16th century.

Etruscan helmet, 500 B.C.

Japanese helmet, 18th century.

Italian helmet, 16th century.

Flemish parade shield, 15th century.

French shield with swords, 16th century.

Full armor had many disadvantages. Because it was so expensive to make, only the well-to-do noble or knight could afford a suit of armor. Even worse was its great weight. A special servant or knight-in-training called a squire had to help the knight put on his armor and mount his horse. Drawings from the Middle Ages show knights being hoisted onto their horses by derricks or cranes. If the knight was thrown to the ground by his enemy, he was usually unable to struggle to his feet. His opponent could then easily kill him with his sword or spear.

▶ THE DECLINE OF ARMOR

Gunpowder (invented centuries before by the Chinese) reached Europe about the end of the Middle Ages. A foot soldier with a gun could now pierce the heaviest armor that a man was able to carry on his body. Armor began to lose its usefulness. However, early explorers of the American continent continued to use armor against Indian arrows. But by the time of the American Revolution, armor appeared only in fancy-dress uniform.

▶ ARMOR IN MODERN FORM

In World Wars I and II, metal helmets were used to protect the head and neck from pieces of flying metal. Lightweight flexible aluminum body armor was tested in the Korean War. Fliers in World War II and in Korea wore thick coveralls padded with fiberglass. These gave protection from cold as well as from shell fragments. Some police officers wear bulletproof vests made of molded fiberglass, thin metal disks, or synthetic fabric.

Today a new type of armor has been designed to help astronauts explore outer space. Space suits are thickly padded and are laced to fit tightly from neck to toe. A helmet, covering the entire head, is fitted with earphones, microphones, and a supply of oxygen. With such careful protection, astronauts are able to face the great strains of rocket launching and space travel. As long as people must protect their bodies against enemy weapons and the forces of nature, they will try to design better armor.

JAMES HOERGER
John F. Kennedy School (Great Neck, New York)

ARMY. See UNITED STATES ARMY; CANADIAN ARMED FORCES.

ARNOLD, BENEDICT (1741–1801)

No other American is remembered in quite the same way as Benedict Arnold. He was a brave soldier, a patriot—and a traitor.

Arnold was born in Norwich, Connecticut, on January 14, 1741. At the age of 14, he ran away from home to fight in the French and Indian War. Later he became a captain in the Connecticut militia. When the Revolutionary War began in 1775, Arnold was already an experienced soldier. He helped Ethan Allen capture Fort Ticonderoga. Then Arnold proposed a daring plan to capture Quebec, the key to British Canada. The attack on Quebec failed, but Arnold proved himself a heroic soldier. He was promoted to the rank of brigadier general in 1776. That same year Arnold and a small fleet bravely fought off a larger British force on Lake Champlain. Although his fleet was destroyed, Arnold's efforts delayed the British plan to invade New York.

In 1777 General John Burgoyne marched south from Canada. This was part of the British invasion attempt. Arnold played a major role in bringing about Burgoyne's surrender at Saratoga.

In June, 1778, Arnold was placed in command of Philadelphia. There he married Peggy Shippen, the daughter of a wealthy Loyalist. Life in Philadelphia was gay, but very costly. Soon Arnold was deeply in debt. In 1779 he was charged with using his position for personal profit and employing soldiers in his command as personal servants. A court martial cleared him of most of the charges, but recommended that the commander in chief reprimand him. General Washington issued the reprimand, but softened it with the promise of a high position in the future.

Meanwhile, Arnold had begun a traitorous correspondence with British General Sir Henry Clinton. Arnold gave him important military information. He did this in anger because he felt that the Continental Congress had not given him the promotions he deserved. He was also desperate for money. The court martial and reprimand increased his anger.

In 1780 Arnold was given command of West Point. He immediately entered into a plot to surrender this strategic post to the

Benedict Arnold delivers the secret plans of the American fort at West Point to British Major John André.

British. In return Arnold was to be made brigadier general in the British Army. He was also promised money.

British Major John André met with Arnold on September 21, 1780. As André was returning on horseback to New York, some American soldiers stopped and searched him. They found incriminating papers hidden in his stocking. When Arnold learned that André had been captured, he fled to a British ship.

The British gave Arnold about £6,315 and the command of a small British force. He fought against Americans in Virginia and Connecticut. In 1781, after the war ended, he left for England with his wife and children. He died there on June 14, 1801, an unhappy man, distrusted by the British as well as the Americans.

Reviewed by RICHARD B. MORRIS
Editor, *Encyclopedia of American History*

ART

Art is one of mankind's oldest inventions. It existed long before a single farm was planted, before the first villages were built. Art was already thousands of years old when writing appeared; in fact, the letters of the first alphabets were pictures. People were probably shaping objects and scratching out images even as they turned their grunts and cries into the first systematic spoken languages.

Indeed, man was making art before he knew what art was. He seems to have made art without questioning why—as if making art was simply something that human beings did in the natural course of their lives.

And man is still making art; he has never stopped. Just about every people, every society, from the oldest to the youngest and from the most primitive to the most advanced, has created works of art. No wonder that the sum of all this creation is called "the world of art." Art is a world in itself, a world as round and full and changeable as the world we live in, and like the planet Earth, a whole of many distinct parts. Removing a wedge from the whole and studying it is like touring a country or visiting an era in the past. One wedge describes the ideals of the ancient Greeks. Another defines the interests of the French in the Middle Ages. Still another demonstrates the ideas that shaped the Renaissance in 15th-century Italy. Another reflects the traditions that had meaning in 18th-century Japan, or 10th-century China, or 17th-century India. But seen as a whole, the world of art reveals a broad picture of all of humanity; it summarizes the ideals, interests, and ideas of all people in all eras. The world of art tells us what has been on men's minds in generation after generation, from the dawn of man to the present day.

Art, then, is a product of the human mind and a mirror of that mind—a record of human progress. And like the mind, and like the societies that progress has created, art is rich, complicated, and sometimes quite mysterious. It is as ever-changing as man.

▶ THE MEANINGS OF ART

Actually, most people do know what art is. The trouble comes when they try to define it. No one definition satisfies everyone's idea. No one definition seems broad enough to cover every object in an art museum. And some definitions are too broad—they may apply to everything in the museum, but they also apply to many things that clearly are not art.

Despite the difficulty of defining art, we can make certain observations that help us to understand what art is. Art is a man-made product that expresses the uniqueness of the maker, of the society to which the maker belongs, of all mankind, or of all of these. The product appeals to the intellect and to the senses, especially to the sense of beauty. The

A painted carving from an Egyptian tomb of about 2500 B.C. shows cattle being led across water.

product can assume a variety of forms—a musical composition, a ballet, a play, or a novel or poem. This article, however, deals only with the "fine" arts: drawing, painting, sculpture, and architecture.

It is his intellect that makes man unique. Men have created religion, science, and technology to make their struggle for survival easier. They have created art to measure the worth of these and all human enterprises against the quality of life. European medieval art dealt almost exclusively with religion. Italian Renaissance art reflected the growing interest in the sciences. Much Oriental art conveys the idea of a harmonious, well-ordered universe. Twentieth-century art is very much a product of the age of technology.

Art—or at least great art—almost always gets at the truth. Great artists are expert observers and their work reflects life as they see it.

An example can be drawn from the illuminated manuscripts of Europe in the Middle Ages. Many of these hand-written, richly illustrated documents were created by monks. The monks were part of the Church, one of the most powerful forces in medieval life. They were certainly unlikely to point out what was wrong with medieval life, or to encourage an overhaul of the political system. Yet, simply because their work reflected the truth of their times as they saw it, these artists left a revealing record of the values of life in that era.

A typical manuscript illustration may depict the construction of a church or cathedral, since church-building was one of the most important activities in Europe between the 12th and 15th centuries. Or it might show a leading nobleman and his entourage, out surveying his lands. The figure of a priest or a nobleman will be drawn larger and possibly in greater detail than the other figures; moreover, he will generally be placed in the foreground. The other faces in the manuscript probably all look exactly alike, as if cast from a single mold. Yet the various details of the church or castle may be shown in great detail.

What do such pictures tell us about life in the Middle Ages? They tell us that power was concentrated in the Church and in the feudal system. The cleric or nobleman is large and important, as befits an agent of power. As for the other people—they were the great mass,

not exactly faceless but all the same, interchangeable, lacking identities of their own. The illustrations seem to be saying that if you have seen one common man, you have seen them all.

By the 15th century that attitude was changing. In many of the paintings by Andrea Mantegna (1431–1506), the architectural setting is depicted with detail as great as that in any medieval illustration. But now the buildings are simply background. Human figures are the important thing—all the human figures. The responses of the people—all of whom look different, all of whom have identities—are part of the subject matter. The pictures are not only about events; they are about the effects of events.

The medieval monks revealed a truth, and so did Mantegna. It was not true in Mantegna's time that all people, peasants as well as noblemen, were truly highly valued. But in theory the preciousness of the individual was recognized.

▶ART AS A RECORD

The earliest art that we know about was painted on the walls of caves during the Old Stone Age—roughly 20,000 years ago. Most of the pictures depict animals—bison, reindeer, ibex—the animals that cavemen hunted and depended on for survival. We cannot be completely sure why men painted these images, but we can make a fairly good guess. We know that today, when primitive peoples are discovered in the world and confronted with modern civilization, they often refuse (after the first time) to be photographed. Shown a snapshot of themselves, they claim that their spirit has been stolen. In other words, the spirit has been taken from the body and transferred to a shiny piece of paper. Assuming that cavemen had similar beliefs about the relationship between spirit and image, we can guess that they created likenesses of their prey in order to capture its spirit. Having taken the spirit, the hunters found it easier to take the body. And since early men were very good hunters, whose mastery of weapons gave them an advantage over much stronger creatures, they must have believed that the magic worked.

Here, already, man was demonstrating his uniqueness; through his intellect he was mas-

Right: Illustration from *The Belles Heures of Jean, Duke of Berry* (1410?), by Jean, Herman, and Pol de Limburg. Metropolitan Museum of Art, Cloisters Collection, New York. Below: *The Adoration of the Shepherds*, by Andrea Mantegna. Metropolitan Museum of Art, New York.

ter of his world. His aims were simple—to hunt well, to survive easily. But the earth warmed, game began to dwindle, and survival became more difficult. Man taught himself to plant and harvest, and realized that working with other men made farming easier and better. But that, in turn, added a new difficulty: he had to learn to live in communities. Again he put his brain to work and came up with laws and ethics to live by—and with weapons and strategies with which to defend himself.

Finally, about 5,000 years ago, the first great civilizations began emerging from man's intelligent struggle for survival. And with them came monumental art—art created to proclaim the greatness of a civilization and to last forever. In Egypt and Mesopotamia gigantic pyramids were erected, the tombs within decorated with carvings and paintings showing the great deeds of the rulers buried there. Clearly, these ancient peoples had no intention of ever disappearing. Even their utensils and vessels were meant to last eternally.

Mesopotamian and especially Egyptian art dwelt on the achievements of rulers. This was so mainly because the rulers were thought to be gods, or at least to have intimate contact with gods. And it was fitting, too, because the ruler was regarded as the living embodiment of the nation: Pharaoh and Egypt were one and the same. The individuality of the human being was seldom even recognized, much less celebrated.

Then came the Minoans and Mycenaeans and the Greeks, and man had his day. The early statuary of the Aegean peoples was said to represent gods and goddesses, but the forms were becoming ever more recognizably human. This in itself seems to indicate that people were beginning to appreciate their own importance. Like the ancient Hebrews, they proclaimed themselves made in their gods' image —not perfect, perhaps, but nonetheless godlike. By the Classical Age (5th century B.C.) in Greece, even that pretense was dropped. Greek sculptors began portraying spear bearers and charioteers with bodies as perfect as those of the gods Apollo and Dionysus.

Greek art idealized the human form. We do not believe that there were no Greeks with pot bellies or bowlegs; but we can conclude that the Greeks thought enough of themselves to find great satisfaction in showing themselves as ideal beings. And so we admire the Greeks not so much for what they were, but for the ideals they set up for themselves.

The Greeks' high regard for the individual is also reflected in their architecture. Their buildings were not like pyramids—massive tombs, useless to the living except to overwhelm—but temples and public buildings designed for people to use. Greek architects took great pains to proportion their structures so that people could use them comfortably: the ceilings are never so high, the rooms never so massive that a person feels small or lost within. This is another example of how we use art, which expresses ideals, to evaluate a people of the past.

Roman art, like Roman civilization, was based to a large extent on the Greek model. But the Romans carried their concern with the individual a step further. One Roman statue is a representation of an old, big-nosed citizen with a stern expression on his face. No one would call it an idealized portrait. Yet, as one studies it, the face gradually appears handsomer; it seems to reflect great character, wisdom, integrity. With such works the Romans are saying that the individual need not meet prescribed standards to be beautiful.

When the barbarian invasions into western and southern Europe became too troublesome for the Romans to deal with, the Emperor Constantine (280?–337) moved his capital eastward to the site of the old city of Byzantium. The new capital was called Constantinople, in his honor. Constantine also was the first Christian emperor, and thus his eastern empire, called the Byzantine Empire, became the first Christian civilization. There the traditions of ancient Greek and Roman art were remolded to fit the needs of Christianity. Under the Emperor Justinian (483–565), Constantinople was built up as the first great Christian city. The proportions were still Greek and Roman—it was a city for people. But after Justinian's death, political troubles and pressure from barbarians in the West and Muslims in the East slowed artistic development.

After Constantine left Rome, the barbarians had completed their sweep of Western Europe. By the time they had taken over, they were convinced that they had inherited a civilization superior to their own. Thus they began to imitate the Romans—and indeed, they even called themselves Romans. They adopted Christianity, taught themselves Latin, and tried to imitate the Romans' artistic achievements. However, the barbarians did it too quickly, before they had had a chance to absorb the real meaning of Western culture. The result was almost a standstill of civilization. It is this period that has been named the Dark Ages.

However important the Dark Ages may have been to the development of European civilization, they were a disaster for the development of the idea of individual human dignity. The barbarians had been pagans and nomads for centuries. Suddenly, and in one sweep, they expected to become Romans simply by taking on the trappings of Rome and Constantinople.

Thus the barbarian leaders imposed Chris-

Right: *The Gilder Herman Doomer,* by Rembrandt. Metropolitan Museum of Art, New York. Below: *The Musicians,* by Caravaggio. Metropolitan Museum of Art, New York.

Above: *The Beach at Sainte-Adresse*, by Claude Monet. Metropolitan Museum of Art, New York. Below: *The Voyage* (1949), by Robert Motherwell. Museum of Modern Art, New York.

tianity not by conversion or education, but by proclamation. Having traveled endlessly, they had never learned to make monumental art, nor had they had any reason to. The art that they had created was very beautiful, but it consisted mainly of portable objects such as weapons and utensils intricately carved with animal figures and abstract designs.

When they tried to become Christian Romans, the barbarians found that they lacked the Romans' skills. For example, during the Dark Ages, the arts of bricklaying and stone-building seem to have been utterly lost. Depiction of the human figure almost ceased. And even as the "darkness" began to fade from Western Europe, these skills had not been mastered.

Charlemagne realized it. Anxious to create a civilization as great as the Byzantine, the emperor set out to build fine stone churches to rival those of the East. But he had to send to Constantinople for stonemasons. The first Western monuments were quite modest—nothing compared to the magnificent palaces and churches of Byzantium—but they were at least a start.

For two centuries Western European building improved very gradually. Then, in the middle of the 12th century, a new and monumental style of architecture called Gothic (the name was given to it much later) suddenly appeared. All over France, Germany, and England, grand cathedrals rose, one after another, each more lavish than the others. All of the art of this period, which lasted into the 16th century in some parts of Europe, was devoted to decoration of the cathedrals. (The one exception was the illuminated manuscript, but even these were often placed in cathedrals.) Columns were surrounded with statues; doorways were richly carved; beautiful stained-glass windows colored the sunlight pouring in; carefully cut and polished wood formed the altars; huge, heavy tapestries hung between chapels; mosaic tiles formed mazelike patterns on the floors. It was as if all the long-lost creative forces had been rediscovered for the glorification of the Church.

What did all this mean to the common man? Actually, it meant a great deal. The medieval peasant loved his cathedral and used it; he went there often for social as well as religious rituals. The cathedrals were not at all like the great pyramids, which were useless to the people except as symbols.

Gothic architecture, like medieval manuscript illustrations, tells us a great deal about how society regarded the common people. The Gothic cathedral is high, heaven-reaching, enormously empty. Inside, one cannot help feeling small and humble. And all the statues—the saints on the columns, the demons over the doors—are watching and warning.

Early in the 15th century, a new building was erected in the city of Florence. It had low ceilings and moderate-sized rooms. It was built according to the same proportions that ancient Greek builders had used. It was not a great church but a home for the orphaned and neglected children of that Italian city.

The Foundling Hospital, as it was called, sent out a clear signal. It told the poor and humble people that they were important, and that their comfort right here on earth was as

Seven-Footed Beastie, by Alexander Calder. Collection of Mr. and Mrs. Austin Bruggs, Connecticut.

important as their faith in a life after death. And since it was built by the rulers of Florence, the building demonstrated that the state could care for the dignity of the individual.

First in Italy and then throughout Europe, the human being and his uniqueness became a main concern of art. This attitude, known as humanism, is what distinguished the Renaissance from earlier periods. It is what made the Renaissance go down in history as a great age for mankind. And again, it was in art that the spirit of humanism was expressed most clearly.

Humanism affected not only the content of art but the very way in which art was created. For if art said that people were individuals, worthy of recognition for their beliefs, were not the people who made art very special individuals, deserving credit for their accomplishments? So, with the Renaissance, the artist took on a new importance. And the recognition that the artist received added a new facet to art.

In Eastern lands, as in the West, art—from its earliest days—was an ever-growing record of what was most important to man. Early Japanese painting tended to be delicate, airy, and romantic—reflecting the graceful life of the Japanese court. Later, when Japan was ruled by militaristic emperors, art became harsher and more realistic. In the 18th and 19th centuries, the Japanese woodcut (a great influence on Western artists) appeared. Woodcuts, which are inexpensive to reproduce, were meant to reach a wider audience—to bring beauty within reach of the hardworking common man.

In India, where millions of people lived in incredible poverty, religion often represented an escape from unpleasant reality, so statues of gods and goddesses were lifelike and vital.

In China, with its respect for traditions and reverence for nature, art and architecture were supposed to follow the Chinese idea of the order of the universe. Even writing was considered an art.

▶ ART OF THE ARTIST

Art since the Renaissance has remained a record of mankind and a reflection of the ideas that concern men's minds. But since the Renaissance this record has come down to us in a series of very personal statements.

Michelangelo believed that the truth of any matter existed in nature. The artist's job was to seek that truth and capture it in his art. He once described sculpture as the act of "liberating the figure from the marble that imprisons it." In other words, the forms that he depicted so dramatically in his work already existed; his job was to find them and free them. So he made a practice of searching the marble quarries for his stones. (Other sculptors simply ordered slabs of certain sizes and shapes.) Then he would go to work, chipping away until the forms were revealed. But great as he was, even Michelangelo did not always succeed. His unfinished *Saint Matthew* was abandoned when he realized that the marble would never "give up" its prisoner. He surely could have completed it in some way, but he chose to stop working when he realized that it would not come out the way he had envisioned it. By admitting defeat, in a sense Michelangelo was saying that there are certain truths that can be sought but never fully revealed.

The Italian painter Caravaggio sought the truth in everyday occurrences, such as the pleasures of making music. Even in his paintings of religious events, he clothed the participants in the apparel of his own time, and placed them in commonplace settings, such as taverns. Saints were often pictured as poor people with plain garments and bare feet. Caravaggio seemed to be saying that all men, even the most humble, have value.

In the Netherlands in the 16th century, peasant life dominated the subject matter of a number of artists. It was this tradition, continued into the next century, that climaxed in the work of Rembrandt.

In a very special way, Rembrandt's subject matter was the soul of man. He painted religious subjects, portraits of prosperous Dutch citizens, and he painted simple portraits of poor people and of himself. But whatever he painted, his figures always appear lit from within, as if they were filled with all the suffering—and the beauty—of mankind. His work may represent the peak of humanism. For Rembrandt is telling us that with all the pain, corruption, and helplessness that characterize man's life, man's spirit is still filled with all the glory and good of God's light.

The 17th and 18th centuries were the "age of kings" in Europe. The courts of the European nations dominated much artistic activity. Many artists were dependent on the kings and aristocrats who ruled the continent. And yet great artists can never be slaves—except to the search for truth. As the abuses of the monarchs stirred the common people to greater and greater resentment, the artists often joined in the protests.

Francisco Goya was a favorite of the court of Spain. The king and his family treated the artist as if he were one of them. Yet one of his portraits of the royal family reveals a fat, expressionless king; a crude, sour queen; and frightened or empty-headed children. When Napoleon's armies came to Spain in 1808, Goya not so secretly cheered them on. Napoleon, however, did not introduce the liberal reforms that Spain needed, and his troops behaved badly to the Spanish population. So Goya turned his talents to an assault on the French. His paintings and engravings include works that are savage attacks on the French invaders, and even more savage—and lasting —attacks on war itself.

Another Spaniard, Pablo Picasso, made a similar statement 130 years later. His well-known painting *Guernica* tells the story of the Spanish Civil War as directly as any text. And it is not only about a destroyed Spanish city; it is about war.

The 19th century and our own have seen a remarkable increase in the speed at which civilization changes. We have come through an Industrial Revolution into an age of technology into a space age. The artist has kept pace with all the changes and tried to record the truths these changes have brought.

We do know that the ways in which artists approach art have been in a state of constant re-evaluation in the last 150 years. The impressionists began a process that led to a breakdown in the importance of subject matter. With these French artists came an interest in the technique used to apply paint to canvas. Concern with forms for their own sake led to cubism and then to abstractionism, in sculpture as well as painting. And in the 1960's and 1970's painting and sculpture seemingly came together in a search for new forms—for a new art that can serve as a whole environment.

What is the truth of our own age, as expressed in art? That question cannot yet be answered. It leads to other questions such

Grand Central Tower silhouetted against Pan Am Building, New York.

as these: What do artists mean when they depict huge figures that resemble characters in a comic strip? What does a perfectly rendered soup can tell us about our society? What is the importance of a huge skyscraper built to last only 20 years?

As we study the art forms of our age, each of us can draw our own conclusions about them.

DAVID JACOBS
Author, *Master Painters of the Renaissance*

See also AFRICAN ART; DESIGN AND COLOR; ORIENTAL ART AND ARCHITECTURE; names of individual artists, as REMBRANDT; names of individual countries, as ITALY (Italian Art and Architecture); names of periods and styles, as BAROQUE ART AND ARCHITECTURE or PREHISTORIC ART; and names of art forms, as COLLAGE, INDUSTRIAL DESIGN, PAINTING, or SCULPTURE.

ARTHRITIS. See DISEASES.

CHESTER ALAN ARTHUR (1829-1886)

21ST PRESIDENT OF THE UNITED STATES

ARTHUR, CHESTER ALAN. On July 2, 1881, President James A. Garfield was shot in the back by an insane man. For 2 months the President lay between life and death. On September 19 the country was shocked to hear that Garfield was dead and Vice-President Chester Alan Arthur was the new president of the United States.

Arthur was a handsome man. Tall and broad-shouldered with a ruddy complexion, Arthur impressed people with his dignified bearing. He was courteous and friendly. His manners were elegant, and he dressed so well that he was known as a dude.

But many people considered the handsome vice-president unfit to be president. Arthur had long been associated with the spoils system. Under this system men received government jobs for their services to a political party, whether they were honest and able or not. The maniac who killed President Garfield explained that he did so because he had been refused a government job. People were alarmed that Arthur, a product of the spoils system, had become president. In fact, the new president was not sure of his fitness for the office. "I hope—my God, I do hope it is a mistake," he exclaimed when the news came.

▶ A MINISTER'S SON

Chester Alan Arthur was born October 5, 1829, in Fairfield, Vermont. He was the oldest son in a family of seven children. His father, William Arthur, was a Baptist minister and teacher who was born in Northern Ireland.

The Arthur family moved about a great deal. The Reverend William Arthur was a man of strong convictions and did not hesitate to speak his mind to his congregations. As a result, he did not stay in one place very long. But Chester's education was never neglected. And he soon showed an ability to get on with people that later was to prove very useful in politics.

At the age of 15, Arthur entered Union College, in Schenectady, New York. He helped pay for his college expenses by teaching school during winter vacations. He studied hard and, in 1848, graduated with honors.

Arthur then studied law. But he continued to teach to support himself until 1853, when he went to New York City to begin his career as a lawyer.

The future president first gained prominence when he became involved in the slav-

WHEN CHESTER ALAN ARTHUR WAS PRESIDENT

The American Red Cross was founded in 1881 by Clara Barton. New York's Brooklyn Bridge, which spanned 487 meters (1,595 feet) and was then the longest bridge in the world, was completed in 1883. The United States Navy began construction of a steel fleet to replace its old wooden warships.
Chester Alan Arthur's birthplace was in Fairfield, Vermont.

ery question that was soon to lead to civil war. William Arthur had been opposed to slavery, and Chester shared his father's feelings. He sympathized with the Negroes and took part in two important cases in their defense. In one his law firm gained freedom for eight Negroes accused of being runaway slaves.

The other case dealt with the problem of segregation. It arose when Lizzie Jennings was not allowed to ride on a streetcar in New York City because she was black. Arthur won $500 for her in damages. And the court decision stated that Negroes had the same right to ride on New York streetcars as anyone else.

▶ARTHUR ENTERS POLITICS

Like most lawyers of the time, Arthur also took part in politics. In 1860 he helped organize the New York State Republican Party, and he supported its candidate for governor. As a reward the governor made Arthur engineer in chief and then quartermaster general of New York State. During the Civil War Arthur's position was very important, for all Union Army volunteers were equipped by the state before they were sent on to the Army. Arthur proved skillful and honest in providing thousands of New York soldiers with food, shelter, guns, tents, and other equipment.

▶COLLECTOR OF NEW YORK

Arthur's work for the Republican Party brought him to the attention of Senator Roscoe Conkling, the political boss of New York State. Arthur became Conkling's lieutenant and worked with him to win the election of Ulysses S. Grant in 1868. For his help President Grant in 1871 appointed Arthur collector of customs for the port of New York.

The collector was in charge of the New York Custom House, which received most of the customs duties of the United States. He also had the power to distribute more than 1,000 jobs. Under the spoils system these jobs went to faithful Republicans. They were expected to work for the party as well as for the Custom House. In the years that Arthur held the position, he simply followed the old system, although he himself remained an honest and able administrator.

In this newspaper cartoon of the 1880's (above), President Arthur turns his back on his old crony, Boss Roscoe Conkling. The woman represents the Republican Party. After President James A. Garfield was assassinated in 1881, Chester Arthur was inaugurated as 21st president at his home in New York City (below).

But many people were becoming angry about the inefficiency of the spoils system. They wanted a merit system, under which officeholders would be chosen on the basis of ability. In 1877 Rutherford B. Hayes, a believer in the merit system, became president. Hayes ordered an investigation of the New York Custom House, and in 1878 Arthur was dismissed from his post. The conflict caused a deep split in the Republican Party. The supporters of the old system became known as Stalwarts. The reformers were called Half-Breeds.

▶ VICE–PRESIDENT

In 1880 the Republicans who met to pick a new candidate for president were still bitterly divided. The delegates voted 36 times before they agreed on a candidate whom no one had expected—James A. Garfield, a Half-Breed. However, Senator Conkling was Garfield's political enemy. And to gain the support of the Stalwarts, the Garfield men nominated Arthur for the vice-presidency. The Republicans won in a close election. Ten months later Garfield was dead, and Arthur became the 21st president of the United States.

The new president was faced with many of the unsolved problems of former presidents Hayes and Grant (*at rear*).

▶ PRESIDENT ARTHUR SURPRISES MANY PEOPLE

As president, Arthur surprised both his friends and enemies. Arthur wished to make a good record for himself and was eager to be renominated and re-elected. He knew that he would never gain the support of reform and independent voters if he acted simply as a tool of Boss Conkling.

Arthur therefore determined not to let his administration be disgraced by the spoils system. He also tried earnestly to deal with some of the serious political problems the nation faced. But he was not so successful as he wished because he never had the full support of Congress.

For many years the Senate and the House of Representatives had gained power at the expense of weak presidents. Even such a strong personality as Abraham Lincoln had trouble with Congress. And his successors—Johnson, Grant, and Hayes—had let themselves be dominated by powerful Congressional leaders. Arthur was especially defenseless. He had become president by accident, and he did not command the support of any strong group in Congress.

Furthermore, Congress was itself divided. Both the Democratic and Republican parties were split into warring groups like the Stalwarts and the Half-Breeds. Some questions, such as the tariff (the tax on goods imported into the country), also divided the legislators. Other issues, such as the currency, set farmers, laborers, and manufacturers fighting one another.

Most important of all, the country was expanding and growing rich. Many people thought only of what they could get for themselves. Their representatives did not vote according to what was best for the nation as a whole. Instead they voted for laws that would gain the most for their supporters. Under such conditions it was difficult even for an able president to work out a good national policy. Arthur tried his best. But his achievements were limited.

The Pendleton Act and the Merit System

Before Arthur took office, it became known that some postal officials had collected money illegally in arranging mail routes. They were brought to trial in the famous Star Route cases. They were never convicted, but the trial made many more Americans aware of the evils of the spoils system.

With President Arthur's support, Congress now tried to introduce the merit system. In 1883 Arthur signed a law that helped take thousands of government jobs out of politics. This was the Pendleton Act. It required candidates for many government jobs to pass tests before they could be accepted. Men who qualified were protected against being dismissed for political reasons. The Pendleton Act was the beginning of the present United States Civil Service.

Too Much Money and a Chinese Problem

During the 1880's the United States had an unusual problem: there was too much money in the treasury. In one year the government collected $80,000,000 more than it spent. This kept money out of circulation, hurt business, and caused prices to fall. Arthur wanted to solve the problem by lowering the tariff. Congress, however, refused to do so. It preferred to spend the money on a "pork-barrel" bill. This was a law that authorized federal funds to be spent on river and harbor improvements. Such a law won votes for the congressmen and senators of the favored states. Arthur rejected the bill even though he knew that this would make him unpopular. But Congress passed it over his veto, and the tariff problem was not solved during Arthur's term in office.

Congress also passed the Chinese Exclusion Act of 1882 against the president's wishes. Its aim was to prevent Chinese from immigrating to the United States. Arthur opposed the bill because it violated a treaty between China and the United States. His opposition forced Congress to rewrite the law so that it had fewer harsh restrictions against the Chinese.

▶ NOT ALL WAS POLITICS

In 1859 Arthur had married Ellen Lewis Herndon, the daughter of a Virginia naval officer. Mrs. Arthur died in 1880, before her husband became president. Each day President Arthur honored her by placing fresh flowers in front of her picture.

The President's favorite sport was fishing. He was considered one of the best salmon fishermen in the country. Arthur was also fond of good food and companionship. He enjoyed the dinners to which he was invited and hated to leave. Since none of the guests could politely leave before the President, the dinners sometimes lasted until midnight.

Arthur liked elegant surroundings, and he had the White House completely redecorated. He installed new plumbing, a new bathroom, and the first elevator in the White House. His sister, who acted as hostess, helped him make it Washington's social center.

▶ ARTHUR IS REJECTED BY THE REPUBLICANS

In 1884 the Republicans did not renominate Arthur for president. The Half-Breed reformers were still not satisfied with him, and his old Stalwart friends, of course, were now against him. James G. Blaine was nominated and later lost the election to Democrat Grover Cleveland.

Arthur returned to his old law practice. But his health was failing. On November 18, 1886, at the age of 56, he died at his home in New York.

Chester Arthur was an honest and courageous president. But the political situation of his times did not permit him to deal successfully with the country's great problems. The greatest achievement of his administration was the Pendleton Civil Service Act. However, he will be best remembered as the spoils system politician who became president by accident, and who proved himself a better man than anyone expected.

OSCAR HANDLIN
Harvard University

ARTHUR, KING

In romance and legend, in music and art, King Arthur and his Knights of the Round Table are among the world's best-known heroes. For centuries they have been favorites of storytellers in many different countries.

The tales, as they are most often told today, are set in Arthur's court at Camelot, in a castle with noble towers and a great hall. In the great hall stood the Round Table, where only the best and most valiant knights could sit. Because the table had no head and no foot, all the knights seated round it were of equal rank. Each knight had his own seat with his name carved on it. The knights were bound by oath to help one another in time of danger and never to fight among themselves.

The tales tell of the wise and courteous Sir Gawaine; the brave Sir Percival; Sir Lancelot, who loved King Arthur's wife, Guinevere; the traitor Sir Modred, who seized the throne and tried to wed Queen Guinevere; the noble Sir Bedivere, who received Arthur's last commands before he died; and Sir Tristram, the knight of many skills. One seat at the Round Table had no name on it. It was reserved for the knight who found the Holy Grail, the cup supposedly used by Christ at the Last Supper. The seat was finally won by Sir Galahad, the purest and noblest knight.

Religion and magic run through all the stories about Arthur and his knights. On the side of good was the mighty magician Merlin, who was Arthur's adviser. On the side of evil was the wicked sorceress Morgan le Fay.

THE STORY OF ARTHUR

Briefly, the story of King Arthur and his knights as it is told in Sir Thomas Malory's *Morte Darthur* really begins with the death of Arthur's father, King Uther of Britain. A time of strife and civil war followed until Uther's nobles gathered in the church to pray to God to show them who their rightful king should be. As they came out of the church they saw a sword stuck into an anvil mounted on a great stone. Written on the sword in gold was a legend saying that whoever could pull the sword out of the stone would be the next king of England. All the nobles tried, but none could move it.

Although Arthur was the King's son, he was not with his father when he died. Shortly after Arthur's birth he had been given to Merlin the magician for safekeeping. Merlin had known that Uther's death would cause a struggle for power among the nobles. Arthur's life would be in danger. Merlin gave the baby to Sir Ector and his wife to bring up as their own, not telling them it was King Uther's son.

Some months after the sword appeared in the stone, a great tournament was held and Sir Ector and his son Sir Kay and the boy Arthur all attended. When Sir Kay discovered that he had left his sword at the inn where they were staying, he sent Arthur after it. The inn was locked up, since everyone had gone to the tournament, so Arthur stopped in the churchyard, where he had seen the sword stuck in the stone without knowing what it meant. He easily pulled the sword out. Thus, after further proof, Arthur became king.

His reign was full of victories. Many of these he owed to another sword, an enchanted one called Excalibur. Here is Malory's tale, adapted by Mary MacLeod, of how he got it.

Leaving Sir Pellinore, King Arthur and Merlin went to a hermit, who was a good man, and skilled in the art of healing. He attended so carefully to the King's wounds, that in three days they were quite well, and Arthur was able to go on his way with Merlin. Then as they rode, Arthur said, "I have no sword."

"No matter," said Merlin, "near by is a sword that shall be yours if I can get it."

So they rode till they came to a lake, which was a fair water and broad; and in the midst of the lake, Arthur saw an arm, clothed in white samite, that held in its hand a beautiful sword.

"Lo," said Merlin, "yonder is the sword I spoke of."

With that they saw a damsel rowing across the lake.

"What damsel is that?" said Arthur.

"That is the Lady of the Lake," said Merlin, "and within that lake is a rock, and therein is as fair a place as any on earth, and richly adorned. This damsel will soon come to you; then speak you fair to her, so that she will give you that sword."

Presently the damsel came to Arthur, and saluted him, and he her again.

"Damsel," said Arthur, "what sword is that which yonder the arm holdeth above the water? I would it were mine, for I have no sword."

"Sir Arthur, King," said the damsel, "that sword is mine; the name of it is Excalibur, that is as much as to say *Cut-Steel*. If you will give me a gift when I ask you, ye shall have it."

"By my faith," said Arthur, "I will give you what gift ye shall ask."

"Well," said the damsel, "go you into yonder barge, and row yourself to the sword, and take it and the scabbard with you, and I will ask my gift when I see my time."

So King Arthur and Merlin alighted, and tied their horses to two trees, and went into the barge, and when they came to the sword that the hand held, Arthur lifted it by the handle, and took it with him. And the arm and hand went under the water; and so they came to the land, and rode away.

Arthur married Guinevere, the daughter of a king whom he helped in battle, and set up his court at Camelot. There he gathered the most chivalrous princes of all the lands to be his Knights of the Round Table. Accounts of their adventures—their tournaments, their battles, their quests for the Holy Grail—make up the rest of the Arthurian legends. Mary MacLeod's adaptation of Malory's book describes one of their tournaments.

Then on the morrow the trumpets blew to the tournament for the third day.

The King of North Wales, and the King with the Hundred Knights, encountered with King Carados and with the King of Ireland; and there the King with the Hundred Knights smote down King Carados, and the King of North Wales smote down the King of Ireland. Sir Palamides came at once to the help of the fallen knights, and made great work, for by his indented shield he was well known. Then King Arthur joined him, and did great deeds of arms, and put the King of North Wales and the King of the Hundred Knights to the worse. But Sir Tristram with his black shield came to their help, and quickly he jousted with Sir Palamides, and there by fine force he smote Sir Palamides over his horse's croup.

Then cried King Arthur, "Knight with the Black Shield, make thee ready to me!" and in the same wise Sir Tristram smote King Arthur.

By force of Arthur's knights, the King and Sir Palamides were horsed again, and the King with an eager heart, seizing a spear, smote Sir Tristram from one side over his horse. Hot-foot, from the other side, Sir Palamides came upon Sir Tristram, as he was on foot, meaning to override him, but Sir Tristram was aware of him, and stooped aside, and with great ire he got him by the arm, and pulled him down from his horse.

Sir Palamides arose lightly, and they dashed together mightily with their swords, and many Kings, Queens, and lords stood and beheld them. At the last, Sir Tristram smote Sir Palamides upon the helm three mighty strokes, and at every stroke he gave him, he cried, "Have this for Sir Tristram's sake!" With that, Sir Palamides fell to the earth, grovelling.

Then came the King of the Hundred Knights, and brought Sir Tristram a horse, and so he was mounted again. Then he was aware of King Arthur with a naked sword in his hand, and with his spear Sir Tristram ran upon King Arthur; the King boldly awaited him, and with his sword he smote the spear in two. At this Sir Tristram was so astonished that King Arthur gave him three or four great strokes before he could get out his sword, but at last Sir Tristram drew his sword, and assailed the other, pressing hard.

Now the great crowd parted them; then Sir Tristram rode here and there, and fought with such fury that eleven of the good knights of the blood of King Ban, who were of Sir Lancelot's kin, were that day smitten down by Sir Tristram. All people, of every estate, marvelled at his great deeds, and all shouted for "the Knight with the Black Shield!"

The uproar was so great that Sir Lancelot heard it, and getting a great spear he came towards the shouting.

"Knight of the Black Shield, make thee ready to joust with me!" cried Sir Lancelot.

When Sir Tristram heard him say this, he took spear in hand, and both lowered their heads, and came together like thunder; Sir Tristram's spear broke in pieces, and Sir Lancelot by ill fortune struck Sir Tristram on the side, a deep wound nigh to death. But yet Sir Tristram left not his saddle, and so the spear broke. Though sorely wounded, Tristram got out his sword and rushed at Sir Lancelot and gave him three great strokes on the helm, so that sparks flew out, and Sir Lancelot lowered his head down to his saddle-bow. And therewithal Sir Tristram departed from the field, for he felt himself so wounded that he thought he should have died.

When Arthur was away from Camelot, Modred tried to take over his kingdom. Arthur returned and defeated him in battle, killing him with his own hand. As Modred fell he lifted up his sword and wounded Arthur mortally. Arthur's body was mysteriously carried away to the island of Avalon. One day, according to legend, he would return.

▶ **SOURCES OF THE LEGENDS**

The book that is the chief source today for all the legends about Arthur and his knights was written by an Englishman, Sir Thomas Malory. It was printed in 1485 and was one of the first books to come from the press of the first English printer, William Caxton. Although the tales were written in English, the title of the book, *Morte Darthur* (Death of Arthur), is French and most of the tales were adapted from the French.

Tales about Arthur were particularly popular in France during the 12th and 13th centuries. Originally, however, the Arthurian tales came from Celtic sources—from myths belonging to the Irish and British races and from early accounts of the history of Britain.

The first of these histories to mention Arthur was written in Latin by Nennius, a 9th-century Welsh priest. He tells of a Celtic military commander named Arthur who in the 6th century won 12 battles against the Saxon invaders of Britain. This is the original Arthur and it is all we know of him. Legends grew up around him, however, and he became a popular Welsh hero. When some of the Celtic people migrated from Britain to France, they carried the tales about Arthur to their new neighbors, the French and the Normans. Wandering minstrels spread the tales even farther as they visited the courts of Europe and followed European armies into lands of the eastern Mediterranean.

About this same time, in the 12th century, another Welsh priest, Geoffrey of Monmouth, wrote down some of these tales in a book called *Historia Regum Britanniae* (History of the Kings of Britain). Although he pretended that the book was a translation into Latin of "a very old book in the British language," it was actually his own creation. He made Arthur into a king and surrounded him with nobles and barons from western Europe.

In 1155 a Norman monk named Wace translated Geoffrey's *Historia* into French, adding material from other sources and leaving out parts. His *Roman de Brut* contains the first mention of the Round Table. In turn, Wace's poem was used by a priest named Layamon, who was the first to write about Arthur in English.

Between 1170 and 1181 a Frenchman, Chrétien de Troyes, wrote poems based on the Arthurian legends that were highly regarded for their style. His material was probably taken from Celtic origins. He is an important source for the story of the Holy Grail.

The Arthurian legends have attracted many English writers since Layamon—in the 15th century, as we have seen, Sir Thomas Malory; in the 19th century Lord Tennyson, Algernon Swinburne, Matthew Arnold, and William Morris; and in the 20th century Edwin Arlington Robinson and T. H. White.

In music the most famous composer to make use of the Arthurian legends was Richard Wagner. In art John Singer Sargent's mural paintings in the Boston Public Library depict the quest for the Holy Grail.

Reviewed by CAROLYN W. FIELD
The Free Library of Philadelphia

ARTICLES OF CONFEDERATION. See UNITED STATES (History and Government).
ARTIFICIAL RESPIRATION. See FIRST AID.

Women (*left*) work in gardens in front of modern skyscraper in Singapore. Terraced rice fields (*right*) are carved into the mountain slopes of Luzon, the Philippines.

Sand mountains in the Rub'al Khali, a great desert in Saudi Arabia.

ASIA

Asia is the largest continent in the world. It extends about 7,100 kilometers (4,400 miles) from the Ural Mountains in the west to the Pacific Ocean in the east. And it runs north and south about 9,600 kilometers (6,000 miles) from the cold Arctic areas in the far north to the tropical regions at the equator. The continent covers about one third of the earth's land surface, and it is the home of more than half of the world's people.

For many centuries the peoples of Asia have had a high level of civilization. Asia has a history older than that of Europe and North America. The continent is sometimes called the cradle of civilization. Evidences of the earliest form of human society exist there. Asia is also the birthplace of many of the world's great religions, including Buddhism, Christianity, Hinduism, Islam, and Judaism.

During the 18th and 19th centuries a large part of Asia fell under the domination of European countries. This began a period of colonialism. In the 20th century, however, the people of Asia began to fight for their free-

Young Buddhist monks of Thailand (*above*), where 95 percent of the people are Buddhists. Hindus (*right*) bathe in the sacred Ganges River near the holy city of Banaras in India.

The Kanchenjunga, one of the highest peaks in the Himalayas, is holy to many people in the former nations of Tibet and Sikkim. Here is the mountain as seen from Darjeeling, India.

dom. Today virtually all its people have gained their independence.

Asia is a continent of extremes. It has the highest mountain in the world—Mount Everest. It also has the lowest spot on the surface of the earth—the Dead Sea. In this vast continent almost every kind of climate can be found. Temperatures rise as high as 49°C (120°F) in parts of southwestern Asia, while in northern Siberia they fall as low as −70°C (−94°F).

Parts of Asia are overpopulated, and many people do not have enough to eat. But the continent is changing. Through education and economic growth, many Asian nations are trying to provide better lives for their peoples.

▶ THE LAND

An immense land mass stretches from the eastern shores of the Atlantic Ocean halfway around the world to the western shores of the Pacific Ocean. This is sometimes called Eurasia. But most people think of this vast area as two continents. Europe is the western part. Asia occupies the larger, eastern part. The Ural Mountains, the Caspian Sea, and the Black Sea serve as the dividing line. On the east, Asia is separated from North America by the narrow Bering Strait and the wide Pacific Ocean. Lying off the southeastern shore of the Asian mainland are the many islands of the Philippines and Indonesia. These islands are also a part of Asia. Like a chain, they help to join Asia with Australia. Southwest of Asia, across the Red Sea and beyond the Arabian Sea, lies Africa. Directly south of Asia is the Indian Ocean. To the north is the Arctic Ocean.

Close to the center of Asia, just north of India, are the Himalayas. These are the highest mountain ranges in the world. They extend for hundreds of kilometers. The Himalayas are part of a chain of mountains that runs across central Asia from Turkey to China. Several of the most important ranges are the Hindu Kush, the Sulaiman, the Karakoram, the Tien Shan, and the Kunlun.

Asia's coastline is roughly 80,000 kilometers (50,000 miles) long. It begins at the shores of the Kara Sea, north of the Arctic Circle. It goes eastward along the northern coast of the Soviet Union and around the Bering Strait. It extends down the eastern coasts of Siberia, Korea, and China and then westward around the Indochinese, Malayan, Indian, and Arabian peninsulas. Finally it goes through the Suez Canal and ends on the shores of the Mediterranean and Black seas.

Off the east coast of Asia, the Pacific Ocean is divided into a number of seas. From north to south they are the Bering, Okhotsk, Japan, Yellow, East China, and South China seas. The northern Indian Ocean is divided into the Bay of Bengal and the Arabian Sea. The Mediterranean Sea separates Southwest Asia from Europe. The island of Cyprus, which lies very close to Europe, is considered a part of Asia. The important lakes (inland seas) include the Aral, Baikal, Balkhash, and Koko Nor, deep in the interior of Asia. Many great rivers cross Asia. Among the most important are the Amur, Hwang Ho (Yellow River), Yangtze, and Si Kiang (West River) in eastern Asia; the Mekong, Chao Phraya (Menam), Salween, and Irrawaddy in Southeast Asia; the Brahmaputra, Ganges, and Indus in southern Asia; and the Tigris and Euphrates in southwestern Asia.

Between the frigid north and the tropical south are several desert areas that stretch from east to west across Asia. They are found primarily in southwestern Asia, the Soviet Union, and China. Countries like Saudi Arabia, Iraq, Iran, and Pakistan receive little rainfall. Semidesert areas, often called steppes, run across the southern and central Soviet Union and Mongolia. These are large, flat, treeless land areas. Farther north is the tundra—an expanse of permanently frozen ground with no trees and little vegetation.

Regions of Asia

Asia is sometimes divided into the following regions: East, Inner, South, Southeast, Southwest, and North.

East Asia. East Asia, or the Far East, is one of the centers of Asian civilization. It consists of China, Korea, and a number of island groups, including Japan and Taiwan (Formosa). The region is well out of the tropical zone in which South and Southeast Asia lie. Therefore, it has all the seasons—hot, cold, dry, and rainy.

Historically and geographically, East Asia is dominated by China. This one country takes

COUNTRIES OF ASIA

COUNTRY	CAPITAL	AREA (km²)	AREA (sq mi)	ADMISSION TO THE UN
Afghanistan	Kabul	647,497	250,000	1946
Bahrain	Manama	622	240	1971
Bangladesh	Dacca	143,998	55,598	1974
Bhutan	Thimbu	46,620	18,000	1971
Burma	Rangoon	678,033	261,789	1948
Cambodia (Kampuchea)	Pnompenh	181,035	69,898	1955
China, People's Republic of	Peking	9,596,961	3,705,390	1971
Cyprus	Nicosia	9,251	3,572	1960
India	New Delhi	3,287,590	1,269,340	1945
Indonesia	Jakarta	1,904,347	735,269	1950
Iran	Teheran	1,648,000	636,294	1945
Iraq	Baghdad	434,924	167,925	1945
Israel	Jerusalem	20,770	8,019	1949
Japan	Tokyo	377,459	145,737	1956
Jordan	Amman	97,740	37,738	1955
Korea				
North Korea	Pyongyang	120,538	46,540	Nonmember
South Korea	Seoul	98,484	38,025	Nonmember
Kuwait	Kuwait	17,818	6,880	1963
Laos	Vientiane	236,800	91,429	1955
Lebanon	Beirut	10,400	4,015	1945
Malaysia	Kuala Lumpur	332,633	128,430	1957 (Malaya)
Maldives	Male	298	115	1965
Mongolia	Ulan Bator	1,565,000	604,248	1961
Nepal	Katmandu	140,797	54,362	1955
Oman	Muscat	212,457	82,030	1971
Pakistan	Islamabad	803,940	310,402	1947
Philippines	Manila	300,000	115,830	1945
Qatar	Doha	11,000	4,247	1971
Saudi Arabia	Riyadh	2,149,700	830,000	1945
Singapore	Singapore	581	224	1965
Sri Lanka (Ceylon)	Colombo	65,610	25,332	1955
Syria	Damascus	185,180	71,498	1961 (readmitted)
Thailand	Bangkok	514,000	198,456	1946
Turkey	Ankara	780,576	301,381	1945
United Arab Emirates	Abu Dhabi	83,600	32,278	1971
Vietnam	Hanoi	329,556	127,242	1977
Yemen (Aden)	Madinat al-Shaab	332,968	128,559	1967
Yemen (Sana)	Sana	195,000	75,290	1947

up over 75 percent of the region's territory. Three important rivers of East Asia begin in and flow through China. They are the Hwang Ho (Yellow River) of North China, the Yangtze River of Central China, and the Si Kiang (West River) of South China. Korea is a large and mountainous peninsula in northeastern Asia. Japan consists of four main islands off the east coast of Korea and Soviet Siberia. Taiwan lies off the southeast coast of China.

Inner Asia. This is a rather imprecisely defined region that is sometimes also called Central Asia. Included within it are Tibet and the Sinkiang-Uighur Autonomous Region of western China. (The people of Sinkiang are related to the people living in Soviet Central Asia.) Mongolia is often considered a part

of Inner Asia too. The region consists mainly of high plateaus, mountains, grasslands, and deserts. The entire area of Tibet, for example, is one great plateau about 4,500 meters (15,000 feet) high. The mountains of Inner Asia gradually slope down to the north toward Siberia. These high mountains act as a wall shielding India from the cold winds of the north. Because of its dry climate and poor soil, this region has a small population.

South Asia. South Asia includes India, Pakistan, Bangladesh, Afghanistan, Sri Lanka, the Maldives, and the small Himalayan countries of Nepal and Bhutan. This whole area of Asia is sometimes called the Indian subcontinent. It extends from the Himalayas south to the sea, forming a huge triangle that sticks out into the Indian Ocean. The Arabian Sea is on one side of it and the Bay of Bengal on the other. South Asia can be divided into three parts. One part is the northern section at the foot of the Himalayas. Another is the fertile plain along the Ganges and Indus rivers. The third is the triangle-shaped Deccan Plateau.

Southeast Asia. Southeast Asia includes the countries of Burma, Thailand, Laos, Cambodia, Vietnam, Malaysia, Singapore, Indonesia, and the Philippines. Most of the region has a tropical climate. Four important rivers flow through mainland Southeast Asia. They are the Mekong, the Chao Phraya (Menam), the Salween, and the Irrawaddy.

Southwest Asia. The region of Southwest Asia is frequently called the Near or Middle East. It includes the countries of Turkey, Iran, Syria, Lebanon, Israel, Jordan, Iraq, Kuwait, Saudi Arabia, Yemen (Aden), Yemen (Sana), the Sultanate of Oman, the United Arab Emirates, and the island-nation of Cyprus. The Suez Canal is considered to be the dividing line between the continents of Asia and Africa. Therefore, the Sinai Peninsula, which lies east of the canal, is also considered to be part of Asia.

Southwest Asia is generally a dry and hot area. Its temperatures are the highest in the world. Sometimes they reach 49°C (120°F) along the coasts of the Arabian and Red seas. There is little rainfall in the region. But a stretch of rich soil in the shape of a semicircle exists between the Mediterranean Sea and the Persian Gulf. It is called the Fertile Crescent. Here the Tigris and Euphrates rivers give water to the farmers. Many people believe that the oldest civilizations in the world were once located here.

North Asia. This region extends from Europe across northern Asia to the Pacific Ocean. It includes Siberia and the area known as Soviet Central Asia (the Turkmen, Uzbek, Tadzhik, Kirghiz, and Kazakh Soviet Socialist Republics). Hence the region is also known as Soviet Asia. Some scholars include the Mongolian People's Republic in North Asia. The region comprises about one third of all Asia. But only 3 per cent of Asia's people live there. The region can be divided into three parts: the desert to the south; the central steppes (semidesert); and the northern forest areas (taiga). North of the forest belt lies the cold arctic region. The land is rich in mineral resources.

Natural Resources

A continent as huge as Asia is bound to have many natural resources. But when we consider its enormous population, the riches of Asia no longer sound quite so bountiful. Until recently poor mining methods and the difficulty in reaching some of these natural resources limited their proper use. Since World War II modern methods and better transportation have been slowly introduced. As a result, the natural resources of Asia have begun to play an increasingly important role in the development of the continent.

Minerals. Asia is a continent rich in mineral wealth. A large part of the mineral deposits, however, remain in the ground unmined. Furthermore, the deposits are not equally distributed. Coal, iron, and copper are found in East Asia. Tin is mined in Southeast Asia. Coal, iron, and manganese are found in South Asia. Turkey has large chromium and copper deposits. Some platinum is mined in the Ural Mountains, and manganese in the Caucasus Mountains. Siberia has rich deposits of nickel, bauxite, aluminum, and iron. China has the world's largest deposits of tungsten and anthracite coal. India is rich in mica, and Malaysia is rich in tin. Southwest Asia, particularly the Persian Gulf area, is the main oil resource center of Asia—and of the world. It is estimated that over one half the world's supply is in the ground there. Other major oil areas are the Caucasus Mountains of Soviet Asia and the islands of Indonesia.

Soils and Vegetation. A major portion of Asia has poor soils. The interior of Asia is too high, dry, and cold for good soil. Nor are the tropical and subtropical soils of Asia very fertile. The more fertile places are located along the river valleys and some coastal areas. Soils on the island of Java are fertile because of their volcanic origin.

Vegetation in Asia ranges from the cold tundras along the northern coast to the tropical rain forests of Southeast Asia. Between these two extremes are found many forests, steppes, and desert areas.

Among the continent's major natural resources are its forests. Large parts of Soviet Siberia, of the mountain regions of western

China, and of Southeast Asia are covered by dense forests. In the tropical and subtropical forests of Southeast Asia trees of high commercial value, such as teak and mahogany, grow. Because of a lack of good highways and railroads to the interior of many parts of Asia, most of these forests are not fully used.

Wildlife. Many animals, some of which are now extinct, had their origin on the Asian continent. A rhinoceroslike prehistoric creature, said to be the largest mammal that ever lived, once existed in Asia. Today Asia is the home of a variety of wild animals such as bears, hyenas, leopards, tigers, and wolves. In southern Asia, a number of poisonous snakes are found. The multicolored king cobra is a dangerous killer. The python is seen mostly in Malaysia and Indonesia. It sometimes grows to more than 9 meters (30 feet) in length. The thick-skinned crocodile lives in India and Malaysia, where many other kinds of reptiles exist. The blind porpoise (susu) lives in the Ganges River. The unusual dugong (sea cow) is also found in southern Asia. The giant panda lives in the bamboo forests of interior China. It is a heavy, bearlike animal with a distinctive black and white fur. Many types of monkeys roam the Asia continent. The gibbon, a small ape with long arms and no tail, is found in Malaysia. In the low, swampy forests of Borneo and Sumatra, many unusual kinds of monkeys are often seen.

Many animals are used today as beasts of burden or for food and clothing. Huge elephants carry people and timber in the jungles of Southeast Asia. In Tibet the shaggy, silken-haired yak is a work animal and an important kind of livestock. Wild oxen in India grow to heights taller than human beings, and when tame are used to plow land. The water buffalo is found in China, India, and Southeast Asia. This strong animal pulls the heavy plows through the muddy waters of rice paddies. The reindeer moves in herds through the wilderness of Siberia and often is used to pull sleds in the snow. Its hide is made into clothing and its flesh is an important source of food. The two-humped Bactrian camel travels the deserts of Central Asia. This hardworking animal is able to go for long periods of time without water.

Livestock such as cattle, sheep, and pigs are found chiefly in China, India, Pakistan, and Turkey. India is estimated to have about one quarter of the world's cattle, and China has enormous numbers of pigs and sheep. Nomadic herding is a way of life for several million people in Southwest Asia. These people move with their sheep and goats in search of food and water.

Waterpower. Asia's water resources are abundant. In the absence of coal and oil, many Asian countries have turned to water for power. But up to World War II, only in Japan were water resources used to any extent. Today hydroelectric projects such as the Damodar Valley of India, the Shihmen of Taiwan, the Chao Phraya (Menam) of Thailand, and the Yarmuk-Jordan Valley of Southwest Asia are beginning to help Asian countries meet their power needs.

Climate

Asia has most of the varieties of climates known. A large part of the continent is cold and dry in the winter and warm and dry in the summer. Because the continent is very large, many places are far from the sea. As a result, the center of Asia is never touched by the winds that bring moisture from the oceans. Most of Central Asia is alternately cold and warm, but always dry.

Temperature. The high mountain ranges that cross Asia act as a huge wall. They keep the cold arctic winds from blowing to the south and the hot winds of the south from blowing north. Therefore, average temperatures in the areas north of these mountains are lower than they would normally be at the same latitude elsewhere in the world. Siberian winters, for example, are among the coldest on earth. The average January temperature is about −51°C (−60°F). In the town of Verkhoyansk, in northeastern Siberia, the winter temperature may drop to about −73°C (−100°F). The hottest parts of Asia are in the southwestern region. The area around the Persian Gulf is one of the hottest in the world. Land temperatures often reach 49°C (120°F). At times the water temperature in the Persian Gulf reaches 36°C (96°F).

Rainfall. Rainfall in Asia is also affected by the size of the continent and its mountain ranges. Many regions have much rain, while others remain dry. Winds that carry moisture from the ocean bring rain to the near side of the mountains. This means that the far side of the high mountains is dry and has little rainfall. Examples of this uneven rainfall can be seen throughout Asia. Parts of Southwest Asia receive as little as 100 millimeters (4 inches) of rain a year, while northeastern India is one of the wettest regions on earth. In 1978, Southeast Asia was hit by heavy rains. The rains caused widespread flooding that damaged crops and left many persons homeless. Parts of southern China also receive much rainfall. Most of the rest of the continent of Asia tends to be dry.

Winds. Many parts of Asia are subjected to very strong winds that dry up the streams and the moisture in the ground. One of these winds is called the Seistan. It blows through Iran for about six months of the year at extremely high speeds. Many of the deserts in Central Asia have similar winds. Winds from the plateau of Tibet and from Central Asia have blown thousands of tons of soil (loess) hundreds of kilometers eastward to China. The heating and cooling of the land in interior Asia causes great masses of air to rush in and out of this area. Because of the height and location of the mountains, the winds usually move in an east-west direction.

CHIEF CITIES IN ASIA
(by population)

Over 7,000,000

Calcutta, India	Shanghai, China
Peking, China	Tokyo, Japan

3,000,000 to 7,000,000

Bangkok, Thailand	Madras, India
Bombay, India	Manila, Philippines
Delhi, India	Rangoon, Burma
Istanbul, Turkey	Seoul, South Korea
Jakarta, Indonesia	Teheran, Iran
Karachi, Pakistan	Tientsin, China
Lüta (Dairen and Port Arthur), China	

1,500,000 to 3,000,000

Ahmadabad, India	Osaka, Japan
Ankara, Turkey	Pusan, South Korea
Baghdad, Iraq	Pyongyang, North Korea
Bangalore, India	Saigon (Ho Chi Minh City), Vietnam
Changchun, China	
Chungking, China	Shenyang, China
Dacca, Bangladesh	Sian, China
Harbin, China	Singapore, Singapore
Hyderabad, India	Surabaya, Indonesia
Lahore, Pakistan	Taipei, Taiwan
Nagoya, Japan	Wuhan, China
Nanking, China	Yokohama, Japan

The monsoons of the Indian Ocean are seasonal winds. For about six months each year they blow from northeastern India across the peninsula, carrying hot air out to the Indian Ocean. From June to September they reverse their direction and blow from the southwest. They then carry rain to the land, creating the wet monsoon season. If these returning winds do not carry enough rain, then crops fail and famine may result. The people of South and Southeast Asia depend upon the wet monsoon to farm. The monsoon areas of Asia are the southwestern coast of India, northeastern India, the Indochinese and Malay peninsulas, and the northern islands of the Philippines.

▶**THE PEOPLE**

Asia is considered to be the cradle of three different civilizations. This explains why the people who live in this vast continent differ from region to region. But as a whole, the Asian peoples of today share two common characteristics. They are rich in cultural traditions, and they are now trying to hasten their economic and social development.

Population

Asia's population is very large, and it is growing very rapidly. Asians now make up more than half of the world's population. The continent has a high birthrate, and its death rate is constantly declining. Modern medicine, sanitation, better diets, and other improvements in living standards have helped to increase the average life span of most Asian people. At the present rate of growth, it is estimated that the population of Asia will double by the early years of the 21st century.

Asia's large population is not spread out evenly over the continent. More than 90 percent of the Asian people live in three regions—South, Southeast, and East Asia. More than one half of Asia's land lies in North and Inner Asia. But very few of Asia's people live there. The government of the Soviet Union has tried to encourage people to colonize Siberia. But this has generally failed because Siberia is a land of too many hardships. China has had more success in settling less hospitable parts of the country. Of the Asian nations, China and India have the largest populations. It is estimated that China will be the

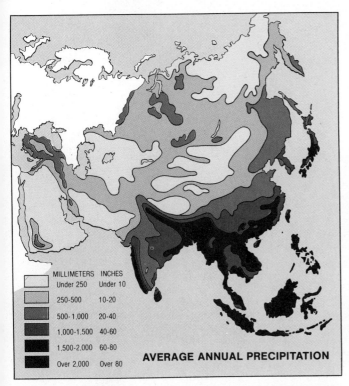

MILLIMETERS	INCHES
Under 250	Under 10
250-500	10-20
500-1,000	20-40
1,000-1,500	40-60
1,500-2,000	60-80
Over 2,000	Over 80

AVERAGE ANNUAL PRECIPITATION

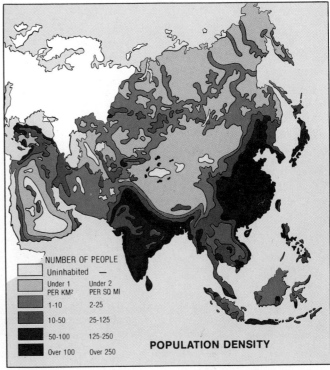

NUMBER OF PEOPLE

Uninhabited	—
Under 1 PER KM²	Under 2 PER SQ MI
1-10	2-25
10-50	25-125
50-100	125-250
Over 100	Over 250

POPULATION DENSITY

first country in history to reach the billion mark.

Population densities vary widely in Asia. In less populated Southwest Asia, there are fewer than 25 people for each square kilometer (60 per square mile). But in South, Southeast, and East Asia, the highest population densities in the world are found. Often the population is much more concentrated then the national population density figures show. For example, a great deal of the soil in India is poor. People live only in the fertile areas, usually along riverbanks or seacoasts. The average population density in these areas can be as high as four to six times the overall population density of the entire country. With an average population growth rate of 1.8 percent a year, the Asians add about 40 to 50 million people a year to the world's total population.

Major Cities

Although the majority of Asians live in rural areas, Asia has some of the largest cities in the world. Tokyo and Shanghai rank among the world's largest cities. There are many Asian cities with populations of over 1,000,000, and quite a few with over 3,000,000. A great

many large cities—such as Bombay, Calcutta, Hong Kong, Jakarta, Karachi, Shanghai, Singapore, and Yokohama—are situated close to natural transportation routes. Almost all of Asia's largest cities are located in East, South, or Southeast Asia. Southwest Asia has many cities, too, but none so large as the great cities of China, India, and Japan. The largest cities in Southwest Asia are Istanbul and Ankara, in Turkey, and Baghdad, in Iraq. Cities like Damascus and Jerusalem, while smaller, are rich in religious and cultural tradition.

Way of Life

Most Asians live in villages. The family is the center of an Asian's life. The family takes care of the young, the sick, and the old. When a young man marries, he brings his bride back to his father's house to live. Very often the whole family lives under one roof. Children are wanted very much because they work with other members of the family in the fields.

In spite of the primitive tools used for farming, production is often very high. But too many Asians are trying to live off too little cultivated land. As a result, the standard of living is low. The average yearly income in

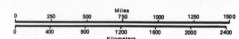

Miles

Kilometers

Lambert Azimuthal Equal-area Projection

 NATIONAL CAPITAL

 TUNDRA

CONIFEROUS FOREST

DECIDUOUS FOREST

 TROPICAL FOREST

 STEPPE (SHORT GRASS)

 DESERT

MOUNTAIN VEGETATION

INDEX TO ASIA MAP

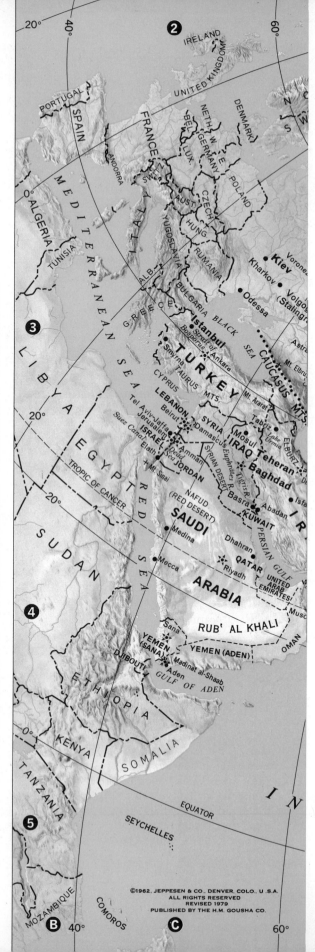

ASIA

ASIA

CANADA

Greenland

Arctic Ocean

North Pole

90°

120°

60°

80°

0°

30°

60°

90°

West Spitsbergen

Novaya Zemlya

Barents Sea

Atlantic Ocean

Arctic Circle

70°

60°

50°

40°

30°

Murmansk

Vorkuta

Archangel

UNION OF SOVIET

S

Ural Mountains

Europe Asia

Perm

Sverdlovsk

Magnitogorsk

Leningrad

★ London

Baltic Sea

Berlin

Moscow ★

EUROPE

Paris ★

★ Madrid

Kiev •

Kharkov

Odessa •

Volgograd
(Stalingrad)

Astrakhan •

Aral Sea

★ Rome

Black Sea

Europe Asia

Caspian Sea

Mediterranean Sea

Europe
Asia

Istanbul

Baku

Ashkhabad

Bukhara •

Samarkand •

Smyrna

★ Ankara

TURKEY

Tabriz •

Nicosia

CYPRUS

Aleppo •

SYRIA

LEBANON

Beirut ★

★ Damascus

★ Teheran

Meshed •

IRAN

AFGHANISTAN

ISRAEL

Jerusalem ★ ★ Amman

Baghdad ★

Suez Canal

Cairo •

JORDAN

Petra

IRAQ

Kandahar

Abadan •

Persepolis

Kerman •

KUWAIT
★ Kuwait

Jahrum •

AFRICA

BAHRAIN
Manama •
Doha ★ QATAR

Persian Gulf

Abu
Dhabi

Gulf of Oman

SAUDI

UNITED ARAB EMIRATES

Muscat ★

Tropic of
Cancer

★ Riyadh

Red Sea

Mecca •

ARABIA

OMAN

20°

Sana ★

YEMEN
(Sana)

YEMEN (Aden)

Arabian

Madinat al-Shaab

★★ Aden

Gulf of
Aden

Socotra

10°

Map by J. Donovan

Alaska
(U.S.)

180°

150°

120°

Aleutian Is.

International Date Line

Attu I.

Kamchatka Peninsula

Sakhalin

Kurile Islands

Pacific Ocean

S I B E R I A

S O V I E T   S O C I A L I S T   R E P U B L I C S

Yakutsk

Tomsk

Krasnoyarsk

Lake Baikal

Irkutsk

Omsk

Novosibirsk

Karaganda

L. Balkhash

Alma-Ata

Tashkent

Kashgar

Ulan Bator

Karakorum

MONGOLIAN PEOPLE'S REP.

Urumchi

SINKIANG-UIGHUR
AUTONOMOUS REGION

PEOPLE'S REPUBLIC OF CHINA

Lanchow

Sian

Chengtu

Chungking

Harbin

Changchun

Shenyang

Fushan

Anshan

Vladivostok

Hokkaido

J A P A N

Sendai

Tokyo

Nagoya

Yokohama

N. KOREA

Pyongyang

S. KOREA

Kyoto

Kobe

Osaka

Seoul

Taegu

Pusan

Hiroshima

Liita
(Darien & Port Arthur)

Peking

Tientsin

Taiyuan

Tsinan

Nanking

Chengchow

Wuhan

Wenchow

Foochow

Amoy

Shanghai

Nagasaki

Okinawa (Japan)

Marianas Isls

Guam

Taipei

TAIWAN

Canton

Kowloon

MACAO

Victoria
HONG KONG

REPUBLIC OF THE
PHILIPPINES

Luzon

Hainan

Manila

Mindanao

Bamian
(Bamiyan)

Kabul

Srinagar

KASHMIR

Islamabad

Jammu

PAKISTAN

Lahore

Amritsar

Harappa

Sukkur

Mohenjo-Daro

Karachi

Tibet

Mt. Everest

Lhasa

Thimbu

BHUTAN

HIMALAYAS

NEPAL

Katmandu

Delhi

New Delhi

Jaipur

Agra

Kanpur

Ahmadabad

Nagpur

INDIA

Bombay

Pune

Hyderabad

Bangalore

Madras

Cochin

Calcutta

Dacca

BANGLADESH

Mandalay

BURMA

Luang Prabang

Rangoon

Vientiane

LAOS

V I E T N A M

Hanoi

Hue

THAILAND

Bangkok

CAMBODIA

Pnompenh

Saigon
(Ho Chi Minh City)

South China
Sea

M A L A Y S I A

Sarawak

BRUNEI

Sabah

Bandar Seri Begawan

Malaya

Kuala Lumpur

SINGAPORE

Strait of Malacca

Borneo
(Kalimantan)

REPUBLIC OF INDONESIA

Celebes
(Sulawesi)

Sumatra

Jakarta

Java

Bandung

Surabaya

TIMOR

Bay of
Bengal

Andaman
Islands

Nicobar
Islands

Sea

SRI LANKA
(CEYLON)

Colombo

MALDIVES

Indian Ocean

Equator

Marketplace in front of a religious shrine near Patan in central Nepal, an independent kingdom of Asia.

Snake charmers in an Indian village not far from the city of Bombay.

Above: Nomads of Mongolia live in tents called yurts. Below: Hong Kong is very crowded. Government apartment buildings provide housing for some of its many people.

The tomb of the conqueror Tamerlane in Samarkand, erected in 1404. Once Tamerlane's capital, Samarkand is now a city in Soviet Asia.

some Asian countries is less than $150 a person. The threat of floods and droughts in the countryside and the lure of new industries have combined to send large numbers of rural people to the cities. This creates problems of unemployment and overcrowding in the cities. Jobs and housing are not always easy to find. This movement of population away from the rural areas has caused a breakdown in the traditional Asian way of life. Factory workers in the city no longer view their families in the villages as the center of their lives. They are more concerned with higher wages, better working conditions, and the benefits that the government can provide.

Asian dwellings vary in style and material from region to region. In the colder northern regions, people live mostly in houses built of baked bricks, stones, or a combination of clay and straw. Bamboo and thatch palms are popular building materials in the tropical south. The nomads of Southwest and Central Asia often live in tents that they can pack up and take with them when they move with their herds. In Asia's growing cities, many people live in tall apartment buildings.

The Asian diet is generally lower in calories than that of the European or American. With the exception of the nomads of Southwest and Soviet Asia, Asians generally eat less meat and dairy products than other peoples. Because of their religious beliefs the Hindus do not eat meat and the Muslims do not eat pork. On the other hand, the peoples of East Asia, notably the Chinese, eat almost everything without taboo. Their cooking is world-famous for variety and good taste. The Asian diet is based mainly on grains. Wheat is the most widely used in the north, and rice in the south. The soybean is an important foodstuff in East Asia, while dairy products are popular with the peoples of Southwest and Soviet Asia. Asians living along the seacoasts or riverbanks also catch fish.

Races

Asia is a land of many races. Various Mongoloid peoples—the Chinese, Japanese, Koreans, Mongols, and Tibetans—live in East Asia. Mongoloid people have yellow skin and straight, black hair. Together, the various Mongoloid peoples make up the largest race in the world today. Malay people occupy the islands of Indonesia and the Philippines. They are sometimes known as the brown race because of their generally dark complexion. The people of mainland Southeast Asia are a Malay-Mongoloid mixture.

The Turkic peoples occupy the area extending from western China to Turkey, including the entire Central Asia region. The peoples of Southwest and South Asia are mostly of Caucasian stock. But they do not all have the white skin of the Caucasian race. This is particularly true in South Asia where most people have dark complexions.

Languages

The peoples of Asia have many languages and writing systems. There is at least one major language group for each of the five principal regions. In South Asia there are two

Nepalese girl of Indian descent.

An Arab of Kuwait.

Young Turkish girl.

Indonesian woman.

Chinese children of Taiwan.

Burmese Boy Scout.

major language groups—the Indo-Aryan and the Dravidian. The Indo-Aryan group may be divided into at least 150 subgroups, including Hindi, Urdu, Bengali, Punjabi, Singhalese, and then again into hundreds of dialects. There are also many languages and dialects in the Dravidian group, which includes Tamil, Telugu, Kanarese, Malayalam, and many other subgroups. Persian, Afghan, and Pushtu, spoken in Iran and Afghanistan, belong to the Indo-Aryan group.

Most languages of East Asia and mainland Southeast Asia, such as Chinese, Thai, Tibetan, and Burmese, belong to the Sino-Tibetan language group. Japanese and Korean are sometimes classified in the Ural-Altaic group of northern Asia. Malay, the major language of Malaysia, and the languages of the Philippines, such as Tagalog, Bisaya, and Ilokano, belong to the Malayo-Polynesian group. The major languages of Southwest Asia, such as Arabic and Hebrew, are Semitic languages, while those of Turkey and Soviet Asia, such as Kazakh, Osmanli Turkish, and Uzbek, are Ural-Altaic languages.

Because of the many languages and dialects used, many people in Asia often do not understand the language spoken in the next town or village. This is particularly true in India, where English is still the language used by educated people for communication. Russian, of course, serves the same purpose in Soviet Asia.

Religions

Asia is the home of the world's great religions. Three important religions have come from Southwest Asia: Judaism, Christianity, and Islam. The oldest is Judaism. Its ideas and philosophy are found in the Old Testament of the Bible. With the appearance of Jesus Christ, Christianity was born. From this origin in Palestine, Christianity spread to Europe and the Western Hemisphere. The last major religion to appear was Islam, in about the 7th century A.D. Its founder was Moham-

med. Today it is the dominant religion in Southwest Asia. While these three religions have many differences, they are similar in their belief that there is but one God. This type of religion is called monotheism.

South Asia has given birth to two of the great religions of the world. They are Hinduism and Buddhism. Along with Islam they are the major religions of Asia. Hinduism is one of the oldest religions in the world. The Hindus believe in many gods. This kind of belief is called polytheism. The majority of Indians are Hindus today. Buddhism first appeared in India in the 6th century B.C. It began as an attempt to reform Hinduism. Its leader was Gautama Buddha. In time Buddhism came to accept many of the ideas of Hinduism. After the 2nd century A.D., Buddhism declined in India. Today it is a major religion in East and Southeast Asia.

Three important religions were born in East Asia. Two, Taoism and Confucianism, were founded in China, and the third, Shintoism, in Japan. Along with Buddhism they are the most important religions in this region. Confucianism is not, however, a religion in the same sense that Islam, Judaism, Christianity, and Hinduism are religions. It stresses duty to family and state and does not have any strong idea of God. In reality Confucianism is a set of rules for good conduct. Hence, it is often referred to as ethical rather than religious. This is the basic difference between Confucianism and the rest of the major faiths.

Buddhist monks in a 14th-century monastery in the city of Chiangmai, in northern Thailand.

CHIEF RELIGIONS OF ASIA (in order of number of followers)		
Hinduism	Buddhism	Taoism
Islam	Shintoism	Judaism
Confucianism	Christianity	

Art and Literature

The traditions that guide Asian artists are centuries old. Asians took a long time to develop their art and are slow in changing it. The kinds of events that have often altered styles in Western art, such as wars or new governments, have seldom influenced Eastern artists. In Asia art has been influenced by the art that came before it, and by very little else.

The major countries of Asia have styles of art that are very different from each other. For example, India, Cambodia, Thailand, and Indonesia have produced art that emphasizes the human body. Figures representing Buddha and many-armed dancing women are among the most common subjects. But in China real and imaginary animals and landscapes have dominated art. The Asians of the Indian subcontinent created sculpture more than any other kind of art. The Chinese and Japanese have worked a great deal in sculpture too, but they have also created many paintings.

Chinese artists were interested more in how they felt toward a landscape than in what the landscape really looked like. This kind of thinking has had a great influence on Western art in recent times. The Chinese have also been masters of calligraphy (the art of beautiful writing) for 2,000 years.

Asian literature is also as old as the continent's civilizations. Parts of the Old Testament of the Bible, for instance, were originally written about 1100 B.C. The Vedas (Books of Knowledge) of early India date from about 1000 B.C. China has one of the most extensive literatures of the world, with an unbroken tradition of some 3,000 years. Because of language differences each region or country eventually developed its own type of literature quite independently of the others. Some of the important ones are the Arabic, Persian, Burmese, Thai, Malay, Korean, and Japanese literatures.

Education

The scholar has always been a respected member of the community in Asia. Asia's tradition of learning is very old indeed. In China, for example, the most revered person of all times is Confucius, a scholar and teacher. The first Chinese university was created in 124 B.C. By the time of the birth of Christ it had grown to 30,000 students.

University students in China. Education is an important part of the country's modernization program.

But before the 20th century, education was a privilege enjoyed only by the well-to-do. In spite of Asia's great tradition of learning, most Asians could not read or write. Not until the latter half of the 19th century did most Asian countries begin to adopt the goal of universal education for all of their people.

The raising of the educational level takes a very long time. This is particularly true in countries where children are needed at home to work in the fields or to help support their families in other ways. Not long ago, less than half of all Asian children between the ages of 5 and 14 attended school at the primary level. Less than one fourth of all children attended school at the secondary level, and very few young people were enrolled in universities.

But almost all Asian governments are trying to improve education. The number of children enrolled in all levels of school has increased rapidly since World War II. Many Asian countries have passed compulsory school attendance laws. And almost all of them have policies designed to keep children in school longer. Fees that prevented many children from attending school have been gradually abolished or lowered. More teachers are being trained. Today there is a college in almost every major Asian city. Some cities—such as Lahore, Manila, Nanking, New Delhi, Peking, and Tokyo —have several universities each. The academic standards of many of these universities compare favorably with those of the best universities in Europe and the United States.

THE ECONOMY

More than two thirds of the people of Asia are engaged in agriculture. Most Asian farms are small. The use of modern farm equipment is widespread in only a few regions, such as Soviet Asia and Israel. Since World War II, the countries of Asia have been trying to increase farm production to keep up with their fast-growing populations. Asian governments have developed many programs, such as the cultivation of more land through irrigation projects. They have introduced better fertilizers, insecticides, improved seed varieties, and modern machinery.

Industrialization has been the major goal of almost every economic development program that has been carried out in Asia since the end of World War II. Today nonagricultural production is beginning to rival farming in some Asian countries. Japan is one of the great industrialized nations of the world. And many Asian cities are developing into important manufacturing centers.

Agriculture

Rice, which needs a warm and wet climate to grow, is the major crop in the southern regions of Asia. Southeast Asia, eastern India, southern China, Korea, and Japan are the important rice-growing areas. Farther north, in the drier regions, many cereal grains, such as wheat, barley, and millet, are grown. China, northern India and Pakistan, and Soviet Asia are major wheat- and corn-growing areas. Other important Asian agricultural products are rubber, produced in quantity in Southeast Asia and Sri Lanka; tea, in Sri Lanka, India, Japan, and China; sugarcane, in India, Taiwan, and the Philippines; cotton, in China, India, and Soviet Asia; soybeans and tobacco, in China; jute, in Bangladesh; silk, in China, Japan, and India; coconuts and copra, in the Philippines, Indonesia, India, and Sri Lanka; palm oil, in Malaysia; groundnuts, in India and China; dates, in Southwest Asia; and fruits, in Israel, India, and Southeast Asia.

Nomadic herders in Southwest and Central Asia depend largely on their livestock. Many small farmers throughout Asia raise poultry for food. India and Soviet Asia produce much cheese and butter, and Soviet Asia and China lead in beef, pork, mutton, and lamb. Wool is a major product in Central Asia.

Manufacturing

The chief industrial centers of Asia are Japan, northeastern China, India, and Turkey. Japan is the most highly industrialized nation in Asia. Today it leads the world in shipbuilding. It leads Asia in the production of steel, aluminum, automobiles, cement, textiles, paper, wood pulp, electronic equipment, and many other industrial products. It exports such items as electronic equipment, television sets, automobiles, and textiles to most of the world. Its closest rivals are China and India—but they are a distant second. India is second to Japan in Asia in the manufacture of textiles, automobiles, and electrical appliances. It is increasing its production of iron, steel, aluminum, and other products under a series of government plans. China is the third industrial area of Asia. Much of its industry is in Manchuria. China is trying to industrialize quickly, stressing the development of heavy industry. Other nations, such as Pakistan, Saudi Arabia, the Philippines, Israel, Burma, South Korea, Indonesia, Singapore, and Malaysia, are also developing industry.

Mining

The most important mining operations are found in Japan, India, China, Southwest Asia, and Soviet Asia. China leads Asia in the mining of coal, tungsten, and iron ore. India is first in manganese and mica. Japan leads in sulfur and zinc production. Turkey is the center of a rich chromium industry, while Malaysia and Indonesia mine much bauxite. Tin is mined in Malaysia, Indonesia, China, and Thailand. Southwest Asia—especially Iran, Iraq, Kuwait, and Saudi Arabia—produces much of the world's supply of petroleum. Indonesia, China, and Soviet Asia are also major producers of oil.

Fishing

Fishing is an important industry in Asia. Japan is the world's leading producer of processed fish, and China ranks second. Japan's fishing industry is one of the most modern in the world. It is equipped with floating canneries that process the fish right after they are caught. Most of the world's leading pearl fisheries are found in Asia, especially in Japan. Japan and the Soviet Union have large whaling fleets.

Umbrellas are made and sold in a village near Chiangmai in northern Thailand.

Filipino women weaving mats. These women belong to the small Moro, or Muslim, population of the island republic.

Fabric (*above*) that has been dipped in dye is hung to dry in Lahore, one of Pakistan's largest cities. Modern factory (*below*) in People's Republic of China.

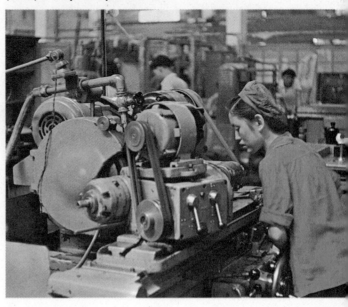

Lumbering

The Soviet Union is the world's leading producer of sawed wood, and a large part of its lumbering is done in Soviet Asia. Japan is the world's third-largest producer of sawed wood. In spite of its rich forest resources, Asia as a whole has a shortage of lumber. Many Asian countries are now carrying out reforestation programs—that is, the planting of trees for future use. Reforestation projects also help prevent floods and soil erosion.

Transportation

Geography has hindered the development of both transportation and trade in Asia. The great size of the continent and its many lofty

Jute for making burlap or twine is soaked in water in southern India.

Chinese farmers hard at work in the rice fields of Taiwan.

Near Kuala Lumpur, capital of Malaysia, a woman strips bark from a rubber tree.

Fishing near the Pescadores Islands in the Formosa Strait.

IMPORTANT DATES

About 3200 B.C. Beginnings of civilization: Sumerians develop cuneiform writing; early urban culture in the Indus Valley; China emerges from the Stone Age.

About 1750 B.C. Hammurabi, King of Babylonia, introduces world's first uniform code of laws.

About 1500 B.C. Shang dynasty: written records kept by Chinese.

About 14th cent. B.C. Phoenicians develop the first alphabet.

13th cent. B.C. Moses leads the Exodus, receives the Ten Commandments.

1028– 256 B.C. Chou dynasty: beginning of China's Iron Age.

600– 300 B.C. Upanishads written: crystallization of the caste system in India.

563? B.C. Birth of Buddha.

551? B.C. Birth of Confucius.

6th cent. B.C. Cyrus the Great founds the Persian Empire.

274– 232 B.C. Asoka unites two thirds of India; rules according to Buddhist laws; sends out missionaries.

202 B.C.– A.D. 220 Han dynasty in China: height of ancient Chinese civilization; paper and porcelain invented.

4 B.C. Birth of Christ.

330 Constantine I moves the capital of the Roman Empire to Byzantium, which he renames Constantinople (Istanbul).

618– 906 T'ang dynasty in China: China most advanced nation on earth; printing invented; administration centralized.

622 Beginning of the Muslim era; Mohammed (570–632) flees from Mecca to Medina and organizes the Commonwealth of Islam.

632– 1100 Growth of Arabic civilization under the influence of Islam.

960– 1279 Sung dynasty in China: beginning of modernity; diffusion of learning; use of tea spread; use of compass; gunpowder developed.

998– 1030 Muslims invade Punjab: mixing of Hindu and Muslim cultures.

1096– 1290 Era of Crusades: increased contact between East and West.

1206– 1227 Genghis Khan (1162–1227) establishes the Mongol empire, conquers large parts of Asia and Europe.

1250– 1350 Thai people—from China—establish what is now Thailand.

1260 Kublai Khan becomes emperor of China.

1271– 1295 Travels of Marco Polo bring first detailed knowledge of Asia to Europe.

1368– 1644 Ming dynasty drives out Mongols, reunifies China.

1369– 1405 Tamerlane conquers much of Southwest Asia, invades India.

1453 Constantinople captured by the Ottoman Turks: end of the Eastern Roman Empire; beginning of the Ottoman Empire.

1498 Vasco da Gama sails to India, opens water route to the East.

1514 Portuguese make first landing in China.

1521 Magellan claims Philippines for Spain.

1526 Mogul Empire in India founded by Baber.

1549– 1551 St. Francis Xavier introduces Christianity in Japan.

1600– 1868 Tokugawa period in Japan: growth of industry, commerce; development of arts; ban on all foreigners begins a long era of isolation.

1644– 1912 Manchu dynasty in China.

1756– 1763 Great Britain becomes dominant power in India after the Seven Years' War.

1839– 1842 Opium War (Anglo-Chinese War).

1853– 1854 Commodore Perry lands in Japan: end of Japanese isolation.

1857– 1858 Sepoy Rebellion (Indian Mutiny) in India.

1868 Meiji Restoration begins in Japan.

1869 Suez Canal opens.

1894– 1895 Sino-Japanese War: Japan wins Formosa.

1898 Spanish-American War: United States takes over the Philippines and Guam.

1900 Boxer Rebellion in China.

1903 Trans-Siberian Railway completed.

1904– 1905 Russo-Japanese War: Japan emerges as World power.

1911– 1912 Revolution in China led by Sun Yat-sen: China becomes a republic.

1923 Turkey becomes a republic under the leadership of Mustafa Kemal (Atatürk).

1931 Japan invades Manchuria.

1937 Japan invades North China.

1941 Japan attacks Pearl Harbor.

1945 First atomic bombs dropped on Hiroshima and Nagasaki; Japan surrenders; World War II ends.

1946 Jordan and the Philippines receive their independence.

1947 India, Pakistan gain independence.

1948 Gandhi assassinated; Israel created; Burma and Ceylon became independent; North and South Korea established as separate states.

1949 The Communists, led by Mao Tse-tung, take over China: Nationalist government retreats to Formosa; Indonesia gains independence.

1950– 1953 Korean War.

1954 The French pull out of Indochina after 7½ years of war; North and South Vietnam, Laos, Cambodia established; SEATO organized.

1955 Bandung Conference of 29 African and Asian states.

1957 Malaya gains independence.

1959 Tibetans revolt against China; Dalai Lama flees.

1960 Cyprus gains independence.

1961 Kuwait gains independence.

1962 Border clashes between China and India.

1963 Malaysia formed.

1964 People's Republic of China becomes first Asian nation to set off nuclear explosion.

1965 Maldives and Singapore gain full independence.

1967 Yemen (Aden) gains independence.

1971 Bangladesh separates from Pakistan; People's Republic of China enters United Nations.

1975 Vietnam War ends; civil war in Lebanon; Sikkim incorporated into India.

1976 North and South Vietnam united.

1979 U.S. recognizes People's Republic of China; Vietnam invades Cambodia; China invades Vietnam; Egypt and Israel sign peace treaty; monarchy overthrown in Iran.

mountain ranges and vast deserts have discouraged road builders and traders for centuries. Up to recent years some areas of Asia, such as Mongolia and Tibet, were almost impossible to reach. But the introduction of modern means of transportation after World War II resulted in some dramatic changes in the pattern of trade.

Transportation in Asia has been easiest along or near the coasts. People traveled by sea and along the great rivers that have been the only real avenues of transportation in a large part of Asia for centuries. But many of the seaports of Soviet Siberia are icebound for the better part of the year. In parts of Asia transportation is still a matter of using old caravan trails. Merchants still cross the deserts of Southwest and Central Asia on camels, although the camels are gradually being replaced by vehicles designed for desert travel.

After the coming of the Europeans, railroads were built—in the late 19th and early 20th centuries. Some new lines were built after World War II, and others are now under construction. Very often the tracks are of a different width in each country. This makes it impossible to join together many parts of Asia by rail. Several railroads are located along the coastal region and do not penetrate the interior or join regions together. There is only one railroad that connects eastern and western Asia. This is the double-tracked Trans-Siberian railroad joining Europe with the Pacific coast of Asia. There is no railroad between the two largest countries of Asia—India and China. Today India, China, and Japan have the most highly developed rail systems in Asia. The Soviet Union is expanding the rail network in Central Asia, in spite of great difficulties caused by the harsh climate and rugged land. Asian governments own most of the railroads. They are increasing the amount of track yearly as part of their industrialization programs.

The roads and highways of Asia are generally poor. The few cars and trucks used in commercial transportation are found in the large cities. But production of cars and trucks has steadily increased in the years since World War II. Japan and India have the most automobiles in use, and they lead Asia in the building of all types of motor vehicles.

Since World War II, most Asian countries have used air transport more and more. The airplane is the best means of transportation over the desert and mountain areas. Jet planes are rapidly opening up the interior of Asia. Airways now join all the important cities of Asia to Africa, Australia, Europe, and North and South America. The leading airlines of the West fly regularly to Asia. In addition, a number of Asian nations have developed their own airlines.

Trade

As transportation improves, the pattern of trade in Asia also changes. The old picture is that of Asia selling its raw materials to the United States and Europe and in return importing manufactured products. Today Asia is manufacturing many of these consumer products for itself. And Asian nations today often process their own raw materials for sale in the world's markets.

But Asia's raw materials continue to form a large part of its exports. Malaysia and Indonesia provide much of the world's rubber, and Southwest Asia provides much of its oil. Most of the world's tea is produced in India, China, Indonesia, and Sri Lanka. Asia is the world's largest producer of rice. Malaysia is the world's leading exporter of tin, and China is the leading supplier of tungsten.

▶ HISTORY

The history of Asia began in three great river valleys—the Tigris-Euphrates in Southwest Asia, the Indus in South Asia, and the Hwang Ho (Yellow River) in East Asia. In these three areas, civilizations developed that give Asia its special place in the world today.

Early Civilizations

The Tigris-Euphrates valley in Southwest Asia was the birthplace of several important early developments. From 3500 B.C. to 600 B.C., there was a brilliant succession of achievements. The Sumerians, Babylonians, and Assyrians developed writing, law, and commerce. The code of Hammurabi (about 1800 B.C.) was one of the first written law codes in the world. Around 600 B.C., the Persians established an empire that extended from the shores of the Mediterranean to northern India. Kings such as Cyrus the Great and Darius the Great were noted leaders.

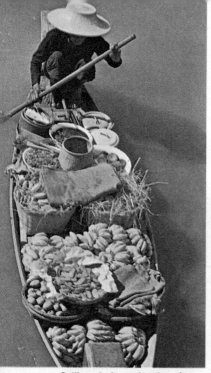

Selling fruit and other items from a boat in Thailand.

Winding road through the famous Khyber Pass is an important link between Pakistan and Afghanistan.

Pedicabs and bicycles (*left*) are part of a Javanese street scene. In Yemen (Aden) camels (*right*) are often used to transport goods.

A painted elephant (*above*) at a festival in Mysore, India. A monorail (*right*) links central Tokyo, Japan, and Haneda Airport.

Left: Men rest on a park bench across from government buildings in Kuala Lumpur, Malaysia. Right: Modern apartment houses in Tel Aviv, Israel.

The ruins of Harappa and Mohenjo-Daro are signs of early civilization in India. In about 1500 B.C., Indo-Aryan invaders came through the mountains of northwestern India to establish the Hindu civilization. Traces of this early beginning remain to this day, and the tradition of Hinduism is still one of the important influences in modern India.

Along the Hwang Ho (Yellow River) in China grew the first civilization in East Asia. The development of this civilization dates back to about 1500 B.C., to the period of the Shang dynasty. The Shang were the ruling family. The political history of China from this point until 1912 is a succession of dynasties. The last one was overthrown in 1912.

Period of Development and Expansion

After 500 B.C., several great religions and empires grew up in Asia. In 334 B.C., Alexander the Great began his conquest of Southwest Asia and northern India. His invasion brought South Asia into direct contact with Greek civilization. Meanwhile the first great Indian empire, the Maurya (321 B.C.–184 B.C.), was established over much of the subcontinent. It created the first real unity in India. The great leader Asoka supported Buddhism and brought peace to this region.

Farther east, in China, the Han dynasty (202 B.C.–A.D. 220) established an empire and extended its influence into Central and Southeast Asia. Under its great ruler Wu Ti, the Han adopted Confucianism. During this period other great religions took form. Christianity appeared in Southwest Asia, and Buddhism began to spread to East Asia.

The 7th century saw the rapid rise of still another major religion, Islam. Its followers, the Muslims, conquered most of North Africa, Southwest Asia, and northern India. The Crusades (European attempts to drive the Muslims out) were largely unsuccessful. In East Asia, China flourished under the T'ang and Sung dynasties from about A.D. 600 to 1200. In the 13th century Genghis Khan, the Mongol conqueror, gained control of much of Asia, from China to Russia.

Period of Colonialism

With the arrival in India of the Portuguese explorer Vasco da Gama in 1498, Europeans actively entered the life of Asia. Aware of Asia's many riches, the Europeans began to carve out their own colonial empires. In the 16th century, the Portuguese entered India and the Spanish entered the Philippines. They were accompanied by Christian missionaries such as Francis Xavier. The English, French, and Dutch joined in the search for colonies in the 17th century. France and England entered India, and the Dutch entered the island of Java. By the 18th century India and parts of Southwest Asia were under colonial rule. The picture was completed in the 19th century, when the rest of Southeast Asia was occupied by European countries. By the end of the century only a handful of Asian countries still remained independent—China, Japan, Korea, Thailand (Siam), Turkey (the Ottoman Empire), and Iran (Persia).

Nationalism and Independence

With the opening of the 20th century, the Asian peoples began movements for freedom. This desire for self-rule and national unity is called nationalism. It has been the most important political force in Asia during this century. Men like Sun Yat-sen and Mohandas Karamchand Gandhi led these movements. In 1912 the Chinese overthrew the Manchu dynasty (1644–1912) and established the first republic in Asia. Thereafter Asian nationalism began to grow rapidly. It reached its height in the years after World War II, when the following nations were born: Mongolia in 1945; Jordan and the Philippines in 1946; India and Pakistan in 1947; Burma, Ceylon (now Sri Lanka), Israel, and North and South Korea in 1948; Indonesia in 1949; Cambodia, Laos, and North and South Vietnam in 1954; the Federation of Malaya in 1957; Cyprus in 1960; Kuwait in 1961; Malaysia in 1963; the Maldives in 1965; Singapore (seceded from Malaysia) in 1965; Yemen (Sana) and Yemen (Aden), in 1967; and Bangladesh (formerly East Pakistan) in 1971. In 1976, following the end of the long Vietnam War, North and South Vietnam were united as a single country.

Some of these nations have Communist governments, while others are pro-Western. Most of the Asian countries have adopted a neutral, or nonaligned, policy in their relations with the Western and Communist worlds. This policy of nonalignment was first officially announced at the important Bandung Conference, held in Indonesia in 1955. It was a sort of declaration of independence for Asian and African countries seeking to free themselves from American and European colonial influences. Prime Minister Jawaharlal Nehru of India and Premier Chou En-lai of the People's Republic of China were the dominant figures at this meeting. These countries not only reaffirmed their independence but also agreed to live together in peace and co-operation.

This has been most difficult to do. Since Bandung there have been three Arab-Israeli wars in Southwest Asia (1956, 1967, and 1973), two wars between India and Pakistan (1965 and 1971), a border war between India and China (1962–1963), civil war in Lebanon and Iran, skirmishes along the Chinese-Soviet boundary, and war on the Southeast Asian mainland. The Vietnam War ended in 1975, but in recent years tensions have developed between China and Vietnam and between Cambodia and Vietnam and Thailand. Israel and Egypt signed a peace treaty in 1979, but differences between Israel and some of its neighbors in Southwest Asia persist.

During the years ahead, the countries of Asia can be expected to play an increasing role in world affairs. Japan is one of the world's leading industrialized nations, and the People's Republic of China is a major power. India's vast size and population make it dominant in south Asia, and events have proved how vital the oil-producing countries of Southwest Asia are to the world economy.

The most important goal of Asian nations today is to develop their economies as quickly as possible. Nowhere is this more evident than in China, where the government has established new ties with the West to modernize its industry. The Asian people want better health care, more education, and a fair share of the world's wealth. They are making their needs known and are willing to work hard through their different political and economic systems to achieve their aims.

EDWARD W. JOHNSON
Montclair State College
Reviewed by HYMAN KUBLIN
City University of New York

See also articles on individual Asian countries; SOUTHEAST ASIA; MIDDLE EAST.

ASSYRIA. See ANCIENT CIVILIZATIONS.
ASTHMA. See DISEASES.
ASTRONAUTS. See SPACE TRAVEL.

These stone archways at Stonehenge, in England, could be used to determine the seasons.

ASTRONOMY

Astronauts walk on the moon. Robot observatories land on Venus and Mars. Other space probes study Jupiter and Saturn and send their findings back to earth. These exciting adventures in space are a part of the science of astronomy.

Astronomy deals with everything beyond the earth—the sun, moon, planets and their moons, and other objects in the solar system. It is concerned with the billions of stars that make up our galaxy and with the billions of galaxies that make up the known universe. Astronomy is the oldest of the sciences. It goes back thousands of years in history.

Drawing copied from the Stone of Denderah, an ancient Egyptian sky map. It shows many familiar constellations, including those making up the Zodiac (shown in color).

THE ORIGINS OF ASTRONOMY

Drawings of the **phases** of the moon (the seeming changes in its shape) have been found in caves in Spain. These drawings are about 10,000 years old. About 6,000 years ago people in various parts of Europe set up huge stones that could be used to mark the places of the rising and setting of the sun and moon. One especially well-known group of these stones is at Stonehenge, in southern England. It is a ring of stone archways. In this primitive observatory, the seasons of the year can be determined by the movement of the sun and moon as seen through the archways.

People in ancient Egypt, Babylonia, China, Mexico, and other parts of the world also studied the night skies. The earliest astronomy records we have were made on clay tablets in Babylonia about 3,000 years ago. They were made by **astrologers**, or high priests who carefully studied the movements of the sun, moon, and planets in the night sky. They believed that these movements revealed what was going to happen on the earth. In those days people thought that the stars and planets controlled the lives of human beings. Even today there are people who believe in astrology, but there is no scientific proof for its claims.

Although the ancient astrologers were wrong, their work did lead to the first careful studies of the heavens and to the development of the science of astronomy. For example, Johannes Kepler (1571–1630), the great German astronomer, was employed by Emperor Rudolph II partly as an astrologer.

Some of the clay tablets of Babylonia were astronomical tables. These tables made it possible to work out exactly the time when **eclipses** (shadowing) of the moon and sun would occur. People believed that eclipses were a bad omen. The astrologers, who could predict the time of eclipses, were looked upon as powerful, important people.

At the same time people were discovering that astronomy had many uses and that some of these uses were of great importance. The position of the sun as it rose and set was used to mark out the length of the day. Astronomy was used to give accurate time, to mark the length of the year, and to draw up the first calendars. Travelers in the desert and seafarers used the sun by day and the stars by night to find their way.

▶GREEK WORLD SYSTEMS

Many ancient peoples studied astronomy, but we know most about the astronomers of Greece. This is so because some of the books they wrote have come down to us.

At first the Greeks thought that the earth was flat. Then, about 500 B.C., the Greek mathematician Pythagoras suggested that the earth was a **sphere** (globe) and that the stars hung around it on a celestial (heavenly) sphere. He was right about the earth but wrong about the stars. There are stars throughout space, but there is no celestial sphere. According to Pythagoras, the earth traveled around a central fire once every day. The sun, moon, and planets also moved around this central fire.

Like Pythagoras, Aristotle, one of the greatest scientists of ancient Greece, thought that the earth was round. But he believed wrongly that the earth stood still, while the rest of the universe moved around it. Ptolemy, another Greek thinker, also worked out a system in which the earth was the center of the universe.

Geocentric (earth-centered) systems like those of Aristotle and Ptolemy raised questions that were hard to answer. For example, there are times when the planet Mars seems to reverse its usual movement through the sky and to travel backwards. Today we know that both Mars and the earth orbit the sun. Sometimes the earth overtakes and passes Mars. This is when Mars seems to move backwards. But if you believe that the earth is standing still, the backward, or **retrograde**, motion is very hard to explain.

Ptolemy tried to explain retrograde motion with the complicated idea that each planet,

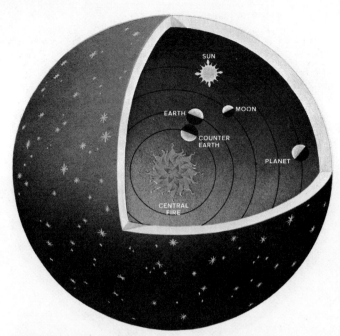

Pythagoras believed that the earth, sun, moon, and planets traveled around a great central fire. All were enclosed in a hollow sphere, or globe, hung with stars.

while circling the earth, also moved in another, smaller cycle called an **epicycle**. Yet epicycles did not completely explain the observed motions of the planets, so more epicycles were added. Even then the system could not account for all the observed motions. Despite these faults, the system was accepted, and it survived for nearly 1,400 years.

▶DISCOVERIES ABOUT THE SOLAR SYSTEM

By the year 1500 people had begun to take a fresh interest in astronomy and science. Nicolaus Copernicus (1473–1543), a Polish astronomer, put forth the correct idea of the solar system in his book *On the Revolutions of the Heavenly Bodies.*

First, he stated that the earth and the other planets move in circular orbits around the sun. Second, a planet moves faster if it is in a small orbit and near the sun. Copernicus also said that the earth turns on its axis once every 24 hours. As a result, the sun and stars appear to rise and set each day. The Copernican theory was much simpler than Ptolemy's. We know today that Copernicus was correct, except for his idea that the planetary orbits are circles.

Johannes Kepler improved the system of Copernicus. He discovered three important laws that govern the motions of the planets. First, the orbit of a planet around the sun is not a perfect circle, but an ellipse—a flattened

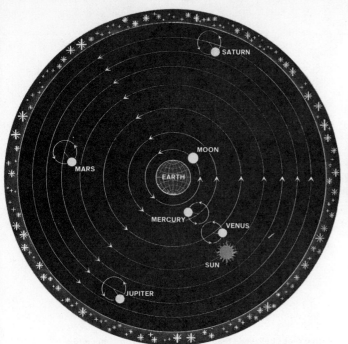

Ptolemy thought that the earth was the center of the universe. The sun and planets circled the earth. Planets also moved in smaller circles, called epicycles.

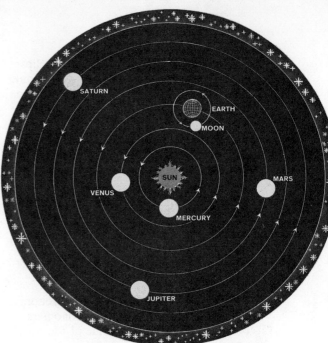

Copernicus was the first to realize that the earth, moon, and planets orbit the sun. However, he was wrong in believing that the orbits were perfect circles.

circle. Second, a planet moves faster when it is near the sun than when it is farther away. Third, the larger the planet's orbit, the longer it takes to go around the sun.

Kepler was able to work out his laws by using the observations of Tycho Brahe (1546–1601), a Danish astronomer. Brahe devoted his whole life to measuring the positions of the stars and the planets in the sky. He did this without the help of the telescope, which had not yet been invented.

The work of Galileo Galilei (1564–1642), an Italian scientist, gave strong help to the new astronomy. He supported the Copernican system and attacked the old ideas of the Greeks. Shortly after the telescope was invented in Holland, Galileo built his own.

With his telescope, Galileo was able to observe mountains and valleys on the moon, the four brightest moons of Jupiter, and the rings of Saturn. He also saw that the planet Venus went through phases, like the moon. He observed dark spots on the sun, and he noticed that each day the spots were in a new position. From observations he concluded that the sun rotates on its axis.

Isaac Newton was born in England the same year that Galileo died. Newton discovered the law of universal gravitation and the laws of motion. The work of this great English sci-

entist made it possible to understand the workings of the solar system. The sun is a very large object, and it exerts a tremendous gravitational pull. This pull keeps each planet in its orbit around the sun. The moon orbits the earth for the same reason. By the time Newton died in 1727, much of astronomy had become an exact science. And people realized that the planet earth was only one part of the universe.

The Planets

To the ancient astronomers, Saturn appeared to be the most distant planet, at the edge of the universe. That belief continued until the year 1781. In that year William Herschel (1738–1822), a German-born musician living in England, discovered a planet beyond the orbit of Saturn. At the time, Herschel was an amateur astronomer. Using a homemade telescope set up on the sidewalk in front of his home, he observed a speck of light that moved from night to night. Herschel at first thought it was a comet. But other astronomers worked out the orbit of the moving light, and Herschel's discovery was recognized as a planet. It was named Uranus.

Neptune was discovered with the aid of mathematics. In the years following the discovery of Uranus, astronomers were puzzled by its failure to move as expected. Up to 1822, the planet seemed to move too quickly; then it lagged. By the 1840's, it was suspected that the peculiar motion was caused by the gravitational pull of an even more distant planet. Two astronomers, working independently, calculated where the suspected planet must be. They were John C. Adams, of England, and Urbain J. J. Leverrier, of France. In 1846, Johann Galle, a German astronomer, found the planet just where Adams and Leverrier had predicted it would be. The planet was named Neptune.

Pluto was discovered by Clyde W. Tombaugh, a United States astronomer, in 1930. He completed the search begun by Percival Lowell, another U.S. astronomer, who had predicted the existence of the planet. It was a long, hard job. Photographic plates were exposed to the sky at night and examined during the day. Ninety million star images were examined before one tiny, shifting point of light was found. This was Pluto. It seems to be at the edge of the solar system—5,900,000,000 (billion) kilometers (3,666,000,000 miles) from the sun.

In the 18th century, astronomers thought that there was an undiscovered planet between Mars and Jupiter. They began a search of the space between the two planets. In 1801, Giuseppe Piazzi, an Italian astronomer, discovered a small body that he thought to be the missing planet. Its name is Ceres. Later many more small bodies were found between Mars and Jupiter. They are called asteroids or planetoids. There are at least 40,000 of these, and most of them are chunks of stone or iron.

Comets

Every few years a great comet, bright enough to be seen without a telescope, appears in the sky. Comets are a part of the solar system. Like planets, they move in elliptical orbits around the sun. Some comets have extremely long orbits, so that they are very far from the sun a large part of the time.

One of the most famous comets was observed in 1682 by Edmund Halley, a British astronomer. It was later named for him. Halley calculated the comet's orbit. He was able to predict that it would return every 76 years, and it has done so, last being seen in 1910. The period of time varies slightly because of the pull of the planets.

NICOLAUS COPERNICUS

TYCHO BRAHE

JOHANNES KEPLER

GALILEO GALILEI

ISAAC NEWTON

Some scientists think that a comet is a frozen ball of ice and dust, perhaps 5 to 10 kilometers (3 to 6 miles) in diameter. When the comet is far from the sun, the ice remains frozen. But the comet does come nearer to the sun, at least for a short time. Then the sun's light and heat cause the ice to evaporate (form gases). These gases are the glowing head, or **coma**, of the comet, which may appear as bright as the brightest stars. The solar wind (electrically charged particles from the sun) blows back some of the gas to form the comet's tail, which may be over 100,000,000 kilometers (60,000,000 miles) in length.

The Moon

In 1969, astronauts set foot on the moon for the first time. They and the astronauts who followed them brought back samples of the moon's rocks. Some of these rocks were up to 4,600,000,000 (billion) years old. The great age of the rocks strengthened a theory held by many scientists. They believe that the entire solar system—the sun, the planets, and their moons—was formed that long ago from vast clouds of dust and gases whirling through space.

The moon's surface is covered with millions of craters of all sizes. The craters were formed over billions of years as rocks in space fell onto the moon. The impacts dug the craters and threw up the fine rock dust that covers the moon's surface.

Other places on the moon have large, dark, flat areas that were once thought to be seas. We know now that these areas are lava that long ago flowed from the moon's interior and became solid. Today the moon is a dead place, without air, water, or life.

The Sun

The sun is the star nearest to us. It is a giant ball of gases. Many studies have been made of the sun, and it is now kept under constant observation. Some of the most interesting studies have had to do with sunspots. These are dark spots that can be observed on the sun's surface. The spots are storms that occur in the hot, swirling gases of the sun. In 1826, Heinrich S. Schwabe, a German astronomer, began to count sunspots. He counted them for 43 years—and was rewarded with the discovery of the sunspot cycle. He found that

In England Herschel built his own reflecting telescope for studying the sky. In 1781 this musician and amateur astronomer discovered the planet Uranus.

about every 11 years the sunspots were very numerous and the sun was in a disturbed state. In 1851, Johann von Lamont, a Scottish-born German astronomer, made a very important discovery. He found that disturbances in the earth's magnetic field took place most often when the sun showed spots. He opened the way for later scientists, who are still studying the effects of the sun on the earth's magnetic field and upper atmosphere.

These effects are due to the fact that the interior of the sun is too hot for ordinary atoms to exist. An ordinary atom has a center, or **nucleus**, that contains one or more positively charged particles called **protons**. Negatively charged particles, called **electrons**, move in orbits around the nucleus. The positive charges of the protons exactly balance the negative charges of the electrons, so the atom is said to be **electrically neutral**.

Temperatures within the sun reach many millions of degrees. This unimaginable heat rips electrons from some atoms of the sun's gases, so that they are no longer neutral. The charged particles are called **ions**. Ionized gases from the sun are blown out into interplanetary space. This flow is the **solar wind**. It streams past the earth, changing the shape of the earth's magnetic field. It also causes the glowing auroras (the northern and the southern lights) when it reaches the top of the earth's atmosphere.

What makes the sun hot? One old idea was that it burns like a flame. Another was that it gives off heat by contracting slowly. In this century, scientists have shown that the sun's enormous heat is produced deep in its interior, by nuclear fusion. The process of fusion is the coming-together (union) of atomic nuclei. On the sun, the union is mainly that of the nuclei of hydrogen atoms, joining to form helium nuclei. Heat and light are given off during this process. It is the same process that takes place in the explosion of a hydrogen bomb. Scientists are working to find ways to control the fusion process, so that its heat may be used to generate electricity.

▶ **DISCOVERIES ABOUT THE STARS**

The stars are like our sun (which is also a star). They are globes of extremely hot gas heated by nuclear reactions in their interiors. It took a great amount of work to establish this fact because the stars are so far away. The closest star to us, other than the sun, is Alpha Centauri. It is about 40,000,000,000,000 (trillion) kilometers (25,000,000,000,000 miles) away.

Binary Stars

William Herschel discovered that some stars have other stars as close companions. Such stars are called binaries. ("Binary" means "made up of two things.") Binary stars revolve around each other. Studies of pairs of stars gave astronomers the times of revolution and the sizes of orbit. From these figures they were able to calculate the masses of the two stars. That is, they could say how much the matter in the stars weighed.

Variable Stars

In 1783, John Goodricke, an English amateur astronomer, was studying the star Algol. He noticed that it changed its brightness. A year later he noticed a regular change in the light from another star, Delta Cephei. Goodricke had discovered two important types of variable stars. Algol is an **eclipsing variable**.

This means that its light dims when a dark companion moves between it and the earth. Delta Cephei is a **pulsating star**. It expands and contracts within a period of about a week. That is why the amount of light from it dims and brightens. Pulsating stars like this one are called **Cepheid variables**.

Some variable stars show a sudden change of brightness. This occurs when an explosion blows off the outer layer of the star. A star that was invisible to the unaided eye may then become very bright in the sky. For this reason such a star is called a **nova**, or new star. Sometimes the exploding star is almost completely destroyed. It is so bright that it is called a **supernova**. Many old records tell us of these stars. There was a brilliant supernova in the year 1054 that was watched by Chinese astronomers for more than a year. Today

The Crab nebula, a bright cloud of gas, was observed as a supernova by Chinese astronomers in A.D. 1054. A pulsar at the center of the nebula may be the remains of a star that exploded. The pulsar emits 30 flashes of light and 30 pulses of radio waves each second.

it is called the Crab nebula. Without a telescope a nova can be seen in the sky about once every ten years. If you know the constellations well enough, you have a good chance of discovering one.

The Classification of Stars

Scientists find it useful to classify (put into some kind of order) the things that they study, whether melons or mice, seas or stars. One classification of stars is based on their temperatures. For most stars, it was found that there is a relation between the temperature of the star and its brightness. Hot stars are brighter than cool stars. Star colors range from bluish white for the hottest stars, through yellow for average stars, to red for the coolest. When stars are arranged on a chart on the basis of temperature and brightness, most of them fall into a pattern called the "main sequence," running from the top left down to the lower right. On this chart, our sun is in the middle. It is an average star.

This classification of stars was first suggested by Ejnar Hertzsprung, a Danish astronomer. His work was improved upon by Henry N. Russell, a United States astronomer. The chart based on their studies is called the Hertzsprung-Russell chart.

How Stars Die

A star may exist for billions of years, but it does come to an end as its fuel supply runs down. The star may explode, hurling much of its gas into space. What remains of the star may collapse into a small, dense (tightly packed) form called a **white dwarf star**. Larger stars may collapse into extremely dense forms known as **neutron stars**. A hand-sized piece of a neutron star would weigh millions of tons if it could be brought to earth.

In 1967, radio astronomers in Cambridge, England, discovered objects that sent out regular bursts, or pulses, of radio waves. These objects, far out in space, were named **pulsars**. Soon other astronomers were able to detect light coming from the same places in space. The light varied with the same rhythm as the radio pulses. Scientists believe that pulsars may be neutron stars and that the pulsing light and radio waves may come from "hot spots" on the rapidly rotating stars.

There is indirect evidence that there are stars even denser than neutron stars. Scientists believe that the enormous gravitational pull of such a star would prevent the escape of all matter and of energy such as light or heat. Such a star could not be seen in the sky, and it is given the name **black hole**.

▶ DISCOVERIES ABOUT THE UNIVERSE

The word "universe" includes everything that exists in space. Early people thought the universe was no bigger than the earth they lived on and the stars they could see above. In the 1700's the known universe was the huge structure of billions of stars that make up the Milky Way galaxy. Today we know that the universe extends for billions of light years in all directions beyond the Milky Way. A light year is the distance that light travels in one year, moving at a speed of nearly 300,000 kilometers (about 186,000 miles) per second.

Galaxies

The Milky Way is a hazy band of light that arches across the night sky. Its glow is due to thousands of stars that can be seen distinctly

The Hertzsprung-Russell chart. The great majority of stars—among them the sun, Sirius, and Spica—are in the group labeled "main sequence." A smaller number of stars—such as Aldebaran, Rigel, and Betelgeuse—are giants or supergiants. Another group, the white dwarfs, are small but very hot stars.

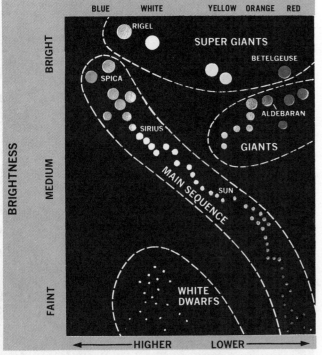

only through a telescope. To the ancient Greeks this hazy band looked like a flow of milk. They gave it a name that we translate as the Galaxy, or Milky Way. The whole Galaxy contains at least 100,000,000,000 (billion) stars. One of them is the sun, for our star is part of the Galaxy.

Other galaxies have been discovered beyond our own. They are sometimes called "island universes." The United States astronomers Heber D. Curtis, Harlow Shapley, and Edwin P. Hubble pioneered in the work on other galaxies. In 1925, Hubble classified galaxies according to their shape. He divided the galaxies into groups that are called spiral, barred spiral, elliptical, and irregular. You can see illustrations of these groups in the article UNIVERSE in Volume U.

Quasars

In the early 1960's, astronomers first observed the objects in space that later became known as quasars. These objects emit extremely strong radio waves. When seen through a powerful telescope, a quasar looks like a fuzzy star. By the 1980's, hundreds of quasars had been observed.

Quasars are a mystery in many ways. Some scientists believe that they may be enormous galaxies moving away from us—the most distant objects ever observed, at the boundary of the known universe.

The Beginning and the End

When and how did the universe begin? Will it ever end? Scientists have developed many theories in attempts to answer these questions.

Since the 1920's, much evidence has been found showing that the galaxies are all moving away from each other at enormous speeds— that is, the universe is expanding. The theory now accepted by most astronomers states that about 15,000,000,000 (billion) years ago, the expansion began with the explosion of a single superdense atom. According to this "big bang" theory, that primitive atom contained all the matter that makes up the universe. From present evidence it is not possible to tell whether the expansion will go on forever. It may be that after billions of years the gravitational attraction between the outrushing galaxies will bring them to a stop, then pull them together to form a new superdense atom.

▶ THE TOOLS OF DISCOVERY

The story of the universe is told by waves of radiation—light waves, radio waves, and other kinds of waves and rays that reach us from space.

Tools That Use Light

Light is one form of radiation. The earliest astronomers, of course, had only their eyes to detect light from space. But later scientists and engineers developed a great variety of instruments to do what eyes alone cannot do. These optical instruments could detect extremely faint light, measure its strength, and analyze and record it. ("Optical" means "making use of light.")

Telescopes. Astronomers use optical telescopes to collect the faint light of distant stars and galaxies and to enlarge the view.

Credit for the invention of the telescope, in 1608, is usually given to Hans Lippershey, of Holland. The next year Galileo made a telescope of his own. He used it to study the night skies. Both of these instruments used a glass lens to collect the light. Such telescopes are called **refracting telescopes**, or **refractors**. The largest modern refractor is at the Yerkes Observatory in Williams Bay, Wisconsin. Its lens is just over 1 meter (40 inches) in diameter.

A second type of telescope is the **reflector**. It was invented by Isaac Newton. It makes use of a mirror, instead of a lens, to collect the light. The largest reflector has a mirror 6 meters (236.2 inches) in diameter. It is in the Soviet Union.

Cameras. The first photograph of the moon was made in 1840 by John W. Draper, a United States doctor. Photography was in its earliest stages, and Draper's task was difficult. Since then the camera has become the most important tool for making astronomical records.

Spectroscopes. Nobody has been on the sun. Yet scientists know exactly which chemical elements make up that seething ball of gases. The device that makes this possible is the spectroscope.

A beam of light from the sun contains all the colors of the rainbow. If the beam is passed through a triangular piece of glass called a prism, it is broken into a band, or **spectrum**, of these colors. To study the light of the sun, a star, or a galaxy, light collected by a telescope is passed through a spectroscope. The instrument produces a wide spectrum, in which thousands of light and dark lines can be seen. Josef von Fraunhofer (1787–1826), a German scientist, was the first to study the dark lines in the sun's spectrum. They are called "Fraunhofer lines" in his honor.

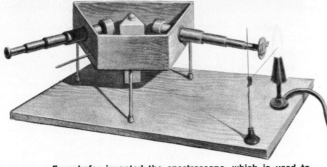

Fraunhofer invented the spectroscope, which is used to identify the elements present in the source of light.

Gustav R. Kirchhoff (1824–87), another German scientist, discovered that each chemical element produces its own pattern of lines. Hydrogen makes one pattern, sodium another pattern, and so on. So study of the spectrum of light from a distant object reveals its chemical composition. The spectroscope can also be used to tell how fast and in which direction the object is moving.

In practice, a camera is attached to the spectroscope. The combination, called a spectrograph, produces photographs of the spectra. The photographs can be kept for study at any time.

Photometers. Look up at the night sky, and you will observe that there are some very bright stars, some less bright, and some so dim as to be barely visible. Actually, there are thousands of times as many stars that are too dim to be seen by the unaided eye. But astronomers must study these stars and learn just how much light they give off. To do this, the astronomer attaches a light meter, called a photometer, to the telescope. It measures the strength of incoming light with great accuracy. Photometers are also used to measure the brightness of photographic images of the stars.

Some Newer Tools of Discovery

Light is one form of radiation. Up to the early 1900's, scientists learned all that they knew about the universe with the help of their eyes and optical instruments.

Today scientists still rely heavily on light. But they also get a great deal of their information from other kinds of radiation. Among these are heat and radio waves and ultraviolet, gamma, and X rays from objects in space.

Satellites and Space Probes. Some kinds of radiation from space never reach the earth, and other kinds are greatly weakened. This happens because the earth's atmosphere absorbs some radiation. So scientists make use of artificial satellites and space probes to carry their instruments far above the atmosphere. The information gathered by the instruments is changed into radio signals and sent to the earth for careful scientific study.

Radio Astronomy. Scientists are exploring space by detecting the radio waves produced by some natural objects. For example, the sun at times sends out strong radio waves. These are produced when charged particles swirl around a region of sunspots. The planet Jupiter sends out powerful radio signals, thought to be caused by storms in its magnetic field. Stars and galaxies send out radio waves. There are also thousands of "radio stars." These are not easily seen or photographed through optical telescopes, but they were detected by radio telescopes.

One radio star is what remains of the supernova seen by the Chinese in 1054. Another is the remains of a supernova in the constellation Cassiopeia. A third, in Cygnus, is caused by two huge galaxies that have collided or have undergone a gigantic explosion.

A radio telescope consists of a huge antenna, usually bowl-shaped, and a radio receiver. The antenna collects radio waves, in the way that the mirror of an optical telescope collects light waves. The waves are strengthened in the receiver and recorded. The first radio telescope was built in 1931 by Karl G. Jansky, a United States scientist and engineer.

Radar Astronomy. In radio astronomy, radio waves from space are detected on earth. In radar astronomy, radio waves produced on the earth are aimed at a nearby astronomical object—the moon, for example. The waves are sent out through an antenna like the antenna

How far away is that star?

Even the nearest stars are trillions of kilometers away. But star distances can be measured through their **angle of parallax**. A simple exercise will help you to understand the principle of this method of measurement.

Close your left eye and hold your index finger about 15 centimeters (6 inches) in front of your nose. Notice which part of the wall is behind the finger. (It helps if there are pictures or other objects hanging on the wall or close to it.) Now, holding your finger still, close the right eye and open the left one. Did you see that the finger seemed to shift to the right across the wall? The seeming shift is called parallax. It happens because your eyes, being a small distance apart, see things from a different viewpoint.

Repeat the experiment, but this time hold your finger as far in front of you as you can. The seeming shift is smaller this time. Now have somebody stand near the wall, holding up a finger, while you stand across the room and sight the finger, first with one eye, then with the other. This time the shift is very small. So you have seen that the farther away an object is, the less its parallax is. We can say the same thing in this way: If the parallax of an object is small, its distance is great. So, if we measure the parallax of an object, we can find how far away it is.

In measuring a star's distance by the parallax method, the star itself is the "finger." The astronomer observes and measures its shift. You had the wall to judge by. What can astronomers use? They use stars even farther away than the one whose distance they want to know. Of course, this cannot be done by closing one eye, then the other.

A very big separation of viewpoints is needed—one of millions of kilometers. How can that be done?

The earth moves in an orbit around the sun, taking one year for the trip. If we take a photograph of a star in July, let us say, we see it against a background of certain more distant stars. If we photograph the same star again in January, one-half year later, the earth will have moved to the other end of its orbit, more than 300,000,000 kilometers (nearly 200,000,000 miles) from the first viewpoint. Now the star will be photographed against a very slightly different background of more distant stars.

Even with this tremendous separation of viewpoints, the shift is very tiny. For the nearest star, the shift is about as big as a dime seen from 5 kilometers (3 miles) away. It takes extremely delicate instruments to measure the shift.

Imagine lines drawn from the earth to the place where the star was seen at half-year intervals. These lines form an angle, which is called the angle of parallax. Knowing the angle and using some mathematics, the astronomer works out the distance of the star.

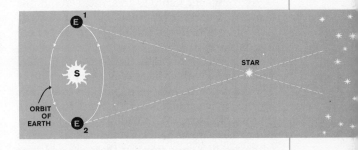

used in radio astronomy. The waves bounce off the moon, and they return to the earth, like an echo. The same antenna that sent them out may be used to detect the reflected signals. Knowing how fast the waves travel, the scientist can calculate how far away the moon is. Modern astronomy radars are sensitive enough to show very accurately the altitude of various places on the moon's surface.

Radar astronomy has been used to map the surfaces of Mars, Mercury, and the moon and of Venus beneath its thick clouds.

X-Ray Astronomy. An exciting new branch of astronomy makes use of x-ray radiation from space. Instruments carried in satellites have detected X rays and gamma rays (a very short type of X ray) coming from the sun. There are also other sources of X rays in the sky that are much farther away. Some of these sources, such as the Crab Nebula, are probably collapsed supernovas. Others may be places where X rays are produced as material in space is pulled into black holes.

Computers. Astronomy has always needed mathematics as a tool. And long, involved calculations were a part of every astronomer's work. Now the computer has largely replaced pencil and paper. Problems that would take days or weeks of calculation can be solved by a computer in a fraction of a second.

Computers in observatories can be programmed to take information directly from telescopes, photometers, and other instruments and to store it for future study. A computer can also control the operation of a telescope or of instruments aboard a satellite or space probe.

How far away is that galaxy?

The parallax method works well for stars, especially for the nearer ones. But it is of no use if we want to measure the vastly greater distances to galaxies outside our own. In the early 1900's, Henrietta Leavitt, a United States astronomer, made a discovery that led to such measurements. She was studying stars of a type called Cepheid variables. These stars go through regular changes of brightness, from dim to bright and back to dim, over a period of time. The period of any particular star is always the same. Leavitt found that those Cepheids that had the greatest maximum brightness took the longest periods of time to go through their variations. For example, a Cepheid with a period of two weeks has a greater maximum brightness than a Cepheid with a period of one week.

Imagine that you are watching the taillight of a car driving away from you in the dark. As the car gets farther away, the light seems to get dimmer. If you had a very sensitive photometer, of the kind used in astronomy, you could measure exactly how much dimmer the light becomes as the car gets farther away from you. Using that measurement and a simple mathematical rule, you could work out exactly how far away the car is at any moment. That mathematical rule applies to all light, whether it comes from a taillight, the sun, or a star.

Now let us suppose that astronomers are trying to learn the distance of a certain galaxy. If they can find a Cepheid variable star among the many stars in that galaxy, they observe the length of its period. As we saw, this tells them what the star's true maximum brightness is. Of course, the great distance makes the star look much less bright than it really is. The astronomers measure this apparent brightness accurately. Now, knowing the true maximum brightness of the variable and its apparent brightness, the astronomers can calculate its distance. Knowing that distance, they also know the distance of the galaxy the variable star is in.

▶ IS ANYBODY OUT THERE?

Astronomers know a great deal about the universe. But one question is still unanswered: Are there intelligent forms of life anywhere but on the earth?

Our sun is one of billions of stars that make up our galaxy, the Milky Way. And the Milky Way is one of the billions of galaxies that make up the known universe. It is hard to believe that we are alone. With trillions on trillions of stars, there must be many that have planets with earthlike conditions. If there is intelligent life, we might expect that "they" would look outward, as we do, wondering whether there is intelligent life elsewhere. Our scientists have already beamed simple radio messages into space. Perhaps someday we will receive a light or radio signal from an intelligent source in the depths of space.

▶ CAREERS IN ASTRONOMY AND SPACE SCIENCE

Modern astronomy and space science are exciting fields of work. The picture of the astronomer as a person forever peering through a telescope is long gone. Today's astronomers are men and women with a choice of dozens of interesting specialities.

Some astronomers are experts in the solution of complex mathematical problems. Others specialize in the development of new theories. Those who have an interest in physics or electronics may go into radio astronomy or work with the small observatories that are placed on satellites and space probes. Other astronomers teach, write, or lecture about astronomy. Some write science fiction. An interest in history has led some astronomers into the field of archeoastronomy. They use their knowledge of astronomy to help other scholars find out more about ancient peoples.

Girls and boys who are considering astronomy as a career should be prepared to study mathematics and science. As undergraduates in college, they will study general astronomy. As graduate students, they will specialize in one of many fields such as planets, stars, the sun, or galaxies. Then they will be ready to take part in the search for greater understanding of the universe.

GERALD S. HAWKINS
Center for Archeoastronomy
University of Maryland

See also COMETS, METEORS, METEORITES, AND TEKTITES; CONSTELLATIONS; ECLIPSES; GRAVITY AND GRAVITATION; MARS; MOON; OBSERVATORIES; PLANETARIUM; PLANETS; QUASARS AND PULSARS; RADIO AND RADAR ASTRONOMY; SOLAR SYSTEM; SPACE EXPLORATION AND TRAVEL; STARS; SUN; TELESCOPES; TIME; UNIVERSE.

ATHLETE'S FOOT. See DISEASES.

ATHLETICS. See OLYMPIC GAMES; PHYSICAL EDUCATION; articles on individual sports.

ATLANTA

Atlanta, the capital of Georgia, rose from the ashes of the Civil War to become the center of trade, transportation, and industry in the southeastern United States. Today nearly 2,000,000 people live in the Atlanta metropolitan area.

Atlanta is located in the northwestern part of Georgia. Transportation has played an important part in its history. The city was founded in 1837 at the end, or terminus, of the Western and Atlantic Railroad. At first it was simply called Terminus. The name was changed to Atlanta in 1845.

During the Civil War, Union General William T. Sherman recognized Atlanta's importance as a Confederate supply center. His troops took the city in 1864, and most of its buildings were burned. But Atlanta was rapidly rebuilt. It became the state capital in 1868. By 1900, the city was prosperous and growing. But it was small in comparison to cities like New York and Chicago. Then, during the 1960's, Atlanta became a major city, its skyline studded with skyscrapers.

Banking, retailing, and tourism are important to Atlanta's economy. Its factories produce textiles, automobiles, steel, paper, furniture, and food products. One of Atlanta's most famous products, the soft drink Coca-Cola, is sold around the world.

Atlanta is still a transportation center. Railroads and highways crisscross and encircle the city. Its airport is one of the busiest in the United States. In 1979 the city opened the first section of a high-speed rail system that will link the downtown area with the suburbs.

The heart of Atlanta is an intersection called Five Points. Office buildings, hotels, banks, shops, and restaurants spread out from this point. Peachtree Street, Atlanta's best-known street, runs to the north. The gold-domed state capitol stands to the south. East of Five Points is the grave of civil-rights leader Martin Luther King, Jr.

Atlanta is a center of education and culture as well. Georgia State University and Georgia Institute of Technology are among its institutions of higher education. Several colleges and universities are clustered at Atlanta University Center, west of Five Points. The city's symphony orchestra and its ballet, opera, and theater companies perform at the Atlanta Memorial Arts Center, which also houses an art school and the High Museum of Art.

There are many things to do and places to go in Atlanta. Atlanta Stadium is home to the city's professional baseball and football teams. There are also professional basketball and hockey teams. Fernbank Science Center has a planetarium and a forest preserve. Historical displays can be seen at Swan House. Wren's Nest, the home of Joel Chandler Harris, author of the Uncle Remus stories, is open to the public. And Grant Park, one of the largest of the many parks, has a zoo. The Cyclorama, a huge circular painting of the Battle of Atlanta, is also in Grant Park. It is a vivid reminder of Atlanta's past.

JOHN RAYMOND
The Atlanta *Constitution*

See also GEORGIA.

Peachtree Center, a modern office and hotel complex, has become a symbol of Atlanta's growth.

ATLANTIC OCEAN

The Atlantic Ocean is a huge body of water second only to the Pacific Ocean in size. The Atlantic furnishes fine trade routes and fishing grounds for four continents—North America, South America, Europe, and Africa. It was the first ocean to be crossed by ships and airplanes.

The Atlantic Ocean may have been named for the mythical land of Atlantis. According to legend, Atlantis was suddenly swallowed up by the sea and disappeared ages ago. Another legend names the ocean for the Atlantides. These water nymphs were the daughters of Atlas. Their home was the Atlantic Ocean beyond the Atlas Mountains.

Size and Location. The Atlantic Ocean is 31,830,000 square miles (82,440,000 square kilometers) in size. But if we include all its gulfs, bays, seas, and the Arctic Ocean, the Atlantic covers about 41,000,000 square miles (106,000,000 sq. km.), or more than one fifth of the earth's surface. The Atlantic extends from the Arctic to the Antarctic regions, touching the Americas on the west and Europe and Africa on the east. At its broadest point, between Florida and the Strait of Gibraltar, the Atlantic Ocean is more than 4,000 miles (6,400 km.) wide. At its narrowest, between the bulge of Brazil and Dakar, Senegal, it is about 1,850 miles (2,980 km.) wide.

Ocean Bed and Islands. The Atlantic Ocean has an average depth of about 12,800 feet (3,900 meters). Its bottom is covered mainly with an ooze made up of the shells of tiny ocean animals. The deepest place is in the North Atlantic, north of Puerto Rico. Here in the Puerto Rico Trench, the ocean reaches down 27,510 feet (8,385 m.).

The ocean bed of the Atlantic is divided into two valleys by the mid-Atlantic ridge. This is an S-shaped ridge running from north to south and rising about 6,000 feet (1,830 m.) from the ocean bottom. Where the ridge rises above sea level, it forms the islands of the Azores, Saint Paul Rocks, Ascension, Saint Helena, Tristan da Cunha, and Bouvet.

Shorelines and Coastal Waters. Compared to the fairly straight coast of the South Atlantic, the North Atlantic has a very irregular shoreline. The greatest indentations are on the European side of the ocean. These are formed by the Baltic, North, Mediterranean, and Black seas. The coastal waters on the American side include Hudson Bay, the Gulf of Saint Lawrence, the Gulf of Mexico, and the Caribbean Sea. Water from most of the great river systems of the world flows into the Atlantic. These rivers—the Saint Lawrence, Mississippi, Orinoco, Amazon, La Plata, Congo, Niger, Nile, Don, Dnieper, Danube, Po, Loire, Rhine, and Elbe—give the Atlantic the largest drainage area of any ocean. Such drainage, from about half of the world's land area, includes many dissolved minerals and makes the Atlantic the saltiest of the oceans.

Currents and Temperature. The North and South Atlantic have several strong currents that affect the climate of nearby land. The direction of these water currents is similar to that of the wind currents. In the North Atlantic they flow in a clockwise direction; in the South Atlantic, counterclockwise. The Gulf Stream of the North Atlantic carries warm water northward from the tropics along the eastern coast of the United States and turns northeast toward Europe. There it keeps many northern European harbors free from ice the year around and makes western Europe warmer than areas of the same latitude in eastern North America. The cold Labrador Current starts in the Arctic Ocean and flows southward along the eastern coasts of Greenland and eastern Canada till it meets the Gulf Stream. It is the Labrador Current that gives northern New England and eastern Canada their cold climates and brings icebergs and fog to endanger shipping in that area. In the South Atlantic the warm Brazil Current travels southward from the equator along the eastern coast of Brazil.

The Sargasso Sea is a part of the Atlantic lying between 20 and 40 degrees north latitude and extending from the West Indies to the Azores. This is a region of relatively still water and still wind, where sailing vessels were often becalmed.

DANIEL JACOBSON
Michigan State University

ATLANTIC PROVINCES. See NEW BRUNSWICK; NEWFOUNDLAND; NOVA SCOTIA; PRINCE EDWARD ISLAND.

ATLASES. See MAPS AND GLOBES; REFERENCE BOOKS.

ATMOSPHERE

The earth is surrounded by a thick blanket of air. This is its atmosphere. The word "atmosphere" comes from two Greek words meaning "a sphere of vapor" (or gas). Earth's atmosphere is made up of about 20 gases. The two main ones are oxygen and nitrogen. It also contains water vapor and dust particles.

Other planets have atmospheres, but theirs are not like ours. Venus, for example, has a very thick atmosphere of carbon dioxide. Clouds floating on top of the carbon dioxide contain droplets of sulfuric acid.

Earth's atmosphere is one of the things that make it a planet of life. It is the air we breathe. It shields us from certain dangerous rays sent out by the sun. It protects the earth from extremes of heat and cold. And it serves us in many other ways.

▶ WHAT OUR ATMOSPHERE IS MADE OF

With water vapor and dust particles removed, air is a mixture of colorless gases.

A gas called nitrogen makes up almost four fifths of air. Nearly one fifth of air is oxygen. Oxygen is the element that almost all life must have. For example, we use it to turn food into energy. Another gas in the atmosphere is carbon dioxide. Though it occurs in very small amounts, it is vital to life on the earth. Green plants use this gas in manufacturing their food. The air contains traces of still other gases. Helium and hydrogen are found in very small amounts. So is ozone, a special form of oxygen. Among the other gases are argon, krypton, neon, and xenon.

The water vapor in the air is water in a gaseous form. Water vapor is found mostly in the lower part of the atmosphere. Winds pick it up from the surfaces of bodies of water and carry it through the air.

In addition, the lower atmosphere is filled with countless specks of dust. These are tiny particles of matter from soil, fires, plants, salt spray, volcanoes, or meteors. Most are too small to be seen. But if you look at a sunbeam, you can see some of the dust particles in the air. The sunbeam is actually the reflection of sunlight on the specks of dust.

Water vapor condenses around dust particles, forming clouds and fog.

▶ AIR HAS WEIGHT AND PRESSURE

Air is matter, and like all matter, it has weight. Weight is the measure of the pull of gravity on matter. If a scale registers 10 kilograms when a stone is placed on it, this means that gravity pulls the stone with that much force. Similarly, earth's gravity pulls on each particle of gas and dust in the atmosphere. Because our atmosphere is a vast ocean of air, it has considerable weight. If it could somehow be compressed and put on a set of scales, it would weigh about 5,700,000,-000,000,000 (quadrillion) metric tons.

The air presses down on us and against us from all sides. Something like a ton of air is pressing against you at this moment. You are not aware of this because air pressure within your body balances the pressure of the air outside.

Air pressure is 1.036 kilograms per square centimeter (14.7 pounds per square inch) at sea level. It is greatest there because that is the bottom of the atmosphere. At higher altitudes the pressure is less. That is why the cabins of high-flying planes are pressurized. They are designed to maintain the air pressure our bodies must have.

▶ LAYERS OF ATMOSPHERE

Our atmosphere is made up of several layers, each different from the others. The layers are the troposphere, stratosphere, mesosphere, thermosphere, and exosphere. Together they form a blanket hundreds of kilometers thick.

The Troposphere

This bottom layer of the atmosphere is where we live. It is also the layer that we know most about. Atmospheric layers vary in thickness. For example, the troposphere is about 20 kilometers (12 miles) thick above the equator and about 8 kilometers (5 miles) thick above the poles.

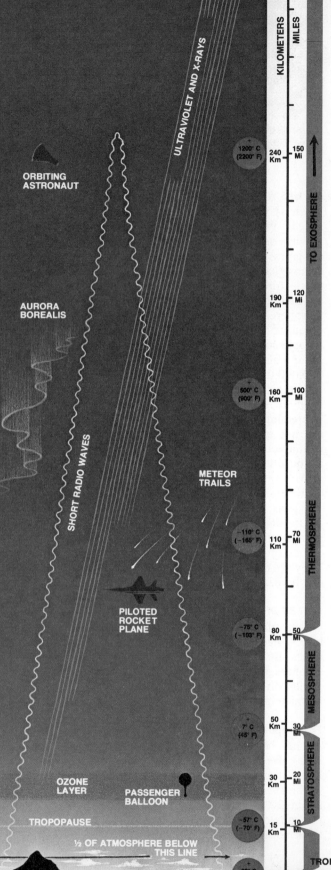

KILOMETERS | MILES

ORBITING ASTRONAUT

ULTRAVIOLET AND X-RAYS

1200° C (2200° F) 240 Km 150 Mi

TO EXOSPHERE

AURORA BOREALIS

190 Km 120 Mi

SHORT RADIO WAVES

THERMOSPHERE

METEOR TRAILS

500° C (900° F) 160 Km 100 Mi

−110° C (−165° F) 110 Km 70 Mi

PILOTED ROCKET PLANE

−75° C (−103° F) 80 Km 50 Mi

MESOSPHERE

7° C (45° F) 50 Km 30 Mi

STRATOSPHERE

OZONE LAYER **PASSENGER BALLOON**

30 Km 20 Mi

TROPOPAUSE

−57° C (−70° F) 15 Km 10 Mi

½ OF ATMOSPHERE BELOW THIS LINE

TROPOSPHERE

20° C (68° F)

MT. EVEREST 9 km (5½ mi)

GREATEST OCEAN DEPTH 11 km (7 mi)

Layers of the atmosphere differ in the way they absorb radiations from the sun and thus differ in temperature. Charged particles (ions) in the thermosphere reflect radio waves. In this diagram only the reflection of short-wave radio transmission is shown. Other radio waves are reflected at lower altitudes.

One half of the earth's atmosphere is squeezed into the first 5.5 kilometers (3½ miles) by the weight of the layers above. Here the molecules (particles) of gas are packed most closely together. Here the pressure and oxygen that we need exist. Most of the earth's people live within about 1.5 kilometers (1 mile) of sea level. But scientists have learned that people can go about 5.5 kilometers up before they must use pressure suits and oxygen masks.

Most of our weather takes shape in the troposphere. Winds pick up water vapor, from which clouds and rain form. Air currents move up and down, while winds blow north, south, east, and west, carrying warm or cold air.

Instruments carried aloft in balloons have proved that the temperature in the troposphere drops steadily as one goes higher. There is a drop of about 2 degrees Celsius for each 300 meters (3.5 degrees Fahrenheit for each 1,000 feet). At the top of the troposphere the temperature approaches −57°C (−70°F). The warmest air in the troposphere is near the earth's surface. This is so because the sun heats the earth and the earth gives off heat that warms the air. The sun does not warm this region of the atmosphere directly.

Near the top of the troposphere, temperatures suddenly level off. The leveling-off marks the tropopause, which is the boundary between the troposphere and the stratosphere.

Winds reach their greatest force at the level of the tropopause. Most of the fast-moving winds called jet streams are found here. They move along fairly regular routes—depending on the season of the year—at speeds up to 500 kilometers (300 miles) an hour. High-flying planes often ride these winds to pick up extra speed.

Weather scientists now think that the jet streams play a major role in the earth's weather and climate. But they are still exploring what happens on the earth when a jet stream shifts its course.

The Stratosphere

The second layer of air is the stratosphere. Its lower regions are swept with strong winds and are icy cold. The air is dry and clear.

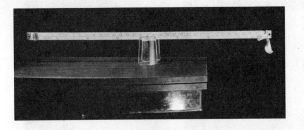

DOES AIR HAVE WEIGHT?

To answer that question, weigh the same balloon twice—once when empty and once when filled with air. First make a scale by hammering a thin nail through the exact center of a yardstick and balancing the yardstick between two drinking glasses. If the yardstick does not balance perfectly, bend a paper clip or small piece of wire around the end of the stick that needs more weight. Slowly move the wire toward the center until the stick is in balance. With a rubber band attach a large empty balloon to one end of the stick. Rebalance the stick by adding wire or paper clips to the other end (*upper photo*). Mark the *exact* spots where the balloon and the wire weight are. Then remove the balloon, blow it full of air, close it with the rubber band, and reattach it to the same spot on the stick (*lower photo*). Notice that the wire weight no longer balances the balloon. The balloon is heavier because of the weight of the air within it.

Most of the moisture and dust have been left behind. The air is also much thinner. With fewer air particles to reflect the sun's light, the sky darkens to violet. Farther up the violet becomes black. Stars can be seen 24 hours a day, and the sun blazes in a black sky.

At a height somewhere between 20 and 35 kilometers (12 and 22 miles), the winds of the stratosphere have died away and the air suddenly turns warm. The warming is caused by a layer of ozone, which is a form of oxygen. This gas absorbs most of the sun's ultraviolet rays. One result of the ozone's action is a band of warm air. Another result is that few ultraviolet rays reach the earth. Small amounts of ultraviolet rays are good for us, but large amounts would literally broil us.

The Mesosphere

Above the ozone layer, the air becomes even thinner, and the temperature again falls. Beginning at a height of about 50 kilometers (30 miles) and extending up to about 80 kilometers (50 miles) is the mesosphere. At the top of the mesosphere temperatures may be lower than $-75\,°C$ $(-103\,°F)$.

The Thermosphere and the Exosphere

The thermosphere reaches a height of perhaps 400 kilometers (250 miles). It is remarkable for electrical activity and a great range of temperatures. At the bottom of this layer, temperatures are below freezing. At the top they exceed $1200\,°C$ $(2200\,°F)$.

Atoms and molecules of gas in the very thin air of the thermosphere are bombarded by radiations from the sun. They are broken into smaller, electrically charged particles called **ions**. The region where this happens is referred to as the **ionosphere**. Here electric currents can flow, as they do in a neon tube or fluorescent light.

The ionosphere reflects radio waves. This allows radio communication between widely separated places on earth. For example, radio waves beamed from North America bounce off the ionosphere and reach Africa. Without the bounce, the waves would simply continue out into space because they do not follow the curve of the earth's surface.

The exosphere lies above the thermosphere. It is the outermost layer. Very few particles reach this great altitude. And some that reach it escape the earth's gravitation and become part of the gases in space.

▶ HOW THE ATMOSPHERE HELPS US

The earth's atmosphere serves us in many ways. Without it our planet would be as barren of life as the moon.

For example, the sun's rays blaze on the surface of the unshielded moon. Yet in a shadow or by night all this heat vanishes. The temperature drops quickly from a high of

Step 1

Step 2

Step 3

Step 4

DOES AIR HAVE PRESSURE?

Obtain a tin can of the type shown above. Make sure the can is clean inside. When the screw cap is off, the pressure inside equals the air pressure on the outside. Pour about 1 cup of water into the can (Step 1). With the cap still off, place the *open* can on a stove and heat the water until it boils (Step 2). The rising steam drives most of the air out of the can; the pressure of the steam on the inside now counterbalances the pressure of the air on the outside. Then quickly remove the can from the stove—taking care not to burn your hands. Screw the cap on tight and cool the can under running water (Step 3). The steam inside condenses into water, which collects on the bottom of the can. Since there is little air or steam present in the can, the pressure inside is greatly reduced. The outside pressure of air pushing against the walls crumples the can (Step 4).

about 120°C (250°F) to −185°C (−300°F). This does not happen on the earth because the atmosphere keeps about 50 percent of the sun's radiation from reaching the earth's surface. The radiation that reaches the earth warms our planet but does not make it boiling hot. At night the blanket of air keeps the heat from escaping too quickly. Compared with the moon, the earth's temperature changes very little. This even temperature and the screening out of dangerous rays from the sun are two of the things that make the earth a planet of life.

The atmosphere also spreads heat all over the earth with its winds. Winds carry hot air away from the tropics to colder regions. They carry cold air away from polar regions to the tropics. Without winds the tropics would be too hot and the rest of the earth too cold.

▶ OTHER EFFECTS OF THE ATMOSPHERE

In many ways the atmosphere helps make the earth a pleasant place to live. Because it carries sound waves, we hear voices and music. It spreads light into places that would otherwise be inky black. It gives us a blue sky and brilliant sunsets. Let us see why.

Rays from the sun are white light, but white light contains all the colors of the rainbow. As the white light passes through the gases and dust of the atmosphere it is broken up and scattered into colors.

The blue and violet part is usually more scattered than the other colors, and so we have a blue sky. Near the horizon the sun's light passes through a part of the atmosphere that includes many tiny dust particles. These particles absorb colors from the white light. The colors that get through are the reds and oranges of sunset and sunrise. Sometimes there is an unusual amount of moisture in the air when the sun is shining brightly. The result is a rainbow, made when the particles of moisture break up sunlight into all its colors.

▶ EXPLORING THE ATMOSPHERE

There is much that we do not yet know about the earth's atmosphere. How are gases exchanged between layers? How do the jet streams work and how do they affect our climate and weather? How will the world's climate be affected if we keep adding more smoke, dust, and combustion gases to the atmosphere? Today—with rockets, satellites, and high-altitude balloons—scientists have powerful tools to explore the atmosphere and to find the answers to these questions.

Reviewed by S. ICHTIAQUE RASOOL
Office of Space and Terrestrial Applications
NASA

See also EARTH, OUR HOME PLANET; WEATHER AND CLIMATE; WINDS AND WEATHER.

ATOMIC BOMB. See NUCLEAR ENERGY.
ATOMIC ENERGY. See NUCLEAR ENERGY.

ATOMS

At one time or another almost everyone has taken apart a toy or a clock to see what made it work. The result is simply a collection of parts—of wheels, metal bands, screws, and pins. Some people can figure out how to put the parts together again, to rebuild the toy or clock. And a few people can even work out ways to make entirely new devices out of the toy or clock parts.

Modern scientists have learned to do very much the same kind of thing with matter. **Matter** is anything that takes up space and has weight; it can be a solid, a liquid, or a gas. (Light and heat do not have weight and so they are not classed as matter.) All matter can be split into smaller and smaller pieces. For example, it can be split into molecules. A **molecule** is the smallest piece that keeps the characteristics of the original substance. For instance, a sugar molecule is the smallest piece that is still like sugar.

With special equipment a molecule can be broken down into still smaller parts. These are **atoms.** A sugar molecule breaks down into 12 carbon atoms, 22 hydrogen atoms, and 11 oxygen atoms.

If all those atoms are put back together properly, they will again form a sugar molecule. But by arranging carbon, hydrogen, and oxygen atoms in different groups, still other substances can be made; alcohol and starch are two of them. To put it another way, molecules of sugar, alcohol, and starch are formed of the same three kinds of atoms. But the proportions and arrangement of atoms vary. And it is the proportions and arrangement that determine which molecule will be made.

This one example shows why atoms are called the building blocks of matter. All the kinds of matter in the world are made from only about 100 kinds of atoms.

Curiously, the idea of the atom is far from new. About 2,500 years ago certain Greeks began to wonder what would happen if they took a piece of wood and kept cutting it into smaller and smaller pieces. Could they go on forever making smaller pieces? They decided that this was impossible. Eventually there would be a tiny piece (too small to be seen) that could not be divided. They reasoned that everything in the world was made out of such tiny particles.

Today we have a more complicated idea of the atom. We know that objects are not made up of simple particles but of molecules that are built up out of atoms. We know that atoms themselves are made of still tinier particles. But traces of the Greek idea remain. We still think of atoms as the building blocks of matter, and the word "atom" itself

Models of three molecules show that they are made of the same kinds of atoms. But the proportions and arrangements of the atoms determine what kind of molecule is made.

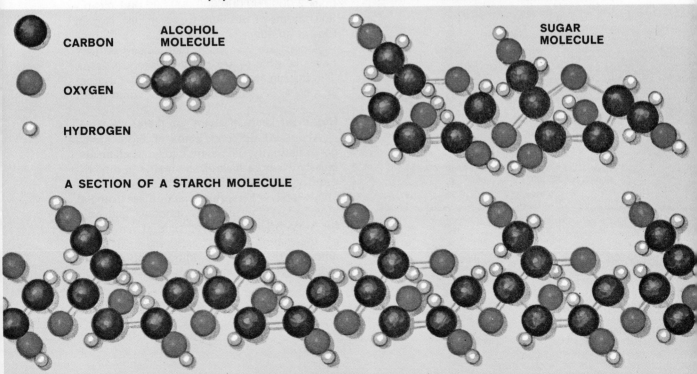

CARBON

OXYGEN

HYDROGEN

ALCOHOL MOLECULE

SUGAR MOLECULE

A SECTION OF A STARCH MOLECULE

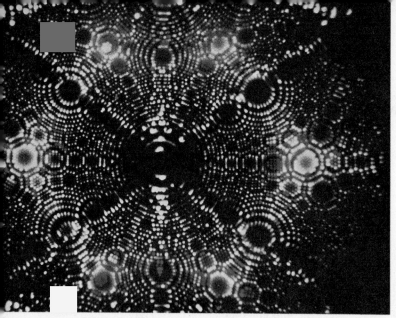

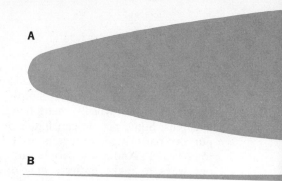

A

B

Photograph (*left*) shows the pattern of atoms in the point of a tiny needle made of tungsten metal. Atoms themselves cannot be seen, but here their patterns are projected by an electron microscope that magnifies 1,300,000 times. Each set of concentric circles represents an atom on or near the needle's surface. To understand how small the actual point is, compare the enlargements of (A) an ordinary pin and (B) the tungsten needle.

comes from a Greek word meaning something that cannot be cut or divided into smaller parts.

▶ **BASIC FACTS ABOUT THE ATOM**

Atoms are so small that they cannot be seen under the most powerful optical microscopes. Yet scientists are able to tell one kind of atom from another. They have learned to measure the size of atoms and the weight of atoms. They have learned about the particles that make up atoms.

The following questions and answers sum up some basic facts about atoms.

How big is an atom?

An atom is smaller than anything you can imagine. Even a speck of dust is gigantic when compared to an atom. It would take about 2,500,000 atoms, placed side by side, to stretch across the head of a pin.

Atoms are also lighter in weight than anything you can imagine. It would take more than 2,000,000,000,000,000,000,000,000 (sextillion) atoms of uranium to weigh just 1 gram ($\frac{1}{28}$ of an ounce).

Atoms are so small that scientists may never be able to see the details of an atom. The instruments they use show how an atom acts on various materials, not the atom itself.

How many kinds of atoms are there?

About 90 different kinds of basic atoms occur naturally. These are known as **elements**. Nearly 20 more have been created in the laboratory, and scientists expect to be able to create a few others. But most of these artificial atoms exist only in small amounts and only for very brief periods of time. Even a few of the natural atoms exist in such small amounts that they are known mainly from laboratory-made samples.

THE 20 MOST COMMON ELEMENTS ON EARTH

Estimated % of Matter by Weight	Element	Atomic Number	Atomic Weight
50	Oxygen	8	15.999
26	Silicon	14	28.09
8	Aluminum	13	26.98
5	Iron	26	55.85
3	Calcium	20	40.08
3	Sodium	11	22.99
2	Potassium	19	39.10
2	Magnesium	12	24.31
	Hydrogen	1	1.008
	Titanium	22	47.90
	Chlorine	17	35.45
	Phosphorus	15	30.97
	Carbon	6	12.01
Less than 1	Manganese	25	54.94
	Sulfur	16	32.06
	Barium	56	137.34
	Nitrogen	7	14.01
	Fluorine	9	18.99
	Chromium	24	52.00
	Strontium	38	87.62

Do atoms combine?

Most atoms do not exist singly in nature but are found combined in molecules.

When atoms of the same kind combine with one another, they form molecules of the **chemical elements**. About 90 such elements exist naturally—one formed from each kind of basic atom. But most of our world is made up of only about 20 elements (see table on page 484).

When atoms of different kinds combine, the molecules form **chemical compounds**. Compounds are made up of two or more elements. Water, for example, is a compound made up of the elements hydrogen and oxygen.

We rarely see a pure element. Most elements are seen in pure form only in the laboratory. One exception is diamond, which is pure carbon. Most of the materials around us are either compounds or mixtures. Gold rings, copper wires, aluminum pans—all have small amounts of other elements mixed in.

Although only about 90 elements exist in nature, they combine to make up the many thousands of different materials in the world. The elements are like the letters of the alphabet. There are only 26 letters. Yet millions of words are made by combining them in different ways. The compounds of matter are like the words, but they are made up of elements instead of letters.

What holds matter together?

The molecules that make up the world of matter are bound to one another by electrical charges. Molecules are bound together most tightly in solids. They move back and forth constantly, but in solids they normally do not move out of their positions. The binding force in liquids and gases is weaker, so their molecules can move about more freely.

▶THE STRUCTURE OF ATOMS

Although atoms have never been seen, scientists have put together a picture of the atom based on its effects on other matter.

In some ways an atom resembles a tiny solar system. At the center of the atom is a **nucleus.** Tiny particles of matter called **electrons** spin around the nucleus, somewhat as the planets spin around the sun.

The nucleus consists of two kinds of particles strongly bound to each other. These

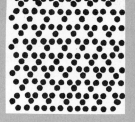

In solids, atoms or molecules are tightly bound together by forces of attraction.

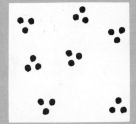

In liquids, the forces of attraction are less and atoms or molecules are able to slide around.

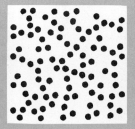

In gases, attraction is so slight that atoms or molecules move about freely and quickly.

This diagram compares the three states of matter.

Diagram of oxygen atom shows basic parts of all atoms. Electrons spin around nucleus of protons and neutrons.

particles are called **protons** and **neutrons**. The protons and neutrons can be split into still smaller particles. But protons and neutrons, along with electrons, are considered to be the three main kinds of particles making up atoms.

An atom is enormous compared to the size of its nucleus. Imagine an atomic nucleus the size of a pea. In such an atom some of the

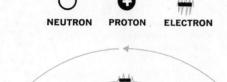

NEUTRON   PROTON   ELECTRON

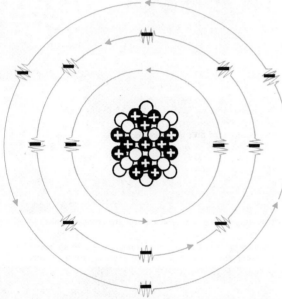

Atoms of two common elements—aluminum (*above*) and oxygen (*below*)—are shown for contrast. The aluminum atom has 13 electrons (negative charges); the oxygen atom has 8. The nucleus of an aluminum atom has 13 protons (positive charges) and 14 neutrons (no charge); the oxygen atom has 8 of each. The sum of the particles in the nucleus gives the atomic weight; the number of protons alone gives the atomic number.

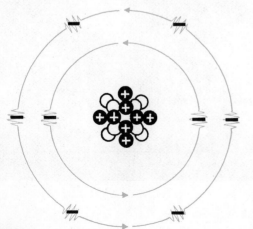

electrons would be moving at a distance of 400 meters or more (about ¼ mile) from the nucleus.

What are the main kinds of atomic particles like?

A proton is a particle of matter that carries a positive charge of electricity.

A neutron is a particle of matter that weighs about the same as a proton. But a neutron has no electrical charge.

An electron is a particle of matter much lighter than a proton or a neutron. It weighs about 1/1800 as much as one of those.

Each electron carries a negative charge of electricity. The same amount of electricity is carried by each proton, but the proton has a positive charge. Since there is one electron for each proton in the nucleus, the positive charges of the protons cancel out the negative charges of the electrons. This balance means that the atoms making up the world of matter are electrically neutral.

Are there any other atomic particles?

Even before the discovery of the three basic particles, scientists had predicted that still other particles would be found. Experiments have shown that there are about 100 other particles. Among them are mesons, positrons, and neutrinos. All these particles, along with the three basic ones, are called **subatomic particles**. Unlike electrons, protons, and neutrons, most subatomic particles exist only for very brief periods. They are formed when atoms are broken apart in laboratories or in nuclear reactors. They also occur naturally in cosmic rays.

How does one kind of atom differ from another?

All atoms are made up of the same kinds of particles—electrons, protons, and neutrons. Atoms differ from one another in the number of particles they are made of. For example, oxygen has 8 electrons, 8 protons, and 8 neutrons; aluminum has 13 electrons, 13 protons, and 14 neutrons. These differences are expressed as atomic number and atomic weight.

Atomic Number. Scientists list atoms in an arrangement known as the **periodic table**. An atom's place on the table is based on how many protons an atom has. This is called its

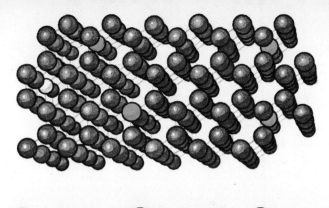

C-12   C-13   C-14

Model shows atoms arranged in a form of carbon. The most common carbon atom has an atomic weight of 12 and is called C-12. Mixed in with the many C-12 atoms are a few heavier carbon atoms, C-13 and C-14. They bring average weight of carbon atoms to a little over 12.

atomic number. Atoms of different natural elements have different numbers of protons. The periodic table arranges atoms from hydrogen (the simplest, with one proton) to uranium (the most complicated natural element, with 92 protons).

Each atom has the same number of electrons as protons. So the atomic number also tells how many electrons an atom has.

Atomic Weight. An atom's weight is concentrated in its nucleus, which is made up of protons and neutrons. All protons weigh the same, no matter what element they are in. So do all neutrons. And one neutron weighs about the same as one proton. Thus, an atom's weight can be expressed by adding the number of protons and neutrons together. Hydrogen, for example, has one proton and no neutrons; its atomic weight is 1. The ura-

nium atom has 92 protons and 146 neutrons; its atomic weight is 238.

Atomic weights of many of the common elements can be expressed as whole numbers. But scientists have discovered that in many cases different atoms of the same element actually vary in weight. When a great number of atoms of any single element are weighed, the result is an average weight that is not a perfect whole number. For example, the weight of the most common atom of the element carbon is 12.00000. But because some carbon atoms are a little heavier, the average weight is 12.01115.

How can atoms of the same element vary in weight?

All atoms of a given element have the same number of protons and electrons. But the atoms of a given element do not always have the same number of neutrons; atoms that differ in their number of neutrons are called **isotopes.**

Isotopes differ in weight among themselves. For example, the most common hydrogen atom—with one proton and no neutrons—has an atomic weight of 1. But a few hydrogen atoms have a nucleus containing a neutron as well as a proton. Such a hydrogen atom is called deuterium. It is an isotope that weighs twice as much as an ordinary hydrogen atom, but in most other ways it is exactly like the ordinary atom. It has the same atomic number because it has the same number of protons. And it has the same chemical properties.

The hydrogen atom (*left*) and its isotopes are represented here. Isotopes are atoms of the same element that differ in weight; weight varies with the number of neutrons. A hydrogen atom has no neutrons; its isotope deuterium (*center*) has one neutron and its isotope tritium (*right*) has two.

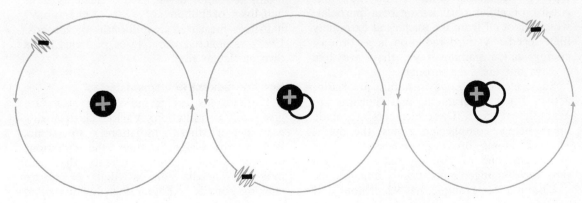

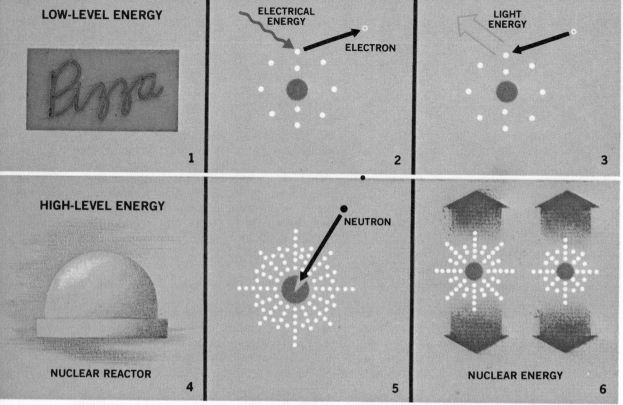

LOW-LEVEL ENERGY	**ELECTRICAL ENERGY**	**LIGHT ENERGY**
Pizza	ELECTRON	
1	**2**	**3**
HIGH-LEVEL ENERGY	NEUTRON	
NUCLEAR REACTOR		**NUCLEAR ENERGY**
4	**5**	**6**

The difference between low- and high-level atomic energy. In the low-level reaction in a neon sign (1), electricity dislodges an electron from an atom of neon gas (2). As the electron falls back into orbit, light is given off (3).

In the high-level reaction in a nuclear reactor (4), a neutron enters a uranium atom (5) and splits its nucleus (6). Two other atoms are formed, and a great deal of nuclear energy is released as heat.

The various isotopes of which elements are made are identical in atomic number and chemical properties. There are more than 1,000 different known isotopes. Most of them have been created by scientists, and generally they have very short lives. Their nuclei (plural of "nucleus") quickly lose particles and become stable, ordinary atoms.

What are radioactive atoms?

Radioactive atoms are unstable atoms. Their nuclei split up and produce various types of radiations. Some of the radiations consist of alpha particles or beta particles, which shoot off from the nucleus at extremely high speeds. A third radiation is a form of energy called gamma rays; they are like X rays but are even stronger.

Some elements found in nature are radioactive. Radium, uranium, and thorium are examples of these. These elements are made up of heavy, complicated atoms; the nuclei of such atoms break down easily. These atoms continue to give off radiations until they have changed into more stable atoms.

Uranium, for example, has 92 protons and

146 neutrons. Through millions of years the nucleus loses particles, until it has 82 protons and 124 neutrons—the same number as an atom of the element lead. That is, it has changed from an atom of uranium into an atom of lead. Lead is a heavy, complicated atom, but its particles are arranged in such a way that it is a stable atom.

All radioactive elements lose particles and break down. The rate at which an element breaks down is measured by its **half-life**. The half-life is the time it takes for half of the atoms to break down. Some elements have half-lives of billions of years. Others have half-lives measured in millionths of seconds. Every radioactive atom loses particles at its own particular rate.

How are radioactive atoms detected?

Particles lost by a radioactive atom are given off as radiation. Various instruments can detect these radiations. In some, such as the **Geiger counter**, the radiations produce small electric currents that can move a needle on a dial or cause clicking sounds. Another instrument, called the **cloud chamber,** has water vapor in a transparent chamber. When radiations pass through the water vapor, the vapor condenses and forms visible droplets along the tracks of the rays. A **scintillation counter** is another instrument that indicates the presence of radioactive radiations; it catches them as light flashes, or scintillations, on a chemically treated screen, where they can be counted.

What is "atom smashing"?

To study the structure and behavior of atoms, scientists use equipment that can speed up subatomic particles and make them very energetic. These energetic particles can then be shot at atoms of other elements. The bombardment breaks down the nuclei of the target atoms into more particles. This process is called "atom smashing."

Machines that smash atoms are generally called **particle accelerators** because they force the nuclear particles to travel at very high speeds. An accelerator like the **cyclotron** whirls the particles around faster and faster and then lets the particles smash into some element. The **linear accelerator** shoots particles in a straight line to a "target" element.

In early atom-smashing experiments, scientists discovered that certain atoms can take part in what is called a chain reaction. As a nucleus is split, it releases particles that cause other nuclei to split. These in turn release still more nucleus-splitting particles, and so on. Each step releases a little energy, but the whole chain releases large amounts of energy. In a nuclear reactor a controlled chain reaction is used to provide heat energy for making electricity.

What is the difference between atomic energy and nuclear energy?

Nuclear energy is one kind of atomic energy. There are many kinds of atomic energy. Any energy released from atoms and their particles can be called atomic energy. Strictly speaking, electricity is a form of atomic energy because it involves the flow of electrons. The energy released from burning coal is also a form of atomic energy because it involves shifts in electrons among atoms.

Like certain other forms of atomic energy, electricity and coal burning are considered

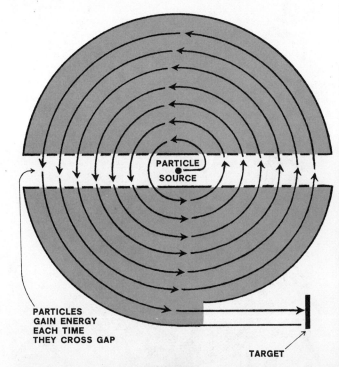

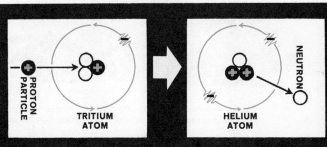

Upper diagram shows basic action of cyclotron, one kind of particle accelerator. Through the use of electricity and magnetism, particles are sent spiraling outward and around (arrows indicate path). Eventually particles are released to smash into a target. Lower diagram shows target. Proton (a particle) enters an atom of the gas tritium. A neutron is given off by the nucleus. The extra proton remains, and an electron is picked up to balance it. The result is a new atom, an isotope of helium.

low-level energy. Such forms of atomic energy do not involve the nucleus of the atom. The nucleus is the source of high-level energy, like that in a power-generating reactor. Because this high-level energy comes only from the nucleus of the atom, scientists prefer to call it nuclear energy.

Reviewed by J. A. L. ROBERTSON
Chalk River Nuclear Laboratories
Ontario, Canada

See also ELEMENTS; NUCLEAR ENERGY.

AUDUBON, JOHN JAMES (1785–1851)

In the early 1800's John James Audubon was living on the American frontier. Like other frontiersmen, he wore his hair long and dressed in buckskin. But he was a different kind of pioneer. His work was the lifelike painting of birds in their natural surroundings.

Audubon was born on his father's plantation in Les Cayes, Santo Domingo (now Haiti), on April 26, 1785. The father, a trader and sea captain, returned to France in 1789, taking his son with him. In the town of Nantes, young Jean Jacques—the French for John James—went to school, but his real interests were the outdoors and painting. He roamed the French countryside, drawing the birds he saw. At 17 he was allowed to study for a few months with the famous artist Jacques Louis David. This was the only formal training he ever received.

In 1803 John was sent to live at Mill Grove, an estate his father owned near Valley Forge, Pennsylvania. There he became engaged to Lucy Bakewell, a neighbor's daughter. After a short time he quarreled with his father's estate agent and went back to France. He returned to Pennsylvania in 1806 and tried to operate a lead mine at Mill

Shown are two of Audubon's bird paintings: (*above*) meadow larks nesting in a field; (*below*) great-footed hawks with wild ducks they have just caught.

Left, self-portrait of Audubon at the age of 37. Right, Audubon's painting of snowy owls.

Grove. Failing at that, Audubon later moved to Louisville, Kentucky, where he set up a general store. In 1808 he married Lucy and took her to Louisville. But the store soon failed, as did all the other business ventures that Audubon tried. Instead of attending to business, he was usually off exploring the wilderness.

At first Audubon hunted for food and sport, but he became more and more interested in studying birds. He sketched them in the wild. Then, to get more detail, he began to bring specimens home. He wired them in lifelike poses and made his paintings in watercolor and chalk.

By 1819 Audubon was bankrupt, but he no longer cared about business. He now had only one aim: to complete his collection of bird paintings for publication.

In 1821 he traveled down the Ohio and Mississippi rivers, searching for birds and earning a little money by painting portraits. When he arrived in New Orleans, he sent for his wife and two sons. Lucy became a governess, and was the main support of the family for the next 12 years.

Audubon began a search for someone to publish his work. Reproduction of his paintings required engraving skills then almost unknown. Also, no publisher could undertake such an expense unless there were "subscribers"—purchasers willing to pay in advance. In 1826, having failed to find a publisher in America, Audubon went off alone to England. He was well received there, but he enjoyed even greater success in Edinburgh, Scotland, where he was acclaimed as an artist and a naturalist.

In London that same year, Audubon finally found financial support; he also found an engraver who could reproduce his bird paintings. During the next 11 years, his *Birds of America* appeared in four large volumes, one of the rarest and most ambitious works ever published. Between 1831 and 1839 he also wrote five separate volumes of text to accompany the engravings. In addition to the life histories of nearly 500 bird species, this work contained many of Audubon's personal impressions of the American frontier.

His books brought him money as well as fame, and in 1841 Audubon was able to buy a Hudson River estate, now New York City's Audubon Park. He worked on a book and paintings of the animals of North America, which his sons completed after his death on January 27, 1851. His interest in all wildlife is honored by today's Audubon societies. Audubon's paintings are still valued for their scientific accuracy. And he has never been surpassed for portraying birds in lifelike poses in their natural surroundings.

JOHN S. BOWMAN
Author and Science Editor

AUGUST

The Roman emperor Augustus named the eighth month August in honor of himself.

In the Northern Hemisphere, August is often hot and humid. Lawns need careful attention or they will become overgrown with weeds. In fact, the Anglo-Saxons called August *Weod-Monath*, or "weed-month."

August is fair and carnival time in many towns and villages. Some English and Scottish towns observe August 1 as "harvest home," a summer holiday which celebrates the bountiful produce of the season. Church altars are decorated with vegetables, fruits, and sheaves of yellow and white corn. It's an old Celtic custom, which had its origin hundreds of years ago when the early Britons gave thanks to their pagan gods and goddesses for a plentiful harvest.

Goldenrod blooms in meadows and along roadsides. Apples begin to ripen on the trees. The wheat fields show that harvest time is near. Flowers of late summer and early fall—marigolds, asters, and chrysanthemums—bloom in many gardens.

Although there are no major holidays in August, the entire month is a holiday. For August is the last full month of summer vacation. Children take advantage of this time before the new school year. Cars packed with happy sightseers head for beaches, parks, and recreation areas.

Picnic grounds and swimming pools are crowded. Sailboat races and regattas end the summer festively. August is the ideal time to enjoy the outdoors. The weather is perfect for camping and hiking trips.

August is a time to explore the world of nature and discover the many wonders of summer's last days. Chipmunks and squirrels scurry about the woods, hunting for nuts. At lakesides frogs and turtles patiently watch for food. Some birds are already gathering for their flights to warmer climates.

Bird song may be stilled, but the insect world takes over. The buzzing, humming, and murmurs of crickets and katydids, locusts, and meadow grasshoppers sound like a concert in full swing.

At night the sky is alive with shooting stars (Perseid meteors). The last hot days of vacation are called the "dog days." They take their name from the Dog Star, Sirius, seen in the eastern skies during August.

But the threat of changing weather lurks behind all the splendor of summer's last display. Along the Atlantic coast, people watch for the beginning of the hurricane season.

In the Southern Hemisphere, August is the last month of winter. There the seasons are reversed, and people are looking forward to spring weather.

Place in year: 8th month.
Number of days: 31.
Flower. Poppy.
Birthstone: Sardonyx; peridot.
Zodiac signs:
  Leo, the Lion
  (July 23-August 22),
  and
  Virgo, the Virgin
  (August 23-September 22).

Historical Firsts

August

1 First federal census in the United States completed, 1790.

6 Hiroshima bombed by the United States Army Air Force. First use of an atomic bomb, 1945.

7 Robert Fulton's steamboat the Clermont sailed up the Hudson River and became the first commercially successful steamboat, 1807.

First Lincoln penny issued, 1909.

15 Panama Canal officially opened to world commerce, 1914.

22 The Savannah, first American steamship to cross the Atlantic Ocean, was launched, 1818.

Birthdays

August

1 Richard Henry Dana, American writer, 1815.
Maria Mitchell, American astronomer and professor, 1818.
Herman Melville, American writer, 1819.
William Clark, American explorer, 1870.

2 Pierre Charles L'Enfant, French architect and city planner, laid out Washington, D.C., 1754.
John Tyndall, British physicist, 1820.

3 Rupert Brooke, English poet, 1887.

4 Percy Bysshe Shelley, English poet, 1792.
Knut Hamsun, Norwegian writer, 1895.

5 Guy de Maupassant, French writer, 1850.

6 Alfred, Lord Tennyson, English poet, 1809.

9 Izaak Walton, English writer, 1593.
John Dryden, English poet, 1631.

10 Herbert Hoover, 31st president of the United States, 1874.

13 Fidel Castro, Cuban premier, 1927.

14 John Galsworthy, English writer, 1867.

15 Napoleon I, French emperor, 1769.
Sir Walter Scott, Scottish writer, 1771.
Ethel Barrymore, American actress, 1879.
Edna Ferber, American writer, 1887.
Thomas Edward Lawrence (Lawrence of Arabia), British soldier, archeologist, and writer, 1888.

15 Princess Anne of England, 1950.

17 Davy Crockett, American frontiersman, 1786.

18 Virginia Dare, first English child born in America, 1587.

19 Orville Wright, American inventor, 1871.

20 Benjamin Harrison, 23rd president of the United States, 1833.

21 Princess Margaret of England, 1930.

22 Claude Debussy, French composer, 1862.

25 Leonard Bernstein, American conductor and composer, 1918.

27 Confucius, Chinese philosopher, 551 B.C.
Theodore Dreiser, American writer, 1871.
Lyndon Baines Johnson, 36th president of the United States, 1908.

28 Johann Wolfgang von Goethe, German writer, 1749.
Count Leo Tolstoi, Russian writer, 1828.
Sir Edward Burne-Jones, English painter, 1833.

29 John Locke, English philosopher, 1632.
Oliver Wendell Holmes, American physician and writer, 1809.
Maurice Maeterlinck, Belgian playwright and poet, 1862.

30 Lord Ernest Rutherford, British physicist and professor, 1871.

31 William Saroyan, American writer, 1908.

Historical Events

August

1 Colorado became the 38th state to be admitted to the Union, 1876.

3 Christopher Columbus began his famous voyage from Spain in search of a westerly route to the East Indies and eventually reached the New World, 1492.

4 John Peter Zenger acquitted of libel—a victory for freedom of the press in the American colonies, 1735.

8 The Spanish Armada defeated by the British Navy, 1588.

9 Richard M. Nixon resigned as president, 1974.

10 Missouri became the 24th state to be admitted to the Union, 1821.

14 End of fighting, World War II, 1945.

15 South Korea became a republic, 1948.

16 Bolivia became independent, 1825.

19 American ship Constitution won naval battle with the British Guerrière, 1812.

21 Hawaii became the 50th state to be admitted to the Union, 1959.

24 Massacre of St. Bartholomew. Under orders from Charles IX, Catholic king of France, numerous Huguenots, or Protestants, were massacred, 1572.

25 Uruguay became independent, 1825.

26 19th Amendment to the United States Constitution gave women the right to vote, 1920.

AUGUSTINE, SAINT (354–430)

Saint Augustine, whose Latin name is Aurelius Augustinus, was born in the year 354. His parents were Monica, a Christian, and Patricius, a man who worked for the Roman Government. At the time of Augustine's birth, the family lived in Tagaste, a small Roman market town in northern Africa.

As a young man Augustine was often in trouble. He later admitted this in some of his writings. His parents sent him to school in Madaura, a city 30 miles from Tagaste, hoping the busy life of a student would keep him out of trouble. He studied Greek, Latin, and philosophy.

In 370 he went to Carthage, the center of learning in Africa, where he continued his studies and opened a school. During his years at Carthage, Augustine tried to find a way to worship God and to live his life. He held different beliefs about religion and philosophy, but no one belief satisfied him completely.

In 383 he traveled to Italy. After spending some time in Rome, he settled in Milan. There he taught school and came under the influence of Saint Ambrose, the resident bishop. Ambrose instructed Augustine in the Christian faith, and after 3 years he decided to become a Christian.

Augustine returned to Tagaste in 388, where he lived a quiet life of prayer and studied to become a priest. He was ordained a priest in 391 in Hippo, becoming famous for his preaching, writing, and holiness. Beloved by the people of Hippo and revered by scholars throughout the Christian world, Augustine had enemies, too, especially those who tried to attack the teachings of the Church. He was made bishop of Hippo in 395 and continued to preach and to write until his death in 430, when barbarian tribes invaded the city.

During his lifetime Saint Augustine was the most respected Christian thinker of the age. Today he is still considered one of the most important religious leaders of all times. He did more than study, preach, and write; he directed the building of many schools, churches, orphanages, and hospitals. He is best remembered, however, for his writings.

Saint Augustine wrote more than 200 books, 300 letters, and 400 sermons. The most famous of his works are *The City of God* and the *Confessions of Saint Augustine* (390). *The City of God* consists of 22 books that defend Christianity and the Catholic Church. In the *Confessions* Augustine retraces his life—the stormy early years, the search for faith, how he became able to live with God and with himself. Augustine was the first to use "confessions" as a form of autobiography, or life story. His frankness, keen mind, and self-knowledge make this autobiography one of the greatest ever written.

Saint Augustine's feast day—the day on which the Catholic Church honors him—is August 28.

JOANNE DRISCOLL

Reviewed by MSGR. JOHN PAUL HAVERTY
Secretary of Education
Archdiocese of New York

AUSTEN, JANE (1775–1817)

The English novelist Jane Austen was born on December 16, 1775, at the parsonage in Steventon. Her father educated her and her older brothers and sister and took other pupils as well. The family was a close and happy one. They often read aloud together in the evening or put on plays in the parlor or in a nearby barn.

Jane began writing when she was very young—plays, novels, and even a history of England. They were short, humorous works that she read to her family. Several of her adult novels were already finished when the first one, *Sense and Sensibility,* was published in 1811. *Pride and Prejudice* (1813), *Mansfield Park* (1814), and *Emma* (1816) followed. By then Jane was living with her mother and sister near her brother Edward in Hampshire. Her father had died in 1805.

Two of Jane Austen's novels—*Northanger Abbey* and *Persuasion*—were published in 1818 after her death. They were the first to include her name as the author. Jane Austen died after a long illness on July 18, 1817.

AUSTRALIA

Australia is a continent and an independent country located in the Southern Hemisphere between the Pacific and Indian oceans. It is a land of startling differences. Most of its people live in cities among tall office buildings, steel mills, automobile plants, and busy factories. Yet there are lonely lands in the north and the center occupied only by the aborigines, Australia's first inhabitants. Lush tropical forests—with animals, flowers, and birds found nowhere else in the world—cover the northeastern coast. Vast grasslands, dotted with flocks of sheep and herds of cattle, stretch across parts of the interior as far as the eye can see. To complete the picture of contrasts, much of inland Australia is desert—dry, barren, and uninhabited. And in the southeastern part of the country, the snow lies for seven months of the year on the high Australian Alps and the Tasmanian mountains.

The Commonwealth of Australia is made up of six states. Five are on the mainland—New South Wales, Victoria, Queensland, South Australia, and Western Australia. The sixth is the island state of Tasmania. There are also two territories on the mainland. In the north is the large Northern Territory, which was granted full internal self-government in 1978. In the southeast is the small Australian Capital Territory (ACT), which includes Canberra, the federal capital.

Australia also administers a number of small island territories. They include Norfolk Island in the Pacific and the Cocos Islands and Christmas Island in the Indian Ocean. Formerly, Australia was responsible for the administration of the Territory of Papua and New Guinea. In 1975, Papua New Guinea became an independent nation and, like Australia, a member of the Commonwealth of Nations. Australia, like many other nations, claims a large area of Antarctica, but territorial claims to Antarctica are not recognized internationally.

The Sydney Opera House and the Sydney Harbour Bridge are especially striking at night.

AUSTRALIA

★ State capital
Perspective map by J. Donovan

▶ THE PEOPLE

The ancestors of the aborigines are believed to have settled in Australia more than 30,000 years ago. But it has been less than 200 years since the first Europeans, coming from England, founded the colony that became the Australian nation. Since then, the development of the new land has been remarkable. Today Australians live in a country with an advanced political and industrial structure and enjoy one of the world's highest standards of living.

How Australians Live

Most Australians live near the coast, mainly in the southeast, south, and southwest, where the climate and soil are best suited to their needs. Life for most Australians is agreeable. Few are so rich that they need not work, and few are so poor that they cannot afford to live comfortably. History, climate, and natural inclination combine to give Australians an easygoing, informal manner. This dates back to pioneer days, when individual character and ability—rather than family status or possession of wealth—stood out in the struggle with nature. Their homes and apartments are well built and are usually equipped with modern electrical appliances. The majority of Australians own their own homes. A large proportion of them own automobiles and television sets.

City Life. The main centers of population are the state capitals—Sydney, Melbourne, Brisbane, Adelaide, Perth, and Hobart. The cities have treelined streets, lovely parks, large department stores, and supermarkets. Sydney has been compared with San Francisco, while Melbourne has been compared with large cities in Britain.

Everyday life in the cities is much like life in any modern city. Men and women leave home in the mornings to go to offices or factories, while the children go off to school. Most Australians have two free days each week, and there is ample time for outdoor activities.

Like most Australians, the city people are involved in sports. Public tennis courts, golf courses, and bowling greens are found in all cities. Swimming, surfing, and yachting are popular throughout the year in cities near the sea. Horse racing is very popular. Spectator sports are well attended. Many people come

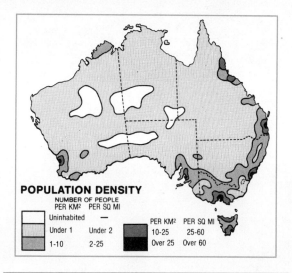

POPULATION DENSITY

NUMBER OF PEOPLE
PER KM²   PER SQ MI

Uninhabited	—	
Under 1	Under 2	
1-10	2-25	

PER KM²	PER SQ MI
10-25	25-60
Over 25	Over 60

FACTS AND FIGURES

COMMONWEALTH OF AUSTRALIA is the official name of the country. The continent is called Australia. The name of both the country and the continent comes from *terra australis incognita,* or "the unknown southern land."

CAPITAL: Canberra.

LOCATION: Southern Hemisphere, between the Pacific and Indian oceans. **Latitude**—10° 41′ S to 39° 08′ S (mainland only) or 43° 39′ S (including Tasmania). **Longitude**—113° 09′ E to 153° 39′ E.

PHYSICAL FEATURES: Area—7,686,900 km² (2,967,909 sq mi). **Highest point**—Mt. Kosciusko, 2,227 m (7,305 ft). **Lowest point**—Lake Eyre, 12 m (39 ft) below sea level. **Chief rivers**—Murray, Darling, Murrumbidgee. **Chief mountain peaks**—Mt. Kosciusko, Mt. Bogong, Mt. Ossa, Mt. Woodroffe.

POPULATION: 14,000,000 (estimate).

LANGUAGE: English.

GOVERNMENT: Independent, self-governing federation. **Head of state**—Queen of Australia, represented by governor-general. **Head of government**—prime minister. **International co-operation**—Commonwealth of Nations; United Nations; Australian, New Zealand, United States Council (ANZUS); Colombo Plan; Organization for Economic Co-operation and Development (OECD).

NATIONAL ANTHEM: "Advance Australia Fair." ("God Save the Queen" is played for viceregal occasions.)

ECONOMY: Agricultural products—wheat, oats, wool, beef, mutton, fruit, sugarcane. **Industries and products**—iron and steel, motor vehicles, heavy machinery, electronics equipment, electrical appliances, chemicals, shipbuilding, aircraft, textiles, food processing, tobacco, wood products. **Chief minerals**—iron, coal, petroleum, bauxite, lead, zinc, copper, nickel, rutile, zircon, uranium. **Chief exports**—wool, meat, grains, metals and ores, fruit, raw sugar. **Chief imports**—heavy machinery, textiles, paper, timber. **Monetary unit**—Australian dollar.

Weekend surf carnivals are held at beautiful beaches on the long Australian coastline. At Manly Beach near Sydney, teams onshore wait to enter a surfboat race.

into the cities from the country to watch amateur and professional Australian Rules football, cricket, and tennis matches.

Symphony concerts, operas, and other musical events are held in the larger cities. Most large cities have their own ballet companies and art galleries. Australia has produced many world-famous artists, dancers, actors, singers, and musicians.

Country Life. The differences between country and city living are rapidly disappearing as communications bring the city closer to the country and give the country easier access to the city. Sheep raising was Australia's earliest economic activity, and it is still the leading farm activity. Large sheep stations dot the inland plains of the east and southwest. They belong to some of Australia's most distinguished families, who have owned them for several generations. Sheep farmers are called graziers in Australia. With the help of hired workers and wonderfully trained sheep dogs,

which look like small collies, they take care of thousands of sheep.

Shearing crews come to clip the sheep once a year. They are highly skilled, and they travel from station to station in the course of their work. For weeks before their visit, sheep are brought into the station headquarters from the most distant pastures. A good shearer can clip as many as 150 to 200 sheep a day.

After shearing, the wool is baled and stored in the woolshed. It is then taken to market for auctioning. Picnics, dances, horse races, and other celebrations are held after the auction. These events are especially festive if the wool has brought good prices at the auction.

Some of the larger sheep stations form complete little communities. Most large stations have houses for the owner and the help, vegetable gardens, a dairy, storage sheds, and a tool-repair shop. Some of the larger stations even have their own one-room schools and power plants to generate electricity.

Smaller farms are found in the irrigated areas and nearer the cities. Most of them belong to farmers of British descent, but some farms belong to or are run by Australians of German or Italian descent. Wheat is the leading crop on the larger farms. Fruits, vegetables, hogs, chickens, and dairy products are produced on the smaller farms.

Life in the Outback. The sparsely settled interior of Australia is known as the outback. Cattle raising is the chief economic activity. Ranches, called stations, vary in size from about 10 square kilometers (4 square miles) to more than 25,000 square kilometers (10,-000 square miles).

The loneliness of life in the outback is rapidly disappearing. Most stations have their own airstrips for use by their own and other planes. Trucks, with trailers often linked together like railroad cars, transport cattle to market much faster than they could be moved by the older method of droving (driving them in herds). And ranch workers on their horses are giving way to crews in trailer trucks.

Outback children are far from any school. Some children go to boarding schools in the cities, but most listen at home to a program called School of the Air. Assignments are given out over the radio, and the children mail in their homework to be graded.

The radio also helps when people become ill. In the early days many sick people died because there were no hospitals or doctors nearby. But today the Royal Flying Doctor Service makes doctors and dentists available throughout the outback. The flying doctor can be called in by radio in an emergency. Some of the doctors fly vast distances every year to care for their scattered patients.

Radio also reduces some of the loneliness of life for people in the outback. It provides most of their entertainment, and people sometimes use it to chat with their neighbors, who are often too far away to visit easily.

The New Australians. Nearly one out of every four persons in Australia has settled there since 1947. Most of these postwar immigrants are from the United Kingdom. The rest of the new Australians are mainly from Italy, Greece, the Netherlands, Germany, Yugoslavia, Poland, and Austria. Efforts to help the newcomers become a part of Australian society have been highly successful.

Two-way radios often provide school instruction for children in the Australian outback.

A member of the Royal Flying Doctor Service visits a patient in central Australia.

The Australian Government has established special schools for aborigine children.

The Aborigines. The Australian aborigines live mainly inland and in the remote northern coastal areas. Most of them no longer live the nomadic tribal life of their ancestors. They total some 100,000, but fewer than half are considered pure-blooded. The aborigines belong to an ethnological group known as Australoids. Before European influence reached them, they moved continually from place to place, hunting animals and gathering food.

The aborigines have the right to enroll and vote in federal elections. Except for those who have chosen to live as tribal nomads, all are entitled to the full range of social benefits available to other Australians. There are special government welfare, housing, and education programs designed to assist aboriginal people, particularly those living in remote areas. A significant number of aborigines continue to live on government reservations, where their traditional way of life is protected.

Language

English is the language spoken in Australia, but it is spoken with a distinctive accent— not English or cockney, as is sometimes mis-takenly believed. The Australians have enlivened the language with a rich variety of their own expressions—so much so that their conversation is sometimes hard for an English-speaking foreigner to follow.

Education

Education is compulsory in Australia. Children must begin school when they are 6 and stay until they are at least 15. Children in Tasmania must stay in school until they are 16. Most children start in infants' classes at the age of 5. There are government-supported, or state, schools in all populated parts of the country. Australia also has many private schools. As in England, the leading private schools are called public schools. The school year begins in late January or early February and ends in mid-December. This time of the year is summer in the Southern Hemisphere.

Elementary school studies include languages, social studies, arithmetic, health education, nature study, reading, and art. Games such as cricket, Australian Rules football, soccer, rugby, and basketball are taught as part of physical education classes. Swimming, tennis, hiking, camping, and singing are popular out-of-school activities. Children in most schools, both state and private, wear their own school uniforms.

Australia has more than 15 universities and a number of colleges that offer courses leading to undergraduate and advanced degrees. Since 1974, students wishing to attend universities and colleges have not had to pay tuition. The Australian National University is mainly for graduate students, but undergraduate courses are given there.

Religion

The majority of Australians belong to various Protestant churches. The largest of these is the Church of England, followed by the Methodist, Presbyterian, Lutheran, and Baptist churches. Many Australians are Roman Catholics. There are also smaller numbers of Jews, Muslims, Buddhists, and members of the Orthodox Eastern Church.

The Arts in Australia

Australia's early poets, novelists, and short-story writers were Europeans who found both the country and the society unfamiliar. For this reason it was some time before Australia's literature truly reflected the Australian environment and developed national characteristics.

There is now a growing body of clearly Australian literature. Among the contemporary poets who have achieved recognition are Kenneth Slessor, Judith Wright, A. D. Hope, and Douglas Stewart. The work of the "bush balladists" is still remembered. These were the poets who wrote about Australia through the eyes of the pioneers who were developing it. Foremost among them was Andrew Barton (Banjo) Paterson (1864–1941). He wrote the final form of the ballad "Waltzing Matilda," which has practically become the national song of Australia.

The short story has been a vital form of literary expression since Henry Lawson turned the campfire yarn into a work of art. Among the best-known contemporary short-story writers are Hal Porter, Gavin Casey, Alan Marshall, Geoffrey Dutton, D'Arcy Niland, and Olaf Ruhen.

The novel in Australia has developed its own character since the publication in 1917 of *The Fortunes of Richard Mahony* by Henry Handel Richardson. Among the contemporary Australian novelists whose works have had worldwide distribution are Patrick White, who won the Nobel prize for literature in 1973, D'Arcy Niland, Jon Cleary, Ruth Park, Morris West, Peter Mathers, Colleen McCullough and David Ireland.

There are public art galleries in all state capitals and in the larger provincial towns. The Melbourne National Gallery, one of the best endowed, has the nation's finest collection of works by masters of the Italian, Dutch, Flemish, French, Spanish, and English schools.

As with literature, art in Australia began as a reflection of European values of form and light. Most of the early paintings were by European artists with fond memories of their homelands. In the latter half of the last century, Swiss painter Louis Buvelot became one of the first to master the Australian landscape. Following him was a group of painters—Arthur Streeton, Tom Roberts, and others—who found the techniques of impressionism an ideal medium for the naturalistic painting of Australian scenes. After the impressionists came another school, including Hans Heysen

---

SOME AUSTRALIAN WORDS AND PHRASES

beano	a feast
billabong	a waterhole
billy	can for boiling water
bludger	idler
bush	forest country
dinkum	honest, true, genuine
ear basher	a talkative bore
galah	a silly, talkative person
give him the drum	tell the true facts
go crook	get angry
grizzle	to complain
larrikin	a hoodlum
never-never	back country
nong	a stupid person
no-hoper	useless person
ratbag	someone not to be taken seriously
ropeable	extremely angry
spine bashing	reclining
squatter	owner of a large sheep station
wake-up	someone sharp; no fool
whinge	complain
yacker	hard work

and Elioth Gruner, who painted the country's scenery more formally.

In recent years, landscape styles have become either starker or more complicated. Notable contemporary artists are Russell Drysdale, Sidney Nolan, Arthur Boyd, John Passmore, and Donald Friend. The best known is probably William Dobell, an exuberant romantic with a fine sense of color and superb technique. There is also a vigorous abstractionist movement in Australia.

An interesting development in Australian painting was the emergence of a school of aboriginal painters. These artists took quickly to watercolor technique when it was introduced to a mission station at Hermannsburg, west of Alice Springs. Their works have been exhibited and have found ready sale in Australia and overseas. Albert Namatjira, who died in 1959, was the best known of the aboriginal painters.

In music and drama many Australian artists have become internationally famous. The beautiful voices of opera singers Dame Nellie Melba and Dame Joan Sutherland have delighted music lovers throughout the world. The music of composers Percy Grainger and Arthur Benjamin has also won international recognition. The acting of Cyril Ritchard and Erroll Flynn and the piano concerts of Eileen Joyce attracted large audiences. Ray Lawler, whose play *Summer of the Seventeenth Doll* was produced in London and New York, is a leading Australian playwright. Jazz musicians Ray Price and Don Burrows and popular singers such as the Bee Gees, Olivia Newton-John, and Helen Reddy have also won popularity with audiences all over the world.

▶ THE LAND

Australia is the world's largest island and its smallest continent. Its total area is about the same as that of the United States, excluding Alaska and Hawaii.

The vast country in which the Australians live extends from Cape York (in Queensland) in the north to Southeast Cape (in Tasmania) in the south, and from Steep Point (in Western Australia) in the west to Cape Byron (in New South Wales) in the east. Asia is the continent nearest to Australia. The numerous islands of Indonesia form stepping-stones between the two continents. To the west of Australia stretches the vast Indian Ocean. The icy shores of Antarctica lie to the south. New Zealand is to the east.

Natural Regions

Australia's major landforms are low plateaus and broad, level plains. Unlike Europe, Asia, or the Americas, Australia has no very high mountains or deep valleys.

Three natural regions extend as broad bands from north to south across the continent. These are the Eastern Highlands, the Central Lowland, and the Western Plateau.

Eastern Highlands. The long range of hills and low plateaus along Australia's eastern coast is known as the Eastern Highlands, or the Great Dividing Range. Australia's highest point, Mount Kosciusko, is in the part of the highlands known as the Australian Alps. The eastern slope of the mountains is too steep for farming and is mainly forested. The western slope is gentler and is divided into large wheat farms and sheep stations. Rivers flowing to the east are short and swift, while rivers flowing westward are longer and often slow and sluggish.

Off the east coast of Queensland is the Great Barrier Reef. The Great Barrier Reef is the world's largest coral formation. It runs along the coast for 2,000 kilometers (1,250 miles). It is separated from the mainland by shallow, sheltered water. A few islands in this stretch of water have become popular resorts. The area is the home of many rare forms of sea life and is a favorite spot for skin diving.

Central Lowland. The Central Lowland is a broad, flat interior basin that stretches from the Gulf of Carpentaria in the north to Spencer Gulf in the south. It occupies about one third of the continent.

The northern section around the Gulf of Carpentaria is very narrow. It is covered with scrub and grass vegetation and is used mainly for raising cattle. The rivers flow only during the wet season.

In the southern section is Lake Eyre, a vast depression that is the lowest point in Australia. Lake Eyre has no outlet. Most of the time it is a large expanse of dried, salty mud. But in unusually rainy years it becomes filled with salty water. Warm, slightly salty water, which is trapped within the rock layers be-

The red monoliths of Mount Olga, in the Northern Territory, are part of a national park.

low the ground, rises to the surface when wells are bored deep into the water-bearing rocks. Ranchers have drilled thousands of wells in this region to get water for their sheep and cattle.

In the southern section of the Central Lowland are the Murray River and its three chief tributaries—the Darling, Lachlan, and Murrumbidgee. The Murray is Australia's most important river. It flows for 2,600 kilometers (1,600 miles) from its source in the Australian Alps to its mouth near Adelaide. The Darling is longer, but it is less important because it often runs dry in drought years. The Darling joins the Murray at Wentworth. Between the Murray and the Lachlan is the Riverina, one of Australia's leading farming and grazing regions.

Western Plateau. The Western Plateau is a vast upland region that occupies more than half the continent. The interior of the plateau is made up of the Great Sandy Desert, the Gibson Desert, the Great Victoria Desert, and the Nullarbor Plain.

Alice Springs and Kalgoorlie are the only important towns in the interior of the plateau. Alice Springs is a thriving cattle center at the end of the railroad line from Adelaide. It serves as the railhead for the surrounding cattle country. Kalgoorlie is the center of Australia's gold-mining industry. All the water for Kalgoorlie and nearby mining towns is piped far across the desert from the Helena River, a tributary of the Darling River just east of Perth.

A few places on the edge of the plateau receive rainfall regularly. One such region is the scrub-and-grassland country of the north around Darwin. Cattle raising is the leading industry in this region. The second nondesert region, known as Swanland, is in the southwest near Perth. Swanland receives enough rain in winter for wheat and sheep farming. The Eyre Peninsula, jutting out into the Indian

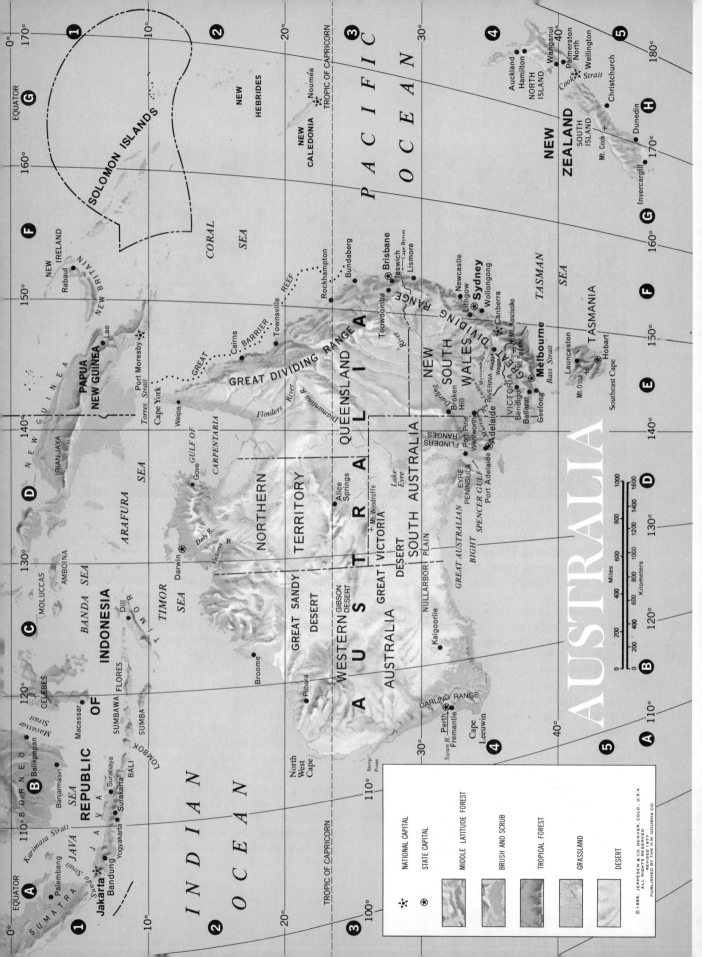

AUSTRALIA

SOLOMON ISLANDS

NEW HEBRIDES

Nouméa
NEW CALEDONIA

TROPIC OF CAPRICORN

PACIFIC OCEAN

NEW ZEALAND

Auckland
Hamilton
NORTH ISLAND
Wanganui
Palmerston North
Wellington
Cook Strait
Christchurch
SOUTH ISLAND
Mt. Cook
Dunedin
Invercargill

TASMAN SEA

CORAL SEA

Rabaul
NEW IRELAND
NEW BRITAIN
Lae
Port Moresby
PAPUA NEW GUINEA
N E W   G U I N E A
IRIAN JAYA

Rockhampton
Bundaberg
Brisbane
Ipswich
Cape Byron
Lismore
Newcastle
Lithgow
Sydney
Wollongong
Canberra
Mt. Kosciusko

NEW SOUTH WALES

GREAT DIVIDING RANGE

Cairns
Townsville
BARRIER
GREAT
REEF

GREAT DIVIDING RANGE

QUEENSLAND

Toowoomba

Darling River

Broken Hill
Wentworth
Wagga Wagga
RIVERINA
VICTORIA
Bendigo
Ballarat
Mt. Buffalo
Geelong
Melbourne
Bass Strait
Launceston
TASMANIA
Mt. Ossa
Hobart
Southeast Cape

TASMAN SEA

Cape York
Weipa
GULF OF CARPENTARIA

Flinders River
Diamantina R.

NORTHERN TERRITORY

Alice Springs
+ Mt. Woodroffe

Port Pirie
Port Augusta
Adelaide
FLINDERS RANGES
SOUTH AUSTRALIA
Lake Eyre
EYRE PENINSULA
SPENCER GULF
Port Adelaide

GREAT AUSTRALIAN BIGHT

Darwin
Daly R.
Victoria R.

GREAT SANDY DESERT

GIBSON DESERT

WESTERN AUSTRALIA

GREAT VICTORIA DESERT

NULLARBOR PLAIN

Broome

Pilbara

Kalgoorlie

DARLING RANGE
Swan R. Perth
Fremantle
Cape Leeuwin
North West Cape
Steep Point

Macassar
Balikpapan
Banjarmasin
B O R N E O
CELEBES
MOLUCCAS
AMBOINA
BANDA SEA
INDONESIA
Surabaya
Surakarta
Yogyakarta
J A V A
FLORES
SUMBAWA
SUMBA
BALI
LOMBOK Strait
Dili
T I M O R
TIMOR SEA
ARAFURA SEA

REPUBLIC OF

Palembang
Bandung
Jakarta
S U M A T R A
JAVA SEA
Macassar Strait
Sunda Strait
Karimata Strait
110°E

I N D I A N   O C E A N

TROPIC OF CAPRICORN

EQUATOR

0° 10° 20° 30° 40° 50°

110° 120° 130° 140° 150° 160° 170° 180° 170°

A B C D E F G H

1 2 3 4 5

Legend

✧ NATIONAL CAPITAL
⊛ STATE CAPITAL

MIDDLE LATITUDE FOREST
BRUSH AND SCRUB
TROPICAL FOREST
GRASSLAND
DESERT

Miles
0 200 400 600 800 1000
Kilometers
0 200 400 600 800 1000 1200 1400 1600

Ocean west of Spencer Gulf, is another non-desert region.

Climate

Because Australia lies in the Southern Hemisphere, winter comes in July and summer in December. People often sunbathe on the beach or swim in the ocean during the Christmas holidays.

Temperature. The one third of Australia that lies north of the Tropic of Capricorn has tropical temperatures. Darwin, on the north coast, has average monthly temperatures of around 27°C (80°F).

The rest of Australia has a moderate climate. Summers are generally hot and winters mild. Winters are often warm enough for Australians to enjoy tennis, lawn bowling, and even surfing. It is warm enough during the winter for cattle and sheep to stay outdoors, so farmers do not have the expense of building barns to shelter their animals.

Rainfall. Most parts of Australia do not receive enough rainfall. In some places droughts occur occasionally. In other places they occur seasonally. A particularly severe drought, affecting every state in Australia, occurred in 1978. Lack of rainfall is one of the major reasons for Australia's small population.

Only one sixth of the continent—a belt of land along the north, east, and south coasts —receives more than 1,000 millimeters (40 inches) of rain a year. Wide areas in the interior receive less than 250 millimeters (10 inches) of rainfall each year.

Australia's humid lands extend in a belt along the east coast and parts of the northern and southeastern coasts. The southeastern coast and the island state of Tasmania have a marine type of climate. Rain falls throughout the year, and snow is common on the higher mountains.

Southeastern and southwestern Australia have a Mediterranean climate. Rainfall is distributed throughout the year. But more rain falls during the winter. Summers are warm and sunny.

The northern coast has a monsoon climate. Rain falls only in summer, when the moisture-bearing northwest monsoon blows onto Australia from Asia. Summers are hot and sticky, and grass and trees grow rapidly. Rivers often flood. Winter is almost completely rainless, and the country becomes dry and parched. Pastures dry up, and cattle must find what grass they can in the few moist places discovered by the cattle drovers.

Farther inland are somewhat drier areas that receive between 250 and 750 millimeters (10 and 30 inches) of rain a year. The rain falls evenly throughout the year in the east. But the northern areas, like the humid monsoon areas along the northern coast, receive most of their rain in summer and are dry during the winter. The semi-arid regions in the south and southwest receive most of their rain in winter and are dry during the summer.

Australian Wildlife

Australia has an extraordinary collection of birds and animals. Many of them are found only there. Early explorers were so surprised by the emu and the kangaroo that they described the continent as the land where birds "ran instead of flying and animals hopped instead of running."

Australia is the home of two of the world's most primitive mammals—the duckbill, or platypus, and the spiny anteater. They belong to the group of mammals known as monotremes, the only mammals that lay eggs. The duckbill (platypus) is a furry creature. It has webbed feet and a long snout shaped somewhat like a duck's bill. The spiny anteater looks like a porcupine.

Australia is famous as the home of the

WILDLIFE of AUSTRALIA

Buctel

Labels on map: SEA TURTLE · CROCODILE · CORAL · GIANT CLAM · DEVILFISH · CUSCUS · DINGO · WATER BUFFALO · BUDGERIGAR · CLOWNFISH · SEA STAR · PARROT · EMU · FRILLED LIZARD · REGENT BOWERBIRD · RABBIT · SUGAR GLIDER · COCKATOO · SHARK · KANGAROO · SPINY ANTEATER · KOALA BEAR · KOOKABURRA · LYREBIRD · PLATYPUS · MARLIN · FAIRY PENGUIN · TASMANIAN DEVIL

marsupials, or pouched mammals. A newborn marsupial is extremely tiny and spends the first months of its life in a pouch on the underside of its mother's body. The kangaroo is perhaps the best known of Australia's marsupials. There are more than 40 different kinds of kangaroos in Australia, in many different colors and sizes. The big red kangaroo and the gray kangaroo may be as tall and heavy as a human adult. A smaller kangaroo, known as the wallaby, is about the size of a large dog. The smallest variety is the rat kangaroo. Australia's famous koala is also a marsupial. The koala is a quaint creature that resembles a teddy bear. It spends most of its life in eucalyptus trees and feeds only on the leaves of these trees. Sugar gliders, sometimes called possums, are unusual animals that glide from tree to tree.

Among other animals found in Australia is the dingo, a wild dog that was probably brought to Australia by the aborigines. It is yellowish brown and has a bushy tail.

The kangaroo shares the Australian coat of arms with the emu, Australia's largest bird and also one of the largest in the world. Like the ostrich, the emu cannot fly but is a swift runner. The cassowary is related to the emu and can sprint at high speeds. Another curious bird is the kookaburra, a large kingfisher that is often called the "laughing jackass." The bush country rings with its rowdy laughter. The brolga, an Australian crane, is sometimes called the "native companion" because many people working in the forests and outback have a tame brolga around the camp. Other Australian birds are graceful lyrebirds, brilliantly colored parrots, and the great white cockatoo. Black- and white-backed magpies are rarely absent from the skies of southeastern and southwestern Australia.

Two animals introduced by the Europeans have run wild in Australia. These are the buffalo, brought from India, and the European rabbit. Buffalo were brought to the north coast as work animals early in the 19th century. They escaped and multiplied and now inhabit the swampy river valleys around Darwin and the Gulf of Carpentaria. Each year hunters shoot thousands of them for their thick hides.

Rabbits were introduced more than 100 years ago. There are now so many of them in Australia that they are pests. Australian sheep farmers wage constant war against the rabbits because they destroy much valuable grass. Many properties are surrounded by rabbit-proof fences, and one whole corner of the continent has been shut off by a long fence to keep out the rabbits. For many years the farmers have laid poison bait and plowed up large underground rabbit colonies. They introduced a disease called myxomatosis (or "myxo"). This disease is deadly to rabbits but harmless to other animals. But many rabbits have now developed resistance to the disease, and Australians are seeking a more effective way to solve the rabbit problem.

Natural Resources

Australia is rich in some natural resources and poor in many others. The most valuable agricultural resource is the vast grassland in east central Australia. Thousands of sheep and cattle are grazed on these pastures. They supply most of the meat and wool that Australia sells to the rest of the world. Australia also has very abundant mineral resources, many of which have been discovered only in recent times. Principal among them are iron ore, coal, bauxite, and petroleum.

Australia's soils are relatively poor. Usually they need to be fertilized for crop production. More serious is a shortage of water over most of the continent. But Australia has taken bold steps to help overcome this problem. The capacity of its water storage facilities has been greatly multiplied. The most remarkable undertaking is the Snowy Mountains Hydro-electric Scheme. This vast project, which also produces electricity, stretches across the Australian Alps in southeastern New South Wales. It is one of the greatest achievements of its kind in the world. By means of a system of dams and tunnels, it makes possible the storage of huge amounts of water behind nine major dams and greatly increases the quantity of water available for irrigation. Water from coastal rivers is diverted through a series of tunnels so that it flows into the inland river systems of the Murray and Murrumbidgee. The water is used to generate electricity in a number of power stations. Other major projects are being carried out in all the states to increase the supply of irrigation water and electricity.

Softwoods are scarce in Australia, but there are large amounts of hardwoods in Swanland and the Great Dividing Range. The native eucalyptus tree and the wattle tree are especially common. Large plantations of North American pine and other softwood trees have recently been established. They should provide enough softwood to meet the needs of the future.

▶ THE ECONOMY

Australia is a major producer and exporter of agricultural products. Mining has long been an important part of the Australian economy. Manufacturing has been expanding. It now contributes about one fourth of the total annual value of production and employs about one fourth of the working population.

Much of Australia's iron ore comes from mines like this one in Western Australia.

Manufacturing

Australia's manufacturing industries have grown very rapidly since World War II. But there continues to be a heavy reliance on imported manufactured goods. They make up about three fourths of the country's total imports.

Since World War II the industries that have developed most are those associated with rapid technological changes and rising standards of living. Those that have grown at the fastest rates are the engineering industry and the manufacture of vehicles, construction materials, and chemicals. Products of these industries have been able largely to replace imports. Factories today are turning out—and often exporting—a wide range of goods. These include diesel-electric locomotives, motor vehicles, agricultural and earth-moving equipment, roller bearings, machine tools, cathode-ray picture tubes, synthetic fibers, electronic equipment and appliances, power cables, fiberglass, plastics, fertilizers, pharmaceutical and veterinary products, and petrochemicals.

One of the most important factors in the nation's industrial development is the prosperity of its iron and steel industry. The Broken Hill Proprietary Company Limited (BHP) and its subsidiaries produce nearly all Australian steel. This company, the largest in Australia, has expanded rapidly. In addition to iron and steel, it manufactures alloy steels, wire, and other metal products.

In spite of its small population, Australia has a large domestic market for automobiles. The motor vehicle industry in Australia employs more people than any other industry. It meets almost all the local demand for motor vehicles, and vehicles are also exported.

Australia also has major shipbuilding and aircraft industries. Other notable industrial groups are textiles, food processing, tobacco, and wood products.

Investment from overseas, most of it coming from the United States and the United Kingdom, has played a significant part in the development of Australia's manufacturing and mining industries.

Agriculture

Australia has more than one sixth of all the sheep in the world and produces nearly one third of all the world's wool. The merino is the most important breed of sheep. It produces more wool than any other breed. The sheep country is mainly in Victoria, New South Wales, Western Australia, and Queensland.

Australia is also a large producer of meat. More than half of all the meat is beef. Lamb and mutton and a small amount of pork make up the remainder. Most of the beef comes from the large cattle stations in the tropical north country, but some beef cattle are also raised in the sheep areas. Australians eat more than half of the meat produced. The rest is exported in chilled, frozen, or canned form. The United States is an important customer. Japan and a number of European countries, including Britain, also buy large amounts of Australian meat.

Dairying is important near the cities along the eastern and southern coasts, where fresh milk is needed daily. The dairy farms are much smaller than the northern cattle stations. Butter, cheese, and other dairy products are produced for home use and for export.

Wheat grows well in eastern and southwestern Australia. The wheat farms are usually very large and mechanized. Many wheat growers also keep sheep as an additional source of income. The sheep are put to graze on the stubble after harvest. Australia exports the greater part of its wheat. Most of the wheat is bought by such countries as China, India, Egypt, Japan, and Chile. Oats are another major grain crop.

Fruits are abundant in several places. Pineapples and tropical fruits are grown on the north Queensland coast. Peaches, plums, and citrus fruits flourish near Perth. Apples, plums, and peaches come from Tasmania and from irrigated areas in the Riverina. The Barossa Valley near Adelaide is the center of the Australian wine-making industry. Sugarcane is grown along the northeastern coast of Australia. Well over half the sugarcane crop is exported.

Mining

Australia has been an important mineral producer since gold was first discovered in the 1850's. For many years gold was the most important metal, but now it is outranked by several other minerals. The area around Kalgoorlie in Western Australia is the major gold-mining center.

Vast sheep stations like this one have long been important in the Australian economy.

Iron ore, chiefly from the Pilbara region of Western Australia, has become the nation's most valuable mineral product. Deposits in Western Australia are estimated to total nearly 25,000,000,000 (billion) tons. Most of Australia's iron ore is exported to Japan, which in recent years has replaced Britain as Australia's principal trading partner.

Coal is second in importance among Australia's mineral products. Black coal is mined in New South Wales and in Queensland. Brown coal (lignite) is mined in Victoria. Coal is used to generate much of Australia's electricity, and large quantities are exported to Japan and other countries.

Since the end of World War II, the production of oil has become one of Australia's major industries. Most of the oil comes from a vast field off the coast of Victoria, in Bass Strait. Other fields are located west of Brisbane and at Barrow Island, off the northwest coast of Western Australia. Australia now produces enough oil to satisfy most of its domestic needs.

Since 1960, Australia has become the world's largest producer of bauxite, which is used to make aluminum. Nearly all the bauxite is exported. Bauxite is mined at Weipa, Queensland; in the Darling Range in Western Australia; and at Gove, Northern Territory. Other important minerals include lead and zinc, at Broken Hill and Mount Isa; copper, from Mount Isa; nickel, near Kalgoorlie in Western Australia; and mineral sand concentrates of rutile and zircon, from the eastern seaboard. There are also vast reserves of uranium near Darwin in the Northern Territory.

Transportation and Communications

Transportation is well developed. Roads are extensive along the coast. Many of the roads in the outback are unpaved. These red clay roads can be clearly seen from the air. Australia is one of the most highly motorized countries in the world, with more than 450 motor vehicles for every 1,000 people. Trains are fast and modern. Australia also has one of the largest domestic aviation networks in the world. More than 9,000,000 passengers, as well as considerable amounts of freight, are carried each year on flights within Australia. The outback is particularly dependent on air service as a means of transportation.

Australia is in direct air communication with the major cities of the world. Qantas, Australia's overseas airline, operates services from Sydney to countries around the world. Several other international airlines have regular services to Australia.

The government maintains Australia's internal telegraph and telephone service. The government also operates a network of radio and television stations. Short- and long-wave radio stations are scattered throughout the country. Individually operated voice radios bring distant neighbors closer together in the sparsely settled north. Television is available in the larger cities. There are both state and commercial television stations in operation. The larger cities have two or more daily newspapers, and there are many local ones in smaller towns.

▶ AUSTRALIA'S STATES AND TERRITORIES

In 1901 the six self-governing colonies of New South Wales, Victoria, Queensland, South Australia, Western Australia, and Tasmania joined together in a federation. The colonies became states, and the federation was called the Commonwealth of Australia.

New South Wales

Almost four of every ten Australians live in New South Wales, Australia's most populous state. Most people live along the east coast, and more than one half are in Sydney, the capital and largest city. Sydney is also the largest city in Australia. The state of New South Wales is filled with contrasts. People can ski in the mountains in the southern part of the state or visit an almost tropical beach in the north.

New South Wales is Australia's leading industrial state. Most manufacturing is located along the narrow coastal plain. Sydney is the most important center. Other industrial towns include Newcastle and Wollongong. A great variety of products, from ships and motor vehicles to television sets and other household appliances, are made in New South Wales. Coal deposits have greatly helped the state's industrial development, and it is expected that the Snowy Mountains Hydroelectric Scheme will attract even more industries in the future.

The farmlands of New South Wales are nearly all west of the Great Dividing Range.

In the New England region at the western foot of the highlands are the best wheat and grazing lands. Beef cattle are important in the drier northwestern sections of the state. A dam on the Murrumbidgee—the Burrinjuck Dam—and a dam on the Murray River—the Hume Weir—provide irrigation water for the dry lands in the southeast. Rice, citrus fruits, grapes, tomatoes, and other vegetables are grown in the irrigated fields.

Victoria

Victoria is the second smallest state in area and the second largest in population. Most people live in the south. Melbourne is the capital and largest city. Other important towns include Geelong and Ballarat.

Sheep and wheat are the chief products in the southwest and on the plains in the northwest. Cattle raising is the leading activity in the drier foothills of the Eastern Highlands. Many cattle are sent up to pastures in the mountains for the summer. Citrus fruits, grapes, peaches, and apricots are grown on irrigated lands along the Murray River. Truck and dairy farmers supply people in Melbourne and Geelong with fresh fruits, vegetables, and milk.

Large deposits of black and brown coal have helped Victoria's industrial development. Most of the brown coal is compressed into briquettes that are used to make electricity. Some is made into gas, which is sent by pipeline to Melbourne. There are also large hydroelectric power stations in the state.

Queensland

The tropical northeastern corner of Australia is in Queensland, Australia's second largest state. Queensland has long stretches of beautiful beaches. Its coast is a popular vacation spot for people from the southern states.

In spite of its size, Queensland has a population smaller than that of either New South Wales or Victoria. Most people live along the narrow coastal plain in the east, while the dry interior of the state is thinly populated.

The climate along the east coast is hot and humid. Sugarcane, cotton, bananas, and other tropical crops are the leading products. Gold is mined along the coast. Brisbane, the capital and largest city of the state, is located in the

Part of the Snowy Mountains hydroelectric complex in the Australian Alps.

southeast. Few people live along the northern and northeastern coasts, where the rainy summers and dry winters of the monsoon climate make life and farming more difficult.

The vast interior of Queensland is sparsely populated. Some sheep and wheat are raised on the Darling Downs in the southeast, and cattle raising and mining are the leading industries elsewhere. Underground water is the one reliable water source. Artesian wells line all the stock routes between the grazing grounds and the railheads.

Mining communities are widely scattered. Copper, silver, lead, zinc, black coal, and bauxite are mined.

South Australia

Most of South Australia's people, farms, and industry are in the southeastern part of this third largest state. Adelaide is the capital and largest city. Woomera is the site of a rocket range and orbital tracking station.

Most of South Australia is too dry for farming. Some wheat is grown east of the Flinders Range and along the eastern margin of Spencer Gulf, but elsewhere all farming depends on irrigation or underground sources of water. From the irrigated lands along the lower course of the Murray River come large quantities of apricots, pears, peaches, nectarines, and grapes. Some of the grapes are used to make

This aborigine stockman works on one of Australia's huge cattle stations.

wine, and some are dried for raisins, sultanas, and currants. Figs, citrus fruits, and plums are also produced. Beef and dairy cattle are raised on irrigated pastures, and sheep graze on the natural grasslands.

Some of Australia's most unproductive desert lands occupy the remainder of the state. Isolated cattle stations, strung along the railroads to Perth and Alice Springs, and occasional training centers for aborigines are the only signs of civilization.

South Australia has valuable mineral deposits. Iron ore is mined and shipped to the New South Wales steel mills. Coober Pedy is the site of one of the world's largest opal mines.

Western Australia

Nearly 300 years ago Europeans first touched at the northern coast of what is now the state of Western Australia. They described it as a rugged, dry, and inhospitable land. Their description still fits all but the southwestern corner of the state. Barren desert stretches across this largest state of the commonwealth. Only occasionally is the view broken by an isolated mining town or a lonely cattle station.

Nearly all of Western Australia's people and most of the state's wheat farms, sheep stations, and fruit orchards are crowded into a small section in the southwest. This section is known as Swanland, after the Swan River.

Swanland is connected with the cities in eastern Australia by a railroad across the empty Nullarbor Plain.

Perth, the capital and largest city of Western Australia, is located on the banks of the Swan. Fremantle, the ocean port for Perth, is Australia's largest west coast port and the one nearest to Europe. Albany is an important station for whaling fleets that fish in the Antarctic and southern Indian oceans. Other ports are associated with Western Australia's important pearling and fishing industry.

Gold was first discovered in the Kalgoorlie region in 1893, and mining towns sprang up overnight. The towns are in the middle of the desert and depend on Perth for all their water. Pilbara is the center of an important iron ore industry.

Tasmania

Tasmania, the island state, is sometimes called the apple isle because it produces most of Australia's apples. It is also famous for its rugged scenery and for the delicious scallops caught along its rocky coasts. At the foot of Mount Wellington is Hobart, the capital and largest city of the island. Other important centers are Launceston and Devonport. A ferryboat connects Devonport with Melbourne on the mainland across Bass Strait.

Tasmania is one of the few places in Australia that have adequate rainfall all year. Tasmania is Australia's leading producer of hops, apples, pears, and berries of different kinds. Potatoes also flourish in this climate and are grown as a specialty in some areas.

The abundance of water has greatly aided the industrial development of the state. Hydroelectric plants are located at many places throughout the island. Many industries that use large amounts of electricity have been attracted to this source of power. There are zinc-refining centers, aluminum smelters, and pulp and paper mills. Tin, copper, lead, and tungsten are other important mineral products of Tasmania.

Northern Territory

The Northern Territory, which became self-governing in 1978, is the least populated and least developed part of Australia. Crocodiles and wild buffalo still live in some of the marshy swamps along the coast. Darwin, the capital, is the only large settlement in the north. Over 90 percent of the city was destroyed by a tropical cyclone in 1974, but rebuilding began at once. Alice Springs, generally called Alice or the Alice, is the only town in the south.

The climate along the coast is hot and wet in summer but too dry for farming in winter. Cattle raising on large stations and mining are the leading industries. Some rice is grown on experimental farms. Copper, gold, uranium, and mica are mined.

▶ AUSTRALIA'S CITIES

Most of Australia's people live in the six capital cities of the states and in Canberra, the federal capital. About half of all Australians live in Sydney and Melbourne.

Sydney

Sydney, on the east coast, is Australia's largest city and the capital of New South Wales. It was founded on January 26, 1788, and was the first European settlement in the country. Sydney is the home of one fourth of all Australian industry and is the center for Australia's engineering, chemical, and oil-refining industries. Sydney has an excellent harbor and is Australia's leading seaport. Many people enjoy sailing, and the harbor is dotted with boats.

From the air, Sydney looks like a city of red roofs. Almost all of the older buildings have roofs made of terra cotta tile. The business district is an interesting mixture of old and new. Many buildings, such as the State Parliament House, St. James Church, and the Supreme Court Building, are reminders of the 19th century. But office and apartment buildings made of concrete and glass are rapidly replacing some of the older structures. The Sydney Opera House, opened in 1973, is strikingly modern in design. The city also has many lovely parks and gardens. A separate article on Sydney appears in Volume S.

Melbourne

Melbourne is Australia's second largest city and the capital of Victoria. It is considered the financial center of the nation. From 1901 to 1927 it was the seat of the federal government. Its harbor is the most important on the south coast and the natural outlet for the production

The downtown area of Sydney, with many high-rise buildings, borders the city's fine natural harbor.

of the southeastern part of the country. Old stone buildings and arcades line the streets in the older parts of Melbourne. They give the city an Old World appearance that often reminds visitors of cities in England.

Melbourne's industrial district lies south of the city and along the coast. The factories manufacture heavy engineering products, power-station equipment, electrical goods, wool and cotton textiles, clothing, and chemicals. Melbourne is closely tied with Geelong, an industrial city to the south. A separate article on Melbourne appears in Volume M.

Brisbane

Brisbane, on the east coast, is Australia's third largest city and the capital of Queensland. It is the only large Australian city with a subtropical climate. Numerous parks and gardens make Brisbane one of Australia's most beautiful cities. Brisbane is the principal export center for the state's wool, meat, wheat, sugar, and mineral products. Textiles, shoes, and clothing are produced in the city. During World War II many hundreds of Americans used Brisbane as the headquarters of United States forces in Australia. A monument in the city commemorates the friendly co-operation between the two countries.

Melbourne is a highly industrialized city as well as an important port.

Adelaide

Adelaide, the capital of South Australia, is Australia's fourth largest city. Performers from all parts of the world visit Adelaide to take part in the Adelaide Festival of Arts, which is held every two years. The city is also Australia's largest wine-exporting center. Wine from the Barossa Valley is loaded onto oceangoing ships at Port Adelaide on St. Vincent Gulf.

Perth

Far to the west of Adelaide is Perth, Western Australia's capital. It is the major west coast city and Australia's fifth largest city. It is said to be Australia's most beautiful city and reminds many Americans of cities in southern California. Its port, at the mouth of the Swan, is Fremantle. Perth and Fremantle process and ship the wool, wheat, fruit, meat, and dairy products of Western Australia. There are also railroad shops, a cement plant, oil refineries, and various light industries.

Hobart

Mount Wellington makes a beautiful background for Hobart, the capital city of Tasmania. Hobart, founded in 1804, is Australia's second oldest city. The city is surrounded by a small but flourishing agricultural area. Fruit, hops, dairy products, wool, and hides are exported through the city. Nearby are large hydroelectric power stations that generate electricity for use in Hobart's flourishing pulp-and-paper industry. Zinc and other metals are smelted near Hobart.

Canberra

Canberra, the national capital, is an important seat of learning and scientific achievement as well as a city of public administration and a center of diplomacy. The site was selected in 1908, and in 1911 an international competition was held to choose a plan for the city. An American architect, Walter Burley Griffin, submitted the prizewinning plan. Construction of the city began in 1923, and four years later the parliament moved from Melbourne to Canberra. Now all branches of the federal government are located in Canberra. An area of 2,432 square kilometers (939 square miles) around the city is designated as the Australian Capital Territory.

Residential suburbs surround a central core where the government buildings, embassies of other nations, and the Australian National University are located. Today the Australian National University is one of the principal centers of nuclear research in the country. It is regularly visited by scholars from other countries. A separate article on Canberra, with information on the Australian Capital Territory, appears in Volume C.

▶ GOVERNMENT

Australia is an independent, self-governing nation. The federal government in Canberra conducts national affairs. Each state has its own parliament. Australia was the first country to use the secret ballot. Every Australian citizen over 18 years old is required to vote.

Legislative authority rests with the Federal Parliament, made up of the Senate and the House of Representatives. Each state has ten senators, and each territory has two. The House of Representatives is elected on the basis of population. Its membership is required to be, as nearly as possible, twice that of the Senate. The governor-general is the Queen's representative in Australia, but the actual head of the government is the prime minister. The prime minister is the leader of the governing party or parties in parliament and is assisted by a cabinet. In 1975, parliament and the prime minister were unable to resolve a bitter dispute. The governor-general, for the only time in Australia's history, used his authority to remove the prime minister from office.

The High Court of Australia is the judicial branch of the federal government. It interprets the constitution and settles disputes between the states. State governments administer state affairs. Town and city councils manage the affairs of smaller state localities.

▶ HISTORY

Even in medieval times there were stories about a large continent in the Southern Hemisphere. But Europeans had never seen it. They wondered what it was like and whether it was inhabited. They called this land *terra australis incognita,* or "the unknown southern land."

Discovery and Exploration

The Dutch were the first Europeans to visit Australia. They sighted it while making their journeys between the Netherlands and the island of Java, a Dutch colony in what is now Indonesia. Ships sailing from the Netherlands to Java used to go around the southern tip of Africa (the Cape of Good Hope) and then sail across the Indian Ocean with the westerly winds. Many navigators sailed too far east before turning north toward Java and found themselves on the west coast of Australia. They later gave the name New Holland to this western part of the continent.

Parliament House and the parade ground in Canberra, Australia's capital city.

But the Dutch did not know how far east this southern continent extended, and in 1642 Captain Abel Janszoon Tasman was sent out to discover what lay in the east. Tasman sailed too far south and failed to see the mainland, but he did visit the island now called Tasmania in his honor. He named this island Van Diemen's Land. Tasman then continued eastward to New Zealand. Later he explored Australia's north coast and gave Dutch names to places like Groote Eylandt.

No careful explorations of the continent were made for another century or so. Then in 1770 the English captain James Cook sighted the east coast of Australia and named it New South Wales. He visited Botany Bay, near what is now modern Sydney, and reported back to England that the bay and much of New South Wales looked good for settlement. In London the British Government was concerned about the Revolutionary War in America and did not listen to his suggestions. For many years the British had been sending convicts to the American colonies to relieve overcrowded jails in England. When the colonies won their independence, the British looked around for another place to send their convicts. It was decided to send some to Botany Bay on the coast of New South Wales.

Early Settlement

In May, 1787, the first group of convicts and a few soldiers left Portsmouth, England, for the trip to Australia. Eleven ships and about 1,500 men made the trip. The ships reached Botany Bay in mid-January, 1788.

But a few days after their arrival the governor of the group decided that Sydney Harbour, a little farther north, was a better place for a colony. He took the fleet there and established a colony known as Port Jackson. This colony later became the city of Sydney.

More convicts followed, and new penal colonies were established in other parts of the continent. Hobart, on Tasmania (then known as Van Diemen's Land), was established in 1804. Another colony, which later became the city of Brisbane, was begun at Moreton Bay, on the eastern coast, in 1824. Albany, in southwestern Australia, was founded in 1826.

The coastline of Australia was only vaguely known at this time. In fact, not until 1798 did George Bass, a naval surgeon and explorer, sail along the south coast. He proved that Tasmania was an island. The strait separating the island from the continent was named Bass Strait in his honor. And not until 1801 did Matthew Flinders, a captain in the Royal Navy, discover and chart Kangaroo Island and Spencer and St. Vincent gulfs along the south coast.

Life was very difficult for the early convicts and for the soldiers in charge of the colonies. The colonies depended on ships from England for all their food and supplies. Farming was difficult, and there were few tools. It was at this time that Captain John Macarthur began breeding fine merino sheep for their wool, at Camden, near Sydney. He sent his first batch of wool to England in 1807. The wool industry flourished and later became Australia's most important industry. The merino, originally a native of the dry and dusty plains of Spain, was to prove well suited to life in Australia's interior.

Many convicts earned their freedom and stayed on in Australia, but at first free English settlers were outnumbered in all of the penal colonies. As more settlers saw the opportunities of the new continent, several free colonies, quite apart from the penal colonies, were founded. The first free colony was the Swan River colony, established in 1829 in southwest Australia. In 1835 a second free settlement, called Doutta Galla, was established in the south; its name was changed to Melbourne in 1837.

For 25 years the New South Wales colony was restricted to a narrow stretch of lowland along the east coast. Then in 1813 three explorers—Gregory Blaxland, William Lawson, and William Charles Wentworth—found a way across the Blue Mountains behind Port Jackson. They were the first Europeans to see the vast plains beyond the Great Dividing Range. Two years later Bathurst, the first inland settlement, was established.

Other explorers went farther inland. In 1824 Hamilton Hume came across a river in the interior that he called the Hume River. In 1829 Captain Charles Sturt explored the Darling and, not knowing that he had rediscovered Hume River, renamed the Hume River the Murray River. In 1836 Major Thomas Mitchell explored the Darling River and the grassy plains of the Riverina.

Close behind the explorers came the sheep herders, always on the lookout for new grazing lands. Some of Australia's most distinguished families are descended from these early sheep herders. Most of the early graziers were squatters. They had no legal title to the land and just settled, or squatted, wherever they saw good pasture.

Later explorers made longer journeys into the desert and the north. One of them was Edward John Eyre, who in 1841 came upon

IMPORTANT DATES

1642	Tasman discovered and named Van Diemen's Land (Tasmania).
1770	New South Wales claimed for Britain.
1788	First colony, Port Jackson (Sydney), founded.
1797	John Macarthur began raising merino sheep.
1798	Bass sighted Bass Strait.
1803	Flinders circumnavigated Australian coast.
1813	Blue Mountains crossed.
1829	Swan River colony begun.
1851	Gold discovered in Victoria and New South Wales.
1853	Van Diemen's Land became Tasmania.
1862	Stuart crossed Australia from south to north.
1891	First federal convention.
1898	Second federal convention.
1901	Commonwealth of Australia formed.
1914– 1918	Australia fought in World War I.
1939– 1945	Australia fought in World War II; Japanese planes bombed Darwin (1942).
1945	Australia became one of original members of U.N.
1950	Australia contributed forces to U.N. command in Korean War.
	Australia became member of Colombo Plan.
1951	ANZUS Security Treaty between Australia, New Zealand, and United States signed.
1965– 1972	Australian troops fought in Vietnam War.
1970	Celebration of 200th anniversary of Cook's landing.
1974	Darwin destroyed by tropical cyclone.
1975	Governor-general dismissed prime minister.
1978	Northern Territory granted self-government.

the great salt lake in central Australia that now bears his name. Another was Friedrich Wilhelm Ludwig Leichhardt, who in 1844 and 1845 traveled overland from Brisbane to the north coast. John McDouall Stuart in 1861 and 1862 journeyed from Adelaide in the south to near the site of Darwin in the north.

Nationhood

The six early colonies grew and became states of modern Australia. The original colony of New South Wales occupied almost all the eastern half of the continent when it was founded in 1788. Three other colonies were later separated from New South Wales. One was Tasmania, which became a colony in 1825. Another, Victoria, became a colony in 1851, and a third, Queensland, was separated in 1859. Western Australia grew up around the Swan River colony, founded in 1829. What became the Northern Territory was originally a part of South Australia. The six colonies all became self-governing during the latter half of the 19th century.

The independent colonies soon realized the need to act together on certain matters. And toward the end of the 19th century, they began to see the need for unification. A first constitution was drawn up in 1891, and a second in 1898. The constitution was approved by the British Crown, and on January 1, 1901, the six separate colonies became states in the new Commonwealth of Australia.

History Since Independence

The new government soon established a system of tariffs, or duties on imports. This protected domestic markets from foreign competition, as well as serving as a form of taxation. The government also set up an immigration policy that encouraged British settlers to come to Australia.

With the outbreak of World War I in 1914, Australia joined forces with Britain and its allies. In World War II, Australia again took part on the side of Britain. Its forces fought first in the Middle East and then in the Pacific, nearer its own shores, when Japan entered the war in 1941. Japanese planes bombed the city of Darwin in 1942.

Since World War II, the Australian government has devoted much effort to breaking down the isolation of the remote areas of the nation by expanding transportation and communication facilities and establishing programs like the Royal Flying Doctor Service and radio and correspondence schools. The Department of Aboriginal Affairs was created to improve opportunities for the aborigines.

Increased demand and a scarcity of imports during World War II provided a major stimulus to Australian industry. In the economic boom that followed the war, Australia was faced with a shortage of labor. The government undertook a program to assist immigrants from many countries to come to Australia. Under the program, more than 3,000,000 immigrants have settled in Australia. But in the late 1970's, a marked decrease in the rate of population growth caused renewed concern for Australia's national and economic security. The country also lost its preferential trading status with Britain when Britain entered the European Communities in 1973.

Australia has become increasingly active in world affairs since World War II. It is a charter member of the United Nations. In 1950 it helped establish the Colombo Plan, an international effort designed to assist developing nations in southeastern Asia. In that same year, Australian troops were sent to Korea as part of the U.N. command. Australia signed the ANZUS defense pact with the United States and New Zealand in 1951 and joined the now-defunct Southeast Asia Treaty Organization (SEATO) in 1954. Australian troops were sent to Vietnam in 1965 but were withdrawn in 1971 and 1972 because of public controversy.

A significant proportion of Australia's national income each year is allocated to assisting the developing countries, especially those in the South Pacific region. Australia is an active member of the South Pacific Forum, which promotes co-operation among its members in the South Pacific. In 1978, in a further attempt to increase regional co-operation, a meeting of regional heads of government of the Commonwealth of Nations was held in Sydney.

CHARLES M. DAVIS
Formerly, University of Michigan
Reviewed by AUSTRALIAN NEWS
AND INFORMATION BUREAU

AUSTRIA

Charlemagne, the founder of the Holy Roman Empire, established a number of military districts in eastern Europe during the 8th century. One of these he called the Ost Mark, or Eastern March. The Ost Mark later became known as the Ost Reich, or Eastern Empire. From this ancient name we get the modern German name for Austria—Österreich. Austria grew, and by the 16th century it had become so large that its emperor ruled all of modern Austria, Belgium, the Netherlands, Czechoslovakia, Hungary, Spain, and all the Spanish colonies in America as well as parts of Italy and Yugoslavia. Today Austria is once again a small country. Wars, revolutions, and political changes have destroyed the empire and reduced the country to a fraction of its former size.

FACTS AND FIGURES

FEDERAL REPUBLIC OF AUSTRIA is the official name of the country. Austria is called Österreich in German, which means "Eastern Empire."

CAPITAL: Vienna.

LOCATION: Central Europe. **Latitude**—46° 22′ N to 49° 01′ N. **Longitude**—9° 22′ E to 17° 10′ E.

PHYSICAL FEATURES: Area—83,849 km² (32,374 sq mi). **Highest point**—Grossglockner, 3,798 m (12,460 ft) above sea level. **Lowest point**—Lake Neusiedler, 113 m (370 ft) above sea level. **Chief waterway**—Danube River.

POPULATION: 7,514,000 (estimate).

LANGUAGE: German.

GOVERNMENT: Federal republic. **Head of state**—president. **Head of government**—chancellor. **International co-operation**—United Nations, Organization for Economic Cooperation and Development (OECD), Council of Europe, European Free Trade Association (EFTA).

NATIONAL ANTHEM: *Land der Berge, Land am Strome* ("Land of the mountains, land on the river").

ECONOMY: Agricultural products—wheat, rye, oats, barley, potatoes, sugar beets. **Industries and products**—textiles, machinery, iron and steel, oil refining, chemicals, dairy products, tourism. **Chief minerals**—magnesite, graphite, gypsum, iron ore, petroleum, natural gas, bauxite, salt, talc, lignite, copper, lead, zinc. **Chief exports**—iron and steel, lumber, machinery, tools, paper, aluminum, electric current. **Chief imports**—machinery and transport equipment, coal, coke, wool, cotton. **Monetary unit**—schilling.

▶ THE PEOPLE

Austria's people have a mixed ethnic background. The population has remained about the same since the founding of the Austrian Republic.

Language. German is the official language of Austria. It is spoken by almost everyone. The non–German-speaking people in Austria are mainly Slovenes, Croats, and Hungarians. Most of these people live along the borders of Hungary and Yugoslavia. They all speak German as their second language. German is used in the public schools, but many country people still speak local dialects at home.

Religion. Most Austrians are Roman Catholics. The saints' days and church holidays of the Roman Catholic Church are important holidays in Austria. A small number of people belong to various Protestant churches. Austria had about 84,000 Jews before World War II, but by the end of the war only a small number remained. Many thousands were killed by the German and Austrian Nazis, and thousands more fled Nazi persecution.

Education. Austria has an excellent school system. School is compulsory for all children between the ages of 6 and 14. All children must attend elementary school, or *volksschule,* for 4 years. Students may then go on to several different kinds of secondary schools. If they wish to prepare for college, they attend *gymnasiums.* Trade schools, art schools, and technical schools train students for non-academic careers. Austria has four very fine universities. They are located in the cities of Salzburg, Graz, Innsbruck, and Vienna. The University of Vienna, founded in 1365, is the oldest and best known. Many foreign students attend summer-school sessions at these universities.

Dress. Austrians in the large cities wear modern dress. But for holidays and special occasions, people sometimes put on traditional local costumes. The women wear colorful dresses with aprons and elaborately embroidered headdresses. Men and boys wear short leather pants, called *lederhosen,* and simple shirts and jackets made of homespun linen or a coarse woolen cloth called *loden.*

Innsbruck, a well-known resort in the Tyrol Mountains, has been the site of the winter Olympic Games. It is built on the Inn River, a tributary of the Danube.

Overhead view of the capital city of Vienna, one of the cultural centers of the world. In the foreground is the famous Burgtheater, one of the city's many fine buildings.

Special Events. Religious holidays and other festivals are joyful occasions in Austria. These are the days when precious folk costumes are worn with an air of gaiety. In some regions, for example, there is the boisterous festival for scaring away the winter. The villagers wear ugly masks and make as much noise as they can with bells and drums.

Weddings are very special occasions in the villages. These are days of much singing and dancing. One of the most exciting dances to watch is the *Schuhplattler*. In this dance the men slap first their thighs, then their knees, and then the soles of their feet while the girls twirl around them in their bright dresses. They dance to the music of the zither or the violin. The musicians play faster and faster toward the end of the dance until the dancers are out of breath.

A favorite holiday throughout Austria is December 6, or Nikolo Day. This is the day when Saint Nicholas, or Nikolo (Santa Claus), visits Austrian children. The night before, the children always remember to leave their shoes where Nikolo will find them. In the morning the good children find presents in their shoes, but the bad children find only lumps of coal and potatoes. Krampus, a black-faced devil who is half human and often half horse, is supposed to accompany Saint Nicholas on his travels. Bad children are especially afraid of Krampus. It is said that he carries a broom to spank very bad boys and girls.

In January and February, *Fasching* (carnival season) is celebrated in many cities, towns, and villages. Elaborate costume balls are often part of the festivities.

Sports. Sports are popular throughout the year in Austria. Mountain climbing, swimming, water skiing, and sailing are favorite summer sports. The cold, snowy winters are wonderful for skiing and skating. There are hundreds of ski resorts in the mountains. Skiing is so much a part of the Austrian way of life that schoolchildren take ski courses between February and April as part of their school work. At this time of year, whole classes go to the Alps with their teachers for a week of skiing.

Soccer is Austria's most popular spectator sport. Large cities have huge stadiums and regularly scheduled soccer games. Like baseball players in the United States, soccer players are great heroes to Austrian children. Even the smallest Austrian village has its own amateur soccer team. Weight lifting, wrestling, and automobile and motorcycle racing are other popular sports.

Cultural Life. Austria is often called "the land of music" because so much of the world's great music was written by Austrians or in Austria. The greatest period of Austrian music, from about 1730 to 1830, produced Joseph Haydn, Wolfgang Amadeus Mozart, Ludwig van Beethoven (who lived in Vienna most of his life), and Franz Schubert. The two giants of music in the 19th century were Johannes Brahms, who spent the last 20 years of his life in Vienna, and Anton Bruckner. The Strauss family (especially Johann, Jr., and Johann, Sr.) made the Viennese waltz world-famous. Gustav Mahler continued the great Viennese tradition into the early 20th century. Arnold Schoenberg and Alban Berg were two of the leading modern composers. Austria is also the birthplace of one of the most famous Christmas carols—"Silent Night." It was written on Christmas Eve, 1818, by Franz Gruber and Joseph Mohr.

Vienna is the home of the world-famous Vienna Philharmonic orchestra, the Vienna State Opera, and the Vienna Boys' Choir. Three music festivals that are held in Austria each year attract thousands of music lovers from all over the world. The Vienna drama and music festival is held in June. The Salzburg festival, held in August, features the works of Mozart (who was born in Salzburg) and other composers. The Bregenz festival, also held in August, specializes in light opera.

Tickets to operas, concerts, and plays in Austria are often sold out weeks in advance. Even rehearsals are usually well attended by students. When the old Vienna Opera House was bombed during World War II, thousands of desperately poor Austrians contributed small amounts of money to restore the building.

Austrians are also proud of their many museums, art galleries, and famous buildings. Priceless art treasures brought to Austria in imperial days are now on public display.

One favorite Austrian pastime is to visit the cafés or coffeehouses. People gather in the coffeehouses to meet their friends, chat, read the newspapers, and enjoy delicious coffee and pastries. Coffee has been popular in Austria since the 17th century.

Science and Invention.   Austria is prominent in the realm of the sciences. Sigmund Freud, Alfred Adler, Ernst Mach, Gregor Johann Mendel, and Otto Rank are among Austrians who have made outstanding contributions to modern science. A number of Austrians (including persons born in Austria-Hungary) have been awarded the Nobel prize for their contributions to scientific research. Their names appear in the article NOBEL PRIZES, in Volume N.

Austrians have also helped in the development of such inventions as the typewriter, the sewing machine, the automobile, the slow-motion camera, and the screw propeller.

▶ **THE LAND**

Austria is wedged between seven other countries. Liechtenstein, Switzerland, and the Federal Republic of Germany (West Germany) are to the west. Czechoslovakia is to the north. Hungary is to the east. To the south are Italy and Yugoslavia.

Austria has five natural regions—the eastern Alps, the Alpine Foreland, the Granite Uplands, the Vienna Basin, and the Styrian Basin.

The Alps.   The Alps cover two thirds of the country. There are three main divisions of the Alps—the Northern Limestone Alps, the Central Alps, and the Southern Limestone Alps. The highest mountains are in the Central Alps. Austria's highest mountain, the Grossglockner ("great bell"), is located there. Deep valleys lie between the main ranges. Most of the people of the Alpine region live in these valleys.

Alpine Foreland.   The Alpine Foreland lies between the Alps and the Danube River in the provinces of Salzburg, Upper Austria, and Lower Austria. It is a region of fertile hills and valleys where cattle graze and vegetable crops are grown. The cities of Salzburg and Linz are both in this region.

Granite Uplands.   Just north of the Danube River are the rolling, forest-covered hills of the Granite Uplands. They occupy the parts of the provinces of Lower Austria and Upper Austria that lie north of the Danube River.

Vienna Basin.   The Vienna Basin, in eastern Austria, is the heartland of Austria. It con-

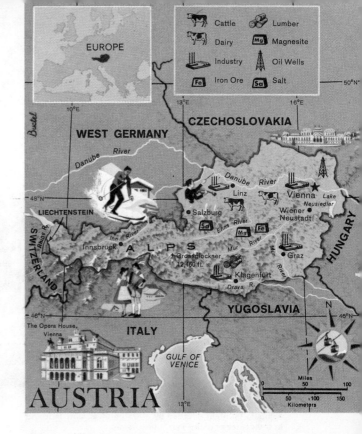

tains all of Austria's best farmlands. It is also the center of Austrian industry. Vienna lies in the middle of the Vienna Basin.

Styrian Basin.   The Styrian Basin, in the province of Styria, is south of the Vienna Basin. It is quite fertile. Grain crops and fruit are grown in its broad valleys.

Rivers and Lakes

The Danube is Austria's most important river. When the sun is not shining, the Danube looks brown and muddy and very different from the beautiful "Blue Danube" for which Johann Strauss, Jr., named one of his great waltzes.

Other important rivers are the Inn, Salzach, and Enns. All are tributaries of the Danube. These rivers are fed by melting glaciers in the Alps, and they flow too swiftly for river traffic. But they are an important source of hydroelectric power. Power from the rivers is used in Austria and is exported to neighboring Italy, Yugoslavia, and West Germany.

Austria has many beautiful natural and artificial lakes. The artificial lakes are in the Alpine region, where many rivers have been dammed for hydroelectricity. The largest natural lake is Lake Neusiedler.

A public fountain guarded by a statue of a saint is found in the center of many Tyrolean villages.

In mountainous Austria every bit of farmland is carefully tended.

Climate

Austria is the meeting place of three of Europe's major climatic regions. Northern Austria has an Atlantic, or marine west-coast, type of climate. This type of climate has mild, rainy winters and cool, moist summers. Southern Austria has a Mediterranean type of climate with hot, dry summers and mild, rainy winters. Eastern Austria has the hot summers and cold winters of the continental climate.

All three climatic regions meet in the mountains. Because of their height the mountains have their own climatic characteristics and are noted for their snowfall in winter. The foehn is an unusual feature of the mountain climate. It is a warm, dry wind that blows from the high mountains in middle and late winter. Like the chinook in western Canada, the foehn literally "eats up" the snow from the ground. Farmers are delighted to see the snow disappear from the mountains. It means that they can soon drive their livestock up to the mountain pastures for the summer. But they also fear the avalanches that sometimes hurtle down the mountainside when the melting snow becomes dislodged. The people of Austria call these terrifying snowslides the "white killers" of the Alps.

▶ **THE ECONOMY**

About half of Austria's people work in manufacturing, handicrafts, and construction. Only a small number are engaged in agriculture and forestry.

Agriculture and Forestry. Because Austria is very mountainous, only a small part of the land area is cultivated. The best soils for farming are found in the Alpine Foreland and in the Vienna and Styrian basins. Most of the land suitable for farming in the Alpine region is in the Alpine valleys. The valley bottoms and sunny slopes are crowded with small farms. Most farms throughout Austria are small or medium sized. Grains, potatoes, and sugar beets are the leading crops.

Cattle and sheep graze on the Alpine Foreland and in summer on the high, grassy Alpine meadows. They provide large quantities of meat, milk, butter, and cheese.

The middle slopes of the Alps are forested. Austria's forests provide valuable lumber and the raw materials for making paper.

Industry. Industry has grown rapidly since the end of Word War II. A number of basic industries were nationalized by the Austrian parliament in 1946. Today about half of the gross national product (the total value of goods and services produced in a year) comes from industry and construction. Oil refining and the making of textiles, machinery, iron and steel, and chemicals are among the leading industries. Tourism is especially important. Millions of visitors come to Austria each year, particularly to Vienna and various Alpine resorts.

Mineral Production. Austria has a number of valuable mineral resources. It is the world's leading producer of magnesite and an important producer of graphite and gypsum. Most of Austria's iron ore comes from the Erzberg ("Ore Mountain") in Styria. Bauxite (the source of aluminum), salt, talc, lignite (brown coal), copper, lead, and zinc are mined in other parts of the country. Austria has deposits of petroleum and natural gas but must import ever-increasing amounts of these important resources. Most of the oil is imported from Trieste, through the Adriatic-Vienna pipeline.

Transportation and Communication. Austria is served by an excellent system of electrical and diesel railroads and modern highways. These highways now cross the Alps and link all parts of Austria with the rest of Europe. Austria is also joined to the outside world by airlines. The Danube is an important waterway. New locks on the river not only store water in basins for the production of hydroelectric power but also have greatly eased navigation.

Austria's up-to-date communication system is owned by the government. There are many radio stations, and the first television station was opened in 1957. The telephone company in Vienna offers more special services than almost any other telephone company in the world. One number provides the exact tone of note A over middle C, by which callers can tune their musical instruments. Other numbers answer with the most popular song of the day, recipes, and stories. A new story is recited over the telephone each morning.

▶ **CITIES**

Many people in Austria live in cities. Vienna, like all the great European capitals, has a style of its own. Its location on the Danube River at the edge of the east European plain has made the city important throughout history. Today it is not only Austria's largest city and capital but the cultural center of the nation.

Graz, Austria's second-largest city, has so many parks and gardens that they cover more area than the city's buildings. Linz is a busy river port and rail and highway junction. It also has many steel and chemical plants. Innsbruck is known as a site of the winter Olympic Games. The spa of Baden, near Vienna, attracts many visitors to its famous hot springs. The city of Salzburg is considered one of the world's most beautiful cities. It is located on both banks of the Salzach River and is surrounded by mountains. Its music festival and *Fasching* attract many visitors. The huge fortress of Hohensalzburg overlooks the city. The city of Klagenfurt is both a popular resort and a busy industrial center. Other noted Austrian resorts include Semmering and Bregenz (on scenic Lake Constance).

▶ **GOVERNMENT**

Austria is a democratic federal republic made up of nine independent provinces. The provinces are named Burgenland, Carinthia, Lower Austria, Upper Austria, Salzburg, Tyrol, Styria, Vorarlberg, and Vienna.

The president of Austria is elected for a 6-year term. The president, who is the head of state, appoints the chancellor and, on the chancellor's recommendations, the ministers of government. The chancellor and ministers are responsible to the National Council. The National Council and the Federal Council make up the Austrian parliament.

▶ HISTORY

The discovery of ancient burial grounds at Hallstatt shows that people mined and traded salt during the early Iron Age in Austria. The first invaders, the Celts, continued the mining of salt at Hallstatt and at Salzburg.

By about 100 B.C. the Romans had penetrated the region. They made themselves complete rulers by about A.D. 10. Pannonia, as the Romans called the area, was an important frontier for the Romans against invasions from the east. One of their camps, Vindobona, grew into the city of Vienna.

From about A.D. 400 the Roman Empire grew too weak to defend its distant frontiers. Austria was overrun by invaders from the east. It was not until the time of Charlemagne in the 8th century that a stable government was established. In 976 the Holy Roman Emperor Otto II gave part of Austria to Leopold Babenberg. The Babenbergs ruled Austria for about 300 years. When the last of the Babenbergs died, Austria fell to Bohemia (now part of Czechoslovakia). The Bohemian king was defeated in battle by Rudolf of Habsburg.

Rudolf and his descendants governed Austria from 1278 to 1918. In 1273 Rudolf was chosen emperor of the Holy Roman Empire. His defeat of the Bohemian king in 1278 added the Duchy of Austria to his realm. Over the centuries the duchy grew into an empire that included most of east central Europe.

The Habsburgs, who ruled Austria until World War I, treated the country as their personal property. They stayed in power by arranging the marriages of their sons and daughters to the children of other rulers, by winning wars, and by making profitable deals with other countries. The history of Austria between 1278 and 1918 is largely the history of the Habsburgs.

"Kaiser Max." One of the greatest of the early Habsburgs was Maximilian I—"Kaiser Max." Maximilian was the real creator of the Habsburg empire. In 1477 he married Mary of Burgundy, who later ruled the Netherlands and parts of France. These lands were thus drawn into the Habsburg empire. Maximilian saw to it that his son Philip married Juana, heiress to the throne of Spain, so that Spain and its colonies in the New World were also brought under Habsburg rule. Maximilian's grandson Ferdinand married Anne, who later became heiress to the thrones of Bohemia and Hungary, bringing these two states into the Habsburg domain.

When Maximilian died in 1519, his grandson Charles V, then 19, became the ruler of more territory than any European monarch has ever had before or since. The Habsburg empire stretched across all of central Europe and included Spain as well. In 1522 Charles made his younger brother Ferdinand the ruler of Austria.

A Century of Wars. The Habsburgs were always fighting to protect their empire. In the 16th century Turkey conquered the eastern part of Hungary and held it for part of the 17th century while Austria was busy fighting the Thirty Years War. This was a fierce but not continuous religious struggle that raged throughout Europe from 1618 to 1648. After the Thirty Years War, Austria turned its attention to the Turks. In 1699, after two wars, the Turks withdrew their forces from Hungary.

In 1701 the Habsburgs were at war again. The last Spanish Habsburg had died, and Louis XIV of France claimed the vacant throne for his grandson Philip of Anjou. England, Austria, and the Netherlands lined up against France. This was called the War of the Spanish Succession. The war ended in a compromise. The grandson of the French King Louis XIV became king of Spain. England took some of the Spanish colonies. The Spanish Netherlands (Belgium) became the Austrian Netherlands, and Austria took states in Italy.

Once the Habsburgs almost lost their own Austrian Empire. In 1740 Austria's King Charles VI died. He had no sons and only one daughter, Maria Theresa. The law said that a daughter could not inherit her father's throne. But Charles wanted the Habsburgs to keep on ruling Austria. Before he died, he passed a law, called the Pragmatic Sanction, that made Maria Theresa the legal heir to the Austrian throne. Many foreign rulers tried to take the throne from Maria Theresa. The War of the Austrian Succession followed. Maria Theresa lost the province of Silesia but held on to the rest of her kingdom.

Maria Theresa followed the Habsburg habit of making political marriages for their children. She arranged the marriage of her daughter Marie Antoinette to Louis XVI of France. This ill-fated queen was beheaded by the guillotine during the French Revolution.

Joseph II, Maria Theresa's son, helped his mother to rule. When she died in 1780, he became king. Joseph freed the serfs and cut down the power of the nobles. His Edict of Tolerance granted religious freedom to Protestants and Jews in Austria.

Nineteenth Century. In the first half of the 19th century, Austria's foreign minister, Prince Klemens von Metternich, was more powerful than his rulers. To keep on friendly terms with France, he arranged the marriage between Napoleon and Austria's Archduchess Marie Louise in 1810. The peace that followed the marriage gave Metternich time to form an alliance against Napoleon. Austria, Russia, Prussia, and England combined to defeat Napoleon in 1815. Until 1848 Metternich was Europe's leading statesman.

By the 1850's the Austrian people were growing prosperous. New factories and railroads were built, and trade with other countries increased. The arts and sciences also flourished.

For 68 years, from 1848 to 1916, Austria was ruled by Francis Joseph. He was a good-natured man, well loved by his subjects. But Francis Joseph was the unfortunate ruler at the time when the Habsburg empire began to collapse.

During the 19th century many of the conquered peoples of the Austrian Empire began to demand greater self-government for themselves. The Magyars in Hungary, the Slavs in Bohemia, and the Serbs in the Balkans all wanted to be free of Habsburg rule. Their constant struggles seriously weakened the Habsburg monarchy. In 1867 Francis Joseph had to make Hungary an equal partner in his empire. The new empire was called Austria-Hungary. But other peoples had to wait until 1919 for their freedom.

War and Its Aftermath. World War I began in 1914. It was touched off when the Austrian Archduke Francis Ferdinand, heir to the throne, was assassinated. Austria, allied with Germany, lost the war. On the day of the armistice, November 11, 1918, Emperor Charles, the last Habsburg monarch, abdicated. Austria became a republic.

Many new countries were carved out of the old Austro-Hungarian Empire. Austria was cut down to an eighth of its former size. A new country, Czechoslovakia, was formed. Hungary became independent. Bosnia became part of Yugoslavia. Smaller parts of the empire went to Italy.

The small new Republic of Austria was in trouble from its creation. A quarter of the population lived in Vienna, cut off from the former territories of the empire. The economy was weak. Little Austria was an easy target for the Nazi dictator Adolf Hitler. In 1938 Germany took Austria without firing a shot.

World War II began the next year. Austria was forced to fight on Germany's side. The Germans were defeated in 1945. The United States, Britain, France, and the Soviet Union then occupied both Germany and Austria.

In 1955 the occupation forces finally withdrew from Austria. The nation regained its independence and declared its permanent neutrality.

In the years since, Austria has restored almost all of its war-damaged historic buildings, maintained stable government, and achieved remarkable economic growth. The country has continued to reaffirm its policy of neutrality in world affairs. Perhaps the best example of the success of this policy was the choice of an Austrian, Kurt Waldheim, as secretary-general of the United Nations in 1972. Waldheim was elected for a second term in 1976.

GEORGE W. HOFFMAN
University of Texas at Austin

Reviewed by KURT HAMPE
Former Director, Austrian Information Service
See also VIENNA.

AUTOBIOGRAPHY. See BIOGRAPHY, AUTOBIOGRAPHY, AND BIOGRAPHICAL NOVEL.

Autographs

Asking your friends to write in an autograph album may start you on a hobby that will last the rest of your life. There are two million autograph collectors, and every year they spend enormous sums to add signatures, letters, and documents to their collections. Your hobby need not be expensive, though. It all depends on what autographs you collect.

The word "autograph" comes from the Greek words *autos*, meaning "self," and *graphos*, "written." Sports stars who write their names for you on a tournament program or piece of paper are giving you their autographs. So are performers who sign your theater programs and authors who sign your copies of their books.

Many collectors prefer to solicit signatures and letters from celebrities in person or by mail. If you write to famous persons for their signatures, be sure to enclose self-addressed, stamped envelopes for the replies. Signatures are very interesting, but letters are more dramatic and usually more valuable. It is often a good idea to ask your correspondent an interesting question. The greatest autograph collection in the United States is in the Morgan Library in New York City. It was started by the financier J. P. Morgan (1837–1913) when he was only 12 years old and began writing to Methodist Episcopal bishops for their signatures.

The ancient Romans collected autographs, and letters of Virgil and Caesar were prized. In Europe during the Renaissance, students collected the autographs of their friends in pocket-size albums called *alba amicorum* (albums of friends). Today autograph collectors gather documents, letters, diaries, manuscripts, and composers' original scores.

The most popular collection in the United States is a set of the presidents' autographs. These can be either simple signatures cut from documents or letters handwritten and dated while the president was in office. In England and other European countries there is a similar interest in kings and queens, emperors, presidents, and dictators. It is not always easy to obtain an authentic presidential signature. Many presidents have used "proxy signers"—persons who have learned to imitate the signatures of other persons to relieve them of some of their work. Nowadays, too, electrical devices that make it possible to sign letters automatically—with one's own pen—have reduced the number of original signatures.

Another popular collection is that of the autographs of the signers of the U.S. Declaration of Independence. The two rarest signatures are those of Button Gwinnett and Thomas Lynch, Jr. Button Gwinnett was killed in a duel with his political rival 9 months after signing, and Lynch died when he was only 30. A letter of Button Gwinnett's was once auctioned off for $51,000. A complete set of signers' autographs was sold in 1978 for $195,000. But documents of many signers—Robert Morris, for instance—are available for less than $100.

Authors' original manuscripts are also particularly prized. Today many writers give their collected works to universities or other institutions so that the works will be kept together and preserved. If this had been done in earlier times, we would not have lost all of Shakespeare's original manuscripts. Even his signature is scarce. Only six authentic ones are known to exist. If another authentic signature were to turn up, it would sell for at least $1,000,000.

Books that are collected for their autographs fall into four types. Signed books have only the author's signature in them. Inscribed books include names of both author and owner of the book. The owner asks the author to write both their names. An inscription might read "To Ben Martin from Rosa Lopez." A presentation book is one the author presents to someone, writing in it to show it is a gift. The fourth type is quite different. It is valued for its association with something or someone that interests the collector. Usually it is a book that has belonged to a famous woman or man and has a signature or inscription inside to prove it.

When autographs are put on the market to be sold, they are classified as follows:

Cut Signature—a signature torn or cut out of the flyleaf of a book or from a letter.

D.S. (Document Signed)—a signature on a document that is more or less intact.

L.S. (Letter Signed)—a letter dictated to a secretary and signed by the author.

A.L.S. (Autograph Letter Signed)—a letter written personally in longhand and signed by the author. This is the most valuable.

Other factors deciding the value of an autograph are rarity, quality, and demand.

Some autographs sold during the 1970's, mainly at auctions, brought these prices:

A handwritten letter signed by Richard Nixon as president—$6,250; a short handwritten speech by John F. Kennedy—$8,000; a Paul Revere expense account, signed by John Hancock—$70,000.

Of course, what the letter is about has a great deal to do with its value. It does not even have to have been written by a famous person. The correspondence and diaries of people of no public importance who lived during unusual times, such as a soldier describing his experiences during the Civil War, may give valuable information or shed new light upon the happenings of those times.

In caring for your collection, it is wise to follow a few simple rules: Never attempt to make major repairs yourself, but be sure to take care of small breaks and tears to prevent further damage. Use thin strips of ordinary tissue paper applied with common white library paste on one side of the tear only and, if possible, not over writing. Never use glue or tape. Fold as little as possible. Remove clips and pins. Avoid direct light, heat, and dampness. Keep letters flat in folders and the folders flat on a shelf so the letters will not slip down and wrinkle.

Whatever type of collection you have, you will find many other enthusiastic collectors who will trade with you. Dealers will help you buy and sell autographs and check whether an autograph is authentic. Their catalogs give important information on available autographs and their prices. Many museums and libraries have excellent autograph collections you will wish to see.

Reviewed by CHARLES HAMILTON
Author, *Collecting Autographs and Manuscripts*

WILLIAM SHAKESPEARE
1564-1616

MARTIN LUTHER KING, JR.
1929-1968

BABE RUTH
1895-1948

WOLFGANG AMADEUS MOZART
1756-1791

LOUIS PASTEUR
1822-1895

SIMON BOLIVAR
1783-1830

FRANCIS DRAKE
1540?-1596

ISAAC NEWTON
1642-1727

CHARLEMAGNE
742-814

JEANNE D'ARC
1412-1431

MARK TWAIN
1835-1910

REMBRANDT
1606-1669

AUTOMATION

For thousands of years people have been busy devising tools and machines to make their work easier. Primitive people had little besides their bare hands to work with. Then the development of hand tools made it possible for people to cut and shape wood, stone, and metal. The next great step was combining mechanisms like the lever, the wheel, and the inclined plane into machines that would grind flour, press wine and oil, and raise water to irrigate farmland. For hundreds of years slaves or animals provided the power for these crude machines. Then the forces of nature were harnessed to the waterwheel and windmill. Later, the steam engine ended people's dependence on winds that sometimes did not blow and streams that sometimes dried up or froze. Automation is the latest stage in this process of substituting machines for people.

▶ WHAT IS AUTOMATION?

The word "automation" is used so loosely that even experts cannot agree on just what it means. Basically it is the technique of making a machine or a process self-regulating and self-controlling. The technique of automation has been applied to many tasks in factories, offices, homes, and transportation, to say nothing of its many military uses.

Automation is not the same thing as mechanization, which is using machines instead of hand labor. Machines can perform many tasks that are impossible to do by hand, and they can do the work faster and more accurately. But workers are still needed to operate the machines. With automation the machines either operate themselves or are controlled by other machines, without a human operator. Of course, human beings must make the machines, install them in the proper order, set the controls, and keep them running properly. But once the machines have been put in working order, they will keep on doing the jobs they have been "instructed" to do until they are shut off or break down.

Automation may mean performing a single job automatically, such as sorting filing cards or filling cement sacks. It may also mean linking together a group of automatic machines performing different operations to form an automated production line. Some processes, such as oil refining, may be completely automated from start to finish. Others, such as airplane construction, may be partly automated. Certain parts, such as engine blocks or wing panels, may be made automatically, but they must be assembled under human direction.

Whenever a process can be broken down into simple, repetitive operations, automation is possible. If the saving in labor costs is greater than the cost of automated equipment, then it is almost certain that the process will be automated sooner or later.

But not all things can be done by automation. Machines will not replace people in tasks that involve the use of judgment, imagination, artistic creation, and personal care or service. Examples are making business decisions or designing airplane engines; painting a picture or writing a prize-winning movie scenario; and arguing a court case or counseling a troubled child. There are also certain unskilled jobs, such as those performed by messengers and janitors, that it probably would not pay to automate.

How Automation Works

All automation involves three basic components: a **machine** to perform work, a **control** to detect and measure error, and **feedback** to correct the error. The heating system of a house is an example of a simple automated system. Here the machine is the automatic furnace, which is mechanically supplied with fuel and is lighted by an electric spark or a pilot flame. The control is the thermostat, a combination of a thermometer that measures the temperature of the air in a room and a switch that turns itself on and off. When the temperature in the room falls below the temperature the thermostat has been set for, the switch turns on the furnace. And when the room temperature rises to the level of the thermostat setting, the switch turns off the furnace. The error is the difference between the setting and the actual temperature in the room. Feedback takes place when the thermostat reacts to the error and turns the furnace on or off as needed.

If the room temperature is higher than the thermostat setting, this is also an error. However, the thermostat is not designed to respond to this "negative error." It merely remains off until the temperature sinks again.

What Is Feedback?

Feedback simply means the sending back of information about the work to the control unit so that the control will "know" what to do. Although the use of feedback in industry is fairly new, its principles have been known for a long time. In fact, feedback occurs everywhere in nature. If you should step into a shower that is too hot, feedback flashes the sensation to your brain so that you can either jump out or turn on more cold water. You are using feedback to read this page. After you have read one word, a control center in your brain tells the muscles in your eye to move to the right for the next word. If the next word is a very long one and your eye only moves a short space, your brain judges the error and orders the muscles in your eye to move a little further. All of this happens in a split second. When you finish the page, you reach to turn it. As your hand moves closer and closer to the edge of the page, your eye watches it, just as a crane operator watches the hook at the end of the cable. If your hand moves too far, your eye judges the error and feeds it back to your brain, which then controls the muscles in your arm. This may sound extremely complicated; yet you do it thousands of times a day without even thinking about it.

Since automation is a way of doing or making things, it may be used for any number of purposes that have nothing in common. Automation can be used to aim a battleship's guns and keep them on target during combat, to land a spacecraft on the moon, to keep supersonic airplanes flying on course at the proper speed and level, to manufacture automobile parts, to let a person dial a telephone number thousands of kilometers away without the help of an operator, or to do most of the work in a business office. Even some home appliances have been partly automated. There are washing machines that automatically fill themselves with water of the right temperature, wash the clothes, change the water, rinse the clothes, and partially dry them.

▶ AUTOMATION AT WORK

The many varieties of automation result from using many different kinds of machines, with an endless combination of control and feedback mechanisms.

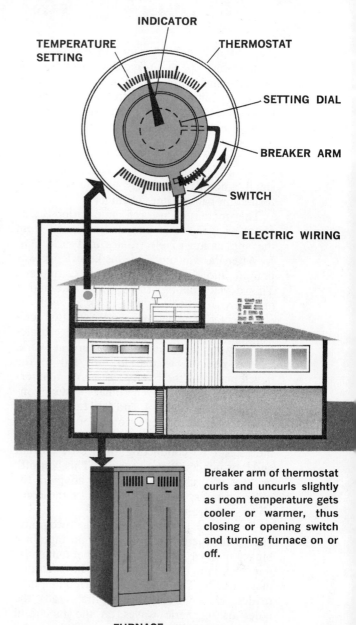

Breaker arm of thermostat curls and uncurls slightly as room temperature gets cooler or warmer, thus closing or opening switch and turning furnace on or off.

Home heating system is a simple and familiar example of automation. Thermostat reacts to changes in room temperature and turns furnace on or off as needed.

Although the basic ideas of automation were known years ago, they could not be put to use in manufacturing (except in a few limited ways) until the time of World War II. Instruments capable of measuring most kinds of error automatically and methods of feeding the information back to the machines' controls had not been developed. It is not difficult to apply automation to simple tasks like regulating the heating system of a house. The thermostat is nothing more than an electric switch that opens and closes itself at the proper temperature. But to measure the diameter of an engine cylinder to 0.025 millimeter ($\frac{1}{1000}$ inch) and feed information back to a cutting tool is something very different. Such delicate work could not be done until the development of electronics. With electronic devices, it became possible to measure very small amounts accurately and feed this information back to the machine.

The increased use of automation came about as a result of knowledge gained from the application of electronics in World War II. After the war much of this knowledge was poured into the development of computers. This development permitted the automation of many repetitive office tasks as well as complicated engineering and scientific calculations. Much was learned about electronics by studying these early computers at work.

This new knowledge in turn led to the development of the binary system of numbers for use in computers. The binary system contains only two digits, 1 and 0. The computer indicates numbers by groups of electronic tubes or transistors. Each tube or transistor indicates 1 by conducting an electric current and 0 by not conducting current. This "on-off" or "yes-no" characteristic was adapted for machine tools, along with some of the computer's electronic circuitry.

To control a machine tool, a "program" (set of instructions) is recorded on tape in a binary-number code. The numbers may be punched into the tape or may be recorded magnetically. The tape is then placed in a tape reader, an electronic device that reads the holes or magnetic waves on the tape and operates small electric or compressed-air motors called **servomotors**. The servomotors are built into the machine tool. They move the work or the tool into the correct position for the job indicated by the tape. To do this, the operation of the machine has to be broken down into a series of simple step-by-step operations. For instance, the speed of a lathe can be set in steps of 100 revolutions per minute. Other instructions in the same program may govern the number of passes the cutting tool will make and the depth of cut. The same tape can be used over and over to turn out thousands of identical parts.

A truly spectacular example of automation in the factory is the manufacture of automobile parts. One automated production line, for instance, takes in a rough block of metal and delivers it at the other end as a finished automobile engine block.

The engine block makes many stops while passing down the line. At each stop, or "station," several different tools go into action. Special transfer machines move the block from station to station. They pick up the block from one machine tool and place it in the next one in exactly the right position for the work to be done. By the time the block comes off the line, 555 separate operations have been performed on it. Holes have been drilled in it at exactly the right places. They have been finished to perfect smoothness, tested for correct size, and inspected for defects. All of this work has been carried out by machines, without the aid of human beings.

Many of the operations involved in making engine blocks and other metal parts for automobiles had been done by automatic machines for years before transfer machines were invented. But the blocks had to be moved from machine to machine by human workers. The transfer machines were the important new addition that transformed a series of unco-ordinated automatic operations into a truly automated process.

As long as the job can be broken down into steps and is repetitive, the computer can take the place of the machinist. In some cases it can do things that no human operator can do. In a milling machine the piece to be worked on is fastened to a table that has three possible motions: back and forth, right and left, and up and down. Each of these motions can be performed in steps of less than 0.025 millimeter. A computer can direct the three motions instant by instant, so that in a few minutes the workpiece can be shaped into forms that the most expert machinists could not duplicate even after many hours of work.

In some automated plants computers control the entire production line. These are plants where the job involves a continuous, non-stop process like refining oil or rolling steel ingots into plates, rather than a series of separate operations like the steps in machining an engine block. Because it can operate under conditions that no human being could

With automation, industrial machinery can be operated from a control center.

cope with, automation has now replaced most workers in up-to-date oil refineries.

Electronic instruments constantly measure the process and feed back information to the computer. The measured quantities are compared with the correct settings on the computer's program. If there is an error (for example, in the thickness of a steel plate or the flow of oil), the computer will correct it by sending a new signal to the rollers or the valves that are not set correctly.

At first the programs for the computers were punched on cards or tape. However, the high speed at which most plants of this type operate made it necessary to use magnetic tape instead. Punched cards or tapes are still used as the master set of instructions. Information is transferred from them to the magnetic tapes. If a change in any part of the program is necessary, it can simply be made on one or more cards and a new magnetic tape can then be made—or new sections can be spliced in to replace the outdated ones.

Some forms of automation are used in the storage, arrangement, and retrieval of information. Almost any kind of information can be recorded on punched cards or computer tapes and stored in so-called data banks. This information can be retrieved almost instantly with the aid of a computer. Typical items in a data bank are scientific information and statistics, such as population figures.

Automation is also being applied to the circulation systems of a few libraries. When you withdraw a book from such a library, a machine records the call number of the book and your library-card number. This information is stored in a computer that the librarian can use to find out quickly and as often as he wants what books have been charged out of the library. The computer will also print overdue notices on postal cards to be sent to the borrower. It can also print a list of books on any subject that a borrower wants to check up on. The actual work of taking books from the shelf and returning them to their proper place is still done by hand. But the computer automatically supplies the information on book borrowing in a fraction of the time the librarian would need to check a file of cards.

In an office or a bank, a computer can take the place of many filing clerks and bookkeepers. For instance, checks cashed in a bank can be put into a computer that will subtract the amount of each check from the correct account and then sort the checks for further handling. At the end of the month, the computer will print up statements to send to all the bank's customers from the information it has stored in its electronic "memory."

Stores make use of automation to help the management decide when to reorder the items sold in the stores and how many of each kind ought to be kept on hand in the warehouse. Each time an item is sold—a kitchen pot, a baseball mitt, an easy chair, a pair of nylon stockings—the sales clerk tears off the stub of the price tag and puts it into an envelope. Once a month all the stubs are mailed in to the head office. There they are run through a computer. Each stub is punched with holes in a code that indicates such things as the type of item, its size, and its price. Other information fed into the computer tells the time when this item was last ordered and how many were ordered then. With this information the computer decides when it is necessary to reorder that particular item and how large a quantity to order. This sort of work was done by human beings for hundreds of years. But the computer does it faster and with fewer mistakes.

▶ HISTORY OF AUTOMATION

Automation is as up-to-date as space flight, yet some of the ideas behind it are nearly 200 years old. The governor that James Watt invented in 1784 to keep his steam engines running at a constant speed is one of the first examples of the automatic control of machinery. This governor consisted of two metal balls attached to a vertical shaft driven by the engine. As the shaft turned, the balls, driven by centrifugal force, tended to fly outward. The balls were also linked mechanically to a lever that opened and closed the throttle of the engine. If the engine was running too fast, the balls would fly out and cause the lever to close the throttle and let less steam into the engine. With less steam the engine's speed dropped and the balls moved closer together. When the engine's speed had dropped far enough, the governor would cause the throttle to open wider and let more steam in.

Even before Watt, some people had hit upon the idea of making machines control themselves. Some windmills were built with a small auxiliary set of sails mounted at the tail end of the main shaft. This auxiliary set of sails, which looked somewhat like the tail rotor of a helicopter, kept the main sails pointed directly into the wind at all times.

In 1801 a French weaver named Joseph Marie Jacquard invented a loom that would automatically make cloth with complicated patterns woven into the material. Jacquard's loom was controlled by cards with holes punched in them. As each card moved into place it would adjust the loom for part of the pattern. The idea of giving orders to machines by using cards with holes punched in them is still used in computers.

A big step toward automation was taken near the end of the 19th century. Working out the results of the United States census had become very difficult because of the number of people and the amount of information required. The director of the Bureau of the Census devised a system for handling this huge and complicated task by machine. He used punched cards like Jacquard's. The holes on each card were arranged in a code pattern that stood for all the information the census takers gathered. For instance, a man's age, the city where he lived, and the number and ages of his children might all be shown by holes punched in a particular position on the card. The cards were fed into machines that added up the data and gave the correct totals.

Faster ways of doing arithmetic have been sought since man began to use numbers. The first mechanical calculator, the abacus, was invented over 2,000 years ago, possibly by the Egyptians. It is still in use in China and Japan. In a contest during the 1950's, a Japanese student with an abacus defeated a U. S. Army sergeant with an electric calculating machine.

Over the centuries several people tried to make a calculator that would work with gears like a machine instead of with beads sliding on wires like the abacus. One of these experimenters was the great 17th-century French mathematician Blaise Pascal. Most of these machines failed because parts could not be made accurately enough.

Early in the 20th century, machines to do

accounting problems in business offices were perfected. These machines were cranked by hand. In 1930 a gear-driven calculating machine that was powered by an electric motor was invented.

The first electronic computer was devised during World War II by scientists at the University of Pennsylvania. This machine was called the Electronic Numerical Integrator and Calculator (ENIAC). It was designed to solve the extremely complicated problems encountered in gunnery. Since ENIAC, the trend in computers has been toward reduced size, cost, and use of energy. One of today's microprocessors weighing less than half a kilogram can do the same work as ENIAC—and do it 20 times faster. The modern instrument uses 20,000 transistors and can be held in your hand, whereas ENIAC had 18,000 vacuum tubes and filled an entire room.

▶ HOW AUTOMATION AFFECTS OUR LIVES

By making it possible for machines to replace people, automation has created what amounts to a revolution in our ways of doing things. Like all revolutionary discoveries, automation has brought with it both good and bad.

On the good side, automation does away with much of the drudgery in work. Machines are taking over more and more of the repetitive, routine tasks that people find boring and unpleasant. Manufacturers thus need fewer

workers to turn out the same quantity of goods. Many products are better made because the electrical and mechanical controls of automated equipment are more accurate than the human hand and eye. Total production increases in some cases, which may lower the cost of producing each item and make goods cheaper. In some automated industries, the workweek has been shortened, and people have more leisure time.

In places where it is difficult or unsafe for people to work, tasks can be automatically controlled by machines. For example, many of the jobs necessary to the operation of nuclear plants have been automated.

On the bad side, many people who have been earning a living at routine, repetitive tasks may be left without work when machines

The old way: Mexican boys spin wool laboriously by hand. The new way: automated spinning machines run themselves.

Men below once prepared stock-market reports for a news service. Now their work is done by computers above.

in the case of people who have spent years learning a skill and do not want to lose their years of experience by starting out as beginners in a new field. These problems are part of the larger problem of unemployment.

The work force of the future will have fewer unskilled jobs. The need will be for more scientists and engineers to design automated factories and more skilled technicians to keep them running. Workers will need more education to be able to do their jobs properly, particularly in electronics and mechanical engineering.

Working conditions are very different in the automated factory. No longer are there large numbers of workers performing heavy tasks by physical strength or watching machines to see that they are working properly. Instead, whole plants are operated by only a few people who are seated at a central control panel. Maintenance technicians replace worn parts and adjust the controls of the machines.

People who are enthusiastic about automation point out that every step in the improvement of machines has put some people out of work but that in the long run there has been an increase in the total number of jobs. Other people point out that there is no guarantee that this will always be true. And history shows that when automation does create new jobs, it takes time for these new jobs to develop.

HAROLD I. SHARLIN
U.S. Department of Commerce

See also COMPUTERS; MANUFACTURING; TECHNOLOGY; UNEMPLOYMENT AND UNEMPLOYMENT INSURANCE.

replace them. Some of these people can be retrained to work in industries that have not yet been automated. Others will find new jobs in fields related to automation, such as building and repairing automated machines or making electronic parts. And some may find jobs in the expanding field of service industries.

Programs have been set up by governments and businesses to retrain people who have lost their jobs because of automation. But no satisfactory plan has been worked out for helping those persons who lack the necessary ability to learn a new trade. Another problem is seen

AUTOMOBILE MODELS

How would you like to own a large fleet of motor vehicles—everything from luxury cars and racing cars to trucks and vans, from motorcycles and buses to vehicles with four-wheel drive? You might even have automobiles that represent important developments in automobile history. Owning such a fleet is possible—in miniature—for those who build and collect automobile models.

▶ HOBBY WITH A HISTORY

Toy cars became a hobby a few years after the first cast-metal models were produced in the early 1900's. Some of these toys were very realistic, and people wanted to collect them. The first kits to build model cars did not appear until the 1930's, and they were merely blocks of wood with wheels. Plastic model car kits appeared after World War II. During the 1950's and 1960's, automobile dealers offered assembled plastic models of new full-sized cars. Because these models are rare, they have become valuable and are considered collector's items.

The first model automobiles with internal-combustion engines were built from metal kits in the 1930's. In such models fuel is burned inside the engines to produce power. These cars were guided by rollers that followed elevated rails on a wood or concrete racetrack. A few cars were guided in a circle with control lines like those used for some model airplanes.

Model racing cars with electric motors did not become widely available until the 1950's.

The first of these racers were guided by rails. But the system of using a slot, or narrow opening in the track, to guide the car became universal by 1960. The slotless system, in which cars are guided by a curb or wall, appeared in the early 1970's.

Radio control was developed for use in model cars with fuel-burning engines by 1965. The combination of rechargeable batteries, electric motor, and radio controls was not perfected until about 1975.

▶ TYPES OF MODELS

More models of automobiles are sold than any other single type of hobby miniature. There are models of every imaginable type of full-size vehicle. Most of these are available as metal or plastic ready-built models or as plastic kits to be put together at home. There are also hundreds of different powered racing models that duplicate the action as well as the appearance of full-size automobiles.

Hobbyists refer to the size of a model, when compared to the size of the real vehicle, as its **scale**. The scale is expressed as a proportion (such as 1:43) or as a fraction (such as $\frac{1}{43}$) of the size of the real vehicle. The larger the fraction, the larger the model. A $\frac{1}{43}$ scale model of a Chevrolet Corvette is about the size of a credit card; a $\frac{1}{8}$ scale model of the same car is about the size of a briefcase. The smallest size, $\frac{1}{87}$ scale, is known as HO scale.

Collector's Cars

Unpowered, ready-built model cars are by

A 1/25 scale model of a classic car, the Stutz Bearcat.

This 1/16 scale 1957 Chevrolet has working doors.

Electric slot racers can reach scale speeds of over 640 kilometers (400 miles) an hour.

far the most popular hobby models. These vehicles can range from postage-stamp-size racing cars, molded in plastic and selling for about $1, to desk-size all-metal models selling for about $3,000. The most popular collector's cars are metal models with some plastic detail pieces, in ¼₃ scale.

Most plastic model kits must be glued together and painted. But there are kits available with simple snap-together construction. Both types of kits include full interior, engine, and chassis details, such as windshield wipers, chrome trim, and hoods and doors that open and close. Sometimes model builders will modify (change) parts from other kits to fit the car they are building. The most common scale for American models is ¼₅, but there are hundreds of kits available in sizes ranging from ⅛₇ to ⅛ scale.

Racing Cars

The two main types of model racing cars are tabletop racers, which run on special tracks, and radio-controlled models, which are usually raced outdoors.

Tabletop Racers. The racing of slot and slotless model cars requires almost as much "driving" skill as racing full-size automobiles. Slot cars must stay in a narrow opening, or slot, to get the electric power needed to race. The cars must be drifted or skidded through the turns without going too fast, or they might spin out and leave their slots.

Slot cars are driven by an electric motor that turns gears to drive the rear axle. A transformer is needed to convert household current to the 12-volt direct current needed for the motor. Metal strips on each side of the slot are rubbed by metal pickup strips, called shoes, on the bottom of the slot car. This carries the electric power from the track to the motor. Hand-held controllers are used to change the speed of the cars.

Slot car tracks range from simple ovals to figure eights. Accessories, such as a lap counter and a grandstand, may be added to the set.

Slotless cars are also powered by direct current. The cars have metal pickup shoes similar to the ones on the slot cars. Imbedded in each lane of a slotless car track are three metal strips. One strip is shared by two cars and serves as a ground, to prevent an electrical shock. The remaining two strips provide power to the cars. This allows independent control of the two cars, even though both may be in the same lane. Cars are able to change lanes by moving from one set of strips to another.

Slotless cars must be steered in order to change lanes for passing. Hand-held controllers, similar to the ones used for slot cars, are used. On each side of the track is a molded plastic fence. The cars rub against this fence and are guided by it around the turns. Because slotless cars can change lanes, more accessories are available. Detours and pit stops can be added to the track.

Radio-Controlled Racing. In radio-controlled racing, a hand-held transmitter sends radio signals to a receiver in the car. These signals make the car speed up, slow down, turn right or left, stop, or go into reverse.

Most radio-controlled cars are powered by battery-operated electric motors. Batteries that can be recharged are available, so the

Slotless electric tabletop racing cars are guided by the "curbs" around the insides and outsides of the turns.

cars can be raced many times on one set of batteries. Some cars have internal-combustion engines for power. The most popular size for radio-controlled models is $\frac{1}{12}$ scale. The large cars, known as **hobby cars**, are $\frac{1}{8}$ scale and can exceed speeds of 50 kilometers (30 miles) an hour.

More expensive radio-controlled cars have transmitters and receivers that use different radio frequencies. This allows up to 14 cars to be raced at one time. In the United States, operators of these larger transmitters must obtain permits from the Federal Communications Commission. The transmitters for many of the smaller cars, known as **toy cars**, are not powerful enough to require a permit. The hobby racing cars have controls that respond instantly to any movement of the levers on the transmitter. With practice, you can duplicate all the maneuvers of a real racing car.

Both electric- and gasoline-powered radio-controlled cars can be raced outdoors. Paved parking lots and school yards are ideal. In many cities, there are also special rental tracks for these cars. Radio-controlled cars with electric motors can be raced indoors, but they need an area at least the size of a tennis court. Radio-controlled dune buggies and other off-road vehicles are raced in the dirt.

ROBERT SCHLEICHER
Author, *Model Car Racing:
Tabletop & Radio Control*

A 1/12 scale electric-powered radio-controlled racing car.

The start of the Indianapolis 500. Cars begin race in eleven rows of three. Starting positions are determined in time trials during the days before the race.

AUTOMOBILE RACING

When automobile racing began in the 1890's, the speeds were like those of a fast horse and buggy. The first major race, held in 1895, was from Paris to Bordeaux, France, and back. The winner averaged only 24 kilometers (15 miles) an hour. But the speeds of racing automobiles increased every year. By the 1960's, the racing automobile was nearly as fast as some kinds of airplanes.

Automobile racing includes events and classes for almost every kind of four-wheeled vehicle. The racing rules and formulas are established so that the vehicles in each class perform as much like the others as possible.

Racing takes place on many kinds of tracks. There are oval tracks, drag strips, and twisting tracks built around oval tracks. There are also cross-country races on public roads or on the dirt and sand. If a car is designed for one type of track, it can sometimes be raced on other tracks if minor changes are made in the car.

The emphasis in automobile racing has shifted away from pure speed. Race car designers now concentrate on improving the cornering speeds, braking, and fuel economy of their machines. Top speeds on a straight course have not increased much since the 1960's. But racing cars are getting around the tracks faster. This is because of improvements in tires, design, brakes, and aerodynamics (the study of the way in which air affects moving objects). It can be said, then, that winners of races are determined by the abilities of the drivers, the car designers, and the mechanics.

Modern racing cars have been made safer with stout metal frame bars, nonexploding fuel tanks, and built-in fire extinguishers. Race courses are now usually lined with safety barriers to help stop cars that go out of control. Safety helmets and fireproof driving suits provide more protection for the driver. But racing is still a dangerous sport, and the driver must be highly skilled.

▶ GRAND PRIX RACING

Grand Prix racing and sports-car racing are the only forms of automobile racing that are popular worldwide. The Grand Prix cars are meant to be the best road-racing machines. The top Grand Prix class is Formula One. It has this name because the cars must be built according to a set formula. The overall winner of Grand Prix Formula One races is really the "world champion" because many countries compete only in this type of racing.

The Grand Prix cars look and perform very much like the cars that race in the famous Indianapolis 500. But they have smaller engines, better brakes, and more cornering speed. They have only one seat, are very low to the ground, and have no fenders. In the past, Grand Prix races were held on public roads. The roads were closed to regular traffic until the race was over. Today the only public roads used for Grand Prix racing are those of Long Beach, California, and Monaco. All other races are held on tracks. Whether held on public road courses or on race tracks, Grand Prix races are from about 240 to 400 kilometers (150 to 250 miles) in length.

SPORTS-CAR RACING

No other mass-produced vehicle is as fast as a sports car over winding and twisting roads. Race courses that imitate such conditions are called road race tracks. These tracks are used for both production and prototype classes of sports-car racing. The production cars are regular sports cars. They are rebuilt for more reliability. But the parts are all regular parts. Only a roll bar and an open exhaust system are allowed as modifications of the cars that the public can buy. The prototype sports cars are built almost exactly like Grand Prix cars. They have a special body and engine not found in sports cars for sale to the public.

There are several sports-car classes, which are based on engine size. Sports-car races range from 30-minute regional races to international endurance events like the 12-hour race at Sebring, Florida, and the 24-hour race at Le Mans, France.

SPEEDWAY RACING

The most common type of speedway track is oval and measures about 1.6 kilometers (1 mile) around. Many classes of cars—such as Midgets, Sprint cars, Quarter Midgets, and Indianapolis-500-style "Championship" cars —race on oval tracks. All but the "Championship" cars often compete in regional or local racing series that include both paved and dirt tracks.

The "Championship" cars have a single-seat cockpit, a powerful engine in the rear, and no fenders. Throughout the year, "Championship" cars compete in races, some as short as 160 kilometers (100 miles) and some as long as 800 kilometers (500 miles). "Championship" racing climaxes at the Indianapolis (Indiana) Motor Speedway each Memorial Day weekend at the end of May. The famous Indianapolis 500 race (so named from its length of 500 miles) is held at that time on the speedway's 4-kilometer (2½-mile) oval track.

STOCK-CAR RACING

There is something especially exciting about

Above: Formula One cars roar through the curving streets of Monaco during a Grand Prix race.

Above: Tightly bunched stock cars vie for lead position.
Below: During "pit stop" at Indianapolis 500, mechanics make repairs and fill fuel tank in a matter of seconds.

Smoke pours out from engine and tires as dragster begins its run.

watching a race when the automobiles look like the family car. In racing, such automobiles are called stock cars. There are many different stock-car classes. A stock car can be the latest model of a car manufacturer, or it can be an old model called a jalopy. Some stock cars can reach 290 kilometers (180 miles) an hour on the banked turns of the large paved oval tracks. Jalopies are often the stars of the races held on dirt track ovals at county fairs. In some countries, stock cars are raced on road race tracks.

The rules for most classes of stock-car racing specify that only the outward appearance of the car and some of the major parts must be truly "stock," or standard. All the other parts—including the wheels, brakes, and moving engine parts—are special racing parts. A tubular steel frame is welded inside the "stock" body to protect the driver and to provide the extra strength needed for faster cornering speeds.

DRAG RACING

Short races in which automobiles accelerate to top speed on straight courses have become very popular. These races are called drag races in the United States and sprint races in many other countries. Drag racers accelerate from a standing start to very high speeds on a 0.4-kilometer (¼-mile) track. There are drag-racing classes for just about every type of automobile from compact sedans (enclosed cars) to hot-rod roadsters (open cars) and from stock to "hopped up" cars. Some specially built "dragsters" are about twice as long as normal passenger cars. Often they have no fenders. The fastest drag racers can

reach speeds of more than 360 kilometers (225 miles) an hour in less than six seconds.

THE LAND SPEED RECORD

Racing enthusiasts used to have areas closed off on weekends for speed contests. Today only a few areas are left. The most famous is Bonneville Salt Flats near Wendover, Utah. Most of the world's land speed records have been set there. Malcolm Campbell went 484.5 kilometers (301.1 miles) an hour in 1935. Craig Breedlove reached 966.4 kilometers (600.6 miles) an hour in 1965, and Gary Gabelich drove 1,001.5 kilometers (622.4 miles) an hour in 1970. In 1979, Stan Barrett went 1,190.1 kilometers (739.7 miles) an hour.

OFF-ROAD RACING

Vehicles with four-wheel drive—such as Jeeps, dune buggies, and special rear-engine racing machines—compete in a variety of automobile races on the dirt, off regular roads. The best-known off-road vehicle races are those on the dirt roads and trails of Baja, Mexico. Similar natural courses are sometimes laid out around the outside of paved race courses. Off-road vehicles also compete on many of the dirt track ovals. Or they use the same types of twisting dirt or sand tracks with jumps that motorcycles race on. There are even some "sand drag" acceleration races for off-road vehicles, where sand dunes or beaches are the race courses.

ROBERT SCHLEICHER
Author, *The Model Car, Truck
& Motorcycle Handbook*

See also KARTING.

AUTOMOBILES

On Christmas Eve, 1801, the hissing and clanking of a steam-powered carriage shattered the silence of the English countryside. At the throttle of this strange vehicle was its inventor, Richard Trevithick. He had designed and built it. According to many automobile historians, this was the first practical use of mechanical power to move a vehicle. Trevithick's carriage held eight passengers and is believed to have traveled at about 13 kilometers (8 miles) per hour. It had huge wheels, a horizontal boiler, and a tall smokestack. The carriage was little more than a novelty. Trevithick eventually took it apart and sold the engine to a mill owner.

Motorists today would hardly recognize the ancestors of their swift, sleek automobiles. But the basic idea and purpose of the automobile can be seen in early 18th- and 19th-century steam road vehicles.

What is an automobile? It is a self-propelled land vehicle that is capable of carrying passengers or freight over a roadway or smooth ground. The truck is basically an automobile that has been adapted to carry heavy loads. Unlike a train, an automobile can travel without the aid of rails. An automobile's power source is some form of motor, or engine. Power generated by the engine is transferred to the wheels and turns them, thus propelling the vehicle along the ground.

▶ HISTORY

No one person invented the automobile. Many individuals living and working in different countries and at different times contributed to its development. Many of the discoveries that went into the creation of the automobile were small in themselves. But together they were important.

The pioneers of the motor vehicle worked under discouraging conditions. They often were denounced and ridiculed. Their experiments were frequently dangerous, and tragic accidents occurred. Many a hopeful inventor saw the work of years end in failure. Others, whose machines worked successfully, had to stop their experiments because they could not get financial backing. But we owe the modern automobile to the knowledge that these people painfully acquired.

The Beginnings. The idea of a self-propelled vehicle has existed since almost the beginning of recorded history. In the Bible the prophet Nahum spoke of chariots that "shall rage in the streets . . . run like the lightning." Homer's *Iliad* describes the labors of the great god Vulcan at his fiery forge, striving to build golden-wheeled chariots that would be "self-moved."

The first recorded use of a self-powered vehicle was in 1769. Nicolas Cugnot, a French military engineer, designed and built an awkward but workable three-wheeled vehicle powered by a steam engine. The vehicle was intended as a tractor for hauling heavy cannon. It had a short career. It went out of control during a trial run and crashed against a wall. In 1770, Cugnot improved his design and built the more powerful tractor shown in this article.

Around 1784, William Murdock, an assistant to the brilliant James Watt, built a model road vehicle powered by a small-scale copy of one of Watt's steam engines. The model performed well, but Murdock never built a full-sized version. Watt apparently felt that the experiments might distract Murdock from his regular job of installing Watt's large pumping engines at mines. And he discouraged Murdock from further development of road engines.

Only a few years after Trevithick's brief success, the American inventor Oliver Evans built a steam-powered dredge that was equipped with wheels so that it could move on land. To demonstrate to the public that steam could move land vehicles as well as boats, Evans drove his machine around Philadelphia's Center Square for several days. Then he put it to work dredging the waters around the docks in the Schuylkill River. Evans hoped the demonstration would persuade rich people to back him in manufacturing steam vehicles. But most people of his day did not think that his invention was practical.

After the work of Trevithick and Evans, steam-powered vehicles rapidly gained popularity in England. A number of companies were formed to operate steam-powered passenger coaches. But these early steam coaches soon ran into opposition. Stagecoach and railroad operators resented and feared their competition. Farmers disliked them, and turnpike owners charged them extra-high fees to make up for the damage they supposedly did to the roads. Beginning in 1831, the British Parliament passed a series of very strict laws regulating the use of self-propelled vehicles. The climax was the Red Flag Act of 1865. It was so called from one of its provisions, which required a person to walk ahead of all "road locomotives" with a red flag to warn of their approach. The various laws imposed such high taxes and so many limitations that steam coaches could not operate without losing money. This greatly curbed automobile development in England until the Red Flag Act was repealed in 1896.

Meanwhile, experimenters on the European mainland and in the United States were pushing ahead. Building on the work of earlier scientists and engineers, the French engineer Jean Joseph Étienne Lenoir completed a workable internal-combustion engine in 1860. This one-cylinder engine ran on coal gas ignited by an electric spark. The Lenoir engine was designed as a stationary power plant for factories. But a small model was used experimentally in 1863 to power a road vehicle.

About 1865 an Austrian inventor, Siegfried Marcus, built and road tested a simple four-wheeled vehicle with an internal-combustion engine that used a liquid fuel. Ten years later he produced a second liquid-fueled vehicle. It ran successfully and is now preserved in a museum in Vienna.

In 1876 the direct ancestor of today's automobile engine was built by the German engineer Nikolaus A. Otto. Otto's engine used the four-stroke principle of operation—intake, compression, power, and exhaust. Automobile engines of today continue to operate on this principle. Otto's original engine, like Lenoir's, operated on coal gas, but it was soon adapted for use with other fuels. Otto's invention provided a relatively light and powerful engine that was important to later developments.

During the time from 1880 to 1900, the concept of the automobile slowly emerged. It was still mostly a rarity and a rich person's novelty. But people were beginning to take it seriously as a method of transportation. Most of these early automobiles were powered by steam or electricity. But the internal-combustion engine was soon to take its place as the standard automobile engine.

Why the Gasoline Car? The electric car was superior to the steamer or the gasoline car in several ways. It ran quietly and smoothly, without the vibration and smelly fumes of its rivals. It was easy to control. It did not require a complicated system of gears and clutches to transmit power to the wheels or to run in reverse. There were few moving parts to wear out. But it had a fatal defect. It could not carry with it an adequate power source. The batteries ran down—usually after a distance of about 30 to 60 kilometers (20 to 40 miles)—and had to be recharged. It was obviously more convenient to add a few liters of gasoline to a fuel tank than to recharge or replace a heavy, cumbersome battery. Besides, batteries large enough to power an automobile were very costly. Another count against the electric automobile was its generally low speed —20 kilometers (12 miles) an hour was a good speed for most electric cars in 1900.

Steam-driven cars were even more popular than the electrics in the late 1890's and early 1900's. More than 100 different makes of American steamers were placed on the market in those years. Steamers offered more power than the electrics, absolute silence, and a remarkably smooth performance. But their drawbacks were serious. It took a long time to build up steam, and doing so was a complicated procedure. Owners feared—largely, without foundation—that a boiler explosion or accident might result from the open fire under the boiler. Today, the best remembered of the steam cars are the Stanley steamers. They were made in Newton, Massachusetts, from the late 1890's well into the 1920's by Francis and Freelan Stanley, who were identical twins. In 1906 a Stanley steamer set a new world's land speed record at Ormond Beach, Florida. It hurtled across the sands at 205.3 kilometers (127.6 miles) an hour. By the time the last steamers were made in the mid-1930's, some very efficient and dependable machines were being produced.

The internal-combustion engine is much more complicated than either the steam engine or the electric motor. It has many more moving parts that can wear out. In its early days, it was tricky and temperamental. It frequently broke down or simply refused to work. But there are good reasons why it eventually became the standard power plant for automo-

1770 CUGNOT

1886 DAIMLER

1892 DURYEA

1901 OLDSMOBILE

biles. With all its failings, it produced more power in relation to its weight than the other types. When it broke down, it was relatively easy to repair. Its cruising range was limited by the amount of fuel in its tank but not by the availability of water or the endurance of batteries.

Gottlieb Daimler and another German, Karl Benz, are usually credited with being the earliest builders of successful automobiles with internal-combustion engines. Each produced a motor car in 1886. Daimler's greatest contribution was his light, reliable, medium-speed gas engine. The design formed the basis for the modern automobile engine. It is quite certain that Daimler's first machine was intended mainly for testing an all-purpose engine that could be used in boats, trains, airplanes, and the like. But Benz concentrated on the idea of

a vehicle fitted with a gasoline motor. He worked intensively on a design combining the motor, body, chassis (frame and wheels), and other parts into a well-planned unit.

In the early 1890's a French engineer, Émile Levassor, produced a chassis to fit Daimler's engine. The resulting vehicle, called a Panhard-Levassor, is regarded by many historians as the forerunner of the modern automobile. It was the first motor vehicle in which the frame was made separately from the body and suspended from the axles by springs. It also was the first to have the engine in front and the now-standard clutch-and-gear transmission.

Whatever source of power they used, the pioneer automobile designers had to overcome a common problem—the rear wheels had to turn at different speeds when rounding a curve.

In a horse-drawn vehicle, this was not a problem because each wheel revolved individually. But it was a different story when the wheels were turned by power. Some designers tried to meet the problem by connecting only one wheel to the engine. Some of the early steam coaches had a separate engine for each driving wheel. Neither of these solutions was really satisfactory. The problem finally was solved around 1880 by the invention of the differential gear by Amédée Bollée of France, who designed it for his steam coach.

The first automobiles were primitive by today's standards. Passengers rode high above the ground in open bodies, exposed to wind, rain, dust, and mud. Before the electric starter was introduced in 1912, a motorist had to hand crank an auto to get it going. Motorists had to contend with an awkward steering device like the tiller of a small boat, unreliable tires, and the absence of garages and service sta-

tions. At night, oil lamps had to be lighted by hand. But the many inconveniences did not discourage potential buyers. Many people believed that the automobile represented a new frontier for the 20th century. The fact that a person could have independent transportation by mechanical means was considered a miracle of modern technology.

Competition Plays Its Part. People always have been fascinated by contests centered on getting from one place to another—whether by foot, horse, chariot, or some other method—in the fastest time. As soon as early builders of horseless carriages had succeeded in making their vehicles run, they looked around for other such machines against which they might engage in contests of speed.

It is not surprising that motor racing started in Europe. Only there did enough machines exist, and only there were roads good enough. The first such contest was the Paris-Rouen

1907 RAMBLER

1912 BUICK

1918 MODEL T FORD

1924 DODGE

1931 CHRYSLER

1938 LINCOLN ZEPHYR

1947 STUDEBAKER

1954 CADILLAC

trial of 1894. It was not so much a race as a trial of reliability. It was staged to test the dependability of the vehicles, as well as their speed, over a 125-kilometer (78-mile) course. Nineteen cars started. All but four finished— a remarkable achievement for the period. A steam-powered De Dion-Bouton won.

America's first automobile race was run on Thanksgiving Day in 1895. The course was about 90 kilometers (55 miles) long, from Chicago to Evanston, Illinois, and back. The night before the race a blizzard swept through the area. The five contestants faced huge snowdrifts and rutted, frozen roads. Conditions were so difficult that some observers said the run would not have been possible with a horse-drawn vehicle. A gasoline-powered, American-built Duryea won the event.

The race focused attention on the horseless carriage in a very special way. It showed dramatically that the automobile was a practical means of transportation within the grasp of the ordinary citizen.

Following the 1895 race, contests of an amazing variety were staged. There were road races, through choking clouds of dust; climbs, up steep hills and mountains; sealed-bonnet contests, in which hoods could not be raised; events that pitted specialized speed machines against one another or tested the reliability of stock cars; and so on. Those early races subjected the automobile to fierce competition. That helps explain why the American automobile improved rapidly in its first few decades.

Car manufacturers in the United States had another reason for rapid improvement of their automobiles. For hundreds of years Europe had had a good system of roads. Some of them, paved with brick, had been built by the Romans in the 3rd century B.C. They linked many of western Europe's important cities. The situation was entirely different in the United States. As recently as 1904 all the hard-surfaced roads in the country laid end to end would have totaled only about 65,000 kilometers (40,000 miles). Most roads were narrow, filled with ruts, and often so muddy that cars had to be pulled out by horses. Car builders had to adapt their vehicles to the poor roads. As a result, early American automobiles were more rugged, more powerful, and more dependable than most European cars.

▶ **AUTOMOBILE MANUFACTURING**

There were only 8,000 automobiles in the United States in 1900. The country had fewer skilled workers than Europe. But it had advantages that would make it the automobile-

AUTOMOBILES OF THE 1970'S

VOLVO (Swedish)

MUSTANG (American)

JAGUAR (British)

FIAT (Italian)

VOLKSWAGEN (German)

CHEVROLET (American)

TOYOTA (Japanese)

CITRÖEN (French)

PINTO (American)

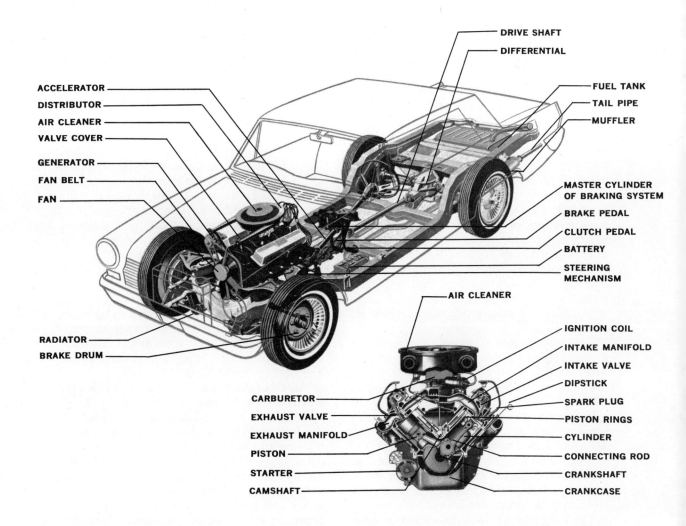

ACCELERATOR
DISTRIBUTOR
AIR CLEANER
VALVE COVER
GENERATOR
FAN BELT
FAN
RADIATOR
BRAKE DRUM

DRIVE SHAFT
DIFFERENTIAL
FUEL TANK
TAIL PIPE
MUFFLER
MASTER CYLINDER OF BRAKING SYSTEM
BRAKE PEDAL
CLUTCH PEDAL
BATTERY
STEERING MECHANISM

AIR CLEANER

CARBURETOR
EXHAUST VALVE
EXHAUST MANIFOLD
PISTON
STARTER
CAMSHAFT

IGNITION COIL
INTAKE MANIFOLD
INTAKE VALVE
DIPSTICK
SPARK PLUG
PISTON RINGS
CYLINDER
CONNECTING ROD
CRANKSHAFT
CRANKCASE

manufacturing center of the world. It had practically all the raw materials needed to build an automobile, plenty of fuel for both factory and car, and a good supply of labor. And there was a great potential market for the finished product.

Two brothers, Charles E. and James F. Duryea, are considered to have been the first Americans to make and market a successful gasoline automobile. James Duryea completed the first Duryea automobile in 1893, in Springfield, Massachusetts, working from his brother's design. Their second car was the winner of the 1895 Chicago race mentioned earlier. The $2,000 prize money helped the brothers establish the Duryea Motor Wagon Company. In 1896 the company produced 13 automobiles.

The Olds Motor Vehicle Company established a factory in Detroit, Michigan, in 1899. The company, started by Ransom E. Olds, became the first in the United States to produce and sell cars on a large scale. In 1901, the firm made 425 cars. This was mass production on a scale never seen before. The success of the Olds operation did much to establish Detroit as the "Motor Capital of the World."

Although Olds was the first company to produce cars in quantity, Henry Ford is considered the founder of modern automobile mass production. Ford built his first gasoline-powered automobile in Detroit in 1896. In 1903 he formed the Ford Motor Company. In the first three months, the Ford Company turned out 150 cars. By the end of September, 1904, it had built and sold 1,708 cars.

Until 1908, Ford had been producing a

variety of models that were low, medium, and high priced. But in October of that year he brought out the the famed four-cylinder Model T. Its success eventually led him to drop all other models. More than 10,000 Model T's were sold in the first year.

To keep prices down, Ford decided to produce the car in large volume. In 1912 he began buying huge quantities of parts and announced that he intended to build 75,000 identical Model T automobiles. This was the first time that automobile manufacture had been truly standardized. It meant that a spark plug, a wheel, or a gear from one Model T would be interchangeable with the same part in any other Model T.

Ford's methods were soon adopted by other manufacturers, and they have been used ever since. Nearly every automobile on the highways today is a mass-produced, standardized automobile.

The manufacture of today's automobile is a combination of ideas—the public's idea of what kind of car it needs and the manufacturer's idea of what kind of car will best fit this need. When the manufacturer finally decides to start work on a new model, these ideas begin to take shape. Engineers, stylists, and designers decide how the car should look and perform. From highly detailed sketches and drawings, a full-scale clay model of the car is built. Exact measurements of the model are taken, and blueprints are drawn.

The blueprints are then placed in the hands of hundreds of specialists who plan the production. Step by step the specialists build the car from the ground up. They design and make working models of the various parts that will go into the car. Engineers re-design or improve engines or, if necessary, design an entirely new engine to suit the car. Other engineers experiment with various types of frames, axles, gears, brakes, and other components to see which will perform best under the most grueling conditions. Many of these parts are seldom seen by the car's owner. But their construction and operation are vital to comfort and safety.

Styling engineers select paint finishes and interior fabrics and trim and design the instrument panel and other accessories. Production specialists work on the methods, machines, and tools to make the car. If a new part has been designed for the car, they must figure out how much it will cost and how quickly it can be made.

Eventually a prototype, or sample version, of the car makes its appearance. It has taken months—sometimes years—of painstaking research, design, and engineering to produce the prototype. But two vital questions still must be answered before it goes into production. First, will it perform satisfactorily, and second, is it a car that the public wants?

The sample car is put through a great many tests to see whether anything is wrong with it. It is placed in special "torture" chambers, where it is frozen and thawed, drenched by tons of water, shaken, and twisted until all the flaws have been spotted and corrected. When the laboratory tests have been completed, the prototype car is driven over a proving ground or test track, where it is subjected to far more severe punishment than the average automobile will undergo. Day after day it is driven up and down steep hills, through mud baths, and over the worst kinds of roads.

All this testing leads to changes in design, when necessary, and to more testing. Even when the car is placed in production, samples are frequently taken directly from the assembly line and put through the same tests. The parts from which the car is assembled go through a constant inspection and testing process. This system, which most manufacturers call **quality control**, not only leads to improvements in the car but assures them that it is being built properly.

While the prototype is undergoing its many tests, production engineers are planning how to manufacture the car in quantity. They design machines that will turn out the various parts of the car. Some of these machines, such as those that stamp out the roofs or fenders, take up as much space as an ordinary house and stand several stories high. Other machines are set in rows, or banks, and parts such as engine blocks are automatically moved from one machine to another as different drilling and grinding operations are performed.

Before large-scale production starts, engineers must figure out the most efficient way to assemble the cars. They know that each machine must do its work in harmony with other machines, so that the proper number of parts are produced at the right time and delivered

Assembly-line workers get ready to connect automobile body to engine and chassis.

to the proper place. Often they will build a miniature factory—complete to the last conveyor belt, machine, and worker—to aid them in their planning. Today's mass production of automobiles takes split-second timing, and the scale models help the planning engineers avoid costly mistakes.

At last production begins. Modern automobile production is very much like a great river. The main river is fed by side rivers, which are fed by streams, and so on, back to the points where snow melts and rainfall trickles into gullies to form brooks.

The "main river" of the automobile industry is the assembly line, an endless moving belt that carries parts. As a basic part, such as an engine block, passes certain points, other parts are added, either by automatic machines or by workers. "Feeder" assembly lines bring the parts to specified locations in time to be added to the basic unit. There are many sub-assembly lines feeding parts and assembled units, such as carburetors, into the main assembly line. There are some 18,000 parts in the average automobile, ranging in size from the roof and engine hood to the tiny screws used in the speedometer. Nearly every part has been transported on an assembly line before it becomes a part of the finished automobile.

Once the sub-assemblies have been completed, they are ready to be fitted together into major pieces of the car. There are three such major pieces, or assemblies. They are the **chassis**, which includes all the underpart of the car—the frame, wheels, and other components, such as the brake system—the **engine**, and the **body**.

The exact methods of the final assembly vary widely among automobile manufacturing companies, but the basic pattern is similar.

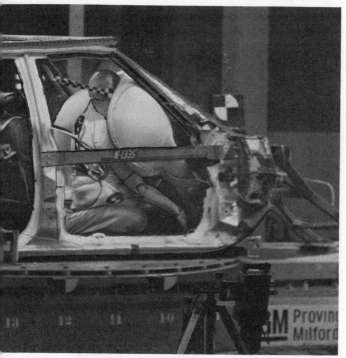

An experimental collision in a test vehicle. An air bag inflates to protect the human-sized dummy.

First the two sub-assembly lines carrying the chassis and the engine meet and the two assemblies are fitted together. Then the chassis-and-engine assembly is joined to the body to produce a nearly completed car.

This operation, called the "body-drop," is one of the most dramatic spectacles in automobile manufacturing. The conveyor brings the chassis and engine into position. Then the body is slowly lowered from an overhead balcony or assembly line. Guided by workers, the body settles gently onto the chassis, and the two are fastened together with bolts.

Some companies use an integrated, or single-unit, type of construction, with the body and chassis welded together to make one instead of two major assemblies. Some companies use both systems, depending on the type or size of vehicle that is being manufactured.

Many smaller but necessary operations are performed and parts added as the car moves on. Seats and floor mats are installed, and the electrical system is connected. Heater hoses are hooked up, and various pieces of trim are added. Finally, at the end of the line, gasoline is pumped into the tank, and water is added to the radiator. An employee slides behind the wheel, starts the engine, and drives the car off the line. But the car is not ready for its first owner yet. Inspectors swarm over the car, adjusting headlights and checking details such as wheel alignment and the operation of door latches and window controls. At last the car is ready for the road.

▶ ECONOMIC IMPACT OF THE AUTOMOBILE

The automotive industry is one of the world's biggest producers and merchandisers. At the same time it is one of the greatest buyers. It consumes large quantities of raw materials of all kinds, including nearly one fourth of the annual steel output of the United States. One out of every seven wage earners in the United States is connected with the industry. In Canada it is one of the largest manufacturing employers.

According to figures of the U.S. Department of Commerce, one out of every six businesses in the United States is an automotive business. The many people employed by these businesses are distributed throughout the 50 states. They work for motor vehicle and parts manufacturers; automotive retail and wholesale dealers and service businesses; commercial bus, truck, and taxi lines; highway construction companies; and petroleum refineries.

Even greater is the employment that the automotive industry creates indirectly by the business it does with other industries. Motor vehicle manufacturers spend as much as 50 cents out of every dollar they make to buy materials and equipment from other companies. One major automobile manufacturer, for example, buys various items from some 31,000 different firms. This great volume of business keeps many thousands of people employed.

The supplier system of the automotive industry can be described as an economic chain reaction. Each supplier has its own suppliers, who in turn buy from other producers, until the chain finally reaches the suppliers of the basic materials—the farms, mines, and mills in every part of the country.

An even greater chain reaction takes place when the automobile rolls off the final assembly line. Hundreds of trucking firms do nothing but haul new cars from the factory to the dealers. The dealers themselves employ staffs of salespeople and mechanics, and their advertisements bring earnings to newspapers and radio stations. Nationwide networks of service stations supply gasoline and oil to keep cars running. Service stations in turn purchase their supplies from oil companies. Cars need regular servicing if they are to perform properly, and this keeps an army of mechanics busy. Worn and damaged parts must be replaced, and this creates business for parts' manufacturers and suppliers. The automotive sales and service industry, including filling-station sales, amounts to $120,000,000,000 (billion) or more a year for the United States alone.

Motor transportation touches our lives at almost every point. Products go to market by truck. Children go to school by bus. Construction of highways, bridges, and buildings depends on trucks and other automotive equipment. The fire and police departments would be paralyzed without fleets of motor vehicles. Even garbage is collected and carried off by specially equipped trucks.

For years motor touring has been a major industry in almost every state of the United States and every province of Canada. Roadside businesses—such as drive-in theaters, restaurants, motels, and shops—depend for their existence on automobile travelers. Using an automobile is so much a part of people's lives that there are drive-in banks and even drive-in church services. People in the United States own about 40 percent of the world's cars, trucks, and buses. Japan is in second place in the number owned. Other countries that rank high are West Germany, France, Italy, the United Kingdom, and Canada.

▶ HOW AUTOMOBILES ARE CHANGING

Automobiles are essential to the economies and the way of life of many countries. Yet the large numbers of vehicles on the roads have caused safety, environmental, and energy problems. Since the late 1960's, pressure has been brought to bear on automobile designers and engineers to solve these problems. Such pressure has had important effects on the shape and mechanical design of automobiles being manufactured today.

Air Pollution. Automobiles are important contributors to air pollution. Exhaust emissions from the burning of fuel and evaporation from the gasoline system can release harmful chemicals into the atmosphere. These chemicals include hydrocarbons, nitrogen oxides, and carbon monoxide.

Beginning with 1968 models, automobiles sold in the United States have been subject to federally prescribed clean-air standards. Intensive research has led to steadily cleaner

---

Why is the engine of an automobile usually up front?

Some early automobiles had engines under the seat or in the back, but many automobile builders copied the design of horse-drawn carriages and put the engine where the horse had been. Technical factors had an effect, too. It was found that it was easier to keep the engine from overheating at the front end of the car, since the onrushing air helped cool it. And control linkages from the dashboard were less complicated to arrange with a front engine. A number of rear-engine cars are built now, but engineers still find it easier to design cars with the engine in front.

emissions. By the end of the 1970's, cars produced 90 percent less hydrocarbons than the uncontrolled vehicles of the early 1960's. Systems were devised that routed engine exhaust back into the cylinders, where they were burned. Catalytic converters were later added. These are units through which hot exhaust gases are circulated and cleaned. It was also found that emission control could be aided by adjusting the mixture of air and gasoline in the carburetor and making other engine modifications.

Fuel Supplies. A new approach to automobile design has also become necessary because of a dwindling gasoline supply. The saving of fuel has become a major goal of car makers. Since lightweight cars need less gasoline than heavy cars, one trend has been toward smaller size and reduced weight of automobiles. New compact and subcompact (smaller than compact) cars have been designed and built. Manufacturers drastically cut the weight of cars by using plastics and lightweight metals in place of heavier metals such as steel.

Smaller, more compact engines are being designed. Diesel engines are becoming more popular. Engineers are working with designs of turbine engines that will use less fuel. Work is under way to see whether the cars of tomorrow could be powered by steam or electricity, by a mixture of gasoline and alcohol (called gasohol), by hydrogen gas, or even by coal gas.

Engineers also have created a variety of electronic devices to help conserve fuel. For example, an electronic carburetor containing a microprocessor (a tiny computerlike device) is being tested. It monitors the amount of oxygen in exhaust gases. And it can adjust the mixture of fuel and air in the carburetor so that fuel is burned efficiently and with as few pollutants as possible. Another example is a small computer that has a display panel on the car's dashboard. It can calculate average speed, average fuel consumption on a trip, driving distance on the gas remaining in the tank, and engine speed and temperature. Such devices add to the efficiency of the automobile.

JAMES J. BRADLEY
National Automotive History Collection
Detroit Public Library

See also ENGINES; INTERNAL-COMBUSTION ENGINES; MASS PRODUCTION; TRANSMISSIONS; TRANSPORTATION; TRUCKS AND TRUCKING.

A technician checks one of the 18 batteries in an experimental electric-powered car.

The Boeing 747 is the world's largest passenger plane. It can hold nearly 400 people.

AVIATION

For thousands of years people dreamed of having the ability to fly. Mythology and folklore are filled with tales of supernatural beings who could fly. Yet as recently as the year 1900, most people thought that anyone who took the idea of a "flying machine" seriously was an impractical dreamer. Now flying is a part of everyday life. In fact, it is so much a part of our lives that we tend to take it for granted.

Aviation has brought truly revolutionary changes, especially since World War II. For one thing, the airplane has shrunk the world in terms of travel time. No place in the world is more than 24 hours away from any other by air. A traveler can board a plane in New York and arrive in London in less than four hours. This trip would have taken several days on the fastest ocean liner before World War II. (It took Columbus 70 days to sail from Spain to the West Indies.) It is not unusual for business executives to fly to a meeting several hundred kilometers away—and return home the same day. A letter mailed in the city of Quebec, in eastern Canada, will reach Vancouver, on Canada's west coast, in a day by airmail. It would take the same letter several days to cross the continent by ground transportation.

Airplanes also are useful to industry. They speed goods from factories to waiting customers in a fraction of the time it would take by train or truck. Airplanes take vaccines, antibiotics, and other lifesaving drugs, as well as food, to victims of earthquakes, floods, and other disasters. Airplanes can deliver fresh tropical fruits to northern markets. Vital machinery and parts can be carried quickly to isolated mining camps and construction sites. Ranchers and farmers use airplanes to round up cattle and to spray crops. The growth of aviation has led to new occupations calling for special skills and has created new job opportunities.

Aviation has made other changes, too. It has made war more devastating than was ever imagined in the past. Supersonic bombers and missiles can carry deadly weapons to any spot on the globe. Isolation is no longer a defense. On the bright side of the picture, aviation is bringing the peoples of the world closer together and helping them to understand one another better. And aviation makes it possible for the leaders of nations to meet quickly face to face to settle emergencies. Finally, the airplane and its "child," the space vehicle, have opened new areas for exploration and discovery in outer space.

Because aviation is largely concerned with airplanes, this article will concentrate on their story. Helicopters, gliders, and balloons are each discussed in separate articles, in volumes H, G, and B.

An airplane is a heavier-than-air craft that is powered by one or more engines. It is too heavy to float through the air like a balloon. It can fly only because of its engine or engines, which give it forward thrust, and its wings, which convert part of the forward motion into lifting force.

The Airframe

An airplane's structure is made up of six basic components, or parts. Each of these components is vital to safe operation. Every airplane must have wings to support it in the air against the force of gravity. It must have an engine to provide power. It needs a landing gear to take off and land safely. A fuselage, or body, is necessary to house the pilot and crew members and to carry passengers and cargo. Stabilizers must be provided to keep the plane steady in the air. Control surfaces are necessary so that the pilot can control the direction of flight. These basic components, minus the engine, make up what is called the airframe.

The Wing. An airplane wing usually is relatively flat on the bottom and curved on the top. It is this shape that gives the wing its lifting power. Air passing over the curved top moves faster than air passing under the relatively flat bottom. This creates a difference in pressure, so that the wing is pushed up from beneath. The faster the wing is passing through the air, the greater the lifting effect will be.

The distance from the leading edge to the trailing edge of the wing is called the **chord**. The distance from wing tip to wing tip is the **span**.

For many years the standard shape for aircraft wings was more or less straight, with a certain amount of taper from fuselage to wing tip. But the development of aircraft that could fly near or above the speed of sound brought new problems. It was found that wings extending straight out from the fuselage could not stand the stress of extremely high-speed flight. New shapes had to be developed. Near-sonic and supersonic aircraft use swept-back (V-shaped) or delta (triangular) wings.

Even stranger shapes have been tested by engineers. One type featured extremely short wings that gave the craft the appearance of a barbed arrow. Another design, going to the opposite extreme, was made up almost entirely of a flying wing.

The Fuselage. Most modern airplane fuselages are built with **semi-monocoque** construction. *Monocoque* is a French word meaning "single shell." In a monocoque fuselage, most of the stresses are carried by the shell, or skin. Small airplanes are often built with monocoque construction to save weight. But monocoque construction is not strong enough or rigid enough for large cargo planes or airliners. Lengthwise bracing and stiffeners are added. This is called semi-monocoque construction.

Because modern jet passenger planes fly at high altitudes where the air is extremely thin, the cabin must be **pressurized**. That is, the pressure of the air inside the cabin must be only a little lower than it would be on the ground. Otherwise, the passengers would suffer from a lack of oxygen. The fuselage must be strong enough to withstand the difference between outside and inside pressure. It must also be airtight so that the air will not leak out. Tobacco smoke and odors are removed through the plane's ventilating system.

The Stabilizers. At the tail end of the fuse-

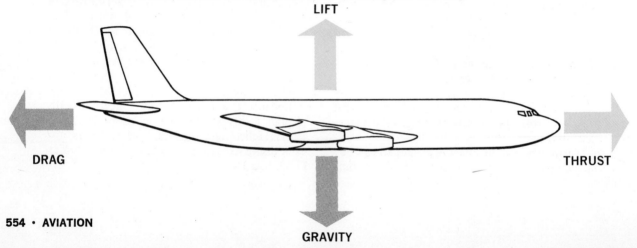

Four forces—lift, thrust, gravity, and drag—act on every plane in flight. For the plane to stay airborne, lift must be greater than gravity, and thrust must be greater than drag.

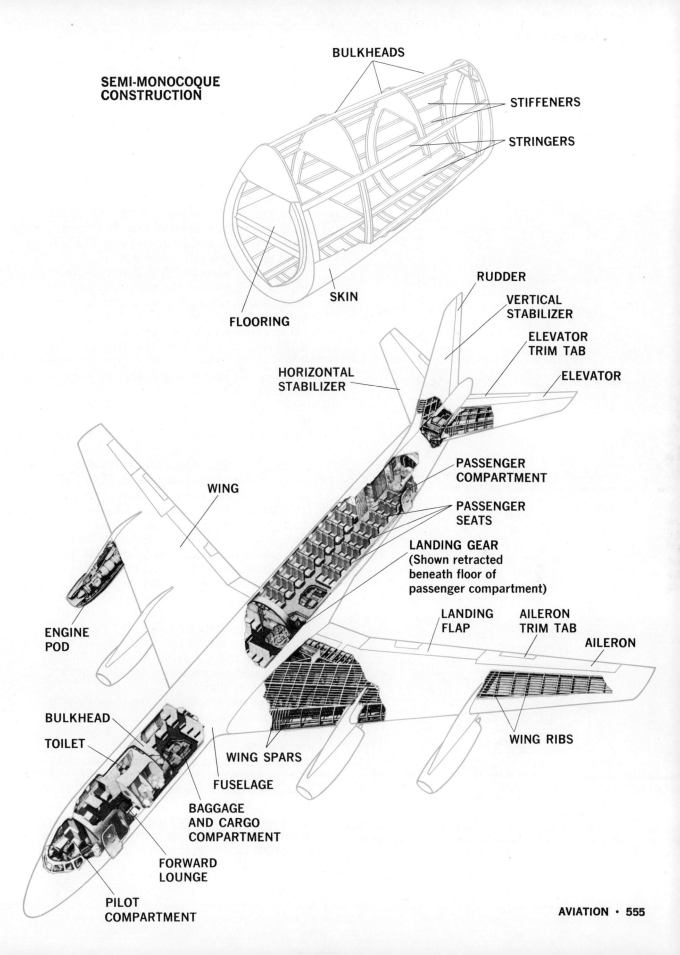

SEMI-MONOCOQUE CONSTRUCTION

BULKHEADS

STIFFENERS

STRINGERS

SKIN

FLOORING

RUDDER

VERTICAL STABILIZER

ELEVATOR TRIM TAB

ELEVATOR

HORIZONTAL STABILIZER

PASSENGER COMPARTMENT

PASSENGER SEATS

LANDING GEAR
(Shown retracted beneath floor of passenger compartment)

WING

ENGINE POD

LANDING FLAP

AILERON TRIM TAB

AILERON

WING RIBS

BULKHEAD

TOILET

WING SPARS

FUSELAGE

BAGGAGE AND CARGO COMPARTMENT

FORWARD LOUNGE

PILOT COMPARTMENT

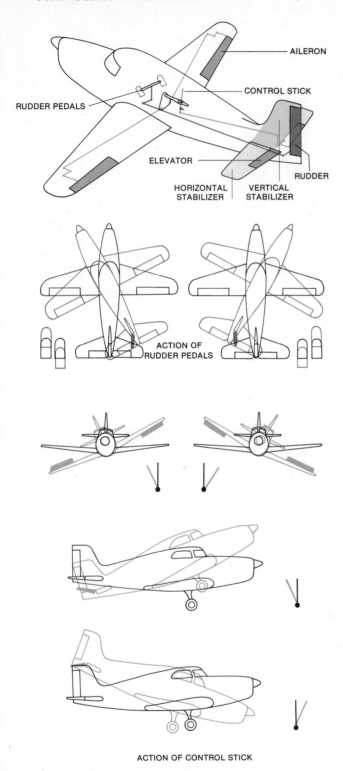

AILERON

CONTROL STICK

RUDDER PEDALS

ELEVATOR

RUDDER

HORIZONTAL STABILIZER

VERTICAL STABILIZER

ACTION OF RUDDER PEDALS

ACTION OF CONTROL STICK

Black outlines indicate plane in straight, level flight. Colored outlines show what happens when control surfaces are moved to steer plane.

lage are two stabilizers, or tail fins, to keep the airplane steady in flight. The vertical stabilizer prevents the airplane from yawing (swinging from side to side). The horizontal stabilizer prevents the plane from pitching (dipping up and down). If the stabilizers are properly designed, the airplane will remain steady even if the pilot's hands are off the controls for a moment.

To prevent the airplane from rolling, the wings are usually built so that they form a shallow V when seen from the front. This tilting of the wings is called **dihedral**.

The Control Surfaces. The control surfaces are hinged flaps that the pilot can move to change the direction of flight. There are three main control surfaces on an airplane.

The **ailerons** are located on the trailing edge of the wing near the wing tips. They are connected so that when the aileron on one wing moves up, the aileron on the other wing moves down. This makes the plane bank (tilt) to the left or right. In large airplanes and some small planes, the pilot operates the ailerons with a wheel mounted on the control column. In other planes the pilot simply manipulates the control column, or "stick." The wheel is turned, or the stick is moved from side to side. If the pilot turns the wheel or moves the stick to the right, for instance, the left aileron goes down, and the right aileron goes up. Air pushes against the upturned right aileron and forces the right wing down. At the same time, air striking the downturned left aileron forces the left wing up.

The **elevators** are located on the trailing edge of the horizontal stabilizer. When the pilot pushes the control column (stick) forward, the elevators go down, and the tail of the plane goes up. This points the plane's nose downward, and the plane descends. Pulling back on the column moves the elevators up, and the plane climbs.

The **rudder**, which steers the plane right or left, is on the trailing edge of the vertical stabilizer. It is controlled by two foot pedals in the cockpit. When the right pedal is pushed, the rear end of the rudder moves to the right. The pressure of the air against the rudder pushes the tail of the plane to the left. This turns the plane's nose to the right. When making a turn, the pilot uses the ailerons together with the rudder. The plane banks, much as a bicycle rider leans over in rounding a corner.

In small airplanes the control surfaces are worked by cables connected directly to the control column and rudder pedals. Large airplanes have hydraulic or electric boosters to help move their control surfaces. But at very high speeds, the force of the wind is sometimes too great for even this powerful machinery. **Trim tabs** are used to counteract the force of the wind. These are small flaps attached to the trailing edges of the control surfaces. They are linked to the control cables so that they automatically move in the opposite direction to the control surface. Thus, when the pilot moves the elevator upward, the trim tab of the elevator moves downward. Air striking against the downturned trim tab helps push the elevator up.

Trim tabs can be set to hold the control surfaces in position for straight, steady flight. An airplane may have a tendency to turn toward the left. The pilot can correct this by adjusting the trim tab on the rudder. Trim tabs, then, are on the elevators, rudder, and ailerons.

The Landing Gear. The landing gear supports the plane on the ground or on the water. It allows the plane to speed up to its takeoff and to slow down and stop after landing.

Most of the weight of the airplane rests on the two main landing gears, which are usually located directly under the wings. A third landing gear is located at either the nose or the tail of the fuselage. Modern airplanes have their weight concentrated forward and their wings fairly far back along the fuselage. Therefore, they usually have the third landing gear in front. This arrangement is known as **tricycle** landing gear. The landing gear causes a good deal of drag in high-speed flight. To prevent this, many landing gears are designed to retract (fold into the wings and fuselage of the plane) after takeoff.

Airplanes that take off from and land on water are called seaplanes. They have pontoons (floats) instead of wheels. Amphibians have landing gear that contains both wheels and floats. They can operate from either land or water. Planes that must operate in snowy areas, such as northern Canada or the Antarctic, often are equipped with skis.

Power and Propulsion

The heart of the airplane is its engine or engines. The engine provides the power to lift the plane off the ground, keep it aloft, and get it to its destination.

There are two types of airplane engine, piston and jet. The piston engine is the older type. An aircraft piston engine works in the same way as the familiar automobile engine, but its design is quite different. The jet engine gets its power from the forward thrust of the violently expanding gases produced when fuel is burned.

The first airplanes had liquid-cooled engines like those of automobiles. After World War I, designers trying to reduce the weight of the engine developed the air-cooled engine.

The air-cooled engine is lighter than the liquid-cooled engine because it does not have the extra weight of radiator, hoses, fans, cooling fluid, and circulation pumps. But it has one disadvantage. An air-cooled engine must be built so that the greatest possible area is exposed to the onrushing air. This causes drag. Liquid-cooled engines do not need a large cooling surface. They are more compact and streamlined than air-cooled engines.

Because of their lightness, air-cooled engines replaced liquid-cooled engines for most uses by the 1930's. But liquid-cooled engines continued to be used in some military fighters and bombers—where high speed and the ability to maneuver were very important—until jet engines took their place in the 1950's.

The supercharger is an essential part of the piston airplane engine. It is a compressor that supplies extra air to the engine to enable the fuel to burn properly. Without a supercharger, piston-engined airplanes would be unable to operate in the thin air of high altitudes.

Air-cooled engines usually have the cylinders arranged in a circle around the crankshaft. Engineers call this a radial arrangement. Designers have built radial engines with as many as 36 cylinders, but the usual number is 9 or 18. In small planes the engines have fewer cylinders. They often are built in a flat "pancake" form with horizontally opposed cylinders. This causes less drag.

Jet Engines. A jet engine burns its fuel in an enclosed space called a **combustion chamber.** The burning produces hot gases that rush out of the rear opening of the engine at high speed. The rearward rush of the gases pushes the engine (and the plane it is attached to) forward. The gases race past a fanlike device called a **turbine**, making it turn. The turbine is mounted on an axle. As the axle turns, it turns another set of fans, called the **compressor**, at the front end of the engine. The spinning compressor packs enormous amounts of air into the combustion chamber, providing the oxygen needed for continuous burning of the fuel.

In the modified jet engines called the turbofan and the turboprop, the turbine has a second job to do. In the turbofan, the turbine turns a set of huge, fanlike bladed wheels. The fans force air out through special ducts at very high speed. This provides extra thrust without burning extra fuel. In the turboprop engine, the turbine turns a propeller. The propeller provides about 90 percent of the thrust.

Jet or Piston—Which Is Better? Piston engines are more efficient than jet engines. That is, they develop more power per liter of fuel. They also are easier to control. They operate better at speeds below 650 kilometers (400 miles) per hour. The disadvantages of piston engines are that they require frequent overhauling and need special high-grade gasoline, which is expensive.

Jet engines use more fuel than piston engines, but they have a higher power-to-weight ratio. A jet engine is capable of producing 2½ times as much power per unit of weight as a piston engine can produce.

Jet engines are less expensive to run than piston engines, for they run on cheaper fuels, such as kerosene. They have other advantages, too. They cost less to manufacture than piston engines. They are easier to overhaul because they have fewer moving parts. And they become more efficient the faster and higher they operate. Jet airplanes can cruise at much higher altitudes than piston-engine planes. Thus they can take advantage of the reduced drag in the stratosphere.

Jet engines have almost entirely taken the place of piston engines for high-speed, high-altitude flight. But piston engines will probably be used for many years for short-range passenger planes, cargo planes, and sports planes.

The Propeller. A propeller does not look much like a wood screw, but it works on the same principle. The whirling blades bite into the air and screw their way forward, pulling the airplane along with them. The angle at which the blades strike the air determines how big a bite they take and how much pulling power they produce. The flatter the angle of the blades, the smaller the bites. Small bites give high pulling power but low forward speed.

Early airplane propellers had fairly flat blade angles that could not be changed. This was like driving a car with only one forward speed—low gear. The flat blade angle was satisfactory as long as planes flew relatively slowly. But it was not practical for high-speed flying because the engine would have had to turn too fast.

To solve the problem and provide the airplane with a "high gear," the variable-pitch propeller was invented in 1923. The blades of the variable-pitch propeller can be partly rotated so that they have a flat angle for takeoffs and a steep angle for normal flight. The angle of the blades is changed by controls operated by the pilot. A newer development is the constant-speed propeller, which automatically adjusts the angle of its blades to maintain a constant forward speed as the engine speed changes.

▶**AIRPLANE DESIGN**

Designing an airplane is a complex task. Hundreds of engineers may be needed to design a new type of plane. The people who plan the shape of the airframe are experts in aerodynamics (the branch of science that deals with air in motion and bodies moving through the air). Stress analysts calculate the forces that will act on each part of the plane during flight, takeoff, and landing. Other designers are materials experts. They select the best materials for the various parts of the airframe and decide how sturdy each part must be to withstand the forces on it. Another group of experts designs the various control, hydraulic, electrical, and air-conditioning systems.

Before a new airplane can be designed, the designers must know what the customer requires. The customer (usually a commercial airline or a government) furnishes a list of performance specifications. The list includes details about everything that the airplane must be able to do.

For instance, for a jet airliner the specifications may state that the plane must be able to carry 150 passengers and a crew of 10, fly a distance of 8,000 kilometers (5,000 miles) nonstop at a cruising speed of 1,000 kilo-

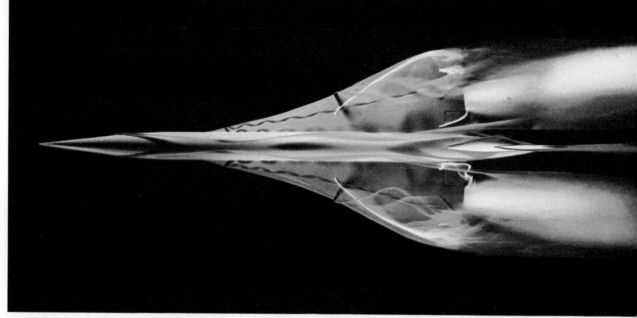

Colored smoke in a wind tunnel shows airflow around a model of a newly designed plane.

meters (620 miles) per hour, and operate at an altitude of 12,000 meters (40,000 feet).

The specifications would be quite different for a local-service passenger plane, a military fighter or bomber, or a small private plane. The specifications for all types of planes would also state the distances within which the airplane must be able to take off and land and the types of special radar and navigation equipment that it would carry.

Once the requirements are known, the rest is up to the designers. They figure out the size and shape of airframe and the type of engine that will do the job best.

Many combinations of different wing and fuselage shapes, rudder and elevator arrangements, and types of landing gear are possible. But no matter what type of airplane is being planned, the designers must keep certain basic requirements in mind. First of all, the airplane must be safe to fly, since human lives will depend on its performance. It must operate reliably, without breaking down. It must cost as little as possible to operate and to keep up. Because safe operation depends on frequent and thorough inspection and maintenance, airplanes must be as easy to inspect and overhaul as possible.

The materials used in constructing the plane are tested to make sure that no part will bend or break in flight. Planes may be equipped with certain duplicate systems for control and navigation, to be used in case some of the equipment fails.

Weight and drag are the aircraft designer's worst enemies. Every extra bit of weight means that the plane will need more power to do its job. This, in turn, means that it will have to carry more fuel, which leaves less room for passengers and cargo. A heavier airplane needs longer runs for taking off and landing. It is also harder to maneuver.

The chief practical problem the designers face is how to make the airplane as light as possible without weakening it. Aluminum alloys, plastics, and other light, strong materials have helped solve the problem to some extent, but it is still one of the major challenges in airplane design.

Drag is the resistance of the air to objects passing through it. Drag is a problem because a great deal of power is used up in overcoming it. The faster an airplane flies, the greater the drag. At speeds of several hundred kilometers an hour, even a scratch in the metal skin or a slightly protruding rivet head causes drag. Streamlining does away with a large part of the drag but cannot eliminate it entirely.

Wind-Tunnel Testing

Before the final design of the airplane is decided on, scale models of the proposed design must be tested in a wind tunnel. A wind tunnel is a long, closed passage through which air is blown at high speed to represent the conditions of actual flight.

If changes are necessary, the wind-tunnel tests will reveal which parts of the design need

A large airplane has many instruments that provide flight information. These instruments are located on panels in front of and above the pilot and copilot.

changing. The model is redesigned and tested repeatedly until its performance is satisfactory in every way. When the tests are successful, the practical work of building the plane can begin.

▶ INSTRUMENTS AND NAVIGATION

The pilot's compartment contains many instruments that provide information needed to fly the plane. The bigger the plane, the greater the number of instruments. In a large commercial airliner, instruments are arrayed in banks on the control panel in front of the pilot's and copilot's seats, on the flight engineer's instrument panel, and even on the ceiling.

Aircraft instruments are divided into two groups—engine instruments and flight or navigation instruments. As a safety measure, there are duplicate sets of navigation instruments in all but the smallest planes. Some large planes may also have duplicate sets of engine instruments so that both the pilot and the flight engineer can see how each engine is running. The flight engineer is a special crew member whose job is to keep track of the performance of the engines and adjust the engine controls while the pilot or co-pilot handles the actual flying of the airplane.

Engine Instruments

There are many engine instruments, but six are particularly important. These are the ones that measure the number of revolutions per minute that the engine makes, the temperature and pressure of air entering the engine, fuel pressure, oil pressure, and engine temperature. Jet planes have a special gauge that measures the temperature of the exhaust gases in the tailpipe, rather than the temperature inside the engine. And we must not forget the gauge that shows how much fuel is in the tanks.

Flight Instruments

The pilot depends on flight instruments to provide four basic types of information—heading (the direction in which the plane is flying), altitude, speed, and attitude of the plane in relation to the ground. With this knowledge, a pilot can fly high-speed aircraft in heavy air traffic in almost any kind of weather.

What are the basic flight instruments? First of all, there is the compass, which indicates the heading of the airplane. The magnetic compass gives a true reading in straight, level flight, but it has a tendency to err when the airplane is making a turn. For this reason, large airplanes also use a gyrocompass, which is not affected by turns.

Altitude is shown by the **altimeter**. There are two types of altimeter. The pressure altimeter works by measuring the outside air pressure. The pressure of the atmosphere decreases at a fairly regular rate the farther one rises above sea level. But it is affected by changes in temperature and other factors, and these must be taken into account to get an accurate reading. Outside air temperature is shown by the air temperature gauge.

No such corrections are necessary with the radio altimeter. This is an electronic instrument that sends out a radio beam to the ground and measures the time it takes for the beam to be reflected back to the plane.

The speed at which the airplane is moving through the air is measured by an **airspeed indicator**. The heart of this instrument is a flexible diaphragm that expands as air enters it. The air enters through a specially designed tube called a Pitot-static tube, usually mounted on the nose of the airplane. The faster the plane is moving, the more the diaphragm expands. Since the airspeed indicator works by air pressure, the pilot must allow for changes in air pressure to obtain the true airspeed.

Because the airplane is flying in a sea of air that is constantly moving, its speed in relation to the air (airspeed) is not the same as its ground speed (speed in relation to the earth's surface). A plane flying 480 kilometers (300 miles) an hour against a head wind of 80 kilometers (50 miles) an hour will have an actual ground speed of 400 kilometers (250 miles) an hour. If the plane flies at the same airspeed but with a tail wind of the same force as the head wind, it will cover 560 kilometers (350 miles) of ground an hour.

When winds blow from the side instead of directly ahead or behind, they push the airplane sideways off its intended course. This is known as **drift**. Drift is one of the chief causes of error in air navigation. The amount of drift can be calculated by observing the ground through a **drift meter**. This is a periscope tube equipped with a special grid scale.

Other important instruments include the rate-of-climb indicator, the turn-and-bank indicator, and the artificial horizon. The last two instruments let the pilot know the attitude of the plane with respect to the earth's surface even when darkness, heavy fog, or clouds prevent the pilot from seeing the ground.

Air Navigation

The simplest and oldest method of navigating an airplane is called **pilotage**. With this method the pilot learns the plane's location by spotting landmarks on the ground and checking them against a map. Pilotage worked well enough when planes flew in the daytime at relatively low speeds and altitudes, so that landmarks were easy to see. It cannot be used very well at night or when fog or clouds obscure the ground. It is not practical, either, for high-speed or high-altitude flying. Today it is used mostly in flying small private planes for pleasure in good weather.

The development of flight instruments made it possible to navigate airplanes by **dead reckoning**, without the need for being able to see landmarks. To navigate by dead reckoning, the pilot must be able to tell by the instruments the direction in which the plane is headed, the altitude and airspeed of the plane, and the outside air temperature. With this basic data, the pilot can estimate the plane's position on a flight map without seeing the ground. But this method is no longer generally used because errors in the functioning of the instruments and changes in winds aloft make it unreliable.

The development of radio and electronic navigation equipment greatly simplified the task of guiding an airplane on its course. A great step forward in the history of commercial aviation was the laying out of regular air routes, or airways, between major airports in the United States and Canada. At intervals along these airways there are radio range stations, which send out radio signals marking the route. The locations and frequencies of these radio range stations are given on flight maps. Instruments in the cockpit tell the pilot whether the plane is right or left of course and indicate the direction to the radio station.

Most airplanes are equipped with automatic radio compasses that indicate the direction from which a radio signal is coming. If lost, the pilot can find the way to an airport by tuning the plane's radio compass to the frequency of the airport's radio range transmitter. The indicator needle shows the way to the station. This is sometimes known as "homing in" on a radio station. The pilot also can pinpoint the position by tuning in on two or three stations and plotting the signal directions on a map. The airplane's position will be the point on the map where the directional lines cross.

The old-style radio ranges have been replaced by a more effective device called VOR. (VOR stands for Very-high-frequency Omnidirectional Range.) The VOR station sends out 360 courses, spaced 1 degree apart, radiating out from the transmitter like the spokes of a wheel. The pilot may select and fly any of these courses. An indicator in the cockpit shows the position of the airplane in relation to the VOR station at any time. A second device, called DME (Distance Measuring Equipment), is coupled to the VOR receiver in the airplane. It shows the exact distance from the airplane to the VOR transmitter.

VOR is more accurate than the radio compass, and it operates even under bad radio conditions. Another advantage is that the VOR transmitter sends out signals in all directions. The old-fashioned radio range transmitter sent out beams in only four directions.

Tacan (*tactical airborne navigation*) is a still newer radio navigation system that works like a combination of VOR and DME. Tacan operates at longer range. Its range is about 315 kilometers (195 miles). VOR's range is from 64 to 240 kilometers (40 to 150 miles), depending on the plane's altitude.

For very long distances, another radio system, called loran (*long range navigation*), is used. Loran signals can be transmitted as far as 1,200 kilometers (750 miles) during the day and about twice as far at night. Loran is used by ships at sea as well as by airplanes flying over the ocean. It is very accurate, and positions can be calculated within 0.8 kilometer (½ mile).

Sometimes, planes must make extremely long flights in areas where there are no radio aids to navigation. On such flights dead reckoning might be inaccurate. The plane's position is then determined from the sun, moon, and stars. This is called **celestial navigation**.

The Autopilot

Automation has come to flying as it has to other fields. Automatic pilots are standard equipment in most commercial aircraft. Increasing numbers of military aircraft are being equipped with these electronic brains.

The automatic pilot, or autopilot, is based on two gyroscopes that are connected to the airplane's controls. When the airplane deviates from level, straight flight, the gyroscopes detect the change. By means of electrical servomotors, they move the controls and return the plane to level, true flight.

Some airplanes have complex autopilots that are connected to a computer. The pilot sets the computer to fly the airplane at a certain speed and altitude. Radio signals or the gyrocompass guides the course. If the information fed into the computer by the various flight and navigation instruments shows that the plane is changing its speed, banking to one side, starting to nose down or up, or going off course, the computer will correct these errors by adjusting the controls. The autopilot can also be "locked into" the instrument landing system of an airport so that the airplane will be automatically guided along the correct approach course down to a point just above the runway.

▶ AIRPORTS

In the earliest days of aviation, there was no need for airports. The light wood-and-cloth airplanes could take off and land in any level, open field. Cow pastures and meadows were favorite landing strips.

The situation began to change as flying gained popularity in the 1920's. Airplane landing fields were opened at the edge of almost every city and large town in North America. Along one side of the grass-covered airfield would be hangars for storing and repairing the airplanes and perhaps also a lunch counter for the mechanics and pilots. Because airplanes of those days had to take off and land directly into the wind, the airfield always had a wind sock on a high pole to indicate wind direction. No flying was done at night, so there were no runway lights.

In contrast to the airfield of the 1920's, the modern airport is almost a city in itself. There are many buildings and services for the convenience and comfort of passengers, their friends, and other visitors. There are waiting rooms, restaurants, barbershops and beauty parlors, post offices, banks, gift and souvenir shops, florists, and even bowling alleys. A large airport may have its own bus system to transport passengers from one building to an-

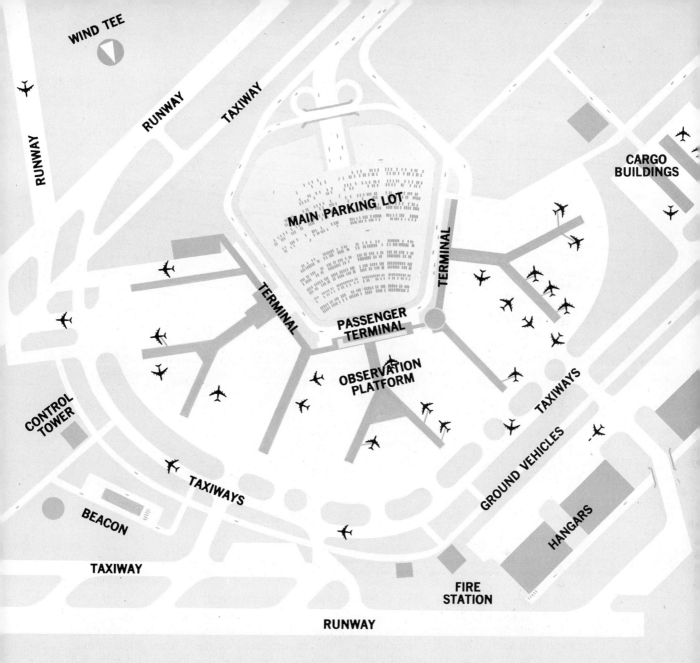

WIND TEE

RUNWAY

RUNWAY

TAXIWAY

RUNWAY

MAIN PARKING LOT

CARGO
BUILDINGS

TERMINAL

TERMINAL

PASSENGER
TERMINAL

OBSERVATION
PLATFORM

CONTROL
TOWER

TAXIWAYS

GROUND VEHICLES

TAXIWAYS

BEACON

HANGARS

TAXIWAY

FIRE
STATION

RUNWAY

A modern airport is designed for maximum convenience and efficiency. Runways, access roads, and buildings are laid out to keep planes, traffic, and passengers moving smoothly.

other or to and from the airplanes. There are also hangars where the planes are serviced and separate freight buildings.

But the heart of the airport is still the area where the planes take off and land—the runways. Jet planes require very long runways—sometimes as much as 3 kilometers (2 miles) in length. The runways are paved with concrete to withstand the impact of these very heavy planes, which hit the ground at speeds

of up to 240 kilometers (150 miles) an hour. Taxiways link the runways with one another and with the terminal buildings.

Drainage systems keep the runways from being flooded during rainy weather. Snowplows and salt spreaders keep them clear and ice-free in winter. Underground storage tanks hold vast supplies of fuel and oil. Emergency fire and ambulance crews are always on duty in case of accidents. Elaborate systems of ap-

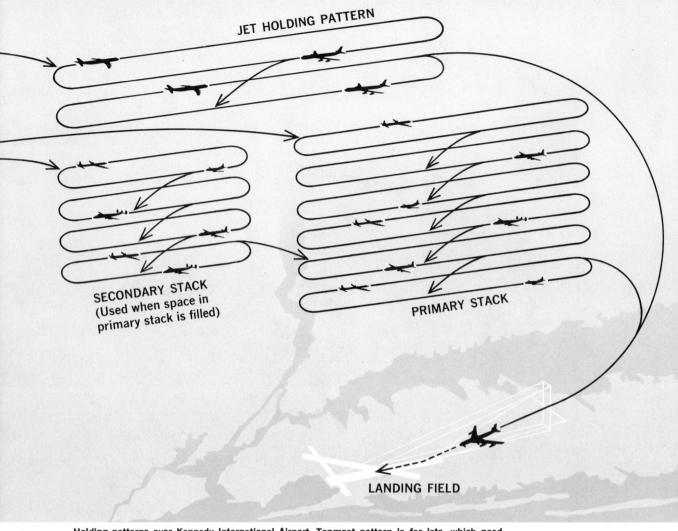

JET HOLDING PATTERN

SECONDARY STACK
(Used when space in
primary stack is filled)

PRIMARY STACK

LANDING FIELD

Holding patterns over Kennedy International Airport. Topmost pattern is for jets, which need more room than piston planes. Stacking levels are about 610 meters (2,000 feet) apart.

proach and landing lights guide pilots safely in at night and in bad weather.

If the runway is the heart of an airport, the control tower is its nerve center. It is from there that all approaches, landings, and takeoffs are directed by two-way radio. Only very small airports do not have control towers.

Whenever possible, airports are located away from densely populated areas. One reason is to avoid the risk of airplanes crashing into tall buildings when visibility is poor. As a safety measure all tall structures near airports (such as factory chimneys, buildings, and bridges) carry red warning lights at night. Engine noise, particularly from jets, is another serious problem. By locating the airport away from thickly settled areas, the number of people affected by the noise is kept down.

▶ AIR TRAFFIC CONTROL

One of the most serious problems in aviation has been the constant increase in the number of airplanes. In the United States alone, there are more than 66,000,000 takeoffs and landings every year.

The large number of planes occupying the airways at any one time makes necessary a system for preventing collisions. In the United States the job of air traffic control is handled by the FAA (Federal Aviation Administration), a government agency. Besides being in charge of controlling the movement of airplanes in flight, the FAA supervises the upkeep and improvement of radio navigation aids.

All flights in the United States and Canada are divided into two classes—VFR (Visual

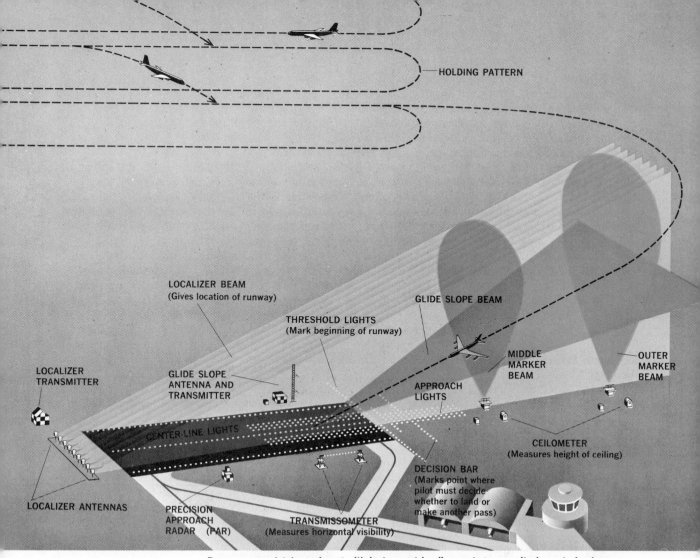

LOCALIZER BEAM
(Gives location of runway)

THRESHOLD LIGHTS
(Mark beginning of runway)

GLIDE SLOPE BEAM

HOLDING PATTERN

MIDDLE
MARKER
BEAM

OUTER
MARKER
BEAM

LOCALIZER
TRANSMITTER

GLIDE SLOPE
ANTENNA AND
TRANSMITTER

APPROACH
LIGHTS

CENTER-LINE LIGHTS

CEILOMETER
(Measures height of ceiling)

LOCALIZER ANTENNAS

DECISION BAR
(Marks point where
pilot must decide
whether to land or
make another pass)

PRECISION
APPROACH
RADAR (PAR)

TRANSMISSOMETER
(Measures horizontal visibility)

Runways completely equipped with instrument landing systems permit planes to land even when visibility is very poor.

Flight Rules), in which pilots can see where they are flying, and IFR (Instrument Flight Rules), in which pilots must rely on instruments. The FAA and its Canadian equivalent, the Department of Transport, regulate all IFR flights made on the established airways and all takeoffs and landings, whether instrument or visual, at commercial airports.

Air traffic control is so complicated that it is divided into two different branches. These are called Air Route Traffic Control (ARTC) and Approach Control. Military aviation has a separate control system.

To reduce the danger of collisions between aircraft, each airway is divided into 300-meter (1,000-foot) levels. Aircraft flying north or east fly at odd-numbered levels. Aircraft flying west or south use even-numbered levels. As a

further safety measure, each plane flying by IFR must keep a distance of at least ten minutes' flying time horizontally and 300 meters (1,000 feet) vertically from all other IFR aircraft. The vertical distance is doubled for jets flying at 8,800 meters (29,000 feet) and higher. ARTC centers keep in constant touch with pilots by radio to make sure that all traffic is moving safely.

Before beginning a flight, all commercial pilots must submit a flight plan to the nearest ARTC center. The flight plan will state the destination of the flight, the airways that will be followed, the intended altitude and speed of flying, and other information. The ARTC controller can disapprove the flight plan if the airway level or route the pilot has chosen is too crowded or if there is bad weather along the route. In such cases, alternate levels or routes are suggested to the pilot.

Before the pilot can take off, permission must be given by the airport control tower. The pilot is then given clearance (permission to take off) and instructions to get clear of the airport area and proceed on course.

On an IFR flight, the pilot must report at regular checkpoints to ARTC controllers along the route. If traffic or weather conditions change, the controller can order the pilot to change course or fly at a different altitude. If the plane runs into unexpected rough weather, the pilot can request a change of course or altitude.

When the airplane nears the end of its flight, ARTC turns the pilot over to the local Approach Control center. The job of Approach Control is to direct the pilot as the airplane comes into the air traffic pattern near the airport. At busy airports, each airplane is carefully followed on radar. If traffic is heavy, the pilot will be ordered to fly a "holding pattern" —that is, to circle in a definite area until the way is clear for a landing. At very busy airports it is a common practice to "stack" the planes by having them circle the same area at different levels. Each time the runway is clear, the lowest plane lands, and all the others move down one level.

The actual business of landing is handled by an airport traffic control tower. The FAA operates the control tower at every civilian airport in the United States, except for a few private airports. The FAA also operates the equipment that guides airplanes for instrument landings in bad weather. Whether flying IFR or VFR, the pilot cannot land until given permission by the control tower.

▶ **THE AVIATION INDUSTRY**

The aviation industry is made up of all the companies whose business is the building or operating of aircraft and spacecraft. This includes the manufacturers of airframes, engines, instruments, control systems, helicopters, missiles, rockets, and all other types of aviation equipment. It also includes commercial airlines and airports. Because it includes the designing and building of spacecraft, it is often called the aerospace industry.

Aircraft manufacturing is a highly specialized business. Some companies build nothing but airframes. Others specialize in engines, control systems, or instruments. Even the largest manufacturer would not be able to make all the special parts and equipment that go into a modern airplane. It is cheaper to buy them from other manufacturers.

Manufacturing airplanes is complicated and exacting work. Three or more years may be required to design a new type of airplane and another two or three years to build the first actual working version. Testing may take another two years.

The aircraft manufacturing industry needs scientists, engineers, and highly trained workers. When the plane is ready to go into production, skilled technicians are needed to make the parts, and mechanics are needed to assemble them. Aeronautical engineers need at least four years of college, and even technicians and mechanics will find additional courses in mathematics and engineering helpful.

Air transportation is the other major part of the aviation industry. First in importance are the commercial airlines. These are officially defined as public carriers, operated for profit, that provide regularly scheduled flights for passengers or cargo. They must meet very strict government safety requirements. The government also regulates passenger fares and freight rates.

In addition to scheduled airlines, there are charter, or nonscheduled, airlines. They fly whenever they have enough business, rather than on a regular schedule. Charter airlines must meet the same safety requirements as scheduled airlines. There are also air taxi services and helicopter carriers that shuttle passengers between airports and cities.

Passenger and cargo carriers are the workhorses of the aviation industry. But the largest number of airplane buyers in North America fall into the category of general aviation. This group includes all the small and medium-sized private craft that are used for sport flying, flying lessons, forest-fire spotting, and crop dusting and other farm purposes. Company planes for business travel also come under this category.

The development of satellites, shuttle orbiters, and other spacecraft is an exciting and growing branch of the aviation industry, although it is largely in the experimental stage.

Governments are the main customers and will continue to be for years to come.

In the United States and many other countries, the government is the largest single customer of the aviation industry. Many manufacturers would go out of business without government orders for military aircraft. The government also helps the airlines by paying them to carry mail.

Careers in Aviation

Of all the careers in aviation, that of a pilot has always seemed the most glamorous. The qualifications for this job are strict because human lives depend on a pilot's fitness. To qualify for a commercial pilot's license, applicants must be in normally good health, with at least 20/50 vision in each eye, correctable to 20/20. They must not be color-blind. They must be able to hear a whisper at 2.5 meters (8 feet), because pilots often depend on radio communication. They must be at least 18 years of age. They must pass written government examinations on air traffic rules, meteorology (the study of weather), air navigation, and the principles of flight. They must have at least 200 hours of flying time in a powered aircraft, including solo flights and instrument flying instruction. They also must pass other flight tests. Holders of a commercial pilot's rating are qualified to fly cargo planes as pilot in command. They may not fly passengers on regularly scheduled flights except as copilot.

The captain, or pilot in command, of an airliner must hold an air transport rating. The requirements for this are stricter than those for the commercial rating. Pilots must be at least 23 years old and high-school graduates. They must pass more difficult physical and mental tests. And they must have at least 1,500 hours of flying experience.

A college degree is not required for pilots, but it is desirable. Mathematics, science, and engineering are especially helpful as an academic background.

Actual training in flying must be taken in a government-approved flying school or in military service. The airlines do not train pilots.

Many young people choose careers as flight attendants. Flight attendants do not have to pass any government examinations, but they must meet the airline's qualifications. These qualifications vary from airline to airline. But in general, the flight attendant must be at least 20 years old and a high-school graduate. Some airlines also require two years' experience in business or two years of college or nursing training. Flight attendants must present a good appearance and have vision of at least 20/100, correctable to 20/20. Important personal qualifications are an interest in doing things for others and the ability to treat people with tact and poise. The airlines give successful candidates an intensive training course that includes first aid, baby care, food service during flight, and general information on flying, navigation, communication, parts of the airplane, and emergency procedures.

There are many other jobs related to aviation. Mechanics, electronics specialists, instrument repairers, dispatchers, meteorologists, reservations and ticket agents, and cargo personnel are needed by most airlines and some business aircraft operators. Mechanics, electronics specialists, and meteorologists are usually trained in special schools or colleges. The others generally receive on-the-job training.

▶ HISTORY OF AVIATION

One of the earliest legends of flying is the Greek myth of Daedalus and Icarus. Daedalus, a skillful artisan, made artificial wings of wax and feathers for himself and his son Icarus. Icarus, delighted with the way the wings worked, carelessly flew too near the sun. The sun's heat melted the wings. Icarus plunged into the sea and was drowned.

The earliest actual attempts at flight were based on the story of Daedalus and Icarus. A few adventurous individuals strapped on artificial wings that they tried to flap like a bird's wings. Others, who were bolder, launched themselves from high towers. All these attempts failed.

With the rebirth of science in the 1500's and 1600's, educated people realized that humans do not have the strength to fly by flapping artificial wings. Experimenters turned to mechanical devices to make up for a human being's lack of muscle power. But they were still chained to the idea of a craft with flapping wings, or ornithopter (from Greek words meaning "bird wing"). Some small models of ornithopters were built that could actually fly for short distances. But models large enough to hold a person simply did not work because no good source of power was available. But the idea of flight with flapping wings has continued to fascinate inventors. Even today, experimental ornithopters, powered by gasoline engines, are being built.

Around 1500 the Italian artist and inventor Leonardo da Vinci designed a small, primitive helicopter powered by a spring. A model is believed to have been built and flown, but Leonardo apparently looked on it as no more than a toy.

As scientific knowledge grew, a few people toyed with the idea of vessels that could float in the air. But most of their plans were impractical. The first to succeed were two French papermakers who were interested in science, the brothers Joseph Michel and Jacques Étienne Montgolfier. In 1783 the Montgolfiers launched a series of hot-air balloons, including some that carried passengers. In the same year a French physicist, Jacques A. C. Charles, made a successful trial of a hydrogen-filled balloon.

Following these experiments, a ballooning craze swept Europe and North America. Trick balloon ascents became a popular feature at

fairs. Incidentally, the parachute was developed by balloonists who jumped as part of their act. Balloons quickly found more serious use for military and scientific observations. But balloons were not the solution for practical air transportation. They could lift heavy loads into the air, but there was no way of controlling the direction of their flight. They floated along wherever the winds happened to blow them. The future of aviation lay with power-driven heavier-than-air craft.

Pioneers of Aviation

If anyone deserves the title "the founder of aviation," it probably is Sir George Cayley, a 19th-century English scholar and inventor.

Cayley studied the flight of birds. He noticed that some birds, such as gulls, could soar through the sky for long distances without moving their wings. He believed it was possible to build a machine that would carry people and glide through the air in a similar way. In the early 1800's he built model gliders and experimented with them until he could make them sail smoothly in the air.

Cayley also thought of making wings with curved surfaces for better passage through the air and of using rudders and elevators to control the flight of the craft. His designs formed much of the basis for later airplane construction.

Other people took up Cayley's ideas and began to design gliders. Otto Lilienthal, a German, had great success with his designs. His first glider, built in 1891, was made of wood strips and cloth. The pilot hung from a frame in the center of the wing. Lilienthal took off in his glider by running down a hill with it until he was moving fast enough for the wind to lift the craft. He controlled the direction of flight by moving his body to one side or the other. Lilienthal built large gliders and made over 2,000 flights in them. He was killed in 1896 while testing one of his new gliders.

Power-driven model airplanes were being flown by the middle of the 19th century. The first was a steam-powered model designed and built by John Stringfellow, an English engineer. Other experimenters used clockwork, electric motors, or compressed air. But steam remained the most popular source of power until the end of the 19th century. Tiny steam

Lilienthal's glider was made of wood strips and cloth. The pilot hung from a frame in the center of the wing. He would move his body to help control the flight.

The Wright brothers' two-winged plane had the engine set on the lower wing.

engines worked well enough in small model airplanes. But steam engines large enough to power a full-sized plane were too heavy to be practical. The development of the internal-combustion engine, light yet powerful, gave aviation its real start.

The American astronomer Samuel Langley almost won the honor of perfecting the power-driven airplane. After years of patient experiments and trials with models, he completed a full-size airplane called the *Aerodrome* in 1903. Langley's gasoline-powered machine was to be launched from the top of a house-boat in the Potomac River. But a supporting post on the airplane caught in the launching mechanism, and *Aerodrome* crashed into the river. The machine was fished up and repaired, but the same kind of accident wrecked the second launching. Langley was savagely attacked by the newspapers. Discouraged, he stopped his experiments.

On December 17, 1903, just two weeks after Langley's second failure, the Wright brothers made the first successful powered flights in a heavier-than-air craft. Orville and Wilbur Wright were bicycle builders in Dayton, Ohio. The news of Lilienthal's glider experiments had roused their interest in flying. They devoted their spare time to reading all the books they could find about flight and to designing and building gliders.

In September, 1900, they tested their first glider at Kitty Hawk, North Carolina. From 1901 to 1903 they continued to make improve-ments on their gliders and to test them at Kitty Hawk. Then they decided that they had learned enough to attempt powered flight. They built a small, light gasoline engine, installed it in a glider, and connected it to two propellers with bicycle chains. They called their airplane the *Flyer*—the name of the bicycles they made. The aircraft had biplane wings, a front elevator, and a rear rudder. The pilot rode lying down on his stomach. There were no ailerons on the wings with which to make the plane bank. Instead, the pilot bent the wing tips up or down by manipulating cables.

On December 17, 1903, the brothers each flew the plane twice. The first flight lasted 12 seconds. The fourth, covering 260 meters (852 feet), lasted 59 seconds. These were the first powered, controlled flights ever made.

The Wright brothers' achievement started the Age of Aviation. The main task now was to develop and improve the primitive airplane that the Wright brothers had used. Many people were eager to take part in this work. The French were especially excited about aviation. French inventors had been trying for some years to develop an airplane. Several years later Wilbur Wright demonstrated the brothers' aircraft in France. This increased the already intense interest in airplanes there.

More and more enthusiasts built and flew their own airplanes. These early pioneers worked with nothing to guide them but the uncertain experience of other experimenters.

They were learning the science of airplane construction and flight by trial and error.

The planes they flew would look strange to modern eyes. They were frail constructions of wood and cloth, braced by outside struts and wires. The temperamental engines often went dead in midair. They were dangerous to fly in bad weather. Many of these early airplanes were biplanes—that is, they had two sets of wings, one above the other. Alberto Santos-Dumont, a Brazilian-born aviation pioneer, made the first officially observed successful European flight in a powered biplane in 1906. Santos-Dumont, who lived in France, had earlier conducted experiments with motor-powered dirigibles.

Airplane research in Canada began in 1907, when Alexander Graham Bell established a laboratory at Baddeck, Nova Scotia. Bell was particularly interested in the multicellular box-kite wing, which looked like a honeycomb standing on its side and had great lifting power. He also experimented with conventional wings.

In 1909, Louis Blériot, of France, became the first person to fly a plane across the English Channel. He made the flight in a monoplane

Blériot was the first person to fly across the English Channel. He took off from Calais and landed at Dover.

that he had designed himself. Blériot had added several new features to his airplane. The pilot sat in the middle of the fuselage, instead of lying down, and controlled the flight with a control stick and pedals, just as airplanes are flown today. The rudder and the elevators were at the rear of the plane. Blériot's design became the standard for later airplane builders.

World War I quickly brought many improvements to aviation. Until that time governments had not taken a serious interest in aviation. Flying had been considered the sport of a few daredevils who were using unreliable contraptions. But when fighting started, it was realized that airplanes could be useful for observing the enemy and directing artillery fire and, later, as fighters and bombers. The various governments pushed airplane development programs, and impressive progress was made. At the beginning of the war, most planes flew at about 100 kilometers (60 miles) per hour. At the war's end, engines five times as powerful were being used, and fighter planes could fly more than twice as fast as those used at the start of the war.

When the war was over, aviation returned to being a sport. Newspapers and wealthy private citizens sponsored air races and long-distance flights. An English newspaper offered a prize of £10,000 for the first aviator to fly nonstop across the Atlantic Ocean. This prize was won by two English flyers, John Alcock and Arthur Whitten Brown, who flew from Newfoundland to Ireland in 1919.

During the 1920's, other pilots flew over the Andes mountains, across the Pacific Ocean, over the North and South poles, and around the world. The motive was not always prize money. Many of the aviators made the flights for the excitement and honor of being first.

The 1920's and 1930's also saw the Far North opened up by aviation. Until then, vast areas of northern Canada and Alaska had been considered out of reach for most people. The airplane changed this. Adventurous "bush pilots," many of them former pilots from World War I, flew their small, light planes almost everywhere. They flew mail and medicines to isolated missions and government outposts. They flew heavy machinery to wilderness mining camps. They flew passengers and supplies to any place where a landing could

Lindbergh became famous after crossing the Atlantic Ocean in *The Spirit of St. Louis*.

be made. Where highways and railroads could not penetrate, the bush pilots did. Thousands of square kilometers of wilderness were surveyed by prospectors from bush pilots' airplanes. For the first time in history, vast areas were accurately mapped and isolated communities could be supplied.

Airplanes improved steadily as pilots and builders gained experience. Biplanes were replaced by faster monoplanes. Wood-and-cloth construction gave way to aluminum and stainless steel. Streamlining was improved with the invention of retractable landing gear. The speed of airplanes kept increasing. In 1920 the world speed record was 303 kilometers (188 miles) per hour. By 1940 it had risen to 755 kilometers (469 miles) per hour.

One of the most famous aviators of the 1920's was Charles A. Lindbergh. He accomplished what many pilots before him had tried unsuccessfully to do—a nonstop flight from New York to Paris. Lindbergh made the flight all alone in May, 1927, in his single-engined monoplane, *The Spirit of St. Louis*. The flight took a little over 33 hours.

Lindbergh's flight aroused widespread interest in aviation in the United States. This interest helped the growth of commercial aviation in that country. Lindbergh's success made flying seem safer to many people, and they were willing to take a chance on flying themselves.

The growth of passenger airlines brought a need for more safety devices. De-icers were added to airplane wings to keep ice from becoming dangerously thick and heavy. Fire-extinguishing systems were installed, and new instruments and radio aids were developed to improve navigation and to allow safe night flying. In the 1930's one of the most famous passenger airliners was the DC-3, built by the Douglas Aircraft Company. This plane could carry 30 people at 290 kilometers (180 miles) an hour for distances of 3,200 kilometers (2,000 miles).

World War II brought a rapid development of airplanes, as had World War I. The power of piston engines was doubled, and the average speed of fighter planes was increased from 480 kilometers (300 miles) to 725 kilometers (450 miles) per hour.

The outstanding aviation development of the war period was the jet engine. An English air force officer, Frank Whittle, had invented the engine in 1936, but progress was slow in perfecting it until the war came. The first jet-powered airplane was the German Heinkel He-178, which made a flight in 1939. But a practical jet fighter plane was not developed until 1944. This was the Lockheed P-80. A

Why can't people use artificial wings and fly like birds?

Birds' entire bodies are specialized for flight. They have extremely large and powerful breast muscles to move their wings, and a keel-like, projecting breastbone to give these powerful muscles a firm attachment. Parts of the body that are not used in flying, such as legs, are reduced in size. Birds are also light in relation to their size; much of their bulk consists of feathers. Hollow bones further cut down total body weight.

People are specialized for life on the ground. They lack the body features that enable birds to fly. To fly with artificial wings, people would have to be built somewhat like turkeys.

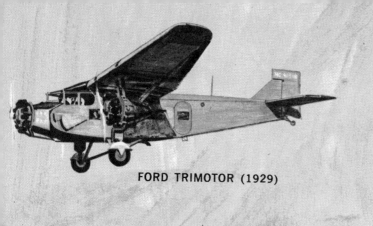

FORD TRIMOTOR (1929)

DOUGLAS DC-3 (1936)

LOCKHEED P-38 (1939)

BELL MODEL 47 EXPERIMENTAL
HELICOPTER (1950)

BOEING B-17-G FLYING FORTRESS (1943)

DOUGLAS DC-7 (1953)

DASSAULT MIRAGE IIIE (FRANCE, 1961)

GENERAL DYNAMICS F-111A (UNITED STATES, 1964)

HAWKER-SIDDELEY HARRIER (UNITED KINGDOM, 1966)

MIKOYAN MiG-23 "FOXBAT" (SOVIET UNION, 1965)

TUPOLEV TU-144 SUPERSONIC TRANSPORT (SOVIET UNION, 1968)

The pilot turns this biplane upside down during an acrobatic maneuver. This is an example of stunt flying.

This plane is designed for mountain flying. It has a reserve supply of fuel, for use in an emergency.

These planes can land and take off on water. They provide air service to places that otherwise are hard to reach.

few German jet craft appeared in combat in World War II. But it was not until the Korean War (1950–53) that jets were used in great numbers.

The jet engine has revolutionized both civilian and military aviation. It has made possible such feats as a transatlantic flight in six hours in subsonic aircraft—and a little over three hours in a supersonic plane. The first jet airliner was Britain's Comet, which began operating in 1949. Since then a great variety of powerful and fast jet and turboprop airliners have been produced.

Another development of World War II was the helicopter. Designers of several countries were able to build helicopters that flew. But it was the Russian-born American engineer Igor Sikorsky who in 1939 turned the helicopter from a curiosity into a practical machine.

A more recent development is the VTOL (Vertical TakeOff and Landing) craft. It can take off and land in as small an area as a helicopter and can fly as fast as an airplane. Some VTOL craft operate by tilting the engines up. Others tilt the entire wing with the engines.

▶ LOOKING TO THE FUTURE

As aviation continues to progress, improvements will be made in aircraft, engines, navigation aids, and electronic equipment. Most new airplanes will probably have a slightly shorter and plumper shape. Their engines, both piston- and jet-powered, will be quieter and more fuel-efficient. Airliners will have more automatic systems and will be able to fly higher and farther on less fuel than older jet planes. Some experts predict that a second generation of supersonic airliners will appear. Others say that unless there is a technical breakthrough that will allow more passengers to be flown in them, the airlines of the world will not purchase any more than the few now flying. Instead, designers will concentrate on making subsonic aircraft more efficient.

New developments in the design of aircraft wings show promise for making commercial airplanes stronger and more efficient. Stronger metals now being developed will allow the wings to withstand the high stresses imposed on them. The wings on today's jets create too much drag. A new wing shape, called the

MILESTONES OF AVIATION

1783 Jacques-Etienne and Joseph Montgolfier of France launched first successful balloon (June).

In October Jean François Pilâtre de Rozier, French doctor, made first manned ascent, in hot-air balloon designed by the Montgolfiers.

1785 Jean Pierre Blanchard, French balloonist, made first successful voyage across English Channel; also made first air voyage in United States, in 1793.

1804 First winged glider made by Sir George Cayley, English aviation pioneer.

1848 John Stringfellow (English) constructed first successful power-driven model airplane.

1852 Henri Giffard flew steam-driven airship over Paris.

1891 Otto Lilienthal began his glider experiments in Germany.

1903 Wright brothers made first sustained, controlled flights in powered heavier-than-air craft at Kitty Hawk, North Carolina.

1909 Louis Blériot (French) flew across English Channel. First crossing ever made in an airplane.

1910 First radio communication from airplane in flight to ground made by J. A. D. McCurdy (Canadian).

1911 Galbraith P. Rogers flew across United States, New York to California; flying time, 49 days.

Eugene Ely accomplished first landing on deck of a ship.

1912 Harriet Quimby flew across English Channel, first woman to perform this feat.

1918 First airmail route established in United States.

1919 First crossing of Atlantic by air, accomplished by U.S. Navy seaplane, from Newfoundland to Portugal via the Azores; flying time, 54 hours.

First nonstop air crossing of Atlantic made by two English airmen, Captain John Alcock and Lieutenant Arthur Whitten Brown.

First international airmail, between London and Paris.

1923 Two U.S. Army pilots made first nonstop transcontinental flight, New York to San Diego, California, in 26 hours, 50 minutes.

1924 U.S. Army Air Service pilots completed first round-the-world flight, which was also first transpacific flight and first westbound Atlantic crossing; flying time, 175 days.

1926 Lieutenant Commander Richard E. Byrd and Floyd Bennett flew across North Pole, May 9.

1927 Charles A. Lindbergh made first solo nonstop transatlantic flight, New York to Paris; flying time, 33 hours, 30 minutes.

1929 Lieutenant James H. Doolittle, U.S. Army, made first "blind" flight, using instruments only.

Commander Richard E. Byrd and crew made first flight across South Pole, November 29.

Fritz Opel of Germany flew first rocket plane.

1930 Frank Whittle, an Englishman, patented a design for a jet engine.

1931 Wiley Post and Harold Gatty flew around the world in 8 days, 15 hours, 51 minutes.

Clyde Pangborn and Hugh Herndon flew nonstop from Tokyo, Japan, to Wenatchee, Washington—first nonstop Pacific crossing.

1932 Amelia Earhart became first woman to fly Atlantic solo.

1939 First flight by jet aircraft made, in Germany.

1947 Captain Charles Yeager, USAF, made first supersonic flight, in X-1, a rocket-powered plane.

1949 A USAF B-50, *Lucky Lady II*, completed first nonstop round-the-world flight.

1962 Joseph A. Walker, civilian pilot, flew X-15 at record speed of 6,693 km (4,159 mi) per hour.

Major Robert White, USAF, set world aircraft altitude mark of 95,935.8 m (314,750 ft) in X-15.

1963 Sam Miller and Louis Fodor made fastest round-the-world trip: 46 hours, 28 minutes.

1965 Commander J. R. Williford, U.S. Navy, made longest direct helicopter flight—3,388.46 km (2,105.49 mi).

1967 First nonstop crossing of North Atlantic made by two USAF helicopters.

1969 First flights of Supersonic Transports (SST's)—Soviet TU-144 and Anglo-French Concorde. They can fly at speeds up to 2,250 km (1,400 mi) per hour.

1970 Boeing 747's (Jumbo Jets) in commercial use.

1976 Concorde began first passenger-carrying supersonic service, between London and Bahrain, and between Paris and Rio de Janeiro.

1977 NASA's Space Shuttle Orbiter completed the landing phase of its test program.

The Lockheed L-1011, powered by three jet engines, is designed to carry about 240 passengers.

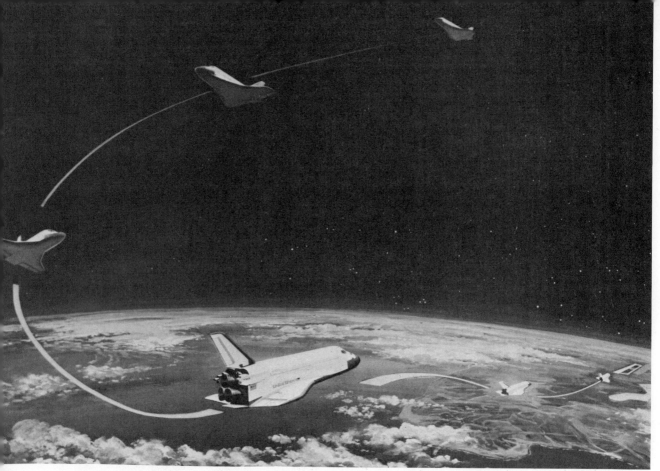

The space shuttle is designed to carry a crew and cargo to and from a satellite. It is launched from a launchpad, like a spaceship. It returns to earth like an airplane, on a runway.

supercritical wing, has been designed. It slices through the air with less turbulence.

Today, much commercial aviation is automated. On-board computers already are used to determine the best route, altitude, and throttle settings. They also give continuous readings as to position above the earth's surface at any moment. In the coming years, computers and other equipment will increase the amount of automation in flight. Pilots will be able to monitor the plane's performance through newly designed instruments and small television screens. Engine performance and fuel consumption will be automatically recorded and relayed back to maintenance bases, where specialists will determine what parts may need replacement or repair.

Satellites will probably play a part in future commercial operations. With their ability to remain in stationary orbits, they may be used by pilots to obtain precise readings on a plane's position at all times, without relying on ground stations.

Helicopters and other VTOL aircraft will be improved through the use of more efficient rotors and thrust devices. One of the important problems to be solved in this area is that of noise. The powerful engines needed to lift an aircraft vertically are relatively loud.

Transportation into outer space will continue to develop. In the United States, attention has been focused on the Space Shuttle Orbiter. This airplane-like craft is comparable in size and weight to a modern airliner. It is designed to carry people and equipment to and from orbiting space stations. Upon return to earth, it will make an airplane-like landing on a runway.

C. V. GLINES
Editor, *Air Line Pilot* magazine

See also AERODYNAMICS; BALLOONS AND BALLOONING; GLIDERS; HELICOPTERS; INTERNAL-COMBUSTION ENGINES; JET PROPULSION; NAVIGATION; RADAR, SONAR, LORAN, AND SHORAN; ROCKETS; SUPERSONIC FLIGHT; TRANSPORTATION; UNITED STATES AIR FORCE.

AZTECS. See INDIANS OF NORTH AMERICA; MEXICO.

HOW TO USE THE INDEX

When travelers visit a large city, they use maps or guides to find their way about. When you want to find information in an encyclopedia, you need a guide, too. The Index is your guide to all the information in THE NEW BOOK OF KNOWLEDGE.

The entire Index is contained in Volume 21 of your set. In addition, each volume of THE NEW BOOK OF KNOWLEDGE contains the corresponding alphabetical division of the Index.

USING THE INDEX

When you look something up in this encyclopedia, you should always refer to the Index first. It will tell you where you can find what you want to know. And sometimes, if you need just one key fact, it will tell you all you want to know.

The Index brings together all the references to information about a particular subject. It tells you where that subject—and every subject related to it—is discussed. In most cases when you use the Index to look up a topic, you will find along with it a short definition or identifying phrase. This brief definition explains a term that may be unfamiliar to you and helps you make sure you have found the topic you are looking for. Because it includes these definitions, the Index is called a Dictionary Index. You will also find throughout the Indexes in the individual volumes about 5,000 brief biographies and summaries of subjects not included in the main articles.

HOW THE INDEX IS ARRANGED

Suppose the subject you want to find out about is anthropology. If you look it up in the Index, this is what you will see:

Anthropology (an-thro-POL-ogy), study of human beings and human culture **A** 300–09
  archeology related to **A** 349, 364
  blood groups studied **B** 258
  Mead, Margaret **M** 191
  Mexico City's National Museum of Anthropology **M** 252
  prehistoric people **P** 442–46
  races, human **R** 29–32
  research methods **R** 182
  See also Ancient civilizations; Prehistoric art

The subject you are looking up, **Anthropology,** is called the **heading** and is in boldface type. In parentheses next to the heading there is a **pronunciation guide** (an-thro-POL-ogy). This is provided for all heading words that may be difficult to pronounce. (The pronunciation guide is explained in the opening pages of Volume 21.)

Next to the pronunciation guide are a few words that identify the topic—"study of human beings and human culture." These words are called the **identification**. A volume letter (in boldface type) and page numbers follow the identification—**A** 300–09. The letter **A** tells you in which volume the article on **anthropology** is and 300–09 tells you on which pages of the **A** volume you will find the main article on anthropology. The heading, its identification, and its volume and page numbers together make up the **entry**.

Beneath the entry there is a list of additional references to your subject. These references are called **subentries**. They are indented and arranged in alphabetical order. The subentries refer to all the important information about your subject throughout the set. Unless you look in the Index, you may not think of all the points about your subject that have been cov-

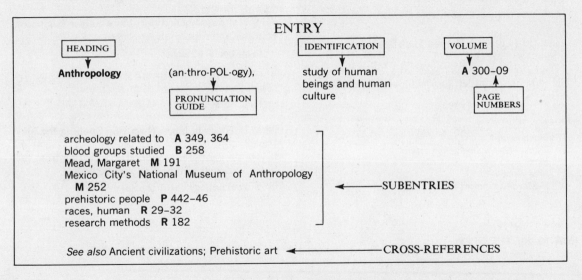

ENTRY

HEADING
Anthropology

(an-thro-POL-ogy),
PRONUNCIATION GUIDE

IDENTIFICATION
study of human beings and human culture

VOLUME
A 300–09
PAGE NUMBERS

  archeology related to **A** 349, 364
  blood groups studied **B** 258
  Mead, Margaret **M** 191
  Mexico City's National Museum of Anthropology **M** 252
  prehistoric people **P** 442–46
  races, human **R** 29–32
  research methods **R** 182
        ←——SUBENTRIES

See also Ancient civilizations; Prehistoric art ◀————CROSS-REFERENCES

ered in the encyclopedia. (Subentries, in turn, may appear as main entries in other parts of the Index under their own initial letters.)

In the case of **Anthropology** there are only a few subentries. But if you look up a broad topic, such as **Vocations,** you may find dozens of subentries. Subentries are helpful if you want to review the whole of a particular field.

Finally, in the last line of the **Anthropology** listing, you come to the words *"See also,"* followed by two Index headings. The *"See also"* listings are called **cross-references**. They tell you where to look to find more information related to your subject. Cross-references are guides to Index entries, not to article titles.

Pictures are noted in the Index only if they fall on a page that is different from the main entry or if they are to be found in a different article.

Bohr, Niels, Danish atomic physicist **B** 300; **C** 216;
    pictures **C** 215, **P** 232
Bridges **B** 395–401
    Tower Bridge, London, picture **E** 305

Maps are not noted in the Index. If you look up a country, state, or province article, you will find at least one map, often with its own index, included within the pages of the article.

Parentheses are used to enclose pronunciation guides. They are also used to enclose initials, alternative forms of names, and dates.

Initials: **Air Route Traffic Control** (ARTC)
Alternative forms of names:
    Aaron, Hank (Henry Louis Aaron)

Dates: Life dates are given in parentheses when there is a brief biographical sketch.

Montessori (mon-tes-SOR-i), **Maria** (1870–1952), Italian educator and physician, b. near Ancona. Dr. Montessori was the first woman in Italy to obtain a medical degree. She developed methods of teaching children that emphasized the child's initiative and freedom of expression. Her methods have influenced teaching practices for 3- to 6-year-olds all over the world. English translations of her books include *The Montessori Method* and *Advanced Montessori Method.*

Dates are also used to distinguish between persons of the same name:

Adams, Charles Francis (1807–86), American diplomat
Adams, Charles Francis (1866–1954), American lawyer

Dates are also given for historical events that are summarized briefly in the Index.

    Atlantic Charter (August, 1941)

What Shall I Look For?
Think of the specific word about which you need information and look for that. Go directly to the name you usually use for the thing you want. If you want to find out about baseball, turn directly to **Baseball** in the Index. You do not have to hunt first under **Sports,** although you would find baseball listed there too.

How Do I Look Up a Person's Name?
Look for the last name, just as you do when you use the telephone book.

    Blake, William, English poet and artist **B** 250b

How Do I Look Up Names That Begin with "Mac" or "Mc"?
Names beginning with "Mac" and "Mc" are placed in alphabetical order, just as they are spelled.

    MacArthur, Douglas
    Macbeth
    Mac Cool
    Machine age
    Macy, Anne Sullivan
    Maze
    Mba, Leon
    McBurney, Charles

What If the Person Is Known by More Than One Name?
Some persons are known by more than one name. Such entries are listed by their best-known names— **Buffalo Bill; Twain, Mark; Napoleon.** But if you should look under the person's official name, a cross-reference will tell you the right place to look.

    Bonaparte, Napoleon see Napoleon I
    Clemens, Samuel Langhorne see Twain, Mark
    Cody, William F. *see* Buffalo Bill

How Do I Look Up Names Beginning with "Saint" or "St."?
Saint is always spelled out. Place names beginning with Saint are listed under **Saint.**

    Saint Louis, Missouri

But the names of saints are listed according to the name. "Saint" is placed after the name.

    Paul, Saint

What If There Is More Than One Spelling for My Topic?
If you use a different (but correct) spelling from the Index, you will also find a *"see"* reference.

    Archaeology *see* Archeology

How Are the Headings in the Index Arranged?
Because this is a Dictionary Index, it is arranged like a dictionary, letter by letter.

Mink
Minneapolis
Minnesingers
Minnesota

What If a Heading Is Made Up of More Than One Word?
Even when headings are made up of more than one word, they are still arranged alphabetically, letter by letter.

New Amsterdam
Newark
Newbery, John
New Castle

When there is a comma in the heading, the letter-by-letter arrangement goes through to the comma only—so that all the same names will be brought together.

Black, color
Black, Hugo
Black, Joseph
Blackball
Black Hills
Black market

What About Words in Parentheses, Titles, and Roman Numerals?
The alphabetical arrangement of headings is not affected by words in parentheses, titles, or Roman numerals. Just look up the heading as if it did not contain these added words or symbols.

Adler (OD-ler)**, Alfred**
Adler (AD-ler)**, Felix**

Gregory, Saint
Gregory, Lady Augusta
Gregory, Dick

John, Saint, apostle of Jesus Christ
John I, II, and III, books of the Bible, New Testament
John, king of England
John II, king of France
John XXIII, pope

How Do I Look Up a Heading That Begins with a Number?
If a number is the first word in a heading, the number is spelled out and put in its alphabetical place.

Seven Cities of Cibola
Seven seas
Seven Sisters
Seventeenth Amendment, to the United States Constitution
Seven wonders of the ancient world

When numbers appear in any other place in a heading, they come before letters.

Carbon
Carbon-14
Carbon black

Do I Look Up "A," "An," and "The"?
"A," "an," and "the" are not used in alphabetizing. If any one of these words is part of the title of a book or play, the word is put at the end of the title.

Big Wave, The
Midsummer Night's Dream, A

How Are Initials Indexed?
You will find initials in their proper alphabetical order. A *"see"* reference along with them will lead you to the heading for which the initials stand.

CIA *see* Central Intelligence Agency

How Do I Look Up the Abbreviation "Mt."?
Mount is always spelled out and is placed after the name.

Everest, Mount

The word "lake," too, as a geographical term, is placed after the name.

Michigan, Lake

But you can look up the names of forts, towns, and rivers just as you would say them.

Fort Dearborn
Lake Placid
Mississippi River
Mount Vernon

How Do I Look Up a Poem?
Poems are listed individually by name and also by their authors.

To Autumn, poem by John Keats **K 200**

Keats, John
    "To Autumn" K 200

How Do I Look Up a Story?
If the story you are looking for has been included in its complete form, you will find it listed under the heading **Stories, told in full.** If the story you want is part of a longer work, you will find it listed individually by its name.

Oliver Twist, book by Charles Dickens, excerpt

Other listings similar to **Stories, told in full** are **Experiments and projects; Hobbies; How to.**

A, first letter of the English alphabet **A** 1
See also Alphabet
A-1, term meaning "first-class" **A** 1
AA see Alcoholics Anonymous
Aa (AH-ah), lava **V** 378, 379
AAA see Agricultural Adjustment Administration
AAA see American Automobile Association

Aachen (AH-ken), a city in West Germany in the state of North Rhine–Westphalia. The city is in a coal-mining region southwest of Cologne, near the Belgian and Dutch borders. It is known as Aix-la-Chapelle to the French. An industrial and commercial city, Aachen produces steel, textiles, electrical machinery, and other manufactures. It is also noted for its baths, established by the Romans near sulfur springs. Charlemagne made Aachen his northern capital and built its cathedral, which contains his tomb. Until the 16th century, it was the coronation city of the holy Roman emperors. Aachen was the first major city to be captured by the Allies (1944) in World War II. The population is about 242,000.

Aachen, Treaties of see Aix-la-Chapelle, Treaties of
Aalto (AHL-to) **Alvar Henrik,** Finnish architect and designer
modern architecture **A** 386a
stadium for the Polytechnical School, Otaniemi, Finland, picture **A** 386c
AAM (air-to-air missiles) **M** 344, 348
A & P see Atlantic and Pacific Tea Company, Great
Aardema, Verna, American writer
illustration by Leo and Diane Dillon for Why Mosquitoes Buzz in People's Ears **C** 248a
Aardvark, African, mammal **M** 66; picture **M** 69
Aardwolf, hyenalike animal **H** 308
Aarhus, Denmark **D** 112

Aaron (A-ron), in Old Testament, brother of Moses and first Jewish high priest, said to have lived sometime between 16th and 13th centuries B.C. He rebelled against Moses and built a golden calf, an idol, which Moses destroyed.
Moses and Aaron **M** 468
See also Golden Calf

Aaron, Hank (Henry Louis Aaron) (1934–   ), American baseball player, b. Mobile, Ala. In 1974 he hit his 715th home run, breaking Babe Ruth's lifetime record. By the end of his career, he had set a new lifetime home run mark of 755. Aaron played for the Milwaukee (later Atlanta) Braves of the National League from 1954 to 1974. He was the league's batting champion (1956, 1959), Most Valuable Player (1957), and home run leader (1957, 1963, 1966–67). He played one season (1975–76) with the Milwaukee Brewers of the American League and then returned to the Braves as a vice-president. **B** 78; **N** 102; picture **B** 76

Aar River, Switzerland, picture **S** 498
AAU see Amateur Athletic Union of the United States
Abaca (ab-a-CA), plant fiber **R** 332
Abacus (AB-a-cus), device for counting **A** 2–3; **N** 392
an early office machine **O** 55
first computing machine **C** 449; pictures **C** 451
Japanese soroban **J** 27

Abadan (ah-bah-DAHN), a port city in southwestern Iran on Abadan Island, near the Iraqi border. It is located on the delta of the Shatt al Arab, a river that empties into the Persian Gulf. Abadan is one of the world's largest petroleum-refining centers. Its refineries are connected with Iran's rich oil fields by pipelines. A huge refinery, established in 1909, is controlled by the National Iranian Oil Company. Abadan's population is over 300,000.

Abalone (ab-al-O-ne), also called ear shell, a mollusk found along coastlines in many parts of the world. It has beautiful red, green, or black shell, used to make mother-of-pearl buttons or ornaments. Picture **S** 148
gastropods **O** 278

Abbai (ob-I), name for Blue Nile in Ethiopia **E** 299
Abbate, Niccolo dell', Italian painter **R** 171

Abbe (AB-be), **Cleveland** (1838–1916), American meteorologist, b. New York, N.Y. He issued first daily weather reports in United States. Their popularity led to formation of U.S. Weather Bureau, which he organized. He was responsible for adoption of U.S. standard time.

Abbey Theatre, Dublin, Ireland **D** 299; **I** 394; **T** 161
Yeats, William Butler **Y** 344

Abbott, Douglas Charles (1899–   ), Canadian public official, b. Lenoxville, Quebec. Abbott was elected to the House of Commons (1940) and later was minister of national defense and of finance. From 1954 to 1973 he was a judge of the Canadian Supreme Court. In 1974 he became head of a parliamentary advisory commission.

Abbott, Sir John Joseph Caldwell (1821–93), Canadian statesman, b. St. Andrews, Quebec. He was dean of the Faculty of Law at McGill University (1855–80) and a leading authority on commercial law. He served in the Legislative Assembly of Canada and the House of Commons (1859–74, 1881–87) and was appointed to the Senate (1887). He was mayor of Montreal (1887–89), Conservative Party leader, and prime minister (1891–92).

Abbott, Robert Sengstacke (1868–1940), American publisher, b. St. Simons Island, Ga. He founded (1905) and edited Chicago Defender, a weekly newspaper devoted to interests of blacks. The paper's strong editorials greatly encouraged migration of southern blacks to northern industrial centers.
NAACP, history of **N** 97

Abbreviations A 4–6
amateur radio **R** 63
how filed in libraries **L** 186
knitting and crocheting **K** 278
Postal Service abbreviations **P** 410
shorthand systems based upon **S** 164
states see state articles
used as slang **S** 194
See also individual letters of the alphabet

ABC Powers, term derived from initials of Argentina, Brazil, and Chile. These nations were closely allied before World War I and formed board (1914) to settle differences between United States and Mexico.

Abdomen, part of the body **D** 212
CAT scan, picture **X** 341
doctor's examination of **M** 208h
insects **I** 262, 263
Abdul-Hamid II, sultan of Turkey **T** 329

Abdul-Jabbar, Kareem (1947–), American basketball player, b. New York, N.Y. He has been named Most Valuable Player of the National Basketball Association five times (1971, 1972, 1974, 1976, 1977). Abdul-Jabbar is 218 cm (7 ft 2 in) tall. He led UCLA to three national titles (1967–69). Playing for the Milwaukee Bucks of the NBA, he won the Rookie of the Year award in 1970 and led the Bucks to the NBA title in 1971. He was traded to the Los Angeles Lakers in 1975. A Muslim, he changed his name from Lew Alcindor in 1971. Picture **B** 90a

Abdullah ibn Hussein, king of Jordan **J** 139
Abdul Rahman, Tunku see Rahman, Tunku Abdul
à Becket, Saint Thomas, English churchman see Becket, Saint Thomas à
Abel see Cain and Abel

Abel (A-bel), **John Jacob** (1857–1938), American physician and chemist, b. Cleveland, Ohio. He is noted for his studies on chemical composition of animal glands, tissues, and fluids. In the course of research he discovered crystalline form of insulin, essential in treating diabetes, and adrenaline (epinephrine), a substance that raises blood pressure.

Abel (OB-el), **Niels Henrik** (1802–29), Norwegian mathematician, b. Findoe. His proofs and theorems of algebraic equations have caused him to be known (with K. G. Jacobi) as creator of higher trigonometry.

Abelard (AB-el-ard), **Peter** (1079–1142), French philosopher and theologian, b. near Nantes. His fame as lecturer and teacher attracted students from many countries, but his philosophy offended the Church and he was condemned for heresy (1140). His marriage to Heloïse displeased her uncle Fulbert, who was responsible for a physical attack upon Abelard. After the attack Abelard withdrew to a monastery and Héloïse became a nun. Their letters and love story have become famous.

Aberdeen, Scotland **S** 87
Aberdeen, South Dakota **S** 324
Aberdeen Angus, breed of beef cattle **C** 147

Aberhart, William (1878–1943), Canadian political leader, b. Seaforth, Ontario. He formed Social Credit Party of Alberta and was premier of Alberta (1935–43). He supported program of social credit advocating return of government profits to consumers in form of dividends.

Abernathy, Ralph David (1926–), American minister and civil rights leader, b. Linden, Ala. He succeeded Martin Luther King, Jr., as president of the Southern Christian Leadership Conference (SCLC) in April, 1968. He served in that post until 1977. In May, 1968, he led the Poor People's March on Washington, D.C.
　　See also Poor People's March; Southern Christian Leadership Conference

Aberrations, of lenses **L** 148–49
Abhorrers, name of an early English political party **P** 378
Abidjan (ab-id-JON), capital of Ivory Coast **I** 489, 492; pictures **D** 119, **I** 490

Abigail, in Old Testament (I Samuel), wife of Nabal and, after Nabal's death, wife of David. Story relates that when David was marching with his armies against Na-

bal, Abigail met him with a supply of provisions and thus subdued his anger and prevented the fight.

Ability
Ability grouping, of students **E** 78
Ablation, removal, as by evaporation, or vaporization
Able-bodied seamen **U** 183
ABM see Safeguard anti-ballistic missile
Abolitionist movement, in black American history
Abomey (ah-BO-may), capital of early kingdom of Dahomey **B** 140
Abominable Snowman **H** 129
Aborigines (ab-or-IJ-in-ese), Australian native people

Abortion, the ending of a pregnancy before the embryo or fetus (unborn child) is able to survive on its own. If an abortion happens naturally, because of a physical problem of the mother or baby, it is called a *spontaneous abortion* (miscarriage). When the life or health of the mother or baby is in danger, doctors may perform an *induced therapeutic abortion*. An abortion performed for any other reason is called an *elective abortion*. Some people believe that elective abortion is murder. Others say that it is a private matter between a woman and her doctor. In 1973 the U.S. Supreme Court ruled that a woman has the right to an elective abortion during the first three months of pregnancy. During the second three months, states may enforce certain health regulations, such as demanding that the abortion be performed in a hospital. After that time, abortion is legal only when a woman's life or health is in danger.

Abracadabra, supposedly magical word used to invoke aid of good spirits in preventing or curing disease or misfortune. When inscribed on an amulet worn around the neck, it was supposed to ward off evil spirits. Word was first used by Sammonicus, a 2nd-century physician.

Abraham, father of the Jews **A** 6b; **J** 102
Abraham, Plains of, Quebec **F** 462
Abraham Lincoln Birthplace National Historic Site, Kentucky **K** 221
Abraham's Sacrifice, etching by Rembrandt **D** 358
Abramowitz, Shalom Jacob see Mendele Mocher Sefarim

Abrasives (a-BRAI-sives), materials used for grinding and polishing **G** 387–89
   grinding machines **T** 219
   optical glass grinding **O** 174–75

Abruzzi (a-BRU-tzi), **Duke of the** (Luigi Amedeo Giuseppe Maria Ferdinando Francesco, Prince of Savoy Aosta) (1873–1933), Italian explorer, mountaineer, and naval officer, b. Madrid, Spain. He led North Pole expedition aboard ship *Stella Polare,* attaining farthest northern latitude (86° 33′ N) of any explorer up to that time (1899–1900). He made first ascent of Mt. Elias, Alaska (1897), commanded Italian Navy in Adriatic during World War I, and developed colonization programs for Italian Somaliland.

Abruzzo, Ben, American balloonist **B** 32

Absalom, in Old Testament (II Samuel 13–19), son of King David of Israel. He rebelled against his father and was slain by Joab, David's captain. John Dryden's satirical poem ''Absalom and Achitophel'' makes use of the story of Absalom.

Absaroka (ab-SA-ro-ka) **Range,** Rocky Mountains, picture **W** 333
Absentee ballots, for voting in elections **E** 113
Absolute magnitude, of stars **S** 406
Absolute music **M** 532
Absolute zero **H** 90; **M** 177
Absolution, forgiveness **P** 435
Absorbent papers **P** 53

Absorption, process by which one substance takes in (absorbs) another substance or energy. Liquids, gases, sound, light, and heat are absorbed by porous solids, liquids, and gases. It is also the process by which digested food passes into the bloodstream.

Absorption refrigerating system **R** 137
Abstinence syndrome, in narcotic withdrawal **N** 13
Abstract art, modern art movement **M** 397
   African sculpture **A** 76; pictures **A** 74, 75
   collage **C** 376–77
   concern with form **A** 438g
   Dutch **D** 362
   France **F** 432
   Germany's Blue Rider group **G** 171
   Kandinsky, Wassily **K** 166
Abstract expressionism, art movement **P** 31, 32; **U** 122
   modern art **M** 397
Abstract words **S** 118
Abu Dhabi, capital of the United Arab Emirates **U** 64a

Abu Dhabi, largest of the seven formerly British-protected sheikhdoms that make up the United Arab Emirates along Persian Gulf. The traditional economy, centered around fishing and pearling, has been replaced by oil production (since 1962). The principal city, Abu Dhabi, located on the coast, becomes an island during high tide. **U** 64a, 64b

Abundant numbers **N** 379–80
Abu Simbel, site of ancient Egyptian temples **D** 21; **E** 100; pictures **A** 363, **E** 90d, 101
Abyssal (a-BISS-al) **plain,** flat area of ocean floor **O** 28–29
   deep-sea vessels and underwater exploration **U** 17
Abyssinia *see* Ethiopia

Abyssinian cats **C** 142; picture **C** 144
Abyssinian wild ass **H** 244
A.C. *see* Alternating current
Acacia (ac-A-sha), tree **A** 328; **P** 283
Academic dress **U** 205–06

Academic freedom, principle advocating freedom to teach or learn whatever is thought to lead to truth, without fear of coercion. It protects teachers and scholars from loss of position or other persecution because of ideas they may express.

Academy, school in Athens started by Plato **P** 332

Academy of Motion Picture Arts and Sciences (AMPAS), an honorary organization composed of people in the motion picture industry. Each year it presents Academy Awards (''Oscars'') to those who have made outstanding contributions in such areas as acting, writing, and directing. The academy was founded in 1927. It has headquarters in Beverly Hills, Calif., and publishes the *Academy Bulletin.*

Academy of Science, Canberra, Australia, picture **C** 87

Acadia (a-CAY-dia), French name for area now Nova Scotia and New Brunswick, Canada. It was fought over by French and English from 1610 to 1713, when a treaty granted England possession. In 1755 English expelled all French settlers (Acadians) who would not take oath of allegiance to England. Deported Acadians, many of whom settled in Louisiana, are immortalized in Henry Wadsworth Longfellow's poem *Evangeline.*
   Canada, early history of **C** 69, 70; **N** 138, 138g, 344a, 344h

Acadia National Park, Maine **M** 41
Acadians, original French habitants of New France, now Canada **C** 48; **N** 138g, 344g, 344h
   Maine settlers **M** 38
   See also Cajuns

Acanthus, prickly plant found in tropics and southern Europe. Some varieties have white or rose-colored thorny flowers, while others have no flowers. Plant usually grows to about 1 m. Its graceful design was copied by ancient Greeks in their architecture (Corinthian columns). Picture **F** 505

A cappella (oc-ap-PEL-la), musical term **M** 532
   choral music **C** 277
Accelerando, musical term **M** 532
Acceleration, change in speed of an object **M** 470–71
   gravity and gravitation **G** 322–23
   human body, effects on **S** 340j
   law of falling bodies **F** 34
Accelerators, in chemistry
   plastics **P** 327
Accelerators, particle *see* Particle accelerators
Accelerometer (ac-cel-er-OM-et-er), instrument to show changes in speed **N** 68; **S** 340g
Accents, in music **M** 532
Accents, in poetry **P** 353–54
Accents, marks of stress in pronunciation **P** 478
Accessories, things added to give style
   interior decorating **I** 301–02
Accidentals, in music **M** 532
Accident insurance *see* Insurance, accident
Accidents
   alcoholism is a leading cause of **A** 148

first-aid treatment for **F** 157–63
National Traffic and Motor Vehicle Safety Act, 1966
  A 550
occupational health and safety **O** 16–17
safety **S** 3–7
workers' compensation **W** 253
Accompaniment, in music **M** 532
Accordion, folk music instrument **F** 330; **K** 240; picture **K** 239
Accounting and bookkeeping **B** 311–14
insurance **I** 297
mathematics **M** 168
See also Calculators; Computers
Accra (AC-cra), capital of Ghana **G** 196; picture **G** 194
AC-DC (universal) **motors** **E** 139
Ace, hole in one, in golf **G** 255
Aces, fighter pilots in World War I **U** 159
Acetate (AS-e-tate) **fibers** **N** 424, 428
Acetic (a-CE-tic) **acid,** in vinegar **F** 349
Acetone (AS-e-tone), flammable chemical formed by fermentation **F** 91
Acetylcholine, transmitter agent in the nervous system **B** 365
Acetylene (a-CET-il-ene), gas **G** 60, 61
automobile headlights **L** 285
fuel **F** 490

Achaeans (a-KEE-ans), a people of ancient Greece. They originally migrated into northern Greece and settled in Thessaly. About the 13th century B.C. they moved southward into the Peloponnesus, which they dominated until displaced by other Greek-speaking tribes, particularly the Dorians. In Homer's *Iliad* the Greeks who fought in the Trojan War are usually referred to as Achaeans. Their region in Greece was called Achaea.
Trojan War **T** 293

Achard (OC-hart) **Franz Carl,** German chemist **S** 456
Achebe, Chinua, Nigerian novelist **A** 76c, 76d

Acheson, Dean Gooderham (1893–1971), American lawyer and statesman, b. Middletown, Conn. He was undersecretary of treasury (1933), assistant secretary of state (1941–45), and secretary of state (1949–53) under Truman. He played an important role in founding NATO. His book, *Present at the Creation: My Years in the State Department,* won the Pulitzer Prize (1970) for autobiography.

Acheson, Edward, American inventor
carborundum **G** 388–89
Achievement tests **T** 117, 120
counseling tests in guidance **G** 399
examinations for college entrance **E** 348, 349
Achievers, of Junior Achievement, Inc. **J** 157–58
Achilles (ack-ILL-ese), in Greek mythology **G** 366
Achilles playing dice, painting on a Greek vase, picture **A** 227
Iliad **I** 69
Achilles heel **G** 366

Achilles tendon, a long cord of tissue that connects the calf muscle of the leg to the heel bone. It is the strongest tendon in the body and gives the leg the elasticity needed to lift the heel while walking. The achilles tendon is easily injured, especially in athletics.

Achondroplasia *see* Dwarfism
Acid dyes **D** 371

Acid rain, rain or other precipitation that contains sulfur and nitrogen oxides, as well as other chemical pollutants. Acid rain forms when chemicals from power plants, factories, automobiles, and other sources combine with moisture in the air. When this mixture falls to earth, it has been known to poison fish and other aquatic life and to damage buildings and stone statuary. Some environmental studies have also linked acid rain to crop and forest damage and pollution of drinking water.

Acids **C** 216
canning of food **F** 346
fatty acids **O** 76, 79
tests for (experiments) **C** 217
See also names of acids
Ackia Battleground Monument, Mississippi **M** 358

Aclinic line, or **magnetic equator,** imaginary line on earth's surface, lying close to geographical equator. At any point along this line attraction between North and South magnetic poles is balanced, and a magnetic needle will show no dip.

ACLU *see* American Civil Liberties Union
Acne **D** 205
Aconcagua (oc-on-CA-gua), highest peak in Andes **A** 253, 391; **M** 499; **S** 276; picture **S** 275
Aconite (monkshood), plant **P** 322
Acorns, fruit of oak trees
Acorn Area Indians of North America **I** 174–75
Acoustic microscope **M** 288
Acoustics (a-COO-stics), science of the behavior of sound **S** 260–61
How do musical instruments make sounds? **M** 544
noise control **N** 270
Acquired characteristics, in biology
Lamarck's theory of evolution **E** 344
Acre, measure of land **A** 96; **W** 111
Acronyms, words formed from the initial letters in a phrase or title **A** 4
Acropolis (a-CROP-o-lis), highest area of a Greek city **A** 374
Athens, picture **E** 327
Acrostics (a-CROST-ics), word games **W** 236
Acrylic (a-CRIL-ic) **fibers** **N** 425
Acrylic (plastic) **paint** **P** 30
Acta Diurna ("Acts of the Day"), public announcements in ancient Rome **N** 197–98

Actaeon (ac-TE-on), in Greek mythology, hunter who happened upon Artemis (goddess of the hunt) bathing in a river. Angered and offended, Artemis changed him into a deer, and he was hunted down and eaten by his own hounds.

ACTH, stands for adrenocorticotrophic hormone, a chemical substance produced in the human brain by anterior pituitary gland. It is taken from the same gland in cattle, mainly for use in treatment of rheumatoid arthritis. It stimulates the adrenal gland to produce cortisone.

Acting **T** 156
charades **C** 187–88
how to put on a play **P** 335–41
importance to Oriental dance **D** 292, 293
pantomimes with the dance **D** 35
Acting president, duty of the vice-president **V** 325

Actinide (AC-tin-ide) **series,** of rare earth elements **E** 159

Actinium (ac-TIN-ium), element **E** 154, 159

Action and reaction, Newton's third law of motion **M** 471

Action painting, work of some abstract expressionists **M** 397

    painting in the United States **P** 31

    Pollack, Jackson **P** 387

ACTION Programs, activities of the United States government agency for volunteer help **A** 7

    Peace Corps **P** 101

Actium, battle of, 31 B.C. **M** 100

Activating enzymes B 296

Act of Settlement, 1701, England **E** 225

Act of Union see Acts of Union

Actors and actresses P 336

    Barrymore family **B** 67-68

    Chaplin, Charlie **C** 186b-87

    circus performers, pictures **C** 301, 303, 304

    motion picture industry **M** 472-488c

    Shakespeare, William **S** 130b-33

    star system in motion pictures **M** 473

    theater **T** 156-57

Actors' Equity Association (AEA), a trade union of actors, dancers, chorus members, and other performers in the legitimate theater. It was the first union to include a clause in its contracts providing for arbitration of all disputes. It was founded in 1913 and has its headquarters in New York, N.Y.

ACTP see American College Testing Program

Acts of the Apostles, The, book in the New Testament **B** 160; **C** 279-80

Acts of Trade and Navigation, British U 129

Acts of Union

    England and Ireland, 1801 **E** 228; **I** 390; **P** 265

    England and Scotland, 1707 **E** 225; **S** 89

    Upper and Lower Canada united, 1841 **C** 73; **Q** 16

    Wales and England, 1536 **W** 4

Actuaries, mathematics experts in insurance companies **I** 297

    mathematics **M** 167-68

Acuff, Roy, American singer **C** 524b

Acupuncture, medical treatment **M** 208a, 208b

    anesthesia **A** 259

Acute angles, in geometry **G** 124; diagram **G** 125

ADA see Americans for Democratic Action

Adagio, musical tempo **M** 532

Adam, Adolphe, French composer **F** 447

Adam, James and **Robert,** Scottish architects and furniture designers **A** 317; **E** 240; **F** 507

    chair, picture **D** 67

    design for Drury Lane Theatre, London, by Robert Adam, picture **E** 240

Adam and Eve, in the Old Testament (Genesis), first man and woman and parents of human race. Adam (from Hebrew word for "life") was created by God in His image out of dust. Eve (from Hebrew word for "mother of all living") was made by God from one of Adam's ribs. They were placed in Garden of Eden but were expelled for eating forbidden fruit of the tree of knowledge of good and evil. They had three sons: Cain, Abel, and Seth.

    earliest palindrome **W** 236

Adam and Eve, sculpture by Brancusi **S** 104

Adamawa Highlands, Nigeria **N** 254

Adam de la Halle (ad-ON d'la OLL), French poet-musician **F** 444

Adams, Abigail Smith, wife of John Adams **A** 8, 12; **F** 165

Adams, Adrienne (1906–), American illustrator of children's books, b. Fort Smith, Ark. Among books she illustrated are *Thumbelina, The Shoemaker and the Elves, Mouse House,* and *The Ugly Duckling.* **C** 244

Adams, Brooks, American historian **A** 18

Adams, Charles Francis (1807–86), American diplomat **A** 18

Adams, Charles Francis (1866–1954), American lawyer **A** 18

Adams, Charles Francis, Jr. (1835–1915), American economist **A** 18

Adams, Henry, first of the Adams line **A** 18

Adams, Henry Brooks (1838–1918), American historian, b. Boston, Mass. A grandson of John Quincy Adams, he was secretary to his father, Charles Francis Adams, during his term as U.S. minister to Great Britain (1861–68). He taught history at Harvard University (1870–77), where he instituted the seminar method of study and edited the *North American Review.* His writings include *History of the United States* in 9 volumes, *Mont-Saint-Michel and Chartres,* and *The Education of Henry Adams.*

    American literature, place in **A** 207

Adams, James Truslow (1878–1949), American historian, b. Brooklyn, N.Y. He won the Pulitzer prize for history (1921) for *The Founding of New England,* part of a trilogy with *Revolutionary New England, 1691–1776* and *New England in the Republic, 1776–1850.* He was also editor of the *Dictionary of American History* and *Atlas of American History.* **A** 214a

Adams, John, 2nd president of United States **A** 8–11; picture **V** 325

    Adams family **A** 18

    casting vote of vice-presidents **V** 326

    favored Independence Day celebrations **I** 112

Adams, John Couch, English astronomer **P** 278

    astronomy, history of **A** 473

Adams, John Quincy, 6th president of United States **A** 12–15

    Adams family **A** 18

    Clay, Henry **C** 335

Adams, Léonie Fuller (1899–), American poet and educator, b. Brooklyn, N.Y. She was a lecturer at Columbia University (1947–68) and was poetry consultant to Library of Congress (1948–49). In 1969 she received the Brandeis medal for poetic achievement. Her works include *Those Not Elect* and *This Measure.*

Adams, Louisa Johnson, wife of John Quincy Adams **A** 13; **F** 166–67

Adams, Maude (Maude Kiskadden) (1872–1953), American actress, b. Salt Lake City, Utah. She is noted for her roles in J. M. Barrie's plays, especially *Peter Pan,* and for her role as Juliet in Shakespeare's *Romeo and Juliet.* She retired (1918), returned briefly to the stage, and later taught dramatics at Stephens College, Columbia, Mo.

Utah, famous people from **U** 253

Adams, Richard, English novelist **E** 267
Adams, Samuel, American Revolutionary patriot and statesman **A** 16–17
Adams family **A** 18
Committees of Correspondence **R** 196

Adams, Samuel Hopkins (1871–1958), American magazine writer and novelist, b. Boston, Mass. He was a reporter on New York *Sun* (1891–1900) and was on staff of *McClure's Magazine* (1903–05). He wrote a famous series exposing quackery in patent medicine (1905). This series was in part responsible for passage of first Pure Food and Drug Act. His works include *It Happened One Night* and *The Incredible Era*.

Adam's apple, bulge in front part of throat. Part of the larynx, it is especially prominent in men. Name comes from legend that part of the apple became stuck in Adam's throat when he ate the forbidden fruit.
speaking mechanism **S** 377

Adams family, of Massachusetts **A** 17–18
Adams National Historic Site, Quincy, Mass. **M** 144
famous people from Massachusetts **M** 147
Adams National Historic Site, Quincy, Massachusetts **M** 144
Adamson Act, 1916 **W** 179
Adams-Onís Treaty (Transcontinental Treaty of 1819) **T** 109, 272
diplomatic triumph for Adams **A** 13
No-Transfer Principle in Monroe Doctrine **M** 427
Adana (a-DA-na), Turkey **T** 326
Adaptability
behavior of animals **A** 286–87
Adaptation, in biology **L** 214–27
anthropological findings **A** 306–07
birds **B** 209–10, 221–23
cactus **C** 3–4
camels **C** 34
camouflage of fishes **F** 193; pictures **F** 192
evolution theory **E** 346
home areas of plants **P** 304
insects **I** 274–76
lizards **L** 319–20
mammals **M** 63–64
pinnipeds **W** 5–8
whales **W** 151
See also Ecology; Estivation; Hibernation; Life; Plant defenses; Protective coloration
Adaptive radiation, in biology
birds **B** 209–10
Addams, Charles, American cartoonist **C** 128
cartoon, picture **C** 127
Addams, Jane, American social worker **A** 19
peace movements **P** 105
Addends, in arithmetic **A** 398
Addiction, to drugs **D** 328, 329–30
the life of addicts **N** 13–14
See also Alcoholism
Adding machines **C** 449; **O** 55–57
Addis Ababa, capital of Ethiopia **E** 300; pictures **A** 69, **E** 296, 298
Addison, Joseph, English essayist **E** 258, 292; **M** 14
Addition, in mathematics **A** 398–99
abacus **A** 2–3
algebra **A** 158–59

decimal fractions **F** 401
fractions **F** 399
OR computer circuits **C** 454
use of binary numeration system for computers **C** 456
using base-4 system **N** 400
Additives, chemicals
food preservation and processing **F** 348
food regulations and laws **F** 350–52
for lubricants **L** 371
gasoline **G** 63
Address, forms of, in speaking and writing **A** 19–21
See also Letter writing
Addressing machines **O** 58
Ade, George, American journalist and humorist **H** 280
Adelaide, capital of South Australia **A** 511, 514
Adelie (ad-A-le) penguins **P** 121–24; pictures **H** 185, **P** 370
through the year with birds **B** 212, 213
Adelita, Mexican song **N** 27
Aden (A-den), city of Yemen (Aden) **Y** 347

Adenauer (OD-en-our), **Konrad** (1876–1967), German statesman, b. Cologne. He was chief mayor of Cologne and a member of Prussian Upper House (1917–33) and president of Prussian Council of State (1920–33). He was a member of Provincial Diet and Provincial Committee of Rhine Province (1917–33) but was removed from office by Nazis and imprisoned twice. Reinstated as chief mayor of Cologne in 1945, he was one of founders and leaders of Christian Democratic Union. Adenauer was chancellor of German Federal Republic (1949–63). Pictures **E** 111, **P** 456a

Adenoids, lymph tissue in nasal passages **D** 209
Adenosine (ad-EN-os-ene) **triphosphate,** or ATP **B** 198, 296–97; **P** 222
Adeodatus I, Saint, pope **R** 296
Adeodatus II, pope **R** 296
Adeste Fideles (ad-EST-ay fid-AY-les), or "O Come, All Ye Faithful" **C** 122
Adhesion, in physics **L** 310; **P** 233
Adhesives **G** 242–43
bonding of plywood **F** 504
Ad hoc committees, of organizations **P** 80
Adiabatic cooling, of air **C** 358
Adirondack (ad-ir-ON-dack) **Mountains** **N** 213; picture **N** 215
Adja, African people **B** 139
Adjectival clauses, in sentences **P** 91
Adjectives, words that modify nouns **P** 91

Adler (OD-ler), **Alfred** (1870–1937), Austrian psychiatrist, b. Penzing-Vienna. Originally a close associate of Sigmund Freud, he later disagreed with basic Freudian ideas and developed theory that inferiority complex is root of most psychological problems. He spent much time in United States (after 1925) and finally settled in New York City (1935). He lectured and taught at several medical schools and founded School of Individual Psychology, Vienna. He started *Journal of Individual Psychology* and was author of numerous works, including *The Science of Living* and *The Pattern of Life.*

Adler (AD-ler), **Felix** (1851–1933), American scholar, lecturer, and founder (1876) of Society for Ethical Culture, b. Alzey, Germany. He came to United States in 1857. He taught Hebrew and Oriental literature at Cornell University (1874–76) and was professor of ethics at Columbia University (1902–33). Adler started first free

Adler, Felix (continued)
kindergarten in New York, N.Y., and was active in movements to create better housing and to eliminate child labor.

Adler, Mortimer Jerome (1902–), American author and educator, b. New York, N.Y. In 1974 he was appointed chairman of the board of editors for *Encyclopaedia Britannica*. Adler was associate professor and then professor of philosophy of law at the University of Chicago from 1930 to 1952. He became co-editor of the Great Books of the Western World series in 1945 and director of the Institute for Philosophical Research in San Francisco in 1952. His books include *How to Read a Book, The Difference of Man and the Difference it Makes,* and *Time of Our Lives.*

Adler, Ruth (1915–68), American author and illustrator of children's books, b. Sullivan County, N.Y. She has illustrated books, including *Electronics* and *Magic House of Numbers* (written by her husband). She collaborated with her husband, **Irving Adler** (1913–), on such books as "Reason Why" series, *The Earth's Crust,* and *Oceans.* Both are known particularly for works on science and mathematics.

Adler (AD-ler) **Planetarium and Astronomical Museum,** Chicago, Illinois **M** 513
Administrator (feminine: administratrix) of a will **W** 174
Admiralty Court, Canada **C** 78
Admiralty Islands, Papua New Guinea **I** 425
Admiralty law *see* Maritime law
Adobe (ad-O-be), sun-dried bricks **B** 391
houses **H** 173–74
pueblo, picture **A** 302

Adoff (ADE-off), **Arnold** (1935–), American author and anthologist, b. New York, N.Y. As a teacher Adoff was concerned by the lack of black literature for young readers. He began collecting the works of black poets for use in his classroom. His collections grew into poetry anthologies such as *I Am the Darker Brother* (1968) and *My Black Me* (1974). He has also written a biography, *Malcolm X* (1970), and books of poetry for children.

Adolescence (ad-ol-ES-cence) **A** 22–24
acne **D** 205
drug abuse **D** 329, 331, 332
juvenile delinquency **J** 162–64
values **V** 268a
See also Family

Adonis (ad-ON-is), in Greek mythology, handsome youth loved by Aphrodite and Persephone and ordered by Zeus to spend half the year with each goddess. He was killed by a boar while hunting.

Adoption **A** 25–26; **S** 225
orphanages and foster-family care **O** 227
Adoration, prayer of **P** 434
Adoration of the Kings, The, painting by Leonardo da Vinci **L** 153
Adoration of the Magi, painting by Botticelli, picture **N** 39
Adoration of the Magi, painting by Gentile da Fabriano **U** 2
Adoration of the Magi, painting by Rubens **D** 356
Adoration of the Shepherds, The, painting by Mantegna **A** 438a

Adoula (ad-OO-la), **Cyrille,** prime minister of Congo (Kinshasa), now Zaïre **Z** 366d
Adrar des Iforas (od-RAR days e-fo-RA), mountains in North Africa **M** 57
Adrenal (ad-RE-nal) **glands** **B** 279–80, 297
Adrenocorticotropic hormone *see* ACTH
Adrian I, pope **R** 296
Adrian II, pope **R** 296
Adrian III, Saint, pope **R** 296
Adrian IV, pope **R** 297
Holy Roman Empire **H** 163
Adrian V, pope **R** 297
Adrian VI, pope **R** 297
Adriatic Sea **O** 45

Adsorption, process by which a solid or liquid substance holds on its surface (adsorbs) another substance. In gas masks activated charcoal, an adsorbent, holds poison gas molecules, allowing wearer to breathe in pure air. Adsorption is often confused with absorption, in which one substance takes in another.

Adularescence (ad-u-la-RES-cence), in gemstones **G** 70

Adult education, studies for adults. Enrollments in such studies are increasing rapidly, spurred by the idea that education should be a continuing, or lifetime, experience. Courses range from crafts and technical skills to academic subjects. They are offered by colleges and universities, local schools, public libraries, government, and private groups.
Denmark **D** 107, 110
recreation for older citizens **O** 100

Adulteration, of food **F** 351
Ad valorem (ad va-LO-rem) **tariff** **T** 25
Advection fog **F** 288–89
Advent, religious season **R** 155, 290

Adventist, member of a religious group believing that hope of world lies in second coming of Christ. Advent movement was founded by William Miller (1782–1849), a New England Baptist who predicted that the world would come to an end in 1843, at which time Christ would appear. Many Adventist churches with differing views were organized in the 19th century. The largest, the Seventh-Day Adventist Church, does missionary work throughout the world.

Adventure clubs, of Camp Fire, Inc. **C** 38; picture **C** 39
Adventures of Augie March, The, book by Saul Bellow **B** 136
Adventure stories
early rogue, or picaresque, novels **N** 345–46
Adverbs, words that modify verbs, adjectives, or other adverbs **P** 91–92
Advertising **A** 27–34
book publishing **B** 331, 334
commercial art **C** 424–27
communication **C** 441
consumer education **C** 494b
department stores **D** 120
difference between it and public relations **P** 507
Goodyear blimp, picture **H** 107
how radio broadcasting is financed **R** 56
illustration and illustrators **I** 92, 95
mail order **M** 31
modeling, fashion **M** 384–85
newspaper circulation **N** 200, 204

photography **P** 205
posters **P** 404; picture **B** 173
radio programs **R** 60
smoking ads banned on radio and television **S** 203
television **T** 70, 70b, 71
trade and commerce **T** 243
trademarks **T** 244–45
See also Opinion surveys
Advertising agency **A** 30, 32–33, 34
Advocates *see* Lawyers
Adze, tool, pictures **T** 210b
AE *see* Russell, George William
AEC *see* Atomic Energy Commission
Aegean (e-GE-an) **civilization** **A** 438b; **P** 15–16; **S** 94
Aegean Sea **O** 45
Greek islands **G** 333
Aegina (e-JY-na), Greece, picture **G** 336
Aeneas (an-E-as), hero of Vergil's *Aeneid* **A** 35
Aeneid (an-E-id), epic poem by Vergil **A** 35; **V** 304–05
Trojan War **T** 293

Aeolus (EE-ol-us), in Greek mythology, the ruler of the winds. He lived in the Aeolian Islands, where the winds were kept. In the *Odyssey*, Aeolus gives a bag of wind to Odysseus (Ulysses) to help speed his ship home after the Trojan War.

Aeration, method of purifying water **W** 68
Aerial acts, in a circus **C** 304; picture **C** 301
Aerial Lift Bridge, Duluth, Minn., picture **B** 401
Aerial perspective **P** 158
Aerial photography **P** 206
Aerial roots, of plants, picture **P** 291
Aeries, eagles' nests **E** 2
Aerobics, book on physical fitness by Dr. Kenneth Cooper **J** 120b
Aerodynamics, science of air in motion **A** 36–41
airplane design **A** 558–60
birds, flight of **B** 204–05
glider flight **G** 238–39
helicopters, how they fly **H** 105–06
hydrofoil boats **H** 304–05
supersonic flight **S** 469–73
Aeromedicine, part of space program **H** 248
Aeronautical engineering **E** 206
Aeronautics *see* Aviation
Aerosol containers
fluorocarbons used in **G** 62
household pest control **H** 260–63
insecticide bombs **I** 258
Aerospace Defense Command, of U.S. Air Force **U** 161
Aerospace industry **A** 566–67
photography **P** 208
Aerospaceplanes, future space vehicles **R** 262
Aerotrain, new development in transportation **T** 267
Aeschylus (ESC-il-us), Greek dramatist **A** 229; **D** 294; **G** 351
Aesculapius (es-cu-LAPE-ius), legendary Greek doctor **M** 203
serpent wand of, picture **M** 208c
Aesop (E-sop), Greek author of fables **F** 2–3; **H** 280
"Ant and the Grasshopper, The" **F** 5
"Four Oxen and the Lion, The" **F** 5
"Lion and the Mouse, The" **F** 4
Aesthetics (es-THET-ics), or **esthetics,** the branch of philosophy that studies beauty **P** 192
Aetna, Mount *see* Etna, Mount

Afars, African people **D** 236b, 237
Afars and the Issas, French Territory of the *see* Djibouti

Affenpinscher (AHF-en-pin-sher), an alert and lively toy breed of dog known in Europe since the 16th century. The name Affenpinscher comes from two German words that mean "monkey terrier." The wiry, black coat is short on the body but longer on the legs and face, giving the dog its monkeylike appearance. It stands about 25 cm (10 in) at the shoulder and weighs about 3.5 kg (8 lb). It has cropped ears and a docked tail. Picture **D** 260

Affettuoso, musical term **M** 532
Affinity, chemical **D** 370

Affirmative action, policies or programs designed to overcome the effects of past discrimination. U.S. President Lyndon B. Johnson first used the term in 1965 in ordering federal contractors to take "affirmative action" in hiring members of minority groups. The principle was later broadened to include educational institutions, some of which reserved a set number of places for minorities. These quota systems were challenged in a court case, *The Regents of the University of California* v. *Bakke.* Allan P. Bakke, a white man, charged that he was denied admission to a university medical college because of a rigid quota system. The U.S. Supreme Court ruled in 1978 that admissions plans favoring minorities are constitutional but that quota systems are not because they discriminate against whites. Bakke entered the college that year.

Afghan hound, a large dog of the hound group. The current breed was developed in the mountainous countryside of Afghanistan. The Afghan hound is still used there as a hunting dog. It first appeared in the United States in 1926. The Afghan hound stands about 69 cm (27 in) high and weighs about 27 kg (60 lb). Its thick, silky coat may be gray, black, or light brown. It has high-set hipbones, a long, narrow head with a flowing topknot, and a long tail that curls into a ring at the end. Picture **D** 254

Afghanistan (af-GHAN-ist-an) **A** 42–45
Communism **C** 445
flag **F** 239
AFL-CIO *see* American Federation of Labor–Congress of Industrial Organizations
Africa **A** 46–69
art *see* African art
birds of **B** 226
Congo River **C** 465
conservation programs **C** 488
dance **D** 32
doll making **D** 268
education **E** 80, 82; **T** 43
family, picture **F** 45
flags of African countries **F** 235–37
food specialty, couscous **F** 335; picture **F** 337
French empire **F** 412–13
immigration **I** 103
life, plant and animal communities **L** 258
literature *see* African literature
mountain peaks, highest in Africa **M** 494
music *see* African music
Negro history **N** 89–91
Nile River **N** 260–61
poverty **P** 424–424b
prairies **P** 430–33

Africa (continued)
proverbs **P** 487
Sahara, desert **S** 8
Spanish enclaves **S** 356
Stanley and Livingstone, explorers of **S** 400
teachers **T** 43
waterfalls, selected list **W** 57
World Wars I and II **W** 275, 290
See also names of countries
Africa Hall, Addis Ababa, Ethiopia **E** 300; picture
E 298
African Americans *see* Black Americans
African art A 70–76
decorative designs on homes, picture **A** 60
use by Modigliani **M** 403
African hunting dog D 250; picture **D** 251
African kingdoms, early N 90–91
Africa, history of **A** 67
Benin **N** 256
Dahomey **B** 140
Fulani-Hausa **N** 256
Kimbundu, in Angola **A** 261
Mali **M** 58
Yoruba empire of Oyo **N** 256
Zimbabwe, ruins of, picture **Z** 368d
African literature A 76a–76d
A Story, A Story, folktale, picture from **C** 248
African music A 77–79; **N** 253–54
African violet, plant **H** 268–69
African warthogs, wild pigs **H** 211; **P** 248
African wildcat C 141; picture **C** 140
Afrikaans (af-rik-AHNS), language spoken by South African people of Dutch descent **A** 55; **N** 8a;
S 268
Afrikaners, South Africans of Dutch descent **S** 268
Afro-Americans *see* Black Americans

Afro-Asian bloc, an informal voting group in the United Nations made up of Arab, African, Asian, and some South American nations. The group, formed during the 1950's, supports development of poorer countries and is opposed to colonialism. The bloc's growing U.N. membership gives it an important voice in world affairs.

Afro-Brazilian dance L 69
Afro-Cuban dance L 69
Afterburners, in turbofan engines **J** 86
Agades, Niger **N** 251

Aga Kahn (OG-a kahn), spiritual leader of Ismaili Muslim sect. He claims descent and spiritual authority from Mohammed through his daughter Fatima. Shah Karim Khan (1936–) became Aga Khan IV upon the death of his grandfather Aga Khan III in 1957. He married Sarah Croker Poole (1969), making her Begum Aga Khan.

Agam, Vaacov, Israeli painter
Double Metamorphosis II, painting **P** 32; picture
P 31
Agamemnon (ag-a-MEM-non), drama by Aeschylus
D 294
Agamemnon, in Greek mythology **G** 365–66; **T** 293
Iliad **I** 69
Agapetus I, Saint, pope **R** 296
Agapetus II, pope **R** 297
Agar-agar (OG-ar-OG-ar), a gum obtained from algae
A 157; **R** 185
Agassiz (AG-as-se), **Elizabeth Cary,** wife of Jean Louis Rodolphe Agassiz **A** 80
Agassiz, Jean Louis Rodolphe, Swiss-born American geologist and naturalist **A** 80

ice age findings **I** 19, 20
Agassiz, Lake, ancient glacial lake **M** 76, 324–25;
N 324
Agate, chalcedony quartz **Q** 7
Agate Fossil Beds National Monument, Nebraska **N** 81
Agatho, Saint, pope **R** 296
Age *see* Aging
Aged, the *see* Old age

Agee, (AY-gee) **James** (1909–55), American writer, b. Knoxville, Tenn. His novel *A Death in the Family* won a Pulitzer prize in 1958. With photographer Walker Evans, he produced *Let Us Now Praise Famous Men* (1941). This was a study of Depression tenant farmers, told in words and pictures. Agee was an influential film critic during the 1940's. Later, he turned to writing film scripts, including *The African Queen* (1952) and *Night of the Hunter* (1955). His film works were collected in a two-volume set, *Agee on Film* (1958, 1960). **A** 213

Agents (brokers), in wholesale selling **S** 116–17
Agents provocateurs (oj-ONT prov-oc-a-TER), spies
S 389
Age of Bronze, The, sculpture by Rodin **R** 283
Age of Exploration and Discovery E 374–75, 387–90
geographical expeditions **G** 98
Age of Fishes, Devonian period in geology **F** 181–82
Age of Kings, 17th and 18th centuries in Europe
A 438f–438g
Age of Mammals F 388–89
Age of Reason H 136
American literature **A** 197–98
Age of Reptiles F 383, 387
dinosaurs **D** 172, 180–81; chart **D** 174
Ageratums (a-GER-a-tums), flowers **G** 46; picture
G 50
Aggregation, a form of group behavior **F** 201–02
Aghlabites, Tunisian dynasty **T** 312
Agincourt (AJ-in-court), **Battle of,** 1415 **H** 282
Aging A 81–87; **L** 210–11
age of fish **F** 185–86
cell aging and division **C** 159
clam shell showing stages of growth, picture **S** 149
horses' teeth **H** 236
How long do insects live? **I** 265–66
old age **O** 96–101
percentages of older people in populations
P 395–96
stroke, brain damage **D** 207–08
trees **T** 274
Agitato, musical term **M** 532

Agnes, Saint, Christian martyr and patron saint of young girls, lived during 3rd century. She is thought to have been executed when only 12 or 13 years old. According to legend, a young girl could learn whom she would marry by following certain rituals on St. Agnes' Eve (January 20). The legend was used by Keats in his poem "The Eve of St. Agnes."

Agnew, Spiro T., American public official **M** 128; pictures **N** 262d, **V** 331
Agnon, Shmuel Yosef (Samuel Joseph Czaczkes), Hebrew novelist **H** 103

Agnosticism (ag-NAHS-tuh-siz-um), a philosophical belief that people cannot make judgments about things that can never be understood or proved, particularly the existence of God. The term dates from the 19th century when T. H. Huxley stated that any knowledge of God was impossible because of the limited nature of the human mind. He coined the word *agnosticism* from two Greek words meaning "no knowledge."

Aiken, Conrad Potter (continued)
Collected Poems (1954), he was appointed to Chair of Poetry in the Library of Congress (1950–52). His novels include *Blue Voyage* and *Great Circle*.

illustration by Milton Glaser for *Cats and Bats and Things with Wings* **I** 97

Aikido (i-ki-DOE), a Japanese self-defense method based on jujitsu. Two opponents face each other on a mat. The attacker tries to draw the defender off balance and then throw the defender to the mat with painful joint locks. Roles are reversed in alternate rounds.

Ailerons (AIL-er-ons), of airplanes **A** 556; diagram **A** 555

Ailey (AY-lee) **Alvin** (1931–   ), American choreographer, b. Rogers, Texas. A leading figure in modern dance, Ailey is director of the Alvin Ailey American Dance Theater, which he founded in 1958. He worked with choreographer Lester Horton and appeared in Broadway shows before starting his own company. Many of Ailey's dances are set to jazz or gospel music. Among his best-known works are *Blues Suite* (1958), *Cry* (1971), and jazz ballets that celebrate the music of Duke Ellington. **D** 34

Ainu (I-nu), a people of Japan **I** 434, 436; **J** 24, 42
Air **A** 479–82
    aerodynamics **A** 36–41
    air conditioning **A** 101–03
    balloons inflated with hot air **B** 30
    Boyle's law **B** 354; **C** 209–10
    chemical formulas of its chief gases **C** 198
    chemistry, history of, first theories **C** 206
    cloud formation **C** 358–59
    compressed air **W** 71
    deodorizers **D** 117
    dust **D** 346–48
    gases **G** 58–59
    International Geophysical Year, findings **I** 317
    jet streams **J** 88–91
    lift, in airplane flight **A** 38
    liquefaction of gases **L** 308
    matter, states of **M** 170–71
    pollution **A** 108–11; **E** 272f–272g
    pressure *see* Air pressure
    resistance to falling bodies **F** 33
    Why does air move? **W** 184
    winds **W** 184–87
Air, compressed *see* Compressed air
Air, liquid *see* Liquid air
Air-age maps, in North Pole-centered azimuthal projection **M** 93

Air bags, a passive restraint system designed for automobiles, to protect passengers from injury. The bags, mounted in the dashboard or steering wheel, would be automatically inflated by a gas canister when the automobile is involved in a collision. A 1977 ruling by the U.S. Department of Transportation requires air bags or automatic seat belts on all new cars by 1984. **A** 550

Airbrakes **R** 88
Air-breathing missiles **M** 345
Air conditioning **A** 101–03
    air conditioners **E** 119
    air cycle system of refrigeration **R** 137, 138
    heat pumps **H** 99
    spacecraft and space suits **S** 338, 340a, 340L

Aircraft *see* Airplanes; Balloons and ballooning; Gliders; Helicopters; Satellites, artificial
Aircraft carriers **U** 192
Air-cushioned vehicles **T** 267–68

Airedale (AIR-dale) **terrier,** the largest dog in the terrier group. It is used for hunting small game and as a watchdog. Originally bred in the Aire valley of northern England, it was first shown as a breed in 1879. The Airedale is tan with black markings and has a wiry topcoat over a softer undercoat. It has a long, flat head, V-shaped ears, straight legs, and a tail carried up. The average shoulder height is 58 cm (23 in). Airedales weigh from 18 to 23 kg (40 to 50 lb). Picture **D** 255

Airfields *see* Airports
Air Force, Canada *see* Royal Canadian Air Force
Air Force, United States *see* United States Air Force
Air Force Cross, American award, picture **M** 199
Air Force Reserve **U** 162, 165
Air guns **G** 424; **P** 348
Air-launched cruise missiles (ALCM) **M** 349
Airlift, to Berlin, Germany **B** 144; **G** 164
Airline flight attendants **A** 567; **S** 125; **W** 213
Airlines **A** 566–67
    See also transportation section of country, province, and state articles
Airline stewardesses *see* Airline flight attendants

Airlocks, chambers in which air pressure can be regulated to allow passage between differently pressurized sections in a tunnel **T** 318

Airmail **A** 575; **P** 407
Airman's Medal, American award, picture **M** 199
Air mass **W** 76
Air National Guard **N** 43; **U** 162
Airplane models **A** 104–07
Airplanes **A** 553–76
    aerodynamics, theory of flight **A** 36–41
    Concorde **N** 270
    gliders compared to **G** 238
    hydraulic systems **H** 303
    instruments, picture **A** 560
    inventions in air transportation **I** 338
    jet liners, pictures **A** 553, 573, 575; **I** 230
    models **A** 104–07
    "otter aircraft," in Far North, picture **C** 60
    polluting the air; picture **A** 110
    rocket-powered **S** 471-72, 473; pictures **A** 571, **R** 262, **S** 471
    supersonic flight **S** 469–73
    use as farming tool **F** 59
Air plants (epiphytes) **P** 318
Air pollution **A** 108–11; pictures **E** 272a, 272c, 272f
    automobiles are important contributors to air pollution **A** 551–52
    bronchitis and emphysema **D** 194
    cancer **C** 92
    coal **E** 202b
    deodorizers **D** 117
    disease, prevention of **D** 221
    environment, problems of **E** 272f–272g
    lead in gasoline **G** 63
    Los Angeles **L** 345
    smog **F** 289
    See also Dust; Fallout
Airports **A** 562–64; **H** 37
    circular airport of the future **T** 268
    harbor and port facilities in port cities **H** 37

holding patterns, diagram **A** 564
See also transportation section of country, province, and state articles
Air pressure **A** 479; demonstration **A** 482
air pollution affected by **A** 109
barometer **B** 54
deep-sea diving hazard **D** 81, 82
how a tornado causes damage **H** 297–98
pumps, action of **P** 528
tornadoes, how they cause damage **H** 297–98
tunnels, underwater **T** 318
vacuum formed by **V** 263
Venturi effect in aerodynamics **A** 37–39, 40

Air rights, the legal rights to the space above a piece of property. Such space, whether over a building, highway, or railroad tracks, is being used more and more to provide places for new construction. The Pan Am Building in New York City, for example, was built over Grand Central Station. In the United States, air rights belong to the owner of the property below. They are paid for or leased, as are the rights to a piece of land. At times legal disputes about air rights arise when weather control, airplane routes, or the use of a nation's air space are involved.

Air Route Traffic Control (ARTC) **A** 565–66
Air sacs (alveoli), of the lungs **B** 277; **D** 194, 203
Airships **I** 338; **H** 305–06
Goodyear blimp, picture **H** 107
Airspeed indicator, in airplanes **A** 561
Air terminals *see* Airports
Air-to-air missiles (AAM) **M** 344, 348
Air-to-surface missiles (ASM) **M** 344, 348
Air traffic control **A** 564–66
Air University, Alabama **U** 161–62
Aitken, William Maxwell *see* Beaverbrook, Lord
Aix-la-Chapelle *see* Aachen, West Germany

Aix-la-Chapelle (EX-la-shap-ELL),**Treaties of,** three pacts signed by European powers in Aix-la-Chapelle (French name for German city of Aachen). The first (1668) ended War of Devolution between France and Spain. The second (1748) ended War of Austrian Succession, during which Prussia, Spain, Sardinia, Bavaria, Saxony, Poland, and France had tried to seize the Austrian Empire. The third (1818) was an attempt to solve problems that had arisen as a result of French defeat in Napoleonic Wars.

Ajar, Emile, French novelist **F** 443

Ajax (A-jax), name of two legendary Greek heroes of the Trojan War. Ajax the Greater was renowned for his strength and size, and as a warrior was considered second only to Achilles. Ajax and Odysseus (Ulysses) both claimed the armor of the dead Achilles. When Odysseus won the armor, Ajax, insane with rage, slaughtered a flock of sheep and then, in shame, killed himself. He is the subject of a play, *Ajax,* by Sophocles. Ajax the Lesser was punished by the sea god Poseidon (Neptune) for having violated the prophetess Cassandra after the fall of Troy. He was shipwrecked and drowned.
Ajax playing dice, painting on a Greek vase, picture **A** 227

Ajman, state, United Arab Emirates **U** 64a
Ajolotes, lizards **L** 320

Akbar (Jalal-ud-Din Muhammad) (1542–1605), third emperor of Mogul dynasty of India, b. Umarkot. Called Akbar the Great, he came to throne (1556) and extended empire to include much of India, Kashmir, Afghanistan, and Baluchistan. He practiced religious and political tolerance and evolved new religion, Din Ilahi. **I** 133

Akhnaton (or Akhenaten) (Amenhotep IV), king of ancient Egypt **A** 221; **E** 91, 100–01, 102

Akiba (a-KI-ba) **ben Joseph** (50?–132), Jewish scholar, b. Lydda, Palestine (now Israel). He taught at rabbinical school near Jaffa, Palestine, and developed a method of interpreting Bible in which every word and sign has particular significance. His collection of Jewish oral law was basis of Mishnah (first part of Talmud, book of Jewish civil and religious law). He supported Bar Cocheba in revolt against Roman Emperor Hadrian (132) and was executed for disobeying a Roman law that prohibited teaching of Jewish law. He is one of ten martyrs mentioned in Jewish prayer of repentance. **T** 15

Akihito (ah-ki-HE-to), Crown Prince of Japan **J** 48
Akii-Bua, John, Ugandan athlete **O** 116a

Akita, a heavyset, powerfully built dog originally developed to hunt bears in Japan. The Japanese now use the Akita as a guard dog and police dog. The male stands up to 70 cm (about 28 in) at the shoulder. Females are slightly smaller. The Akita has erect, triangular ears and a large curved tail. Its rough outercoat covers a soft, dense undercoat. Akitas may be any color or mixture of colors. Picture **D** 260

Akron, Ohio **O** 72
Soap Box Derby **S** 215
Aksenov, Vladimir, Soviet cosmonaut **S** 345
Aksum, Ethiopia **E** 301
Akureyri (ok-u-RAY-ri), Iceland **I** 43
Al- in Arabic names *see* main part of name, as Azhar University, al-
Alabama **A** 112–27
holiday, Fraternal (Columbus) Day **H** 149
places of interest in black American history **N** 94
Alabama, University of **A** 121
Alabama Claims **G** 296
Alabama River **A** 115, 120
Alabama State Capitol, picture **A** 124

Alabaster, name given to two mineral substances. Modern alabaster, a form of gypsum, is relatively soft and usually white and is used in statues and ornamental carvings. Large deposits of it are found in Italy. Oriental alabaster is a kind of marble and was used in ancient times for making statues.

Aladdin and the Wonderful Lamp, story from *Arabian Nights* **A** 345–46
Alakaluf (a-la-ka-LOOF), Indians of South America **A** 306–07
Alamein, El, Battle of, 1942 **W** 295
Alamo, Battle of the, 1836 **M** 238; **T** 122, 137
Bowie, James, hero of **B** 344
Crockett, Davy, hero of **C** 533
flag **F** 228
Alamogordo (al-a-mo-GOR-do), New Mexico **N** 191

Alanbrooke, 1st Viscount (Alan Francis Brooke) (1883–1963), British general; b. Bagneres-de-Bigore,

Alanbrooke, 1st Viscount (continued)
France. He commanded British 2nd Corps in France at beginning of World War II and played an important role in the evacuation of Dunkirk (1940). He was chief of Imperial General Staff (1941–46). He was made a field marshal (1944) and created 1st Viscount Alanbrooke of Brookeborough (1946).

Aland (OL-and) **Islands,** Finland **I** 425–26
Al-Anon, a program for the family and friends of alcoholics **A** 148

Alarcón (ol-ar-CONE), **Hernando de,** Spanish explorer and navigator who lived during 16th century. He assisted Coronado in expedition into what is now southwestern United States, and he explored Gulf of California and Colorado River (1540–41).

Alarcón, Juan Ruiz de, Mexican-born Spanish playwright **L** 71
   golden age of Spanish literature **S** 369
Alarcón, Pedro Antonio de, Spanish writer **S** 370

Alaric (AL-a-ric) (370?–410), king of the Visigoths; b. Peuce, an island at the mouth of the Danube River. For a time Alaric commanded Gothic troops serving in the Roman army. Elected king of the Visigoths (395), he led them in an invasion of Greece. The Romans made peace by appointing him military governor in the colony of Illyricum (now in Yugoslavia). In 401 he invaded Italy, and after several sieges captured Rome (410). The city was plundered, but its religious shrines were spared. Alaric planned to establish a kingdom in northern Africa, but his fleet was wrecked by a storm and he died soon after.

Alarm clocks **W** 50
Alas, Leopoldo see Clarín
Alaska **A** 128–43; **T** 112; **U** 92–93
   Aleutian Islands **I** 426
   Alexander Archipelago **I** 426
   Eskimo food **F** 339–40
   Eskimo life **E** 284–91
   glacier with terminal moraine, picture **I** 18
   gold discoveries **G** 253
   holiday, William Henry Seward's Day **H** 148
   Katmai National Monument, picture **N** 54
   Mount McKinley National Park, pictures **A** 134, **N** 51
   origin of Alaskan flag **A** 128
   pioneers **P** 262
   Portage Glacier, picture **G** 223
   Pribilof Islands **I** 435–36
   purchase, cartoon **T** 107
   taiga, picture **C** 343
   tundra, picture **C** 344
Alaska, Gulf of **A** 130, 134
Alaska, University of **A** 139
Alaska Highway, North America **A** 138
   British Columbia **B** 405; **C** 61
   part of the Pan American system **P** 50
   Yukon Territory **Y** 365
Alaskan Air Command **U** 162
Alaska Native Claims Settlement Act (1971) **A** 136
Alaskan brown bears **B** 106, 107
Alaskan (Northern) **fur seals** **W** 6–7
   migration **H** 190–91

Alaskan malamute, a working dog. The breed is named for the Malamutes, an Eskimo group. The Malamutes are believed to have developed the breed to pull sleds and as a pack animal. It is a strong dog with a full chest, upright ears, and curling tail. The malamute stands about 63 cm (25 in) high and usually weighs between 34 and 39 kg (75 and 85 lb). Its double coat is coarse on top but oily and wool-like below. The malamute is most often gray or black and white in color. **D** 259; **E** 289

Alaska Peninsula **A** 130, 140
Alaska Pipeline **A** 137
Alaska Range **A** 130, 132; picture **A** 134
Alateen, program for young people who live in an alcoholic family **A** 148
Al-Azhar University see Azhar University, al-
Alba, Fernando Alvarez de Toledo, duke of see Alva, Fernando Alvarez de Toledo
Albacore, fish **F** 215

Albanel, Charles (1616–96), French explorer and Jesuit missionary who spent many years at Tadoussac, Canada. He was a member of first French expedition from Quebec to Hudson Bay (1670–71). On his second trip there (1674) he was captured by English and taken to England. He returned to Canada (1676), and continued missionary work until his death.

Albania (al-BAY-nia) **A** 144–46
   Communism **C** 445
   created by Balkan wars **B** 19
   flag **F** 237
Albanian Labor Party **A** 146
Albany, Australia **A** 512, 516
Albany, capital of New York **N** 222

Albany Plan of Union, first formal plan for unification of American colonies. It was proposed by Benjamin Franklin and adopted in 1754 by Albany Congress, a convention of delegates from the colonies and representatives of Iroquois Indians. The plan called for a grand council, with representatives from each colony, which would deal with problems of taxation, defense, and trade. It was rejected by both Great Britain and the colonies but served as a basis for later plans of unification.
   Franklin, Benjamin **F** 454

Albany Regency, New York political group **V** 273
Albatrosses, birds **B** 228
   locomotion in air, picture **A** 295
   principles of flight **B** 205

Albee (ALL-bee), **Edward** (Franklin) (1928–), American playwright, b. Washington, D.C. He is best known for his drama Who's Afraid of Virginia Woolf? (1962). His plays deal with such themes as loneliness and human cruelty. They are written in a variety of styles and are often darkly humorous. Albee's first play was The Zoo Story (1959). Other works include The Sand Box (1960), Tiny Alice (1964), and two plays that won the Pulitzer prize, A Delicate Balance (1966) and Seascape (1975). **A** 215; **D** 300

Albéniz (al-BAY-neeth), **Isaac,** Spanish composer **S** 373
Albers (OLB-ers), **Josef,** German-born American painter **D** 143
   Bauhaus **B** 105
   Homage to a Square: Silent Hall, picture **D** 142
Albert, antipope **R** 297
Albert I, king of Belgium **B** 131; **W** 271–72; picture **W** 270

Albert I, prince of Monaco **M** 406, 407
Albert, prince of Saxe-Coburg-Gotha, consort of Queen Victoria **E** 226–27; **V** 332
    first Christmas tree in England **C** 291

Albert, Carl Bert (1908–), American legislator, b. McAlester, Okla. A Democrat, he was elected to the U.S. House of Representatives in 1947. He was speaker of the House from 1971 until his retirement in 1977. Before his election he practiced law in Oklahoma.

Albert, Lake, east central Africa **L** 26
Alberta, Canada **A** 146a–147
    Banff National Park **B** 42–43
    Jasper National Park **J** 54–55
    world's largest deposits of tar sands **E** 202b
Alberta, University of **A** 146d
Alberti (ol-BER-ti), **Leon Battista,** Italian architect **A** 380; **I** 467, 477
    Renaissance architecture **R** 164–65
Albert Lasker awards *see* Lasker Foundation, Inc.

Albertus Magnus, Saint (Albert, Count von Bollstadt) (1206?–80), German philosopher, theologian, scientist, and writer, b. Lauingen, Swabia. Called Albert the Great or Universal Doctor, he became a Dominican monk (1223). He was teacher of Thomas Aquinas at Cologne (1248–54) and Bishop of Ratisbon (1260–62). Recognized by contemporaries as one of the foremost scholars of his time, he was noted for work on Aristotle and for his scientific investigations. He wrote *Summa de Creaturis.* He was beatified in 1622 and canonized in 1932. **A** 344

Albigensian (al-bi-JEN-sian) **heresy** **R** 292

Albino (al-BY-no), human being or other animal born without normal color (pigment) in skin, hair, and eyes. An albino's hair is white, and eyes and skin are pink. Condition called albinism is hereditary. Plants also may be albinos.

Albumen, white of egg **E** 88
Albumin, class of simple proteins
    albumin glue **G** 243
Albuquerque (AL-bu-ker-ke), New Mexico **N** 192
Alcaeus (al-CE-us), Greek lyric poet **G** 350
Alcan Highway *see* Alaska Highway
Alcatraz Island, San Francisco Bay
    occupation by American Indians **I** 200b
Alcazar, The, medieval castle in Spain, picture **S** 359
Alcestis (al-CES-tis), in Greek mythology **G** 364
Alchemy, ancient practice of chemistry **C** 193, 207–08
    aging **A** 84
    early distillation processes **D** 226
    zinc used in trying to make gold **Z** 370
Alcindor, Lew *see* Abdul-Jabbar, Kareem
ALCM (air-launched cruise missiles) **M** 349
Alcmene (alc-ME-ne), in Greek mythology **G** 362–63
Alcohol **A** 147; **C** 216
    and driving **D** 321
    beer and brewing **B** 116
    depressants, abuse of **D** 329, 330
    distillation process **D** 226
    fermentation **F** 90
    foundations' wealth compared to spending on **F** 393
    grain, uses of **G** 286
    molecule model of its atoms **A** 483
    thermometers, use in **T** 165
    whiskey and other distilled beverages **W** 159
    yeasts, sac fungi **F** 498
Alcoholics Anonymous (AA) **A** 148
Alcoholism **A** 148

Alcohol, Tobacco and Firearms, Bureau of, an agency within the U.S. Department of the Treasury. It administers laws applying to alcohol, tobacco, firearms, and explosives. It also investigates violations, such as illegal possession of firearms and explosives and failure to pay taxes on alcohol and tobacco products.

Alcott, Amos Bronson, American educator **A** 149
Alcott, Louisa May, American author **A** 149; **C** 240
    Little Women **A** 149; excerpt **A** 149–50
Alcove Springs, Kansas **K** 186
Aldebaran (al-DEB-ar-an), star **S** 407; **C** 491
Alden, John, Pilgrim settler **P** 344
Alderney, one of the Channel Islands, Britain **I** 429

Aldrich, Thomas Bailey (1836–1907), American author and editor, b. Portsmouth, N.H. He served as editor of *Every Saturday* (1865–74), and of *Atlantic Monthly* (1881–90). Although he is remembered chiefly for his novel *The Story of a Bad Boy* and short story "Marjorie Daw," other works include poems "Fredericksburg" and "Elmwood," novels *Prudence Palfrey* and *Stillwater Tragedy*, and nonfiction *Ponkapog Papers.*

Aldridge, Ira Frederick (1805?–67), American actor, b. New York, N.Y. One of the first blacks to achieve stage fame, he was known for his interpretations of title roles in Shakespeare's tragedies *Othello, Macbeth,* and *King Lear.* He made his debut in London in 1826, playing Othello.

Aldrin, Edwin E., Jr, ("Buzz") (1930–), American astronaut, b. Montclair, N.J. A fighter pilot in the Korean War, he worked with experiments in the Gemini-Titan flights before appointment as astronaut (1964). As lunar module pilot of Apollo 11 moon expedition in July, 1969, Col. Aldrin became the second person to walk on the moon. He left the astronaut program in 1971 and retired from the Air Force the following year.
    first astronauts on the moon **S** 339–340a; pictures **M** 452, **S** 340h
    space flight data **S** 344

Aldus Manutius *see* Manutius, Aldus
Ale, a type of beer **B** 116
Aleichem, Sholem *see* Aleykhem, Sholem
Aleijadinho *see* Lisboa, Francisco Antônio
Alekseev, Konstantin *see* Stanislavski, Konstantin
Alemán (ol-ay-MON), **Mateo,** Spanish writer **S** 369
Alemán, Miguel, Mexican president **M** 251
Alembics (al-EM-bics), early distillation devices **D** 225–26
Alencar, José Martiniano de, Brazilian novelist **L** 72
Alençon (ol-on-SAWN), lace pattern **L** 19
Aleppo (a-LEP-po), Syria **S** 508
Alessandri Palma, Arturo, president of Chile **C** 255
Alessandro Filipepi *see* Botticelli, Sandro
Alesund (ALL-es-un), Norway **N** 343, 344; picture **N** 339
Aletsch (OL-ech) **Glacier,** Switzerland **A** 174
Aleutian (a-LEU-tian) **Islands** **I** 426; picture **I** 431
    Alaska **A** 128, 134, 135, 143
    World War II **W** 295
Aleutian Range, Alaska **A** 130, 132

Aleuts, a people of Alaska **A** 136, 143
Alewife, fish
    habitat, feeding habits, uses **F** 215
Alexander V, antipope **R** 297

Alexander, Chief (Wamsutta) (?–1662?), American Indian chief of Wampanoag tribe of New England. He was brother of Chief Metacomet, known as King Philip. According to Indian legend, he was poisoned by English during Indian uprisings that ended in King Philip's War (1675–76).

Alexander I (1777–1825), czar of Russia (1801–25); b. St. Petersburg (Leningrad). He became czar after the assassination of his father, Czar Paul I. At the beginning of his reign Alexander promised social reforms, including emancipation of the serfs and a constitution, but these were never realized. His great struggle with Napoleon led to the invasion of Russia and the burning of Moscow (1812). Alexander took part in the Congress of Vienna (1815) following Napoleon's defeat, and formed the Holy Alliance with Austria and Prussia. During his reign Poland and Finland came under Russian rule. **U** 49
    architecture in the Empire style **U** 54

Alexander II (1818–81), czar of Russia (1855–81), b. Moscow. He succeeded his father, Czar Nicholas I, during the Crimean War. Alexander's greatest achievement was the emancipation of the serfs (1861), which won him the name Czar Liberator. He also initiated reforms in the Army, the government, and the courts, and he introduced local self-government. During his reign Russia gained territory in Central Asia and the Caucasus. The Czar's reforms failed to satisfy the radicals, and in 1881 he was assassinated. **U** 49

Alexander III (1845–94), czar of Russia (1881–94), b. Tsarskoye Selo (now Pushkin). Alexander III's rule was marked by his reaction against the reforms of his father, Czar Alexander II. A nationalist, he tried to Russianize the peoples of Poland, Finland, and the Baltic countries, and he persecuted the Jews. The harsh conditions of the Russian peasants were improved somewhat during his reign, and industrial expansion was encouraged.

Alexander, Grover Cleveland (1887–1950), American baseball player; b. St. Paul, Nebr. He was one of baseball's greatest pitchers. During his 20-year career (1911–30) in the National League (with Philadelphia, Chicago, and St. Louis) he won 373 games, a league record he shares with Christy Mathewson. In 1916 he pitched 16 shutouts, a major league record. He was elected to the Baseball Hall of Fame in 1938.

Alexander, Harold Rupert Leofric George, 1st earl Alexander of Tunis (1891–1969), British field marshal, b. Tyrone, Ireland. During World War II he was in charge of evacuation of Dunkirk (1940) and commander in chief in Middle East (1942). As deputy allied commander in chief in North Africa, he directed invasions of Sicily and Italy (1943). Made field marshal and supreme allied commander of Mediterranean area (1944), he was also governor-general of Canada (1946–52) and British minister of defense (1952–54).
    World War II in North Africa **W** 295

Alexander III, king of Macedonia *see* Alexander the Great

Alexander I (Obrenovich) (1876–1903), king of Serbia (1889–1903), b. Belgrade. The last of the Obrenovich dynasty, he suspended (1894) liberal constitution of 1888 and annulled a series of laws passed by the radical government. Both he and his commoner wife Madame Draga Mashin were assassinated by a group of military officers.

Alexander, Lloyd (1924–), American writer of children's books, b. Philadelphia, Pa. Ancient Welsh legends inspired him to write the tales of Prydain, an imaginary land. He won the Newbery Medal in 1969 for *The High King* and the National Book Award in 1971 for *The Marvelous Misadventures of Sebastian*. **C** 244

Alexander, Martha (1920–), American author and illustrator of children's books, b. Augusta, Ga. She develops her stories by sketching and writing almost at the same time. Her works include *Nobody Asked Me if I Wanted a Baby Sister* (1971) and *I'll Protect You from the Jungle Beasts* (1973). **C** 242

Alexander I, Saint, pope **R** 296
Alexander II, pope **R** 297
Alexander III, pope **R** 297
Alexander IV, pope **R** 297
Alexander VI, pope **R** 297
    Papal Line of Demarcation for the New World **E** 380
Alexander VII, pope **R** 297
Alexander VIII, pope **R** 297
Alexander and the Terrible, Horrible, No Good, Very Bad Day, book by Judith Viorst, picture **C** 248c
Alexander Archipelago, island group, Alaska **I** 426
    Alaska's Panhandle **A** 130
Alexander Graham Bell Association for the Deaf **D** 52

Alexander Nevski (1220?–63), Russian national hero and saint of Russian Orthodox Church, b. Vladimir. He defended Russia against invasions from west and in 1240 defeated Swedes at Neva River, earning the surname Nevski. He became grand duke of Kiev and Novgorod (1246) and of Vladimir (1252).

Alexander the Great, king of Macedonia **A** 151–53; **S** 388
    Aristotle and Alexander **A** 397
    Greek civilization extended by **A** 230
    Soviet Central Asia **U** 46, 47
    submarine experiment **S** 444
Alexandria, Egypt **E** 90d, 90f; picture **E** 90f
    Alexander the Great founds **A** 152
    Pharos, lighthouse, wonder of ancient world **W** 216
    scientists of Alexandria **S** 63–64
Alexandria, Louisiana **L** 360
Alexandria, Virginia **V** 357
Alexandria, Museum of, ancient Egypt **M** 510
Alexandrian Library, ancient Egypt **L** 194
    higher education in the ancient world **E** 65
Alexandrite (al-ex-AN-drite), gemstone **G** 75
Alexis I, Russian czar, picture **U** 48

Alexius I Comnenus (com-NE-nus) (1048–1118), Byzantine emperor (1081–1118), b. Constantinople. Usurping the throne from Nicephorus III, he strengthened the military forces, reinforced the treasury, and through war and diplomacy resisted foreign enemies, including Scythians, Turks, and Normans. He improved relations with the papacy, and the First Crusade (1196–99) took place during his reign. His life is recorded in the *Alexiad*, by his daughter Anna Comnena.

Crusades **C** 538, 539

Aleykhem (a-LAI-kem), or **Aleichem, Sholem** (Solomon J. Rabinovich) (1859–1916), Jewish writer and humorist, b. Kiev, Russia. Considered one of classic modern Yiddish writers, he is remembered for his witty and satiric stories, written in rich idiomatic style, of Jewish life in Russia and America. Aleykhem inherited a large fortune but soon lost it in a publishing venture to encourage young Yiddish writers. He left Russia (1905) and settled in New York. His books include *Adventures of Mottel, The Great Fair*, and *The Writings of a Traveling Salesman*.

Yiddish literature **Y** 350–51

Alfalfa, plant of the pea family, cultivated extensively as food for cattle and horses. Distinguished by its small purple flower, it was originally native to Asia and was probably introduced into Europe by invading armies before birth of Christ. Brought to New World by Spaniards, it is now widely cultivated in western plains of United States. A hardy plant, alfalfa is adaptable to most climatic and soil conditions. It returns nitrogen to the soil but may deplete the soil of certain other elements.

Alfaro (ol-FAR-o), **Eloy,** Ecuadorian political reformer **E** 58
Alfheim (OLF-heim), Norse fairyland **N** 279
Alfieri (al-fi-AIR-i), **Vittorio,** Italian poet **I** 479
Al fine, musical term **M** 532
Alfonso X, the Wise, king of Castile **S** 366–67
  gave Castilian Spanish a phonetic spelling **S** 366
Alfred the Great, king of England **A** 154–55; **E** 216–17
  English literature flourished under **E** 246–47
Algae (AL-ge), flowerless plants **A** 155–57; **M** 280
  eutrophication of water sources **W** 59
  fertilizers stimulate growth and cause pollution **E** 272d, 272e
  food use in future **P** 223, 310
  fossil, picture **F** 382
  lichens **F** 95
  plankton **P** 279–80
Algebra, branch of mathematics **A** 157–59; **M** 156
  Hamilton's algebra **M** 159–60
  See also Arithmetic

Alger, Horatio (1834–99), American author, b. Revere, Mass. He wrote over 100 enormously popular books on the theme of "rags to riches." His stories, such as *Mark the Match Boy* (1869), told of poor boys who combined hard work and honesty to achieve success. The term "Alger hero" still refers to someone who becomes successful by using this formula. A graduate of the Harvard Divinity school, Alger had been a Unitarian minister. But he gave up the ministry in 1866 to devote more of his time to writing.

Algeria A 160–63
  flag **F** 235
  France, history of **F** 420
  oil refinery at Hassi Messaoud, picture **A** 68
Algiers, capital of Algeria **A** 162
Algol, star **S** 409
  study of variable stars **A** 475
Algonkin, Indians of North America **I** 170–71
  present-day life in Quebec **Q** 10a

Alhambra (al-HAM-bra) **palace,** Spain **I** 421; **S** 356
  Court of the Lions, picture **S** 363
  Spanish art and architecture **S** 360
Alhazen (ol-ha-ZEN), Arab mathematician and optical scientist **O** 166; **S** 65

Ali, Muhammad (Cassius Marcellus Clay, Jr.) (1942–), American boxer, b. Louisville, Ky. After winning an Olympic gold medal as a light-heavyweight in 1960, Ali became a professional boxer. He defeated Sonny Liston to win the world heavyweight title in 1964. Ali adopted the Black Muslim religion in the same year and later claimed that his religion exempted him from service in the armed forces. Convicted in court for refusing to serve, he lost his title. In 1971 the U.S. Supreme Court overturned the conviction. Ali was defeated by Joe Frazier in a 1971 title bout but regained the championship in a 1974 fight with George Foreman. He held the title until he was defeated in 1978 by Leon Spinks. Later that year, Ali regained the title in a rematch with Spinks. He is the first fighter to have won the heavyweight title three times. **N** 103
  boxing **B** 353–54

Ali Baba, hero of story "The Forty Thieves" from *Arabian Nights* **A** 346
Alice in Wonderland, book by Lewis Carroll **A** 164–65; **C** 123; excerpt **A** 164
  Tenniel illustration, picture **C** 239
Alice Springs, Australia **A** 503, 513
Alice Tully Hall, Lincoln Center, New York City **L** 298
Alien and Sedition Acts, United States **A** 10–11
  Alien Act and Alien Enemies Act, 1798 **A** 166
Alien Contract Labor Law, 1885 **I** 99–100
Aliens A 166
  See also Citizenship; Immigration and emigration; Naturalization
Alimony, in divorce **D** 236
Alkalies, chemical bases **C** 216
  soaps contain **D** 145
Alkali metals **C** 216, 218; **E** 158
  electron shells, diagram **C** 203
Alkaline earth metals **E** 158
Alkyd (AL-kid) **resins,** types of liquid plastics
  paints **P** 32
Alkylosaurus, dinosaur, picture **D** 177
Alla breve, musical term **M** 532
Allagash (AL-la-gash) **Wilderness Waterway,** Maine **M** 41
Allah (OL-lah), Arabic name for God of Islam **M** 404
Allahabad (al-la-ha-BAD), India **G** 25
All-American Canal, California **C** 19
All-American Soap Box Derby *see* Soap Box Derby
Allargando, musical term **M** 532
All Around the Kitchen, folk song **F** 324
Allegheny (AL-le-gainy) **Front,** escarpment
  a wall blocking overland trails **O** 254
Allegheny Mountains, North America
  canals **C** 86
Allegheny Plateau, eastern North America **M** 118–19; **N** 213; **P** 130–31; **W** 128
Allegheny Portage Railroad National Historic Site, Pennsylvania **P** 138
Allegheny River, picture **P** 130
Allegory, story to explain or teach something **F** 111
  early English literature **E** 248
  early French literature **F** 436
  Everyman, greatest morality play **E** 250
  Pilgrim's Progress **E** 256
Allegretto, musical term **M** 532

Allegri, Antonio see Correggio, Antonio Allegri da
Allegro, musical term **M** 532
Allegro Brillante, ballet, picture **B** 29
Allen, Ethan, American Revolutionary War hero **A** 167; **R** 199; **V** 319–20
Allen, Frederick Lewis, American writer **A** 214a
Allen, Hervey, American novelist **A** 213
Allen, Horatio, American engineer **R** 88–89

Allen, Richard (1760–1831), American clergyman, b. Philadelphia, Pa. A slave who was freed by his master, Allen became a wandering minister and, in 1787, organized the first church for blacks. In 1799 he became the first black minister in the Methodist Episcopal Church. He helped organize the African Methodist Episcopal Church in 1816 and served as its first bishop.

Allen, Woody (Allen Stewart Konigsberg) (1935–), American actor, comedian, and filmmaker, b. Brooklyn, N.Y. His film *Annie Hall* won an Academy Award for best picture of 1977. Allen frequently appeared on television and in nightclubs as a stand-up comedian before concentrating on films. Much of his humor comes from presenting himself as a shy, awkward man fighting a losing battle with the world. His other films include *Play It Again, Sam* (1972) and *Manhattan* (1979). **M** 488c

Allende (ah-YEN-day), **Salvador** (Salvador Allende Gossens) (1908–73), Chilean statesman, b. Valparaiso. A political activist at medical school, he was jailed for opposition to the government. He was elected a national deputy in 1937. With Socialist and Communist support, he ran unsuccessfully for the presidency in 1952, 1958, and 1964. In 1970 he became the first Marxist-Socialist ever elected president of a Western democracy. Allende died in a violent seizure of power by Chile's armed forces in 1973.
    Chile, history of **C** 255

Allentown, Pennsylvania **P** 142
Allergy **D** 190–91
All Hallows' Day **H** 15
Alliance for Labor Action (A.L.A.) **L** 7
Alliance for Progress (*Alianza para el Progreso*), a program of social and economic development for Latin America
    OAS, aims and work of the **O** 211
Alliances, of nations **I** 322
Allied Control Council, over Germany after World War II **G** 163–64

Allied Youth, an organization that sponsors educational programs for junior and senior high school students. Its programs inform young people of the dangers of alcohol and drugs. The organization, founded in 1931, has headquarters in Arlington, Va.

Allies, among nations **I** 322
Allies, in World War I **W** 272, 282
Alligators **C** 533–35; **R** 180–81
    leather from endangered species no longer available **L** 107
    See also Reptiles
Alliteration, repetition of the same first sounds in a group of words **P** 353
    Beowulf **B** 141
All Men are Brothers see *Water Margin, The,* Chinese novel
Allosaurus see Antrodemus

Allotropes, different forms of a chemical element **C** 218

Allouez (ol-WAY), **Claude Jean** (1622–89), French Jesuit missionary to North America, b. Haute Loire. He explored parts of Mississippi Valley and Lake Superior region, where he founded missions.

Alloys **A** 168–69; **M** 176
    aluminum **A** 177
    amalgam **C** 218
    bronze and brass **B** 408–10
    cast iron **I** 404–05
    chemistry, history of **C** 205
    chromium alloys **C** 296
    copper **C** 502–03
    gold alloyed with other metals **G** 248
    kinds of steel **I** 396
    magnesium alloys **M** 22
    magnets **M** 29
    nickel **N** 249–50
    properties of metals changed **M** 232
    silver **S** 182
    soldering and brazing, used in **S** 249
    standard jewelry alloys of gold **G** 248
    tin used in **T** 195
    tungsten and steel alloys **T** 308
    type metal **T** 343–44
    See also Brass; Brazing; Bronze; Metals and metallurgy; Soldering; Welding
Alloy steels **A** 168; **I** 396, 398
All Quiet on the Western Front, novel by Erich Maria Remarque **G** 180
All Saints' Day **H** 15
    Feast of All Saints **R** 154, 290
All Souls' Day, religious holiday **R** 154, 290
    Latin America **L** 51
    Mexico **M** 242
Allspice **S** 382
All-star games, in baseball **B** 78
All's Well That Ends Well, play by Shakespeare **S** 133
All the Friendly Beasts, Christmas folk song **F** 325
Alluvial (al-LU-vial) **deposits** **R** 237
    gold found in **G** 248–49
Alluvial Floodplain, area of Louisiana **L** 350–51
Alluvial soils **S** 234
    Africa **A** 52
    Georgia **G** 134
    North America **N** 291
Alluvium (al-LU-vium), river deposits **R** 237
All-wheel drive, of a truck **T** 296
Almagro (ol-MA-gro), **Diego de,** Spanish soldier **P** 266
    Chile, history of **C** 254
Almanacs, type of reference book **R** 130–31
    Poor Richard's Almanack **F** 452
Almandite (AL-mand-ite), garnet gemstone **G** 71
Almonds **N** 420
Almoravids (al-MO-ra-vids), Berber dynasty
    Moroccan empire founded by **M** 461
Alnico, alloy **M** 29
Alnilam, star **S** 407
Aloha (a-LO-ha) **State,** nickname of Hawaii **H** 56
Alouette (ol-oo-ETT), folk song **F** 322
Alpacas (al-PAC-as), hoofed mammals **H** 212; picture **H** 213
    native to the Andes **A** 253
    wool shawls worn by gauchos **A** 389
Alpha-amylase (al-pha-AM-il-ace), digestive enzyme **B** 294
Alphabet **A** 170–73; **W** 318

Arabic **M** 305
Arabic letters used in Islamic art **I** 417
Braille **B** 252–53
communication advanced by **C** 431
Communists introduce alphabet for Chinese **C** 258
Danish has 29 letters **D** 106
development of languages **L** 38
encyclopedias in unit and split-lettered alphabetical systems **E** 197
flags for the letters (International Code), pictures **F** 245
forming letters in handwriting **H** 31–32
Hebrew **H** 100
Hindi, picture **I** 119
indexes, learning to use **I** 115
Japanese language **J** 28
Latin language **L** 76
letter-by-letter arrangement in an index **I** 115
letters, capitals and lower case, in manuscript and cursive writing, picture **H** 32
letters in several type styles, picture **T** 343
most used letter **E** 1
pronunciation **P** 478
Russian **U** 58
sampler, picture **E** 187
Should it be taught to a preschool child? **R** 108
Welsh alphabet **W** 3
word-by-word arrangement in an index **I** 115
See also Writing; individual letters of the alphabet
Alpha brass, alloy **B** 410
Alpha Centauri, star **A** 475; **S** 405
Alpha particles, of radioactive atoms **A** 488; **R** 67
ions and ionization **I** 353
Alpha rays, streams of alpha particles of radioactive elements **R** 67
radioactive radiation **R** 45
radiations emitted by nuclei **N** 359
Alphubel, mountain peak, Switzerland, picture **S** 498
Alpine glaciers **G** 223; **I** 19–20
flow of ice, diagrams **I** 7, 8
Alpine plants
wild flowers **W** 171
Alpine skiing **S** 184d–184e, 184f, 185
Alps, mountains of Europe **A** 174–75
Alpine regions of Austria **A** 521
Alpine village, picture **H** 169
branches named and located **E** 309
cable cars, picture **G** 103
great mountain systems of the world **M** 499
ibex, picture **G** 244
landforms of Italy **I** 451
Liechtenstein **L** 206–07
Mont Blanc, picture **G** 244
Switzerland **S** 499–500
Al-Razi, Arab physician *see* Rhazes

Alsace-Lorraine (AL-sass luh-RAIN), a historic region of eastern France. France and Germany fought for control of the area through the Thirty Years War, the Franco-Prussian War, and World Wars I and II. The chief cities are Strasbourg, Metz, and Nancy. It is an agricultural area, noted for its wines. Lorraine has rich iron ore deposits.
France, history of **F** 418, 419

Alsted (OL-shtet), **Johann,** German encyclopedist **E** 197

Alston, Charles Henry (1907–77), American artist, b. Charlotte, N.C. He began his career in commercial art. Later he turned to the depiction of black life in America in portraits and murals. After 1950 Alston taught at the Art Students League of New York. His paintings include *Painting* and *The Family.*

Altaic (al-TAI-ic), (Turkic) **languages** **L** 40
Altair (al-TIRE), star **C** 493
Altamira Caves, Spain
cave paintings **P** 14, 440
Alternating current (A.C.), in electricity **E** 134
electric generators **E** 121–22
electric motors **E** 137, 138–39
rectified by diodes (electron tubes) **E** 146
transformers **T** 249
Althing, Iceland's legislature **I** 44; **V** 339
Altimeter, measures altitude **A** 561; **B** 54
Altiplano regions, of South America **S** 276
Bolivia **B** 303, 304
Altitude
climate and altitudes **C** 346
climate control factor **W** 88–89
cloud formation **C** 358
in geometry **G** 125
vertical life zones **Z** 372–73
Altman, Robert, American film director **M** 488b
Alto, musical term **C** 277; **M** 532
Alto-cumulus clouds **C** 360; picture **C** 361
Alto-stratus clouds (AL-to-STRAIT-us) **C** 360; picture **C** 361
Altricial (al-TRI-cial) **birds** **B** 215

Alum, a white solid chemical compound. The most common form contains potassium, aluminum, sulfur, and oxygen. It is widely used in purifying water, dyeing cloth, and making paper and also, in styptic-pencil form, to stop bleeding from small cuts.
used as a mordant in dyeing **D** 369

Alumina *see* Aluminum oxide
Aluminum (aluminium) **A** 176–77; **E** 154, 159
airplanes designed for subsonic flight made of **S** 471
atomic structure **A** 486
canoes made of **C** 99
five-ton ingot, picture **M** 231
metals, chart of some ores, location, properties, uses **M** 227
non-ferrous alloys **A** 168, 169
world distribution **W** 261; diagram **W** 260
Aluminum bronze, alloy **B** 409
Aluminum foil
reflective insulation **I** 291
Aluminum oxide (alumina) **A** 176
abrasive for grinding and polishing **G** 388
Alva, Fernando Alvarez de Toledo, duke of, Spanish statesman **N** 120

Alvarado (ol-va-RA-tho), **Pedro de** (1495?–1541), Spanish soldier, b. Badajoz. A companion of Cortez in conquest of Mexico (1519–21), he held command of Mexico City in Cortez' absence (1520). In Mexican rebellion he is said to have escaped death by jumping across a large gap in the causeway now known as Alvarado's Leap. He was an important figure in siege of Mexico City (1527), and he was governor of Guatemala (1530–32).

Alvarez (OL-va-raith), **Luis Walter,** (1911–   ), American physicist, b. San Francisco, Calif. A professor of physics

Alvarez, Luis Walter (continued)
at University of California (since 1945), he developed ground-controlled (radar) approach system for landing aircraft and did atomic research at Los Alamos (1944–45). In 1968 he received the Nobel Prize for contributions to physics of subatomic particles.

Alveoli (al-VE-ol-i), (air sacs), of the lungs **B** 277; **D** 203
    emphysema **D** 194
Always Prepared, motto of U. S. Coast Guard **U** 175
Alyssum, sweet, flower, pictures **G** 27, 28
A.M., ante meridiem, or before noon **T** 189–90
AM, radio see Amplitude Modulation
Amahl and the Night Visitors, opera by Gian-Carlo Menotti **O** 139–40; picture **O** 141

Amalekites (a-MAL-ek-ites), fierce nomadic tribe of Biblical times. They were traditional enemies of Israelites, who first encountered them during exodus from Egypt and thereafter fought them many times.

Amalgam (a-MAL-gam), alloy **C** 218
    gold and mercury **G** 247
    silver-mercury alloys **S** 182
Amalgamated Clothing Workers of America C 354
Amalgamation (a-mal-ga-MAY-tion), of ores **M** 228
    gold-extracting process **G** 249
Amana (am-AN-a) **colonies,** Iowa **I** 367
Amanitas (am-a-NI-tas), poisonous fungi **F** 499; pictures **F** 500
    destroying angel mushroom **M** 521
Amateur athletics
    Olympic Games **O** 108

Amateur Athletic Union of the United States (A.A.U.), a federation of amateur athletic organizations that serves as the governing body of many competitive amateur sports. It sponsors National Championship competitions, represents the United States in international competition, provides uniform rules, and keeps records. The A.A.U. was founded in 1888. It has headquarters in Indianapolis, Ind., and publishes rule books for various sports and a monthly magazine, *A.A.U. News and Amateur Athlete.*
    gymnastic events **G** 433

Amateur Bicycle League of America see United States Cycling Federation
Amateur Hockey Association I 34, 35
Amateur radio see Radio, amateur
Amateur Radio Emergency Service R 63

Amateur Softball Association of America (ASA), governing body for amateur softball in the United States. It provides standardized rules of play. Founded in 1933, ASA has headquarters in Oklahoma City, Okla., and publishes *Balls and Strikes,* a monthly.

Amateur Telescope Makers (ATM's) **T** 64
Amateur theatricals T 156
    putting on a play **P** 335–41
Amati (a-MA-ti) **family,** Italian violin makers **V** 342
Amazing Stories, science-fiction magazine **S** 84
Amazon ants A 324–25
Amazonite (AM-az-on-ite), gemstone **G** 76
Amazon parrot, picture **P** 180
Amazon River, South America **A** 178–79; **S** 277
    Brazil **B** 380
    houseboat, picture **R** 241

How did the Amazon River get its name? **A** 179
    tidal bores **T** 185

Amazons, in Greek mythology, race of women warriors who lived around the Caucasus, allowing no men among them. Their children were fathered by men from neighboring nations, and sons were either killed or sent back to fathers. Their queen supposedly was killed by Achilles during Trojan war.
    how the Amazon River got its name **A** 179

Ambassadors, highest ranking officers in embassies **F** 369–70
Ambassadors, The, painting by Holbein, picture **N** 36
Amber, fossil resin **R** 184
    discovery of static electricity **E** 123
    "display case" for insects **E** 340; picture **D** 341
    organic gems **G** 76

Ambergris, waxy, grayish-black substance formed in digestive tract of sperm whales. It is usually obtained from slaughtered whales but is sometimes found floating in the sea. It is used to make perfume and is extremely valuable.
    fixatives in perfumes **P** 155
    whale products **W** 147, 152

Ambler, Eric (1909–　), English author of mystery novels and films, b. London. His works are often based on international spying. He served in British Army in North Africa and Italy in World War II. His books include *A Coffin for Dimitrios, Journey into Fear,* and *Dirty Story.*
    spy-adventure stories **M** 556

Ambon, Indonesian Moluccas **I** 221
Ambrogini, Angelo see Poliziano
Ambrose, Saint C 283; **R** 289
    converted Saint Augustine **A** 494
    hymn composer **H** 311
Ambrose light tower, at the entrance to New York harbor, picture **L** 277

Ambrosia, in mythology, the food of the gods. Ambrosia supposedly gave immortality to those who ate it. In modern usage, it is anything extremely pleasing to the taste.

Ambrosia beetles P 285
Ambulances (AM-bu-lan-ces)
    flag **F** 246
    stretcher being transferred, picture **H** 248
Ambulatory, semicircular aisle in church architecture **A** 377
Amen, god see Amon-Re
Amendments to the United States Constitution U 155–58
    civil rights amendments in the Bill of Rights **C** 314
    Eleventh Amendment **J** 56
    First 10, Bill of Rights **B** 179
    Fourteenth Amendment **J** 125
    freedom of religion, speech, and press in First Amendment **F** 457
    how U.S. Constitution has been changed **U** 147–48
    See also Bill of Rights, American
Amenemhet I (om-en-EM-het), king of ancient Egypt **E** 98
Amenhotep III (om-en-HO-tep), king of ancient Egypt **E** 100; **N** 90
Amenhotep IV see Akhnaton

America
    American colonies **A** 180–94
    exploration and discovery of **E** 378, 380, 384–86
    first shown on world map, picture **E** 378
    Vespucci, Amerigo, continents named for **V** 323
    Viking discovery of **V** 339–40
    See also Central America; Latin America; North America; South America; names of countries
America, song by Samuel Francis Smith **N** 24

American Academy and Institute of Arts and Letters (AAIAL), an honorary institution for the advancement of creative work in literature, music, and art. It was formed in 1976 by a merger of the American Academy of Arts and Letters (founded 1904) and the National Institute of Arts and Letters (founded 1898). Its 250 members are chosen on the basis of achievement. AAIL presents annual awards for distinguished work. It has headquarters in New York, N.Y.

American architecture *see* United States, architecture of the
American art *see* United States, art of the

American Association for the Advancement of Science (AAAS), the largest scientific organization in the United States. Its members represent all fields of science. AAAS was founded in 1848. It has headquarters in Washington, D.C., and publishes the weekly *Science.*

American Association of School Librarians **L** 200
American Automobile Association (AAA) **V** 259
American Badminton Association *see* United States Badminton Association
American Ballet Theatre **B** 29

American Bar Association (ABA), an organization of attorneys in good standing who are admitted to practice law before state bars. The ABA seeks high standards of legal education, sound federal and state legislation, uniform laws throughout the United States, and the improved administration of justice. Founded in 1878, it has headquarters in Chicago, Ill., and publishes the *American Bar Association Journal.*

American Basketball Association **B** 90a, 90b
American beech, tree, picture **T** 278

American Bible Society (ABS), a nonprofit organization devoted to the circulation of the Bible and parts of the Bible throughout the world. It translates and distributes copies of the Bible in over 200 languages and in braille. Founded in 1816, it has international headquarters in New York, N.Y., and publishes the *American Bible Society Record.*

American Bill of Rights **B** 177–80

American Book Awards, The (TABA), annual awards for outstanding books written by United States authors. The awards, sponsored by the Association of American Publishers, were established in 1980 to replace the National Book Awards. Two awards, one for a hardcover book and one for a paperback, are made in 13 basic categories, ranging from general fiction and nonfiction to reference books. One award is made in each of the categories of first novel, western, and poetry, whether hardcover or paperback. Additional awards are presented for book design, cover design, and jacket design.

American Bowling Congress (ABC) **B** 345, 348
American Boy, magazine **M** 16
American buffalo *see* Bison

American Camping Association (ACA), an organization of people interested in organized camping. The association has programs in outdoor living skills, ecology, and camp director certification. The ACA was founded in 1910. It has headquarters in Martinsville, Ind., and publishes *Camping Magazine.*

American Cancer Society **C** 92
American Canoe Association **C** 100a
American Checker Federation **C** 191

American Civil Liberties Union (ACLU), an organization that seeks to protect the rights of all people, regardless of color, race, national origin, sex, religion, or political belief. It arranges court test cases and protests restrictions on or violations of rights. The ACLU was founded in 1920. It has headquarters in New York, N.Y., and publishes *Civil Liberties.*

American Civil War *see* Civil War, United States
American College Testing Program (ACTP) **E** 348
American colonies **A** 180–94
    architecture **A** 383–84
    cattle and other livestock **C** 146
    colonial life in America **C** 385–99
    communication **C** 435–36
    Declaration of Independence, events preceding **D** 59
    drama **D** 299
    education and early schools in America **E** 69–70
    flags, historic **F** 228
    French and Indian Wars **F** 458–62
    homes **H** 180–82
    ironworks **I** 405
    Jamestown, Virginia **J** 20–21
    Lafayette's role in American Revolution **L** 22
    literature **A** 195–98
    Oglethorpe founded Georgia **O** 59
    Penn, William **P** 127
    Pitt, William, Earl of Chatham **P** 265
    Plymouth Colony **P** 343–46
    police **P** 373
    political parties **P** 379
    population **U** 131–32
    postal service **P** 407
    prisons and criminals **P** 468
    Raleigh established Roanoke Island **R** 101
    Revolutionary War, events leading to **R** 194–98
    slavery, development of **S** 197–98
    taxation **T** 26
    territorial expansion **T** 105, 108
    thirteen stripes in the flag **F** 247
    United States began as a farming society **U** 128
    westward movement **W** 142–46
    Zenger, John Peter, wins fight for free press **Z** 368a
American Colonization Society **N** 93
    Liberia **L** 167

American Conference, National Football League **F** 365
American crawl, swimming **S** 490–91
American Dental Association **D** 115
American drama **D** 299–300
    American literature, place of drama in **A** 214b–215
American Dream, painting by Robert Indiana **U** 120
American eagles *see* Bald eagles

American Educational Theater Association **T** 162–63
American elk (wapiti) **H** 214; picture **H** 215
American elm, tree, picture **T** 276
  leaf, diagram **L** 115
  Massachusetts, state tree of **M** 134
  North Dakota, state tree of **N** 323
American English **W** 240
  slang **S** 194
American Expeditionary Force (A.E.F.) **W** 279–80
  commanded by Pershing **P** 157

American Farm Bureau Federation (AFBF), a federation of co-operative groups made up of farm and ranch families in all 50 states and Puerto Rico. It promotes educational and legislative programs of benefit to farmers and conducts research in new ways to use farm products. The AFBF was founded in 1919. It has headquarters in Park Ridge, Ill., and publishes *Farm Bureau News.*

American Federation of Arts (AFA), an organization of about 500 art institutions and 2,500 individuals interested in encouraging art appreciation in the United States. It originates and sponsors traveling exhibitions, in the United States and abroad, representing all the visual arts. It was founded in 1909 and has its headquarters in New York, N.Y. The federation publishes *Who's Who in American Art.*

American Federation of Labor (AFL) **L** 4
  child labor laws, supporter of **C** 235
  Gompers, Samuel **G** 263
American Federation of Labor–Congress of Industrial Organizations (AFL-CIO) **L** 7
American Field Service **V** 259
American flag **F** 229, 243–44, 247–48; picture **F** 230
  flag code **F** 231–34
  flying over the South Pole, picture **P** 370
  pledge to *see* Pledge of Allegiance
American folklore *see* Folklore, American
American Folklore Society **F** 314
American Football League **F** 365
American Forestry Association, conservation organization **C** 488
American Foundation for Overseas Blind **B** 254
American Foundation for the Blind **B** 254
American Friends Service Committee (AFSC), relief organization of the Religious Society of Friends **Q** 4a
American Friends Society *see* Quakers
American Fur Company, of John Jacob Astor **F** 522–23

American Gold Star Mothers, a patriotic organization of mothers whose sons or daughters were killed fighting in World Wars I and II, the Korean conflict, Vietnam, or in other combat areas. Founded in 1928, it has headquarters in Washington, D.C., and publishes *Gold Star Mothers.*

American Gothic, painting by Grant Wood **W** 221
American Graffiti, motion picture **M** 488c
American Hall of Fame *see* Hall of Fame for Great Americans

American Heart Association (AHA), an organization devoted to the prevention and treatment of heart and circulatory diseases. With a membership of physicians, scientists, and lay persons, the organization promotes research, education, and community programs.

Founded in 1924, it has headquarters in Dallas, Tex., and is financed by public contributions.

American Hero, The, song by Nathaniel Niles **N** 23
American history *see* America, exploration and discovery of; American colonies; United States, history of the
American holly
  state tree of Delaware, picture **D** 87
American Home Economics Association **H** 166

American Humane Association (AHA), an organization of societies and individuals that acts to prevent cruelty to children and animals. It was founded in 1877 and has headquarters in Englewood, Colo. Its publications include the *American Humane Magazine.*

American Independent Party, United States **P** 381

American Indian Movement (AIM), an organization founded in 1968 that works to help American Indians improve their economic status and fight discrimination. It gained wide attention in 1973, when members helped occupy the village of Wounded Knee, on the Pine Ridge Indian Reservation in South Dakota.
  Indians of North America **I** 200b

American Indians *see* Indians of North America; Indians of South America

American Institute of Architects (AIA), a society of architects concerned with serving the needs of their profession and maintaining high standards of safety in architecture. It offers educational programs for professionals and students and informs citizens of ways in which they can improve local surroundings. The institute presents annual awards for achievement in design. The AIA was founded in 1857. It has headquarters in Washington, D.C., and publishes the *AIA Journal* monthly.

American Institute of Graphic Arts **B** 326
Americanisms, American English
  word origins **W** 240

American Jewish Committee, a national organization of American Jews, founded in 1906. Its aims are to fight prejudice, to protect civil and religious liberties, and to promote understanding through education and human relations. Its publications include the quarterly *Present Tense* and the monthly *Commentary,* an independent journal of opinion and criticism. Headquarters are in New York, N.Y.

American Jewish Congress (AJC), an organization of American Jews dedicated to the unity and survival of Jews all over the world. It is active in helping the people of Israel. Founded in 1918 by Louis Brandeis and other American Jews, it has headquarters in New York, N.Y., and publishes *Congress Monthly* and the quarterly *Judaism.*

American Kennel Club **D** 252, 259, 261
American Labor Party **L** 8
American Lawn Bowling Association **B** 349
American League, baseball **B** 75, 77
  world series records **B** 79

American Legion, an organization of men and women veterans of World Wars I and II, the Korean War, and the Vietnam War. It supports patriotism and national defense and also works for veteran benefits and to help the aged. It was founded in 1919 by World War I veterans. It has headquarters in Indianapolis, Ind., and publishes the *American Legion Magazine*.

American Libraries, official bulletin of the American Library Association **L** 192
American Library Association L 191–92, 200
  book awards **B** 309–310b
American literature A 195–215
  contributions to art of the novel **N** 348–49
  place in the history of the drama **D** 299–300
  See also Canadian literature; Children's literature; Drama; Folklore, American; Humor; Latin-American literature; Literary criticism; Magazines; Short stories; names of writers
American Manual Alphabet, picture **D** 51

American Medical Association (AMA), a national association of physicians. It provides professional information to its members and assists in setting and maintaining standards for medical schools. It also represents the medical profession in dealings with the federal government. Founded in 1847, it has headquarters in Chicago, Ill., and publishes the *Journal of the American Medical Association*.

American Museum of Immigration, Liberty Island, New York **L** 168
American Museum of Natural History, New York City **M** 512; picture **M** 515
American music *see* United States, music of the; Folk music; Jazz; Negro spirituals
American National Red Cross *see* Red Cross

American National Theater and Academy (ANTA), an organization of persons and groups in the professional or amateur theater. It aids in civic, industrial, charity, and university productions. It acts abroad as the U.S. agency for the performing arts, exchange programs, and copyrights. Founded in 1935, it has headquarters in New York, N.Y.
  stimulates appreciation for the theater **T** 162

American Newspaper Guild N 205
American Newspaper Publishers Association N 204–05
American Numismatic (nu-mis-MAT-ic) **Association C** 375

American Nurses' Association (ANA), a professional society of registered nurses. The association sponsors research in all fields of nursing, maintains a library, and gives awards in special areas of nursing. It was founded in 1896 and has its headquarters in Kansas City, Mo. It publishes the *American Journal of Nursing* monthly. **N** 413

American painting *see* United States, art of the
American Party (Know Nothing Party) **P** 380
  Fillmore, Millard **F** 125
American Peace Society P 104
American Pharmaceutical Association D 322
American Philosophical Society F 453; **P** 183; **S** 69–70
American plan, of hotel rates **H** 259
American Popular Revolutionary Alliance (APRA), Peruvian political party **P** 166
American Printing House for the Blind B 253
American Professional Football Association F 365

American Public Health Association (APHA), a professional organization of public and industrial health officials and workers. The APHA is dedicated to promoting and protecting personal, environmental, and public health. It conducts research in public health and the causes of communicable disease. It also sets testing standards for health workers and explores the worth of various medical care plans. Founded in 1872, it has headquarters in Washington, D.C., and publishes the *American Journal of Public Health*.

American Public Welfare Association (APWA), an organization of public welfare agencies, professional staff members, and others interested in public welfare. It was founded in 1930 and has its headquarters in Washington, D.C. The association publishes *Public Welfare Journal*.

American Radio Relay League (ARRL) **R** 62, 63
American Red Cross *see* Red Cross
American Regionalist, art style
  Wood, Grant **W** 221
American Revolution *see* Revolutionary War
American saddle horse H 244
American Samoa S 25-27
  Pacific coaling stations for United States **T** 114

Americans for Democratic Action (ADA), an organization of politicians, people in business, labor leaders and other citizens interested in liberal political ideas. It seeks to "formulate liberal domestic and foreign policies, based on the realities and changing needs of American democracy" and to obtain public support of such policies. The ADA tries to realize its ideas through the major American political parties. Founded in 1947, it has headquarters in Washington, D.C., and publishes *ADA World* monthly.

American Shakespeare Festival Theater, Stratford, Conn., picture **C** 479
American Society for the Prevention of Cruelty to Animals *see* Society for the Prevention of Cruelty to Animals, American

American Society of Composers, Authors, and Publishers (ASCAP), an association of music writers and publishers. It protects the copyrights of members by licensing commercial users of music, such as radio and TV stations and hotels. It also tabulates the number of public performances of a member's work and distributes royalties. ASCAP was founded in 1914 by Victor Herbert, George Maxwell, Nathan Burkan, and others. Its headquarters are in New York, N.Y.

American Society of Genealogists G 76a
American Society of Newspaper Editors N 205
American Sokol Educational and Physical Culture Organization G 433
American Stock Exchange S 433
American Telephone and Telegraph Company T 57
American University, Cairo, Egypt **E** 90d
American upland, class of cotton **C** 522

American Veterans Committee (AVC), an organization of men and women who served in World Wars I and II, the Korean conflict, and Vietnam. Its purpose is "to achieve a more democratic and prosperous America and a more stable world." Founded in 1944, it has headquarters in Washington, D.C., and publishes the *AVC Bulletin*.

American Veterans of World War II, Korean and Vietnam Wars *see* AMVETS
American War of Independence *see* Revolutionary War
American Water Ski Association **W** 63
American Whitewater Affiliation **C** 100a
American Youth Hostels, Inc. **H** 253

America's Cup, yacht-racing trophy (originally called Hundred Guinea Cup). It was won by U.S. schooner *America* (1851) and presented to New York Yacht Club (1857) to be used as an international challenge trophy. Since 1870 it has been sought by numerous challengers, mostly British, but has thus far been kept by American yachts.

America the Beautiful, song by Katherine Bates **N** 25
Americium (am-er-IS-ium), element **E** 154, 159
Americo-Liberians, Liberian descendants of settlers from the United States **L** 164
Amerigo Vespucci *see* Vespucci
Amerindians *see* Indians of North America; Indians of South America
Amethyst (AM-eth-ist), quartz gemstone **G** 74, 75; **Q** 7; picture **G** 73
Amharas, a people of Ethiopia **E** 296
Amharic (am-HARR-ic), official language of Ethiopia **E** 296
Amicable numbers **N** 380
Amiens, Treaty of, 1802 **N** 10
Amin, Hafizullah, president of Afghanistan **A** 45

Amin (ah-MEEN), Idi (Field Marshall Idi Amin Dada) (1925–), Ugandan dictator, b. West Nile. Amin gained international attention when he expelled Asians from the country and was accused of killing Ugandans who disagreed with him. He entered the army at age 21, gained control of the armed forces in 1966, and seized the presidency in a 1971 coup, ousting Milton Obote. In 1979 Amin was overthrown and driven out of the country by Tanzanian troops and Ugandan exiles. **U** 4, 6, 7

Amine, chemical **V** 370b
Amino (a-MI-no) acids, in body chemistry **B** 184, 290–91, 295–96
 chain of molecules, picture **V** 363
 chemical makeup of viruses **V** 370
 genetics **G** 84–85
 proteins in nutrition **N** 416
 structure of antibodies **I** 106
Amir, Arabic title *see* Emir
Amis, Kingsley, English novelist, poet, critic, teacher **E** 267
Amish (OM-ish), religious group, branch of Mennonite Church **P** 128; **F** 290
Amistad Revolt *see* Cinque, Joseph
Amman (OM-mon), capital of Jordan **J** 138; picture **J** 139
Ammeters (AM-met-ers), devices to measure electric current **E** 133
Ammonia (am-MO-nia), gas **G** 59, 61; **N** 262
 absorption refrigerating systems **R** 137
 coal by-product **C** 365
 ocean thermal energy conversion **E** 202d
 structural formula **C** 200
Ammonites, creatures with coiled shells **P** 437
Ammonium nitrate, chemical compound
 explosives **E** 394
Ammunition **G** 414–26
 explosives **E** 390–96
 lead **L** 94

Amnesty and Reconstruction, Proclamation of, 1863 **R** 117

Amnesty International, a human rights organization that won the Nobel peace prize in 1977. It was founded in 1961 to further human freedom by condemning torture and imprisonment because of religious and political beliefs. Its method is to adopt "prisoners of conscience" and plead their cases through mailings and other publicity. The organization has members in more than 30 countries. World headquarters are in London, England. **C** 316

Amoebas (a-ME-bas), one-celled animals **M** 277–78
 a giant amoeba **A** 265
 feeding habits **A** 274
 invertebrates, picture **A** 264
 reproduction **G** 77
Amoebic dysentery, disease **M** 278
Amon-Re (om-on-RAY), ancient Egyptian sun-god **A** 220
Amon-Re, Great Temple of, Karnak, Egypt **A** 371–72; **E** 100
Amortization, of a debt **R** 112
Amos (A-mos), Old Testament book **B** 155
Amos, Hebrew prophet **J** 105
Amoskeag (AM-os-keg) Mills, New Hampshire **N** 153
Amperage (AM-per-age), of electricity **E** 122, 133
Ampère (ON-pare), André Marie **E** 129, 133; **T** 51
 electric motors, history of **E** 140
 experiments in magnetism **M** 28
Amperes (AM-peres), units of measure in electricity **E** 133; **T** 250
Amphetamines (am-PHET-a-means), drugs **D** 330
Amphibians (am-PHIB-ians), aircraft **A** 557
Amphibians, land-water animals **F** 470–78
 evolution of fishes **F** 182–83
 prehistoric animals, development of **P** 437
 three-chambered heart **M** 72
Amphibious ships
 United States Navy **U** 193
Amphibious warfare
 United States Marine Corps **U** 178
Amphitheaters (AM-phi-theaters), outdoor theaters
 Epidaurus, Greece, picture **G** 335
 Greek drama, picture **D** 294
Amphoras, ancient Greek vases, pictures **A** 364; **D** 71
Amplification, of electric currents
 triodes (electron tubes) **E** 148
Amplification, of sound
 electronic music **E** 142h
Amplifiers
 transistors and integrated circuits **T** 254
Amplitude, in physics
 noise, in decibels of sound **N** 269–70
 sound waves **S** 258–59
 strength of waves **T** 253–54
Amplitude modulation (AM) **R** 57
Amsterdam, capital of the Netherlands **N** 116, 118, 119; pictures **H** 180, **N** 115
 early stock exchanges **S** 429
Amsterdam Island, in Indian Ocean, picture **I** 423

Amtrak, quasi-governmental corporation created (1971) by U.S. Congress to take over responsibility of maintaining railroad passenger service between 300 American cities. **R** 80

Amu Darya (om-U DAR-ya), river, formerly Oxus, in western Asia **A** 43, 44
Amulets (AM-u-lets), ornaments to ward off evil **G** 74
pre-Columbian amulet, picture **D** 71
Amundsen, Roald, Norwegian explorer
first Northwest Passage by sea **N** 338; **P** 364, 365
first to reach South Pole **P** 366

Amundsen (OM-un-sen) **Sea**, body of water in South Pacific off coast of Antarctica. It was explored by a Norwegian, Nils Larsen, who named it (1929) after Raold Amundsen, discoverer of South Pole.
Antarctic Ocean, arms of **O** 45

Amur (om-OOR) **River**, Asia **R** 240
beach at Khabarovsk, Siberia, picture **U** 45
Amusements see Recreation

AMVETS (American Veterans of World War II, Korean and Vietnam Wars), a veterans' organization that works to promote peace, encourage patriotism, and improve the welfare of veterans. Its goals include employment of the handicapped. It was founded in 1944 and has headquarters in Washington, D.C.

An, Babylonian god see Anu
Anableps, four-eyed fish, picture **F** 191
Anacletus II, antipope **R** 297
Anacletus, Saint, pope see Cletus, Saint
Anaconda (an-a-CON-da) **Company** **M** 443
Anacondas, snakes **A** 263; **S** 207
Anacortes (an-a-COR-tese), Washington, picture **W** 19
Anadolu, Asian Turkey **T** 324
Anadromous (a-NAD-ro-mous) **fish** **F** 215
Anaerobic bacteria **B** 11
hyperbaric chambers used in treating infections **M** 210
Anagrams, word games **W** 236
Analgesics, substances that relieve pain **N** 13
Analog electronics **E** 144
Analog time display, in solid-state watches **W** 49
Analysis, in chemistry **C** 196, 218
Analytical method, of philosophy **P** 191
Analytic geometry **M** 157
Analyzer, automated, used to perform common medical laboratory tests **M** 202
Anansi, hero of African folktales **A** 76b
Anapests, metrical feet in poetry **P** 354
Anarchism (AN-arc-ism), theory of government **G** 276
Anasazi (ah-na-SA-zi), cliff dwellers **C** 415
Anastasius, antipope **R** 296
Anastasius I, pope **R** 296
Anastasius II, pope **R** 296
Anastasius III, pope **R** 296
Anastasius IV, pope **R** 297
Anatolia (an-a-TO-lia), Asia Minor, now Anadolu, Turkey **A** 238; **T** 324, 325
See also Asia Minor
Anatomic pathology **M** 201–02
Anatomy (a-NAT-omy), **comparative**
body plan of animals **B** 269–70
Anatomy, human, structure of human body **B** 267–83
father of, Andreas Vesalius **B** 189
reproductive organs **R** 179–80
Anatosaurus, dinosaur, picture **D** 177
Anaximander (an-ax-i-MAN-der), Greek philosopher **S** 62
Ancestor worship **R** 145

African art reflects **A** 72
art of the Pacific islands **P** 9–10
China **C** 260
Anchises (an-KY-sese), father of Aeneas **A** 35
Anchorage (ANC-or-age), Alaska **A** 141
Anchors Aweigh, song by Miles and Lovell **N** 25
Anchovies (AN-cho-vies), fishes **P** 163
Ancient civilizations **A** 216–32
African kingdoms, early **A** 67; **N** 90–91
aqueducts **A** 344
art as a record **A** 438b
art see Ancient world, art of the
Asia **A** 466
Aztec Indians of North America **I** 195, 197
bread and baking **B** 388a–388b
Celts **C** 165–66
early history of Greece **G** 338
education systems **E** 61–65
Egypt, ancient **E** 91–92
European civilization, development of **E** 330–32
fairs and expositions **F** 9
food in ancient times **F** 333
grain crops **G** 281
historical writings **H** 134
homes **H** 177–78
Incas, Indians of South America **I** 203–07
masonry of brick and stone **B** 393–94
Maya Indians of North America **I** 197–99
Mediterranean Sea regions **M** 214
Middle East called the cradle of civilization **M** 306
music see Ancient world, music of the
mythology **M** 557–64
science, advances in **S** 60
slavery **S** 195
technology **T** 45–46
Zimbabwe, picture of stone ruins **Z** 368d
See also Archeology; names of ancient races and peoples; names of countries of ancient times
Ancient history see Ancient civilizations
Ancient world, art of the **A** 233–43
art as a record **A** 438b
Egyptian art and architecture **E** 93–103
furniture design **F** 505
Indian art of North and South America **I** 152–57
See also Ancient civilizations; Archeology; Architecture; Prehistoric art; Sculpture; Wonders of the world; names of ancient countries
Ancient world, music of the **A** 243–47
See also Musical instruments
Ancohuma (on-co-OO-ma), mountain in Bolivia **B** 303–04
Ancón (an-CONE), Ecuador **E** 55
Andalusia (an-da-lu-SI-a), Spain **S** 352, 357
folk music **S** 372, 373
Andalusian dialect, of Spain **D** 152
Andaman (AN-da-man) **Islands,** India **I** 426
Andaman Sea **O** 45
Andante, musical term **M** 532
Andantino, musical term **M** 532
AND circuits, of computers **C** 453–54; picture **C** 455
Anders, William A., American astronaut **S** 344
Andersen, Hans Christian, Danish writer of fairy tales **A** 247–49; **C** 238; **F** 21
Andersen Medal, book award **B** 310
"Emperor's New Clothes, The" **A** 249–51
place in Scandinavian literature **S** 52
"Princess on the Pea, The" **F** 26
Anderson, Bill, American singer **C** 525
Anderson, Carl, American cartoonist **C** 128

Anderson, C. W. (Clarence William) (1891–1971), American author and illustrator, b. Wahoo, Neb. He is best known for the realistic drawings of horses that illustrate the many children's books he wrote. Anderson used lithography to achieve his clear and detailed illustrations. His books include *Afraid to Ride* (1957), *Blaze and the Lost Quarry* (1966), *Blaze and the Gray Spotted Pony* (1968), and *The Blind Connemara* (1971).

Anderson, John Bayard (1922–   ), American politician, b. Rockford, Ill. Anderson practiced law and served in the U.S. Foreign Service in West Berlin before winning election to the U.S. House of Representatives in 1960. He ran unsuccessfully for the Republican presidential nomination in 1980 and then became an independent candidate for the presidency. He held moderate views on economic issues and favored many social welfare programs. His supporters included both Democrats and Republicans. **C** 124c

Anderson, Dame Judith (1898–   ), actress, b. Adelaide, Australia. She has lived primarily in United States. Noted for performances of tragic roles in such plays as Eugene O'Neill's *Mourning Becomes Electra* and Robinson Jeffers' *Medea,* she is also famous as a Shakespearean actress.

Anderson, Marian, American singer **A** 251;   **N** 100, 107
Anderson, Maxie, American balloonist **B** 32
Anderson, Maxwell, American playwright **A** 215

Anderson, Robert (1805–71), American army officer, b. Louisville, Ky. He was graduated from U.S. Military Academy at West Point (1825) and served in Black Hawk, Seminole, and Mexican wars. He was in command at Fort Sumter during Confederate attack that marked start of Civil War (1861).

Anderson, Sherwood, American writer **A** 207; **S** 167
Anderson, South Carolina **S** 308
Andersonville National Cemetery, Georgia **G** 139
Andes (AN-dese), mountains of South America **A** 252–53; **M** 499
    ancient Indian civilizations **I** 201–07
    Argentina **A** 391; picture **A** 392
    Bolivia **B** 303–04
    Chile **C** 251, 252
    Colombia **C** 381
    in Peru, picture **M** 498
    landforms of South America **S** 276
    railroad pass, picture **G** 102
    Venezuela **V** 297

Andes, Army of the, a revolutionary force famous in military history for crossing the Andes in January, 1817. The army of about 5,000 men was recruited and trained by Argentinian liberator José de San Martín. After leaving Mendoza, Argentina, the men traveled for 21 days through mountain passes to Chacabuco, Chile. The crossing was dangerous and costly. Although most of the men survived, more than half of their 9,000 mules and nearly one third of their 1,600 horses did not. The army's victory at Chacabuco marked the first decisive blow for South American independence from Spain.
    Chile, history of **C** 254
    flag **F** 239
    San Martín, José de **S** 35

Andesite (AN-dese-ite), a volcanic rock **S** 433
Andorra (an-DOR-ra) **A** 254–55
    flag **F** 237
Andorra la Vella, capital of Andorra **A** 254
Andover, New Hampshire, picture **N** 153
Andradite (an-DRA-dite), gem mineral **G** 75
André, Brother, Canadian churchman **Q** 13
André (ON-dray), **Major John,** English spy **R** 207
    Arnold and André **A** 436
    famous spies **S** 388
    Purple Hearts awarded to André's captors **M** 198
Andreä (on-DRAY-a), **Johann Valentin,** German Lutheran minister **U** 255
Andrea Chénier (shain-YAY), opera by Giordano **O** 140
Andrea del Sarto see Sarto, Andrea del
Andrea Doria, ocean liner **O** 24

Andretti (an-DRET-tee), **Mario** (1940–   ), American race car driver, b. Montona, Italy. He won the Formula One Grand Prix world championship in 1978. Andretti's interest in race car driving began in Italy. He moved to the United States in 1955 and took up stock car driving in 1958. During his career he has been a three-time U.S. Auto Club national driving champion (1965, 1966, 1969) and winner of the 1969 Indianapolis 500.

Andrew, Saint, one of the 12 Apostles **A** 332–33
    Scottish feast of St. Andrew **H** 156
Andrews, Roy Chapman, American zoologist, explorer, and writer **W** 206
Andrews, Texas
    an open-plan school, picture **S** 57
Andreyev (on-DRAY-ef), **Leonid,** Russian author **U** 61
Andrić (AN-dreech), **Ivo,** Yugoslav writer **Y** 355

Androcles (AND-roc-lese), or **Androclus,** Roman slave who lived sometime during 1st century A.D. According to legend, after escaping from his master he befriended a wounded lion. He was later saved from death when the lion chosen to kill him in the arena turned out to be his old friend. George Bernard Shaw's *Androcles and the Lion* was based on this story.

Andromeda (an-DROM-e-da), constellation **C** 493
    spiral galaxy in, diagram **U** 197
Andromeda, in Greek mythology **G** 362
Andronicus, Lucius Livius see Livius Andronicus, Lucius
Andros, Sir Edmund, English governor **C** 466, 480
And Wonder, sonnet by Merrill Moore **S** 256
Anegada, one of the Virgin Islands, British **C** 118
    See also Virgin Islands, British
Anemia (a-NE-mia) **D** 191
    dietetics and study of anemia **B** 182–83
    pernicious anemia **V** 370d
    sickle-cell anemia **D** 199
    thalassemia **D** 199
    transfusion used in treatment **T** 251
Anemometers (an-em-OM-et-ers), instruments to measure winds **W** 84
Anemones (a-NEM-o-nes), **sea,** polyps **J** 74; pictures **J** 72
    damselfish immune to poison, picture **F** 204
Aneroid (AN-er-oid) **barometer** **B** 54; **W** 82–83
Anesthesia (an-es-THE-sia) **A** 256–59
    acupuncture **M** 208b
    drugs **D** 326
    progress in modern surgery **M** 208a
    See also Drugs; Medicine, history of

Anesthetics (an-es-THET-ics) **A** 258; **P** 314
Angel, painting by Fra Angelico **R** 166

Angel, a supernatural being who serves God. People of many different religions believe that angels are messengers from God. According to Christian tradition, there are nine choirs, or groups, of angels. Angels are usually pictured as winged creatures.

Angel dust, drug **D** 330
Angel Falls, Venezuela **S** 277; **V** 298; **W** 56b
Angelfish, picture **F** 192
Angelico (on-GEL-ic-o), **Fra,** Italian painter **A** 259;
  P 20
  Renaissance art **R** 166
Angeli Laudantes ("Praising Angels"), tapestry designed by Burne-Jones **T** 23

Angelo, Valenti (1897-   ), American author and illustrator of children's books, b. Massarosa, Italy. Angelo often uses childhood memories in writing his books. He wrote and illustrated *The Acorn Tree* (1958) and *The Tale of a Donkey* (1966). He also illustrated the award-winning book *Roller Skates* (1936) by Ruth Sawyer.

Angelus, Roman Catholic prayer that may be recited at the sound of the Angelus bell three times daily, morning, noon, and evening; name comes from first line of prayer *Angelus Domini nuntiavit Mariae* ("The Angel of the Lord declared unto Mary").

Anger, feeling of, psychology **M** 220–21
  divorce, attitudes toward **D** 236a
Angerstein (ANG-er-stine), **John Julius,** English merchant and art patron **N** 37
Angiospermae, division of the plant kingdom **P** 292
Angkor, ancient city in Cambodia **C** 31, 33
Angkor Thom, capital of the Khmer Empire **C** 33; picture **S** 335
Angkor Wat, temple in Cambodia, picture **C** 33
Angle of incidence, in physics of light, diagram **L** 261
Angle of reflection, in physics of light, diagram **L** 261
Angles, Germanic people, invaders of Britain **E** 216
Angles, in geometry **G** 124; diagrams **G** 125
Angleworms see Earthworms
Anglican Church, or Protestant Episcopal Church **P** 483–84
  Reformation **R** 134–35
  See also England, Church of
Angling see Fishing
Anglo-Egyptian Sudan see Sudan
Anglo-Norman French language **F** 433
Anglo-Saxon Chronicle **E** 246
  Alfred the Great **A** 155
Anglo-Saxon language **E** 243
  compared with Anglo-Norman French **F** 433
  names **N** 4
Anglo-Saxon (Old English) **literature** **E** 245–47
  Beowulf **B** 141–42
Anglo-Saxons, Teutonic peoples who settled in England **E** 216
  Celtic and Anglo-Saxon art **E** 233–34
  conversion to Christianity **C** 284

Anglund, Joan Walsh (1926–   ), American author and illustrator of children's books, b. Hinsdale, Ill. She is noted for her small, uniquely illustrated books, which often rhyme. Her works include *A Friend is Someone Who likes You* and *Love is a Special Way of Feeling*.

A Friend is Someone Who Likes You, picture from **C** 245

Angola (an-GO-la) **A** 260–61; **P** 402
  Cuban military intervention **C** 551
  flag **F** 235
Angora (an-GO-ra), now Ankara, capital of Turkey **T** 326
Angora goats **C** 151, 152
Angostura, Venezuela see Ciudad Bolívar

Angström (ONG-strem), **Anders Jonas** (1814–74), Swedish physicist, b. Lödgö. He was a founder of spectroscopy—science dealing with light separated into its various colors or wavelengths. His studies of wavelengths of light led to his discovery (1862) of hydrogen in the atmosphere. Angstrom unit (A), used in measuring wavelengths of light, is named in his honor.
  units of measure of light wavelengths **E** 24

Anguilla (an-GWIL-ah), one of the Leeward Islands in the Caribbean Sea, formerly a British colony. In 1967 the islands of St. Kitts, Nevis, and Anguilla became an associated state within the West Indies Associated States, with full internal self-government. Anguilla broke away from the state in 1969. When St. Kitts and Nevis later chose full independence, Anguilla elected to remain a British dependency. **S** 15
  Caribbean Sea and Islands **C** 118, 119

Anicetus, Saint, pope **R** 296
Animal behavior see Animals: intelligence and behavior
Animal bites **F** 161
Animal defenses
  adaptations for self protection **L** 219
  butterflies and moths **B** 472
  frogs, toads, and other amphibians **F** 477–78
  insects **I** 274–76
  lizards' protective behavior **L** 320–21
  mammals **M** 66–67
Animal diseases
  vectors **V** 283
  veterinarians and what they do **V** 324
Animal Farm, novel by George Orwell **E** 267
Animal gods **M** 560
Animal intelligence see Animals: intelligence and behavior
Animal kingdom **K** 249–59
  classes of animals **A** 262, 264
  eggs and embryos **E** 88–90a
  how classification works **T** 30
Animal locomotion see Animals: Locomotion
Animal plankton **P** 280–81
Animals **A** 262–74
  Africa **A** 50, 52; pictures **A** 51
  agents for dispersal of seeds **F** 281–82
  ages of, how to tell, pictures **A** 86
  amphibians **F** 470–78
  Asia's wildlife **A** 451
  Australia's wildlife **A** 505–07
  bacteria distinguished from **B** 9–10
  biological clocks **L** 243–50
  bioluminescence **B** 197
  blood types **B** 258
  body plans compared **B** 269
  cave dwellers **C** 157
  cell structure **C** 162–63
  circus acts **C** 303–04; pictures **C** 301
  cold-blooded **B** 259; **H** 123
  communication see Animals: communication
  conservation of **C** 485–86

Annapolis Valley, Nova Scotia, Canada   **N** 344b, 344d; picture **N** 344e

Annapurna, mountain peak in Nepal, picture **N** 112

Ann Arbor, Michigan
music festival   **M** 522

Annatto (an-NOT-to), yellow dye   **D** 369

Anne, Princess (Anne Elizabeth Alice Louise) (1950–   ), b. London, second child of Queen Elizabeth II of England and Philip, Duke of Edinburgh. She is fourth in line to throne of England. In 1973 Anne married a commoner, Captain Mark Phillips of The Queen's Dragoon Guards, and in 1977 she gave birth to a son.

Anne, queen of Great Britain and Ireland   **E** 224–25

Anne, Saint, mother of Virgin Mary and wife of Joachim. She is often pictured wearing a veil. One of many shrines dedicated to her is Ste. Anne de Beaupré near Quebec City, Canada. She is believed by many to have the power to effect miraculous cures. She is the patron saint of Quebec. Feast day is July 26th.

Annealing, heating-cooling process   **M** 232
bronze and brass   **B** 410
glass   **G** 232
steel   **I** 403
wire   **W** 190a

Anne Boleyn see Boleyn, Anne

Anne in White, painting by Bellows   **U** 118

Annelids (AN-nel-ids), worms   **W** 309–10

Anne of Cleves, 4th wife of Henry VIII of England **H** 109

Annie, musical, picture   **M** 542

Annotations, for books
library catalog cards   **L** 187

Annual rings, of tree growth   **T** 286–87

Annuals, plants   **P** 303
cultivated grasses   **G** 317
gardens and gardening   **G** 29–30, 46

Annuities, insurance   **I** 295

Annular eclipses   **E** 46

Annulment of marriage   **D** 236

Annunciation Day, religious holiday   **R** 154

Annunciation of the Virgin, in New Testament (Luke), announcement by archangel Gabriel to the Virgin Mary that she would bear a son, to be called Jesus. Feast day is celebrated March 25.

Annuu see Samoa

Anoles (a-NO-les), lizards   **L** 318

Anopheles (a-NOPH-el-ese) mosquito   **H** 260; **I** 283

Anorexia nervosa, disease   **D** 191

Anouilh (on-NUI), **Jean,** French playwright   **F** 442

Antananarivo, capital of Madagascar   **M** 4b, 5

Ant and the Grasshopper, The, fable by Aesop   **F** 5

Antarctic, south polar region   **P** 363, 366–71
American claims by exploration   **T** 115
birds of   **B** 226, 228
Ewing-Donn theory of Ice Ages   **I** 24
frigid, or polar zones   **Z** 372
icebergs   **I** 27
ice sheet and ice islands   **I** 11–12
International Geophysical Year   **I** 319–20
penguins, where they live, map-diagram   **P** 121

Antarctica (ant-ARC-tic-a), hub of the Antarctic region **P** 366; picture   **C** 344
Argentina claims in   **A** 390
exploration by Byrd   **B** 481

mountain peaks, highest in Antarctica   **M** 494

Antarctic Ocean   **O** 45

Antarctic Treaty, 1959   **P** 363, 371

Antares (an-TAR-ese), star   **C** 493

Anteater civets, or falanoucs, animals   **G** 93

Anteaters, mammals   **M** 66
Australian wildlife   **A** 505

Anteaters, spiny   **P** 333–34

Antelopes, hoofed mammals   **H** 221
antelope family, pictures   **H** 219

Antennae (an-TENN-e), of animals
butterflies and moths   **B** 468
crustacea   **S** 168, 170
"feelers," of insects   **I** 262–63, 266–69

Antennas, of radar and radio   **R** 34d, 35, 51; picture **E** 143
Apollo tracking antennas   **S** 340g
communications satellites   **E** 142e
radio-astronomy observatories   **O** 10
radio telescopes   **R** 70–72; **T** 64
television reception   **E** 142c

Anterus, Saint, pope   **R** 296

Anthem, musical form   **M** 535

Anthemius of Tralles (anth-E-mius of TRAL-les), Byzantine architect   **B** 485

Anthems, national see National anthems and patriotic songs

Anthers, of flowers   **F** 277; **P** 295; picture   **F** 276

Anthocyanins (an-tho-CY-an-ins), plant pigments **T** 282

Anthony, Susan Brownell (1820–1906), American woman suffragist and reformer, b. Adams, Mass. Born into a Quaker home, she was first a schoolteacher, then an active worker for temperance, abolition, and women's rights. She lectured for equal rights for women, was one of the organizers, with Elizabeth Cady Stanton, of the National Woman Suffrage Association (1869), and was president of the National American Woman Suffrage Association (1892–1900).
woman suffrage movement   **W** 212b

Anthony of Padua, Saint (1195–1231), Franciscan monk and theologian, b. Lisbon, Portugal. He taught theology and preached in France and Italy. According to legend, once when he could not get people to listen to him, he turned and preached to a school of fish, who miraculously gave him their attention. He was canonized in 1232 and is patron saint of Portugal and Padua.

Anthracite, hard coal   **C** 363; **F** 487

Anthrax, disease   **C** 151; **I** 287; **M** 208
bacteria causing disease, picture   **B** 11
disease, conquest of   **D** 215
Koch discovers microbes causing   **K** 293
Pasteur, Louis   **P** 96–97

Anthropology (an-thro-POL-ogy), study of human beings and human culture   **A** 300–09
archeology related to   **A** 349, 364
blood groups studied   **B** 258
Mead, Margaret   **M** 191
Mexico City's National Museum of Anthropology **M** 252
prehistoric people   **P** 442–46
races, human   **R** 29–32
research methods   **R** 182
See also Ancient civilizations; Prehistoric art

Anti-aircraft guns   **G** 426

Anti-aircraft missiles   **M** 348

Antibiotics A 310–16; **D** 212, 217; **M** 208a
  disease, conquest of **D** 217
  drug industry **D** 323
  Fleming's work **F** 249
  genetic strains of microbes produce antibiotics **G** 88
  only drugs that kill microbes directly **D** 327
Antibodies A 316a; **D** 212; **V** 260
  acquired immunity **I** 104–05; **M** 209, 210
  Behring's research **D** 215–16
  control of parasite diseases **D** 188
  medical laboratory tests **M** 202
  rejection of organ transplants **M** 211
  structure and source **I** 106–07
  vaccination and inoculation **V** 260, 261
  virus diseases **V** 369
Anticline, rock formation, with oil deposit, diagram **P** 170
Anti-Comintern Pact, 1936 **W** 286
Anticorrosives *see* Corrosion
Anticosti Island, Quebec **I** 426
Anticyclones, or highs, in meteorology **W** 75, 187
Antidotes, remedies for effects of poisons **P** 356
  first aid for poisoning **F** 160
Antietam (an-TEE-tam), **Battle of,** Civil War battle near Sharpsburg, Va. **C** 324
Antietam National Battlefield Site, Maryland **M** 125
Antifouling paints **P** 33
Antifreeze, chemical **I** 4
Antigens A 316a; **I** 105
Antigonish, poem by Hughes Mearns **N** 274
Antigua, Caribbean island *see* Antigua and Barbuda
Antigua (an-TI-gwa), Guatemala **G** 392; picture **G** 393
Antigua (an-TI-ga) **and Barbuda** A 316b; **C** 118, 119
  flag **F** 241
Antihistamines, drugs for allergic reactions **D** 191, 193
Anti-Lebanon Mountains, between Syria and Lebanon **L** 121; **S** 507
Antilles (an-TILL-es), island group dividing Caribbean Sea from Atlantic Ocean **C** 116–19
Antilles Current **G** 411
Antilles, Greater *see* Greater Antilles
Antilles, Lesser *see* Lesser Antilles
Antilocapridae, American family of hoofed mammals **H** 217
Antimasque, comic dance preceding masque **D** 25

Antimatter, matter in which the electrical charges of the subatomic particles are the opposite of those in matter that makes up the world. An atom of matter has a nucleus of protons and neutrons surrounded by electrons. But an atom of antimatter would have a nucleus of antineutrons and antiprotons surrounded by positrons (positive electrons). When matter and antimatter are brought together, they destroy each other's mass, producing immense energy. Some antimatter has been successfully produced in laboratories under special high-energy conditions. **N** 369

Antimony (AN-tim-ony), element **E** 154, 159; **M** 227
  producing regions of North America **N** 291
Antinoüs, cult figure of ancient Rome
  statue, picture **R** 286
Antioch (AN-ti-ock), ancient city, now Antakya, Turkey
  center of Apostles' missions to Gentiles **R** 288
Antioch College, Yellow Springs, Ohio
  Horace Mann, president **M** 83
Antiochus Epiphanes (an-TY-o-chus e-PIPH-an-ese), Syrian king **H** 35

Antioxidants (an-ti-OX-id-ants), in chemistry
  vitamin E **V** 371
Antiparticles, subatomic particles **N** 369
Anti-perspirants (an-ty-PER-spir-ants) **D** 117
Antipopes, pretenders to the papacy of the Roman Catholic Church **R** 296–97
Antiprotons, subatomic particles **N** 369
Antiques (an-TEEKS) **and antique collecting** A 317–21
  furniture design **F** 505–10
  interior decorating **I** 302–03
Antiquities (an-TI-quit-ies), **popular** **F** 302
Anti-Semitism, hostility toward Jews and Judaism **J** 110
  Union of Soviet Socialist Republics **U** 29
Antiseptics **D** 222
  Lister, Joseph **L** 311
  See also Disinfectants
Antiserums, used to acquire passive immunity A 316a; **I** 106; **V** 261
Antisubmarine weapons **S** 446
Antitoxins, a kind of antibody **D** 200; **V** 260
Antitrust laws **T** 305–06

Antivivisectionist (an-tee-VIV-ih-sec-shun-ist), a person opposed to vivisection, which is the use of live animals for scientific research. Antivivisectionists emphasize the rights of animals. They feel that many experiments are unnecessary and cruel. They believe that substitutes, such as one-celled organisms and human tissue grown in test tubes, can be used instead of animals. Organizations working to regulate experimentation on animals include the American Antivivisection Society and, in England, the National Antivivisection Society.

Antlers
  deer **D** 83; **H** 214
  mammals **M** 67
Antofagasta, Chile **C** 254
Antoinette Perry Memorial Award *see* Tony Award
Antonescu (on-to-NES-cu), **Ion,** Rumanian general **R** 359–60
Antonia: A Portrait of the Woman, documentary motion picture **M** 488c
Antonioni, Michelangelo, Italian motion-picture director **M** 488, 488a, 488b
Antony, Mark, Roman general **M** 100; **R** 303
  Cicero's opposition to **C** 298
Antony and Cleopatra, play by Shakespeare **S** 133
Antonyms and synonyms **S** 504
Antrodemus, dinosaur **D** 174; picture **D** 176
Ants A 322–31
  animal maze tests **A** 283; picture **A** 284
  aphids, "ant cows," picture **P** 286
  bull-horn acacia, home of ants **P** 283
  household pests **H** 261
  how to build an ant observation nest **A** 330
  strength of **I** 273; picture **I** 274
Ant's cows *see* Aphids
Antwerp, Belgium **B** 130
  trade, early development of **S** 428
Anu, Babylonian god **M** 557

Anubis (a-NU-bis), in Egyptian legend and religion, god of the dead, who ruled over graves and supervised burial. He was the son of Osiris, chief Egyptian god and symbol of regeneration, fertility, and life. Picture **M** 560

Anvil, bone in the ear, diagram **B** 285
Anvil-topped cumulo-nimbus cloud, picture **C** 361

Anxiety, emotion

mental illness **M** 224

Anzacs, nickname given to Australian and New Zealand soldiers. The name is formed from initials of Australian and New Zealand Army Corps. The term originally referred only to those who took part in Gallipoli landings (1915) but applied in World War II to all New Zealand and Australian troops.

Anzio, Italy

beachhead battle, World War II **W** 298

Anzus Council, or **Pacific Council,** organization comprised of Australia, New Zealand, and U.S., from whose initials the name is derived. It was established by Tripartite Security Treaty (1951), a pact to provide for mutual defense of the 3 nations and of their possessions in the Pacific.

Aorta (a-OR-ta), artery carrying blood from heart **B** 276

heart action **H** 86a

Aoudad (OWD-ad), a kind of wild sheep **S** 145

AP see Associated Press

Apache (ap-ACH-e), Indians of North America **I** 193–95

Arizona **A** 413
beadwork, pictures **I** 194
Geronimo **G** 189
Indian Wars **I** 214
New Mexico **N** 187
See also Cochise

Apalachee, Indians native to Florida **F** 272

Apartheid (a-PART-ate), racial segregation in Republic of South Africa. The term is Afrikaans for "separateness." Apartheid is a continuation of economic, political, and social discrimination and segregation that existed from the 17th century. It became a political issue when incorporated into Nationalist Party platform (1948). Aim of the white group is establishment of separate homelands for nonwhites. This policy has been condemned by UN General Assembly. **S** 268–69, 273

Namibia **N** 8b

Apartment houses **H** 182–83

ancient Rome **H** 178
Borneo, picture **B** 338
Brasília, Brazil, picture **L** 59
electronically-controlled heating system, picture **E** 143
Habitat, Montreal, pictures **A** 386d; **H** 183
modern architecture **A** 386a
New York City **N** 231; picture **C** 306
Tel Aviv, Israel, picture **A** 468
underground apartments on Florida coast, picture **H** 184
See also Condominium

Apatite, rock

fertilizers **F** 97

Apennines (AP-en-nines), mountain range of Italy **I** 451

San Marino **S** 34–35

Apéritifs (a-per-i-TEEFS), or appetizer wines **W** 188

Apes **M** 418–19; picture **M** 417

ancestors of apes **E** 347
animal communication **A** 280, 281
feet and hands **F** 83–84

Aphelion (a-PHE-li-on), point in comet's or planet's orbit farthest from the sun **S** 241

Mars **M** 105
Mercury's orbit, picture **R** 144

Aphids, plant lice **P** 285–86, 288

ant food **A** 329
prey of ladybugs **I** 257
vectors of plant diseases **V** 284, 285

Aphrodite (aph-rod-ITE-e), Greek goddess **G** 361

Apia (a-PI-a), capital of Western Somoa **S** 23

Apiary (APE-i-ary), colony of bees **H** 202

Apis (A-pis), sacred bull of Egypt **C** 145

Aplodontia (ap-lo-DON-tia), or mountain beaver **R** 277; picture **R** 278

stores hay for winter use **M** 66

Apocalypse (a-POC-a-lips), Biblical book of Revelation **B** 162

Apocrypha (a-POC-riph-a) **B** 152, 156–57, 159

Apodes (AP-o-dese), order of fishes **E** 85

Apogee, point of a satellite's orbit farthest from earth **S** 40, 41

moon's orbit **M** 446

Apollinaire, Guillaume, French poet **F** 441

Apollo, (Phoebus Apollo); Greek and Roman god **G** 360

Roman coin picturing Apollo **A** 232
Temple in Corinth, ruins, picture **G** 340

Apollo, Project, name of U.S. project to put astronauts on the moon **M** 453; picture **M** 454

Apollo 7, 8, 9, 10 **S** 339, 342, 344
Apollo 11, moon landing **E** 370; **S** 339–340a, 340h–340i, 344; pictures **M** 452, **S** 340b–340c, 340h
Apollo 12, moon landing **S** 344
Apollo 13, first in-flight failure **S** 344
Apollo 14, moon landing **S** 345
Apollo 15, moon landing **S** 345
Apollo 16, moon landing **S** 345
Apollo 17, **M** 455; **S** 345
Apollo Soyuz Test Project **S** 345
Lunar Rover, picture **S** 340g
navigation **N** 68, 69; **S** 340f–340g
observatories **O** 14
space suit, life-support system, diagrams **S** 340L
tracking network **S** 340g

Apollodor of Damascus, Greek engineer **E** 208

Apollo-Saturn spacecraft, diagrams **S** 340a, 340h

Apoplexy see Stroke

A posteriori (ay-pos-tir-i-OR-i) ("from later on") **U** 194

Apostles, The, 12 disciples of Jesus Christ **A** 332–33; **C** 279–80, 281

chosen by Jesus **J** 83
New Testament of the Bible **B** 160
Peter, Saint **P** 167
Roman Catholic Church, history of **R** 287

Apostles' Creed **R** 295, 301

Apostle spoons **K** 285

Apostolic (ap-os-TOL-ic) **succession** **O** 228

Apostrophes (a-POS-tro-phese), punctuation marks **P** 532

Appalachia (ap-a-LAY-chi-a), name given disadvantaged region in the Appalachian Mountains in eastern United States. The region consists of parts of 11 states from northern Pennsylvania to north central Alabama.

poverty in the United States **P** 424a–424b

Appalachian Mountains, North America **M** 496; **N** 285

Canada **C** 50; **Q** 10a
formation of **E** 11

Arabian Sea **O** 45
Arabic-Hindu (ARR-a-bic-HIN-du) **numerals** **N** 391–92
Arabic language **L** 39; **M** 305; **S** 44
   common language of early science **S** 64
   Islam, language of **I** 416
   northern Africa **A** 55; **N** 458
Arabic numerals **N** 391–92
Arab-Israeli wars **I** 444–45; **J** 81, 113
   Egypt **E** 92
   Jordan **J** 139
   Lebanon **L** 123
   Nasser, Gamal Abdel **N** 15
   Palestine **P** 40d
   Sadat, Anwar el- **S** 2
   Syria **S** 508

Arab League, a league of sovereign states founded in 1945 to promote the political, cultural, and economic unity of the Arab community. This covenant, based on the Alexandria Protocol, was signed by Egypt, Iraq, Saudi Arabia, Syria, Lebanon, Jordan, and Yemen (Sana). Since then, many other Arab nations have joined. The league is made up of a council in which each country has one vote. Palestine is considered an independent nation and a full member of the League. Egypt was expelled from the Arab League after it signed a peace treaty with Israel in 1979.

Arable land **G** 96
Arab Republics, federation of Egypt, Libya, and Syria **E** 92
Arabs **A** 55
   alchemists **C** 207–08
   drugs, early use of **D** 322
   Iraq **I** 378
   Morocco **M** 458–61
   Palestine **P** 40b
   Saudi Arabia **S** 44–49
   smoking waterpipes, picture **M** 304
   Soviet Central Asia **U** 46, 47
   Syria **S** 505
Arachne (ar-ACK-ne), in Greek mythology **S** 383
Arachnids (a-RAC-nids), a class of animals **I** 283–84
   spiders **S** 383–88

Arafat (AHR-a-fat), **Yasir** (1929–), Palestinian leader, b. Jerusalem. He graduated from Cairo University as an engineer, and also received commando and other military training in Egypt. While working in Kuwait, he joined al-Fatah, an organization of militant Palestinians. A foe of Israel, he is chairman of the Palestine Liberation Organization (PLO).

Arafura (ar-a-FU-ra) **Sea,** part of the Pacific Ocean that lies between New Guinea and Australia, containing Aru Islands, which were Japanese air base in World War II.

Arago (a-RA-go), **François** (Dominique F. J.), French scientist **E** 129, 140
Aragon, ancient kingdom in Spain
   Ferdinand II, king **F** 87
Aragon, Louis, French poet **F** 442
Aral Sea, central Asia **L** 26; **U** 33
Aramaic (ar-a-MAI-ic) **language** **H** 100
   Dead Sea Scrolls **D** 48–49
   in the Bible **B** 152, 153
Aramid, type of nylon **N** 425
Aramis (a-ra-MECE), one of *The Three Musketeers* **D** 342–43
Aransas National Wildlife Refuge, Texas **T** 126

Arantes do Nascimiento, Edson *see* Pelé
Arapaho, Indians of North America **I** 164
Ararat, Mount, in Asian Turkey **T** 324
Araucanians (ar-auc-ON-ians), Indians of South America **I** 210
   Chile **C** 249, 254
Arawak (AR-a-wak), Indians of South America **I** 207–09
   Antigua and Barbuda **A** 316b
   Jamaica **J** 14, 17
   Puerto Rico **P** 516
   St. Vincent and the Grenadines **S** 18d
   Trinidad **T** 292
Arbeau (ar-BO), **Thoinot,** French priest **D** 27
Arbela (ar-BE-la), **Battle of,** 331 B.C. **A** 152; **B** 100
Arbitration
   labor-management relations **L** 16
   provided for in treaties **T** 273
Arbor Day (Arbor and Bird Day) **H** 152–53
   Jewish Arbor Day in Israel **R** 154
   origin in Nebraska **N** 72
Arboretums (ar-bor-RE-tums), plantings of trees and shrubs **Z** 379
Arbutus, trailing, also called Mayflower
   state flower of Massachusetts, picture **M** 134
Arc, of a circle **G** 127

Arcadia (ar-CAY-dia), province of southern Greece. Mythical mountain home of the god Pan, it was almost inaccessible in olden times. Poets have praised the peaceful life of Arcadian shepherds, and so "Arcadian" is often used to describe simple, pastoral living.

Arcadian poetry **I** 479

Arcaro, Eddie (Edward Arcaro) (1916–), American jockey, b. Cincinnati, Ohio. He rode over 4,000 winners (since 1932), making him one of the leading jockeys in racing history, with total purses estimated at over $20,000,000. He was a five-time winner of the Kentucky Derby and only jockey to ride two "triple crown" winners.

Arc de Triomphe, Paris *see* Arch of Triumph
Arcetri (ar-CHAY-tri) **Observatory,** Italy **S** 466
Arch, in architecture *see* Arches
Archaeology *see* Archeology
Archaeopteryx (arc-e-OP-ter-ix), first known bird **B** 207
Archaic Period, of Greek art **G** 344–45; **S** 94–95
Archangel (ARC-angel), Union of Soviet Socialist Republics **U** 33
   main port on the White Sea **O** 49
Archangel Michael, icon by Andrei Rublev **U** 56
Arch bridges **B** 395, 397; pictures **B** 399
Archeoastronomy **A** 476d
Archeology (arc-e-OL-ogy), study of things of the past **A** 348–65
   aerial photography **P** 206
   anthropology related to **A** 300, 307–08
   cave dwellers and their art **P** 439–41
   Celtic tribes **C** 165–66
   ceramics, a source of information **C** 176
   Israel, discoveries in **I** 444
   Pompeii **P** 390
   pre-Columbian collection in Mexico's national museum **M** 253
   prehistoric people **P** 442–46
   recovering dinosaur bones, picture **D** 181
   research methods **R** 182
   Schliemann, Heinrich **S** 53–54
   tree-ring calendars **T** 287

Archives (ARC-ives), place in which public or private records and documents of historical value are preserved.
National Archives, established by U.S. Congress in
1934, is located in Washington, D.C., and holds such
notable documents as Declaration of Independence,
Constitution, and Bill of Rights. Public Archives of Canada, founded in 1872, is located in Ottawa.

Ardizzone (ar-dit-ZO-ne), **Edward** (1900–   ), English author and illustrator of children's books, b. Haiphong,
Indochina (now Vietnam). His first reputation was as an
artist, but he is best-known for his series of books about
Tim and his sea adventures, including *Little Tim and the
Brave Sea Captain*, and *Tim All Alone*, which won Britain's Kate Greenaway Medal (1956).

Argall, Sir Samuel (?–1626), English adventurer. He was
the first to sail the northern route directly from England
to Virginia (1609). Accompanying Lord Delaware to Virginia (1610), he helped replenish the colony's food supplies; kidnapped Pocahontas, thus securing the release
of English captives (1612); and overthrew French colonies in Maine and Nova Scotia (1613). He was deputy
governor of Virginia (1617–19).

Buenos Aires **B** 426–28
cattle raising, picture **S** 289
fascism in **F** 64
flag **F** 242
gaucho barbeque, picture **L** 5
immigration **I** 103
Islas Malvinas (Falkland Islands) **I** 432; **S** 278
life in Latin America **L** 47–61
national anthem **N** 20–21
Pampa, The, picture **G** 314
San Martín, José de, early fighter for freedom **S** 35
sheep ranch in Patagonia, picture **P** 433
Tierra del Fuego, picture **S** 275
Argol see Tartar
Argon, element **E** 154, 159; **G** 59
industrial uses **G** 62
Langmuir's use in light bulbs **L** 35
one of the noble gases **N** 109
use in welding, picture **G** 60
Argonauts (AR-go-nauts), in Greek mythology **G** 364
Argumentation see Debates and debating
Aria (AR-ia), accompanied song for the single voice
M 535; **O** 131–32
popular form in baroque period **B** 65
Ariadne (arri-AD-ne), in Greek mythology **G** 365
in story from *Tanglewood Tales* **H** 75–76
Arianism (AR-i-an-ism), heresy of Arius **C** 283
Arias, Arnulfo, president of Panama **P** 46
Arica (a-RI-ca), Chile
rainfall least in world **R** 94
Aries, constellation **C** 490; sign of, picture **S** 244
Arif, Abdul Rahman, president of Iraq **I** 383
Arif (a-REEF), **Abdul Salam Mohammed,** president of
Iraq **I** 383
Arikara (a-RIK-a-ra), Indians of North America **S** 326
Ariosto (ar-i-OS-to), **Lodovico,** Italian poet **I** 478
Aristarchus (ar-is-TARC-us) **of Samos S** 63–64
Aristocracy (ar-i-STOC-racy), government **G** 274
Aristophanes (ar-is-TOPH-an-ese), Greek dramatist
A 229; **G** 353
ancient Greek comedy **D** 294
Aristotle, Greek philosopher **A** 396–97; **P** 191–92
air theory **E** 351
Alexander the Great and Aristotle **A** 151
ancient civilizations **A** 230
astronomy, early history of **A** 471
biologist of the ancient world **B** 187
contributions to science, summary **S** 63
earth theory **C** 206
encyclopedia, father of the **E** 193
government systems **G** 274
Greek literature **G** 355
his library **L** 194
literary criticism **L** 312
medical advances **M** 203
memory, law of association **P** 493
oratory and rhetoric **O** 180
Aristotle Contemplating the Bust of Homer, painting by
Rembrandt **G** 354
Arithmetic A 398–401
abacus **A** 2–3
binary number system **C** 453, 454, 456
calculators **C** 9
computer circuits **C** 453–54
fractions **F** 397–402
graphs **G** 309–13
interest **P** 149–50
numbers and number systems **N** 384–88
numerals and numeration systems **N** 389–401
percent **P** 148–49

sets **S** 126–27
See also Calculators; Computers
Arithmetic mean, or mean, a kind of average of a set of
numbers **S** 417
Arius (a-RY-us), Greek theologian **C** 283; **R** 289
Arizona A 402–17
Grand Canyon National Park **G** 290–92
Hopi Indians descendents of cliff dwellers
I 190–91
irrigated desert regions, pictures **D** 126
modern church architecture, picture **C** 288
Arizona, University of, at Tucson, picture **A** 410
Arizona Highways, magazine **A** 410
Arkansas (ARK-an-saw) **A** 418–32
Arkansas River, United States **A** 422, 426, 429
Colorado **C** 403
Fryingpan–Arkansas Project **C** 405
Oklahoma **O** 83
Arkansas Toothpick (Bowie knife) **B** 344
Arkansas-Verdigris River Navigation System O 86

Ark of the Covenant, sacred chest containing agreement
between God and Israel made on Mt. Sinai. It was kept
by Israelites during years of wandering in desert. After
they settled in Promised Land, it was placed in King
Solomon's temple in Jerusalem. Today the term refers
to a holy chest holding the scroll of the Torah, or law of
Moses, which is placed along the eastern wall of every
synagogue as a symbol of the original.

Arkwright, Richard, British inventor and early industrial-
ist **C** 520; **I** 236, 238; **T** 140–41
Arlandes (ar-LOND), **Marquis d',** French balloonist
B 30
Arlington House, The Robert E. Lee Mansion, formerly
Custis-Lee Mansion, Virginia **N** 29; **V** 353
Arlington National Cemetery, Virginia **N** 28–30;
V 353
amphitheatre, picture **H** 224
Unknown Soldier **U** 225
Washington, D.C. **W** 32
Arm
bones of the **F** 79
Armada (ar-MA-da), **Spanish,** 1588 **B** 101; **E** 222
Drake defeats King Philip's fleet **D** 290–91
first naval battle fought entirely under sail **S** 159
race for overseas empires created conflicts **E** 388
Armadillos, mammals **M** 66–67; picture **M** 69

Armageddon (ar-ma-GEDD-on), in the Bible, the place of
the final battle between powers of good and evil on judgment day (Revelation 16:16). In modern usage, the
term refers to any great battle.

Armagh, Northern Ireland **U** 73
Armature, framework used in clay modeling **C** 336
Armatures, in electric motors **E** 137–38
electric generators **E** 121, 122
Armed Forces, U.S. see United States Armed Forces
Armed Forces Day H 150
Armenian (ar-ME-nian) **Soviet Socialist Republic**
U 44–45
languages of the U.S.S.R. **U** 28
popular foods **F** 335
Armies
Alexander the Great **A** 151–153
Canadian armed forces **C** 79–82
United States **U** 166–75

Armistead, James, American patriot, b. New Kent
County, Va., dates of life unknown. During the Revolu-

Armistead, James (continued)
tionary War, Armistead, a slave, collected valuable information about British forces at Portsmouth, Va., for Lafayette. For this service the Virginia State Legislature granted him freedom in 1786.

Armistice, an agreement to halt hostilities in a war. A partial armistice or truce usually affects only a single battlefield or other limited area, while a general armistice, which must be agreed to by the heads of the governments involved, suspends all fighting and is often a beginning of peace negotiations.
> New York celebration, Armistice, 1918, picture **W** 280

Armistice Day see Veterans' Day
Armitage, Kenneth, English painter **E** 242
Armonica (ar-MON-ic-a), invented by Franklin **F** 453; picture **F** 452
Armor **A** 433–35
> coats of arms **H** 115–18
> combat arms of United States Army **U** 168–69
> early decorations **D** 73
> knights, knighthood, and chivalry **K** 272–73
> Metropolitan Museum of Art collection **M** 237
> Roman soldiers, picture **R** 305

Armored tanks see Tanks, armored
Armory Show, New York art show, 1913 **P** 30; **U** 122
> modern art in the United States **M** 395

Arms races, reasons for disarmament **D** 186
> between the World Wars **W** 282–85

Armstrong, Edwin, American engineer, picture **E** 147
Armstrong, Louis, American musician **J** 58–59; **N** 102

Armstrong, Neil Alden (1930–   ), American astronaut, b. Wapakoneta, Ohio. A combat pilot in Korea and test pilot before joining the astronaut program, he was command pilot of Gemini 8 (1966). On July 20, 1969, as the only civilian member of Apollo 11 crew, he became the first person to walk on the moon's surface. He has been a professor of aerospace engineering since 1971.
> first astronaut on the moon **E** 370; **S** 339–340a
> space flights and space flight data **S** 344

Armstrong, William H. (1914–   ), American author and educator, b. Lexington, Va. His book *Sounder* won the Newbery Medal in 1970. His other books for young readers include *Barefoot in the Grass: The Story of Grandma Moses* (1970) and *Animal Tales* (1971). He has also written books that help students improve their study skills. **C** 243

Army, Canadian see Canadian Armed Forces
Army, United States Department of the **U** 166–67, 174–75
> national cemeteries **N** 28

Army Air Corps, United States **U** 160
Army Air Corps Song, by Robert Crawford **N** 26
Army ants **A** 331
Army National Guard, United States **U** 175
Army of the Andes see Andes, Army of
Army of the Potomac see Potomac, Army of the
Army worms **P** 289; picture **P** 288
Arnarsson, Ingolfur, Norwegian Viking **I** 44
Arne, Thomas, English composer **N** 27
Arnold, Benedict, American soldier and traitor **A** 436
> Revolutionary War **R** 199, 204, 206–07

Arnold, Matthew, English author **E** 262
Arnolfo di Cambio, Italian architect **I** 463
Arno River, Italy **I** 450, 452

Aromatic plants see Herbs; Spices and condiments
Aron Kodesh (a-RONE KO-desh), in Judaism **J** 119
Aroostook (a-ROOS-took) **River,** Maine **M** 36
> bloodless war, boundary dispute **M** 47; **N** 138g

Arouet, Francois Marie see Voltaire

Arp, Hans (Jean) (1888–1966), French artist, b. Strasbourg, Alsace (then part of Germany but now part of France). He was a founder of the Dada movement in Zurich, Switzerland (1916), and after 1925 a member of a group of surrealist painters in Paris. During the 1920's he did many abstract reliefs on wood but after 1930 devoted himself mainly to sculpture.
> surrealism in modern art **M** 395; **S** 105

Árpád (AR-pod), (?–907), Hungarian national hero. Leader of the Magyar tribe, he was elected prince of all seven Hungarian tribes, and he led nomadic tribes (896?) into region of Danube basin in what is now Hungary. He established the Árpád dynasty (890?–1301), of which Saint Stephen was the first crowned king and King Andrew was the last.

Arpeggio, in music **M** 532
Arpino, Gerald, American choreographer **B** 29
> *Clown,* ballet, picture **D** 33

Arrack, alcoholic beverage from coconut palm **C** 369
Arraignment, in law **C** 527
Arrangement in Grey and Black, painting by Whistler **W** 160
Arrest, for breaking the law **C** 527
> steps in law enforcement **L** 88

Arretine (ARR-a-tene) **ware,** pottery **R** 306
Arrhenius (ar-RAE-nius), **S.A.,** Swedish chemist **C** 215
Arrow and the Song, The, poem by Longfellow **L** 343
Arrow plant, source of Mexican jumping beans **J** 150
Arrowrock Dam, Idaho, picture **I** 58

Arrowroot, edible starch produced from stems of several tropical plants, particularly arrowroot, grown in the West Indies. It is a tasteless whitish powder, often used in cookies, puddings, and crackers.
> St. Vincent and the Grenadines is the world's leading producer **S** 18d

Arrows, in archery **A** 366–68
Arrowworms, or glassworms, sea animals **P** 281
Arroyos, dry river beds **R** 237
Arsenal, building for storing weapons
> Harper's Ferry National Historical Park, West Virginia **W** 135

Arsenic, element **E** 154, 159
> insecticides **I** 257

Arson **F** 153–54
Art **A** 437–438g
> African art **A** 70–76
> American see United States, art of the
> ancient **A** 233–43
> archeology related to **A** 365
> color in art **D** 141, 143
> decorative arts **D** 66–78
> graphic arts **G** 302–08
> modern **M** 386–98
> museums **M** 514–20
> painting **P** 14–32
> prehistoric art **P** 439–41
> religious see Religious art
> sculpture **S** 90–105
> *See also* names of individual artists, such as Rembrandt; of specific countries, as Italian art; of art

periods, as Baroque art; and of art forms, as Painting or Industrial design

Art, ancient see Ancient world, art of

Art, commercial see Commercial art

Art directors
motion pictures **M** 479–80, 481
plays **P** 336

Artemis (AR-te-mis), Greek goddess **G** 360

Arteries, blood vessels **B** 275–76; **D** 212
cholesterol in body chemistry **B** 293
hardening of **D** 195–96
heart **H** 86–86a
pulse and pulse rates **M** 208f

Arterioles, arteries branching from large arteries **B** 279; **H** 86a

Arteriosclerosis (ar-te-rio-scle-RO-sis), hardening of the arteries, disease **D** 195–96

Artesian (ar-TE-sian) **wells W** 123

Art galleries see Art Museums

Arthritis D 192
occupational therapy **O** 18

Arthropods, animals **P** 436

Arthur, Chester Alan, 21st president of United States **A** 438h–441; picture **V** 328
civil service, beginnings of **C** 317

Arthur, King legendary hero of Britain **A** 442–45; **E** 216; **L** 129
English literature, legends based on **E** 247–48
story of the sword, a fragmentary myth **M** 560
Welsh folklore **W** 3

Artichokes, vegetable **V** 289
flowers we eat **P** 308; picture **P** 309

Article, part of speech **P** 90

Articles of Confederation, 1781 **R** 203; **U** 134–35, 145
Albany Plan of Franklin **F** 454
attacked by *The Federalist* **F** 78
need to regulate trade between states **I** 331
Northwest Ordinance, 1787 **W** 143
Ohio established as Northwest Territory **O** 74
weaknesses **U** 135, 145

Articulated buses B 466; picture **B** 465

Articulated diving bell D 81

Artifacts, things used in past eras **A** 348–49, 351, 358, 365
means of dating **A** 359–62

Artificial languages L 40

Artificial limbs, for handicapped persons **H** 28

Artificial pearls P 114

Artificial respiration F 158, 160
first aid for fire victims **F** 153

Artificial satellites see Satellites, artificial

Artificial sweeteners see Sweeteners, artificial

Artigas (ar-TI-gos), José G., Uruguayan leader **U** 239

Artillery, weaponry **G** 424–26
United States Army **U** 171

Art Institute of Chicago, Illinois **I** 80

Artiodactyla (ar-ti-o-DACT-il-a), order of even-toed hoofed mammals **H** 208–09; **M** 62, 68

Artisan, maker of decorative art objects **D** 66

Artist in His Studio, painting by Jan Vermeer **D** 360

Artists' materials D 301, 303
sculpture **S** 90–91

Art museums M 514–20
See also names of museums

Art nouveau, style of decorative art **D** 78
dining room, picture **D** 77
Tiffany lamp, picture **D** 77
watch, picture **D** 78

Arts see Art

Arts and crafts see Decorative arts; Handicrafts

Art song, song created by a composer to a poetic text **M** 538
lied **C** 333
styles of singing **V** 376

Artyukhin, Yuri, Soviet cosmonaut **S** 345

Artzybasheff (art-zee-BAHSH-ef), **Boris** (1899–1965), American author and illustrator, b. Kharkov, Ukraine, U.S.S.R. He illustrated many children's books, including *Seven Simeons: A Russian Tale* (1937), one of the first Caldecott Honor Books. He was also well known as the illustrator of over 200 *Time* magazine covers.

Aruba (a-RU-ba), an island in the Netherlands Antilles off the coast of Venezuela. The island is internally self-governing and sends representatives to the Netherlands Antilles legislature on Curaçao. The chief town is Oran-jestad. Although its economy depends greatly on the re-fining and shipping of Venezuelan oil, Aruba's tourist and chemical industries are growing. The population is about 62,000.
Caribbean Sea and islands **C** 118

Aruego (ay-ar-u-A-go), **José** (1932–), author and illus-trator of children's books, b. Manila, Philippines. He be-gan his career in art as a cartoonist. Then he went on to do humorous drawings of animals in children's books. His illustrations may be seen in *Whose Mouse Are You?* (1970). He wrote and illustrated *The King and His Friends* (1969) and *Look What I Can Do* (1971).

Aryans (AR-i-ans)
cultural life of India **I** 116

Asbestos (as-BES-tos), the name of the fibrous form of several different minerals. This material is extremely important for fireproofing and electrical and heat insula-tion. Its fibers can be used as a woolly filling material or spun and woven into a fabric. It has been discovered that prolonged contact with asbestos fibers can cause cancer.
Canada **C** 58
floor coverings **V** 341
North American production **N** 295
particulate pollutant **A** 111
Quebec, Canada, world's largest producer **Q** 10b

Ascanius (as-CAY-nius), son of Aeneas **A** 35

ASCAP see American Society of Composers, Authors, and Publishers

Ascension Day (Ear of Wheat Thursday), religious holi-day **R** 153–54, 290

Ascension Island, South Atlantic **I** 426–27
turtle nesting grounds **T** 334a

Asch, Sholem, Polish-American Yiddish writer **Y** 351

Ascham (ASC-am), **Roger,** English writer and scholar **E** 250

Asclepius see Aesculapius

Ascorbic acid, or vitamin C **V** 370d

Asen (OS-en), **John I and II,** rulers of Bulgaria **B** 444

Asen, Peter, ruler of Bulgaria **B** 444

Asexual reproduction R 176–77

Asgard, home of the Norse gods **N** 277, 278

Ash, tree of the olive family
leaf, diagram **L** 114
uses of the wood and its grain, picture **W** 223
white ash, picture **T** 277

Ashanti, a people of Africa **G** 194, 197, 198
carved gold weights **A** 72; pictures **A** 70, 73
funeral customs **F** 494

Ashanti Crater, in Africa   C 421
Ashcan school, American painting   U 122
Ashdod, Israel, picture   G 106

Ashe, Arthur Robert, Jr. (1943–), American tennis player, b. Richmond, Va. Ashe played on the 1968, 1969, and 1970 winning Davis Cup teams. He became a professional in 1969. His major singles titles include the national intercollegiate in 1965, the U.S. amateur and U.S. championship in 1968, and Wimbledon in 1975. In 1977 foot surgery interrupted his playing career. He made a highly successful comeback in 1978 but suffered serious illness the following year.   N 103

Asheville, North Carolina   N 318
Ash flows, volcanic eruptions   V 382
Ashikaga, ancient ruling clan of Japan   J 43
Ashkenazic (osh-ken-OZ-ic) ritual, in Judaism   J 118, 119

Ashkenazy (ahsh-ken-AH-zee), Vladimir (1937–), concert pianist, b. Gorki, U.S.S.R. He is noted for his powerful, yet sensitive, interpretations of the music of Beethoven, Chopin, Rachmaninoff, and Prokofiev. In 1956 he won the Queen Elisabeth of the Belgians International Musical Competition in Brussels. In 1962 he shared first prize in the International Tchaikovsky Piano Competition held in Moscow. Ashkenazy became a citizen of Iceland in 1972.

Ashley, William Henry (1788?–1838), American pioneer and politician, b. Powhatan Co., Va. He explored and trapped furs along the Missouri River as far as the Yellowstone River (1822–23), traveled from Nebraska across the eastern Rockies to Wyoming (1824–25), and served in Congress (1831–37).
  Rocky Mountain Fur Company   F 523

Ashmole, Elias, English antiquarian   M 511
Ashmolean Museum, Oxford, England   M 511
Ashoka see Asoka
Ashton, Frederick, English choreographer   B 28–28a
Ashton-Warner, Sylvia, New Zealand writer   N 236
Ashurbanipal (osh-ur-BA-ni-pol), king of Assyria   A 224, 225;   L 192–93
Ashurnasirpal II, king of Assyria   A 240; statue, picture   A 241
Ash Wednesday, religious holiday   R 153, 290
  blessed ashes   R 301
  Easter   E 41
Asia (A-zha)   A 446–69
  Alexander the Great's conquests in   A 151–53
  conservation programs   C 489
  Europe's geographic relation to Asia   E 304
  flags of Asian countries   F 239–40
  immigration   I 103
  Middle East   M 300–08
  mountain peaks, highest in Asia   M 494
  music   O 220d–221
  national dances   D 31–32
  poverty   P 424–424b
  prairies   P 430–33
  rice consumption   R 229
  Siberia   S 173
  Southeast Asia   S 328–35
  teachers   T 43
  theater of the east   T 163

waterfalls, list of important falls with location and height   W 57
  See also names of countries

Asia Minor (known also as Anatolia), peninsula forming western extremity of Asia, including major portion of Turkey. It is bordered on the north by Black Sea, on the south by Mediterranean Sea, on the west by Aegean Sea. It was the first settlement of kingdom of Hittites (about 1900–1200 B.C.) and a principal crossroads of Eastern and Western civilizations in ancient times.
  landforms of Turkey   T 324

Asian kraits, snakes   S 208; picture   S 206

Asimov (AZ-i-mof), Isaac (1920–), American writer, educator, b. Russia. He went to the United States in 1923. He attended Columbia University, where he took his Ph.D. in chemistry. He taught biochemistry at Boston University Medical School but left in 1958 to devote full time to writing. A writer with over two hundred books to his credit, he is able to explain complex scientific processes in terms easily understandable to the lay person. His books range from science fact and fiction to textbooks and major historical works.

Askia Mohammed (OSK-ia-mo-HAM-med), ruler of Songhai   N 90
ASM (air-to-surface missiles)   M 344, 348
Asmara, Ethiopia, capital of Eritrea   E 300
Asoka, king of Magadha (modern Bihar), India   A 468;   I 131
Asparagus   V 289
  stems we eat   P 307; picture   P 306
ASPCA see Society for the Prevention of Cruelty to Animals, American
Aspdin, Joseph, English bricklayer, invented Portland cement   C 168
Aspen, Colorado
  ski resort, picture   C 408
Aspen Festival, Aspen, Colorado   M 551
Asphalt, a tarlike substance
  La Brea Pits, Los Angeles, California   L 345
  petroleum refining   P 174
  road surfaces   R 250
Asphalt tiles, floor covering   V 341
Aspirin, drug   D 328, 329
  treatment of rheumatoid arthritis   D 192

Asquith, Herbert Henry, 1st Earl Of Oxford and Asquith (1852–1928), British statesman, b. Morley, Yorkshire. Educated at Oxford University, he became a barrister (trial lawyer) before entering Parliament in 1886 as a Liberal. He served as home secretary (1892–95), chancellor of the exchequer (1905–08), and prime minister (1908–16). Among the measures adopted by his government was the Parliament Act (1911), which ended the veto power over bills by the House of Lords.

Asroc, missile   U 193
Ass, or donkey
  Abyssian wild ass   H 244
Assab, Ethiopia   E 300–01

Assad, Hafez al- (1928–), president of Syria, b. Qardaha. Assad, formerly commander of the Syrian Air Force and minister of defense, took power in a bloodless coup in 1970 and became president in 1971. In that office he ruled Syria longer than any other leader since independence in 1944 and became a major representative of the Arab cause in the Middle East.   **S** 508

Assassinations, presidential   **P** 448; **V** 325
  Garfield, James A.   **G** 53, 56
  Kennedy, John F.   **K** 211
  Lincoln, Abraham   **L** 297
  McKinley, William, picture   **M** 190
Assassin bug   **V** 283

Assassins, secret Muslim sect, founded in the 11th century, that believed in the murder of its enemies as a religious duty. Its name comes from Arabic word *hashshashin,* meaning "hashish eaters," because the members were thought to be under the influence of that drug when they went on their murderous missions. The sect flourished in Syria and Persia and spread over much of the Near East until subdued by Mongols and Mamelukes during 13th century. Today the word "assassin" is applied to one who kills a political figure or other powerful leader.

Assateague National Seashore, Virginia   **V** 348, 353
Assault, crime   **C** 532c
Assessed value, of property   **R** 112

Assemblage, modern art form in which the artist assembles objects not necessarily intended for artistic use. Such things as scraps of paper, cloth, wood, and metal are used. Assemblages may be either two- or three-dimensional. The French artist César (1921–   ) creates assemblages by welding pieces of metal, as in *Motor 4,* and by compressing parts of automobiles, as in *The Yellow Buick.* Collage is an assemblage in two dimensions.

Assemblage with Rainbow, collage by Kurt Schwitters, picture   **M** 396b

Assemblies of God, Protestant denomination. This pentecostal sect, which does mainly evangelical and missionary work, was founded in 1914. Members believe in second coming of Christ and divine healing.

Assembly, freedom of *see* Freedom of assembly
Assembly language, in computer programming   **C** 457
Assembly-line method, in manufacturing   **M** 84–85; picture   **I** 249
  automobiles   **A** 549–50
  introduced by Henry Ford   **F** 367
Assets, shown in bookkeeping statements   **B** 312
Assimilation, of ethnic groups   **E** 302
Assiniboine-Red River, Canada   **M** 76
Assiniboins (as-SIN-ib-oins), Indians of North America
  Bison Area tribal life   **I** 166
Assist, in baseball   **B** 75
Associated Press (AP), news-gathering service   **N** 200
Associated states, of the United Kingdom   **C** 428
Association of ideas, law of, in psychology   **P** 493
Association of Research Libraries   **L** 177

Association of South East Asian Nations (ASEAN), an organization formed to promote peace, stability, and economic, social, and cultural development in Southeast Asia. It was founded in 1967 with the signing of the ASEAN Declaration (or Bangkok Declaration). The member countries—Indonesia, Malaysia, the Philippines, Singapore, and Thailand—co-operate to solve their common problems. Headquarters are in Jakarta.

Associative properties, of numbers   **N** 387–88
Assonance (AS-so-nance), a kind of rhyme   **P** 353
Assuan *see* Aswan, Egypt
Assumption, The, painting by El Greco   **S** 361
Assumption Island *see* Asuncion
Assumption of the Blessed Virgin Mary, Feast of   **R** 290
Assumption of the Virgin, painting by Correggio   **I** 472
Assurbanipal *see* Ashurbanipal
Assyria (a-SIR-ia), ancient empire of Asia   **A** 224–25
  aqueducts   **A** 344
  architecture   **A** 373
  art   **A** 239–41; picture   **A** 225
  conquest of kingdom of Israel   **J** 104
  libraries, history of   **L** 192–93
  sculpture   **S** 93
  tunnels to carry water   **T** 314

Astaire, Fred (Fred Austerlitz) (1899–   ), American dancer and actor, b. Omaha, Nebr. He is noted for his singing and dancing in such musical films as *Top Hat, The Gay Divorcee, Easter Parade,* and *Finian's Rainbow.* He had nonmusical parts in *On The Beach* and *The Towering Inferno.*   **D** 34

Astatine (AST-a-tene), element   **E** 154, 159
  one of the halogens   **I** 349
Aster, pattern of cell division   **C** 164
Asterism, star effect in gemstones   **G** 70
Asteroids (planetoids), small planets   **A** 473; **P** 274; **S** 239–40, 243
  Mars   **M** 107
Asters, flowers   **G** 51; picture   **W** 170
Asthma, labored breathing caused by an allergic reaction   **D** 190
Astigmatism (a-STIG-ma-tism), eye defect   **L** 150, 265
Astley, Philip, English circus performer   **C** 300
Astor, John Jacob, German-born American merchant and fur trader   **F** 522–23; **O** 256
  Oregon, history of   **O** 207
  real estate fortune   **R** 112

Astor, Lady (Nancy Witcher Langhorne Astor, Viscountess Astor) (1879–1964), first woman member of British Parliament, b. Greenwood, Va., U.S.A. She succeeded her husband, Waldorf Astor, as Conservative member in House of Commons (1919–45). She campaigned for women's rights, temperance, and child welfare.

Astoria, Oregon, picture   **O** 202
  Fort Astoria   **F** 523
Astrakhan fur *see* Persian lamb
Astrida *see* Butare, Rwanda
Astrodome, Houston, Texas   **H** 270
Astrolabes (AST-rol-abes), navigation instruments   **N** 64
  exploration stimulated   **E** 374
Astrology (a-STROL-ogy), the study of stars and planets for revelation of what will happen on earth   **A** 470–71
Astronauts and cosmonauts   **S** 344–45
  first female U.S. astronauts, picture   **S** 347
  food and meals   **F** 342
  navigation in space   **N** 69
  piloted satellites of the future   **S** 43
  rhesus monkey, picture   **M** 420
  using camera, picture   **P** 209
Astronomical (ast-ro-NOM-ic-al) **photography,** or astro-photography   **P** 207–08
Astronomical telescopes   **O** 167

Astronomical unit (A.U.), the mean distance from the earth to the sun—149,600,000 km (about 93,000,000 mi). The unit is sometimes used in astronomy to express large distances.

Astronomy (a-STRON-omy) **A** 470–476d
  comets **C** 418–19
  constellations **C** 490–93
  eclipses **E** 46–46b
  history *see* Astronomy, history of
  Mars **M** 104–11
  measuring the distance of galaxies **U** 202–03
  meteors and meteorites **C** 419–21
  observatories **O** 8–15
  planets **P** 269–78
  quasars and pulsars **Q** 7–8
  radio and radar astronomy **R** 69–76
  Rudolphine tables of fixed stars **B** 361
  satellites, use of **S** 42
  seasons **S** 108–12
  solar system **S** 239–48
  stars **S** 405–11
  sun **S** 458–67
  tektites **C** 421
  telescopes **T** 60–64
  universe **U** 196–204
  See also Comets; Constellations; Earth; Eclipses; Meteors and meteorites; Moon; Planets; Radar astronomy; Radio astronomy; Satellites; Solar system; Space exploration and travel; Stars; Sun; Telescopes; Tides; Universe; names of planets
Astronomy, history of **A** 470–476d; **S** 78–79
  Brahe, Tycho, works of **B** 361
  Copernicus, father of modern astronomy **C** 501
  Galileo's discoveries **G** 6, 7
  Kepler, Johannes **K** 234
Astrophotography (ast-ro-pho-TOG-raphy), or astronomical photography **P** 207–08
Astrophysics **P** 238
  astrophysical observatories **O** 9
  science, history of **S** 76
Asturias, Miguel Angel, Guatemalan writer **G** 391; **L** 72
Asunción (a-soon-ci-OHN), capital of Paraguay **P** 65; picture **P** 62

Asuncion (formerly Assumption) **Island,** located in northern part of Marianas island group in western Pacific. This U.S. trusteeship is an uninhabited volcanic island less than 3 km (about 2 mi) in diameter.

Asvagosha, Indian writer **O** 220e
Aswan (os-WON), Egypt **E** 91
Aswan High Dam, Egypt **D** 20–21; **E** 90d, 90e
  artificial lake engulfs historical sites of Sudan **S** 449
  Egyptian art, concern for **E** 93
Asymmetrical (a-sim-MET-ric-al) **balance,** in design **D** 133
Asymmetry, lack of proportion
  What makes modern music different and unpredictable? **M** 399
As You Like It, play by Shakespeare **S** 133–34
Atabrine, synthetic drug that acts like quinine **P** 313
Atacama (at-a-CA-ma) **Desert,** Chile **C** 251; pictures **D** 126, **G** 106, **S** 276
  nitrate **C** 253
Atahualpa (ata-HUAL-pa), Inca ruler **I** 207; **P** 165, 266

  methods used to control Incas **E** 388
Atatürk, Mustafa Kemal, president of Turkey **T** 326, 329
Atbara (OT-ba-ra) **River,** tributary of the Nile **N** 260
Atchison, Topeka, and Santa Fe Railroad **N** 195
A tempo, in music **M** 532
Aten (OT-en), or **Aton,** ancient Egyptian god **A** 221; **E** 100
Athabasca, Lake, Canada **A** 146c; **C** 52; **L** 26; **S** 38c
Athabasca River, Canada **J** 55; picture **J** 54
Athabasca tar sands, Alberta, Canada **A** 146c, 146d; **C** 56
Athanasius (ath-a-NAY-shus), **Saint,** Bishop of Alexandria **C** 283; **R** 289
Athapascan (ath-a-PASC-an) **language family,** of North American Indians **A** 136

Atheism (A-thee-iz-um), the denial of the existence of God. Atheism holds that everything in the world can be explained on a scientific or material basis rather than as the result of creation by a supreme being. Everything that exists now is said to have come from some form of matter that existed before. The term comes from the Greek word *atheos,* meaning "without God."

Athena (a-THE-na), Greek goddess **G** 361

Athenaeum (ath-en-E-um), literary or scientific association or club. Term is derived from Greek "Athenaion" (Temple of Athena), where poets read their works. Name was also given to school for study of arts built in Rome (2nd century A.D.) by Emperor Hadrian.

Athens, capital of Greece **G** 331, 337; pictures **C** 308, **G** 335
  ancient civilization in Athens **A** 227–28; **C** 308a
  citizenship **C** 311
  Dionysus, Theater of, picture **T** 155
  early form of democracy **D** 104
  education in early Athens **E** 62–64
  hotel, picture **H** 257
  oratory **O** 180
  Parthenon **A** 374; pictures **A** 375, **E** 327, **G** 335
  Pericles, its greatest statesman **P** 156
  Solon, founder of democracy in ancient Athens **S** 252b
  wall-carving, picture **A** 227
Atherosclerosis (ath-er-o-scler-O-sis), hardening of the arteries **B** 293
Athlete's foot **D** 206
Athletics *see* Gymnastics; Olympic Games; Physical education; Sports

Athlone, 1st Earl of (Alexander Augustus Frederick William Alfred George Cambridge) (1874–1957), British army officer and governor-general, b. London. An uncle of the future King George VI, he fought in the Boer War and in World War I. He was governor-general of the Union of South Africa (1923–31) and of Canada (1940–46).

Athos, Mount, religious state in Greece **G** 332
Athos, one of *The Three Musketeers* **D** 342–43
Athus (ot-URS), Belgium
  steelworkers, picture **B** 128
Atkins, Chet, American singer, musician, and record producer **C** 525

Atkins, Tommy, traditional nickname for British soldier, comparable to American "GI Joe." Name originated in British War Office in 19th century as demonstration name used in filling out forms and was made popular through poems of Rudyard Kipling.

Atlanta, capital of Georgia   **A** 477;   **G** 138, 143–44
 Civil War   **C** 326–27
 Memorial Arts Center   **G** 139
 Sherman captured the city   **S** 151
Atlantic, Battle of the, 1940–41   **W** 291
Atlantic and Pacific Tea Company, Great (A & P)   **S** 468
Atlantic Basin, Canada   **C** 51–52

Atlantic Charter (August, 1941), declaration of common principles and war aims by President Franklin D. Roosevelt and Prime Minister Winston Churchill. Charter was signed aboard battleship U.S.S. *Augusta* off coast of Newfoundland. It expressed hope that all men "may live out their lives in freedom from fear and want" and called for general disarmament and the establishment of a permanent peace-keeping structure. Its provisions were endorsed by 15 anti-Axis nations and were later incorporated into United Nations Declaration (1942).

Atlantic City, New Jersey   **N** 166
Atlantic Coastal Plain, United States   **U** 89
Atlantic Monthly, magazine
 Holmes's essays   **H** 160
Atlantic Ocean   **A** 478
 cables, submarine   **T** 52–53
 earthquake belt   **E** 34
 Gulf Stream   **G** 411
 history of, diagram   **E** 11
 hurricanes, months when they occur   **H** 293
 icebergs in the North Atlantic   **I** 25–26
 mid-ocean ridge explored by geologists   **G** 114
 ocean currents   **O** 32–33; diagram   **L** 232
 ocean floor   **O** 28–29
 ocean liner crossings   **O** 20, 23
 tide schedule, typical   **T** 180
Atlantic Provinces of Canada *see* New Brunswick; Newfoundland; Nova Scotia; Prince Edward Island
Atlantides, in mythology, water nymphs   **A** 478

Atlantis, legendary island in Atlantic Ocean, described by Plato as having an ideal state and a highly developed civilization. According to tradition it was destroyed by an earthquake and sank beneath the sea.
 how Atlantic Ocean was named   **A** 478

Atlantis II, ship, floating oceanographic laboratory, picture   **O** 25
Atlas, in Greek mythology   **G** 363;   **W** 243
Atlas, rocket, picture   **R** 255
Atlases, bound volumes of maps   **M** 93
 reference books   **R** 129
 research methods   **R** 183
Atlas Mountains, northern Africa   **A** 46, 160;   **M** 460; pictures   **A** 162,   **M** 458
Atman, Hindu spiritual principle *see* Brahman
Atmosphere, gases enveloping our earth   **A** 479–82
 air pollution   **A** 108–11;   **E** 272f–272g
 clouds   **C** 358–61
 comets   **C** 418–19
 cosmic rays   **C** 511–13
 earth's shield   **E** 24–25
 formation of earth's atmosphere   **E** 19
 how earth's atmosphere is held   **E** 23

International Geophysical Year findings   **I** 316–17
 layers   **E** 16–17
 Mars   **M** 108, 110
 meteors, meteorites   **C** 419–21
 moon lacks   **M** 450, 455
 ozone layer   **O** 271
 planets   **P** 270–78
 research with ballooning   **B** 32–33
 space dust   **D** 347
 sun's atmosphere   **E** 46a–46b;   **S** 461–63
 twinkling layer of air   **S** 409
 weather of the atmospheric layers   **W** 71–72
 See also Air; Meteorology
Atmospheric pressure   **A** 479;   **W** 72
 boiling point affected by   **H** 93–94
 freezing point affected by   **H** 94
 pumps, action of   **P** 528
 See also Air pressure
Atolls, coral islands   **P** 2
 corals   **C** 504
Atomic bomb   **N** 362–63
 Einstein's work on   **E** 105–06
 Hiroshima and Nagasaki, Japan   **J** 48
 man-made radiation belts   **R** 49
 Truman, Harry S, and bombing Japan   **T** 300
 United States Air Force   **U** 160
 World War II   **W** 308
Atomic energy *see* Nuclear energy

Atomic Energy Commission, a federal commission created by Atomic Energy Act of 1946 to provide civilian administration of U.S. atomic energy program. It was officially abolished in 1974. In 1975 its functions were divided between the new Nuclear Regulatory Commission (NRC) and the new Energy Research and Development Administration (ERDA).

Atomic numbers   **A** 486–87;   **C** 201, 218
 elements   **E** 153–59
 nuclear energy   **N** 355
 See also Periodic table
Atomic physics *see* Nuclear physics
Atomic power *see* Nuclear energy
Atomic weight   **A** 484, 487;   **C** 218
 Dalton's theory   **D** 15
 elements   **E** 153–54
 experimental measurements   **C** 212
 isotopes   **C** 203–05
 nuclear energy   **N** 356, 357–58
Atomium, symbol of Brussels World's Fair   **F** 16
Atoms   **A** 483–89;   **C** 218
 alloy structures   **A** 168, 169
 ancient "elements"   **C** 206–07
 atomic shower, International Geophysical Year findings   **I** 312–13
 carbon chains and rings   **C** 106
 chemical structure   **C** 196, 201, 216
 chemistry, history of, theories   **C** 206–07, 212–13
 cosmic rays   **C** 511–13
 crystals   **C** 541–42
 Dalton's theory   **C** 212;   **D** 15
 electricity   **E** 123, 126, 128
 electronics   **E** 143–44
 elements, chemical   **E** 153–59
 ions and ionization   **I** 350–55
 magnetism   **M** 28–29
 matter and atoms   **M** 174–78
 nuclear energy   **N** 352–71
 radiation·   **R** 40
 radioactive dating   **R** 64–66

Atoms (continued)
  radioactive elements **R** 67
  Rutherford's theory **R** 361
Atoms for Peace Plan, 1953 **D** 184
Atom smashing, process for studying atoms **A** 489
Aton *see* Aten
Atonality, in music **M** 400, 532
Atonement, Day of, Jewish holy day **J** 120
ATP, adenosine triphosphate **B** 296–97
  photosynthesis forms this compound **P** 222
Atrium, center hall of a Roman house, picture **R** 306
Atriums, chambers of the heart **B** 276; **D** 196; diagram **B** 276
  coronary circulation of the heart **H** 86a–86b
Atropine (AT-ro-pene), drug **P** 314, 321
Atta, or leaf-cutting, **ants A** 326
Attachés (at-ta-SHAYS), representatives of the armed forces in the Foreign Service **F** 370
Attar of roses
  Bulgaria, major producer of **B** 441
Atterbom, Per Daniel Amadeus, Swedish poet **S** 52
Attica, region around Athens
  Attic dialect becomes common language of Greece **G** 349
  Attic vases **G** 343

Attila (AT-til-a) (406?–453), king of the Huns. He became king in 433, ruling jointly with his brother Bleda until the latter's death (444?). The Huns, an Asian people, had migrated into eastern Europe in the 4th century. Under Attila they conquered most of eastern and central Europe and invaded the eastern Roman Empire, advancing to the gates of the capital, Constantinople (now Istanbul). The destruction wrought by Attila earned him the name Scourge of God. In 451 he invaded Gaul (modern France), but his westward expansion was checked by Roman and Gothic troops at the battle of Chalôns—one of the great battles of history. In 452 he invaded northern Italy. Attila is said to have spared Rome at the entreaty of Pope Leo I. After Attila's death the Hunnish empire disintegrated.
  Chalôns, battle of, 451 **B** 100
  Nibelungenlied and Volsung Saga, legends **L** 130
  See also Huns

Attlee, Clement Richard (1883–1967), Earl Attlee, English statesman, b. London. He was elected to Parliament as Labour member (1922) and became leader of Labour Party (1935–55). He held various posts in Winston Churchill's coalition government during World War II, was British delegate to UN conference in San Francisco (1945), and served as prime minister (1945–51), during which time he helped to bring various industries under state ownership and to institute extensive health and welfare services. He was made a peer in 1955.

Attorney General, member of the cabinet of the U.S. president and head of U.S. Justice Department **P** 448
Attorneys *see* Lawyers
Attractants, substances produced by animals to attract mates *see* Pheromones

Attucks (AT-uks), **Crispus** (1723?–70), American revolutionary patriot, killed in the Boston Massacre. It is thought that Attucks was born a slave (possibly in Massachusetts) and that he escaped and worked on sailing ships. He was in Boston at a time when many colonists were angered by the presence of British troops. A number of fights had broken out between troops and colonists. On the evening of March 5, 1770, a crowd of Bos-

ton men, including Attucks, confronted a small party of British soldiers and pelted them with sticks and stones. The soldiers fired into the crowd. Attucks and four others were killed. A memorial to the five men stands today on Boston Common.
  black American history **N** 92
  Boston Massacre **R** 196

Attu Island, Alaska **A** 128
Atwood, Margaret, Canadian novelist and poet **C** 64
A.U. *see* Astronomical unit
Auburn, Maine **M** 44
Auburn system, of punishment **P** 468–69
Auckland, New Zealand **N** 241
Auctions
  antique furniture, picture **A** 317
  tobacco **T** 201
Audemars, Georges, Swiss scientist **N** 427
Auden, W. H., English-born American poet **E** 266
Audible sounds **S** 259–60
Audiometer, instrument for testing hearing **D** 50; picture **H** 84
Audio signal, television **T** 66, 68
Audio-visual materials and equipment
  education **E** 78
  special services of libraries **L** 173–74, 175–76, 179; picture **L** 181
Audit, in bookkeeping **B** 311
  insurance auditors **I** 297
Audubon (AUD-u-bon), **John James,** American naturalist and painter **A** 490–91; **K** 216
  Audubon Memorial State Park, Louisiana **L** 358–59
  birdbanding started in North America **B** 229
  passenger pigeons, painting **B** 230
  United States, art of **U** 117, 120
  Wild Turkey, painting **U** 118

Audubon Society, National (NAS), an organization devoted to the preservation of wildlife (birds, animals, plants) and the conservation of natural resources. The society is named after John J. Audubon, the famous painter of birds. It was founded in 1905 and has headquarters in New York, N.Y. Its publications include *Audubon* magazine. **C** 488

Aue, Hartmann von *see* Hartmann von Aue
Augean (au-GE-an) **stables,** in Greek mythology **G** 363
Auger (AUG-er) **bits,** tools **T** 214; **W** 230
  auger mining of coal **C** 367
Augsburg Confession, 1530 **P** 483
August, 8th month of year **A** 492–93
Augusta (au-GUST-a), capital of Maine **M** 43–44
Augusta, Georgia **G** 144
Augustin I *see* Iturbide, Augustin de
Augustine, Saint (354–430), early Christian leader and Bishop of Hippo **A** 494; **C** 283–84; picture **C** 282
  father of Latin theology **R** 289
  philosophical system **P** 192
Augustine, Saint (?–604), archbishop of Canterbury **R** 290
  Anglo-Saxons converted to Christianity **E** 216
Augustus, emperor of Rome **R** 303
  Aeneid written in honor of Augustus **A** 35
  heir of Julius Caesar **C** 6
  Latin literature, golden age of **L** 79–80
  Roman coin picturing Augustus **A** 232

second triumvirate with Mark Antony and Lepidus **M** 100

Aukrust, Olaf, Norwegian poet **S** 52

Auks, seabirds, related to gulls and terns, of colder regions of the Northern Hemisphere. Auks are black-and-white birds with short tails, webbed feet, and small wings that they use in swimming.
    extinct great auk **B** 231

Auld Lang Syne, song by Robert Burns **B** 460
Aulos, double oboe of ancient Greece **A** 247
Aurangzeb (AUR-ang-zeb), emperor of Mogul dynasty of India **I** 133
Aureomycin (aur-e-o-MY-cin), antibiotic **A** 312

Auriol (or-i-OL), **Jacqueline** (1917–), French flier, b. Challans. She is considered France's leading woman flier and one of France's top test pilots. In 1955 she became the second woman to break the sound barrier, flying 1,150 km (715 mi) per hour.

Auriol, Vincent (1884–1966), French politician, b. Revel Haute-Garonne. He was Socialist member of the Chamber of Deputies (1914–40) and general secretary of Socialist group in Parliament (1919–36). Imprisoned after German conquest of France (1940), he escaped (1943) and joined French underground, later being active in de Gaulle's Free French movement and becoming first president (1947–53) of Fourth Republic.

Aurochs (AUR-ocks), extinct wild cattle **H** 221

Aurora (uh-ROR-a), in Roman mythology, the goddess of the dawn. In Greek mythology she is known as Eos, the daughter of the Titan Hyperion and the sister of Helios (the sun god) and Selene (the moon goddess). She is said to have ushered in each new day by driving a chariot, drawn by two white horses, across the sky.

Aurora australis (aus-TRAY-lis), southern polar lights **I** 310, 353
Aurora borealis (bo-re-AL-is), or northern lights **I** 310, 353
Auroras, polar lights **I** 310, 353
    International Geophysical Year findings **I** 313–15
    radiation belts **R** 49
    shown in the ionosphere, diagram **E** 16
    solar flares **E** 27
    solar wind **S** 463, 475
Austen, Jane, English novelist **A** 494
    place in English literature **E** 261
    style and themes of her novels **N** 346
Austerlitz, Battle of, 1805 **N** 11
Austin, capital of Texas **T** 133
Austin, Moses, American pioneer miner **N** 366
Austin, Stephen F., American pioneer **M** 366–67; **T** 135

Austin, Tracy (1962–), American tennis player, b. Rolling Hills, Calif. In 1979 she became the youngest player to win the women's U.S. championship. She delighted tennis fans in 1977 by becoming the youngest player in modern tennis to reach the third round of play at Wimbledon. Austin began playing in tournaments as a young child and had won several national titles before entering international competition. She turned professional in 1978.

Austin, Warren R., American statesman **V** 320
Australia (aus-TRAY-lia) **A** 495–517
    aborigines **A** 6a
    Australian words and phrases **A** 501
    Canberra, capital of Australia **C** 87–88
    dependencies **C** 428
    explored by Capt. Cook **C** 494c
    favorite foods **F** 335, 339
    flag **F** 243
    football **F** 366
    gold discoveries **G** 253; **M** 320
    immigration **I** 103
    kangaroos and other pouched mammals **K** 167–75
    Melbourne **M** 215
    mountain peaks, highest in Australia **M** 494
    national anthem **N** 21
    New Guinea **N** 147; **P** 59
    prairies **P** 430–32
    rabbit plague **R** 24
    snakes **S** 208
    Sydney **S** 503–04
    western desert area, picture **D** 125
    winter season, picture **S** 111
    Wollomombi waterfall **W** 57
Australian Alps **A** 502, 507
    Snowy Mountains Hydroelectric Scheme, picture **A** 511
Australian ballot **E** 115
Australian Capital Territory **A** 514; **C** 87
Australian crawl, swimming **S** 490
Australian Elizabethan Theatre Trust **T** 163
Australian region, land region of animal life **L** 234–35
Australian Rules, football, Melbourne home of **M** 215
Austral Islands *see* Tubuai Islands
Australoids, Australian aboriginal people **A** 6a, 500
Australopithecus, early humanlike creature **F** 139; **P** 442; pictures **A** 305, **P** 444
Austria **A** 518–25
    flag **F** 237
    folk dance **D** 30
    German and Austrian literature **G** 174–81
    German and Austrian music **G** 183–89
    German language **G** 172–73
    Hallstatt culture **C** 165–66
    national anthem **N** 21
    Vienna **V** 332a–332b
    World War II, annexed by Hitler, 1938 **W** 286
Austria-Hungary **A** 525; **H** 288
    Czechoslovakia former part of **C** 559, 563
    flag (until 1918) **F** 227
    World War I **W** 271, 281
Austrian music **G** 183–89
    See also names of Austrian composers
Austrian Succession, War of the (1740–48) **A** 525
Authoritarian family **F** 43
Authorship *see* Writing (authorship)

Autism (early childhood autism), a severe mental disorder in children. Autistic children cannot form normal relationships with other people, even their own parents. They often do not speak at all, or they just repeat what they have heard. Autistic children are obsessed with sameness. They may react violently if something, such as a chair, is moved out of its usual place. They may sit for hours staring, while rocking back and forth or performing other rhythmic movements. Autism was first described as a syndrome (a set of symptoms) in 1943 by Dr. Leo Kanner (1894–). It is generally thought to be caused by an inborn defect in body chemistry. Treatment with very high doses of vitamins and operant

PHOTO CREDITS

The following list credits, by page, the sources of photos used in THE NEW BOOK OF KNOWLEDGE. Credits are listed photo by photo—left to right, top to bottom. Wherever appropriate, the name of the photographer has been listed with the source, the two being separated by a dash. When two or more photos by different photographers appear on one page, their credits are separated by semicolons.

A

2 Steven Kest—Shostal Associates
6a Paolo Curto—Bruce Coleman, Inc.
6b Giraudon
7 Jim Pickerell—Action
10 Bettmann Archive
11 Yale University Art Gallery
14 Bettmann Archive
15 Bettmann Archive
27 Forest Service, U.S. Department of Agriculture
28 Metric Commission of Canada; General Foods Corporation © 1979.
29 Foster and Kleiser
31 Carl Perutz; Carl Perutz; J. Walter Thompson Co.
33 Kenyon & Eckhardt
34 Warshaw Collection of Business Americana
41 Ryan Aeronautical Co.; UPI; Boeing Co.
43 Marc Riboud—Magnum
44 Marc Riboud—Magnum; Aloys Michel; Stephanie Dinkins; Marc Riboud—Magnum.
47 John Lewis Stage—Lensgroup; Harrison Forman; John & Bini Moss—Photo Researchers; Carl Frank; George Rodger—Magnum.
51 M. S. Klein—Shostal; George Rodger—Magnum; Hilda Harrison—C. P. Cushing; M. S. Klein—Shostal; George Rodger—Magnum.
54 E. Kollmar—Shostal; Marc & Evelyne Bernheim—Rapho Guillumette; Carl Frank; H. Street—Shostal; Tom Larson—American Museum of Natural History; Marc & Evelyne Bernheim—Rapho Guillumette; Carl Frank.
59 George Rodger—Magnum; E. Kollmar—Shostal; Brian Brake—Magnum; E. Kollmar—Shostal.
60 Louis Renault—Photo Researchers; Pete Turner—FPG; George Rodger—Magnum; Marc Riboud—Magnum.
63 Marc Riboud—Magnum; Marc Riboud—Magnum; Duncan Edward—FPG; Carl Frank; W. R. Donagho—Shostal.
64 Hal Linker—Shostal
66 Inge Morath—Magnum
68 Vincent—AAA Photo; Everts—Rapho Guillumette; Hoa—Qui; Hoa—Qui.
70 W. Bruggmann—E. Leucinger Collection; Lee Bolton.
71 Charles Uht—Museum of Primitive Art
73 W. Bruggmann—Ethnological Collection, Zurich; Lee Bolton—Museum of Primitive Art, New York; W. Bruggmann—In the Possession of the Oni of Ife; Charles Uht—Museum of Primitive Art; Lee Bolton; W. Bruggman—Rietberg Museum, Zurich.
74 W. Bruggmann—Rietberg Museum, Zurich; W. Bruggmann—Rietberg Museum, Zurich; W. Bruggmann—Rietberg Museum, Zurich; Frank Newens—Pitt Rivers Museum, Oxford University; J. A. Lavaud—Musée de l'Homme, Paris.
75 W. Bruggmann—Ethnological Collection, Zurich; W. Bruggmann—Rietberg Museum, Zurich, Von Der Heydt Collection; I. Zafrir—Israel Dubiner Collection, Tel Aviv; University Museum, Philadelphia; Charles Uht—Museum of Primitive Art; University Museum, Philadelphia.
76 Charles Uht—Museum of Primitive Art
76a Marc and Evelyn Bernheim—Rapho Guillumette
77 Peter Larson—FPG; Robert S. Kane.
79 Ken Heyman—Rapho Guillumette
80 Archives, Museum of Comparative Zoology Library, Harvard University
85 Courtesy of Professor V. N. Nikitin—University of Kharkov
86 F. E. Nichy—U.S. Bureau of Commercial Fisheries; By permission, British Museum (Natural History); Smithsonian Institution; Walter Dawn; Reprinted from *Seals, Sea Lions, and Walruses* by Victor B. Scheffer, with permission of the publishers, Stanford University Press, © 1958 by the Board of Trustees of the Leland Stanford Junior University.
90 Shostal; Shostal; Ray Manley—Shostal.
91 Allis Chalmers; H. Armstrong Roberts; Courtesy of Atlee Burpee.
97 Ed Drews—Photo Researchers; Dan Budnik—Magnum; John Lewis Stage—Photo Researchers; Eric Lessing—Magnum.
98 Birnback; Eric Lessing—Magnum; Ned Haines—Rapho Guillumette.
99 Birnback; Stephanie Dinkins; Henri Cartier-Bresson—Magnum; Tom Hollyman—Photo Researchers.

101 Bettmann Archive
104 *Model Airplane News*
106 Robert Schleicher
107 Cioffero—Fundamental Photographs
108 F. Neal—Photo Researchers
110 George Hall—Woodfin Camp; Courtesy of Bethlehem Steel Co.
111 St. Louis *Post Dispatch*—Black Star; De Sazo—Rapho Guillumette.
113 S. A. Grimes; Mem Tierce; Rutherford Platt; Color Illustration, Inc.
114 Douglas Faulkner
119 Douglas Faulkner
123 Ray Atkeson; Douglas Faulkner.
124 Douglas Faulkner
129 John J. Koranda; George W. Merriman; Steve McCutcheon; Color Illustration, Inc.
133 Steve McCutcheon; Bob & Ira Spring.
134 C. J. Ott—Shostal
137 C. W. Sorensen
139 C. W. Sorensen
141 Ward Wells—Shostal
146 Harry Redl—Black Star
146b Malak; George Hunter; Annan.
146f Gene Ahrens—Shostal
146g George Hunter—Shostal; Malak.
156 Walter Dawn; Bruce Hunter—American Museum of Natural History; Walter Dawn; Walter Dawn; Dr. George A. Llano—Courtesy of *Scientific American.*
162 Michel Hetier—Rapho Guillumette; Shostal; G. Mangin—Rapho Guillumette.
169 Revere Copper & Brass, Inc.
174 Bob & Ira Spring
175 Ray Manley—Shostal; Bob & Ira Spring; Swiss National Tourist Office.
178 J. David Bowen; Rene Burri—Magnum.
179 George Holton—Photo Researchers; Davis Pratt—Rapho Guillumette; Davis Pratt—Rapho Guillumette.
198 Bettmann Archive
207 Pictorial Parade
209 Tom Hollyman—Photo Researchers
211 Pictorial Parade
212 Photoworld—FPG
213 Pictorial Parade
214a Erich Hartman—Magnum Photos, Inc.
214b © 1932, 1960 James Thurber. From *The Seal in the Bedroom,* Harper & Row. Originally printed in *The New Yorker.*
215 Bettmann Archive
216 Hirmer Fotoarchiv
218 Editions Tel; Hirmer Fotoarchiv.
220 Lee Boltin; Lee Boltin.
221 Egyptian Collection, Staatlichen Museum, Berlin—Art Reference Bureau; Ancient Egyptian Paintings, Oriental Institute, University of Chicago.
222 Courtesy of Museum of Fine Arts, Boston
224 Archaeological Survey of India—Art Reference Bureau, Inc.; E. Boubat—Agence TOP.
225 Hirmer Fotoarchiv
226 Margot Wolf—Scala, New York; Roland-Ziolo—National Archeological Museum, Athens.
227 Roland-Ziolo—Acropolis Museum, Athens; Scala, New York.
229 Editorial Photocolor Archives; Trustees of the British Museum.
230 Mansell Collection; Snark International.
231 Tetrel; Chase Manhattan Bank, Money Museum.
232 American Numismatic Society; Bill Froelich; Alinari—Art Reference Bureau; Held—Ziolo.
233 By permission of the trustees of the British Museum—Art Reference Bureau
234 Oriental Institute, University of Chicago
235 Hirmer; Editions Tel.
236 John Baker—Shostal; Raymond V. Schoder.
237 Alison Frantz—Art Reference.Bureau
239 Hirmer; Josephine Powell.
240 © British Museum—Art Reference Bureau
241 Courtesy of the Trustees of the British Museum; Louvre—Editions Tel.
242 William G. Froelich; Art Reference Bureau.
243 Staatlichen Museum, Berlin
244 Art Reference Bureau; Courtesy of the Trustees of the British Museum; Tomb of the Leopards, Tarquinia—Art Reference Bureau.
246 Metropolitan Museum of Art, Fletcher Fund, 1956

252 Cornell Capa—Magnum; John Meyer—Shostal; Tom Hollyman—Photo Researchers; C. W. Close—Shostal.
255 Tom Hollyman—Photo Researchers; Peter Wichman—Birnback.
256 Boston Medical Library, Massachusetts Medical Society
257 New York Hospital; Gorman-Rupp Industries, Inc.
261 Harrison Forman
275 Ylla—Rapho Guillumette
276 David Corson—Shostal; Courtesy of Bell Telephone Laboratories, Inc.
277 Allan D. Cruickshank—National Audubon Society; Lynwood Chace.
279 Robert Meyerriecks; Lawrence E. Perkins; Lawrence E. Perkins; Henry C. Johnson.
280 Kitchen Kinne—National Audubon Society
282 FPG
283 Roy De Carava
284 Al Bassy—Three Lions; Dr. Ross E. Hutchins.
285 *The Times,* London—Pictorial Parade
287 Professor Harry F. Harlow—Primate Laboratory, University of Wisconsin
288 Lilo Hess—Three Lions
294 Jacques Six
295 Bel-Vienne—Jacana; G. Holton—Photo Researchers.
296 Eric Hosking; Ray Tercafs—Jacana.
297 Spiderman Copyright © 1979 Marvel Comics Group, a division of Cadence Industries Corp. All Rights Reserved; © MCMLV, Walt Disney Productions, World Rights Reserved; © MCMLV, Walt Disney Productions, World Rights Reserved; © 1979 Hanna-Barbera Productions, Inc.; © Walter Lantz Productions.
298 © MCMLXII Walt Disney Productions, World Rights Reserved; © Walt Disney Productions, World Rights Reserved.
300 Constance Stuart—Black Star; Richard Harrington—Three Lions; Olin's Winchester Western.
301 John Hiney—Photo Researchers; Shostal; Tom Hollyman—Photo Researchers.
302 Shostal; Shostal; Rapho; Shostal.
303 South African Tourist Corp.; Courtesy of American Museum of Natural History; National Film Board of Canada; Marc & Evelyne Bernheim—Rapho Guillumette.
304 Swedish National Travel; Harold Schultz; Wide World; Katrina Thomas—Photo Researchers.
306 Camera Press-Pix; Carleton S. Coon for Alfred A. Knopf, *Origin of the Races.*
307 William W. Bacon III—Rapho Guillumette; Irish Tourist Office; D. Forbert—Shostal; FPG; Bill Brindle—Photo Researchers; Sabine Weiss—Rapho Guillumette; John Moss—Photo Researchers; Marc & Evelyne Bernheim—Rapho Guillumette; Ernest Kleinberg—Rapho Guillumette.
309 © by Chicago Natural History Museum
311 Chas. Pfizer & Co.
314 Chas. Pfizer & Co.
315 New York Academy of Medicine; Chas. Pfizer & Co.; Chas. Pfizer & Co.; Eugene H. Kone—Rockefeller Institute; Wide World.
317 Sotheby Parke Bernet, Inc., New York
318 Pat Zimmerman; *Antiques Monthly,* Tuscaloosa, Ala.; Lee Boltin—Courtesy of Cooper Union Museum
319 Sotheby Parke Bernet, Inc., New York; National Gallery of Art, *Index of American Design;* Lee Boltin—Courtesy of Cooper Union Museum; Lee Boltin—Courtesy of Cooper Union Museum.
320 Antique Coin Bank Collection of the Seaman's Bank for Savings, New York City; Sandak; Corning Museum of Glass.
321 Metropolitan Museum of Art, Gift of William R. Stewart, 1926; Metropolitan Museum of Art, Bequest of A. T. Clearwater, 1933; Metropolitan Museum of Art, Gift of Mrs. Abraham Lansing, 1901; Metropolitan Museum of Art, Bequest of A. T. Clearwater, 1933.
322 Jacques Six; Dr. Ross E. Hutchins.
323 Jacques Six
324 Bruce Coleman Ltd.
325 Bisserot—Bruce Coleman Ltd.
326 Jacana
327- Dr. Ross E. Hutchins
328
331 Rudolf Freund—Nettie King Associates